Martiros SARYAN

Martiros

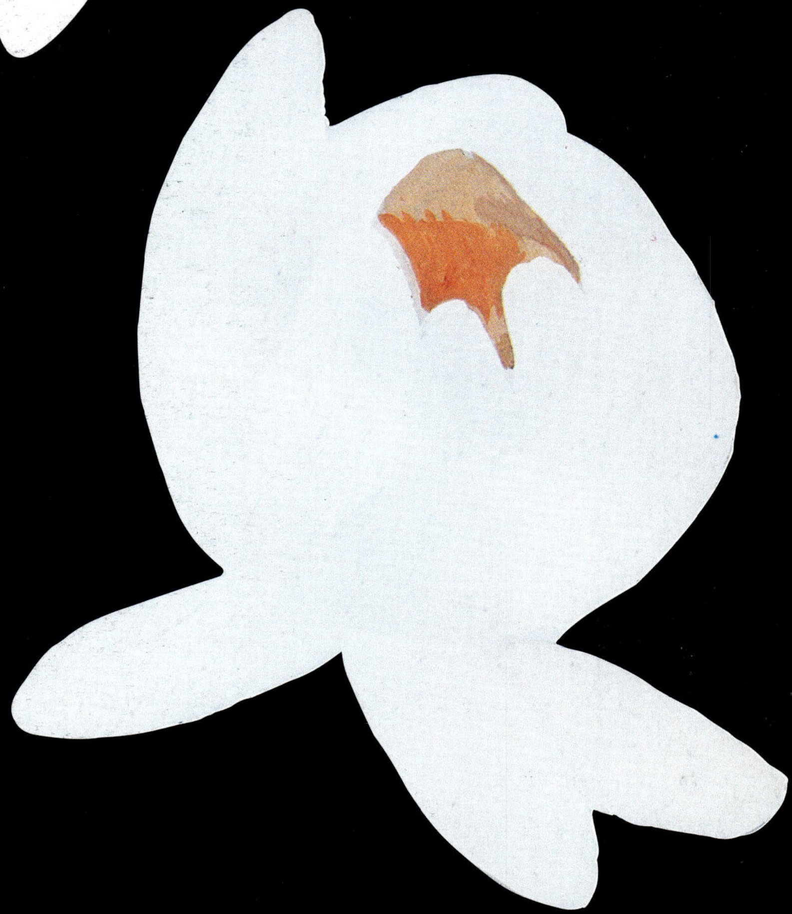

SARYAN

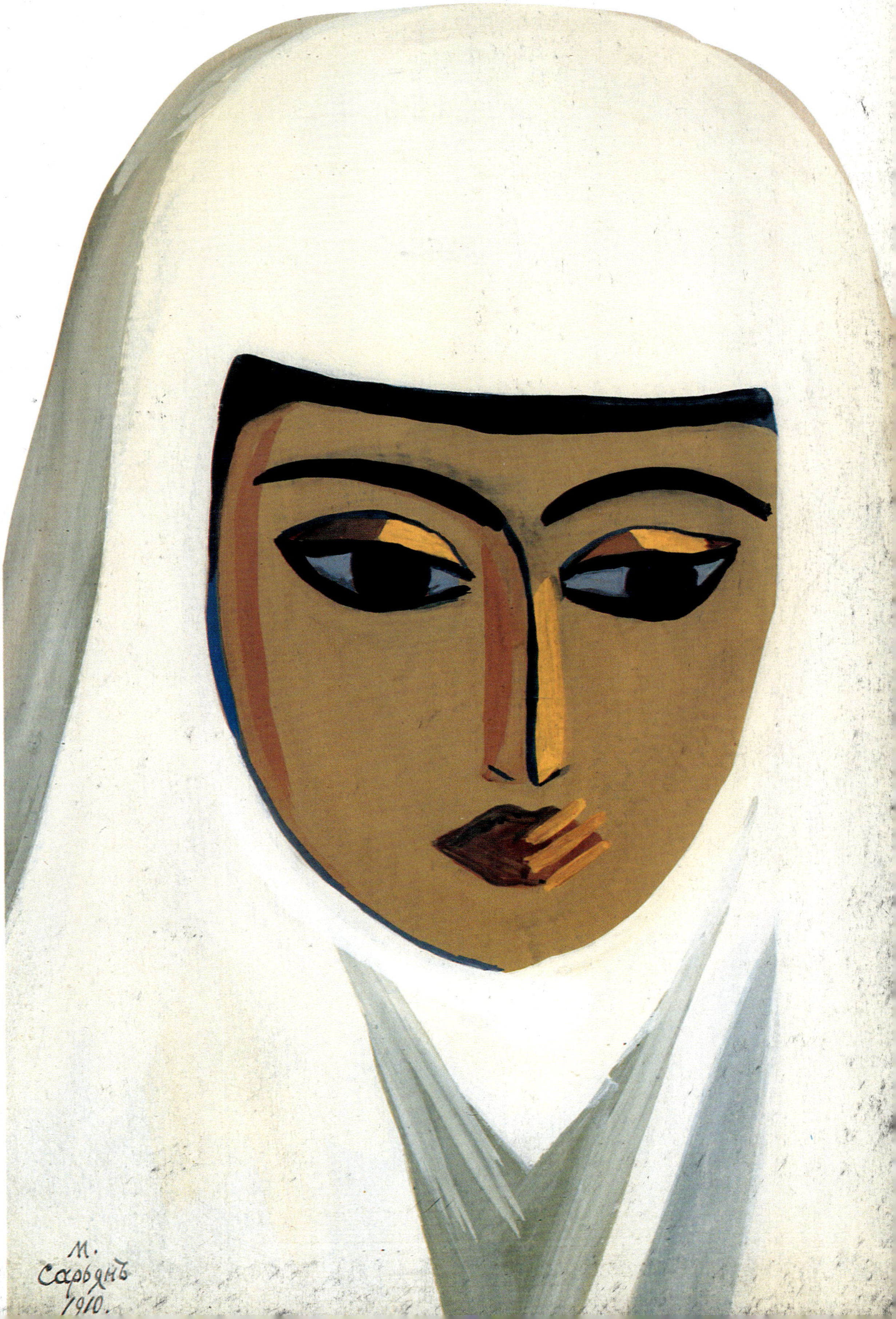

Publishing Director: *Paul André*
Designed by *Sergei Dyachenko*
Edited by *Tatyana Mordkova*
Translated from the Russian by *Paul Williams*
Typesetting: *Nina Sokolova*

Printed and bound in Europe
ISBN 1 85995 320 4

Martiros SARYAN

1880 - 1972

Vera Razdolskaya

Parkstone
PARKSTONE PRESS

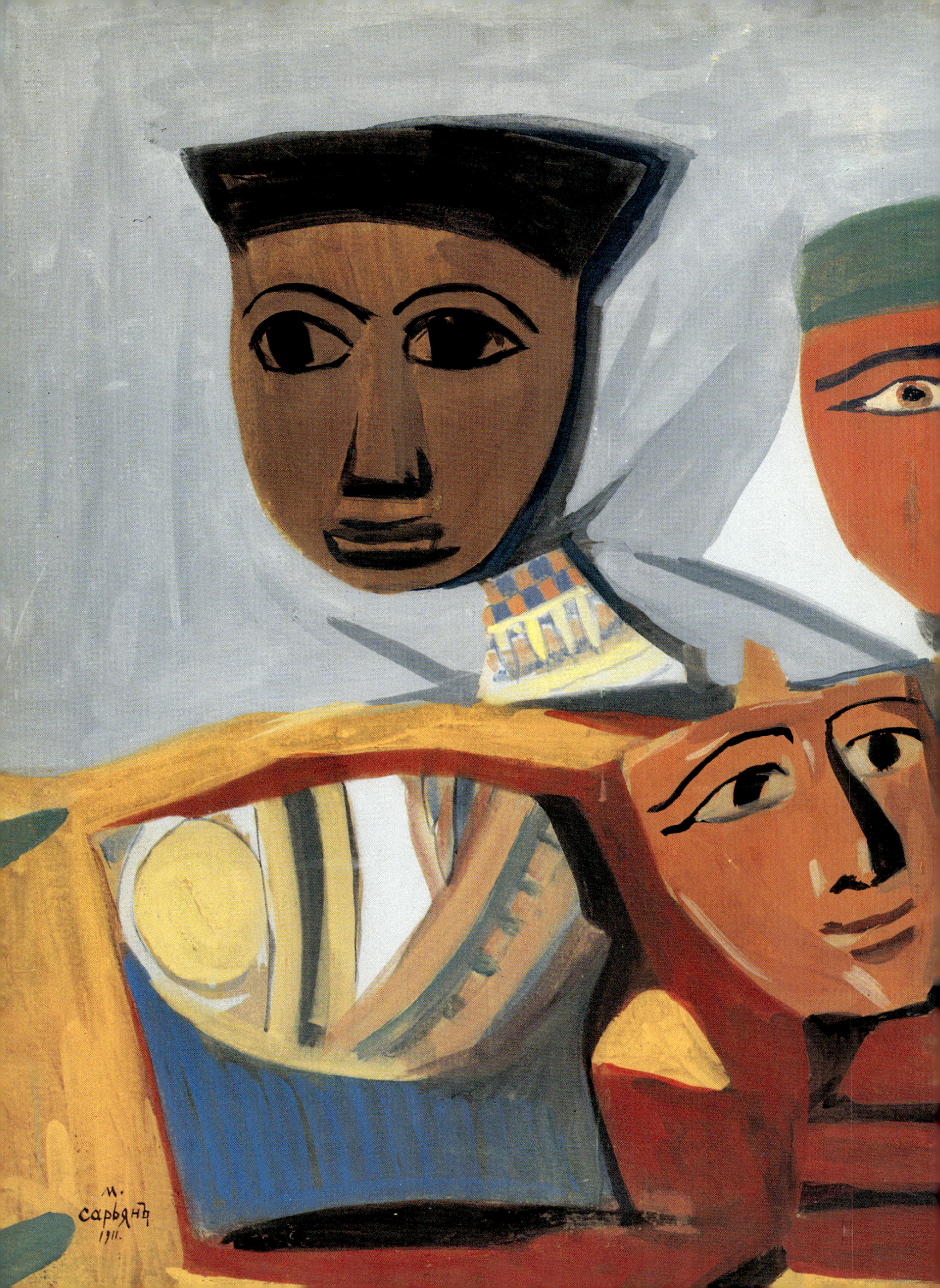
М.
Сарьянъ
1911.

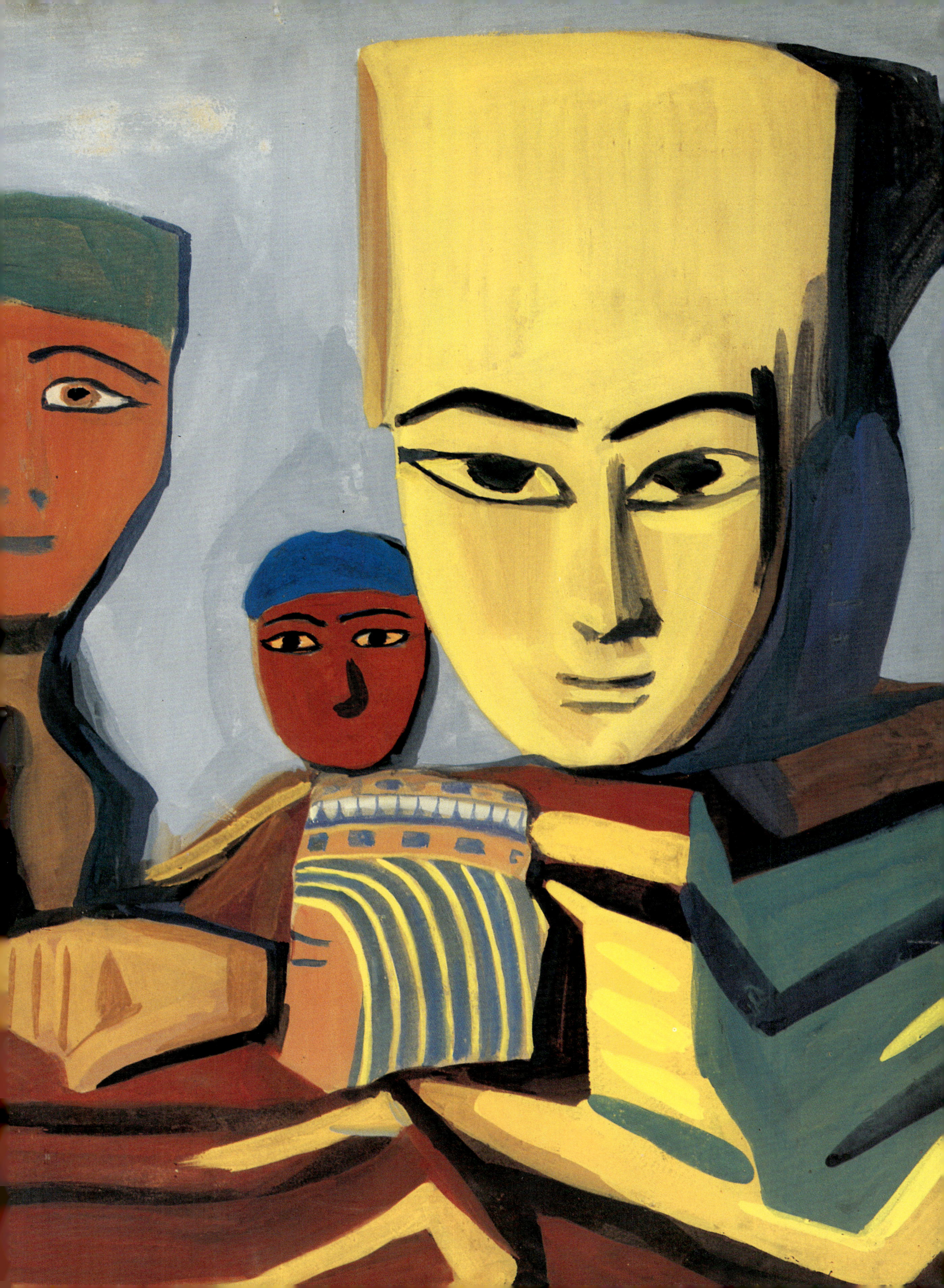

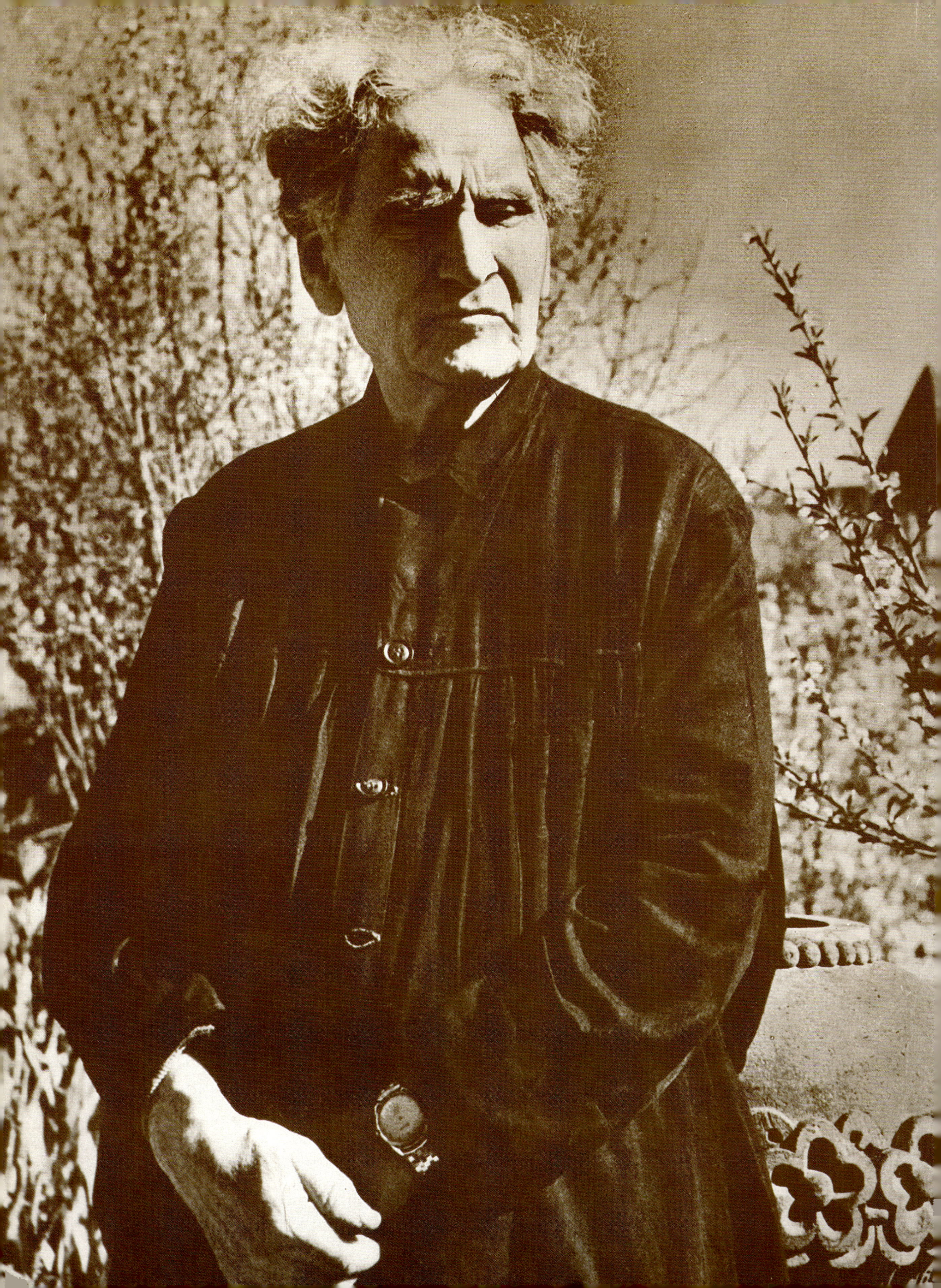

"Art should make a person happy, reinforce his life-affirming ideals, infuse him with strength to struggle with evil and resist death."[1] That sentiment expressed by Saryan might act as an epigram to his œuvre which evolved in a surprisingly harmonious manner, without dramatic contradictions or slumps. The trials and tribulations, of which there were no few in his life, remained the lot of Saryan the man and did not darken his view of the world. The output of Saryan the artist changed over the course of his life, but always retained a joyful intonation.

Saryan's art formed in a period of great uplift and intense aesthetic searchings in Russian art, with which it was closely bound up not only in the early years, but also at the time when he had become the head of the Armenian national school, its premier artist. At the same time, right at the beginning of his creative path, Saryan was able to draw on the experience of Western European, more precisely French, art and so he entered the artistic life of his day at the level of the most advanced tendencies in not only Russian, but European artistic culture. Armenia, and the East in general, Russia and the West all fed his work. And Saryan was able to fuse all this rich variety of impressions and traditions into an integral, profoundly individual style that invariably bore the stamp of his vivid, powerful personality.

← *Lotus*. 1911
Tempera on cardboard. 39 x 48 cm
Art Museum, Ivanovo

← *Persian Woman*. 1910
Tempera on cardboard. 36.5 x 33.5 cm
Martiros Saryan Museum, Yerevan

← *Egyptian Masks*. 1911
Tempera on cardboard. 70 x 82 cm
National Gallery of Armenia, Yerevan

"I do not know when the artist was born in me. Probably back in the days when I listened to my parents' tales about our distant Armenia and took delight in the many colours of butterflies and flowers."[2] In those simple words, spoken late in life, Saryan defined the most important impulses that fuelled his art over many decades. They were provided by his ancestral homeland, inaccessible, yet alluring for the moment, and the natural world. At first the latter was the landscape of the steppes around the Sea of Azov, where the artist spent his childhood.

Martiros Saryan. Photograph, 1959

The Karmravor Church near Ashtarak. Mid-7th century

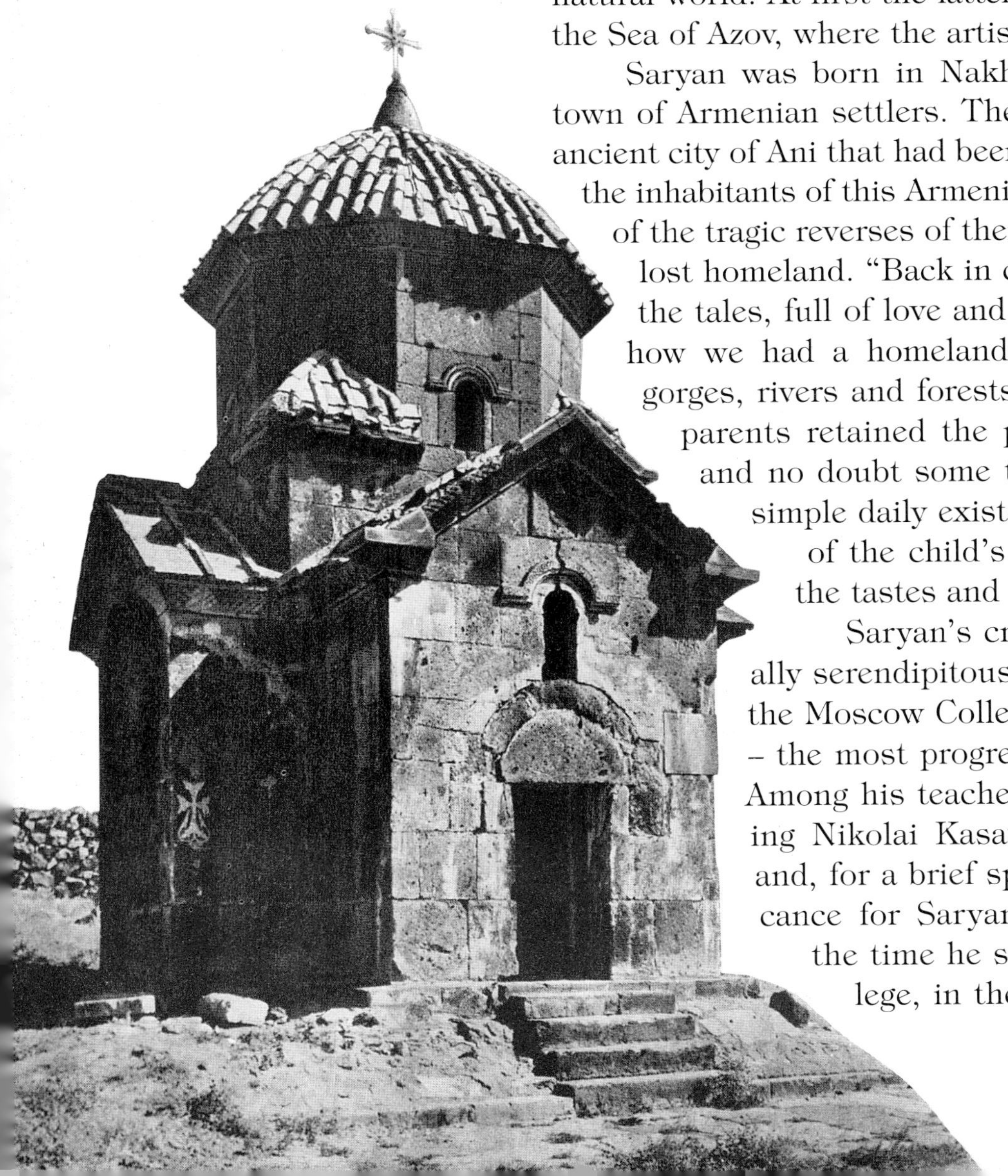

Saryan was born in Nakhichevan-on-Don (now part of Rostov), a town of Armenian settlers. Their distant forebears had long ago left the ancient city of Ani that had been devastated by wars and earthquakes, but the inhabitants of this Armenian colony on the Don retained the memory of the tragic reverses of their nation's fortunes and the bitterness of a lost homeland. "Back in childhood, while still very small, we heard the tales, full of love and longing, told by our father and mother of how we had a homeland – Armenia, tales of its mountains and gorges, rivers and forests, fertile fields and gardens."[3] The artist's parents retained the patriarchal way of life of their ancestors and no doubt some traditional items of folk art adorned their simple daily existence. All this was stored up in the depths of the child's consciousness and imperceptibly shaped the tastes and predilections of the future artist.

Saryan's creative life came together in an exceptionally serendipitous manner. At the age of sixteen he entered the Moscow College of Painting, Sculpture and Architecture – the most progressive school of art in Russia at the time. Among his teachers were many outstanding artists, including Nikolai Kasatkin, Abram Arkhipov, Leonid Pasternak and, for a brief spell, Isaac Levitan. Of tremendous significance for Saryan's professional evolution, however, was the time he spent, after having graduated from the college, in the portraiture studio run by Valentin Serov and Konstantin Korovin. Saryan derived a great deal from Serov "both in terms of the development of daring and in terms of visual form".[4] That perceptive observation by Kuzma Petrov-Vodkin also goes a long way towards explaining Saryan's early maturity. Lessons from Korovin, who was the greatest master of Russian Impressionism, undoubtedly encouraged the development of his gifts as a colourist and his mastery of painterly technique.

Of exceptional importance too was the creative spirit that reigned in the college and especially in the milieu in which Saryan directly circulated. As Pavel Kuznetsov recollected, at the college in the late 1890s "a group of artists began to form: Saryan, Sapunov, Utkin, Sudeikin, Petrov-Vodkin, Matveyev, Karev, Feofilaktov and myself",[5] a group united to a considerable extent by shared aesthetic interests and searchings.

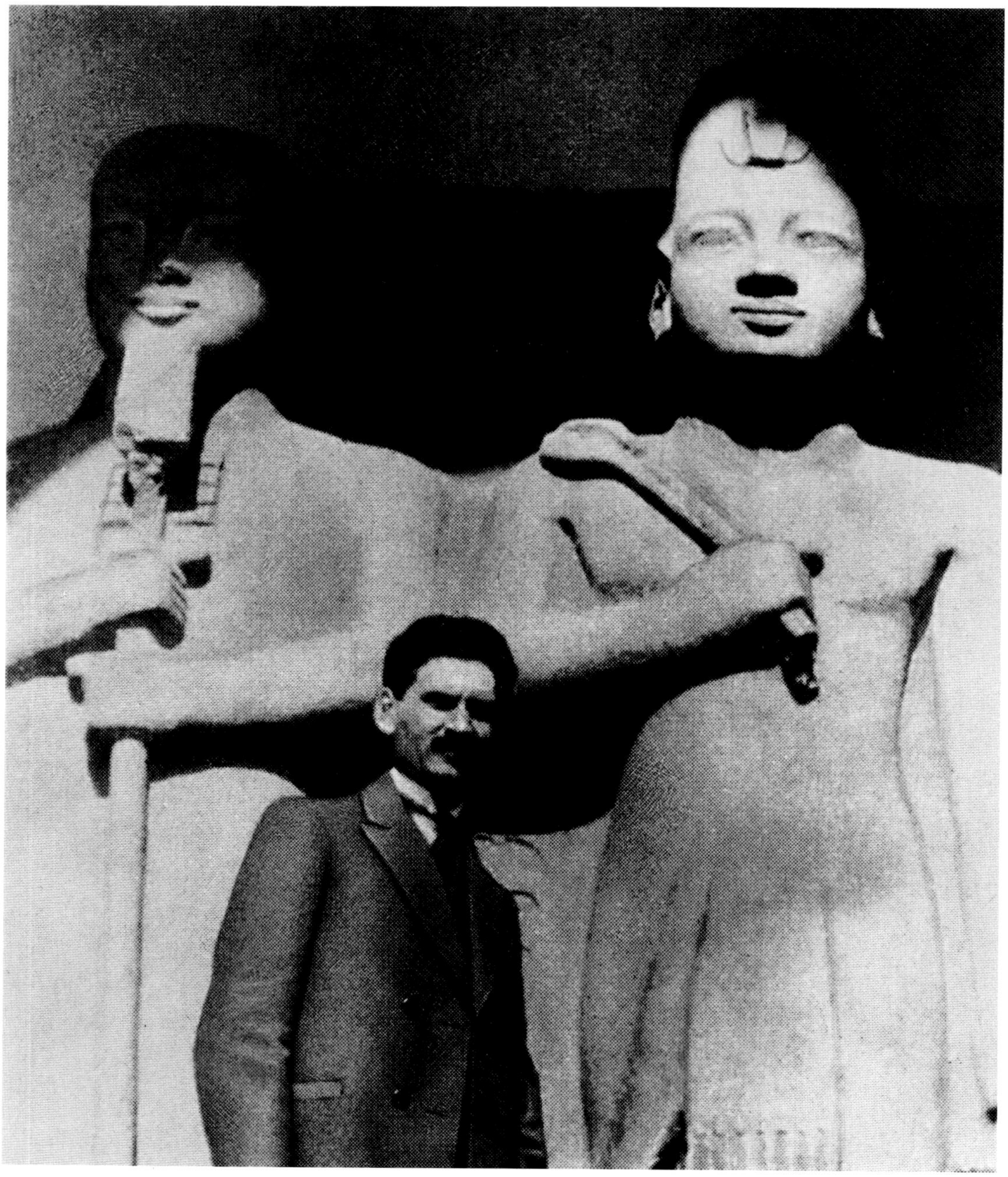

Martiros Saryan in Egypt.
Photograph, 1911

The core was formed by men from the Volga basin – Pavel Kuznetsov, Kuzma Petrov-Vodkin and Piotr Utkin, as well as the sculptor Andrei Matveyev.[6] They had nearly all studied in Saratov under Victor Borisov-Musatov, one of the most enchanting and subtle Russian painters. Thus, while still at college, Saryan came into contact indirectly with the work of an artist who had imported onto Russian soil profoundly, if selectively, perceived tendencies in contemporary French art developed by Puvis de Chavannes, the Impressionists and the Nabis.

Saryan's time in Moscow was of immense significance for him in a wider sense – he lived an exceptionally intense cultural life. The young provincial came into early contact with the most varied aspects of culture – literature, music, the theatre. He also, of course, strove to assimilate the experience of contemporary Russian painting. He was a constant visitor to the Tretyakov Gallery and attended numerous exhibitions that were heterogeneous in content but presented works by leading artists, including Saryan's immediate teachers, not to mention such masters as Vasily Surikov, Mikhail Vrubel and Borisov-Musatov.

"The Moscow school of painting, the artistic life of Moscow in that period and also French art helped us, the young artists, to really solve the many and varied tasks of the painter's art," Saryan later wrote.[7]

But he was also drawn to the south, to the Caucasus and above all to Armenia, the country where they spoke the language of his ancestors.

Saryan made his first journey to Armenia in 1901. Subsequently such trips became an almost annual event. Over a few years he made himself very familiar with the country, its flora and fauna, the life of its people and, of course, its art – not only works of architecture, but also folk art: carpets, stone carving and ceramics. He also undoubtedly had the opportunity to examine frescoes in the churches and miniatures. All of this left a deep impression in the artist's mind, later to become an extremely important element in his work. "My first journey to Transcaucasia, through Tiflis and Lori to Yerevan, was a staggering event for me," Saryan recalled. "It was, you might say, the thing that determined my subsequent course."[8] But the effect was far from immediate.

The artist's first works are highly immature in character and suggest a timid attachment to painting from life. They are primarily portraits, still very constrained in manner, wholly in the Russian realist tradition propagated by the Itinerants – depictions of the artist's mother and his female cousin Sandukht, and a 1902 watercolour self-portrait. These, like the first landscape studies painted in Armenia (for example, the 1902 *Makravank*, executed in a restrained greyish-green palette), do not yet reveal Saryan's individuality, although the landscapes especially testify to a growing professional ability.

Martiros Saryan. Photograph, 1908

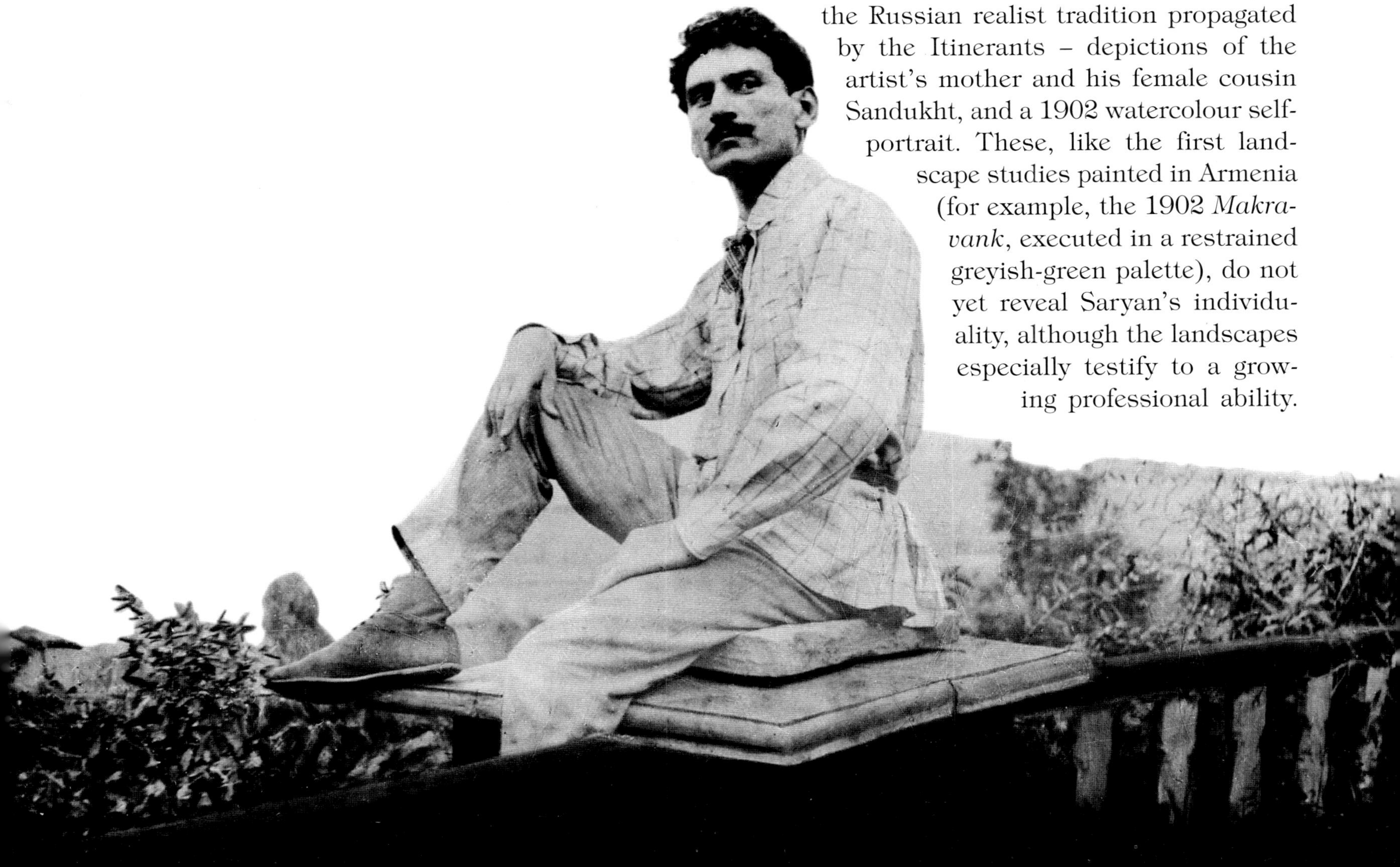

The artist sensed that "it was necessary to struggle within himself with the grey and cloying school and to find his own technique, not using someone else's."[9]

The breakthrough came quite unexpectedly at the turn of the year 1904. As Saryan wrote later: "After a series of studies painted from life, I wanted to tear myself away from that and immerse myself in the realm of the fantastic... What I saw was transformed. To do so I needed to achieve strong and vivid expressiveness."[10] And so those works were born that the artist himself called "fairy-tales", "dreams" or "reveries". For all their individuality and originality, they are undoubtedly connected with

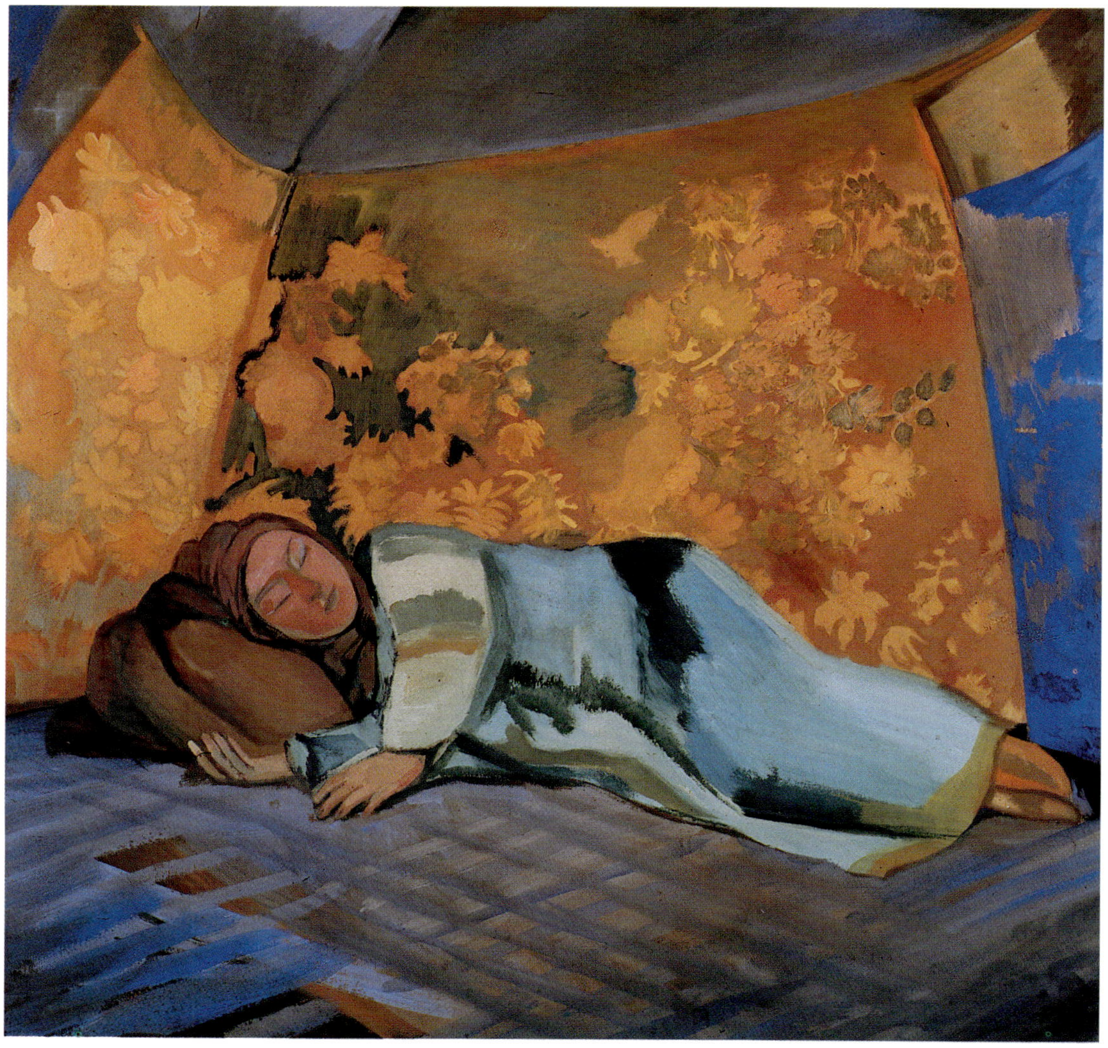

Pavel Kuznetsov. 1878–1968
Woman Sleeping in a Sheepfold.
1911
The Tretyakov Gallery, Moscow

one of the most important tendencies in contemporary Russian, and more generally European, art – Symbolism.

The Symbolist movement, so brilliant and complex in Russian literature, was a much narrower phenomenon in painting, although to a large extent it propagated the same view of the world, the same principles in life and art: a lurch towards the spiritual, a yearning to reject the boring or repulsive prosaic nature of the everyday, to get away from it into the world of dreams and reveries, a striving to root out the secret meaning of things, to penetrate the hidden essence of existence, to express the inexpressible, the obscure, the "unstated". In Russia Symbolism emerged somewhat later than in most other countries, but underwent a more accelerated course of development. At the turn of the century, and especially in the early 1900s, Russian society lived in the expectation of a radical renewal of life, which encouraged an atmosphere of searching for new paths in art as well. This atmosphere caught up young artists and the students of the College of Painting, Sculpture and Architecture. The leader of the group was Pavel Kuznetsov. His nearest associates were his close friends – Saryan and Piotr Utkin. The group also included Nikolai Sapunov, Sergei Sudeikin and the brothers Vasily and Nikolai Milioti. Up until 1904, although they participated in many exhibitions (Saryan had been presenting his works regularly beginning with college exhibitions from 1900), they were to a certain extent diluted in the mass of fellow-participants. They did,

Martiros Saryan with his fellow-students. Photograph, 1904

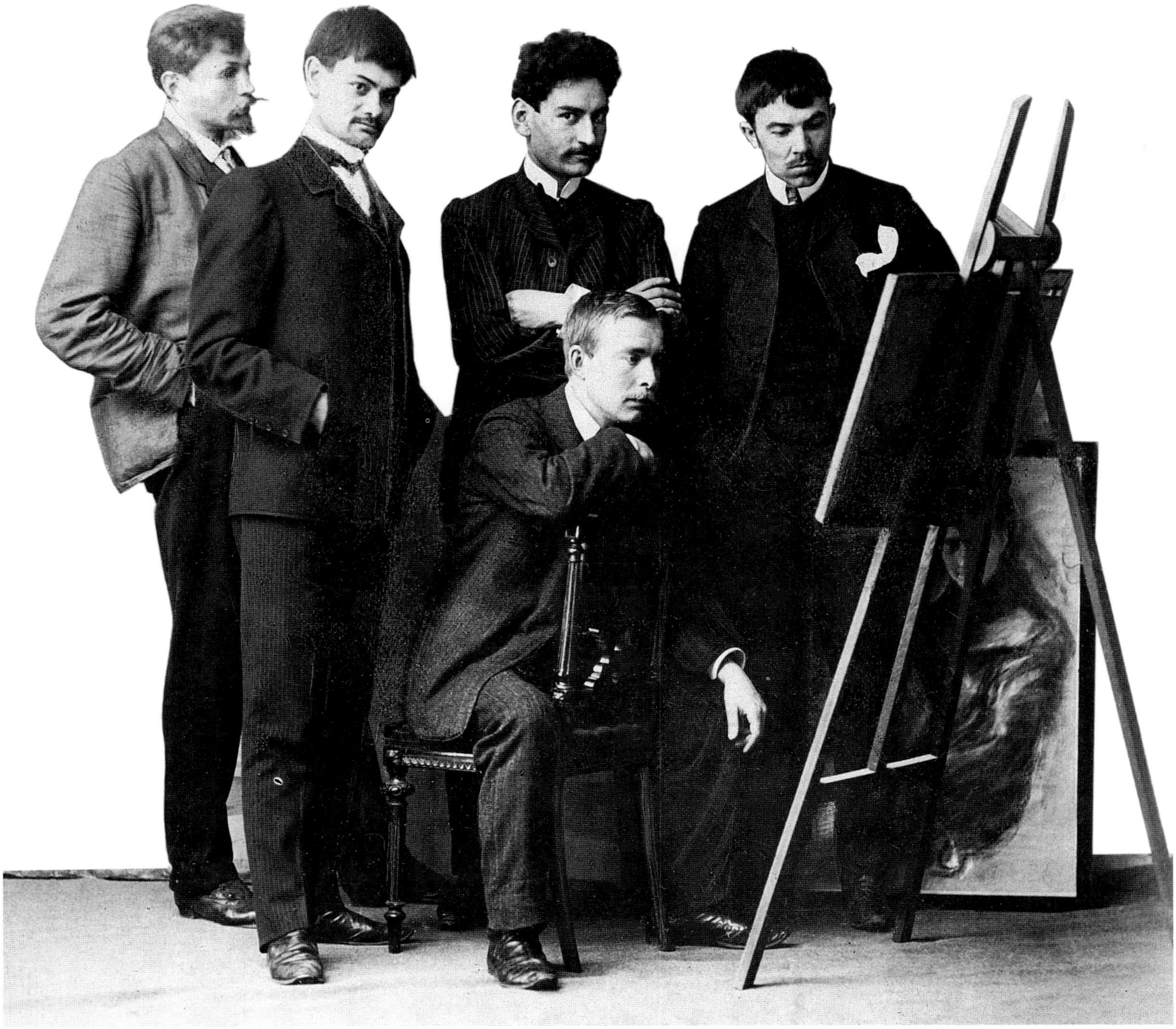

however, attract the attention (at first usually unfavourable) of the public and the critics. The first separate exhibition by some members of the group, entitled "The Scarlet Rose", was held in 1904, but since it took place in Saratov it did not evoke any great resonance. On the other hand, "The Blue Rose", the first great exhibition of young innovators, held in Moscow in 1907, presented the Symbolist movement with a fullness unseen before, or indeed since.[11]

The exhibition included a cycle entitled *Fairy-Tales and Dreams* that heralded a wholly new departure in Saryan's art. "What I depicted was, as it were, a combination of the real, since I did it under the impression

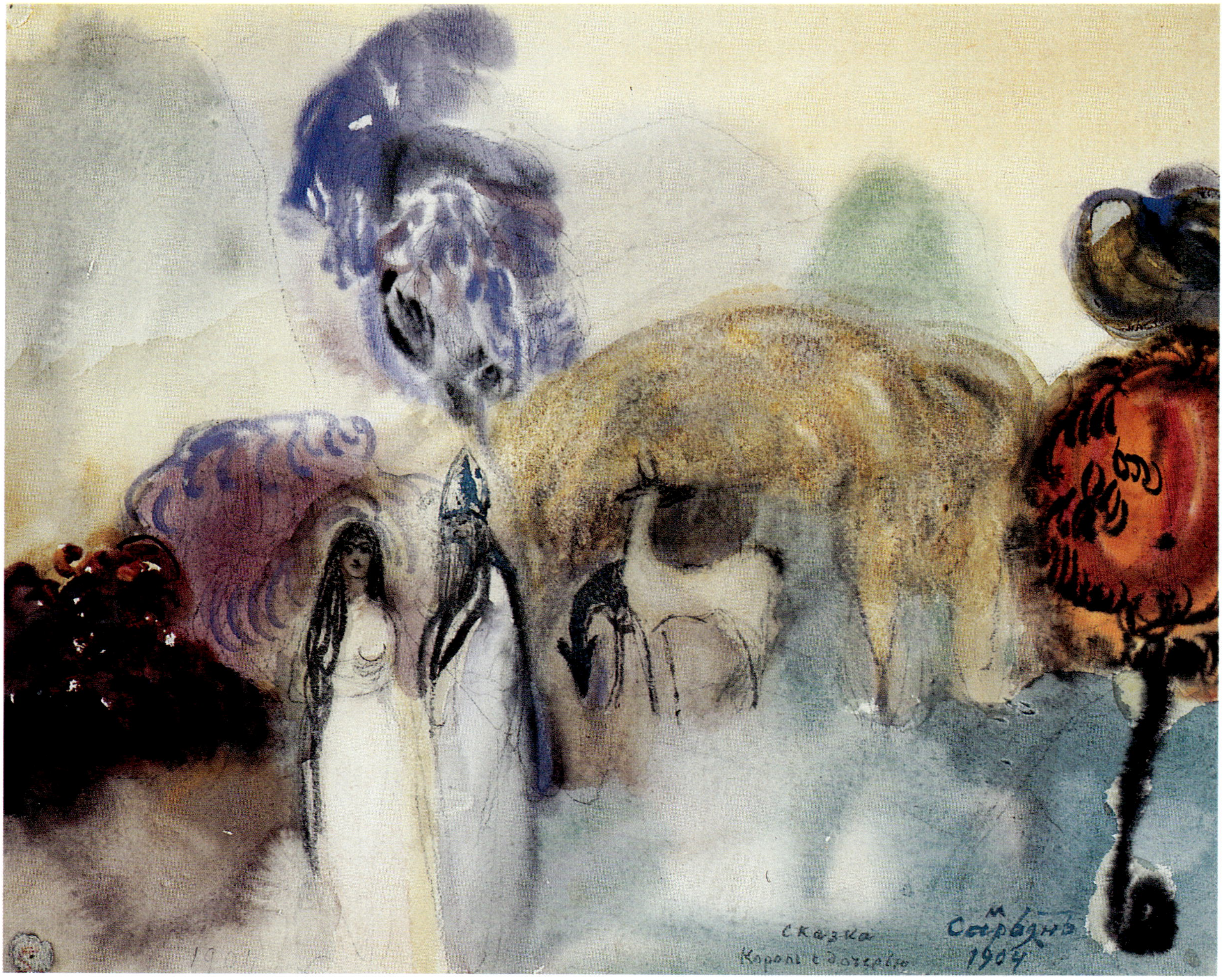

The King and His Daughter. A Fairy-Tale. 1904
Watercolour on paper. 25 x 34 cm
Martiros Saryan Museum, Yerevan

of what I had seen, with fantasy, because I synthesized, changed, intensified the range of colours so as to express my feelings more vividly," the artist would write later.[12]

The first, earlier part of this cycle – mainly watercolours of relatively small dimensions – dates from the years 1903–05. The second was created in 1906–07 in a wider variety of techniques, not only watercolour or gouache, but also tempera and occasionally oils. The two parts are linked by a certain unity of content and mood, although the second does display substantially new tendencies. The titles of these works are themselves indicative: *Eastern Fairy-Tale* (1903), *The King and His Daughter. A Fairy-Tale*, *By the Spring. A Fairy-Tale* and *A Fairy-Tale. By the Tree* (all three 1904), *The Lake of Fairies* (1905) and *Love. A Fairy-Tale* (1906). No matter what the subjects and the titles, however, landscape is a very important element in the image.

Saryan sees nature alive and animated, inhabited by strange, incorporeal personages, elegant animals and exotic birds. The poetic charm of these works lies not only in their inherent fabulous quality, but most importantly in the special melodic structure of their composition and in the beauty of their colour, here more intense, there translucent and tender, sparkling and iridescent with the subtlest shifts of tone and gradation. A moving, intriguing world of beauty, harmony and mystery opens before us.

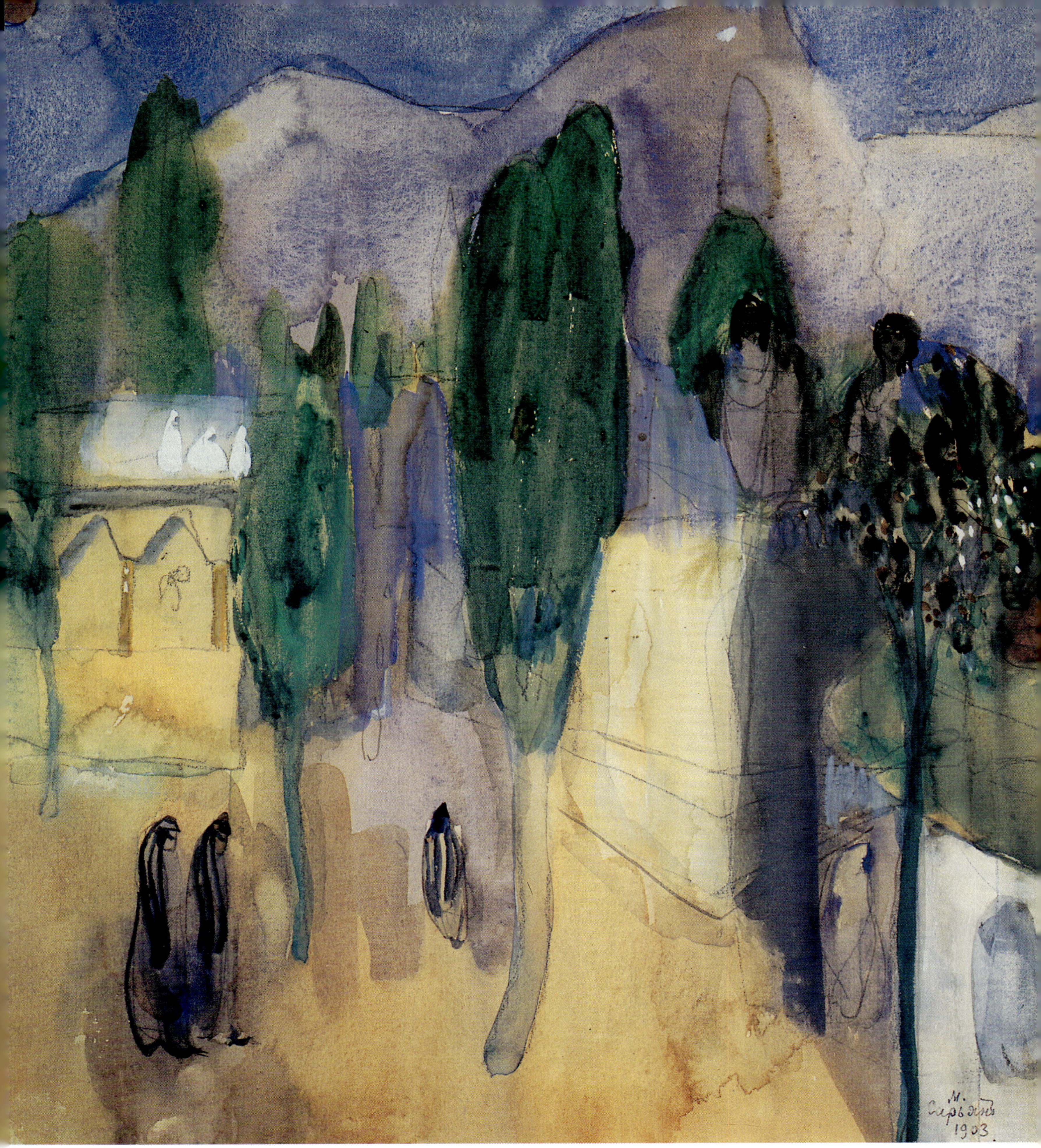

Eastern Fairy-Tale. 1903. Sketch
Watercolour on paper. 23 x 21 cm
Martiros Saryan Museum, Yerevan

→
A Fairy-Tale. By the Tree. 1904
Watercolour on paper. 23 x 33 cm
Martiros Saryan Museum, Yerevan

His poetical perception of the world, and also the very motifs of these works, link Saryan to certain other members of the Blue Rose group.[13] We can recall works by those artists who were closest to him at this time: Pavel Kuznetsov (*By the Fountain*, 1904–05; *Morning*, 1905) and Piotr Utkin (*Dream*). The dominant emotional intonation of many works by those artists – a mood of thoughtful contemplation, dreamy aloofness,

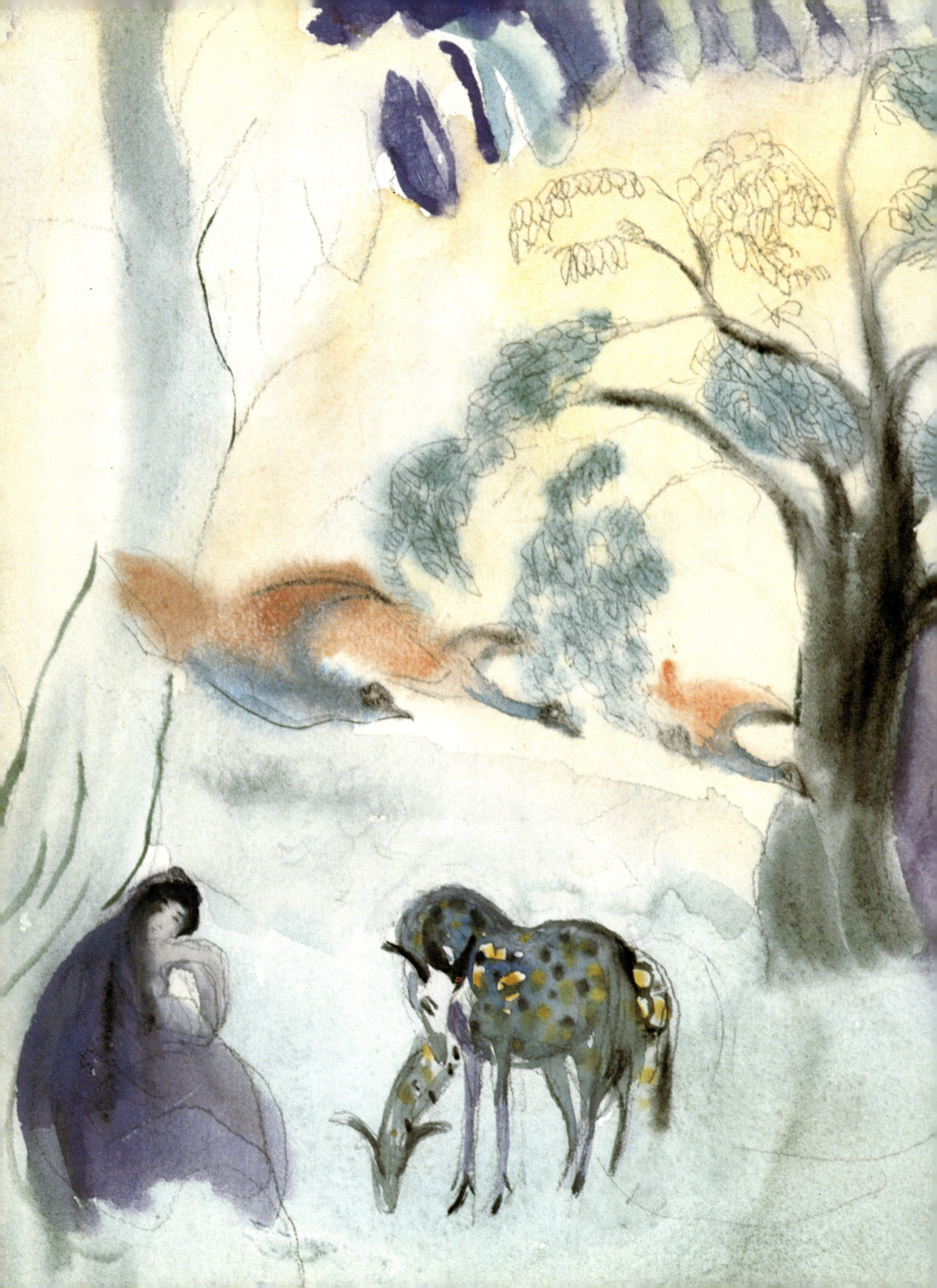

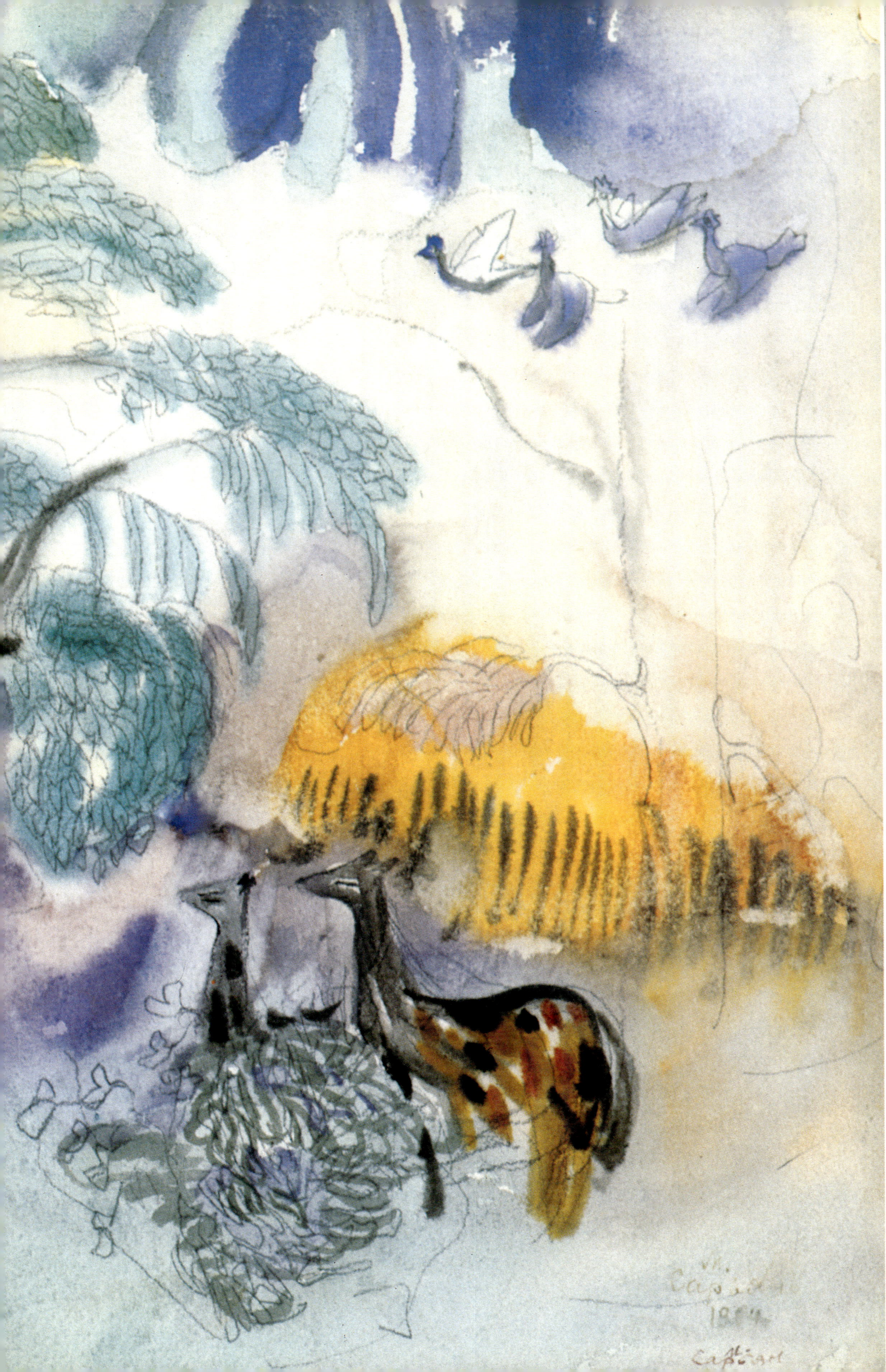

a particular predilection for depicting unstable states of mind, dreams – is akin but not identical to Saryan's. On the other hand, Saryan remained a stranger to the mysticism that permeated many works by the Symbolists, including those of his close friend Kuznetsov. Only on rare occasions does his pantheism take on a mystical aura, as for example in *The Comet* (1907), where the mysterious one-eyed figure seems to be the offspring of another world, or, even more powerfully, in the 1906 work *Man with*

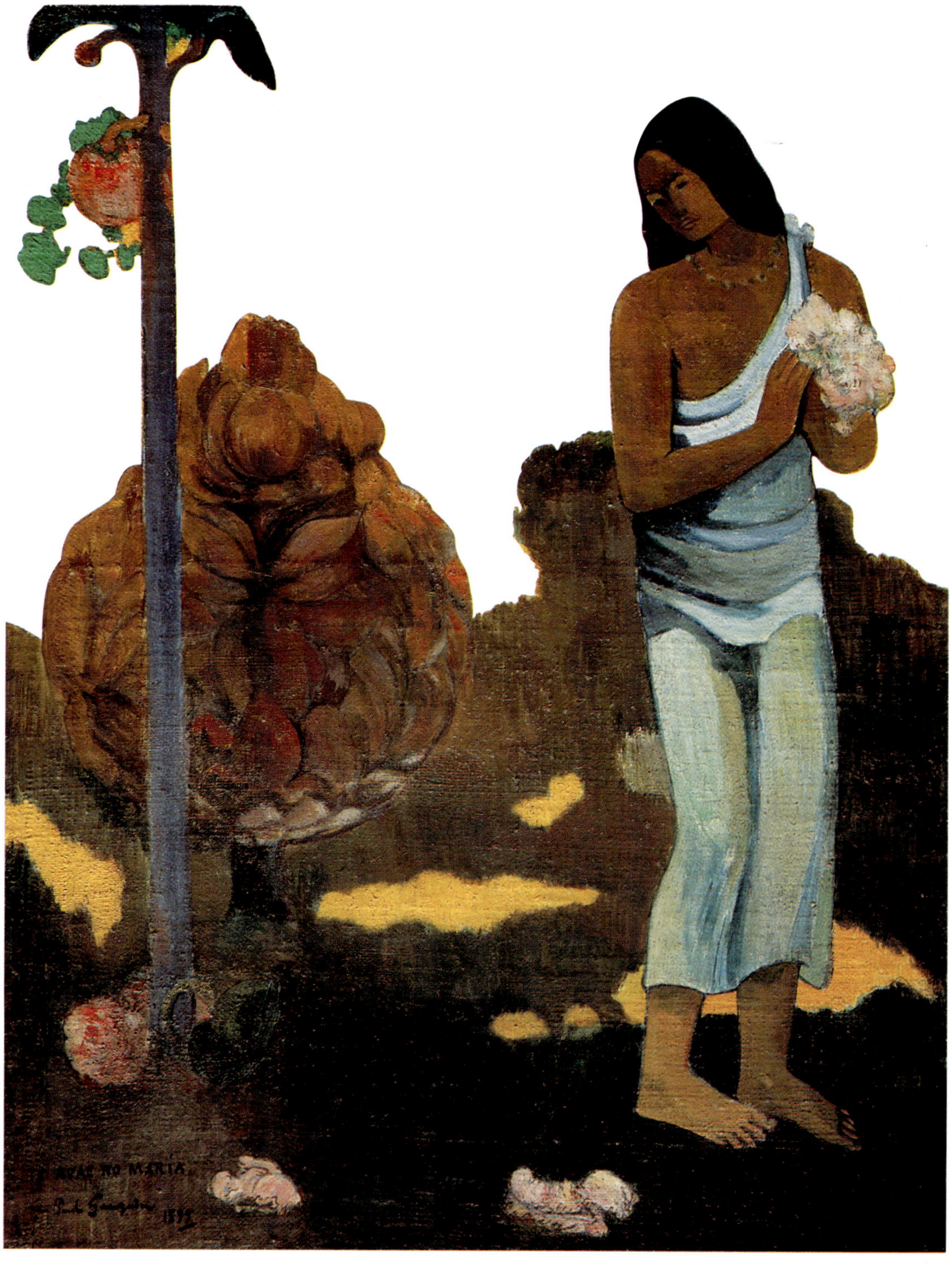

Paul Gauguin. 1848–1903
Woman Holding Flowers (The Month of Mary)
The Hermitage, St Petersburg

Gazelles, in which the spectral city seems to threaten to swallow the figures slowly making their way towards it. Works of this kind were, however, an exception for Saryan. This is not, though, the only facet of the distinctive originality that determined the artist's special place among the Blue Rose group and set him apart from them. His *Fairy-Tales and Dreams*, for all their visionary fantastic quality and ghost-like translucency of colour, express more distinctly the natural aspect; they are more suffused with the "juices of the earth".

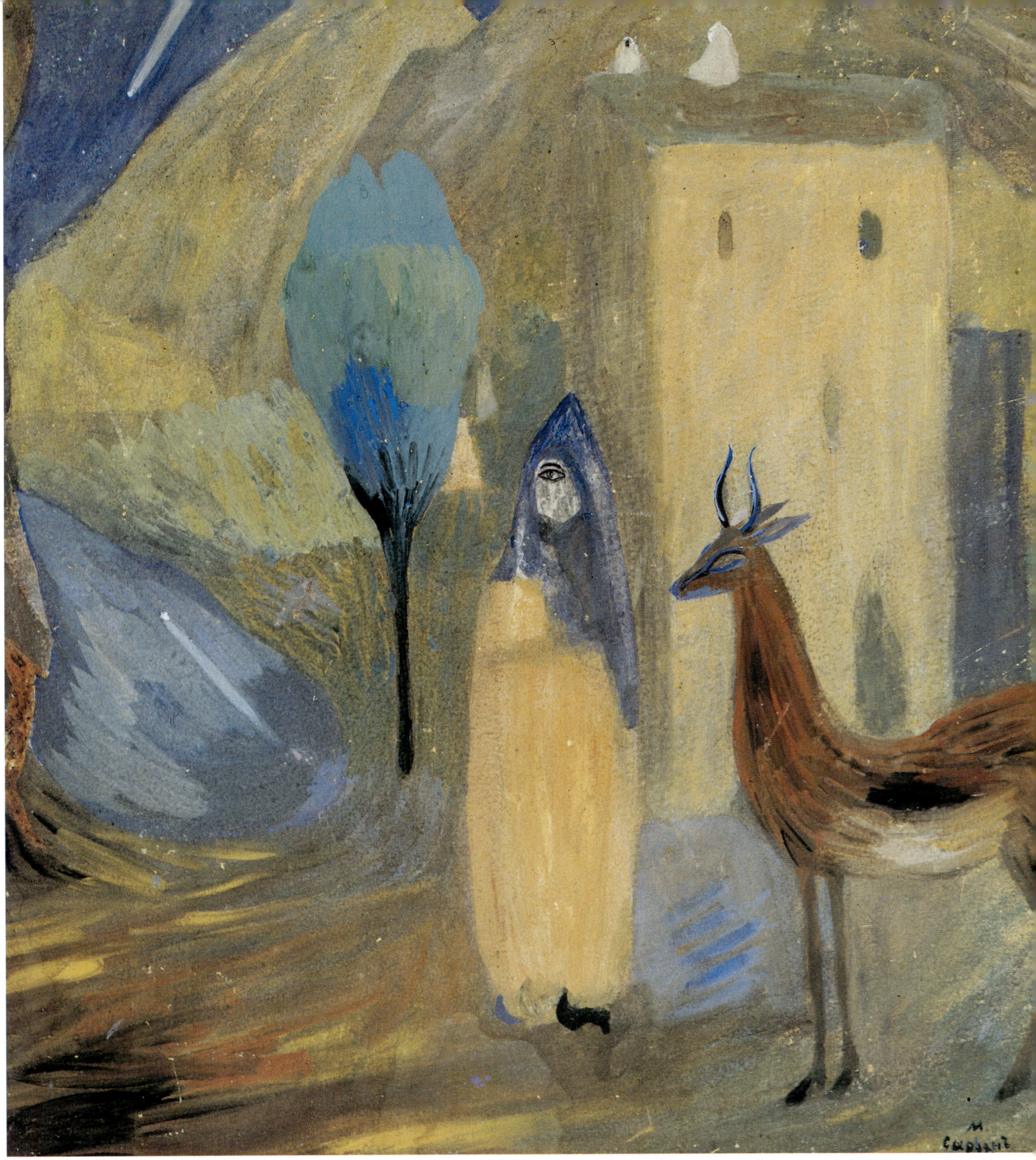

The Comet. 1907
Tempera on canvas. 36 x 30.5 cm
L. Saryan collection, Yerevan

Besides, even in these early works we can feel the artist's perception of the East as a dream. "Saryan's East did not begin with nature, but with the fairy-tale. It is the East reconstructed by Europeans with the aid of Scheherazade."[14] This apt definition by Dmitry Sarabyanov has often been quoted. It is difficult to disagree with it, nonetheless we should not forget that when working on his *Fairy-Tales and Dreams* Saryan repeatedly visited Armenia, and each time he must have discovered something new for himself in its nature and art. It is not simply that the artist introduced

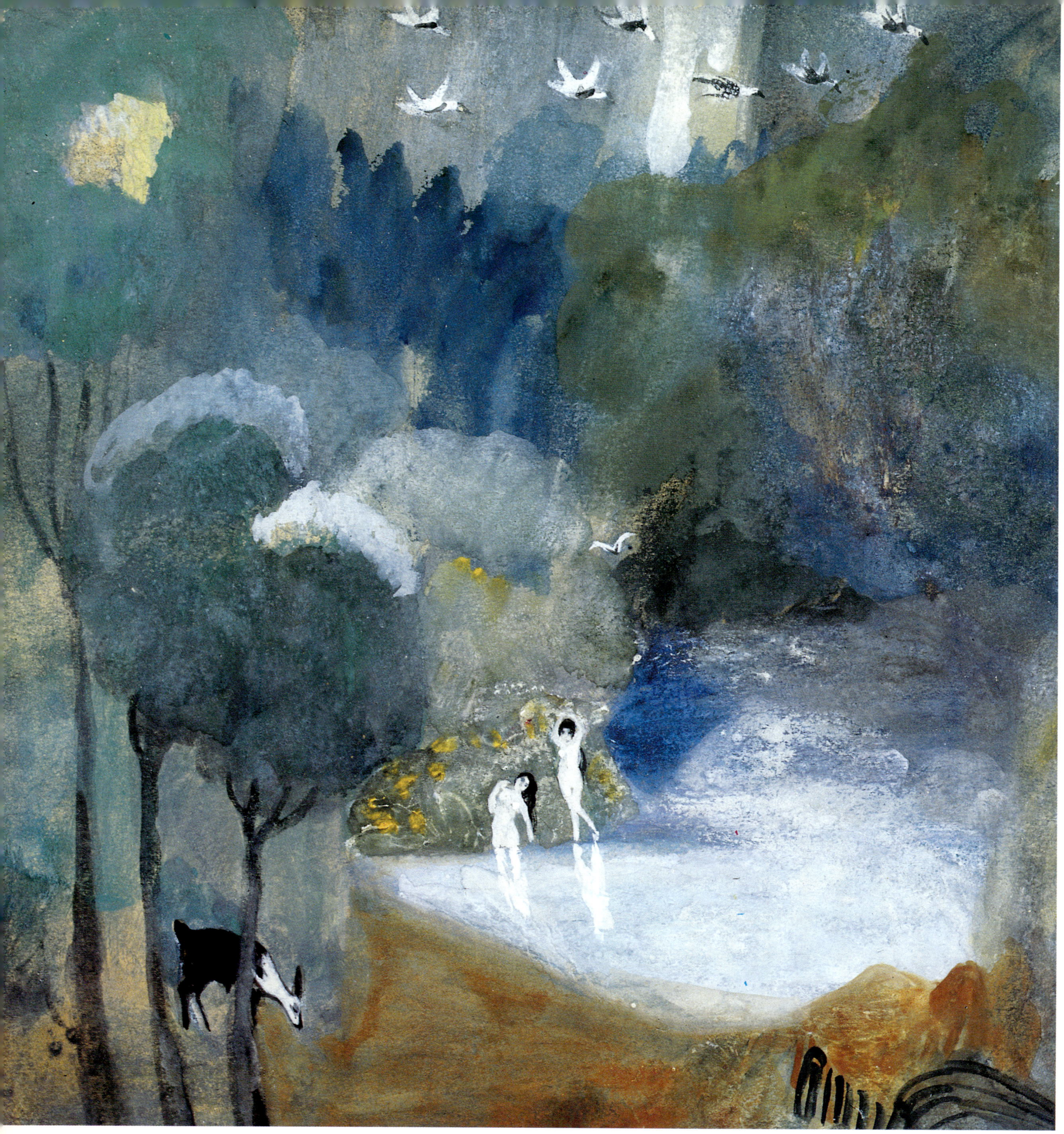

real-life motifs into his fabulous compositions – the outline of a building reminiscent of Armenian monuments, or reminiscences of the Armenian countryside, something that is reflected in the titles of the works themselves (for example, *At the Foot of Mount Ararat*, *Mountains in Bloom. In the Gorge of Akhurian*). The chromatic structure of the *Fairy-Tales and Dreams* with its combinations of golden browns, greens and pale blues recalls, perhaps subconsciously, the colour-schemes of Armenian, and more widely Oriental, carpets or miniatures. "Enamoured of the beauty of the East, I strove after a colourful, flowery manner of painting," Saryan later explained.[15]

The Lake of Fairies. 1905
Gouache on paper. 24.5 x 24.5 cm
The Tretyakov Gallery, Moscow

Of course, the evolution of Saryan's conceptions about colour was also affected by the experience of Russian art, in the present instance above all probably the refined, "musical" structure of Borisov-Musatov's works, and, undoubtedly, by his acquaintance with contemporary French painting, whose significance was underlined on many occasions by the artist himself. Originally this acquaintance was indirect – through his teachers Serov, Korovin and, once again, Borisov-Musatov. Then, from

Piotr Utkin. 1877–1934
Triumph in the Sky. 1907
Perished

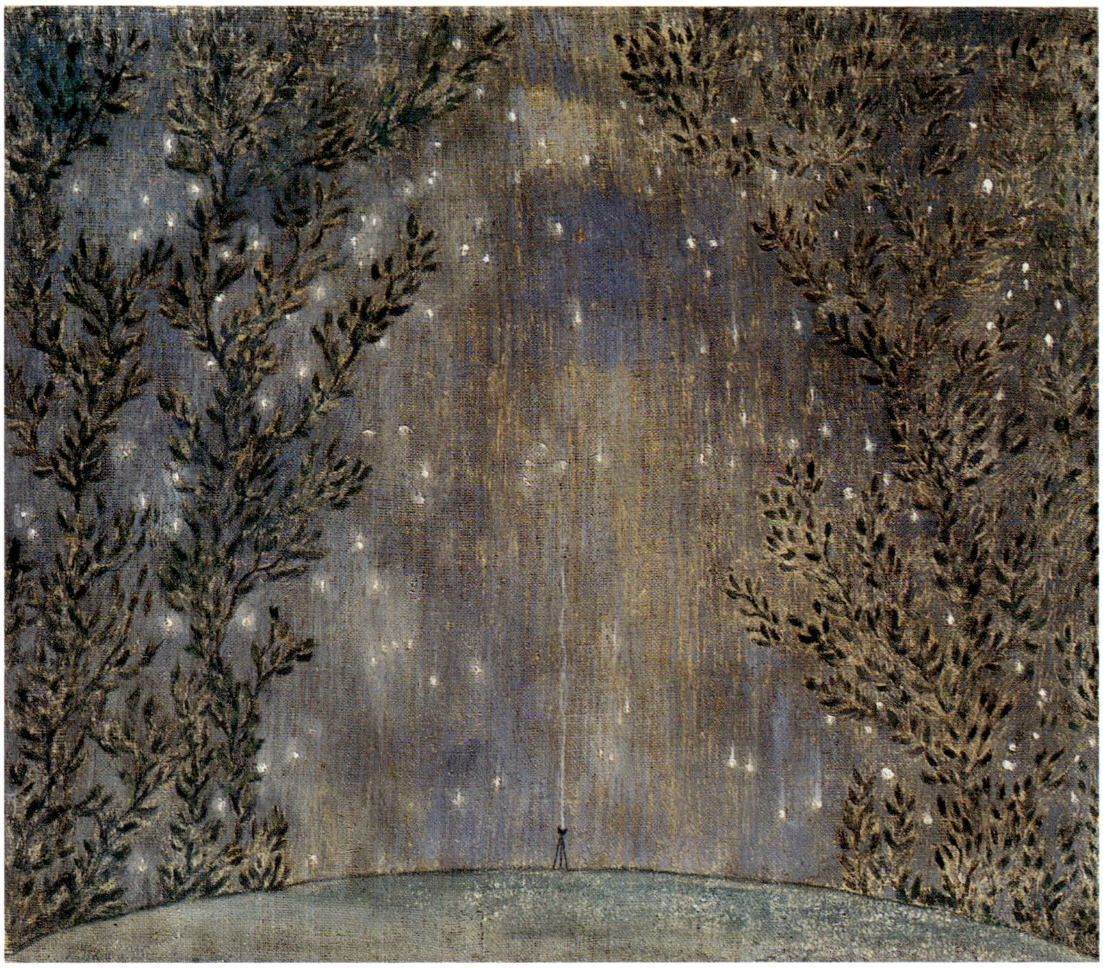

Piotr Utkin. Photograph, 1910s

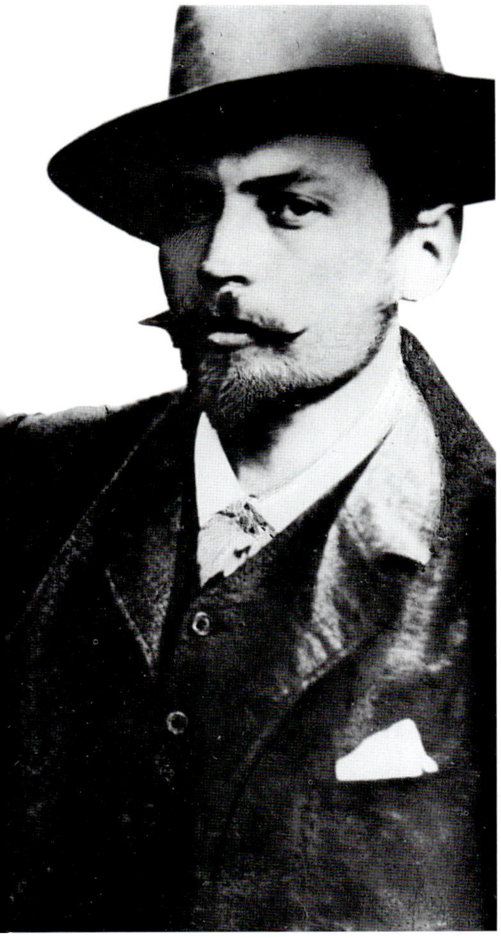

1906–07 onwards, Russian artists were given the opportunity to make direct contact with French painting through Ivan Shchukin's splendid and constantly expanding collection that included a wide range of works by the Impressionists and Post-Impressionists and then those by contemporary artists, above all Matisse. It would be difficult to overestimate too the significance of the joint exhibitions of Russian and French artists organized by the magazine *The Golden Fleece* [*Zolotoye Runo*] in 1908 and 1909. "Acquaintance with the French inspired me even more and persuaded me of the correctness of my course and my views on painting," Saryan said.[16] In this context he stressed the significance of Impressionism, pronouncing it "a great step in the development of world art", without, however, specifying which of the French Impressionists had played a special role in the formation of his own painterly vision. It is, moreover, completely obvious that the artist's evolution was undoubtedly more closely linked with later developments in French art – Post-Impressionism and especially the work of Gauguin.

Saryan's drawing on Gauguin's experience coincided with new, latent tendencies that were ripening in his art. They can first be traced in the thematic motifs and images of the *Fairy-Tales and Dreams*. The best of them were created in 1905–07. Many of them, as before, embody the artist's poetic reveries of "divine" nature "unmade by human hand". But Saryan was too attached to the soil, he was too fond of the sun to remain long a captive of spectral dreams and mirage images. The year 1905, when the watercolours *The Lake of Fairies* and *Mountains in Bloom. In the Gorge of Akhurian* were produced, also saw the creation of the small painting *Charms of the Sun*. It features the same figures noiselessly gliding in long robes, the same trees with round crowns, but the motif is of a completely different character, so too is the emotional intonation. Entirely different from the majority of the *Fairy-Tales and Dreams* cycle is the manner of painting with a more abstract understanding of shape. Of course, the change of technique was also different – Saryan decided on tempera which allows the painter to cover large areas in a single opaque tone, but the choice of technique was obviously dictated by new painterly goals. It was not by chance that tempera became the artist's preferred medium for the next decade. The most striking thing about this painting, however, is the colour scheme. It seems to be on fire with the resonant golden orange colour of the houses, ground and sky, contrasting with the deep green of the trees. Colour here engenders a sense of sunlight and joy, distinct from the more restrained, refined melancholy that marks most of the *Fairy-Tales and Dreams* cycle. This tempera is called *Charms of the Sun*, but the charms are quite earthly and cheerful. Besides this, both the nature of the motif presented and, especially, the intensity of light in the colour have a distinctly Eastern character, more pronounced than in many other works of this period and thus it anticipates the artist's subsequent development. The year 1907 already provided a number of milestones on that course, such as *Beneath the Trees*, or *In the Caucasus. Tiflis* – not a work from life, but one that synthesizes the unique features of the Georgian city, or *Evening in the Mountains*, an even bolder work in terms of its conception of colour and space.

In making this move, the artist drew not so much on the experience of the Impressionists (it had been mastered and taken into account, but never "came to the surface" in Saryan's style even in the preceding years), as on the principles of plasticity and colour expounded by Gauguin. His example undoubtedly helped Saryan in his efforts to simplify and generalize shape, line and colour. Like Gauguin he allotted prime significance to the last and his understanding of colour was in many ways close to the celebrated thesis of the French artist: "Pure colour... And for its sake everything should be sacrificed."[17] Saryan expressed similar thoughts on the significance of colour on several occasions. Gauguin's experience helped him to attain the level of the boldest discoveries in painting and the treatment of shape, blending that experience, as Maximilian Voloshin correctly observed, with the simple, synthetic forms of Eastern art.

The further course taken by Saryan's style was already revealed in some other works from that same year, 1907 – the mysterious and intriguing *Cloth Seller* and, particularly, the painting *By the Pomegranate Tree*. The contrasts of colour reach such height of tension and intensiveness that there is every cause to speak of the artist's Fauvism.

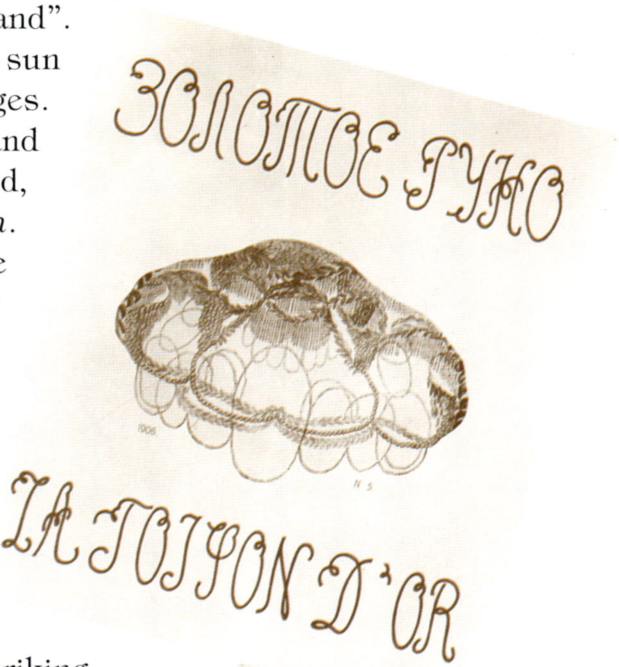

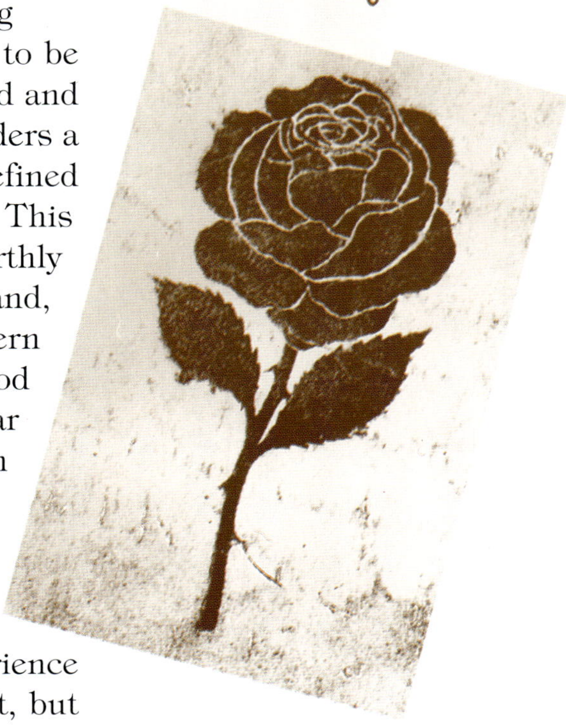

Pavel Kuznetsov. 1878–1968
Cover for *The Golden Fleece* magazine
(St Petersburg, 1906, No 5)

Nikolai Sapunov. 1880–1912
Cover for the catalogue of the Blue Rose
exhibition (Moscow, 1907)

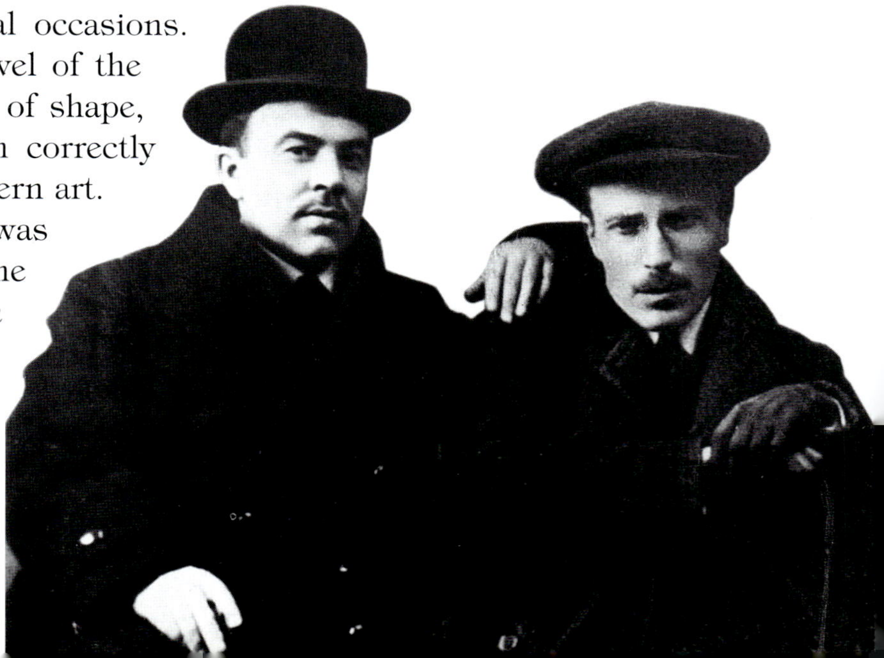

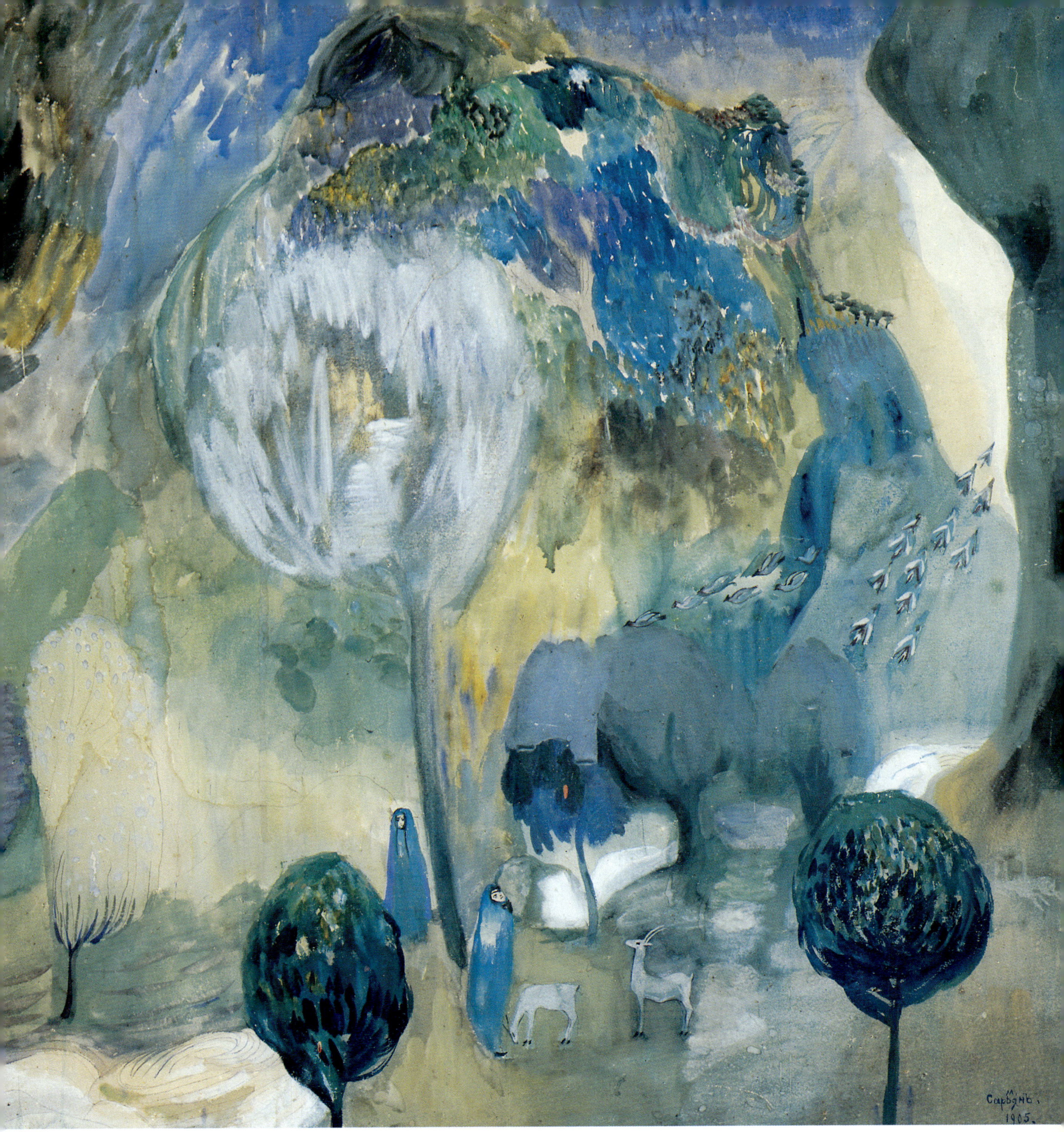

Mountains in Bloom.
In the Gorge of Akhurian. 1905
Watercolour on paper. 67 x 66 cm
Martiros Saryan Museum, Yerevan

Pavel Kuznetsov and Alexander Matveyev. Photograph, 1910s

Also connected to a certain degree with Fauvism is the technique of separate, elongated brushstrokes that imbue the whole painterly fabric with motion in different directions.

The mention of Saryan's Fauvism inevitably raises the question of his ties with parallel tendencies in French art, and above all with Matisse. It is very important to note that Saryan turned to a Fauvist brilliance of colour before he became acquainted at first hand with the latest works by Matisse, Derain or Vlaminck. In 1905, when the artist was creating

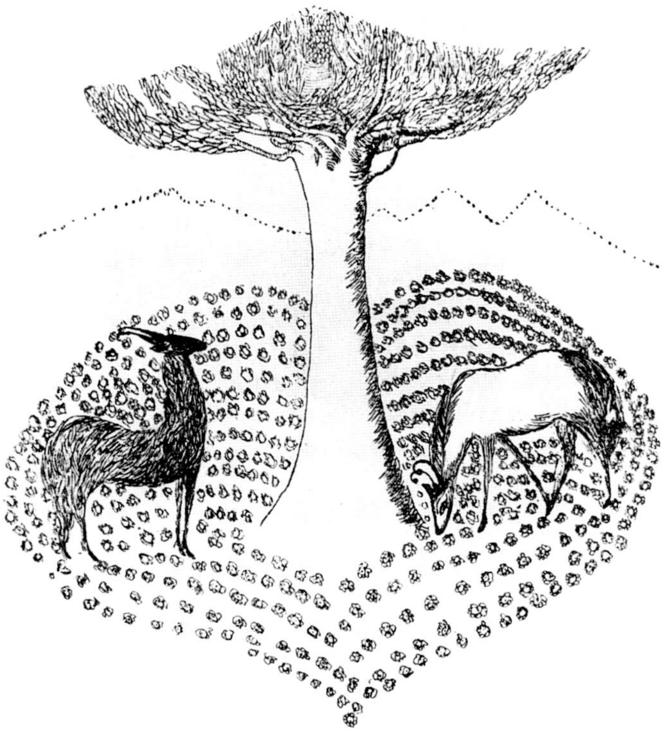

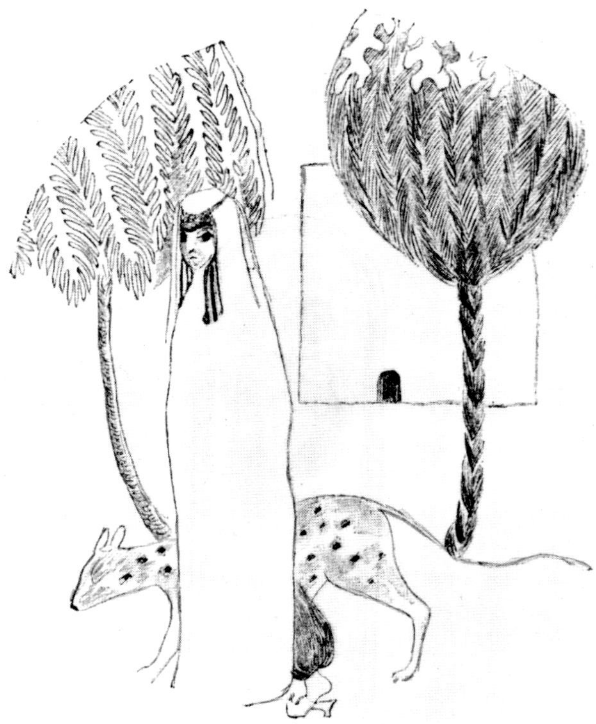

Charms of the Sun, he could not have known them. Fauvism made itself properly felt as a force in French art only at the Salon d'Automne that year, and its spread beyond the borders of France was still something for the future (albeit the near future). Evidently in this instance we should rather be talking about kindred stages of development. Of course common sources were of strong significance: Fauvism in all its manifestations was a development of the painterly conceptions of Cézanne, Van Gogh, and, especially, Gauguin. One and the same impulse gave rise to similar stylistic phenomena. It is interesting that the epithet "wild" (*fauve*), which became an established term with regard to the French artists, was also employed by hostile critics to several works by Saryan.[18]

His Fauvism, however, has a pronouncedly Eastern overtone. Above all the traditions of Armenian art clearly show through in it, especially those of the miniature, which was characterized by resonant colour and a flat simplification of shape, and also carpets with their saturated dyes and astonishing wealth of ornamental and rhythmic motifs. The pomegranate tree in the painting mentioned above seems to be an analogue in its own way to the floral ornament and also to the bright plumage of the birds (in the present instance a peacock) that adorned mediaeval manuscripts.[19] And indeed the personages depicted reveal emphatically Eastern features.

The style of *By the Pomegranate Tree* – colourful, decorative, yet at the same time saturated with emotional expression – came to full fruition in the works of 1908 that completed the Symbolist period in Saryan's career, but by now on an entirely new level regarding the treatment of shape. *By the Sea. A Sphinx* is a tremendous landscape: sea and the earth rising in mountainous ridges to a blue sky – the primary elements of nature, beautiful and mysterious, that is personified in the image of a sphinx with a female face. The tempera work *By the Well. A Hot Day* contains no overtly fantastic motifs, but here too nature appears just as fabulously beautiful and majestic, filled with a sense of the tense rhythm of life. The main compositional element is a mighty tree spreading a deep blue

Gazelles by a Tree. 1907
Indian ink on paper
Location unknown
The drawing was made for *The Golden Fleece* magazine

Girl. Snow Leopard and Trees. 1907
Indian ink on paper
Location unknown
The drawing was made for *The Golden Fleece* magazine

Love. A Fairy-Tale. 1906
Watercolour on paper. 24 x 17 cm
K. Saryan collection, Yerevan

→
Charms of the Sun. 1905
Tempera on cardboard. 18.5 x 31.5 cm
Museum of Fine Arts, Stavropol

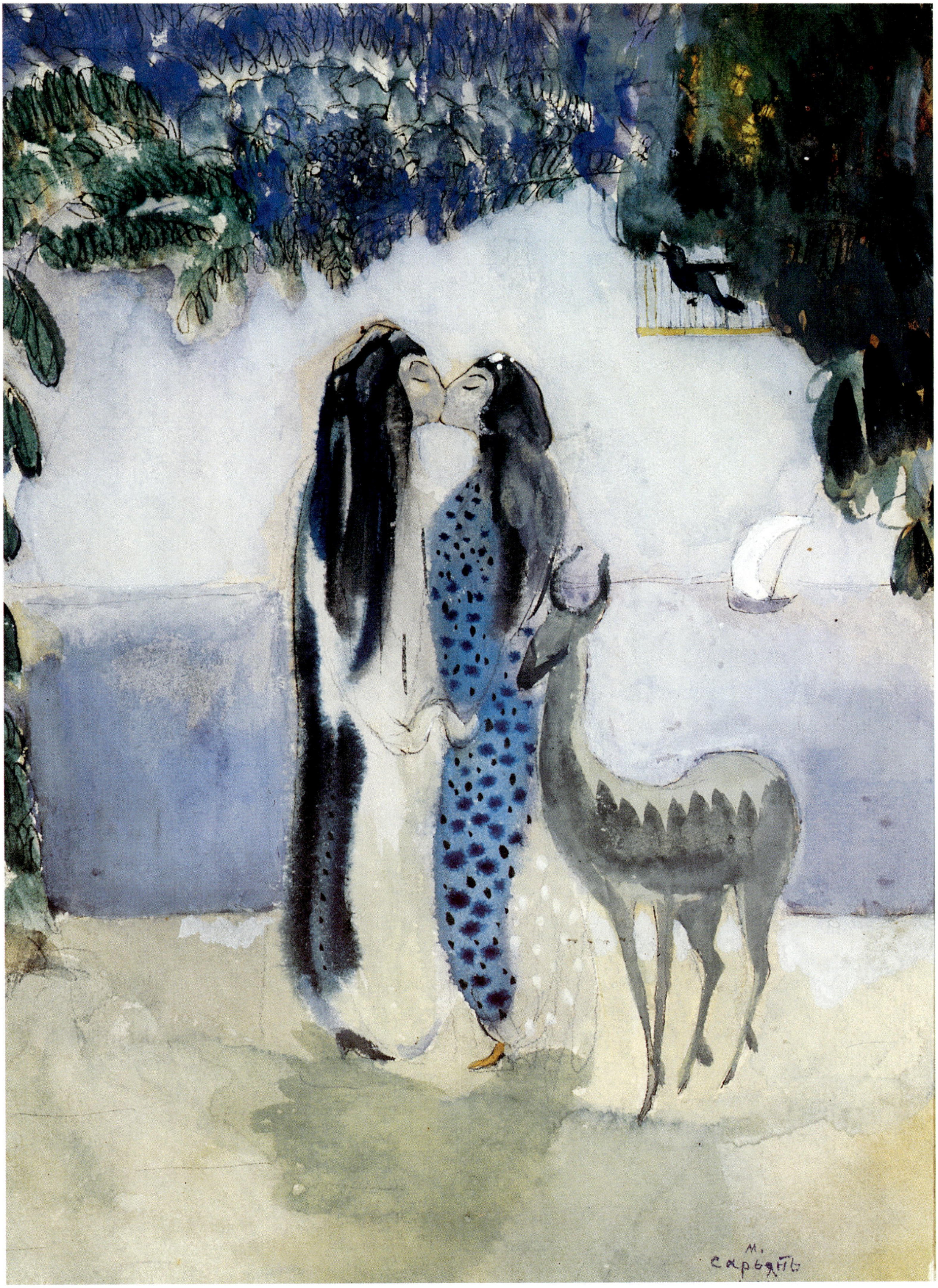
М.
Сарьянъ

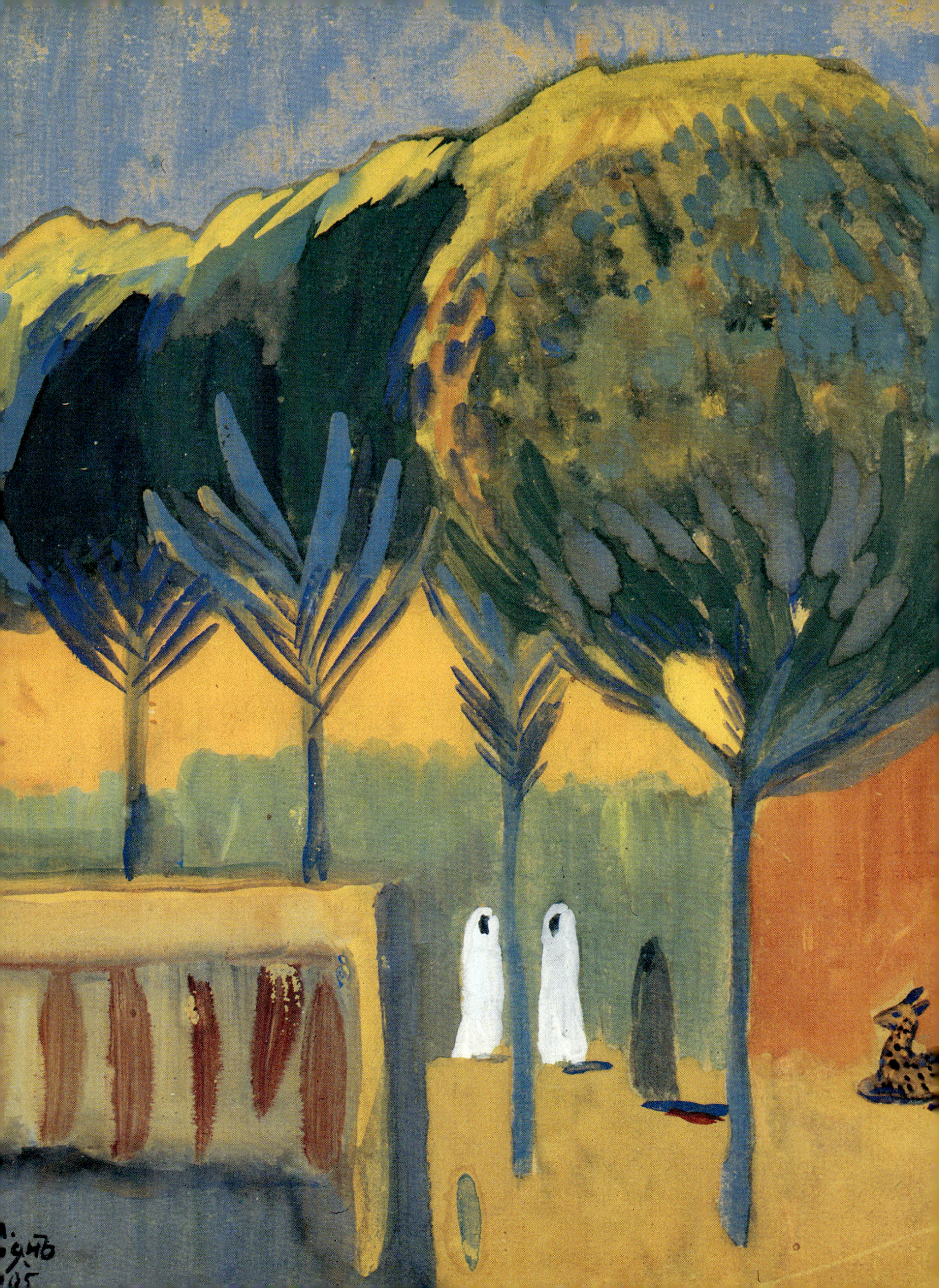

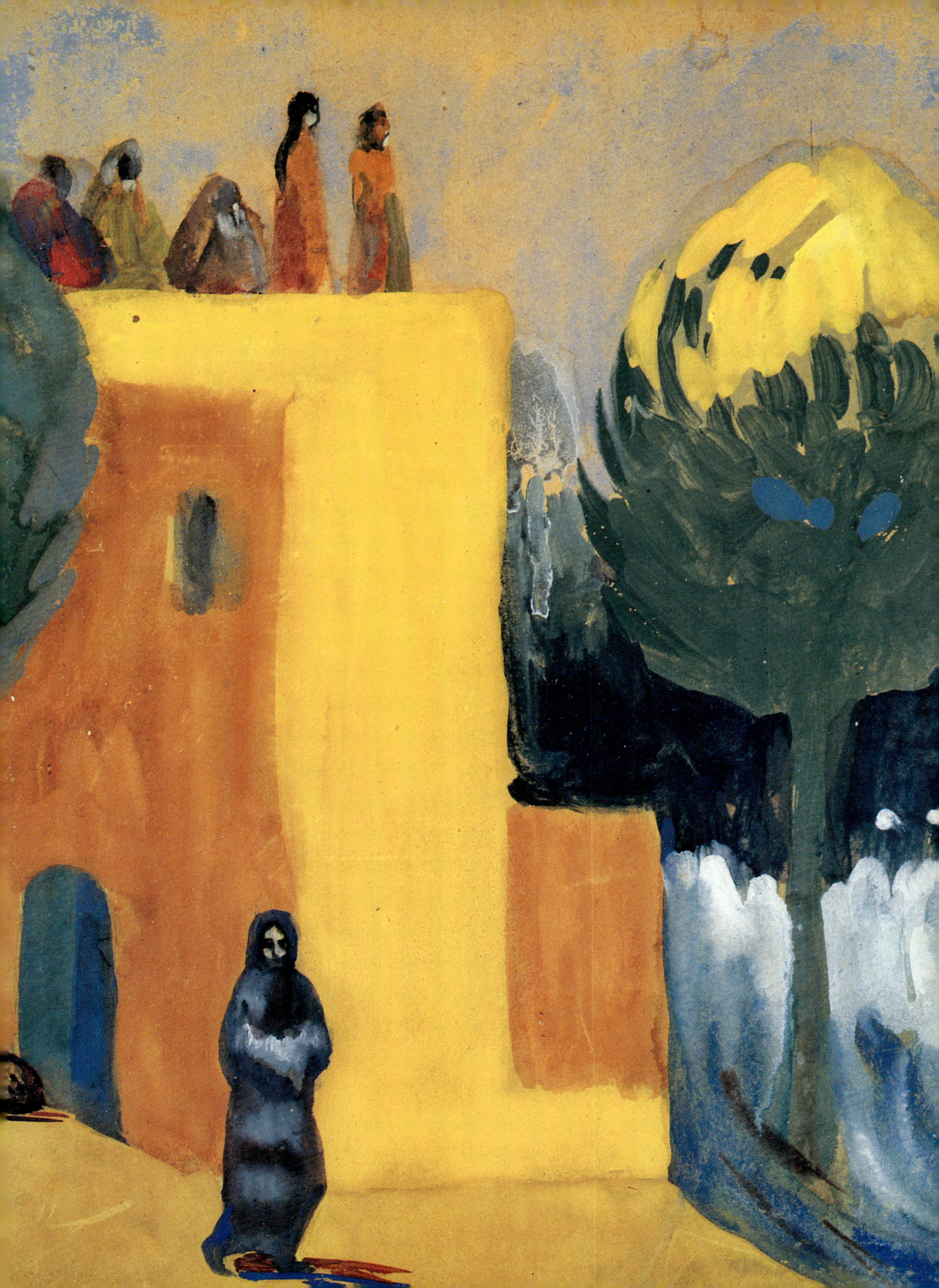

shadow over the ground. An equally dense blue has hidden itself in its luxuriant crown. As in many other works of Saryan's from this period, the tree undoubtedly has a certain symbolic meaning: it is the "tree of life" providing a link between Earth and Heaven, the axis of the universe. Here it also plays the role of an active spatial axis, seeming to tear apart the plane of the painting and to attract its dynamic motifs.

In both these paintings Saryan used the technique of large, elongated brushstrokes that has already been mentioned. It is as if he is drawing with colour, combining in one operation both drawing and painting. In places the strokes have been applied parallel, in others they fan out or merge into spots. Through these methods the artist rendered the pigment texture exceptionally mobile yet at the same time endowed it with an ornamental integrity. The question of merging drawing and painting occupied many artists as far back as the late nineteenth century. Thus, for example, Degas painted as if drawing, especially in his late period. Van Gogh constructed shape with mobile, twisting strokes or dabs. Saryan's brushstroke is different. In itself it is calmer, but in combination with its neighbours it creates a pulsating surface. At its base lie large, abstracted patches that the artist then "whips, spurs and whisks up on end with blows of coloured strokes."[20]

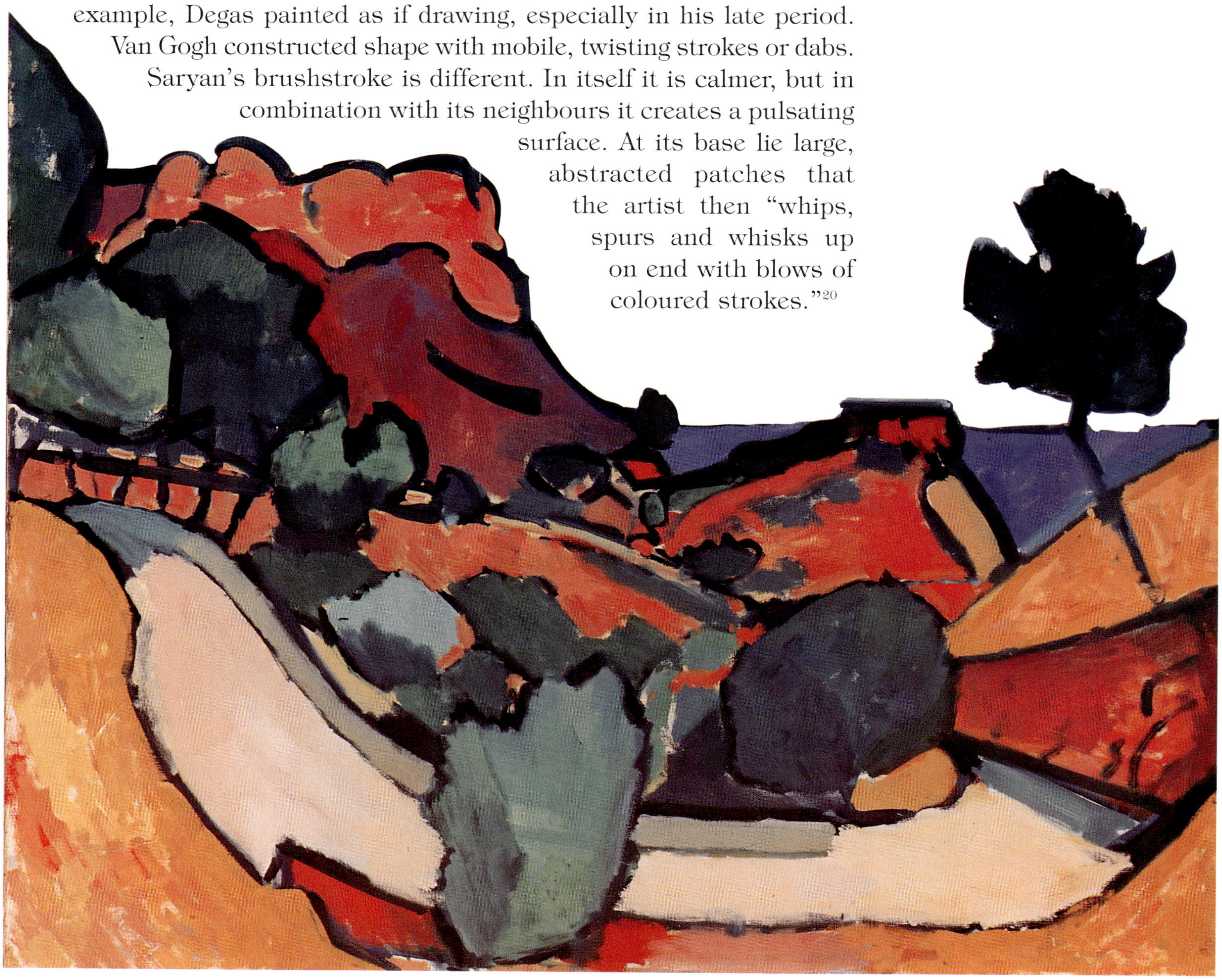

André Derain. 1880–1954
Road in the Mountains. 1907
The Hermitage, St Petersburg

In these works the tendency to simplify also determined the chromatic structure. The artist's palette is reduced to two basic relationships – dark blue and golden yellow, dense and saturated, recreating sunlight and deep, translucent shadow. In some of the works produced in 1907, and more so in 1908, Saryan shifted ever further away from the strivings of the Blue Rose artists (which were, incidentally, themselves far from homogeneous).

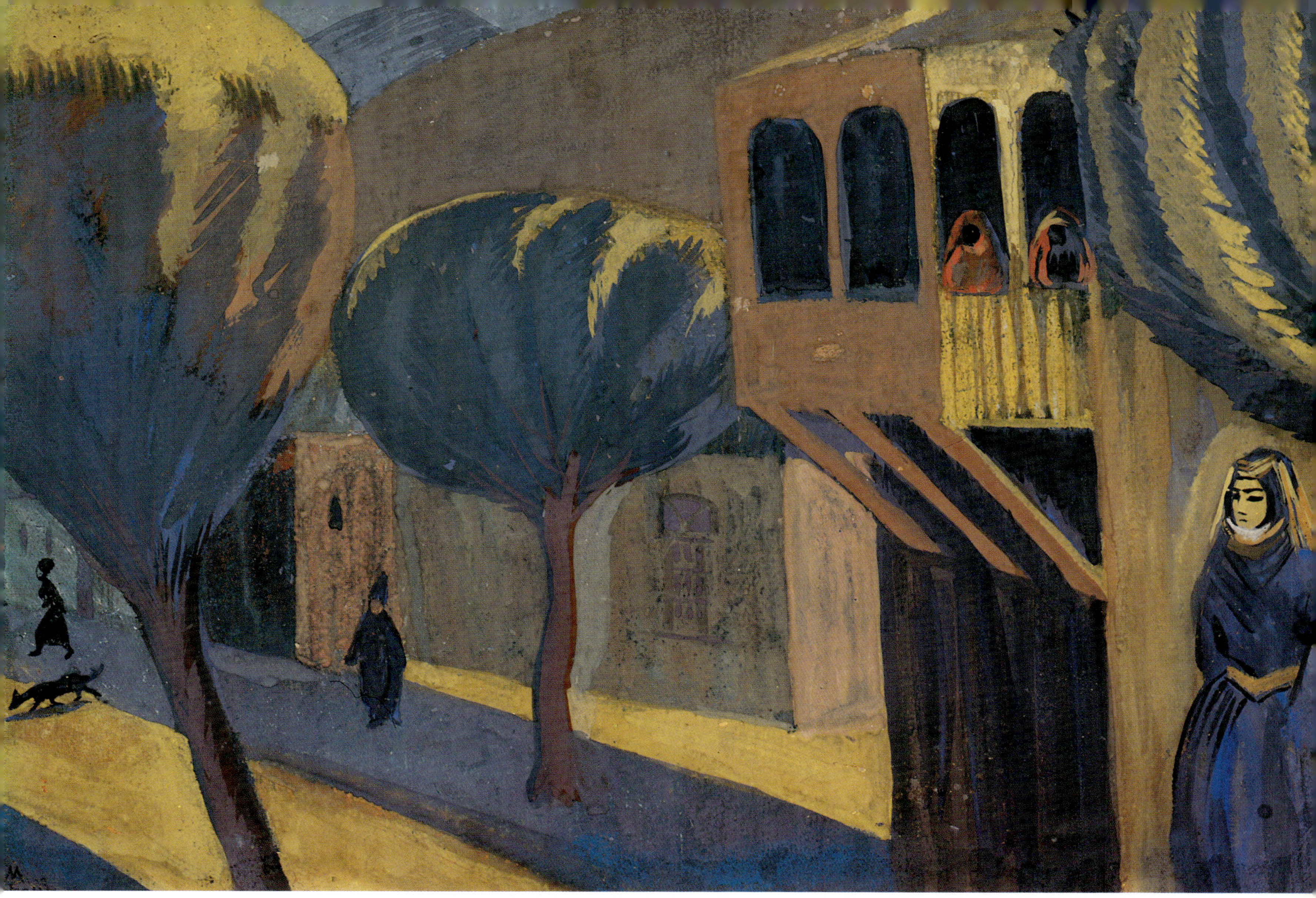

In the Caucasus. Tiflis. 1907
Tempera on canvas. 34 x 48 cm
K. Saryan collection, Yerevan

The moment had come about which the artist later told Voloshin: "I dreamed for a long time about the Caucasus and Transcaucasia and, although I had spent time in the northern Caucasus on several occasions, it did not charm me especially. On the other hand, the central Caucasus and especially the south enchanted me. There I first saw the sun and experienced intense heat. Caravans of camels with bells, nomads coming down from the mountains with tanned faces, with herds of sheep, cows, buffalos, horses, donkeys or goats; the bazaars, the street life of the motley crowd; Muslim women slipping silently by in black and pink veils, in violet baggy trousers, in wooden clogs, looking out from the flat roofs of square yellow buildings; the big, dark, almond-shaped eyes of the Armenian women – it was all that reality of which I had daydreamed back in childhood. I felt that the natural world was my home, my sole consolation; that my delight in contemplating it was different to that in front of a work of art, which only lasts a matter of minutes. Nature, many-faced and many-coloured, forged by a great unknown hand is my only teacher."[21]

What Saryan was talking about had already been presented in vague outlines in many of the *Fairy-Tales and Dreams*, and more strongly in such works as *Charms of the Sun*, *By the Pomegranate Tree* and *By the Well. A Hot Day*. Throughout the second half of the first decade of the century, the poetic dream of the south, the East took on ever more definite and real forms in Saryan's art. Many artists felt the pull of the East at that time. For European art it had already become a tradition. Interest in the Eastern world and its artistic cultures waxed particularly strong in the last decades of the nineteenth century and the beginning of the twentieth, when creative minds were seeking ever more radical methods of regenerating art. In Russia, especially indicative in this context is the course taken by Saryan and the closest of his Blue Rose associates, Pavel Kuznetsov. For the latter contact with the world of the Volga steppes, the life of the Kirghiz and later the Turkmen provided the way out of a crisis and the beginning of a great creative peak.[22] Kuznetsov, however, was a Russian who came to the East and that to a large extent determined the special poetic remoteness of his vision of the East. Saryan was in his blood a man of the East and turning to it was for him a return to the sources, to a specifically national creative consciousness that had preserved stable, vivid archetypes.[23]

The decisive shift in Saryan's evolution coincided with the year 1909. His new style already found final expression in the *Self-Portrait* that dates from the beginning of the year. The head, incorporated into a landscape, is depicted in close-up against the background of mountains. All the means of expression are subordinated to the concept of the image – a monumental synthesis of the human personality and the natural element. The artist does not rule out the portrait likeness, but gives something more – a formula of character and guidelines in life. "A man amid the mountains and valleys, lit by the rays of the great luminary", was Saryan's comment on the painting.[24] The artist often said that he loved the sun more than anything in the world and here he has personified it, as it were, in his own countenance. But the heat of its radiance can only be felt in contrast with the blue shadow. Saryan introduces blue dabs into the dense black of the hair, gives form to the face with them and models the golden patch of the mountain-top with strokes of pale and dark blue, thus making the colour and structure of the head and landscape resemble each other. Russian art had never before seen such boldness of visual

Evening in the Mountains. 1907
Tempera on canvas. 30 x 45 cm
S. Shuster collection, St Petersburg

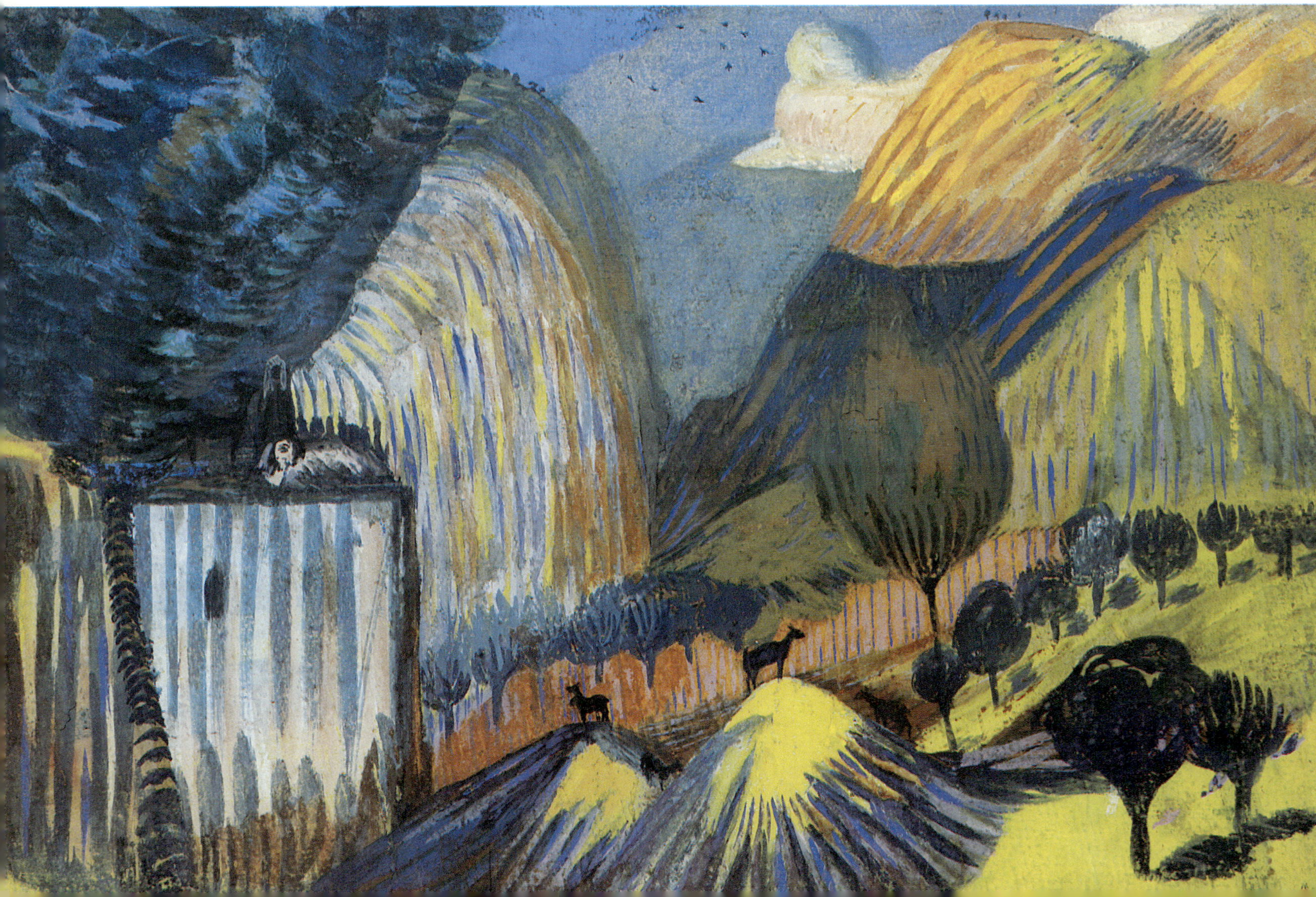

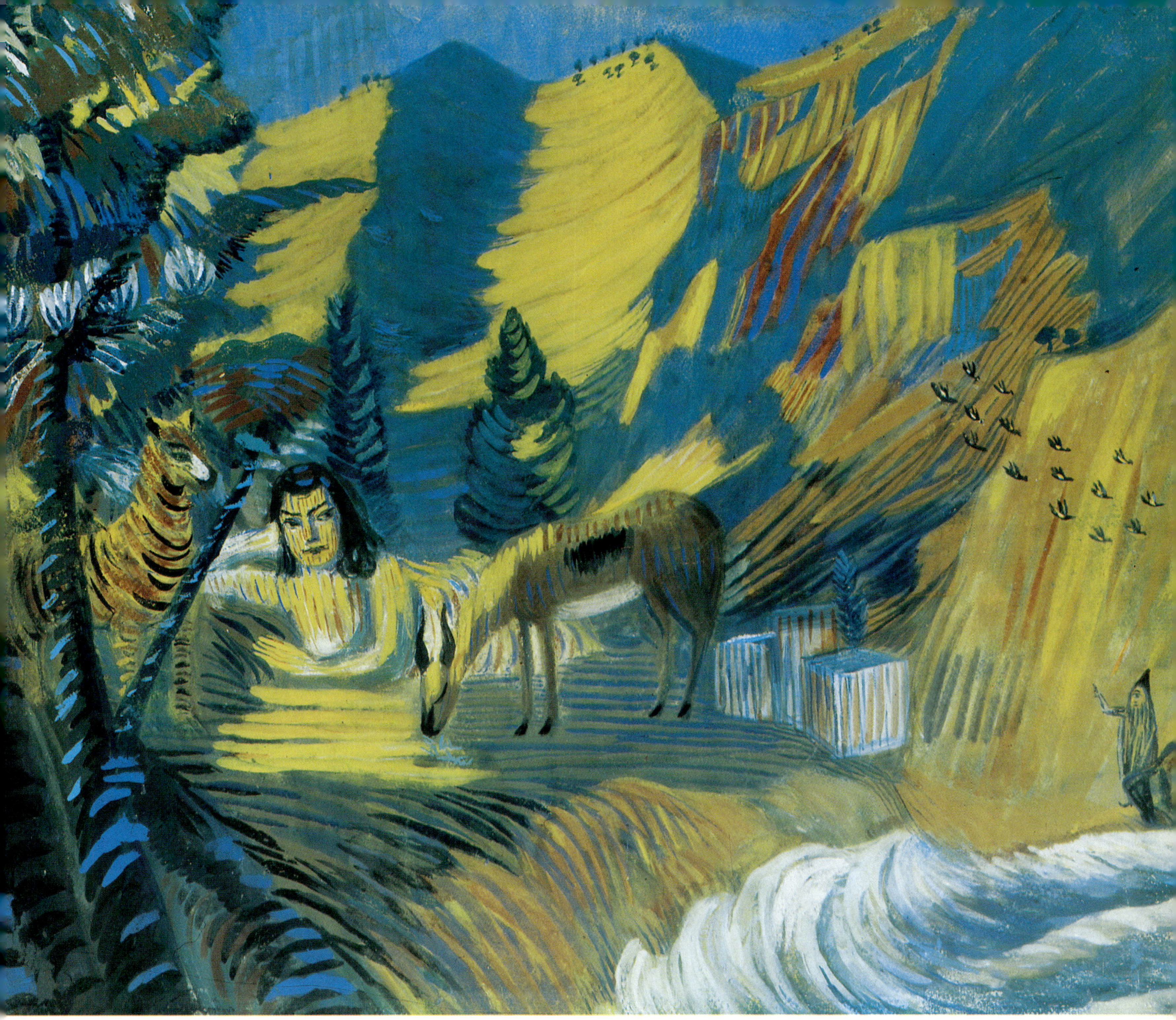

By the Sea. A Sphinx. 1908
Tempera on cardboard. 65 x 73 cm
Martiros Saryan Museum, Yerevan

→
By the Pomegranate Tree. 1907
Tempera on cardboard. 34.5 x 52.5 cm
The Tretyakov Gallery, Moscow

interpretation and painterly approach. Saryan's self-portrait can be compared for emotional and chromatic expressiveness with some of those by Van Gogh, but the essence of the image is entirely different. Saryan's work is devoid of the acute sense of tragedy inherent in the Dutch artist's creations. We have here an embodiment of life-affirming energy, of strong-willed decisiveness – a man unshakeable in his positions on life and art.

This last is confirmed by other works from the same year – *Hyenas*, *Morning in Stavrino* and *Heat. A Running Dog*. In them the landscape is created with a hitherto unprecedented economy of means. In *Hyenas* it is conveyed by simple relationships between greyish and golden-yellow patches, while a blue shadow, repeating the outline of a seated hyena, creates a sense of bright sunlight through the contrast with the ground. The figures of the animals are equally simplified, yet endowed with striking individual expression. Only the fragmentary hatching of the tree still represents a link with the style of the previous works. But already in *Hyenas* the artist was arriving at an integral, abstracted manner that was then developed in other works.

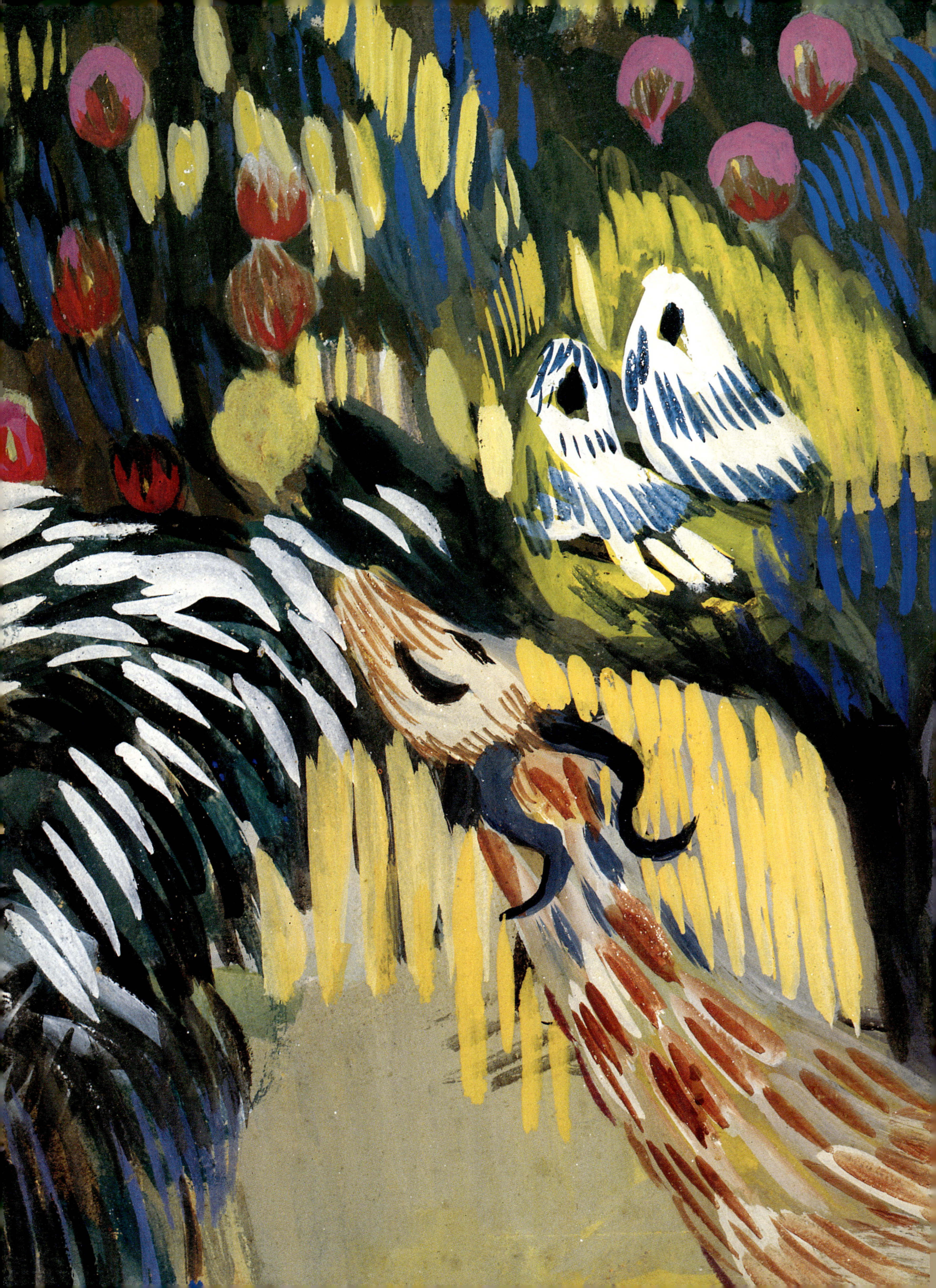

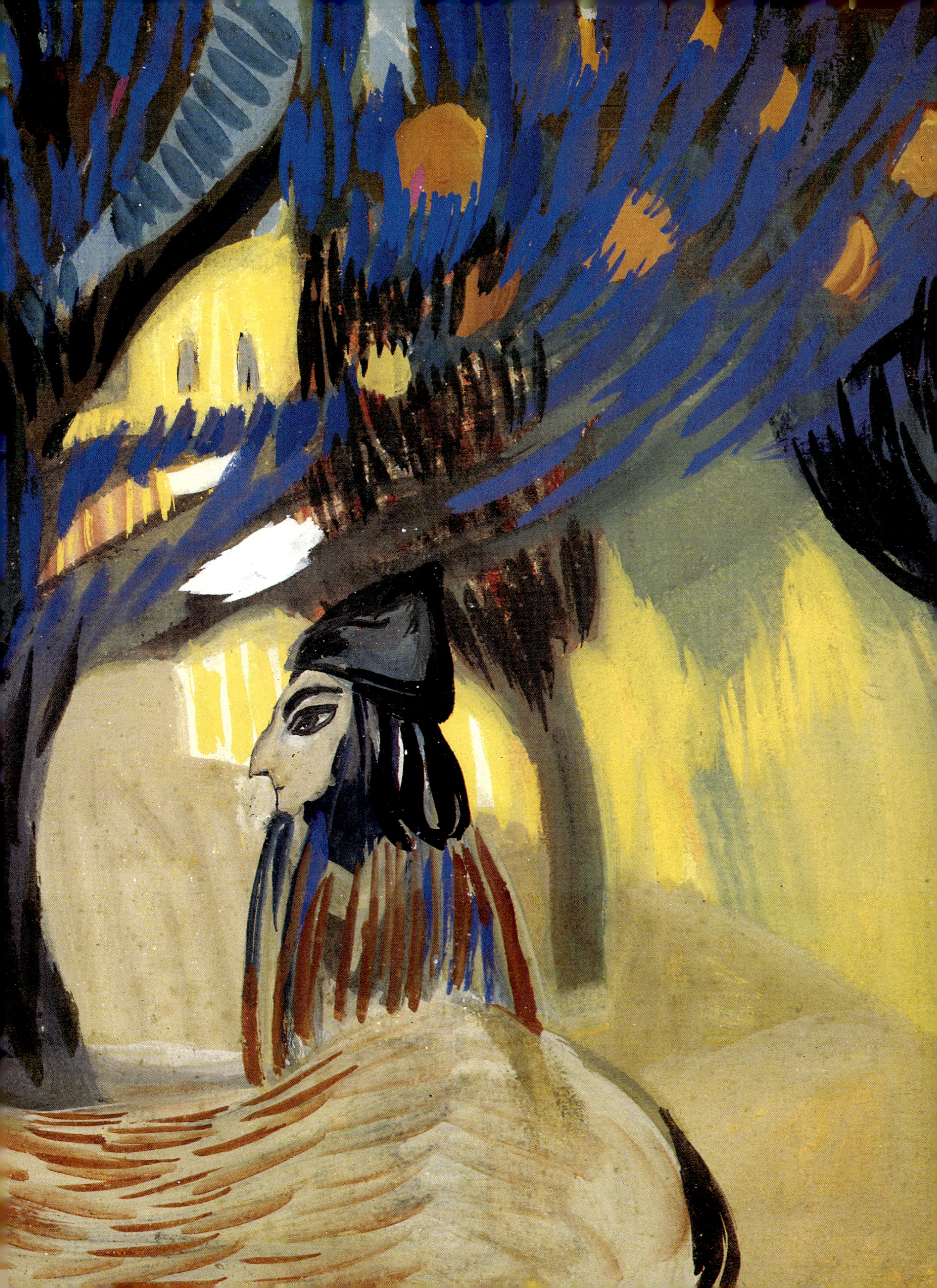

Morning in Stavrino, a composition founded mainly on the relationships of large, in part even geometrized flat shapes, stands out among them for its calm and balance. Finally there is *Heat. A Running Dog* which combines in a distinctive manner balance and dynamism, in which the animal's headlong dash is incorporated into a strict rhythmical structure formed by the symmetrical arrangement of colour patches. Here the line finally loses its significance as the boundary of shape, as shape is

Cloth Seller. 1907
Tempera on cardboard. 24 x 28 cm
S. Piatin collection, Moscow

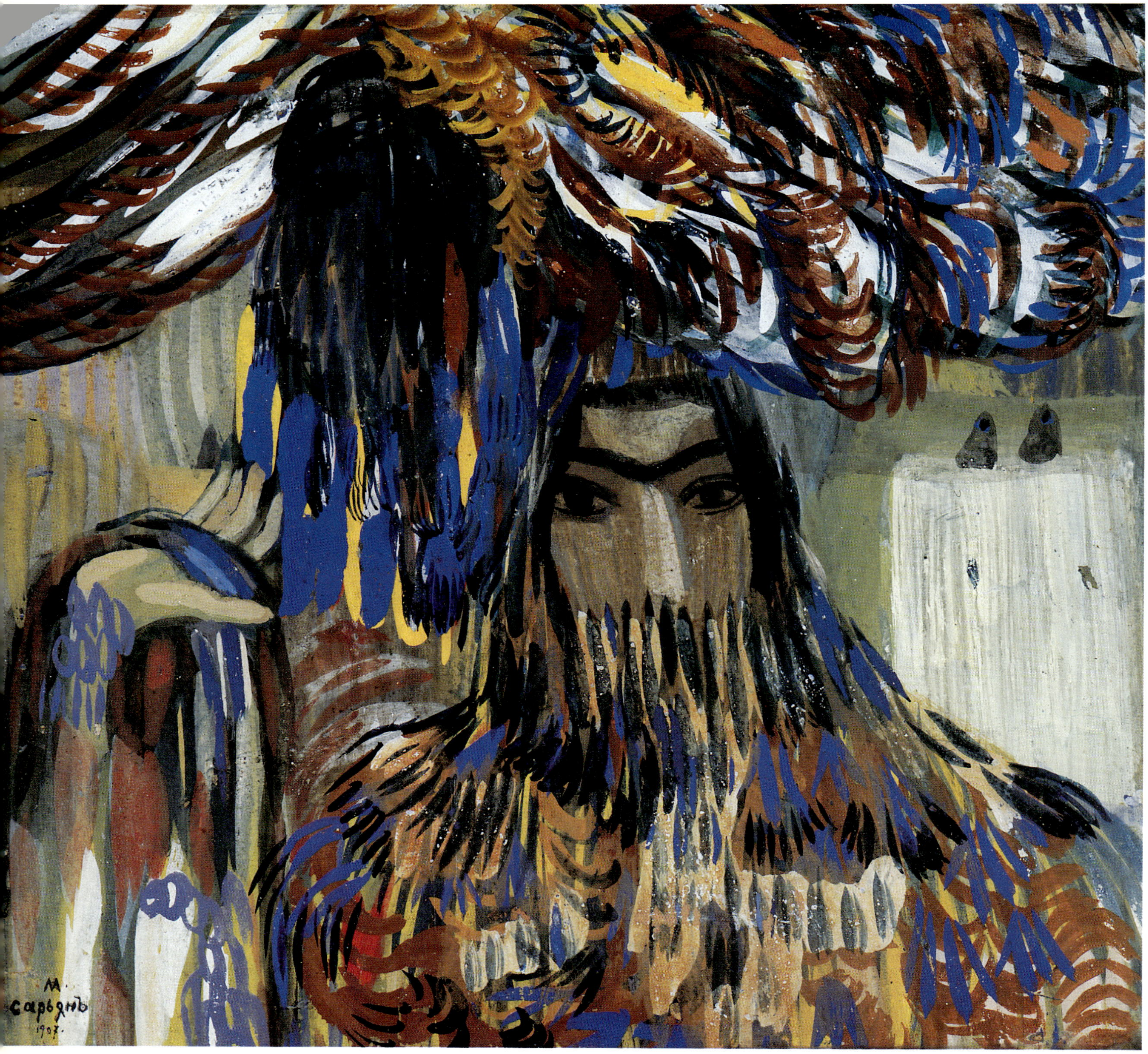

conveyed exclusively by painterly means. At the same time, the constructive basis of the composition becomes ever more evident.

Space in all these works is reduced to a plane articulated by large patches of contrasting tones, but the sense of space is not altogether lost due to the precisely regulated relationship between those patches and the

By the Well. A Hot Day. 1908
Tempera on canvas. 51 x 63 cm
Martiros Saryan Museum, Yerevan

distribution of a few depictive elements. Space is constructed not in depth, but from the bottom up. This was suggested both by the character of the motif and by the undoubted link with the traditions of Eastern art, above all of the miniature, in which just this principle of spatial organization is dominant. Even in those instances when Saryan was not painting mountains, but recreating the steppes around the Sea of Azov (*Morning in Stavrino*, *In the Sambek Grove*), he more often accentuated

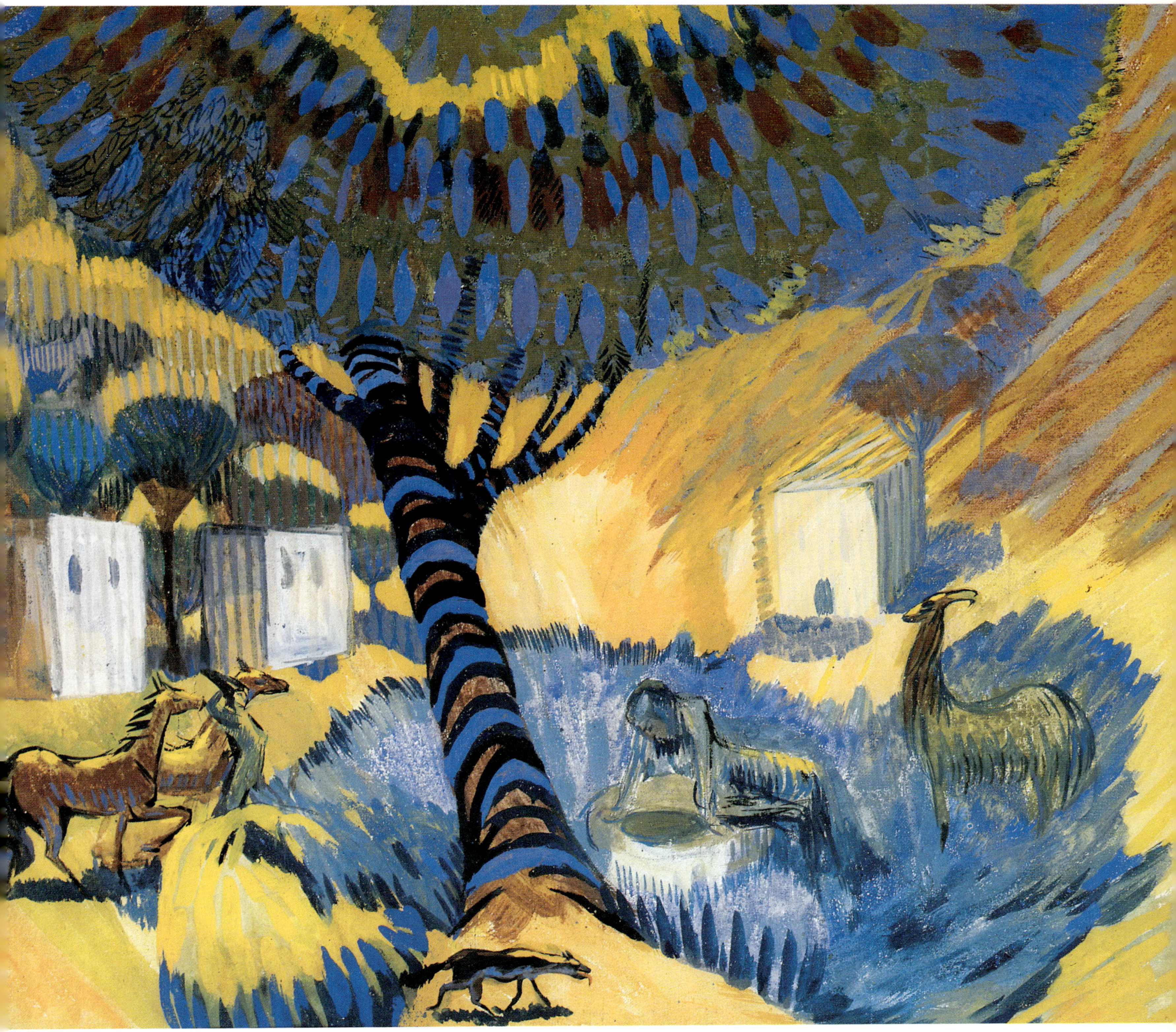

→
Hyenas. 1909
Tempera on cardboard. 67.5 x 99 cm
The Russian Museum, St Petersburg

ascending lines and not those that run horizontally. Saryan's style, as seen in these works, can be considered fully established for the immediate future, although there were still many ways in which it could be perfected. The artist himself defined better than anyone the essence of his creative strivings: "I tried to seek out more stable, simpler forms and

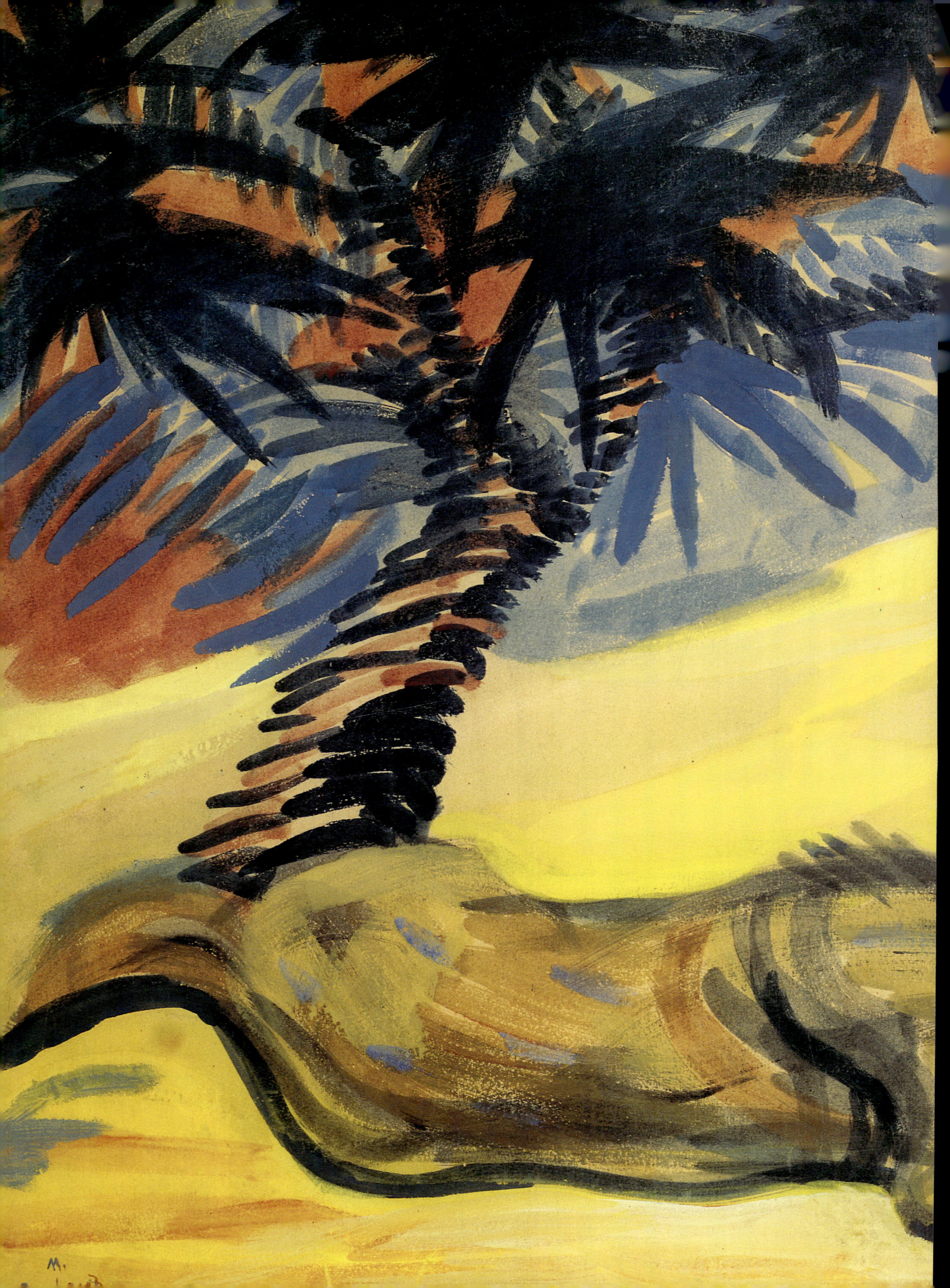

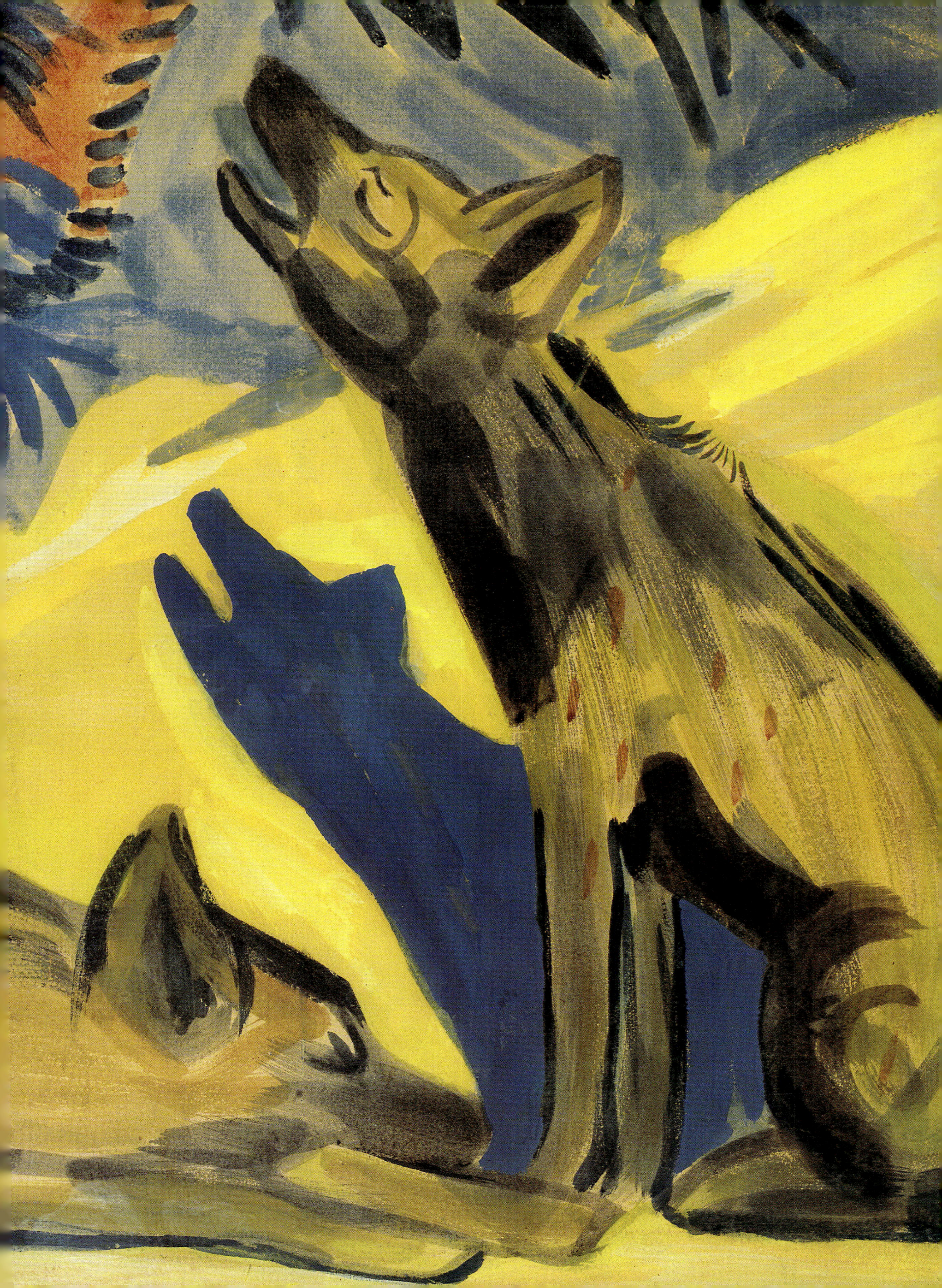

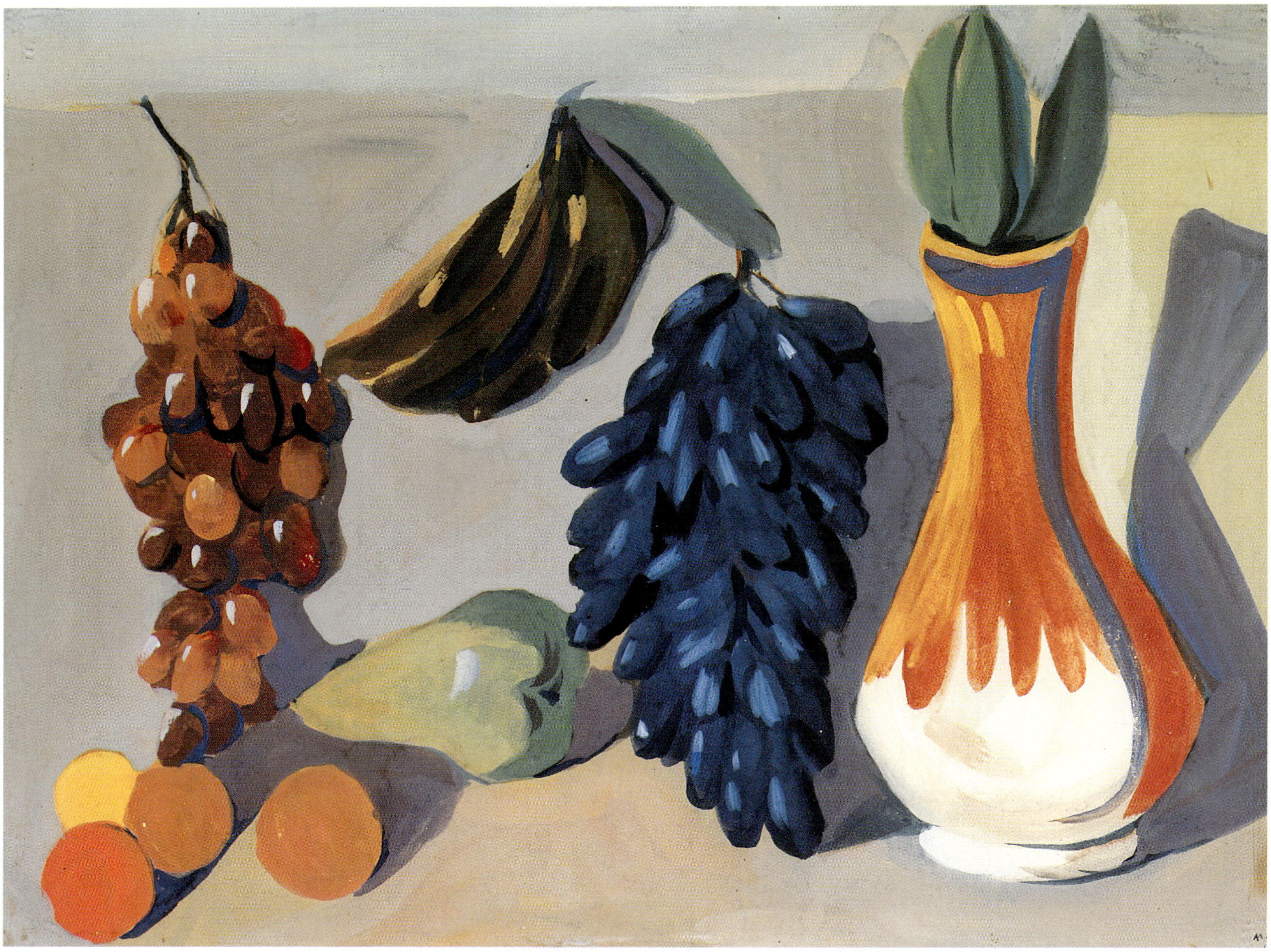

Still-Life: Grapes. 1911
Tempera on cardboard. 43.5 x 64 cm
The Tretyakov Gallery, Moscow

paints to convey the painterly essence of reality. In general my goal was to achieve the greatest degree of expressiveness by simple means, avoiding any sort of agglomeration, in particular to dispose of compromising half-tones... Besides that, my goal was to attain the fundamentals of realism. I am talking about that power of expression that is found in all true works of art from ancient times through to the present day. More accurately about that power to charm which has been achieved in all ages by different means."[25]

Saryan considered the chief means of expression in painting to be colour. He believed that paints, like people, possessed their own unique individuality and out of respect for that he disliked mixing them. "Paints should be like soloists in an ensemble, and not like singers in a choir whom we perceive not individually, but in groups or even all together. What pleasure is there in seeing instead of separate, interesting faces a featureless crowd?"[26]

The artist's understanding of colour changed in the course of his long life, but it always remained of primary importance in his art. In the period in question Saryan strove after particular brightness, resonance and, at the same time, expressivity in his colour. As the decade drew to an end he was already very far from direct observations from life, from Impressionism. Through the experience of Van Gogh and Gauguin he came, as was said earlier, to a personal variant of Fauvism that he went on to overcome.

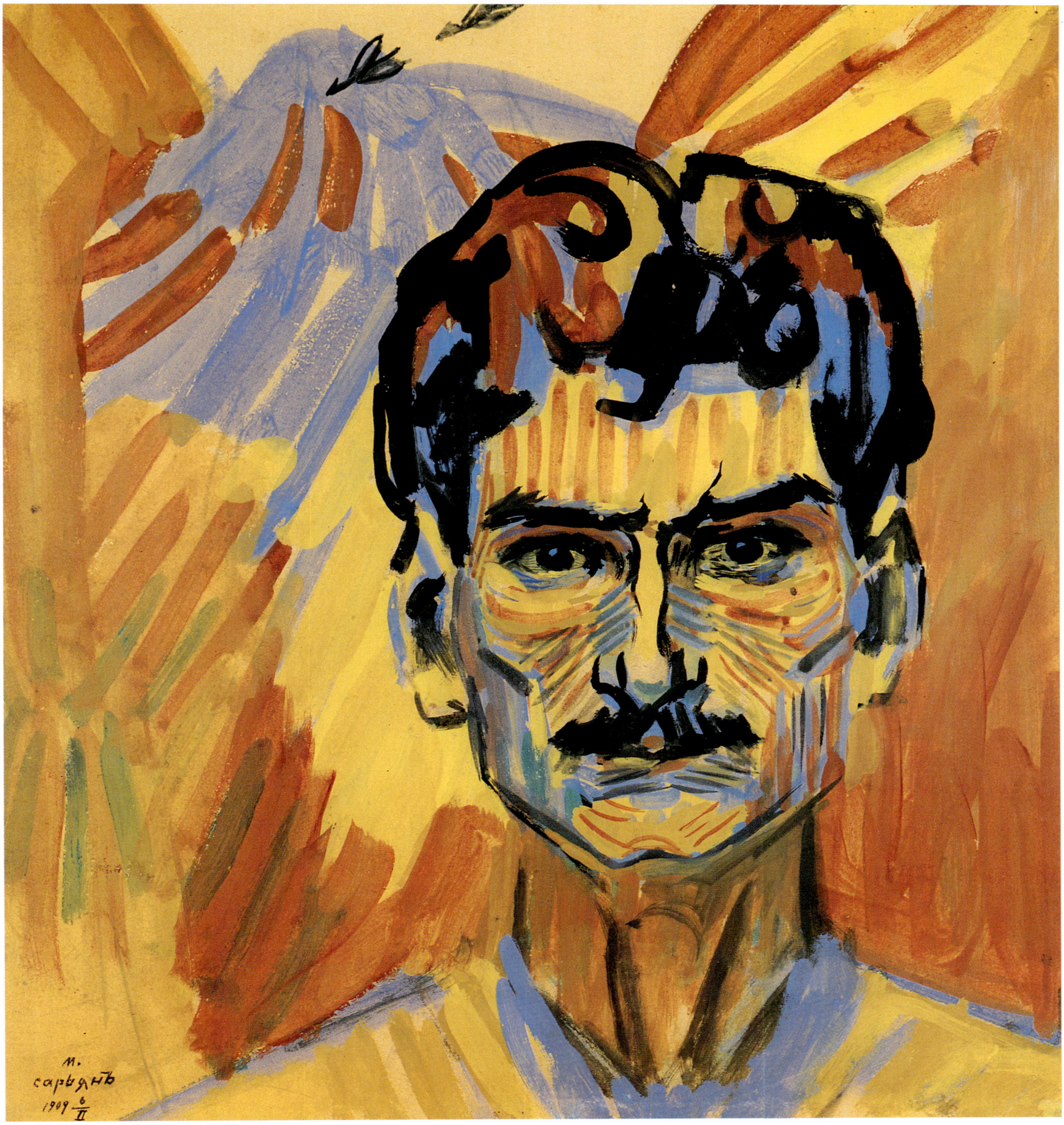

Self-Portrait. 1909
Tempera on cardboard. 47 x 45 cm
The Tretyakov Gallery, Moscow

In this context it is interesting to compare the painting of Saryan and Matisse. The parallels are strongest when we look at their works from the years 1909–14. They consist not only in the use of certain technical devices, but, most importantly, in the affirmation of the special significance of unobscured, resonant colour in the interpretation of the world. The devices themselves were an expression of deeper essential features in the two artists' views of the world. A comparison of what Matisse and Saryan had to say about the nature and aims of their work is sufficient to make their kinship obvious. "In my paintings I always strove to convey a feeling of the happiness of life,"[27] Saryan said, and also "art should make a person happy".[28] Matisse's statement that "a painting should provide deep satisfaction, rest and the purest delight"[29] has a rather different ring to it, but expresses if not the same sentiment, then a closely related one. The differences lie in the artists' individual temperaments and, of course, in the peculiarities of national character and culture. Saryan is more direct and impulsive, Matisse more reserved and austere. For a certain period, however, their creative paths came strikingly close together, although they were far from coinciding.

Scholars have quite often written about the French artist's influence on Saryan. It probably cannot be entirely excluded, but it should be remembered that Saryan first came across Matisse's painting only in 1906 or 1907, in Sergei Shchukin's collection. The noted collector bought his first Matisse in 1906, but that was a pre-Fauve work. Moscow artists became more broadly acquainted with new French painting at the joint exhibitions organized by *The Golden Fleece* magazine in 1908 and 1909. As well as Cézanne, Van Gogh and Gauguin, these also included paintings by Matisse, Braque, Derain, Rouault and Henri Rousseau. This was a real introduction to the lofty achievements and bold experiments of contemporary French artists and could obviously have played some role in Saryan's creative evolution. Even before that, however, in 1907, he created his own proto-Fauve and Fauve works (*By the Pomegranate Tree*). Lines of development ran parallel to some extent as is borne out by "juxtaposing" certain works by Matisse and Saryan.

Steppe Flowers (1909), one of Saryan's early "floral" still-lifes, undoubtedly has features akin to Matisse's *Bouquet of Flowers in a White*

Morning in Stavrino. 1909
Tempera on canvas. 50 x 69 cm
K. Saryan collection, Yerevan

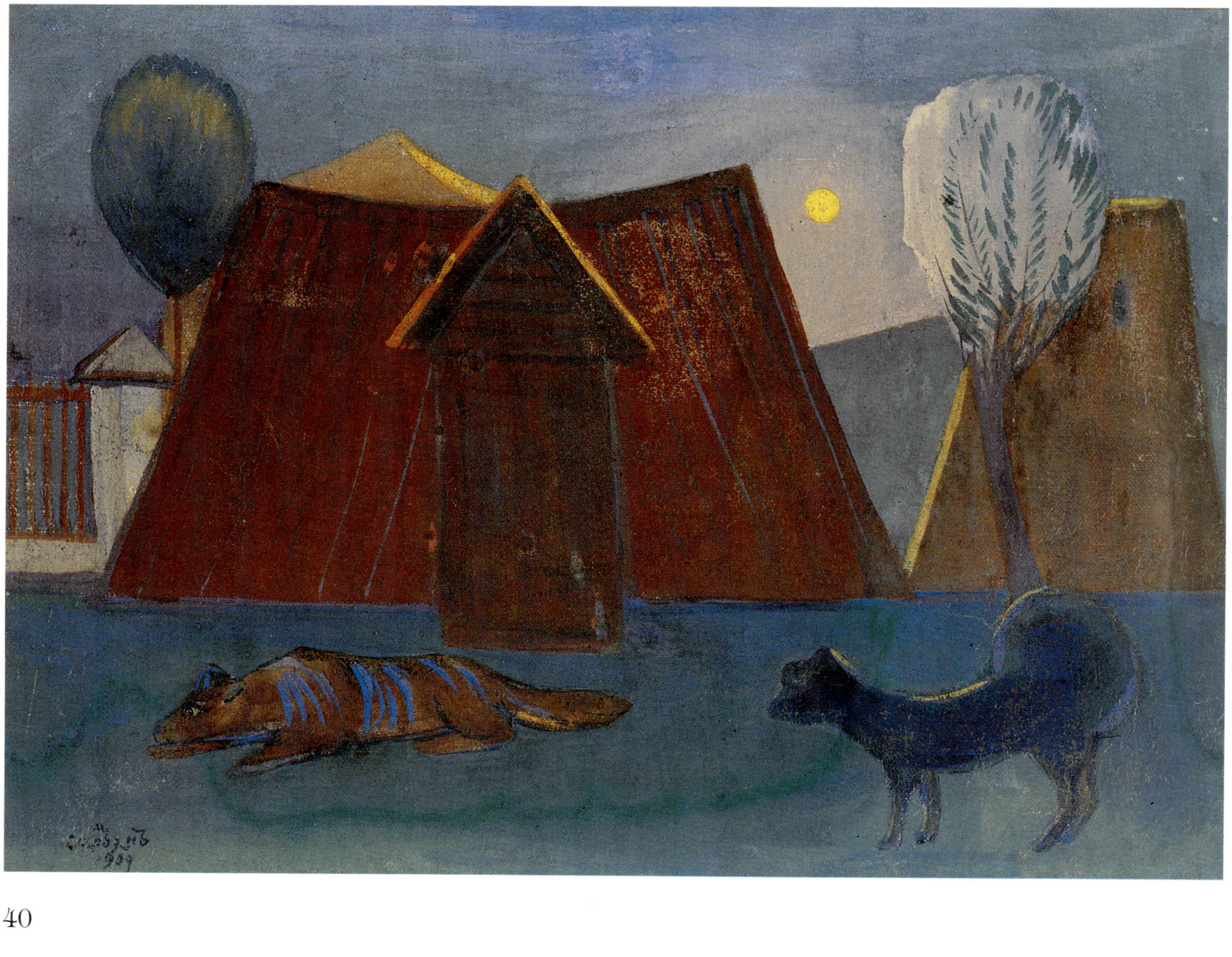

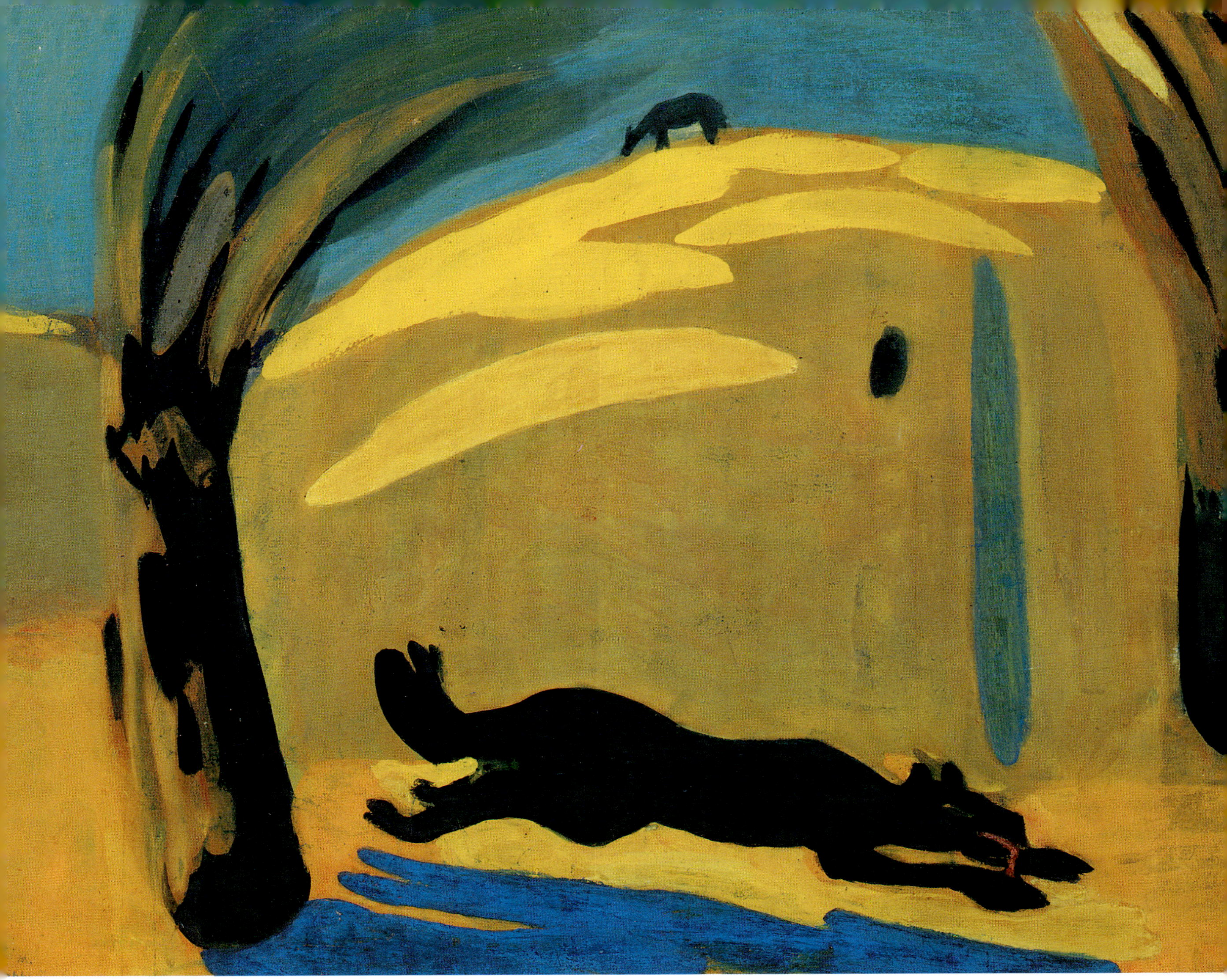

Heat. A Running Dog. 1909
Tempera on cardboard. 56 x 58 cm
D. Dobychin collection, St Petersburg

→
Blossoming Trees. 1910
Tempera on cardboard. 35 x 53 cm
National Gallery of Armenia, Yerevan

Vase (*ca* 1909). Despite the difference in ranges of colour (corresponding to the difference in real life), they are brought together by a similar conception of shape, understanding of the painter's tasks and even the manner of executing individual details.

Less obvious is the similarity of two other still-lifes – Matisse's *Fruit and a Bronze* from 1910 (in which year it was acquired by Ivan Morozov) and *Light Range. Still-Life* which Saryan painted in 1913. The more restrained chromatic harmony of the latter differs strongly from the resonant, dense, contrasting colour of Matisse's still-life. There is, however, undoubtedly something in common in the choice of objects, in the precise compositional organization, in the rhythmical combination of immobile items and the dynamic stripes of the drapes, and, most importantly, in the principle of simplifying shape to which both artists adhered. In Matisse's work the ornamental aspect is more distinctly expressed; the painterly texture of *Light Range* is more subdued. One more significant aspect: Saryan's fruit are more material, they brilliantly express "the joy of ripening fruits", as Osip Mandelstam put it, something significantly alien to Matisse's offerings.

Saryan's subsequent development was to a great extent shaped by his journeys in the Near and Middle East – to Constantinople (1910),

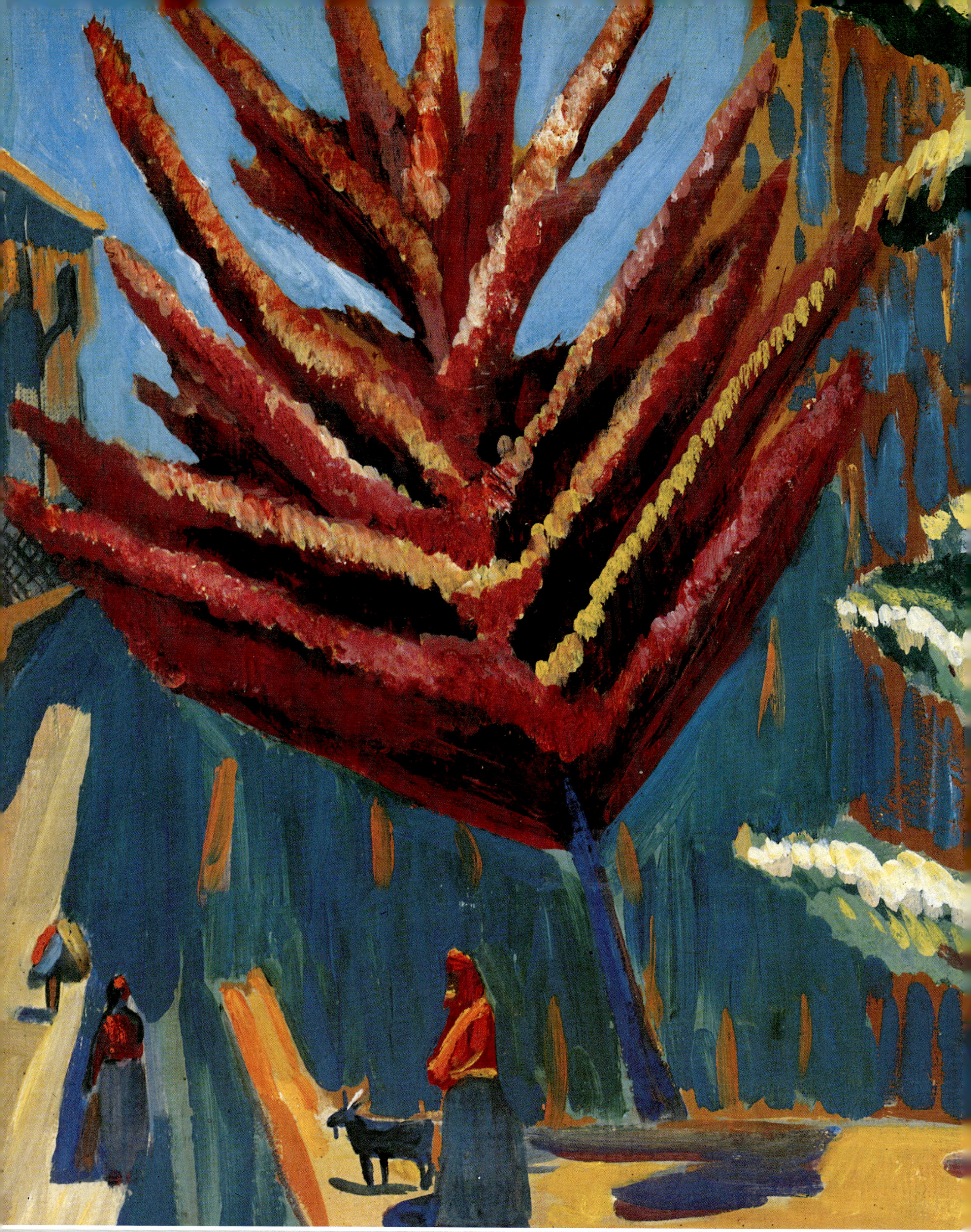

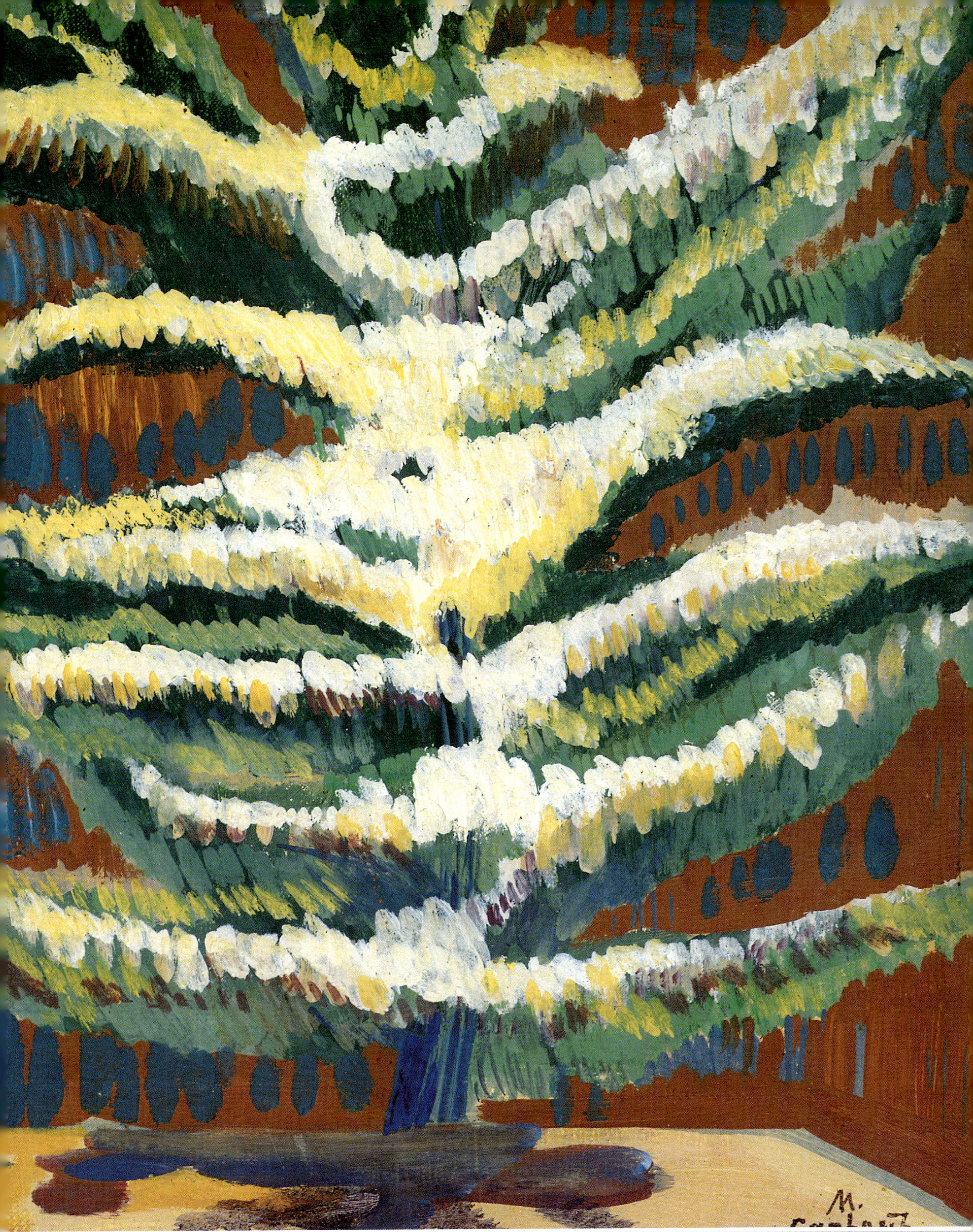

Egypt (1911) and Persia (1913). As the artist himself later recollected, the East became for him "the main theme, the main source of creativity". He strove "to understand the East, to discover its characteristic features, so as to better substantiate my searchings in painting... I wanted to convey the realism of the East, to find convincing features in the depiction of that world."[30]

The pictures of the Eastern cycle were to become the pinnacle of Saryan's output. It was in them that his style, worked out in its basic features back in 1909, acquired a classic finish and perfection.

The artist's memoirs give us an idea of the keen interest evoked in him by new countries, scenery and monuments, but most importantly by the life of the streets, its rhythm, its colour, the bustle of the bazaars, the splendour of flowers and fruit... His alert eye could catch the unique originality, the plasticity and painterly beauty of the most insignificant motifs and they became the occasion for the creation of masterpieces.

In some instances Saryan painted directly from nature. That was the case with *Wisteria* (1910) – with its striking energy of colour one of the most typical, and one of the last, of the artist's pure Fauve works. As a rule though, in Constantinople and on his subsequent journeys, Saryan strolled about the city making brush sketches or pencil jottings, then in the studio he painted from memory, retaining what was most important in what he had seen, without chance detail and trivia. This accorded with his searches after synthesis, recreating not the outward appearance of real life, but its essence, character and expression.

Examples of such works could be *Lemonade Seller*, *Mules Loaded with Hay* and *Fruit Stall*, all dating from 1910. Saryan is interested in the special typicalness of what he sees and he conveys it in movement, silhouette, colour relationships and even in faces. This typicalness became the chief focus of his attention in such works as *Eastern Women* (1910). The two heads on a blue background do not repeat but set off each other, bringing out type and expression with particular acuity. Works like this reveal features of the canon, that set of certain iconographic devices which is so specific to Eastern art. This canon was undoubtedly intrinsic to Saryan's nature, but he introduced into it a sense of the tension

Mules Loaded with Hay. 1910
Tempera on cardboard. 36.5 x 70 cm
National Gallery of Armenia, Yerevan

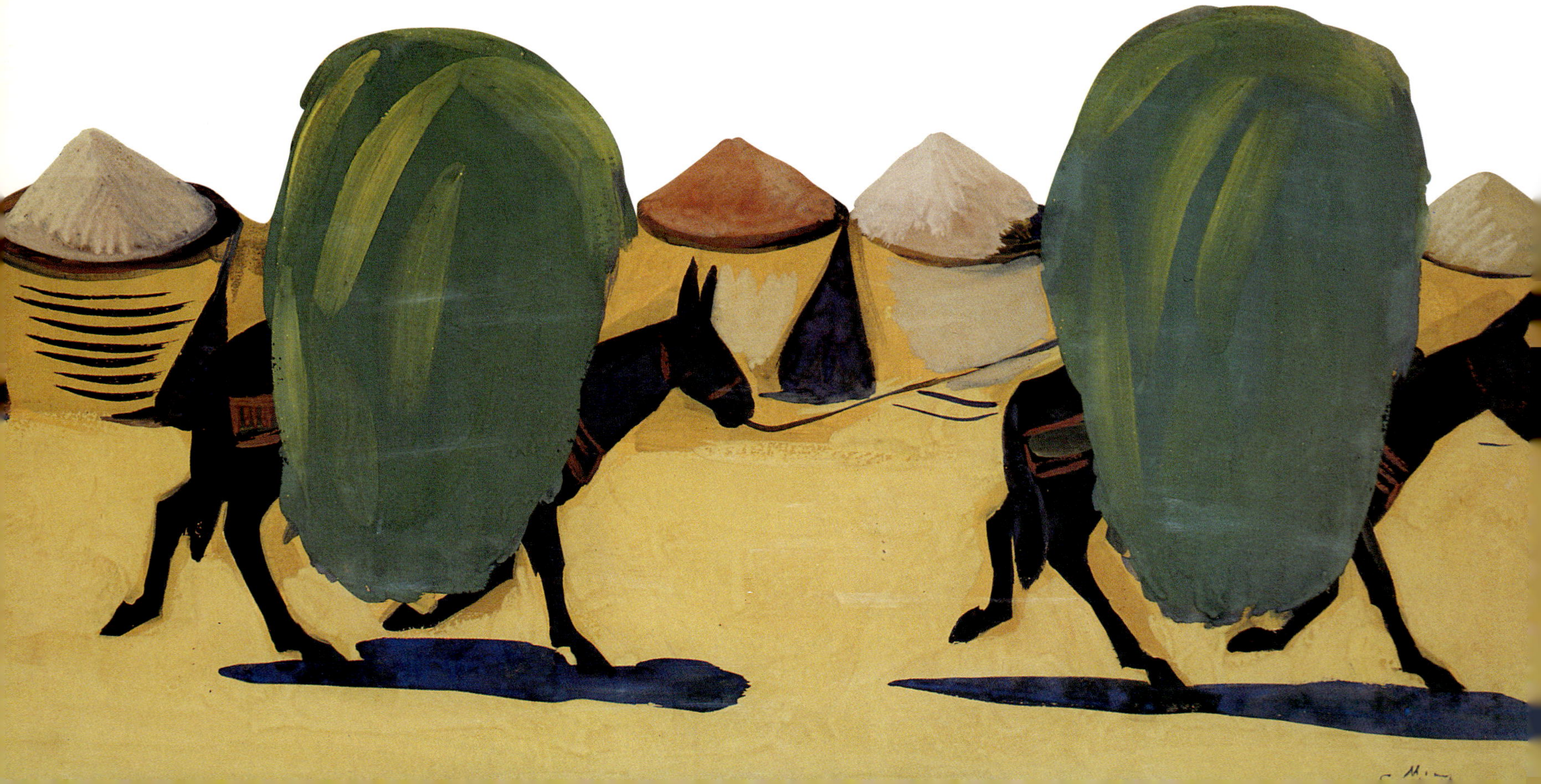

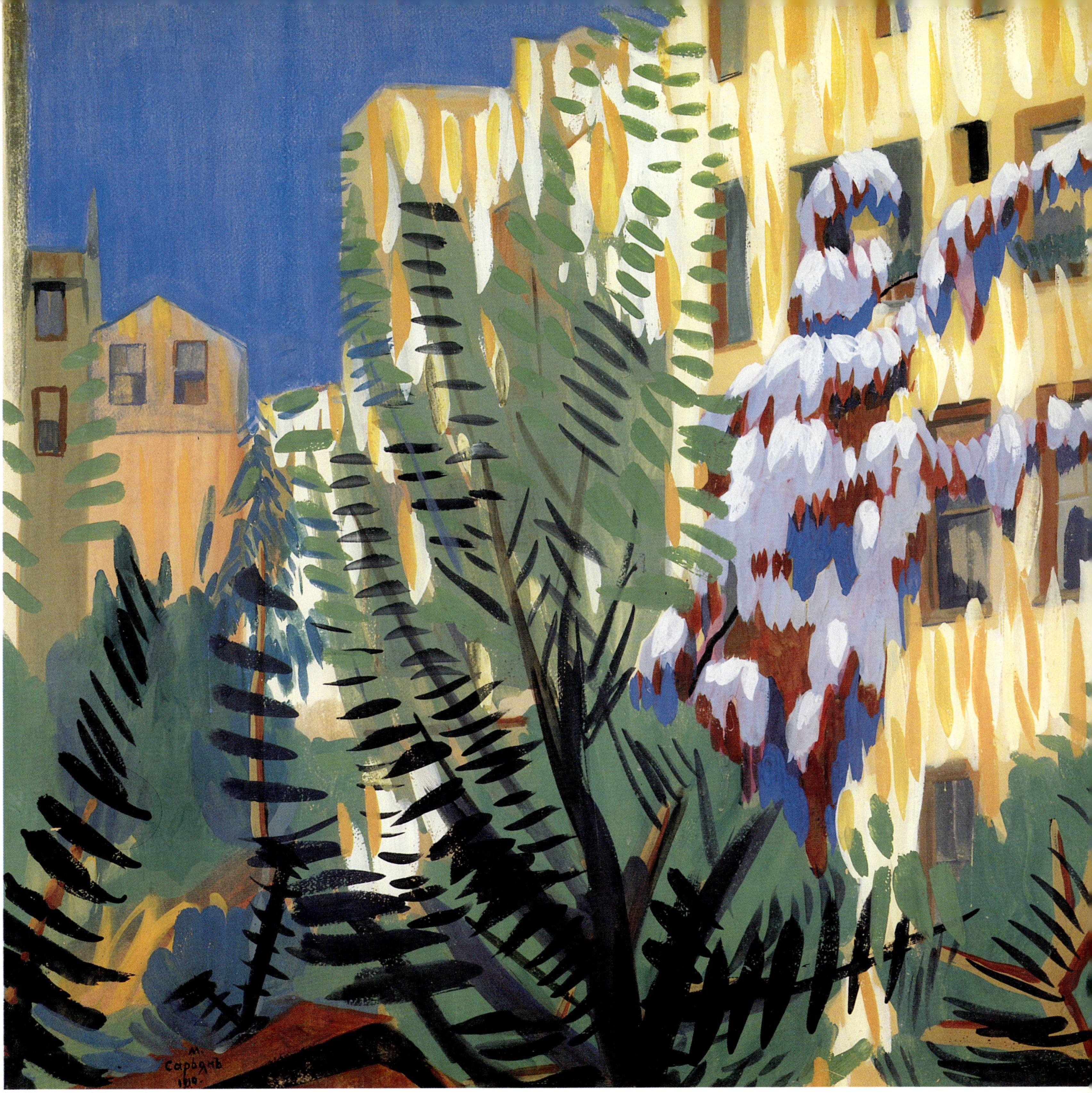

Wisteria. 1910
Tempera on cardboard. 63 x 65 cm
The Tretyakov Gallery, Moscow

→
Street. Noon. 1910
Tempera on cardboard. 66 x 39 cm
The Tretyakov Gallery, Moscow

→
Lemonade Seller. 1910
Tempera on cardboard. 47.5 x 35.7 cm
The Russian Museum, St Petersburg

of life. Equally canonical is his *Persian Woman* (1910), an almost emblematic image of an Eastern beauty, not frozen and cramped though, but animated by the vision of the artist who was able with three dabs of paint on the lips or the judicial insertion of highlights to convey the living expression of an attractive countenance. A girl like this one, but more earthy, is among other no less colourful figures that enliven a Constantinopolitan street in which the sun struggles with shadow turning a wall of the house and the ground golden, while the bright clothes flare out against the background of the dark wall (*Street. Constantinople*, 1910). Saryan was fond of this contrast of light and shade, because it enables the viewer to strongly sense the beneficent power of the sun which the artist had always loved, but whose true value he (like Delacroix before him) discovered in the East.

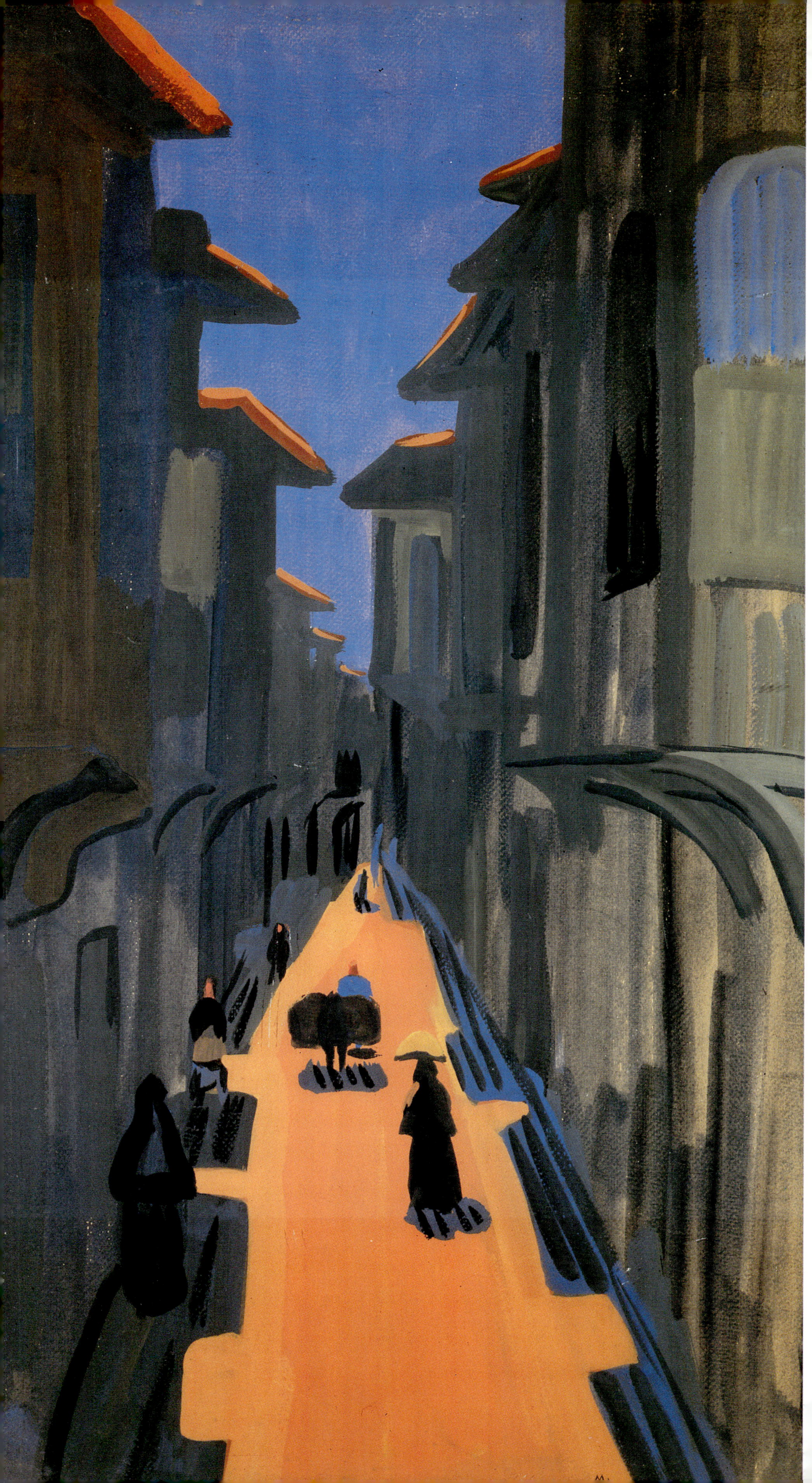

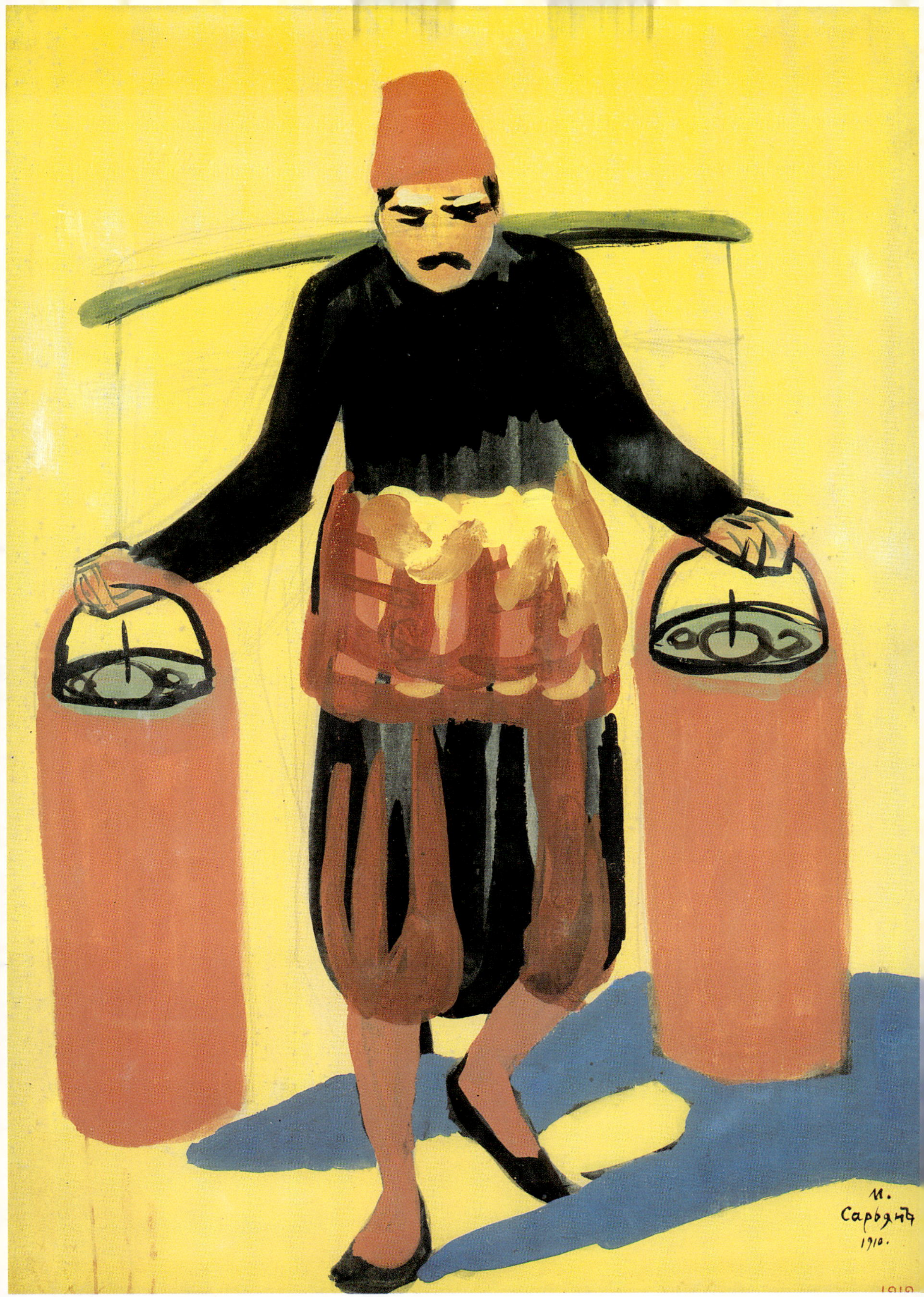
М.
Сарьянъ
1910.

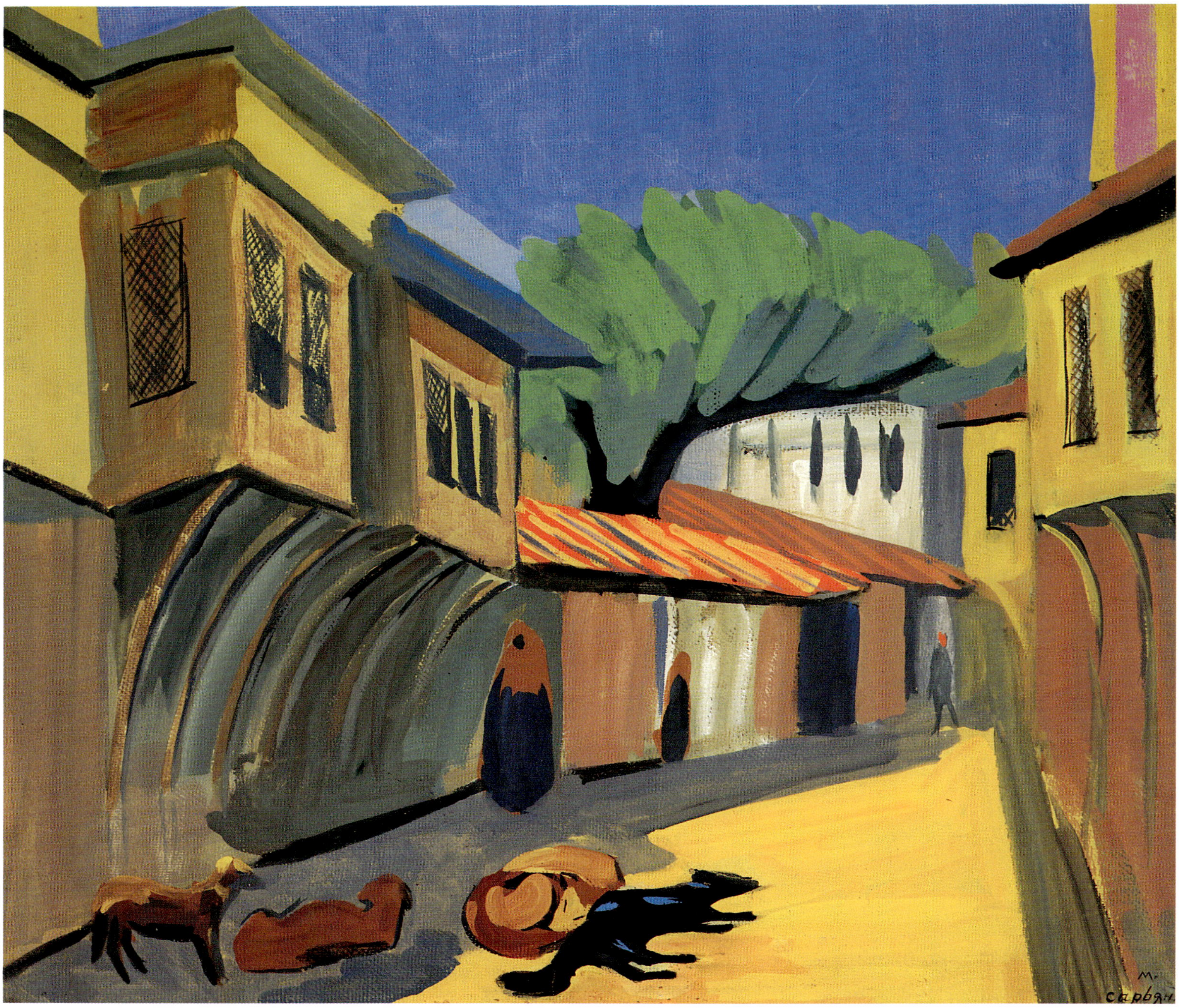

Constantinople. Dogs. 1910
Tempera on cardboard. 59 x 67 cm
The Tretyakov Gallery, Moscow

The classic manifestation of this theme – the antagonism and unity of light and shade – is the painting *Street. Noon* (1910) which is unique for the absolutely perfect balance between composition and expressiveness of colour.

It would be hard to name another painting that so powerfully conveys the sense of sultry heat, the blinding strength of the southern sun that has taken possession of the narrow expanse of the street along which a few people are slowly moving. Thin strips of shadow remain only at the edge of the houses; their dark masses conduct the gaze into the depth. But this depth is deceptive; it comes back towards us in the flood of an extremely blue sky that contrasts sharply with the orange ground. A brilliant analysis of *Street. Noon* has been made by the art-historian Dmitry Sarabyanov, who among other telling observations noted the dual symmetry of this astonishing composition, both vertical and horizontal: "...just like the sides of the street, the blue triangle of the sky and the orange one of the ground between the houses match each other". Commenting on the exceptional importance of the way colour is organized in the painting, the researcher writes: "Two complementary colours – orange and blue – have, as it were, drawn to themselves all the minor

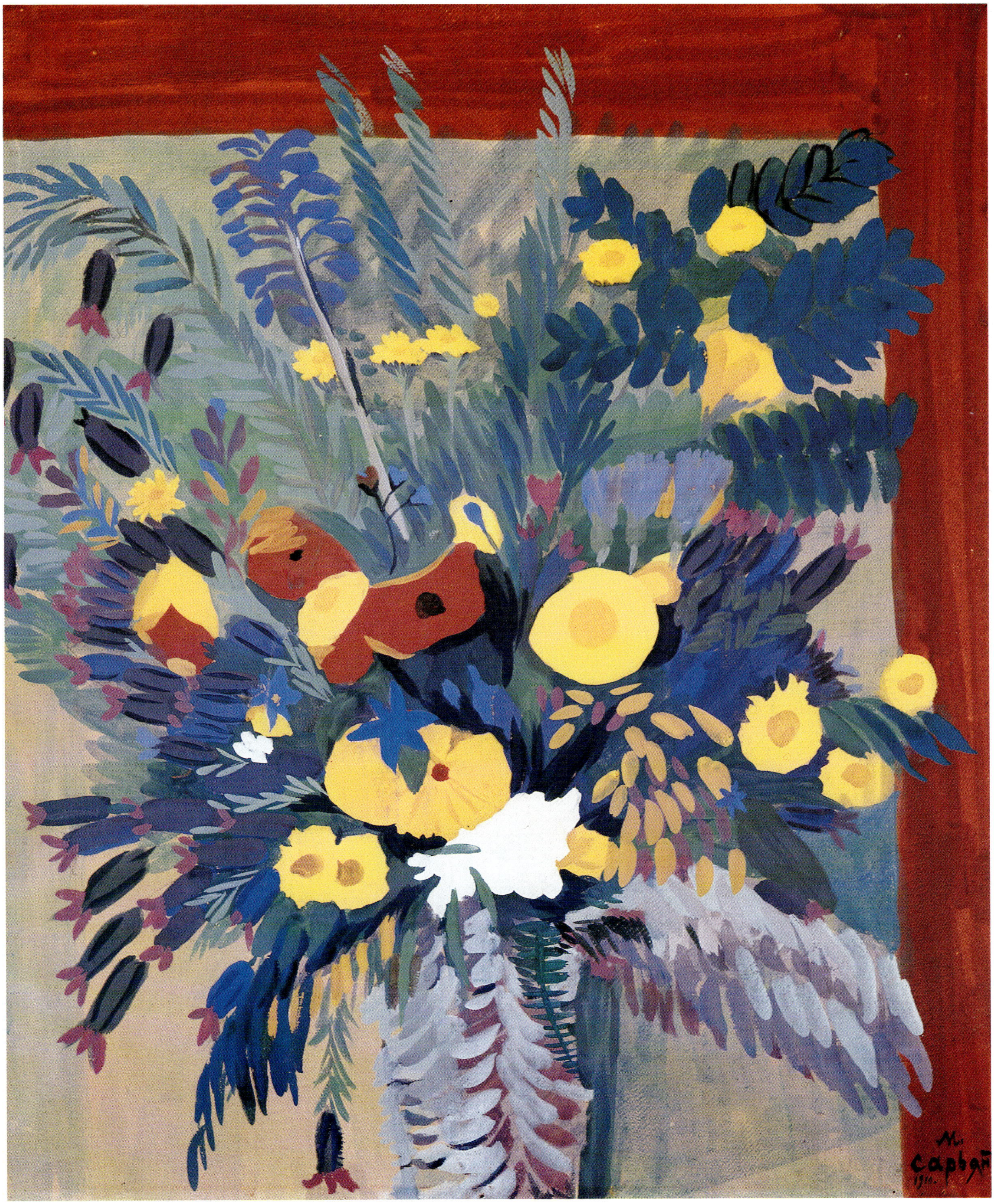

Flowers from Chamlych. 1910
Tempera on cardboard. 67 x 56 cm
R. Drampian collection, Yerevan

vacillations, purged themselves of admixtures... Saryan does not seek vacillations of colour, leaves no traces of brushstrokes, does not set the texture in motion. The simplicity of chromatic relationships, the bold power of contrast – all this becomes a generalized expression of natural qualities, but not an imitation of them."[31]

In this painting the artist completely overcomes the Fauve fragmentation of colour. His style – both in composition and chromatic structure – acquired an economy of expression appropriate to Eastern poetics in the broadest sense of the word. At the same time the keenness of his vision of the real world was not diminished. Quite the contrary, Saryan's gaze became ever more acute and penetrating, picking out the most distinctive elements. *Mules Loaded with Hay*, for example, is a masterpiece in the way it conveys the shape and motion of the animals, their hurried step. In this little painting a sense of immediacy and liveliness, even of a chance recorded instant, is combined with an absolutely deliberate arrangement of composition and space.

Uniquely characteristic are the artist's dogs, the free denizens of the Constantinopolitan streets. Saryan painted them several times, but the synthetic embodiment of this motif was *Dogs. Constantinople* (1910). For all the economy of depiction, each dog is given an individual expression. All together they make up a sort of frieze, carefully thought out in terms of colour combinations and a rhythmic structure that evokes associations with similar frieze-like compositions in Eastern and, above all, Ancient Egyptian art.

Saryan knew that art well and valued it even before his journey to Egypt and had devoted one of his first articles to it, which was printed in the Armenian periodical *Nor kiank* in 1906. He believed that the ancient Egyptians had managed to grasp the world in all its boundlessness, yet at the same time to endow their monuments with clarity and simplicity – qualities that he himself sought and that captivated him in Egyptian masks. Saryan collected them and from this period on began to introduce them into the composition of his own still-lifes and portraits. In the still-life *Egyptian Masks* (1911) he painted them against the background of a grey wall in combi-

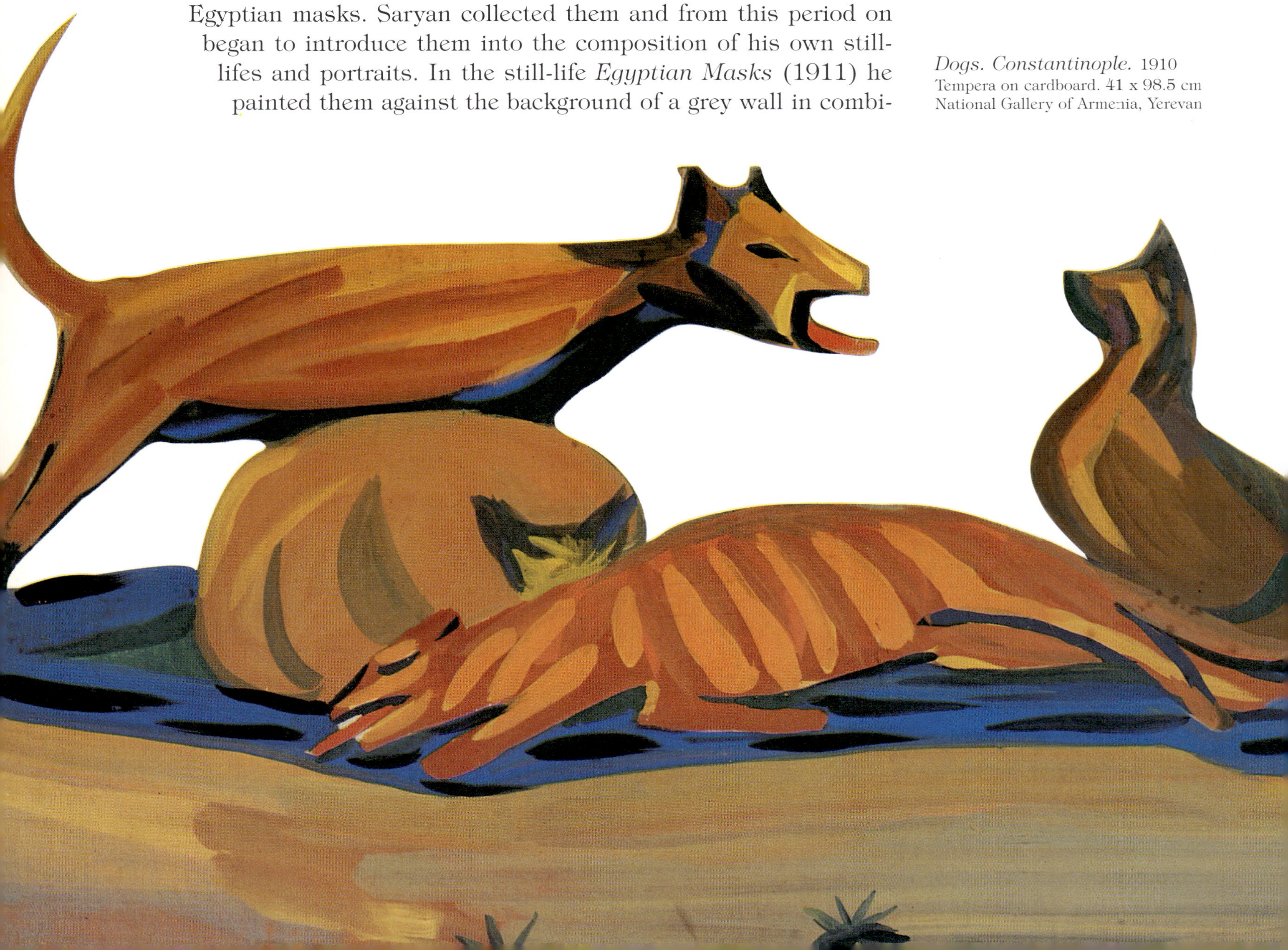

Dogs. Constantinople. 1910
Tempera on cardboard. 41 x 98.5 cm
National Gallery of Armenia, Yerevan

nation with fragments of pottery. For all their seemingly frozen nature, these immobile countenances are striking for the variety and intensity of expression in their wide-open eyes, closed lips and highly lifted brows. In them we can read arrogance, surprise, inquiry. The masks come to life, as it were, and we fall under the power of the magic force that they radiate. They appear to engage us in a dialogue, addressing us from eternity.

The world of the East is presented in the most varied motifs and manifestations in the artist's work. In Egypt he painted the endless desert running away to the sky in rolling waves of sand (*Desert. Egypt*, 1911). The relationship between their yellow-brown hues and the deep blue of the firmament is perceived as the equivalent of the desiccating heat, but even this burnt earth is capable of giving and supporting life. The signs of life – the tree and the figure of a man on a camel – are more than just an animating device; they are indications of the ineradicable, fecund power of nature.

This power also materializes in the glorious fruits that Saryan was now depicting all the time. Possibly the best known still-life of this period is *Grapes* (1911). Alongside the heavy, juice-filled bunches are a few round fruits and a simple vessel containing a green plant. They provide a sort of accompaniment to the main motif, stressing the saturated colour, entrancing succulence and weight of the grapes. The whole depiction presents an integral harmony of colours and shapes organized in a strict, yet natural arrangement. Saryan does not construct a composition in depth, does not strive after a clear division between the surface of the table and the wall. The two form a common, neutral background against which the artist spreads his objects and their shadows that play an important role in the structure of the composition.

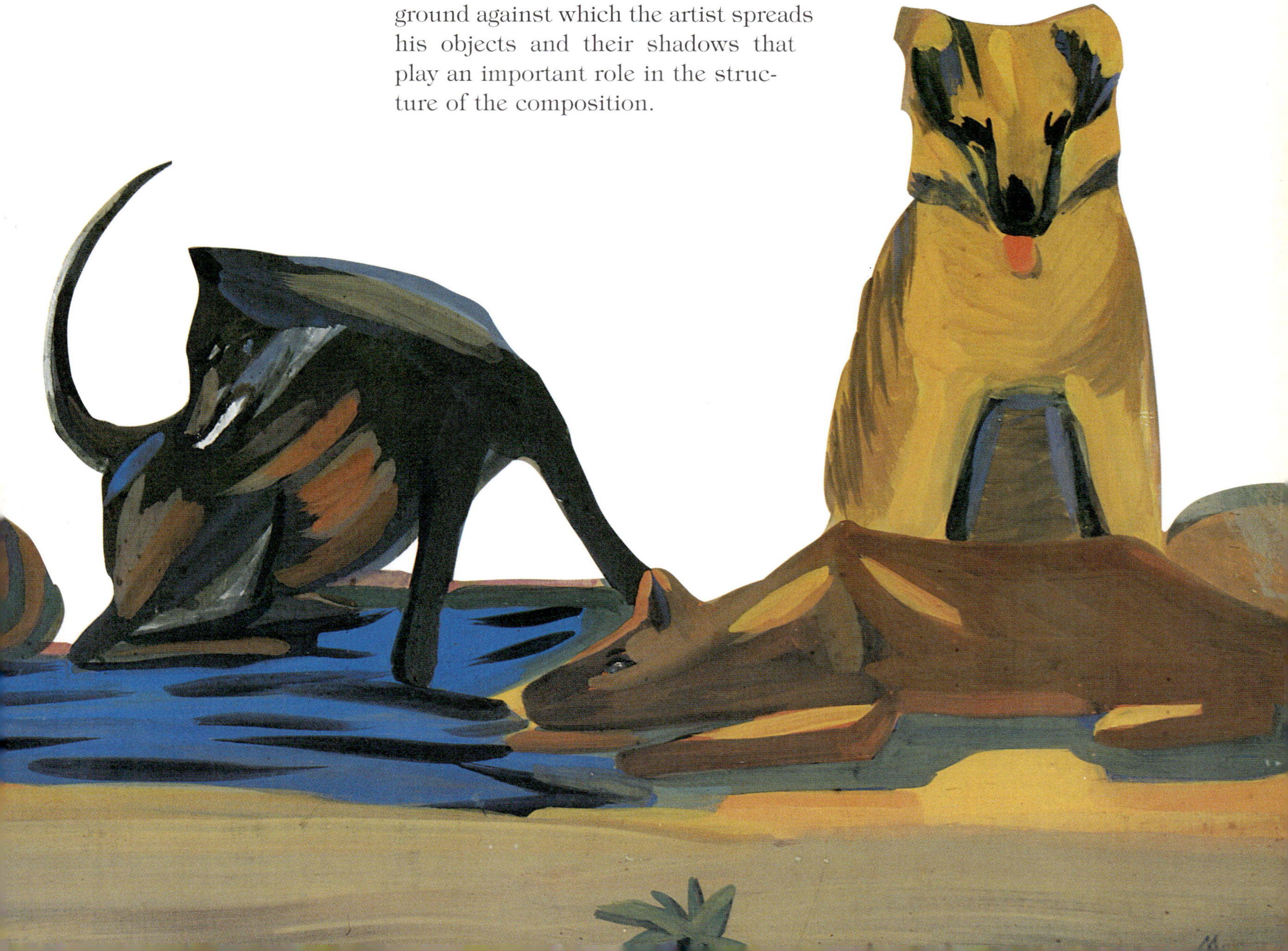

It is hard to say, without ifs or buts, to which particular genre many of the most characteristic paintings of the Eastern cycle belong. There are practically no pure landscapes among them. The artist himself said that he did not like "to paint an empty landscape; the figures of people and animals greatly enliven it."[32] Quite often such figures occupy a very modest place in the space of the painting, but their semantic role is very great. The majority of Saryan's works are images of Eastern life in the broadest

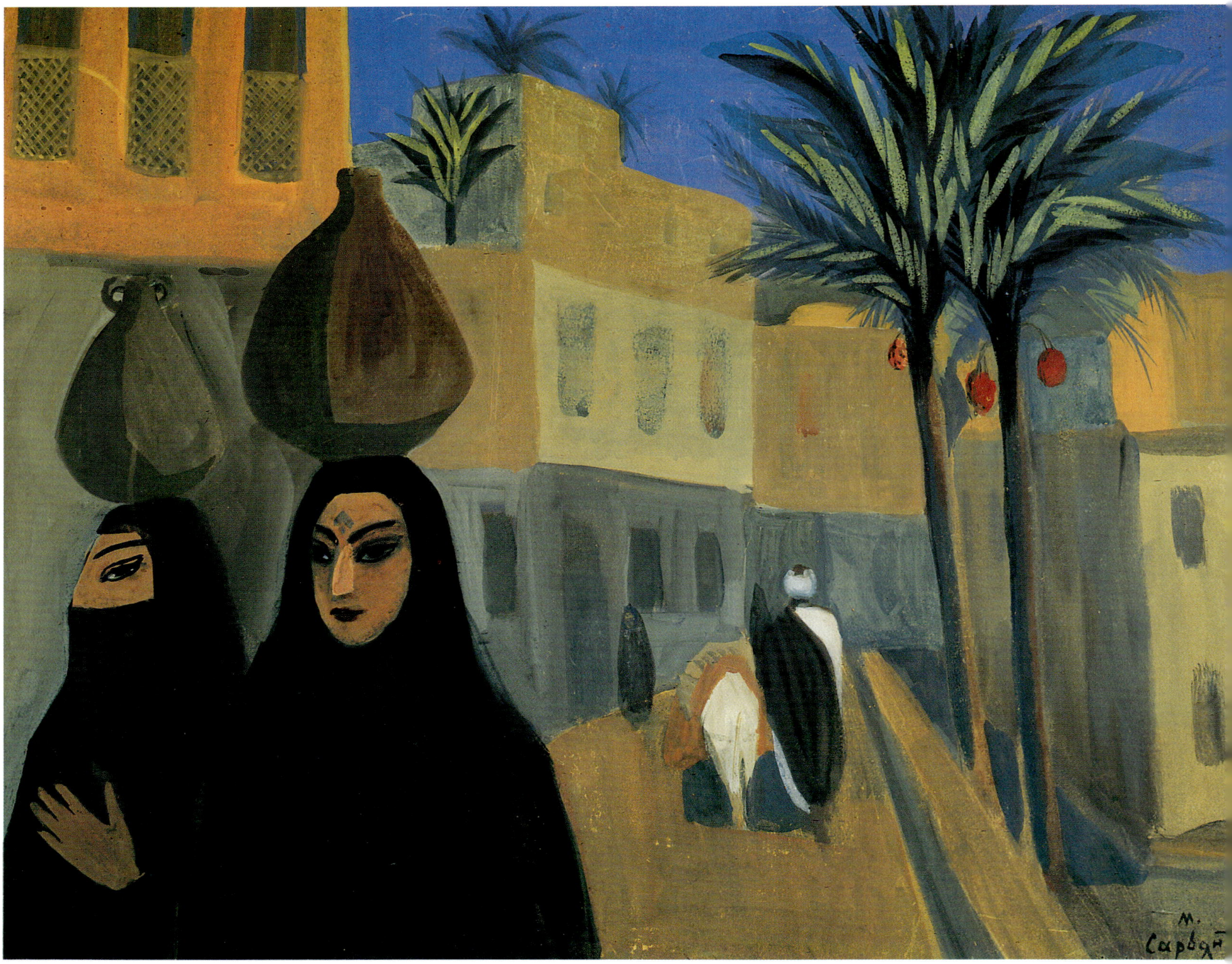

Street in Cairo. 1911
Tempera on cardboard. 48.5 x 64 cm
The Tretyakov Gallery, Moscow

sense. Like no one else, perhaps, he was able to convey the very essence of that life, its rhythms and colours, its charm. Even today many paintings of the Eastern cycle come across as poetic revelations. In them, it would seem, direct, keen observation is given the only possible expression, perfect in its painterly, plastic integrity. In *A Fellah Village* (1911) Saryan places the broad expanse of a street in the landscape format. The fiery colour of the ground fuses with the walls of the houses, which in the shadows take on a contrasting blue-black resonance. That is echoed by other dark patches – the buffalo in the left-hand part of the painting and the female figure by the wall, which are both conveyed by a solid area of black with broad blue brushstrokes giving it form with unerring precision. The combination of "dynamic and static" (Dmitry Sarabyanov) so typical of the artist's work is produced by a balance of patches of colour and shape, enhanced by the palms that frame the composition.

In *Date-Palm* (1911) – an image of the East that has become a classic and is arguably unsurpassed – a closely-related motif is given an even more laconic embodiment. The composition is ideally centralized. The palm with splendid branches spread in a dense blue sky serves as the vertical axis around which all the elements are grouped. In this painting

Dogs in Constantinople. 1910
Tempera on canvas. 104 x 139 cm
Martiros Saryan Museum, Yerevan

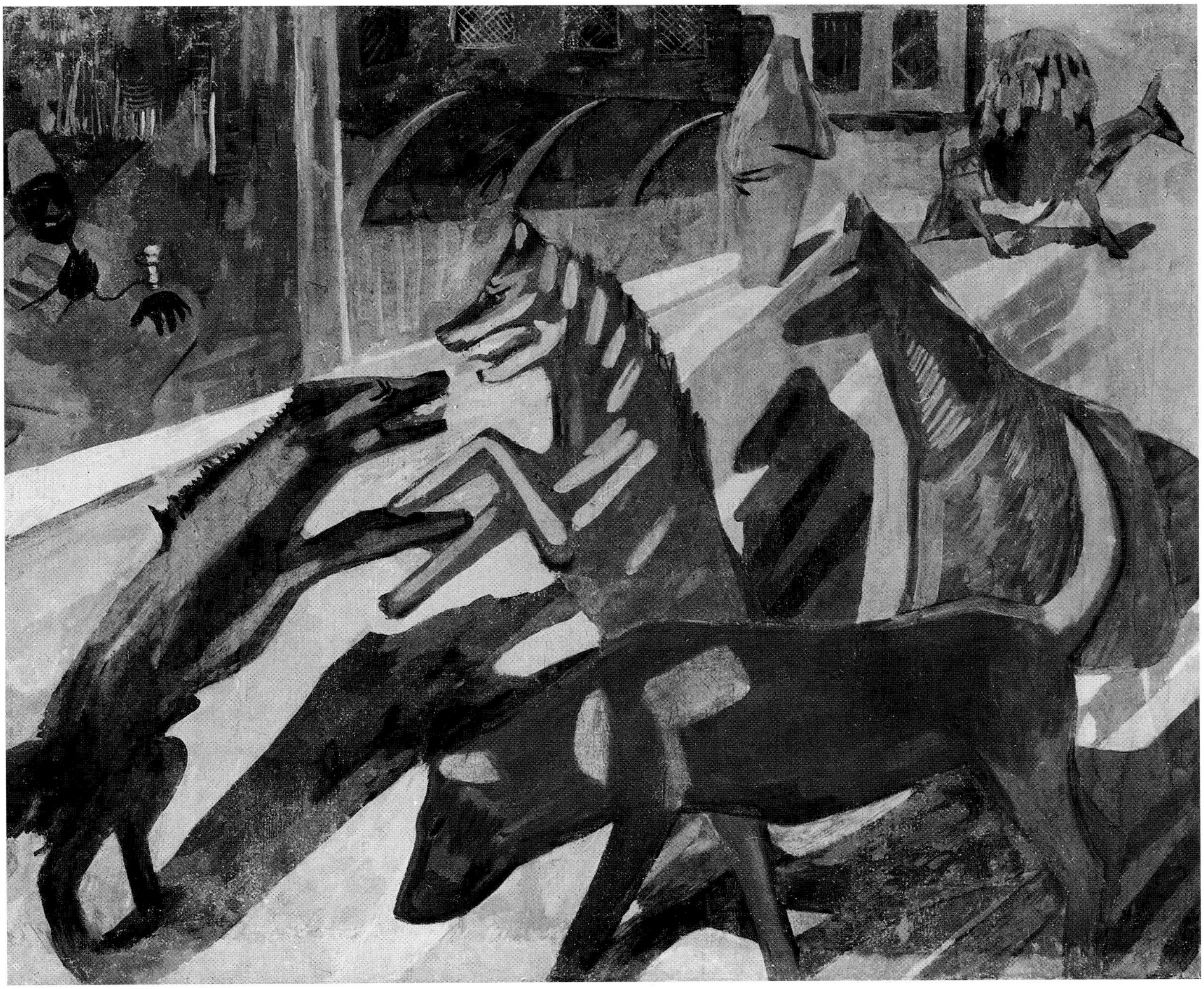

the static principle emerges victorious. An easy languor has seized everything beneath the scorching sun. The calm that reigns here is not disrupted even by the sudden intrusion of a camel's head into the seemingly frozen space. This device is indeed extremely typical of Saryan who, as Nikolai Punin aptly put it, knew how to "break out a silhouette"[33] and so provide a point of reference by which depth can be reckoned in a generally flat composition, introducing movement, unexpectedness, poignancy. Like the majority of the Eastern works, *Date-Palm* exudes the heat of the midday sun, which is expressed in the tense contrast between the sultry colours of the earth, the green of the palm-branches and the dense azure of the sky. The artist had no less subtle an appreciation of the colourful charms of the southern night. This is demonstrated in *Nocturnal*

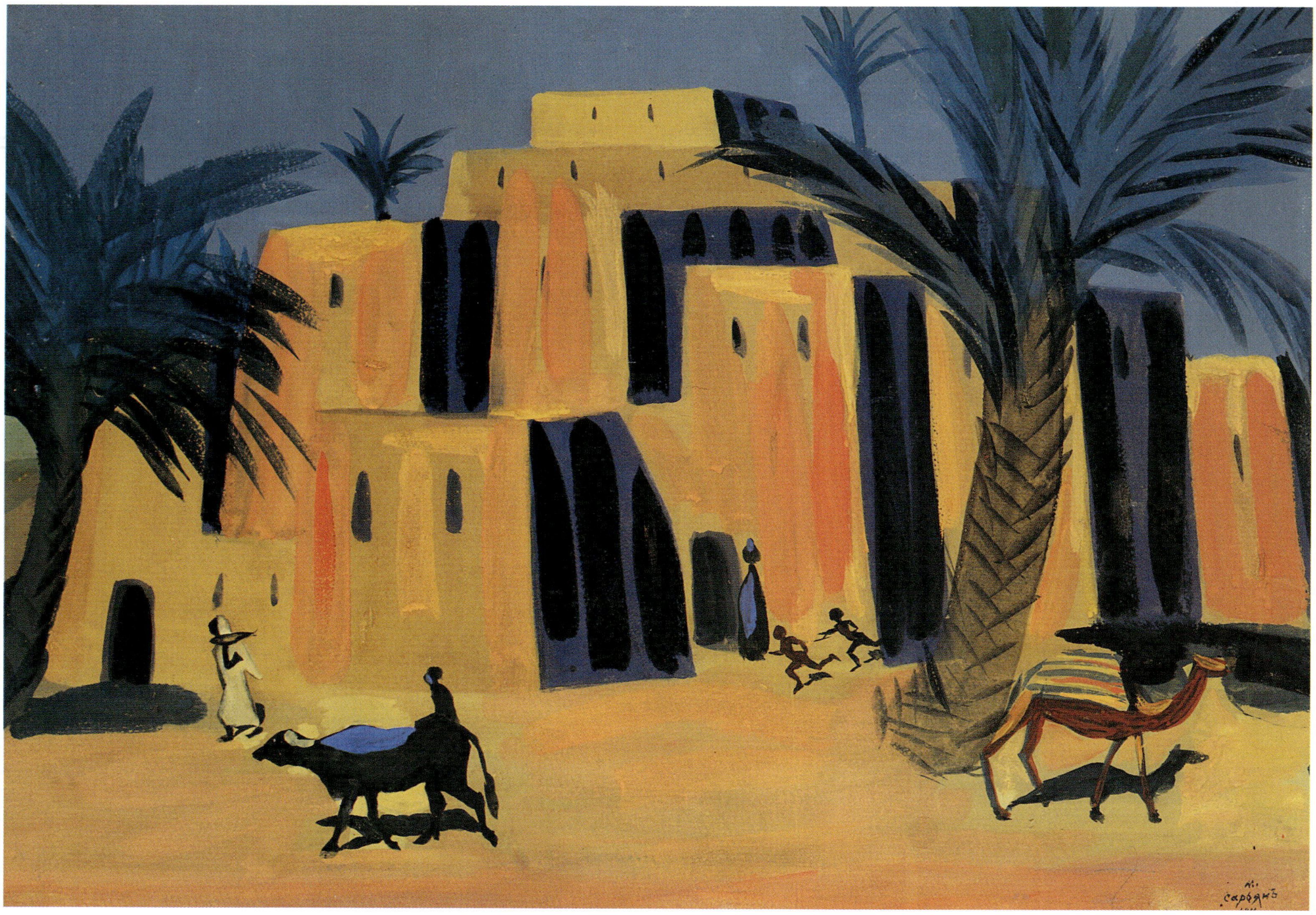

A Fellah Village. 1911
Tempera on cardboard. 49 x 70 cm
Art Museum, Riazan

Martiros Saryan in Egypt.
Photograph, 1911

Date-Palm. 1911
Tempera on cardboard. 106 x 71 cm
The Tretyakov Gallery, Moscow

Landscape (1911) embraced by deep blue that condenses to black in the shadows, the crown of the tree and the figure of the buffalo that, although frozen and immobile, is full of a striking sense of life.

There is no doubt that Saryan's impressions of the East were of great significance for the crystallization of his style. Here too a certain similarity with Matisse can be found.

As it is known, the French artist's interest in the East was firm and enduring. Matisse first visited Morocco in 1906, but it was a short trip that left no noticeable trace in his art. Of particular significance were two fairly long stays in that country, in 1912 and 1913. Matisse's impressions of Morocco were more than just an impulse to creativity, they decisively influenced his style. As the artist himself put it, they helped him "to move away from Fauvism and acquire new links with the real world."[34] We can, then, speak of the existence of common tendencies in the work of both artists, that do indeed reveal themselves in their "Eastern" compositions. There is no call, however, to speak of any sort of borrowings or direct influences. Saryan visited Turkey and Egypt before Matisse and many of his Eastern works had been created before Matisse's Moroccan paintings found their way to Russia.

Talk of overlaps in style between the two artists is, of course, relative, since each reveals vivid individual features even in closely related works.

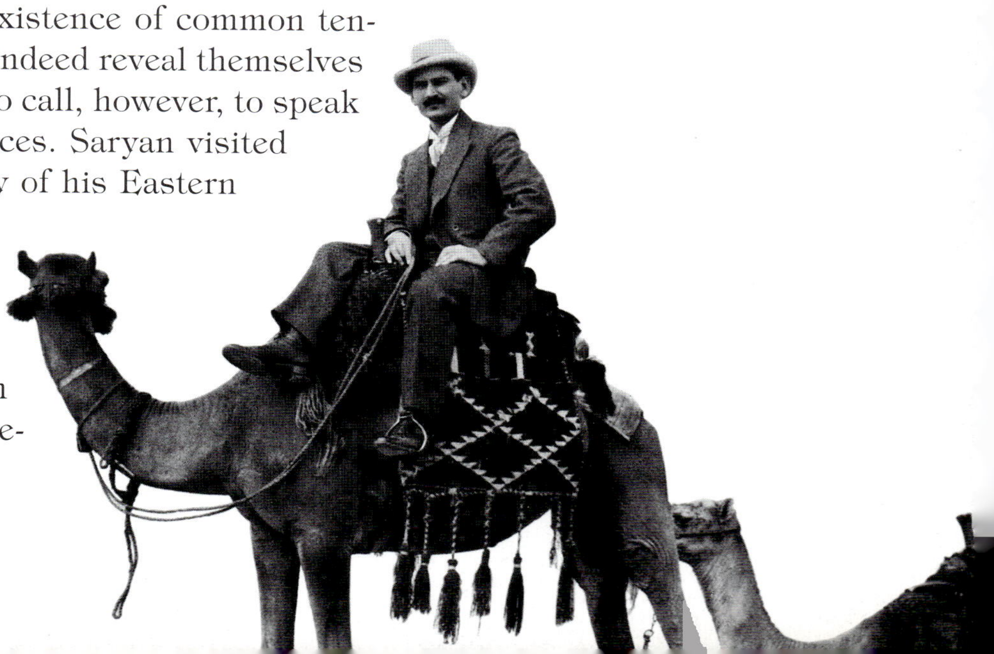

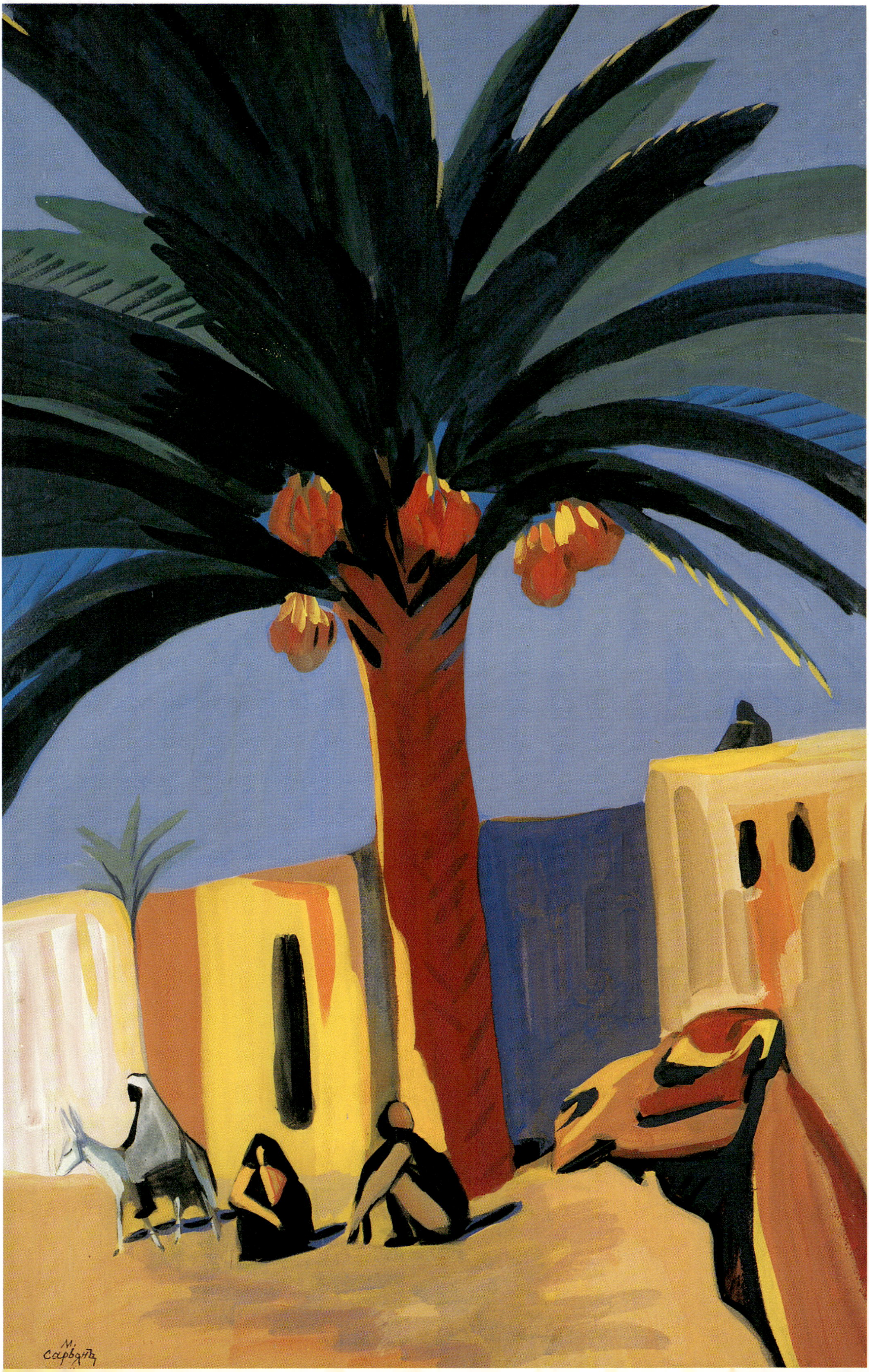
М.
Сарьянъ

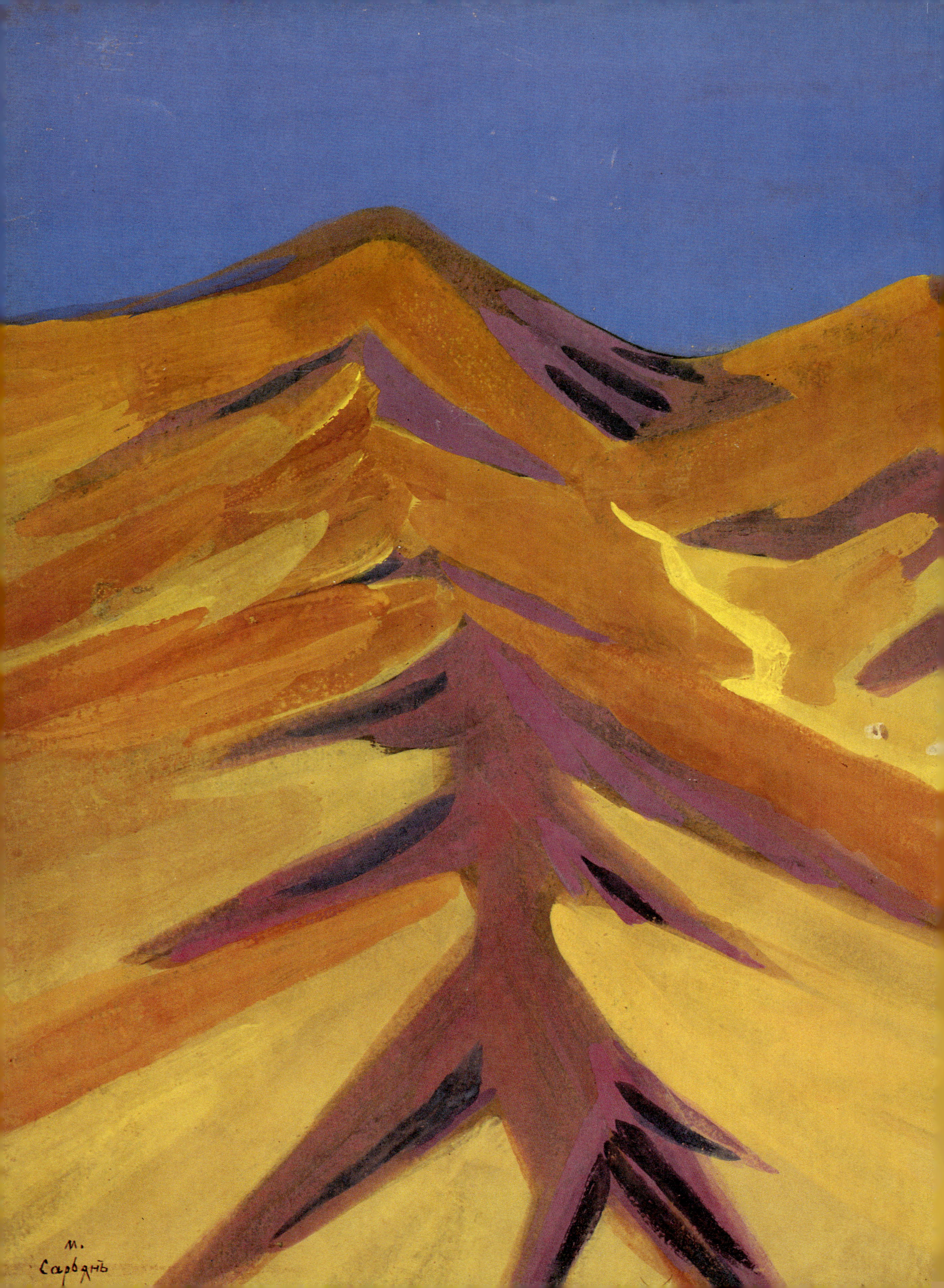

М.
Сарьянъ

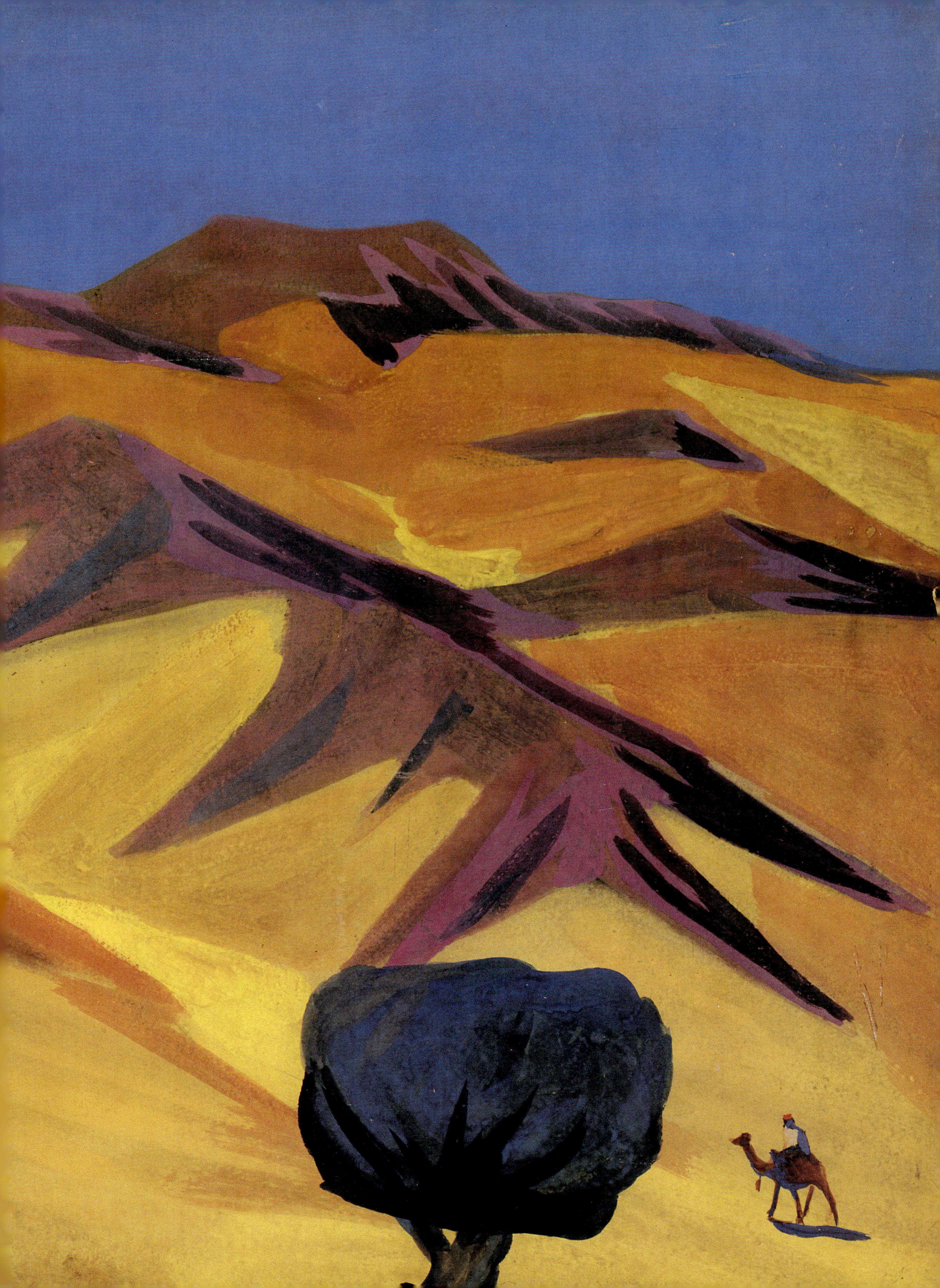

One such pair is Matisse's *View from the Window. Tangiers* (1912–13) and Saryan's *Street. Constantinople*. Both artists construct form and convey spatial relationships by a combination of flat, generalized patches, predominantly of pure colour – blue, gold and green with isolated strokes of red or pink. Saryan is more decisive in his simplification of shape and more active in his use of colour contrasts. Matisse's colour is lighter, more refined; Saryan's is more intensive. On the whole, the French artist's vision of the East is more remote and, probably, more rational. Saryan was more direct, more emotional in his delight in the world around him and at the same time more attentive to its specifics.

This is confirmed by some other examples, including the comparison of Saryan's *Egyptian Women* with Matisse's *Zorah Standing*. Both works date from 1912. Matisse's *Zorah*, for all the enchanting expressivity in the combination of the static figure and the intensity of her gaze, is more abstract in character – it is a poeticized, collective image of an Eastern woman taken out of the real current of life. Saryan's women are more terrestrial. They are full of vital strength. We keenly sense the quickness of their step, the energy of their gestures. Saryan also synthesizes features characteristic of their appearance and manner of behaviour, yet at the same time precisely indicates the individuality of each of them, albeit in simplified form, here too going further than Matisse. He is able to achieve a uniquely

←
Desert. Egypt. 1911
Tempera on cardboard. 51 x 69 cm
National Gallery of Armenia, Yerevan

Greengrocer. 1912
Tempera on canvas. 71 x 88.5 cm
Museum of Russian Art, Kiev

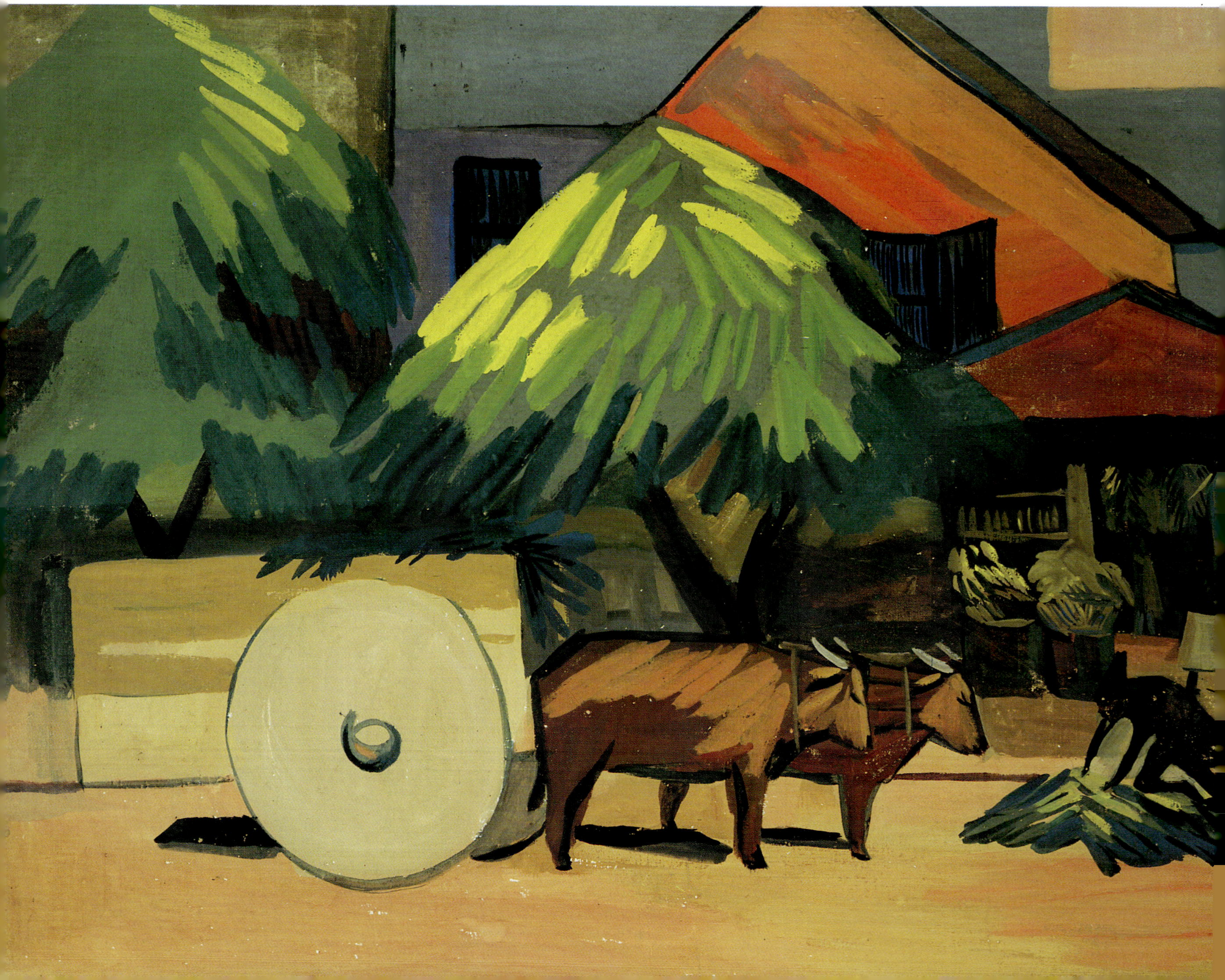

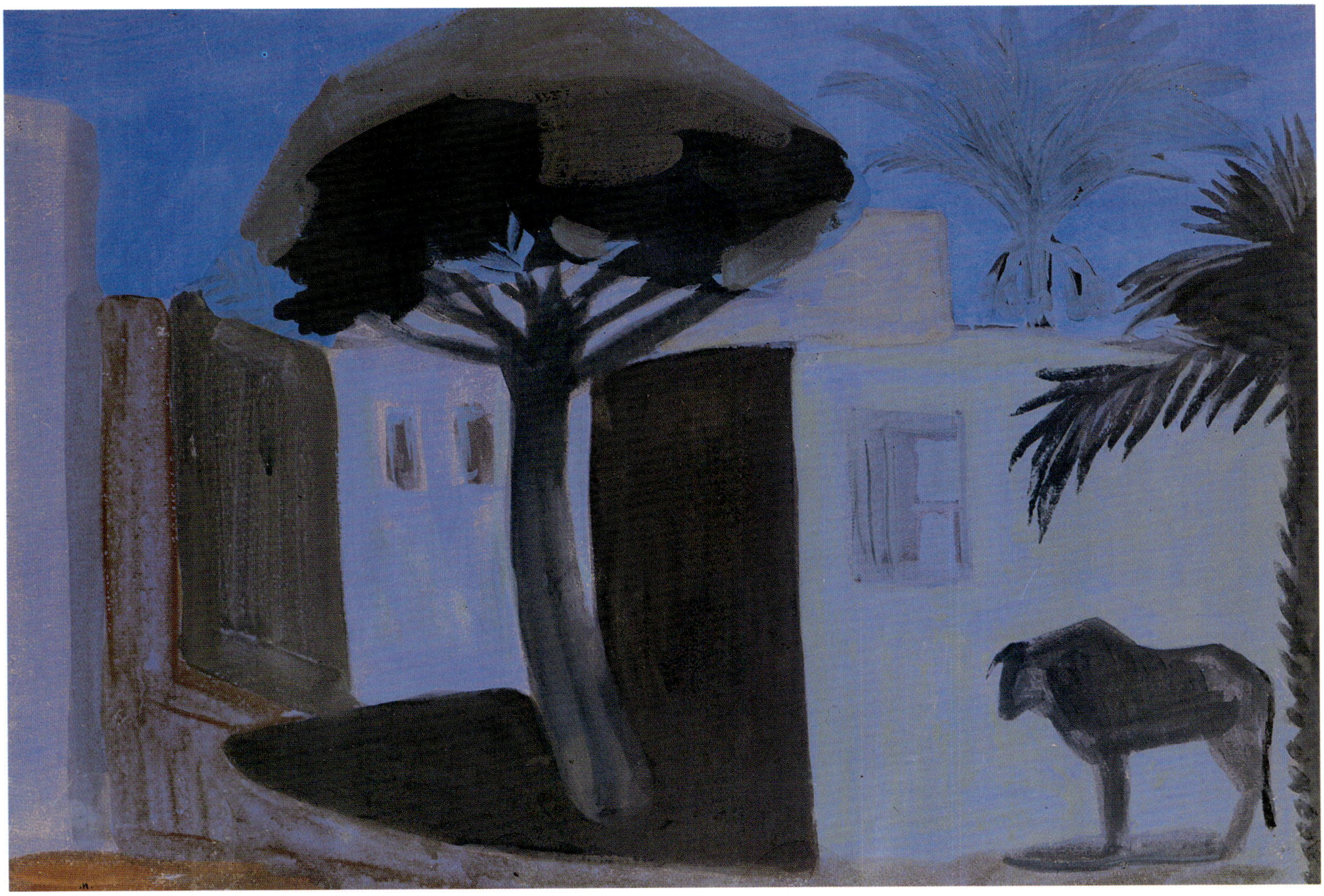

Nocturnal Landscape. 1911
Tempera on cardboard. 47 x 68 cm
L. Saryan collection, Yerevan

specific expression with a single dab of paint, laid on boldly and precisely, or a sharp contrast of colours. We can also note the absence in his work of the ornamental element that characterized many of Matisse's paintings of the early 1910s and expressed itself in the trimmings of the costume in *Zorah Standing* and in another painting now in the Hermitage – *Zorah on the Terrace* (1912–13). At the same time, the sensation of shape, the exceptional significance given to colour in the structure of the image, and the very principle of "drawing with the brush" which both artists follow are undoubtedly evidence of kinship between their stylistic concepts. Yet this kinship is not always strong, as is revealed by a comparison between Matisse's *Arab Coffee-House* and Saryan's *Persia*, both from 1913.

Matisse worked for a long time on this painting, which might be considered one of his most perfect creations, the most poetic and inspired image of the East in his art. It is general knowledge that he moved from impressions from life to ever more abstract and synthetic embodiments of them. In his work, for all the expressiveness of the light languorous poses and silhouettes of the figures, the main thing is to convey a general state of dreamy contentment, self-absorbed meditation. It is poured out, as it were, in the transparent bluish atmosphere with which the incorporeal figures almost merge. In this unsteady haze any attempt at closer definition, even an allusion to identifiable facial features would be an unacceptably dissonant note.

Saryan retained all the keenness and immediacy of observation from life. In his painting (which he called a panel) every figure is given a specific, to some extent even portrait characterization – this is true of the red-bearded old man in a turban and the youth breathing in the smoke from the hookah in self-oblivion. This does not, however, in any way reduce the viewer's perception of the scene as an expression of certain fundamental features of slow-moving Eastern life, its beauty and slightly coarse charm, put over with a barely perceptible touch of humour. It is in this combination of specific characterization and the general that the distinctiveness of Saryan's art lies.

In *Persia* the Eastern colour is enhanced by a skilful, free adaptation of the Iranian miniature traditions. This makes itself especially felt in certain background figures. The Eastern artistic tradition across the widest geographical area – Armenia, Iran, Ancient Egypt – gave much to Saryan. He perceived it in a very organic manner and, with very rare exceptions, was not inclined to stylization. One of the exceptions, the later painting *In Persia* (1915), is an elegant and striking composition, eloquent and

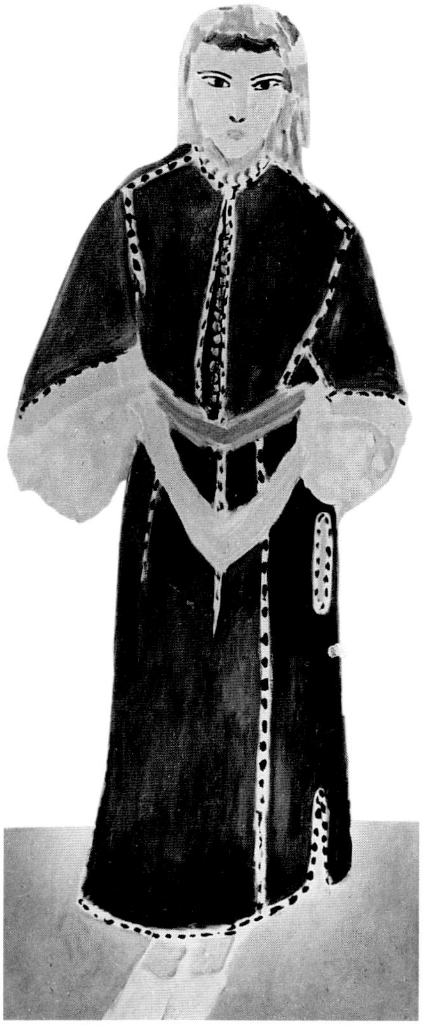

Henri Matisse. 1869–1954
Zorah Standing. 1912
The Hermitage, St Petersburg

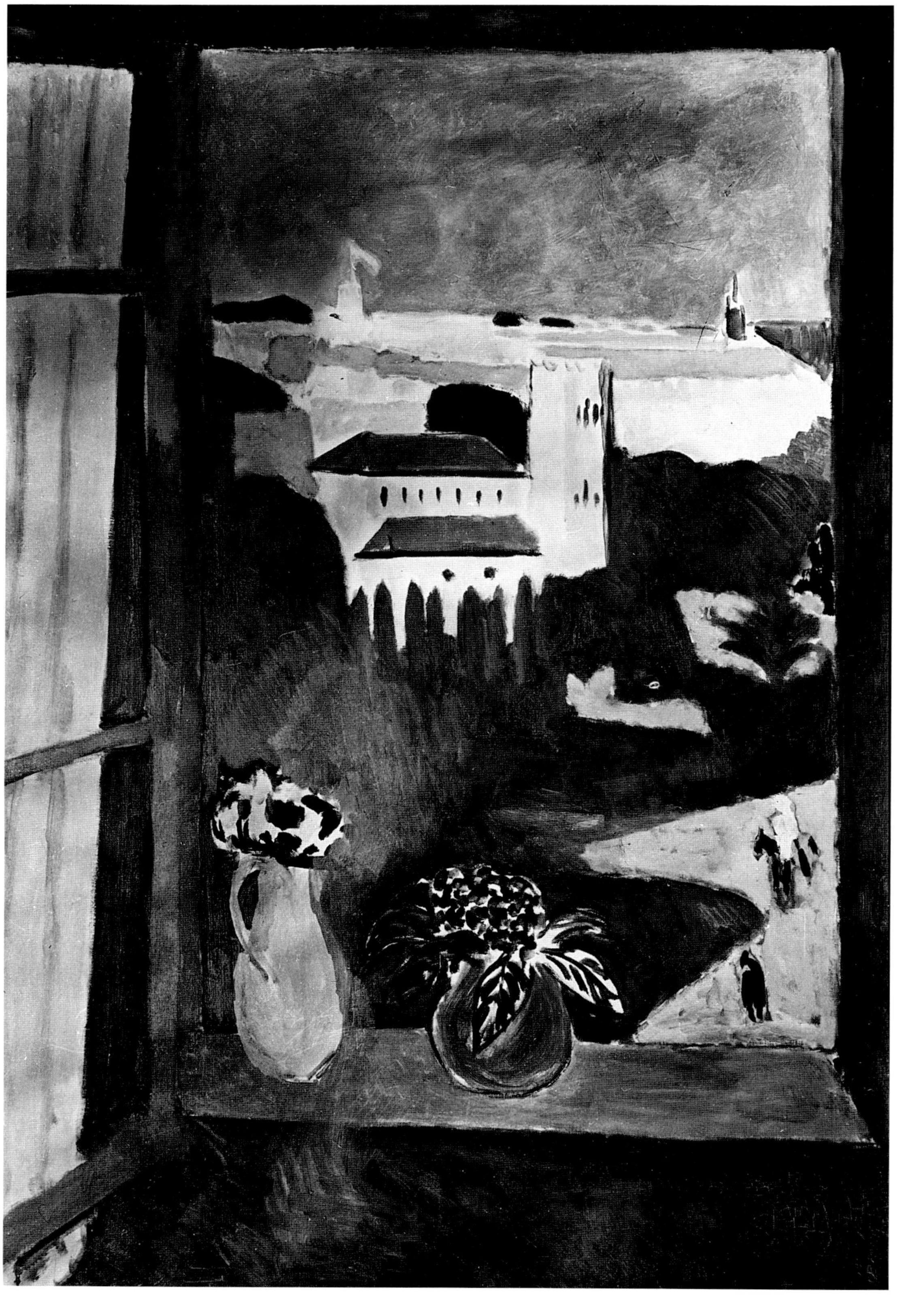

Henri Matisse. 1869–1954
View from the Window. Tangiers. 1912–13
The Pushkin Museum of Fine Arts, Moscow

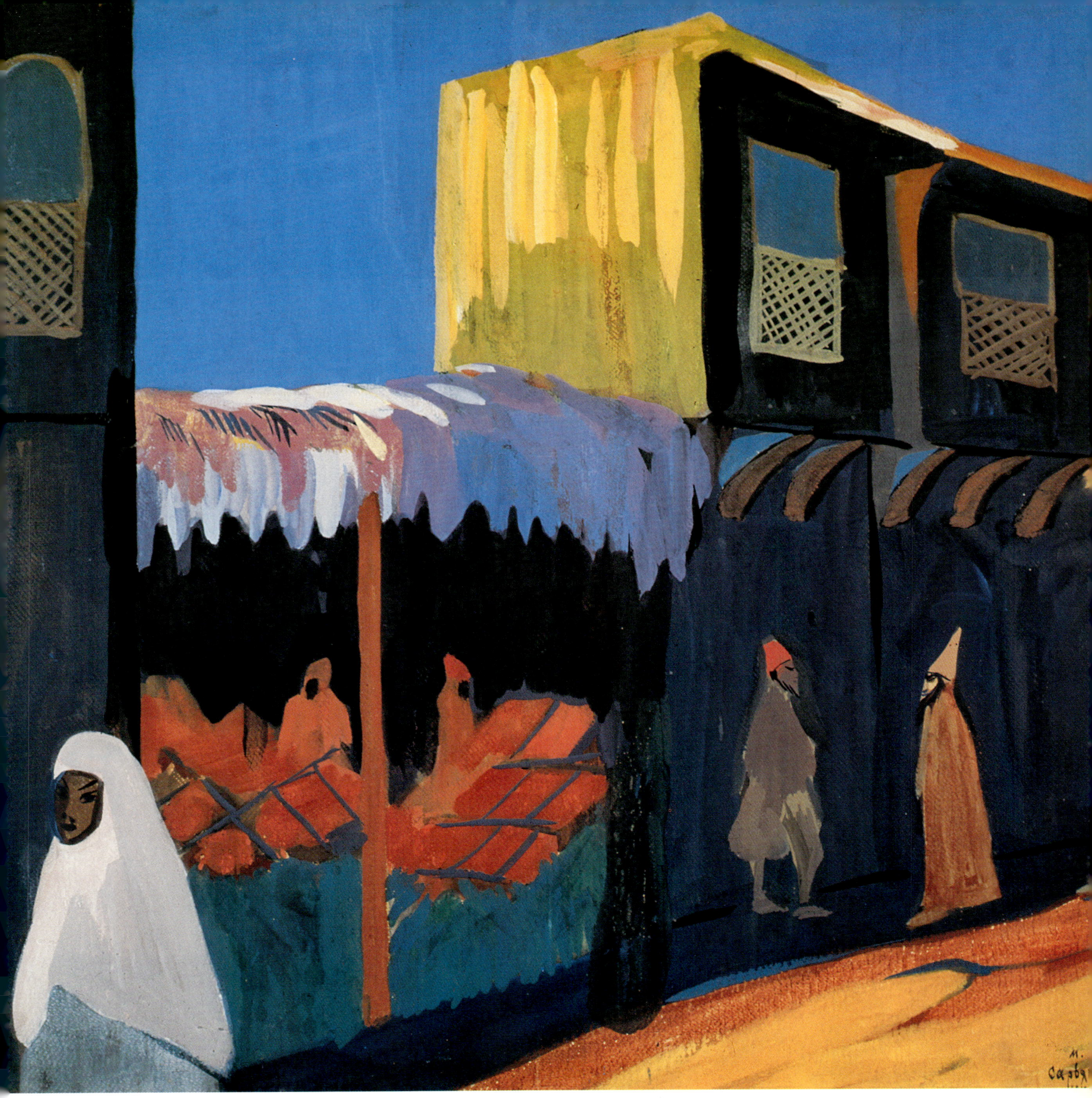

Street. Constantinople. 1910
Tempera on cardboardi, 59.5 x 63.5 cm
The Tretyakov Gallery, Moscow

→
Egyptian Women. 1912
Tempera on cardboard, 76.5 x 53.2 cm
The Russian Museum, St Petersburg

→
Woman Walking. 1911
Tempera on canvas. 68 x 51 cm
A. Arutiunian family collection, Moscow

precise in the details, but too overtly connected with the Iranian miniature in its general structure, in the "stacking" of spatial planes and motifs from different times arranged from the bottom upwards.

Saryan did not sacrifice observation from life even in those instances when it might seem that the abstracted, flat conception of form excluded direct contact with the real world. A brilliant confirmation of this approach is *Woman Walking* (1911). The figure is "sprawled" across the surface. The face is presented in profile, as in Ancient Egyptian art, and also as a patch of paint. Its outline in combination with the sketched-in eye, eyebrow and mouth recreates the character of the real-life original with an accuracy that is at the same time garish and moving.

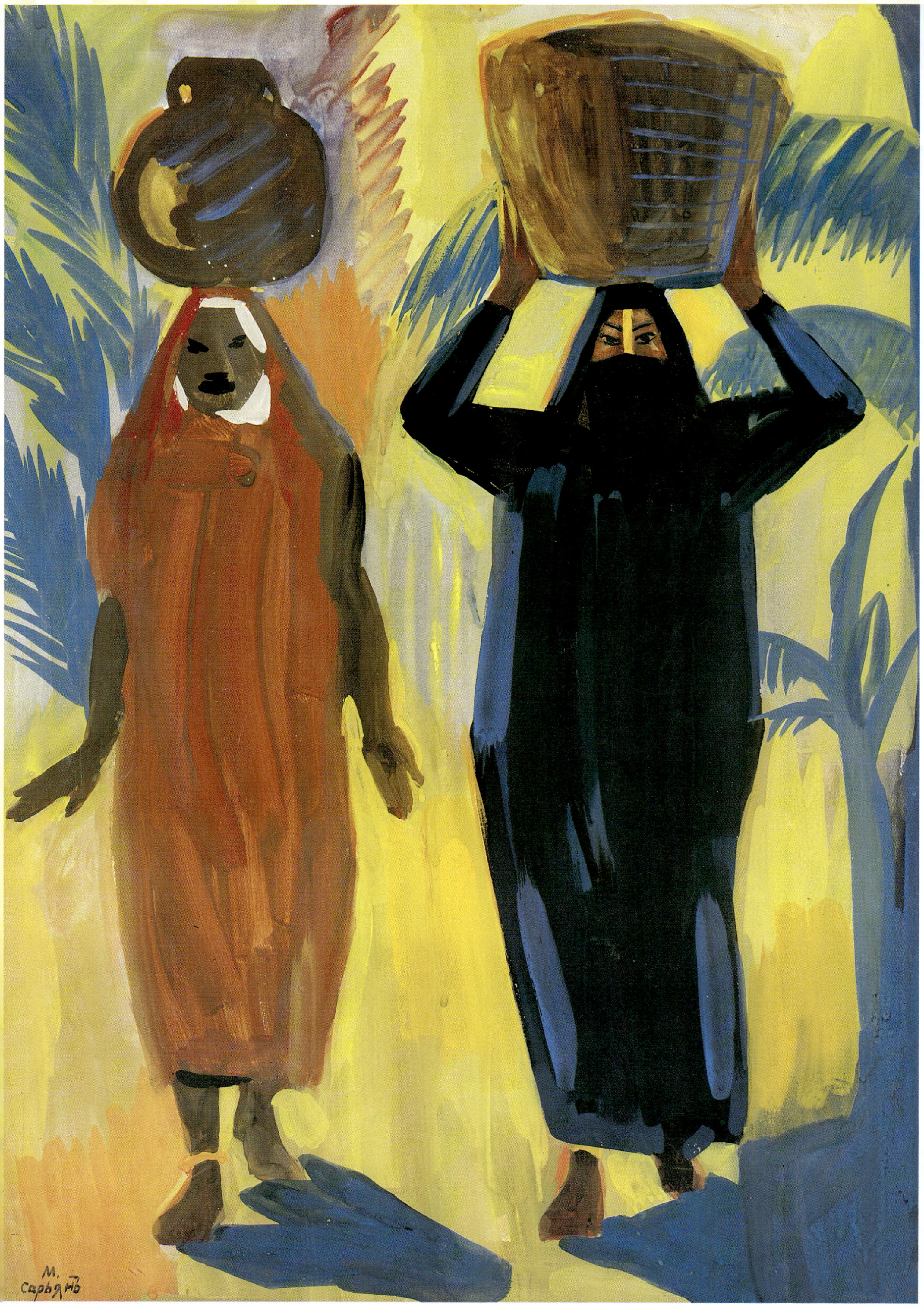
М.
Сарьянъ

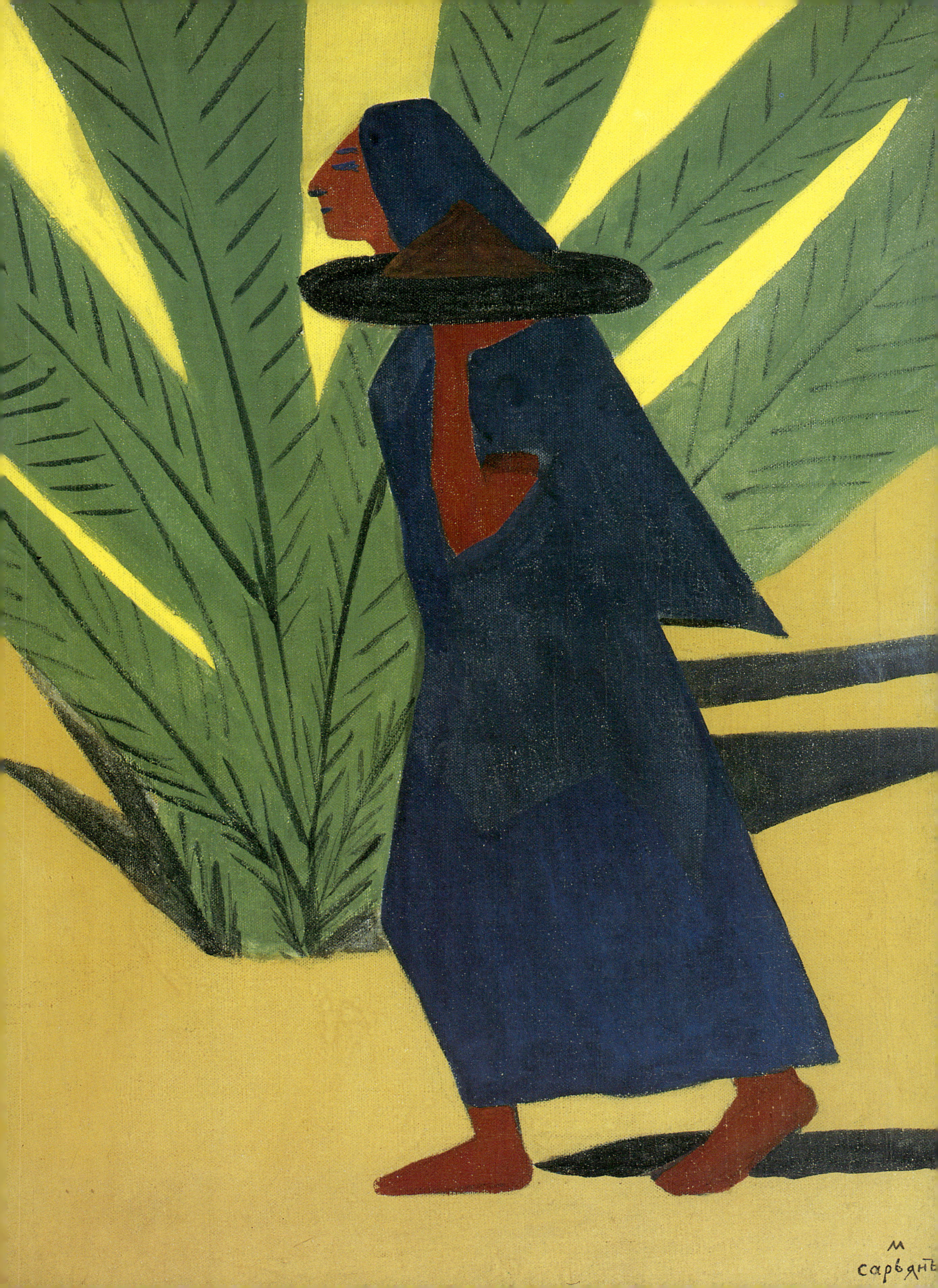
М
Сарьянъ

The elements of depiction are reduced to a minimum – the figure and the palm that serves as its background. The depth is practically not indicated; the golden ground changes its tint and passes into the golden glow of the sky. The contrast with the blue shadows creates a sense of bright sunlight. These shadows are organically linked into the play of colour patches and strike a chord with the green of the palm and the dense blue of the figure. The woman moves towards the sun, cutting the space with

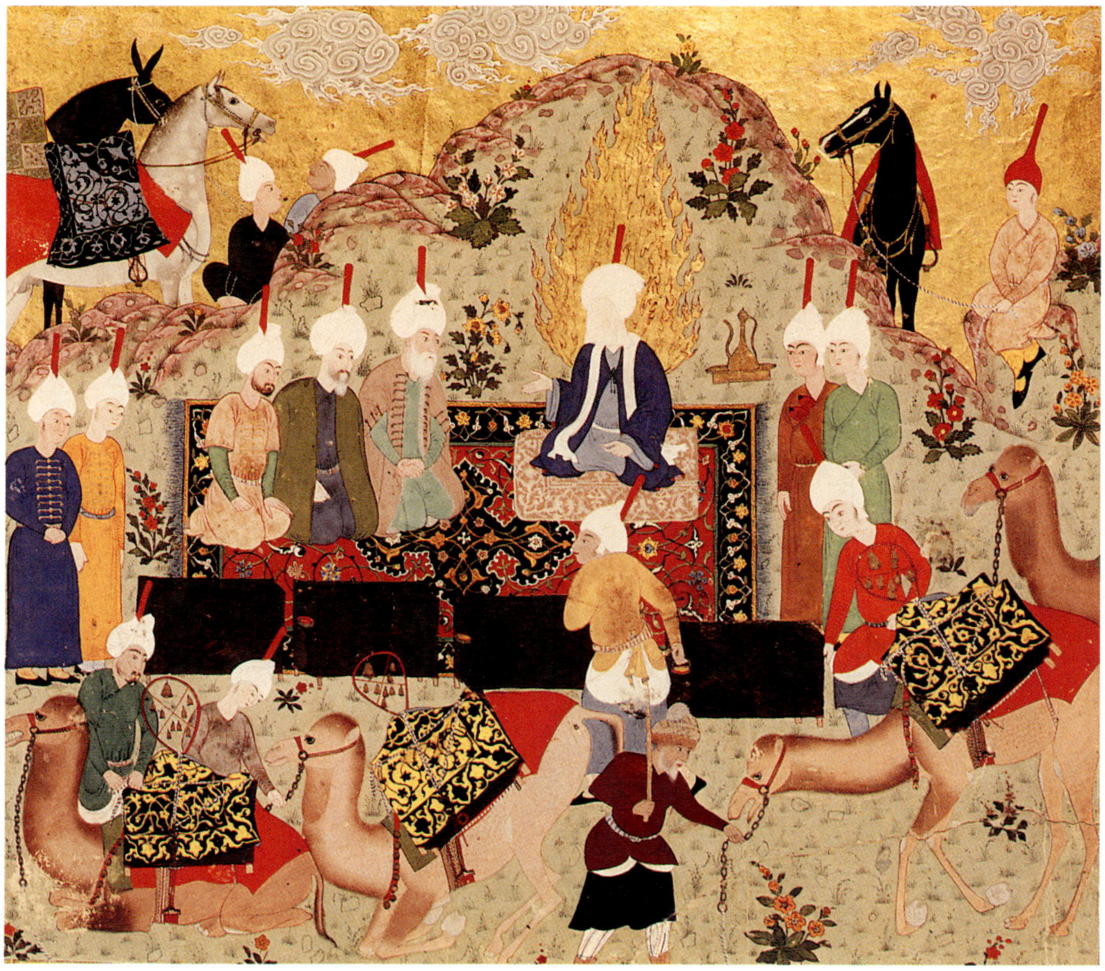

Miniature: *Khurasan Merchants before Muhammad ibn-Ali al-Bakir.* By Qasim ibn-Ali
Iran, Tabriz school
From the manuscript *The Story of the Faithful Imams* by Muhammad ibn-Abu Zaid ibn-Arabshah al-Husaini al-Alawi al-Varamini. 1521
The National Library of Russia, St Petersburg

her sharp profile. The simple motif acquires a broad collective significance. The image of the fellah woman comes across as a plastic symbol of the East with its impenetrable reserve, its contradictory combination of movement and calm. This emblematic quality teeters on the edge of poster schematization, but Saryan does not cross that boundary, primarily due to the sense of the living image that never let him down.

In the intervals between his journeys to the East, the artist worked in Moscow and visited Armenia. He painted landscapes more directly connected with the real world than the paintings of the Eastern cycle, but never simply imitating nature. Saryan was always convinced that "nature provides the material so that the artist made his own, new nature from it".[35] This kind of active interpretation of Armenian scenery can be found in *Morning. Green Mountains* and *Mount Abul with Passing Camels*, both from 1912.

Saryan considered the winter of 1910/11 to have been the first stage of his successes and the beginning of "real recognition". Some of the artist's works were acquired by the Tretyakov Gallery (*Wisteria* and then *Street. Noon*). Throughout the first half of the 1910s (as, incidentally, in the preceding years) he participated in many major exhibitions in Moscow, St Petersburg and other Russian cities. The critics who had originally

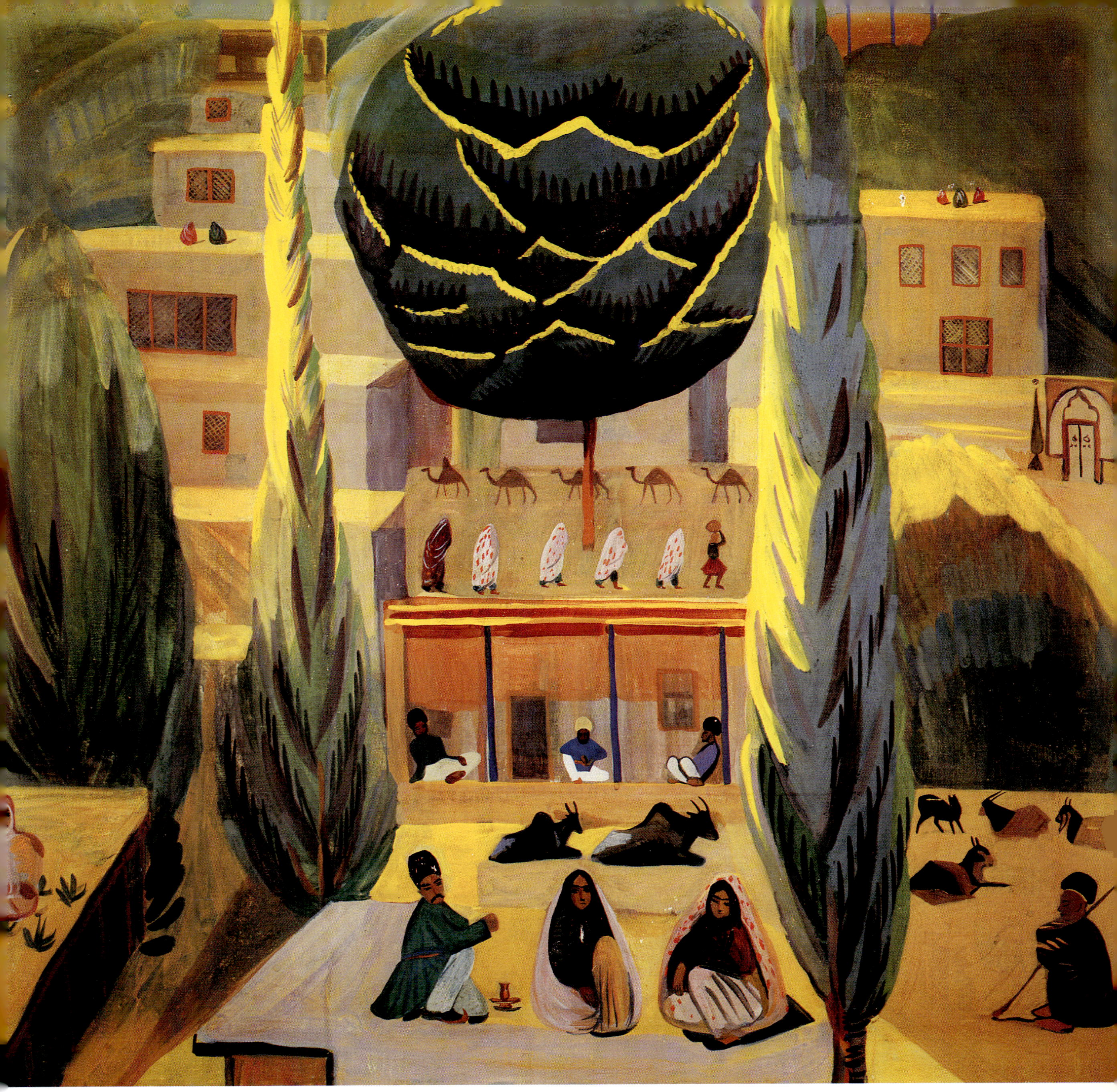

In Persia. 1915
Tempera on canvas. 112 x 120 cm
V. Kunin collection, St Petersburg

been very antipathetic, put off by the artist's bold innovation (the "colouristic alarm-bells of his work", their "merciless brightness"), rated Saryan more and more highly. Pavel Muratov, who as far back as 1908 had noted Saryan's works as the best things in the Russian section of the "Golden Fleece" exhibition,[36] thought very highly of his *Constantinopolitan Observations* at the 1911 exhibition of the Union of Russian Artists.[37] That same year Sergei Makovsky wrote that "of all the 'young ones' – the seekers and the darers – he [Saryan] is perhaps the most original".[38]

As early as 1909 Sergei Shchukin, the great collector and connoisseur of contemporary art, was delighted with Saryan's *Self-Portrait* at the "Golden Fleece" exhibition and commissioned a portrait of his son from him. Compositionally, the portrait of Ivan Shchukin (1911) is indeed similar to the *Self-Portrait*, but the painterly approach is entirely different. For the likeness of Shchukin junior Saryan employed "a purely decorative method".[39] Shape is constructed by large patches of colour; the painted surface is calmer than the dynamic, tense texture of the *Self-Portrait*. The face would come across as a frozen mask were it not for the wide-open eyes disgorging a powerful stream of energy at the viewer. "A cannon! Two cannon!" the artist Serov said of them.

The *Self-Portrait* and the depiction of Ivan Shchukin opened a new period in Saryan's work as a portraitist.

He found no difficulty in producing a likeness, but that was not what the artist considered the main task of portraiture. "I am interested above all in the inner content, the character of the personality and then, of course, its outward manifestations in gestures and facial expression," Saryan said.[40] He considered the most difficult part to be the "art", that is to say finding an artistic form suited to his conception of the model.

The artist's early portraits are not marked by compositional variety, but they are always very active in terms of colour. He painted the head frontally, more often than not close up, cutting the figure off at a more or less low level. Each time a special world opens up before us, full of inner movement and life. Saryan's portraits are distinguished by especially keen assessment of the sitters and a sharpening of their basic characteristic features. And in order to bring out those features he found special paint-

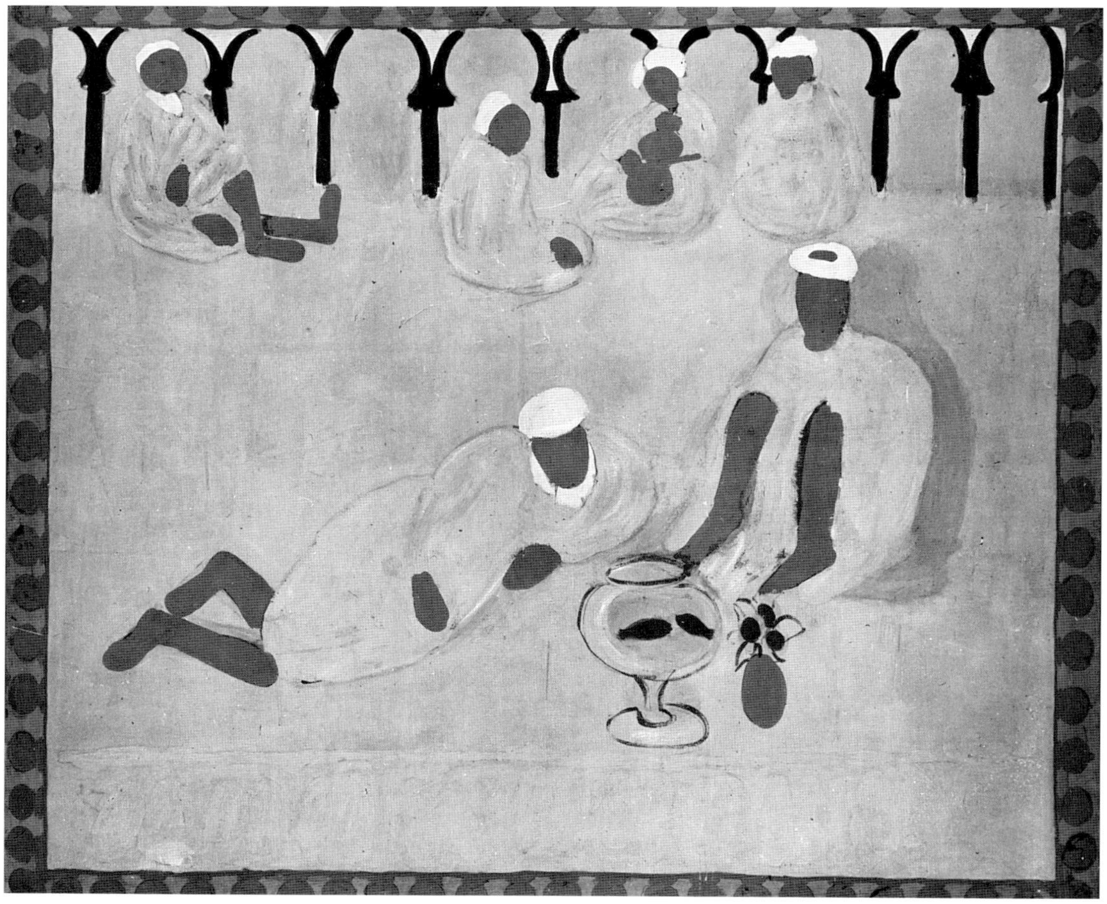

Henri Matisse. 1869–1954
Arab Coffee-House. Ca 1913
The Hermitage, St Petersburg

erly devices and relationships of colour. In the 1912 portrait of the art-historian Garegin Levonian, for example, his active, wilful character and stormy temperament are revealed above all by the energetic modelling of the face with large, dynamic brushstrokes and the contrast between its swarthy tone and the black cap of hair, the glaring white of the collar and the greenish hues of the clothing and background. In the later portrait of Alexander Tsaturian (1915), not only the thoughtful pose and sad look,

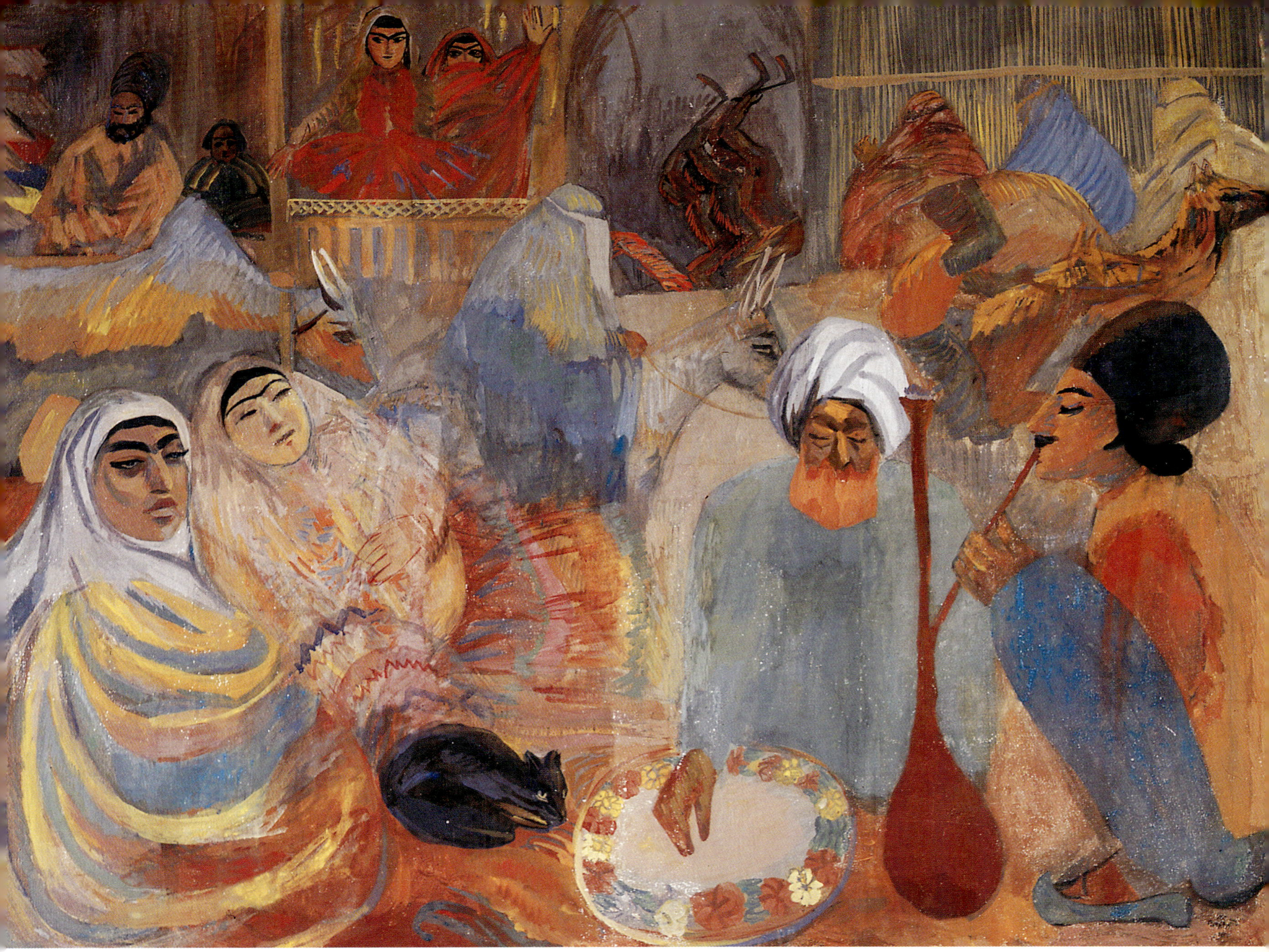

Persia. 1913
Tempera on canvas. 140 x 185 cm
Martiros Saryan Museum, Yerevan

but also the more restrained tonality with the black patches of clothing, hair and beard dominant convey the appearance and character – outwardly calm, but filled with a concealed air of tragedy – of a poet whose muse informed the world of the fate of his people with a piercing sadness. It seems that in this portrait Saryan created a painted equivalent to Tsaturian's poetry, its intonation and mood.

Energy, will-power and inner strength are the dominant features of the 1915 image of Mnatsakan Giulnazarian. Alexander Kamensky gave a convincing interpretation of this little-known portrait by Saryan as "a modern paraphrase of the national heroic epic".[41] "He was unruly, audacious, fiery" – that characterization of Mger of Sasun in Avetik Isaakian's poem would seem to apply equally here.[42]

The subjects of all three portraits, so various in character and cast of mind, undoubtedly evoked profound sympathy in the artist. He had a different attitude to the millionaire Iosif Mantashev, a narrow-minded, superficial, satiated individual, who nonetheless interested the artist on account of his strongly expressed "Eastern colour". Saryan stressed it, painting Mantashev against a background of red drapes with bright flowers, in a dressing-gown that made him look "like an Indian maharajah".[43] In contrast to the other portraits that are full of the intensiveness of psychological or emotional life, the 1915 portrait of Mantashev seems the embodiment of inertness, spiritual immobility and passiveness.

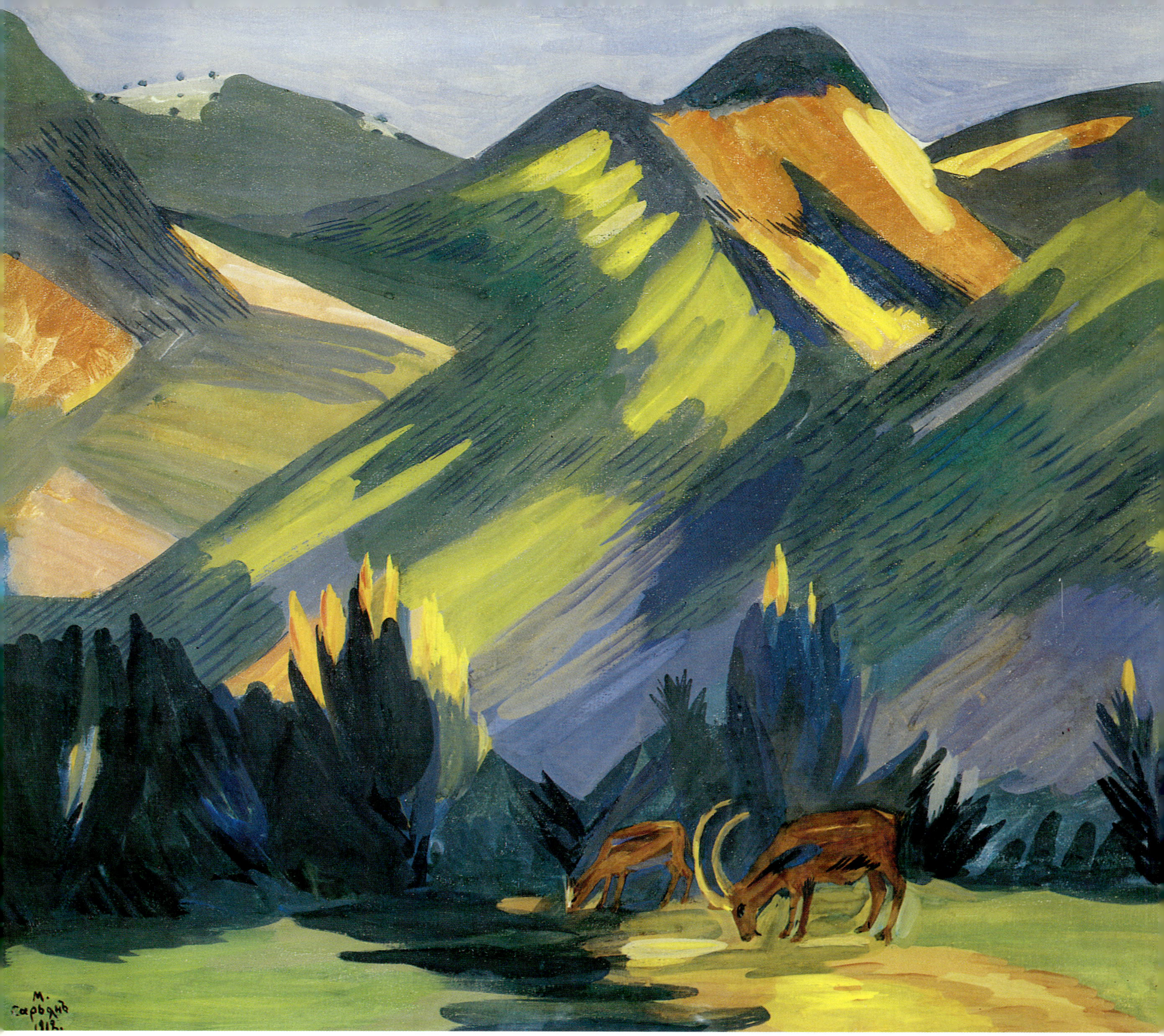

Morning. Green Mountains. 1912
Oil on canvas. 74.5 x 58.5 cm
The Russian Museum, St Petersburg

In Saryan's female images collective features dominate, synthesizing general poetic conceptions of Eastern womankind. One such is the *Persian Woman* already mentioned. Related in some ways is *Head of a Girl* (1912) – a portrait of the artist's cousin Mariam Tazakhulakhian, but that captivating image of a young Eastern beauty places more stress on individual character and the girl's proud awareness of her own attractiveness.

The mid-1910s were a time of transition in Saryan's life and work. Outwardly his affairs were in excellent shape. "Every year brought me successes," the artist recalled, "but my mind was constantly torn by doubt. New thoughts and intentions arose in me."[44] Artistic life in Moscow was becoming ever more motley and chaotic. There was much in it that seemed alien and false to Saryan. He strove to get away from Moscow, to isolate himself and work. Plans for new journeys – to India, China and Japan – were left unrealized due to the outbreak of the First World War. Before that, however, in the spring of 1914, the artist headed to Transcaucasia. "Travelling around my homeland, I obtained from nature answers to questions, which had long bothered me and which were clearer than you will find in any treatise on aesthetics."[45] Saryan painted studies in Yerevan (including *Ararat and Zangu*), a cycle of superb still-lifes *The Flowers of Kalaki*, and a small canvas that was nonetheless grand in terms of spatial sweep – *The Surb-Khach Rocks at Kalaki*. It was as if he rediscovered Armenia for himself and he "worked with great inspiration, learning from nature about composition and painting in a landscape".[46] This was the year that laid the foundations of new tendencies in the artist's work that came to full fruition in the following decade.

A profound shock for Saryan, one which to a certain extent shaped his destiny, was the genocidal attack on Armenians in Turkey. Those who escaped the bloody annihilation sought refuge in Transcaucasia. Saryan,

Mount Abul with Passing Camels. 1912
Oil on canvas. 138 x 142 cm
National Gallery of Armenia, Yerevan

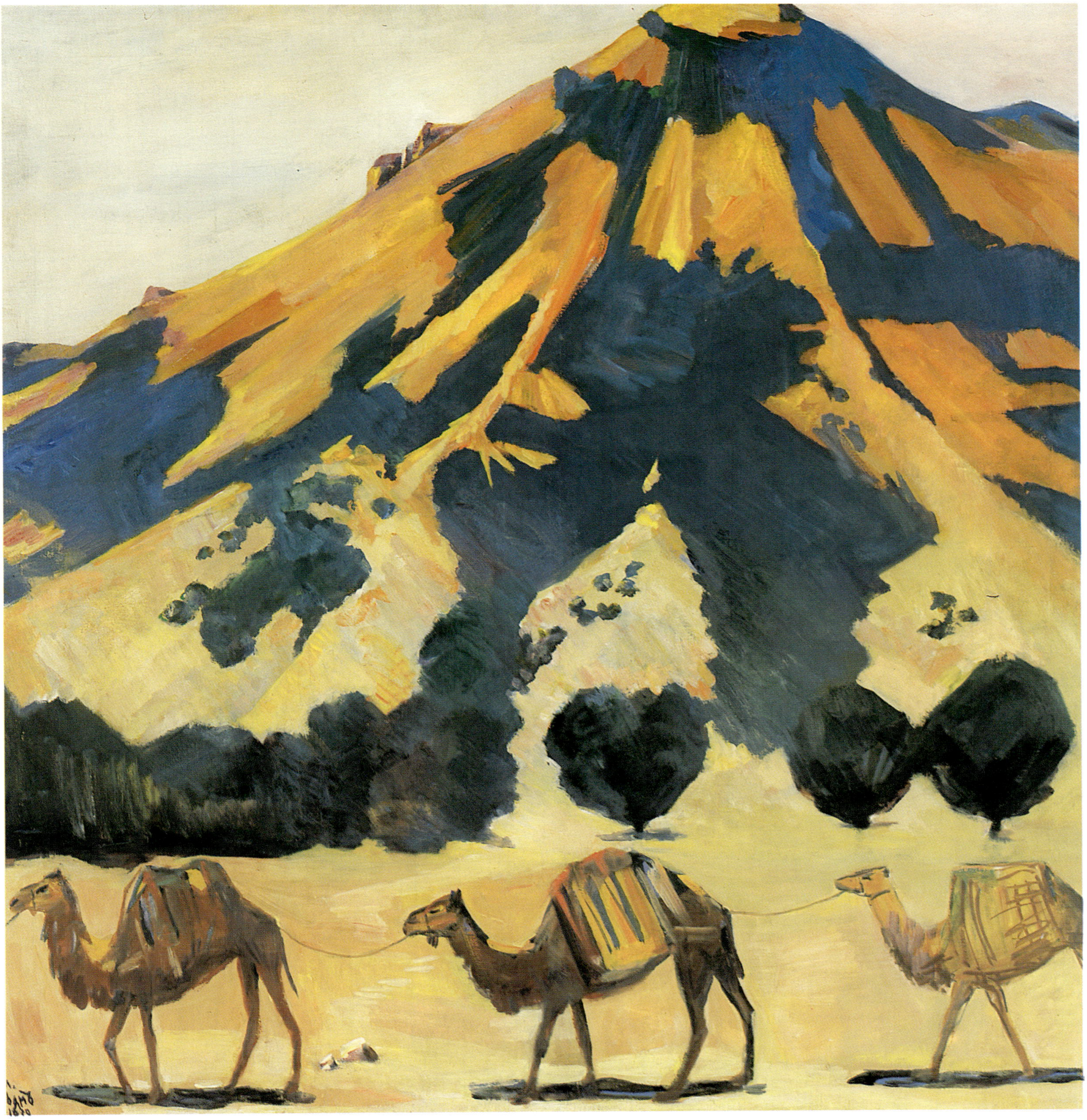

who travelled to Armenia in the summer of 1915 as a member of the Refugees' Relief Committee, found a terrible picture of hundreds dying from exhaustion and disease. "In those days of suffering," Saryan recalled later, "with all my heart, with all my being I became kin to my people. And I would not exist as an artist, if that sense of my homeland had not grown within me. I devoted all my subsequent work to that homeland."[47]

During the war Saryan lived mainly in Tiflis. There, in the spring of 1916, he married Lusik Agayan – an event which undoubtedly encouraged his achievement of a final spiritual balance and a renewal of his vital energy. He took part in the World of Art exhibitions in 1915 and, for the last time, in 1916, when he displayed the portrait of Alexander Tsaturian already mentioned.

Among the relatively small number of works produced in the second half of the 1910s, mention should be made of the splendid still-lifes, including the fairly diminutive *Fruit* and *Wild Flowers*, both from 1916. In contrast to the majority of floral still-lifes, here the colour activity is allocated to the background of the painting, on which one can easily make

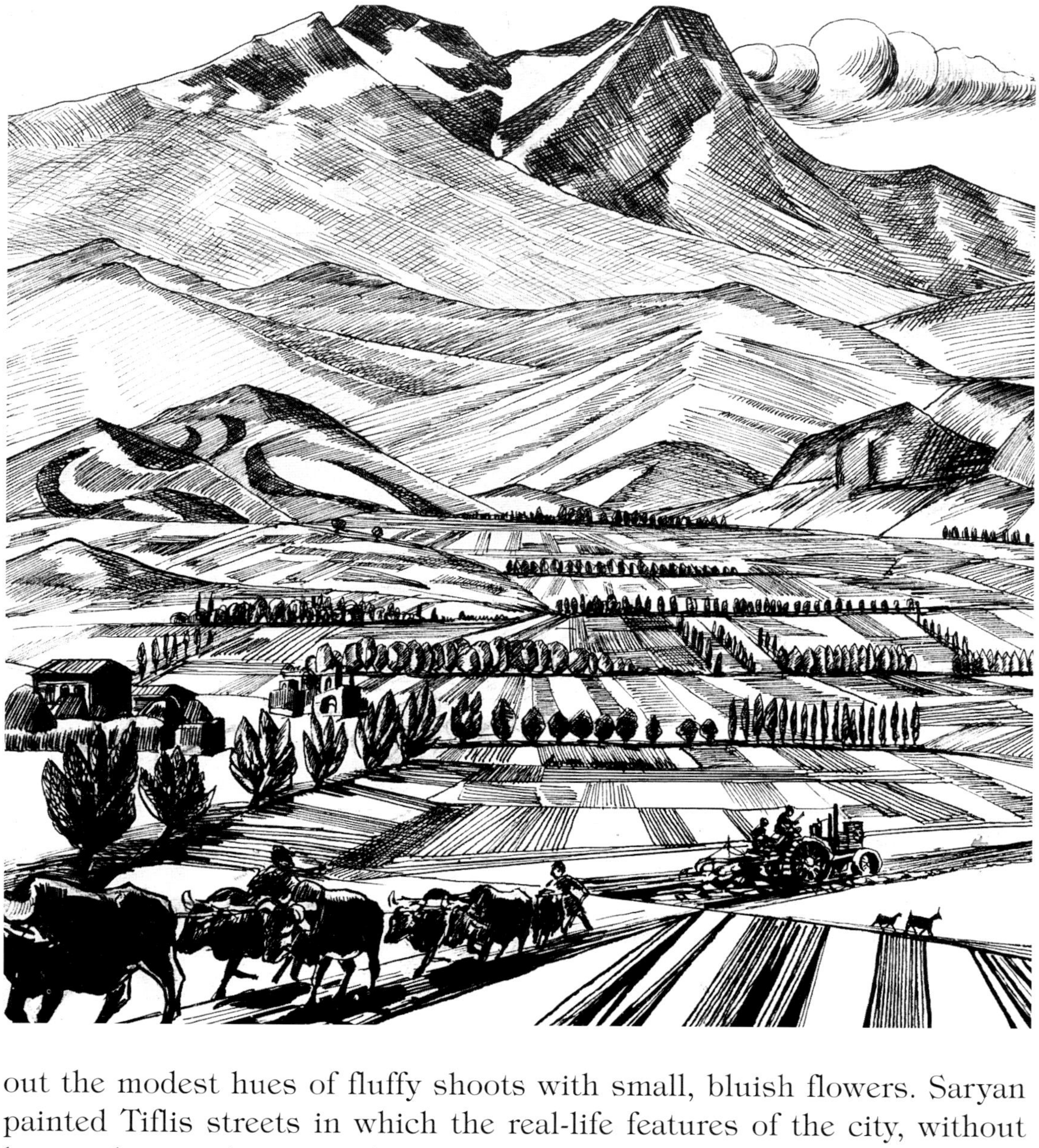

Aragats. 1925
Indian ink on paper. 26 x 25 cm
National Gallery of Armenia, Yerevan

out the modest hues of fluffy shoots with small, bluish flowers. Saryan painted Tiflis streets in which the real-life features of the city, without losing their authenticity, become transformed at times into decorative, colourful fantasies (*Afternoon. Old Tiflis*, 1917). The charm of the Eastern fairy-tale springs up again in all its mysterious delight in the opulent, heady visual "chord" of pinky-reds, yellows and greens in the painting *The Red Horse* (1919).

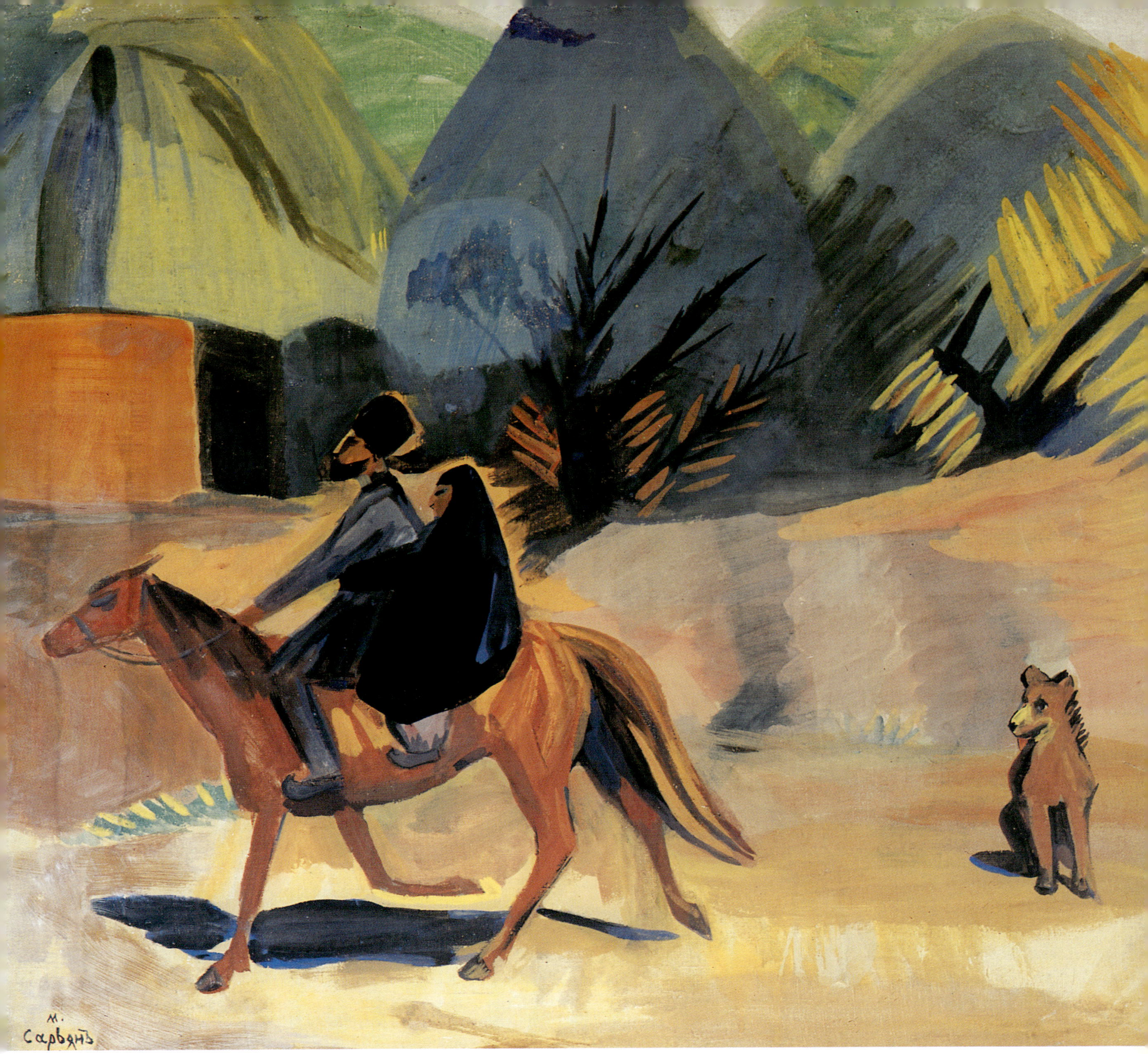

On Horseback. 1912
Tempera on canvas. 59 x 79 cm
National Gallery of Armenia, Yerevan

Nonetheless this was a time of transition in the artist's work. The beginning of a new peak was associated with changes in the historical destinies of Russia and Transcaucasia – with the formation of the Armenian Republic. For Armenians around the world this was an event of tremendous significance. After several centuries without their own state, they finally acquired a real homeland. "After enduring terrible tribulations, the surviving portion of the Armenian people, who had still not had time to dry their tears, began, on a small scrap of land at the foot of Aragats, in the conditions of the just order that had arisen, to lay the foundations of their economic and cultural life."[48]

The greatest representatives of the Armenian intelligentsia – writers, architects, artists – flocked from all corners of Russia and all ends of the Earth to the land of their ancestors, full of the brightest hopes and an unshakeable certainty in its revival. Saryan was among the first. In 1921 he moved to Yerevan for good and devoted himself with immense enthusiasm

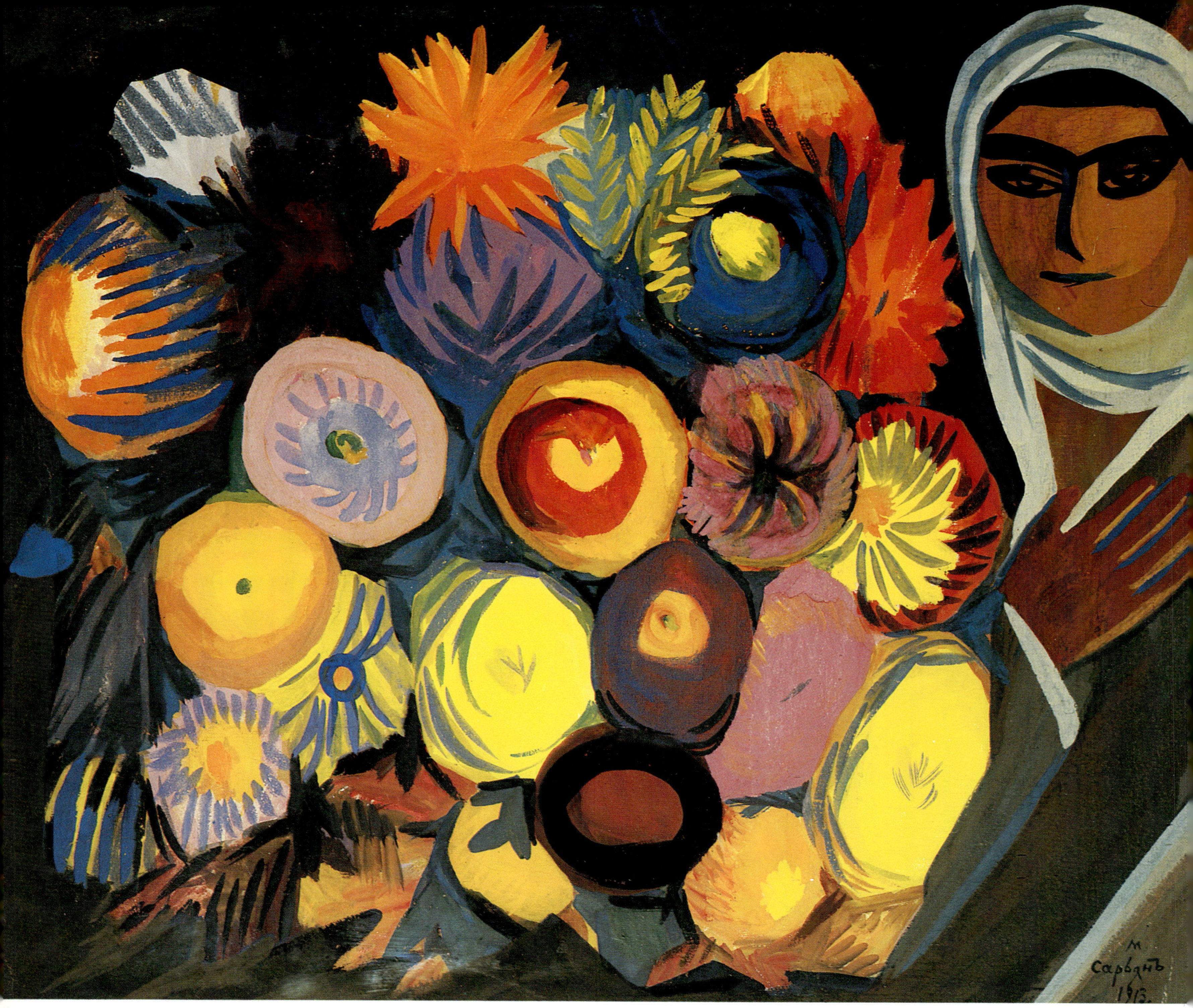

Still-Life. 1913
Tempera on canvas. 55 x 66 cm
The Radishchev Art Museum, Saratov

to the noble and difficult mission of regenerating Armenian culture. As its normal course of development had been broken off long ago and virtually everything had to be built again on the newly acquired land, without forgetting the great traditions that still lived on in surviving monuments, splendid illustrated manuscripts and a rich and varied folk art. And, of course, in literature, the evolution of which had proceeded practically uninterrupted, despite the vicissitudes of history, from the heroic epic of ancient days, through magnificent mediaeval poetry to the poetry and prose of the modern era. Many men of letters were friendly with Saryan, or became so when they moved like him to Armenia.

For the first the artist was immersed in his cultural mission. Thus, he organized the Museum of Archaeology, Ethnography and Fine Arts (later they separated), becoming its first director, and also the Committee for the Protection of Ancient Monuments. Saryan was also one of the creators of the Yerevan Art College and the Union of Artists. Only after two years, when everything had been set in motion and no longer demanded his direct involvement could the artist again devote himself fully to his own creative work.

The year 1923 opened a new period in the artist's career, which was almost entirely devoted to Armenia. This period can be subdivided, with a fair degree of approximation, into separate stages: the 1920s, the 1930s–1940s, and the last two decades of Saryan's life (through to the early 1970s). This division is, however, fairly arbitrary, because, although there was considerable variety in terms of genre and even style, Saryan's art remained quite homogeneous over those five decades. A suitable introduction to it is provided by the artist's own words: "You need to love every tree, every blade of grass in your country. To love your own village, your own city, your own homeland... To love your people... You must nurture within yourself one of the noblest of human sentiments – the feeling of

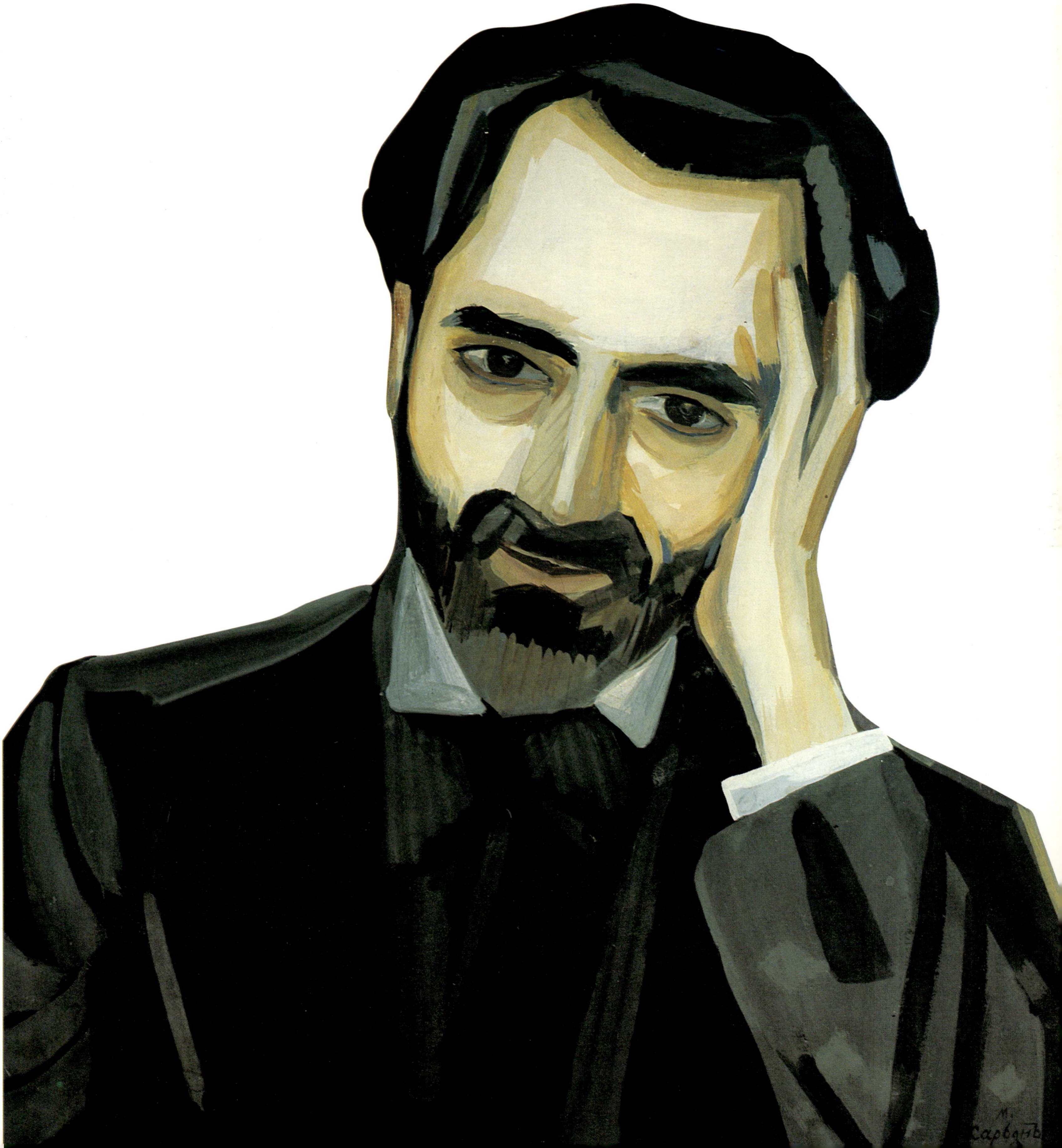

Portrait of the Poet Alexander Tsaturian. 1915
Tempera on canvas. 70.5 x 62 cm
National Gallery of Armenia, Yerevan

patriotism."[49] This feeling filled Saryan's art to the end of his long life. It prompted him to take an especially attentive attitude towards specific motifs of natural scenery and the realia of daily existence and to strive to express their variety and beauty. At this time the artist's method of working changed in comparison with the preceding period (1900–1910s). At the beginning of his career Saryan wanted to "tear away" from the real-life image and immerse himself in the romantic world of fantasy – that is how the *Fairy-Tales and Dreams* appeared. Yet even in them, the break with reality was not absolute. The "attraction of the earth", which Saryan once defined as being a philosophical law as well as a physical one, was something he felt even at that time and that set him apart in many ways from the majority of Blue Rose Symbolists. Subsequently, in the 1910s, in the

Portrait of Mnatsakan Giulnazarian. 1915
Tempera on canvas. 47 x 47 cm
National Gallery of Armenia, Yerevan

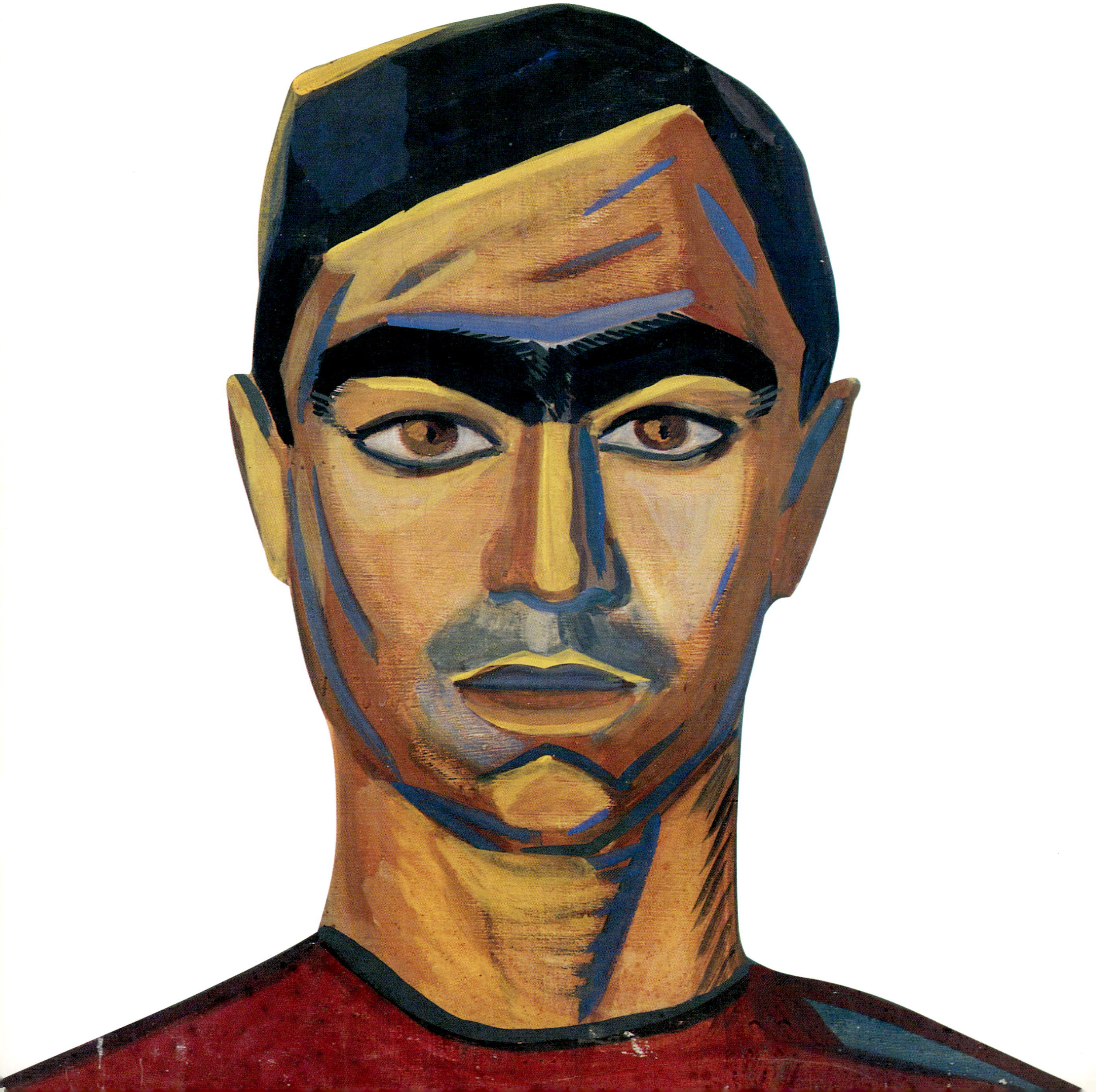

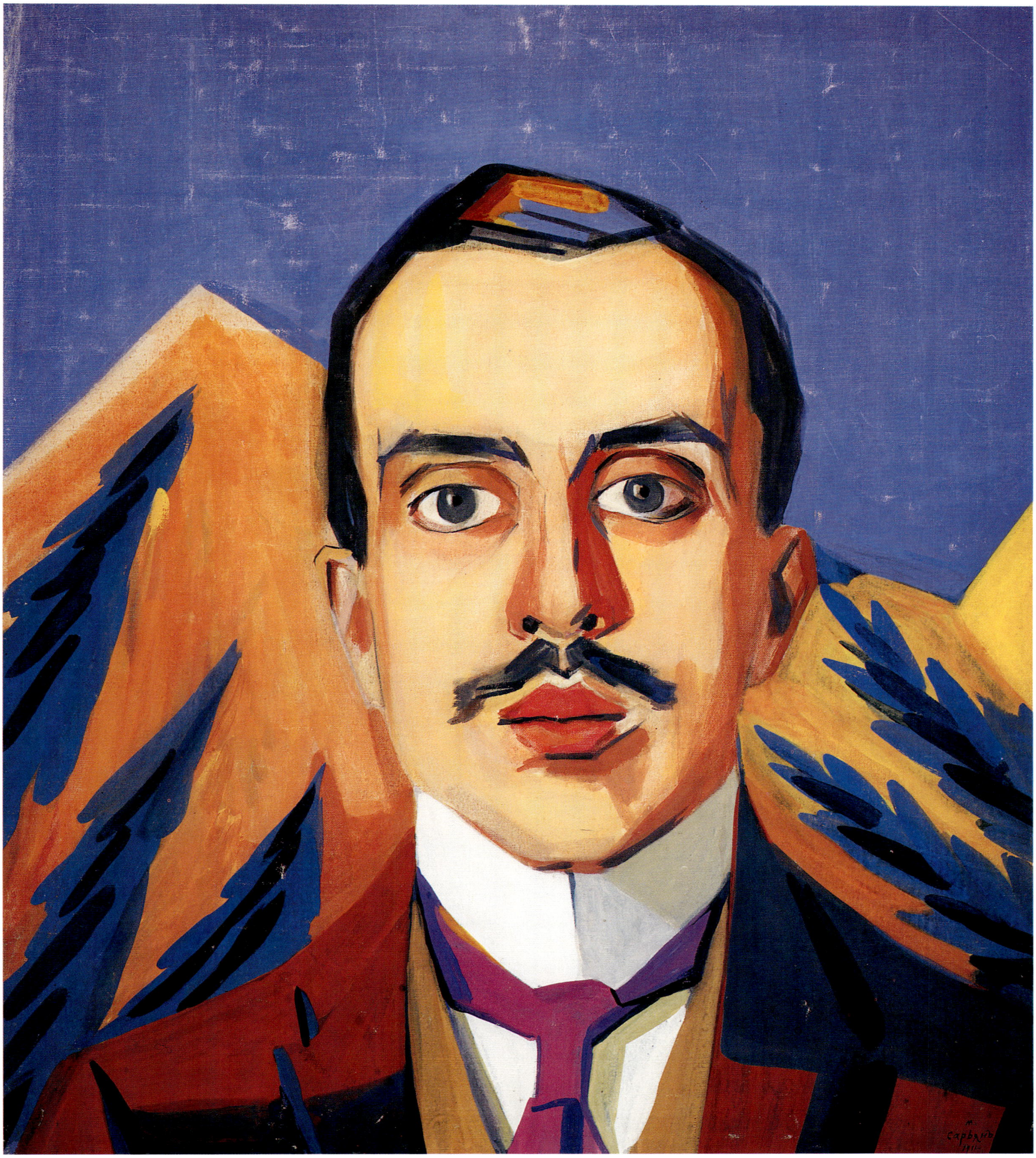

Portrait of Ivan Shchukin. 1911
Tempera on canvas. 95 x 85 cm
I. Afanasyev family collection,
St Petersburg

→
Head of a Girl
(Mariam Tazakhulakhian). 1912
Tempera on cardboard. 69.3 x 51.5 cm
The Tretyakov Gallery, Moscow

programmatic works of the Eastern cycle, Saryan managed to fuse together the real-life impulse and the synthetic expression of its essence preserved in the memory. In Armenia the artist began painting from life and asserted that that kind of work was his greatest pleasure.[50] Let us note, however, that in the things done from life, even in the small studies, one always senses the artist's ability to organize his observations, to subordinate them to a particular concept.

Interestingly, a sort of "return to nature", a striving to express it more specifically, could be found at that time in the work of several major

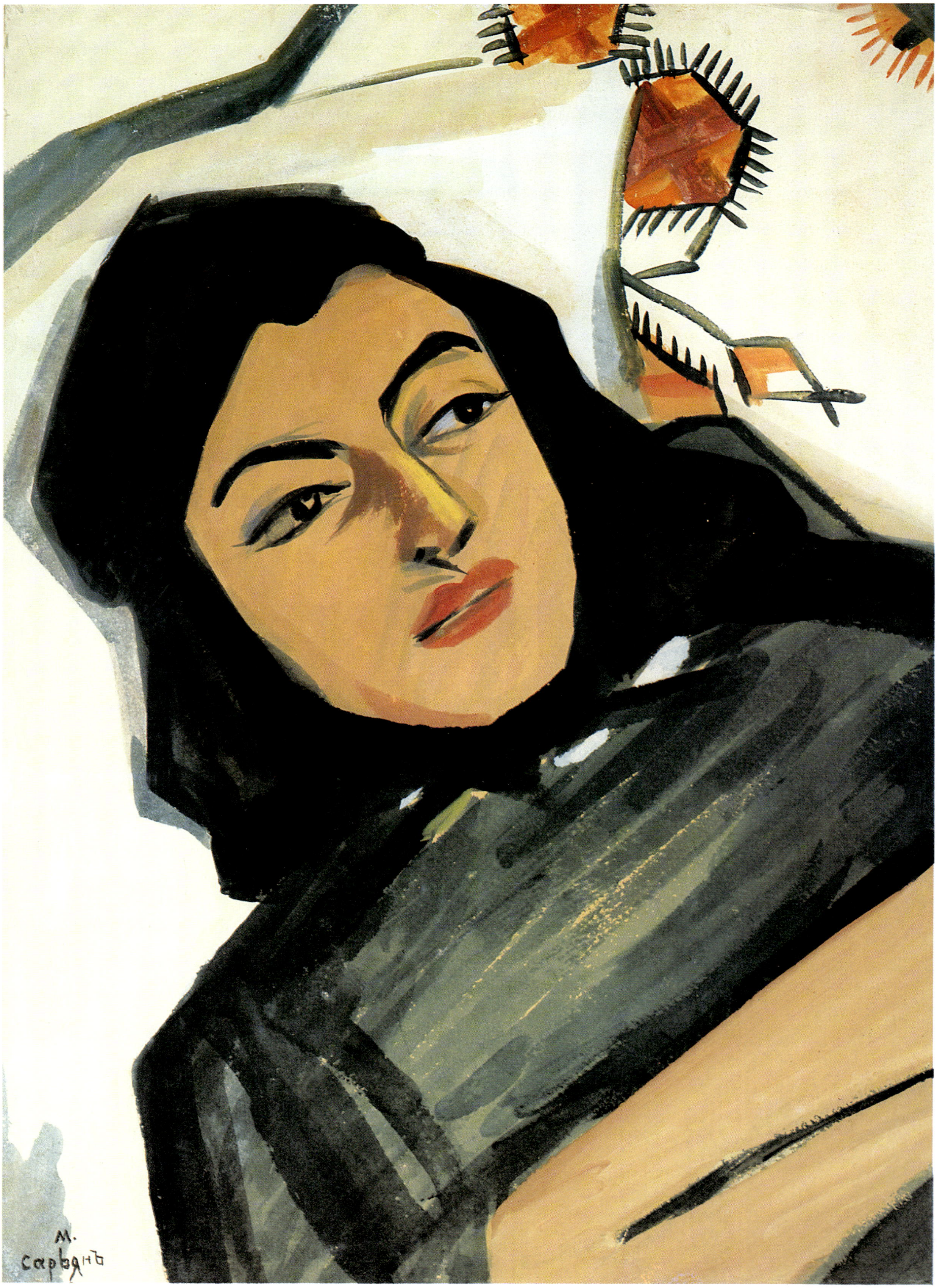
М.
Сарьянъ

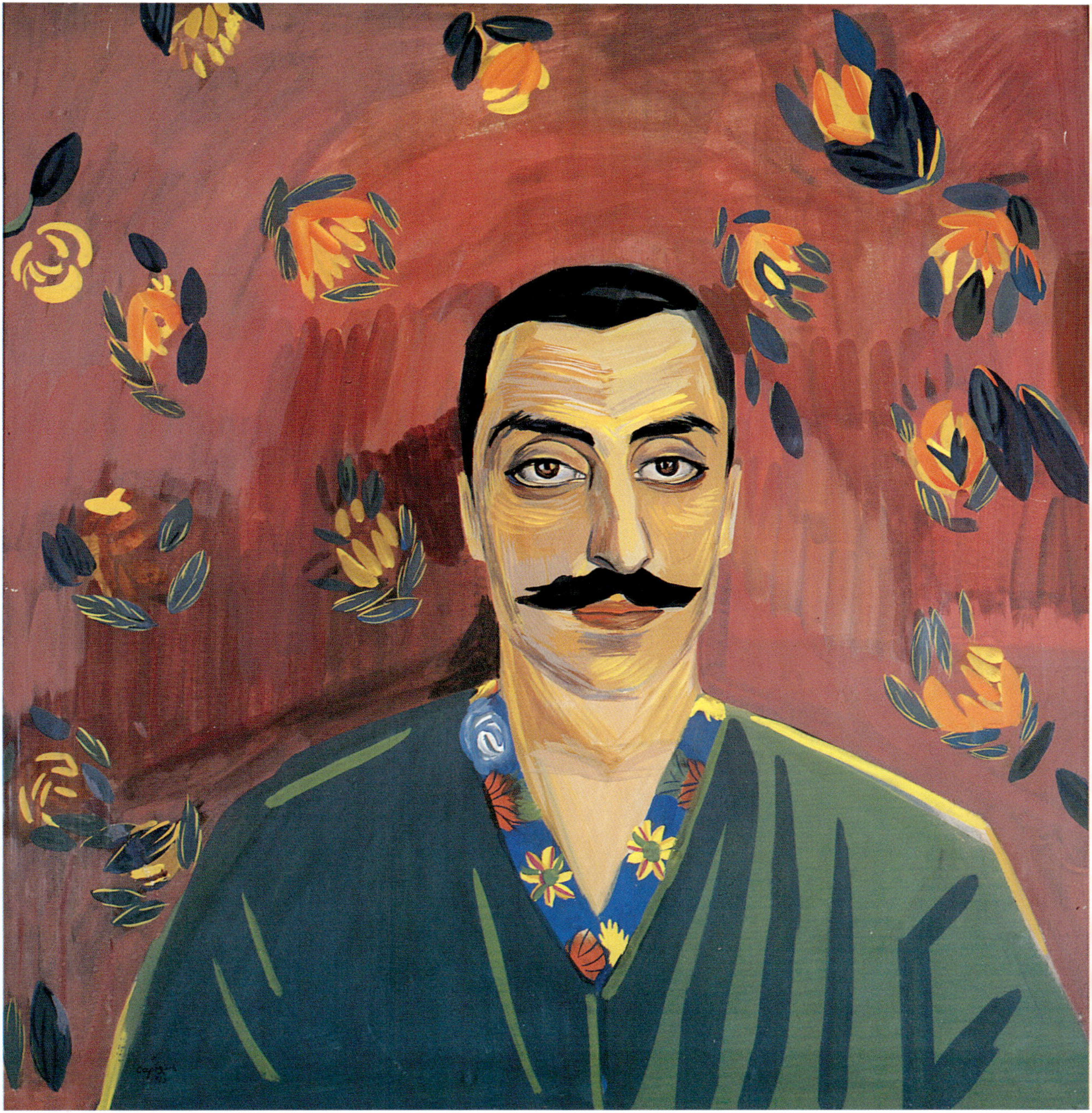

contemporary artists, including the former Fauves, Derain and Matisse. The closeness of Saryan and Matisse in the 1910s has already been commented on. In the 1920s the two artists developed in different directions. Matisse's "East" or south and Saryan's Armenia are far removed from each other in terms of imagery and themes. The actual natural element was of less interest to the French artist and finds expression most often in still-lifes, views from the window and the cultivated Provençal motifs. As for the *Odalisques* and *Nudes* that are so characteristic of Matisse's late output, themes of that kind were wholly alien to Saryan.

The kinship remained, however, in the significance that both artists gave to colour and sometimes in its actual quality. It remained too – and this is probably the most important thing – in the joyful perception of the world that runs through the work of both artists, even in defiance of dramatic changes in their fortunes. In this sense Saryan was probably closer to Matisse than many of his compatriots.

It is interesting that certain Western critics or artists linked their names together on the rare occasions when such people got to see Saryan's works. One such occasion came in 1924 with the artist's participation in the 14th International Biennale in Venice. His paintings drew particular attention in the Soviet section of the exhibition. "Saryan has something that among the Western artists reminds one of Matisse,"

←
Portrait of Iosif Mantashev. 1915
Tempera on canvas. 88 x 88 cm
National Gallery of Armenia, Yerevan

The Surb-Khach Rocks at Kalaki. 1914
Oil on canvas pasted on cardboard. 36 x 47.5 cm
Art Museum, Yaroslavl

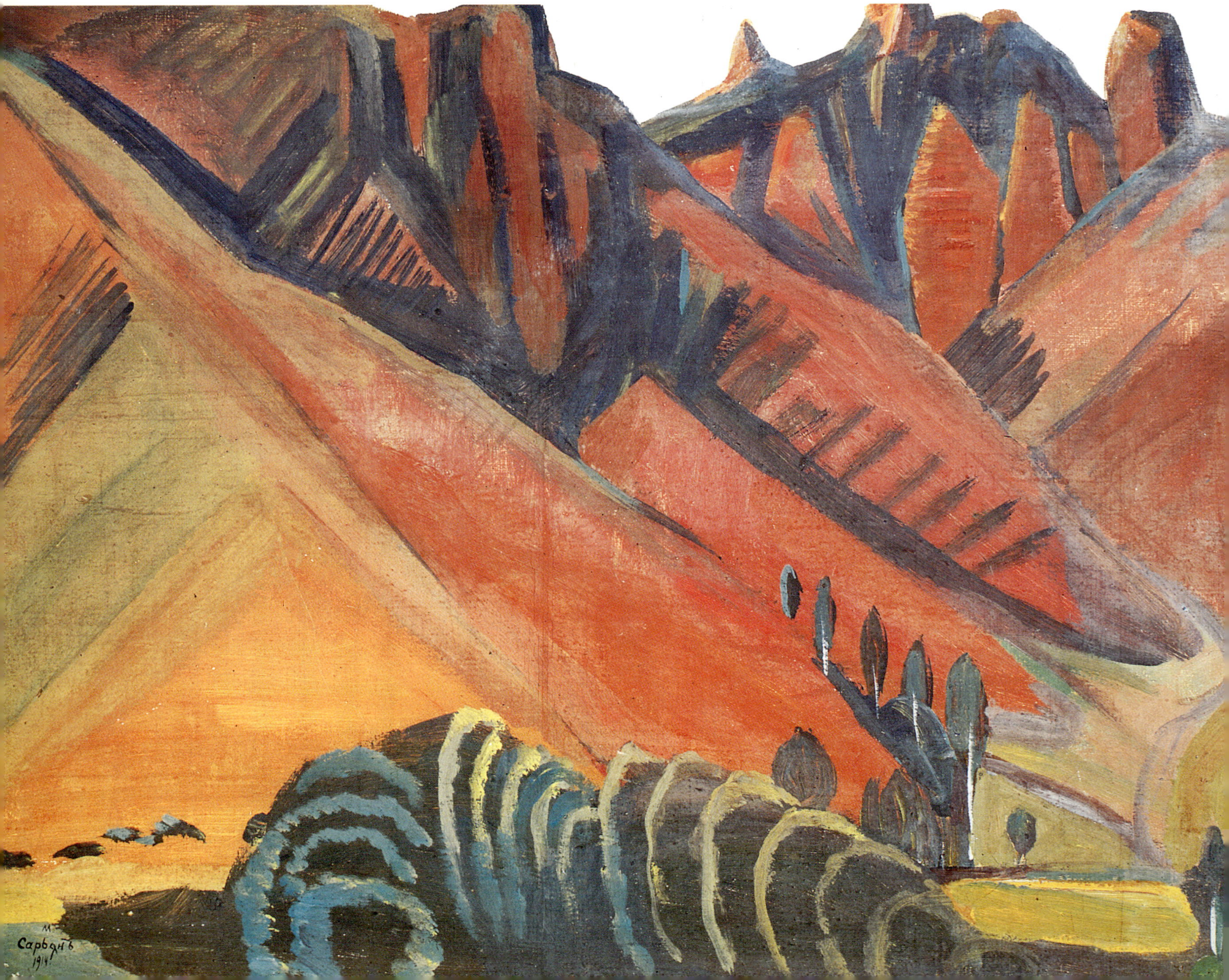

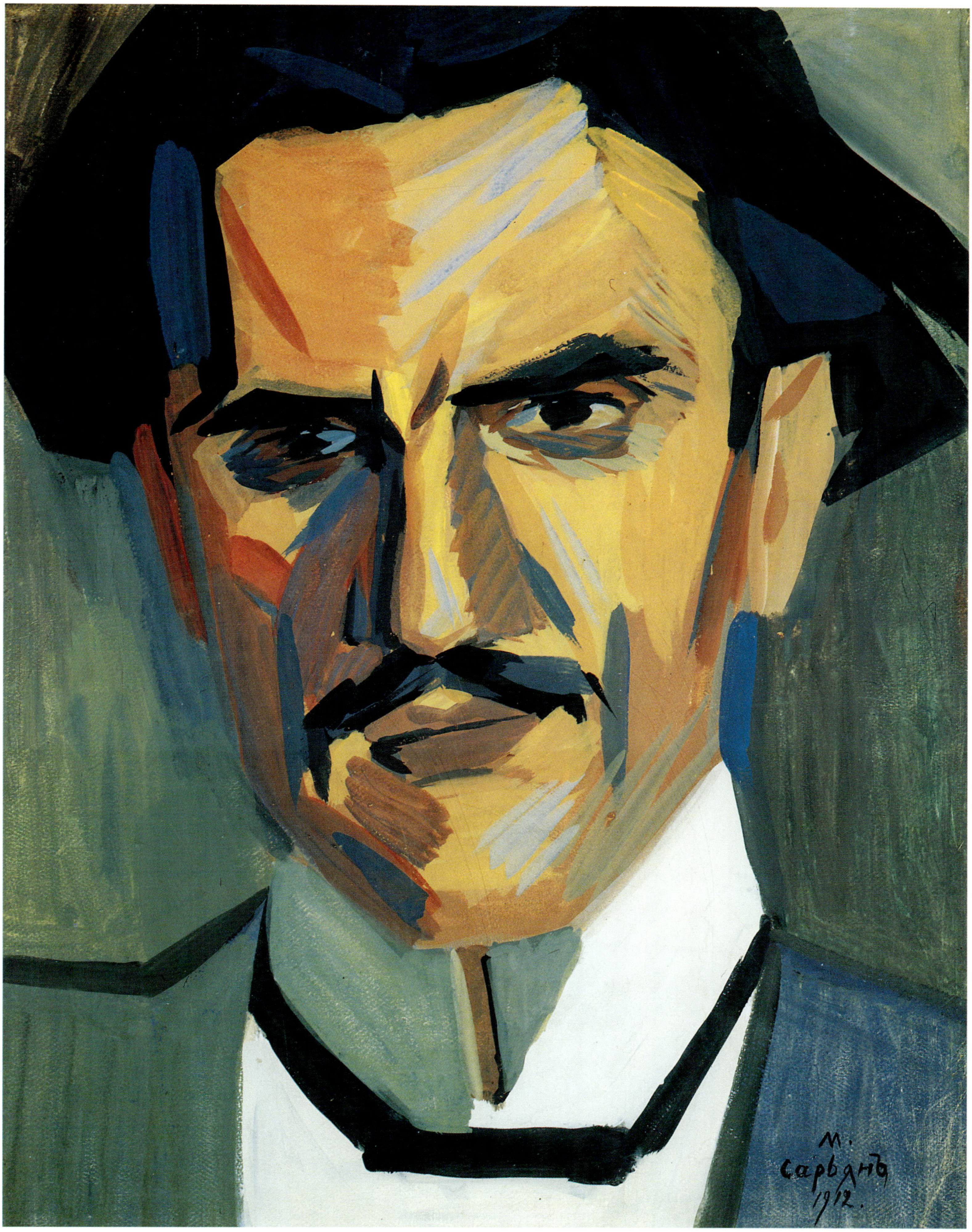

Portrait of the Art-Historian Garegin Levonian. 1912
Tempera on cardboard. 70 x 54 cm
National Gallery of Armenia, Yerevan

→
The Flowers of Kalaki. 1914
Tempera on canvas. 88 x 79 cm
National Gallery of Armenia, Yerevan

→
The Flowers of Asia. 1915
Tempera on canvas. 75 x 57 cm
The Russian Museum, St Petersburg

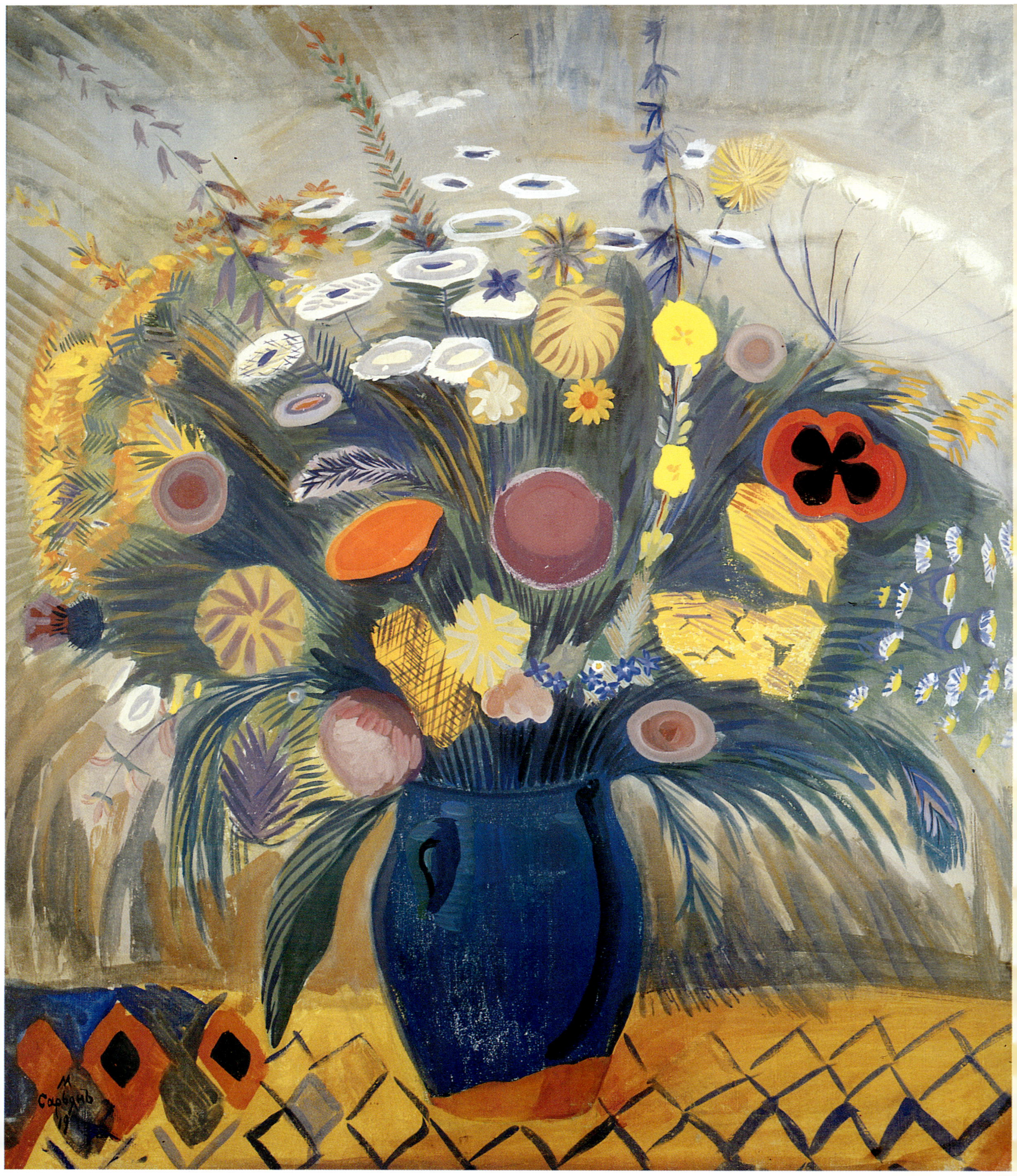

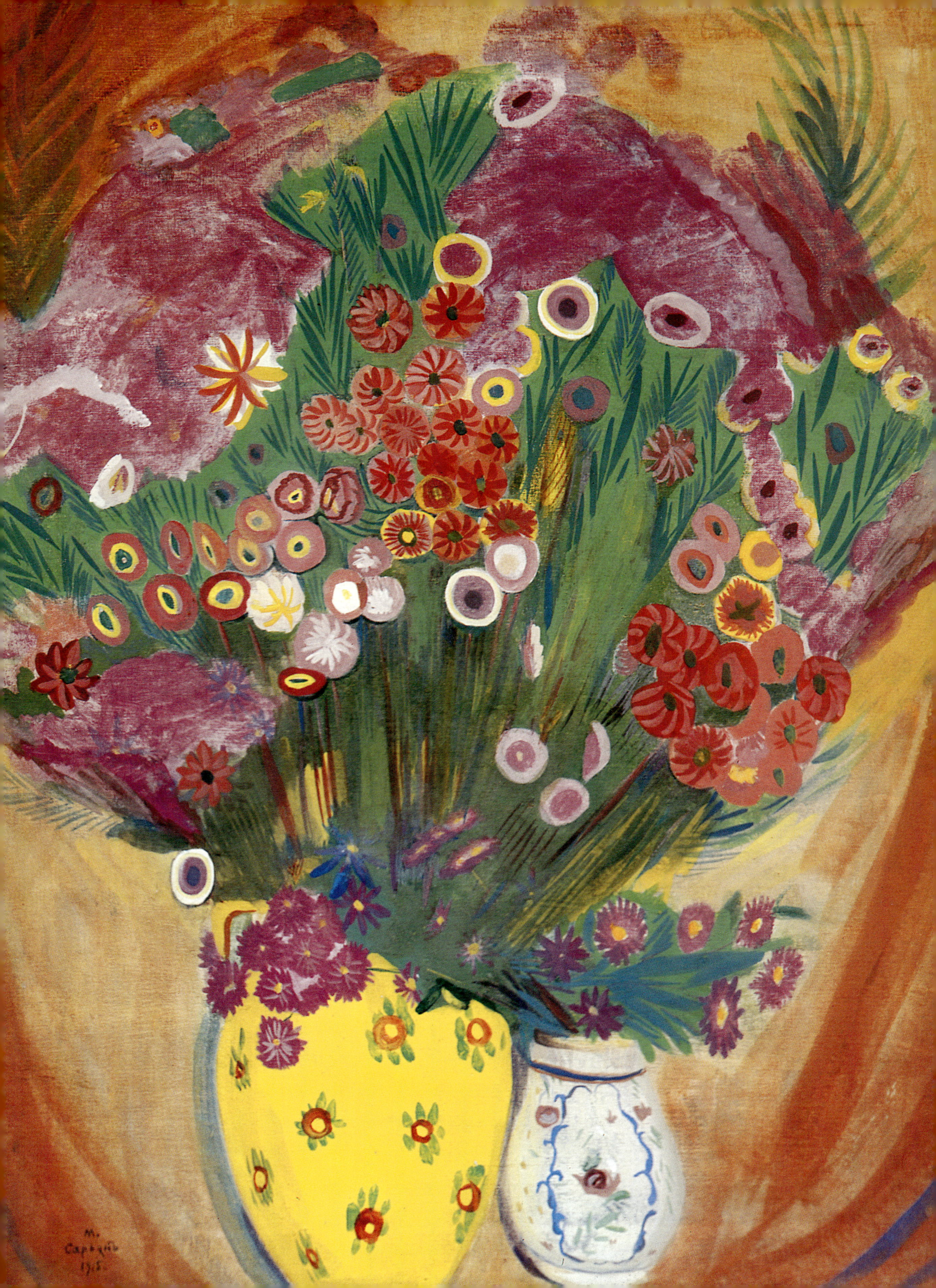

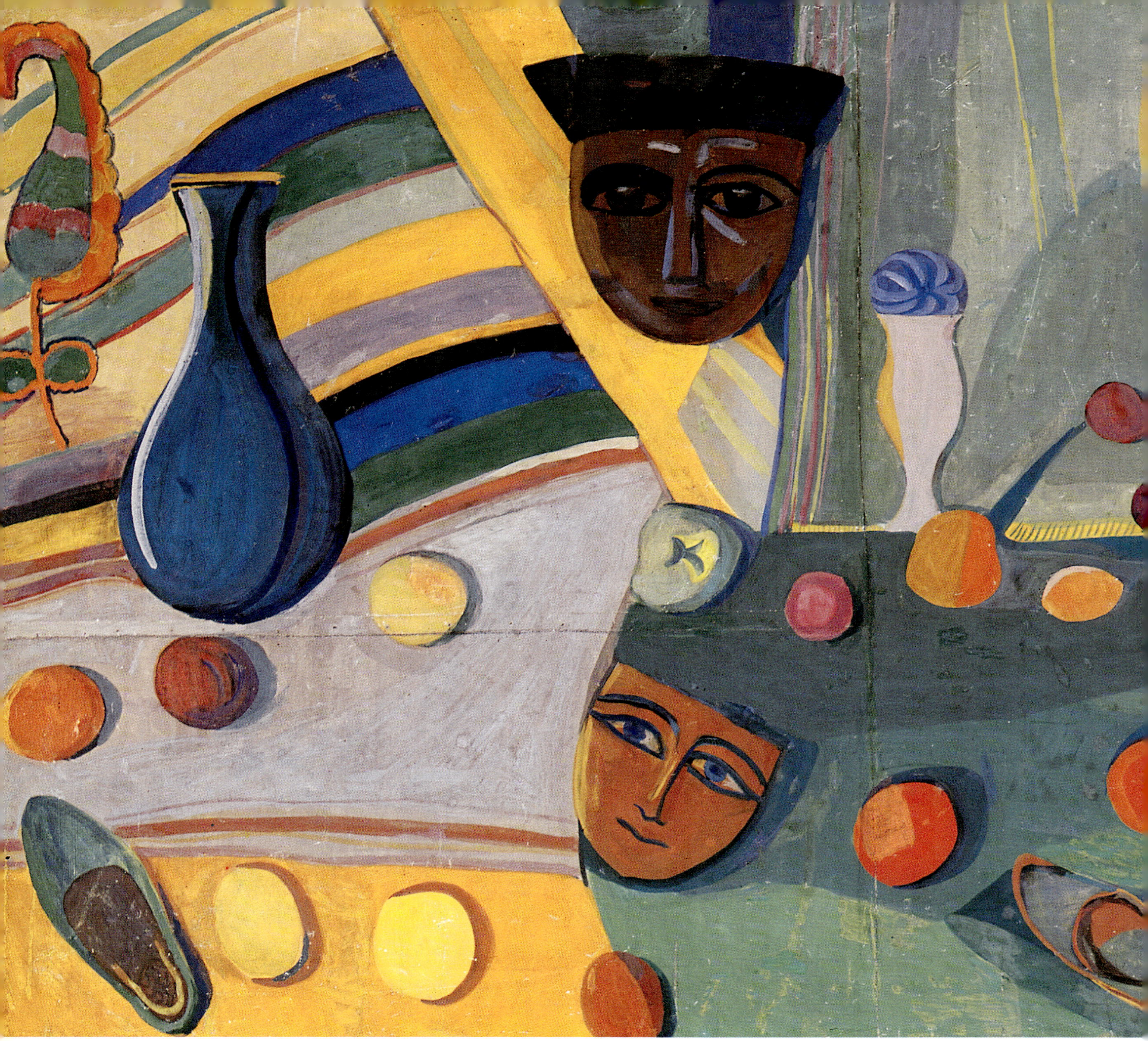

Giuseppe Sprovieri wrote in the newspaper *Il Mondo*. "It is the characteristic features of Orientalism. Incidentally, Saryan differs from the other in his exceptional, direct and clear force, in other words less sober-mindedness."[51] But let us return to those changes that took place in Saryan's art about the middle of the 1920s. The method of working from life, intensified attention to various motifs from the natural world and, more broadly, the life of Armenia often prompted the artist to abandon the garish, lapidary, emphatically abstracted manner of the 1910s. Colour completely retained the leading role in his work, but its nuances took on greater significance, not only the sharp chromatic contrasts, but also their internal differentiation. This determined a change of technique. Tempera ideally suited Saryan's early style. Now he more often painted in oils, and that in turn influenced the evolution of his artistic style. Brushstrokes of different colours or their shades constructed form in greater detail and volume. The artist's painting acquired a third dimension.

Large Eastern Still-Life. 1915
Tempera on canvas. 105 x 231 cm
Martiros Saryan Museum, Yerevan

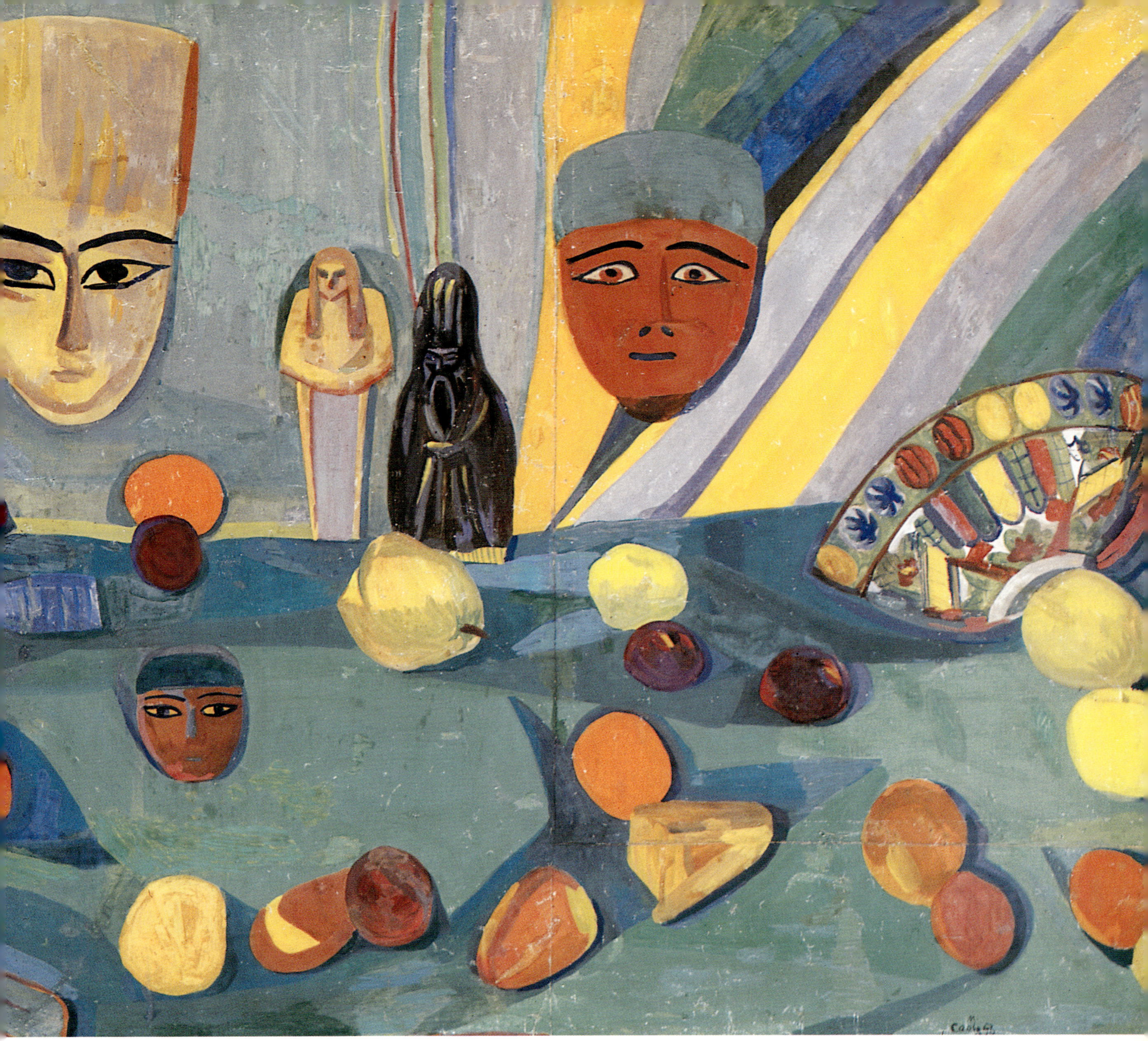

At the same time it would be a great error to draw too much of a distinction between the early and late Saryans. The artist did not break away from what he had already done, but adapted his devices in accordance with a new vision. The impression that he rejected his boldest discoveries is an illusion. He broadened and deepened his earlier experience, in part restricting the intensity of colour, but made up for it with a greater subtlety in chromatic relationships. All of this, incidentally, describes the evolution of the artist's late work only in the most general terms; almost every work is unique in its painterly and plastic structure.

On the whole, Saryan remained true to the fundamental principle of his creative view of the world: "True art was, is and will be not simply illustration, but a great discovery of the world."[52]

Such a discovery were his landscapes of Armenia – a country striking for its special beauty, astonishing variety of colours and shapes and sharp contrast between grim rocks and blooming valleys, between snowy peaks,

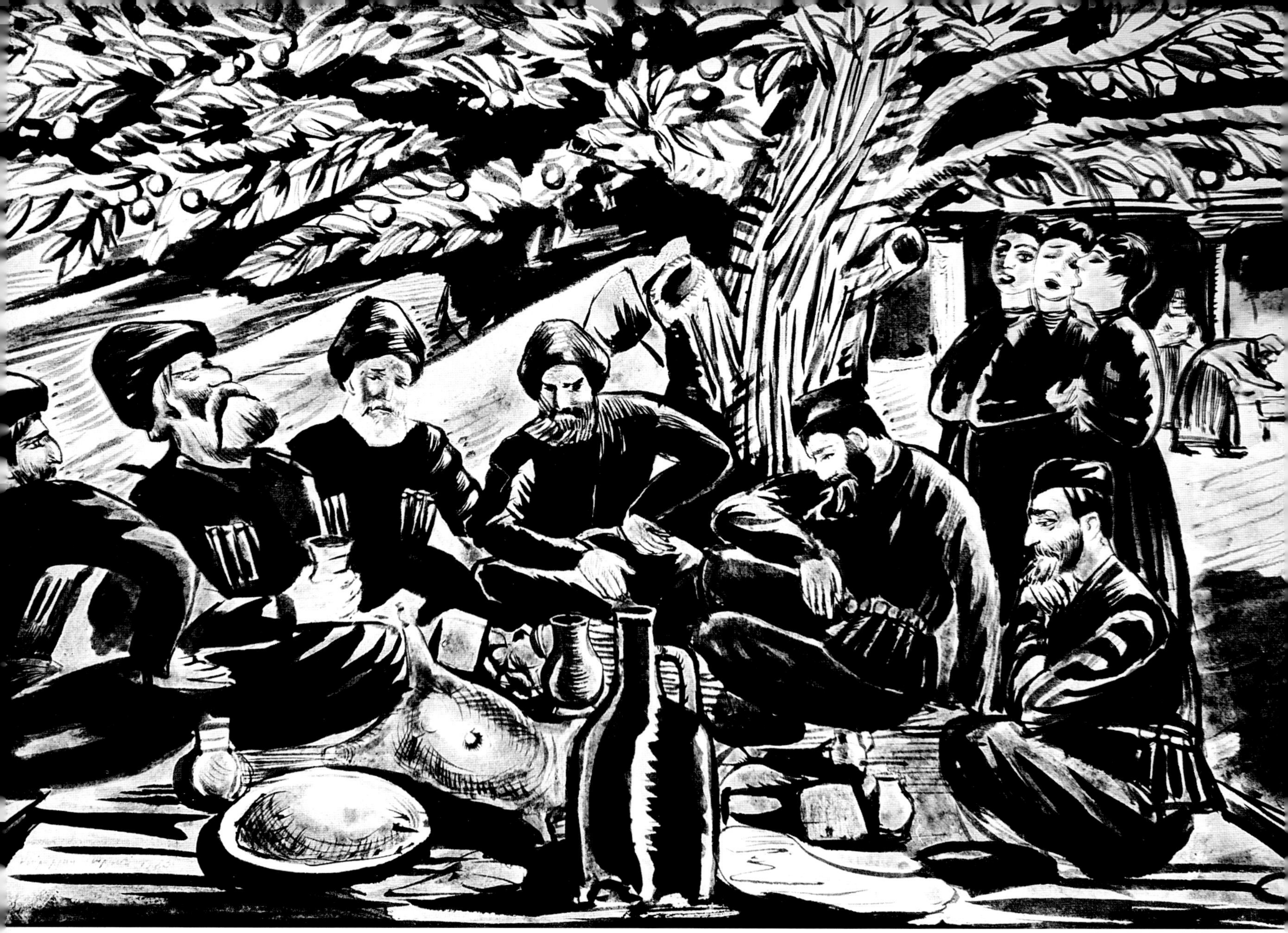

green meadows and deep gorges. Andrei Bely, on first seeing Armenia, perceived it as "a legend of the life of extinct volcanoes". In his splendid essay *Armenia*, he recalled the ancient Armenian tradition that "paradise was created here and not between the Tigris [and the Euphrates]."[53]

Before Saryan, Armenia had been painted by many people, including Gevorg Bashindzhagian, Yegishe Tatevosian, Fanos Terlemezian and Vardges Surenyants, artists with different creative principles and styles. But only Saryan had found the expressive devices that properly accorded with the character of Armenian nature, as if suggested by that nature, but far from simply copying it. He was able to recreate "the sharpness of the transitions, the contrast of tones and the abundance of sun".[54] In that blinding light the ridges of the mountains are alight with an astonishing multiplicity of tones – from snow-white and pale blue to golden-yellow, crimson, green and intense violet. Saryan was the first to capture not only the chromatic richness, but also the special structure, the architectonics of the ancient mountains, the measured rhythm of the mighty slopes descending to the valleys. He profoundly sensed the decorative values of the chromatic and plastic structure of the Armenian landscape. He was able to extract from nature the essence that is not accessible to the fleeting glance. It was again Andrei Bely who wrote: "I have been looking at Armenia for two days now, but I first caught sight of it in Saryan's canvases."[55]

In terms of space encompassed, Saryan's Armenian landscapes cover a truly infinite range – from intimate motifs to majestic panoramas

The Blessing of Old Men. 1923.
Illustration to the poem by Hovannes Tumanian
Indian ink on paper. 24.5 x 33 cm
L. Saryan collection, Yerevan

Buddhist Still-Life. 1919
Watercolour and gouache on paper. 68 x 59 cm
A. Arutiunian family collection, Moscow

→
Still-Life: Fruit. 1916
Tempera on canvas. 33 x 49 cm
Martiros Saryan Museum, Yerevan

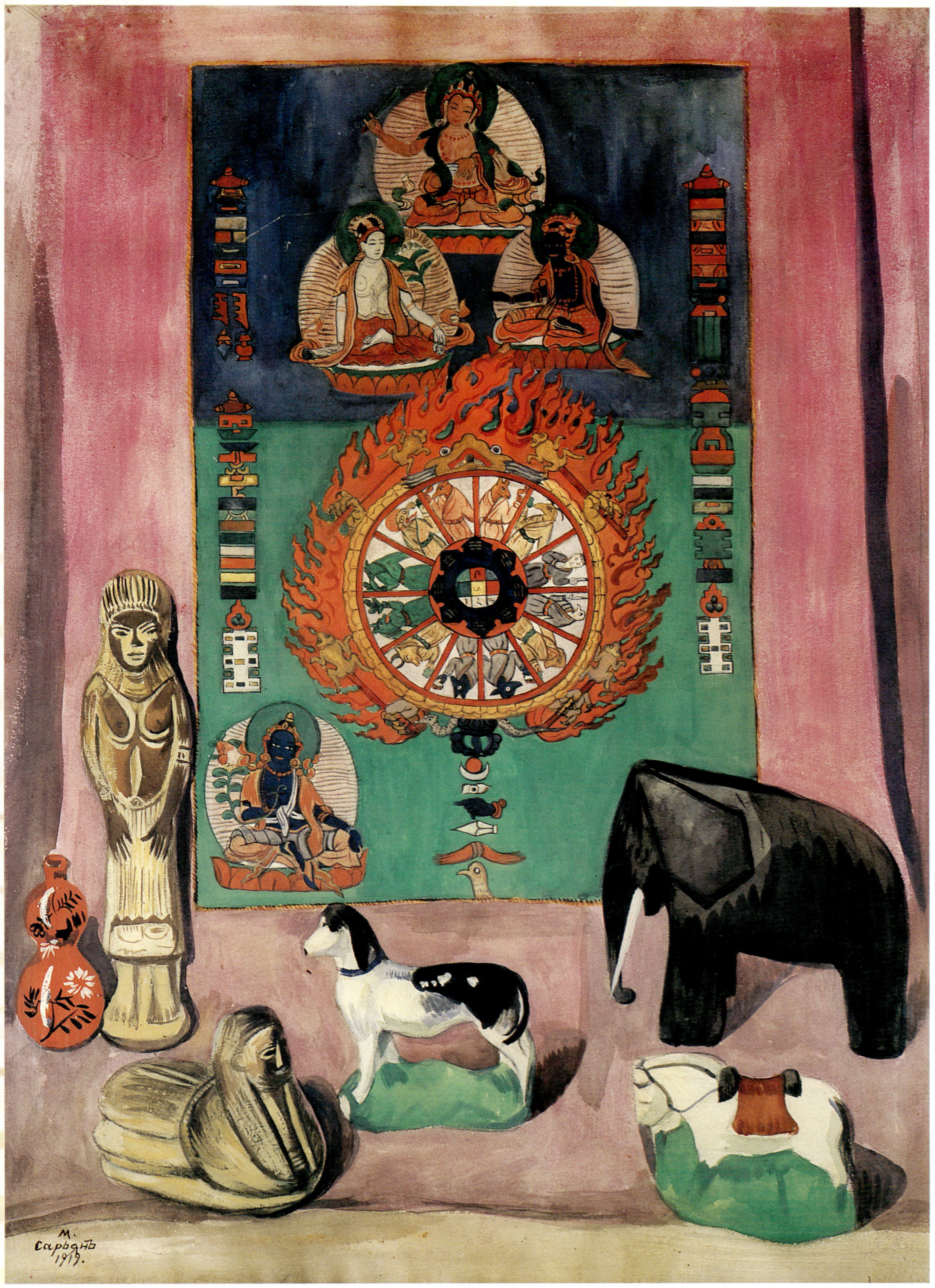
М.
Сарьянъ
1919.

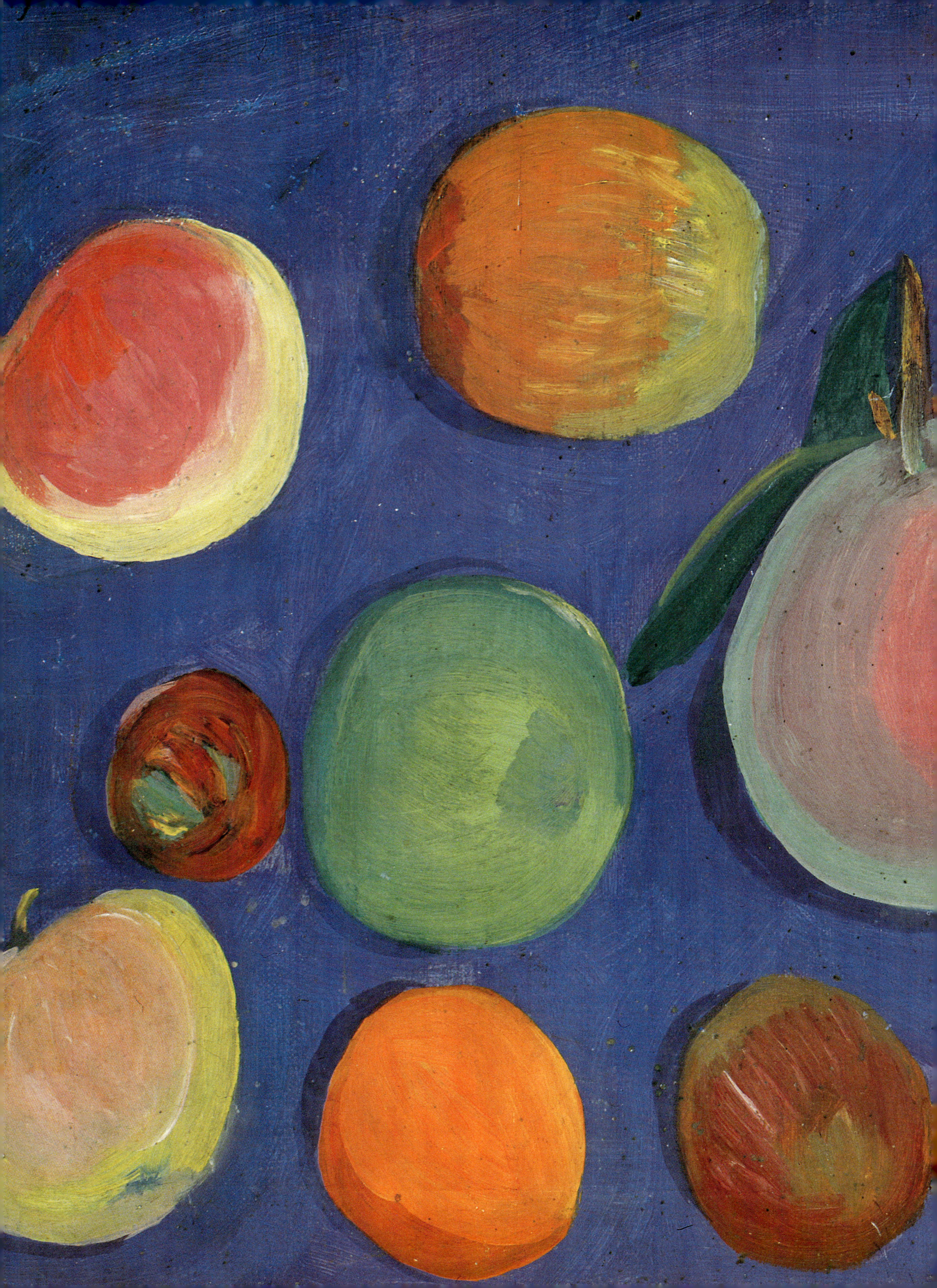

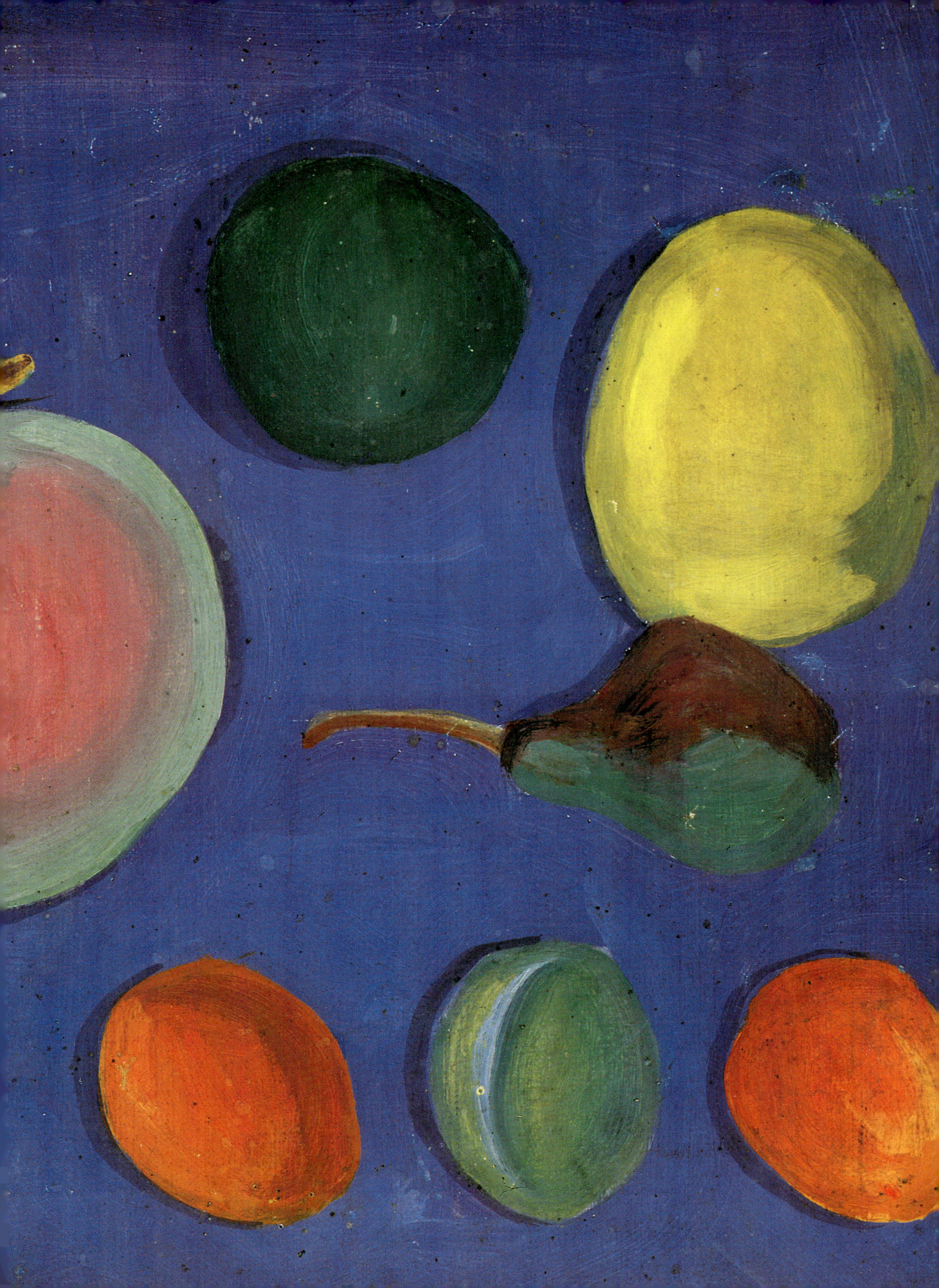

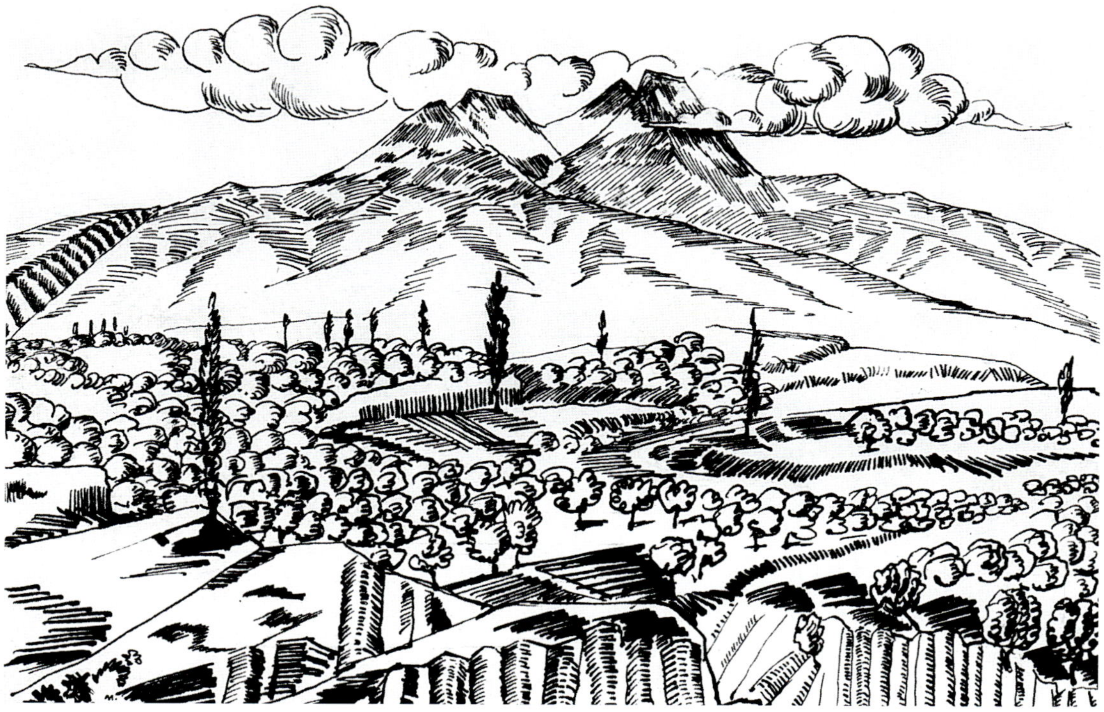

Aragats. 1929. Illustration
to the anthology of Armenian folk-tales
Indian ink on paper. 12 x 17 cm
Martiros Saryan Museum, Yerevan

Aragats in Summer. 1922
Oil on canvas. 27 x 29 cm
L. Saryan collection, Yerevan

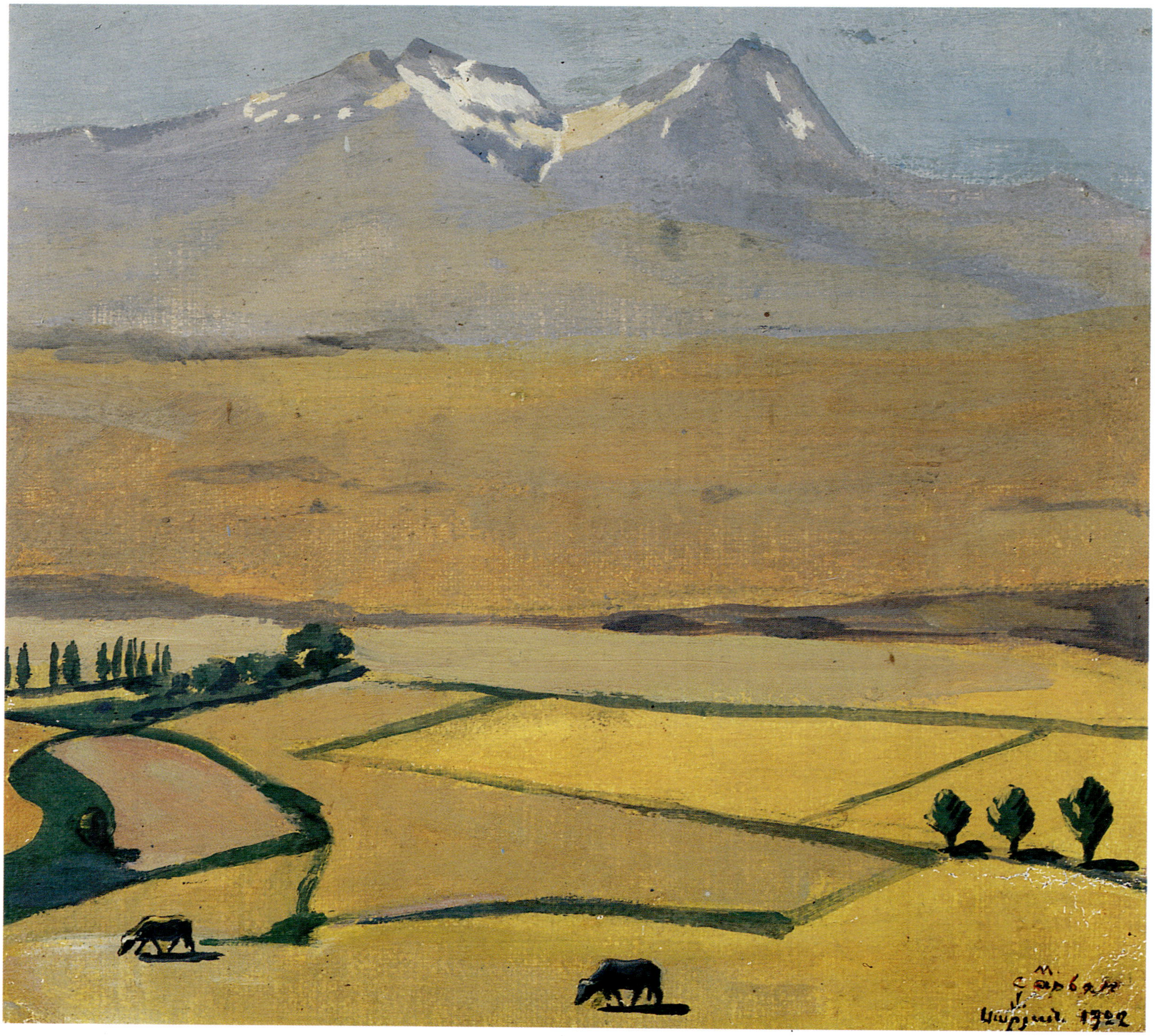

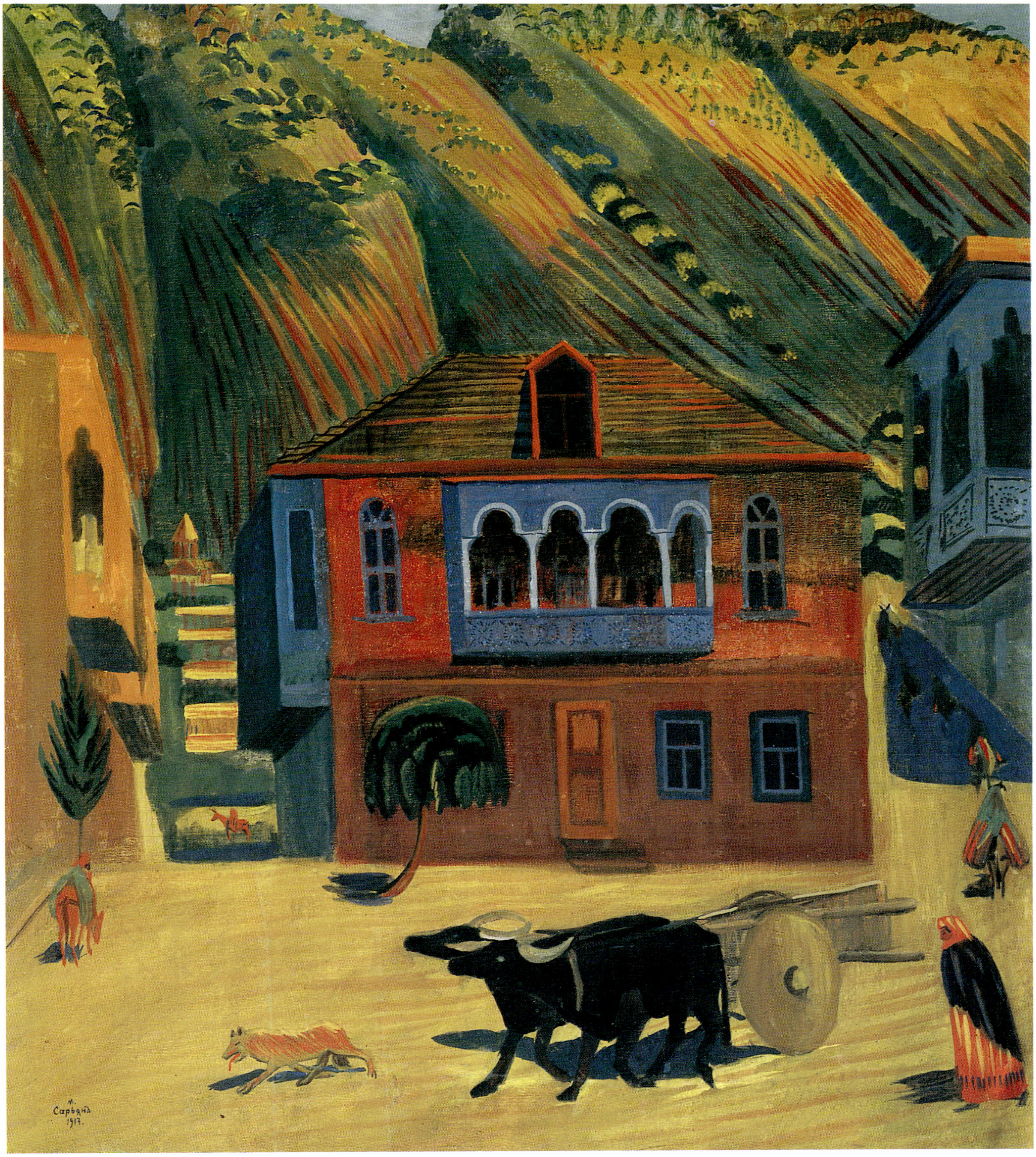

Afternoon. Old Tiflis. 1917
Tempera on canvas. 84 x 75 cm
Art Museum of Georgia, Tbilisi

of valleys and mountains, frequently contained in a very small format. This is certainly true of the diminutive paintings *Aragats in Summer* and *Mount Shamiram* (both 1922). Although no bigger than a modest study, they are absolutely finished works and even have a monumental quality, because the precise vision of the world that never failed the artist is entirely subordinated to his organizing creative will.

In many instances Saryan decisively eliminates insignificant details and subordinates specific observations to a generalizing concept to create a profound, synthetic image of his country. This is the case with his

Mountains. Armenia, *Sunlit Landscape* and *Armenia* (all 1923), *Midday Silence* (1924) and *Aragats* (1945). Differing in the degree of decorative transformation of the world, they are all united by an exceptionally wide spatial compass that at times seems boundless. Pressed and dynamic, the forms seem to rear up before our eyes in the dense blue of the southern sky, pushing it to the upper edge of the picture.

In his landscapes Saryan created a poetic – chromatic and structural – formula of the Armenian terrain and for many years this formula, taken up by his followers, quite simply represented the only way in which the scenery of Armenia could be perceived.

The artist's palette was rich and complex. Gathered there are the colours of the mountains, here glistening blindingly bright in the sunlight, there more restrained and subdued. The painting *Mountains. Armenia* – a classic example of Saryan's synthetic landscape – is constructed on warm-cold relationships of the shades of green, yellow, brown and lilac.

Sunlit Landscape. 1923
Tempera on canvas. 70 x 78 cm
National Gallery of Armenia, Yerevan

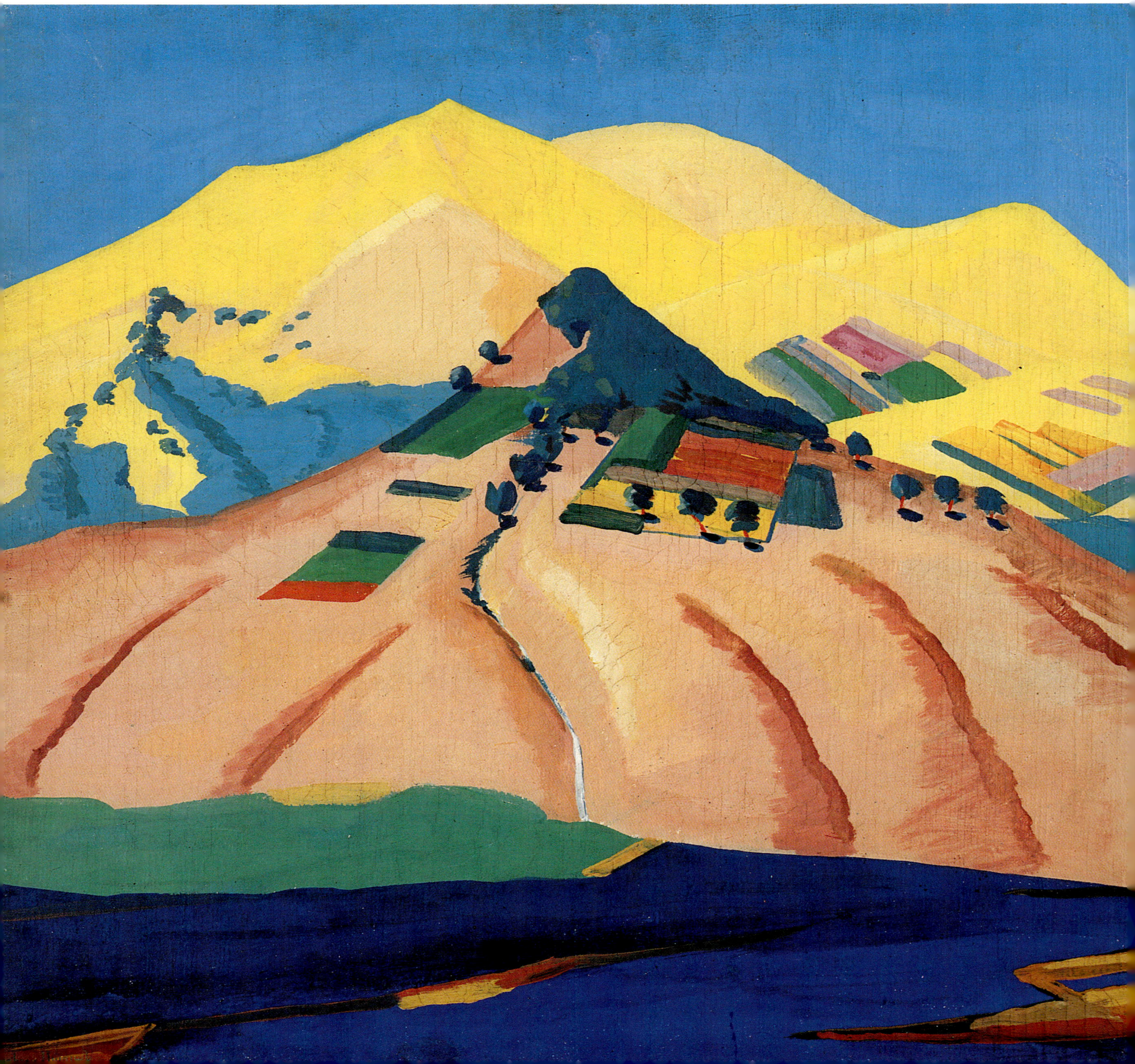

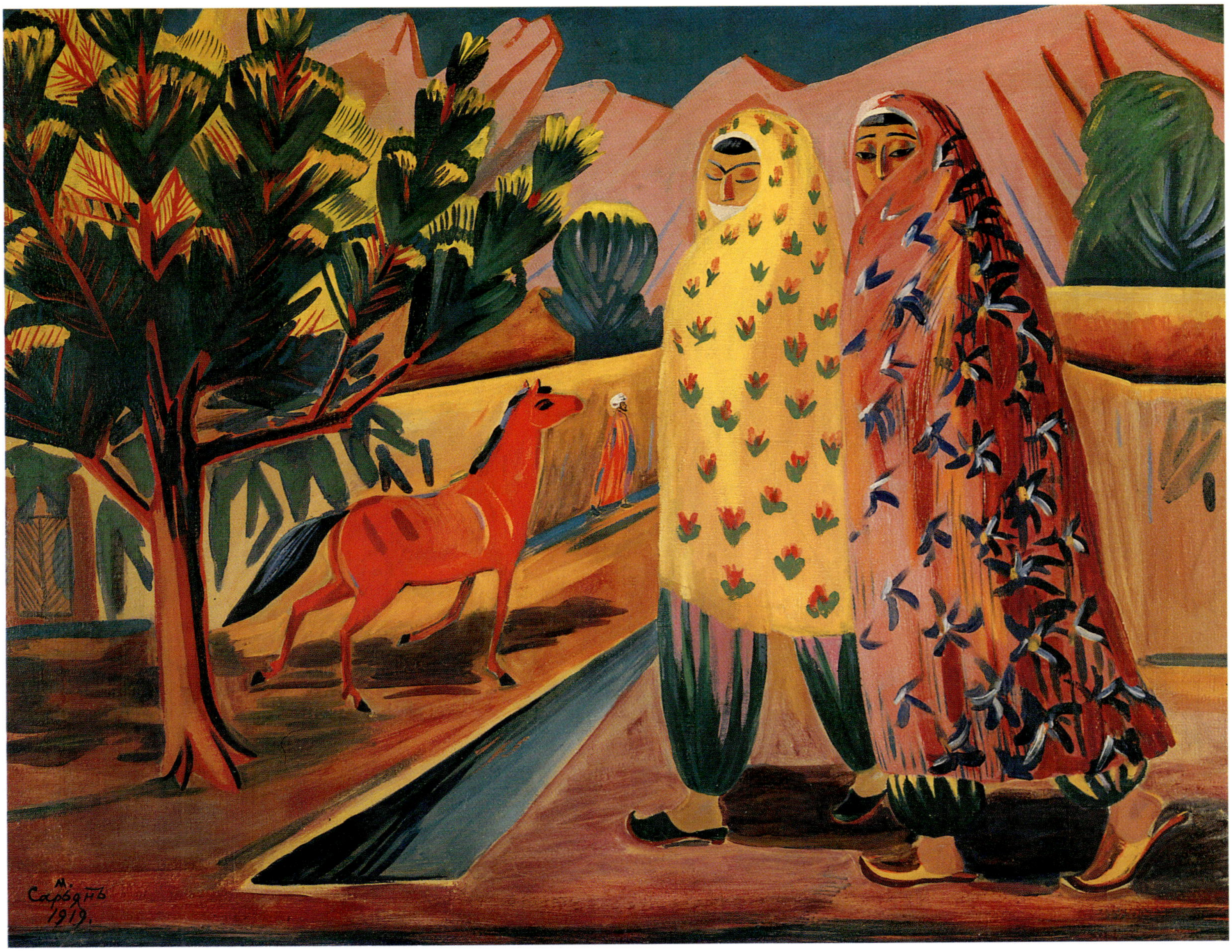

The Red Horse. 1919
Oil on canvas. 104 x 140 cm
A. Arutiunian family collection, Moscow

→
Sunrise over Ararat. 1923
Oil on canvas pasted on cardboard.
23 x 36 cm
I. Lunacharskaya collection, Moscow

→
Armenia. 1923
Oil on canvas. 138 x 103 cm
National Gallery of Armenia, Yerevan

→
My Courtyard. 1923
Oil on canvas. 102 x 68 cm
National Gallery of Armenia, Yerevan

Sunlit Landscape scorches the eye with the contrast of pinky-yellow, blue and green tones. *The Ghegam Mountains* (1926) seem to be afire with the resonant gold of their slopes, cut across by rows of trees and a winding stream with a buffalo that has dropped down to drink. Indications of life are almost invariably present even in Saryan's most decorative landscapes. In his compositions, often constructed on the principle of a headlong vertical rush, the foreground is usually given over to that life – a line of buffalos and a ploughman following the plough; a herd grazing on the mountain slopes or frozen in lazy lassitude beneath the scorching sun; women dancing on the flat roof of a house. All these motifs, modest in size compared to the age-old majesty of the mountains, are organically introduced into the structure of his paintings. Human life in the mountains was Saryan's favourite theme. It is a hard life. The mountains of Armenia are stony and infertile. From time immemorial the peasants had to carry bags of soil up onto their slopes, and only then did they begin to turn green and bring a harvest. It was not without cause that Saryan called one of his late still-lifes *The Fruits of the Stony Slopes of Aragats* (1958). He knew the hard work that had gone into producing the bright, juicy fruit and therefore probably valued them especially highly. The Armenian countryside has many aspects, yet there are certain motifs that have long been perceived as symbols of the land – its highest peaks, Aragats and Ararat. It is between them that the flourishing region of Armenia, the Ararat valley,

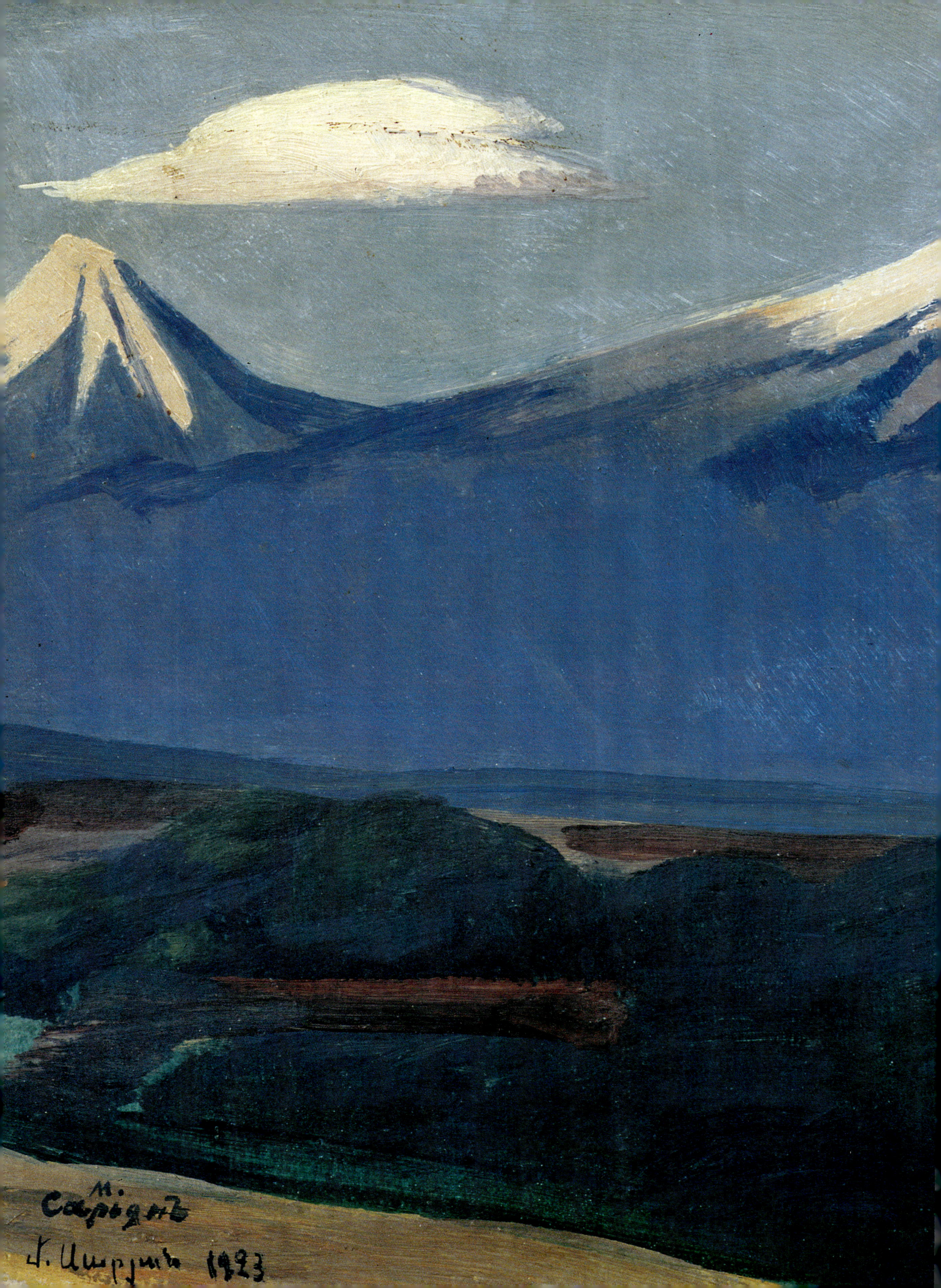
М. Сарьянъ
1923

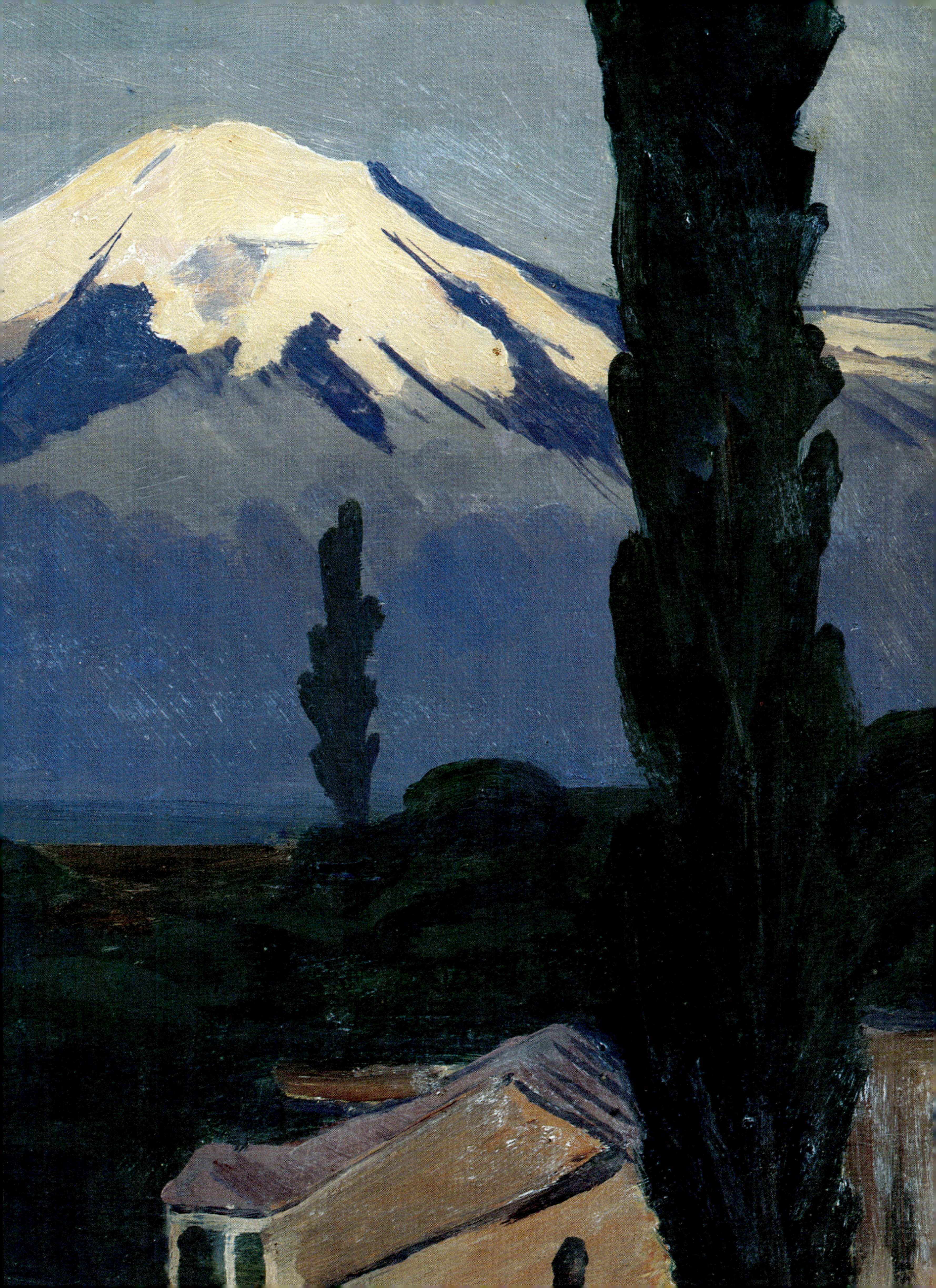

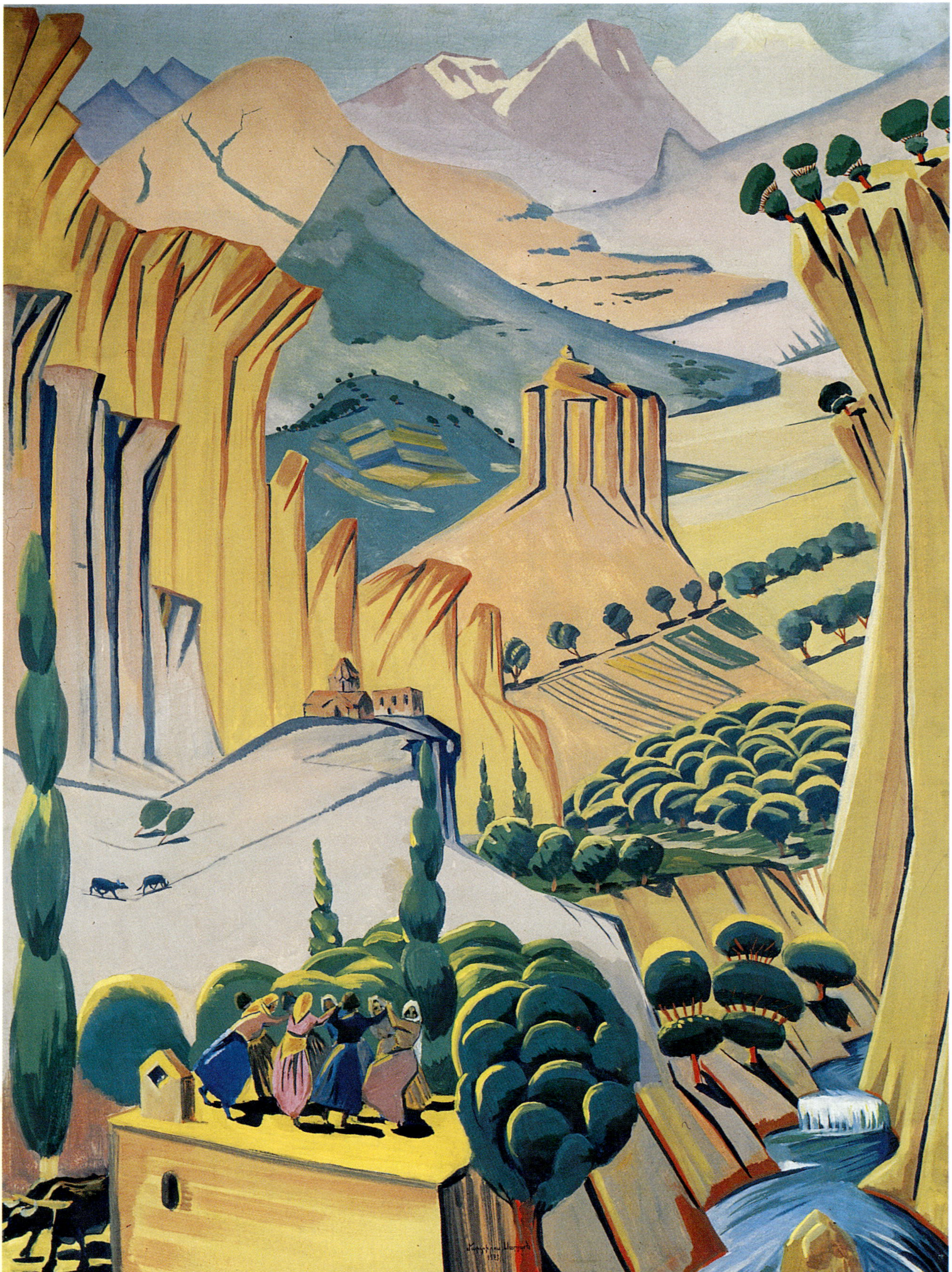

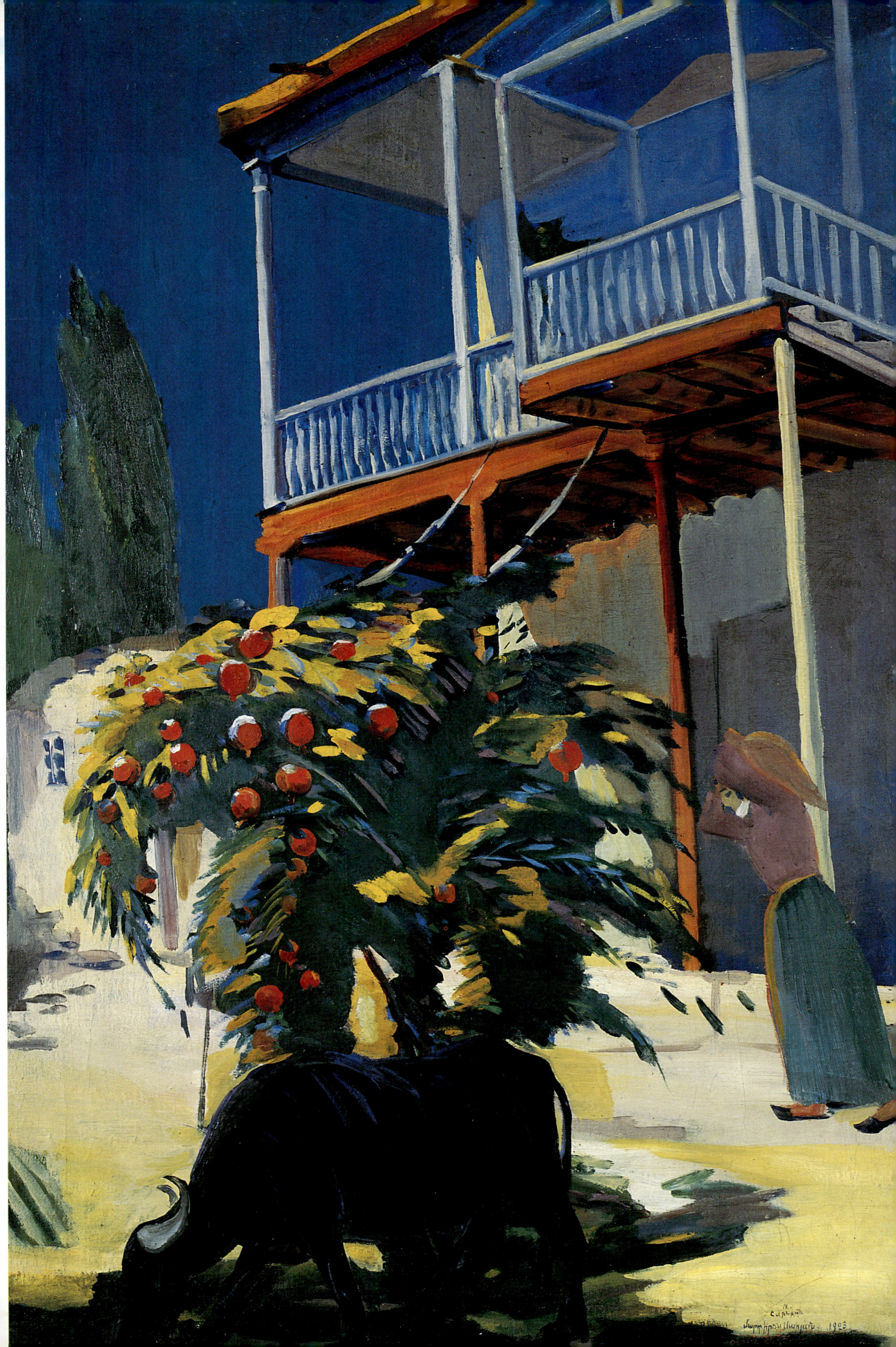

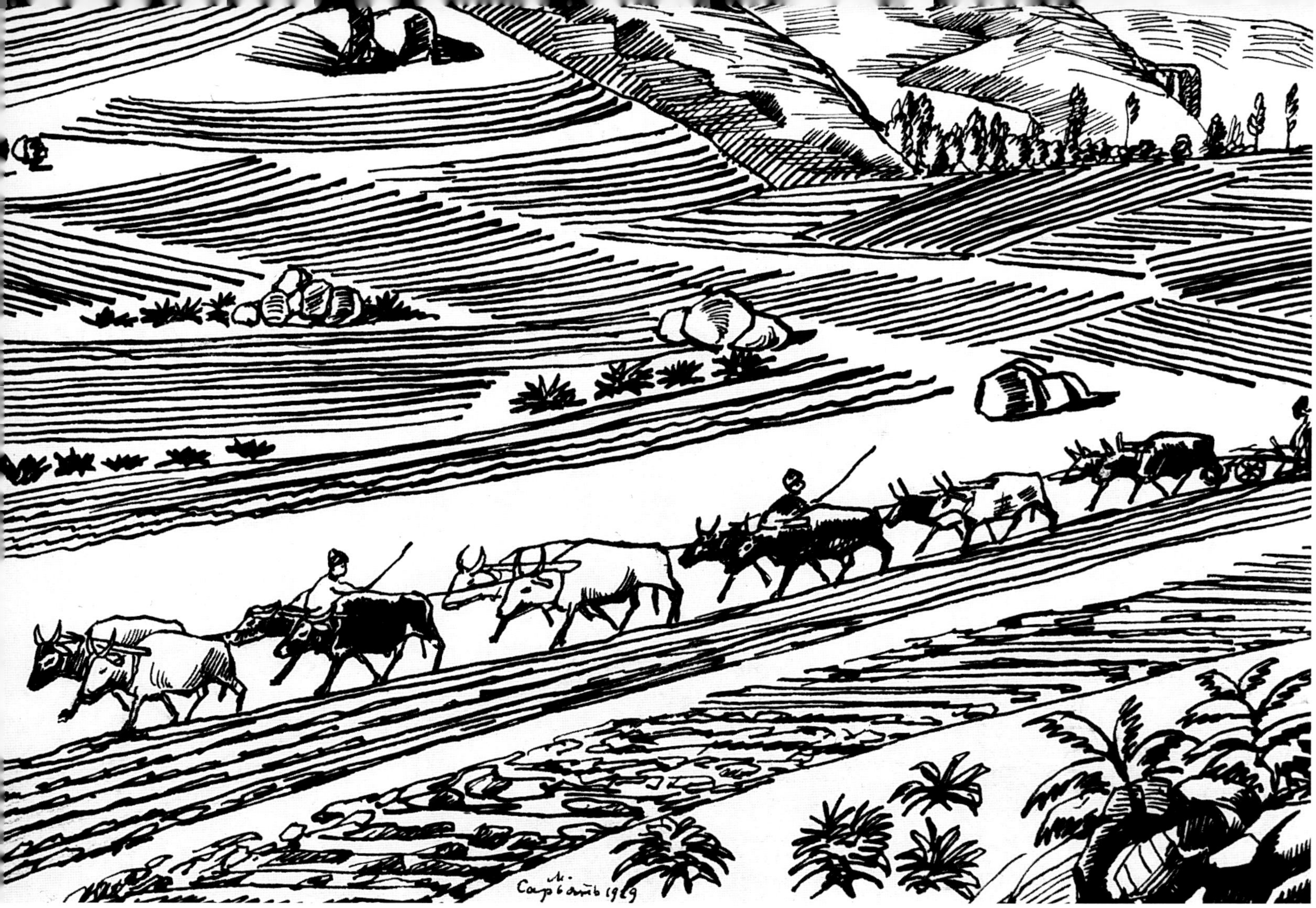

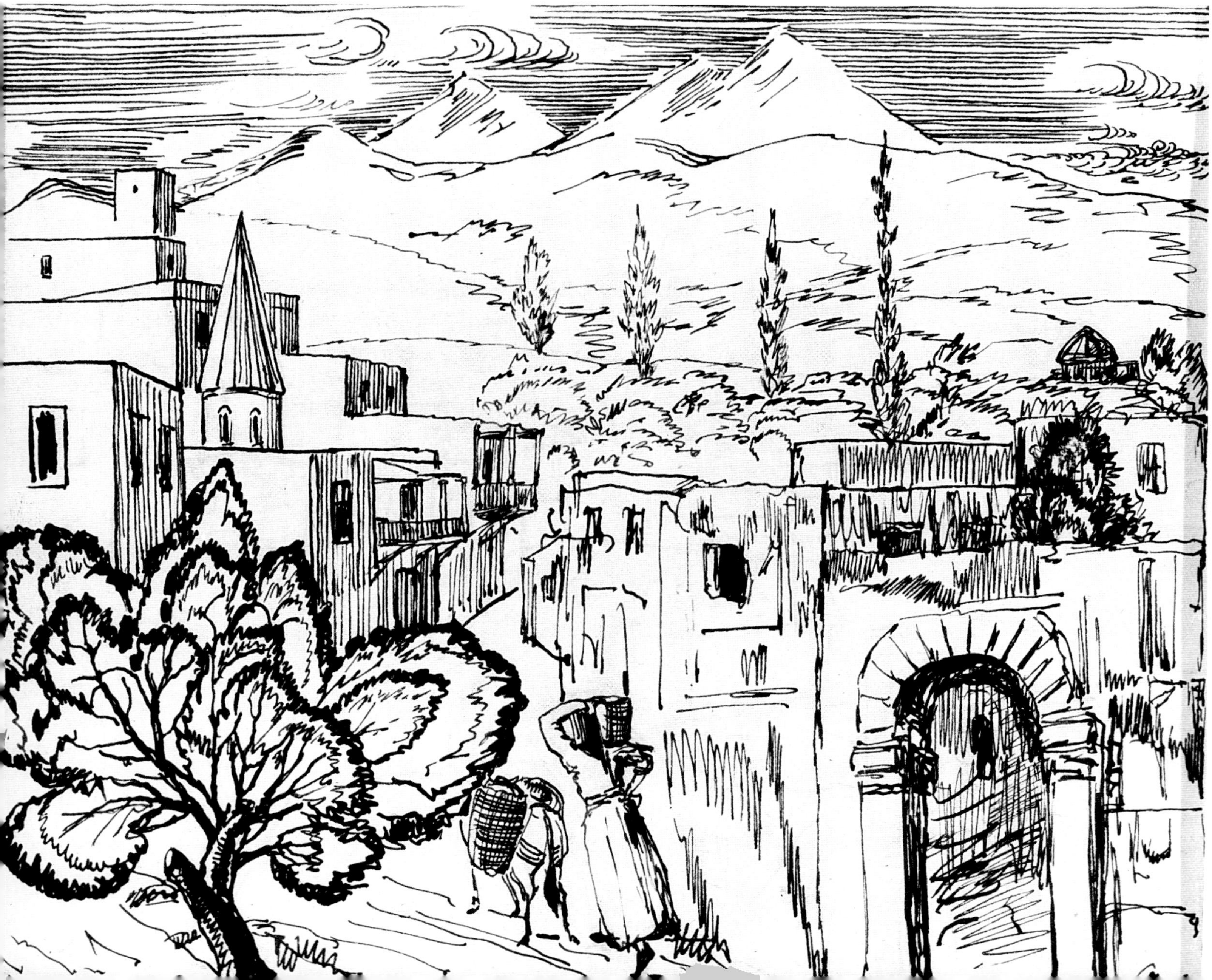

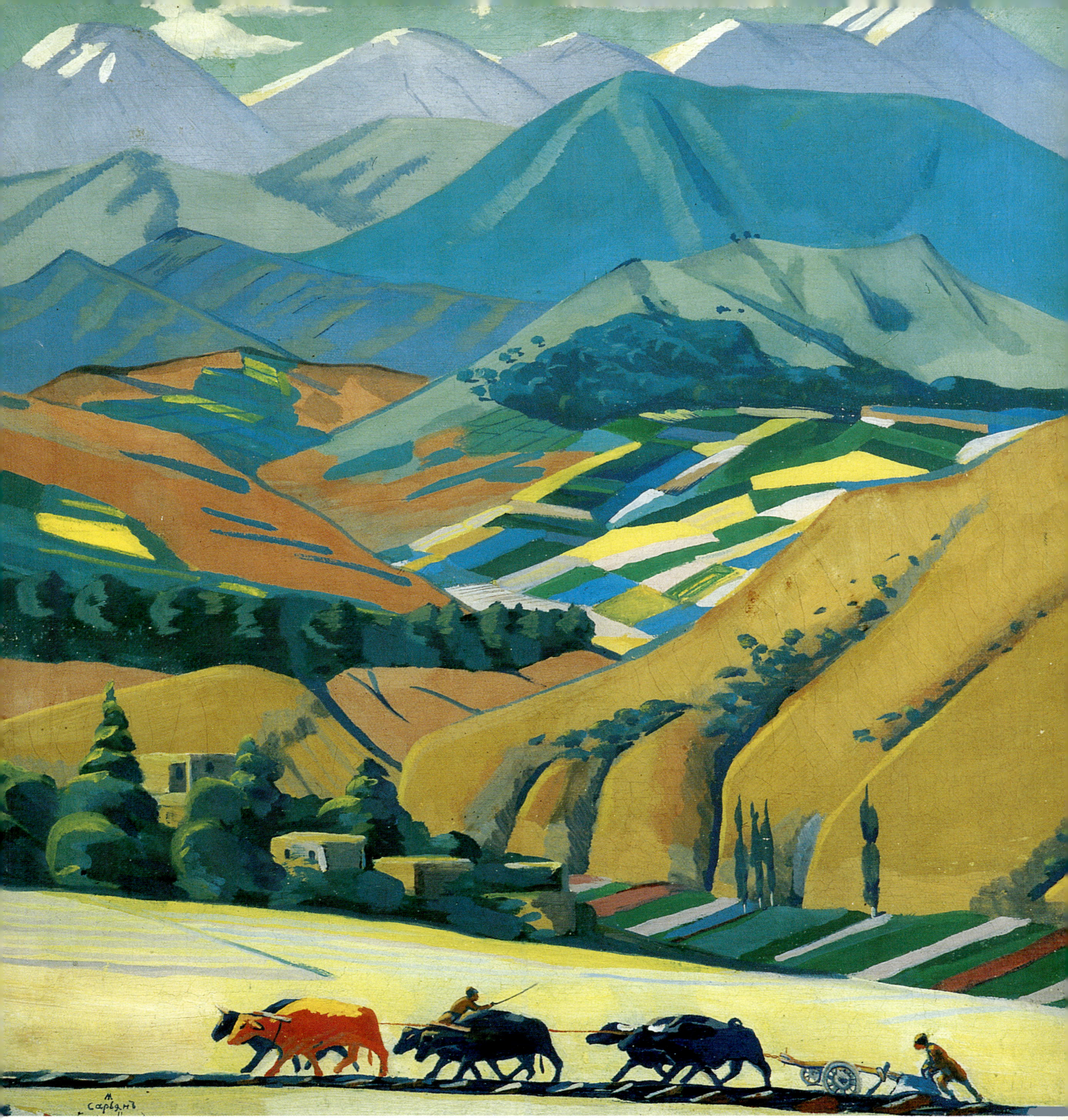

Ploughing. 1929. Illustration
to the anthology of Armenian folk-tales
Indian ink on paper. 17 x 12 cm
Martiros Saryan Museum, Yerevan

Ashtarak. 1934
Indian ink on paper. 11 x 14 cm
Martiros Saryan Museum, Yerevan

Mountains. Armenia. 1923
Oil on canvas. 66 x 68 cm
The Tretyakov Gallery, Moscow

lies. And although Ararat is now outside the national borders, the image of Armenia is inconceivable without that astonishing, legendary mountain with its great and little summits, so perfect and unsurpassed in shape that it seems to have been individually made by some higher power.

Saryan devoted whole cycles of works created over several decades to the two mountains. Such an attachment to one and the same small set of motifs is a feature of the mature creative period of many artists. Suffice it to recall the series of paintings by Monet, Pissarro or Cézanne. Just as the last turned time and again to Mount Sainte-Victoire and

Hokusai to Mount Fuji, Saryan painted Aragats and, especially frequently, Ararat. From different distances, changing his point and angle of view, without striving like Monet to capture momentary, unstable states of light and air, Saryan revealed various facets of his beloved motifs in the course of natural cycles – the seasons or times of the day, subordinating the compositional variants and, most importantly, the colour characteristics to his concept.

In the 1920s he painted Aragats in summer, with golden slopes baked by the sun, and in autumn, in a restrained, greyish range. In his canvases Ararat appears either excessively close or a distant mirage seen from Yerevan and the surrounding heights, in the early morning with its snowy peaks turning rosy in the rays of dawn, or in a hazy autumn afternoon. The greater portion of paintings in these cycles date, however, from the following decades.

The Ghegam Mountains. 1926
Oil on canvas. 70 x 70 cm
Martiros Saryan Museum, Yerevan

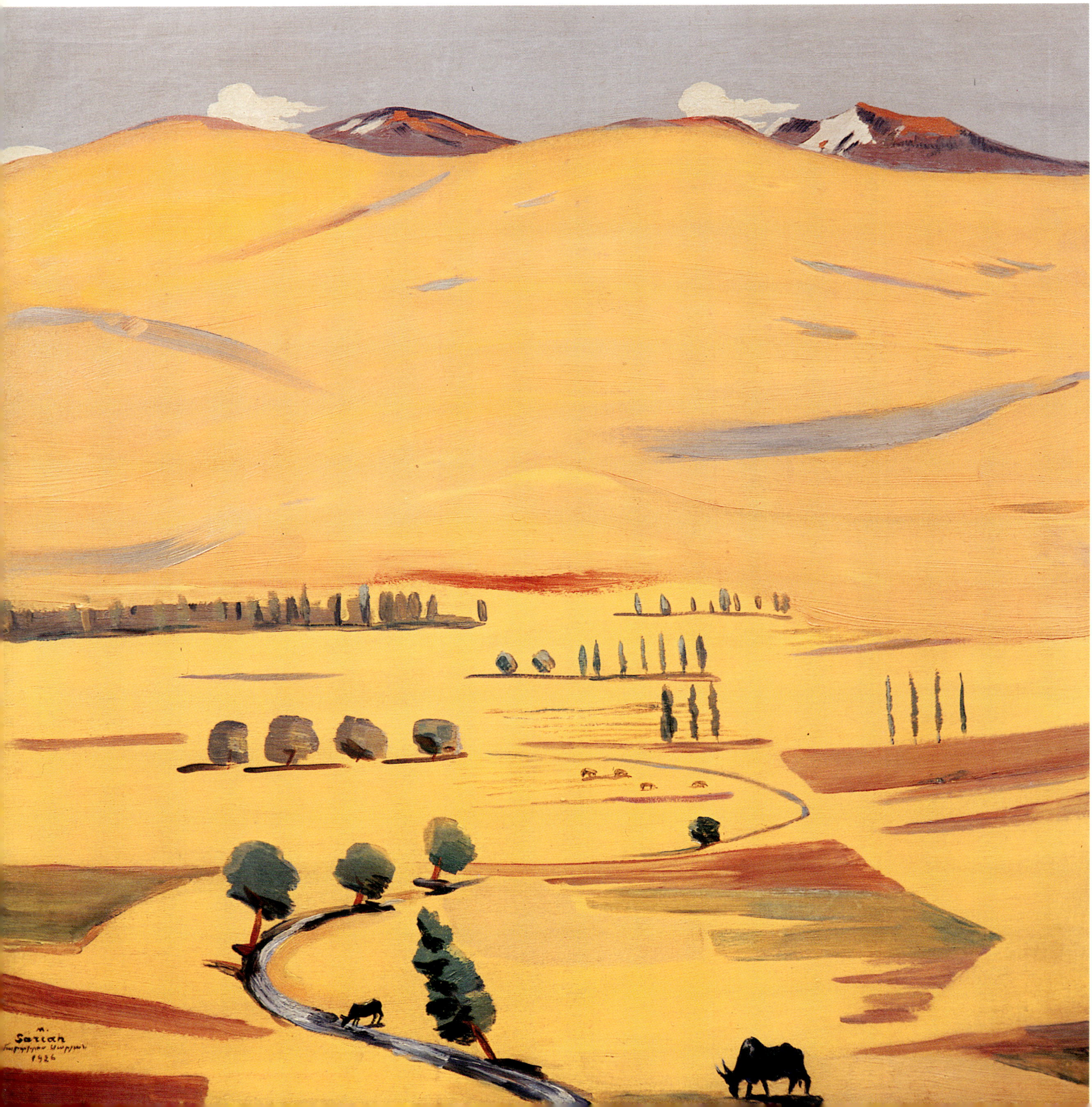

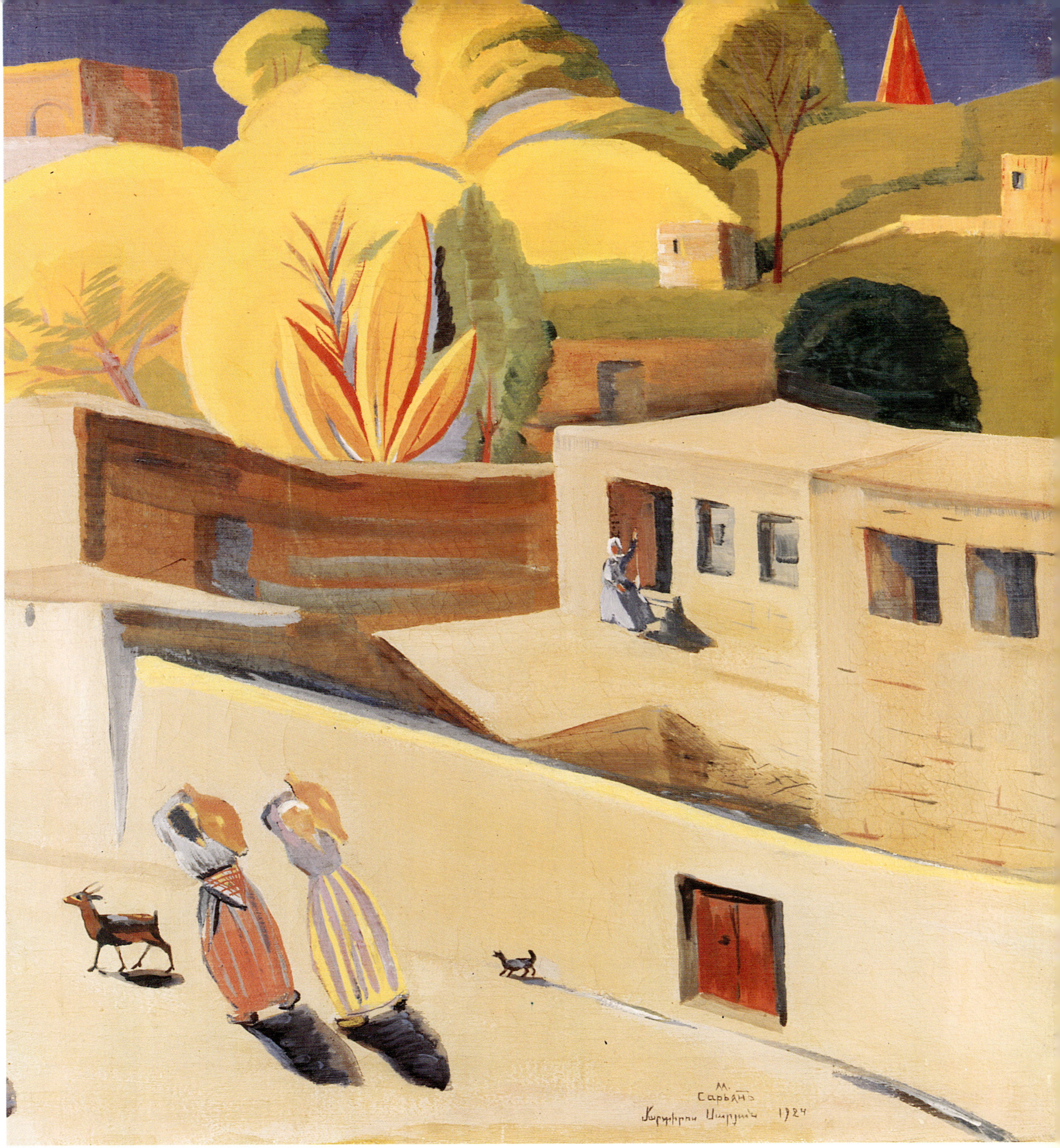

Yerevan. 1924
Oil on canvas. 69 x 69 cm
The Russian Museum, St Petersburg

The artist was far from always faithful to actual topography, though. His works include "imaginary" mountain landscapes, decoratively transfigured by the artist's fantasy yet still retaining a genuine feel of the highlands. Among them are *Gazelles* and *Camels* (both 1926), compositions where the rhythm of the mountain peaks echoes either the rapid running of the gazelles or the measured, tread of the camels.

In 1923 Saryan produced his first large monumental and decorative work – a colourful, poetic image of Armenia as the curtain for the newly-established Sundukian Drama Theatre in Yerevan. Observing all the laws

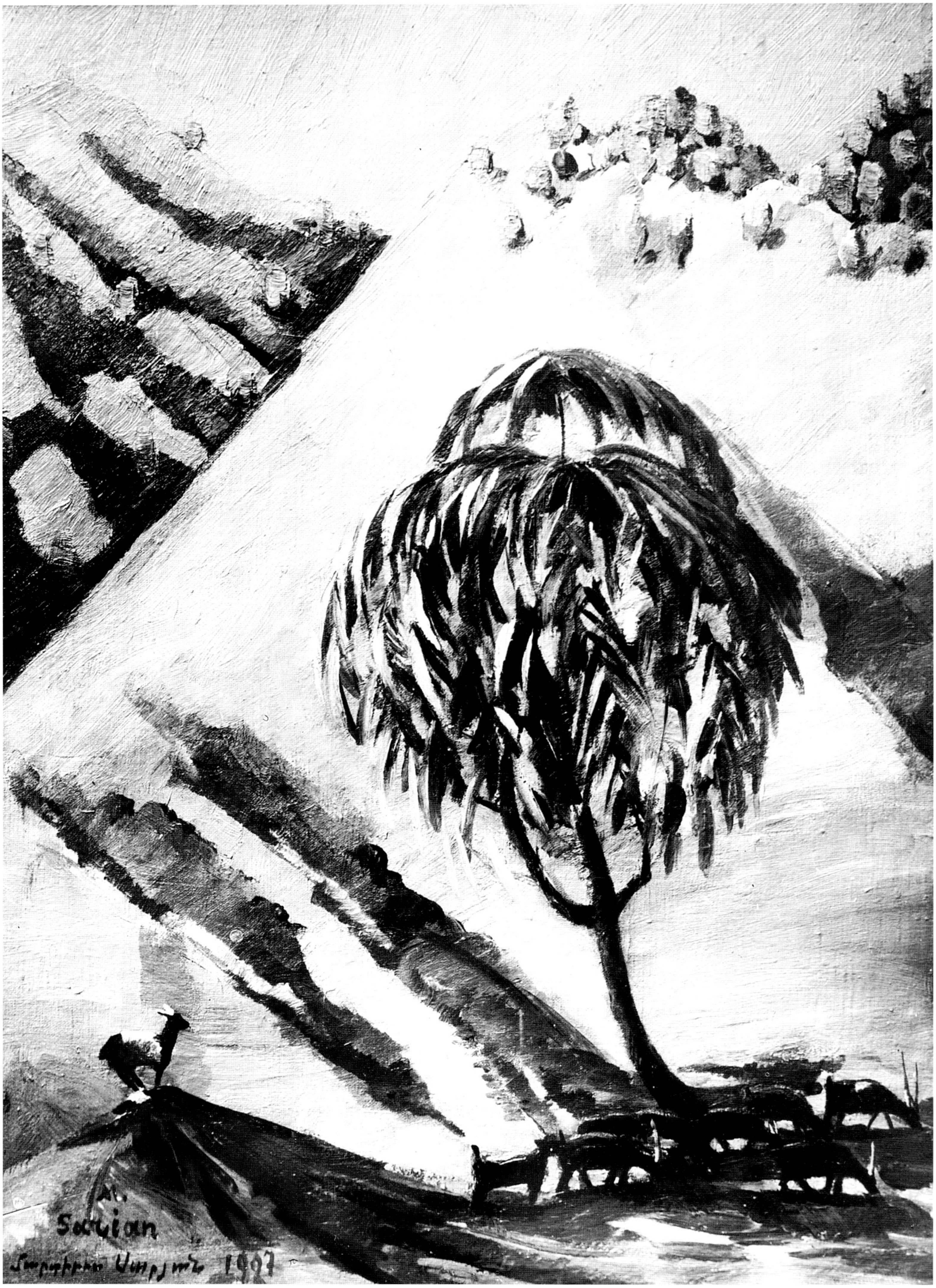
M. Sarian
Մարտիրոս Սարյան

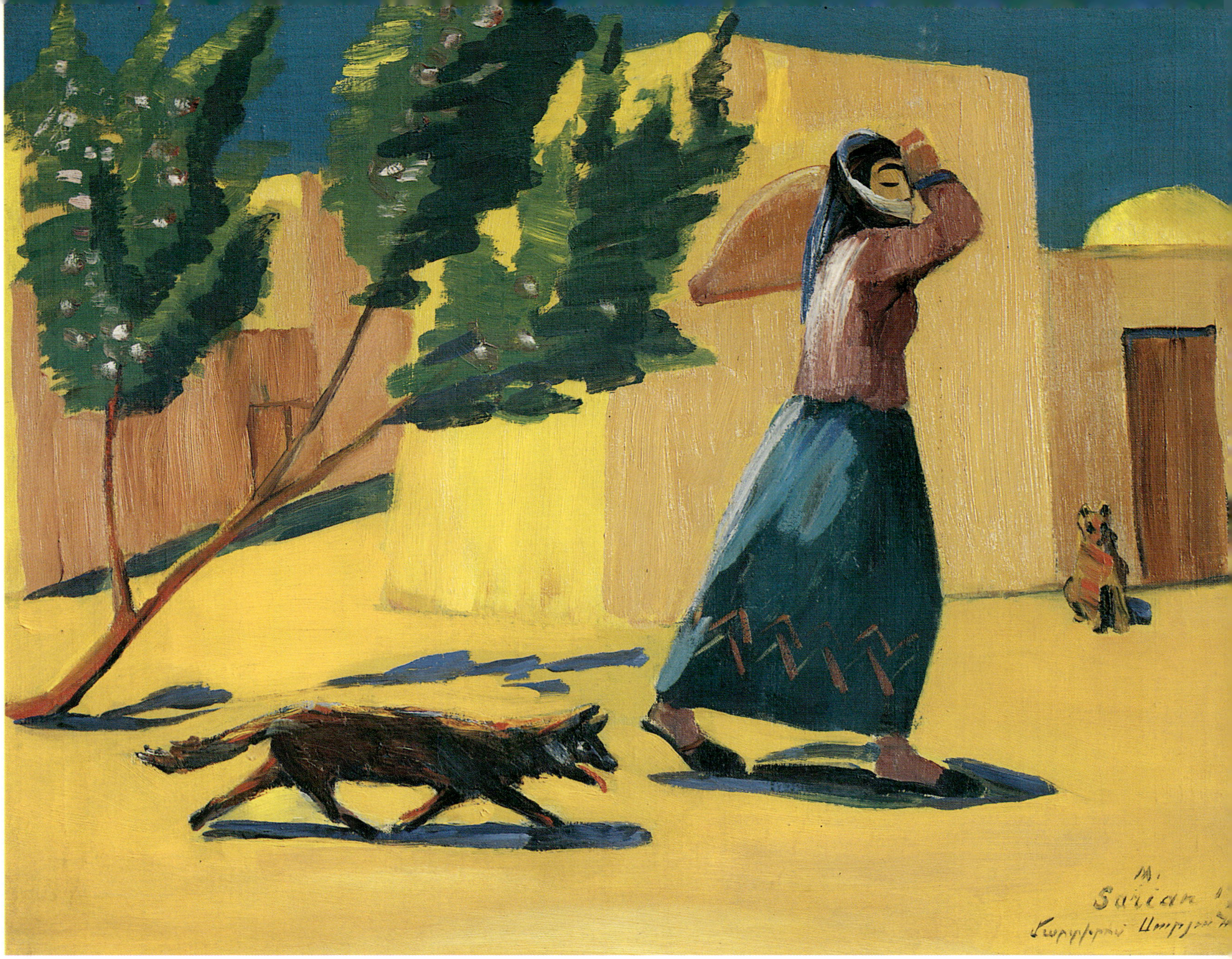

To the Spring. 1926
Oil on canvas. 48 x 64 cm
Martiros Saryan Museum, Yerevan

of monumental art, Saryan managed, despite the flat treatment of the composition, to give a sense of distance, to combine infinite expanses with vivid, specific details. He found room in this work for both an old church on the top of a cliff and one of his favourite motifs – women dancing on the flat roof of a house.

Alongside such large-scale works, Saryan was painting more modest motifs – Yerevan streets with typical wattle-and-daub houses seeming to clamber up the steep slopes; cosy enclosed courtyards. He painted his own courtyard (1923) with a balcony on tall pillars and a pomegranate tree that, according to a biographer, he added himself.[56] A black buffalo and a woman with a pitcher give this typical Yerevan motif character and life.

Such female figures with pitchers on their shoulders, astonishingly expressive in their rapid motion, were one of Saryan's most brilliant discoveries – a sort of pictograph that marks many of his works, notably *Yerevan* (1924), a poetic, colourful image of the old city warmed by the golden glow of the autumnal sun and *To the Spring* (1926), in which the woman with a pitcher is accompanied by a no less expressive dog. With its lapidary idiom and the intensive contrast of sultry orange and dense blue the latter small canvas is reminiscent of the paintings in the Eastern cycle. It was painted in France where the artist was sent on an official working journey in 1926. Saryan spent about a year and a half in Paris, the "artists' capital" of which he had long dreamed. "For me it was

Summer. Goats. 1927
Oil on canvas
Perished in 1928

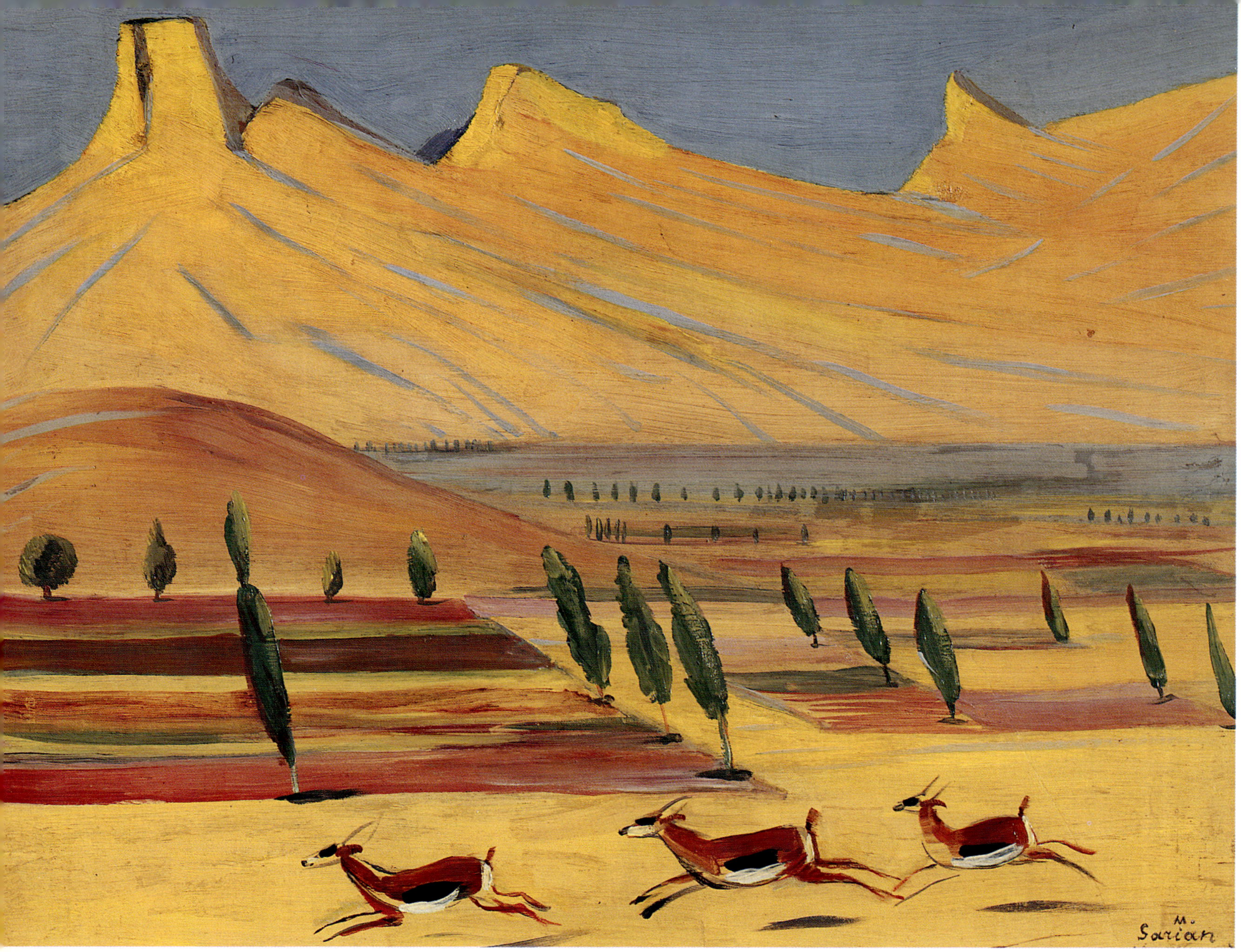

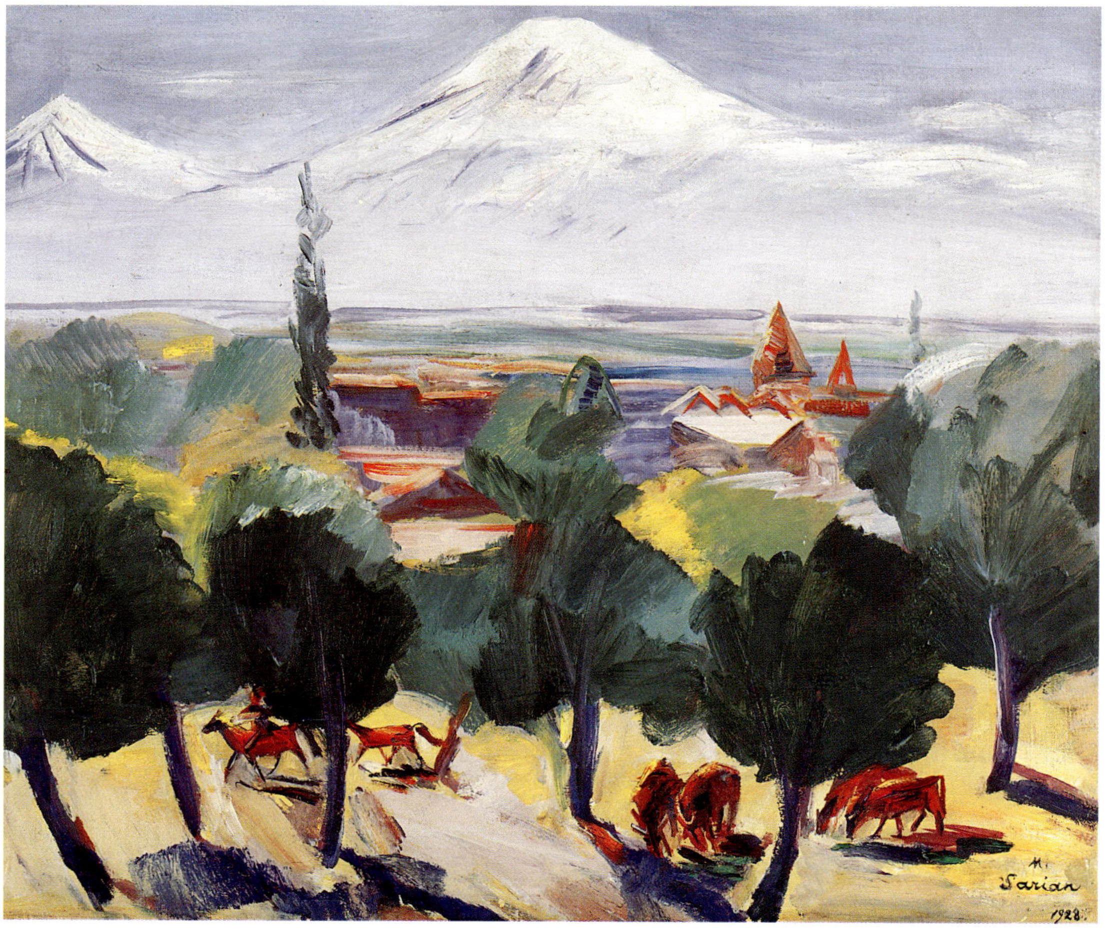

Gazelles. 1926
Oil on canvas. 46 x 61 cm
The Tretyakov Gallery, Moscow

Hazy Autumn Day. 1928
Oil on canvas. 59 x 73 cm
Martiros Saryan Museum, Yerevan

Lake Sevan. 1936
Oil on canvas. 73 x 53 cm
I. Koretskaya collection, Moscow

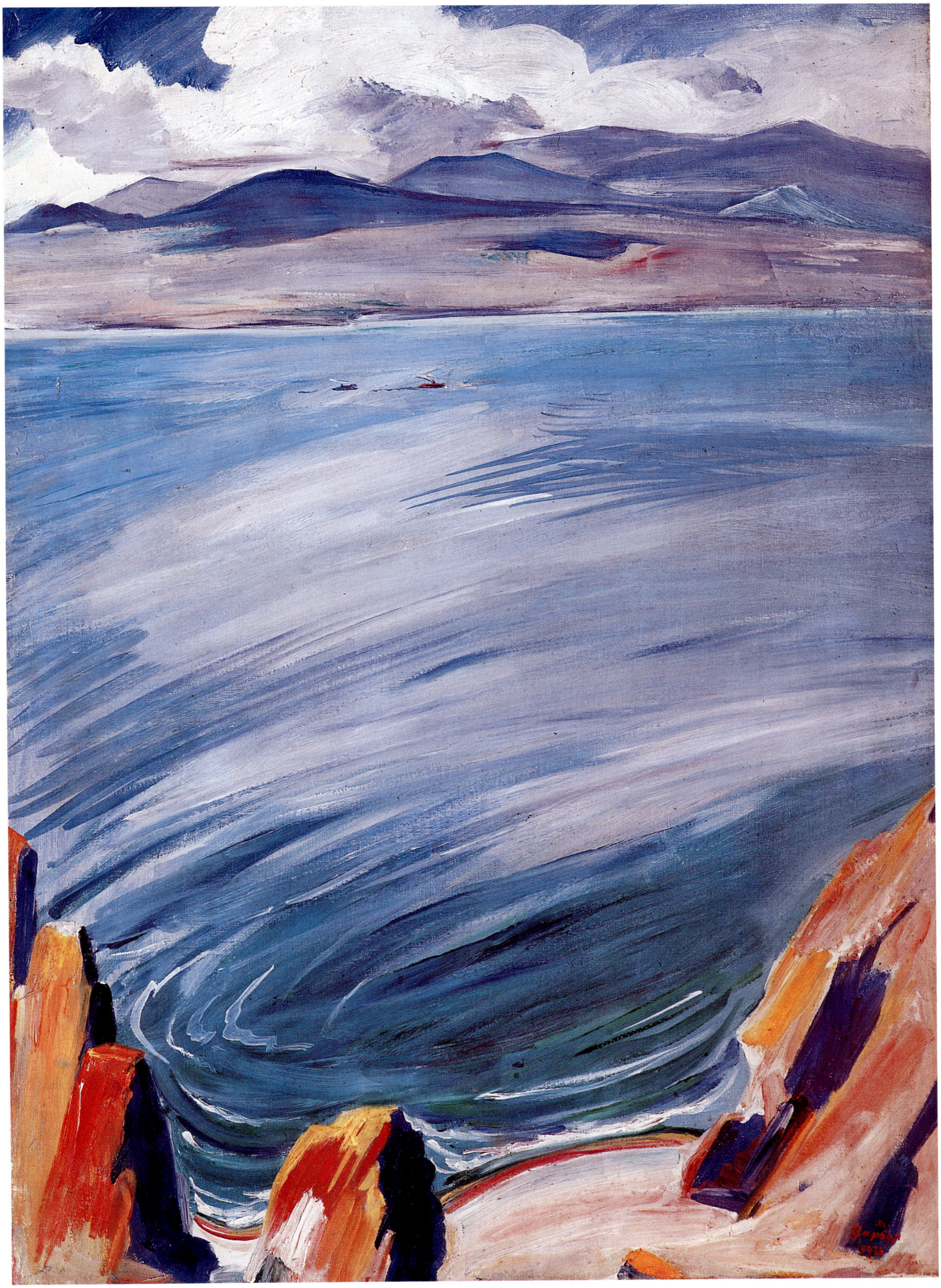
М. Сарьян
1936

important to make direct contact with French art; I studied under the marvellous French artists..." Saryan wrote later.[57] Besides that, he wanted "to somehow gain an understanding of his own possibilities and aspirations."[58] He already had a high opinion of the Impressionists' painting, but in Paris he again felt the charm of their art. This can be traced in paintings and studies produced in France, where, by his own admission, the artist worked enraptured "literally from dawn to dusk". The studies

Room. 1935. Sketch of the stage sets for Armenak Stepanian's opera *Bold Nazar*
Watercolour on paper. 56 x 78 cm
The Bakhrushin Theatre Museum, Moscow

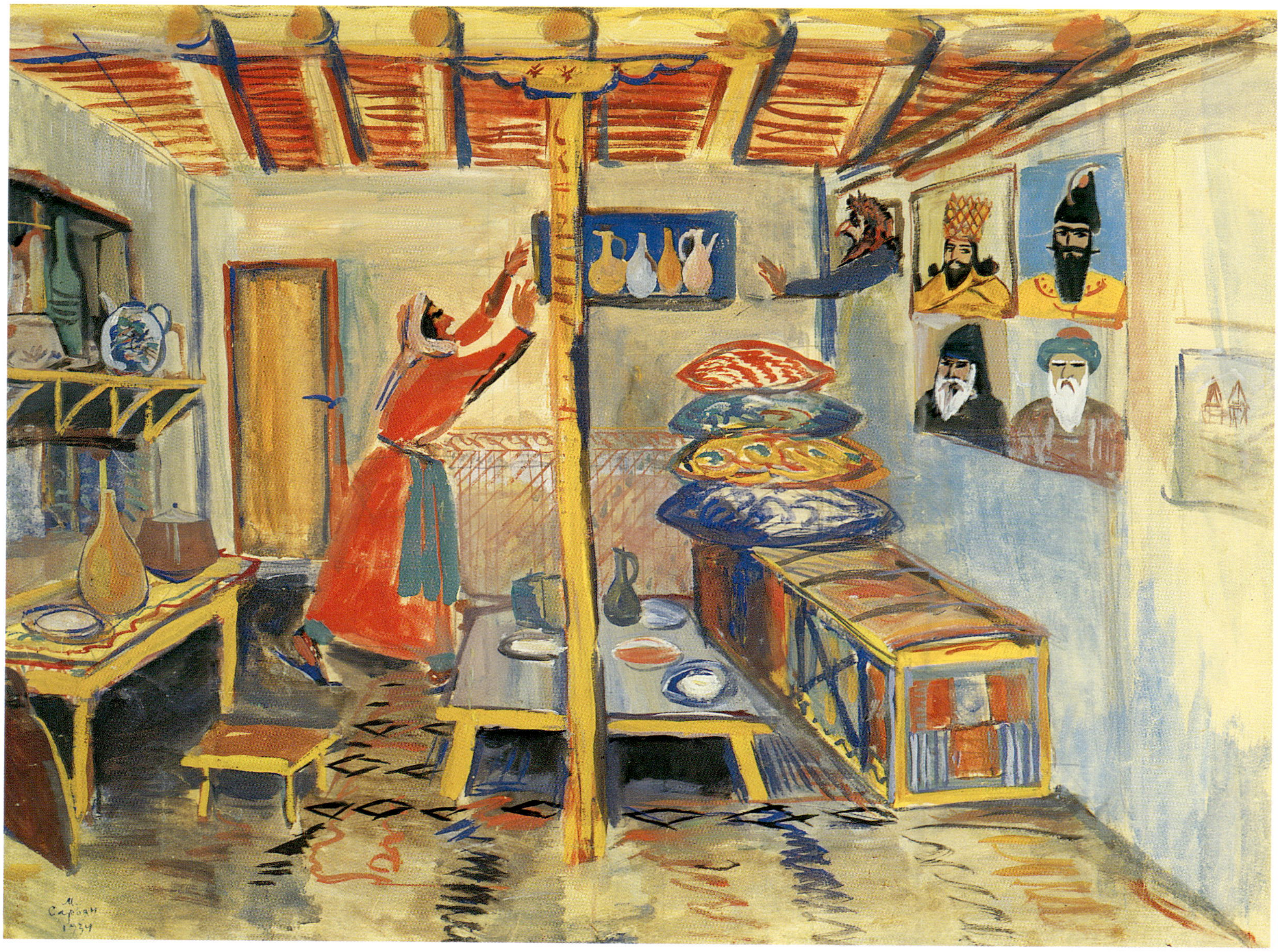

painted on the banks of the Marne, for example, betray a link with the works of Monet, and to an even greater degree Sisley, in the typically Impressionistic character of the motifs, in the use of the landscape format with a strip of water in the foreground and rippled reflections on its surface, in a more fragmentary manner of painting.

The only Parisian townscape – *From the Studio Window. Paris*, a view of the quiet little Rue Broca, not far from the Boulevard Saint-Michel – prompts associations with images of the French capital in the work of later artists, Bonnard or Utrillo, in its intimacy, the lyrical intonation and colour scheme constructed on the relationship of delicate tones conveyed by separate brushstrokes in one place, combined brushstrokes in another. Works like this are, however, exceptions in the artist's œuvre.

In Paris too Saryan painted Armenia – landscapes, at times including genre motifs (*To the Spring* that has already been mentioned), and still-lifes that also had an emphatically "Armenian" colour to them. Indeed

Sketch of Almast's costume for Alexander Spendiarov's opera *Almast.* 1939
National Gallery of Armenia, Yerevan

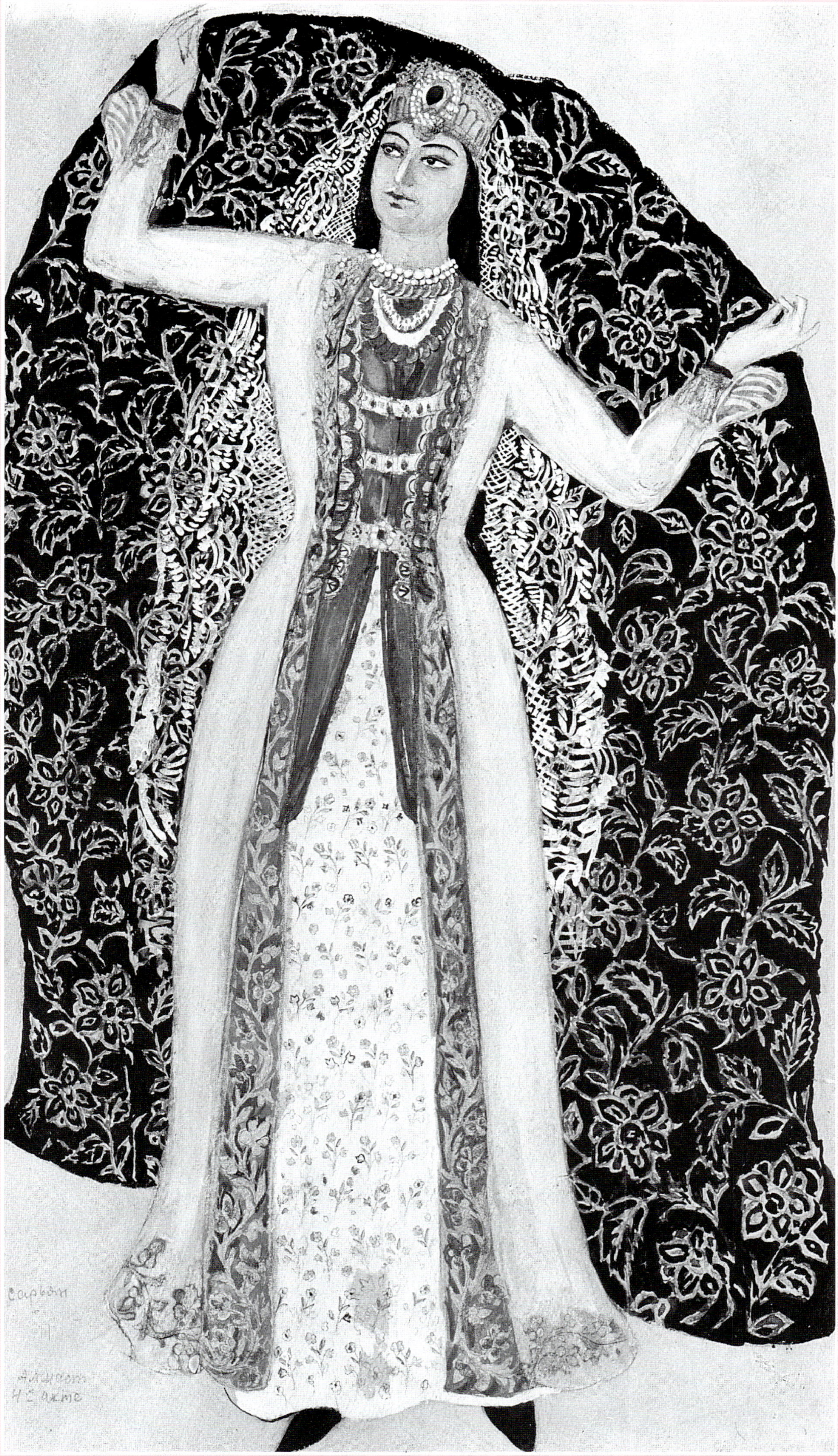
Сарьян
Алмаст
4е акте

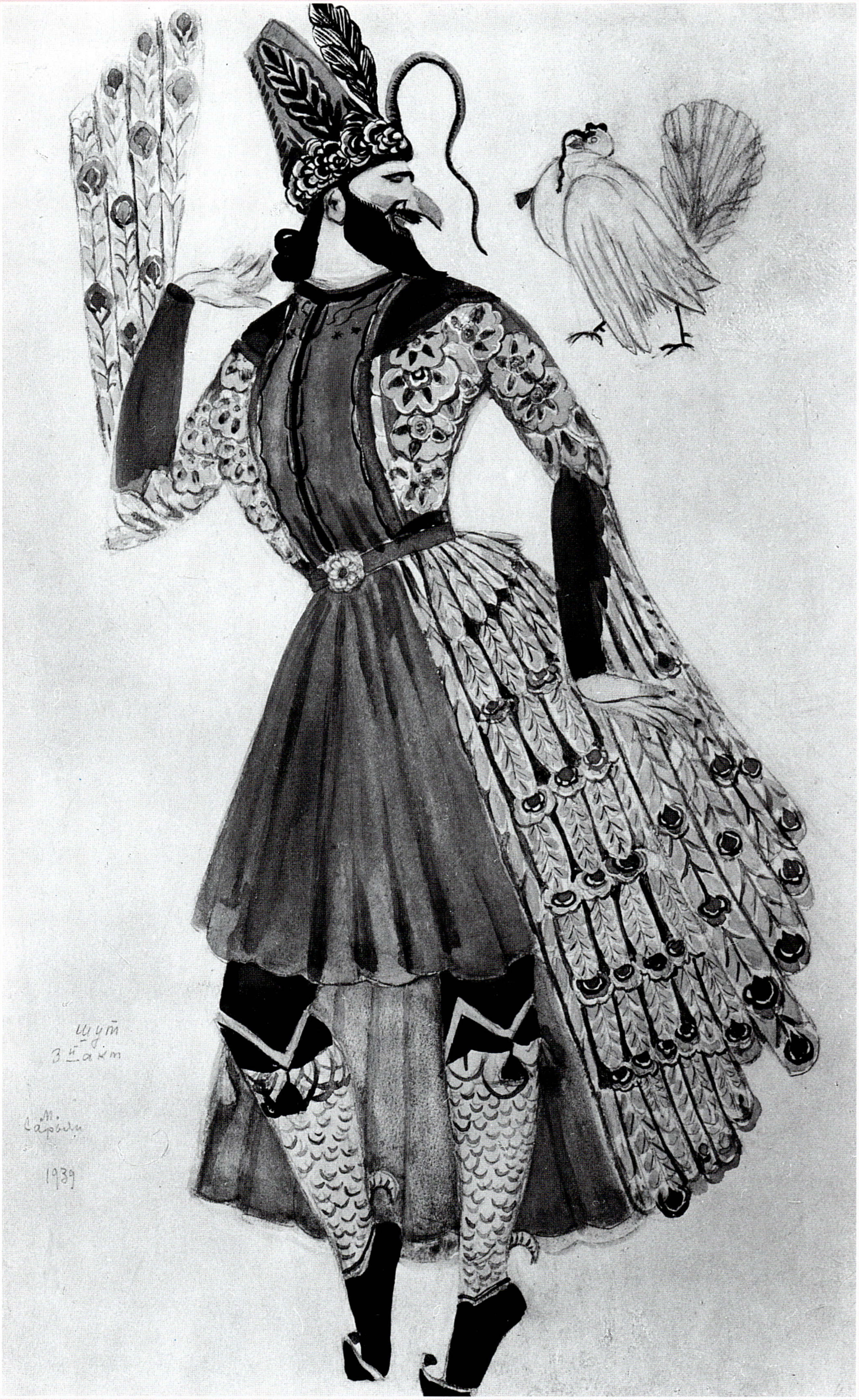
шут
3й акт
М. Сарьян
1939

Sketch of the Jester's costume
for Alexander Spendiarov's
opera *Almast*. 1939
Gouache on paper. 47 x 30 cm
National Gallery of Armenia, Yerevan

even the subjects of the portraits painted in Paris were compatriots of the artist who lived there. It was with them and with the émigré Russians, who included his teacher Konstantin Korovin, that Sarayan chiefly mixed.

Saryan's stay in Paris culminated in a one-man exhibition held at the Galerie Girard. Apart from thirty-six paintings created in France, several canvases that the artist had brought from Armenia were displayed. The foreword to the catalogue was written by the noted art-critic

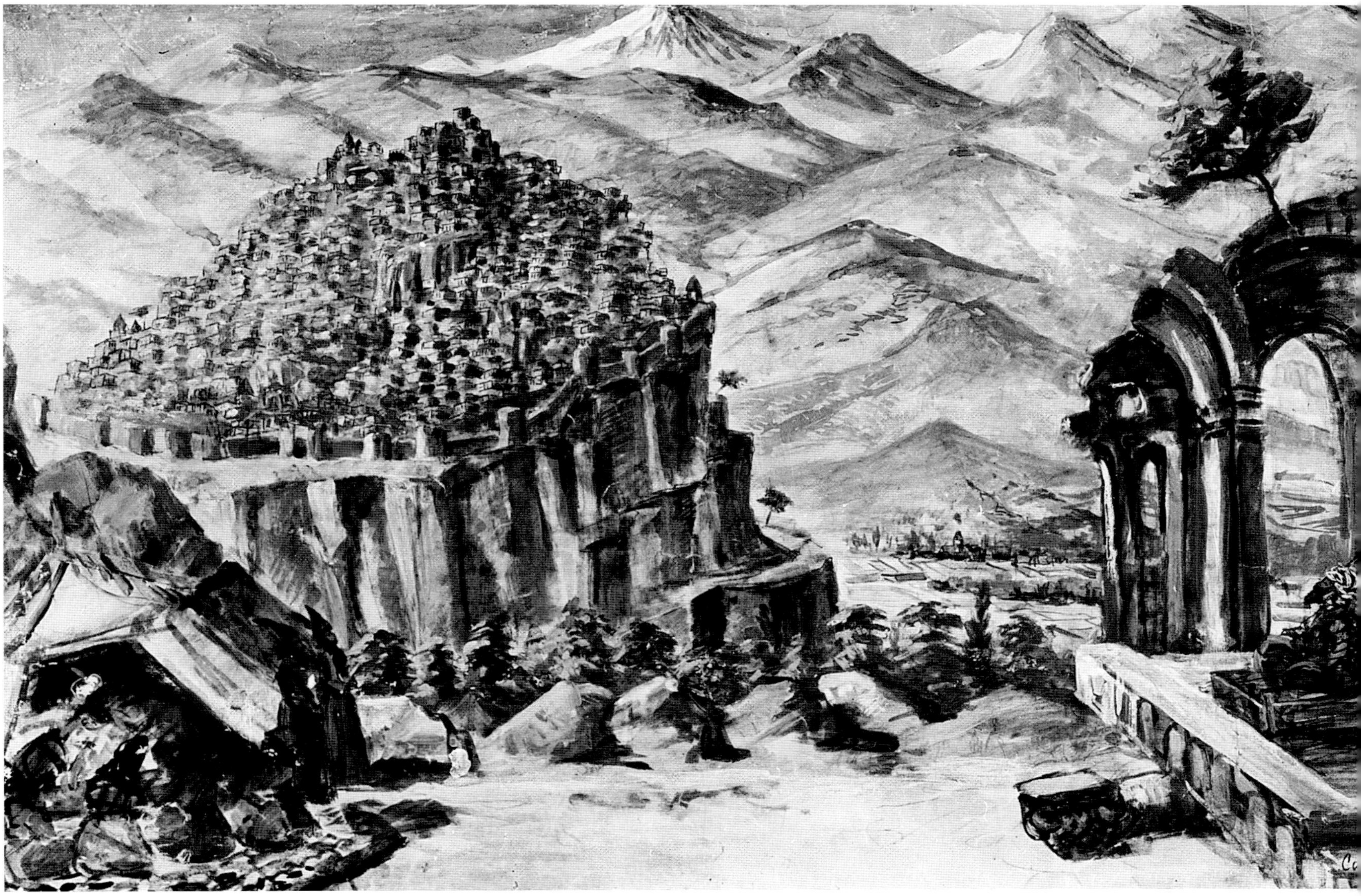

Sketch of the stage sets for the third act
of Alexander Spendiarov's opera
Almast. 1939
Gouache on paper. 35 x 50 cm
National Gallery of Armenia, Yerevan

Louis Vauxcelles. The success of the exhibition inspired Saryan, but fate soon struck him a savage blow. Almost all the works that he sent back to his homeland on a French ship perished when a fire broke out on board. The only things to survive were a few canvases and drawings that the artist took with him on the train and a number of paintings that he sold or gave to people in Paris. These last included *Gazelles* and *The Ghegam Mountains*, which many years later returned to his homeland. We can judge the rest only by photographs. Saryan learnt of the loss of his works when he was already back in Yerevan. "In such a mood," the artist recalled, "I began the second, now entirely settled period of my life. But I overcame my sorrow and continued to work and live with my people and for them."[59]

Can we consider the Parisian period a dividing line in Saryan's œuvre? Was it of significance for his subsequent development? Undoubtedly yes – but only to a certain extent. The new contact with French art encouraged the search for greater tonal integrity, heightened the

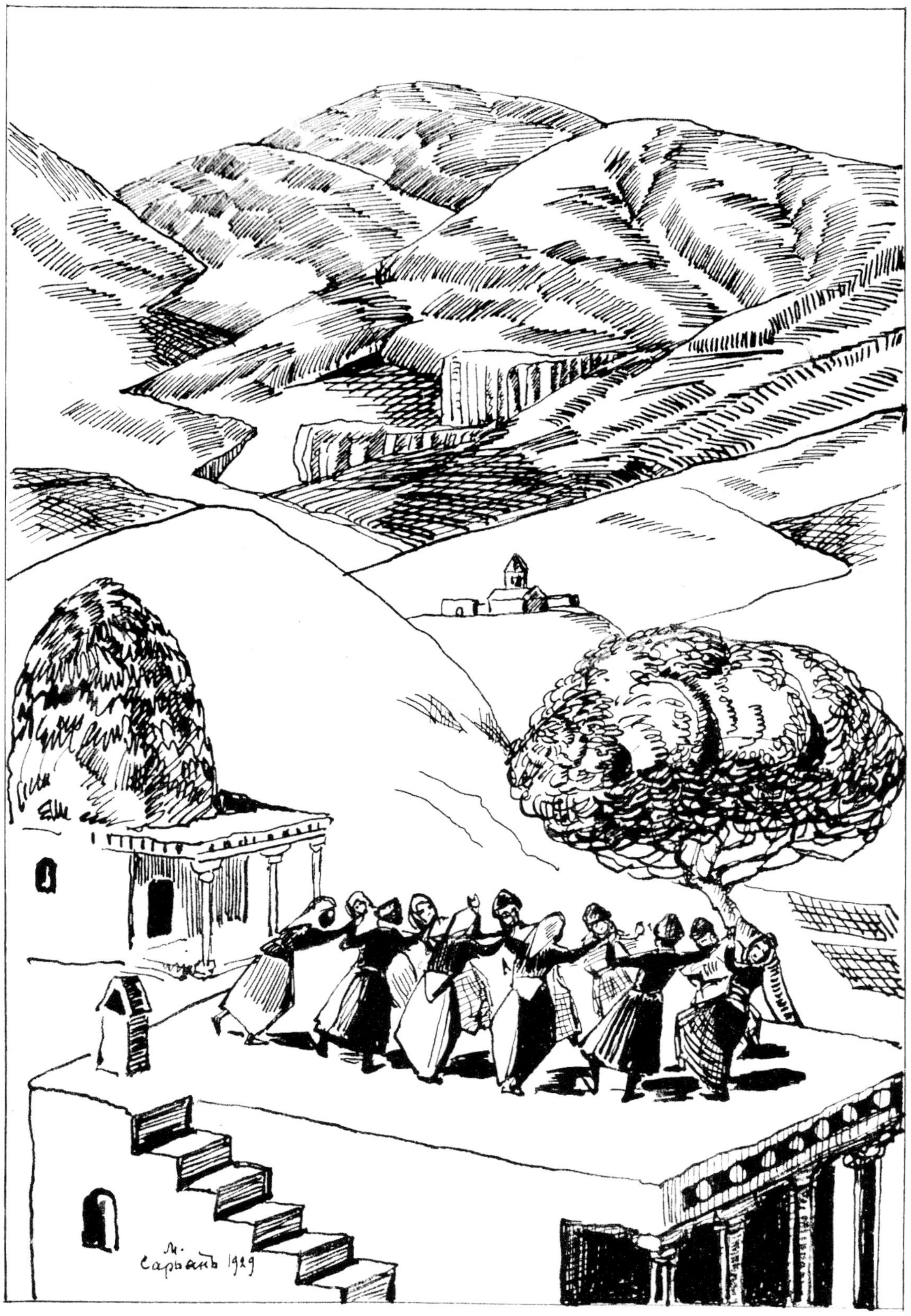

Peasants' Dance. 1929. Illustration
to the anthology of Armenian folk-tales
Indian ink on paper. 17 x 12 cm
B. Okunev family collection, St Petersburg

attention that the artist paid to the light-and-air medium and the great variety of colour shades. It did not, however, affect the basics of his creative world-view and method. "Monumentality, generalization is in the blood of my art," Saryan would tell Alexander Kamensky, a scholar of his work. "While in Paris, and genuinely carried away by the Impressionists, I understood that – somewhat by contrast – with particular force. My artistic convictions resisted, as it were, my own attempts to paint in a more detailed and, if you can put it that way, 'crumbly' manner. The tendency to abstraction remained and emerged victorious."[60]

Saryan's subsequent art did not develop under the badge of his Parisian impressions. It was, above all, a logical continuation of his previous course. Fundamentally he remained "true to his roots" (Yervand Kochar). In comparison with the 1920s, however, the artist's range of

Multicoloured Landscape. 1937.
Design of a fly-leaf for the anthology
of Armenian folk-tales
Tempera on cardboard. 41 x 98.5 cm
B. Okunev family collection, St Petersburg

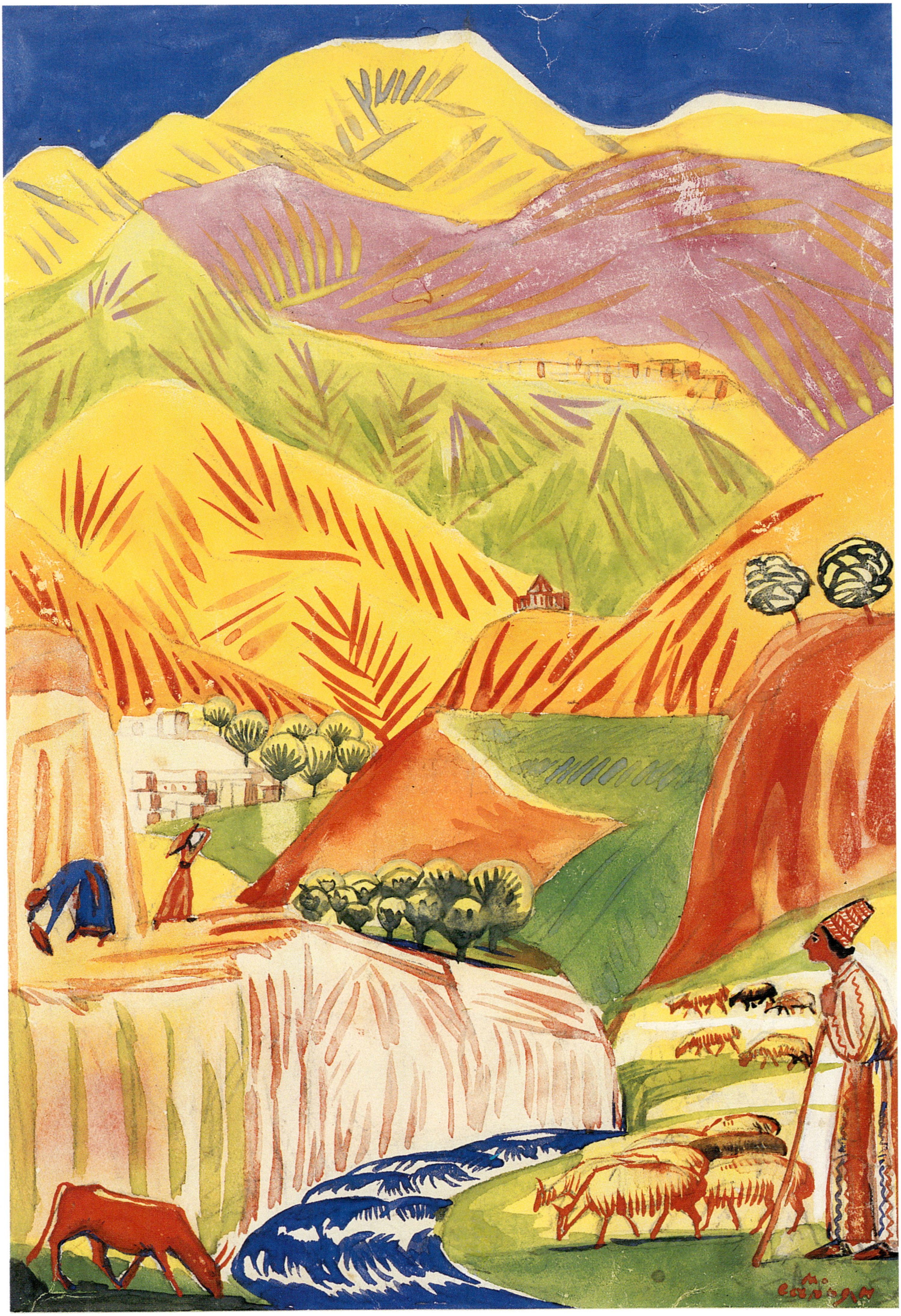

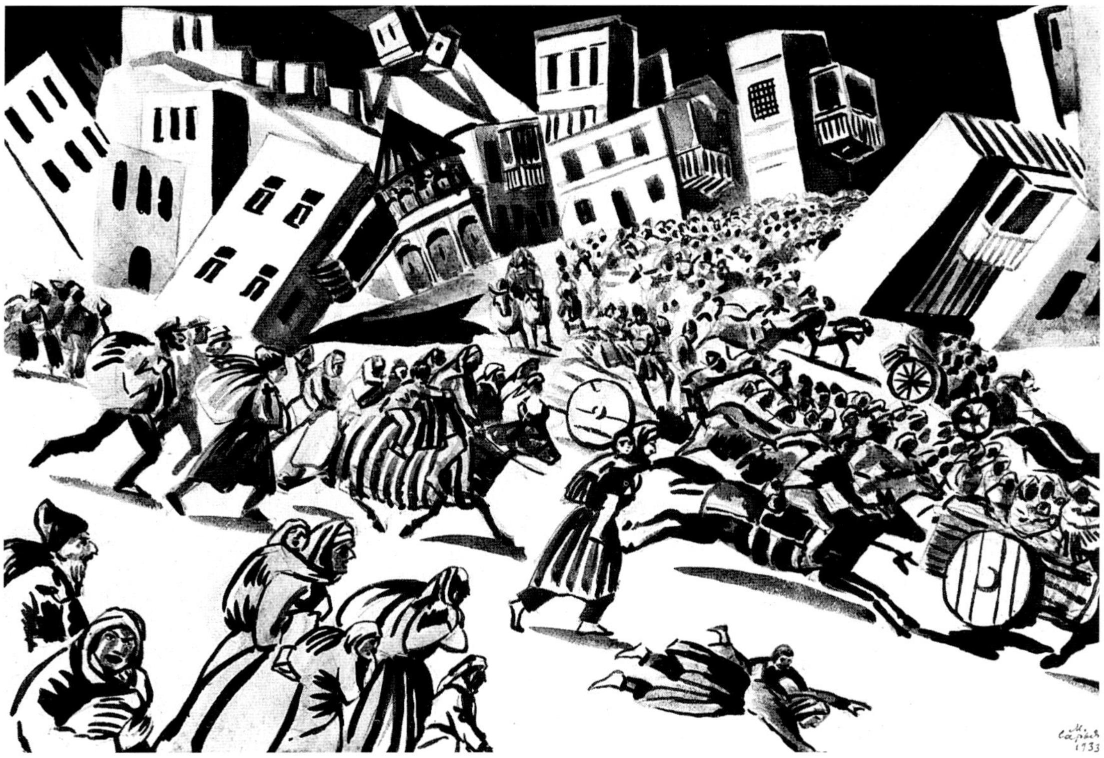

The Flight of the Nairians. 1933.
Illustration to *The Nairi Land* by Yegishe Charents
Indian ink on paper. 20 x 26 cm
Yegishe Charents Memorial Museum, Yerevan

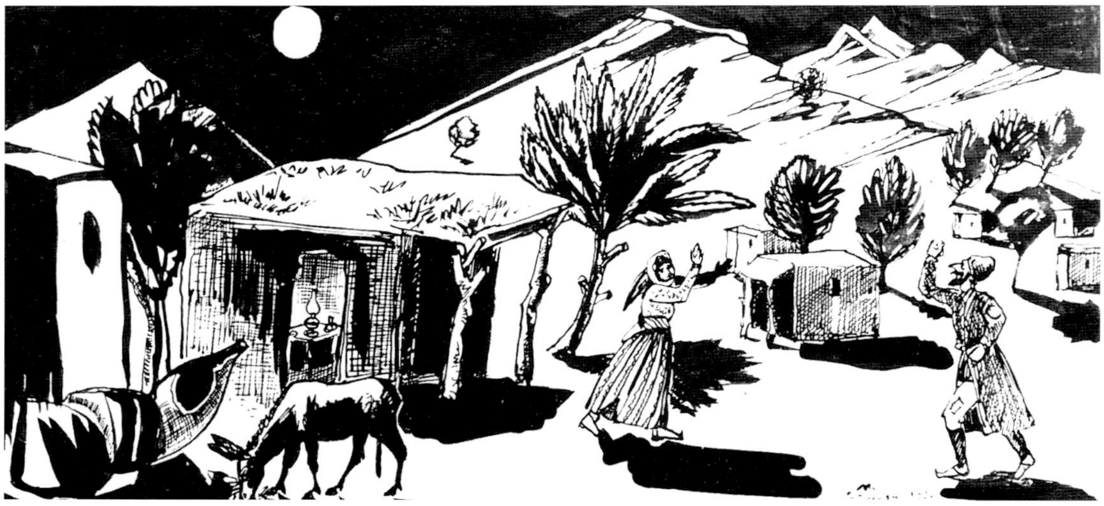

Headpiece to Hovannes Tumanian's fairy-tale *Bold Nazar*. 1936
Indian ink on paper. 15 x 29 cm
Hovannes Tumanian Memorial Museum, Yerevan

interests and genres did expand. Among other things, the 1930s produced many of his best works in stage design and book illustration.

Saryan's decorative gift and his keen feeling for human characters determined the artistic perfection of his work in the sphere of theatrical art as well. For Stanislavsky's 1931 production of Rimsky-Korsakov's opera *The Golden Cockerel* in Moscow he designed only one act, but revealed immaculate taste and an ability to completely match the set and costumes to the drama and music. Later, recalling this production, Stanislavsky wrote that, of all the artists involved in designing it, only Saryan had satisfied him unreservedly. The artist himself spoke of his desire "to introduce painting into the theatre, so that the stage looked like a good painting, alive in colour relationships, and so that it was uncluttered, with no superfluous things."[61] This in many ways contradicted the generally accepted standards of stage design in the 1930s, demands for sets that were true to life and an abundance of "natural" props.

Saryan gave brilliant expression to his understanding of the aims of theatrical art in the Armenian Opera Theatre where he designed productions of *Bold Nazar* by Armenak Stepanian (1935) and *Almast* by Alexander Spendiarov (1933 and 1938–39). In both instances he revealed a splendid feeling for the stage and a profound grasp of the content and

Cover design for Gurghen Maari's *Childhood and Youth*. 1930
Watercolour on paper. 25 x 19.5 cm
Martiros Saryan Museum, Yerevan

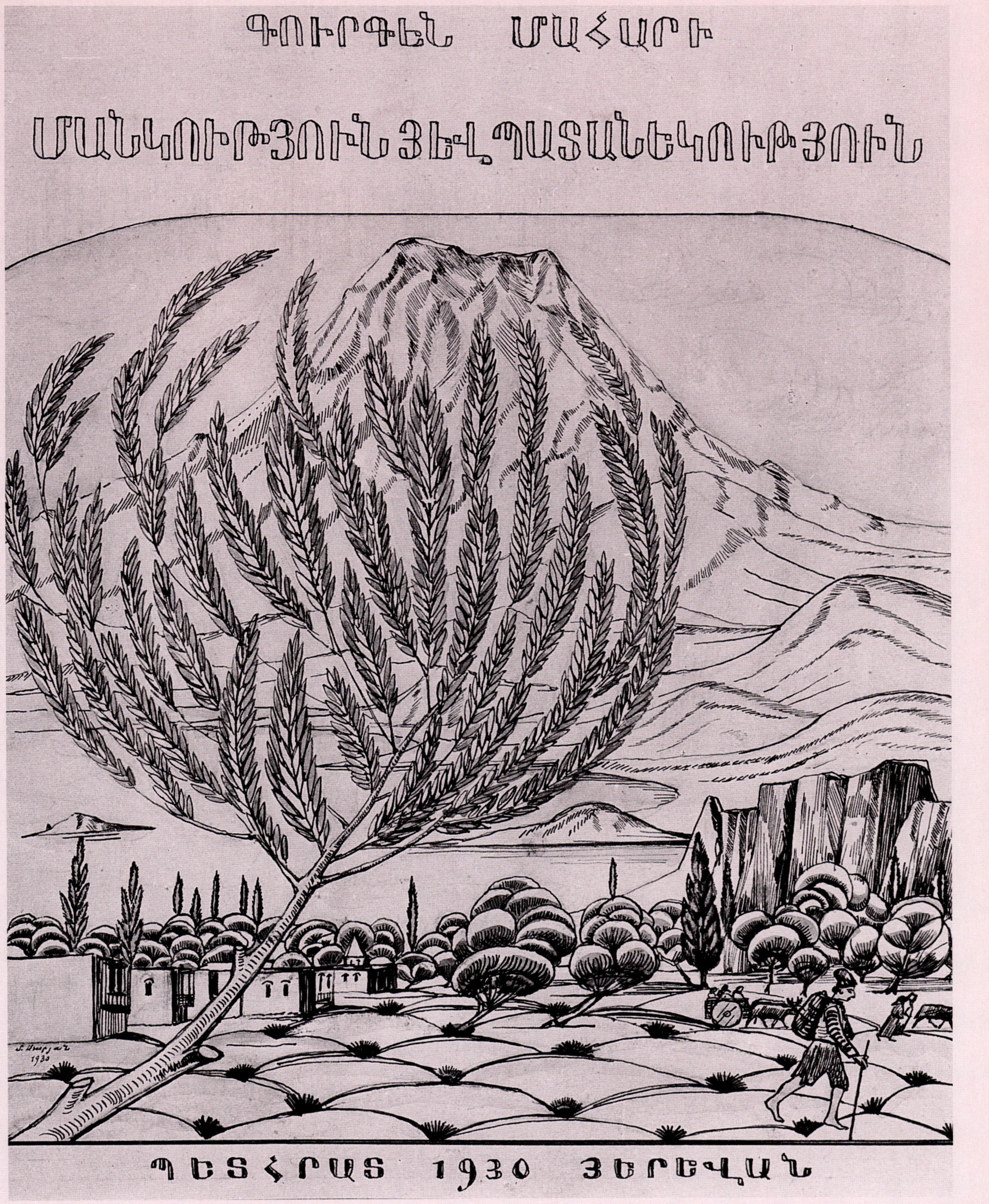
ԳՈՒՐԳԵՆ ՄԱՀԱՐԻ
ՄԱՆԿՈՒԹՅՈՒՆ ՅԵՎ ՊԱՏԱՆԵԿՈՒԹՅՈՒՆ
ՊԵՏՀՐԱՏ 1930 ՅԵՐԵՎԱՆ

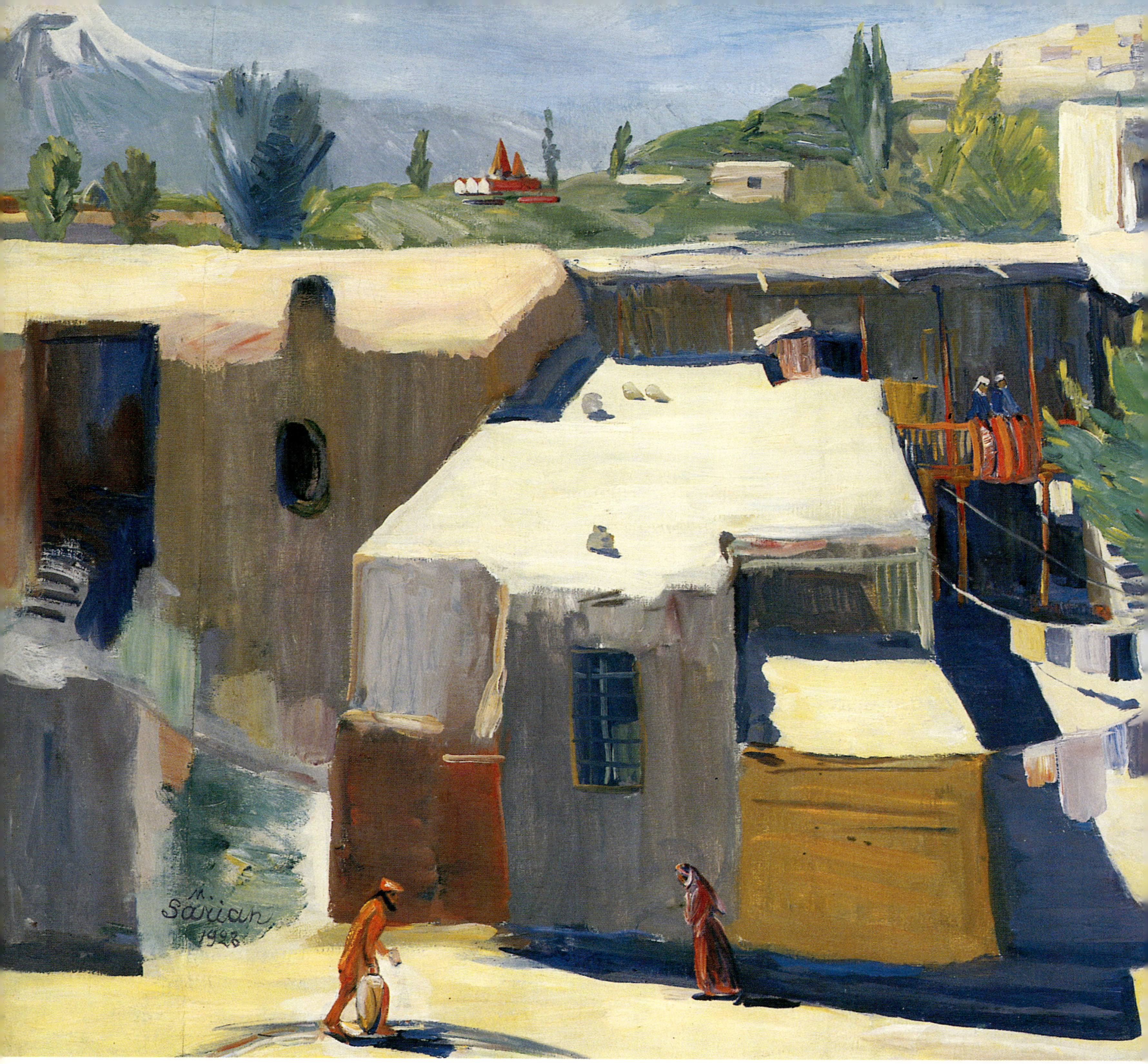

Old Yerevan. 1928
Oil on canvas. 105 x 230 cm
The Tretyakov Gallery, Moscow

style of very different works. His sets to a large extent determined the character of the mise en scène, and the costume designs the appearance and performance of the actors. Saryan designed the sets for *Almast*, a heroic-patriotic opera, in enlarged, monumental forms with a relatively restrained colour-scheme so that the more resonantly coloured costumes would accentuate the performers in dances and movement. The costume designs for *Almast* are true masterpieces. Looking at them, one is put in mind of the theatrical works of Bakst and Golovin, but the ornamental richness and Eastern colourfulness of Saryan's costumes are probably unique. As is the expressiveness of the imagery. Each sketch embodies a finished character with totally individual features, be it the grotesque angularity of the Fool or the snake-like grace of the insidious Almast.

Saryan had just as subtle a sense of book art. He was incomparable as an illustrator of Armenian folk-tales. In his work on them, high artis-

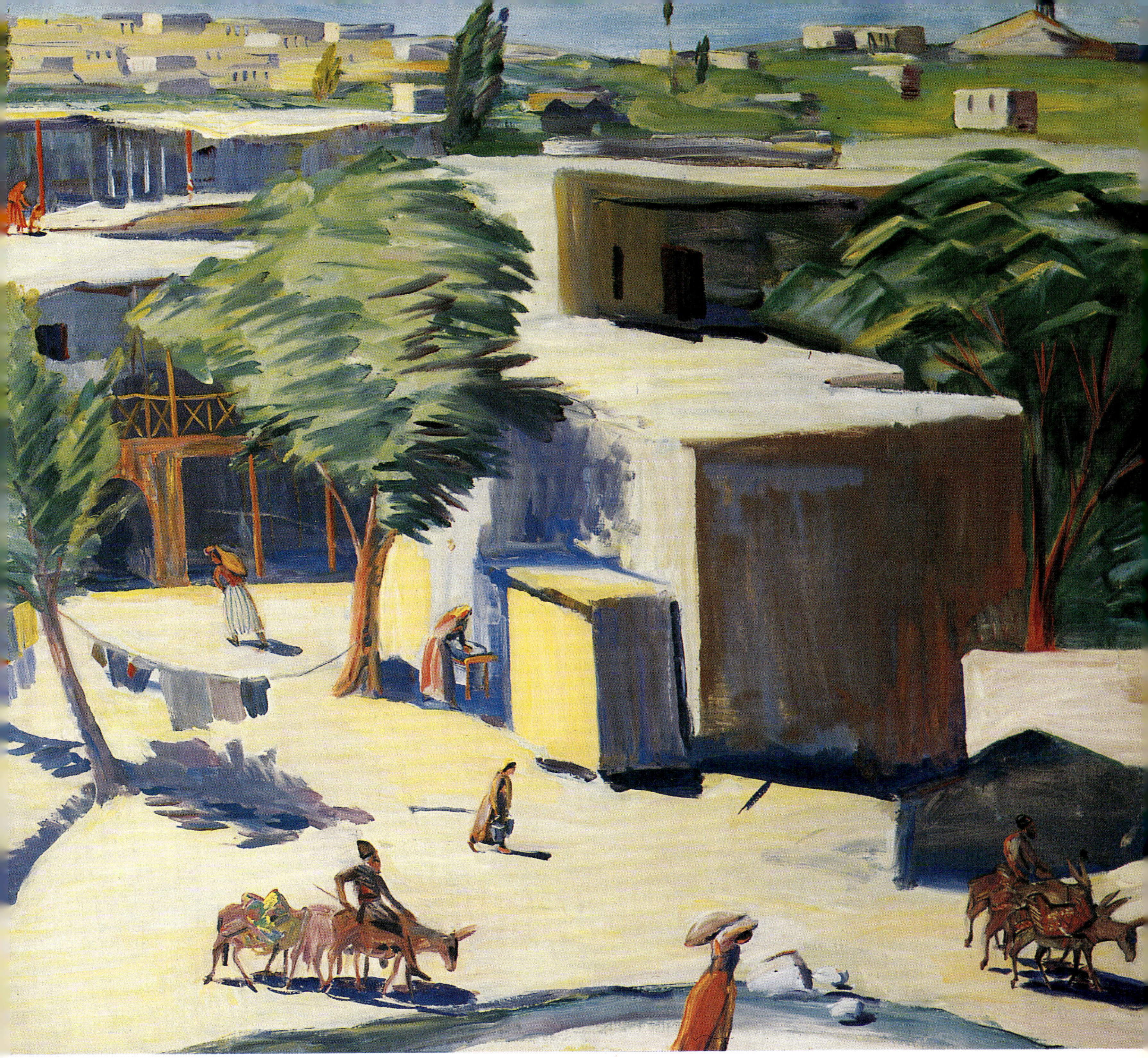

tic culture is inseparable from a profound, incisive grasp of popular life and character, the daily existence and scenery of Armenia, from the national traditions of its art. The illustrations to the folk-tales were executed with an unusual vivacity and humour, as were the drawings for Yegishe Charents's book *The Land of Nairi* or Vaan Totovents's *Life on the Old Roman Road*. A totally different approach is seen in the cover designs for poems by Avetik Isaakian (1929) or Gurghen Maari's book *Childhood and Youth* (1930). Refined, translucent pen-drawings with delicate colour tinting, astonishingly elegant in composition and slightly stylized in manner, express with a special lyricism the poetic charm of the Armenian countryside.

While bound by blood to Armenia, Saryan did not isolate himself from the artistic life of the wider state. In the 1930s his works were displayed at many exhibitions, collective and individual, in different cities of the Soviet Union and abroad. In 1937 the artist was accorded the highest award, the Grand Prix, for the decorative panel he produced for the Soviet Pavilion at the World Exhibition in Paris. The panel – an enormous (about 50 square metres) synthetic landscape of Armenia – was "exceptional in elegance and colourfulness".[62] Saryan continued to create decorative panels, but he still considered the "main line" of his development to be easel painting.[63]

Armenia remained Saryan's chief theme. He was now interpreting it in wider ways than before. Alongside monumental, synthetic landscapes he produced works with more specific motifs, frequently accentuating genre elements. One of the first such works is the painting *Old Yerevan* (1928). Presented on a canvas strongly extended in the horizontal direction is a panoramic view of a typical little Yerevan street. The artist seems to have immersed himself with pleasure in the peaceful everyday course of affairs with mundane concerns and interests, its characteristic, expressive details. Rising proudly above this scene of daily life is the summit of Great Ararat, seen on the horizon in the hazy distance – an embodiment of eternity, existing in an entirely different temporal context, yet connected with the life that has since time immemorial flourished, declined

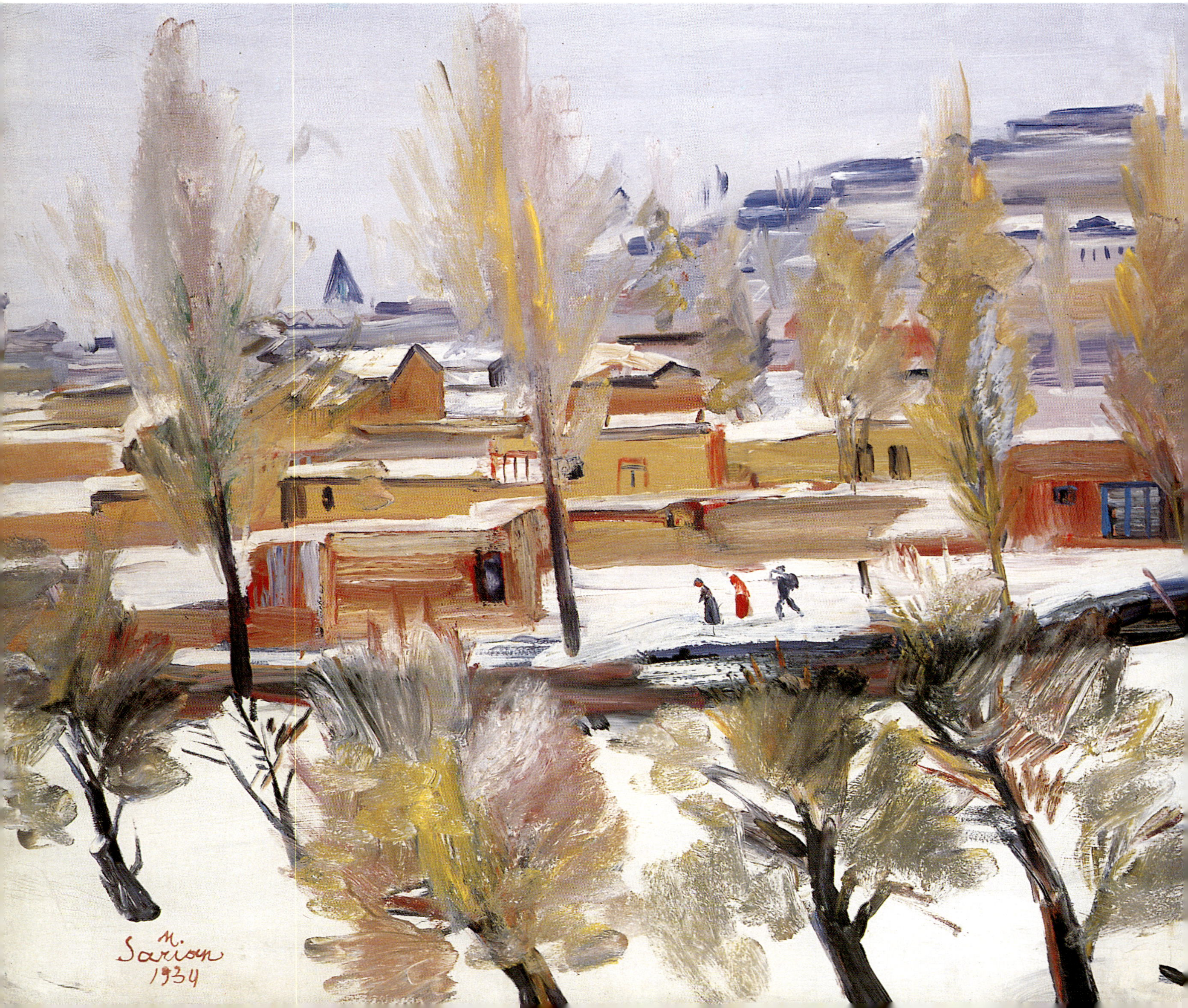

Southern Winter. 1934
Oil on canvas. 69 x 165 cm
Museum of Oriental Art, Moscow

and revived anew at its foot. A few years later Saryan painted another work close in motif, format and composition: *Southern Winter* (1934) – one of the relatively few winter views in his output. The usual appearance of the city is transformed here by a fragile covering of snow and Saryan conveys its barely perceptible changes of colour with astonishing subtlety.

Works like this precisely and vividly recreate the character of the old city, its spirit and distinctive poetic charm. Rapid construction was increasingly crowding in on these quarters and the artist hastened to record their passing delights. But modern development did not escape his attention. We find it in a number of views of Yerevan with stronger genre aspects, such as *Earthmoving on the Construction of the State Theatre* (1931) and *Building a Bridge. Yerevan* (1933). These are not, however, among Saryan's finest works. There was always something truly "folk-traditional", even patriarchal, in his perception of life and this kind of subjects probably did not evoke any real creative response in his soul.

On the other hand, the people of modern Armenia were of tremendous interest to him. His social contacts with them provided the impulse for a new peak in his work as a portraitist. In comparison with his earlier work in this field, there were now a number of substantial differences.

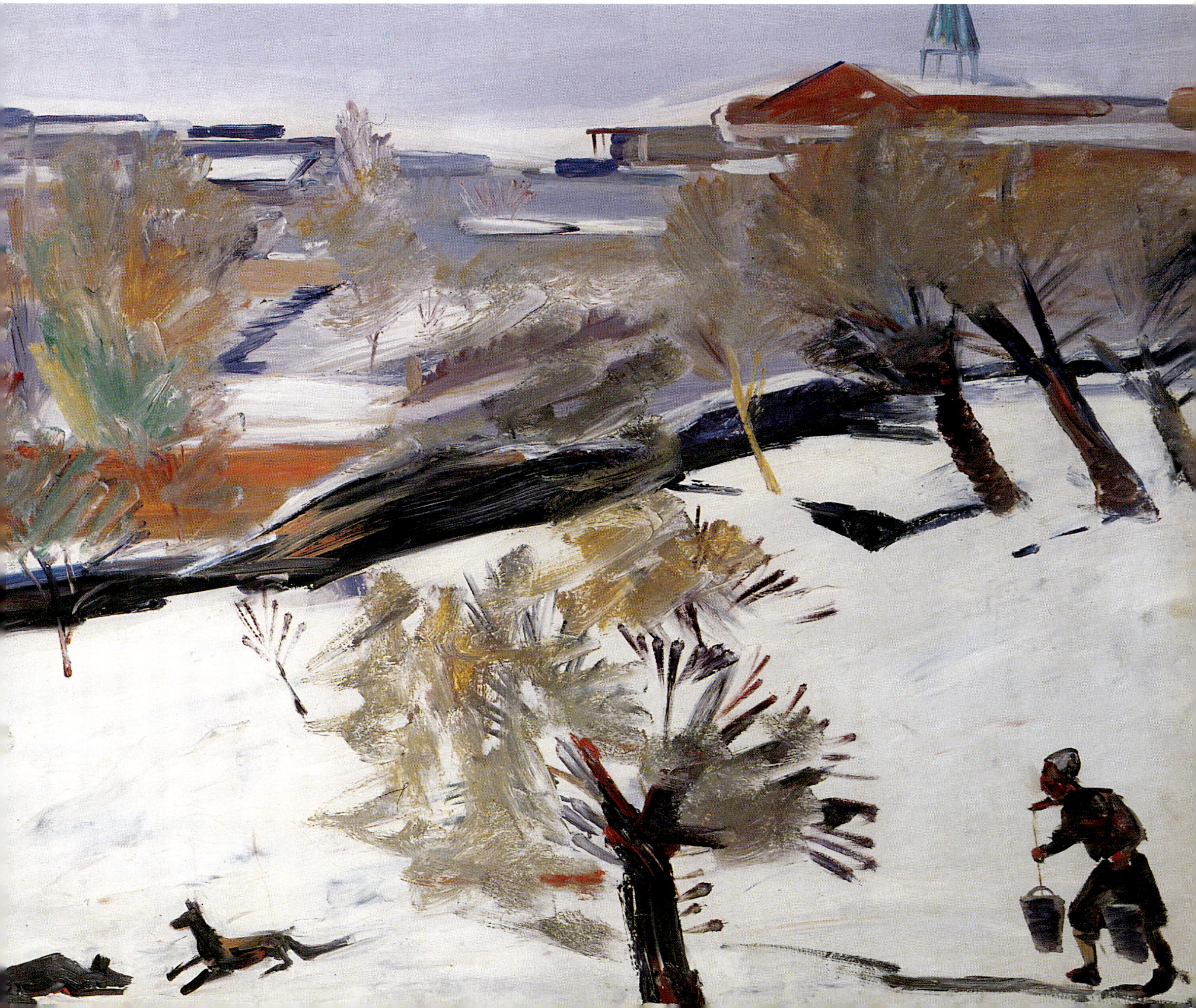

The portraits of the 1910s were remarkable above all for the striking accuracy of the artist's evaluation, the heightening of individual characteristic features of the subject. The late portraits were the result of more prolonged study, a deeper grasp of the personality. The best of them combine the earlier acute presentation of character with penetrating psychological analysis and the emotional expressivity that is invariably present in Saryan's works.

The artist usually painted people close to him in spirit, with rich and complex inner lives. He believed that each person was a new world, dictating its own means of expression, and resolutely avoided clichés. Each time he found new devices, a new chromatic equivalence to embody his idea of the person. This idea had, as a rule, formed before Saryan started work and he therefore painted his portraits quickly, without preparatory studies, in two, three, or even one session. The artist considered conveying a likeness a vital element, but the most important thing for him was "to find in a person's face features that reveal his spirit, to see the sitter not just physically, but spiritually. The skill of the portraitist lies in the ability to grasp what a face expresses and what it conceals... Most important of all in a portrait is just that inner resemblance."[64]

Saryan first met the poet Yegishe Charents in 1921. He painted his portrait in the second year of their friendship. In it the artist abandons the compositional devices of the earlier portraits. Retaining the close-up view of the head with the body cut off at the shoulders, he presents it not frontally, but three-quarters turned and shifted from the centre, which introduces dynamism and tension into the compositional structure. The expressiveness of Charents's unattractive, but very eloquent face is enhanced and stressed by juxtaposition with the mask that Saryan hung on the blue cloth serving as a background. "Charents and I loved those relics of the East," the artist recalled. The wide-open eyes of the mask look into space, while Charents's sharp eagle eye fixes the viewer imperiously. In the context of this portrait the mask is not only intended to set off the living face through the symmetry of its features. Here, as in other works by Saryan, it can be interpreted as a symbol of eternity. It is excluded from the day-to-day flow of life, while Charents belongs entirely to it – he was in the full sense of the word the first poet of modern Armenia. Saryan conveyed with astonishing precision his active, uncompromising character and, at the same time, as the artist said much later, "the drama of his fate". Of course now, knowing of the poet's tragic death in that fateful year of 1937, we involuntarily seek signs of that end in his appearance. Yet it is hard to abandon the idea that the portrait does indeed in some way possess prophetic qualities. And the mask takes on one further meaning – representing the enduring memory of this exceptional individual. "Charents was a legend," Saryan wrote later. "I think of him and I am staggered that that wonder lived in the same city as us, that I sat alongside him and painted him."[65] It was a wonder too that the portrait outlived Charents. Many of Saryan's friends perished in 1937, including those who had sat for him. The paintings shared the fate of

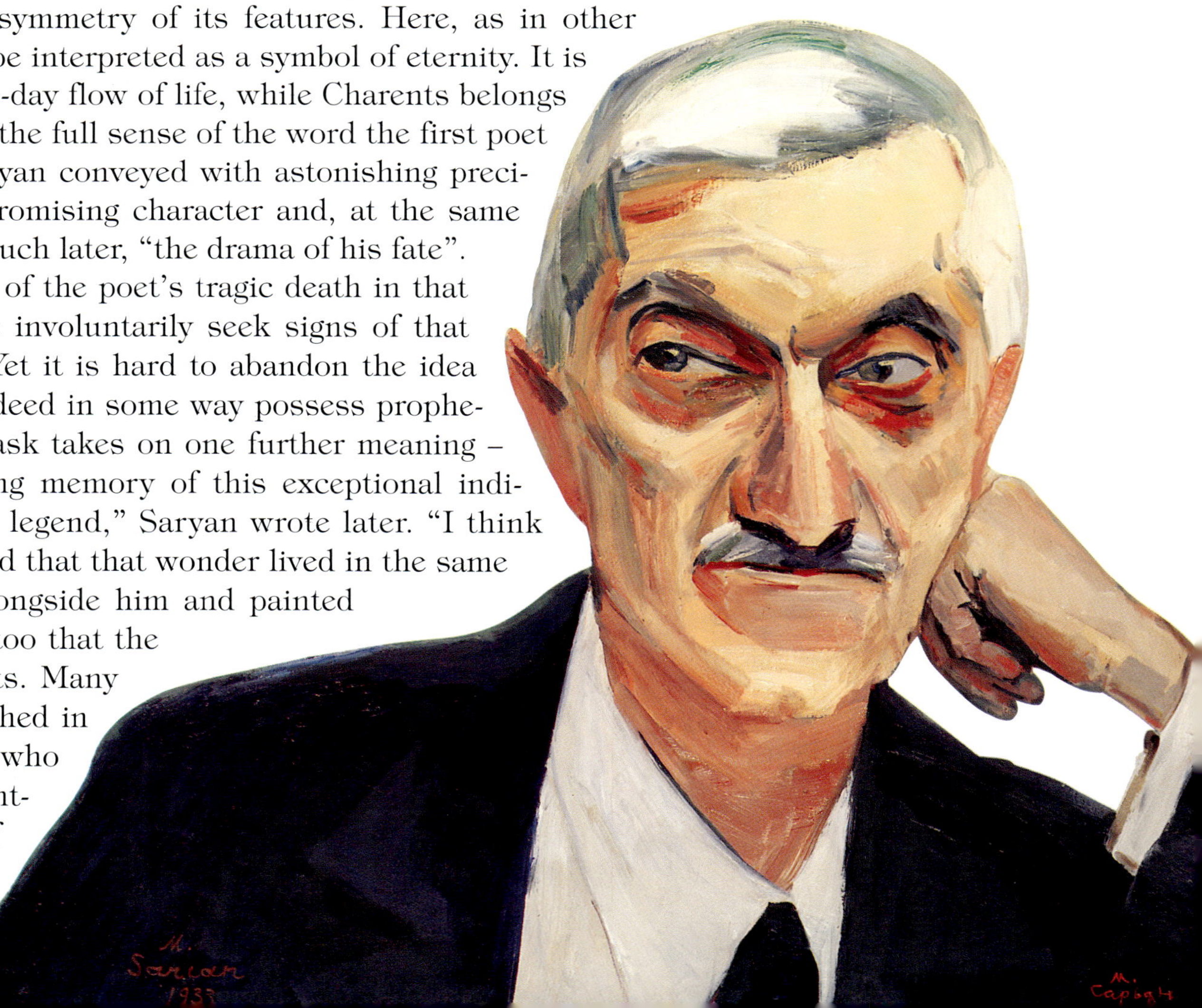

Portrait of the Architect Alexander Tamanian. 1933
Oil on canvas. 73 x 92 cm
National Gallery of Armenia, Yerevan

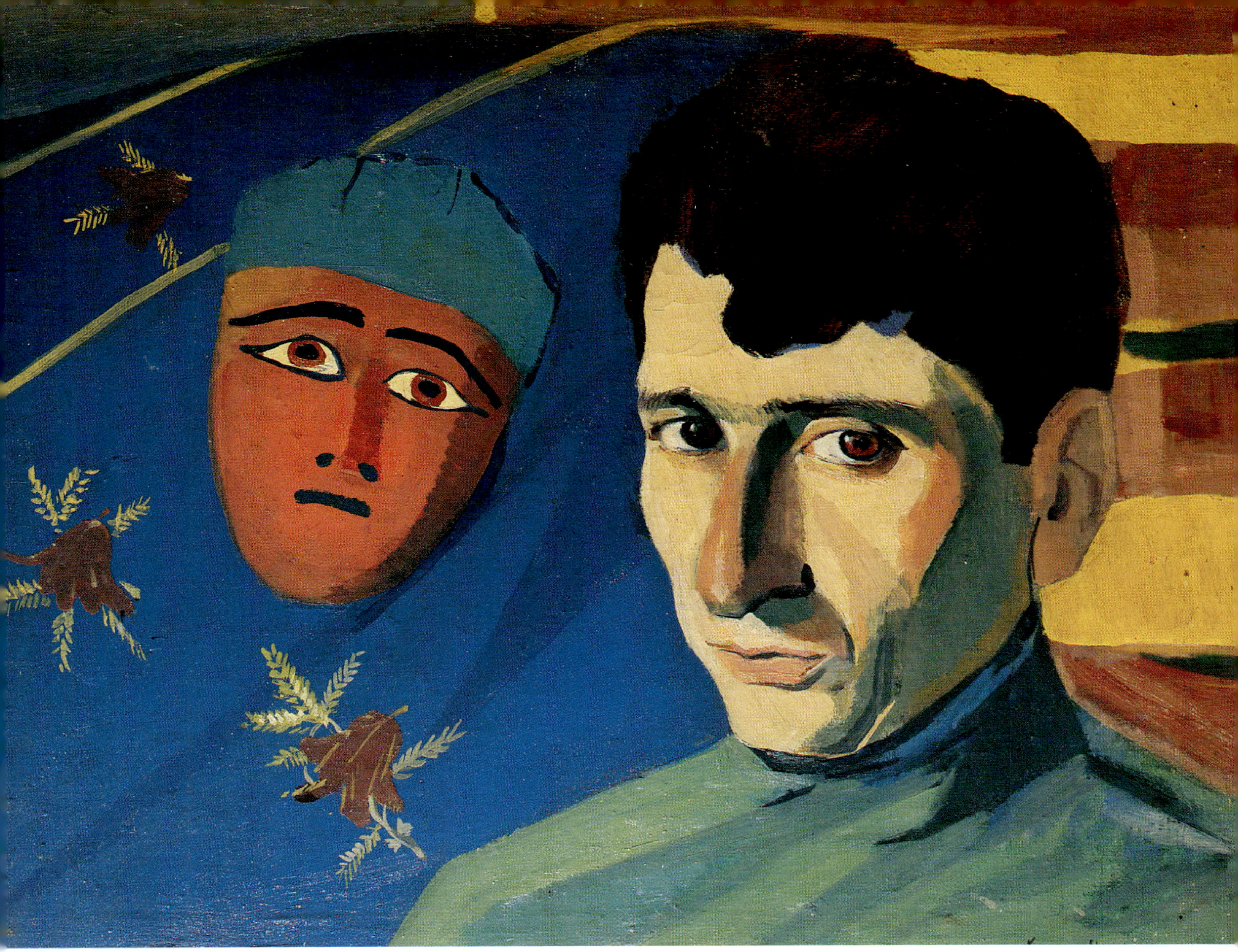

Portrait of the Poet Yegishe Charents. 1923
Oil on canvas. 44 x 59 cm
The Charents Museum of Literature and Art, Yerevan

→
Portrait of Victoria Alabian. 1931
Oil on canvas. 46 x 61 cm
Martiros Saryan Museum, Yerevan

their subjects. The portrait of Charents survived only through the courage of those who kept it hidden for more than twenty years.

A totally different approach – garish and decorative – is seen in the image of the actress Anna Khumashian. Saryan introduced a certain playful tone into it. The depiction of this vivid, temperamental woman has a certain element of orientation towards the viewer and, at the same time, a winning natural vital force.

In 1924 Saryan created a cycle of graphic portraits of Armenian actors. Each of them keenly conveys individual features inseparable from the actor's character – the restrained passion of the tragedian Vagram Panazian; the intense seriousness of Mikael Manvelian, the charm of Arus Voskanian. These confidently and skilfully executed drawings are marked by a certain dryness alien to Saryan's graphic manner as a whole.

The true peak of Saryan's portrait art came in the late 1920s, 1930s and 1940s. Soon after his return from Paris, the artist painted his sons *Zarik and Sarik* (1928) – two children's heads in identical skull-caps against a background of striped fabric. With special, tender attention and delicate touches of the brush, the artist conveys faces that are outwardly similar but at the same time very different in character and expression. To some extent a development of this small study was the painting entitled *My Family* (1929) – the first of the artist's few group portraits.

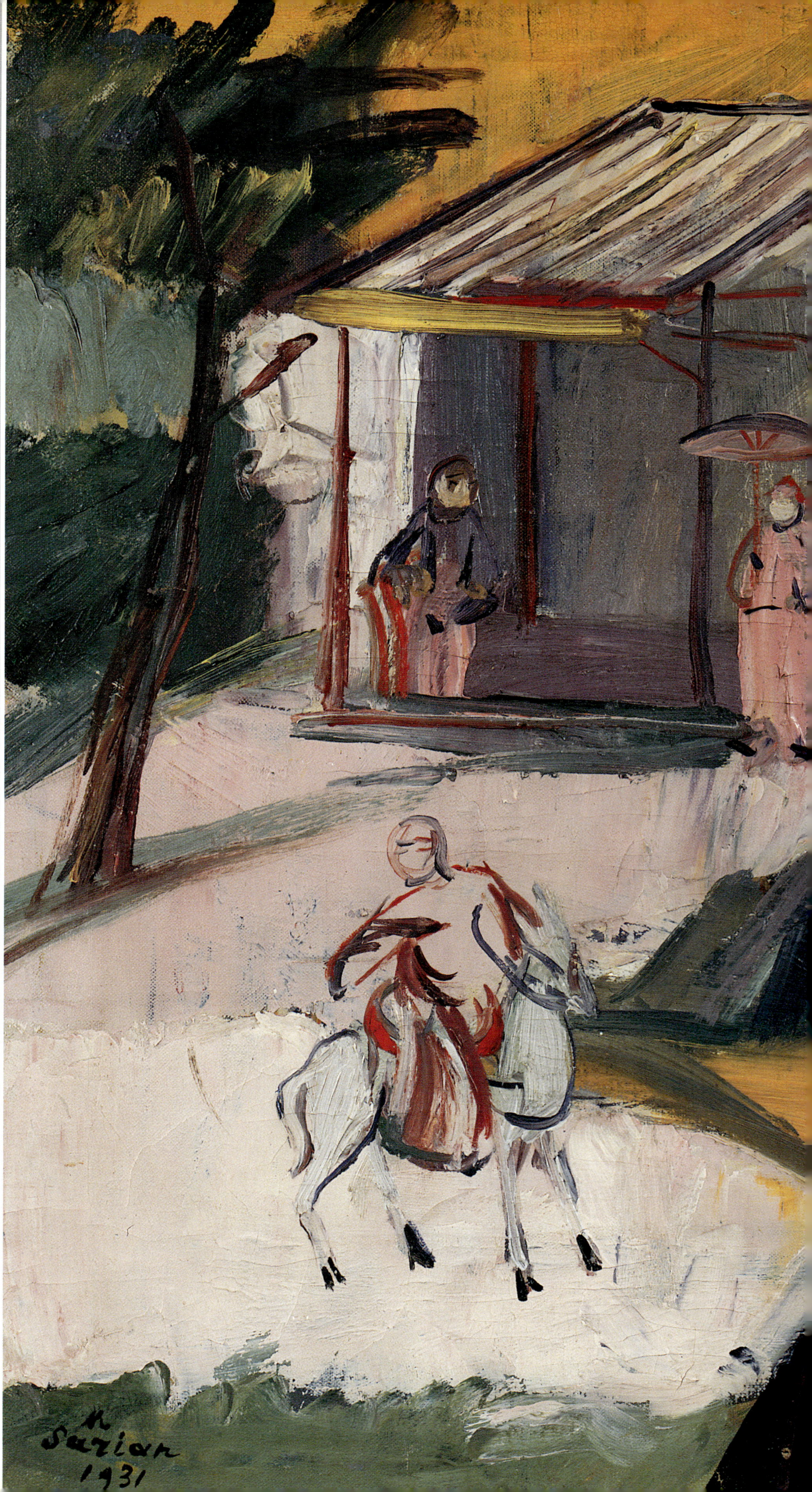
M
Sarian
1931

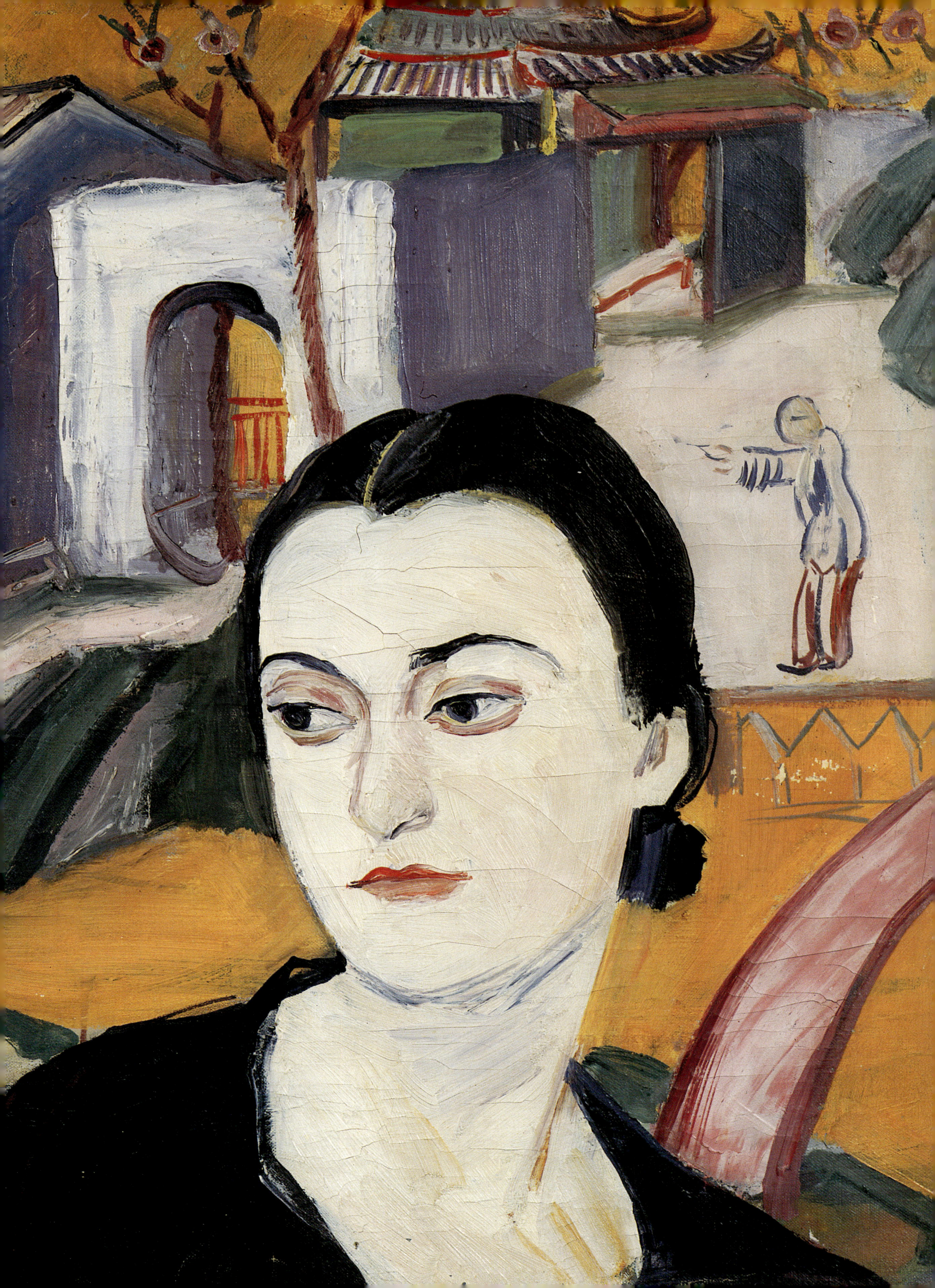

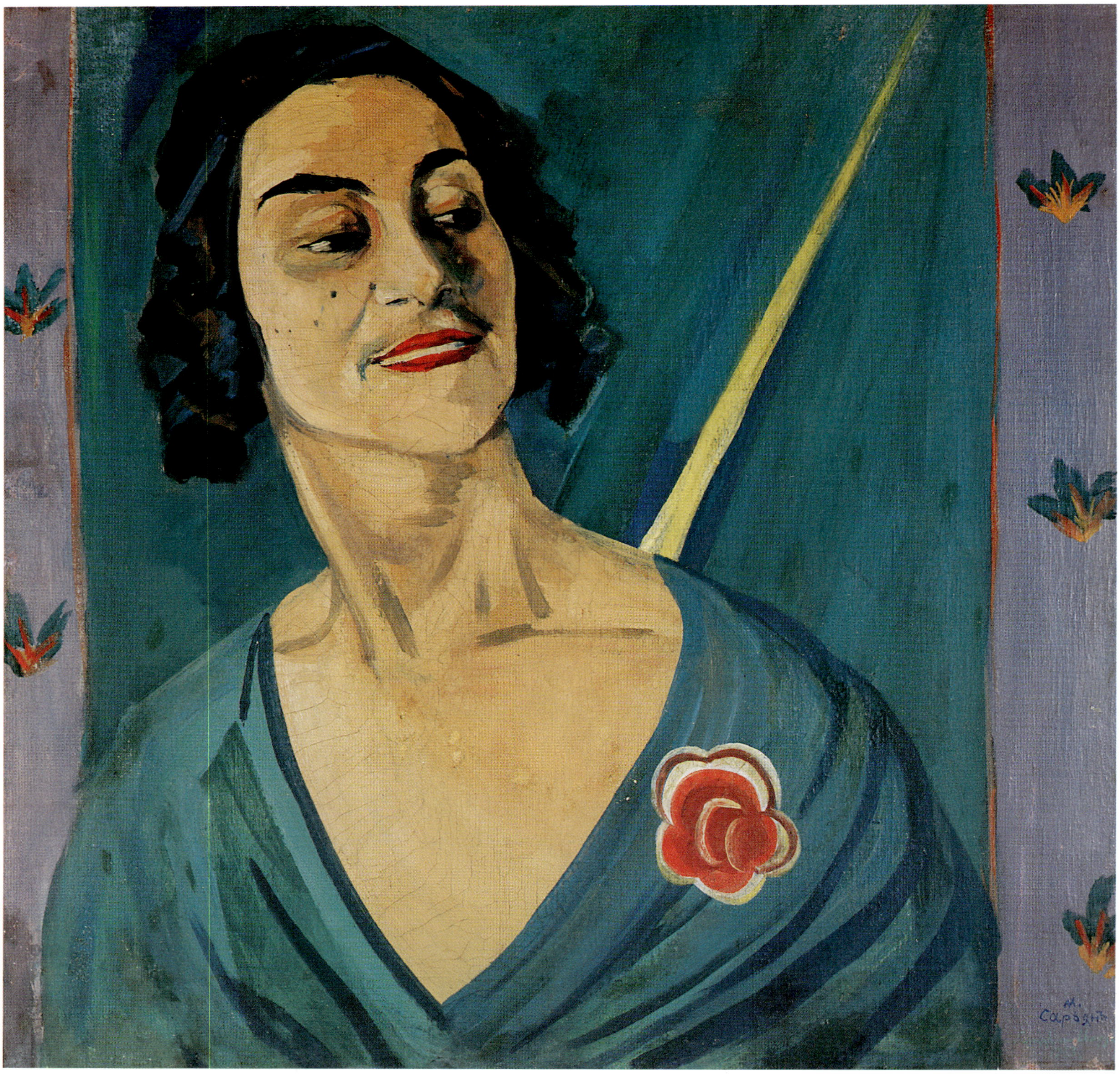

Portrait of the Actress Anna Khumashian. 1923
Tempera on canvas. 68 x 73 cm
National Gallery of Armenia, Yerevan

A natural relaxed atmosphere is here combined with a perfect composition that incorporates organically – in terms of both rhythm and meaning – a photograph of the artist and a mask. The countenance of the mask with its large, almond-shaped eyes reflects, as it were, the living faces. Here it is perceived as an embodiment of the creative principle, of art whose spirit permeated the life of the artist's family.

The moving lyrical tone of the portrait is supported by the refined and restrained chromatic relationships. Dark and pale blue hues determine the colouristic resonance of the painting, gently combining with the warm pinky shades of the faces and background. Only in the foreground do the bright stripes of the rug introduce a necessary accent in this delicate range of colours. Leonid Singer justifiably noted the "fresco-like laconicism" of this portrait and at the same time called it "one of Saryan's most Matissean canvases".[66] In the refinement of colour and its quality, *My Family* can be compared with Matisse's *Portrait of Madame Henri*

My Family. 1929
Oil on canvas. 102 x 80 cm
The Tretyakov Gallery, Moscow

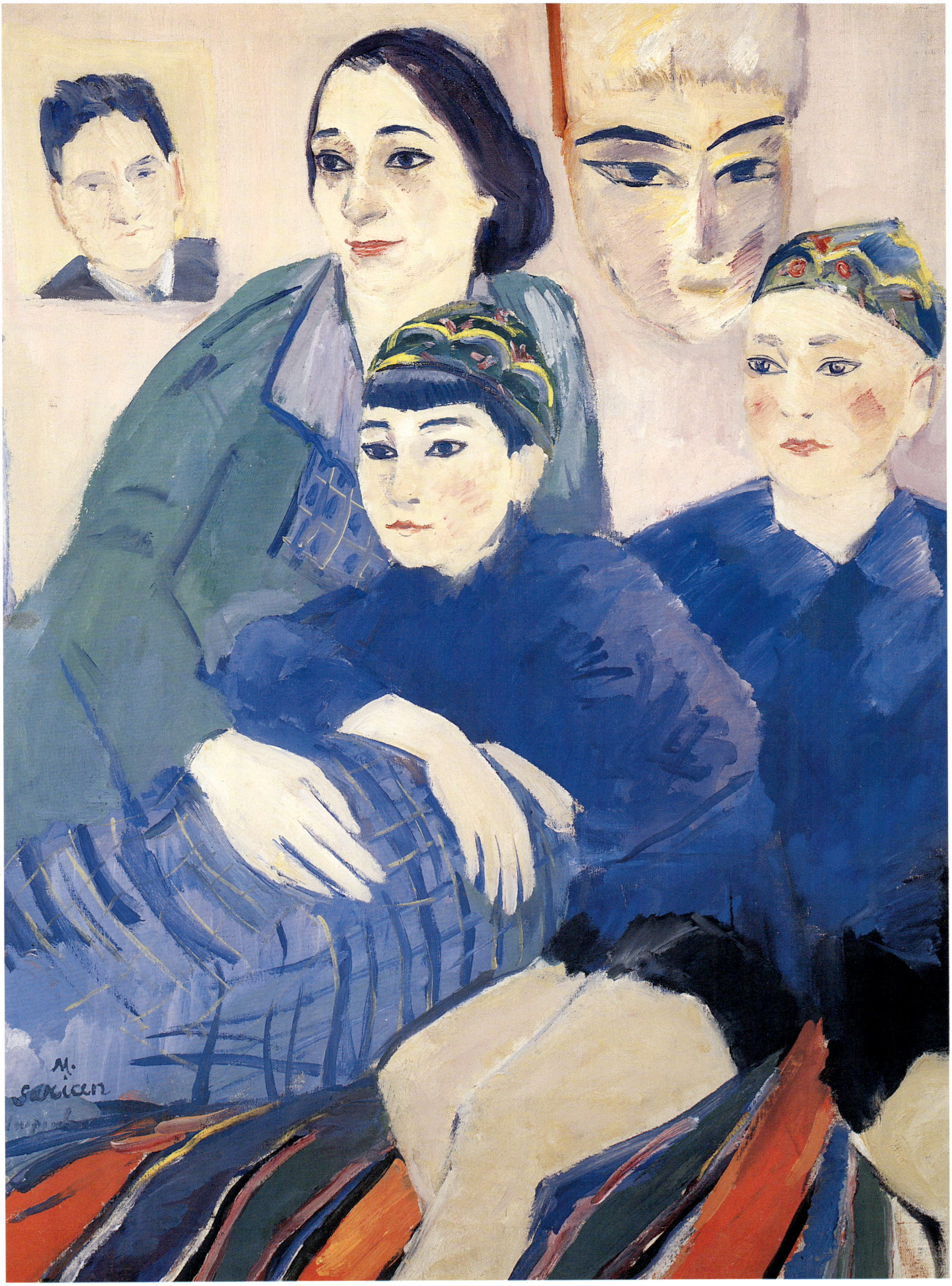

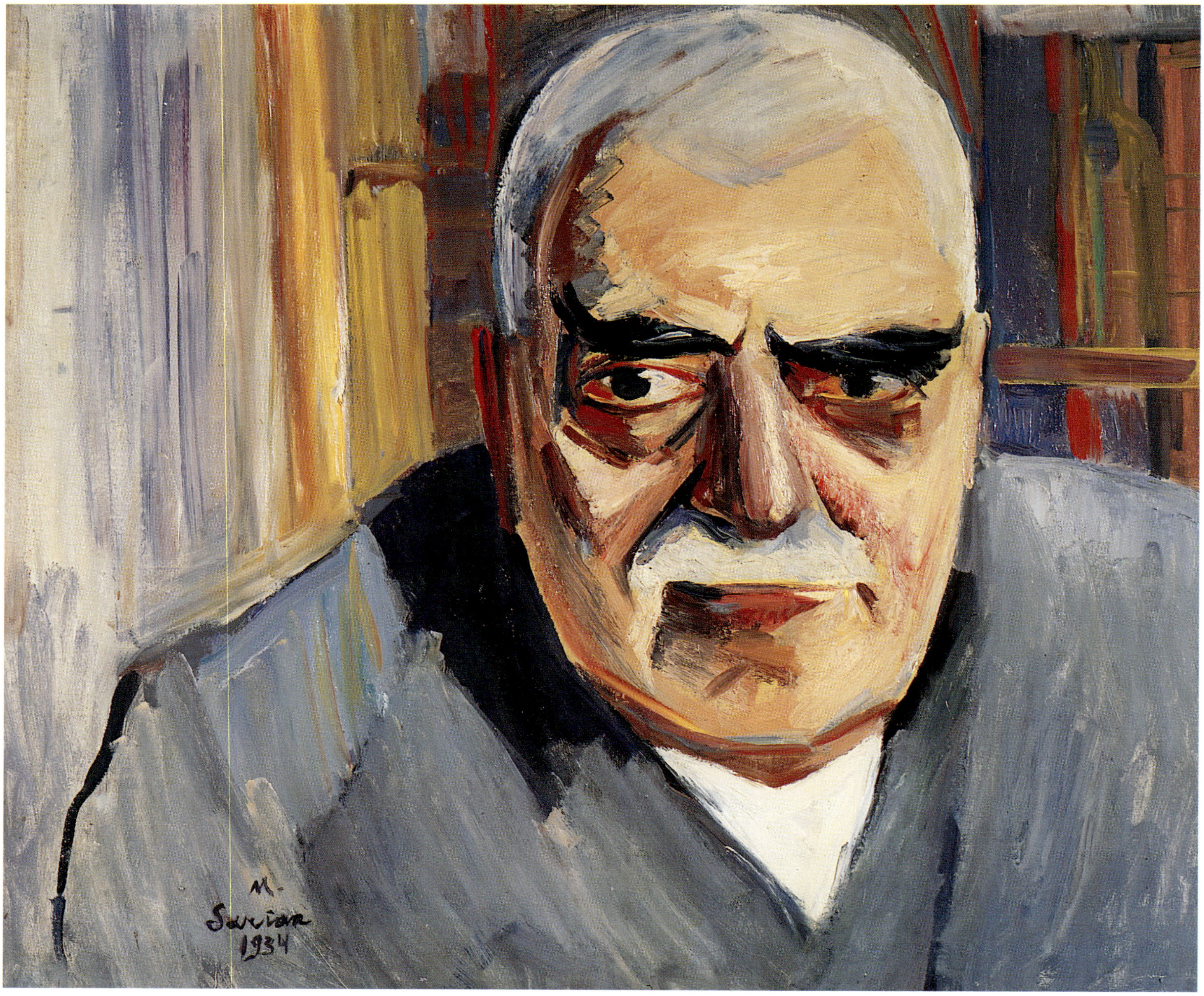

Portrait of the Architect Toros Toramanian. 1934
Oil on canvas. 72 x 90 cm
National Gallery of Armenia, Yerevan

Matisse (1913), now in the Hermitage. Of course Saryan's images do not have that elegance that in its time captivated Apollinaire in Matisse's painting, that degree of the purging of the real-life subject that marks the French artist's work. For all the abstraction of form, Saryan is nonetheless closer to a direct perception of life, but it is just that which fills his canvas with the charm of living expression. The artist numbered *My Family* among his favourite works and wished to produce "a few more paintings like it".[67]

In terms of composition and approach to colour, the portraits of this period are considerably more varied than those of the early years. There are, however, many among them that display exceptional conciseness of expression. In the 1930 portrait of Stepan Agadzhanian pale bluish tones dominate, stressing the swarthy colour of the face. The background is neutral, but, thanks to the mobility of the brushstrokes conveying subtle pinky-silver hues, it seems vibrant and spacious. We can read in the face of the old man, in his slightly dimmed eyes both the bitterness of adversities in life and a concealed melancholy. Agadzhanian was an artist who had outlived his day. His modest fame was overshadowed by that of other painters, above all Saryan's own, and in this portrait we sense the artist's sympathy for his aged colleague.

The same blue-azure dominance, but more resonant, is developed in the portrait of the art-historian Karen Kamsarakan (1935), this time in the background against which the face of a still very young man with clear blue eyes appears. Those eyes are echoed in the light bluish shadows on the face and the darker blue dabs of the background. Saryan intensified the colour in Kamsarakan's face with energetic, reddish brushstrokes, thus stressing the contrast between it and the background and the austere, dark green clothing. The patch of the clothing serves as a sort of frame for the animatedly tossed back head. This expression of ardour combines with the seriousness of the seemingly inquisitive gaze directed at the viewer. The portrait of Kamsarakan is striking for the concentration, even perhaps nakedness, of the expression. It acutely conveys not only the individuality of the subject, but also the time when it was painted, a time of the boldest hopes and expectations, as well as of difficulties and doubts. Two years later Kamsarakan was arrested and shot. His portrait, like Charents's, survived by a miracle. Now looking at the face of this youth with the prospect of a long and interesting life stretching out before him, we, perhaps arbitrarily, seem to detect a hint of tragedy in his mien.

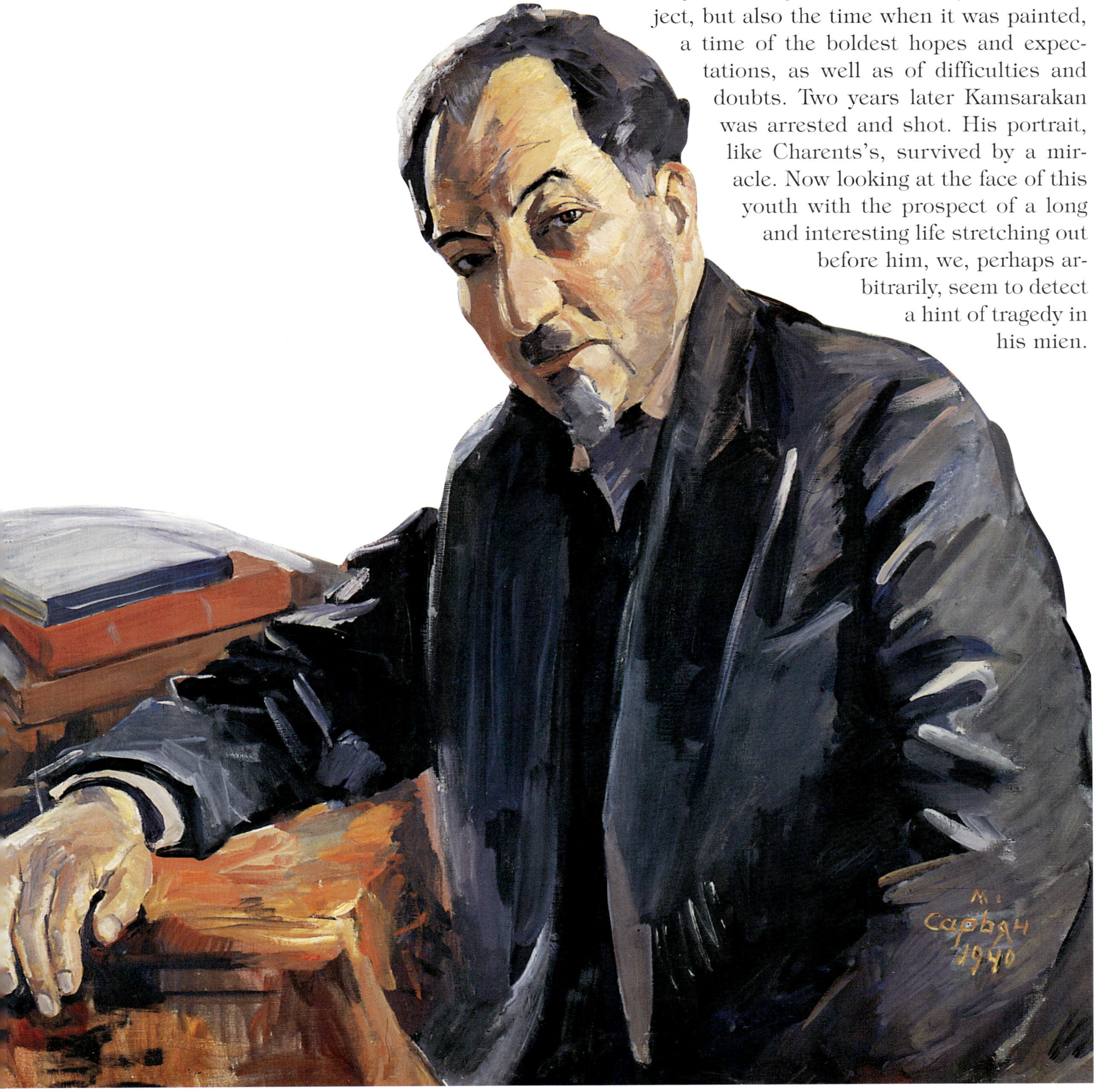

Portrait of the Poet Avetik Isaakian. 1940
Oil on canvas. 89 x 89 cm
National Gallery of Armenia, Yerevan

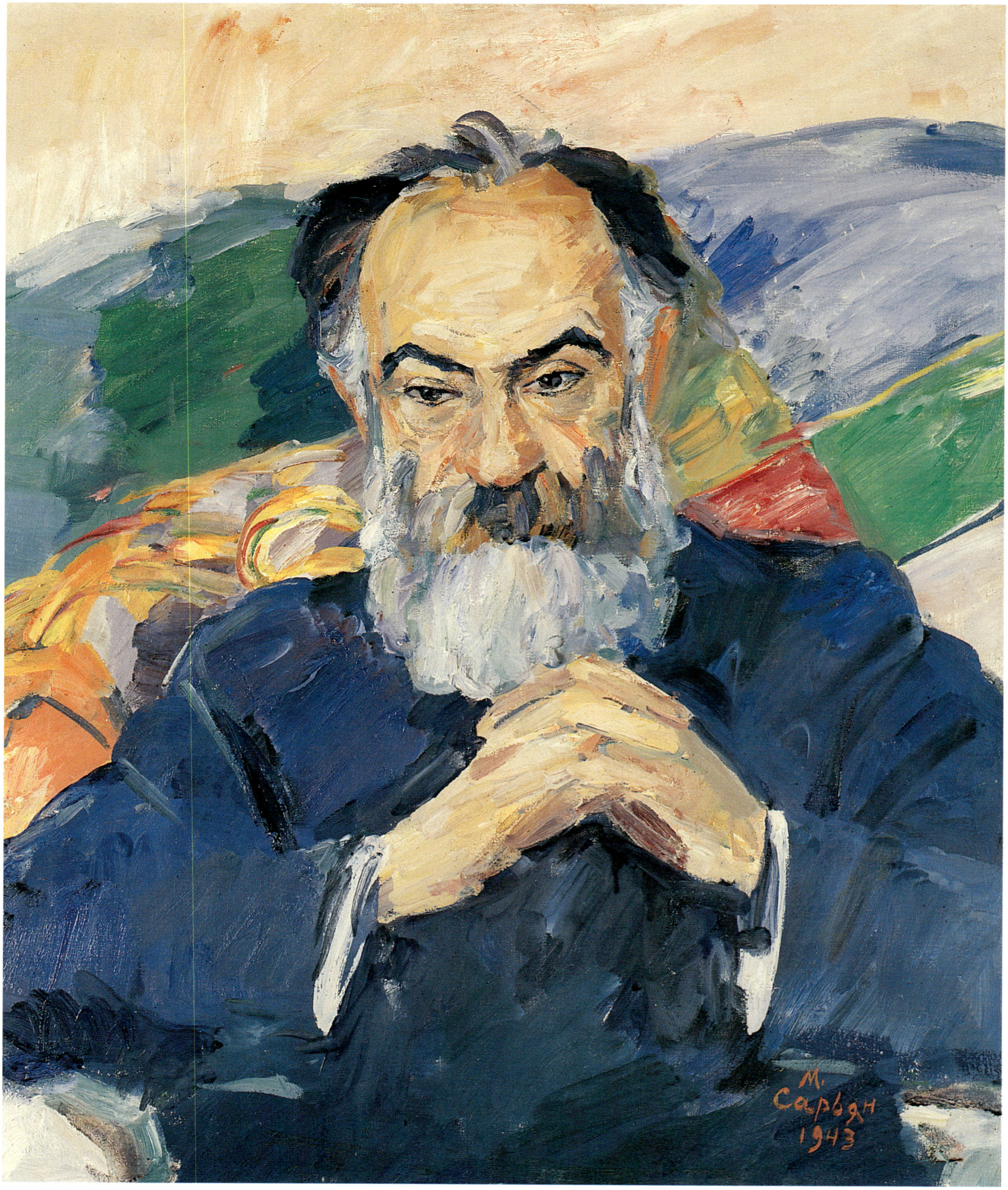

Portrait of Academician Iosif Orbeli.
1943
Oil on canvas. 73 x 64.5 cm
National Gallery of Armenia, Yerevan

Portrait of the Stage-Director Ruben Simonov. 1939
Oil on canvas. 100 x 70 cm
Museum of Oriental Art, Moscow

→
Flowers for the Armenians who Died Fighting in the Great Patriotic War. 1945
Oil on canvas. 196 x 250 cm
National Gallery of Armenia, Yerevan

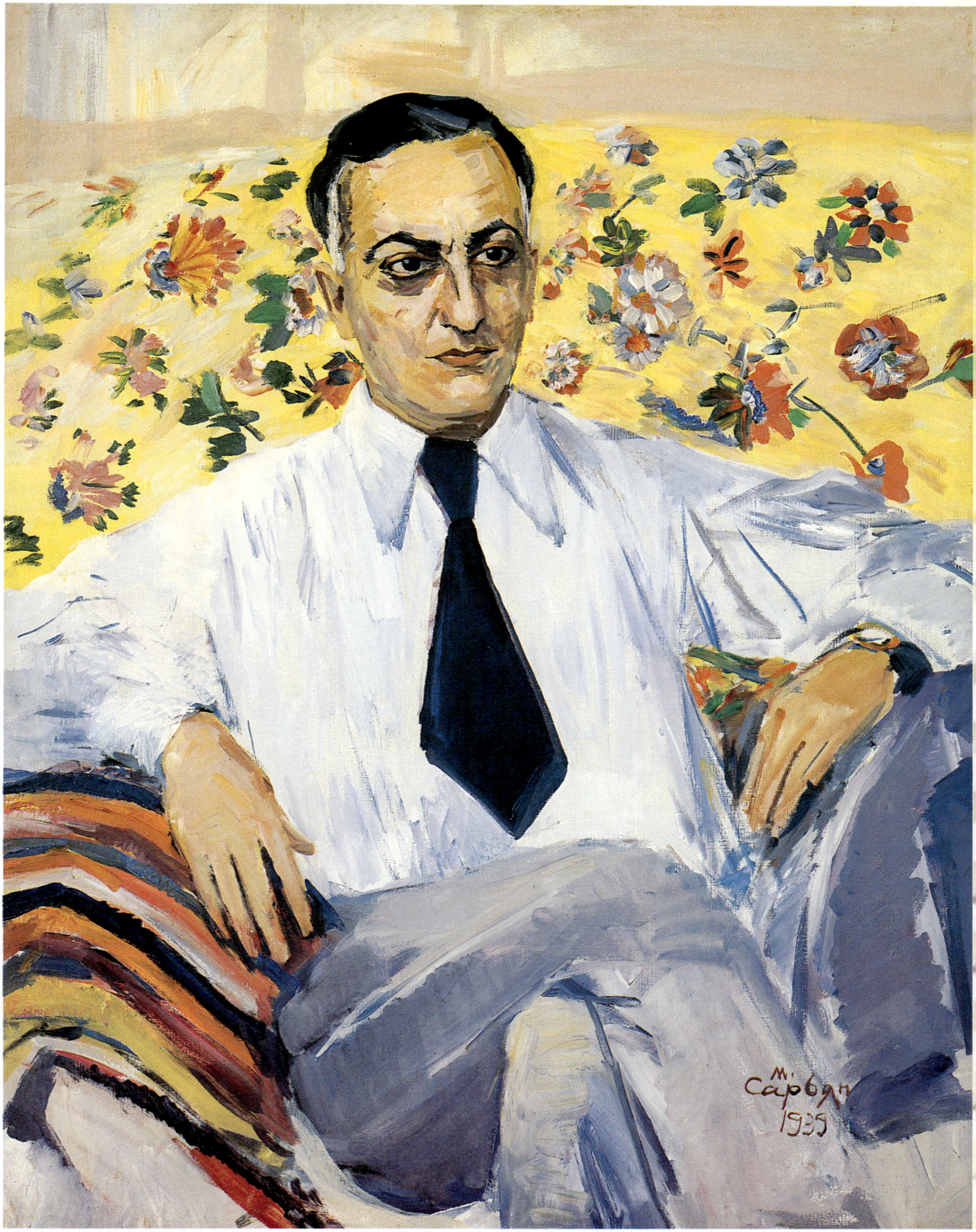
М. Сарьян
1935

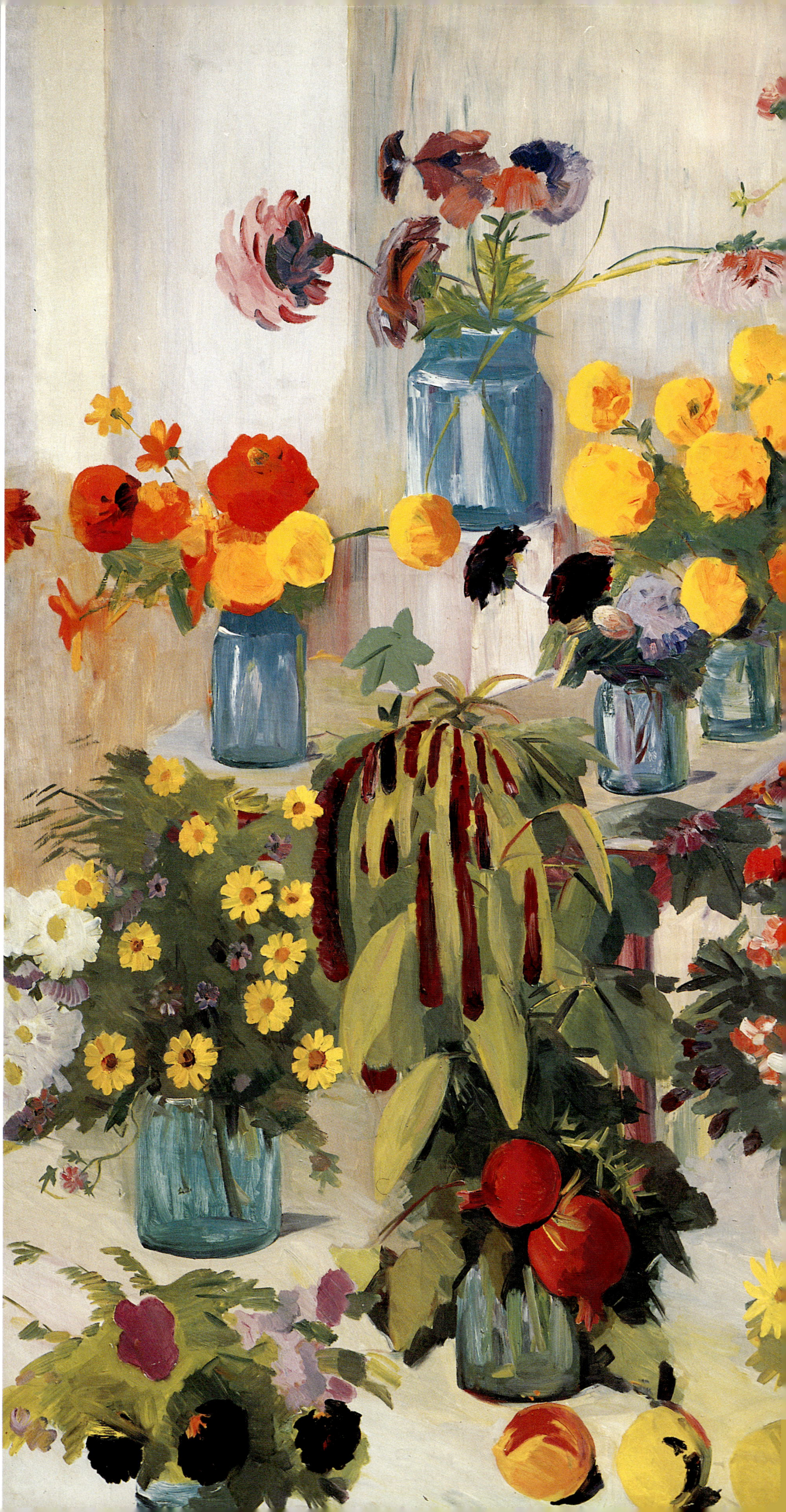

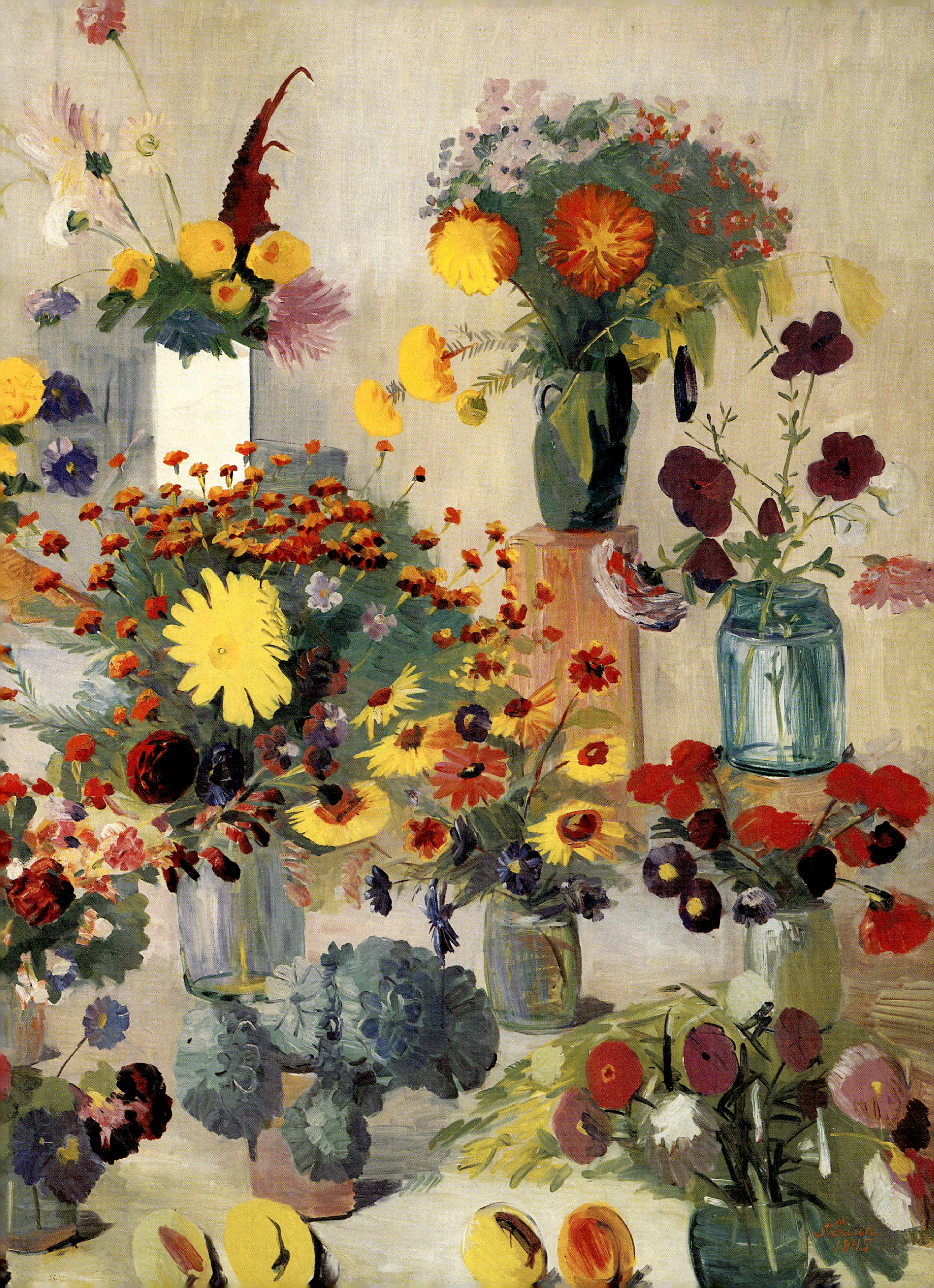

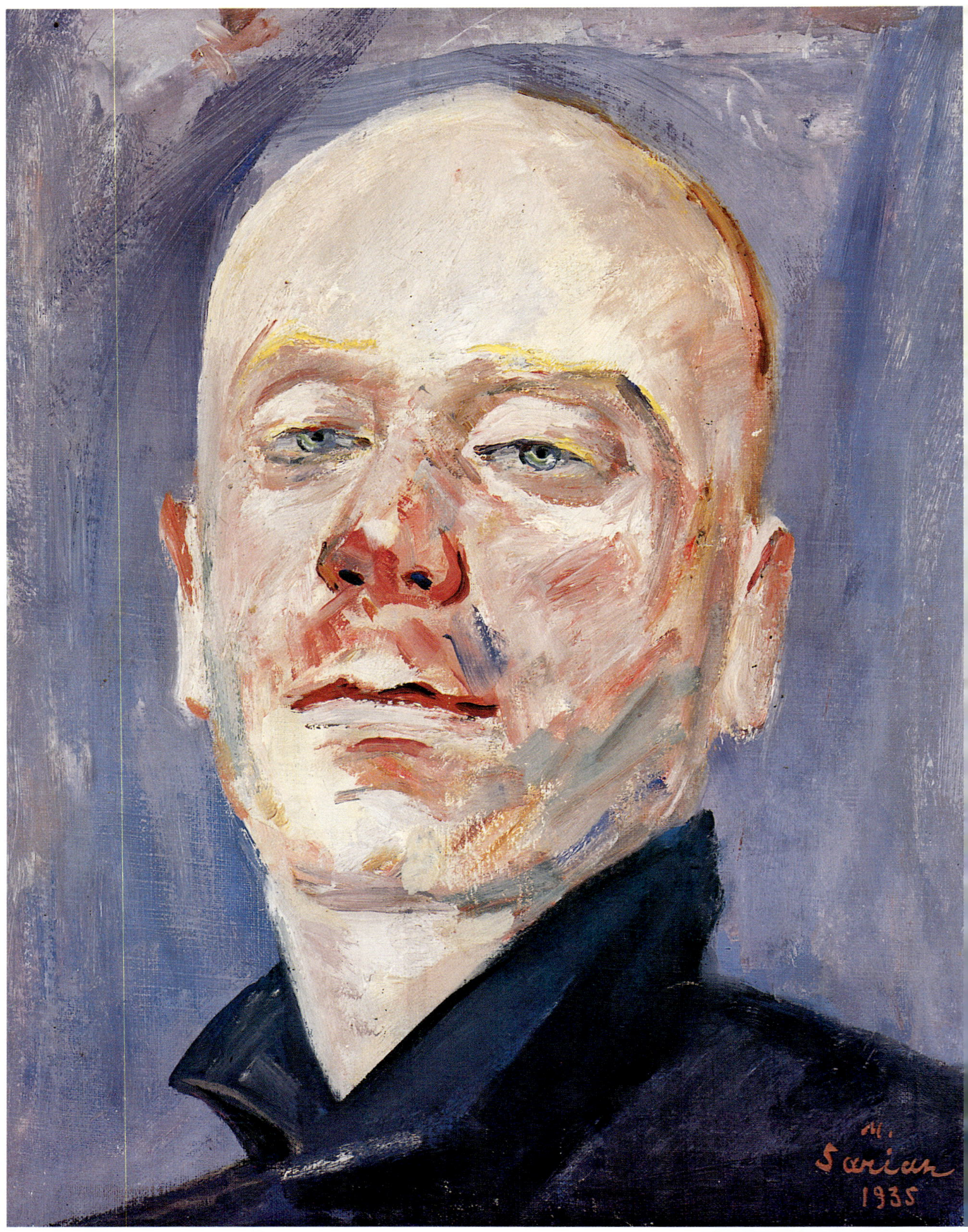
M. Sarian
1935

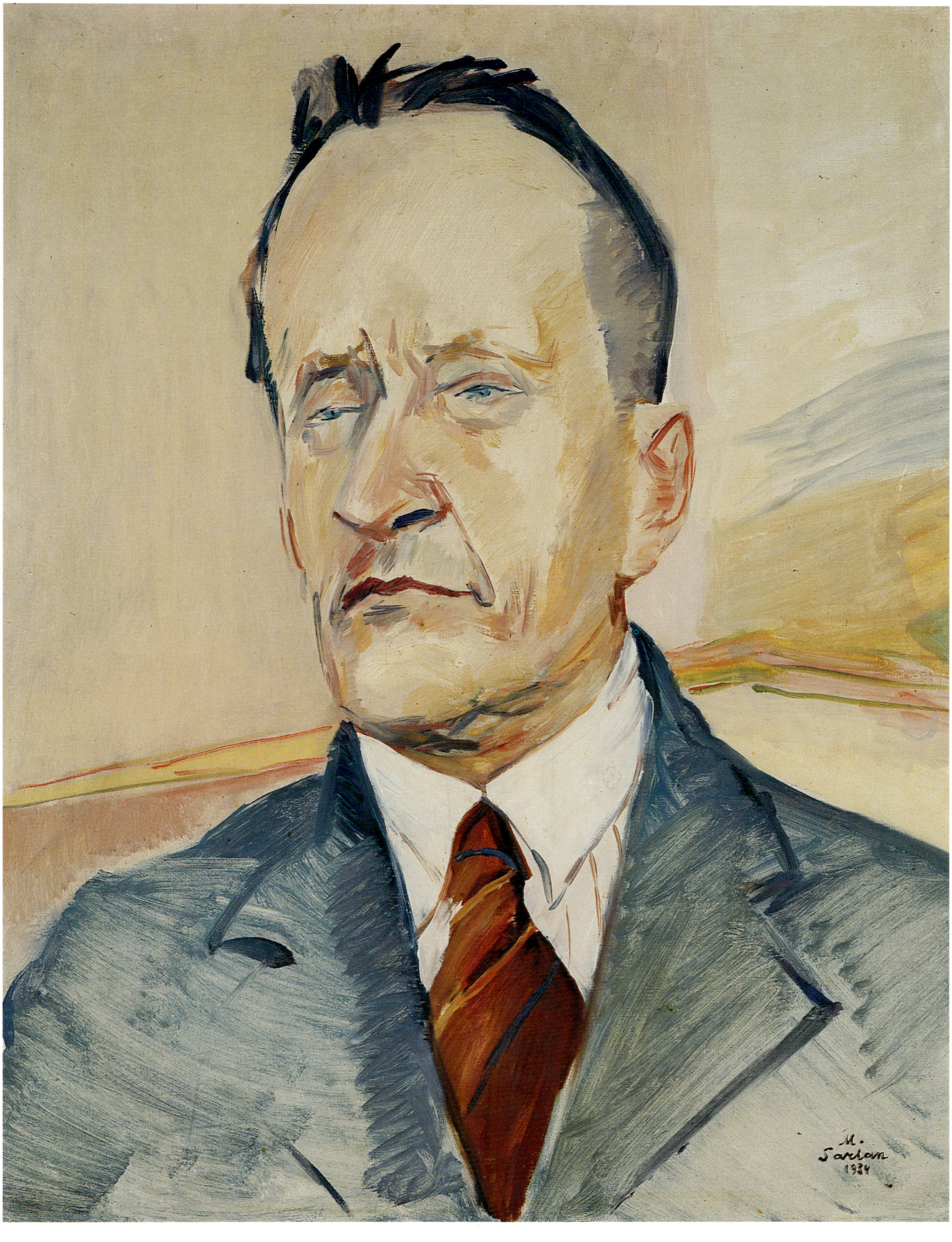

Portrait of Karen Kamsarakan. 1935
Oil on canvas. 45 x 38 cm
Martiros Saryan Museum, Yerevan

Portrait of the Pianist Konstantin Igumnov. 1934
Oil on canvas. 73 x 59.5 cm
National Gallery of Armenia, Yerevan

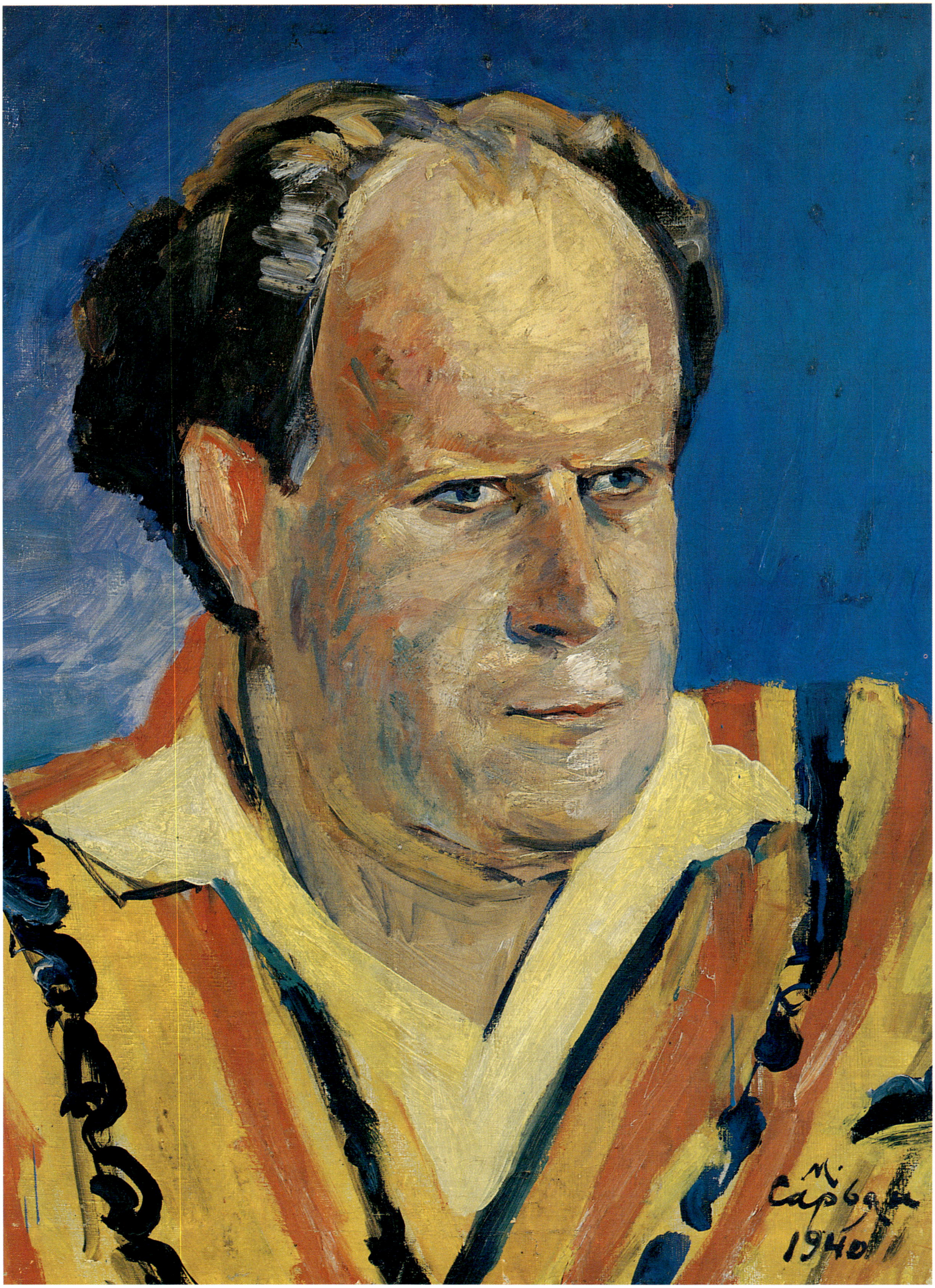
1940

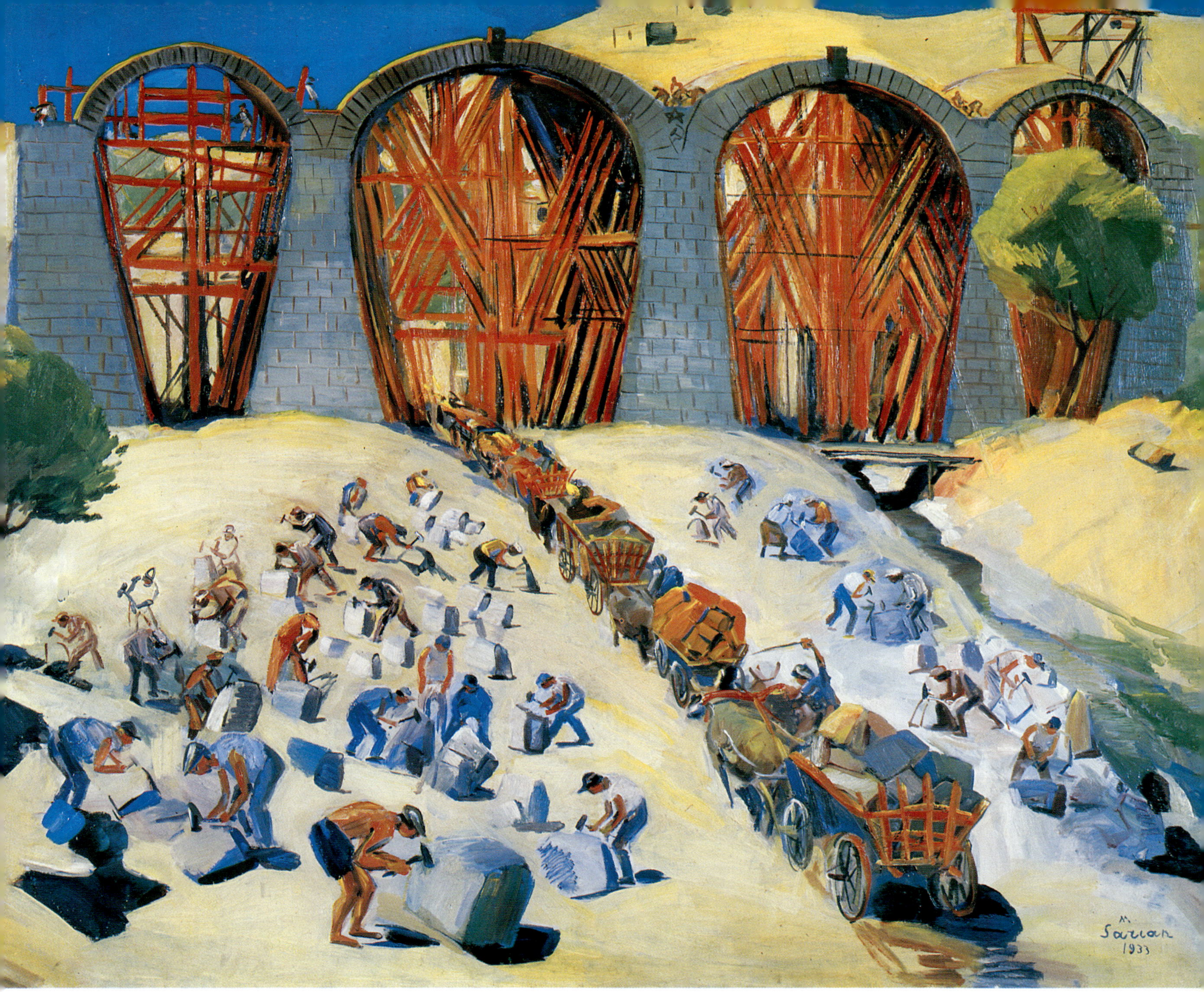

Building a Bridge. Yerevan. 1933
Oil on canvas. 73.5 x 92 cm
National Gallery of Armenia, Yerevan

Portrait of the Film-Director Sergei Eisenstein. 1940
Oil on canvas. 63 x 51 cm
L. Vagarshian collection, Yerevan

Saryan the portraitist was exceptionally active in his perception of the sitter. "If you paint a person," he believed, "you should reveal (I would say 'expose' in all the niceties) him for yourself and be able to see in him both yourself and your attitude to him."[68] In the keenness and incisiveness of characterization some of Saryan's portraits do indeed border on exposure. But those subjects who gave occasion for such treatment did not as a rule attract the artist. He delighted in painting creative individuals with an inner significance and integrity. That is how he presents the architects Alexander Tamanian (1933) and Toros Toramanian (1934) to us. Both portraits are very simple in composition. As usual in such cases the artist concentrates attention on the head, which he depicts larger than life-size here. By this means he affirms the exceptional magnitude of the personality, while the composition as a whole acquires an avowedly monumental character. In the portrait of Tamanian, sharp facial features are conveyed by large, dynamic brushstrokes. Depicted in distant outline on the left, not distracting from the figure, is a scale-model of the Yerevan Opera Theatre, one of Tamanian's most important creations. The architect had done much work in Russia before moving to Armenia soon after Saryan. He became the creator of a new national style in architecture.

The artist stressed the European elegance of Tamanian's appearance, but also the intensive spiritual life concealed behind the outward reserve.

Saryan became acquainted with Toros Toramanian in his youth. This brilliant expert on ancient and mediaeval Armenian architecture made a tremendous impression on him. The artist recollected him being "like the monuments that surrounded him... like some simple sculpture with a beauty of its own."[69] Many years later, when Saryan painted his portrait, this impression was revived in his memory. Toramanian's head and heavy figure really do put one in mind of an ancient statue, monumental and majestic. The sitter was seriously ill, yet still "full of a thirst for life and creative work". The artist succeeded in expressing the indomitable power of the spirit that lit up his already moribund body.[70]

The 1934 portrait of the pianist Konstantin Igumnov was painted in a single sitting, but the prickly brushwork, a certain exaggeration of proportions, a correct, restrained colour scheme say everything about this interesting, complex individual. The keenness of the characterization is taken almost to the point of the grotesque, but no further. Saryan never lost the sense of an integral character and never reduced his perception of a person to a schema or a caricature.

In the artist's compositional portraits, carefully selected details of setting and background acquired an expressive significance. The figure of the poet Avetik Isaakian (1940) is placed in an interior in such a way that he is surrounded by two landscapes of Armenia: one a painting by Saryan

Bzhni. The Fortress. 1946
Oil on canvas. 82 x 60 cm
Martiros Saryan Museum, Yerevan

Self-Portrait: Three Ages. 1942
Oil on canvas. 97 x 146 cm
Martiros Saryan Museum, Yerevan

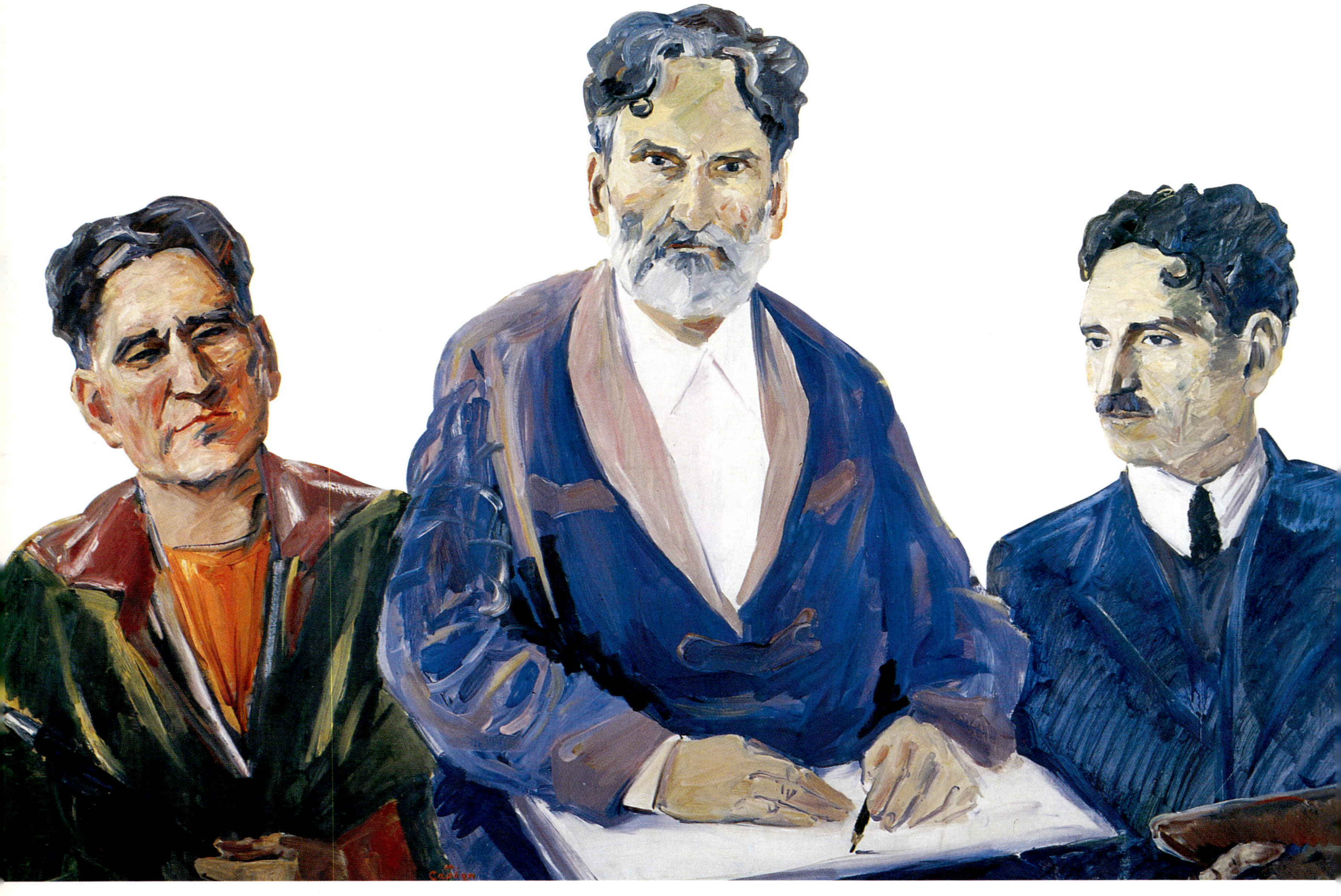

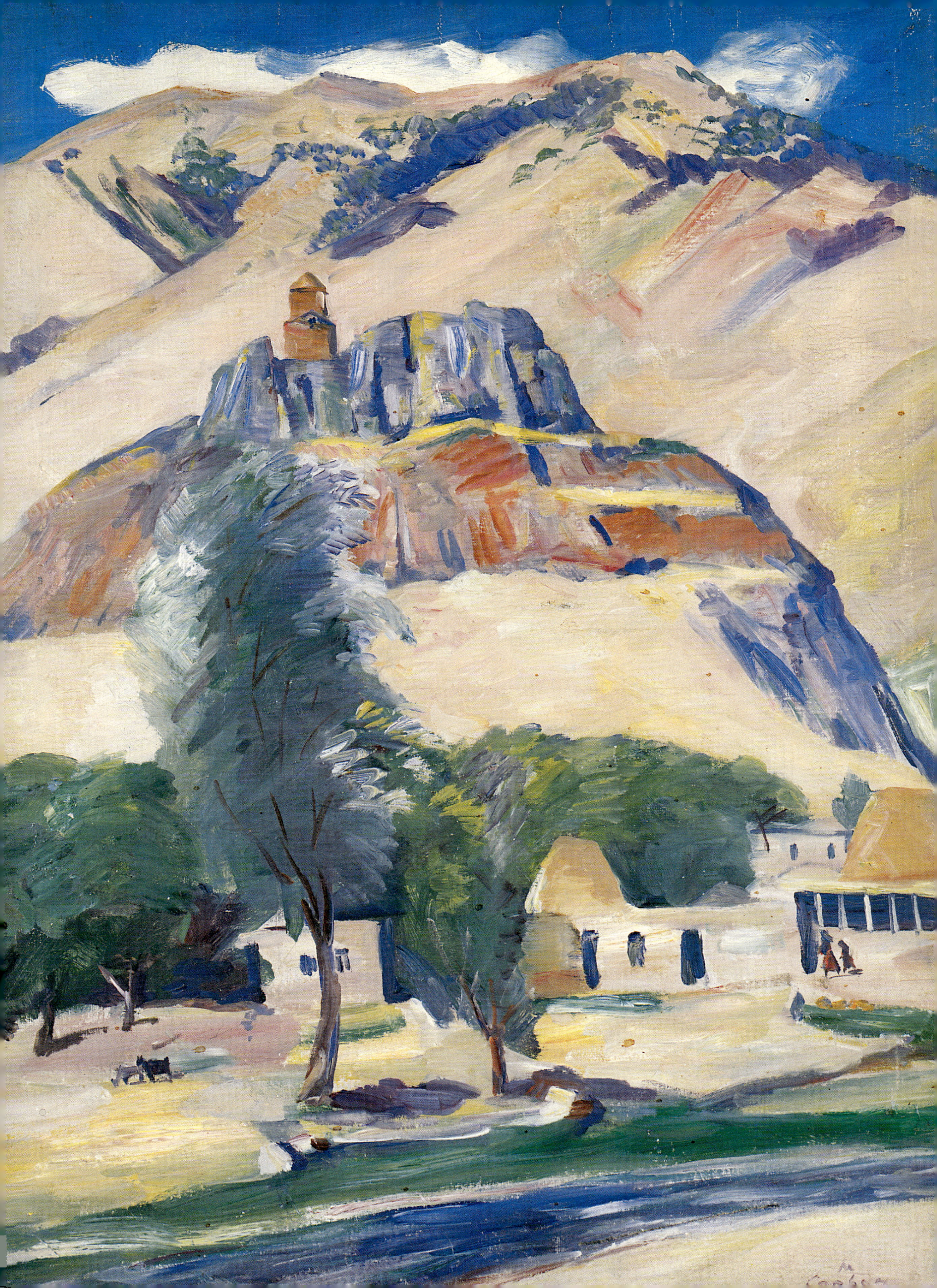

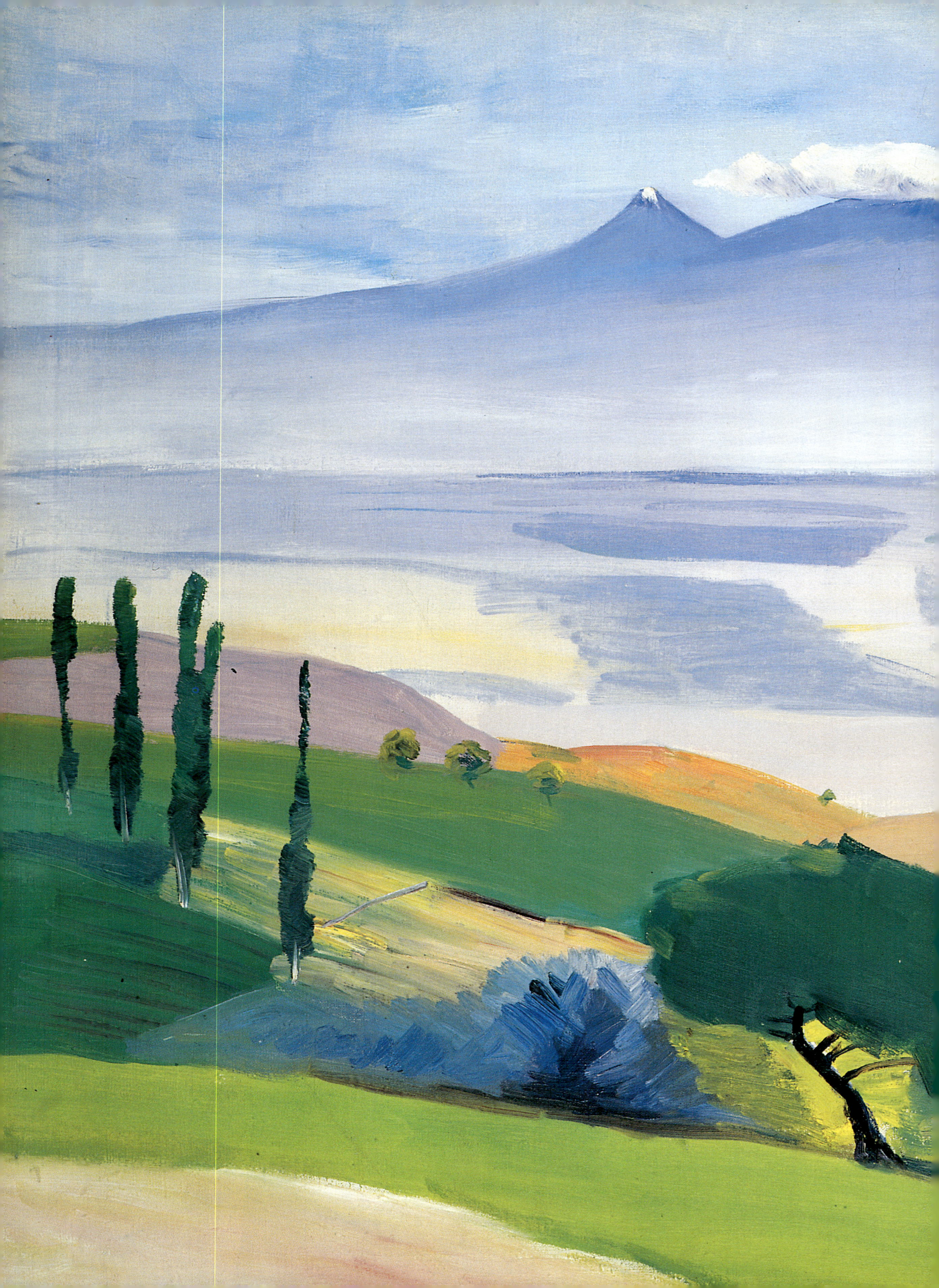

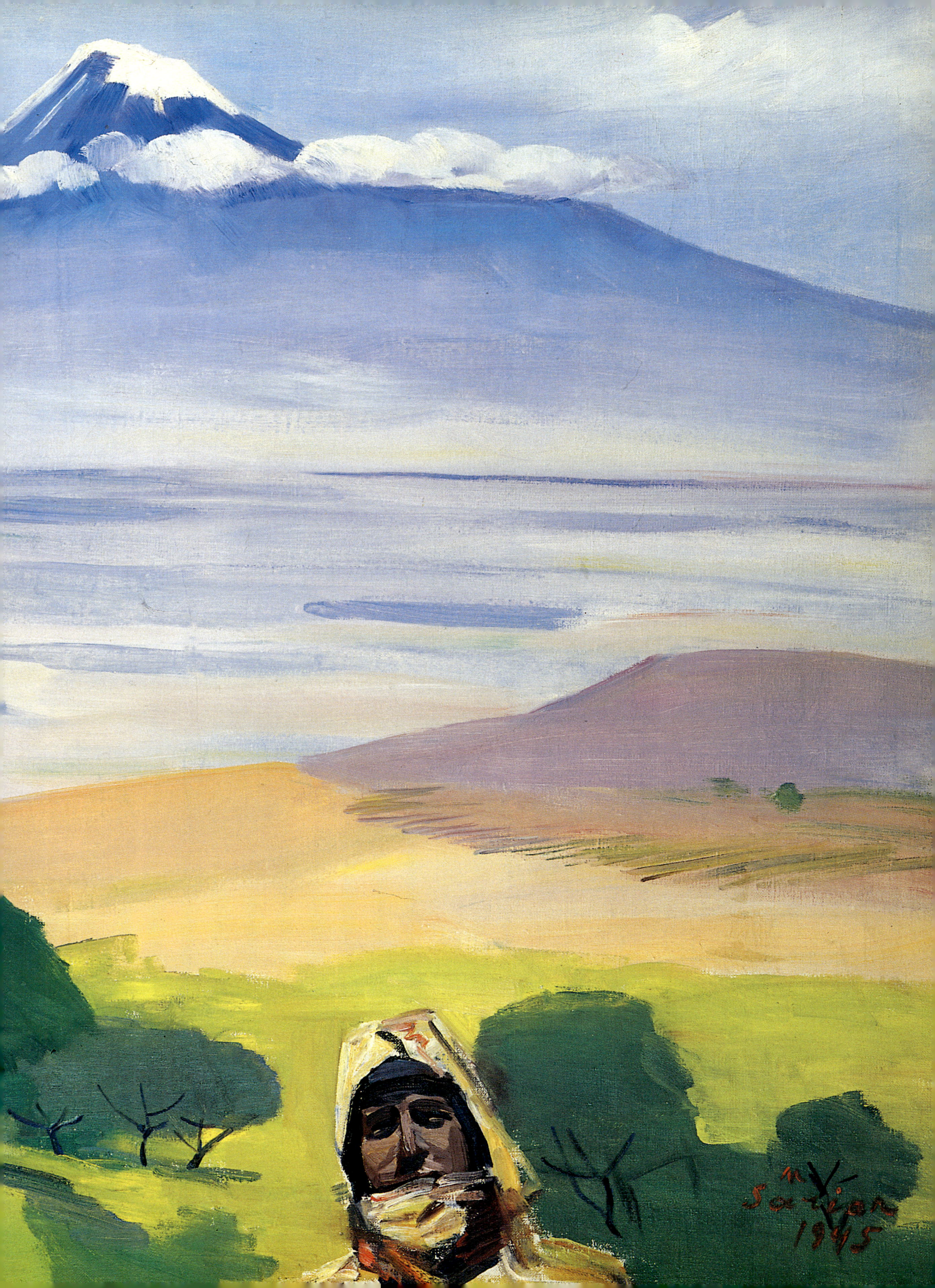
M. Sarian
1945

himself, the other the view of tall cliffs with blossoming trees seen through the window. These two images of the country – one real, the other invented by the painter – are important semantic elements in the structure of the portrait. They echo the splendid verses in which Isaakian sang the praises of his homeland. The artist did not embellish the poet's appearance – his figure is massive, his hand, resting on the table, somewhat coarse, his features large and heavy. Yet for all the lack of outward attraction, the image is full of significance and calm dignity. This is a man who has seen much and lived through much, but has retained a lively interest in the world and in people. A wise and good-natured man.

In contrast to the brave austerity seen in the depiction of Isaakian, the 1939 portrait of the actor and director Ruben Simonov betrays a certain seeking after effect. The background for the figure was a piece of coloured fabric. According to the artist, this "served as a sort of additional key for the study of this man's spiritual organization."[71] The decorative detail does indeed stress the hint of an actor's pose that Saryan caught in Simonov's handsome face and in his bearing.

The portrait of the ballerina Galina Ulanova, made in 1940, strikes one as unexpected. Saryan recreated not her celebrated stage persona, refined, emotionally replete and complex, but her everyday appearance, stressing the strong character of this woman and her wilful determination – features unfamiliar to those who knew her only from the theatre.

The most important means of expression in the majority of Saryan's portraits is colour. He painted the film-director Sergei Eisenstein against an intense blue background that contrasts with the burning tones of the

←
Ararat Valley. 1945
Oil on canvas. 96 x 128 cm
Museum of Oriental Art, Moscow

April Landscape. 1944
Oil on canvas. 54 x 73 cm
I. Bagramian family collection, Moscow

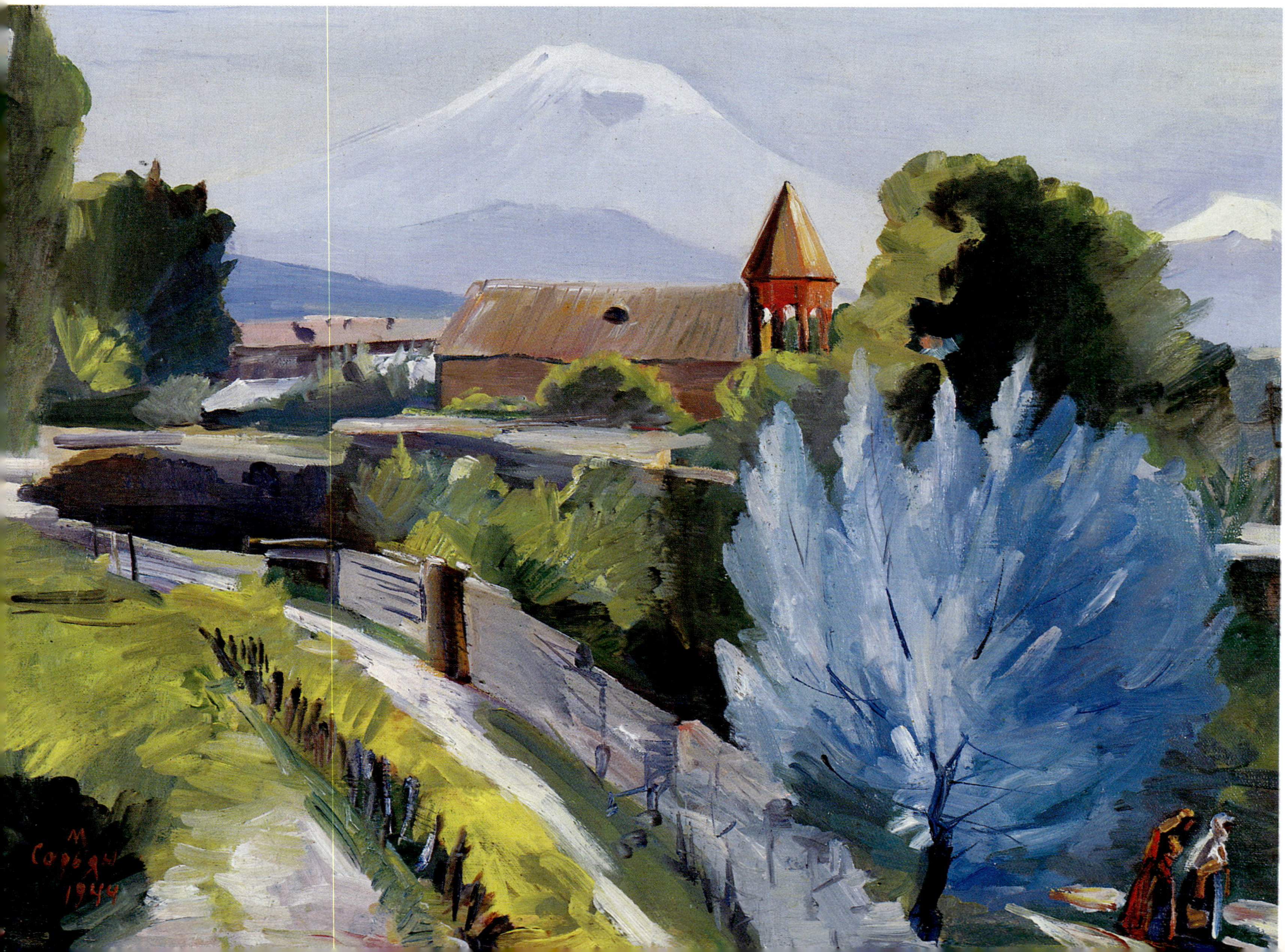

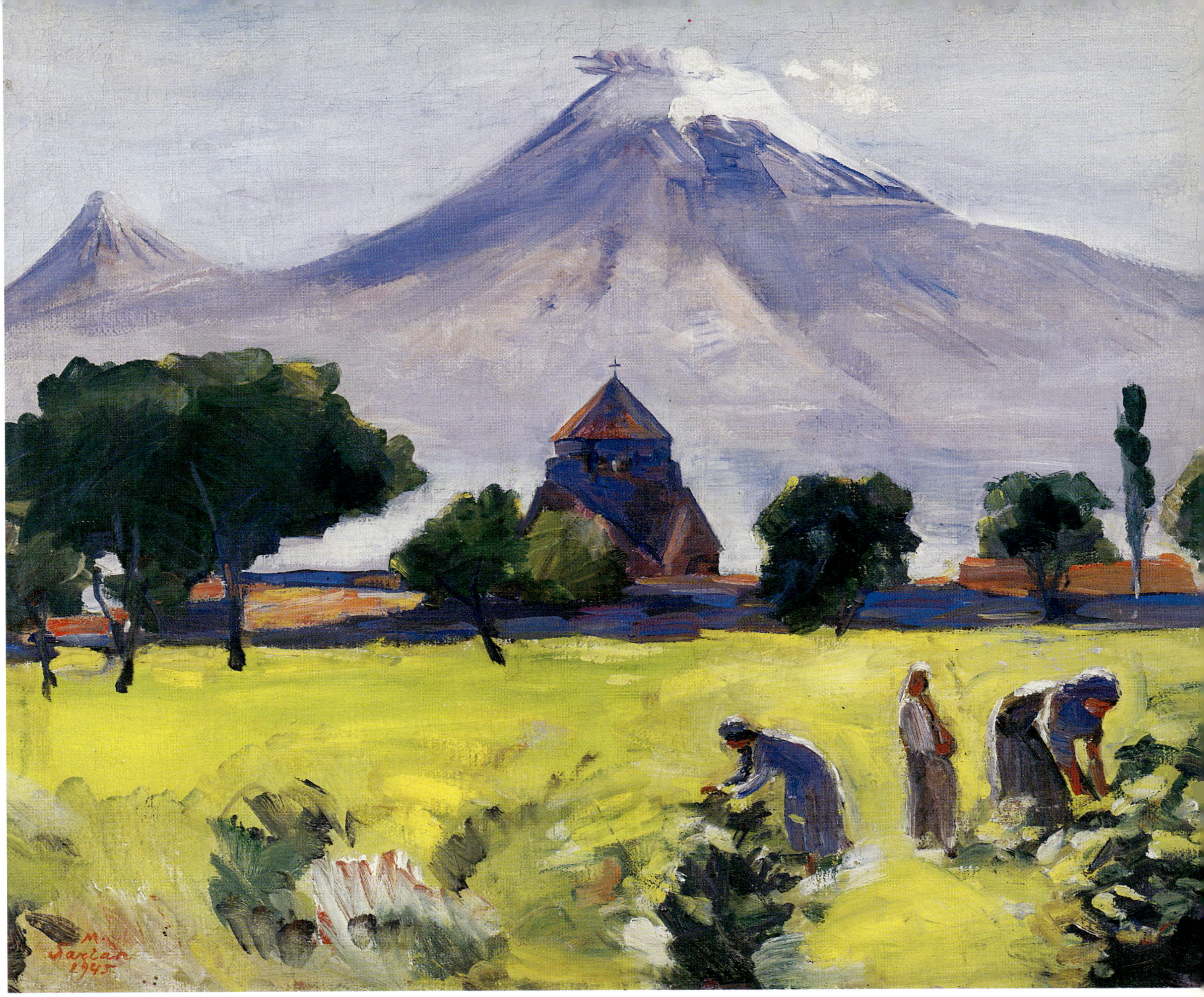

Ararat and the Church of St Hripsimé. 1945
Oil on canvas. 52.5 x 65 cm
Martiros Saryan Museum, Yerevan

→
October in Yerevan. 1961
Oil on canvas. 79 x 102 cm
Museum of Oriental Art, Moscow

face and the bright stripes of the clothing. This contrast comes across as a painterly equivalent to the tense inner life of the sitter. Reflections of that life can be divined in the face moulded with broad brushstrokes, the tightly pressed lips, knitted brows and bulging forehead that seems to pulsate with thought. Saryan superbly conveyed the unique, uncompromising character of the director who so often met with lack of understanding and opposition.

The combination of a background of resonant colours and a dark figure not only introduces an element of Eastern decorativeness into the portrait of academician Iosif Orbeli, but also intensifies the eloquence of the image. It is easy to detect here bitter meditation and alarm (the work was painted in 1943, at the height of the war), coupled with a passionate temperament ready to burst into speech, gesture or motion and destroy the outward stasis of the figure and the deceptive calm of the face.

Self-portraits occupy a special place in the artist's œuvre. The early ones have already been mentioned. A long gap then ensued. In *My Family* the artist's presence is indicated by a photograph on the wall – without this the family would be incomplete, but it can scarcely be described as a self-portrait. Only in 1933 did Saryan paint the first in a series of self-portraits (*Self-Portrait with a Mask*) created in this period of his life.

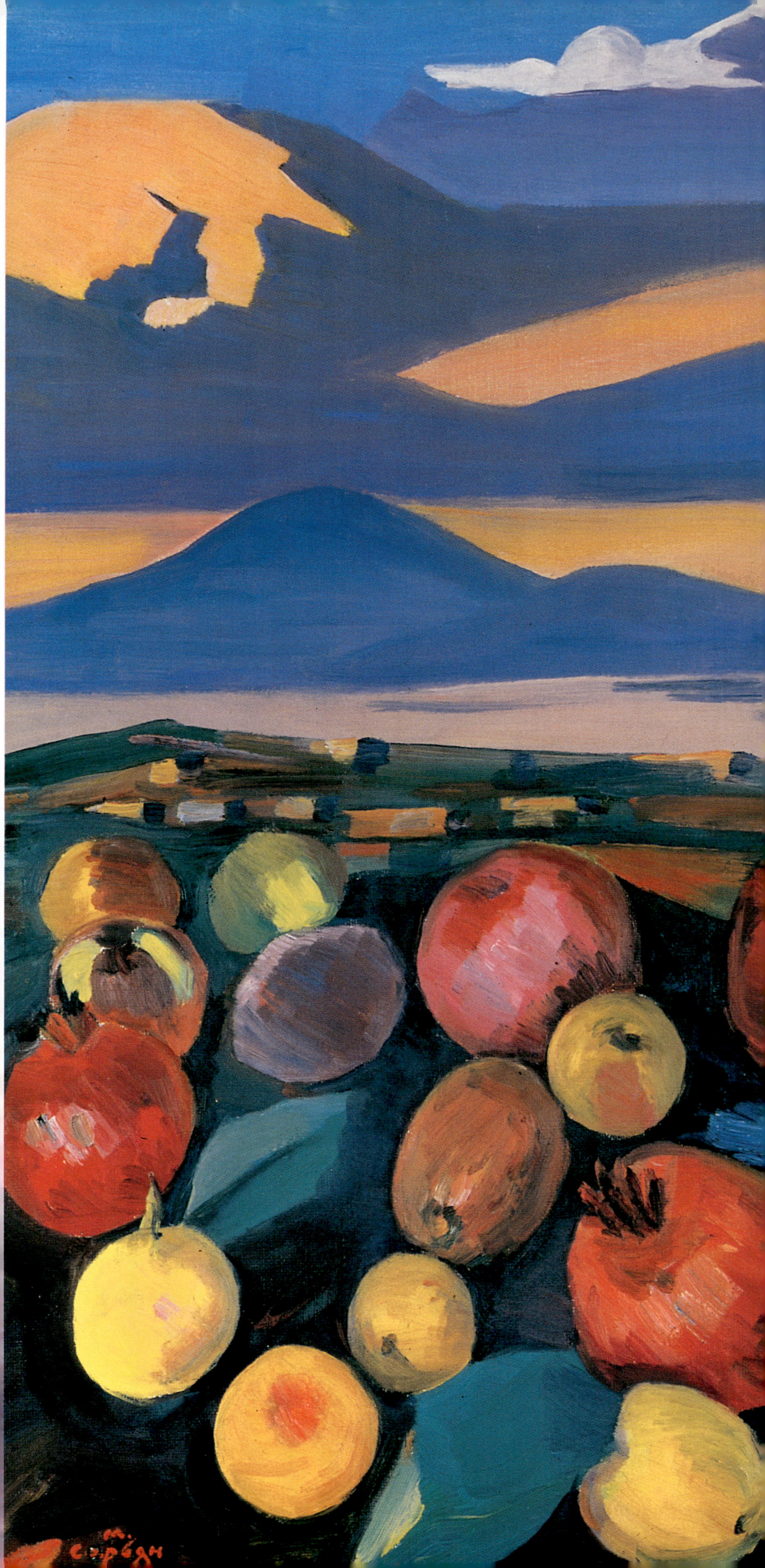
М.
Сарьян

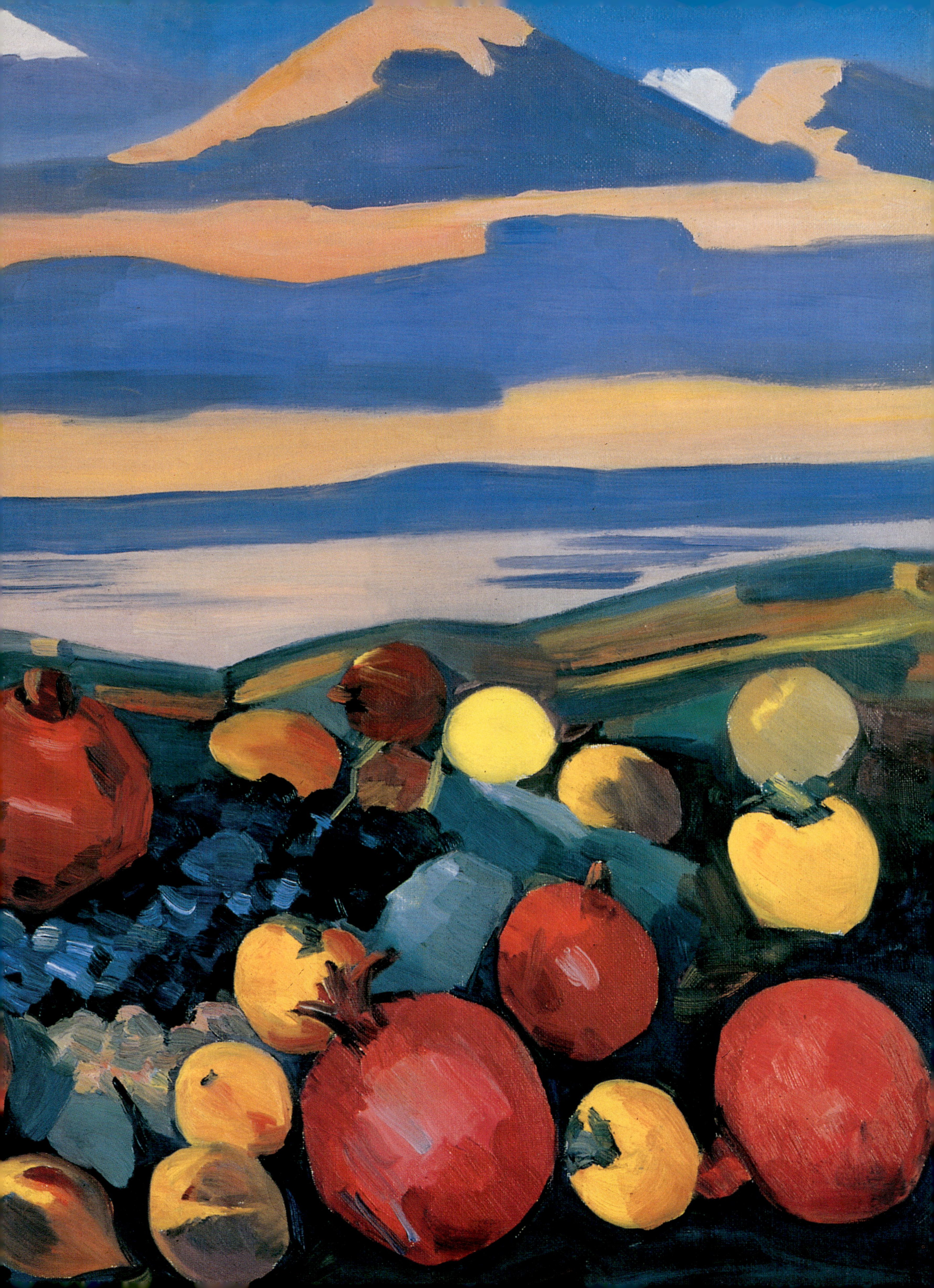

As in the portrait of Charents, Saryan contrasts a living face, conveyed by dynamic, raised brushstrokes, with the smooth, frozen countenance of the mask that nevertheless is full of a distinctive kind of expressiveness. The artist is staring intensely at something outside the canvas. The wide open eyes of the mask are gazing in the same direction, as if sharing his fixed interest in the world. Both countenances represent the transient and the eternal, the living and the artificial, not dead, but rather animated by some

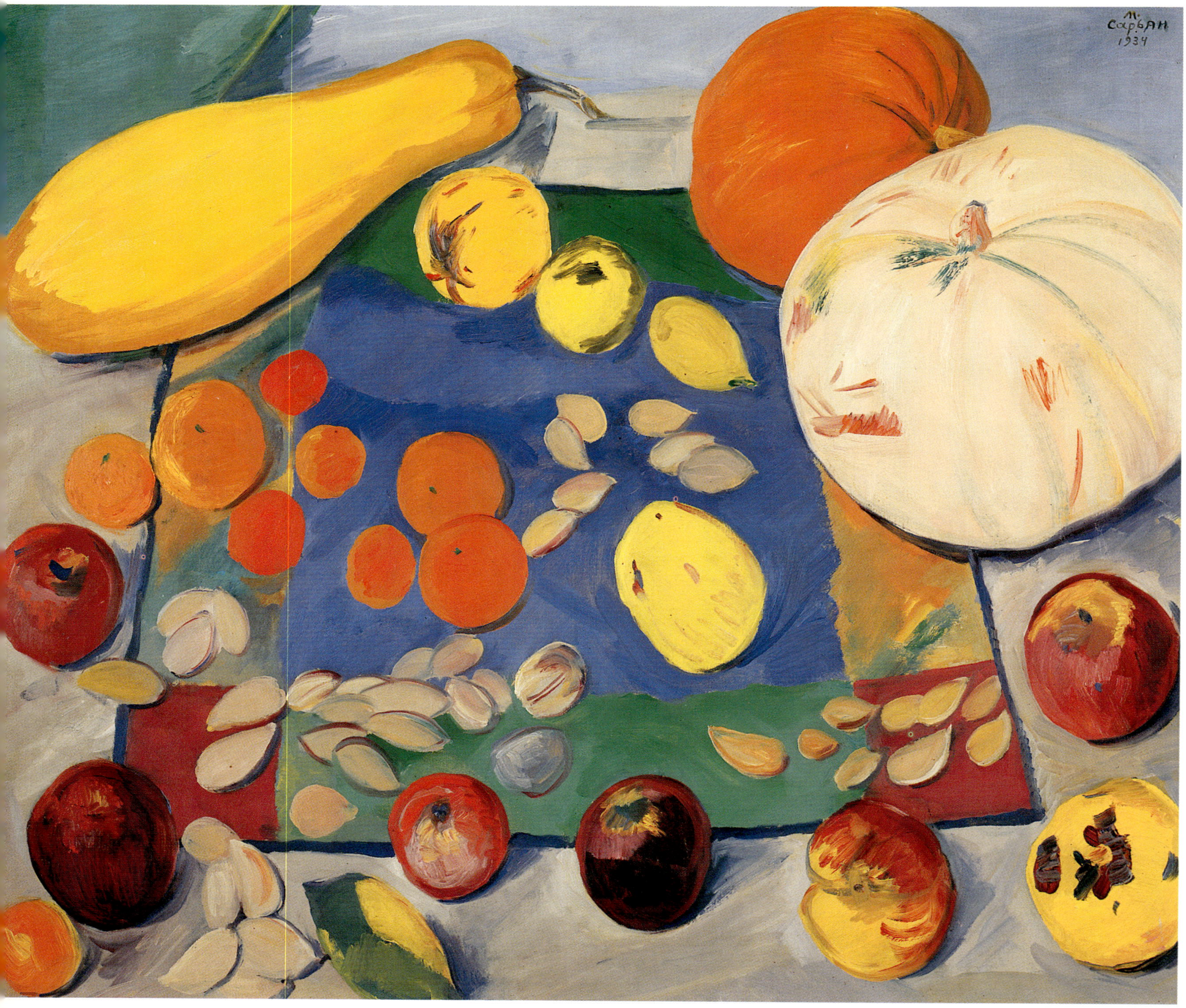

Still-Life: Fruit and Vegetables. 1934
Oil on canvas. 73 x 92 cm
G. Tarverdian collection, Yerevan

secret thought. In no other work by Saryan were man and mask so close, united by some shared inner mystery. The mask here is like the artist's double, participating in his life, capable of absorbing and storing for perpetuity the concentration of his thoughts, the motions of his soul.

In 1942, a time of severe trials for the whole country, Saryan painted himself for the one and only time at work, brush and palette in hand (*Self-Portrait*). The adversities of wartime and concern for his son, who had been called up to the front, not only failed to break the artist's spirit, but seem on the contrary to have opened up new resources within him, strengthening the capacity to defy circumstances that always distinguished this outwardly reserved, yet amazingly courageous man.

Dating from that same year is a self-portrait with a unique conception – *Three Ages*. In it Saryan boldly breaks one of the immutable laws of traditional easel painting, the unity of time and place. On a single canvas he depicted himself at different periods of his life. On the right the

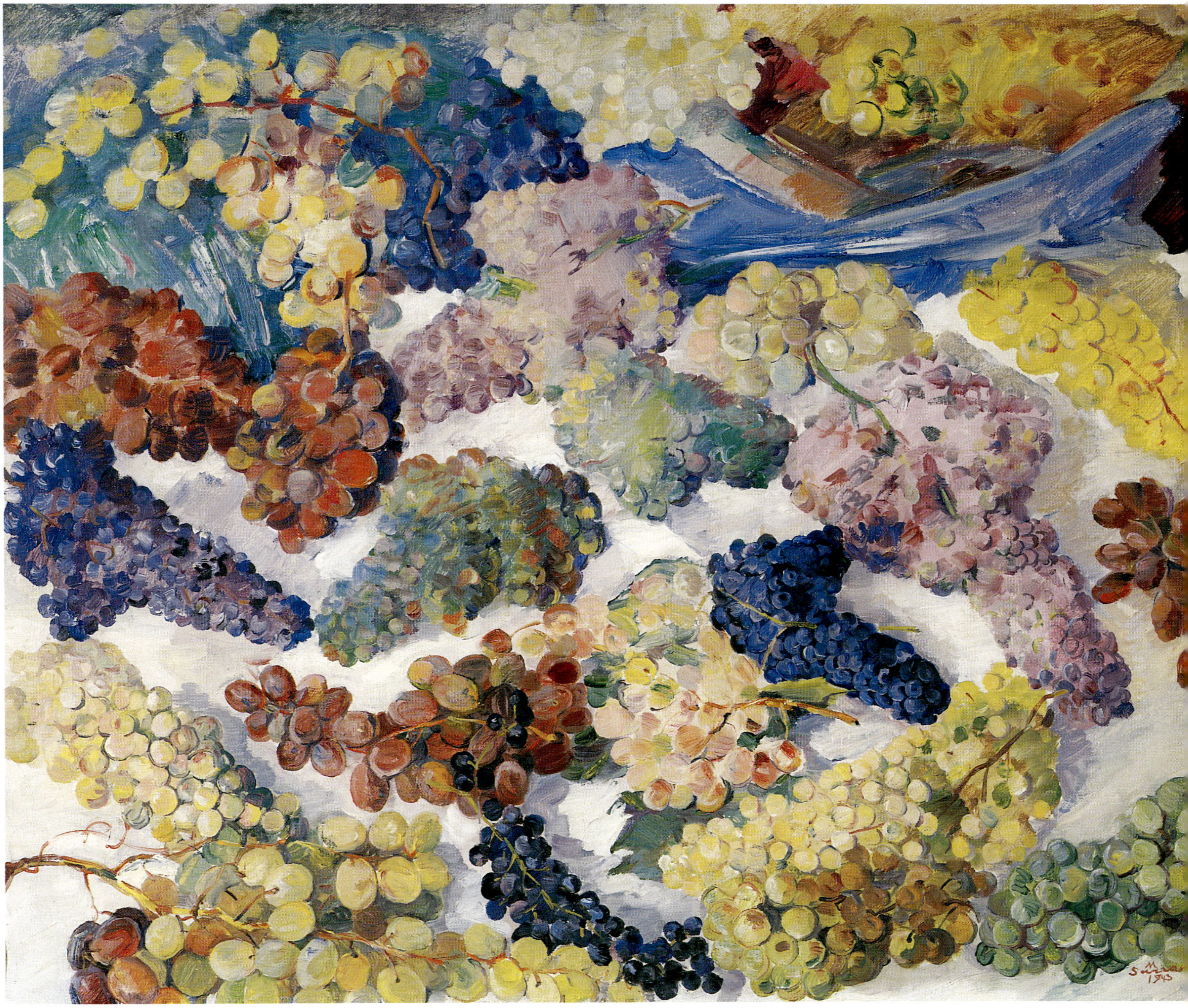

Grapes. 1943
Oil on canvas. 72 x 93 cm
The Tretyakov Gallery, Moscow

artist is still a very young man; on the left he is in his mature years (a sort of parallel with *Self-Portrait with a Mask*). Rising above them in the centre is the figure of an old man, rendered wise by life but still full of strength, who regards the world with a serious, searching look. It is hard to think of another work in the art of that period with so daring a conception. The development of a man's life is here presented in three temporal dimensions, but its apogee is of course the central figure, one of Saryan's most vivid psychological images.

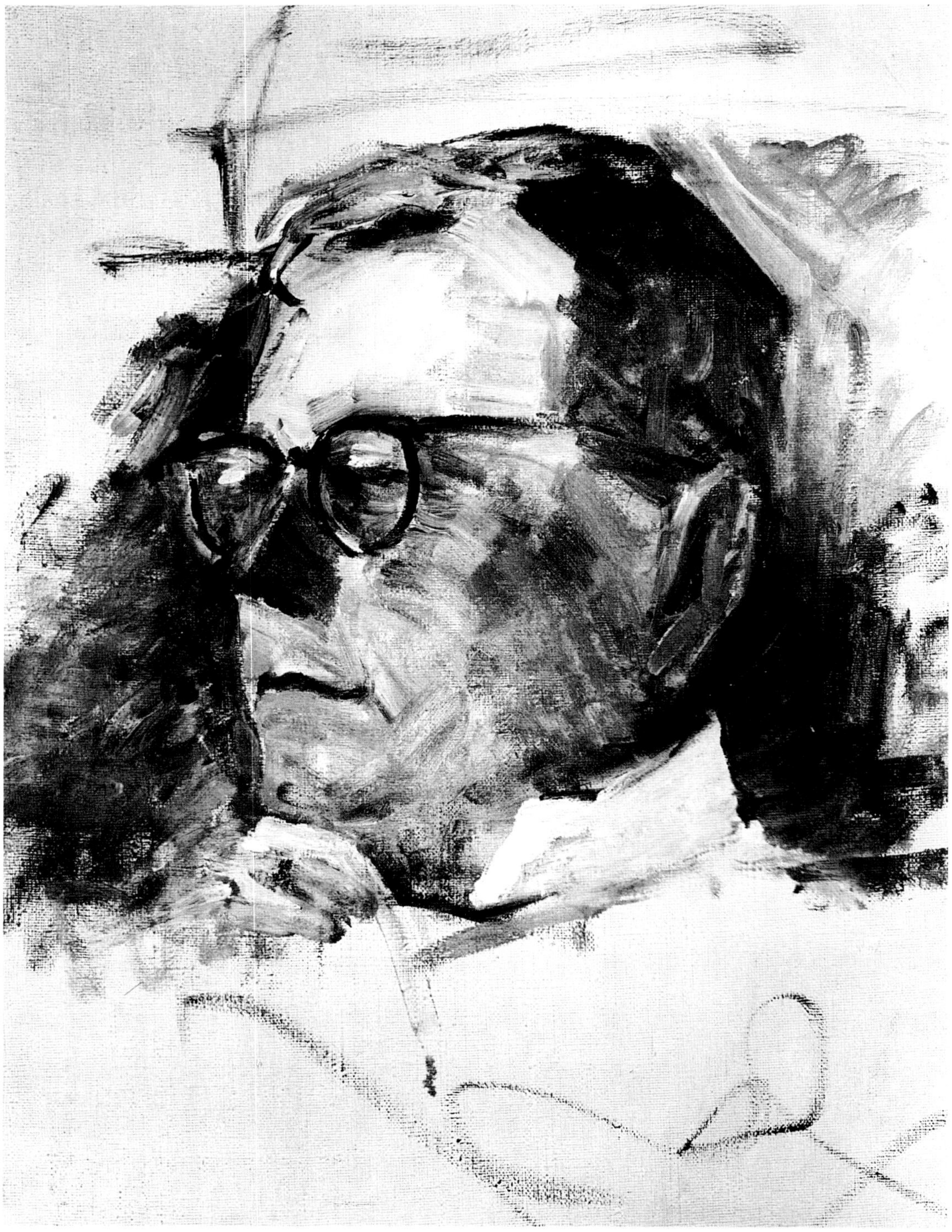

Portrait of Dmitry Shostakovich.
1963
Oil on canvas. 58 x 46 cm
L. Saryan collection, Yerevan

An equally free approach to concepts of space and time can be found in certain portraits of the artist's wife in which she is presented simultaneously in different conditions of life and emotional states. These include the 1935 triple portrait of Lusik Saryan and the 1941 work *From the Artist's Life (A Portrait of Lusik Saryan in Profile)*. In the latter the artist makes skilful use of the reflection of the subject in a mirror, in which we also see Saryan himself. In the foreground there is a photograph of the couple's son, who was by then already in the army. This painting with its seemingly unplanned and fairly complex compositional structure reveals a genre or narrative aspect that was not characteristic of Saryan's art as a whole. At the same time the artist managed to express with astonishing tact the atmosphere of deep mutual attachment that bound his family together, an atmosphere tinged in the present instance with a barely detectable hint of disquiet.

As the generally acknowledged head of the Armenian national school of painting, Saryan was inseparably linked to the artistic culture of the country as a whole, with the complex and at times dramatic course of its development. His fame and authority were indisputable. Yet Saryan, like many other prominent figures in the arts, had at times to endure the attacks of time-serving critics, the mouthpieces of the official opposition to "formalism" and to everything that did not accord with the narrow standards of Socialist Realism. In the best cases, such art was passed over in silence or pushed to the fringes of cultural life. Attempts to distort the meaning of Saryan's work were renewed in the second half of the 1940s and the 1950s, although at that time he was accorded official awards. The artist ignored the unjust and absurd critical assaults with his inherent dignity. They were incapable of shaking or altering his creative principles, yet they did cause quite a degree of moral pain. The award of the Lenin Prize to Saryan in 1961 (in the face of active opposition from many official authorities in the arts) put an end to the attacks from vulgarizing critics. More than that, his art provided a sort of shield for many young artists seeking to assert their own aesthetic vision independent of the generally accepted norms, first and foremost, of course, in Armenia.

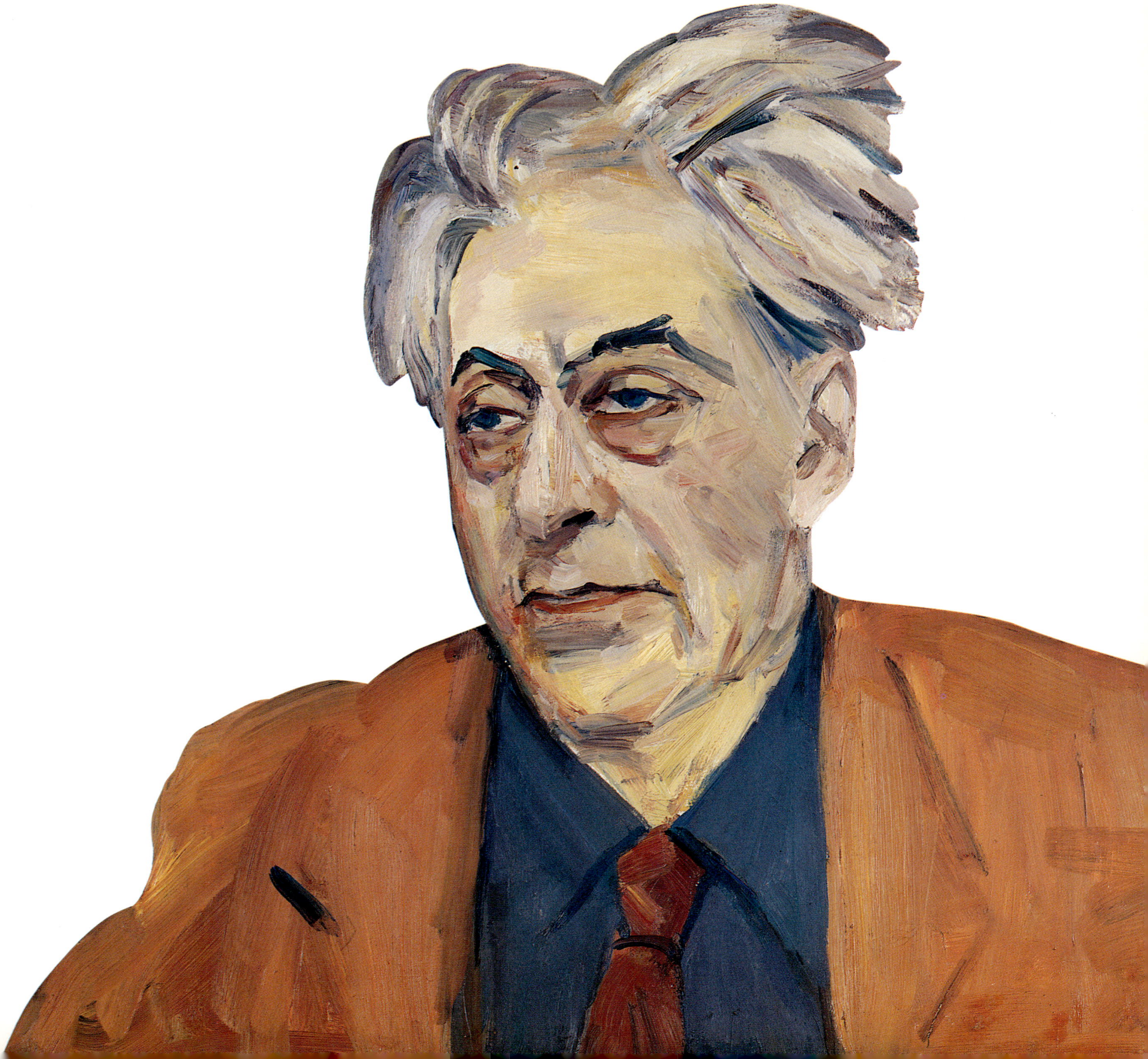

Portrait of Ilya Ehrenburg. 1959
Oil on canvas. 54 x 73 cm
Martiros Saryan Museum, Yerevan

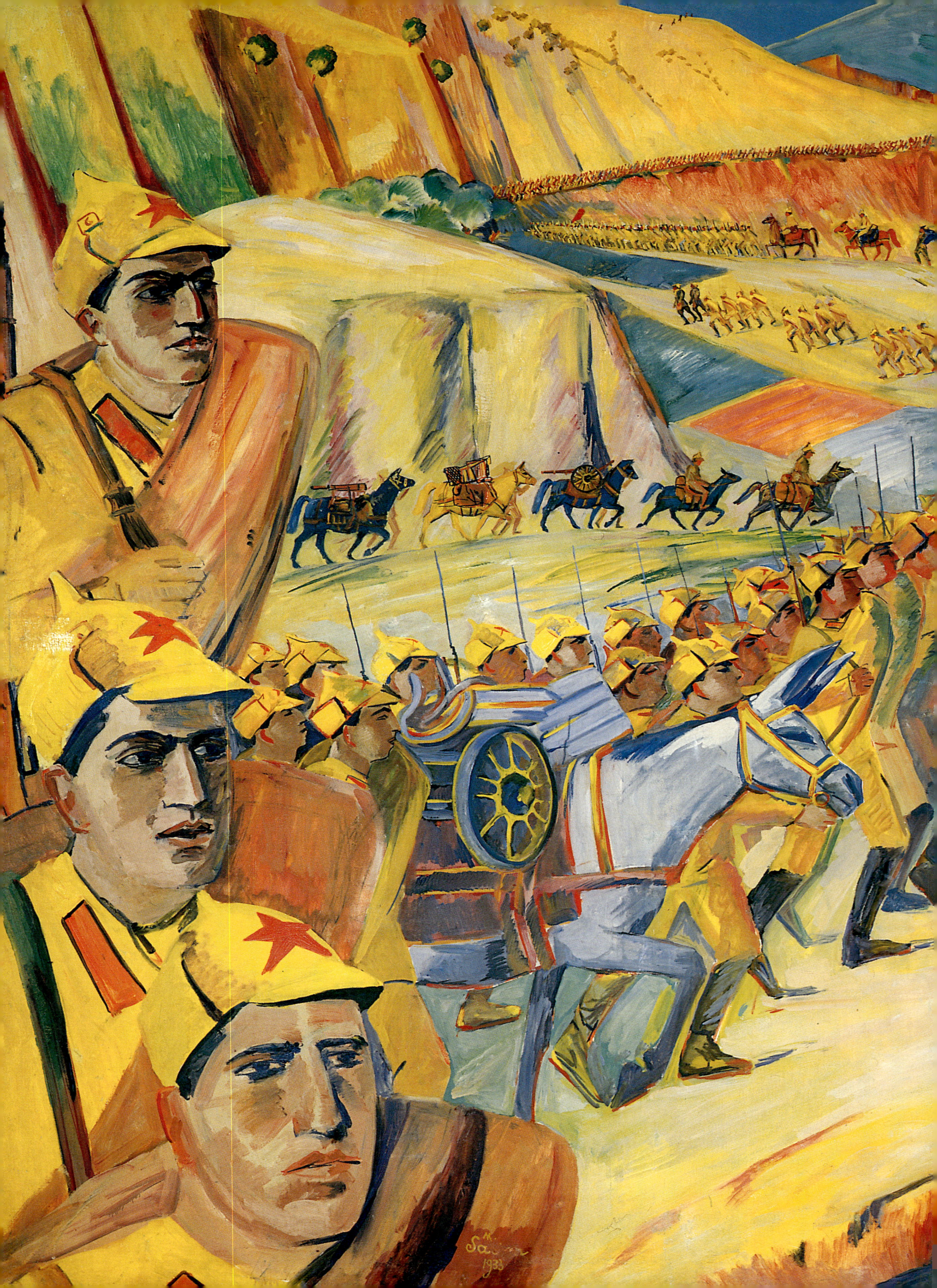

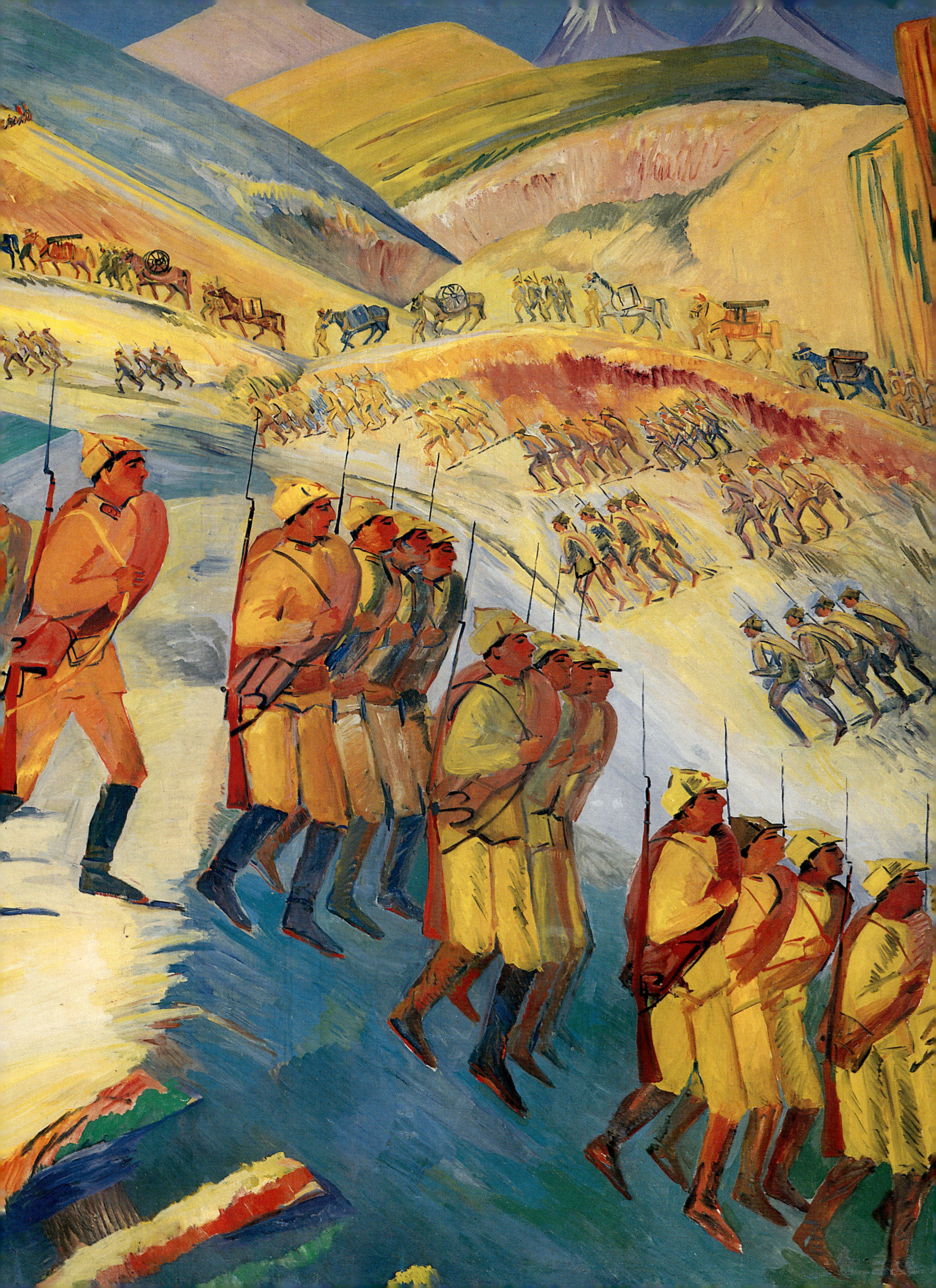

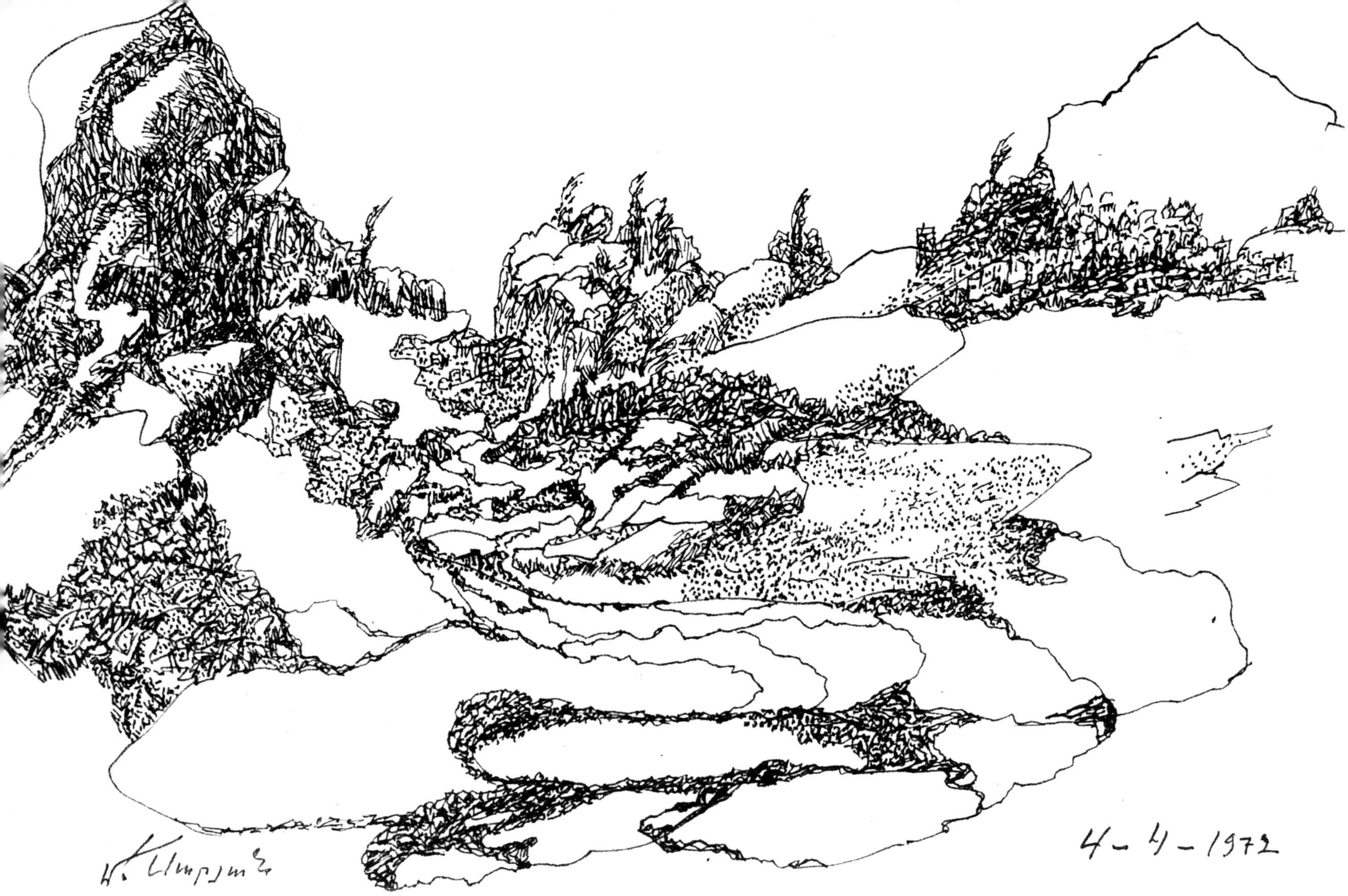
4-4-1972

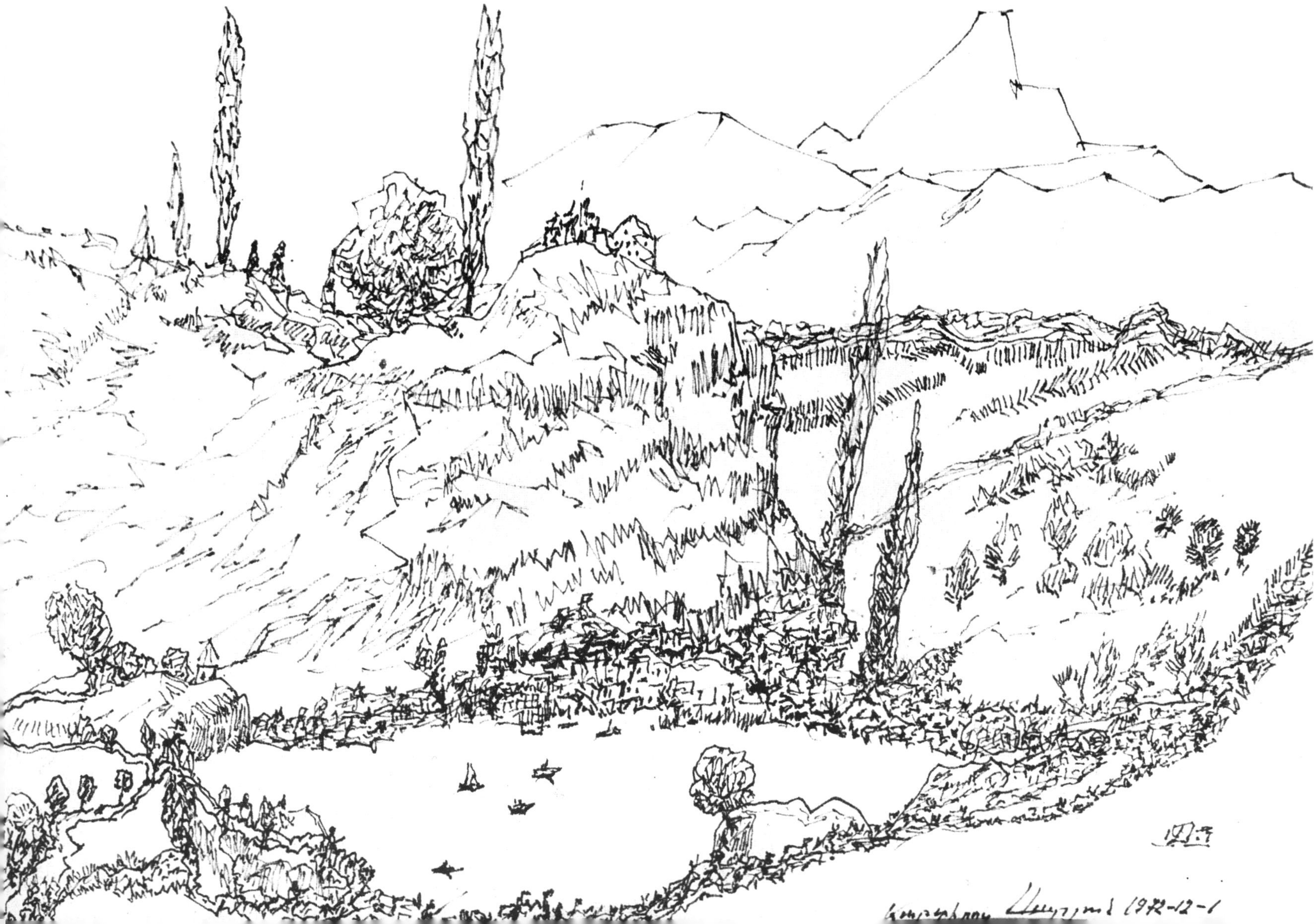
1972-12-1

←
March of the Armenian Detachment of the Red Army. 1933
Oil on canvas. 200 x 290 cm
The Grekov Art Studio, Moscow

Mountainous Landscape. 1972
Felt pen on paper. 21 x 31 cm
L. Saryan collection, Yerevan

Armenian Landscape. 1972
Felt pen on paper. 22 x 31 cm
L. Saryan collection, Yerevan

The Collective Farm of Karindzh Village in the Tumanian Mountains. 1952
Oil on canvas. 100 x 109 cm
Martiros Saryan Museum, Yerevan

Saryan himself had an exceptionally sympathetic attitude towards the young artists who venerated him as Varpet, the Teacher, but did not in any way encourage their attempts to imitate him. "I welcome those who are bold and original!"[72] In the difficult years when all manner of freedom, including creative freedom, was restricted he fought with his art for their right to be daring. Not everyone made full use of that right. Many Armenian artists evolved within the furrow that he had ploughed, with greater or lesser individual deviations from his conceptions. The brightest talents, though, while following him, quickly found their own course, still maintaining links of continuity with the great master. First mention among them must go to Minas Avetisian.

In the last decades of his long life, Saryan retained a fervent interest in the world, the capacity to enjoy its beauty, and a staggering amount of creative energy. Back at the end of the war and in the first post-war years the cycle of paintings devoted to Mount Ararat was extended with

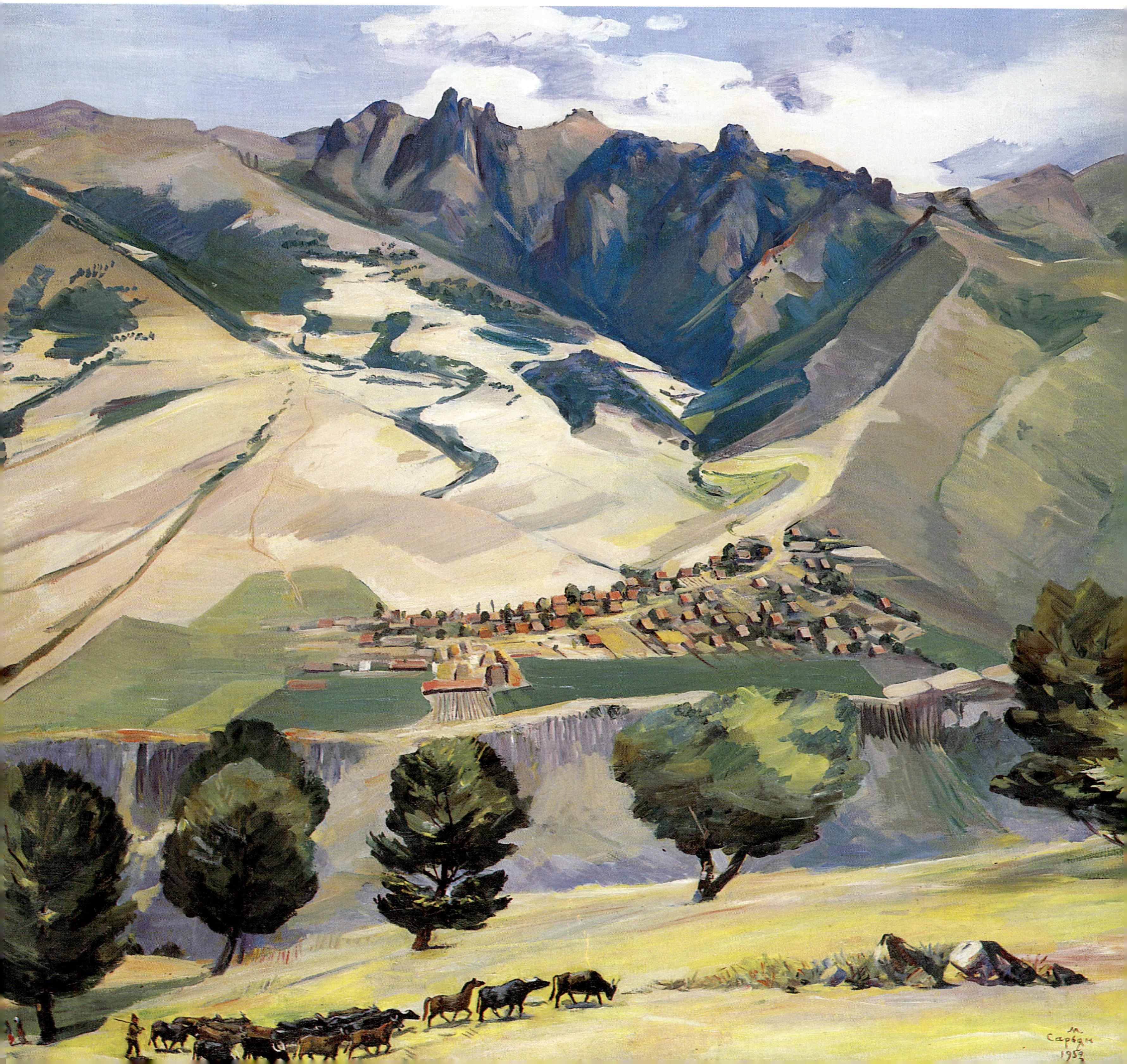

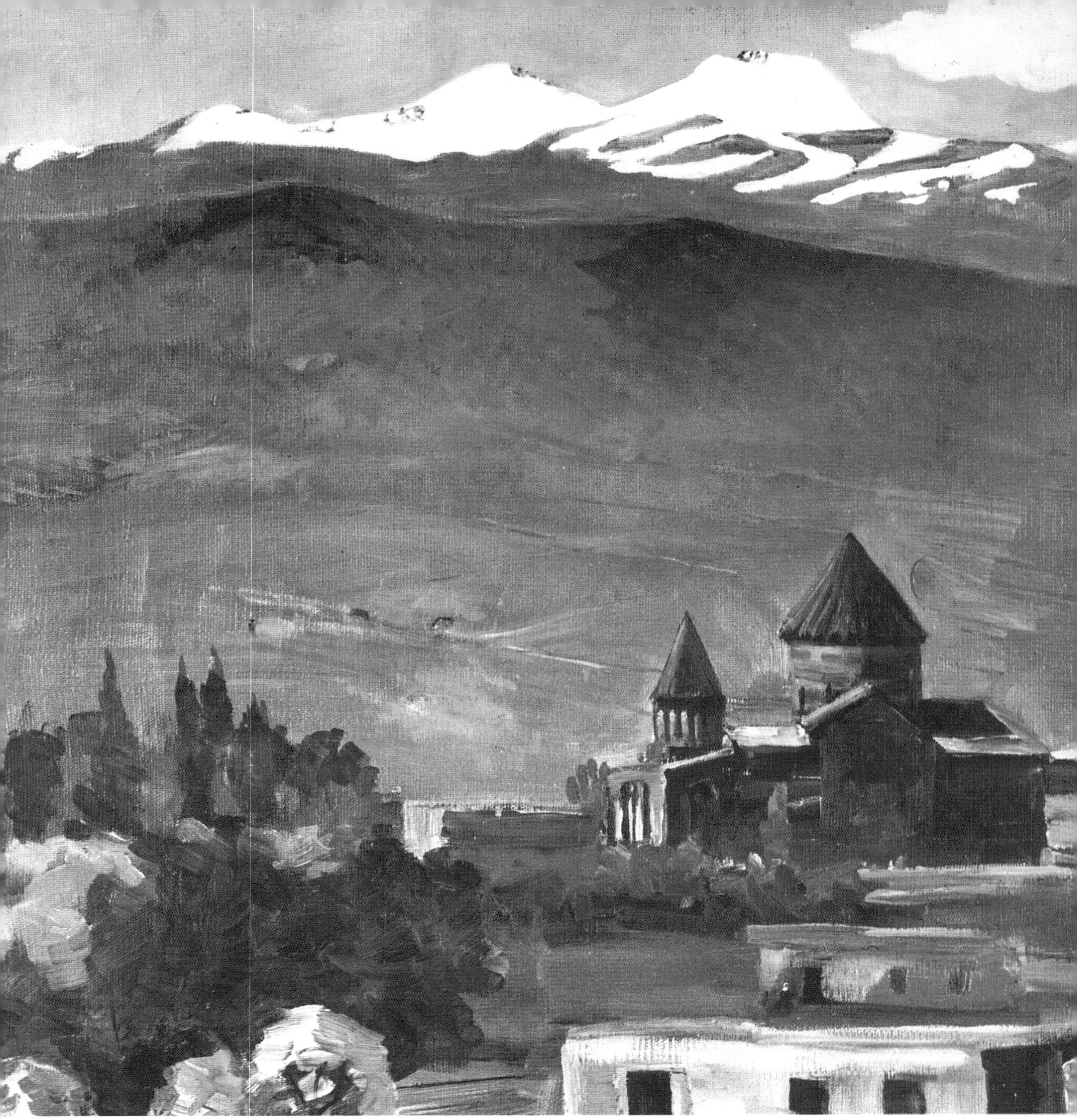

some splendid new works. He painted the mountain in a pale blue haze, distant as a daydream, with the foreground taken by a joyful spring landscape (*April Landscape*, 1944) or a broad expanse of green valley (*Ararat* and *View of Ararat from Dvin*, 1952). The painting *Ararat Valley* (1945) is astonishing for the subtlety of its colour orchestration. The head of a peasant woman that appears "suddenly" in the foreground is a vivid detail, a sort of spatial module establishing both a sense of distance and an unexpected proportionality between the human being and the tremendous landscape culminating in the majestic peaks of the biblical mountain.

Mugni and Aragats in Spring. 1951
Oil on canvas. 53 x 72 cm
A. Alikhanov family collection, Moscow

Khatchkars. 13th century. Photograph

The Church of St Hripsimé in Echmiadzin. 618. Erected by the Catholicos Komitas

→
The Seventh-Century Karmravor Church. Ashtarak. 1956
Oil on canvas. 54 x 73 cm
L. Saryan collection, Yerevan

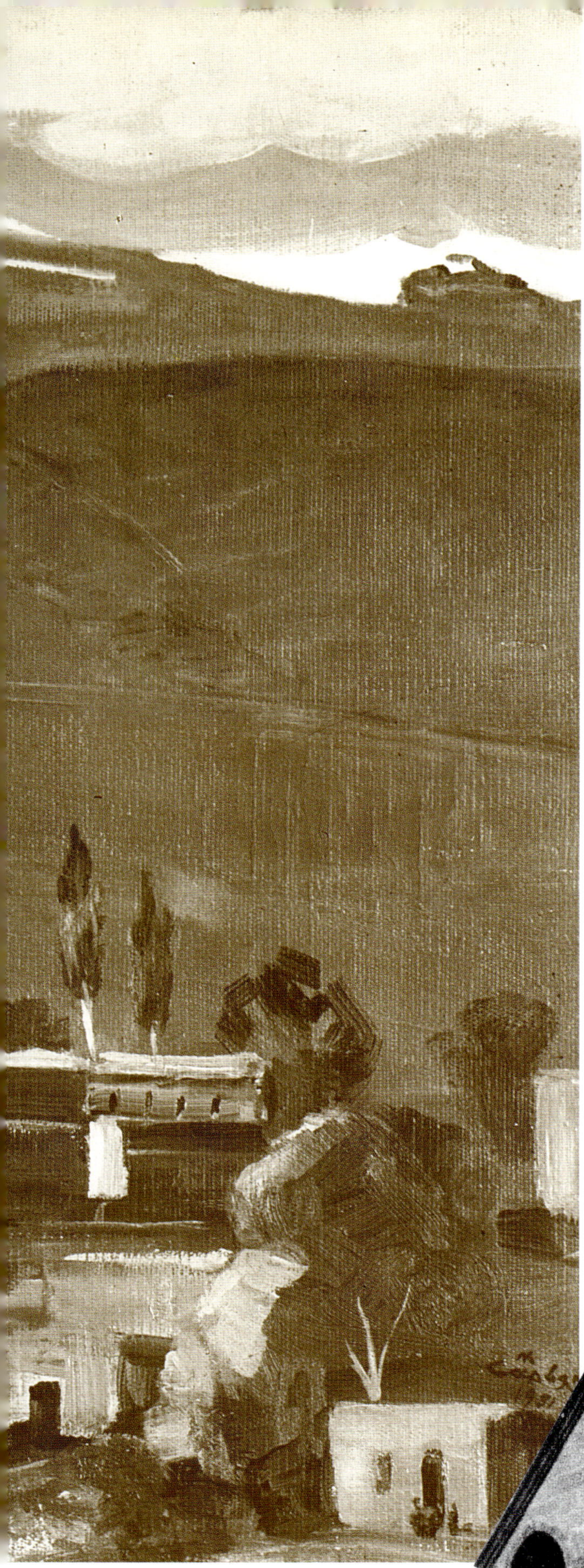

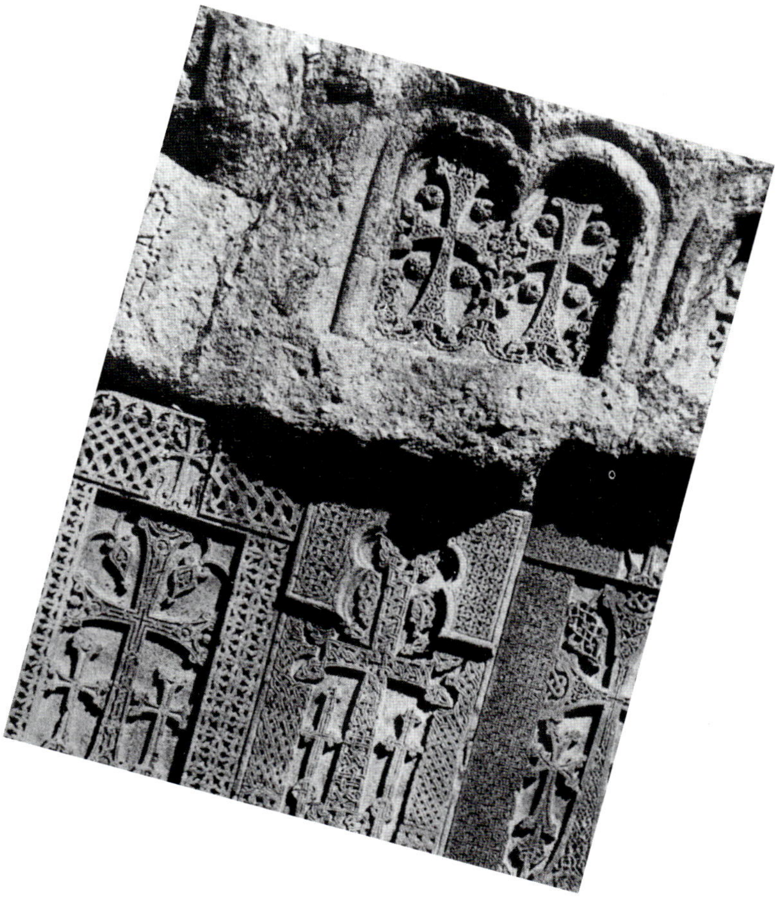

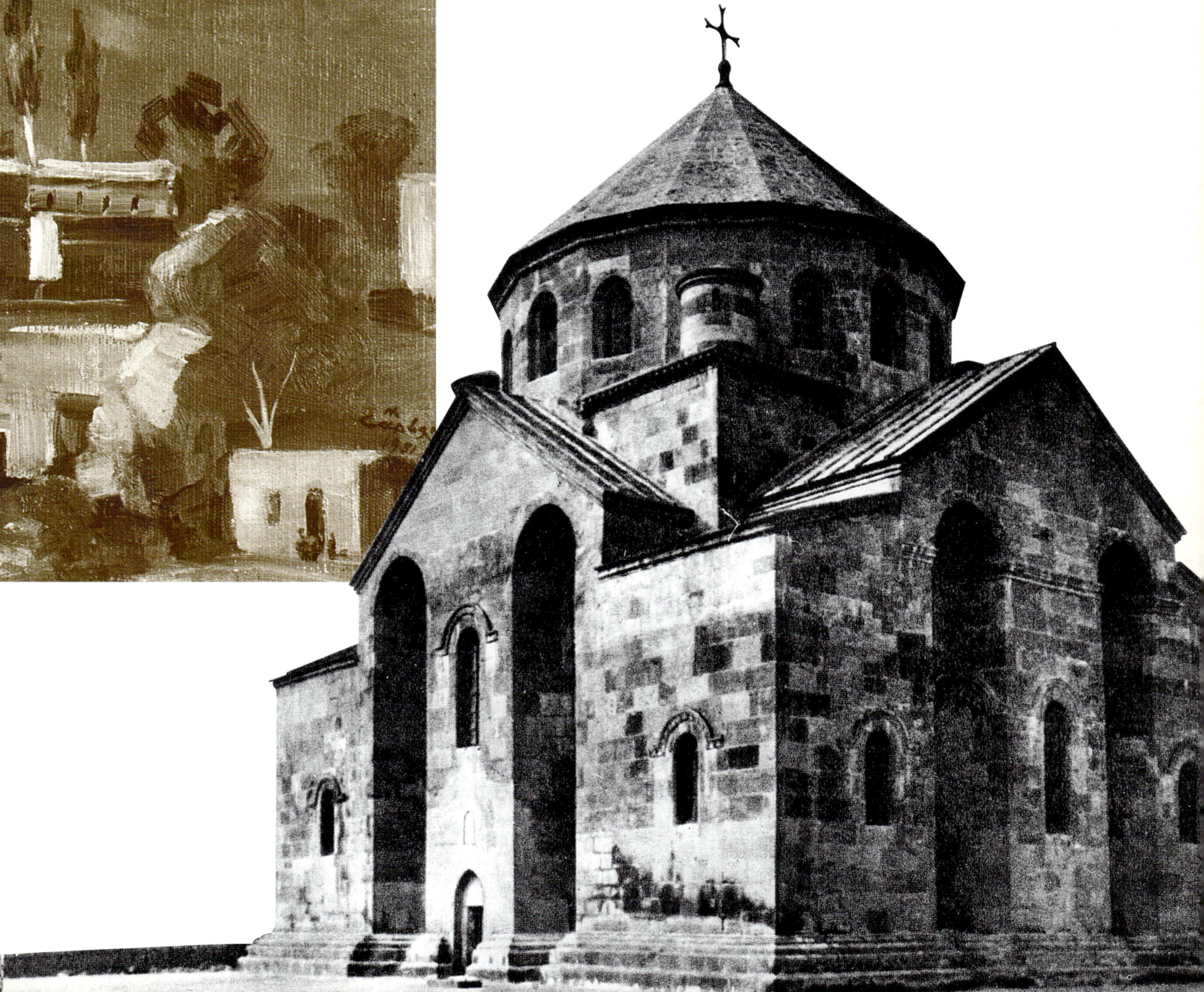

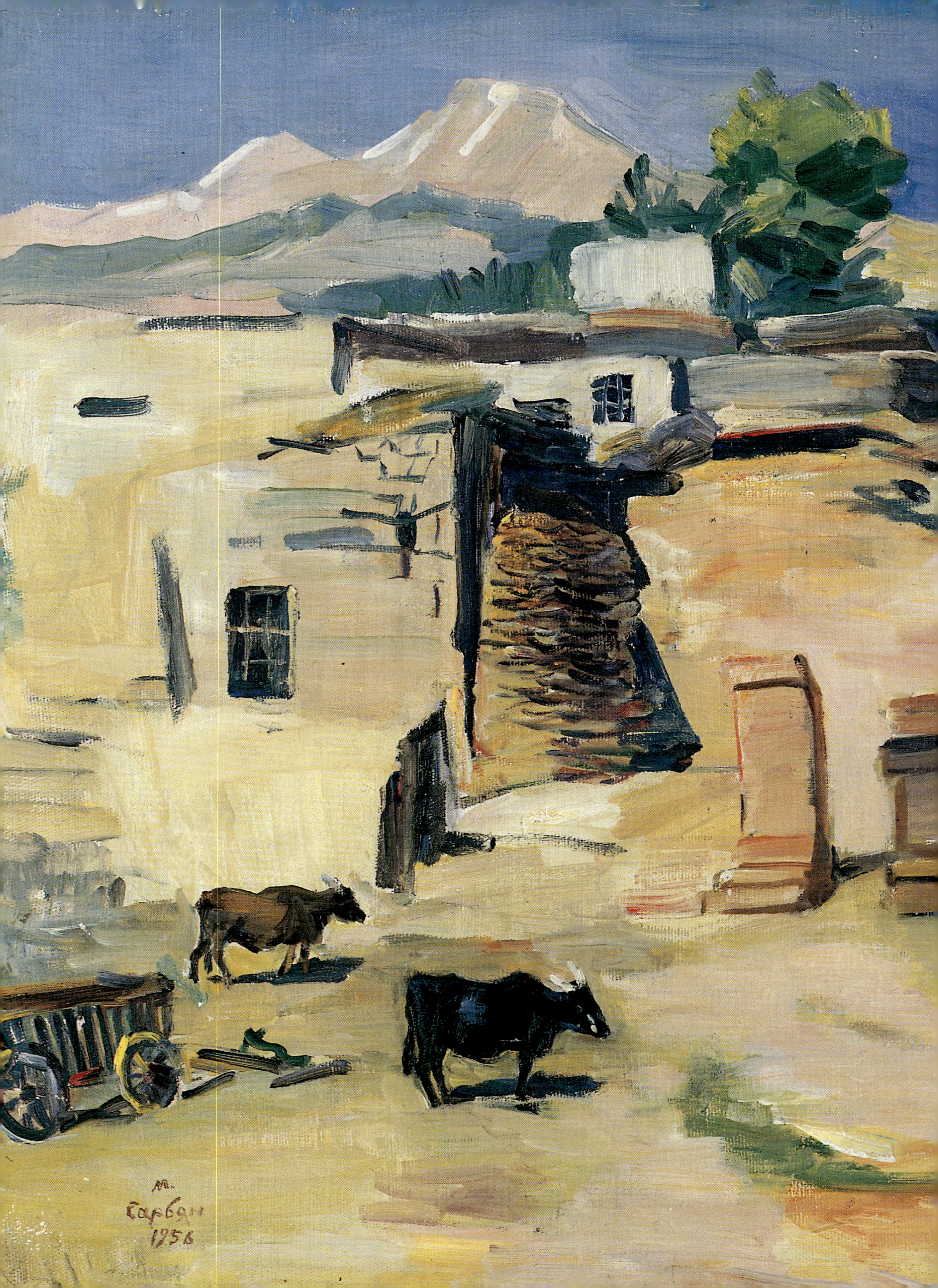
М.
Сарьян
1956

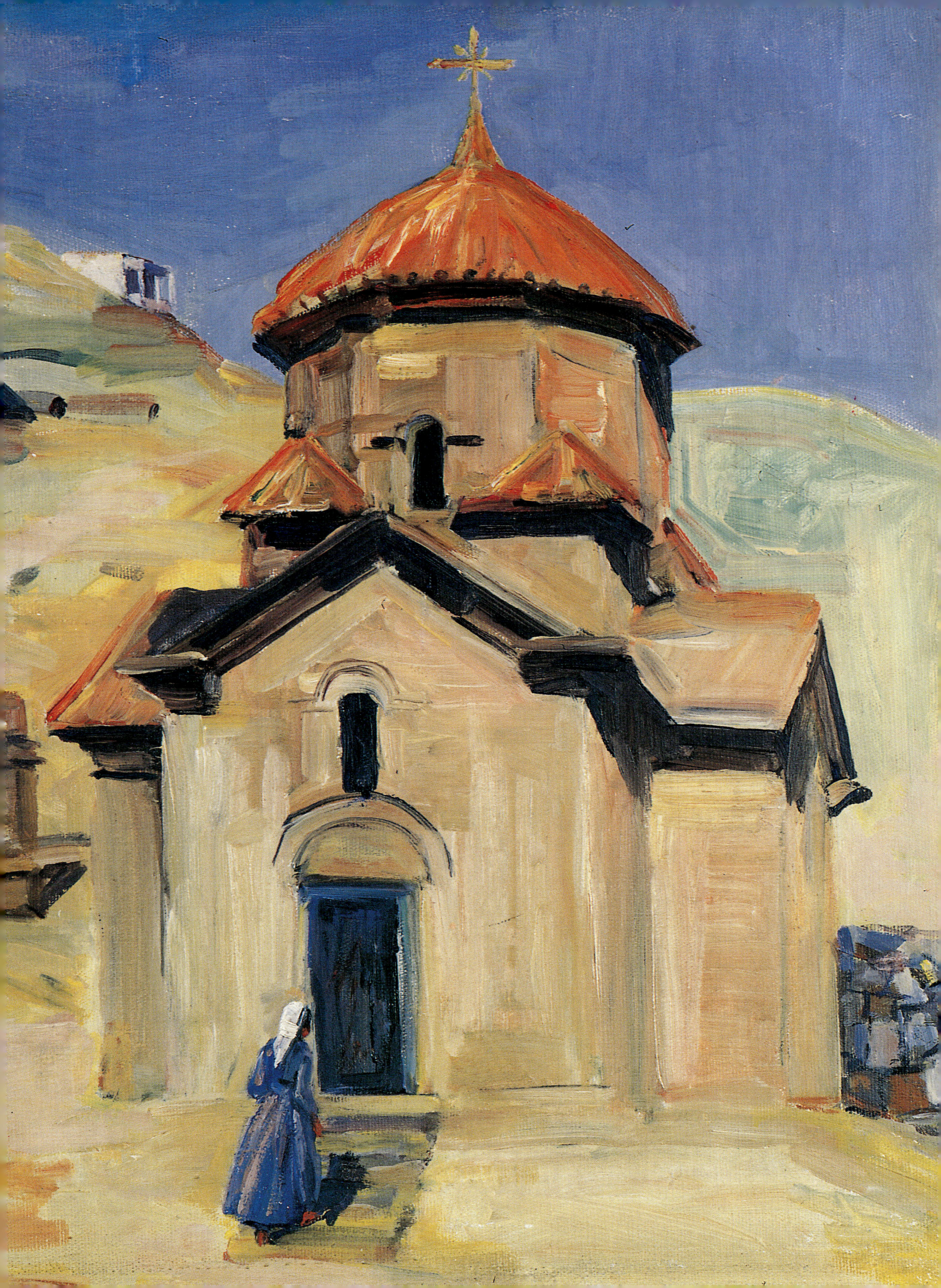

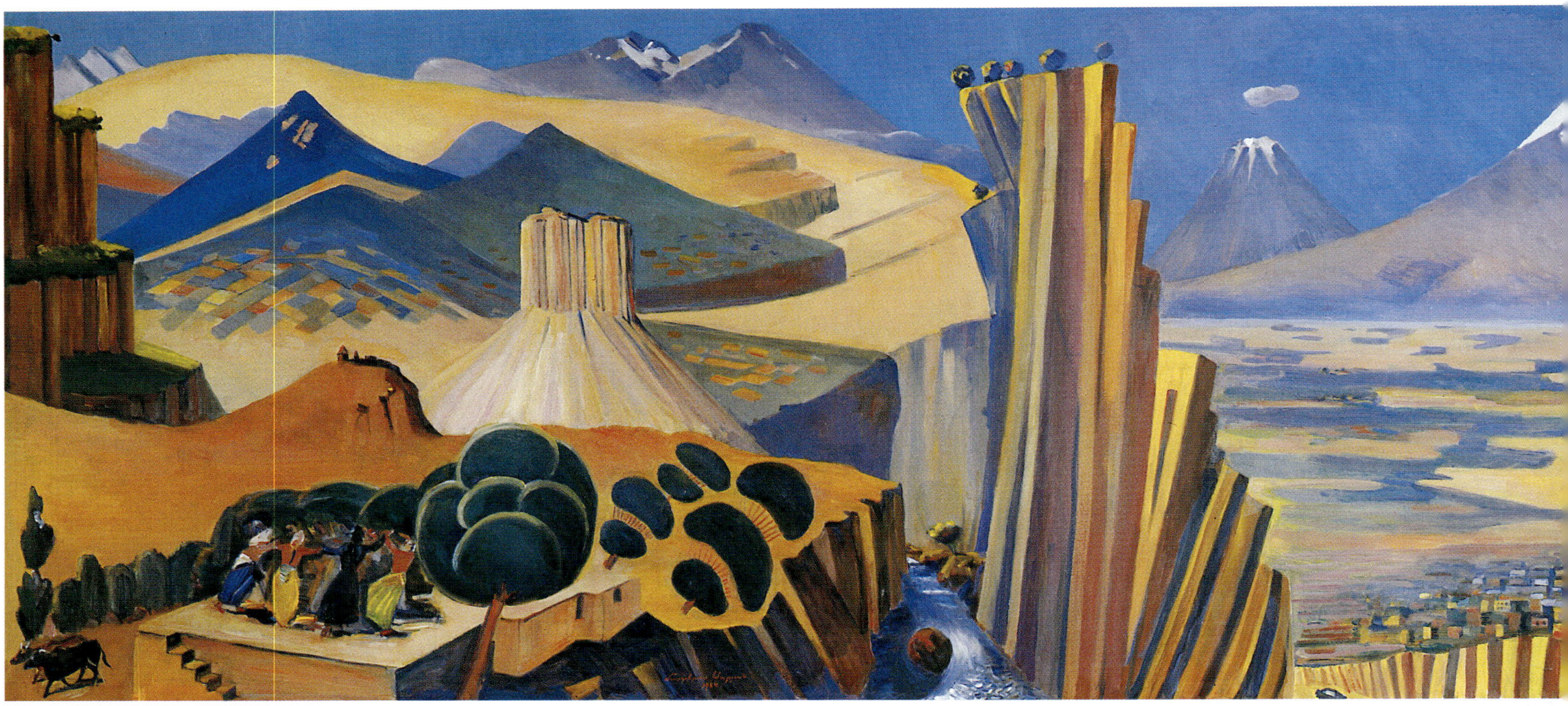

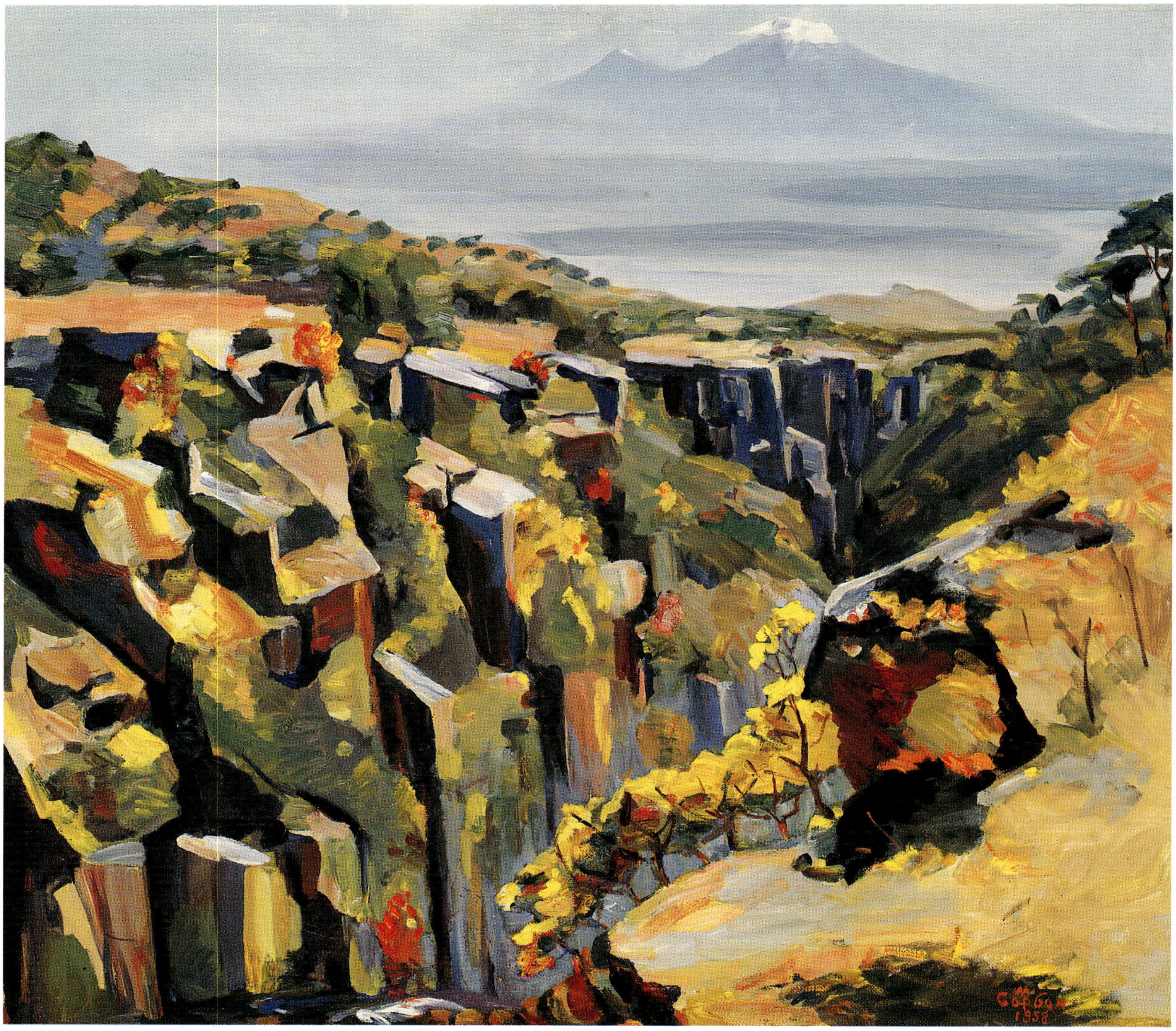

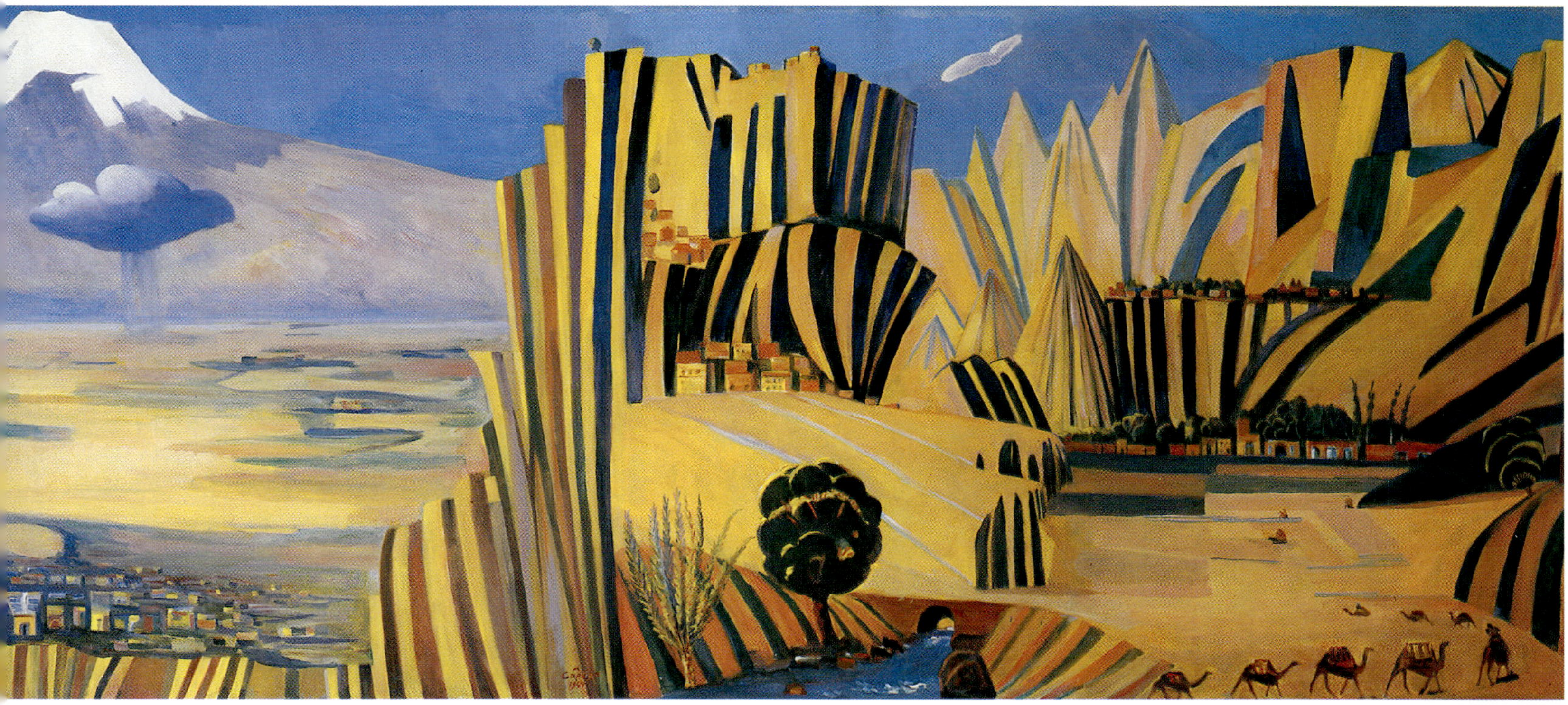

Panel: *Armenia.* 1964
Oil on canvas. 107 x 480 cm
L. Saryan collection, Yerevan

Precipice on the Slope of Mount Aragats. 1958
Oil on canvas. 80 x 100 cm
L. Saryan collection, Yerevan

→ *Flowers of May.* 1947
Oil on canvas. 73 x 92 cm
L. Saryan collection, Yerevan

In another landscape the same Ararat is depicted from closer quarters, the evening sun has coloured its slopes in shades of lilac, intensified by the contrast with yellow-green fields. Standing out clear-cut against the background of Great Ararat is the dark silhouette of the Church of St Hripsimé echoing its harmonious shape.

In this period Saryan quite often included ancient monuments in his landscapes. They fit so organically into the configuration of the mountains, their rhythm and structure, that they seem to be the inspired creation of nature itself. One example is the painting *Bzhni. The Fortress* (1946) with its dizzying flight from the foot of the mountain to the summit, crowned by the ancient temple, and on to the mighty mountain ridge that obscures the sky.

Saryan's still-lifes are invariably connected with the Armenian soil and the material world of Armenia. "The life of nature," the artist said, "is astonishing and mysterious. The seed grows in the soil, grows at the appropriate time, flowers, again gives seed and therefore does not die. Man is the same. He does not die; he is nature itself."[73] The sense of delight in the fertile power of nature and the variety of its manifestations permeates Saryan's still-lifes, such as *Fruit and Vegetables* (1934) and *Grapes* (1943). On each occasion he has carefully thought through the interrelationship of the objects, their decorative harmony that is at times resonant, at others restrained. The composition of many of the late still-lifes, which embraces the whole space of the painting, generates a sense of the special wealth and abundance of natural forms. In *Grapes*, for example, the splendid large bunches are placed on a white tablecloth in such a way that they seem dissatisfied with the amount of space allotted them. They extend not only beyond the surface of the table, but beyond the surface of the painting and in our minds we can continue their motion, full of vital energy.

This centrifugal burst of the material world beyond the bounds of the canvas is also a characteristic feature of many of the floral still-lifes, the most well-known of which is perhaps *Flowers for the Armenians who Died Fighting in the Great Patriotic War* (1945). It was painted immediately after the victory celebrations. On that day many people came to share the occasion with Sarayan and all of them brought bouquets of flowers.

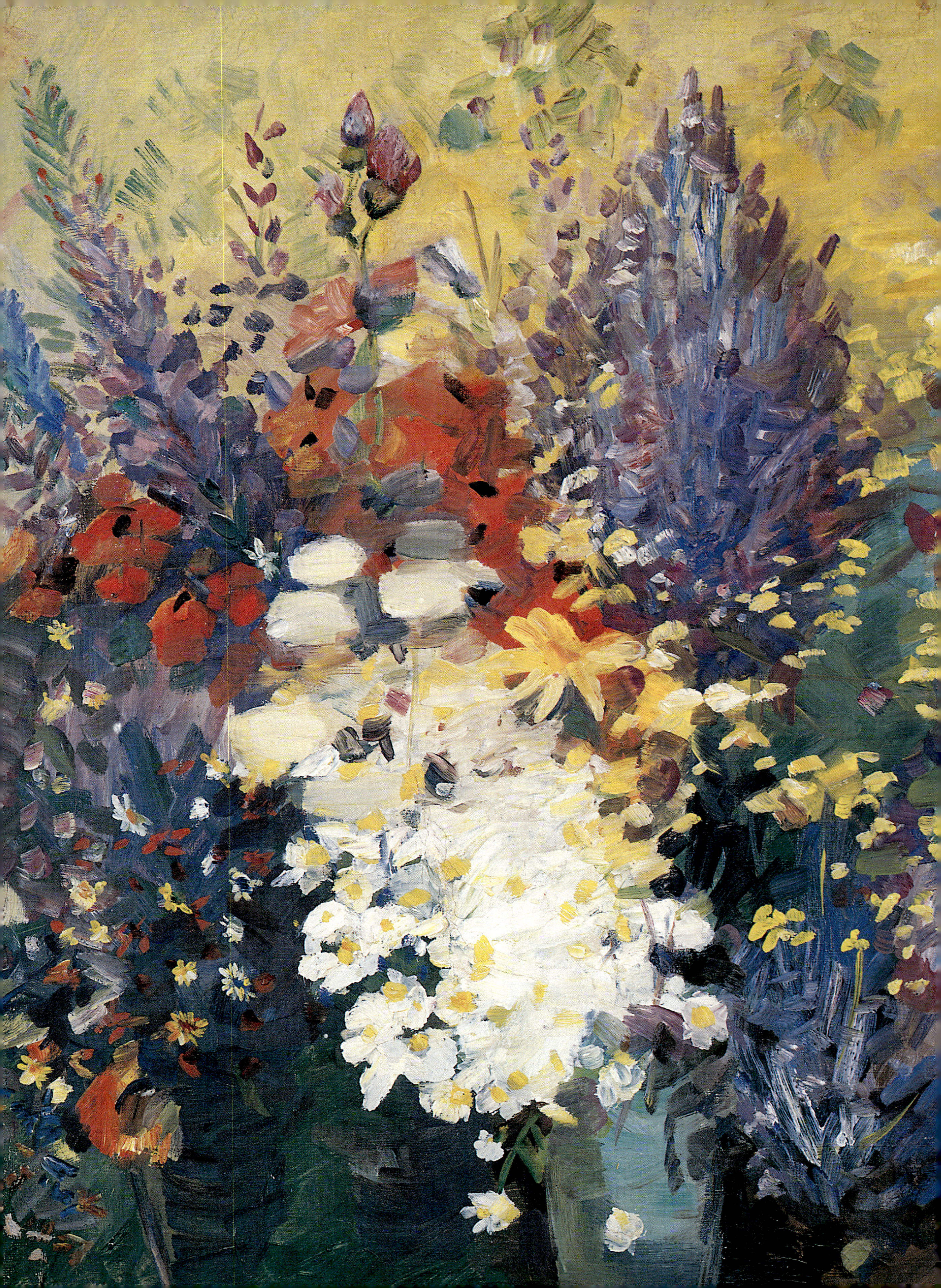

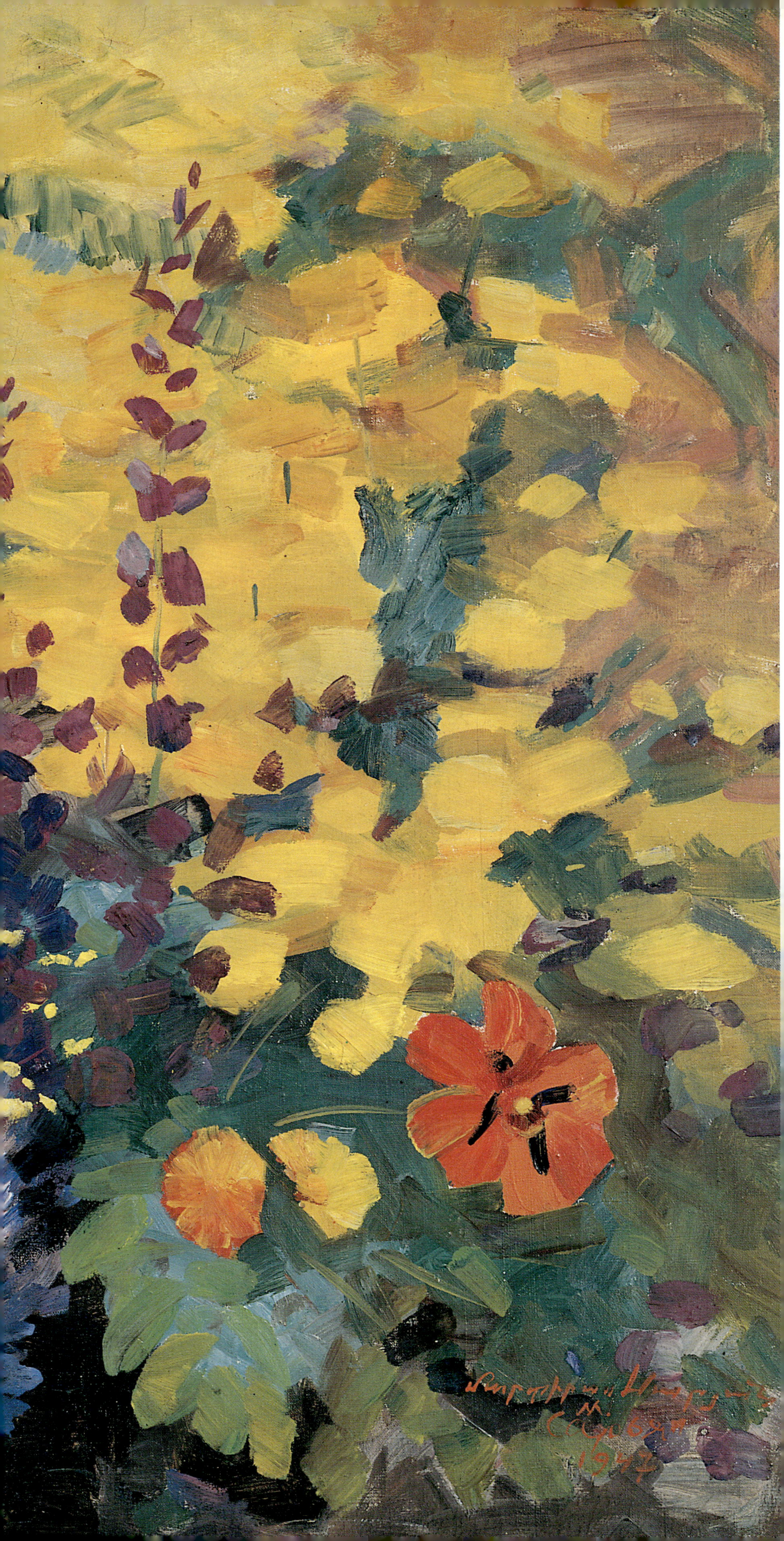
М. Сарьян
1947

The artist decided to put them together, paint them and dedicate the painting to his countrymen who had fought at the front. The different blooms – modest wild flowers and elegant garden varieties – are arranged on a table in simple jars or jugs, seemingly at random, but actually in a considered order, so that the large bright yellow flower in the centre draws to itself this multiplicity of burning colours, bringing it to a unity like a musical chord giving harmony to the chorale. This painting does indeed come across like a festive choral work in honour of the heroes, a tribute of admiration for their great deeds.

In his last years Saryan rarely painted portraits. Those he did are varied in the perfection of their images, but include some splendid works. Above all the portrait of the writer Ilya Ehrenburg (1959) is one of the most profound and psychologically authentic in the artist's œuvre. Its restrained and noble colour scheme accords to the utmost with the image of a tired, aging man, sad, intelligent and ironic, but still concealing a "mutinous and passionate spirit" behind seeming calm.

Saryan created an image of blooming youth in his portrait of his granddaughter Katarine (1963). He painted her against the background of

Portrait of Katarine Saryan. 1963
Oil on canvas. 60 x 79 cm
K. Saryan collection, Yerevan

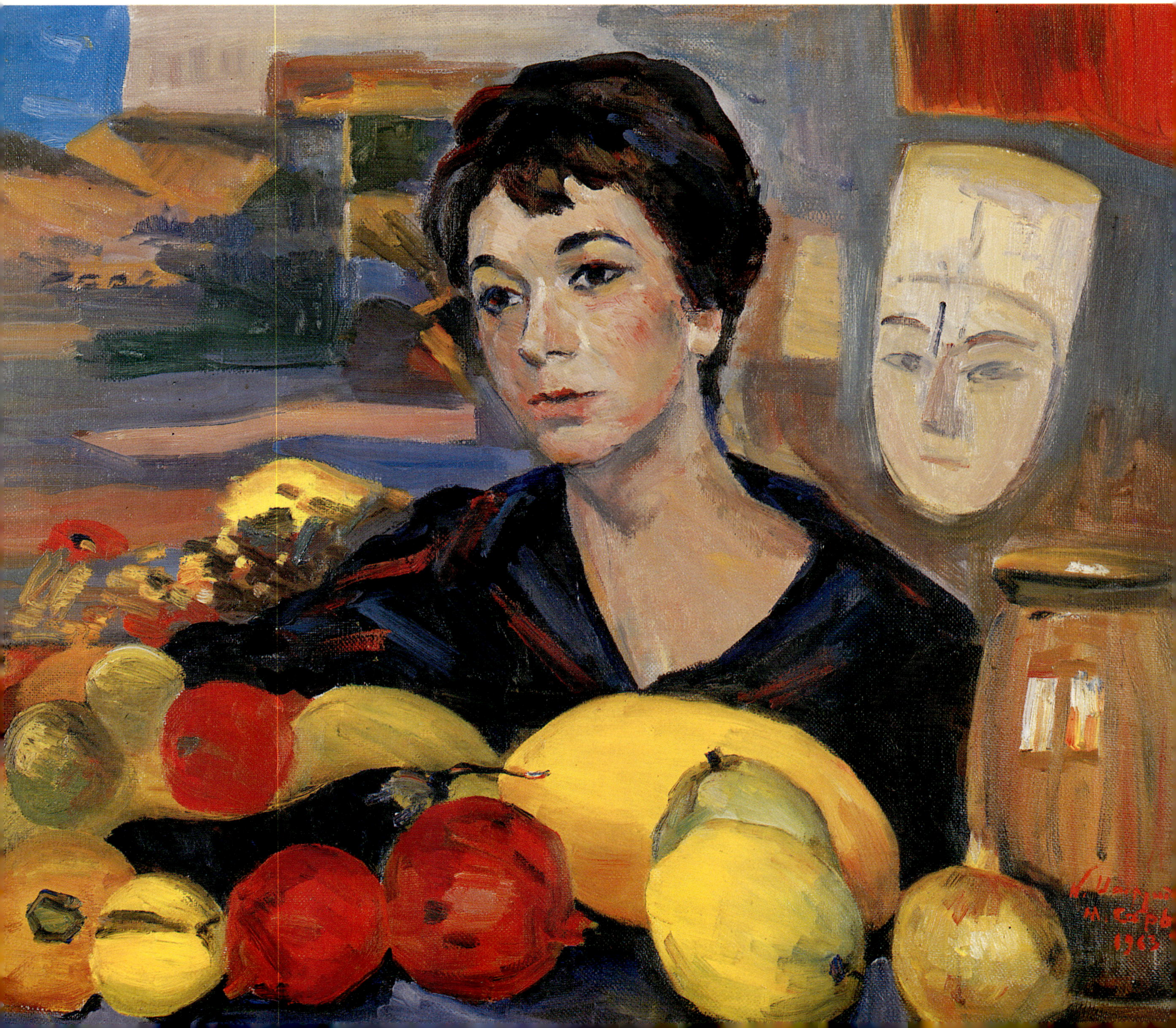

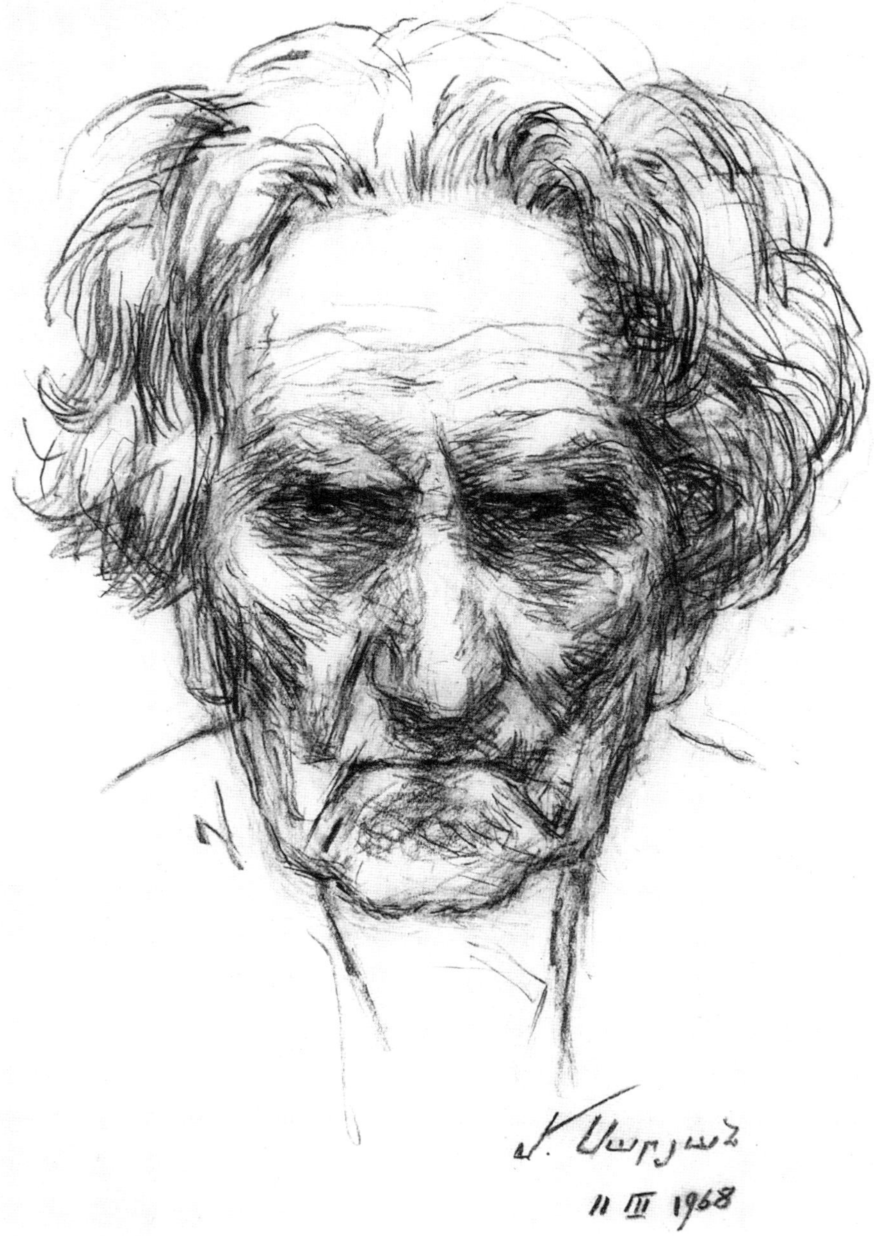

Self-Portrait. 1968
Pencil on paper. 27 x 20 cm
L. Saryan collection, Yerevan

a sparsely indicated landscape, surrounded by objects of which he was so fond and which can so often be found in his still-lifes – fruit, a simple vessel and the mask whose mysterious impenetrability sets off the living charm of the young face. The vivid resonant colours of the fruit and the background introduce a joyful note into the painting, but it is hard not to detect sad intonations of leave-taking in it.

The landscapes produced in the last two decades of the artist's life were as before varied in terms of spatial conception and imagery. There are monumental works synthesizing the rich rhythmic and chromatic variety of the Armenian countryside – *The Collective Farm of Karindzh Village in the Tumanian Mountains* (1952), *Armenia* (1957),[74] and the astonishingly luminescent *A Clear Morning. Biurakan* and *Morning. Ararat and the Valley* (both painted in Biurakan in 1957), and more

→
A Fairy-Tale. 1971
Oil on canvas. 50 x 65 cm
L. Saryan collection, Yerevan

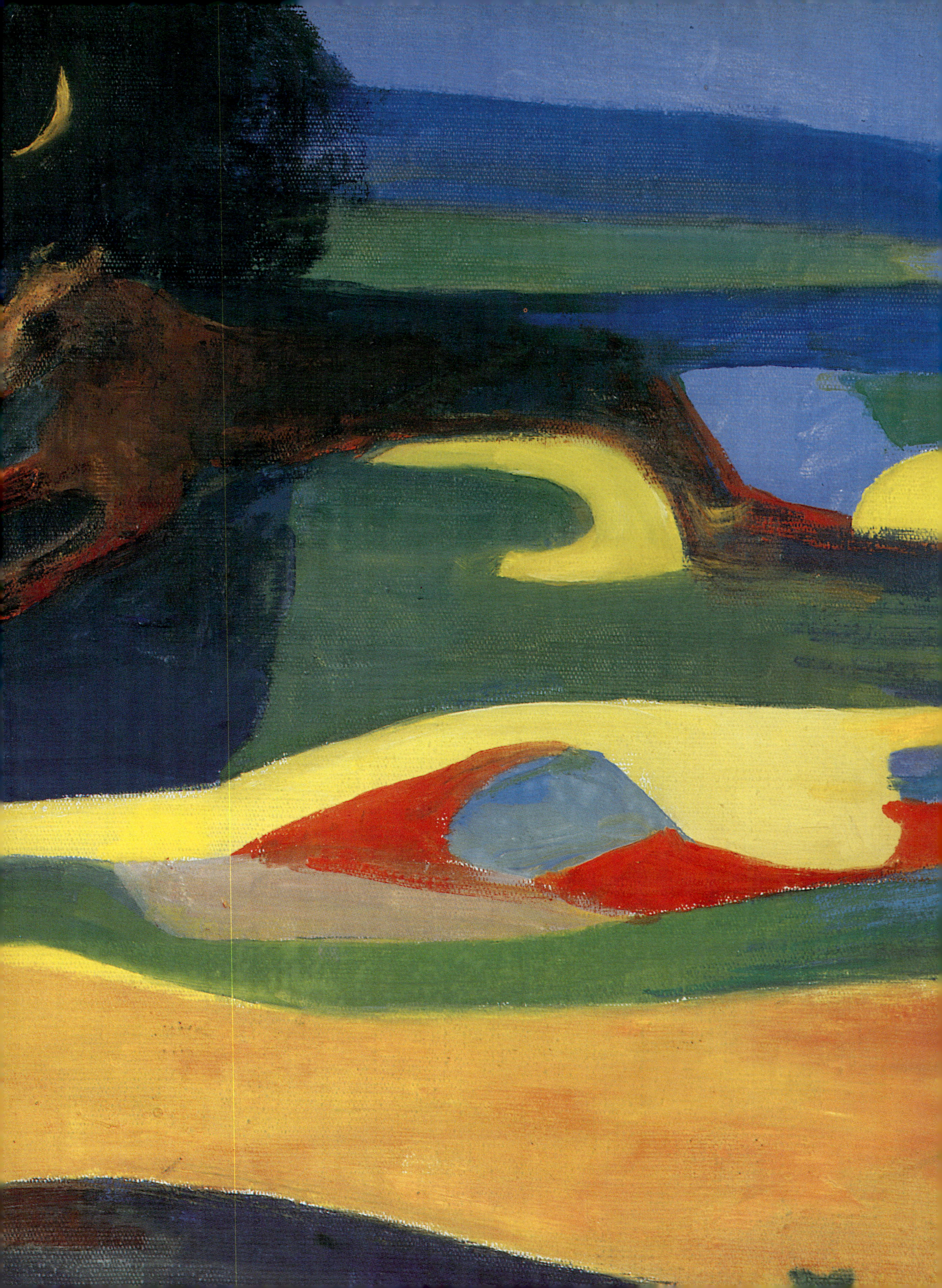

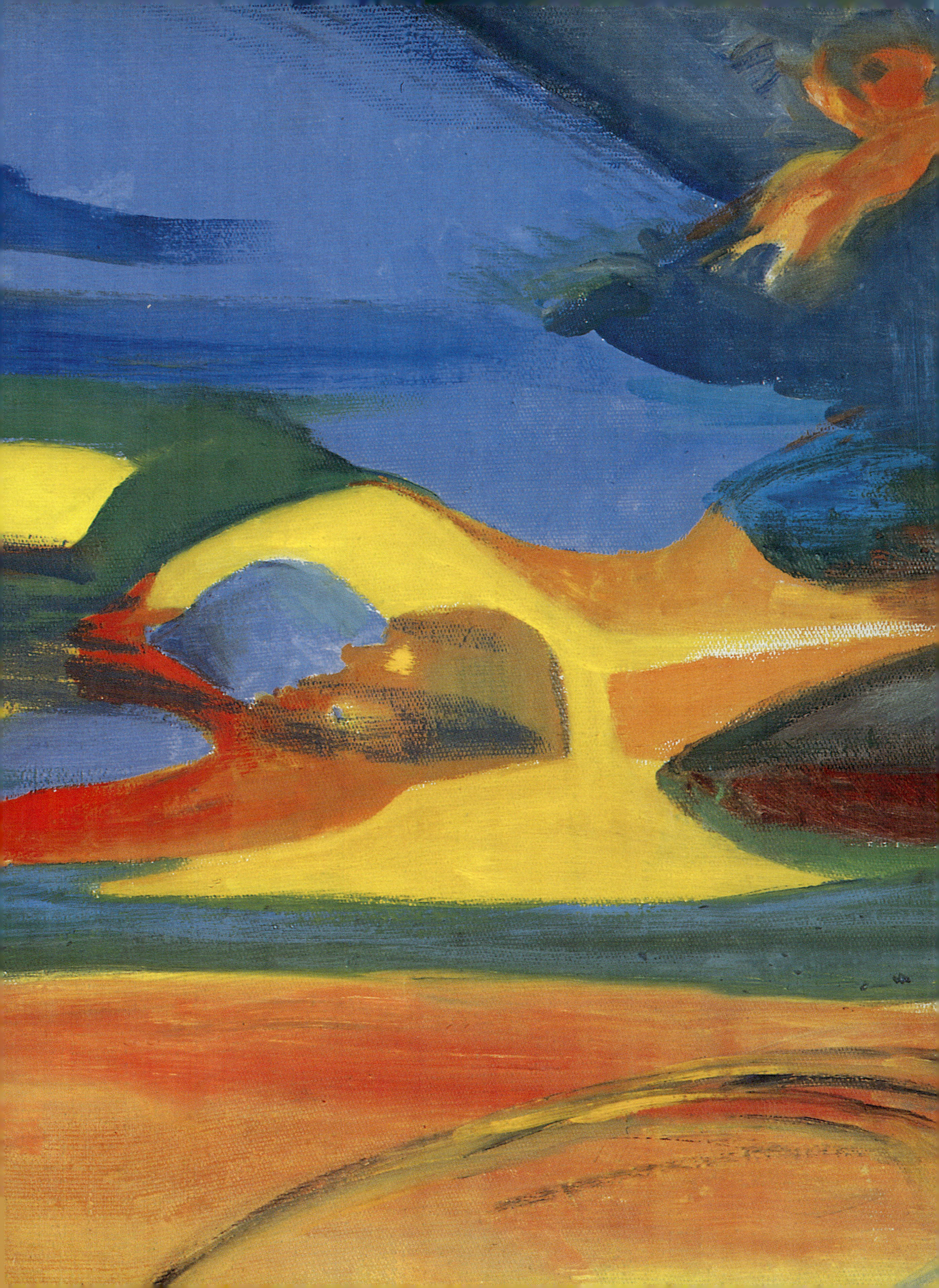

intimate landscapes – *A Corner in Ashtarak* and *The Seventh-Century Karmravor Church. Ashtarak* (both 1956). The year 1958 produced two views of Ararat very different in composition and painterly structure. *Ararat and the Charents Arch* is constructed around the calm relations between the dark silhouette of the arch named after the poet and the lightly and tenderly painted distance with the airy silhouette of the twin peaks. *Precipice on the Slope of Mount Aragats* is on the contrary filled with the tension of forms. The solid ground seems to gape open before us in the pointy ledges of sharply delineated rocks, coloured with flares of the autumnal hues of land and trees. The entire foreground is presented with striking painterly force. Then in the distance this conglomeration of dynamic volumes is opposed to valleys wrapped in translucent shadow and Ararat with its snow-whitened peaks rising into the sky. No one has expressed the poetry and meaning of Saryan's many *Ararats* better than Renato Guttuso: "Ararat is the cradle of the world, the sacred mountain of which Armenians dream and which they can only see, see in order to dream.... And Saryan depicts Ararat in all its reality, gives it a powerful character, but as if he is dreaming it. Saryan takes possession of it, through his painting he joins it to his native land from which it was torn by international treaties. A sense of reality and dream."[75]

Reality and dream are fused into one in Saryan's late decorative panels – the exquisite *Armenia* (1957) iridescent in silvery tones, or *Dance of the Mountains* (1958). In the latter the mountainous terrain, as if permeated by a musical rhythm, takes on a truly planetary character. In his last works (it is no longer easy to call them landscapes) Saryan rejected specific motifs and material forms in order to express ever more general concepts of the earth, the world, the universe. This is the case with *Earth* (1969) and *A Fairy-Tale* (1971) – splendid cosmic visions set down with an unfading sense of chromatic harmony. *A Fairy-Tale* was to be the artist's last painted work. It remained on the easel in his studio in the Saryan House Museum.

A graphic self-portrait from 1968 has preserved the appearance of the artist at the end of his life. The interweaving of impetuous strokes gives rise to the noble head of an old man with a wise and serious gaze. One can read in it both the experience of years lived worthily and a courageous acceptance of the end, as inevitable and natural as life itself. The life that Saryan extolled with such inspiration in his art.

The artist died on 5 May 1972. The numerous exhibitions that have been held almost every year since in many countries of the world have made the significance of his art obvious, a significance that far transcends national borders. As Guttuso wrote in 1975: "Saryan should be seen not only as a great Armenian artist, a national poet of his homeland, but as a powerful and subtle master who occupies an outstanding place among the few true artists of the first half of the twentieth century."[76]

→
Pilgrimage. 1929 Illustration
to the anthology of Armenian folk-tales
Indian ink on paper. 12 x 17 cm
L. Saryan collection, Yerevan

Notes

[1] M.S. Saryan, *From My Life*, Moscow, 1985, p. 74 (in Russian).

[2] *Martiros Saryan: Flowers*. Exhibition catalogue, introduction by Sh. Khachatrian, Moscow, 1987, p. 246 (in Russian).

[3] M.S. Saryan, *From My Life*, p. 13.

[4] K.S. Petrov-Vodkin, *Euclidean Space*, Leningrad, 1982, pp. 107f (in Russian).

[5] Quoted from: A.A. Rusakova, *Symbolism in Russian Painting*, Moscow, 1995, p. 230 (in Russian).

[6] *Ibid.*

[7] Quoted from: *Saryan on Art*, compiled by M. Kazarian and Ya. Khachikian, Yerevan, 1989, p. 132 (in Russian).

[8] Quoted from: *On Saryan: Pages of Art Criticism. Opinions of Contemporaries*, compiled by A.A. Kamensky and Sh. Khachatrian, Yerevan, 1980, p. 458 (in Russian).

[9] Quoted from: M. Voloshin, "M.S. Saryan", *Apollon*, 1913, No 9, p. 14 (in Russian).

[10] Quoted from: *Saryan on Art*, p. 144.

[11] For more details see: A.A. Rusakova, *Symbolism in Russian Painting*, Moscow, 1995.

[12] Quoted from: *Saryan on Art*, p. 162.

[13] Of course, the very idea of a "Blue Rose group" presupposes creative common ground going beyond the limits of the 1907 exhibition.

[14] D.V. Sarabyanov, *Russian Painting of the Late 1900s and Early 1910s: Essays*, Moscow, 1971 (in Russian).

[15] Quoted from: R.T. Drampian, *Saryan*, Moscow, 1964, p. 13 (in Russian).

[16] *On Saryan ...*, p. 460.

[17] *Masters of Art on Art*, vol. 5, pt 1, Moscow, 1969, p. 169 (in Russian).

[18] The critic Sergei Mamontov in a review of the "Golden Fleece" exhibition that appeared in the newspaper *Russkoye slovo* on 30 December 1909.

[19] A direct parallel might be the *khoran* (a decorative element used in the illumination of manusrcipts) in a Gospel created by Toros Toranatsi in 1323.

[20] M. Voloshin, *M.S. Saryan*, p. 16.

[21] *Ibid.*, p. 13.

[22] See: A.A. Rusakova, *Pavel Kuznetsov*, Leningrad, 1977 (in Russian).

[23] As one critic wrote: "Kuznetsov peers at the East, Saryan looks at the East". A. Kairansky, *Utro Rossii*, 21 December 1913 (in Russian).

[24] M.S. Saryan, *From My Life*, p. 84.

[25] Quoted from: M. Voloshin, *M.S. Saryan*, p. 14.

[26] Quoted from: *On Saryan...*, p. 464.

[27] Quoted from: *On Saryan...*, p. 314.

[28] M.S. Saryan, *From My Life*, p. 74.

[29] *Masters of Art on Art*, vol. 3, Moscow, 1931, p. 399.

[30] M.S. Saryan. "On My Life and Work", *Iskusstvo*, 1940, No 2, pp. 80f (in Russian).

[31] D.V. Sarabyanov, *The History of Russian Art in the Late Nineteenth and Early Twentieth Centuries*, Moscow, 1993, p. 137 (in Russian).

[32] M.S. Saryan, "On My Work", *Tvorchestvo*, 1965, No 9, p. 2 (in Russian).

[33] N.N. Punin, "M.S. Saryan", in: *Russian and Soviet Art*, Moscow, 1976, p. 193 (in Russian).

[34] *Henri Matisse*. Exhibition catalogue, introductory article by A. Kostenevich, Moscow, 1993, p. 28 (in Russian).

[35] Quoted from: Sh. Khachatrian, "Saryan's Watercolours and Drawings", in: *On Saryan...*, p. 358.

[36] *Russkoye slovo*, 8 April 1908 (in Russian).

[37] *Apollon*, 1911, No 11.

[38] *Apollon*, 1911, No 1.

[39] M.S. Saryan, *From My Life*, p. 86.

[40] Quoted from: *Saryan on Art*, p. 168.

[41] *Martiros Saryan: Paintings. Watercolours. Drawings. Illustrations. Theatrical Decorative Art.* text and biographical outline by A.A. Kamensky, Leningrad, 1987, p. 112 (in Russian).

[42] A. Isaakian, *Selected Works*, Moscow, 1956, vol. 1, p. 268 (in Russian).

[43] M.S. Saryan, *From My Life*, p. 175.

[44] *Ibid.*, p. 178.

[45] *Ibid.*, pp. 164f.

[46] Quoted from: *On Saryan...*, p. 460.

[47] *Ibid.*

[48] M.S. Saryan, *From My Life...*, p. 214.

[49] Quoted from: *Saryan on Art*, p. 35.

[50] "I love to paint Armenia. To paint from life". See: *Saryan on Art*, p. 165.

[51] Quoted from: *On Saryan...*, p. 77.

[52] Quoted from: *Saryan on Art*, p. 47.

[53] *Ibid.*, p. 15.

[54] *Saryan on Art*, p. 23.

[55] Andrei Bely, *Armenia*, p. 31.

[56] R.G. Drampian, *Saryan*, Moscow, 1964, p. 34 (in Russian).

[57] M.S. Saryan, *From My Life*, p. 265.

[58] Quoted from: *On Saryan...*, p. 470.

[59] M.S. Saryan, *From My Life*, p. 267.

[60] Martiros Saryan: *Paintings. Watercolours. Drawings...*, p. 162.

[61] Quoted from: *On Saryan...*, p. 471.

[62] B. Ternovets, *Four Panels*, quoted from: *On Saryan...*, p. 141.

[63] M. Saryan, "*On My Life and Work*", *Iskusstvo*, 1940, No 2, p. 81.

[64] Quoted from: *Martiros Saryan: Portraits*. Exhibition catalogue, introduction by Sh. Khachatrian, Moscow, 1988, p. 21 (in Russian).

[65] *Martiros Saryan: Portraits*, p. 19.

[66] L. Singer, "Saryan's Painting *My Family*", *Iskusstvo*, 1980, No 2, p. 42 (in Russian).

[67] *Ibid.*, p. 42.

[68] Quoted from: *Saryan on Art*, pp. 65f.

[69] M.S. Saryan, *From My Life*, p. 52.

[70] Toramanian died a matter of days after this portrait was completed.

[71] Quoted from: *Saryan on Art*, p. 160.

[72] Speech at a meeting in Moscow on 14 June 1965. Quoted from: *On Saryan...*, p. 476.

[73] *Martiros Saryan: Flowers*. Exhibition catalogue, introduction by Sh. Khachatrian, Moscow, 1987, p. 247.

[74] Saryan included them in the *My Homeland* cycle that won the Lenin Prize.

[75] R. Guttuso, "Some Words about Saryan" (foreword to the catalogue of the Saryan exhibition in Bologna in 1975). Quoted from the Russian translation included in *On Saryan...*, p. 402.

[76] *Ibid.*, p. 409.

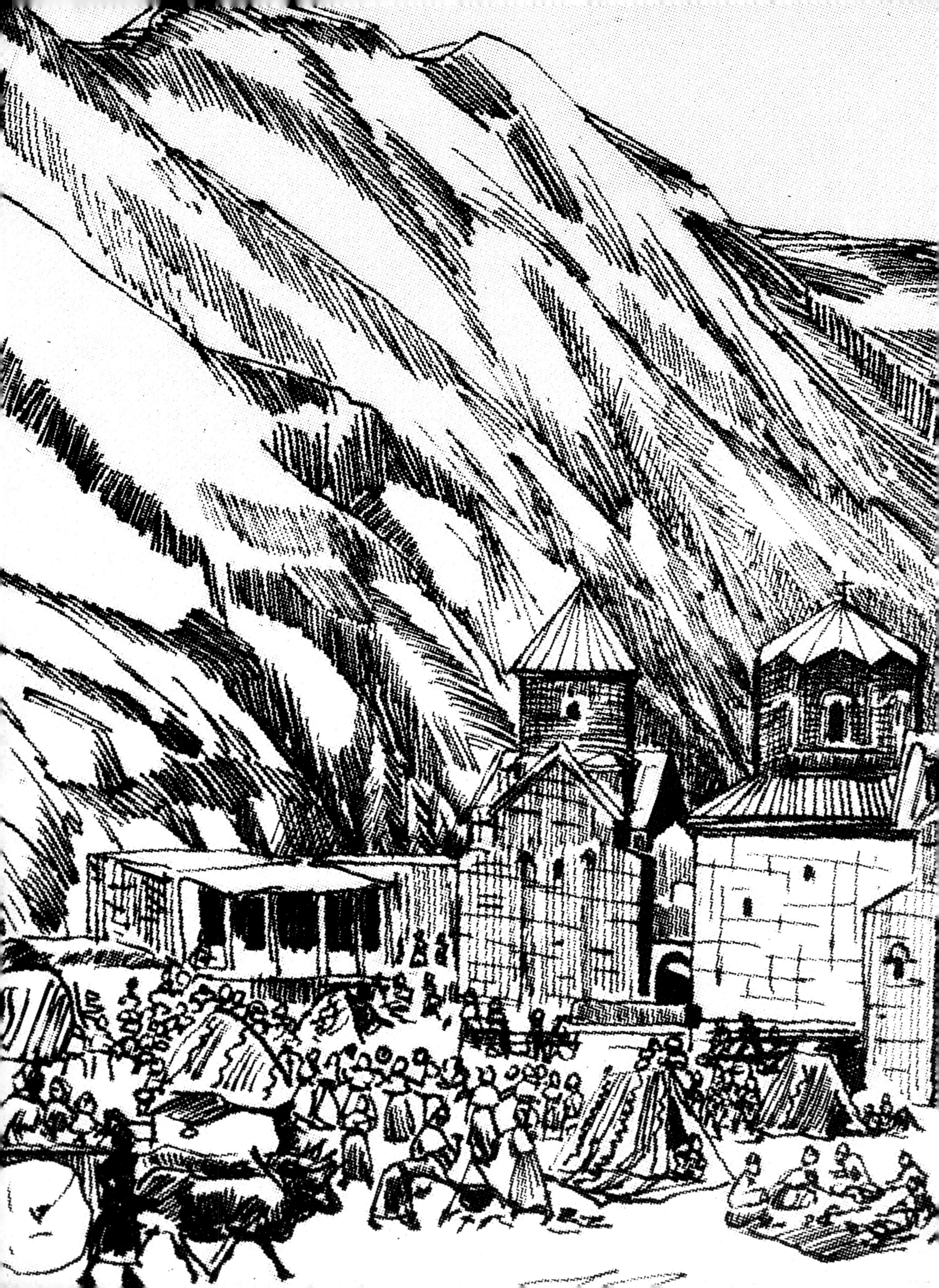

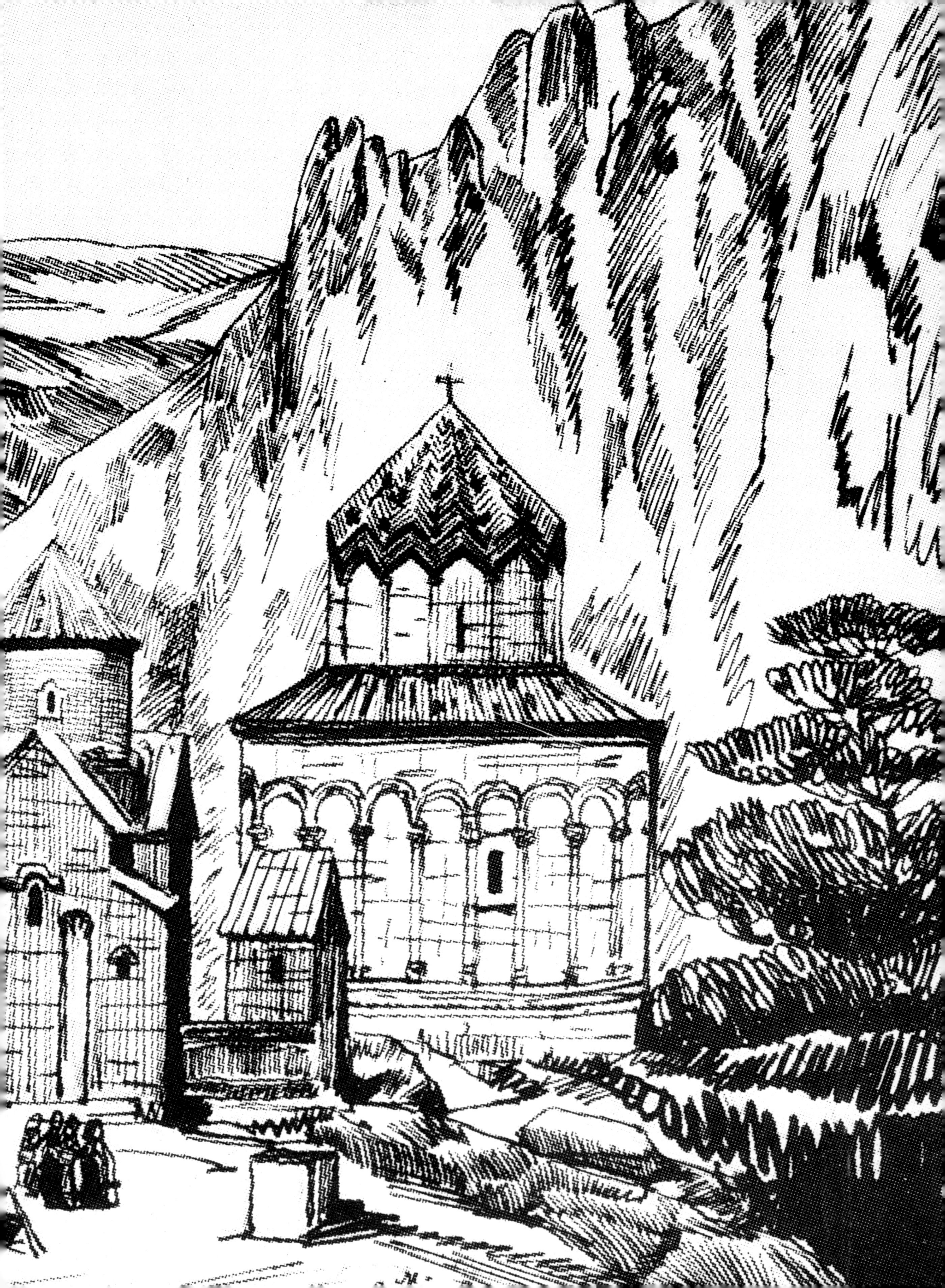

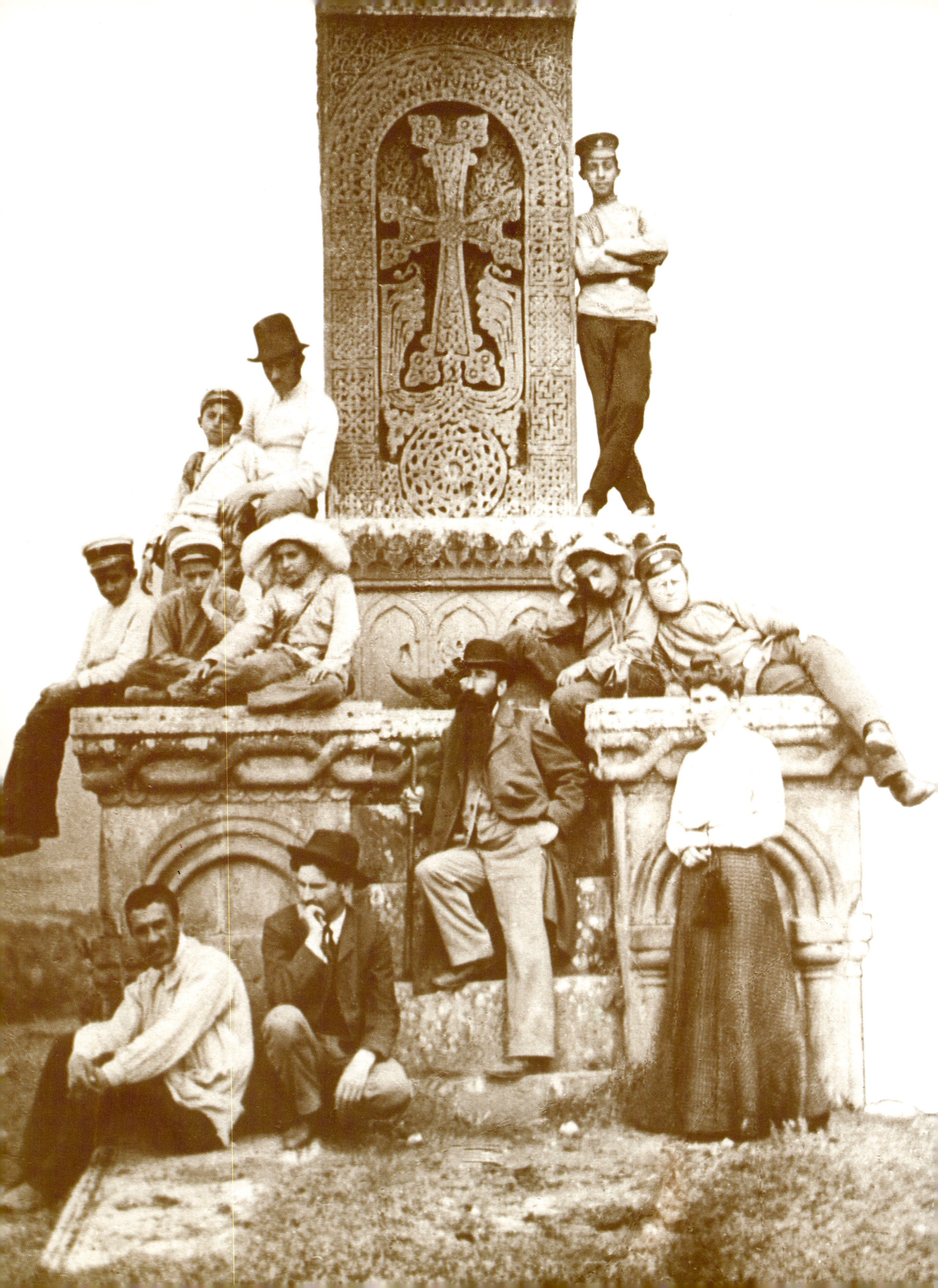

CHRONICLE OF THE ARTIST'S LIFE AND WORK

1880

28 February (16 February Old Style) born in the town of Nakhichevan-on-Don. His father, Sarkis, and mother, Ustiana, have a small plot of land outside the town by the River Sambek, where the future artist spends his early years. He is the seventh of nine children.

1887

Moves into the town of Nakhichevan-on-Don, one of the centres of Armenian culture of the time.

1889–95

Goes to school at the Armenian-Russian municipal college.

1895–96

Works in a newspaper and magazine distribution office.

1896

Hovannes, his elder brother, having provided the money, Saryan travels to Moscow, where he prepares to enter the College of Painting, Sculpture and Architecture. H. Artsatbanian helps him to prepare for the admission test.

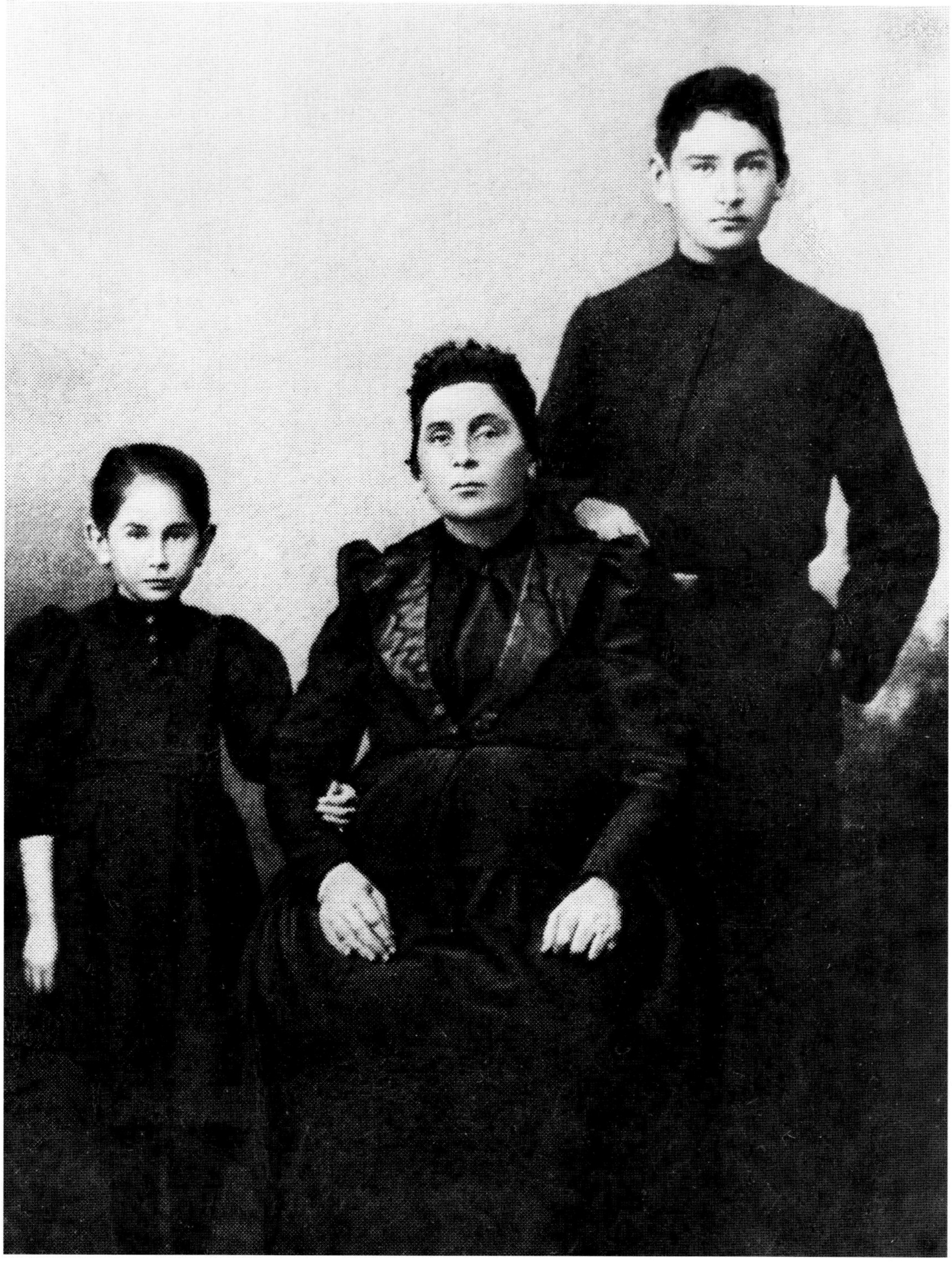

Martiros Saryan (second from left). Sanakhin. Photograph, 1902

Martiros Saryan with his mother and sister. Photograph, 1897

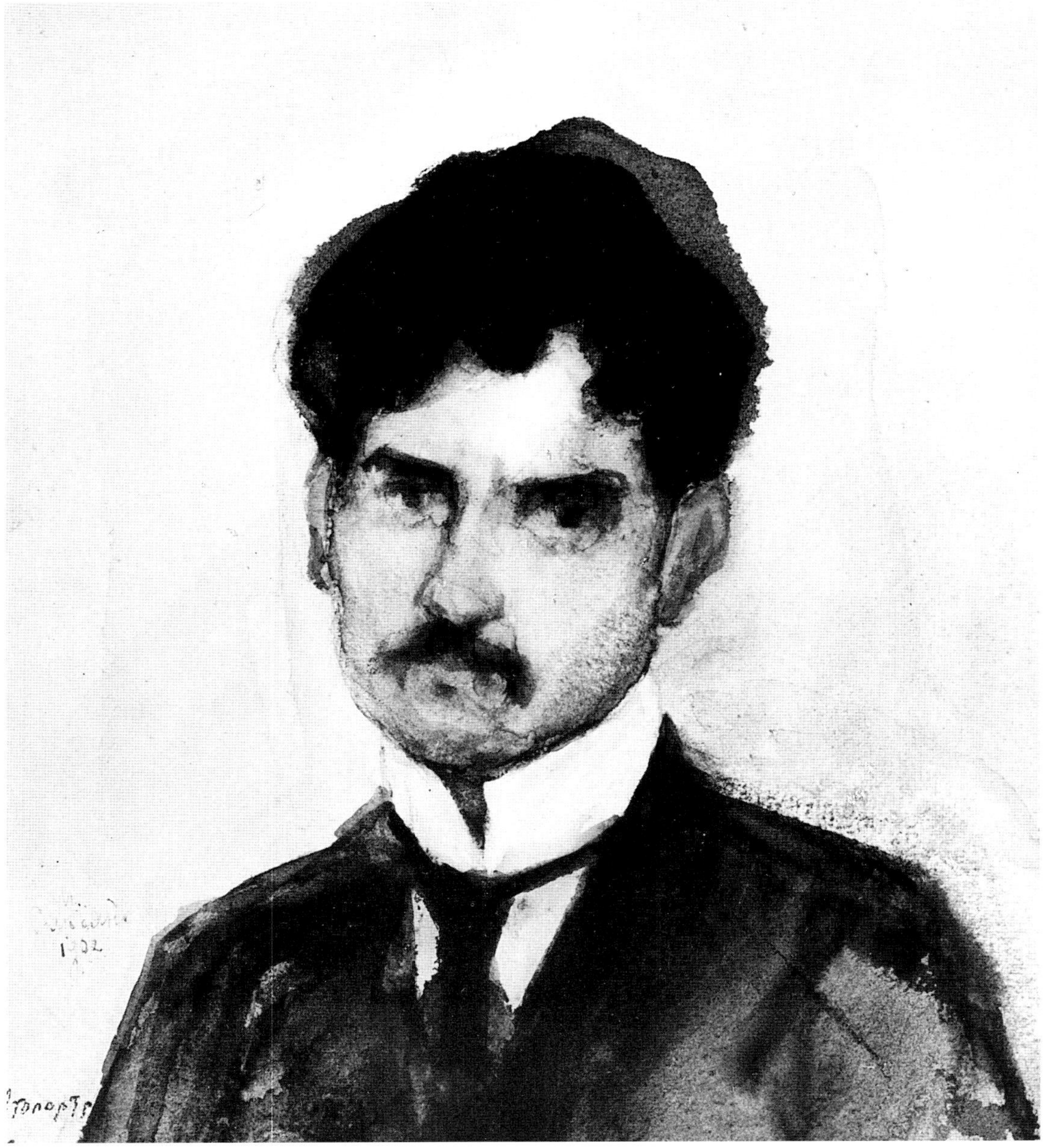

Self-Portrait. 1902
Watercolour on paper. 22 x 20 cm
Martiros Saryan Museum, Yerevan

1897–1903

Studies at the Moscow College of Painting, Sculpture and Architecture, graduating with two silver medals.

1900–02

First journeys, during the summer holidays, to Georgia and Armenia. Visits Ani, the ancient capital of Armenia, where he meets Toros Toramanian, an architect and expert on ancient and mediaeval monuments. Paints his first views of Armenia, *Makravank* and *Mount Aragats*, and other landscapes which serve as the sets for Armenian concerts arranged for the Moscow public.

1900–04

Participates in the exhibitions of the College of Painting, Sculpture and Architecture.

1903–04

Studies in the portrait studio under the direction of Valentin Serov and Konstantin Korovin.

1903–05

Creates the first works in the *Fairy-Tales and Dreams* cycle. Participates in the Scarlet Rose exhibition in Saratov.

1906–07

First acquaintance with new French painting in Sergei Shchukin's collection and at the exhibitions organized by the *Golden Fleece* (*Zolotoye Runo*) magazine. Travels around Georgia and Armenia.
The weekly *Nor kiank* [*New Life*] publishes Saryan's first articles devoted to the art of Ancient Egypt and mediaeval Armenian architecture.

1907

Participates in the Blue Rose exhibition in Moscow.

1908–10

Participates in the exhibitions organized by the magazine *The Golden Fleece* in Moscow.

1910

Travels to Turkey (Constantinople). Participates in the exhibition of the Moscow Association of Artists. His paintings *Wisteria* and *Fruit Stall* are purchased by the Tretyakov Gallery, later so is *Street. Noon*.

1911

Travels to Egypt.

1912

Travels to the north-western parts of Armenia.

1913

Travels to Persia.
The magazine *Apollon* publishes an article on Saryan by Maximilian Voloshin.

1914

Travels to Georgia and Armenia.
Participates in the World of Art exhibition in Moscow.

1915

Moves to Tiflis, Georgia. Then travels to Armenia to participate in the work of the Refugees' Relief Committee
Participates in the World of Art exhibition in Moscow in the autumn.

1916

Returns to Tiflis where he marries Lusik Agayan.
Participates in the World of Art exhibition in Moscow for the last time.

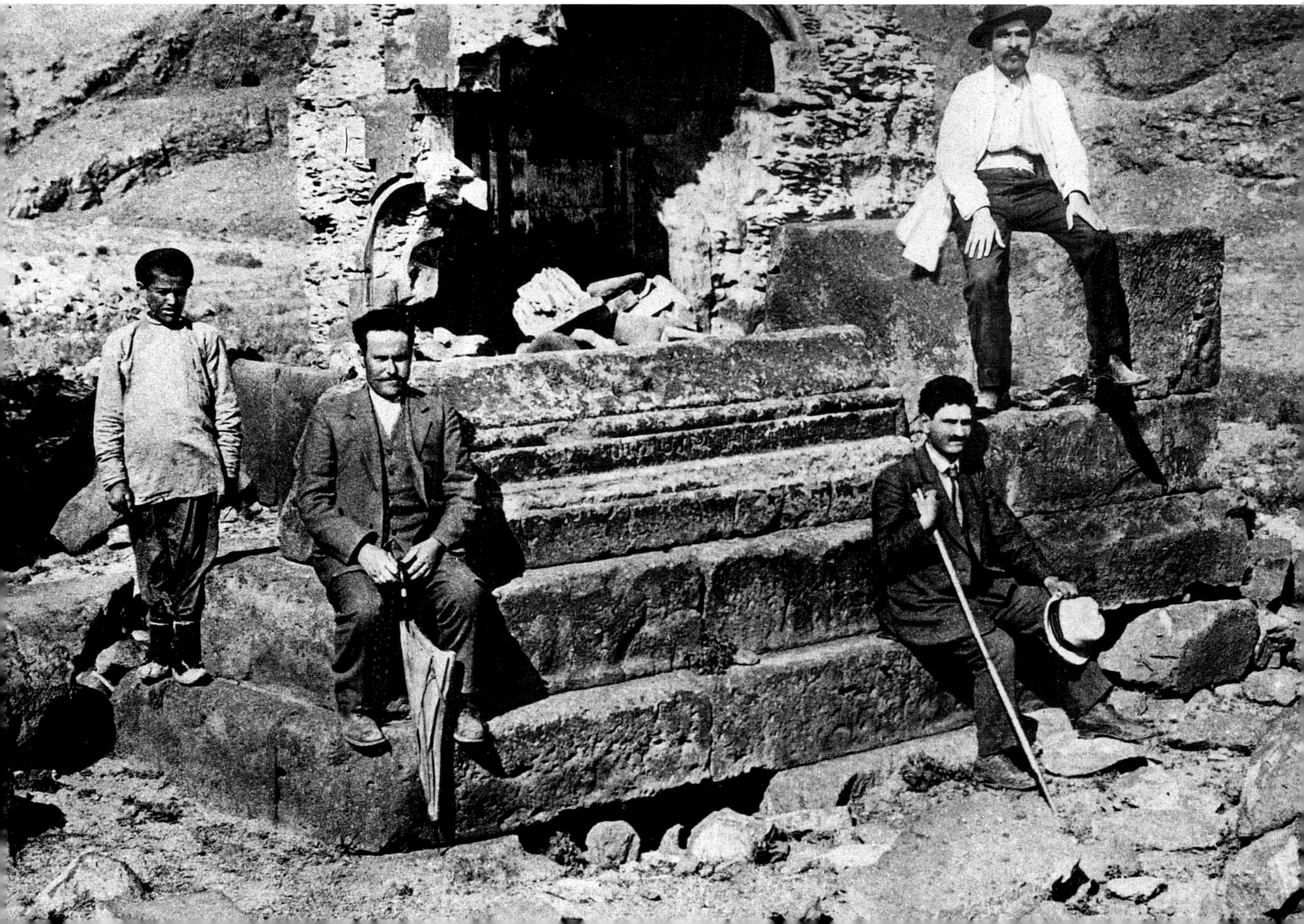

Saryan in Ani. Photograph, 1903

1917

Moves back to Nakhichevan-on-Don. Frequently visits Tiflis. His son Sarkis is born.

1918–19

Organizes the Armenian Local History Museum in Rostov-on-Don. Participates in the Lotus exhibition in Rostov.

1920

His son Gazaros (Lazar) is born.

1921

Moves to Yerevan with his family. Organizes the Museum of Archaeology, Ethnography and Fine Arts. Is involved in the creation of the Yerevan Art College and Union of Artists.

1922–23

Returns to creative work after an appreciable break. Paints landscapes of Armenia.
Creates a curtain for the State Drama Theatre of Armenia, which soon becomes widely recognized as an artistic symbol of the Armenian Republic.

1924

Travels to Italy. Participates in the 14th International Biennale in Venice.

1925

Participates in the Four Arts exhibition in Moscow.

1926

Awarded the title of People's Artist of Armenia.

1926–28

An officially-sanctioned working visit to France.

1929

Participates in the Four Arts exhibitions in Yerevan and Moscow. Produces the cover and illustrations for an anthology of Armenian folk-tales.

1930s

Works for the theatre (*Golden Cockerel*, *Bold Nazar*, *Almast*) and in book illustration. Produces numerous paintings, both easel and monumental works.

Saryan at his one-man exhibition in Paris. Photograph, 1928

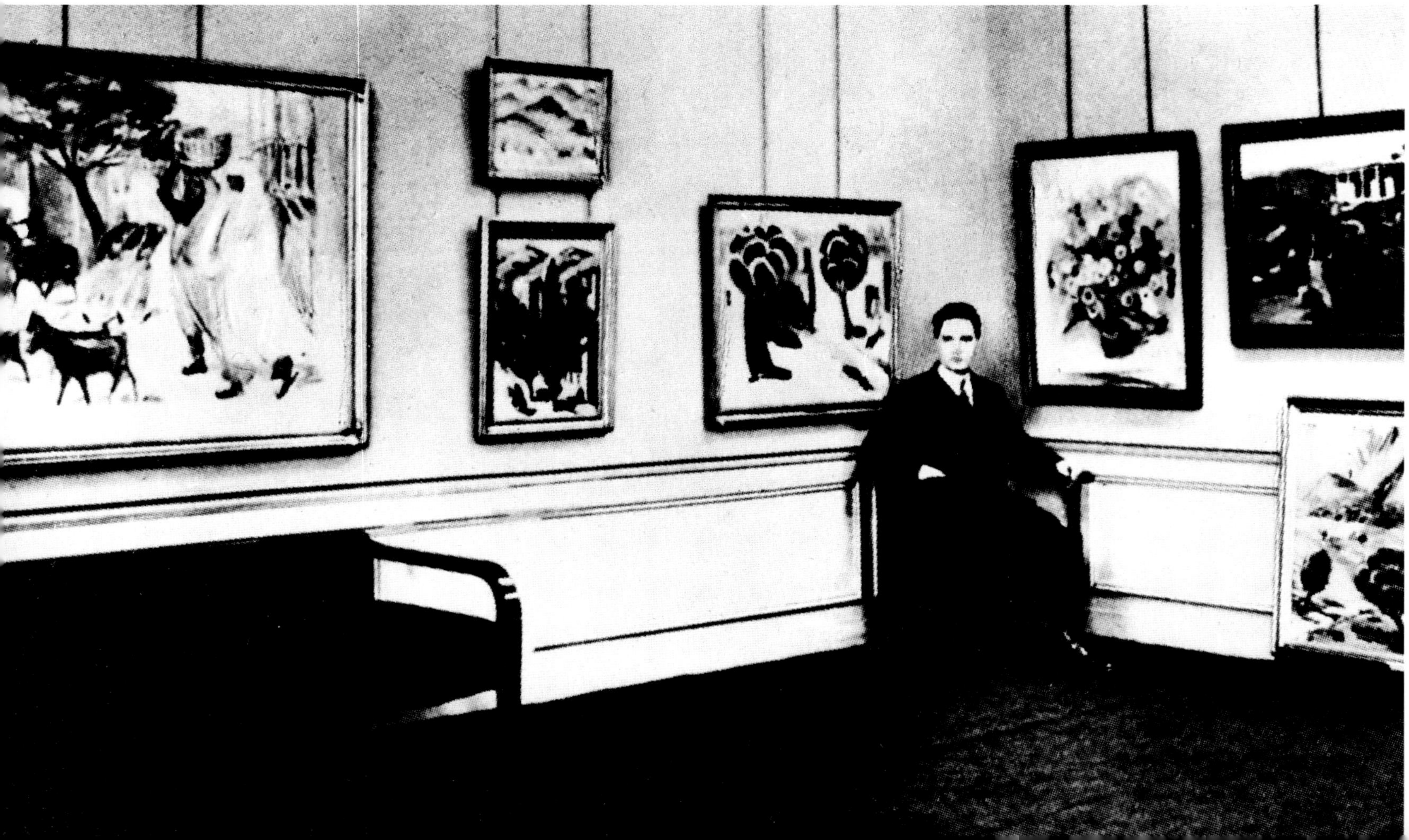

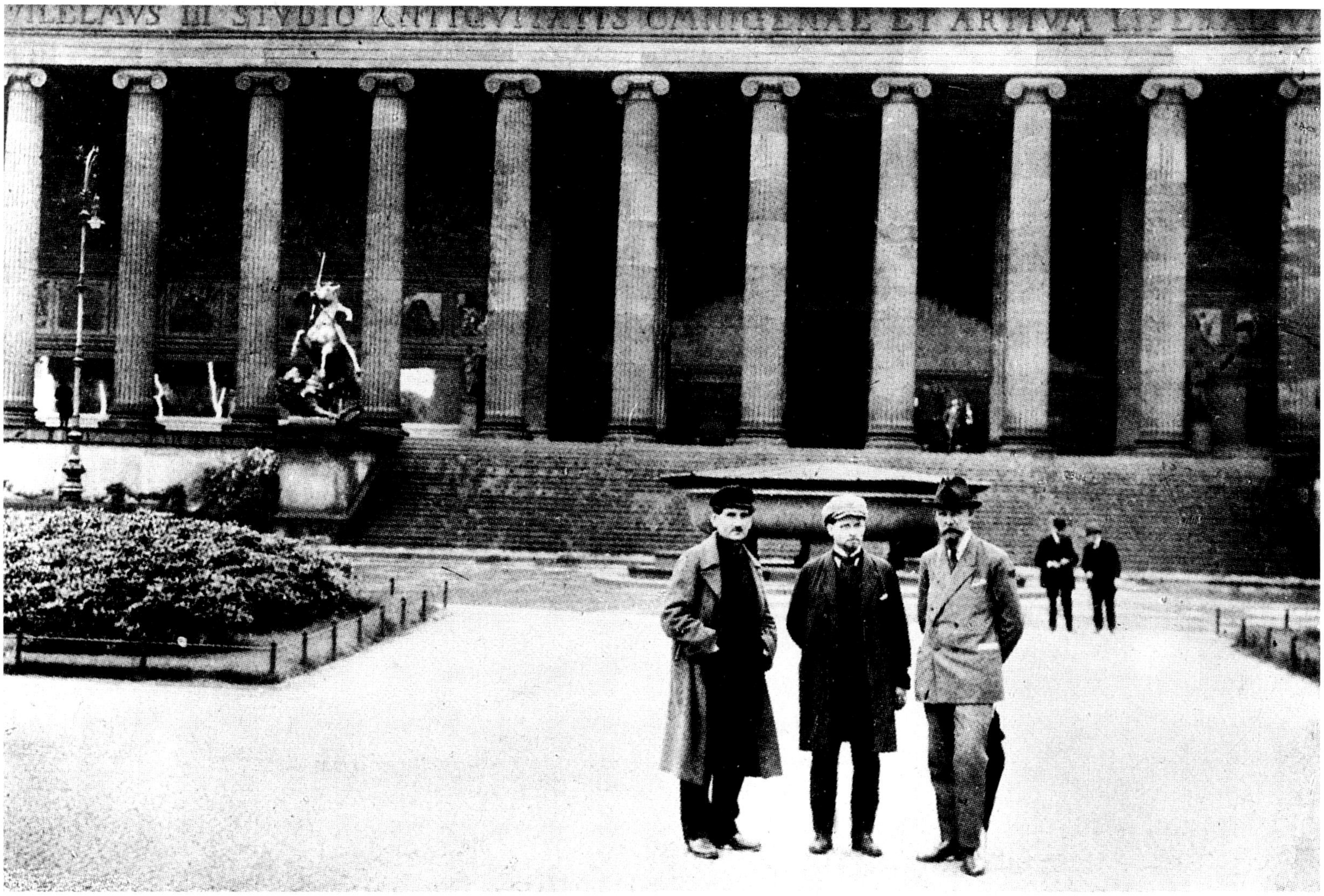

Saryan in Berlin. Photograph, 1924

Participates in many exhibitions in the Soviet Union and abroad (Vienna, Venice, Stockholm, Bern, Zurich, Copenhagen, New York, Philadelphia).

1934

Travels to Ashkhabad. Produces a cycle of paintings on Turkmenian themes.

1936

One-man exhibitions in Moscow and Leningrad.

1937

The Grand-Prix for the decorative panel in the Soviet pavilion at the World Exhibition in Paris.

1939

Creates a monumental panel for the Armenian pavilion at the All-Union Agricultural Exhibition in Moscow.

1940

The periodical *Iskusstvo* (*Art*) (issue 2) publishes the artist's article *On My Life and Work*.

1941

Awarded the USSR State Prize for his design of the opera *Almast* in the Spendiarov Theatre of Opera and Ballet in Yerevan.

1945

Awarded the Order of Lenin and the medals "For the Defence of the Caucasus" and "For Valorous Labour during the Great Patriotic War 1941–45".

1947

Named among the first members of the newly-created USSR Academy of Arts.

1950

Awarded a second Order of Lenin.

1956

Elected a full member of the Armenian SSR Academy of Sciences.

1958

The Grand-Prix at the World Exhibition in Brussels.

1960

The artist's eightieth birthday is widely celebrated in the USSR.

Awarded the title of People's Artist of the USSR.

1961

Awarded the Lenin Prize for the *My Homeland* cycle of paintings. One-man exhibition in Yerevan.

1962

Saryan's elder son Sarkis dies in a car accident.

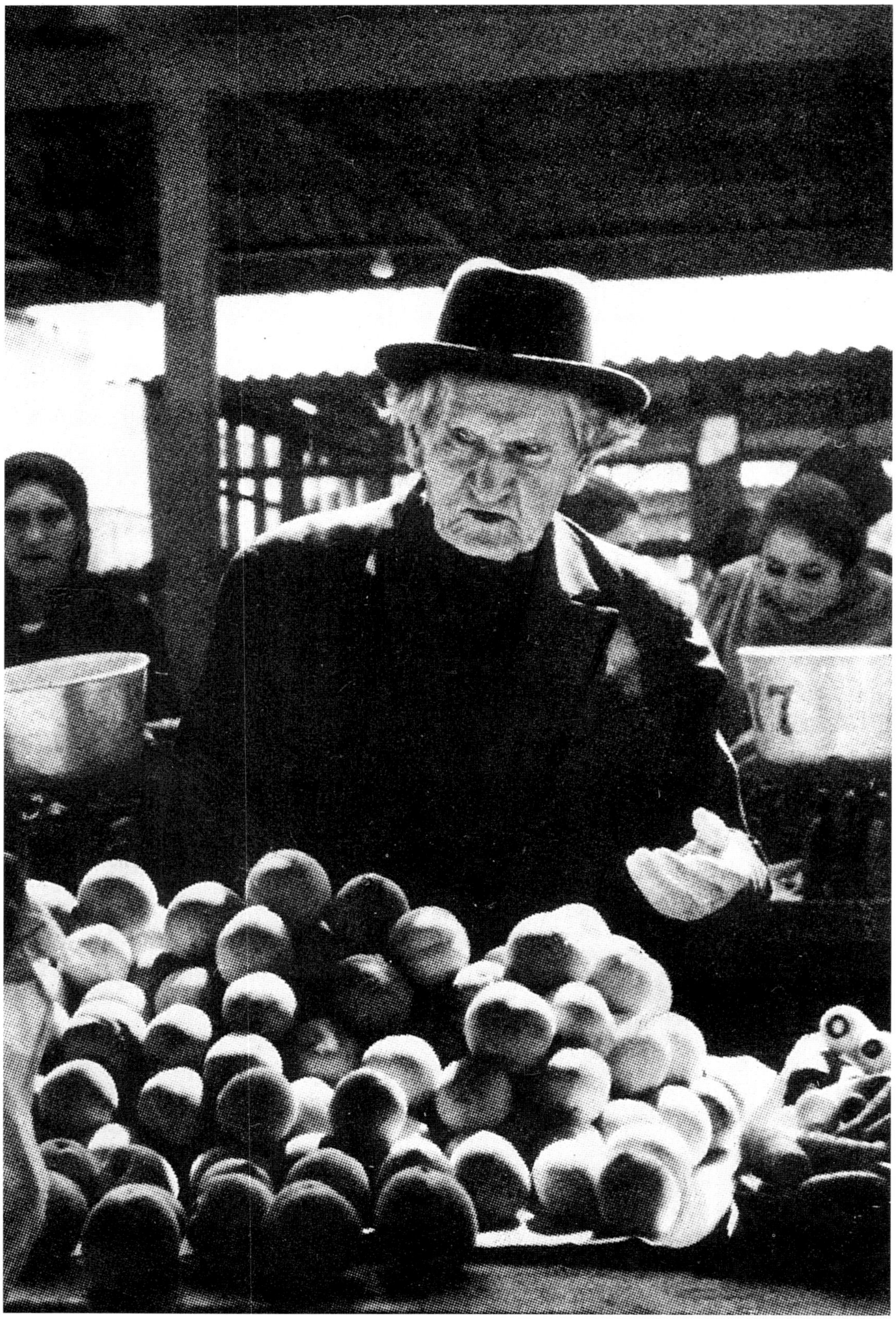

Saryan at the market in Yerevan.
Photograph, 1968

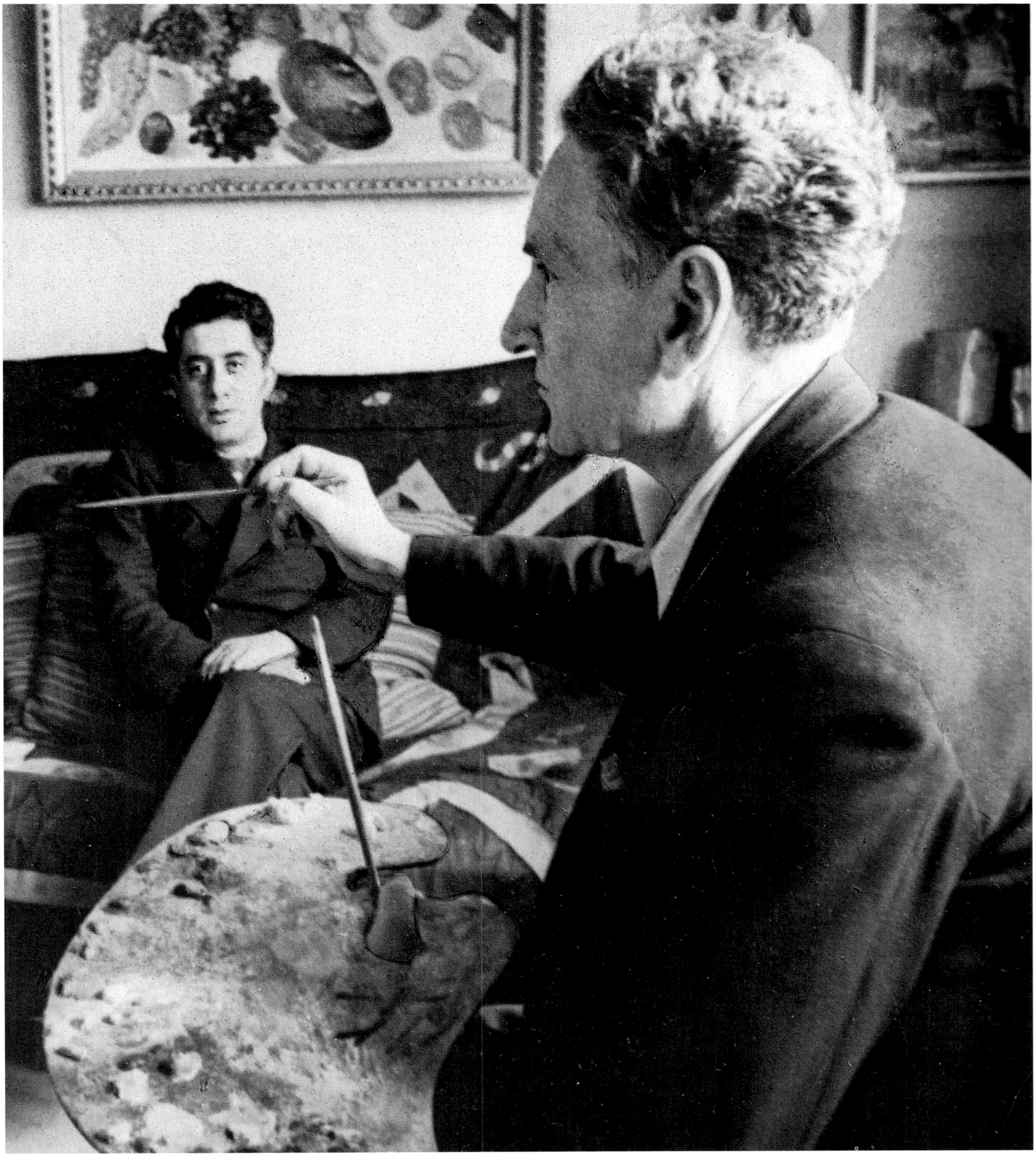

Saryan painting the composer Aram Khachaturian. Photograph, 1944

1964

One-man exhibitions in Moscow and Leningrad (theatre designs and portraits of theatrical figures).

1965

One-man exhibitions in Moscow, Yerevan and Bucharest.

Awarded the title of Hero of Socialist Labour on the occasion of his eighty-fifth birthday.

1966

Awarded the State Prize of the Armenian SSR for his paintings of the 1960s. Saryan's memoirs

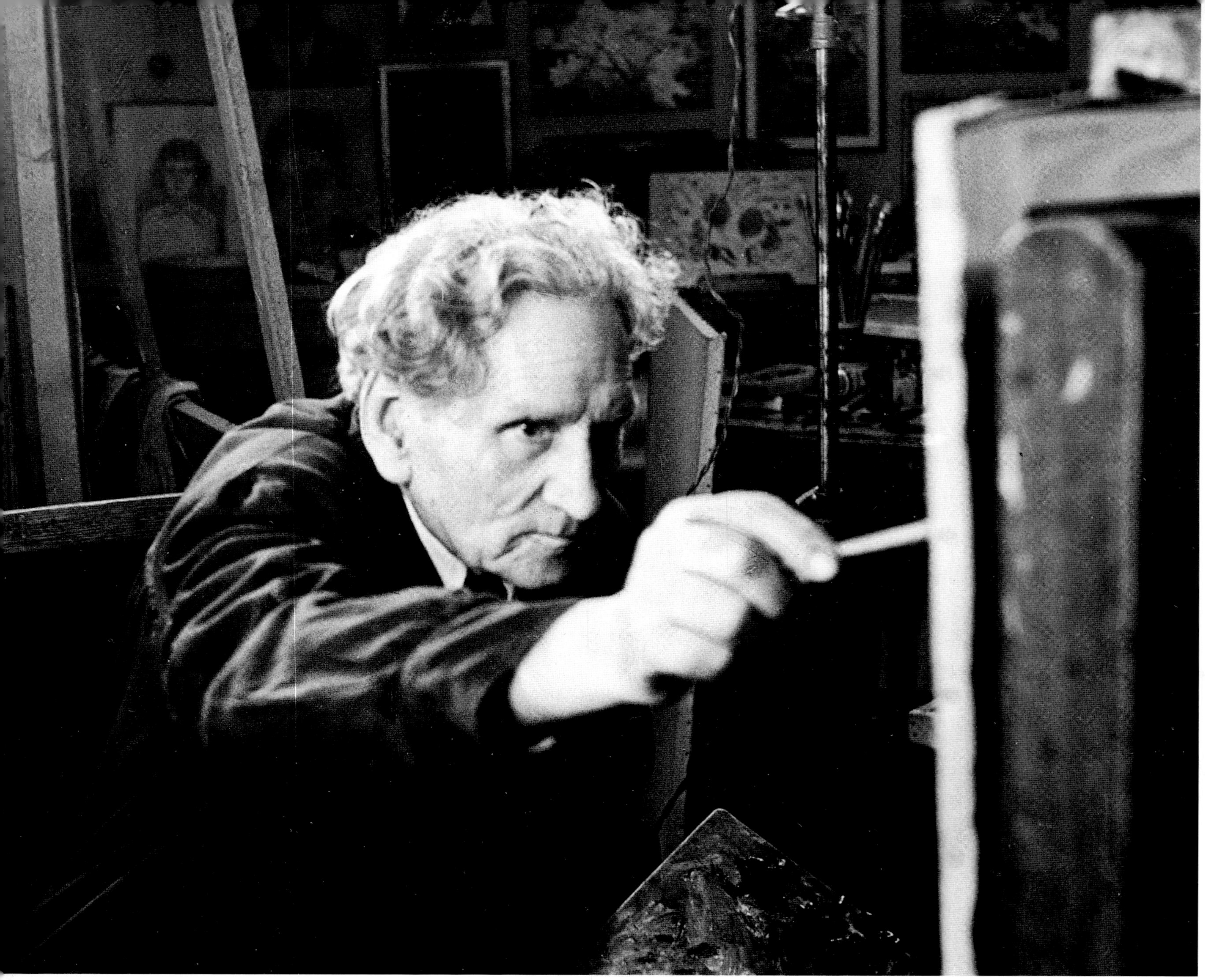

From My Life are published in Armenian in Yerevan. Later Russian, French, Japanese and other translations appear.

1966–69

One-man exhibitions in USSR cities, and also in Romania, Czechoslovakia, Hungary and East Germany.

1967

The Martiros Saryan Museum is opened in Yerevan.

1967–71

Creates his last cycle of paintings and drawings.

1970

The artist's ninetieth birthday is widely celebrated in the USSR and abroad.
Awarded a third order of Lenin.
One-man exhibition of drawings and watercolours in Yerevan.
One-man exhibition in Kiev.

1972

5 May: dies in Yerevan.
11 May: buried in the Yerevan Pantheon.

Martiros Saryan. Photograph, 1965

Saryan's studio. Photograph

→
Earth. 1969
Oil on canvas. 44 x 56 cm
Martiros Saryan Museum, Yerevan

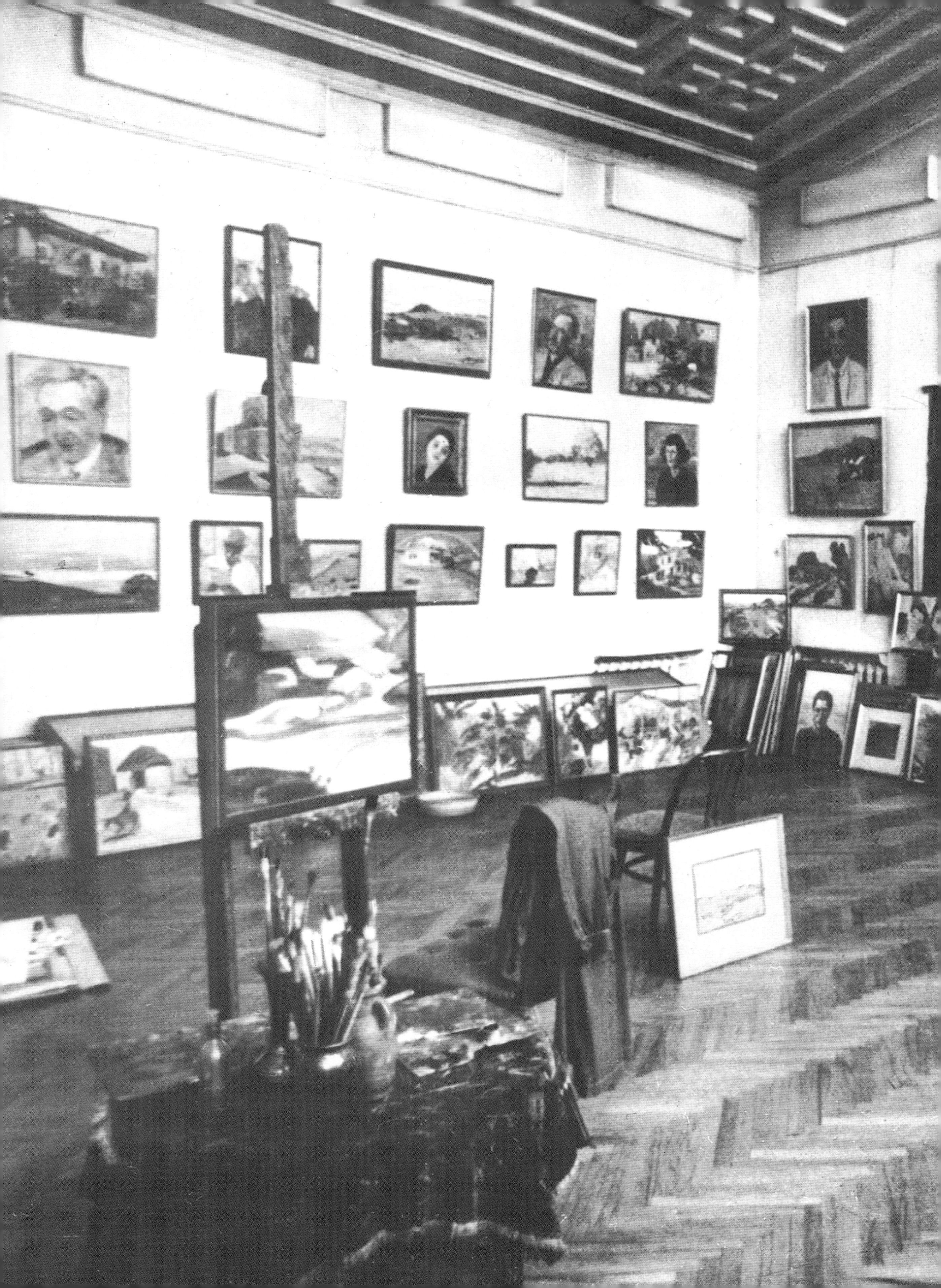

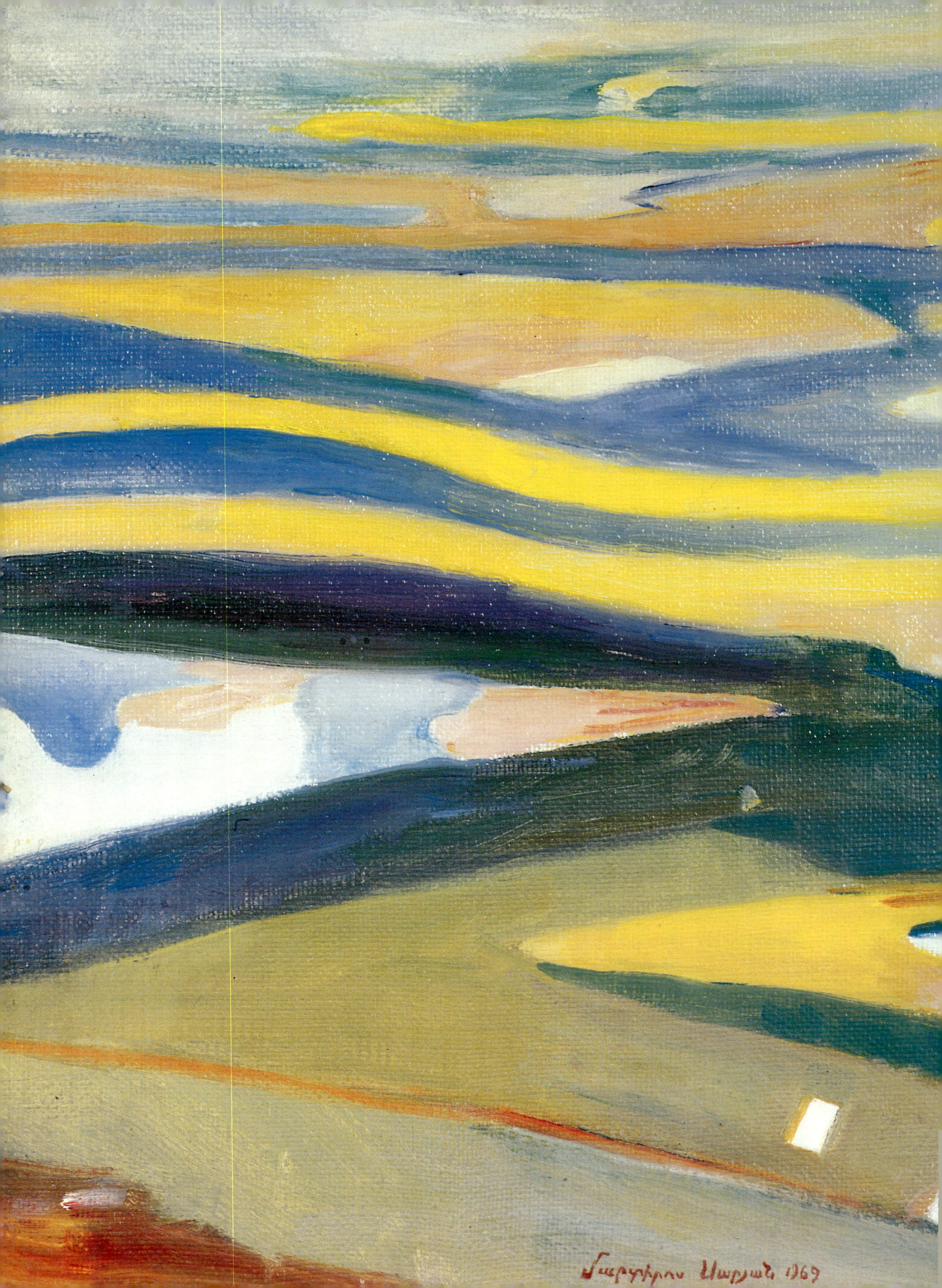
Մարտիրոս Սարյան 1969

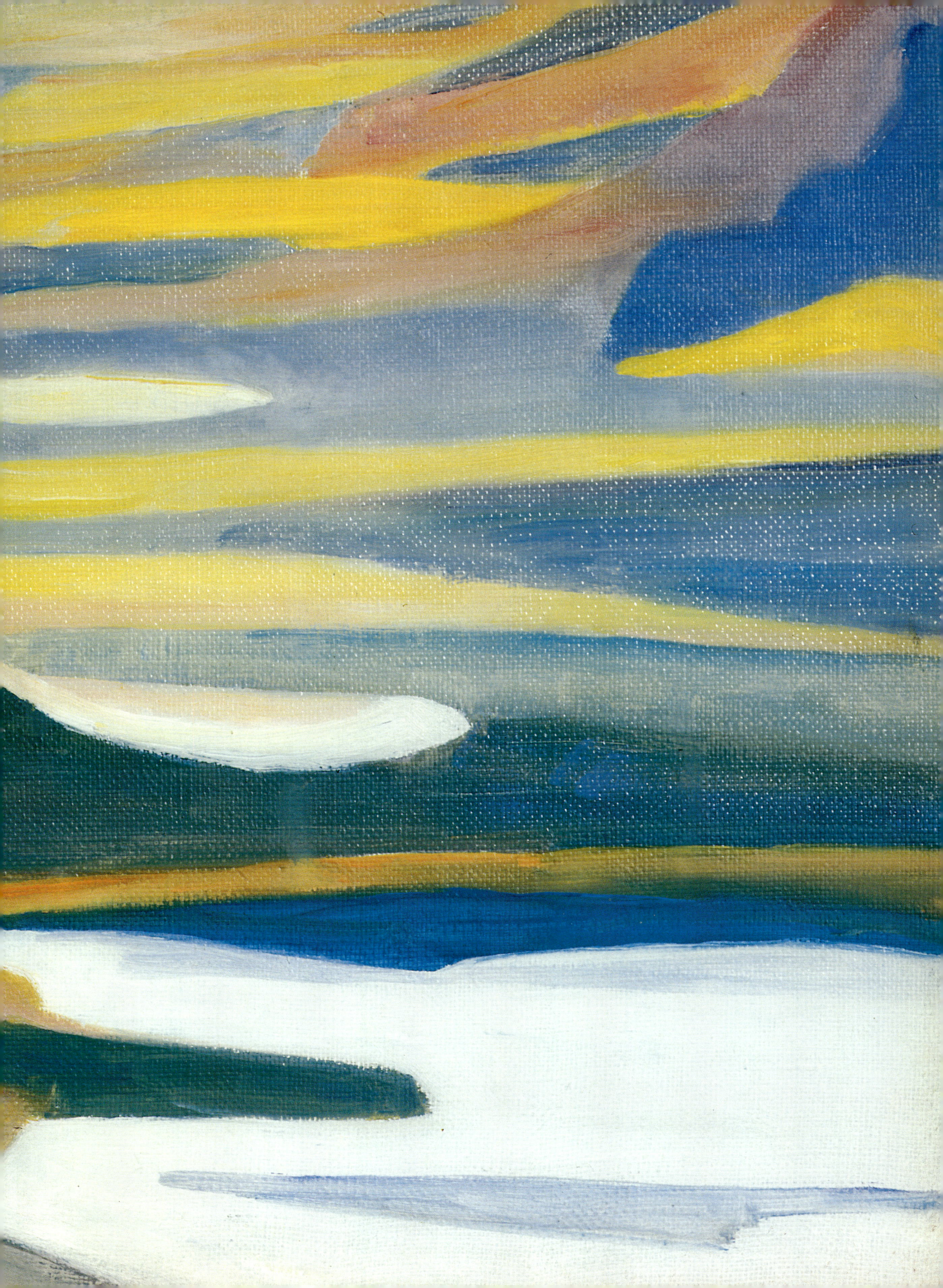

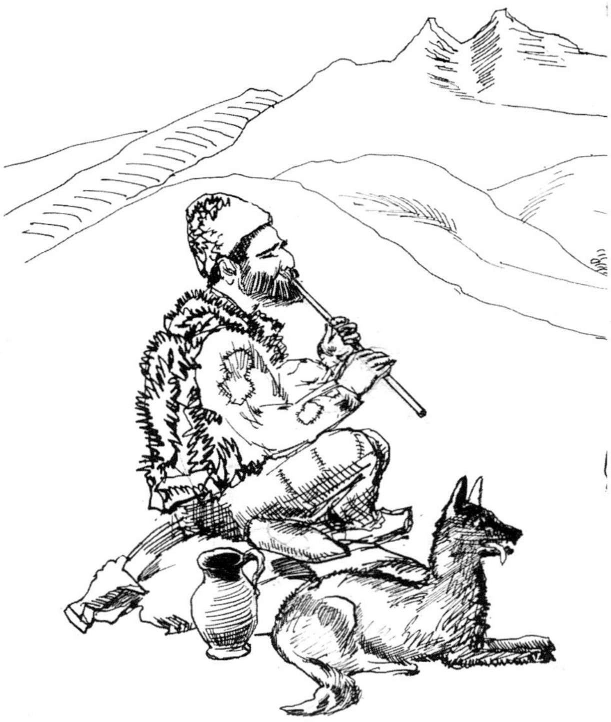

Shepherd. 1929
Indian ink on paper. 21 x 16 cm
A. Akopian collection, Yerevan

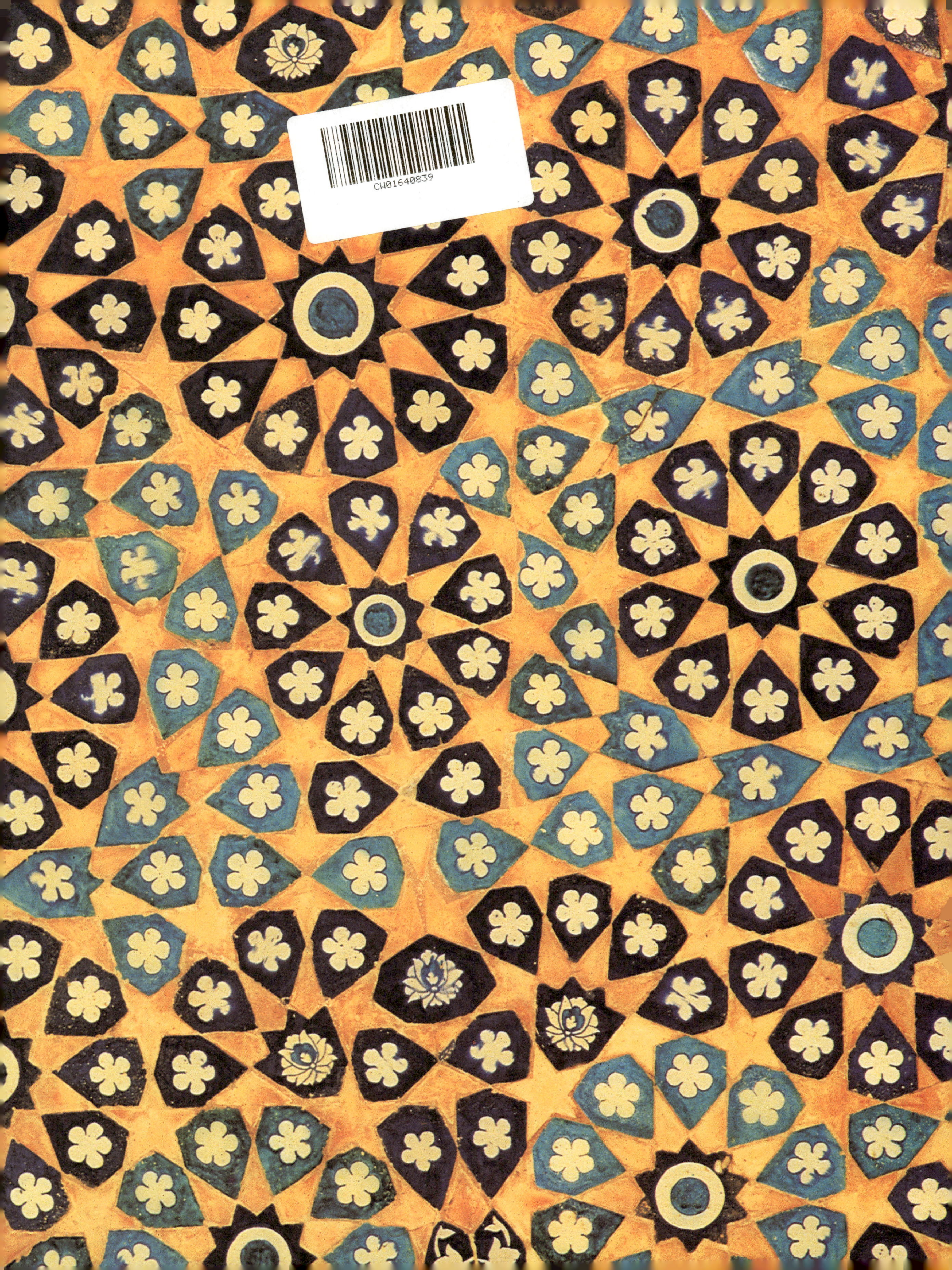

The Art of the Islamic Tile

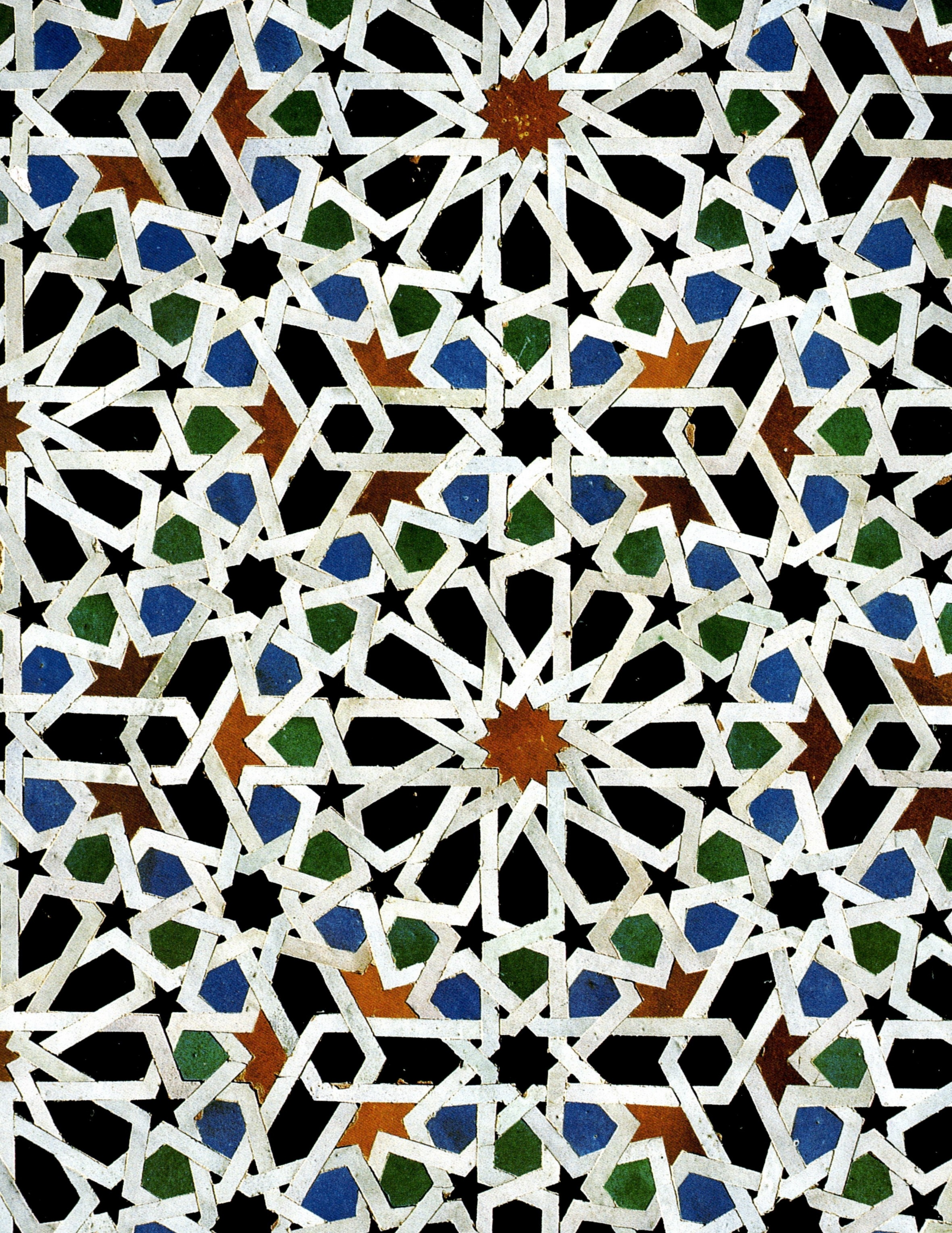

Gérard Degeorge
Yves Porter

The Art of the Islamic Tile

Flammarion

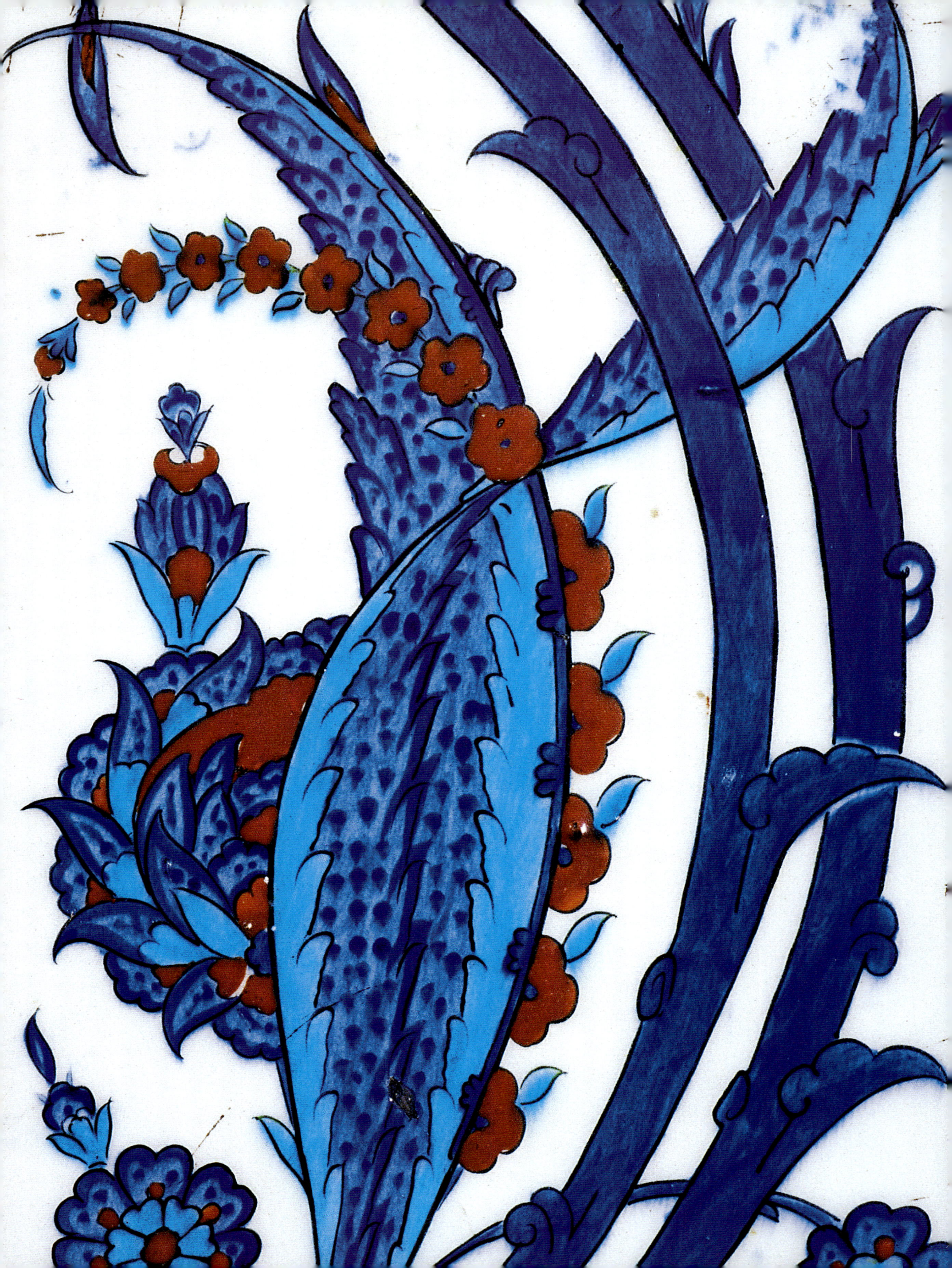

Contents

Foreword

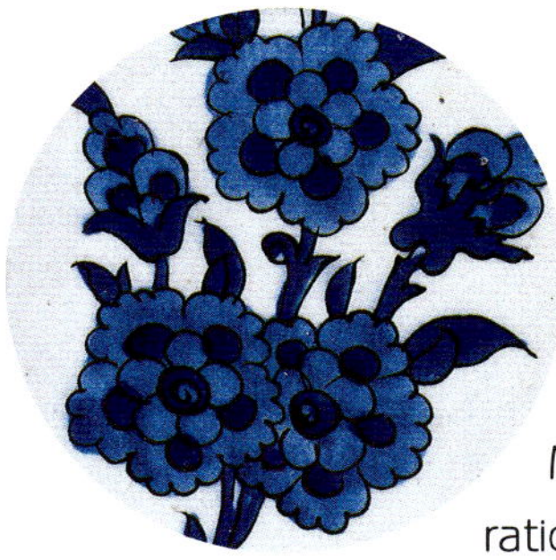

Islamic ceramic tilework is surely one of the most magnificent forms of decorative art in the world. The art form gained widespread popularity extending beyond religious frontiers, and has been highly sought after in the West since the Middle Ages. However, the medium is no less extraordinary when applied as decoration to architectural monuments and the techniques developed for this purpose spread far beyond the confines of the Muslim world. In this realm too, Islamic potters and craftsmen often displayed a skill and ingenuity little short of miraculous. Their work, which can be seen adorning architectural monuments from Morocco to India, not only exhibits a splendid array of decorative designs but also exploits highly sophisticated techniques devised by master potters whose technical expertise can surprise us even today. The architecture of the Islamic world represents a high point in the art of ceramic decoration and exhibits extraordinary variety in form and function, as well as in design.

The buildings that first come to mind when one thinks of Islamic architecture are, of course, the mosque, the minaret, and the *madrasa*, but other constructions—such as princely palaces and residences, as well as mausoleums erected in honor of great kings and humble dervishes alike—should not be forgotten. Moreover, it seems impossible to imagine this *Thousand and One Nights* backdrop without its multicolored coat: onion-like domes enameled in turquoise, slender minarets set with polychrome tiles, palaces and bathhouses where brightly colored tilework provides an enticing vision of sensuous coolness. Like their decoration, these monuments, however, did not appear spontaneously: if the mosque and the palace were already edifices of major importance by the early decades of Islam, the minaret, *madrasa*, and mausoleum seem to have appeared at a later stage and are, moreover, unevenly dispersed over the vast expanse of Muslim territory. Glazed ceramic cladding embellishes the facades and the roofs of all these buildings, endowing them with a kaleidoscope of color. The techniques used in this type of ceramics are often closely linked to those employed in hollow-ware and tableware, and vary according to region and period.

A number of factors account for the somewhat uneven geographical distribution of ceramic architectural decoration in the Muslim world. The first is the traditional construction techniques of the country in which they appear. In regions where brick predominates, a number of technical facilities required for tilemaking already exist. On the other hand, tiles are less well adapted to stonework, so the space allotted to tiling is smaller on stone-built edifices, particularly on the facades of buildings. Another feature that distinguishes architectural ceramics in the Islamic world is of a technical nature: whereas regions to the east had almost universally adopted silica-based paste by the twelfth century, North African countries have kept faith with clay pastes to the present day. Apart from the differences in paste, it is worth noting that some decorative techniques widely used in certain regions were almost totally passed over in others. A good example of this is metallic luster, present in Spain, Iraq, and Iran, but rare or nonexistent in the Maghreb, the Ottoman empire, and India.

In this book, we shall begin by presenting an overview of the formative years of Islamic architecture through an examination of various monuments characteristic of the classical

Muslim world. Following a brief introduction to the materials and techniques employed in the production of architectural ceramics, we will look at the decorative patterns and the craftsmen responsible for these works of art. Most of the book is devoted to a broad panorama of the most important examples of the art of architectural ceramics. These reflect the astounding variety of production in all the many geographical zones over which stretched the vast territory of Muslim control.

Each chapter focuses on a single geographical area from the vast mosaic of the Islamicized world, examining the most representative monuments and the evolution of its characteristic forms and styles. The overview opens with the invention of Islamic stonepaste ceramics in Iraq in the ninth century and the gradual expansion of this technique to the shores of the Mediterranean. We then move on to the pre-Mongol Orient, an area that includes Iran, central Asia, and what is now Afghanistan, from the emergence of the first independent dynasties to the arrival of the Mongols in the thirteenth century. Spain and the Maghreb form a very different geo-cultural bloc, with idiosyncratic architectural forms and ceramic techniques of its own, and is treated over a lengthy chronological period, from the Muslim conquest of Spain (in 711) right through to the modern age (also including Algeria and Tunisia).

The Mongol conquest—with the taking of Baghdad in 1258—signaled an important turning point in the history of the Muslim East. The period following these invasions, marked initially by Mongol then Timurid and Uzbek dynasties, witnessed some of the most remarkable creations in the realm of ceramics. Iran, under the Safavids and Qajars, continued to construct marvels of architectural decoration.

Anatolia, Syria, and Egypt formed another active center, characterized by an architecture primarily of stone, in contradistinction to the Iranian plateau and central Asia. This difference in construction material did not prevent the introduction of ceramic decoration, however, notably in edifices built by the Seljuqs of Rum in Anatolia and then in areas under Mamluk control. Influenced at one and the same time by central Asia and by Mamluk Syria, Ottoman Anatolia was also responsible for some magnificent creations, those of the Iznik workshops being particularly remarkable.

Lastly, the Indian subcontinent, although Islamicized over much of its territory, was still profoundly marked by Hinduism (especially central India), and these specific conditions had their effect on the development of architectural ceramics. Some other regions—Sind and the Punjab in what is today Pakistan—possess an important architectural heritage decorated with ceramics that to date publications have hardly done justice to. We have made a deliberate attempt to remedy this situation by according more generous treatment to this neglected region.

To some, the very notion of giving an account of the whole production of architectural ceramics in such a vast geographical area and in a period stretching over some ten centuries may seem ambitious, even foolhardy. This may explain why few earlier publications have made such an attempt. Although some divergence is inevitable between the unerring poetical vision of the photographer Gérard Degeorge and the more history-centered approach of the author of these lines, both of us express the hope that this dual perspective will provide a complementary, mutually enriching account of this engrossing subject. However, it is not the intention of this volume to furnish an exhaustive catalog of the corpus of architectural ceramics in the Muslim world—such a task would require many volumes. The work concludes with a glossary of the technical terms used in the main text, as well as an extensive bibliography that will allow the inquisitive reader to explore the subject more deeply.

An Introduction to Muslim Architecture

The unheralded and explosive expansion of Islam meant that a substantial proportion of the Arabian Peninsula was converted to the new religion within the Prophet's own lifetime. Nonetheless, an authentic Muslim artistic idiom only arose following the establishment of the Umayyad caliphate (660–750). During this period, the conquered lands began to be Islamicized, adopting the mosque as a place of prayer and Arabic as a common language in all sacred matters. In their earliest large-scale constructions, the Muslims, lacking an architectural tradition comparable to that of the Greco-Roman or Sasanid worlds, naturally owed much to the heritage of Antiquity. Umayyad architecture in Syria and Palestine—civil as well as religious—took its inspiration from indigenous Romano-Byzantine examples. Similarly, the decorative arts derived to a large extent from established Byzantine and Sasanid models.

The collapse of the Damascus Umayyad caliphate and the emergence of ʿAbbasid power that saw the creation of the round city of Baghdad (762) shifted the center of the empire eastward. For that very reason, ʿAbbasid Iraq came under the influence of the building techniques of Sasanid Iran. Racked by schisms, however, the unwieldy territory of the caliphate soon fragmented. As early as 756, Umayyad Spain seceded from the caliphate, while Ifriqiya and Egypt became self-governing respectively in 800 and 868. Then, during the first half of the eleventh century, invaders—Turks from the east and Berbers from the west—gradually wrested power from the Arabs in these regions. These incursions had a profound effect on Muslim history, accentuating the east–west divide. In the artistic realm, this upheaval resulted in the gradual abandonment of "classic" models in favor of novel forms. Thus, the indigenous artistic vocabulary rapidly diversified, taking on—according to the region—different forms that can appear contradictory.

At the time of the birth of Islam, the Arabs already possessed a rich architectural heritage, with monuments situated at the opposite ends of their world, such as the South Arabian temples (Marib, fifth century B.C.) and the tombs at Petra (first century B.C. to first century A.D.). It should also be noted that the Kaʿba in Mecca had already been venerated prior to the Muslim period. Nonetheless, the fledgling community was faced with the task of constructing monuments specific to their new religion. The mosque was of course the first typically Muslim construction. The art of the first centuries of the Islamic period initially arose from sources in Antiquity: Roman, Byzantine, Sasanid, and Arab. The development of a genuine Muslim art, derived from a synthesis of these sources yet taking on unique forms and functions in both civil and religious architecture, followed rapidly.

The Muslim world is essentially characterized by monuments such as the mosque, the minaret, and the *madrasa*. If the mosque is closely allied to Islamic history in general from its onset, the minaret, *madrasa*, and mausoleum, for their part, appeared somewhat later and are spread unevenly throughout the Muslim world.

Mosque and Minaret

The mosque (from *masjid*, "place of prostration") designates the place where Muslim believers gather for prayer. In point of fact, the very first mosque was the Prophet's own house at Medina. The emblematic simplicity of this "primitive" mosque clearly indicates that very few imperatives initially governed the construction of a place of prayer. The only invariable is the ritual orientation (*qibla*) materialized by the *mihrab*, the alcove indicating the direction of Mecca. Even this stipulation arose only in 706, however, when the mosque at Medina was rebuilt under al-Walid I (705–15). The main types of mosque ground plan emerged in the Umayyad period. During the reign of al-Walid I, no less than three types of plan were adopted: that known as "Bedouin" for the mosque at Medina itself, the "Mediterranean" plan for the al-Aqsa at Jerusalem, and the "Syrian" type for the Great Mosque at Damascus. A large proportion of subsequent mosques were derived form these diverse primary models. The templates for mosque construction were thus already in place by the eighth century and differentiation was only achieved by cleverly varying the model of plan and elevation. In the meantime, moreover, the Muslim community had expanded considerably: for this reason, from Spain to Afghanistan to India, the size of congregational ("Friday") mosques increased dramatically.

The minaret—surely the most eye-catching sign of Muslim presence—is still used for the call to prayer today. Its origins remain mysterious, however, though it is certain that the first places set aside for prayer did not possess them. In fact, as a large-scale edifice it appeared relatively late on the scene. Prior to the tenth century, the most famous minarets were found at the mosque of Qairouan (836), the al-Malwiyya at Samarra (849), and the minaret of Ibn Tulun in Cairo (c. 879, rebuilt 1296). The trend toward ever grander minarets seems to have paralleled the appearance of new independent states. The function of the tower was not therefore restricted to simply calling believers to prayer; it also served as an emblem erected to the glory of any number of "commanders" of the faithful. It is worth noting that some of the first architectural ceramics in the Maghreb were to appear on a minaret: that of the Kutubiyya at Marrakech dating from the end of the twelfth century.

The Mausoleum

The last decades of the ninth century saw the adoption of new types of monument, the most important of which was the mausoleum. The first monumental tomb in the Islamic world was probably erected at Samarra: the Qubbat al-Sulaiybiyya. This tomb may have been built for the caliph al-Muntasir, who died in 862; however, recent research seems to suggest that it is in fact the oldest mausoleum erected for a Shi'ite *imam*. The reaction to what was a shift in position with respect to funerary rites (the orthodox attitude to death was previously reflected in burial of the simplest kind) differed depending on the region affected.

At the beginning of the tenth century, dynastic tombs began to appear in Transoxiana and Iran. Subsequently, Shi'ite movements certainly played a role in the development of mausoleums, as in Fatimid Egypt (in Cairo and Aswan, notably). Later, in particular under the Mamluks, tombs were often incorporated into complexes that also included a *madrasa*.

The scale of the tombs and their plans differed widely according to region and epoch, ranging from collective sepulchers, such as those of the Marinids at the Chellah in Rabat, to individual monuments such as the Taj Mahal at Agra, or that of Uljaytu at Sultaniyah. Funerary architecture was probably most in evidence in Iran and central Asia, and later in India. However, although certain dynasties such as the Timurids are noted for their splendid funerary structures, those of others, such as the Safavids, are on the contrary singularly unassuming.

The *Madrasa*

The *madrasa* ("place of teaching") is a higher educational establishment in which instruction is given in the traditional Muslim subjects (chiefly theology and law, but also mathematics, astronomy, and natural science). It was primarily under the Seljuqs (1038–1194) that these institutions became widespread in an effort to combat the Shi'ite influence that had been predominant in the Buyid period (932–1062). At the end of the eleventh century, a number were built by the grand vizier Nizam al-Mulk. Although the great majority have since vanished, it is probable that these *madrasas* were built to a cruciform, four-*iwan* plan. The idea has occasionally been advanced that the shape of this plan stemmed from the four schools of law taught in the institution. In reality, this four-part arrangement, which does seem particularly suited to this function, did not in fact correspond to the way the spaces were actually occupied. Moreover, the *madrasa* developed after this type of ground plan had been adopted for palaces and caravanseries.

Under the impact of the Seljuqs, and in parallel with the evolution of the *waqfs* (endowments for religious institutions), *madrasas* became increasingly numerous during the twelfth and thirteenth centuries, especially in the Middle East, with remarkable examples such as the Mustansiriyya of Baghdad and the al-Firdaus of Aleppo. *Madrasas* were often found within funerary complexes, near charitable institutions (hospital or "dervish monastery," *khanqah*) provided for by one and the same foundation, as was the case with the great Mamluk ensembles at Cairo, by Sultan Qalawun or Sultan Hasan.

Madrasas—preferably transliterated *medersas* as far as Morocco is concerned—are encountered much less frequently in the Maghreb than in the East. However, examples can be found in Tunisia, Algeria, and Morocco, including the *medersas* of the Marinids, which bear witness to the refined taste for decoration of that Moroccan dynasty. The two extreme limits of the Islamic world—India and Spain—are notable for a relative dearth of *madrasas*.

Palace Architecture

The palace, a civil and dynastic structure that was the symbol and locus of power, did not enjoy the protection generally accorded religious edifices. Moreover, such buildings were more often built at the behest of the ruling prince: those who eventually succeeded him had a tendency to neglect or transform the residences of their predecessors. Such factors mean that palaces are generally far less well preserved than religious buildings.

The Muslim world conserves very few palaces dating from before the fifteenth century. Most of these, as at Samarra and in Afghanistan, are known from scattered remains unearthed during archeological excavations. They do give, however, a reasonable idea of how the long-vanished pre-Mongol palaces of Baghdad—known only from written descriptions—might once have looked.

Other groups of buildings, such as the Madinat al-Zahra near Cordoba, have been well conserved in parts and extensively restored. Other scattered examples, such as the Aljafería at Saragossa (eleventh century), the Alhambra at Granada, and the Mandu palace group, only survive because they were occupied at a later point in history. One should not forget those palaces built for Christian princes by Muslim craftsmen, prime examples being the Ziza at Palermo and the Alcazar at Seville (fourteenth century).

The concept of the dwelling space fit for a prince differed widely from India to Spain. The remarkable and practical use of water—with its dual function of irrigating and providing pleasure—and the use of ceramic decoration nonetheless emerge as common features of palace architecture throughout Islamic territories.

The place of ceramics in Muslim architecture also varies considerably from region to region. The domes at Isfahan and Samarkand, which are clad entirely in tiles predominantly turquoise in tone, are strikingly beautiful, yet neither these forms nor the colors are widespread in the Mediterranean area, North Africa, or Spain. In those regions, tilework is largely employed in splendid and infinitely varied paving, something far rarer in the Muslim East. Materials and construction methods are the main factors determining the choice of a particular type of decoration. Ottoman monuments, for instance, are noteworthy for their fine stone carving and for the purity of their architectural lines, created in the main by the use of freestone. Tiles (among them the much sought-after Iznik type) fulfill a purely decorative role in the covered parts of the edifice: in tilework panels beneath a portal, in lunettes above a bay, lining inner courtyards, or in a prayer hall in the mosque.

The possibilities of ceramic facing seemed unlimited. In particular, it could be used to emphasize the architectural lines of a building, highlighting them by means of a contrasting color scheme—by accentuating the vertical thrust of an arch or a vault, for example. Lining walls, tiles recall the rich hangings that decorated the encampments of nomad emirs in ancient times. Cladding great domes, they glint in the sunlight, standing out against the sky; inside, decorating a cupola with a picture of a starry heaven, they seem to encourage the visitor to more elevated, even mystical thoughts.

The addition of color not only rendered the building more visible, but it could also, when necessary, provide a surface on which words could be inscribed, because an inscription in turquoise-glazed bricks is far easier to decipher from a distance than one written in materials of the same "terracotta" hue as the bricks employed in the construction itself.

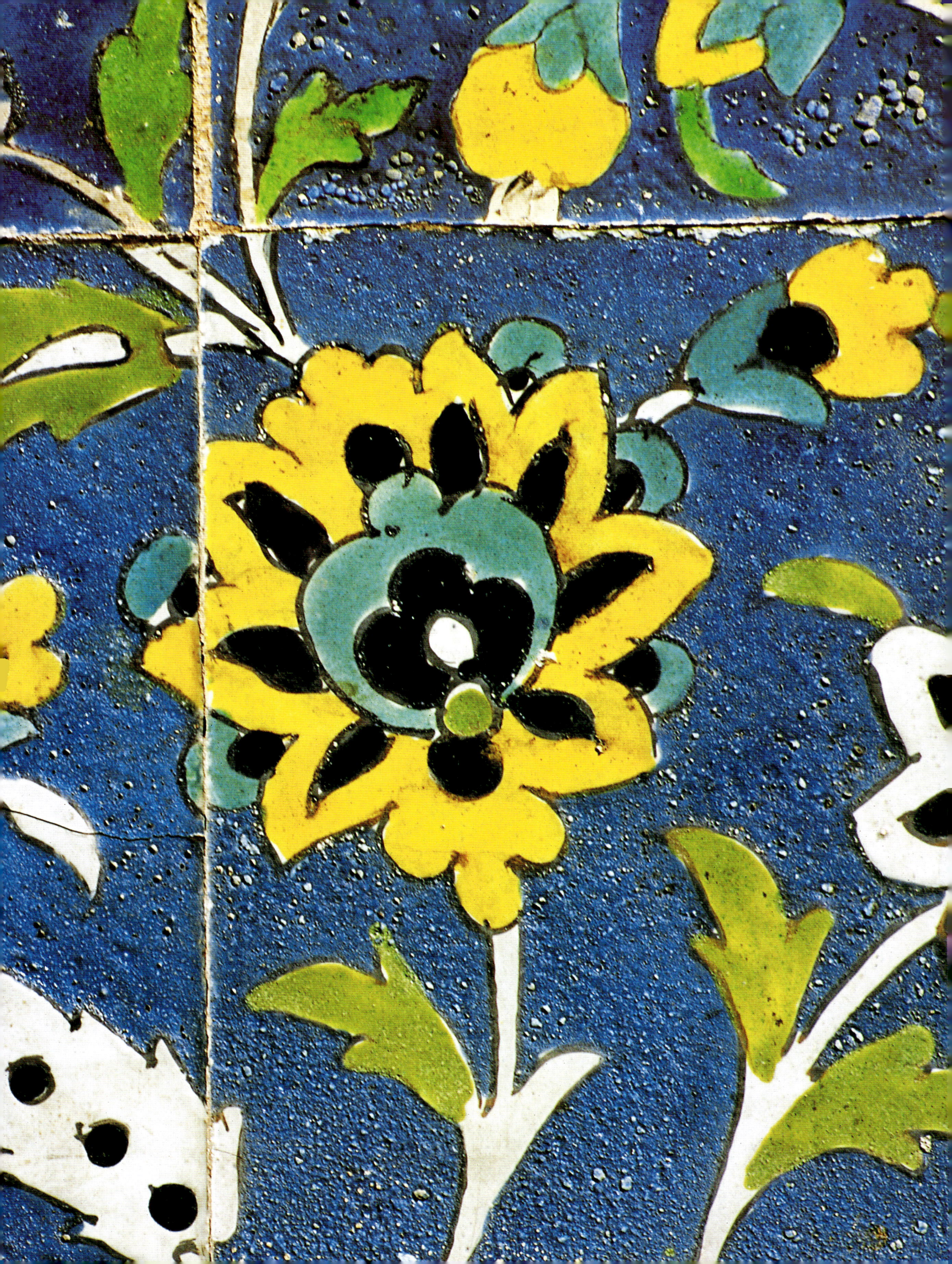

Architectural Ceramics: Techniques, Patterns, and Craftsmen

Oriental Antiquity was well acquainted with a large number of ceramic colored glaze techniques. One might cite third dynasty Egypt, the lands of Mesopotamia (as on the famous Ishtar Gate from Babylon, dating from 600 B.C. and today in Berlin), or the no less celebrated Frieze of the Archers at Susa from the Achaemenid period (now preserved in the Louvre). After centuries of using glazed architectural ceramics, shortly before the Christian era the practice fell into disuse and vanished. Hence, the earliest known monuments in the Islamic world, such as the Dome of the Rock at Jerusalem (692) and the Umayyad Mosque at Damascus (706), are for the most part decorated with true mosaic in the Byzantine tradition. Not until the `Abbasid caliphate and the opulence of Samarra did ceramic tile facing make a timid reappearance. In fact, it was only in the twelfth century that architectural ceramics really took off, soon extending from the edge of the Iranian plateau to the shores of the Atlantic Ocean.

Before studying examples of these ceramics, a number of technical questions should be addressed concerning the types of paste used to make the tiles and the glaze coatings. The information available regarding these techniques is of various kinds. First of all, there exist written texts, the most important of these being the famous treatise of Abu'l-Qasim from Kashan dating from 1300. Other texts, Arabo-Persian treatises on mineralogy for instance, also provide valuable additional information. A number of mainly Ottoman documents, as well as rather vague details given in historical chronicles, also give some idea of the role played by the figures behind the creation of some of the great decorative ensembles of architectural ceramics. More recently, ethnographic research and chemical analyses of ceramic fragments have also furnished elements of comparison that help our understanding.

Pastes and Frits

Architectural ceramics are principally made from two types of paste, the use of which varies according to historical and geographical factors. Initially, the predominant type throughout the Muslim world was the clay-paste glazed tile or brick derived directly from the production processes involved in making bricks. This paste was sometimes rendered opaque with a tin glaze. In the twelfth century, through the efforts of potters in the Muslim East, a new type of paste emerged in which clay is a minor component (10 to 20 percent), the remainder comprising silica (pounded quartz) and frit. The latter is a glass (and hence predominately also composed of silica) fluxed with sodium carbonate. This very hard paste, known as stone-paste, resists high temperatures (1000–1100°C) and is the ideal base for high-fired glaze. The distribution of this stone-paste throughout the Islamic world was uneven, however: only in the east (Egypt, Syria, Iraq, Anatolia, and Iran) was it used to any great extent.

♦ "Black line" polychrome tiles, Friday Mosque, Isfahan (Iran). The decoration is contained within a black line of chromite that prevents the colored oxides from bleeding during firing.

Slips and Glazes

Glaze is a transparent or opaque vitrified material that may be colored by metallic oxides. There are a number of types of glaze, varying according to composition, but also according to the place they occupy on the ceramic.

The first coat over the support (the fired paste, or "bisc") is either known as a "slip" ("engobe") or an "enamel" depending on its composition. The term "slip" is rather imprecise: it covers not a glaze as such, but a clayey substance partially vitrified or not at all, and whose color can range from white through a whole gamut of ochers to black. To obtain a glassy surface, a coat of transparent or colored glaze is necessary. Strictly speaking, the term should therefore be applied only to certain specific processes.

In the case of clay-paste ceramic, the coat applied to the fired ware is a white opaque glaze composed of tin oxide mixed with silica and one or two fluxes (lead, sodium carbonate), and is often known as tin-enamel (tin-glaze). In the case of silica (stone) pastes, tin-glaze and slip are both employed, once again with variations depending on region and period. Any decoration is applied to this coating, which is meant to cover the piece completely. Ornaments can also be obtained by working raw paste (hand-formed or molded decoration) that is subsequently coated in slip or tin-glazed accordingly. If the decor requires color, use may be made of a range of metallic oxides.

Oxides

The major metallic oxides used in ceramics are manganese, iron, cobalt, and copper. These oxides can take high temperatures and are known as "high-firing" or "hard." According to the temperature attained, the firing atmosphere, and their chemical characteristics, these glazes offer a relatively wide range of colors. Long known to potters, these metallic oxides can be employed in conjunction with others, such as chromium or antimony, whose use is less widespread.

Antimony

The oxide of antimony (antimonious oxide, antimony trioxide, Sb_2O_3)—the word comes from the Arabic *`ithmid*—is obtained by calcination (oxidation) in air of a natural sulfide ore, stibnite. Already used

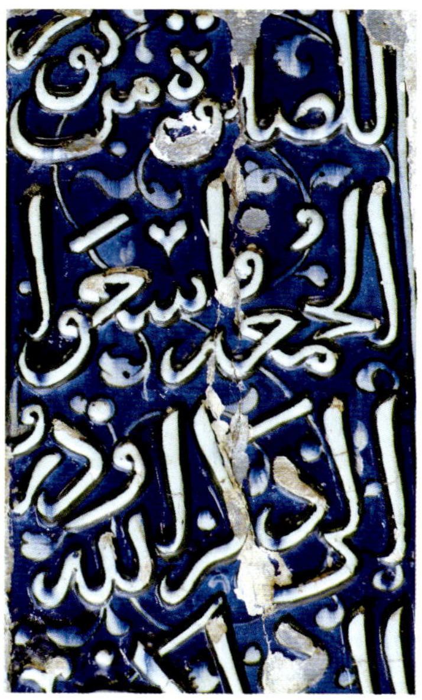

♦ Underglaze-painted stone-paste tile with inscription in relief. Museum of Islamic Art, Cairo.

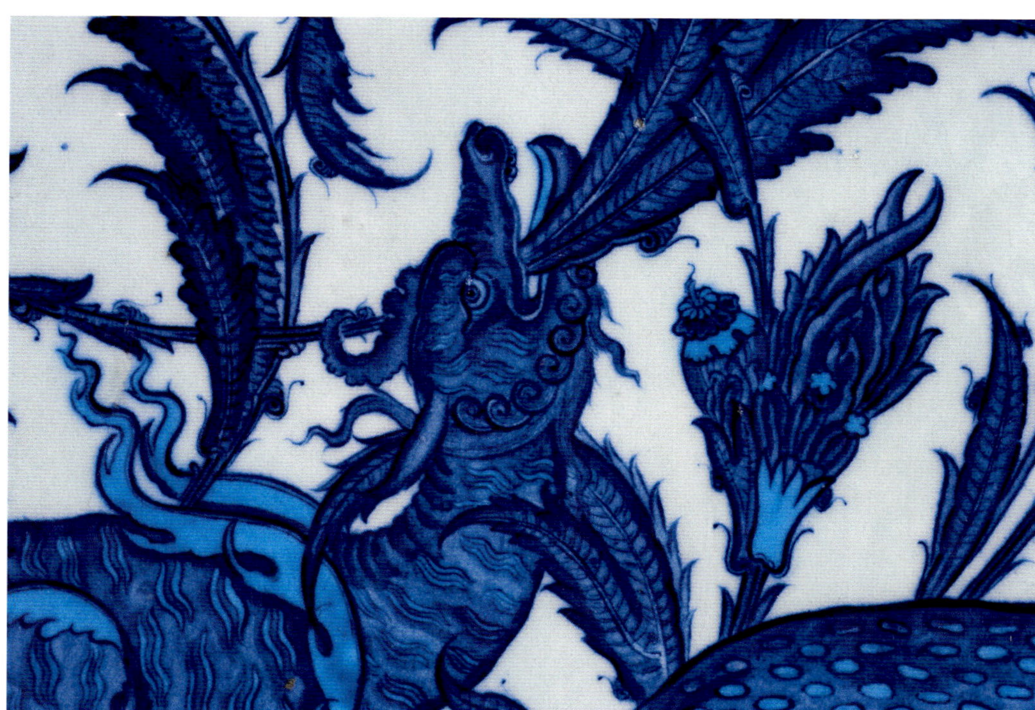

♦ Large underglaze-painted frieze panel (detail), Sünnet Odasi at the Topkapi Saray, Istanbul (Turkey). The monsters in the lower section of the panels derive from the Far Eastern bestiary and are set in a decor in the *saz* style.

FACING PAGE

♦ Iznik tile from the Rüstem Pasha Mosque, Istanbul (Turkey). The colors, especially the famous "Iznik red," are painted on a silica slip and coated in a glaze of perfect transparency.

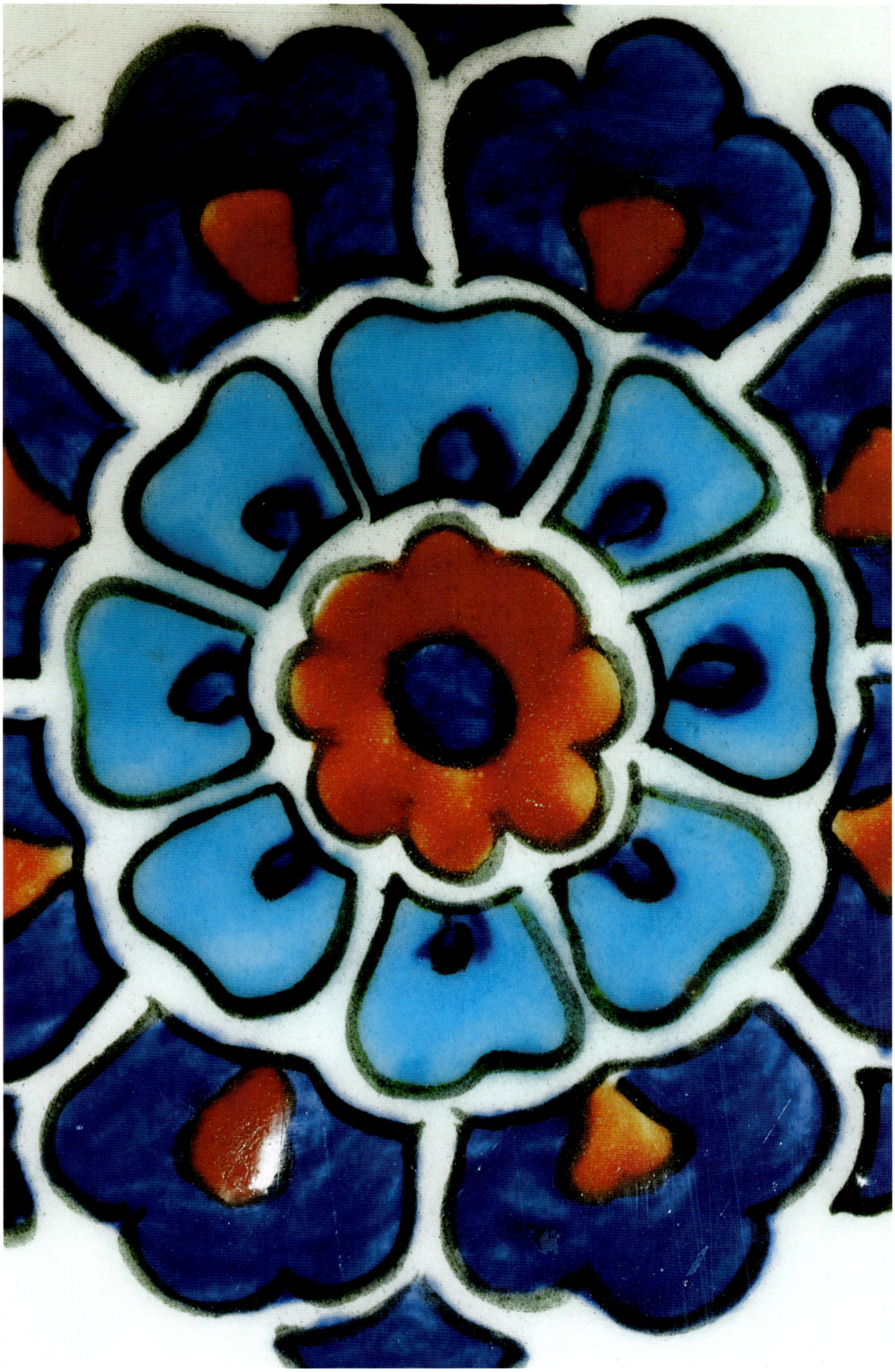

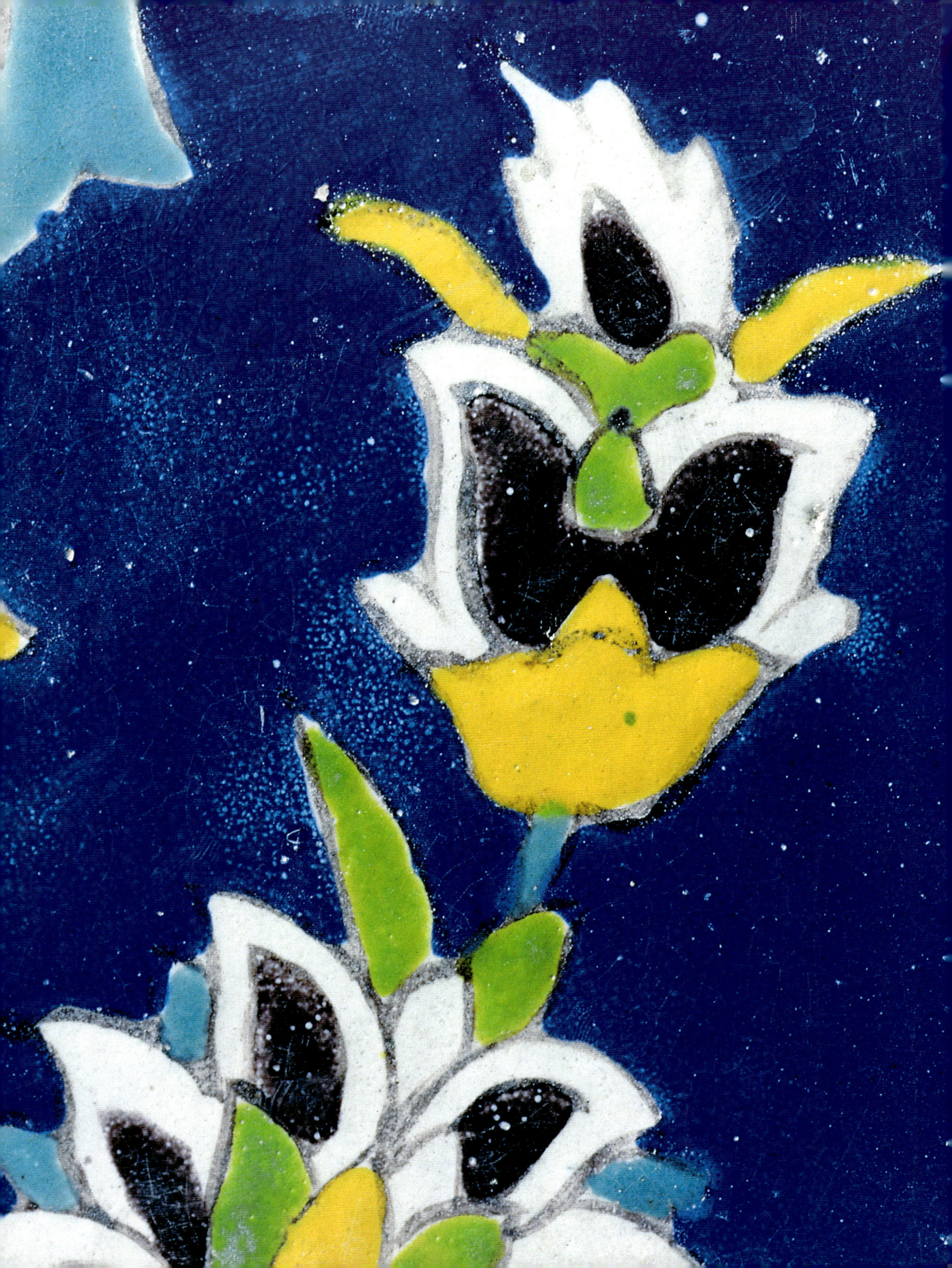

in Antiquity in the manufacture of white-colored glass, antimony oxide is an opacifier that exhibits a bleaching power in certain types of glaze. In ceramics, however, its principal function is as a coloring oxide that combines with lead oxide (antimonate of lead) to give a pale yellow hue that can be deepened with the addition of iron oxide.

Chromium

Chromium oxide is used either in its anhydride state (Cr_2O_3) as a powder of an intense green color, or else, as is more frequently the case, in the form of an iron chromate prepared by oxidation of a combination of iron oxide and chromium oxide that results in a vast palette of yellows and greens. In the form of chromite, it also contributes to polychrome so-called "black line" decorative tilework (see below).

Copper

Copper oxide has been used since early Antiquity and is mentioned in connection with ceramics in the earliest known Oriental treatises. Copper oxide exists in two forms: cuprous oxide (Cu_2O), a reddish powder, and the far more common cupric oxide (CuO), a very heavy black powder obtained by oxidation of the metal in air. This copper oxide is certainly the most frequently exploited stain in the Muslim East. Fusing readily, its prime advantage is that it changes in tone depending on the chemical composition of the glaze with which it is associated: in alkaline glazes devoid of alumina (aluminum oxide), the result is a turquoise blue; alkaline-calcia glazes give an instantly recognizable bluish gray; in lead glazes, an intense, almost bottle green is the rule; lastly it can even be emerald green in color.

Iron

Iron forms a number of different compounds with oxygen. The most frequently employed in ceramics is ferric oxide (red iron oxide, Fe_2O_3), a scarlet powder (produced by the calcination of ferrous sulfate), or black (ferrous oxide, Fe_3O_4), the hydrated form of which is yellow in color. Dissolved in a glaze, its hue ranges from orangey yellow in an oxidizing atmosphere to green in a reductive one. As a slip or natural oxide (hematite), iron oxides can also be used to obtain red, the famous "Iznik red" in particular.

Manganese

Manganese is mentioned in ancient texts—Nasir al-Din Tusi refers to it in his treatise on mineralogy (1255–65): "Manganese is used by glassmakers and ceramists. It is to the frit what borax is to gold, as it makes the glass more liquid."[1] In the East, this stain is employed in its most frequent form as manganese dioxide (i.e., the ore, pyrolusite). When used on clay-paste ceramics under the glaze—in a localized, undissolved surplus—its original black or brown color remains, whereas when dissolved in the glaze the resulting hue is violet.

Cobalt

If nearly all the stains are relatively easy to obtain whatever the region from manganese, copper, or iron oxide, deposits of

FACING PAGE

♦ Detail of a polychrome "black line" tile, Friday Mosque, Isfahan (Iran). The design appears against a cobalt blue ground applied over a white silica slip.

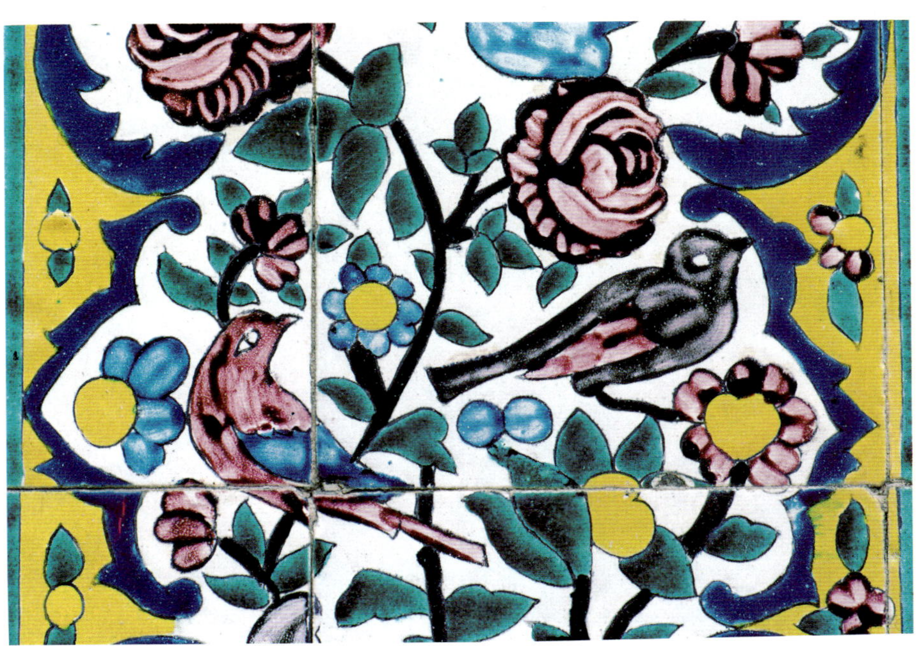

♦ Border of polychrome tiles in a *gol-o bolbol* ("roses and nightingales") pattern. Copper turquoise, cobalt blue, manganese violet, and antinomy yellow on a white silica slip. Khan *madrasa*, Shiraz (Iran), nineteenth century.

cobalt ore are few and far between, with the result that this colorant has long been the subject of long-distance trade. The substantial costs involved are amply compensated for by its outstanding staining power in ceramic ware, since a thousandth part of the oxide Co_3O_4 suffices to stain the whole glaze deep blue.

The use of cobalt to stain glass is attested continuously from Antiquity, but its exploitation in ceramics seems to have been more sporadic. After being employed in ancient pottery (from the fifteenth to the fourth century B.C.), cobalt blue resurfaced in Mesopotamia and Iran on `Abbasid tin-glazed earthenware of the ninth century. There then follows a hiatus in the Iranian region and the Near East between the tenth and twelfth centuries, before cobalt blue became widespread in ceramics in the Islamic world (Syria, Iran), as well as Europe (Spain as early as the thirteenth century). Cobalt deposits in the Kashan region were probably being mined in Antiquity, while in Morocco—even though deposits do exist (at Bou Azzer)—cobalt was being imported from Germany by the mid-nineteenth century.

Decorative Techniques

The simplest technique for decorating ceramics is with a monochrome glaze. Often opacified (particularly in the case of turquoise) by the addition of tin oxide, glazed tiles can either be left smooth or they can incorporate a carved or molded relief design.

Metallic Luster

Paradoxically, luster—one of the most complicated and sought-after techniques in all ceramic decoration—appeared in the ninth century, at the same time as `Abbasid potters were perfecting the manufacture of tin-glazed earthenware. Luster decoration is obtained by reduction of metallic salts applied to the glaze during a final low-temperature firing (at around 650°C) in an atmosphere rich in carbon (reductive atmosphere). An extremely thin layer of metal thus forms on the glaze. This is how Abu'l-Qasim describes the process: "Take one and a half *mans* [approximately 3 kilos] of red and yellow arsenic, one *man* of gold and silver marcasite, one *batman* [half-*man*] of yellow vitriol and a quarter of roasted copper, and mix it to a paste and grind it. A quarter of this is mixed with six *dirhams* of pure silver that has been burned and ground [with sulfur] and is ground on a stone for twenty-four hours until it is extremely fine. Dissolve this in some grape juice or vinegar and paint it onto the vessels as desired, and place them in a second kiln specially made for this purpose, and give them light smoke for seventy-two hours until they acquire the color of two firings. When they are cold, take them out and rub them with damp earth so that the color of gold comes out. Other people add certain preparations like *sirinj* [red lead] and *zanjar* [verdigris] to this enamel. In fact, *shadanaj* stone with roasted silver serves the same purpose. That which has been evenly fired reflects like red gold and shines like the light of the sun."[2]

Low-Fired Decoration

A further technique of decorating on the glaze appeared in Iran in the twelfth century. It allowed less heat-resistant substances (red slips and gold leaf) to be added in the course of a third firing at a lower temperature to high-firing colors such as copper, cobalt, and manganese, which fire around 1000°C.

These procedures increased the color range and were the source of a type of ceramic known as *haft-rang* ("seven-colored") or *mina`i* ("enameled"). This technique was abandoned during the second half of the thirteenth century, although ceramists subsequently employed an associated process known as *lajvardina*, the name deriving from the cobalt (*lajvard*)

FACING PAGE
♦ Detail of a ceramic panel with a carved design, Mausoleum of Shad-i Mulk Aqa in the Shah-i Zinda, Samarkand (Uzbekistan). The high relief (and incisions in the paste) allowed the colored glazes to be kept apart during firing.

FOLLOWING DOUBLE PAGE
♦ Detail of a frieze with an inscription in *sgraffito*, Ben Yussef *medersa*, Marrakech (Morocco). The tiles were first glazed then partially scratched, the pattern appearing from the unglazed ground beneath.

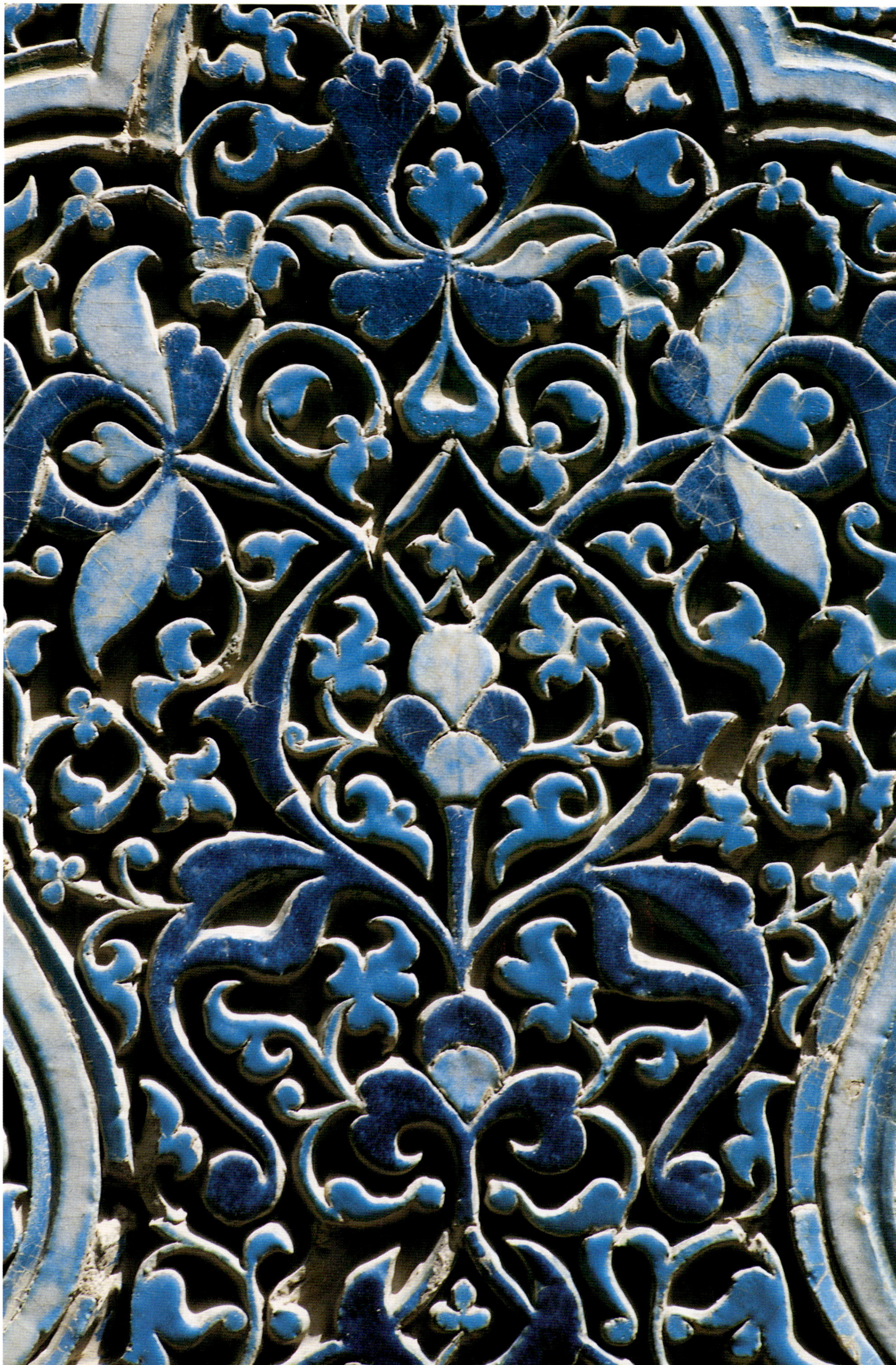

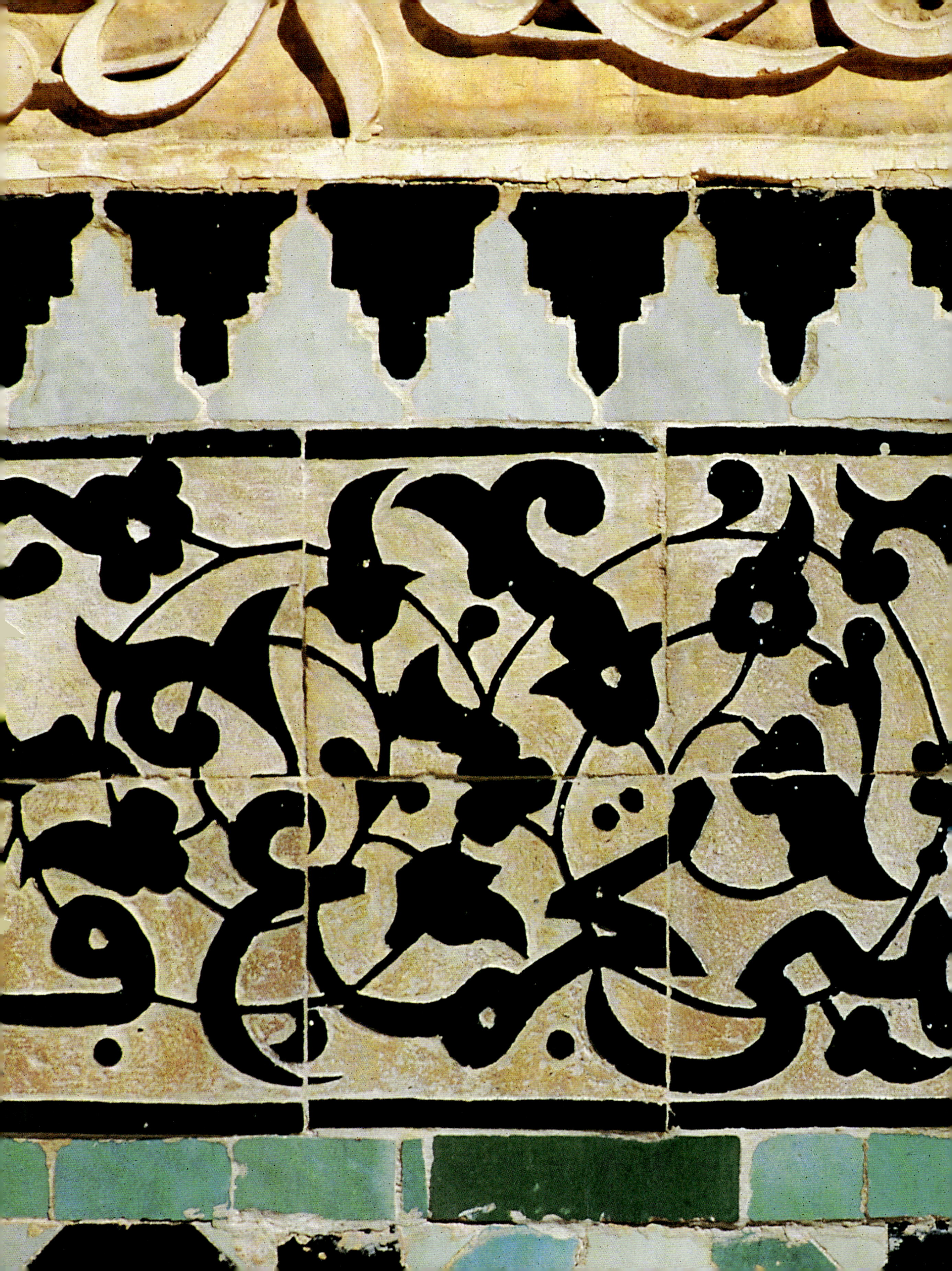

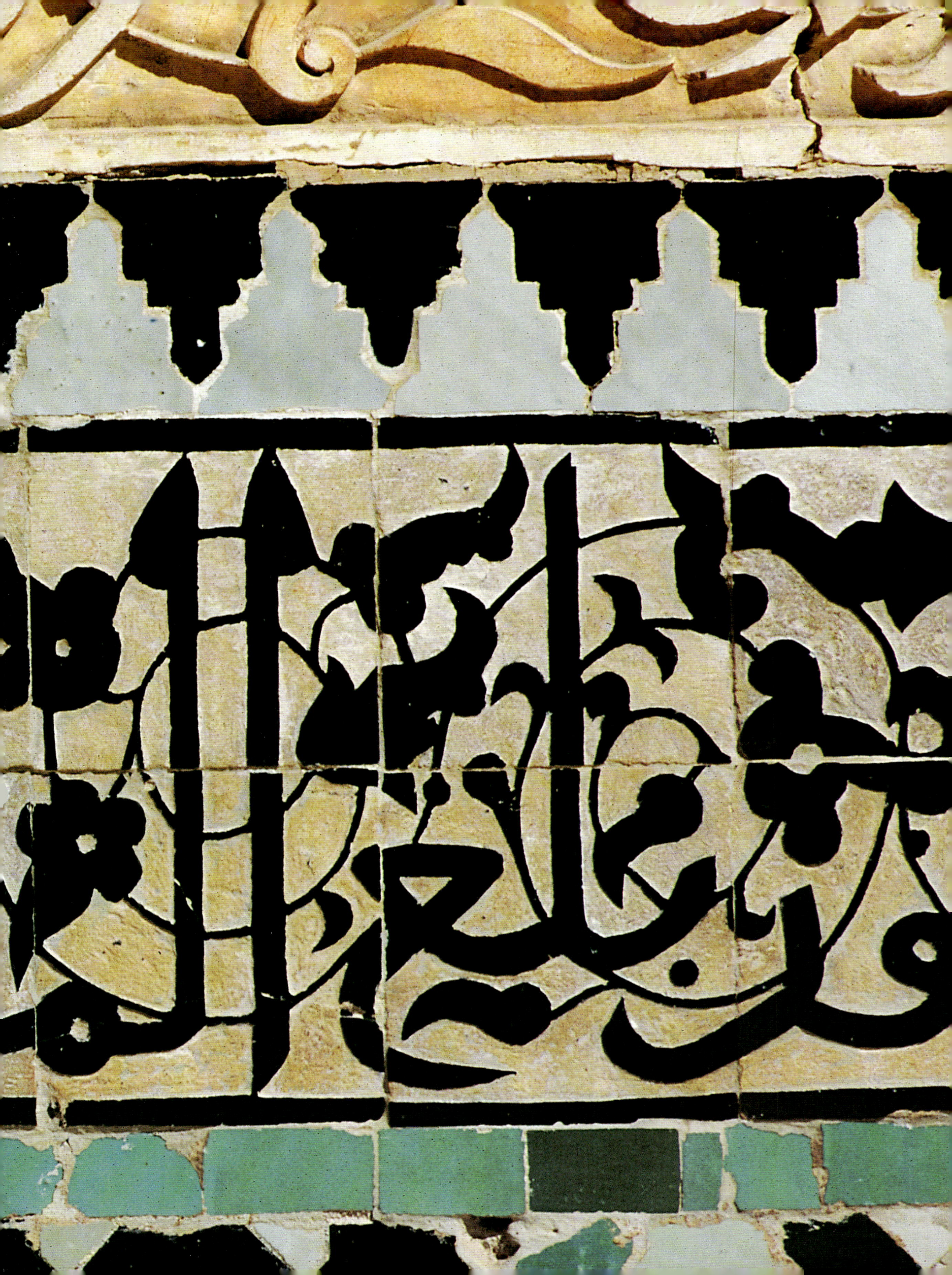

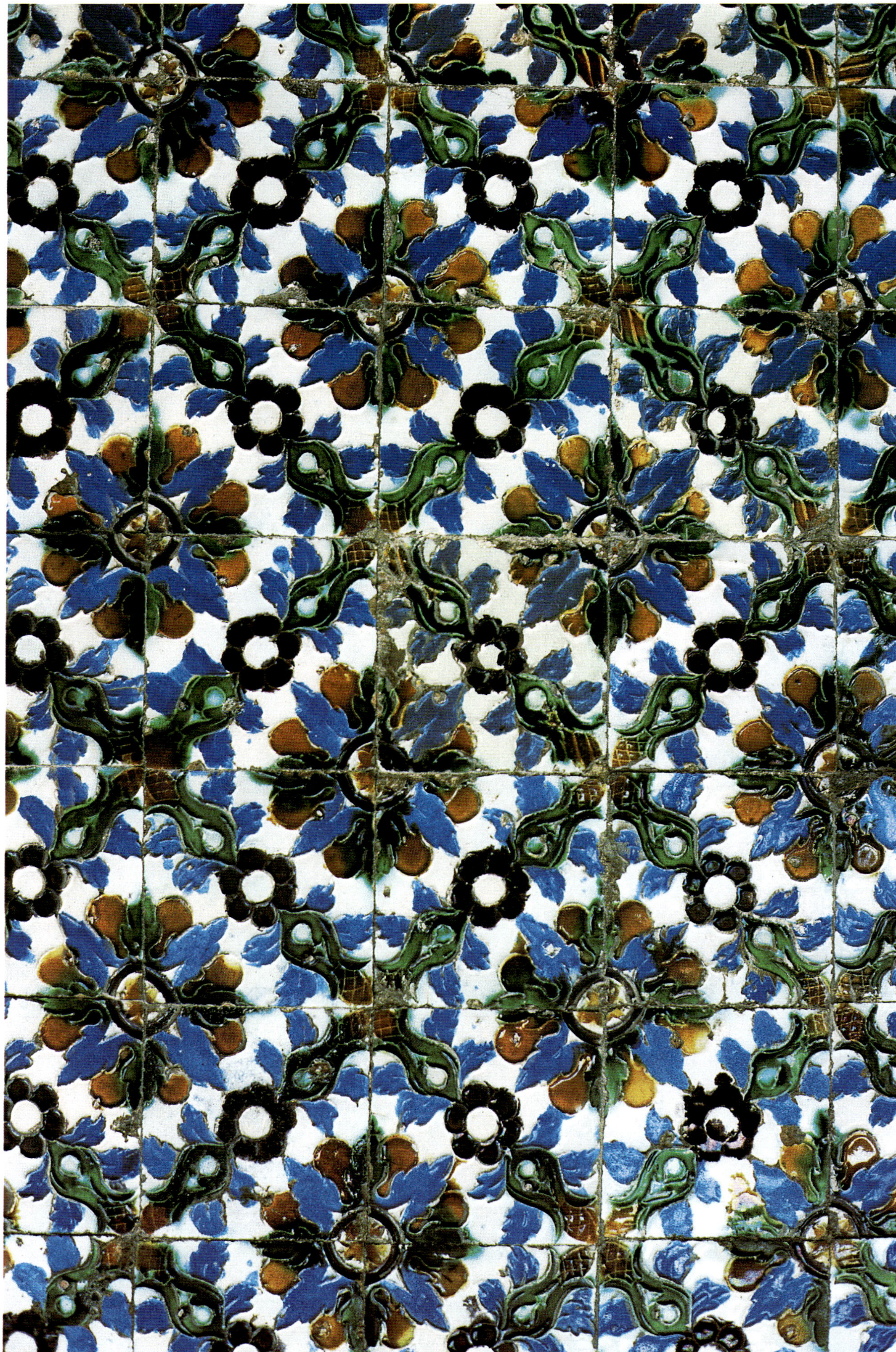

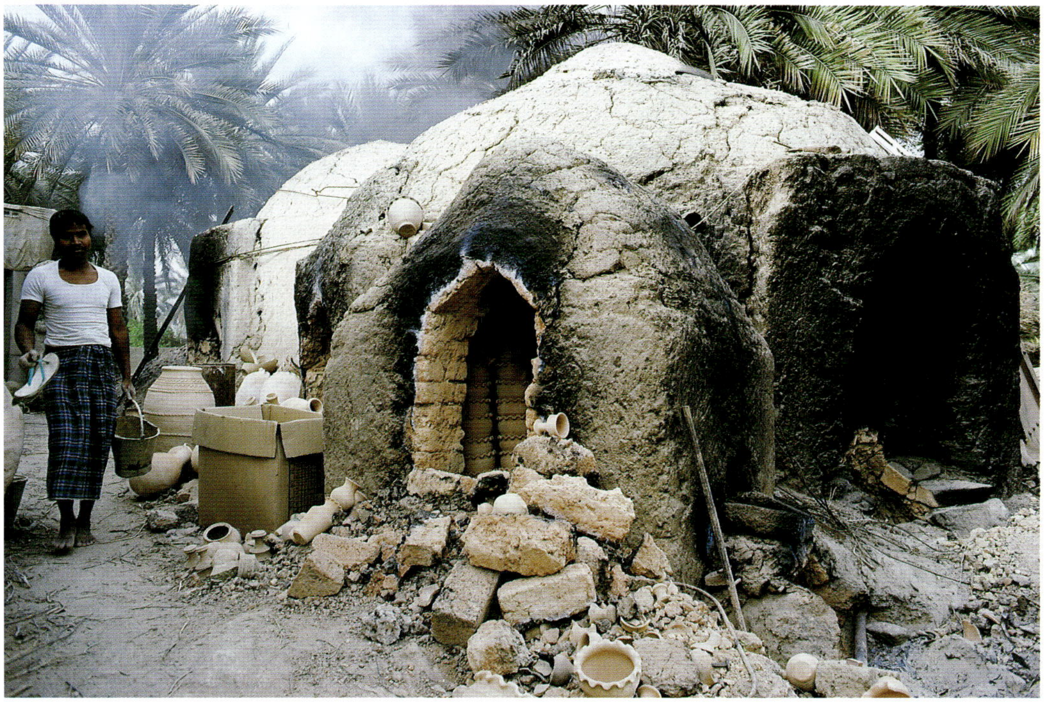

♦ Traditional pottery kiln in Oman.

that imparts the characteristic lapis-lazuli blue. Adopted from the end of the thirteenth to the mid-fourteenth centuries, this technique, like *mina'i*, was applied over the glaze. As in the case of lusterware, pieces that were decorated using low-temperature methods included both architectural tiles and tableware.

In the context of Islamic ceramics, soft-fired decoration cannot strictly be said to mark a technological leap forward. However, the beauty of their designs and the fact that these techniques are described by Abu'l-Qasim make them worthy of interest. The body onto which such decoration is applied is invariably a piece that has already been subjected to hard-firing temperatures. Here is Abu'l-Qasim's description: "If they want to gild[3] transparent or opaque pieces they hammer a *mithqal* of red gold into twenty-four sheets, putting paper covered with plaster between them. They cut them carefully with scissors, and stick them with a pen onto the vessels with dissolved glue, and smooth them with cotton. For red [gold] they mix *qamsari* [i.e. hematite] with ground glaze and embellish with it. For white, they paint with tin white dissolved in glaze; for black, they use *muzarrad* [chromite] mixed with glaze; and for yellow, iron scale dissolved in glaze. Each of these is put in an earthenware capsule into the gilding furnace specially made for the purpose, and fired from morning till night at a low heat. When they are fired the fire is made smaller and the firebox sealed with clay. From time to time samples are tested. All gilded pieces such as writing [inscriptions], etc. are made in this way. Should they want also seven color vessels [*alat-i haft-rang*], which have passed into oblivion in this time—well, God knows what is right. [*variant*: should they want also the seven color vessels, which have passed into oblivion in this time, which are called in the technical terminology of the artificers *lajvardina*, odd ones of them are found in townships and shrines and they make them after the same pattern [as the *haft-rangi*?] and bake them; but God knows the truth of things.]"[4] The passage as quoted is rather puzzling since in fact Abu'l-Qasim is here giving an account of *haft-rangi* technique rather than of *lajvardina*. The phrase in the variant, in which he adds that the technique has "passed into oblivion in this time," compounds the

FACING PAGE

♦ *Cuenca y arista* ("hollow and ridge") tiles with a rosette motif, c. 1538. Casa de Pilatos, Seville (Spain). The colored oxides are molded prior to firing.

confusion by implying that the term *lajvardina* was an equivalent or synonym for *haft-rangi*. Allan nevertheless stresses that this ambiguity is in all probability the fault of a copyist of the "late" version dated A.H. 991/A.D. 1583. Allan also adds that, although the term *lajvardina* is unknown in sources of the Il-Khanid period, it was definitively adopted to designate these pieces with generally dark blue cobalt ground (*lajvard*).[5]

The production of *haft-rang* (or *mina'i*, the more recently coined but accepted term today) took place over a relatively clearly delimited period, the pieces dated between 1179–80 and 1242 corresponding to the final decades of the Seljuqs and the Khwarazm Shahs. As with luster technique, it should be stressed that the majority of known and dated pieces come from the period of the domination of the shahs of Khwarazm. The wider palette and enhanced potential for coloring that the new technique offered was doubtless the reason for decorative artists now signing their works. The name of Abu Zaid appears on a series of pieces dated between 4 *moharram* A.H. 582/March 27, 1186 and *moharram* A.H. 583/March 1187; the same painter seems later to have turned his attention to decorating lusterware.[6]

From "Mosaic" to Polychrome Tiling

During the Seljuq period in Iran and then in Anatolia surfaces of brick buildings were enlivened primarily by turquoise-blue tilework. By the beginning of the fourteenth century, at Sultaniyya, the blue of copper was combined with cobalt and white, and occasionally with black tiling. Yellow started to appear at the end of the fourteenth century. These various color schemes, initially employed as bricks glazed on one face (called *banna'i*), were later obtained by cutting thinner panels that were then arranged into inlaid tile mosaics. This process made it feasible to create the most sophisticated designs and was greatly appreciated in Timurid lands. The same technique—with an almost exclusive preference for geometric patterns—was exploited in the Maghreb, where it was known as *zellij* (giving rise to the Spanish word *azulejo* that nowadays designates all kinds of ceramic tilework). Stemming from the Arabic *qata'a* ("to cut"), the Spanish word *alicatado* is used for mosaics made up of squares cut and assembled. In the Iranian world, the technique was called *kashi-ye mo'arraq*, meaning "inlaid tiles."

One of the main technological difficulties in producing tiles of various colors is the risk that they run and mix during firing. It is for this reason that high-firing colors appeared relatively late on the scene. Polychrome decoration became popular from the second half of the fifteenth century, following a number of often astonishing but tentative experiments during the thirteenth and fourteenth centuries.

Two entirely distinct techniques make use of glazes of more than one color: in the first, often known as *cuerda seca* (from the Spanish name for the process), the solid-color areas are separated by a substance whose composition varies according to region. In the specific case of Spanish ceramics, the demarcation line virtually vanishes during firing and the unpainted area is revealed as a pattern. In the Muslim East, however, the line is composed for the most part of chromite; it turns black and vitrifies slightly during firing.

The second technique concerns underglaze-painted work: the patterns are drawn on the tile in metallic oxides and fixed with a glue, after which they are coated in a glaze that turns transparent at firing. As for earthenware tiles, they are painted over the glaze and are hence known as overglaze-painted ware. Notwithstanding some comments that remain perplexing from the point of view of technological exactitude, the description Abu'l-Qasim gives of polychrome decorated ceramic is of great

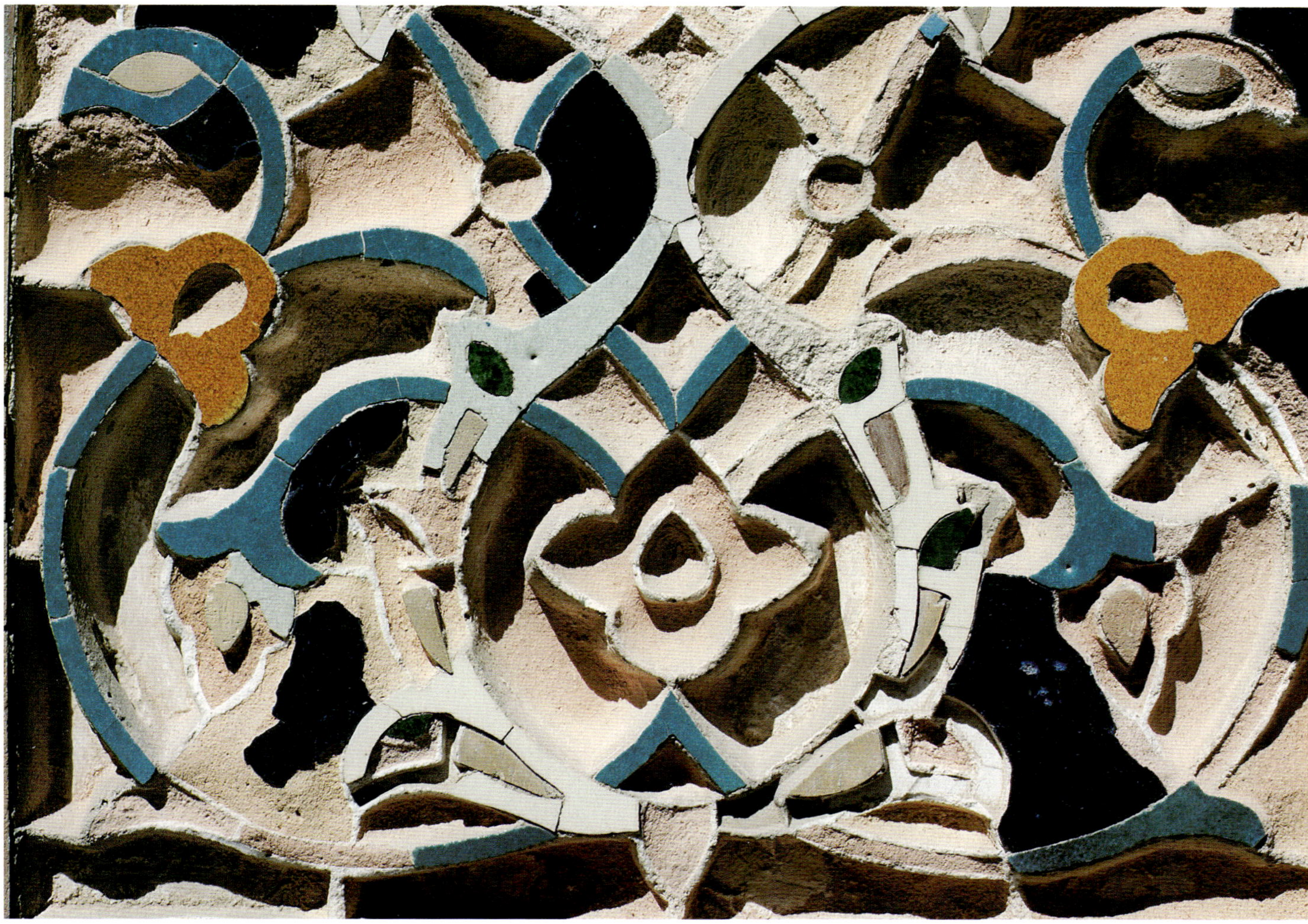

♦ Tilework at the *madrasa* of Ulugh Beg, Samarkand (Uzbekistan), early fifteenth century. The glaze on the motif has partially disintegrated. The body of the ceramic has crumbled in places exposing the mortar that held the elements together.

historical value. In the first place, very few ceramics with this type of decoration dating from the Il-Khanid period have come down to us.[7] In the area of wares, the major representatives of "polychrome" ceramics are a group forming what is known as the "Sultanabad" style from the end of the thirteenth and beginning of the fourteenth centuries. These wares, it should be noted, do not display great chromatic richness: the ground is formed either of a white clay slip or a grisaille, the predominant colors being black, cobalt, and turquoise. The passage in Abu'l-Qasim runs as follows:[8]

> The material for house tiles and writing is made of *bataneh* and *sa-ishkineh* mixed to a dough [paste]—I mean together with glaze frit and clay. There are two types [of glazed tile]: transparent and opaque. The transparent form is also of two types: one for painting on a white ground, and one for painting on a green ground. To paint on a white ground one takes *muzarrad* for black, *sulaimani* [cobalt] for *lajvard* [blue] color, *maghnisiya* [manganese] for red, roasted copper for green, and hammerscale [i.e. iron, for yellow], ground, pounded and sifted. They paint, having mixed each of these with a little *hasa* [and they coat with white frit]. For a green ground they paint with plain *muzarrad*. The vessels are then coated with a glaze frit which has been ground up, finely sifted [mixed with gum-dragon], dissolved in water, and are stood on top of a broad-meshed sieve, which is like the lid of a trough, so that excess of color [glaze] drips away. They are dried in the sun.
>
> If they want a green ground they coat on a mixture of ten parts powdered glaze frit to a quarter of a part of [a *mithqal* of]

FACING PAGE

♦ Close-up of a cut-tile mosaic panel with a floral pattern. Mosque of Wazir Khan, Lahore (Pakistan), 1634–35.

BELOW

♦ Detail of a pattern in cut-tile mosaic with a vegetal arabesque motif (see also preceding page). *Madrasa* of Ulugh Beg, Samarkand (Uzbekistan), early fifteenth century.

roasted copper. The craftsmen call this "*tini*." It comes out of the firing transparent green, like green *mina*. If they use one part of *lajvard* [cobalt] to forty parts of glaze frit it becomes transparent blue like a sapphire. If for every ten [*or*: two] parts of glaze frit they add one part of *maghnisiya* [manganese] it comes out black as *shabeh* [jade], and if they add less it comes out the reddish-purple color of an eggplant.

If they want an opaque color such as turquoise they add for every *man* of ground tin ten *dirhams* of ground roasted cooper and coat this on. If they want *lajvard* color they add ten *dirhams* of *Sulaimani lajvard* and daub and coat the vessels with that. If they want a grayer tone they put in less *lajvard* and add a small amount of red *sirinj* [minium]. If they use an absolutely plain color the vessels come out of the heat white.[8]

Analysis of "Sultanabad"-style ware with which Abu'l-Qasim's text is contemporary demonstrates that a white silica slip is laid on the stone-paste and decorated with black lines with traces of cobalt beneath a transparent, colorless alkaline glaze.[9] If the comparison of text with "Sultanabad"-style ceramics is fairly conclusive, the situation as regards the production of polychrome tiles in the Il-Khanid period is much less clear, as this type of tilework is relatively rare in the Iranian area.

Perhaps the only underglaze "polychrome" tiles known of before this time are those adorning the Kubadabad palace at the Beyşehir complex in Anatolia, dating from 1236 (today housed in the Karatay Madrasa Museum, Konya). In the Il-Khanid period, Iran probably opted for more spectacular forms of architectural ornament, such as large-sized luster tiles or panels decorated with low-fired *mina'i* or *lajvardina* designs.

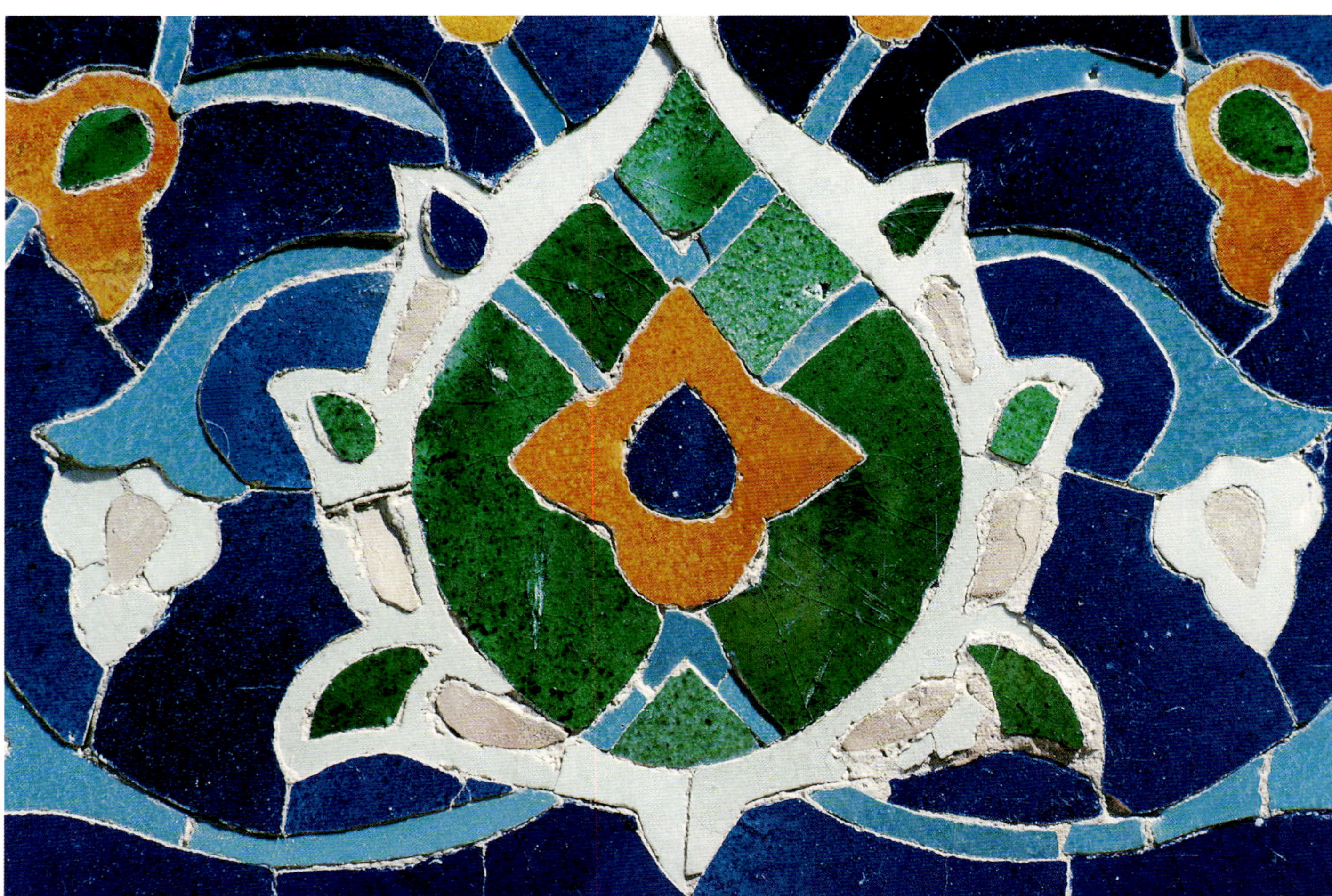

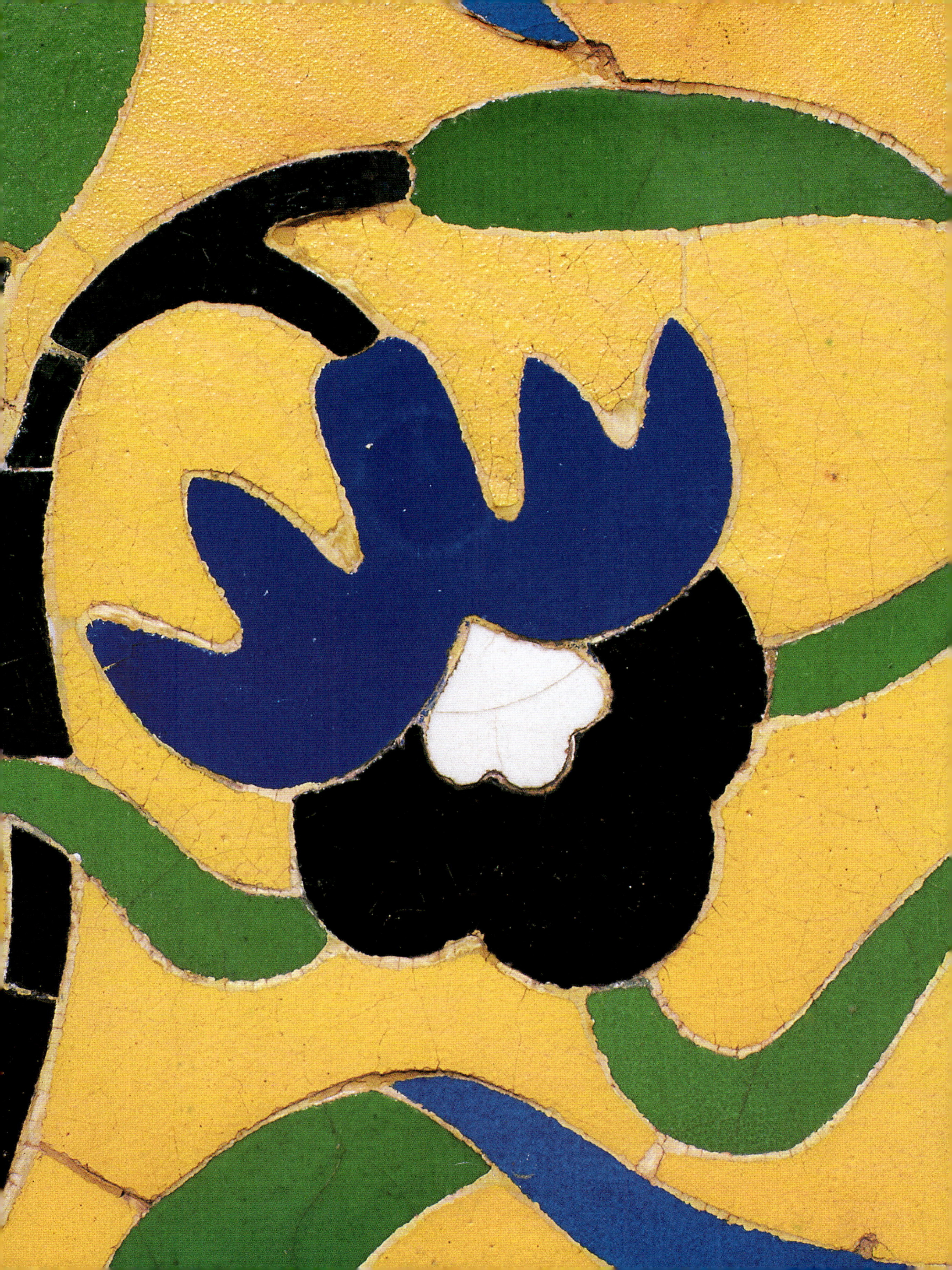

Decorative Designs

On the edifices of ancient Greece and in the temples of India sculpture played a prominent role, while painting fulfilled a similar function on the walls of buildings in the West, but in Muslim architecture it is decorative ceramics that takes pride of place. Indeed, in some instances at least, there is a case for treating such decorative practices, usually considered solely as a craft, as one of the "fine arts" of the Islamic world.

The misgivings of the Muslim world in respect of figurative art are well known. Especially obvious in the realm of religious architecture, this "iconophobia" furthered the development of abstract design. In addition, one of the commonest construction materials, brick, was well adapted to geometrical patterns in architectural decoration; indeed this was an area in which architects and stonemasons from all over the Islamic world proved extraordinarily inventive. With the incorporation of initially turquoise enameled brickwork, builders gradually introduced polychrome into Muslim constructions. It is undeniable that the interplay between geometrical patterns is particularly effective in bringing out architectural forms—the verticals, the soffits of an arch, or the *muqarnas* hanging from a vault, for instance. Occasionally such geometrical patterns meld into calligraphic forms, such as angular Kufic. The geometric motifs themselves—just like those inspired by plant forms—occupy a substantial part of the surface. The diffusion of geometrical patterns was facilitated by a rich scientific environment, with geometry and mathematics being extensively studied throughout the Muslim world. Geometry treatises were even written with the architectural decorator in mind.[10] The recent publication of the "Topkapi Scroll" provides a welcome opportunity to assess one of the very few examples of "cartoons" to have come down to the present day.[11] The geometrical designs derive in part from simple shapes (triangle, square, and hexagon) and in part from more involved forms, such as multi-pointed stars, often linked by intricate geometrical interlacing. In the Iranian region, these interlaced motifs are known as *band-e rumi* ("Rum bands"): this is the type of decoration called *tracería* ("tracery") in Spain. As for the Persian term *hazar-baf* ("thousand weave"), it designates decorative schemes in which plain and stained bricks alternate in patterns reminiscent of basketweave.

Vegetal ornament originally derived from the stylization of the decorative repertory of late Western Antiquity (acanthus leaf), but also from motifs adopted from arts of the Sasanid tradition (outstretched wings). The generic heading "arabesque" often includes all sorts of intricate, palmette interlace motifs. In Spain and the Maghreb, palmette interlace was known as *tawriq* (or *ataurique* in Spain); in Iranian and Turkish lands, the same genus of pattern is designated by the word *eslimi* ("Islamic motif"). When the vegetal patterns take on a more Chinese appearance inspired by Far Eastern decorative models, they were named *khatai* ("from Cathay"; in Turkish, *hatai*). In the Ottoman sphere, these two patterns are occasionally used in conjunction (*eslimi-hatai*) in the form of palmette interlace combined with flowers (peonies and lotus). Also in Turkish lands, the decorative style incorporating large serrated leaves that open twisting and turning in between other motifs is known as *saz*. From the sixteenth century in Ottoman territory—and rather later in Iran and India—the vegetal patterns deployed adopted a more naturalistic appearance. As the eighteenth and nineteenth centuries wore on, there emerged floral motifs inspired by Western herbals mingled with rocaille features derived from the European Rococo.

Decorative schemes depicting animals and human figures are distributed unevenly in the Islamic world. In Turkey, and above all in North Africa, it is certainly

FACING PAGE

♦ The *zellij* technique can be used to clad curved surfaces, as on this pillar at the Glaoui Kasbah at Telouet (Morocco).

♦ Iznik tiles with a floral pattern. *Türbe* of Haseki Hürrem Sultan (1557–58), wife of Suleyman the Magnificent, Süleymaniye complex, Istanbul.

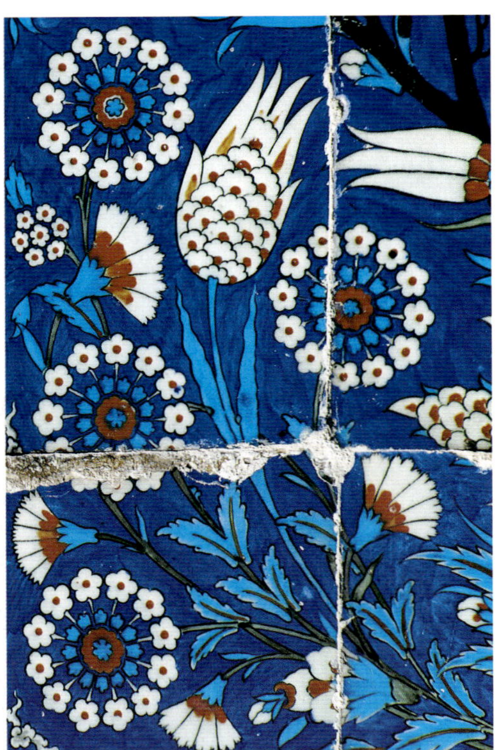

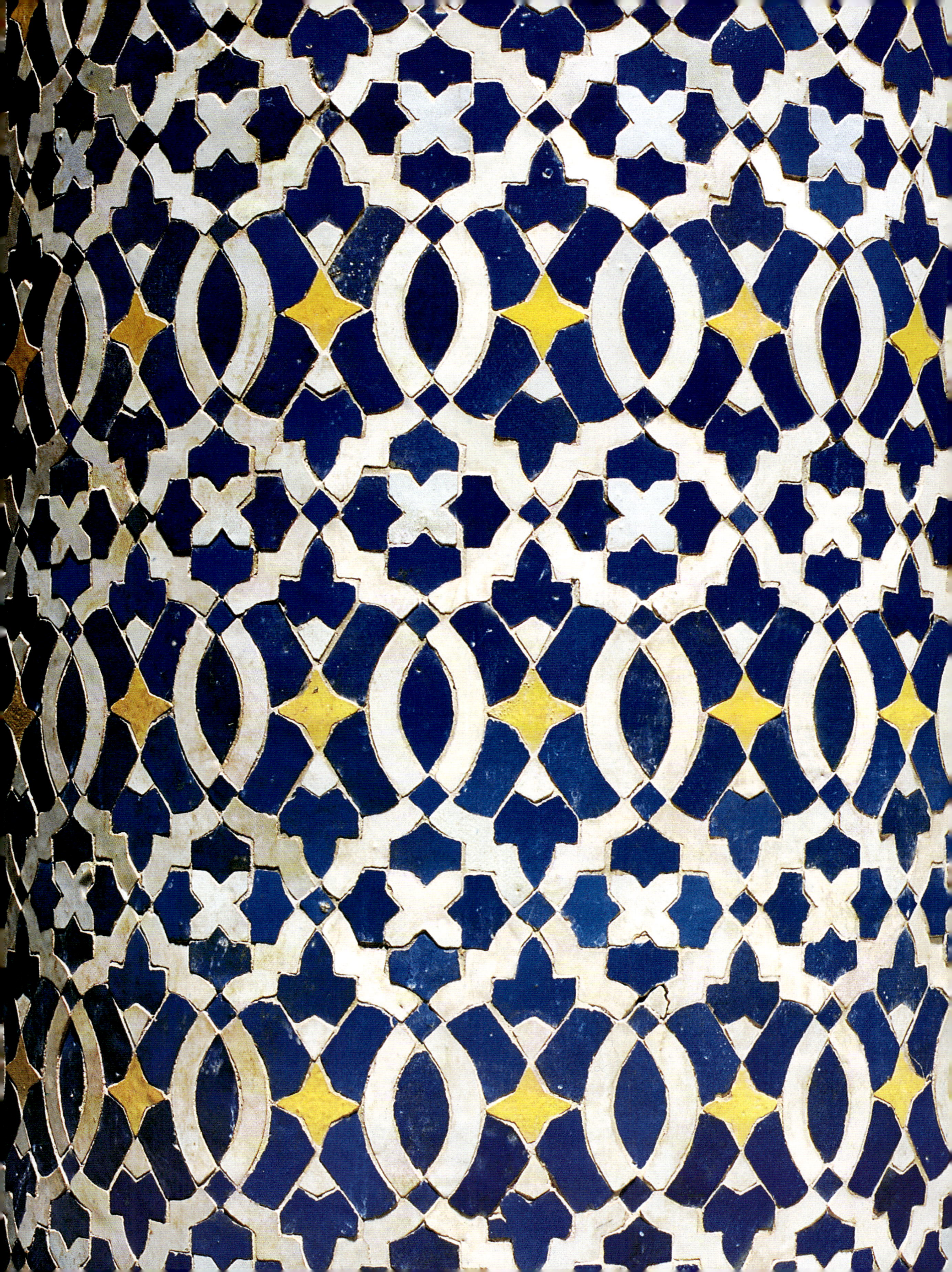

FROM TOP TO BOTTOM

♦ "Black line" polychrome ceramic panel in the Safavid style depicting the story of Farhad and Princess Shirin. Palais d'Orient, Tunis (Tunisia). This panel, together with a number of others, was reassembled in Tunisia in the late nineteenth century.

♦ Detail of assemblage of cross and star stone-paste tiles, luster with touches of cobalt blue and turquoise, from the Ja`far *imamzade* at Damghan (Iran), 1267. Musée du Louvre, Paris (see page 93).

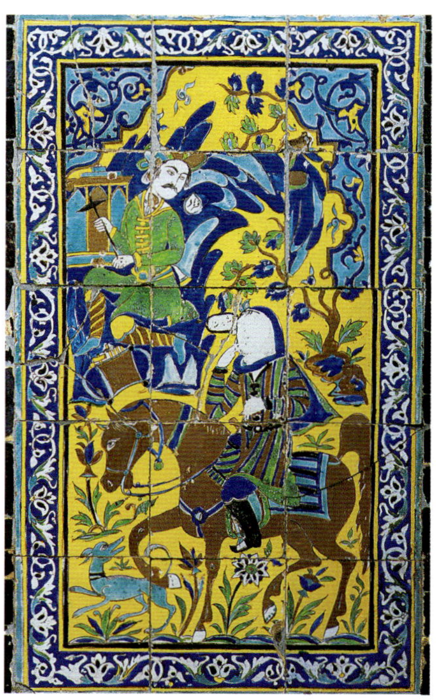

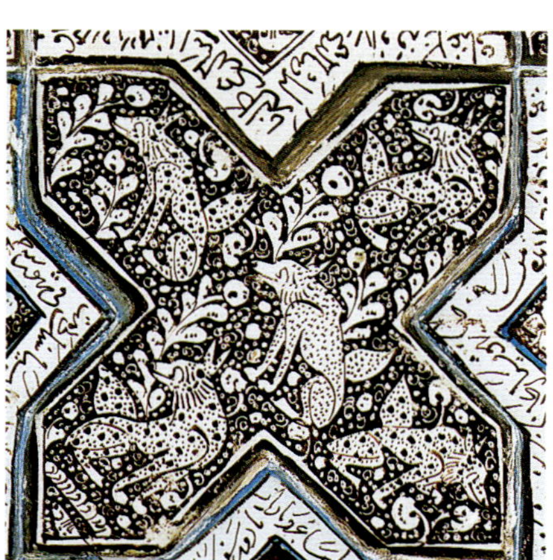

rare to come across living creatures in architectural ornament. In the Turkish world, the limited examples include the star tiles in the palaces of the Seljuqs of Rum and the scattered examples of animals figuring on various tiles of the Ottoman period. The situation is very different, however, in Syria, where from the same period, it is not infrequent to see birds perched up among the plant forms. It is intriguing to note that the very earliest earthenware made in the ninth century in `Abbasid Iraq was adorned with fowl of various species (cockerels, cranes, ducks). Perhaps it was precisely the fact that birds are creatures not bound to the earth that conferred on them their privileged place in Muslim decoration. Symbolic at once of the passage from earth to heaven, of love and faithfulness, or of wealth and the exotic (in the case of parrots and peacocks), birds seemed to have been the animals best adapted to life in what is a priori a non-figurative decorative environment. Other animals, such as lions and some species of deer, do occur occasionally, however. The mosque of the Shah at Isfahan, for example, possesses a remarkable panel adorned with four-footed creatures and birds. This type of decorative scheme is, however, extremely rare in religious buildings.

As for depictions of human beings, they occur over an even more limited geographical range. We have already mentioned the painted stars in the palace of the Seljuqs of Rum; in sanctuaries in Iran from the same period luster or low-fired decoration presenting human figures can also be found. It is above all in the Safavid era in Iran that historiated tiles are most numerous, adorning secular buildings especially. Similarly, the fort at Lahore is representative of figurative art in Mughal India.

Finally there is the most characteristic of all decorative types in Islamic art: calligraphy. The presence of Arabic inscriptions in architecture is one of the rare unifying features of Muslim art generally, although the styles it adopts vary depending on region and period. Angular Kufic has already been mentioned in connection with geometrical decoration, although that script itself possesses numerous variants, such as floriated, plaited, and interlaced. Cursive styles of Arabic originally derived from Naskhi; classified as the six *qalams* ("pens"), the six calligraphic styles (Thuluth, Naskhi, Muhaqqaq, Rayhani, Tawqi`, and Riqa`) were elaborated in Baghdad in the tenth century by the great calligrapher, Ibn Muqlah.[12] Cursive styles diversified relatively rapidly. Thanks to the rhythm imparted by its elongated, vertical strokes, Thuluth is the script most commonly utilized for monumental inscriptions. In the lands of the Maghreb, the *maghribi* style was employed in conjunction with the classical Arabic forms. In the Muslim East, from Turkey to India, monumental inscriptions are formed from a typically Persian style, Nasta`liq, invented at the end of the fourteenth century.

This rapid overview of the various types of decoration serves to demonstrate the extreme variety of Islamic art, as well as the very different esthetic principles prevalent in each region, notably in respect of the use of figurative elements.

Workshops and Artists

The singular rarity of artists' signatures is a remarkable feature of Muslim art, and the situation is no different when it comes to architectural decorative ceramics, the names of artists and craftsmen involved having very seldom come down to us. Analysis of several of the more lavish monuments suggests that a number of individuals were employed in creating the decoration. First there was the architect or project manager, the individual responsible for the construction of the building as a whole. He might be assisted by a designer–decorator, who was responsible for making templates for the decoration

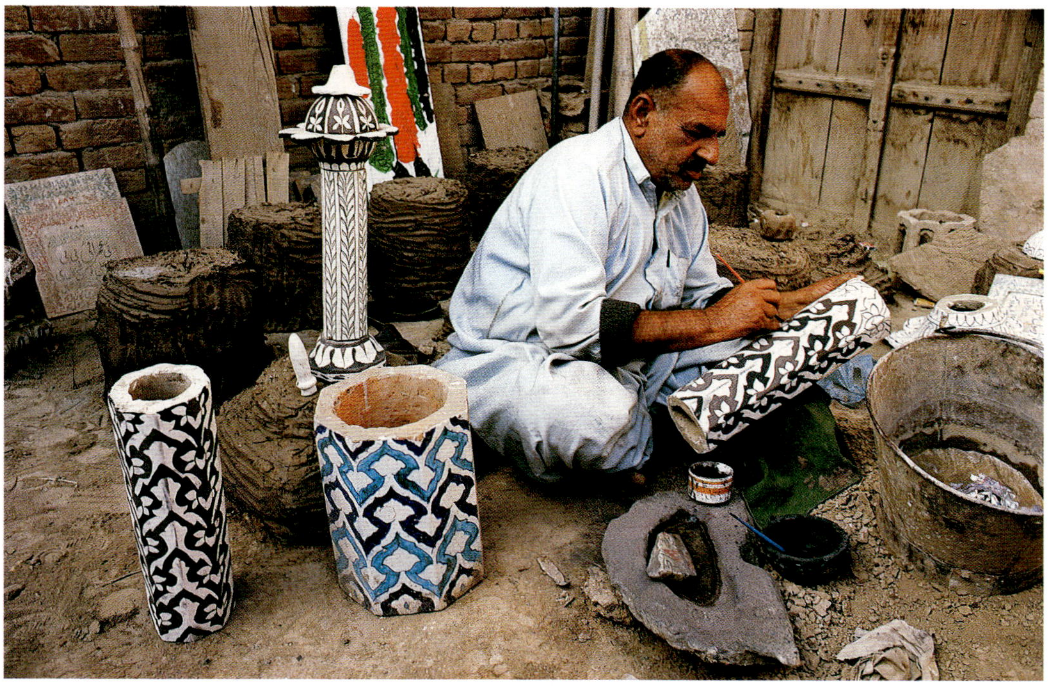

♦ A ceramic craftsman painting the bisc with metallic oxides whose true colors will only be revealed after firing.

and who would collaborate when necessary with a calligrapher for the inscriptions. There then came the master craftsmen in ceramics, who would oversee the execution of the decorative scheme, aided by craftsmen potters, painters expert in decorating ceramics, and terracotta modelers, together with a small army of lesser workers charged with ensuring that the rest of the production chain, from gathering raw materials and fuel to firing and applying decoration, went smoothly. The names of a few of these artisans are known through scattered commemorative inscriptions, signatures on the monuments, or remarks in occasional historical sources. The monuments for which the whole production team is recorded, however, can be counted on the fingers of one hand.

We do know of a few family workshops in which prestigious works in ceramic—such as luster *mihrabs*—were crafted. There is the family of Abu Tahir, for example, which was active over a period of two hundred years, from the twelfth to the fourteenth centuries, its manufacturing activity being centered at the city of Kashan. Other names of potters-cum-decorators are noted in various regions of the Islamic world, for instance Ghaibi al-Tawrizi for decors executed during the Mamluk period at Damascus, or the "masters of Tabriz," who collaborated on the Green Mosque complex at Bursa at the beginning of the fifteenth century. In spite of a few names gleaned here and there, it is impossible most of the time to know precisely how the work that went into these decorations was organized in the workshop. Luckily, there survive a few exceptional records that allow us to gain some idea of the situation in other centers of production. A number of accounting documents pertaining to ceramics manufactories in sixteenth-century Constantinople have recently been published.[13] They document the outlay and scrupulously list the supplies and wages for the workers and master ceramists over a two-year period. This type of record is unfortunately infrequent and in the majority of cases it is not even clear whether the workshops were private concerns or funded directly by the court administration who employed them.

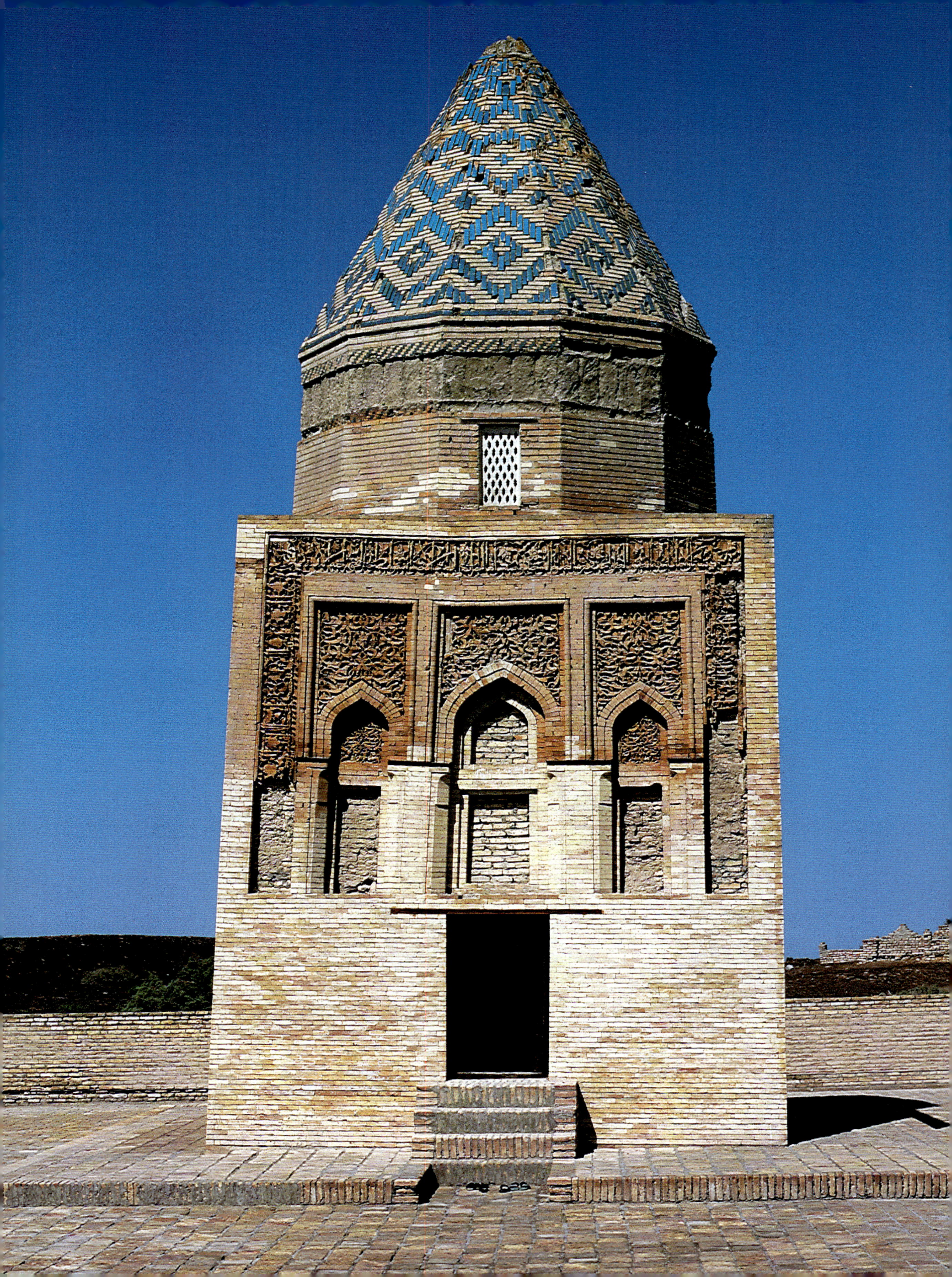

I
The East before the Mongols

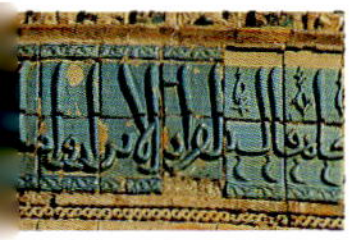

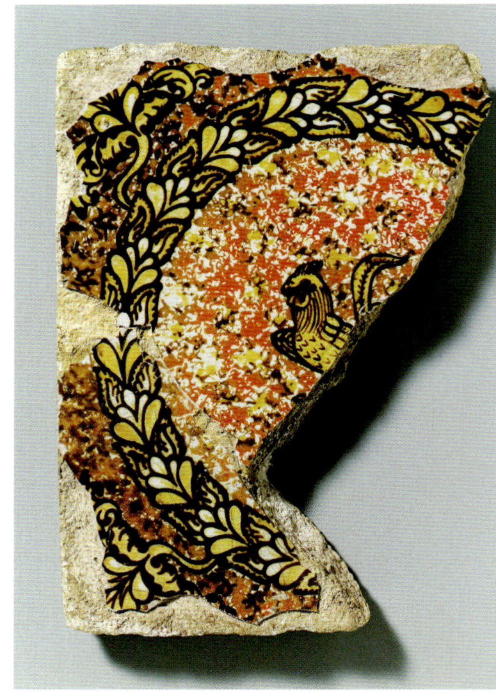

The Rise and Influence of `Abbasid Tin-Enameled Earthenware

♦ Glazed polychrome earthenware luster tile from the palace of al-Mu`tasim, Samarra (Iraq), mid-ninth century. Height 28 cm. Museum für Islamische Kunst, Berlin.

The extraordinary development of the potter's craft during the Samarra period (836–83) gave rise not only to earthenware but also to the techniques of metal luster. The reasons for this upsurge in the ceramic arts are probably to be found in the impact made by the arrival of Chinese porcelain in the `Abbasid court. These magnificent and luxurious objects, especially the Tang white porcelain being produced at that period, served to spur technical research in the search for imitations. In the absence of the necessary raw materials (kaolin, first and foremost) and above all of the specialized know-how to obtain the high temperatures required for firing porcelain, these experiments resulted instead in the production of a clay paste coated in a white glaze opacified with tin, known as tin-enamel or tin-glaze.

It was perhaps due to this wealth of experimentation in ceramics that during the same period a decorative technique that until then had been confined to glass-making began to emerge in pottery: metallic luster. This process seems to have been frequently employed for decorating wares and ceramic artifacts. It is worth noting, however, that whereas in subsequent eras luster is always monochrome, early `Abbasid pieces exploit a broad range of luster hues, from straw yellow through cherry red and olive green to a dark-toned brownish violet. As for tilework on buildings, examples of this practice in the ninth century remain extremely rare. It is once again at Samarra in the palace of Caliph al-Mu`tasim (also known as Jawsaq al-Khaqani) that tilework decorated with polychrome luster appears. Apparently confined to the harem apartments, these tiles are monochrome, the dominant hues being red, yellow, brown, or olive-green. Each one presents a foliage wreath encircling a bird (notably a cockerel in the museum at Berlin, but a crane on one of the fragments in the British Museum), the central field and outer surround of the wreath being flecked in a lighter-hued monochrome in the middle that gets darker toward the edges. According to the reconstitution of the whole ensemble proposed by Friedrich Sarre at the beginning of the twentieth century, these polychrome tiles would have been bordered on four sides by monochrome glazed tiles in the form of a stretched-out hexagon, together forming an octagon. Other luster tiles were simply flecked and doubtless alternated with those decorated with birds as paving. A number of scholars, among them Richard Ettinghausen and Oleg Grabar, have described these bird motifs ensconced in wreaths as being reminiscent of ornaments of Hellenistic origin of the kind found on the baked-clay tile

PAGE 32
♦ Mausoleum of Il-Arslan, Kunya Urgench (Turkmenistan), c. 1172.

ceiling in the synagogue at Dura-Europus, Syria (dating from the third century A.D.). Be that as it may, the exceptional quality of the Samarra tiles is clear, in terms of both technique and imagery, which is characteristic of the eclectic tastes of the period. It should be said, however, that comparison with the use elsewhere of luster tilework during the ninth century is rarely feasible, the most important exception being the decorative scheme on the *mihrab* in the Great Mosque at Qairouan (also known as the Mosque of Sidi ʿUqba).

Founded in 670 by ʿUqba bin Nafi, the mosque at Qairouan in Tunisia was entirely refurbished during the era of Aghlabid domination. Work began in 836 in the reign of Ziyadat-Allah I (817–38) and continued with significant additions, notably in 862 and 875 (the reigns of Ahmad, 856–63, and Ibrahim II, 875–902). The *mihrab* is in the form of a deep semicircular recess flanked by reused Antique columns. Tiles with luster decoration are set into the plasterwork in the extrados of the arch and on the upper reaches of the wall. The origin of these tiles remains a matter for discussion. They can be divided into two groups according to style: the first comprises polychrome decorated tiles incorporating complex motifs, some of which can be recognized as being of Sasanid derivation (for example, the outstretched wings); the second are decorated in monochrome, the patterns (floral, geometric, or calligraphic) being much less complex. A passage from an Arabic chronicle composed at the end of the fifteenth century throws some light on the origin of these tiles: "For the work of the *mihrab*, they brought precious tiles intended for a reception hall which he [the emir] had wished to build, from Baghdad

♦ Great Mosque, Qairouan (Tunisia).

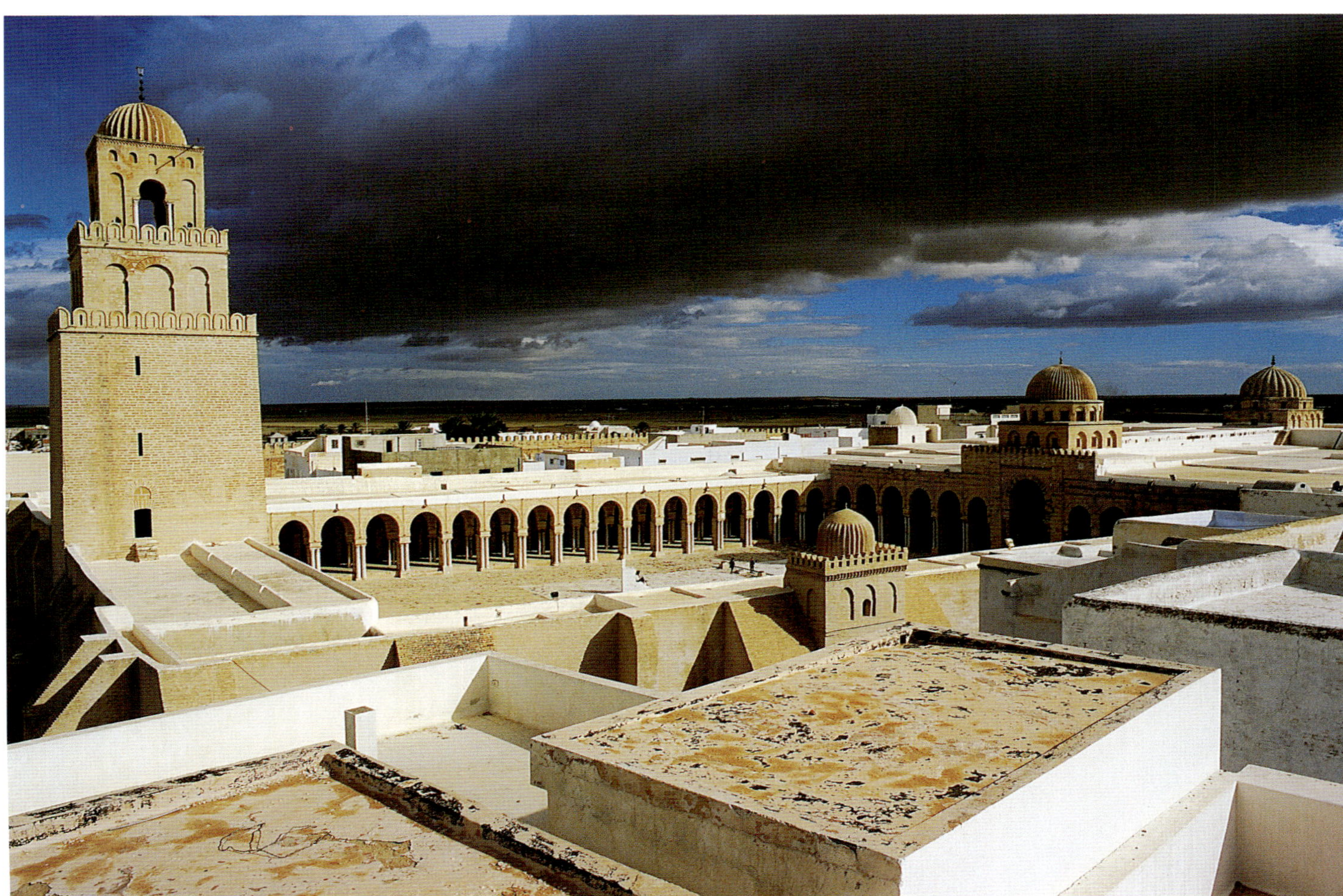

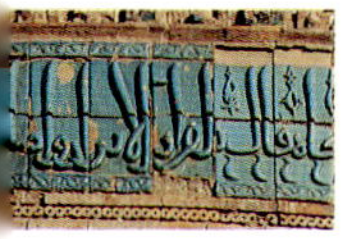

came teak wood for beams and these were made into the *minbar* for the mosque. There also came pieces of marble for the *mihrab* from Iraq and these were assembled in the mosque and the tiles were placed on the face of the *mihrab*. A man from Baghdad made additional tiles and [the mosque] was decorated in this marvelous way with marble and gold and beautiful materials."[14]

According to an account drawn up six centuries after the event, the polychrome tiles came directly from Iraq, while the monochrome group was made on-site by an Iraqi craftsman. However, it should be stressed that there is no conclusive evidence as to where the tiles at Samarra or the polychrome examples at Qairouan were manufactured. According to the most recent research, it seems probable that the main center of production for fine tiles of this type was the town of Basra, in Lower Mesopotamia. This site seems to have manufactured a large number of pieces

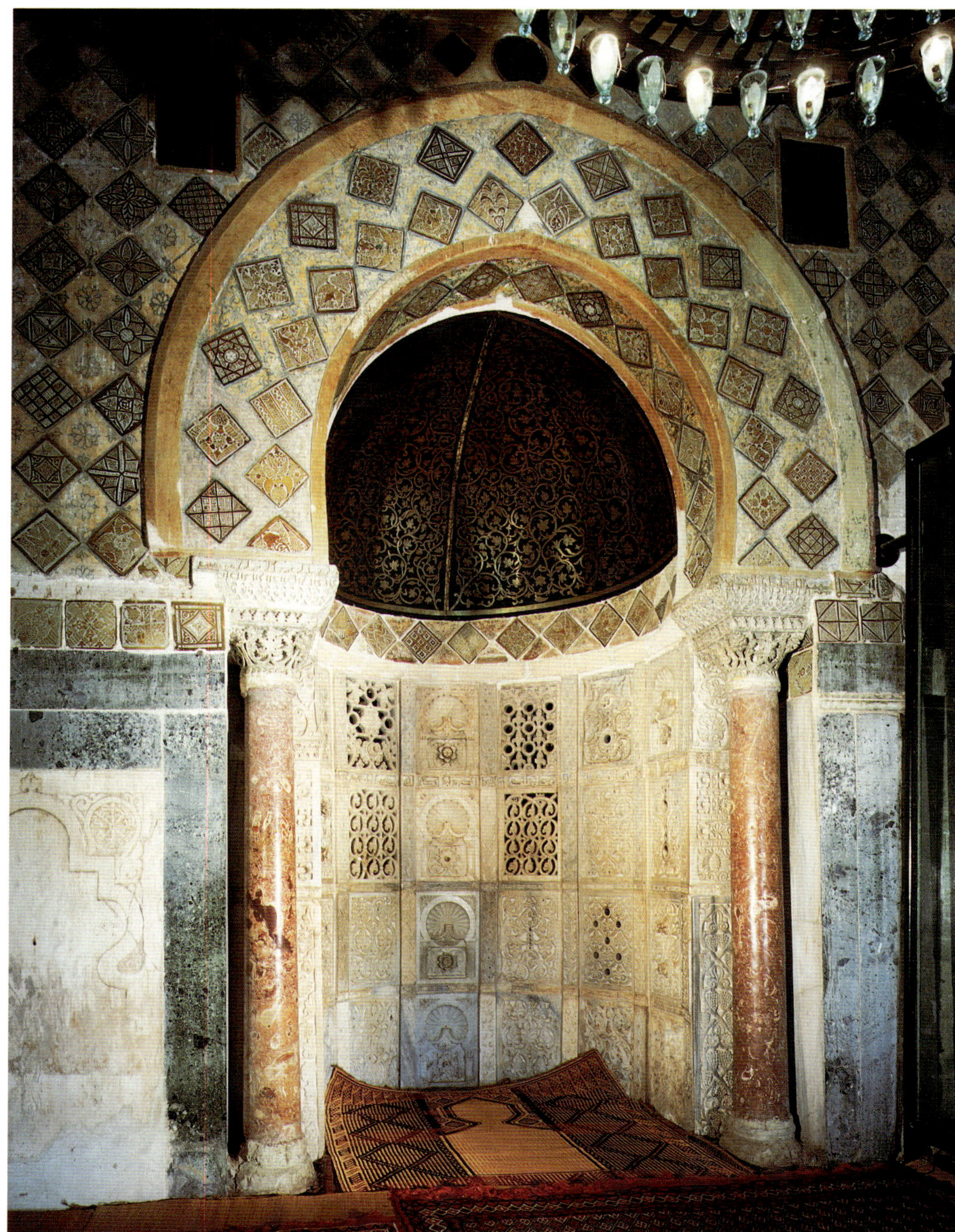

♦ The *mihrab* at the Great Mosque at Qairouan, ninth century, decorated with splendid metallic luster tilework, some of which probably comes from ʿAbbasid Iraq.

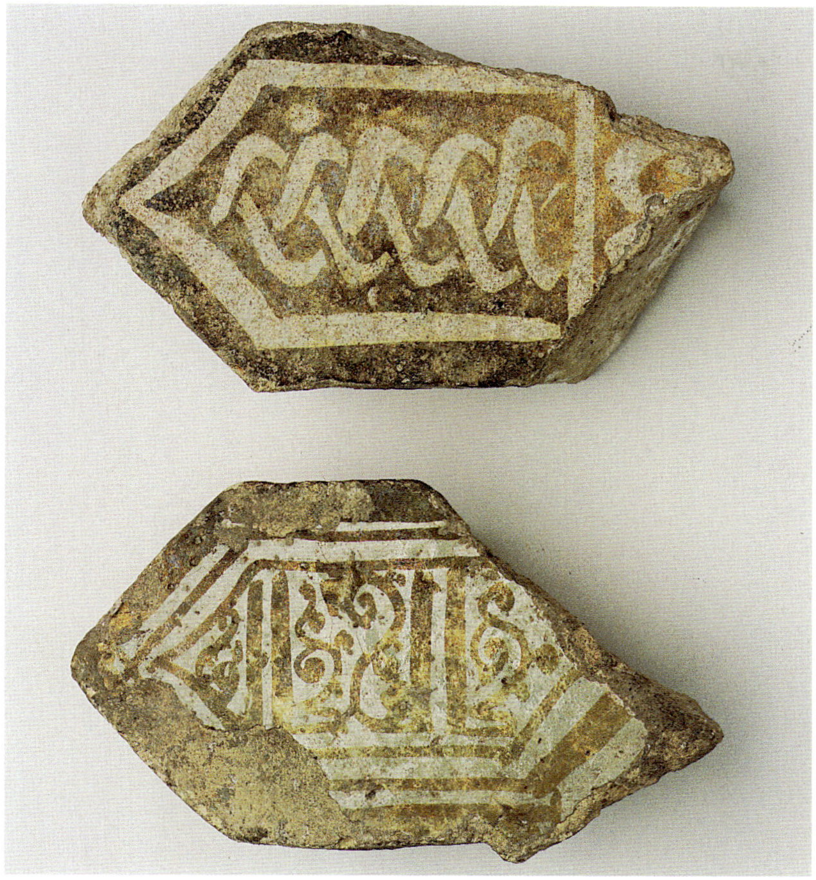

♦ Luster tiles originally from the Qa`la of the Banu Hammad (Algeria, eleventh century). Musée des Arts Décoratifs, Paris.

(primarily tableware), not only in the ninth century, but also throughout much of the tenth. By the end of the century, however, Iraq seems to have ceased producing ceramics with metallic luster decoration.

Curiously, a small-scale production of luster tiles, rather rudimentary in manufacture compared to earlier examples, is attested in the palace complex of the Qa`la of the Banu Hammad, in Algeria. The few fragments unearthed dating from the eleventh century (housed in the Musée des Arts Décoratifs, Paris) are elongated hexagons ornamented with stylized epigraphic motifs (exclamations of well-wishing such as *baraka*, "blessing," and *yumm*, "prosperity"), and elementary geometric patterns.

The manufacture of luster-painted decorative ceramics continued in Fatimid Egypt (969–1171), with stunning results, although the technique is confined essentially to tableware. Egyptian ceramic tilework of this time is very rare and the decorative techniques used (monochrome underglaze *sgraffito*, for instance) are less sophisticated. The few tile fragments found at Sabra Mansuriyya, one of the Fatimid capitals in Ifriqiya, are simply monochrome olive-green glaze.[15]

After a century of opulence that witnessed the construction of a host of gigantic buildings (most especially in Samarra), the tenth century saw a steep decline in caliphate power. Simultaneously, in the east of the region, regional dynasties appeared that were soon busy developing court arts of their own. For the Iranian world, this period is known as the "Persian Renaissance." This era of division was followed in the mid-eleventh century by a period of unification in teh wake of the arrival of the Seljuqs. The latter, in adopting novel architectural models that were to become influential over a vast area, would profoundly mark the Muslim East. After a short "Renaissance" period, the `Abbasid caliphate crumbled with the invasions of the Mongols.

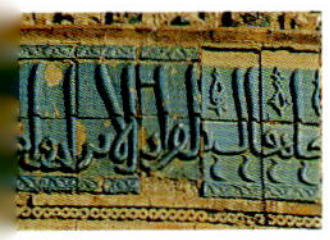

The Iranian East

The foundation of the Samanid emirate (819–1005), with its capital at Bukhara, represents a moment of cultural rebirth for the Iranian world. This can be adduced not only from much Persian literature and writing, but also in architecture, for instance with the tomb of Ismaʿil the Samanid at Bukhara (after 907). Although only unglazed terracotta was utilized in the field of architectural ceramics, the Samanid era did witness an upsurge in the manufacture of ceramic artifacts and tableware, most particularly at Samarkand and Nishapur.

The Ghaznavids, after withdrawing from the Samanid kingdom, went on to found a prestigious principality of their own in what is present-day Afghanistan. Their monuments, which all provide ample evidence of a determination to publicize both their political power and their Sunni fervor, include the site of the Lashkari Bazaar (formerly Bust), a palace complex begun in all probability in the reign of Mahmud of Ghazna. The building of the ensemble was continued by his successors and taken up after the fire of 1149 by the Ghurids, being abandoned forever only following its destruction by the Mongols in 1221. The five- to six-kilometer site along the course of the Hilmand River is one of the very few examples of caliphate architecture in eastern regions to have survived to the present-day. In addition to a number of palaces and pavilions, there are also remains of gardens, and traces of what were temporary constructions. The "south" palace faces a courtyard possessing four *iwans*. The square-shaped throne room contains wall paintings depicting armed guards, a return to a theme typical of traditional Iranian iconography. In addition, these paintings constitute one of the few fresco ensembles from medieval Iran to be conserved.

The plan of the palace of Masʿud III (1099–1115) at Ghazni is similar to that of the Lashkari Bazaar. Ornamentation there is perhaps even richer, especially in the courtyard, where a carved low-relief marble wall panel incorporates arabesque patterns and an epigraphic Kufic frieze. This Persian inscription to the glory of the palace and to the Ghaznavid family is one of the earliest of this type to be preserved. Furthermore, a number of ceramic tiles have been recovered from the site that should probably be assigned to the final phase of its occupation by the Ghurids at the beginning of the thirteenth century. Of various shapes, these tiles are molded with animal and plant motifs under a monochrome lead glaze ranging in color from yellow through bottle green and brown to black.

Also found at Ghazni were minarets of monumental size built by Masʿud III and Bahram Shah (1118–1152) that do not seem to have been associated with a mosque of any kind. They consist of a cylindrical base supporting a lower part with a cross-section like an eight-pointed star and a second, cylindrical tier that has

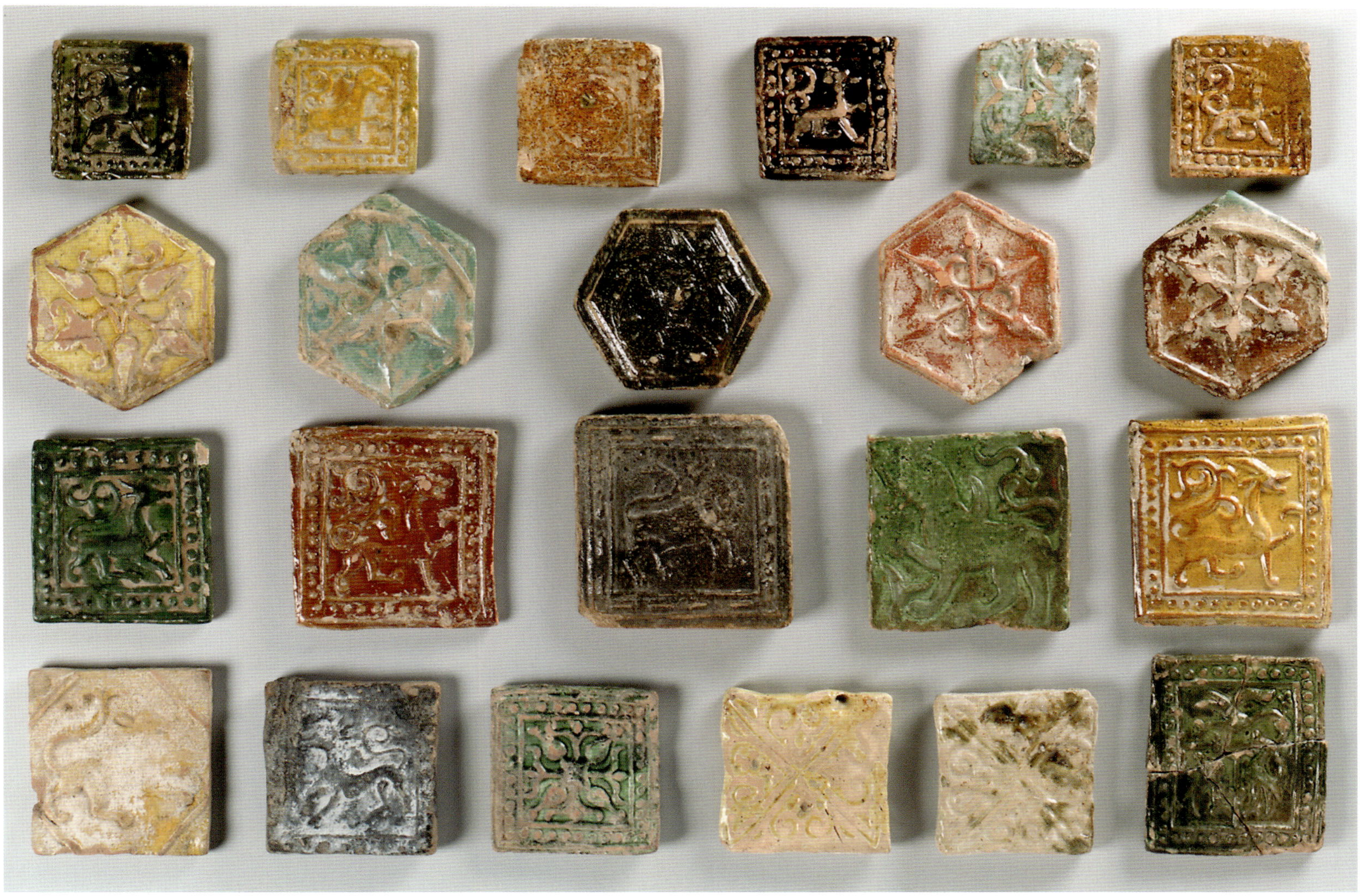

today vanished. They are made entirely of brick with a substantial calligraphic decor in floriated Kufic that lists in particular the titles of the patrons. Other isolated minarets resembling those at Ghazni exist. In a number of cases they would have been attached to a mosque that has since disappeared, while in others the minaret must have functioned as a kind of standard—similar to Hindu "towers of victory" or the triumphal arches of the Romans—serving to crown a military success or exalt the glory of the individual who commissioned it. This seems to have been the case for the minaret discovered in 1957 at Jam in the mountains of Afghanistan, an impressive monument erected by the Ghurid Ghiyath al-Din Muhammad (1163–1202) at his capital, Firuzkuh. The solitary tower seems to have functioned primarily as a commemorative edifice. Its slender form and laudatory inscriptions seem to prefigure the Qutb Minar at Delhi (1199), although there is a crucial difference between the two: whereas the Jam minaret is made of brick with the addition of turquoise ceramic, notably picking out the inscriptions, the edifice at Delhi is entirely of stone (ired sandstone) and is devoid of ceramic ornamentation.

♦ A series of monochrome lead-glazed molded tiles from the palace of Mas˘ud III, Ghazna (Afghanistan), late twelfth to early thirteenth century.

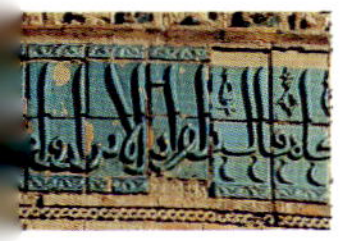

The Qarakhanids

In Transoxiana, the Samanids were definitively unseated by the arrival of the Turkish dynasty of the Qarakhanids (992–1211). These princes continued the architectural work of their Samanid predecessors, although they also brought in new forms. Here too minarets seem to have been enlisted for the purposes of proclamation. In what is today Uzbekistan, for instance, the minaret at Djarkurgan (dated to 1110) comprises a shaft of lobed section standing on an octagonal base. The drum is topped with a Kufic inscription that marked the transition to a second tier (now lost).

The sizable brick-built Kalan minaret at Bukhara is remarkable for its massive form. An inscription furnishes the name of its patron (the Qarakhanid Arslan Shah), its architect, and a date, 1127. Erected outside the mosque, the minaret is linked to it by a walkway. Similar in outline but of slenderer proportions, the 38-meter-high minaret at Vabkent was built considerably later (1197–99), and possesses an important inscription in turquoise glazed ceramic tiles.

Like those of the Samanids, Qarakhanid constructions suffered greatly from Mongol depredations, to the extent that only a few have survived to the present day. The Maghok-i `Attari Mosque (1178–79) in the heart of Bukhara displays total mastery of the art of ornament: the walls of the elegant recessed south front are decorated to right and left with three large rectangular panels of polished brick, which are intricately carved in filigree and finely chiseled. The facade opens up in the middle into a spacious arch the extrados of which displays the remnants of a vigorous inscription band comprising relief-carved clay slabs covered with a monochrome opacified turquoise blue glaze. The letters stand out against a ground formed of leaf scrolls combined with palmettes and fleurons. Contrasting sharply with the surrounding monochrome, the turquoise frieze—in itself a significant ornament—illuminates the whole facade.

Certain monuments, like the mausoleums at Uzgend (Kyrgyzstan), employ mostly carved, unglazed terracotta ornaments with a few discreet dashes of turquoise. The complex is formed by three mausoleums standing side by side, the central one (dating originally from the tenth century) having been clumsily restored. The left-hand mausoleum dates from 1153; the top of the extrados of the arch at the entrance to the one on the right (1186–87) is marked by a turquoise ceramic keystone that provides the only surviving evidence of the technique of glazed ceramic decoration employed in such monuments.

Sadly, many Qarakhanid buildings have today vanished entirely, although occasionally, during archeological excavations, fragments of ceramic decoration are discovered that argue persuasively for the splendor of their architecture.

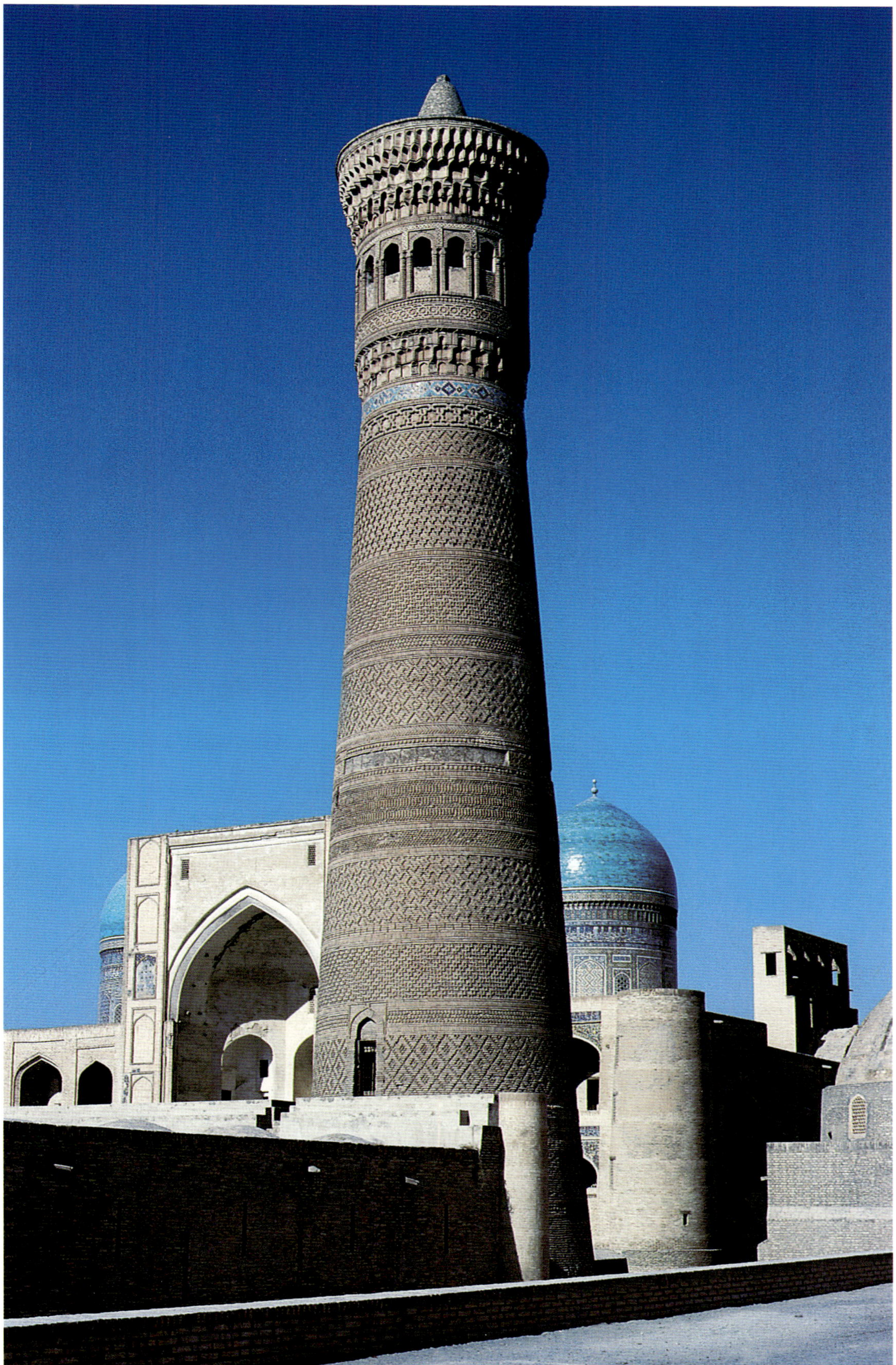

♦ The Kalan minaret, Bukhara (Uzbekistan), dated 1127, is a symbol of Qarakhanid power. Behind the tower appears the facade of the Mir-i ʿArab *madrasa*, 1535–36 (Shaybanid period).

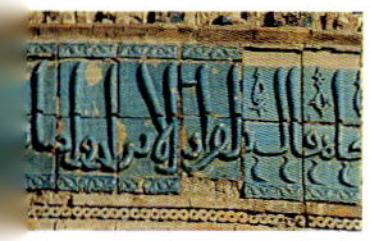

Brick and Turquoise: Seljuq Iran

The Seljuqs, who entered the Iranian world during the first half of the eleventh century, reached Baghdad in 1055. Through repeated incursions into the Near East, their military ambitions, combined with their fervent adherence to Sunnism, created massive upheaval throughout the central Muslim world. In the field of architecture, a continuity with formulae from earlier periods can be discerned in certain types of building, although there was a move toward greater refinement (in stucco decoration) and a predilection for a monumental sense of scale (in funerary architecture in particular). On the other hand, several Seljuq edifices, in reflecting their zealous orthodoxy, are noteworthy for the novelty of their design. The Seljuq era saw the appearance of the "Persian" mosque with its four-*iwan* courtyard, as well as the extraordinary growth of the *madrasa* as an autonomous structure.

Initial forays into polychrome architectural ceramics on facades—provided by turquoise glazed brick—are perhaps to be found at the mausoleum at Radkan in Iran, dated 1020–21. The first glazed ceramic monumental inscription incorporated into a brick revetment is most probably that on the minaret of the Friday mosque at Damghan, dated around 1058. The two tombs at Kharraqan built a few decades later (1067–68 and 1093) are exceptional by the touches of turquoise integrated into the brick decoration. These very early examples were followed by a number of tombs at Maragha in Iranian Azerbaijan, such as the Gunbad-i Surkh (1147) and the "Round Tower" (1167). In the Gunbad-i Surkh (also known as the "Red Tomb"), the inscriptions in plaited Kufic characters executed in turquoise glaze cut slabs laid into the brick facing announce in Arabic: "One day all living beings will perish."

At this time, the use of color in these monuments remained understated, serving simply to bring out the scant inscriptions or emphasize the architectural lines of the construction, without, however, overrunning the entire surface of the walls. Still at Maragha, the later Gunbad-i Kabud (the "Blue Tomb") is dated 1194. Octagonal in plan, this small mausoleum is richly ornamented through the use of unglazed brick, in conjunction with turquoise glazed cut slabs (hence the monument's name) that form a geometrical interlace and an inscriptional frieze above the door recording the date of the building's construction. In the transition zone leading to the drum—which once supported a cupola—a series of *muqarnas*-decorated corbels bears an intricate pattern of stars in turquoise glaze filling each chamber.

Under the influence of the Seljuqs (and that of their vassals, the Qarakhanids), the hitherto spare decoration employing turquoise-colored *banna'i* tilework or brickwork was soon supplanted by the use of

♦ Gunbad-i Kabud, Maragha (Iran), 1194.

pieces of carved or molded ceramic coated in opaque turquoise glaze. Seljuq minarets often differ from their predecessors in having a slenderer shape. That of the Friday mosque at Damghan with its relief inscription under a turquoise glaze has already been mentioned. Dated to 1131, the upper reaches of the cylindrical shaft of the minaret at Sin contains an elegant inscription fringed in turquoise. The minaret at `Ali, Isfahan, dating from the twelfth century, is much more lithe. Its tapering conic shaft that originally soared to a height of 50 meters, provides a striking contrast with the sturdy form of the Kalan minaret at Bukhara (1127). Beneath the overhang of the lower story balcony, turquoise glazed bricks alternate with plain brick, forming geometric interlace patterns and an epigraphic frieze in Kufic.

More sophisticated structurally, the Saraban minaret at Isfahan (built between 1115 and 1130) exhibits two corbeled tiers with *muqarnas* that are ringed with epigraphic bands in turquoise brick. Founded in ancient times, the city of Isfahan was adopted as the Seljuq capital by Alp Arslan (1063–72). At that time, the center of the city huddled round a congregational mosque dating from the `Abbasid era. A brick building with a "Bedouin" plan, it comprised a roof structure resting on cylindrical piers. Between 1072 and 1075, the vizier Nizam al-Mulk added a vast cupola to the mosque in front of the *mihrab*. It was supported by triple squinches borne by a massive structure of square plan. Along the same axis but facing the building, another dome was built in 1088 by Taj al-Mulk. As in Nizam al-Mulk's dome, brick was both the construction material and the sole decorative feature. In 1120, the roof structure was replaced by a series of brick cupolas of incomparable inventiveness and variety. It was also at this time that four *iwans* were added in the courtyard, a feature that was to become characteristic of the Persian mosque (the first four-*iwan* mosque that

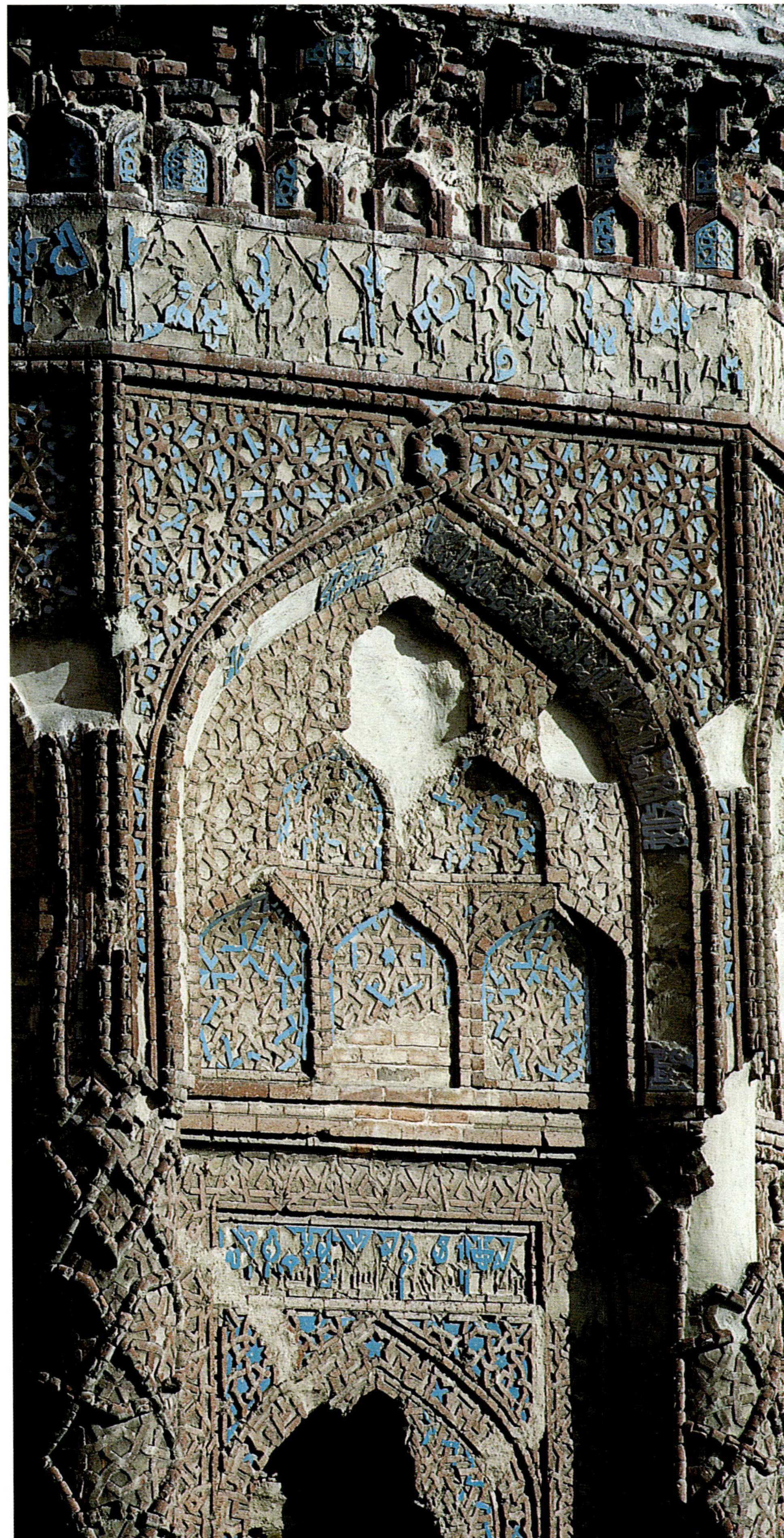

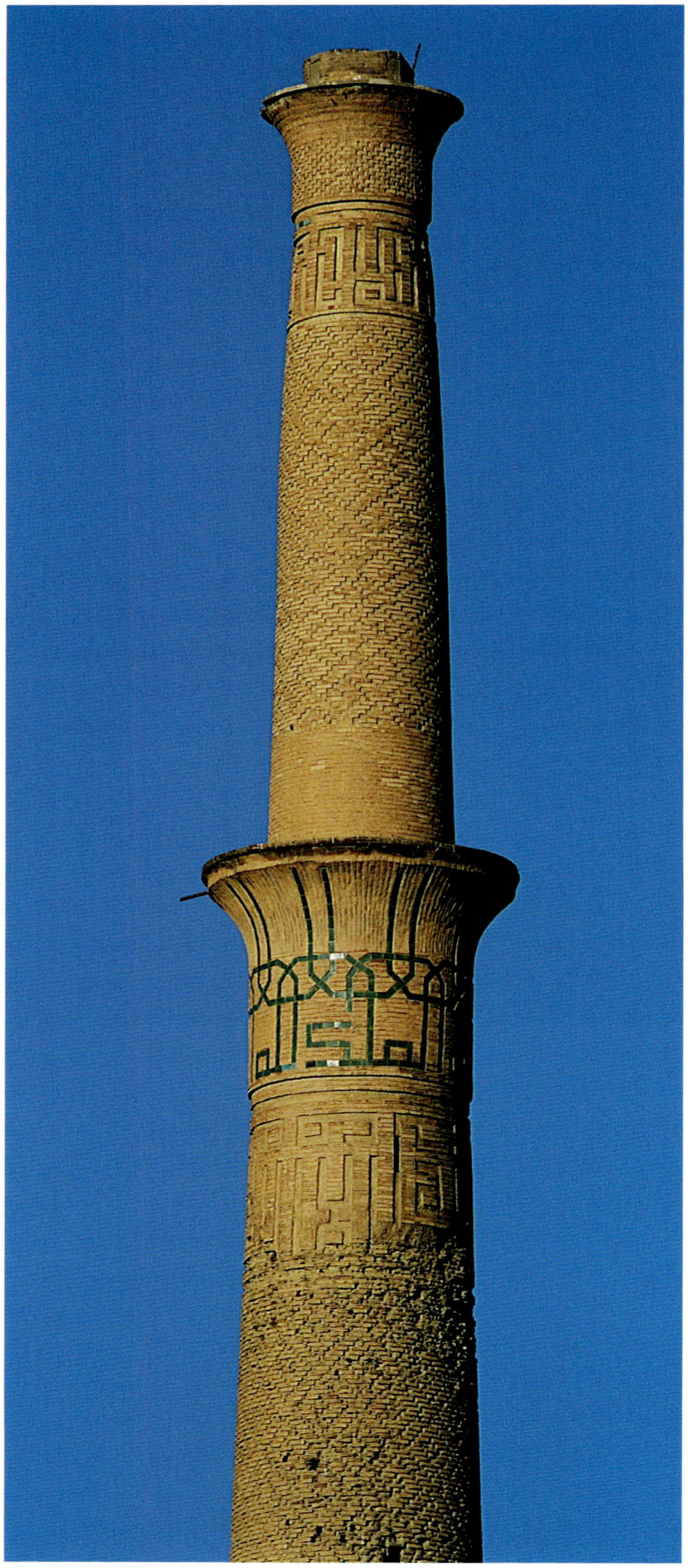

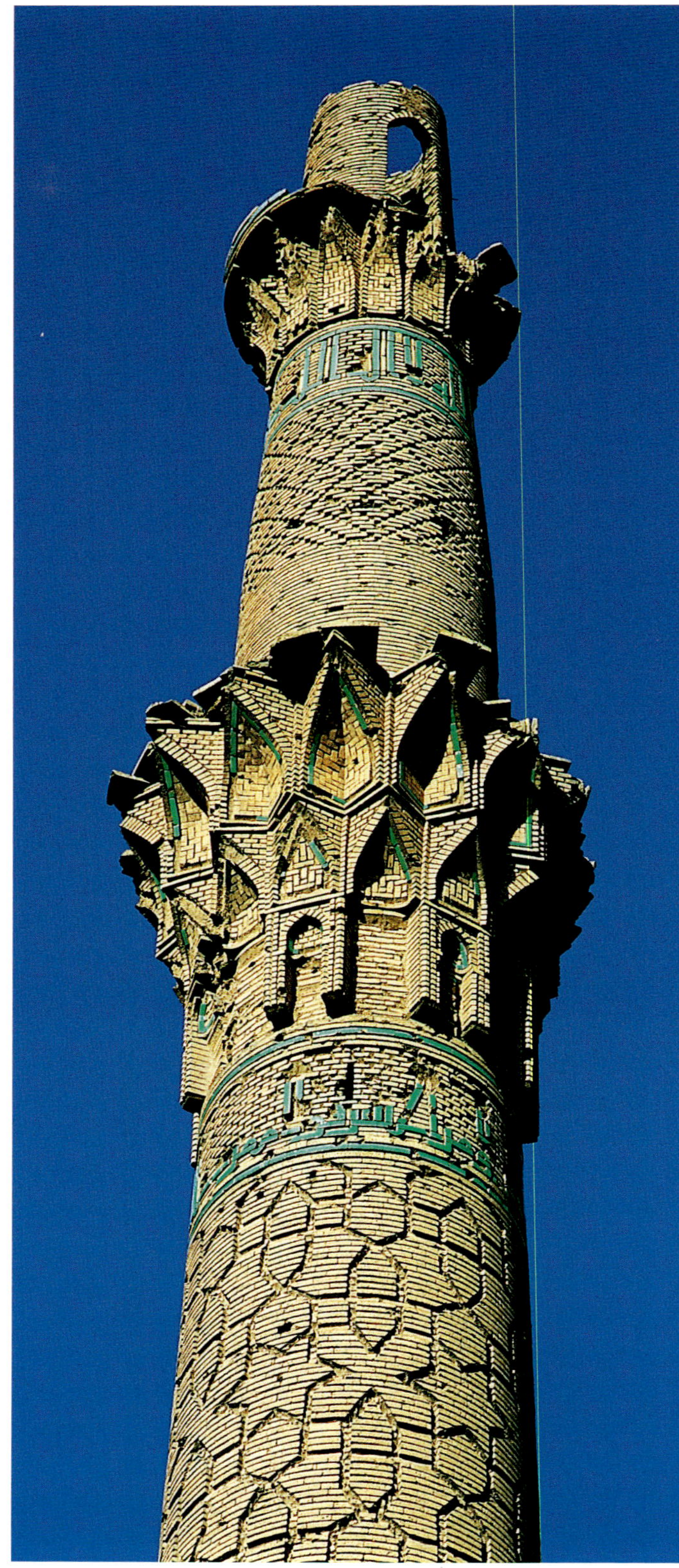

♦ Minaret of the `Ali Mosque, Isfahan (Iran), twelfth century.

♦ Minaret of the Saraban Mosque, Isfahan (Iran), c. 1115–30.

can be dated with any certainty is that of Zavareh, built in 1135–36). Later, in the fifteenth century, the south *iwan* was flanked by minarets. Numerous accretions and transformations enriched this monument still further, most conspicuously in the Safavid era. The ceramic mosaic decorations in the mosque most likely date later than the Seljuq period. The four-*iwan* type of mosque was to spread throughout Iranian territory and was also adopted in the construction of *madrasas*.

The earliest Seljuq *madrasa* is probably the one founded by Tughril at Nishapur around 1046. Other institutions founded by vizier Nizam al-Mulk at Baghdad and Rayy are known by the name Nizamiyya. *Madrasas* must have redounded on the personal prestige of those who commissioned them, but the development of these collegiate schools was linked primarily to the Seljuq policy aimed at seizing the land of the `Abbasid caliphate under Buyid Shi`ite dominion. The purpose of these *madrasas* was thus to instill the tenets of the Sunni faith into future cadres to enable them to administrate the kingdom. These bastions of orthodoxy also served to counter the influence of the Isma`ili sect of the Assassins from Alamut. Although all these constructions have disappeared, they probably conformed to a similar plan based on the model of the four-*iwan* courtyard.

A certain number of Seljuq tombs merely imitated or improved upon preexisting models, compounding the enduring hesitancy between the "tower" and the "square" tomb. The walls of the Gunbad-i `Ali at Abarquh (1056), a rubblework tower built to an octagonal plan, are topped by a brick inscription. Above the inscription, a three-row *muqarnas* cornice (presenting "stalactite" decoration rising in corbels) serves as a base for the hemispherical cupola above. The tomb of Tughril at Rayy (1139–40) rises from a stellar plan reminiscent of the Gunbad-i Qavus, but the transition between the shaft band and the circular cornice bearing the dome (which is now missing) is provided by three tiers of *muqarnas*.

Sultan Sanjar (1118–57) is considered to be the last "great" Iranian Seljuq whose mythical aura endowed him with the status of a literary figure. His tomb at Merv thus had to be appropriately grand and it was indeed the final great Seljuq architectural scheme in the entire Iranian world. It was also the largest tomb of its time, its construction signaling a turning point in the history of the monumental mausoleum. Erected by the architect Muhammad ibn Atsiz from Sarakhs in around 1152, only a few years after the death of Sanjar, the edifice is built on a square plan measuring nearly 39 meters along each side. The cubic elevation is topped by a gallery beyond which extends a series of niches marking the sixteen-sided polygon supporting the cupola. The outer revetment of the bulb dome is missing today, but it was probably of turquoise blue ceramic. The interior comprises a square hall; eight squinches dressed with *muqarnas* extend into prominent ribs toward the cupola, where they crisscross, traces of stucco decoration and paint revealing the lost magnificence of its decoration.

As the twelfth century unfolded, Iranian ceramics underwent a wholesale transformation, as first stone-paste and then, in the last quarter of the century, metallic luster appeared on the scene. These innovations were perhaps an unforeseen consequence of the collapse of the Fatimid caliphate in 1171, when many Egyptian craftsmen had to emigrate. Whatever the reasons, in central Iran the technique of luster painting developed apace. The focus of activity was Kashan, although it is possible that other towns might have sought to emulate the main production center. To date, the oldest lusterware known is a bottle dating to 1179 (British Museum). In the field of architecture, the technique of luster was used in particular for fashioning stars and crosses. These were then assembled into panels that alternate in places with monochrome glaze tiles. It is intriguing to note nonetheless that the overwhelming majority of luster pieces (be they in the form of tiles or tableware) were manufactured after the fall of the Seljuqs, by which time the Khwarazm Shahs had become the dominant power. The most ancient dated luster star of which we are aware has the year A.H. 600, corresponding to A.D. 1203, and is today in the Museum of Islamic Art, Cairo.

The Khwarazm Shahs

At the end of the eleventh century, the dynasty of the Khwarazm Shahs, initially an offshoot of the Iranian Seljuqs, acquired a measure of independence that was consolidated in the following century, especially during the reigns of Il-Arslan (1156–72) and Tekesh (1172–1200). The lands occupied by the Khwarazm were initially confined to a region ensconced between the Caspian and Aral Seas known as Chorasmia. Under Tekesh, and still more so under his successor `Ala al-Din (1200–20), their territory expanded prodigiously and, following the fall of the Seljuqs, soon covered the whole Iranian plateau.

As has already been suggested, it was during this dynasty's reign that the first major ensembles of ceramic decoration employing metallic luster saw the light of day in the Iranian world. Such production, however, seems to have been the fruit of local patronage and concerned the region

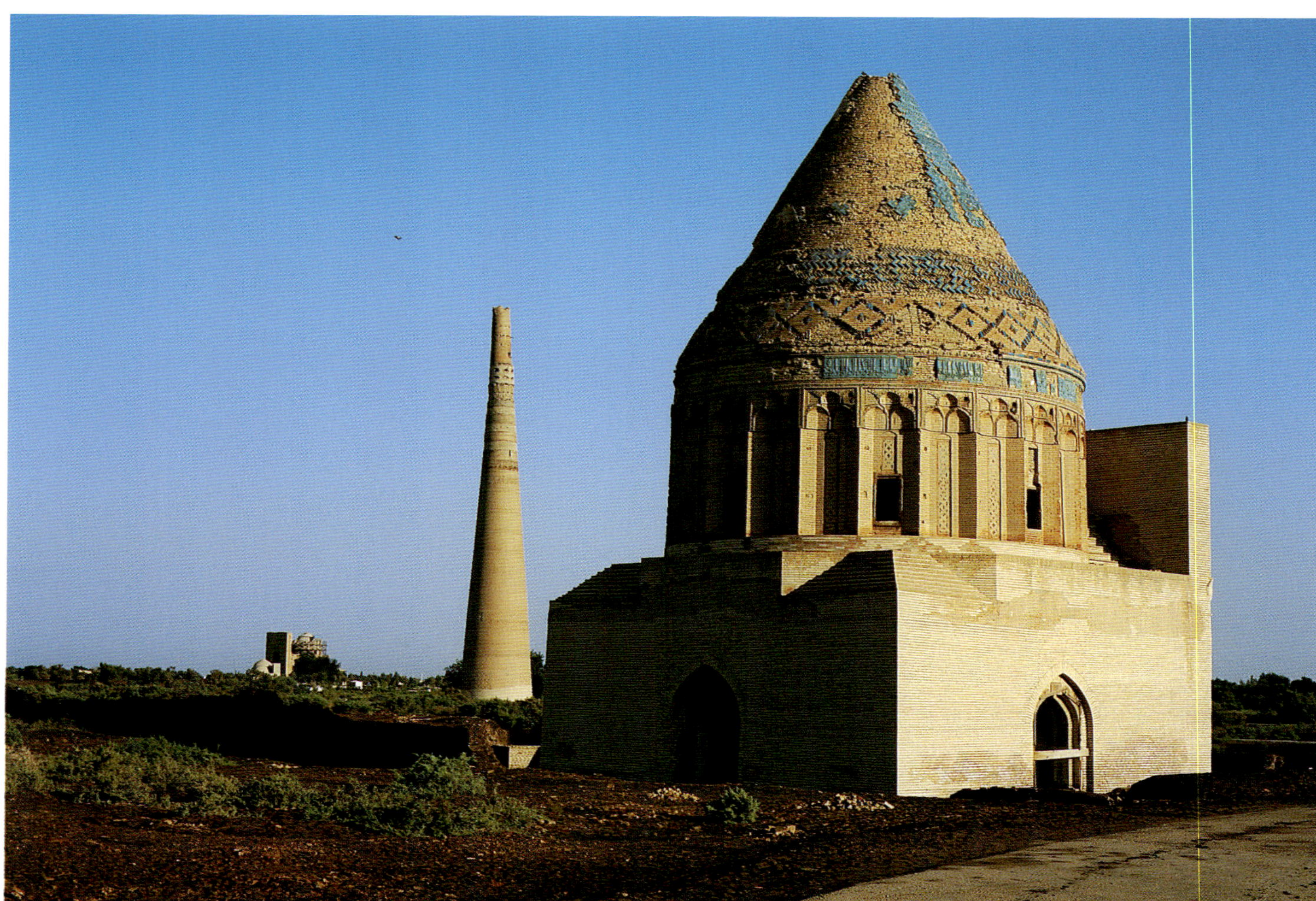

♦ Mausoleum of Tekesh, Kunya Urgench (Turkmenistan), c. 1200. In the background, is the minaret of Qutlugh Temur, fourteenth century.

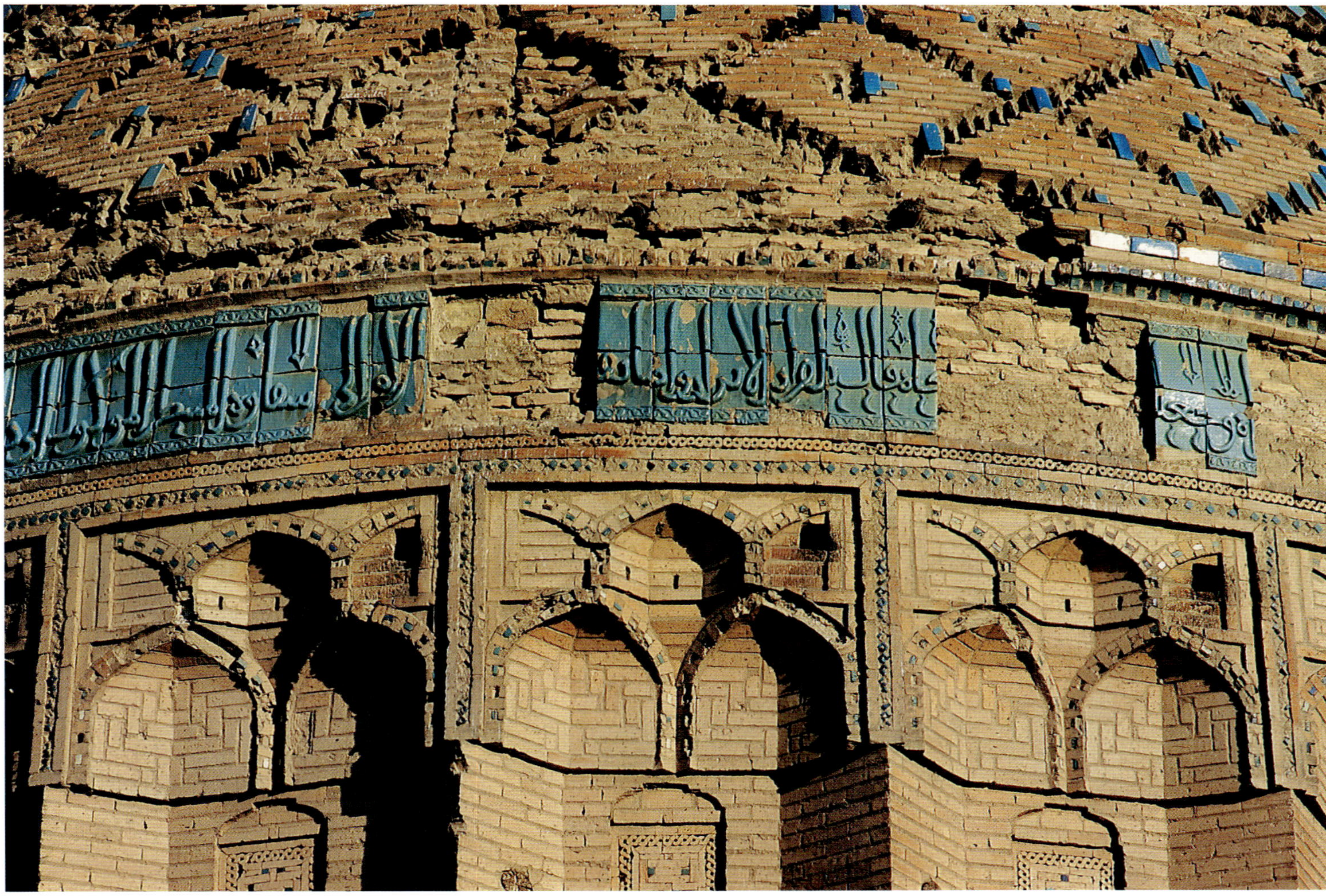

of Chorasmia itself to only a limited degree.

The town of Kunya Urgench is located in the north of what is today Turkmenistan. The medieval site that is now the necropolis is still dominated by the imposing minaret erected in honor of Qutlugh Timur (1321–36). In an outlying area of the necropolis there lies the mausoleum of Il-Arslan, formerly known as that of "Fakhr al-din Razi," whose dodecagonal drum rests on a square base. The three-arched facade is densely decorated with inscriptions and arabesques carved into the terracotta slabs (frieze borders, tympanums, and pediments). An attractive turquoise glazed diaper of diamonds and chevrons decorates the twelve-sided pyramidal dome.

Nearer the minaret stands the mausoleum attributed to Il-Arslan's successor, Sultan Tekesh. This building initiated the large-scale use of relief-decorated ceramic coated in turquoise glaze in the buildings of central Asia. At the outset, the conic dome was totally clad in turquoise-enameled brickwork. The bricks that remain in place in the upper zones are arranged in a chevron pattern; on the lower reaches, in combination with bricks left unglazed, the design forms a series of large diamonds. Immediately beneath the dome, girding the trefoil arcaded drum of the mausoleum, runs a handsomely expansive, strongly carved band of calligraphy in clay slabs with a monochrome turquoise glaze.

Excavations on the same site have unearthed a number of fragmentary *mina'i* tiles that were probably imported to adorn some of the prestigious monuments of the capital before it was submerged beneath the Mongol tidal wave in 1220.

♦ Frieze tiles with an inscription in relief under a turquoise glaze. Drum of the mausoleum of Tekesh, Kunya Urgench (Turkmenistan), c. 1200.

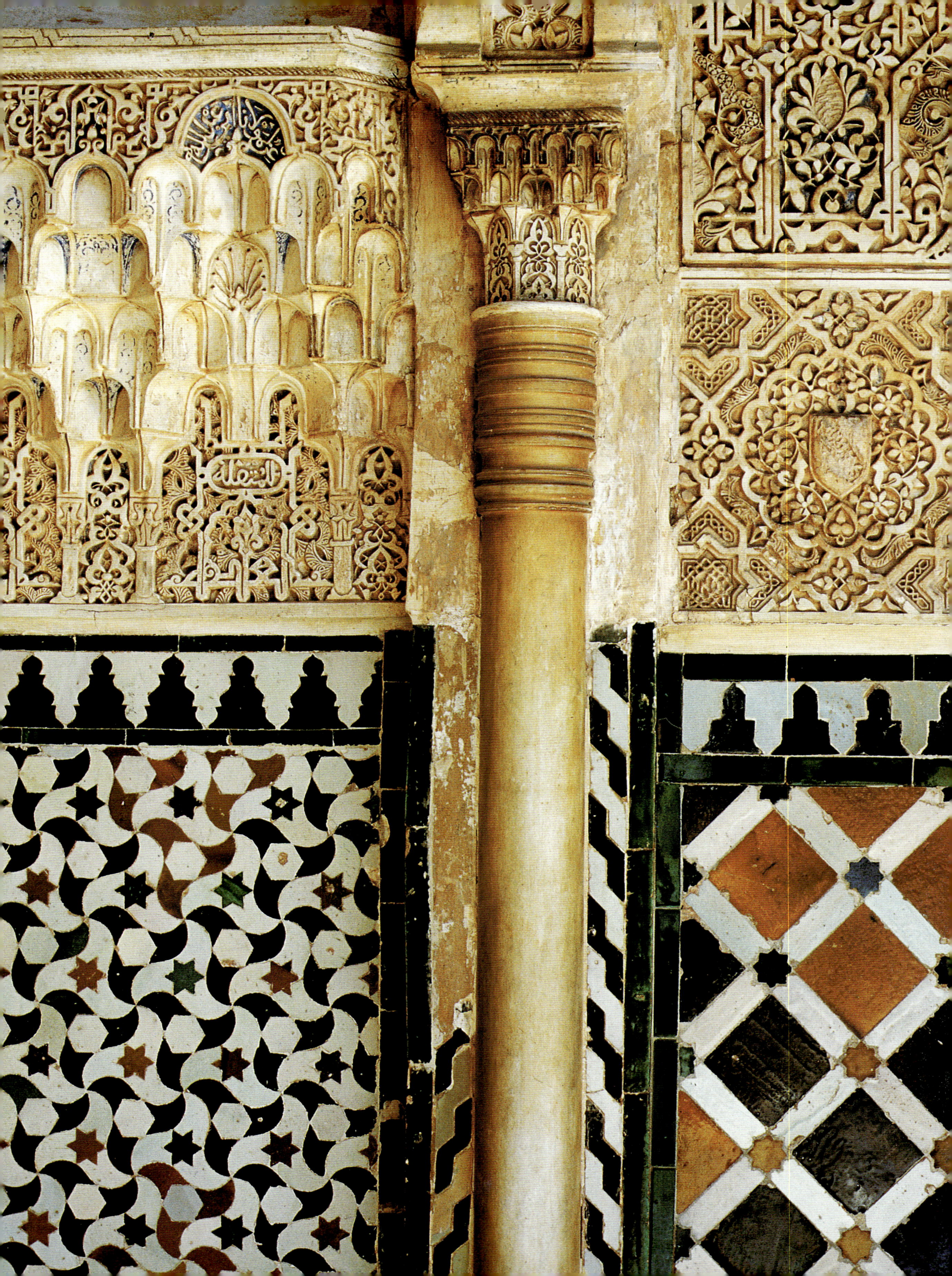

II

The Maghreb and Spain

During Umayyad expansion, the empire of the caliphate grew considerably. The year 711 saw Arab troops simultaneously cross the Straits of Gibraltar and land on the Indian subcontinent. The fall of the Umayyad caliphate in 750, however, marked a schism in the unity of the empire, in particular with the emergence of a separate Umayyad emirate at Cordoba in 756. From that time on, the Muslim West evolved independently from central `Abbasid Islam.

The architecture of Muslim Spain in the emirate (later caliphate) period made use of construction techniques that had been developed at the end of the Roman and Visigothic periods: roof tiles (sometimes lead-glazed) over a framework, and the combined use of stone and brick—most especially in two-color voussoirs. To these tried and tested methods were added new forms, of which the horseshoe ("Moorish") arch framed by an *alfiz* is the most typical. The Berber, Almoravid, and Almohad dynasties also contributed a repertory of forms and decorative types of their own.

Muslim Spain, from Emirate to Taifa Rule

After his proclamation as emir of al-Andalus in 756, `Abd al-Rahman I felt the need to mark his new reign with monuments that would enhance its prestige. He began to build a congregational ("Great") mosque at Cordoba on the "Mediterranean" plan, with eleven naves eleven bays deep opening directly onto a courtyard with a surface area only slightly smaller than that of the prayer hall. A *mihrab* placed at the back of the central nave indicated the direction of Mecca. Due to the pressure of an increasing population, eight additional naves were added in line with the *qibla* between 832 and 848. Then, in 951, `Abd al-Rahman III enlarged the courtyard (*sahn*) and erected a new, far larger minaret on the axis of the *mihrab*. Finally, in 961, al-Hakam II ordered an enlargement of a further eleven bays in the direction of the *qibla*. The *qibli* wall was embellished with a superb mosaic-decorated *mihrab* topped by a cupola adorned in similar fashion. At this time, elements of ceramic architectural decoration also made a tentative appearance. The cornice of the *maqsura* cupola just in front of the *mihrab* presents a band with polychrome elements decorated by the process known as *cuerda seca parcial*. Primarily green and yellow ocher in tone, these elements run along the base of the cupola and present a wavy line formed by the alternation of an arc with two indentations. The *cuerda seca parcial* method consists in applying colored paint directly on to the biscuit (and not on to a priming of white enamel), the colors being kept apart by a dividing line formed of an amalgam of manganese oxide and a fat that burns off during firing.

This phase of the mosque's construction was unquestionably the most spectacular and corresponds to the early flowering of the caliphate, in marked contrast to the rather peripheral and marginal nature of works from the emirate period. A final

PAGE 48

♦ *Zellij* panels with *sharrafa* (crenellated border) crowned by a section decorated in stucco. The Alhambra, Granada (Spain). Patio de la Alberca, fourteenth century.

phase of construction took place in 987 under the auspices of al-Mansur, Hisham II's vizier, but this enlargement took the form of a monotonous line of cursorily decorated columns and capitals over a further eight naves running the entire length of the east wall. The end result is an immense prayer hall (135 by 110 meters) of great depth borne by a veritable forest of columns. In this respect, it is very different from countless other mosques, whose prayer halls are wide but not very deep.

Little short of a city-palace, Madinat al-Zahra was built by `Abd al-Rahman III near Cordoba in 936. It is also one of the few examples of civil architecture dating from

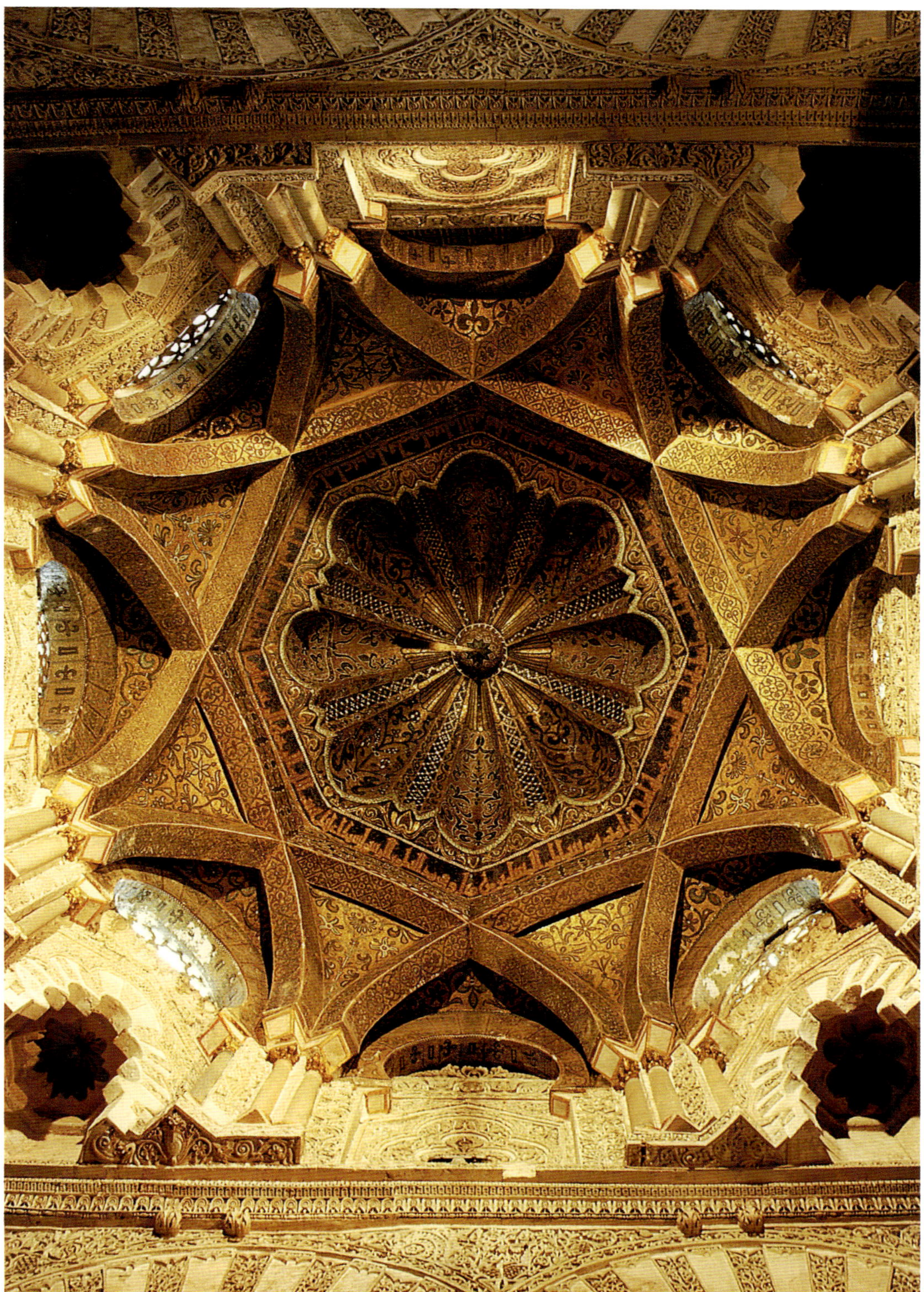

♦ The cupola of the *maqsura* in the mosque at Cordoba (Spain). The cupola (dated 961) is decorated with mosaics and a frieze in *cuerda seca*. This rare example of the use of *cuerda seca* in architecture can be seen in the brightly colored line made up of a series of arcs and double indentations inside the central octagon.

the caliphate period to have survived to the present day. The architectural forms that can be seen in this vast, steeply terraced urban site are close to those found in the Great Mosque of Cordoba, with horseshoe arches, arabesque decoration in stucco and stonework, and *alfiz* flanking the arches. A number of districts of the town have been restored, among them `Abd al-Rahman's audience hall, dubbed the *salón rico* by its discoverers. This hall, with its basilica-like ground plan, has preserved many original decorative features executed by craftsmen who also collaborated on the 961 construction program at the Great Mosque of Cordoba. Like the Corinthian order-inspired capitals, the marble plaques emblazoned with Arabic inscriptions exhibit traces of gilding in places. Such remains are evidence of the splendor of the great palace that was greatly admired by Christian ambassadors. However, the ensemble, comprising palaces, barracks, and gardens, was abandoned when the vizier al-Mansur founded Madinat al-Zahra in 981. Although ceramic ornamentation remained sparse in architecture, the Madinat al-Zahra period was characterized by the massive production of tableware, which was decorated in green and brown, or else in polychromy of the *cuerda seca parcial* type.

Apart from the sections on the cornice of the Great Mosque in Cordoba already mentioned, examples of ceramic architectural decoration during the caliphate period include lead-glazed terracotta elements, which are often shell-like in shape or in the form of a small gadrooned dome. This decorative tradition endured after the fall of the caliphate; a late example of this type of decorative rosette (from a dwelling in Cordoba dated to the eleventh or twelfth century) is preserved in the Museu de Cerámica, Barcelona.

The void left in the Iberian Peninsula by the collapse of the Cordoban caliphate in 1031 was filled by the Muluk al-Tawa`if (party kings). Of the minor powers that emerged at this juncture, that of the Tujibids and Hudids of Saragossa (1019–1142) was one of the most extraordinary. The Aljafería Palace is one of the few monuments to have survived from this period. Encircled by ramparts that are studded with towers, entrance is gained to the building through a single door. The palace itself stands in the middle of the compound and is divided into two parts on either side of a court. Two pools overlooked by arcaded porticos occupy the two far ends of the court, a formal layout that seems to herald the Patio de la Alberca at the Alhambra. The porticos display richly adorned interlacing arches. The north wing houses a central hall flanked by two further rooms, the east one opening onto an oratory of square plan. In one of the corners stands the polygonal *mihrab*, which, in terms of its plan and the arch onto which it opens, recalls the *mihrab* of Cordoba. The heavily restored plaited and floriated Kufic calligraphy is executed in stucco. The inscriptional decoration, as well as the panels with their compound arches and above all the gallery that crowns the hall, are all of a type that was unknown in Cordoba at the time. The present-day appearance of the ribbed cupola covering the room owes much to restoration work undertaken in the nineteenth century.

The art of Muslim Spain, growing out of the creation of the Cordoba emirate, gradually developed to reach a high point during the period of the caliphs, with the construction of Madinat al-Zahra and the enlargement of the Great Mosque of Cordoba under Hakam II. The architectural idiom of the caliphate was readopted by the party kings in many remarkable works (few of which have survived), such as the Aljafería Palace at Saragossa described above. The architectural vocabulary of the Muslim West was to be profoundly altered, however, by the arrival of first the Almoravids and then the Almohads, who introduced the large-scale application of ceramics to architectural decoration.

The Minarets and "Light Towers" of the Berber Kingdoms

The Almoravid and Almohad periods present a fundamental stage in the unfolding history of the western Muslim world. The unification of the Maghreb and Spain that these dynasties achieved between 1090 and 1228 gave rise to the Arab Andalusian civilization, which was distinguished by an outstanding flowering of architecture in the Almohad era, during which the symbiosis between Berber and Andalusian elements reached a peak.

Compared to the Cordoban caliphate and to that of the party kings, the Almoravid and Almohad periods witnessed a number of significant innovations in architecture, such as the systematic replacement of horseshoe arches by lancet or lambrequin ones. Stalactite *muqarnas* also emerged in the Maghreb during the first half of the twelfth century. Whereas in the Muslim East the dome plays a paramount architectural role, in the Maghreb cupolas are often

♦ Qarawiyin Mosque, Fez (Morocco), founded 857. Rooftop view.

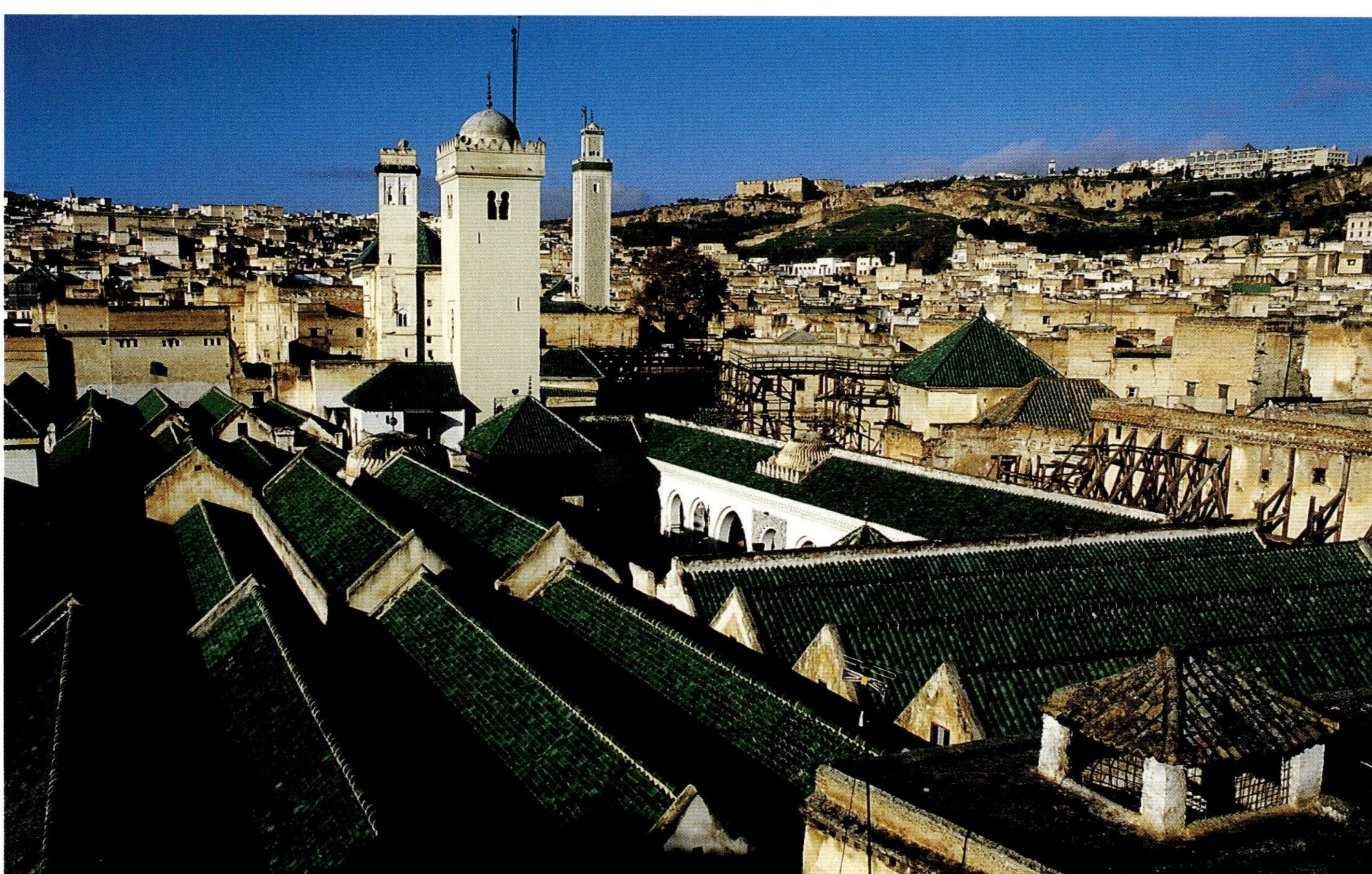

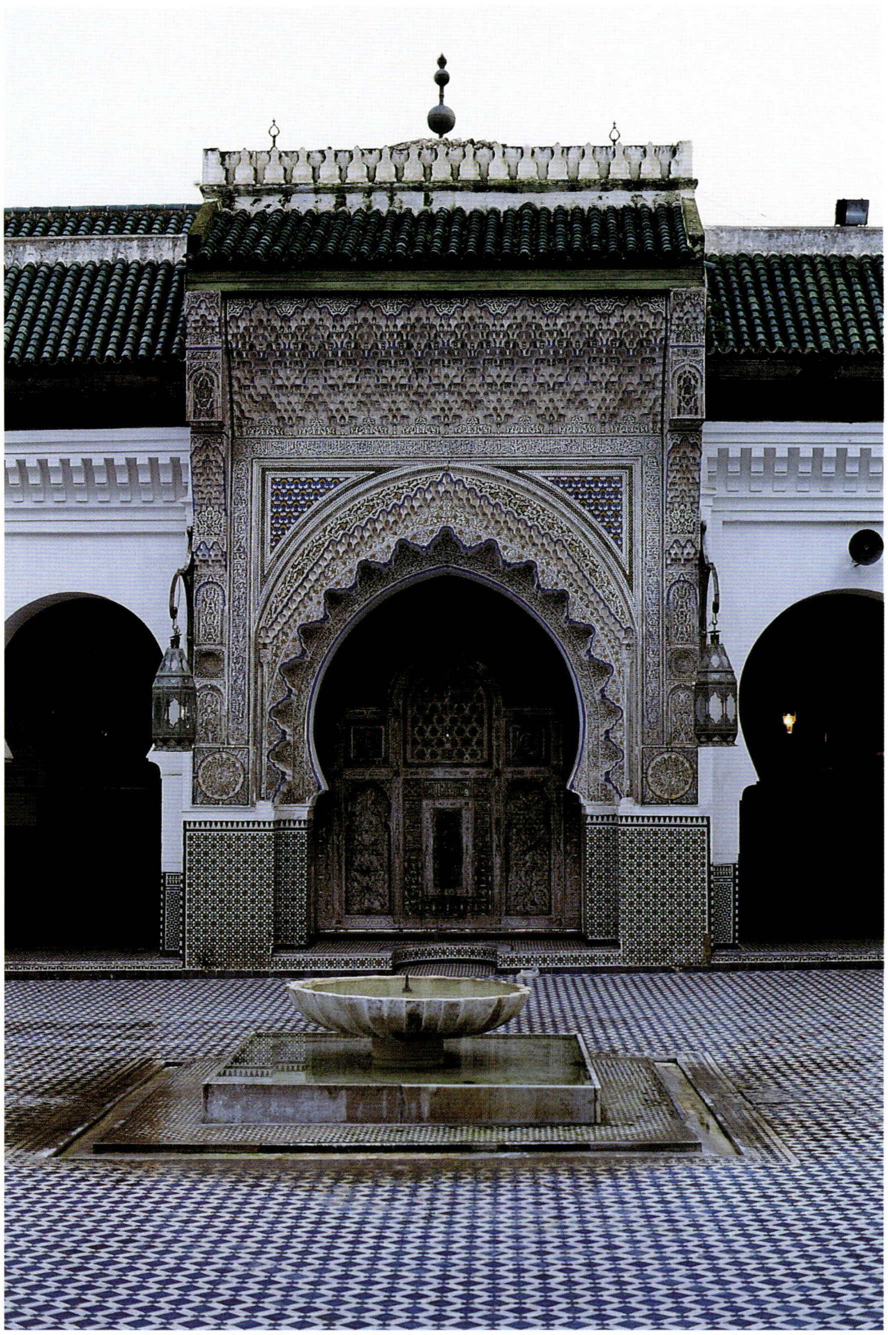

♦ Court of the Qarawiyin Mosque, Fez (Morocco), founded 857, with the fountain for ritual ablutions in the center.

reduced to a purely decorative role, the Qubbat Barudiyin at Marrakech or the lantern of the Great Mosque at Tlemcen being prime examples.

Most mosques in the region comprise a long-sided prayer hall whose naves are either parallel or perpendicular to the *qibla*. Founded in 857, the Qarawiyin Mosque at Fez, for instance, went athrough numerous stages in construction, although the basic structure remained unchanged. After successive programs of enlargement in 956 and 1135, it encompassed a prayer hall nineteen naves deep. The prayer hall opens onto a courtyard surrounded with porticos that were reduced in size as the mosque was enlarged. In the seventeenth century, the final addition of two small outbuildings with fountains on the court side was inevitably reminiscent of the Alhambra at Granada. The tower roofed with green-enameled tiles and the white and green *zellij* paving are virtually all the non-Muslim can see of its ceramic decoration.

The Almoravids

Although only a few Almoravid monuments survive in Spain, the Maghreb is blessed with a significant number, notably at Marrakech and Tlemcen, which illustrate the radical changes brought about by the regime and its shifting cultural references. Yusuf ibn Tashufin founded the city of Marrakech in 1062 and that of Tagrart (Tlemcen) in 1082. The Great Mosque of Tlemcen probably dates from the time of the construction of the city. At the outset, the prayer hall had thirteen naves lying perpendicular to the *qibla*, in which horseshoe arches are still the rule, except for the bay in front of it. The alterations made at later stages, especially under `Ali ibn Yusuf (1106–42), included the lantern placed in front of the *mihrab*, which comprises an openwork stucco cupola supported by squinches enhanced by *muqarnas*. It was under `Ali ibn Yusuf that the territorial and political power of the Almoravids reached its zenith and it was also during his reign that the Great Mosque of Marrakech was built, although only the pool for ritual ablutions, completed in 1120 and known as Qubbat Barudiyin, survives from that time.

The Almohads

In what was plainly a reaction against Almoravid ideology, the Almohads gathered around Ibn Tumart to undermine the ruling power. They took Marrakech in 1141, destroying numerous monuments in the process. It is at Tinmal, where Ibn Tumart began his teaching and is buried, that one of the most original mosques of the Almohad period is to be found. Completed in 1153–54, the mosque has a prayer hall with nine four-bay naves perpendicular to the *quibla*. The naves of the *qibla* and the *mihrab* form a T, while relief is provided by highly elaborate lambrequin arches, a tour de force rendered slightly less demanding perhaps by the nature of the materials: stucco covered bricks for the arches and lime-slaked pisé for the outer walls. The *mihrab* is ensconced in an oblong tower that doubles as a minaret.

The conquest of Marrakech in 1141 and its transformation into an Almohad capital are associated with numerous new building projects. The construction of the Kutubiyya mosque—executed in two phases in 1147 and 1162—signals the adoption of the Almohad minaret. Much larger than the Mosque at Tinmal (88 by 55 meters as against 48 by 44 meters in the latter), the Kutubiyya has seventeen naves lying perpendicular to the *qibla*, with seven bays. Four naves at the east and the west extend on either side of the court to form a portico

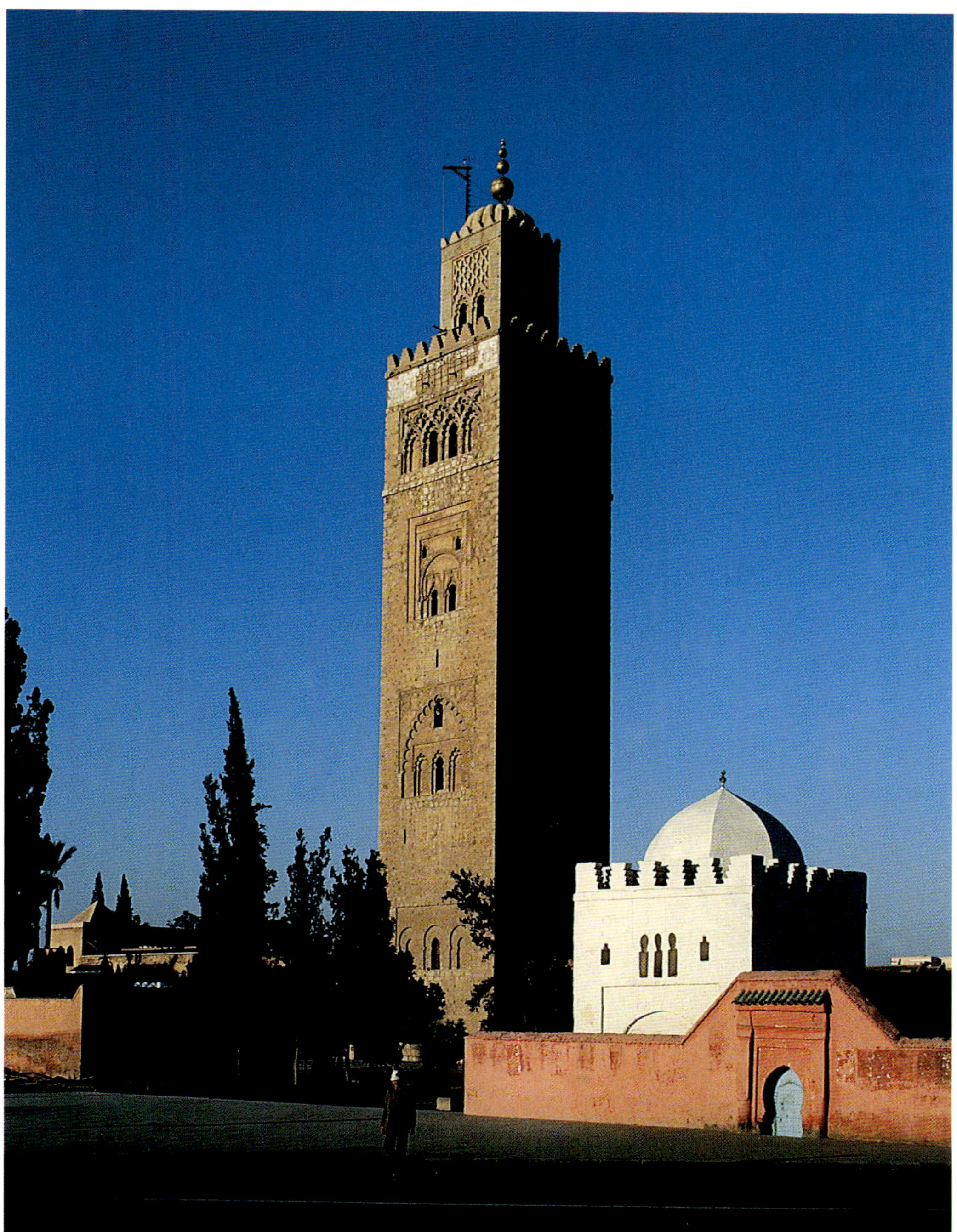

♦ Minaret of the Kutubiyya Mosque, Marrakech (Morocco), end of the twelfth century. Traces of the ceramic tilework, which has today almost entirely disappeared, can just be made out beneath the balcony at the top of the tower.

whose northern side terminates in a wall. Almost all the transverse arches are lobed, while those perpendicular to the *qibla* are lancet. The corner colonnettes on the pillars—absent from caliphal architecture in Spain—are reminiscent of `Abbasid architecture (they are also present in the mosque of Ibn Tulun). Completed prior to 1199, the minaret of the Kutubiyya was probably the first instance of exterior ceramic tile decoration in the Maghreb, although it has unfortunately almost entirely disappeared today.

Almohad minarets are characterized above all by their sheer size—they are often far taller than previous examples—and sober elegance. In general, they possess a large square lower tower, pierced by arches and surmounted by a cubic space topped by a cupola.

Three Almohad constructions with similar characteristics built at the end of the twelfth century represent the "model" of the Maghrebi minaret: that at the Kutubiyya, already mentioned, the Hasan tower in Rabat, and the Giralda at Seville. In later eras, minarets would gradually adopt more or less the same shape as these Almohad monuments, as at the recent mosque in Casablanca. Of a highly original design, the Hasan Mosque in Rabat remained unfinished at the death of its founder, Ya`qub al-Mansur (1199). Had it been completed, it would have been the second largest in the whole Muslim world after that of al-Mutawakkil at Samarra, with a total length of 181 meters. The minaret, also unfinished, would have surpassed all others; the blind arcades at different levels on each side contain various decorative schemes.

The Great Mosque at Seville (1172–82) was replaced in the fifteenth century by the cathedral we see today. There remain only a few sections of the courtyard wall and the minaret, the celebrated Giralda, built between 1184 and 1195. This is probably the most perfect of all Almohad minarets. Its lattice-like decor of interlaced arches derives from the architectural repertoire of the caliphate, but adapted into uncomplicated decorative cladding. The upper reaches as seen today date from the Renaissance; originally it would have been composed of a cubic space surmounted by a gilded copper pinnacle.

Even today, we know little about early attempts at architectural ceramics during the Berber period. We have already cited, for example, those on the Kutubiyya minaret in Marrakech, to which may be added the Torre del Oro and the Giralda in Seville, whose ceramic revetment—now almost entirely disappeared—is attested by J. Gestoso.[16] In the case of the Giralda, it is not inconceivable that the black painted ceramic roundels on the central zone of the minaret might have been added during the restoration work carried out in 1568. Several archeological finds, as well as a note by the chronicler Ibn Sa`id (before 1240), corroborate the use of ceramic tiling predating the Nasrid period. Ibn Sa`id remarks that the pavements of al-Andalus houses "were of most divers colors, replacing the polychrome marble that Easterners use to embellish their residences."[17]

For the history of the Muslim West, the arrival of the Berber dynasties was a turning point exemplified in the field of architecture by the adoption of an idiom quite distinct from that of their predecessors. As has already been observed concerning the Muslim East, minarets in Spain and in the Maghreb acquired a certain monumentality, assuming the role of imposing visual symbols of the new dynasties. Architectural decoration also experienced a revival at this time, in particular due to the new prevalence of *muqarnas*, an impressive array of arch profiles (from lancet and polylobe to lambrequin), and the contribution of ceramics to the color schemes, which added greatly to the decorative refinement of the architecture as a whole. This search for new types of ornament gained pace during succeeding periods.

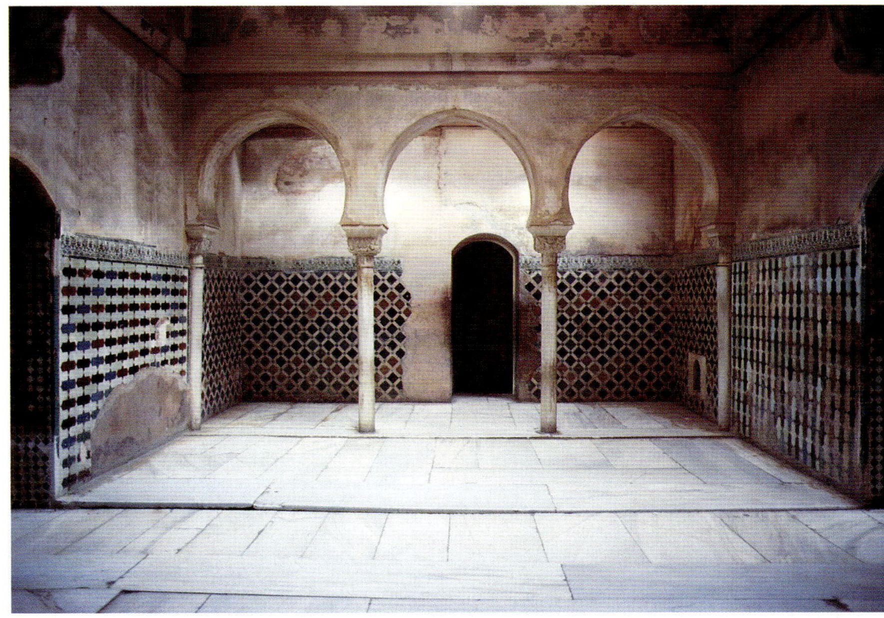

Marinids and Nasrids: Severe Zellij and Luxuriant Palmettes

During the reign of the Marinids in Morocco and the Nasrids in Granada, little innovative progress is discernible in the area of architectural form. All the effort of the creative minds seems instead to have been concentrated on the ornamental, in the form of stucco, wood, and ceramic tiles (*zellij*), a phenomenon particularly well illustrated in Marinid *medersas* and at the Alhambra in Granada.

The Alhambra of the Nasrids

The Alhambra, the most renowned monument of the Nasrid period, is also the best-preserved of all "medieval" Muslim palaces. Started by Muhammad I (1232–72) on a citadel dating back to the ninth century, the oldest surviving part in the central core is probably the Mashwar (council hall), probably built at the time of Isma'il I (1313–25). It was under Yusuf I (1333–54) that work on the hub of the palace was carried out, the Hall of the Ambassadors in the Torre de Comares and the Patio de la Alberca (or Patio de los Arrayanos). This patio, which has a rectangular pool (*birka*) in the center, is the largest in the Alhambra. The court is flanked by porticos on its shorter sides, one of which is dwarfed by the Torre de Comares. The space is given a certain unity

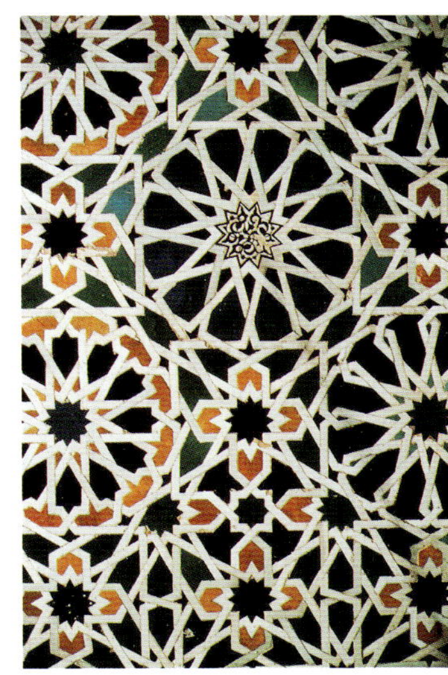

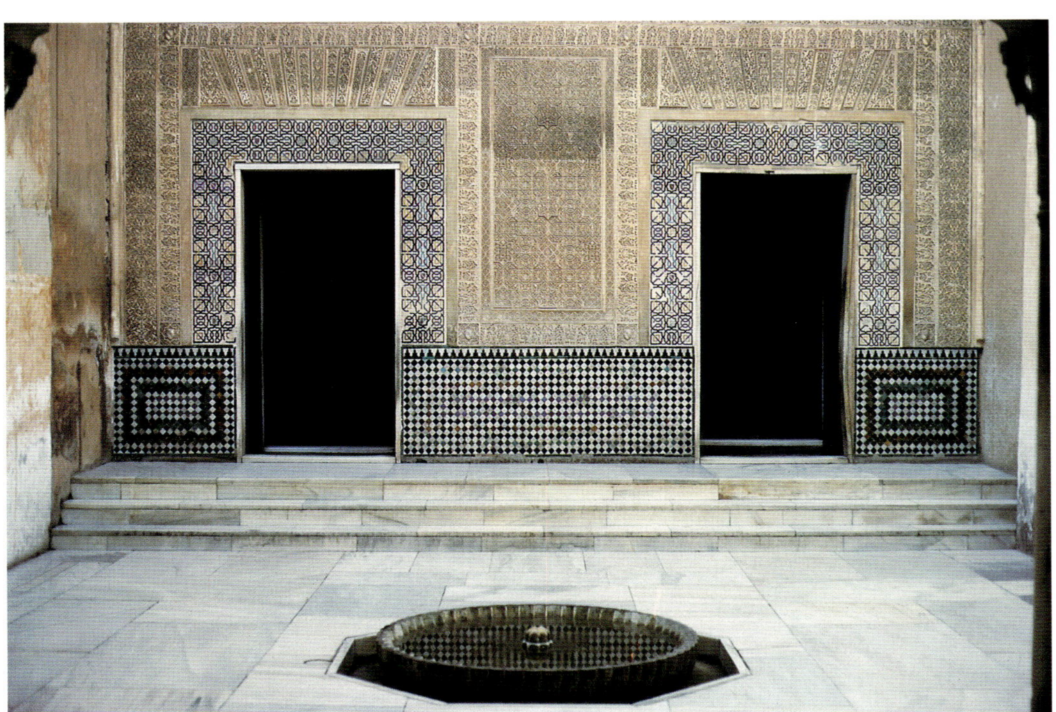

THE ALHAMBRA, GRANADA (SPAIN)

♦ Hall in the *hamman* with dado panels in *zellij* and marble flooring.

♦ Paneling in the Mashwar hall.

♦ Patio in the Mashwar and the facade of the Cuarto Dorado. The dado panels are in checkerboard *zellij*, the upper zones of the wall being stuccoed.

FOLLOWING DOUBLE PAGE

♦ General view. In the center, the Partal; background right, the Torre de Comares.

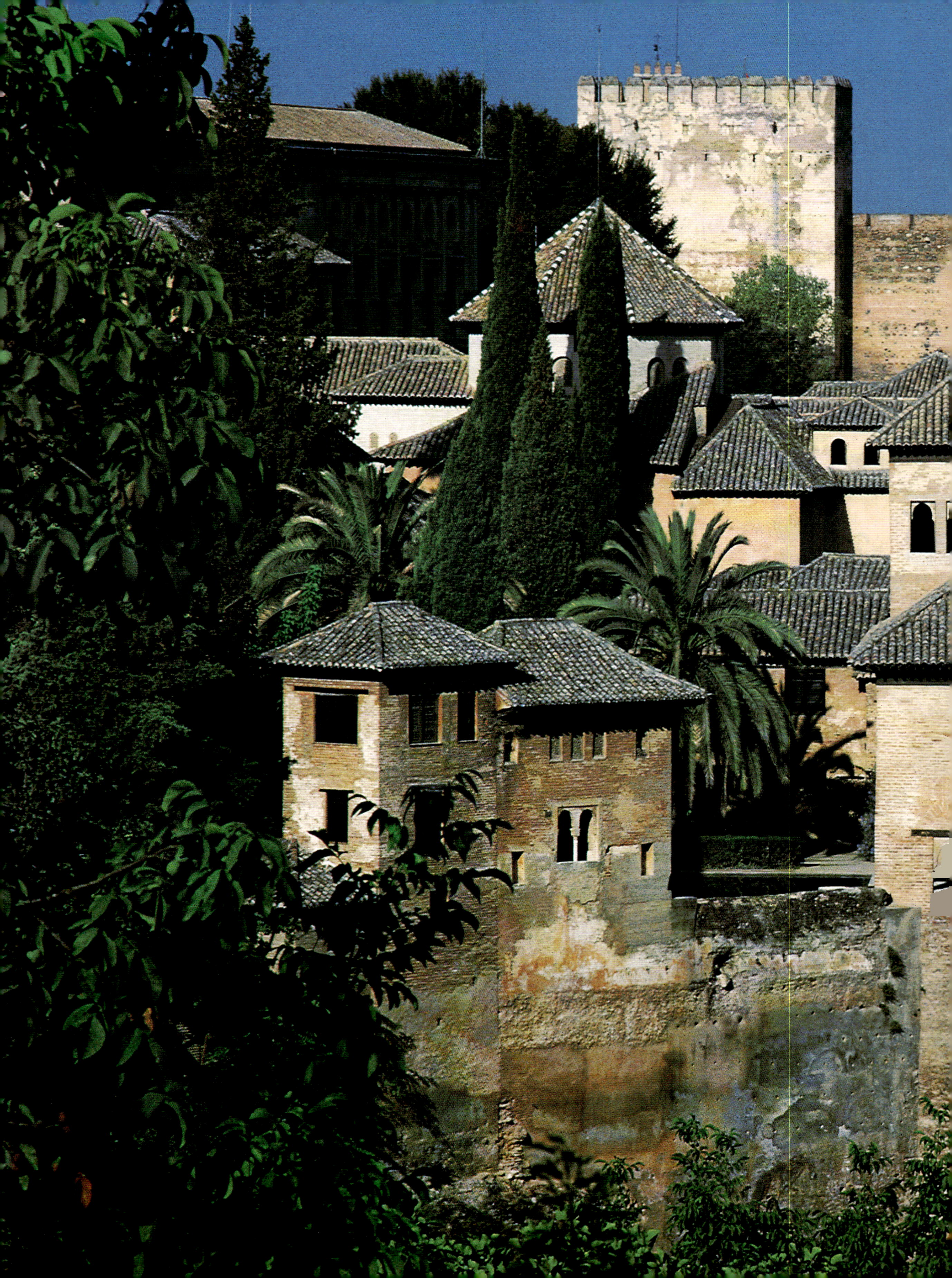

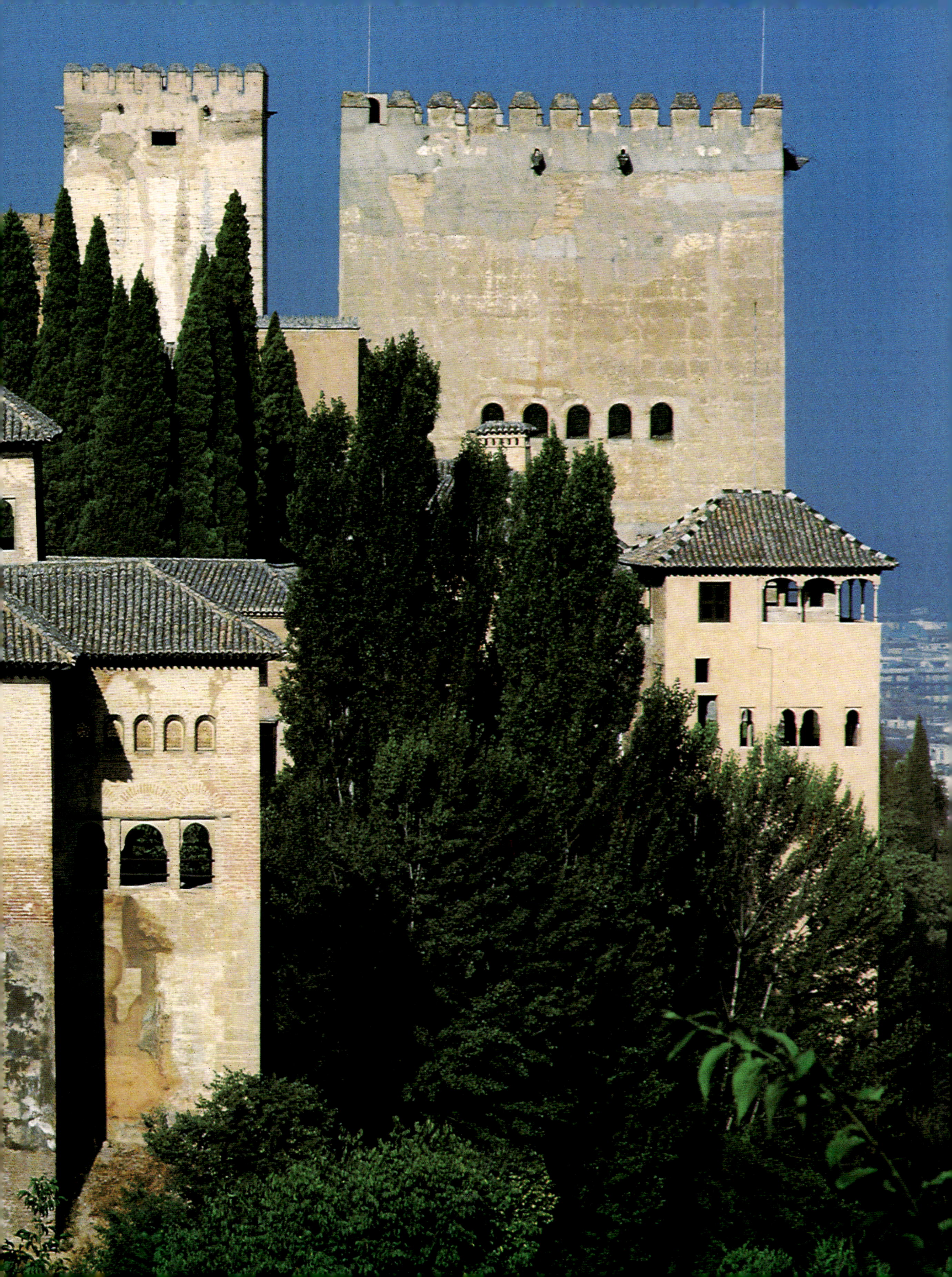

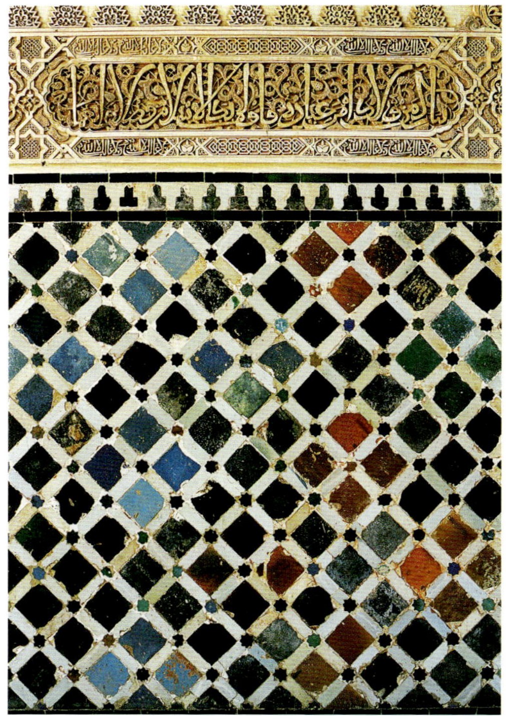

THE ALHAMBRA, GRANADA (SPAIN)

♦ Checkerboard *zellij* wall paneling topped with inscriptional decoration in stucco. Patio de la Alberca.

FACING PAGE

♦ *Zellij* wall paneling with a six-pointed star pattern on a field of whirling indented triangles.

through the balance of vegetation, water, and architecture, as well as through its bilateral symmetry. The Hall of the Ambassadors was most likely a throne room; indeed, the inscription crowning the three windows of the north wall declares: "Long may you live! Thus, when you enter in the mornings and evenings, the mouths of boon, bliss, felicity, and charm greet you in my name. She is the high-domed hall and we are her daughters; however, mine is the preeminence and the honor in rank. We are members among which I am the heart, unchallenged; for the power of the spirit and soul originates in the heart. And if my symbols represent the constellations of her heaven, then in me, and not among them, is the grandeur of the sun. My master Yusuf has decked me (may God support him) in garments of pride and flawless artistry. He made me the seat of the kingdom, and she [the hall] has strengthened the rank with the true light, with the seat and with the throne."[18] A further inscription around the wooden cornice of the superb *artesonado* ceiling includes the *sura* LXVII, "The Kingdom," thus offering confirmation that this hall is indeed a throne room. Like the baths bordering it to the east, this part of the palace dates from the period of Yusuf I. The well-preserved and recently restored baths deploy an astonishing array of cut and inset *zellij* patterns, occasionally in alternation with swathes of white marble. More even than in other parts of the palace, stucco decoration exploits polychromy to the full, allowing the interplay between colors free rein.

The Court of the Lions, dating from the reign of Muhammad V (1354–91), is a rectangle bordered by porticos that on the two shorter sides penetrate into the space in the form of kiosks. The porticos are borne on round-based matchstick colonnettes with composite capitals whose shafts are ornamented in the upper zones with ring banding. The center of the court is occupied by the famous Fountain of the Lions, whose appearance, confirmed by an inscription, evokes the "brazen sea" of Solomon's temple. The fountain feeds into four watercourses arranged crosswise that pass through the gallery and run into adjoining chambers located to the left and right of the longer sides (Halls of the Two Sisters and the Abencerrajes). The cupolas of these two rooms provide a perfect example of Nasrid decorative taste. In reality, the impression that these are cupolas is due entirely to the "stalactite" decoration covering a sharply pointed frame; similarly, the squinches are relegated to a purely decorative, rather than architectonic, function. The overall effect, probably intended to outdo cupolas in the East, is astonishing. Despite the odd throwback, it is far removed from the broad courtyards with *iwans* found in the palaces of Afghanistan or the large quadripartite gardens of the Timurids.

At the end of the Hall of the Two Sisters stands the lyrical Daraxa *mirador* that today opens out onto a small garden. The walls here are still lined with *zellij*, the upper zones being decorated by stucco over which dance lines of poetry especially composed to simultaneously decorate and praise the palace.

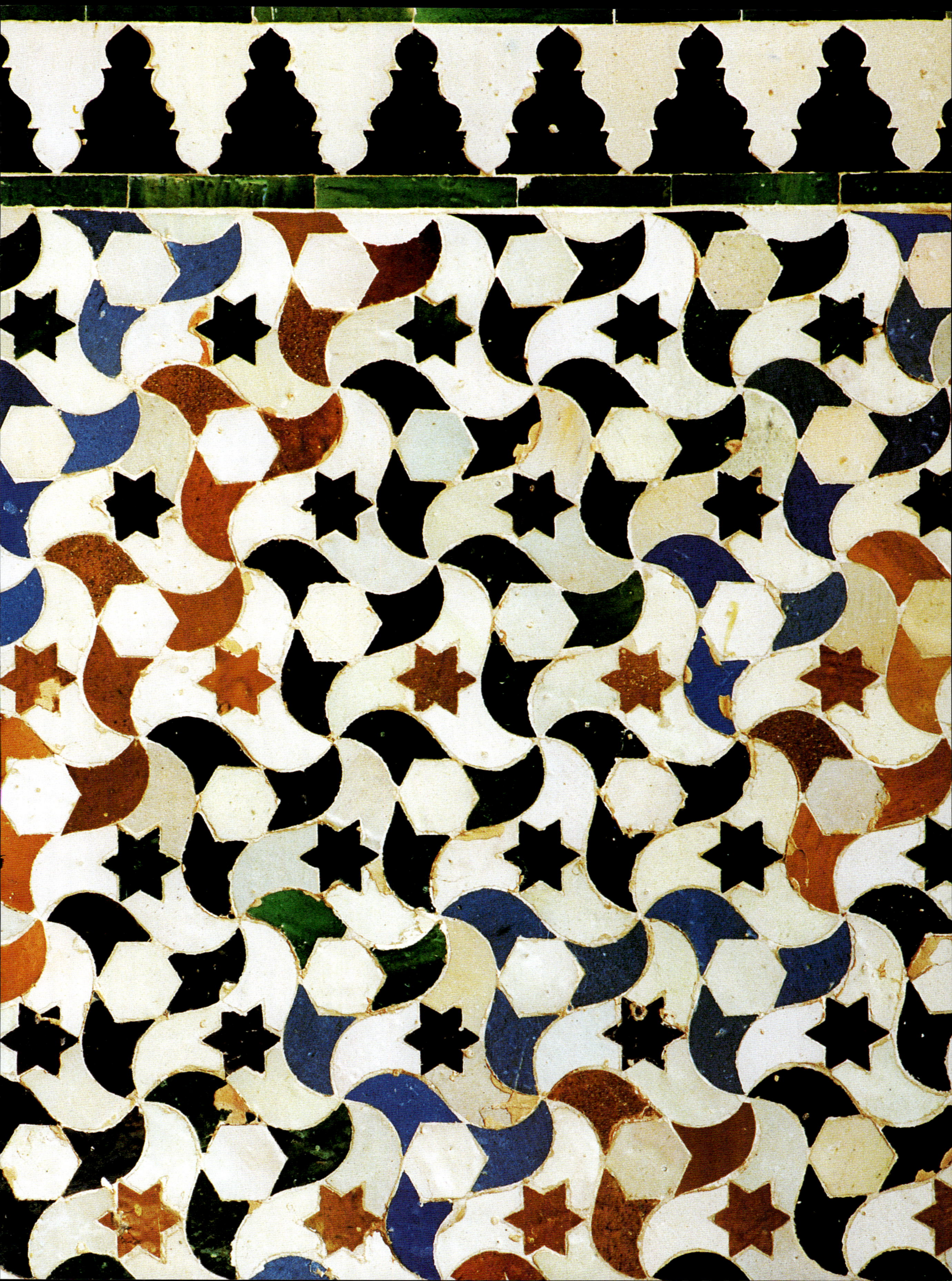

THE ALHAMBRA, GRANADA (SPAIN)

RIGHT

♦ *Zellij* panel with rotating hexagonal and polygonal patterns together with "bat" motifs.

BELOW

♦ *Zellij* panel in a geometric interlace pattern framing a coat-of-arms border (the motto of the Nasrids appears on alternate shields: "There is no victor save God!"). Daraxa *mirador*.

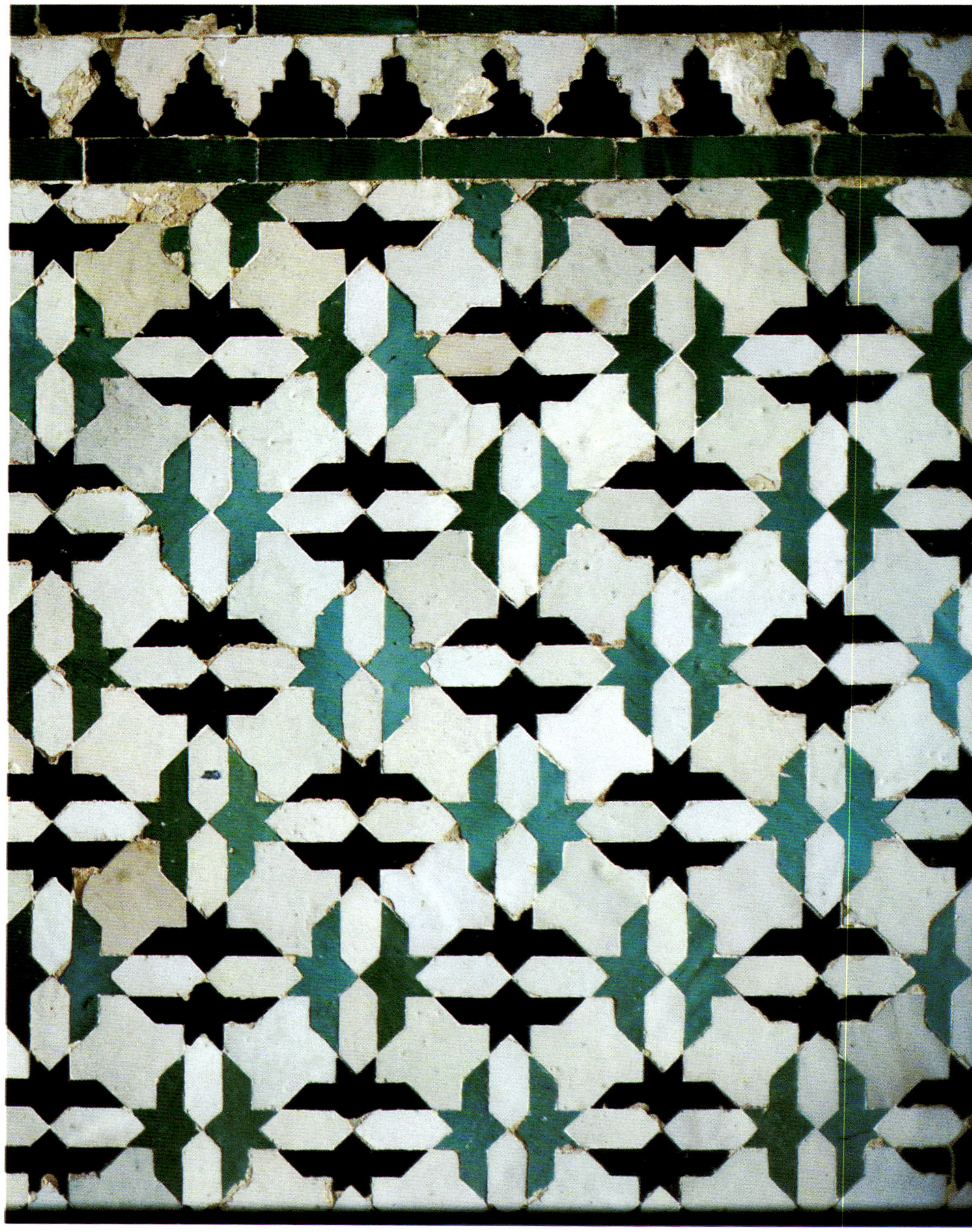

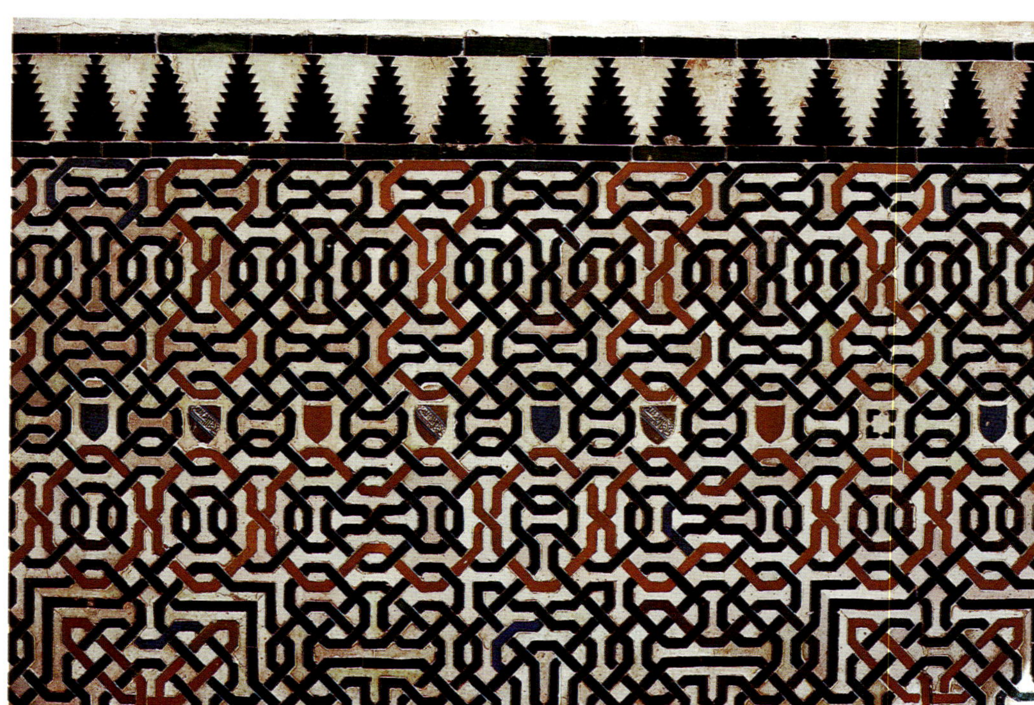

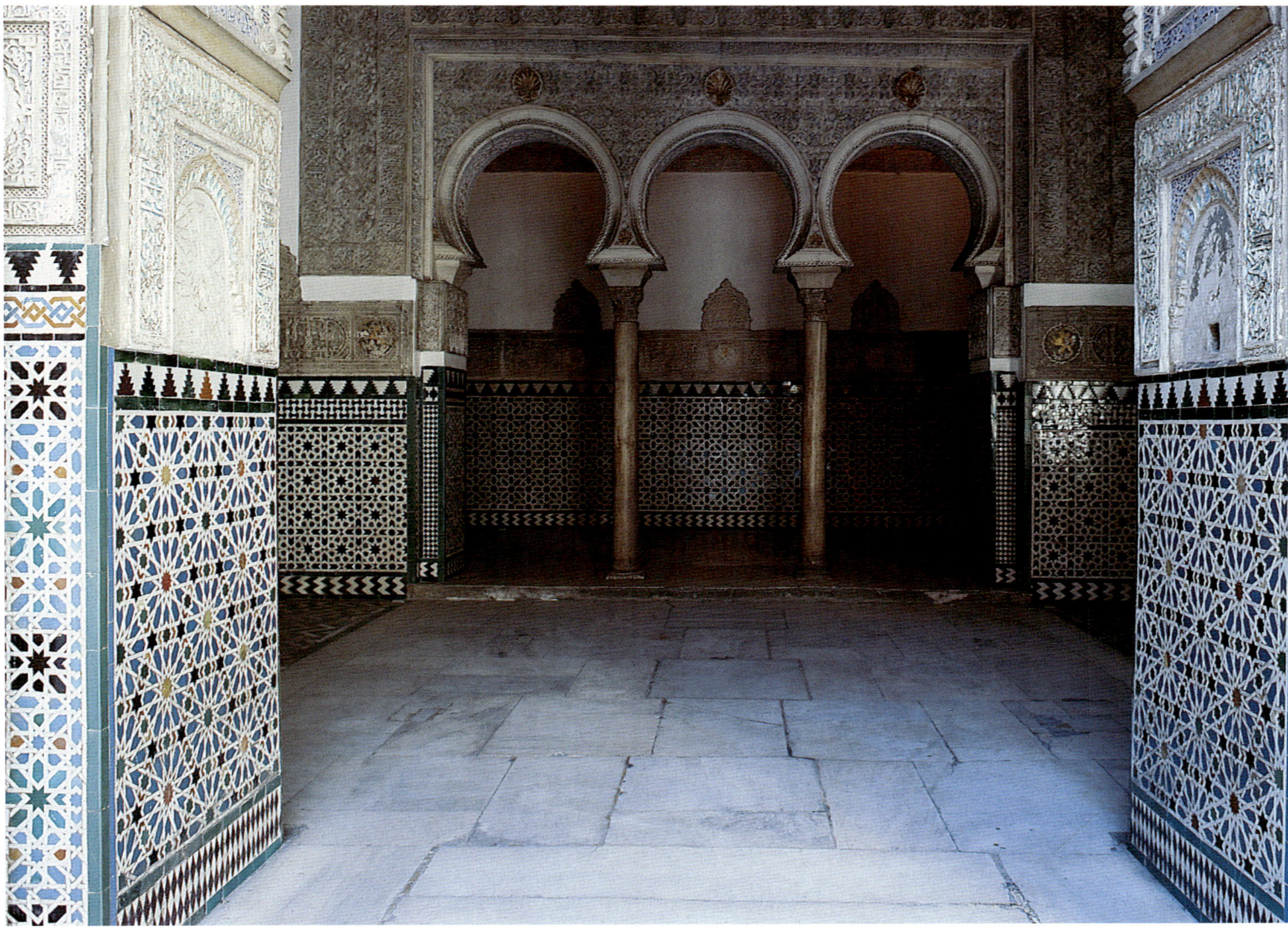

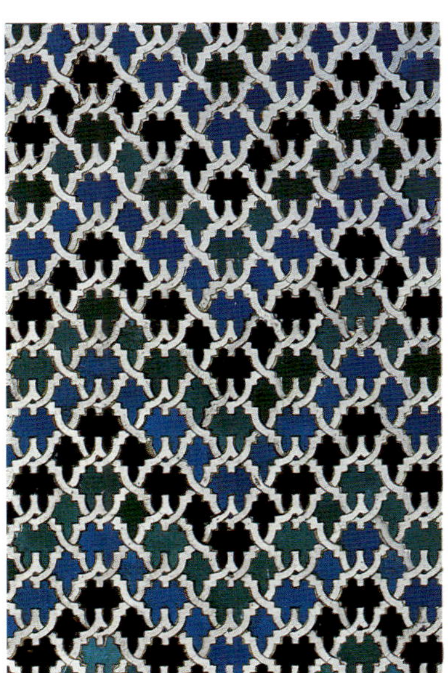

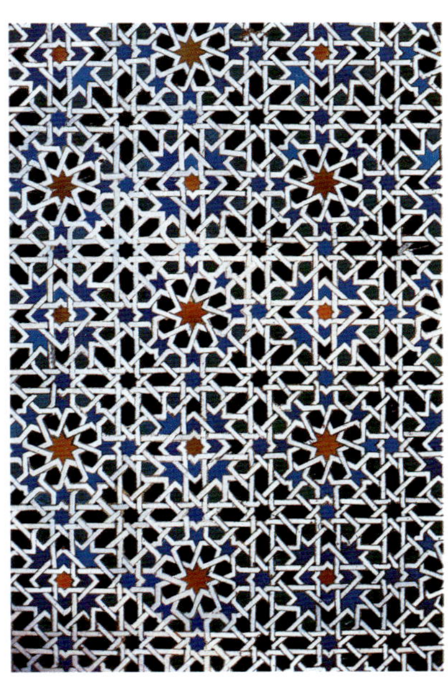

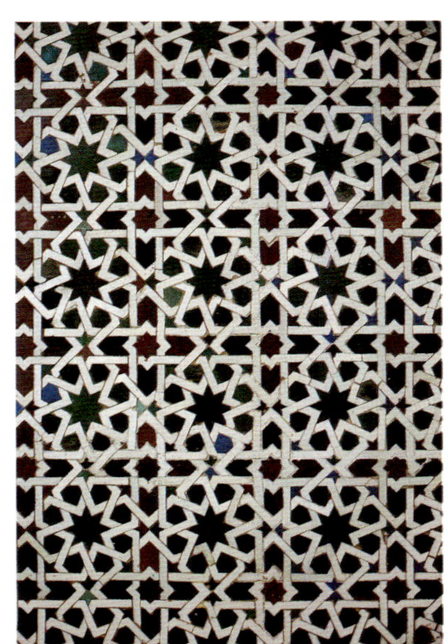

THE ALCAZAR, SEVILLE (SPAIN)

ABOVE

♦ Patio de las Doncellas.

FAR LEFT

♦ Detail of a *zellij* panel with a lattice pattern.

CENTER AND RIGHT

♦ *Zellij* panel with interlace pattern encasing eight-pointed stars.

Contemporary with the Alhambra, the Alcazar at Seville was built by artists from Granada for Pedro the Cruel, king of Castile (1334–69). This remarkably well-preserved palace is the supreme example of Mudéjar art carried out in the Muslim tradition for a Christian patron and contains some of the most beautiful examples of ceramic cladding in the whole Islamic world. Above the second-floor window bays, the facade of the palace of Pedro the Cruel also displays a painted-tile frieze inset into the brickwork. In the main court known as the Patio de las Doncellas, as well as in the chambers encircling it, the splendid *zellij* panels are once again concentrated primarily on the level of the dado; the coats-of-arms of the Nasrid sultans are now joined by the blazons of the kingdoms of Castile and León carved into the stucco above the ceramic paneling. Its magnificent *artesonado* ceiling is adorned with a star pattern reminiscent of that of the Hall of Ambassadors in the Alhambra.

♦ Vine-leaf pattern luster-painted tile. Nasrid Spain, beginning of the fifteenth century. Musée des Arts Décoratifs, Paris.

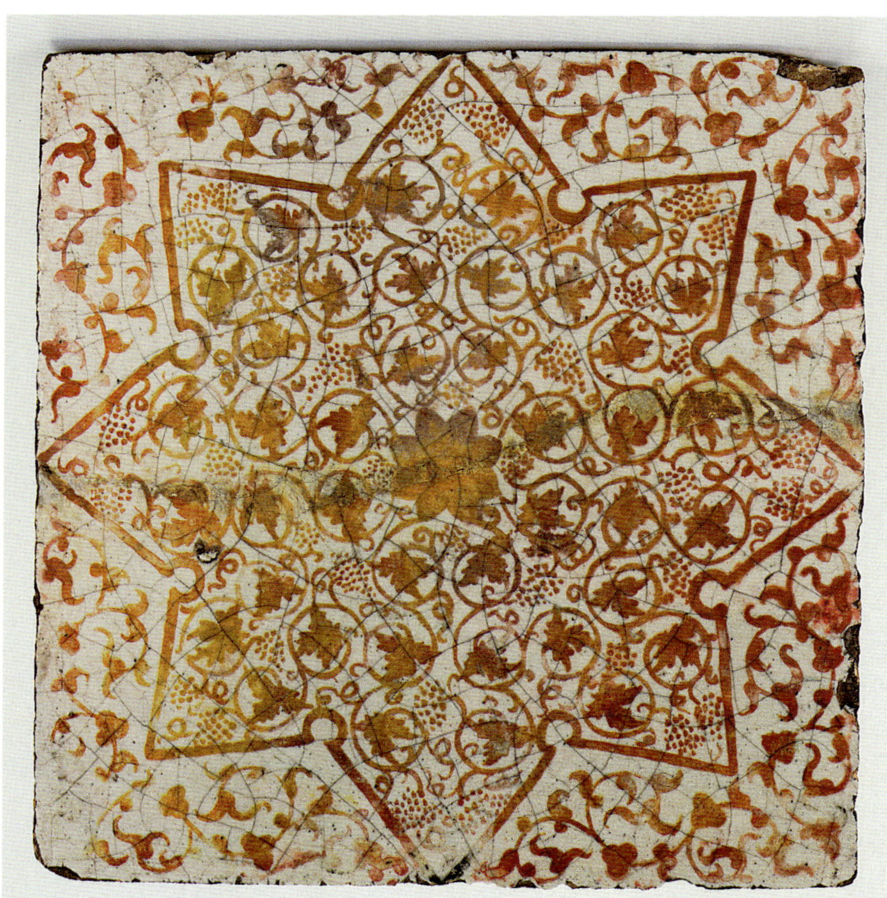

It was completed in 1427 by a master carpenter of the Mudéjar tradition, Diego Ruiz.

In Spain, several techniques were deployed in the making of ceramic decoration, some of which, such as *cuenca y arista* ("hollow and ridge") tilework, were truly novel. The method most generally utilized was the marquetry, or mosaic, of cut tiles, termed *alicatado* in Spain from the Arab verb *qata`a* ("to cut"). One of its first appearances at the Alhambra is probably at the Puerta de las Armas dating from the reign of Muhammad I (1237–73). Most of the wall panels in the Alhambra palace are decorated using this method of assembly, which permits a dazzling array of primarily geometrical and star motifs. The dados are often crowned by a border in the form of an epigraphic frieze; in certain cases, this frieze also takes the form of an assemblage of cut tiles bearing formulas in praise of the sovereign together with the motto of the dynasty: "There is no victor save God!" The Alhambra also affords examples of polychrome tilework of the *cuerda seca* type, as on the spandrels of the Puerta del Vino, although the technique remains relatively rare in the Nasrid era.

Large, painted tiles, their design brightened with metal luster, also remind us that it was under the Nasrid dynasty that some of the most beautiful examples of this type of ceramic—the monumental "Alhambra" vases—emerged. Two examples in particular, both dated to the early fifteenth century, bear witness to the virtuosity of the Nasrid ceramists: the vine-branch tile in the Musée des Arts Décoratifs in Paris and the impressive Fortuny Tablet (Instituto Valencia de Don Juan, Madrid), which measures no less than 108 by 63 centimeters.

As mentioned above, one of most specifically Hispanic techniques in the field of ceramic tiling is represented by pieces molded unfired, and whose partitioned and relief patterns allow metallic oxides of various tints to be contained without fear of bleeding. This method, termed *cuenca*

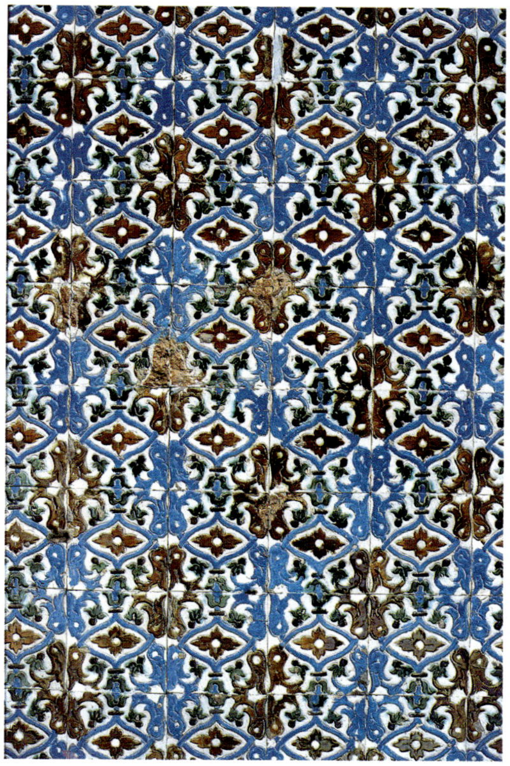

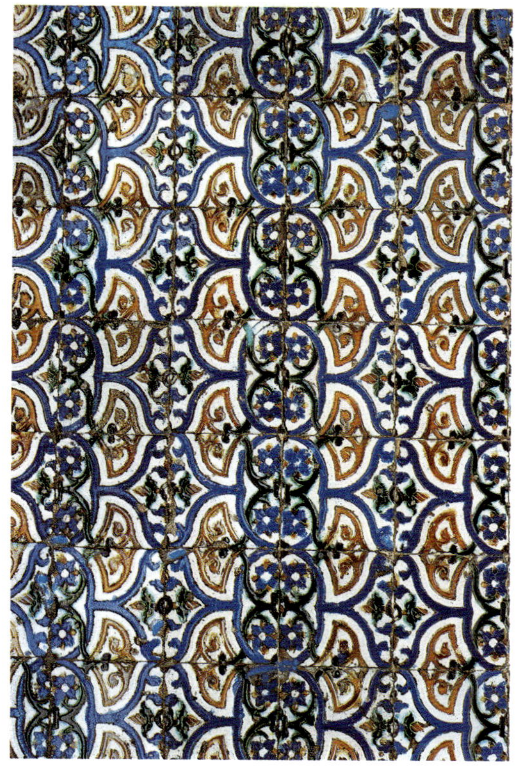

CASA DE PILATOS, SEVILLE (SPAIN), LATE FIFTEENTH–EARLY SIXTEENTH CENTURY

♦ *Cuenca y arista* tiles with a mandorla and palmette pattern, c. 1538.

♦ *Cuenca y arista* tilework with fleuron and fan motifs, c. 1538.

BELOW

♦ Panel decorated with *cuenca y arista* tiles with an iris motif, c. 1538.

y arista ("hollow and ridge"), was particularly highly developed in Seville during the fifteenth and sixteenth centuries. Remarkable examples of these decorations can be admired on the paneling cladding the porticos ringing the court of another splendid palace in Seville, the late-fifteenth- and early-sixteenth-century Casa de Pilatos. Here, the Moorish style of the ceramic dados (dated 1538), the stucco, and the *artesonado* woodwork on the ceilings meld with Italian Renaissance influences, such as the marble gate by the Genoese Antonio Maria D'Aprile, dated 1533.

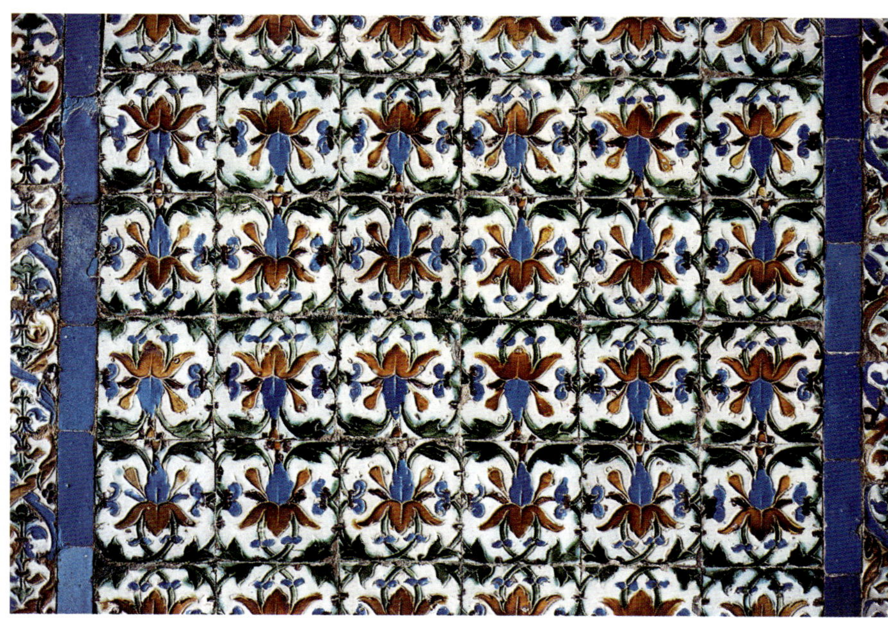

Hispano-Moorish Tiles: Inheritance and Influence

Although recovered by the Christians in 1248, Seville, throughout the Nasrid period, remained under the sway of Muslim artistic models. After the fall of Granada in 1492, followed a few years later by the arrival in Seville in 1503 of Francisco Niculoso (Pisano), an Italian ceramist of great repute, the production of the city turned increasingly to the Italianate style and to creating large pictorial polychrome panels to embellish the many residences and churches. Nevertheless, the impact of Muslim ceramics remained predominant in Mudéjar architecture over large tracts of the Iberian Peninsula. The brick-built towers of Teruel in Aragon, for example—a recent addition to the list of UNESCO's World Heritage Sites—present incrusted patterns of disks, pinnacles, tiles, and other forms in the white, green, and black characteristic of this type of architecture in the thirteenth and fourteenth centuries. Similarly, the external mural Mudéjar decoration in the old cathedral of Saragossa (partially concealed behind the refurbished seventeenth-century frontage) attests to the inclusion of cut-tiles of the Muslim tradition. Certain motifs involve crescent-moon coats-of-arms referring to the power of the Luna family that produced, as well as any number of bishops, the Antipope Benedict XIII (1324–1423).

In addition, Hispano-Moorish tile production was the subject of interchange with northern Europe at least from the fourteenth century; one piece of evidence dated 1369 points to the use of "lateres Saracenorum" (literally, "Saracen tiles") in the flooring of a room in the Palais des Papes at Avignon, southern France.[19] From this date, ceramic tilework paving gradually spread to interiors in France, the tiles being either directly imported or manufactured in situ by "Saracen" craftsmen hired especially, as is attested for Jean de Berry (1384–1416). The only vestiges in France of ceramic tile production in tin-glaze earthenware before this date are those recently discovered in the workshops of the Sainte-Barbe district of Marseille that date from the thirteenth century.[20] It is intriguing to note that, in particular during the eighteenth century, Spanish workshops in Valencia and Catalonia exported painted tiles to North Africa and the Near East (some are even to be found in the harem at Topkapi Palace).[21] It is consequently not so surprising to detect a Valencian or Catalonian flavor in several pieces made in Tunisian workshops such as those at Qallaline.

In the *Medersas* of the Marinids

As has already been pointed out, *madrasas* occupied a less important place in the Maghreb than they did in the Muslim East. From an artistic point of view, however, Marinid *medersas* in Morocco constitute a significant exception. Their construction was motivated by the concern felt by the princes of the dynasty to reach an accommodation with the class of the *ulamas* (the learned) and re-establish a harmonious relationship with the mystic milieus prevalent at that time in Morocco. The complex of the al-Sahrij and al-Saba`in *medersas* exemplifies perfectly the intentions of the Marinid sultans. Created in 1321 by the sultan Abu al-Hasan, this complex originally incorporated—besides the two *medersas*—a reception hall and a garden blessed with a spring that supplied the water required at the two foundations. The entryway to the al-Sahrij *medersa* provides direct access to a court with a sizable rectangular pool that occupies a substantial proportion of the space. Aligned with the entrance, the back of the courtyard leads to the prayer hall. This *medersa*, intended to house students from outlying rural areas, dazzles by its wealth of decoration: the dados are adorned with *zellij* in star patterns and the central zones of the walls are lined with motifs executed in stucco above which run broad and delicately carved timber boards. The flooring is covered with checkerboard tiling.

The al-`Attarin ("of the perfumers") *medersa* at Fez is surely one of the most outstanding Marinid creations. Inaugurated in 1323 by Abu Sa'id `Uthman (1310–31) and completed in 1325, the building faces entirely inward. An L-shaped entryway opens onto a court that occupies most of the surface area; rectangular in shape, one of its shorter sides is taken up by the entrance, the other by the prayer hall. The two longer sides are lined with porticos comprising a pair of pillars and an "Andalusian" colonnette in the Nasrid taste bearing a sturdy architrave. The center of the courtyard, surrounded by marble and colored-tile paving, is occupied by the white marble basin used for ablutions.

The virtually square oratory is crowned with a pyramid roof. Decorated from floor to ceiling, the court is particularly striking: ceramic mosaic panels (*zellij*) surmounted by inscriptions run round the lower reaches of the walls and clad the pillars. The calligraphic friezes were applied using

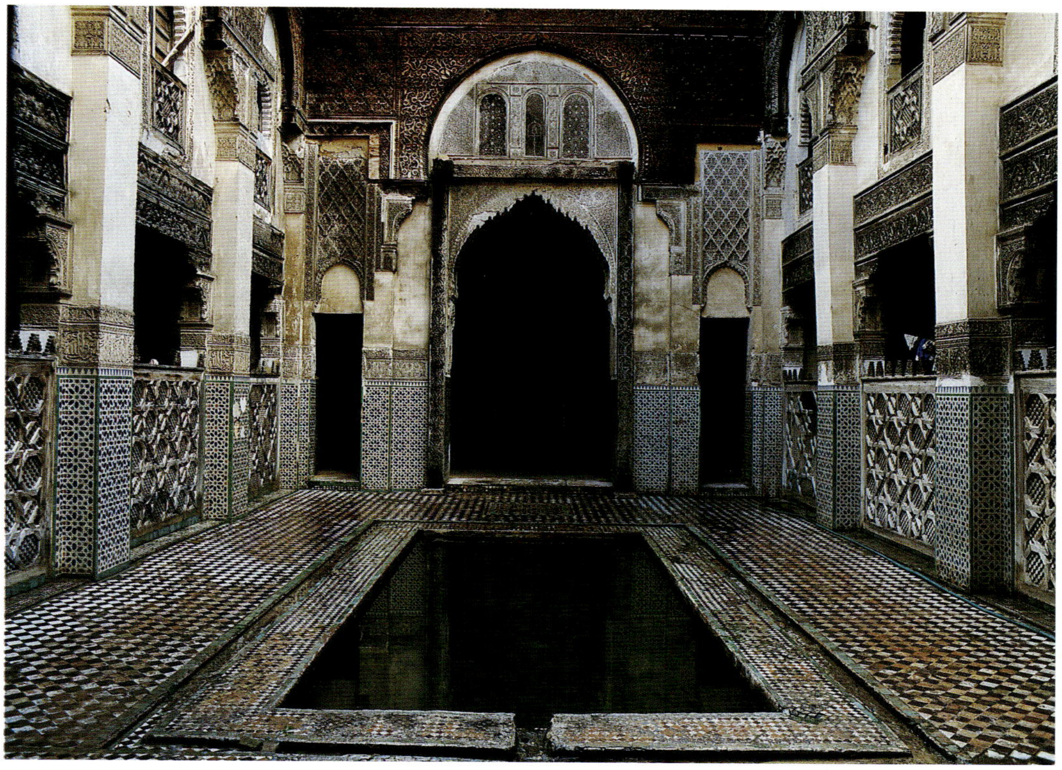

AL-SAHRIJ *MEDERSA*, FEZ (MOROCCO), FOUNDED 1321
♦ The *medersa* courtyard.
♦ *Zellij* panel with geometrical interlace pattern over an eight-pointed star motif.

a special technique employed to great effect in the decoration of Marinid *medersas*. Known in various authorities as *sgraffito*, *sgraffiato*, *esgraffito*, or "incised," the technique consists in scoring into metal oxide on the biscuit to create a pattern in the plain field beneath.

Above the *zellij* dado panels unfold stucco decorations showing leaf-scroll and palmette motifs in a style close to that of the Nasrids at Granada. The parts high up under the roof and also around the windows are dressed in decoratively carved cedar wood. It is perhaps this use of timber and the important role it fulfills in architectural decoration that most differentiates Marinid artistry from that of the Nasrids. Despite its modest proportions, this *medersa* was greeted with great acclaim by its contemporaries. An ancient description of the monuments of Fez describes it as follows: "In the year 723/1323, at the beginning of the month of *sha`ban*, the emir of the Muslims, Abu Sa`id—whom Allah protect and assist—ordered the construction of an important *medersa* at the nearby mosque of Qairouan. It was built under the watchful eye of the blessed Shaykh Muhammad

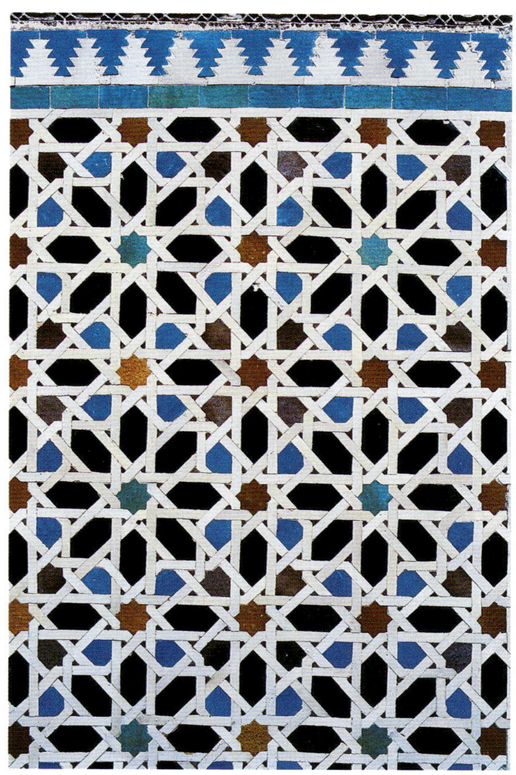

`Abdallah bin Qasim, the *mezwar*. The emir of the Muslims was present during the early foundation works and was accompanied by doctors and pious men, remaining there until the foundations were completely laid out and construction started. This *medersa* is a wonder among the monuments left by these sovereigns. No previous monarch

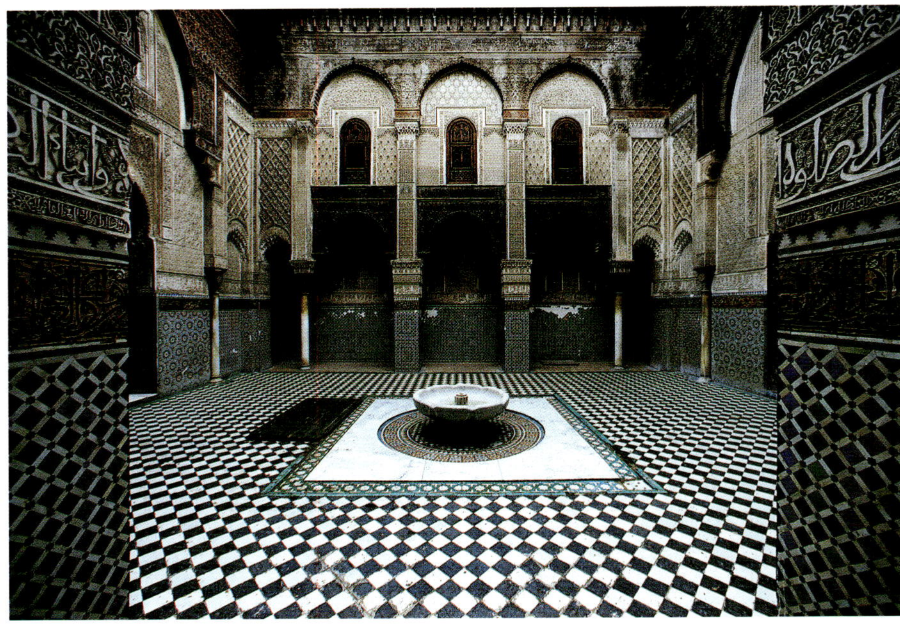

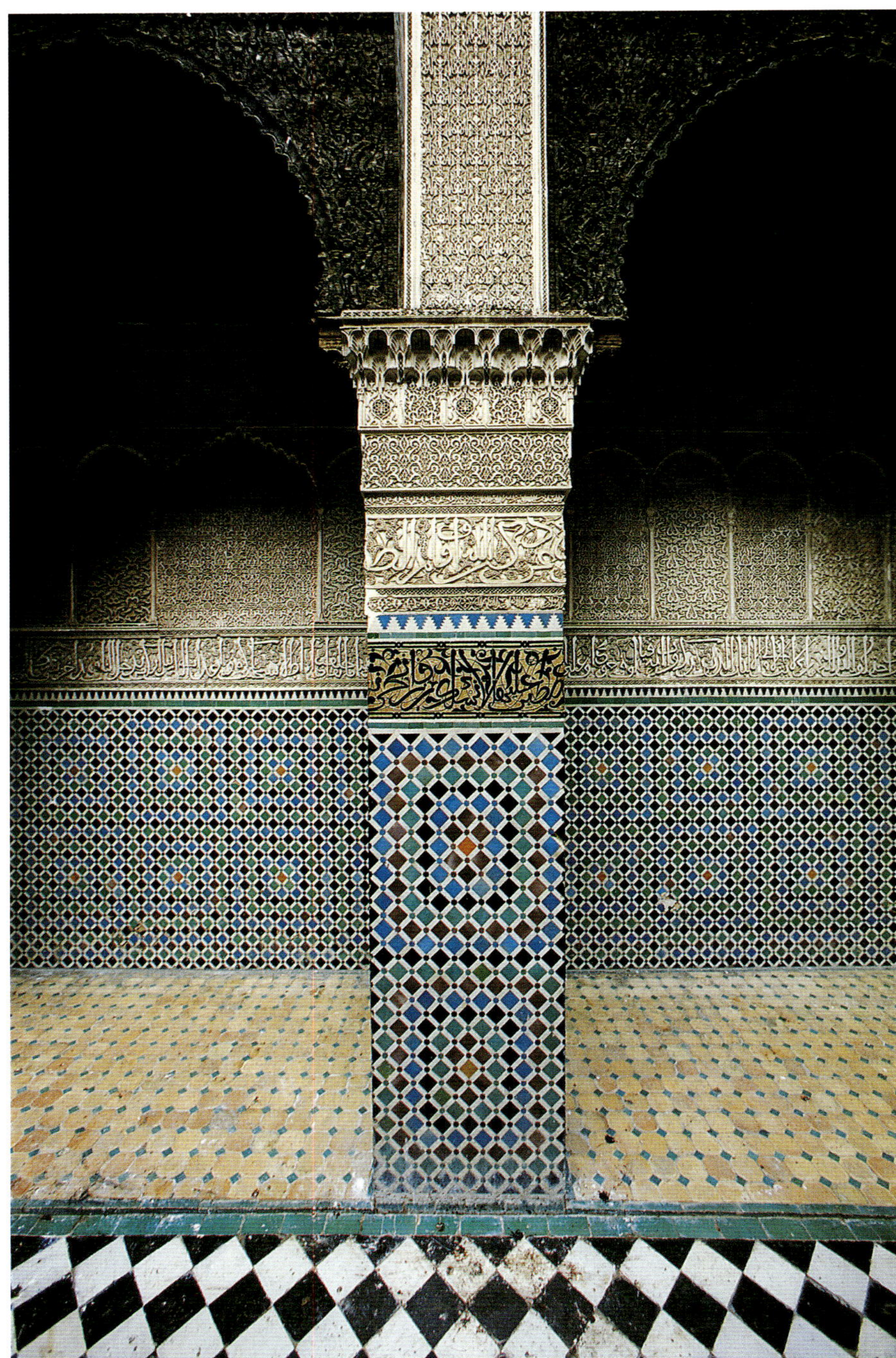

AL-ʿATTARIN *MEDERSA*, FEZ (MOROCCO), COMPLETED 1325

♦ The *medersa* courtyard.

♦ Detail of the *medersa* courtyard showing a checkerboard motif in *zellij* lining the dado and, above, on the pillar, an inscription in *sgraffito* ceramic. The upper reaches of the walls are clad in panels decorated in stucco.

FACING PAGE

♦ *Zellij* panels with a twelve-pointed star inset in a hexagon, above which runs a *sgraffito* ceramic inscriptional band in *maghribi* script topped by an inscriptional frieze intertwined with palmette scrolls (*tawriq*) in stucco.

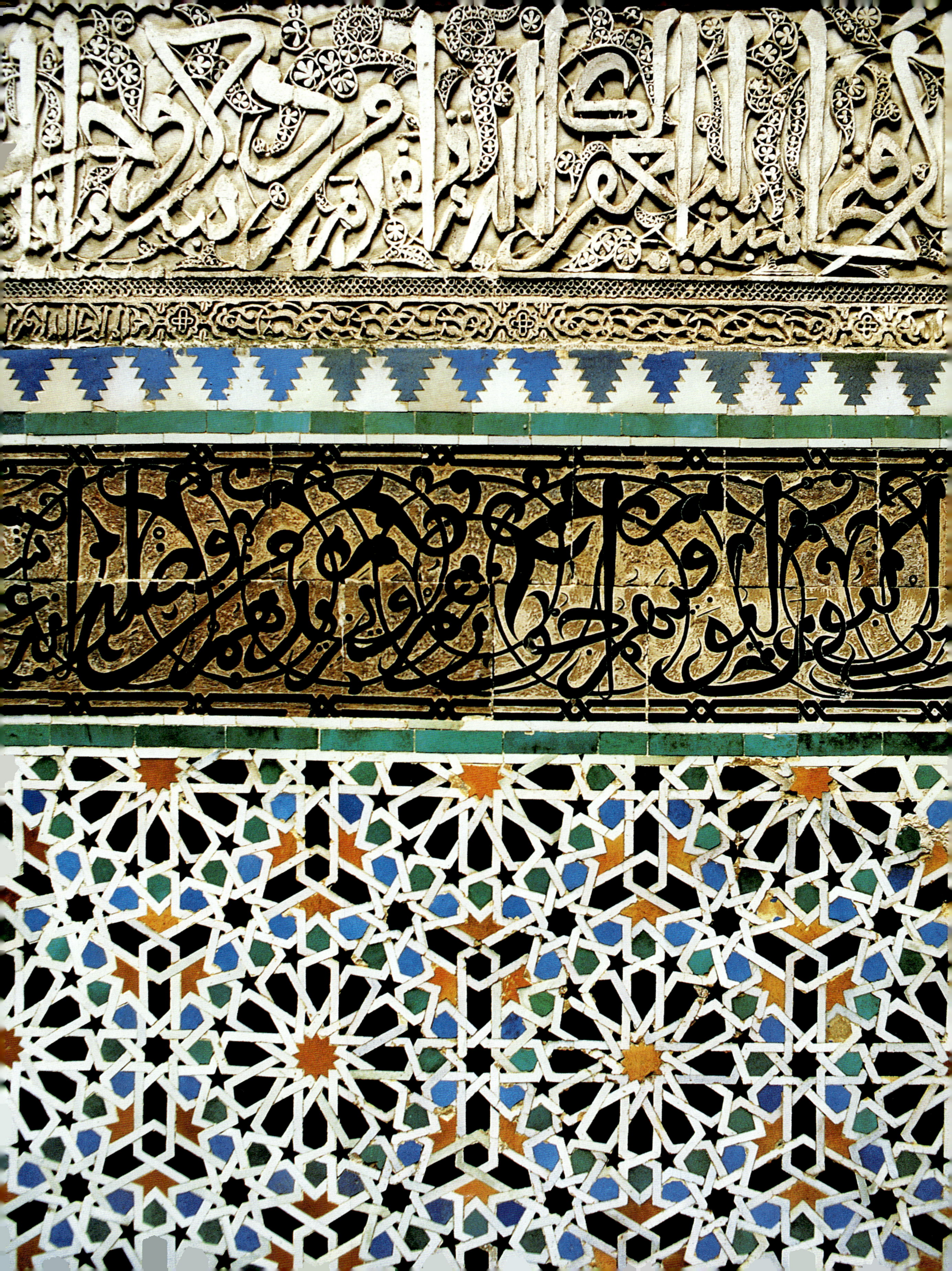

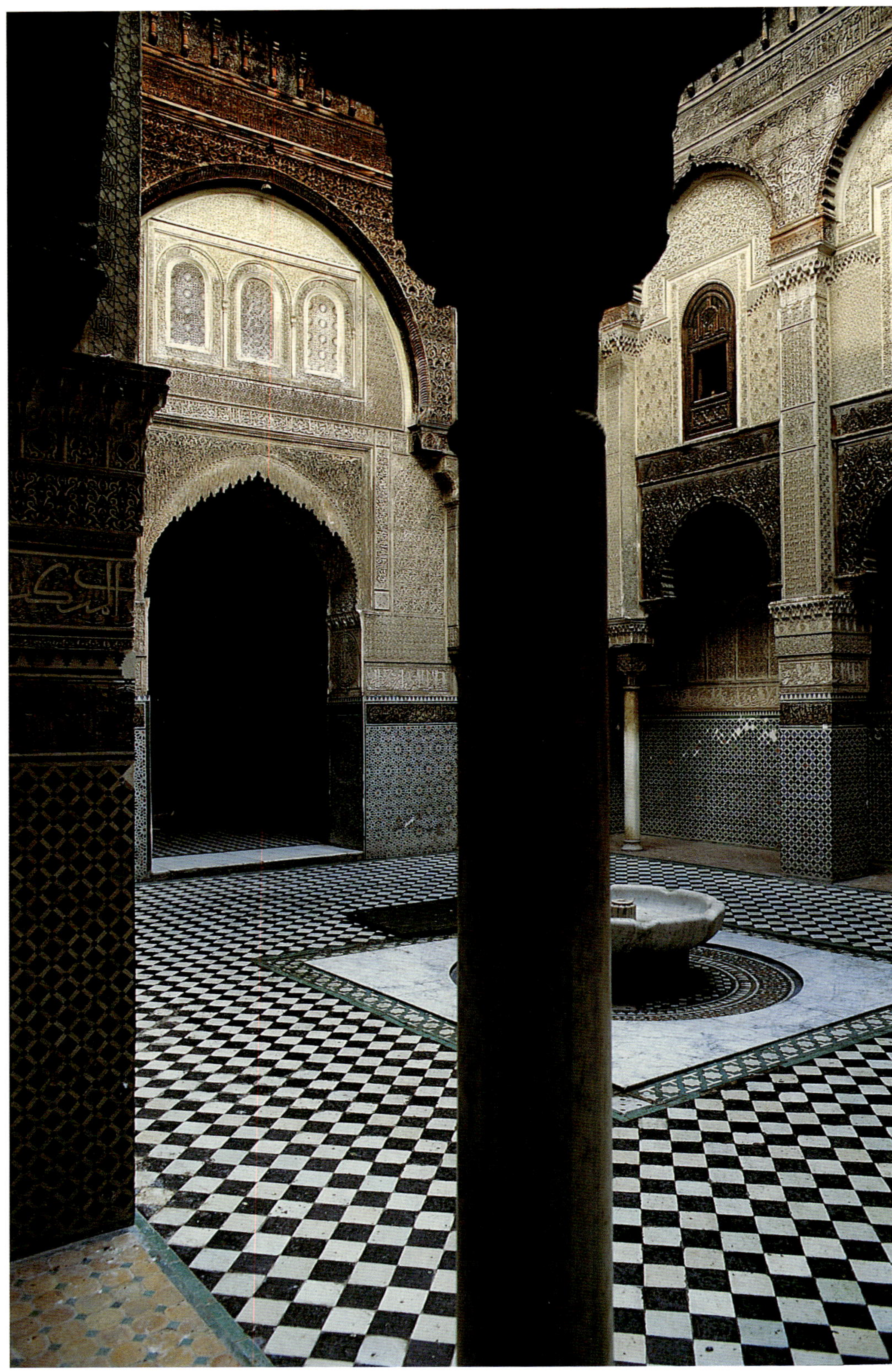

AL-`ATTARIN *MEDERSA*, FEZ (MOROCCO), COMPLETED 1325

♦ The *medersa* courtyard.

♦ *Zellij* panels with a lattice pattern.

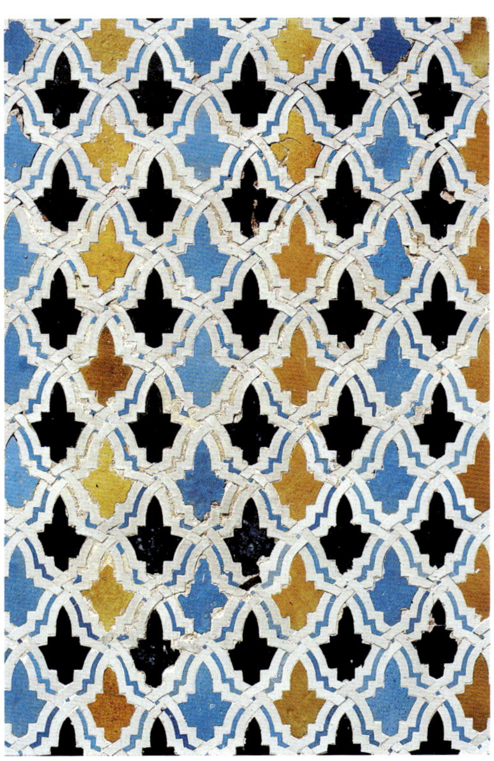

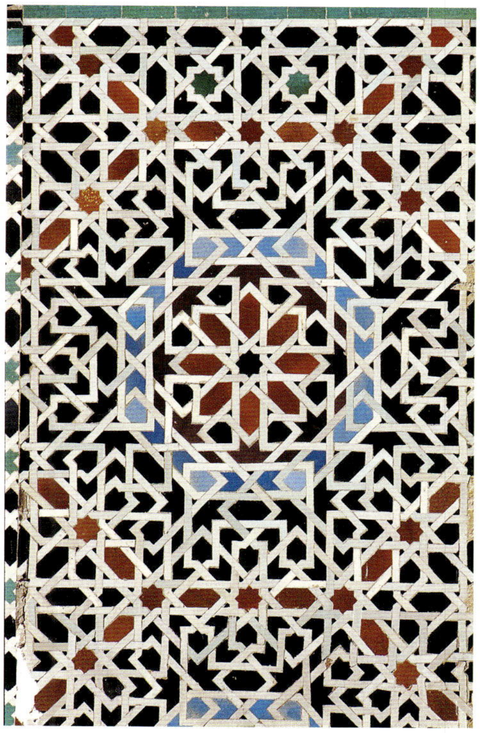

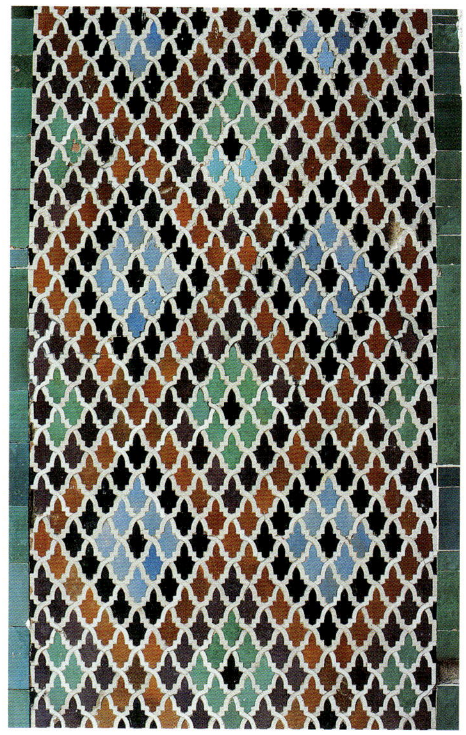

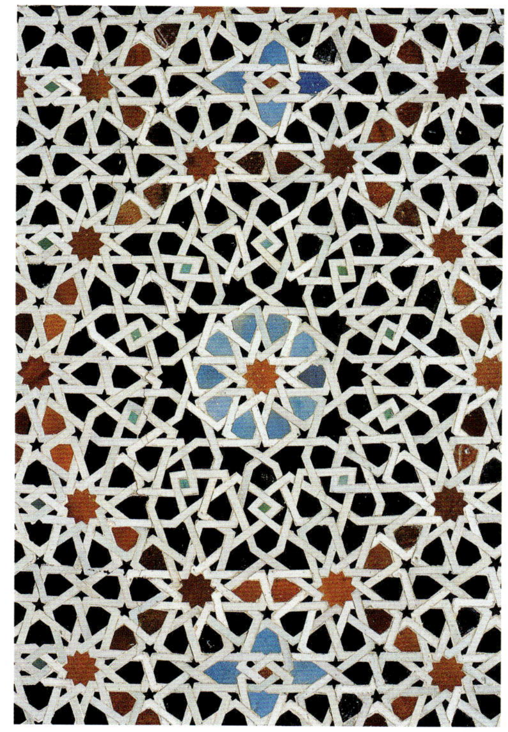

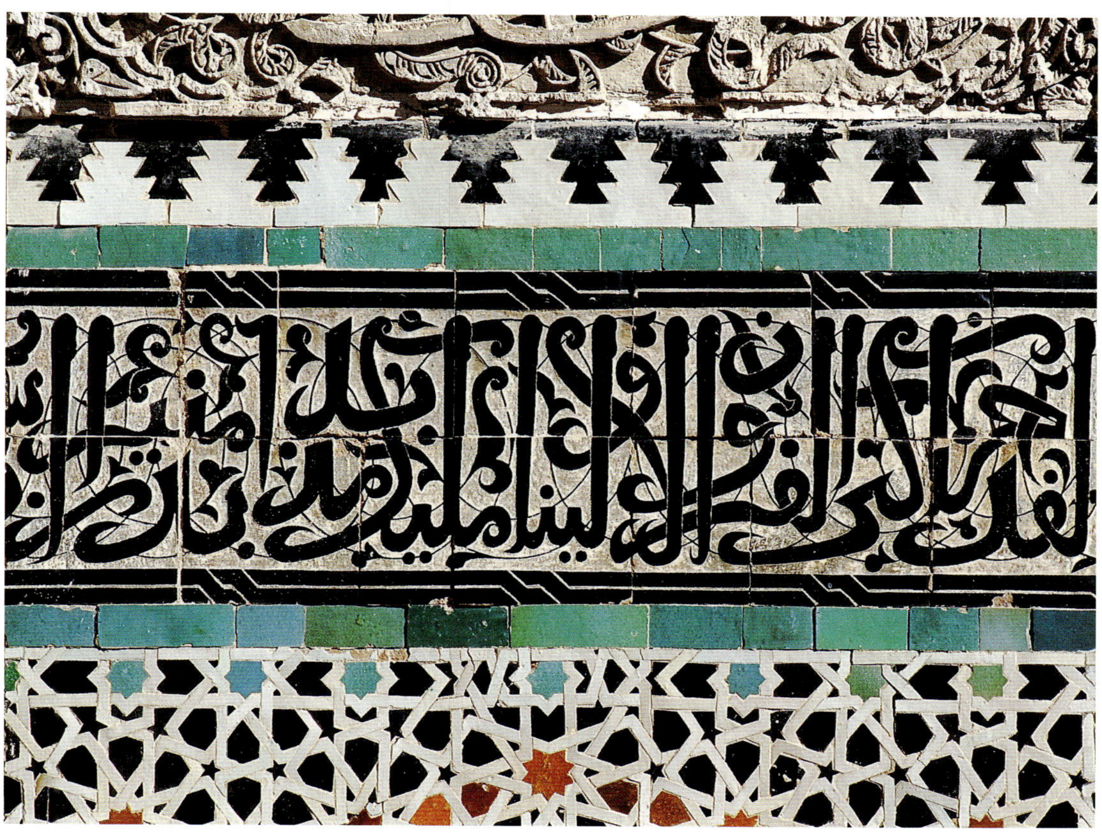

BU ʿINANIYA *MEDERSA*,
FEZ (MOROCCO),
COMPLETED 1355

ABOVE, FROM LEFT TO RIGHT

♦ *Zellij* panels with an eight-branched stellar motif in a pattern of octagons.

♦ Panels of *zellij* tilework in a lattice pattern.

♦ *Zellij* panels with a ten-pointed star motif in an interlace lattice pattern.

LEFT

♦ Top of the dado panel with calligraphic frieze in *sgraffito* ceramic.

has ever built such a thing. He made water run there from an abundant source."[22]

Founded by Abu Inan (1348–59) and built between 1350 and 1355, Bu `Inaniyya in Fez is the largest of the Marinid *medersas*. The building possessed the tallest minaret of its time in the city, partially revetted in *zellij*, as well as containing a curious water-clock. An almost square court paved in marble is framed on three sides by a gallery separated from the court by broad open-work wooden screens; one story houses cells for the students, while on either side of the court lie two study halls reminiscent of the *iwans* of the East, but which are infrequent in Fez. The front of the prayer hall is separated from the courtyard by a modest

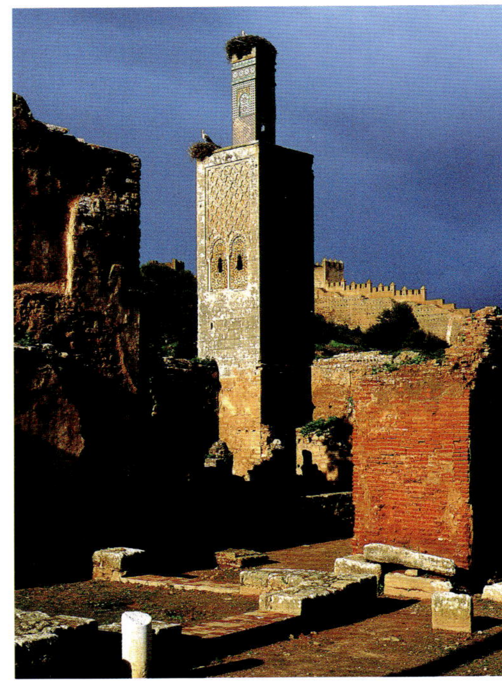

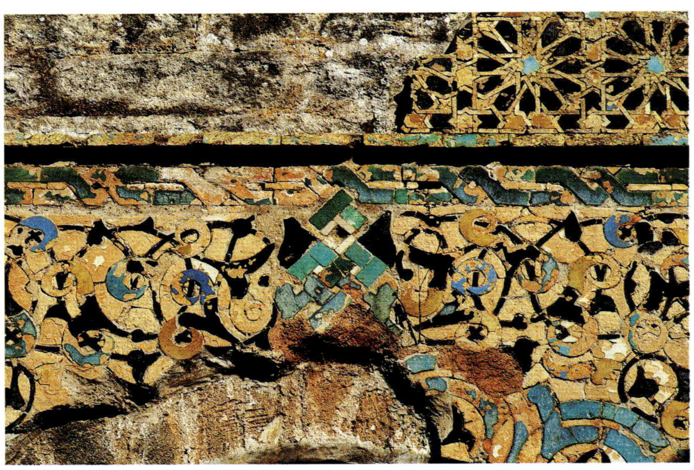

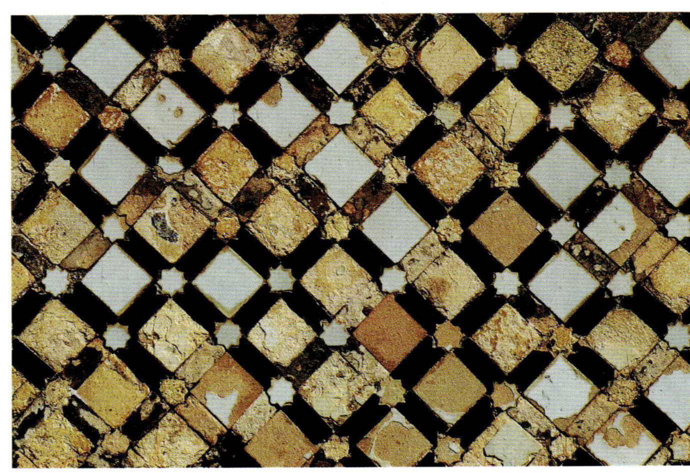

ZAWIYA AT THE CHELLA, RABAT (MOROCCO), FOURTEENTH CENTURY

TOP

♦ Minaret of one of the mosques.

ABOVE

♦ *Zellij* wall decoration showing scroll motifs (*tawriq*) and a border of twelve-pointed stars.

♦ *Zellij* panel with a checkerboard and eight-pointed star pattern.

RIGHT

♦ Tombstones laid with *zellij*.

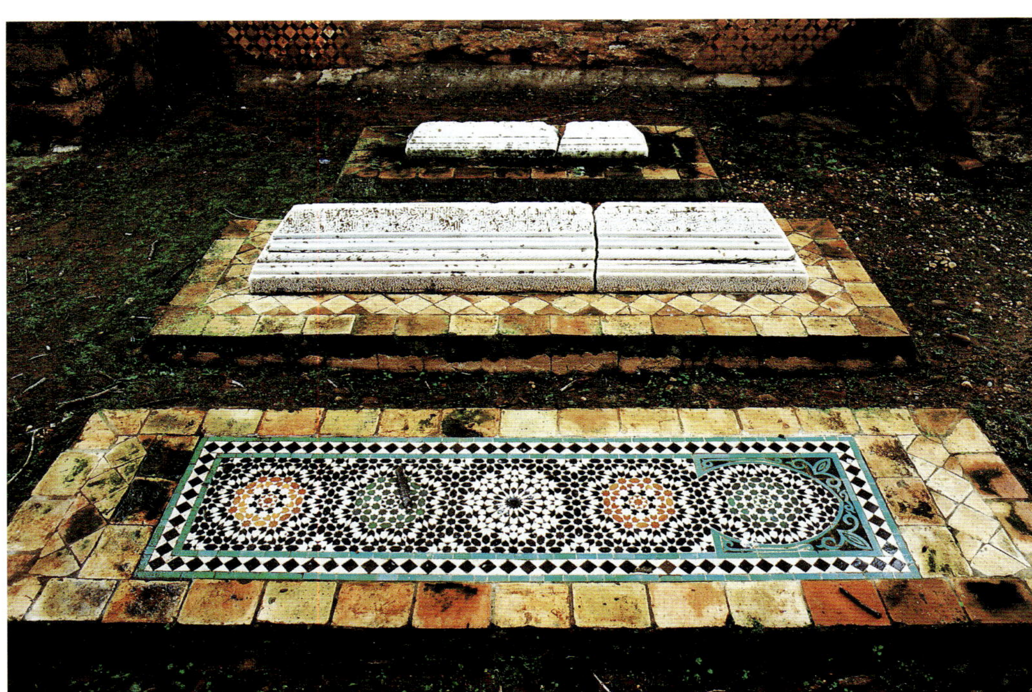

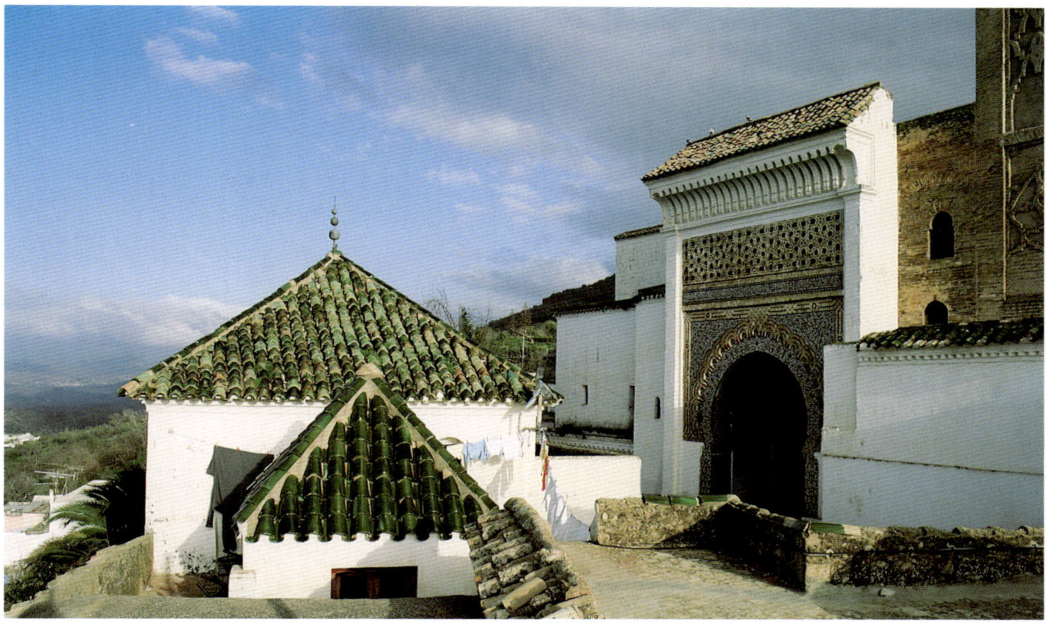

♦ Sidi Bu Medina Mosque, Tlemcen (Algeria), fourteenth century.

canal straddled by two bridges. This watercourse, which can serve for ritual ablutions, crosses Fez and emerges in *medersas* elsewhere. The oratory possesses two naves parallel to the *qibla* and has a ceiling reminiscent of Spanish *artesonados* (coffered ceilings). The *zellij* decorations of the court conform to the same pattern as in the al-`Attarin *medersa*, with cut tiles assembled in a star pattern surmounted by a calligraphic frieze in *sgraffito*.

The Chella *zawiya* in Rabat served as a necropolis for the sovereigns of the Marinid dynasty. In 1338–39, the sultan Abu al-Hasan `Ali had the tombs and the *zawiya* surrounded by a wall designed to look like a fortification. The door is flanked by towers whose sides are raised with *muqarnas* corbels; inside the rectangular enclosure stand two mosques with court and minaret, as well as three mausoleums in a garden steeped in melancholy. *Zellij* decorations burst forth both on the minarets and over the dados of the other buildings.

Lastly, slightly on the fringes of Marinid ceramics, the Tashfiniyya *madrasa* at Tlemcen features a number of elements from the Marinid *medersas* of Morocco. Founded around 1327 by Emir Abu Tashfin, the *madrasa* has undergone more than one restoration, notably during the reign of Sultan Abu al-`Abbas ibn Musa (1430–61). Lucien Golvin provides precise data concerning this vanished monument: "Utterly laid waste today, Tashfiniyya is known to us through two invaluable documents: eyewitness accounts such as the plan drawn up by the architect Duthoit at the time (1873) when its demolition to allow for the construction of the city hall was being carried out, and a watercolor by Danjoy, to which can be added the few vestiges of decoration preserved in the Musée Archéologique at Algiers."[23] As to the decoration, Golvin notes: "In 1873, a fair proportion of the pavement was still in situ: glazed ceramic tiles ran in a square round the basin while a layer of small tiles placed apex-down covered the remainder of the surface."[24] In point of fact, fragments today in the museum at Algiers present another type of revetment executed in sky-blue and black *zellij* in a geometrical interlace pattern forming stars, alternating with a motif of split palmettes lining arcades that conform to the same two-color scheme. Odd as it may seem, these decorations seem closer to those on edifices built by the Seljuks of Rum (at Sivas or Tokat) than to contemporary Marinid *medersas*. Other Marinid constructions at Tlemcen—such as the minarets of Sidi Bu Medina and Sidi Bu Hala and the Mansura Mosque (1303–36)—also contain notable ceramic decorations.

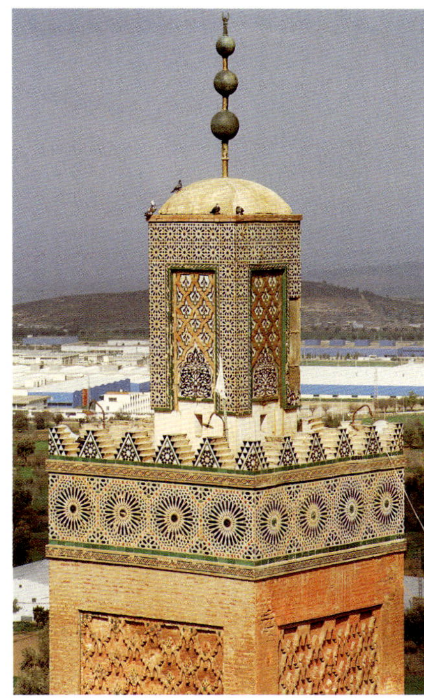

♦ Minaret of the Sidi Bu Hala Mosque, Tlemcen (Algeria), fourteenth century.

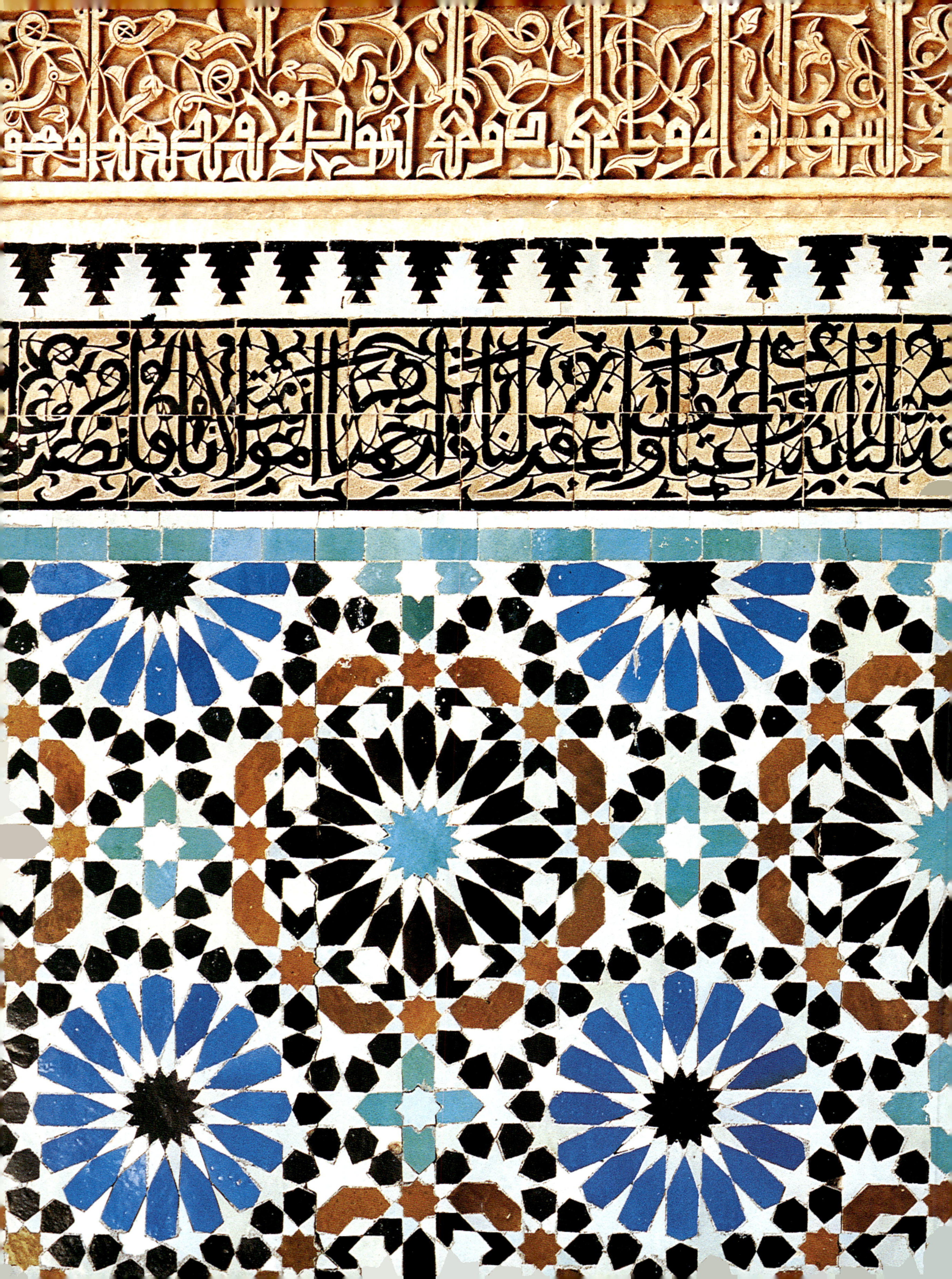

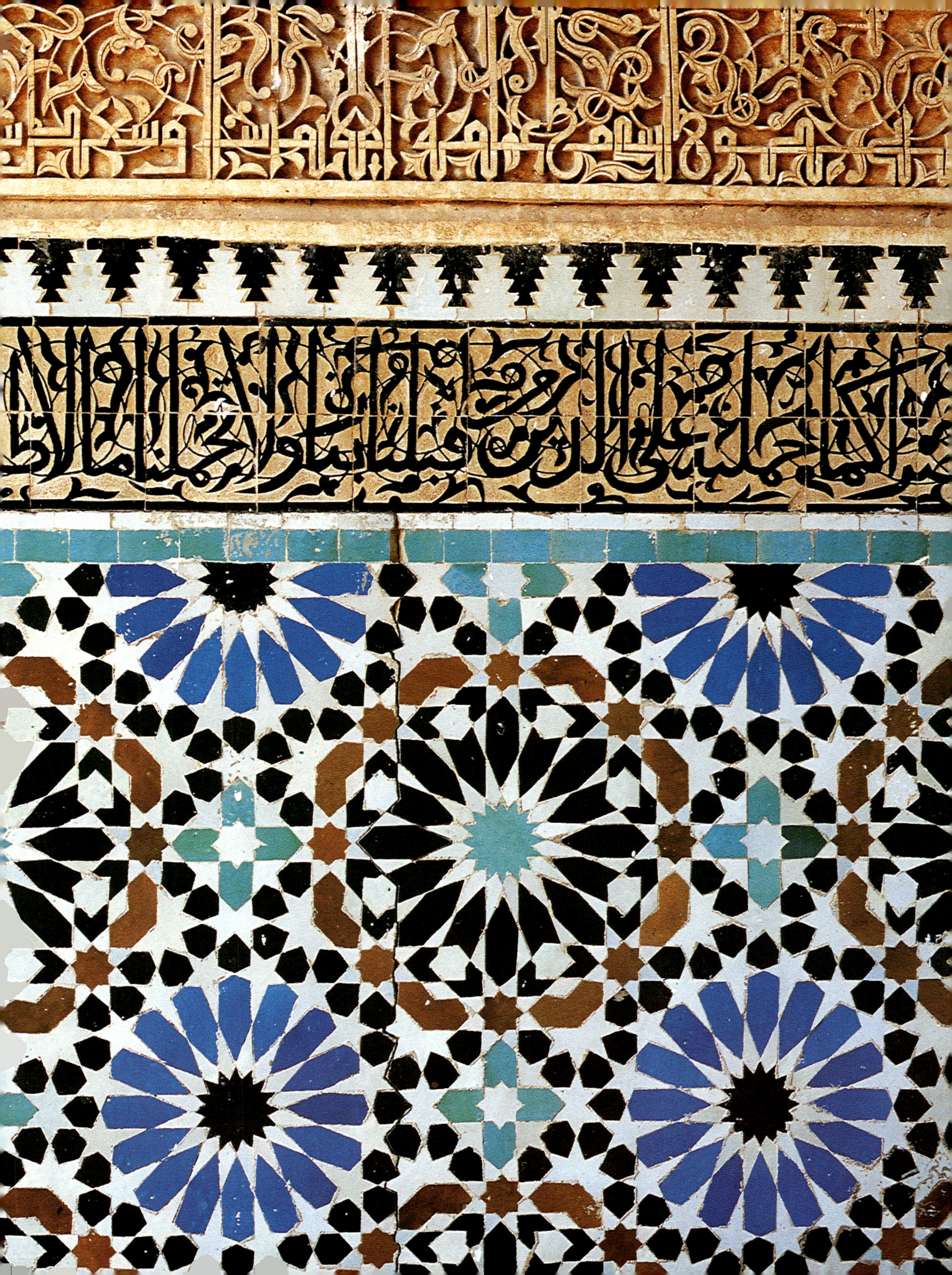

Morocco under the Sa`dis and the `Alawis

PRECEDING DOUBLE PAGE

♦ *Zellij* dados crowned with an inscriptional band in *sgraffito* ceramic and a Kufic script frieze in stucco. Sa`di tombs, Marrakech (Morocco), sixteenth century.

RIGHT

♦ *Zellij* panel with a sixteen-pointed star pattern. Sa`di tombs, Marrakech (Morocco), sixteenth century.

The coming to power of the Sa`dis following the taking of Marrakech in 1525 marks the beginning in Morocco of the era of the sharifs, the Arab dynasties descending directly from the Prophet (*sharif*), whose power has endured down to our own time.

Nothing remains of the first Sa`dian residence in Marrakech, the celebrated Badi` Palace (1578–93), since it was raised to the ground in the eighteenth century by Mulay Isma`il. Its immense site, however, complete with gardens (*agdal*) and vast pools, gives one some idea of this near legendary palace. The best-known monuments of the Sa`dis today, however, are surely their dynastic tombs. Lying not far from the Kasbah of Marrakech, these tombs back against the *qibli* wall of the mosque. Among the many hundreds of tombs comprising the funerary complex, two are particularly noteworthy—that of Muhammad al-Shaykh (died 1557) and that of Ahmad al-Mansur. The latter is the most sumptuous of all and is composed of a small mosque and adjoining mausoleum; like the floors, the dados are lined with *zellij*, above which run stucco bands with an epigraphic design. The central hall, known as "the hall of the twelve columns," is surmounted by an elegant cedar-wood cupola resting on a double sequence of superposed arches and covered without by a four-sided roof clad in green glaze tiles. Architecturally, the Sa`dian period did not add any major innovations to the existing

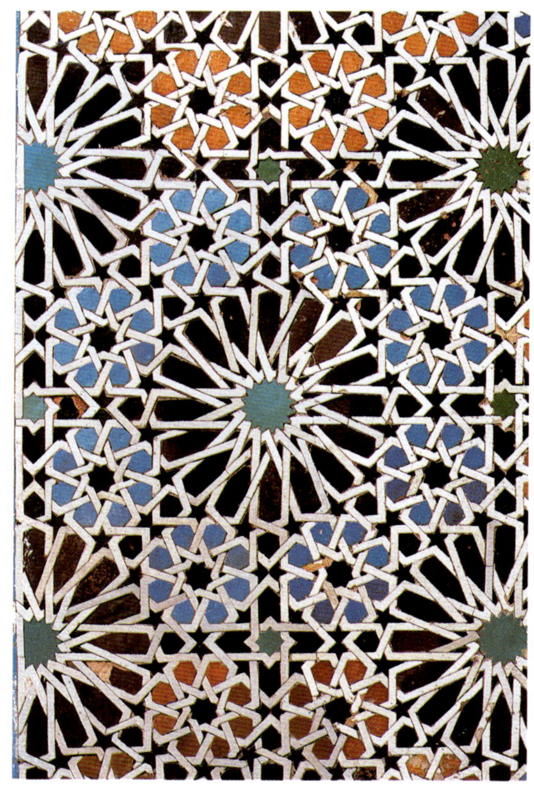

Marinid decorative repertoire. Nevertheless, the harmony of the proportions and the splendid decoration make this monument most attractive.

Still in Marrakech, the Ben Yussef *medersa* was built in 1565 by Sultan Mulay `Abdallah, perhaps on the site of a preexisting *medersa*. Its almost square plan, its generous proportions, and its decorative luxuriance make it one of the most beautiful constructions in all Morocco. As in Marinid *medersas*, the dados decorating the court are composed of extended *zellij* panels with star-shaped motifs topped by a calligraphic frieze of *sgraffito* tiles while, above these,

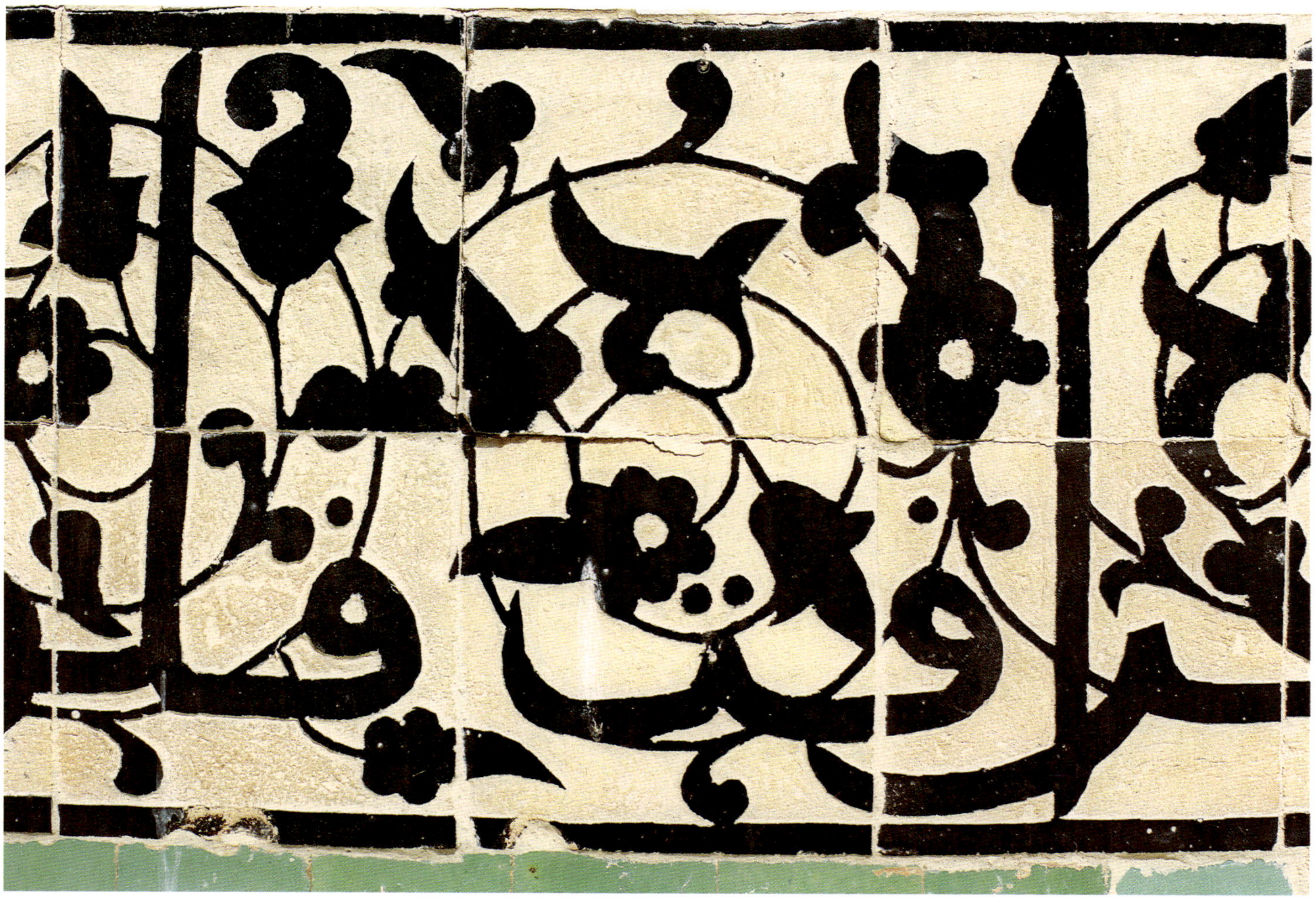

BEN YUSSEF *MEDERSA*, MARRAKECH (MOROCCO), 1565

♦ Detail of the calligraphic frieze in *sgraffito*.

♦ Dado with star-patterned *zellij* crowned with a calligraphic band in *sgraffito* ceramic, above which runs a short inscriptional frieze in stucco.

♦ *Zellij* dado with an eight-branched star pattern.

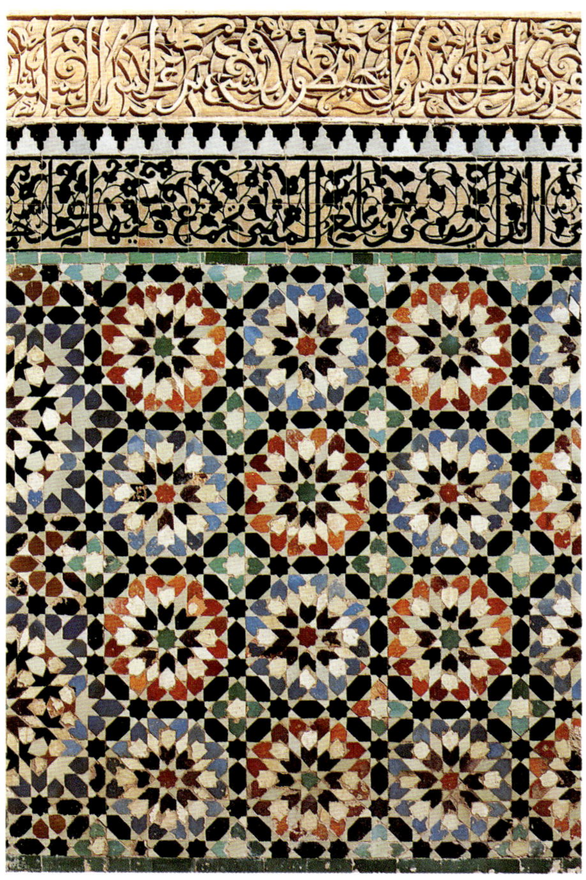

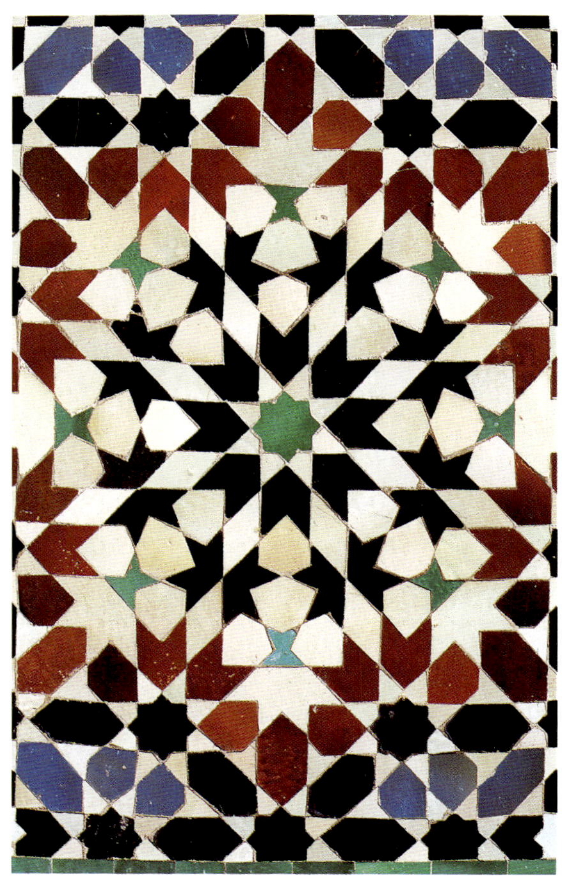

stretches a wide strip of intricately carved stucco. The center of the court is occupied by a large marble basin. The nearby Ben Yussef Mosque dates originally from the Almoravid era, but it was altered in the eighteenth century and again in the nineteenth, to the extent that practically nothing of the initial construction can be said to survive. Its imposing minaret on the other hand still soars 40 meters into the air.

In the mid-seventeenth century, the Sa`dis gave way to a second dynasty of the sharifs, the `Alawis. In the reign of Mulay Isma`il (1672–1727), the capital was transferred to Meknes, a city the sovereign was soon busy embellishing with monuments. The ring of ramparts surrounding the city is punctuated by massive gates, one of the finest being Bab al-Khemis. On it Mulay Isma`il had engraved the following inscription: "I am the door open to all peoples, be they of the East or of the West." Its decoration is particularly remarkable at the level of the spandrels, with black *zellij* tiles framed in green. The mausoleum of the same prince at Meknes, dating from the eighteenth century, is also one of most significant, while the monumental entryway to the complex, the Bab al-Mansur, is equally impressive. The door at the center, flanked on either side by the two projections of the facade, is crowned by a depressed horseshoe arch framed by a broad *alfiz* adorned with a mix of brick and ceramics. The general feeling conveyed by this imposing composition is one of oppressiveness. To the right of the door, the Bab Jama`a en-Nuar is of more modest size and has more harmonious proportions. The interior of the funerary complex presents a pleasing example of the use of *zellij* in a pavement. At the center of the court there is a marble

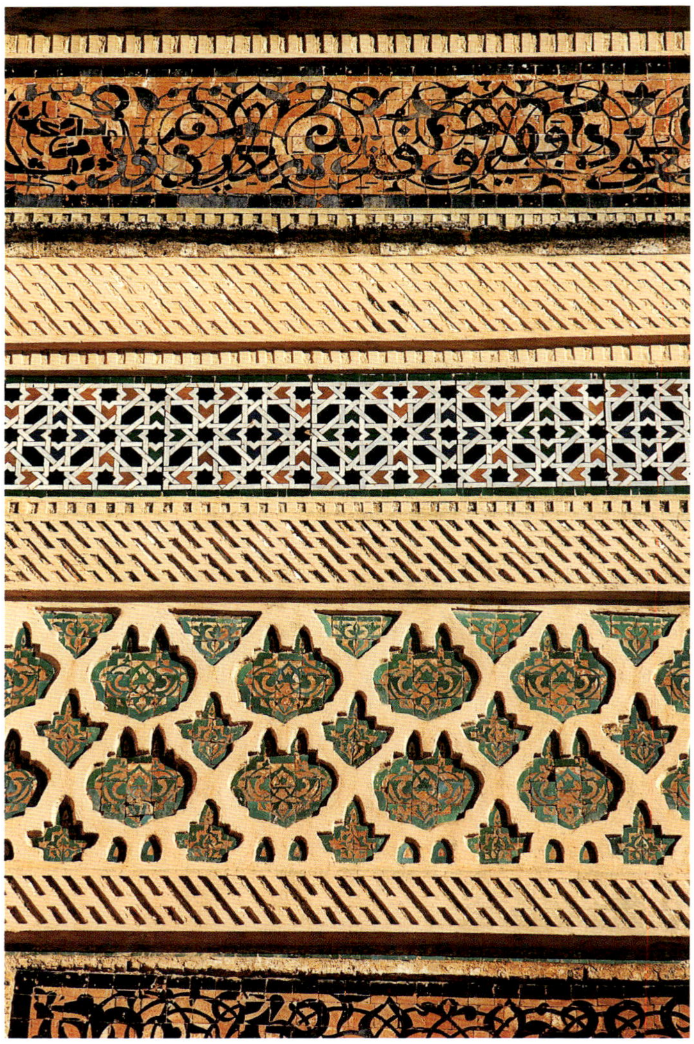

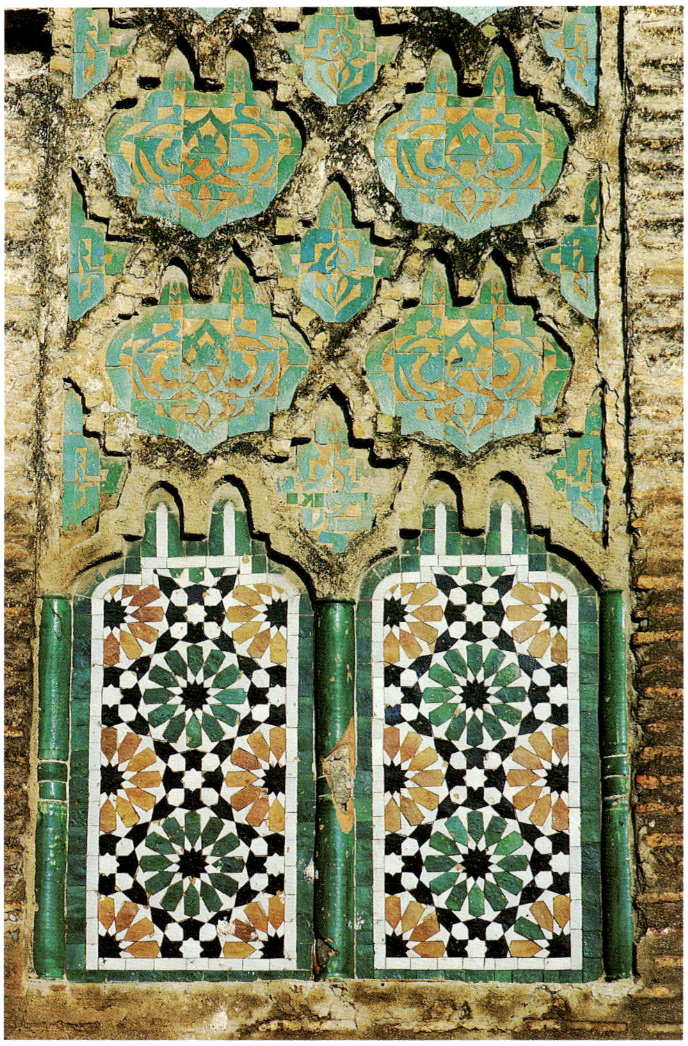

BAB AL-KHEMIS, MEKNES (MOROCCO), EIGHTEENTH CENTURY

♦ Calligraphic frieze on a leaf-scroll ground above bands of stars and latticework set with *zellij*.

♦ Niches and lattices with ceramic decoration.

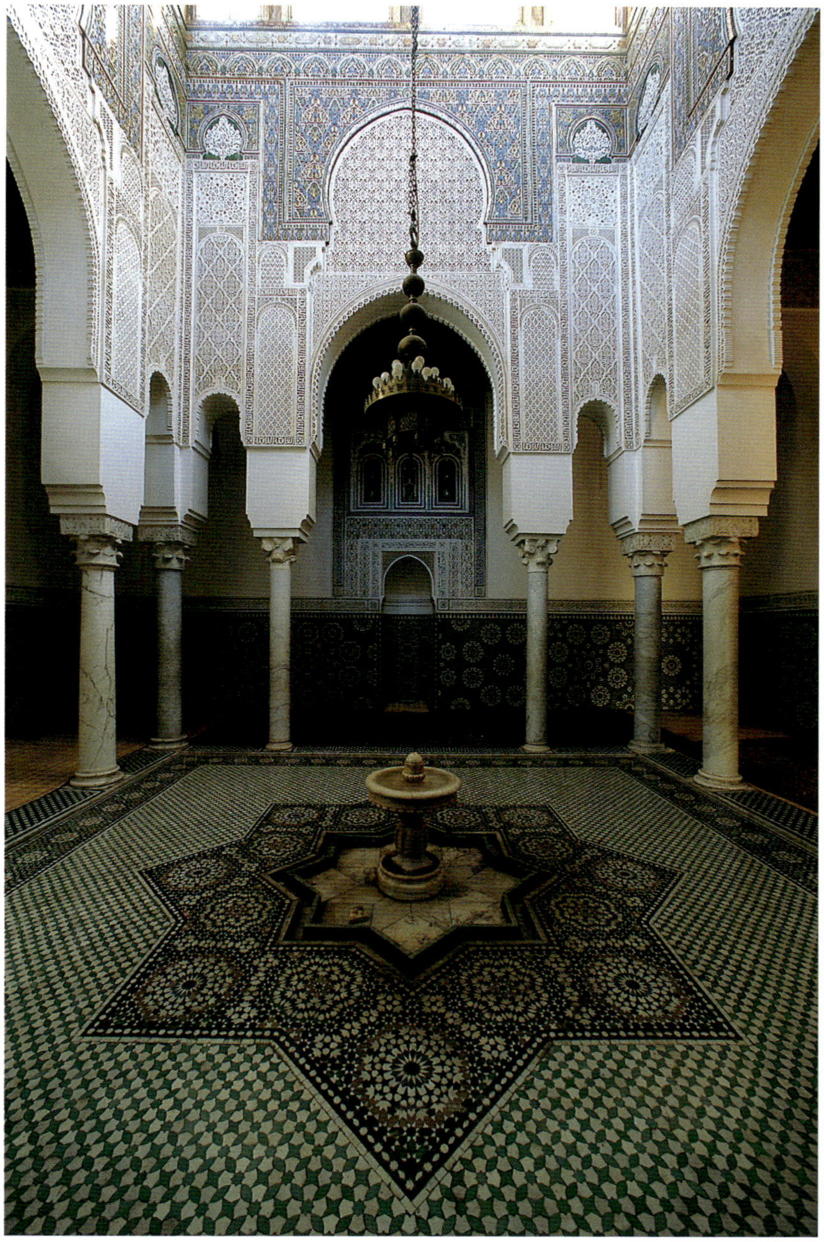

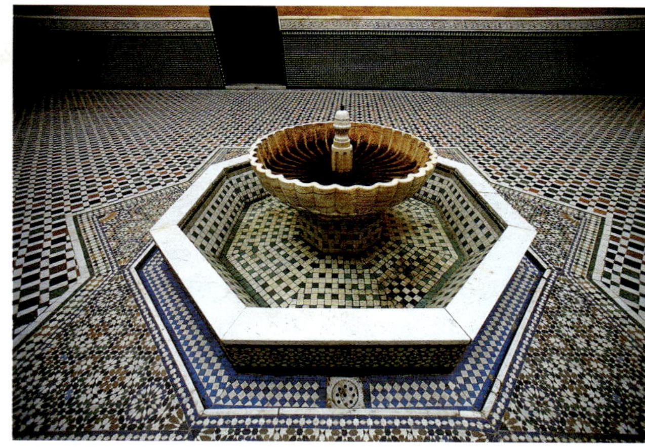

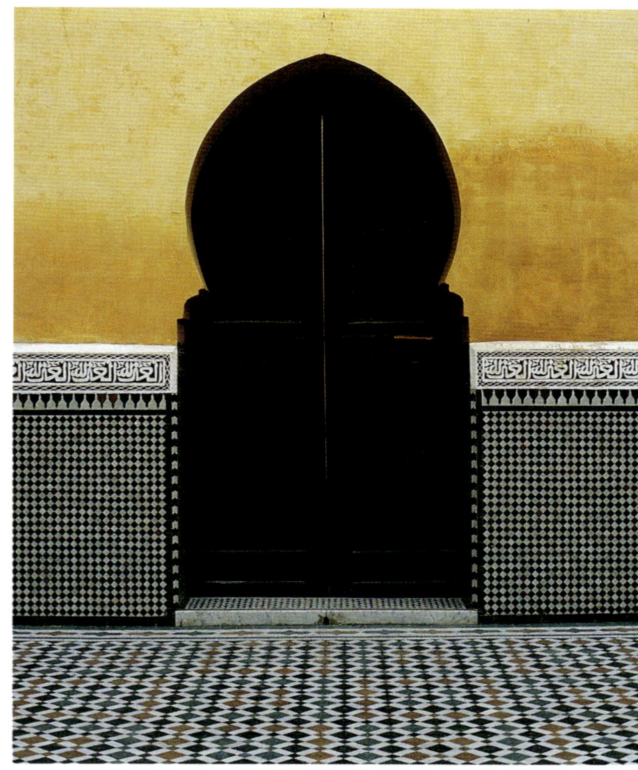

MAUSOLEUM OF MULAY ISMA'IL, MEKNES (MOROCCO), C. 1727

ABOVE LEFT

♦ Inner court paved with *zellij* forming an eight-pointed star around the fountain in the center.

ABOVE RIGHT, TOP

♦ Court of the mausoleum paved entirely in *zellij*.

ABOVE RIGHT, BOTTOM

♦ Doorway in the court. Floor and dado paved in checkerboard *zellij*.

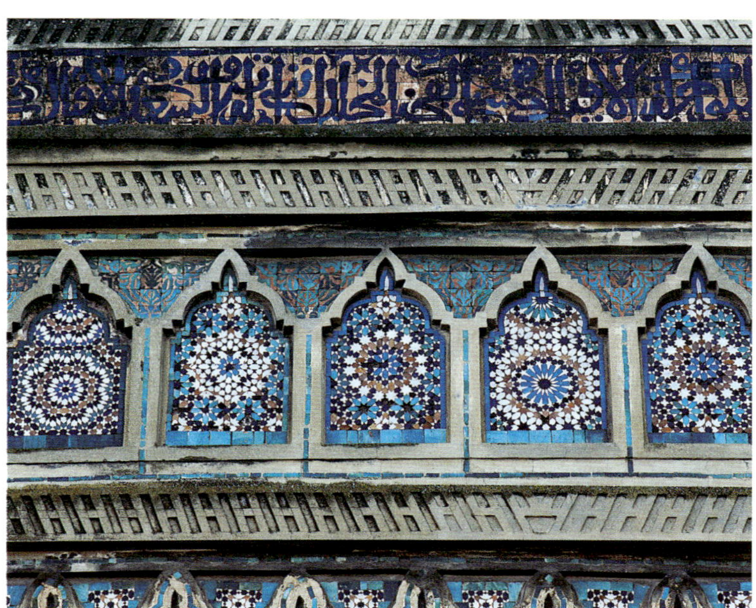

LEFT

♦ Niches and calligraphic frieze set with *zellij*. Bab Jama`a en-Nuar, Meknes (Morocco), eighteenth century.

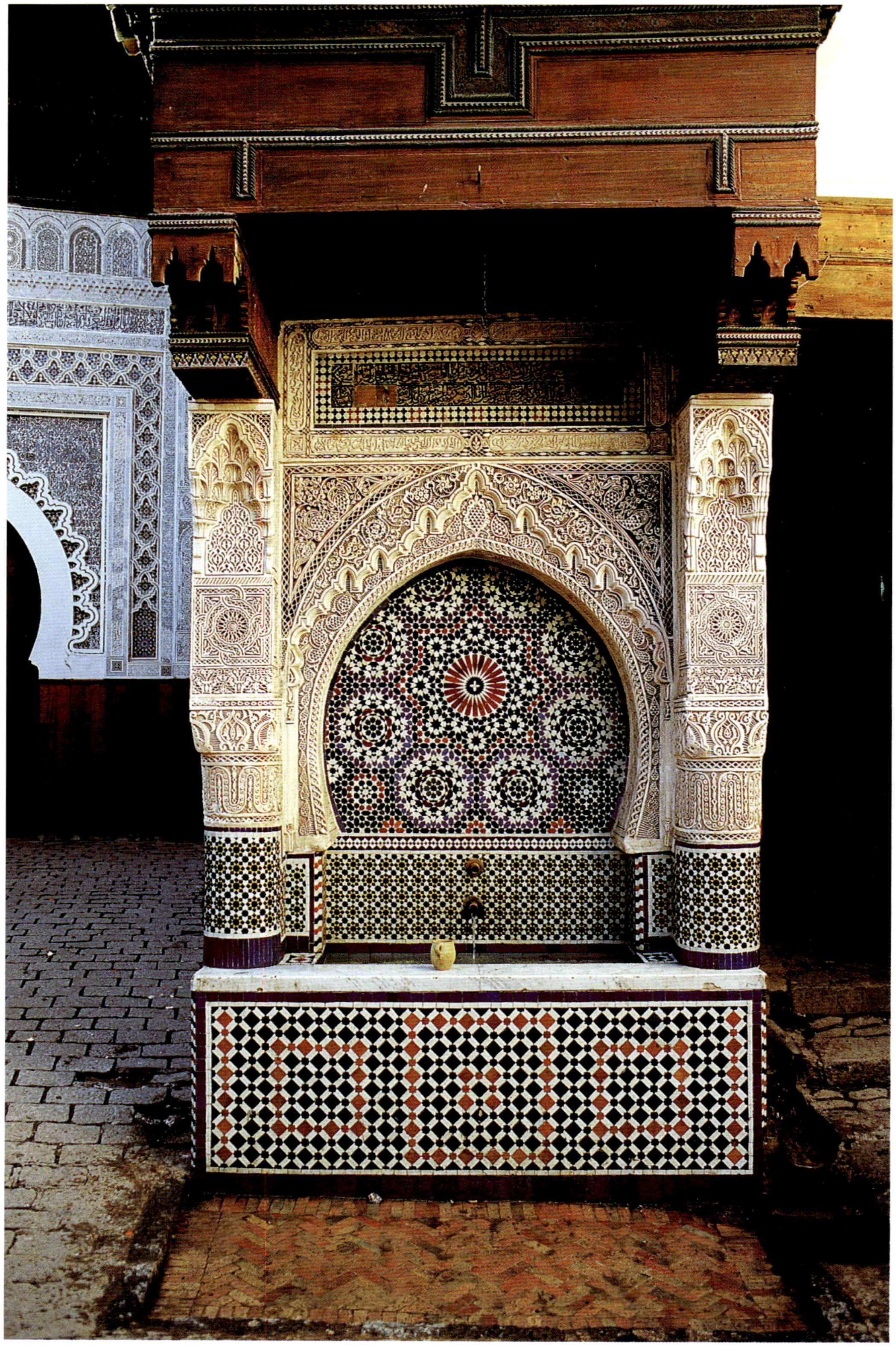

♦ Al-Najjarin fountain, Fez (Morocco), seventeenth century.
♦ *Zellij* panel with sixteen-pointed star motif.

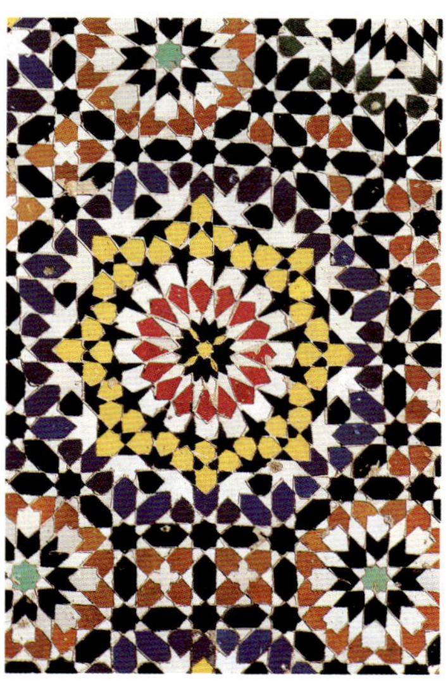

fountain basin within an octagonal pool lined inside with white and green tiling; the pool stands on an octagon inset within an eight-pointed star itself laid with star motifs. Surrounding this central feature, and covering the entire surface of the court, is tile paving which alternates white with ocher, green, and black.

Zellij decorations also appear as ornamentation in smaller public buildings, as well as in fountains, a charming example of the latter being the Al-Najjarin fountain (seventeenth century) located directly in front of the recently restored *funduq* of the same name in Fez.

Although often heavily restored during

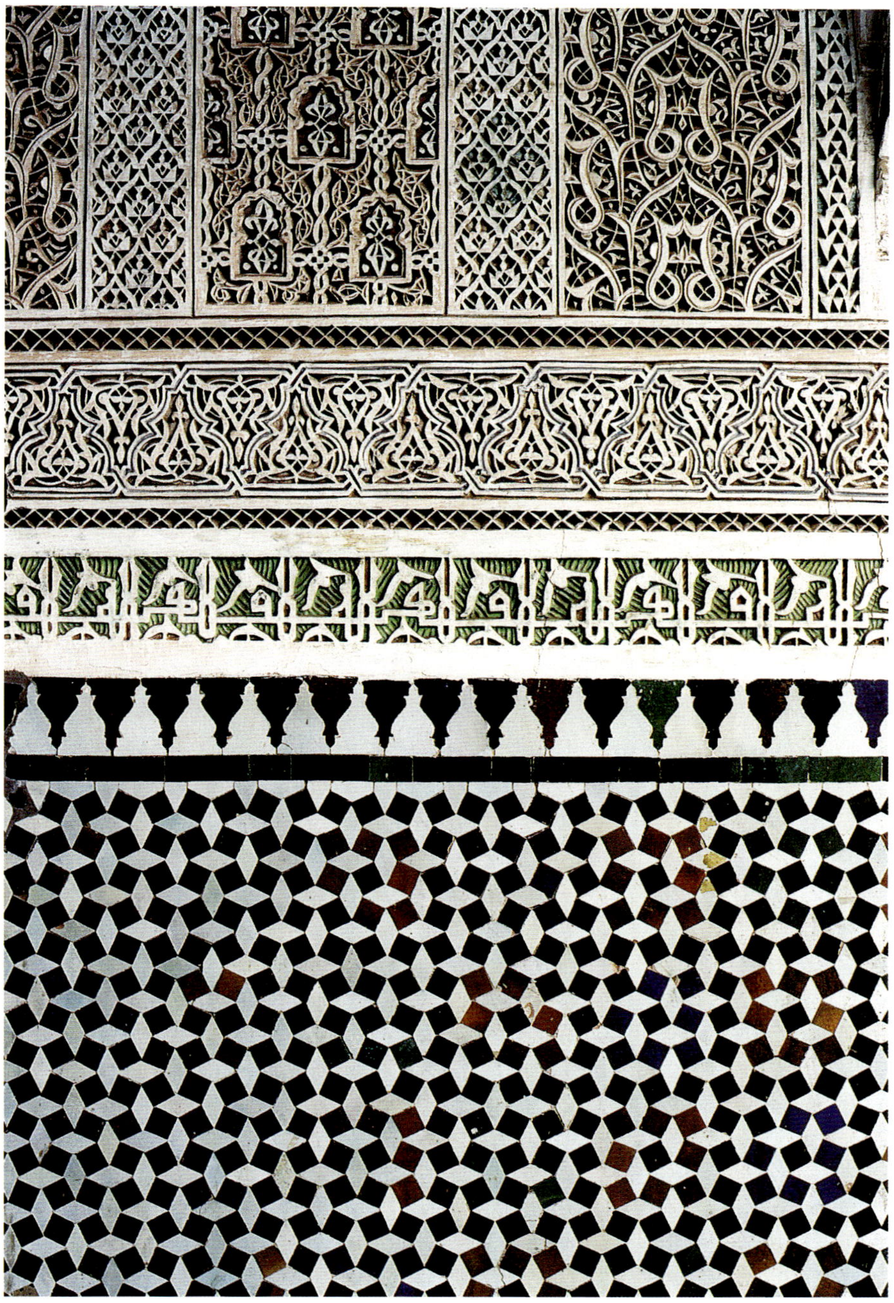

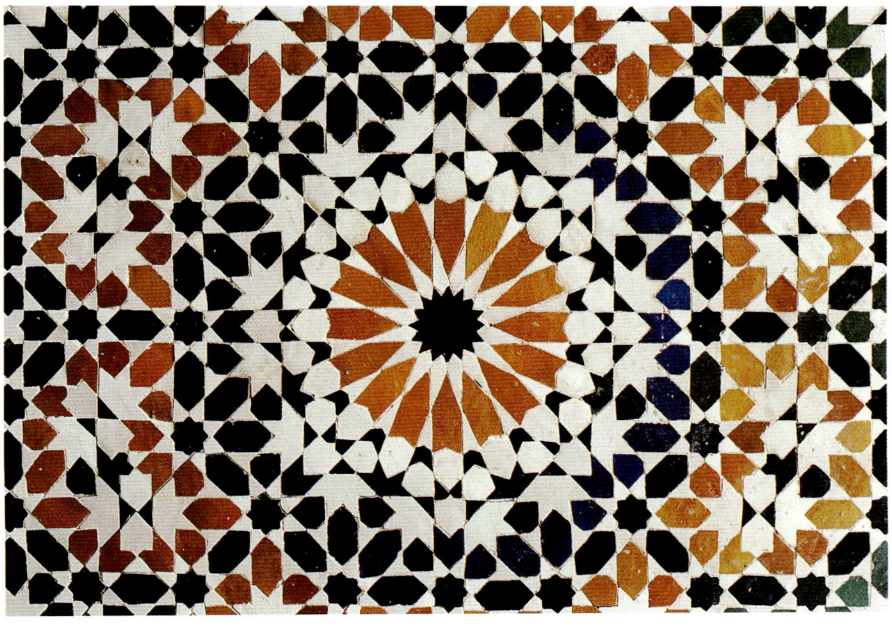

PALACE OF THE BAHIA,
MARRAKECH (MOROCCO),
NINETEENTH CENTURY

♦ Dado with *zellij* in a combination of diamonds and squares topped by a stucco panel.

♦ *Zellij* dado with radiating sixteen-pointed star pattern.

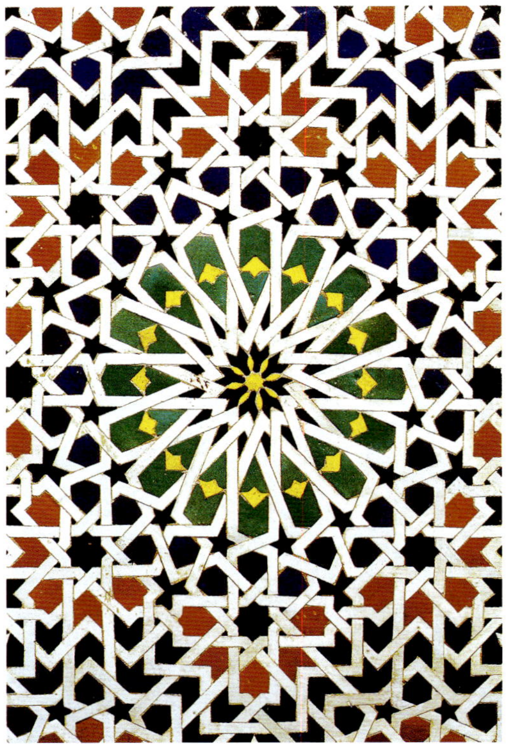

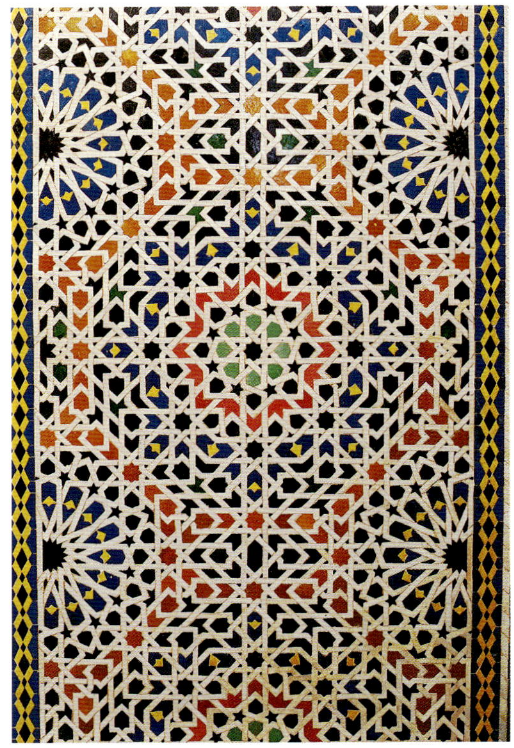

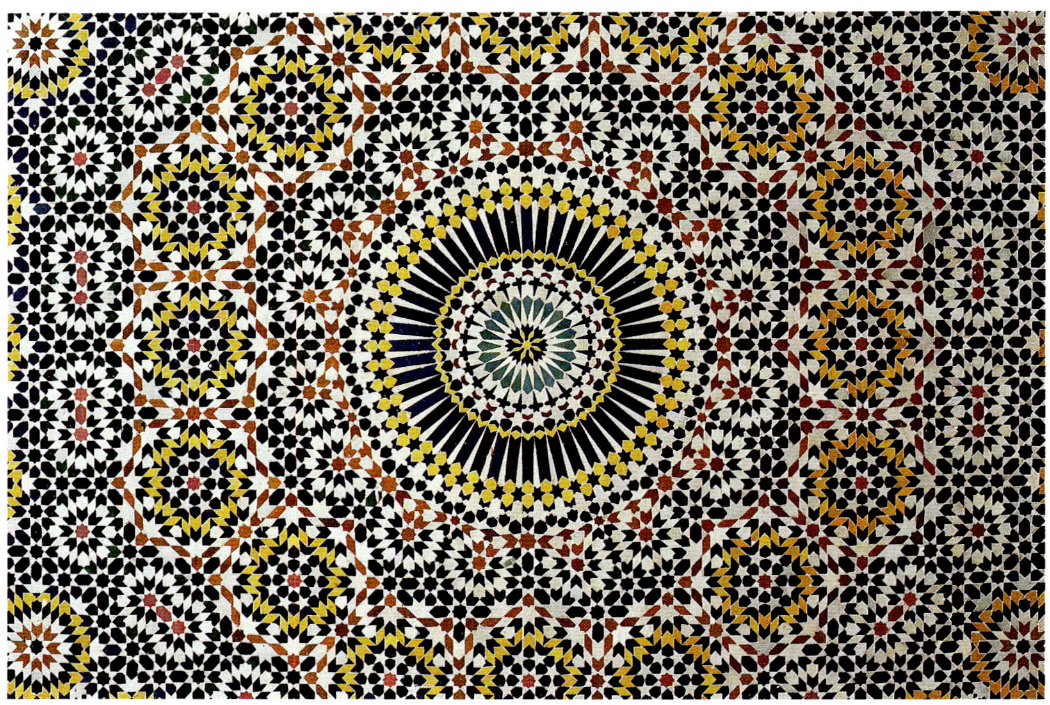

GLAOUI KASBAH, TELOUET (MOROCCO), NINETEENTH CENTURY

♦ *Zellij* panel with radiating eight-pointed star pattern.

♦ *Zellij* with a sixteen-pointed star motif.

♦ Radiating twenty-four diamond motif generating a forty-eight-point pattern.

later occupations, a number of `Alawi palaces have survived, such as Dar al-Bayda and Dar al-Makhzan in Marrakech. These are characterized by their residential feel and their luxuriously appointed internal courtyards-cum-pleasure gardens (*riyad*). Basins, parterres, and fruit tree plantations are connected by paths enhanced by bright notes of colorful *zellij* tilework. Built during the nineteenth century for a vizier of the sultan, the Palace of the Bahia is an immense residence lying close to the royal palaces. Local history recounts how it took so long to build that the expression "Bahia is finally finished" became proverbial to designate the end of any protracted endeavor. The rooms and corridors follow on through each succeeding courtyard and patio, giving a certain impression of aimlessness, although the

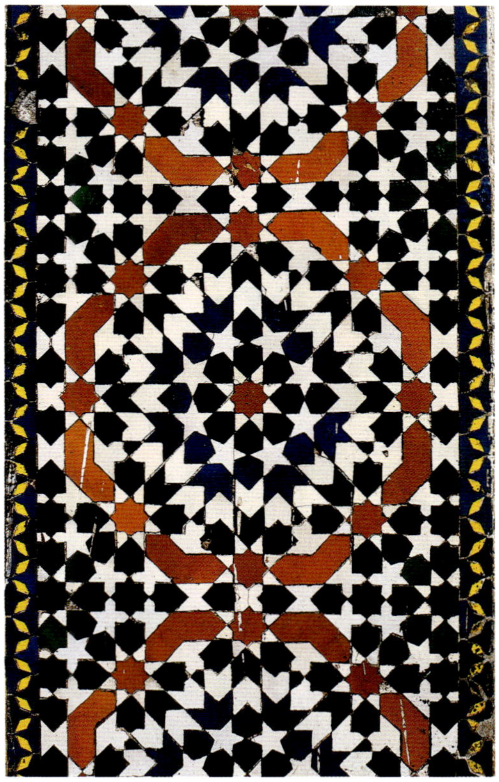

♦ Zaytuna Mosque, Meknes (Morocco). *Zellij* in an eight-pointed pattern set within an octagon.

"apartments of the favorite" are surely one of the supreme decorative achievements of the whole palace.

An attractive example of a *zellij*-ornamented palace is the Glaoui Kasbah at Telouet in the High Atlas. Built in the nineteenth century, this fortress-cum-palace delights with its wealth of decoration all very much in the tradition of Marinid masterpieces of the type.

The creation of the Cordoban emirate in 756 confirmed the split between the Islamic East and West. In the wake of the Berber invasions, over time this schism grew deeper still. Western Muslim architecture thus evolved independently, developing forms and decorative schemes quite distinct from those found in the remainder of Islamic territory. Vaults, *iwans*, and domes, for instance, are almost absent from western Muslim architecture. This difference in conception transpires in other artistic fields, such as the figurative arts—almost completely absent from the Maghreb except for Spain—and calligraphy.

Following the opulence of the caliphate period—perpetuated on a more modest scale in the time of the party kings—Muslim architecture in the West was revived by forms taken from the decorative tradition of the Berber kingdoms. The Marinid and Nasrid dynasties imparted new refinement to ornamentation, which durably influenced the arts of Christian Spain (Mudéjar art) and of Morocco, from the rule of the sharifs down to the present day. Marinid *medersas*, like other ancient monuments such as the Great Mosque at Tinmal, have benefited from restorations executed in accordance with traditional techniques. In connection with these sometimes very recent restorations, Golvin notes: "These joyless observations, however, do nothing to detract from the astonishment we feel at the quality of today's Moroccan craftsmen, heirs to a centuries-old tradition. One has but to see *zellij* makers at work, and more especially the master craftsman who lays out the decoration, to be convinced of the enduring and amazing quality of their handiwork."[25]

Apart from the restoration work to which we have already referred, Moroccan craftsmen continue to distinguish themselves today in contemporary architectural creation, such as the Hassan II Mosque at Casablanca. Built between 1986 and 1993 by Michel Pinseau, the mosque combines traditional forms—as in the 200-meter-high minaret—with ultramodern innovations, like the sliding roof over the oratory. A taste for the traditional arts of Morocco is clearly evident in the timber, stucco, and *zellij* decoration. In Morocco today, the craft of *zellij* is promoted by a host of institutions, such as the national school of arts and crafts at Tetuan set up in 1928. From an invaluable book on the subject published in French in 1992, one can appreciate the endurance of these remarkable techniques, as well as their vivid vocabulary, in particular as regards the names of the various decorative motifs: stars (*khatim*) with a variable number of points (*mkhamsa*: 5; *msadsa*: 6; *tnashri*: 12); *muthamman*, the octagon; and *sharrafa*, the serrated edge.[26]

Modern Tunisia and Algeria

FACING PAGE

♦ Large ceramic panel in the Qallaline style, although the Arabic inscription in the white space at the bottom of the tilework indicates that it was made at Mabeul. Quyi Mosque, Tripoli (Libya).

Ceramic manufacture in Tunisia during "medieval" times is still very little known. Indeed, between the prestigious achievements of first the Aghlabids and then the Fatimids, and the period of Ottoman dominion, originality does not seem to have been the overriding factor in Tunisian ceramic production under the Hafsids. Several monuments of the time are known, notably *madrasas* dating from the fourteenth and fifteenth centuries. All are characterized by a remarkably spare architecture virtually devoid of decoration.

Abu Dham'a al-Balawi, nicknamed Sidi Sahib, was a companion of the Prophet who died in 654 at the time of a military expedition to Ifriqiya. His body was buried at a site that was, a few decades later, to become the town of Qairouan. According to legend, Abu Dham'a would carry about his person some hair that once belonged to the Prophet—hence the European moniker for his funerary mosque, the Mosque of the Barber. In the fifteenth century, the mausoleum consisted of a simple dome. In 1665, during the era of the beys, the monument was rebuilt by Hammuda Pasha, acquiring further additions during the time of Muhammad ibn Murad, between 1685 and 1690.

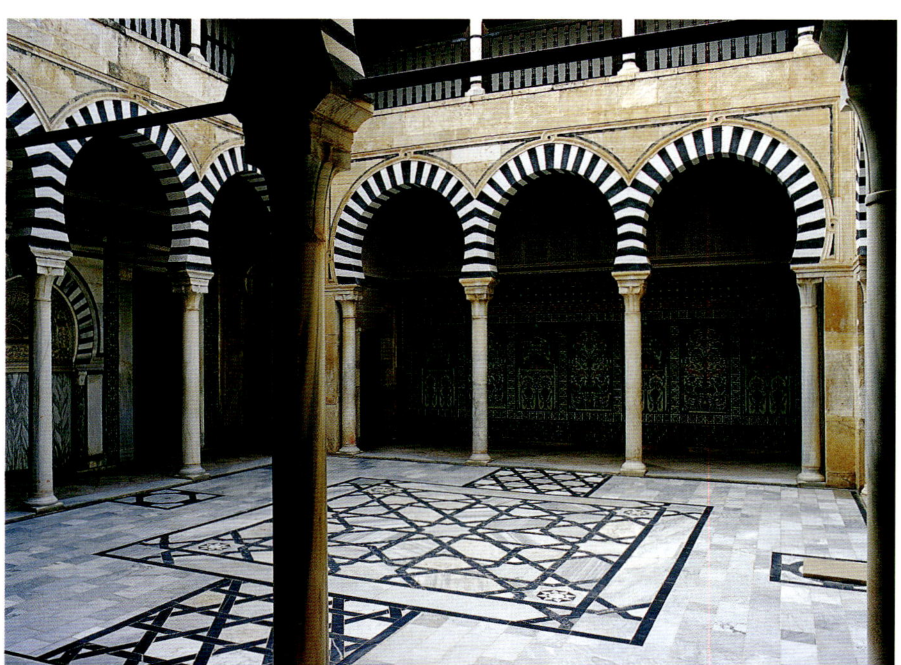

♦ *Zawiya* of Sidi Abid al-Ghariani, Qairouan (Tunisia), founded in the fourteenth century. The dados are lined in Qallaline ceramics.

The most eye-catching elements here are the panels decorating the court and its portico. These panels, combining influences from Ottoman Iznik and motifs derived from the Catalano–Valencian vocabulary, demonstrate the synthesis achieved in the Tunisian workshops between the requirements of the court of the bey, with Ottoman overtones, and the probable arrival, during the sixteenth and seventeenth centuries, of Moriscos from the Spanish Levant. It was primarily Qallaline, a suburb of Tunis which was already active prior to the Ottoman conquest, that gave its name to this type of polychrome tilework, probably as early as the sixteenth century, although it clearly intensified in the following centuries before gradually declining in the nineteenth. Here, as with ceramics from Morocco and Spain, clay paste predominates, the production being primarily earthenware. Moreover, it is interesting to note that certain French regions such as Provence—a thriving market for tiles from Catalonia and

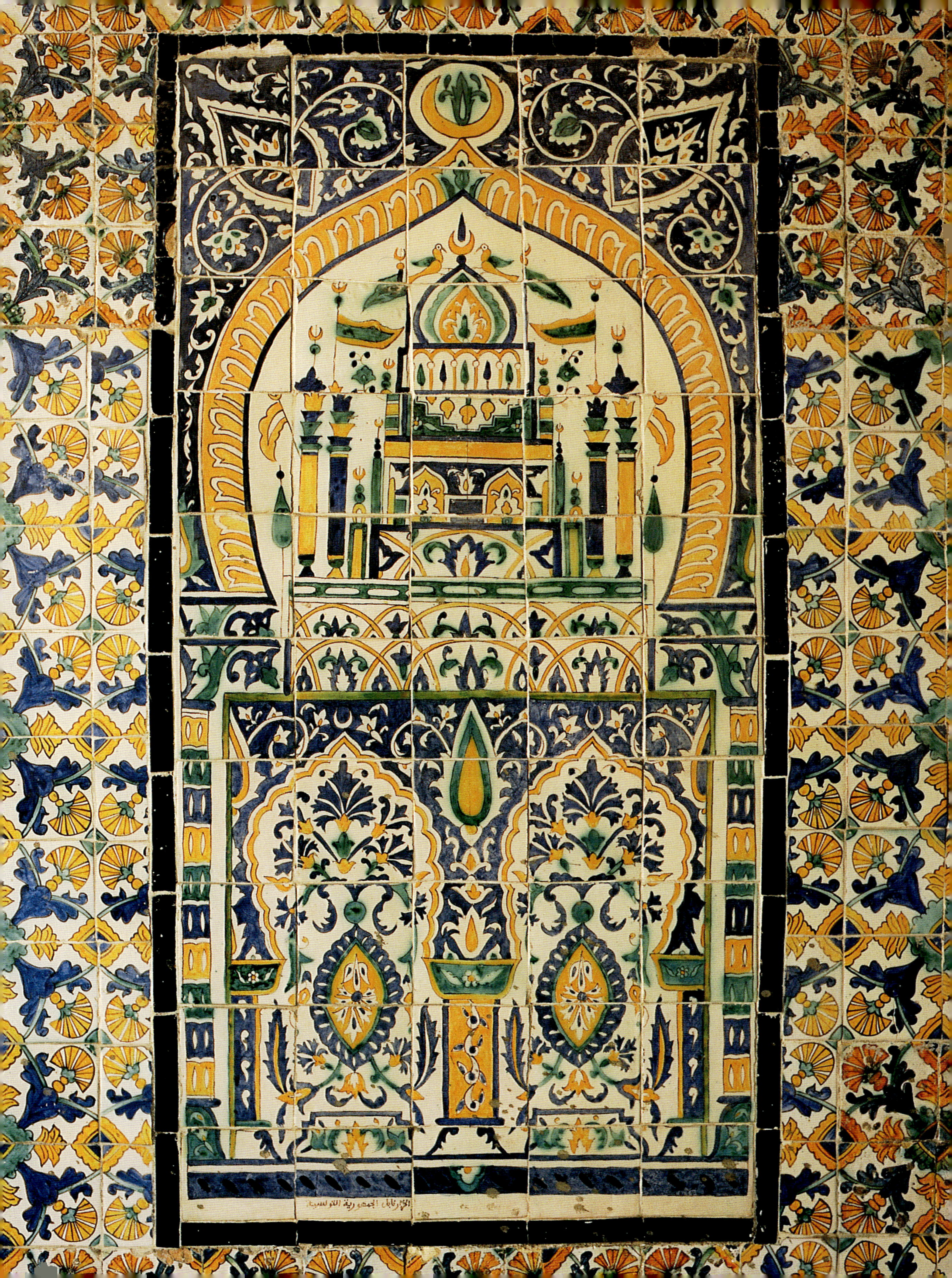
الجمهورية التونسية

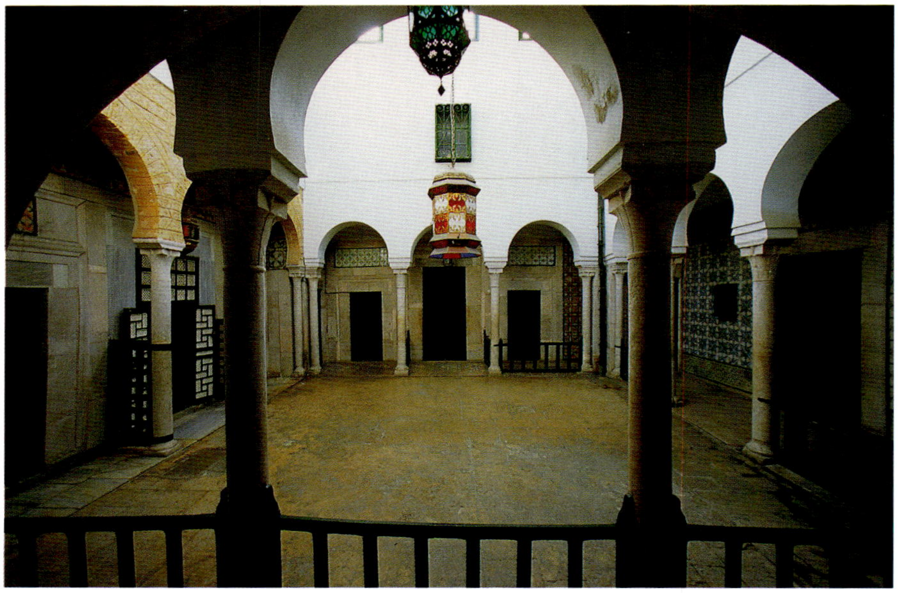

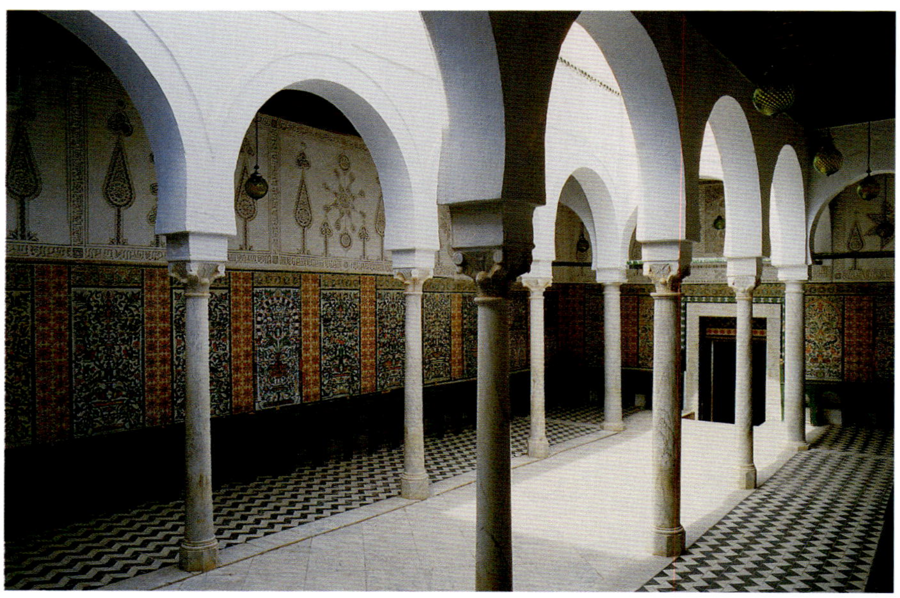

♦ *Zawiya* of Sidi ben Amor, Qairouan (Tunisia). The walls and overdoors are decorated in tilework made for the most part in Qallaline.

♦ *Zawiya* of Sidi Sahab, Qairouan (Tunisia). Dados ornamented with ceramic panels from Qallaline.

FACING PAGE

♦ Courtyard, Dar Jalluli, Sfax (Tunisia), seventeenth century. The walls are decorated with tiles from Qallaline.

♦ Dar Othman, Tunis (Tunisia), nineteenth century. Garden front with panels of ceramics from Qallaline to either side of the door.

Valencia—also obtained ceramics from workshops in Tunisia, where Spanish products were much aped.[27] It is recorded, for example, that a cardinal–archbishop of Aix, a monseigneur de Grimaldi, ordered "6,000 *malons* of three colors from Barbary." It is probable that these tiles came from Tunisia, because at that time Algeria had no workshops making earthenware.[28] For this reason, Tunisian ceramics from Qallaline were widely distributed throughout Algeria and Libya. The Quyi Mosque at Tripoli has panels with architectural decoration framed by scrolling foliage that are practically identical to those found in Tunis and Qairouan.

The *zawiya* of Sidi Abid al-Ghariani was built in the fourteenth century by a Qairouani scholar known by the name of al-Jadidi, who died in 1384. His disciple, Abu Samir Abid, originally from Jebel Gharian in Libya, succeeded him as a teacher in the *zawiya*. Abu Samir Abid in turn died in 1402 and was buried in the monument that has since borne his name. Since its foundation, the *zawiya* has undergone extensive restoration and today houses an association for the protection of the *medina* at Qairouan. The court is encircled by porticos whose walls are covered with tiles added during restoration work.

Other, later religious buildings, such as the *zawiya* of Sidi Amor Abada (or "mosque of the sabers") built in the mid-nineteenth century, also possess particularly fine ceramic panels.

Princely residences, like the Palace of the Bardo at Tunis (or that of the same name in Algiers), built during the second half of the eighteenth century, are also well appointed with tile revetments. The Dar Jalluli Palace in Sfax (seventeenth century) and the Dar Othman in Tunis present some masterly examples of decoration, in particular the courtyard dados lined with tilework. A splendid seventeenth-century dwelling, the Dar Jalluli (today transformed into a museum of popular arts and traditions) is characterized by a wealth of decoration that alternates earthenware tiles with openwork stucco and painted wood. The Bardo at Tunis, which has been restored on many occasions right up to the contemporary period, drew inspiration largely from Ottoman models; it too has since been converted into a museum. This "Ottomanizing" taste also predominates in the construction and decoration of the mausoleum built for President Bourguiba, who died in 1987.

Certain residential buildings in Tunisia testify to a taste for eclectic ceramic decors, ranging from Delft faïence tiles or Barcelona ware to Qallaline panels. There are also surprising figurative compositions of a Safavid style probably dating from the nineteenth

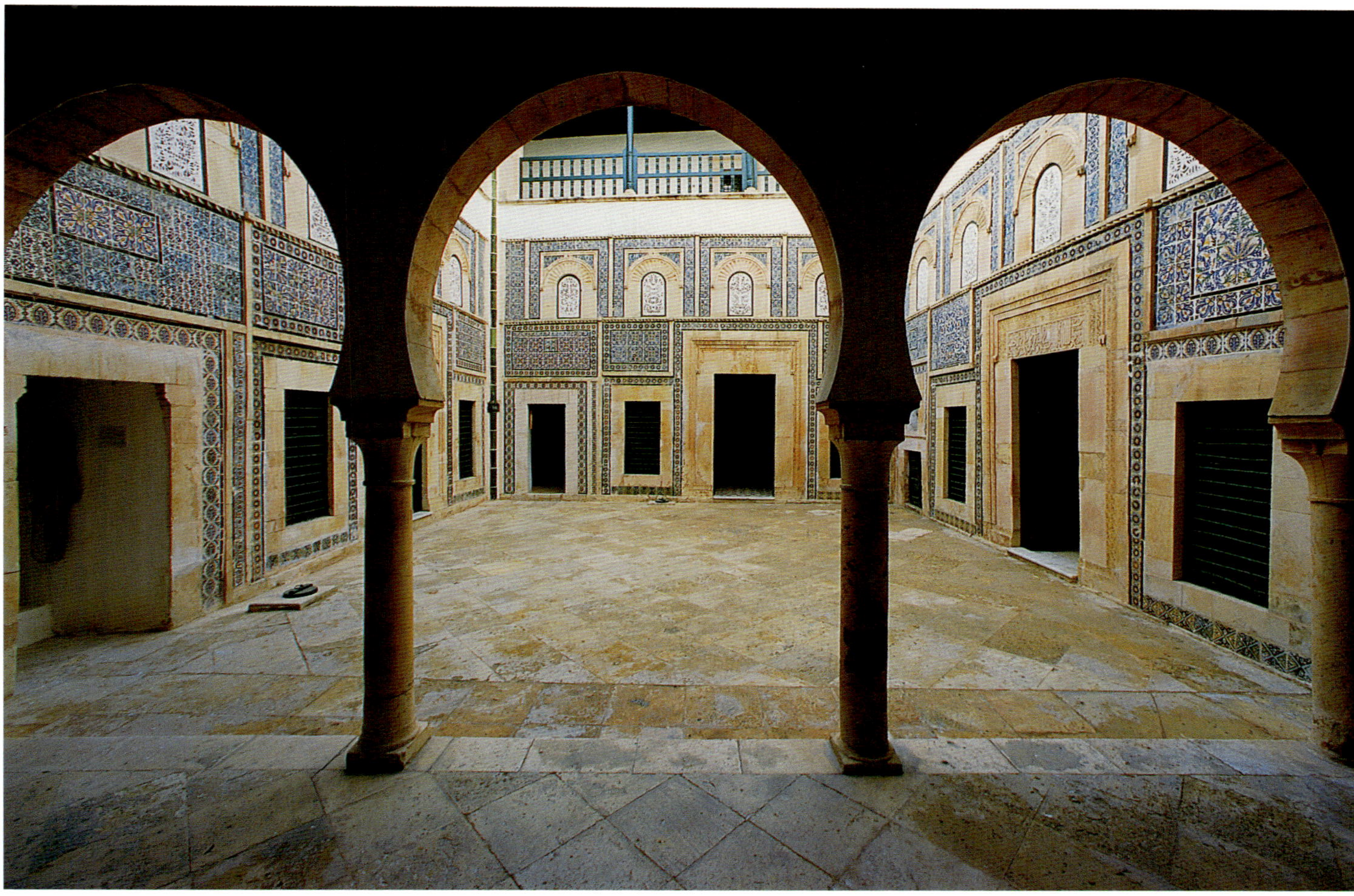

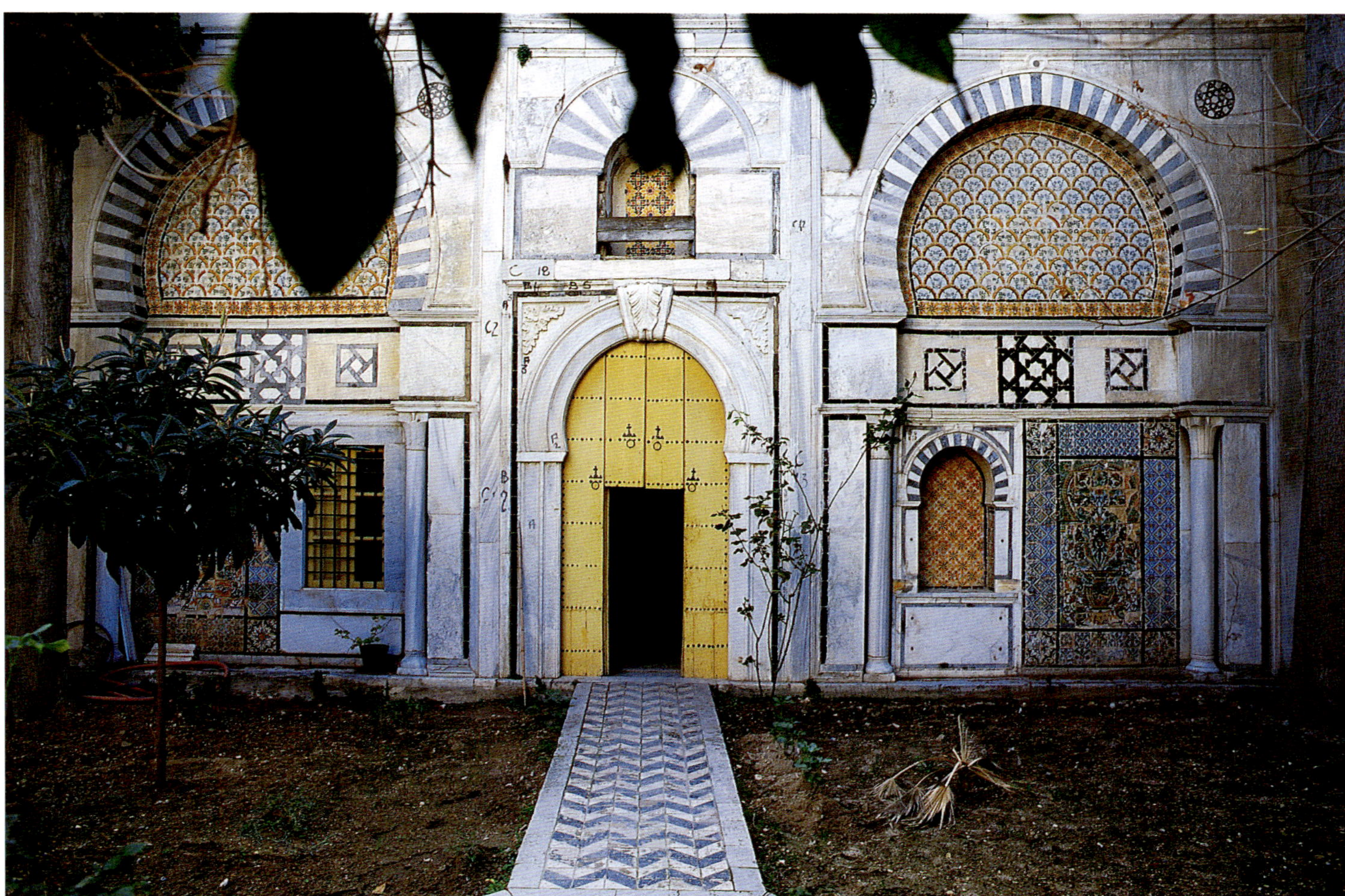

century, such as at the Palais d'Orient in Tunis. These heterogeneous assemblages demonstrate the crucial role played by Maghreb ports in the interchange between East and West, in particular as regards ceramics. It is intriguing to note in this connection that several Persian tiles dating from the Qajar period ended up at Rochefort in the house of a celebrated Orientalist and traveler, the writer Pierre Loti, who may have bought them in Algeria. This diversity of sources was already pointed out by the French Orientalist Venture de Paradis around 1789. He noted: "The great have constructed splendid gardens and superb residences for their harems. These gardens and houses are covered with marble that has been brought in from Genoa and Livorno. Like the floors, the walls are lined with beautiful enameled and painted earthenware tiles of various colors. These tiles come from Tunis and Spain and are named *zelis*. It is one of the industries that has made Tunis prosperous. This manner of lining apartments in a hot climate is most agreeable and cool."[29]

In the 1930s, A. Broussaud noted: "Currently, *faience* is no longer produced in the potters' souk at Tunis. At the Bardo, the Chelma brothers successfully copied old models using historical methods, somewhat improved. They export large quantities of tiles to California. Potters are also trying to revive ancient techniques in Nabeul: some import their paints readymade from France, while others make them on site."[30]

The production of ceramic tiles in Algeria is undoubtedly relatively recent and remains poorly known. Moreover, Broussaud introduces his work on North African earthenware tiles by stating that, "like a happy people, the painted tiles of North Africa have no history."[31] As we have already mentioned, no local workshops dating from before the mid-nineteenth century are known to us, so most Algerian ceramic decoration must have been imported. In fact, it would seem that the European nations paid an annual tribute to the Barbary Coast as an insurance against acts of piracy and it is not impossible that a proportion of these donations might have been paid in the form of ceramic tiles. Thus, the tiles adorning the interior of the patio in the house in which Cervantes is supposed to have been imprisoned in the Hamma at Algiers are stamped on the reverse with the Moustiers mark of the Martres-Tolosane factory.[32] Broussaud also notes the presence of a Marseille tile in the funerary chapel of Sidi Bu Medina in Tlemcen.[33] European travelers often remarked on the abundant ceramic revetments in the area. In 1612, Diego de Haedo published a magnificent description of Algiers, noting: "These halls and courts generally most tastefully built out of brick present for the most part walls embellished with earthenware tiles in various colors; the same applies to the corridors and balustrades within the courtyards that almost resemble monastery cloisters; these buildings, whose upkeep is maintained with the greatest care, are rubbed and washed down every week."[34]

Broussaud mentions a certain number of monuments in Algiers decorated with ceramic tiles, among which the mosque of Sidi Abderrahman (completed in 1700), which incorporates Italian or Spanish glazed earthenware as well as Ottoman pieces dispatched by the sultan from Constantinople.[35] In a similar connection, Broussaud also notes that at Constantine Bey Ahmed decided to build an imposing palace that he wanted to decorate with tin-glazed tiling. "An Italian named Schiaffino procured a great quantity from Livorno and Genoa in exchange for payment in wheat. Another large order was sent to Tunisia and, as if that were not sufficient, the bey had no compunction in purloining the finest tiles he had spotted adorning the houses of some of his wealthier burghers."[36] In the same way, the dado of the *mihrab* wall in the mosque at Constantine—founded in 1726 and which thereafter became a

♦ Large ceramic panel from Qallaline with architectural motifs incorporating birds and plants. Palais d'Orient, Tunis (Tunisia).

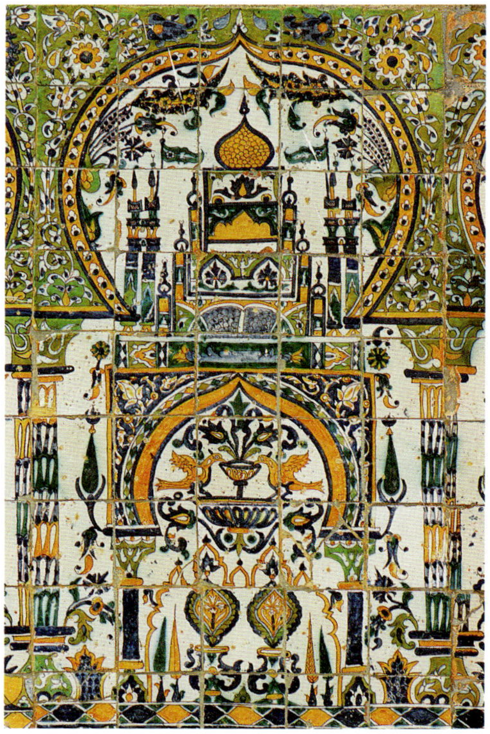

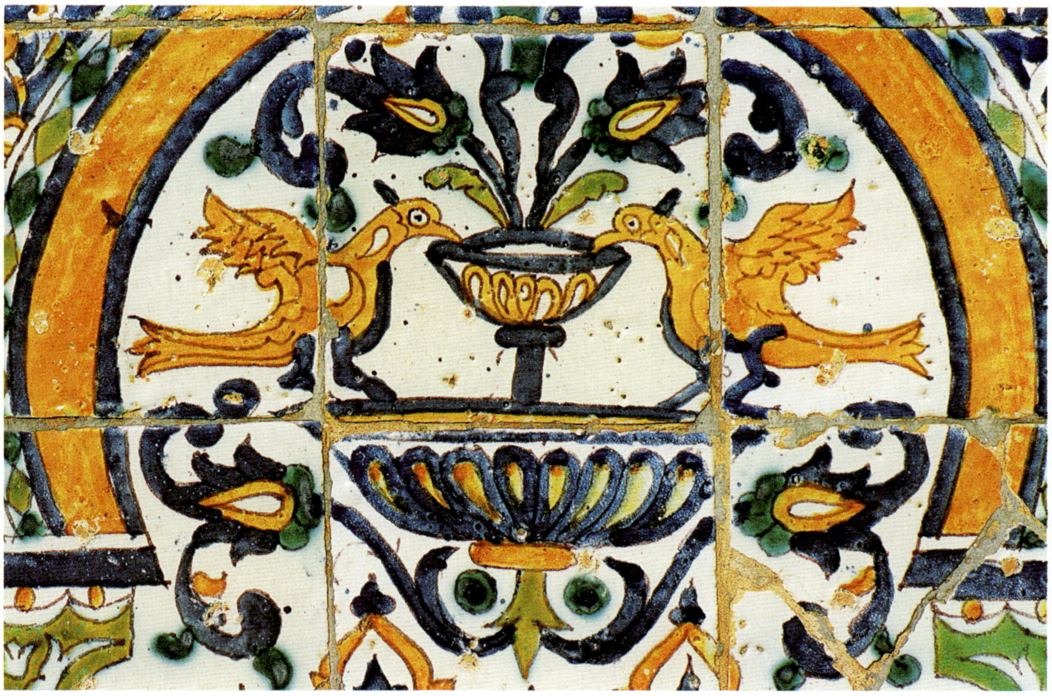

♦ Detail of a ceramic panel from Qallaline depicting two birds drinking at a fountain. Palais d'Orient, Tunis (Tunisia).

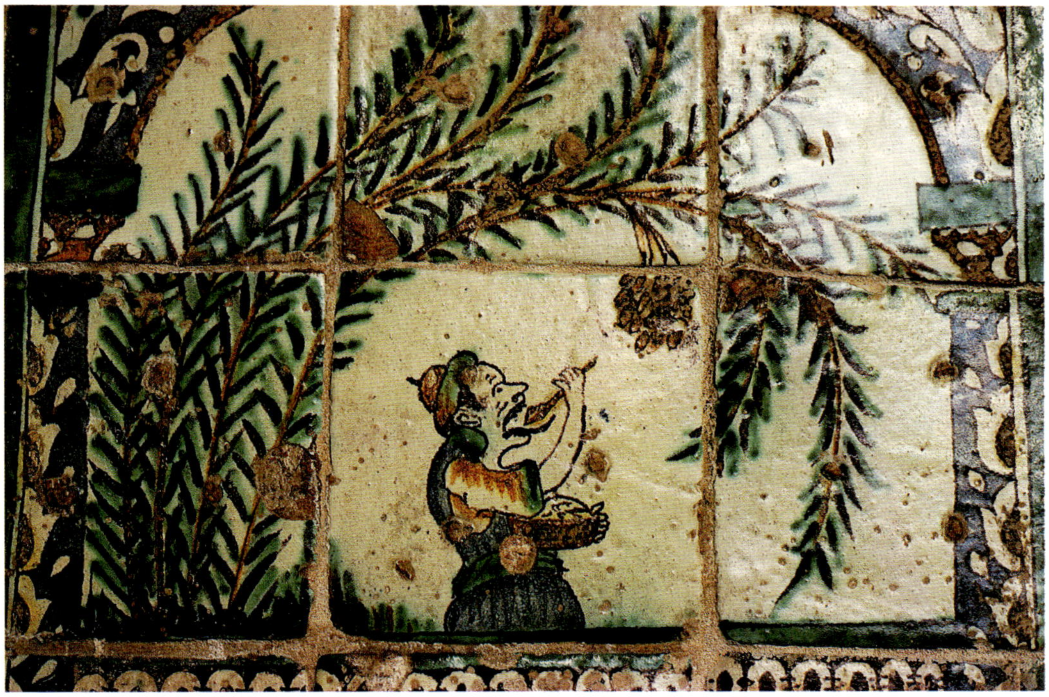

♦ Detail of a panel of earthenware tiles at Qairouan (Tunisia). The caricature at the center is reminiscent of Spanish, possibly Catalan, pieces.

cathedral—is clad with tiles Broussaud describes as "Persian–Tunisian faience."[37]

Some later Algerian buildings deserve a mention, notably the mosque of the Zawiya in El-Hamel to the southwest of Bou-Saada, regarded as one of the most important monuments of nineteenth-century Algerian architecture. Its interior decoration presents a series of ceramic tiles executed by the famous Algerian miniaturist Mohammad Racim (1896–1975). The earthenware tiles are distributed around the drum of the central cupola and on the friezes framing the apertures and windows, as well as on the spandrels. The most exquisite panel is the one in the *mihrab* conch, which bears a commemorative Arabic inscription in Thuluth script on a cobalt ground.[38] Finally, the best-known contemporary Algerian ceramist is undoubtedly Boumehdi, responsible for all the ceramic panels of the Hotel Saint Georges, Algiers, among other projects.

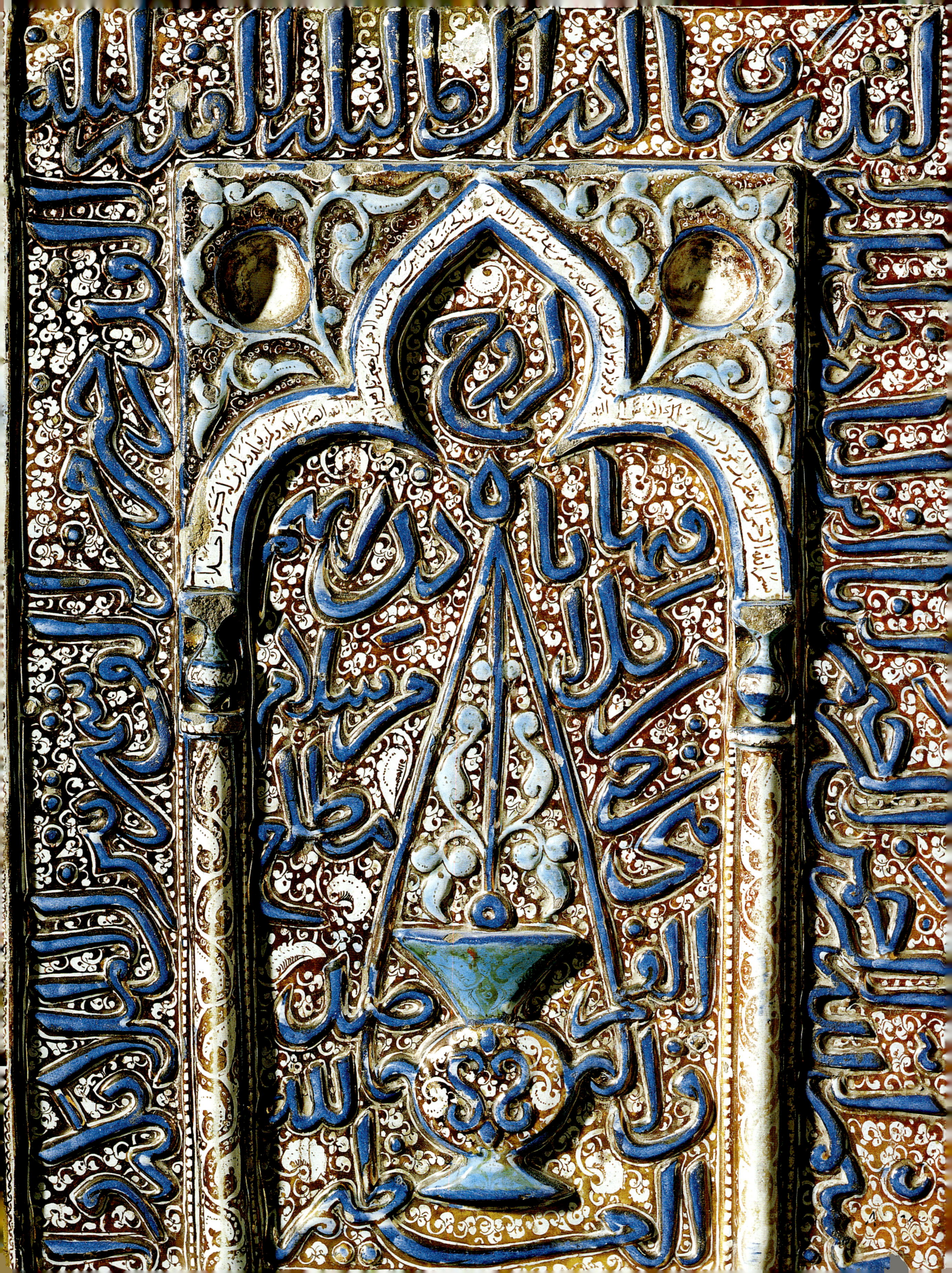

III

Iran and Central Asia, Fourteenth to Nineteenth Century

PAGE 90

♦ Stone-paste ceramic panel in the shape of a *mihrab*. The molded decoration is coated in opaficied glaze with cobalt and turquoise highlights and metallic luster. Kashan (Iran), thirteenth century. 62.5 × 47 cm. Musée du Louvre, Paris.

FACING PAGE

♦ Stone-paste cross and star luster tiles with cobalt and turquoise highlights, originally from the *imamzade* Ja`far at Damghan (Iran), 1267. 78.5 × 49.5 cm. Musée du Louvre, Paris.

Of Cobalt and Gold: Iran under Mongolian Dominion

In the thirteenth century, the East was to experience the dramatic arrival of the Mongols and their steady destructive progress. However, after years of conquest culminating in the capture of Baghdad in 1258, there followed a lull in the strife that historians have termed the Pax Mongolica. By the end of the thirteenth century, and increasingly during the following one, Persian architecture adopted new types of decoration in which ceramics played an increasingly preeminent role. The destruction and massacres often ascribed to Mongol incursions should today be seen in a subtler light. Indeed, to judge by dated ceramic pieces (in particular those decorated in luster), the expected hiatus in production scarcely materialized. The star and cross luster group that at one time decorated the Yahya *imamzade* at Varamin, for instance, is dated 1262 (British Museum). Another panel, with cobalt blue touches in places on the luster decoration, comes from the *imamzade* Ja`far at Damghan and dates to 1267 (Louvre). The production of architectural decoration employing luster tiles intensified at the end of the century with the manufacture of large tiles with relief decoration, such as the sequence of epigraphic friezes in trefoil arches with verses from Firdusi's *Book of Kings*.[39] At least one of these friezes was made in around 1270 to decorate the palace of Abaqa at Takht-i Sulayman. More ambitious, the *mihrabs* (often dated and signed) were built from sizable relief tiles that form spectacular arrays of imposing dimensions. The line of Abu Tahir—the family of potters to which Abu`l-Qasim of Kashan (the author of a celebrated treatise on ceramics) belonged—made its name with masterly works of this type produced almost seamlessly between 1205 (still under the domination of the Khwarazm Shahs) and 1333, by which time the Ilkhanid dynasty was on the wane.

In parallel with the development of luster techniques from the twelfth century onward, other processes, such as *petit feu* decoration, were also being experimented with. The polychromy of this type of decoration, popularly known as *mina`i*, was obtained by the addition of red and white slip in conjunction with gold leaf, which accounts for its ancient name, *haft-rang*, or "seven colors." Although this technique was used more for wares than architectural ornamentation, examples of stars from the twelfth century do exist. In the Ilkhanid period, a technique close to that of *haft-rang* but with a less extensive range of colors was also deployed. This technique is known by the name of *lajvardina*, deriving from *lajvard*, a term denoting the lapis lazuli color (obtained from cobalt oxide) that usually distinguishes this type of production. Examples can be found in the palace of Abaqa at Takht-i Sulayman and at many other sites, be they princely residences or religious buildings. These low-fired tiles were often used in conjunction with other forms of ceramics in alternating designs, for example with a monochrome glaze or luster-painted.

As has been pointed out above, the *lajvardina* and *mina`i* techniques are similar, the two terms applying to different periods and types of decoration. The vogue for

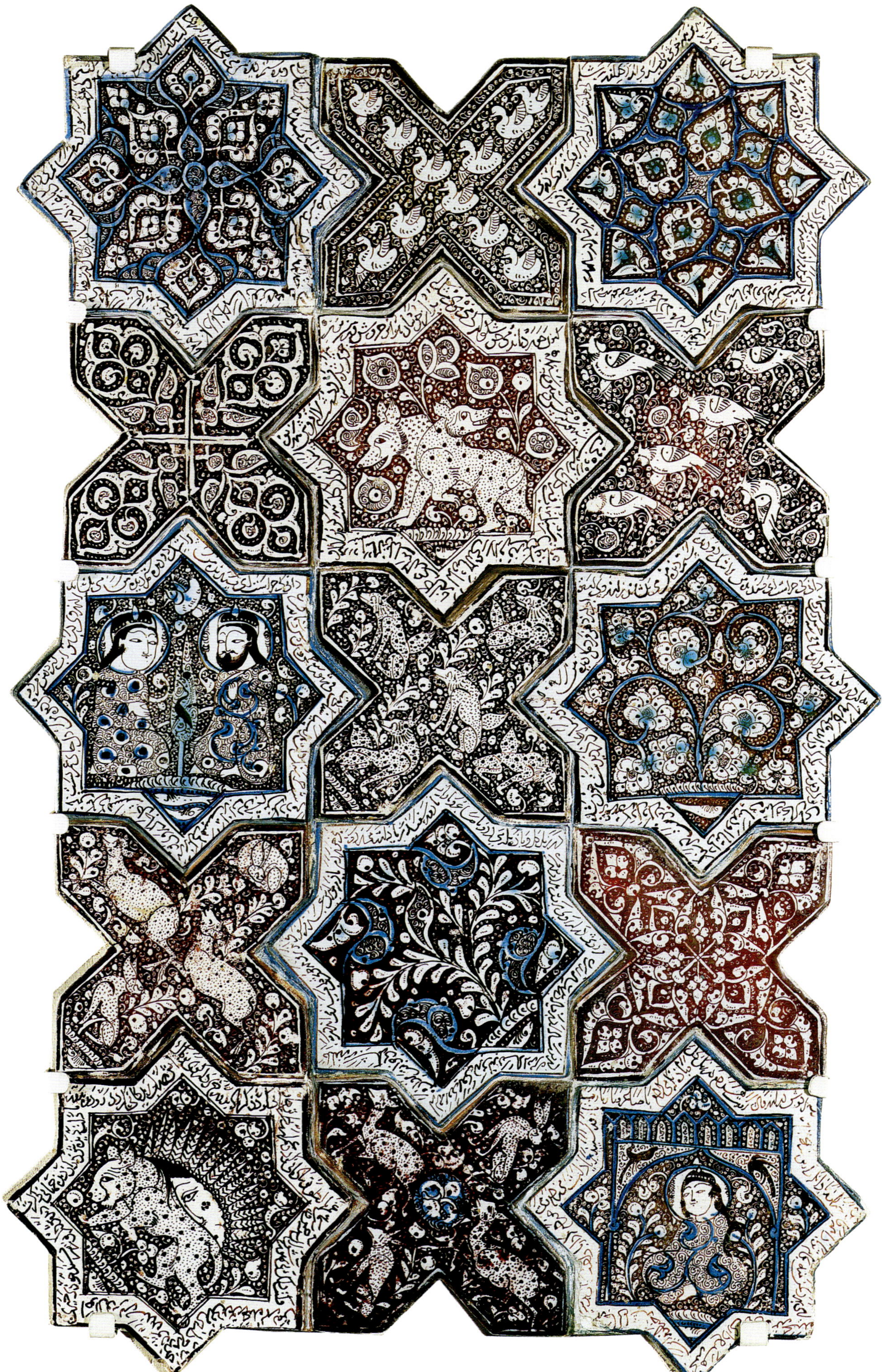

lajvardina seems to have emerged during the last decades of the thirteenth century in the production of both wares and tiles, and its popularity lasted for nearly a whole century, the last pieces of this type dating from 1374.[40] The *lajvardina* technique lingered longer in architectural decoration in central Asia, one of the finest demonstrations being the cenotaph of Qutham ibn `Abbas in Samarkand, which probably dates from the first half of the fourteenth century (see below).

Broadly speaking, architecture in the Mongolian period in Persia (referred to as the Ilkhanid dynasty) continued along similar lines to that of the Seljuq era. The major innovation in architecture was an emphasis on verticality, a tendency reminiscent of European Gothic. This striving toward the vertical was furthered by a reduction in the number of load-bearing points and matched by a corresponding increase in the number of apertures. In general, the chambers tend to be high rather than wide; the *iwans*, narrower and taller, are flanked by minarets and are provided with apertures. The corner colonnettes grow slenderer and are now grouped in greater numbers. Structural force is thus more concentrated, while domes become more elongated. Ceramic tiles appear increasingly in the decor, serving in particular to stress this new-found verticality (on corner colonnettes, for instance). The panels in both exterior and interior walls are recessed, making the walls thinner and forcing the corner piers to bear the weight.

The funerary complex at Natanz was the brainchild of the vizier Zayn al-Din Mastari, who enlarged the burial chamber of Shaykh `Abd al-Samad (died 1299), endowing it with a large mosque, minaret, and hospice, of which solely the superb, intricately decorated gateway with its display of turquoise ceramic alternating with terracotta (1307–8) still stands. Here, rectangular turquoise and cobalt baguettes are arranged into epigraphic panels in an interlocking, labyrinthine Kufic, while a broad band of Thuluth calligraphy stands out in reserve against a turquoise and cobalt checkerboard-patterned ground.

The mausoleum cupola—one of the most elegant examples of this type of work in the Ilkhanid period—is completely carpeted in *muqarnas*. The interior of the

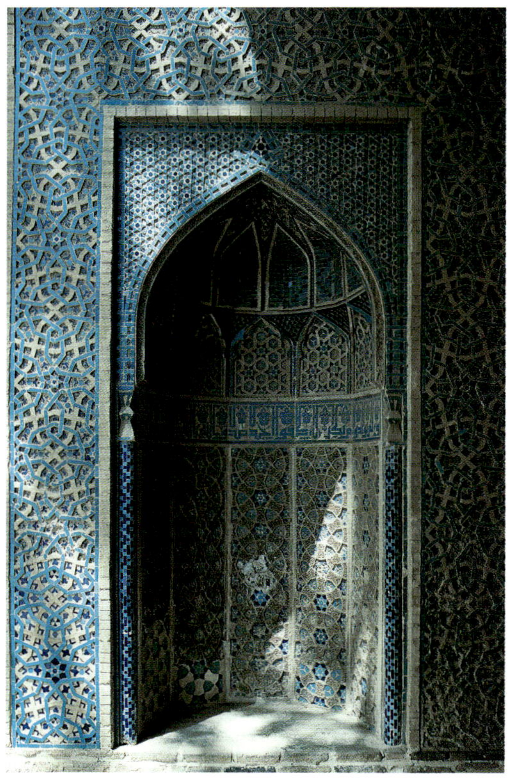

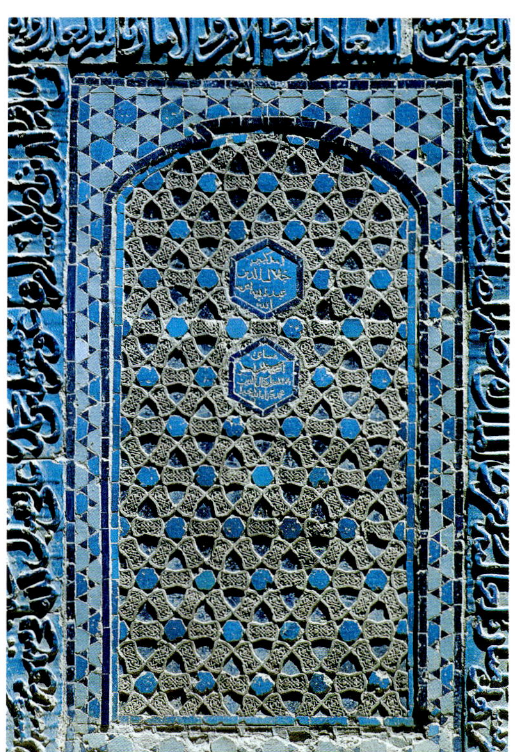

FUNERARY COMPLEX OF SHAYKH `ABD AL-SAMAD, NATANZ (IRAN)

♦ Niche in the facade of the *khanaqah* (1307–8). Untreated terracotta areas alternate with predominantly turquoise cut tilework. At the base of the conch runs an inscription band in plaited Kufic.

♦ Blind arch at the base of the minaret. The two hexagonal tiles are inscribed with the names of the patrons of the building (dated 1324–25): the emir Jalal al-Din `Abdallah and the chief minister Kamal al-Din Muhammad.

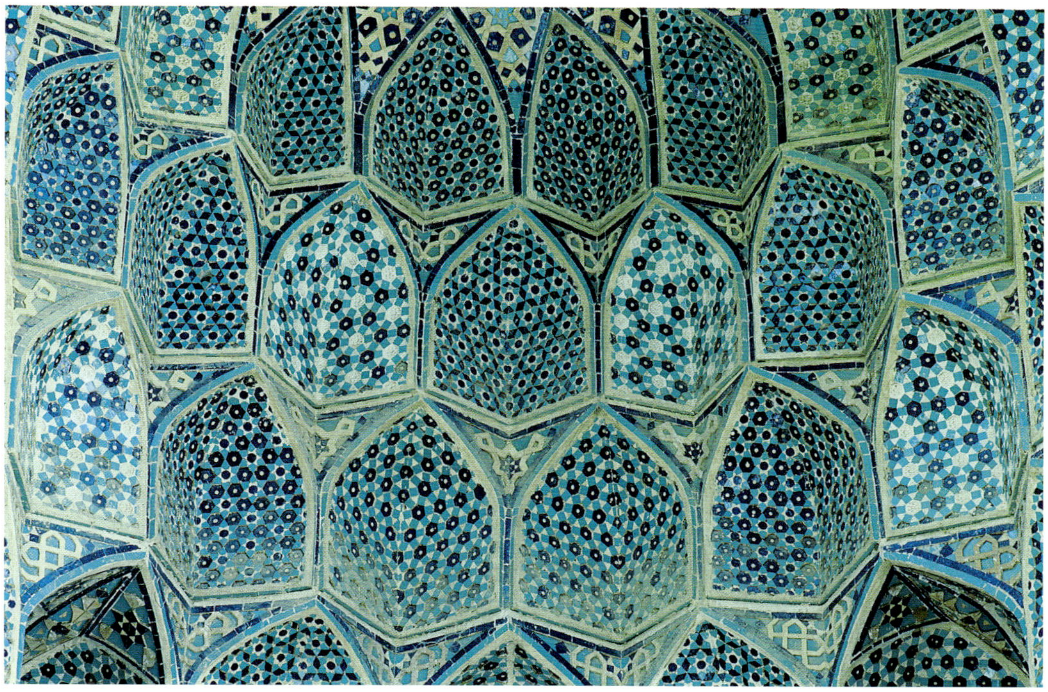

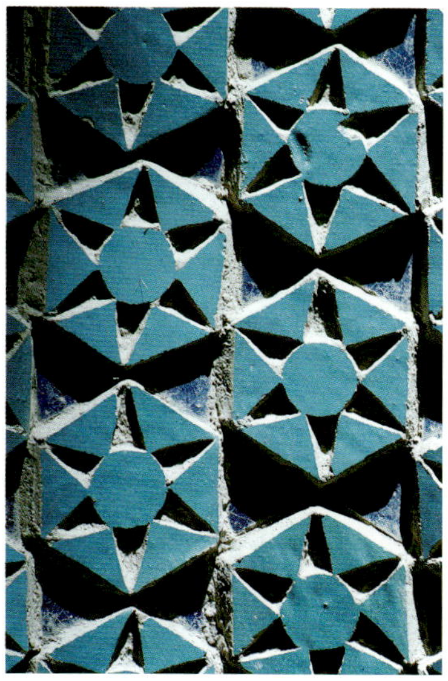

FUNERARY COMPLEX OF SHAYKH `ABD AL-SAMAD, NATANZ (IRAN)

♦ Detail of the *muqarnas* in the *khanaqah* gate (1307–8).

♦ Panel built up from turquoise triangles and circles formed into hexagons that emerge from a ground of cobalt-blue triangles.

mausoleum formerly contained significant examples of decoration in lusterwork tiles, in particular a large epigraphic frieze. Large ceramic tiles also adorned the *mihrab* and cenotaph; the signature of the calligrapher, Hasan ibn `Ali Babawayh, appears on the luster tiles, as well as on the stucco completing the fine decor. A number of tiles from the sanctuary are currently displayed in collections in several of the larger museums; the one that in all probability closed the frieze, bearing the date 1308, is now in the Metropolitan Museum of Art, New York.[41] A little-known tile that probably preceded the one in the Metropolitan is now in the collection of the Musée Granet, Aix-en-Provence.[42]

The main gate to the mausoleum of Bayezit at Bastam (1313) incorporates one of the earliest large-scale ensembles of carved elements partially covered with turquoise glaze; these are arranged in large panels decorated with a repeat or basketweave pattern in Kufic script in the name of `Ali. These panels alternate with broad bands that contrast inlaid turquoise motifs with a geometrical interlace pattern fashioned out of unglazed terracotta.

The mausoleum at Sultaniyah (1307–13) is an original building of surprisingly ample proportions. It is undoubtedly the most beautiful Ilkhanid monument to have survived to the present day, and the best illustration of the architectural innovations of the period. Commissioned by Uljaytu (1304–17), it was originally intended to house the mortal remains of the *imams* `Ali and Husayn. The sovereign had initially envisaged having the relics of the Shi`ite *imams* transported from Iraq (Najaf and Kerbela), thereby ensuring prosperity for the newly founded "imperial" city. Inevitably, the interior decoration contained many references to the Shi`ite *imams* themselves. The project came to nothing, however, and in the end the monument was converted into a tomb for its patron (who in the interim seems to have reverted to Sunnism). The opportunity was thus seized to rethink the decorative program and all references to Shi`ism were carefully expunged.

The edifice is built to a complex plan inscribed within an outer octagon. Devoid of visible buttressing, the external walls are articulated into grandly proportioned internal niches punctuated by arcades and conches. An external, octagonal-shaped vaulted gallery, each side of which is pierced by three arches, serves as a base

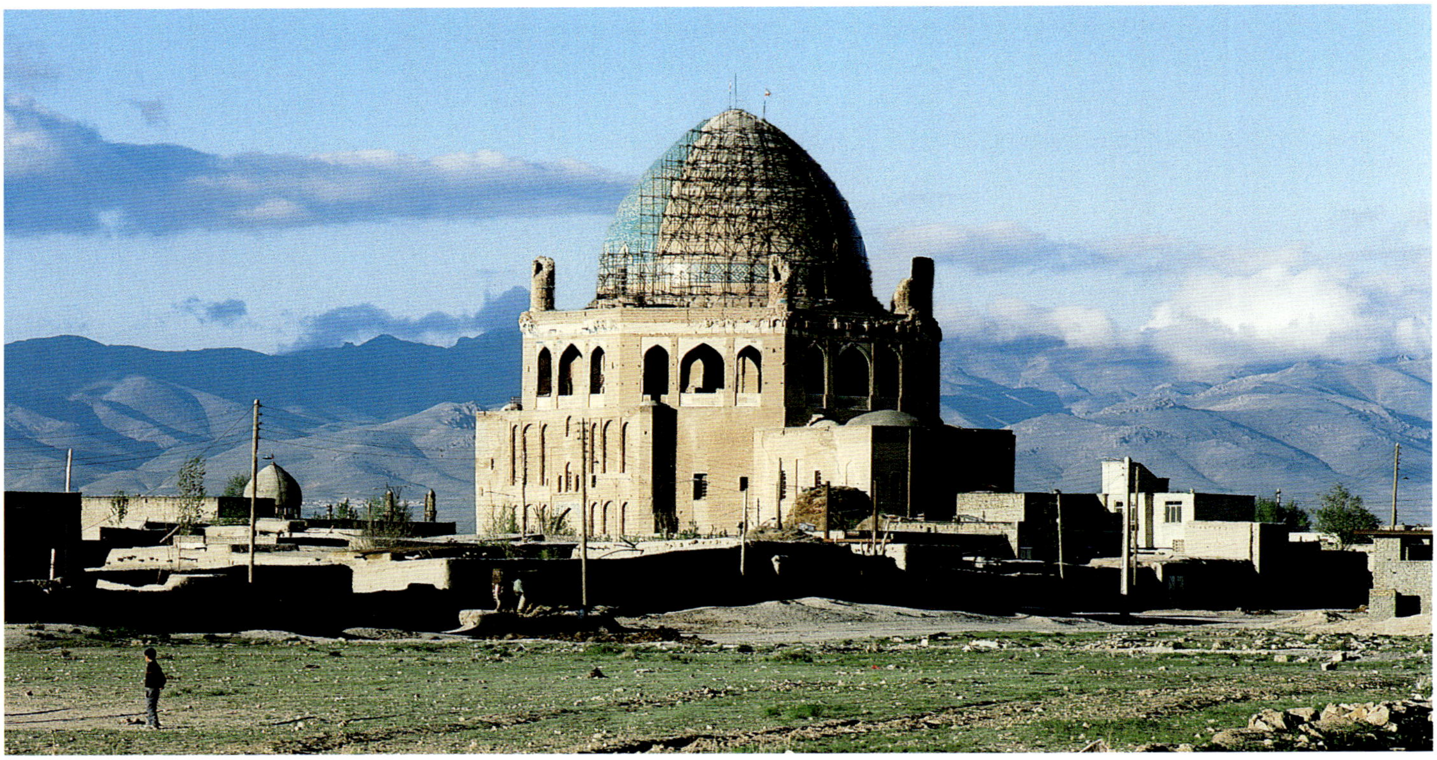

♦ Mausoleum of the Ilkhanid Uljaytu, Sultaniyah (Iran), 1307–13. With its turquoise dome towering over 25 m, the mausoleum is surely the finest monument to be built in Iran under the Mongols.

for the cupola above. The top of the gallery is ringed by minarets placed at each of the eight corners, while the ovoid dome is lined in turquoise tiling. The double-shelled dome (25.5 meters in diameter) seems to prefigure Brunelleschi's great work in Florence. Very few traces of ceramic decoration now survive inside this sumptuous monument. In places, where the second (painted) layer of decoration has fallen away, a few fragments of underglaze tiles can be discerned.[43] The most easily visible remnants (enhanced by recent restoration work) can be found in the external decor. The entire shell is wrapped in turquoise tilework; at the base, a trefoil motif appears in black. Like the string-course girdling the dome, it is embellished with an all-over *banna'i* brick motif spelling out the names of Allah and Muhammad in Kufic script. The eight minarets that stood at the corners of the octagon were also lined in ceramic; the *muqarnas* corbels, like the spandrels of the arches (in particular that of the main entrance), display an opulent decor of cut and inlaid tile mosaic that repeats, on a grander scale, earlier experiments in a similar vein produced in Natanz.

Of a later date, the mausoleum of Baba Qasim in Isfahan (1325–40) is especially notable for its eight-sided pyramidal dome decorated, like the drum supporting it, with turquoise-, cobalt-, and black-colored glazed *banna'i* brick. The main gateway (*pishtaq*), built in 1340, presents a horizontal band with a cut-tile mosaic of Thuluth calligraphy. Above this fans out a gossamer network of *muqarnas* decorated with colored inlay elements—white, turquoise, and cobalt (although novel touches of a brown tone can also be made out)—alternating with unglazed brick. Inside the funerary hall, girdling the top of the wall and just below the squinches, runs a broad Thuluth cut-tile frieze.

For the most part, mosques in the Ilkhanid era reverted to the four-*iwan* plan that had become almost universal during the Seljuq period. The mosque at Varamin (1322–26) southeast of Teheran is a fine example. The verticals of the architecture are emphasized by the use of ceramics, while panels in which turquoise tiles alternate with brickwork adorn the frontage. The Friday mosque at Yazd in central Iran (1325–34) is distinguished by an elegant

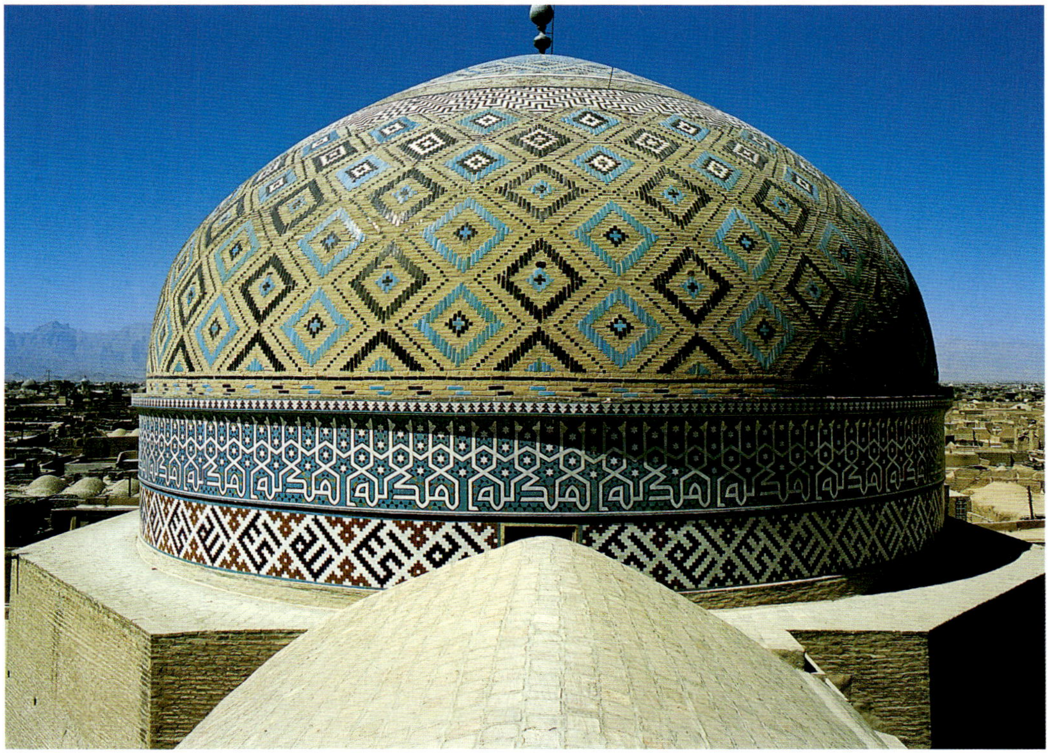

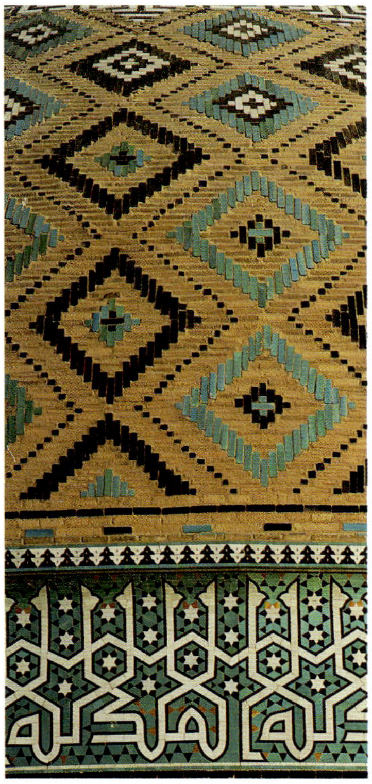

monumental gate clad in cut-tile mosaic and flanked by a pair of minarets. The gate has undergone frequent restoration over the centuries, with the result that it appears still more refined than ever. The interior of the building, in particular the cupola spanning the prayer hall, displays what is probably the most beautiful surviving ceramic decoration in all Ilkhanid Iran. Borne on squinches, the cupola incorporates a star and hexagon pattern of extraordinary quality, the work of Sa`d ibn Muhammad Kaduk al-Banna` Yazdi. Dating to 1375–76, the *mihrab* offers a splendid example of a ceramic mosaic incorporated into the decor of a niche crowned with a semi-vault ornamented with *muqarnas*. In the prayer hall, the remarkable dados are made up of hexagonal turquoise tiles with, in the center of each panel, a rosette with an interlace stellar motif or an oval composition featuring a bouquet.

The Friday mosque at Kerman was erected in 1349, by which time the Mozaffarids had supplanted the Ilkhanids as the real power in the region. The main gateway is noteworthy for its elegant shape: the form of the arch is emphasized by a twist motif clad in tiny elements decoratively arranged into crosses and hexagons. Cut-tile mosaic covers the entire visible surface, alternating with inscription bands and panels composed of geometric and vegetal motifs; brown, a color previously employed rather sporadically, is now extensively used. The *mihrab*, dating from 1375, is a masterpiece of cut-tile mosaic; the elegance of the motifs and the finesse of the design conspire with the wide chromatic range (including brown) to form a marvelously colorful composition that carpets the entire conch.

Lastly, one other remarkable building should be mentioned: the small structure presently standing in the court of the Friday mosque, sometimes called the Masjid-i `Atiq (the old mosque) at Shiraz. It is a stone-built square construction with an inscription hewn out of the stone that stands out against a turquoise cut and inlaid tilework ground (which incidentally provides a date for the building of A.H. 752/A.D. 1351). The monument was erected by a prince of the Inju dynasty (a vassal of the Il-Khani), Abu Ishaq ibn Shah Mahmud, protector of the great poet Hafiz, who was also from Shiraz.[44]

FRIDAY MOSQUE, YAZD (IRAN), 1325–34

♦ Dome of the prayer hall ornamented with colored *banna'i* bricks. The word *Allah* appears on the base of the drum in angular Kufic; above this there runs a broad band of plaited Kufic whose ascenders form stars and hexagons.

♦ Exterior of the dome of the prayer hall (detail).

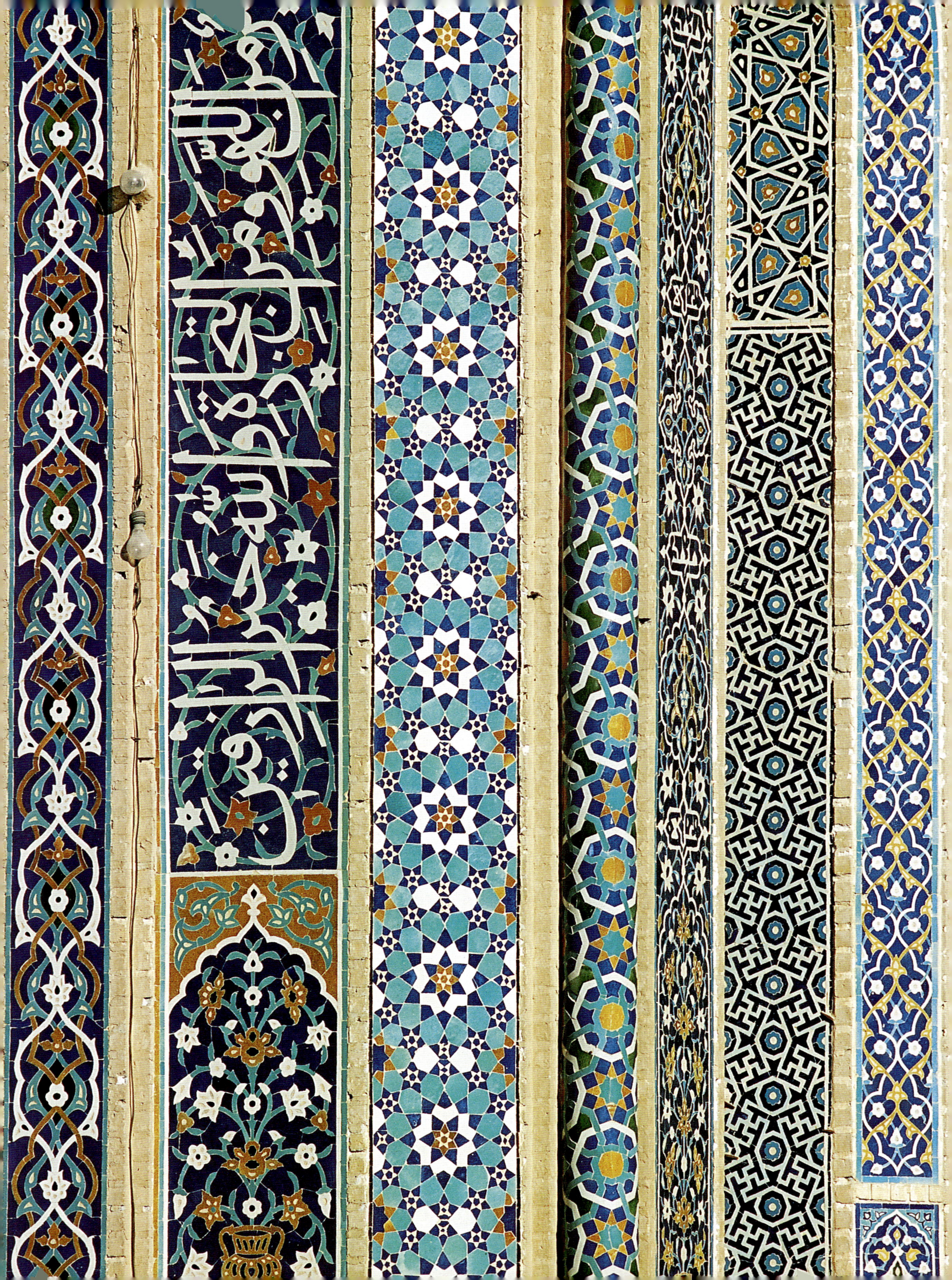

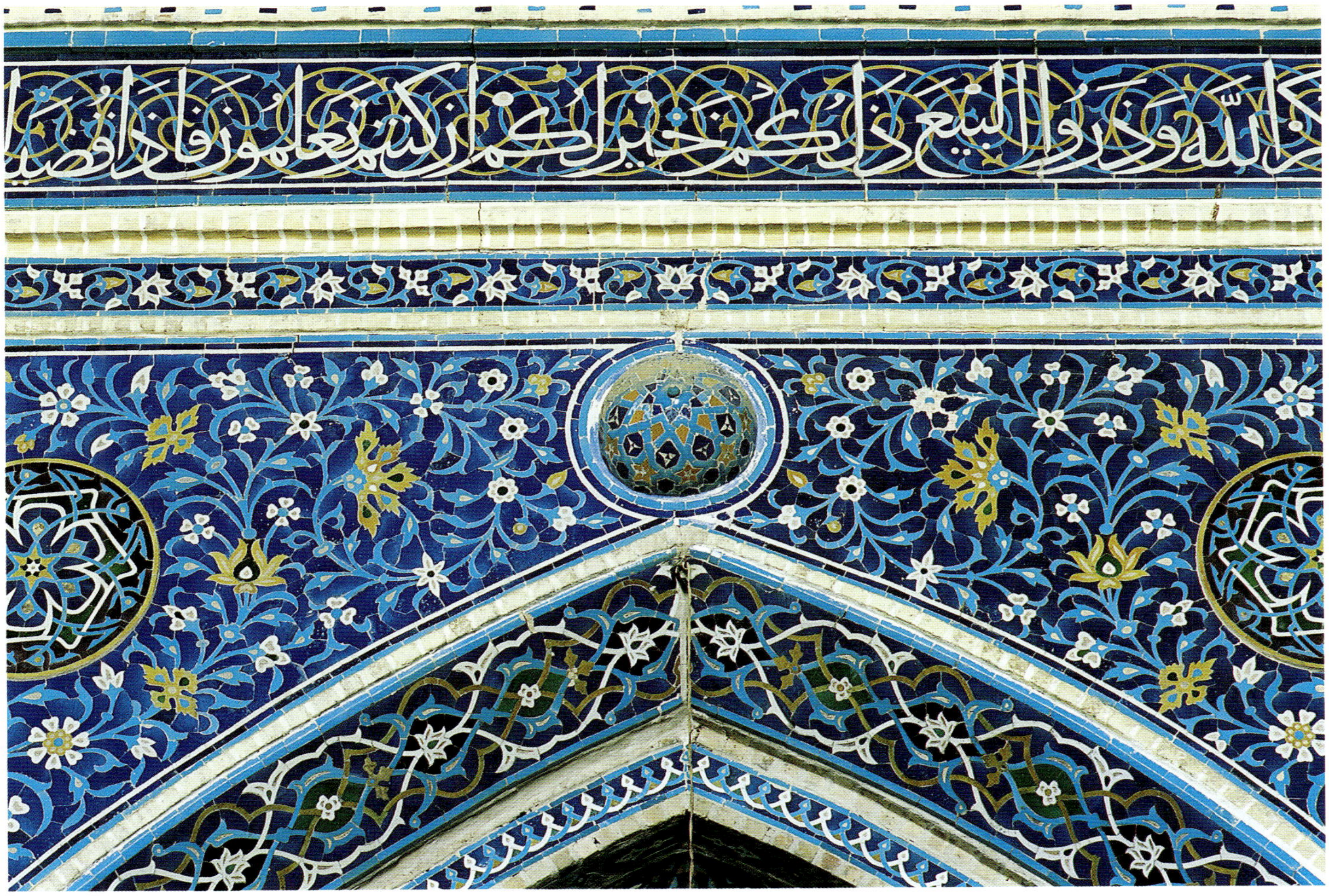

FRIDAY MOSQUE, YAZD (IRAN), 1325–34

ABOVE

♦ Cut-tile mosaic decoration on the facade. Along the top runs a passage from *sura* 62, *al-Jum`a*, "The Congregation."

RIGHT

♦ Cut-tile decoration in a niche in the prayer hall *iwan*.

FACING PAGE

♦ Reveal on the facade clad with cut-tile mosaic. The inscription in Thuluth script quotes the end of *al-Jum`a*: "That which Allah has to bestow is better than any matter of amusement or commerce."

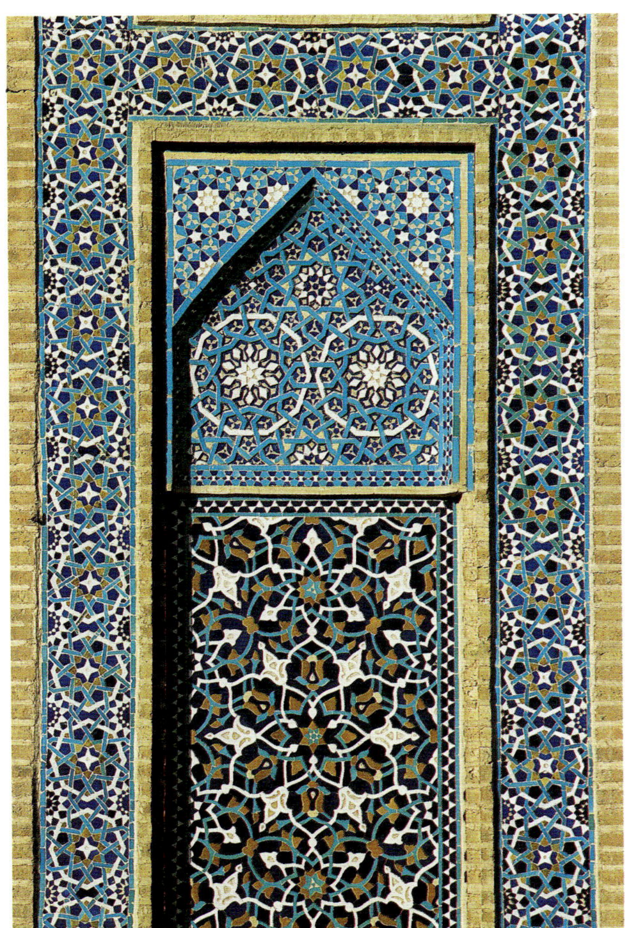

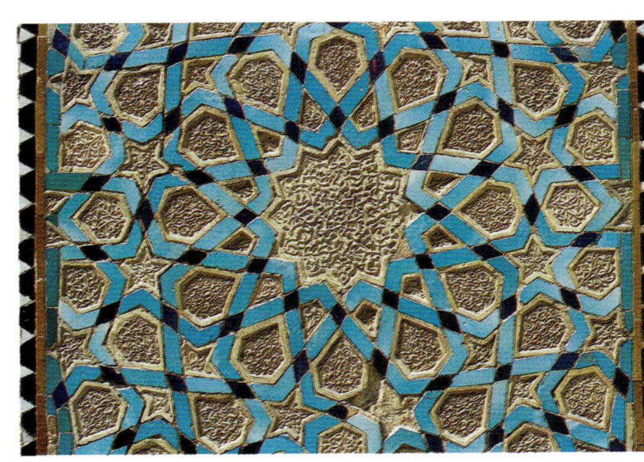

♦ A panel of molded terracotta elements inset into a star and interlace pattern composed of turquoise and black cut tiles.

FRIDAY MOSQUE, YAZD (IRAN), 1325–34

♦ Detail of a cut-tile mosaic (*kashiyi mu`arraq*) in the form of a vase with a spray of flowers.

♦ Dado in an *iwan* in the oratory comprising a ground of turquoise blue tiling and a cut-tile mosaic medallion (*shamsa*).

♦ Interior of the prayer hall cupola, with the signature of the architect, Sa`d ibn Muhammad Kaduk al-Banna` Yazdi.

FACING PAGE, TOP

♦ Cut-tile mosaic of ten-pointed stars amid a geometrical interlocking motif. The Persian inscription in the middle sings the praises of the building.

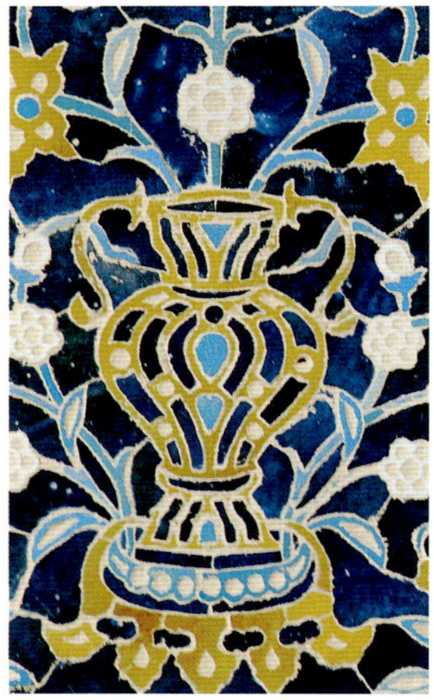

FACING PAGE, BOTTOM

♦ Brick arch, Friday Mosque, Shiraz (Iran), 1351. The spandrels are adorned with an interlace pattern forming a star.

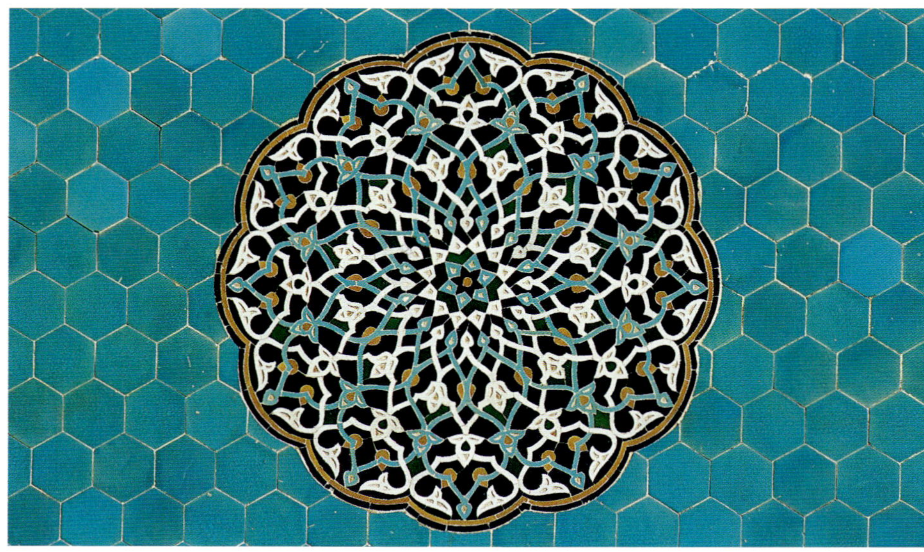

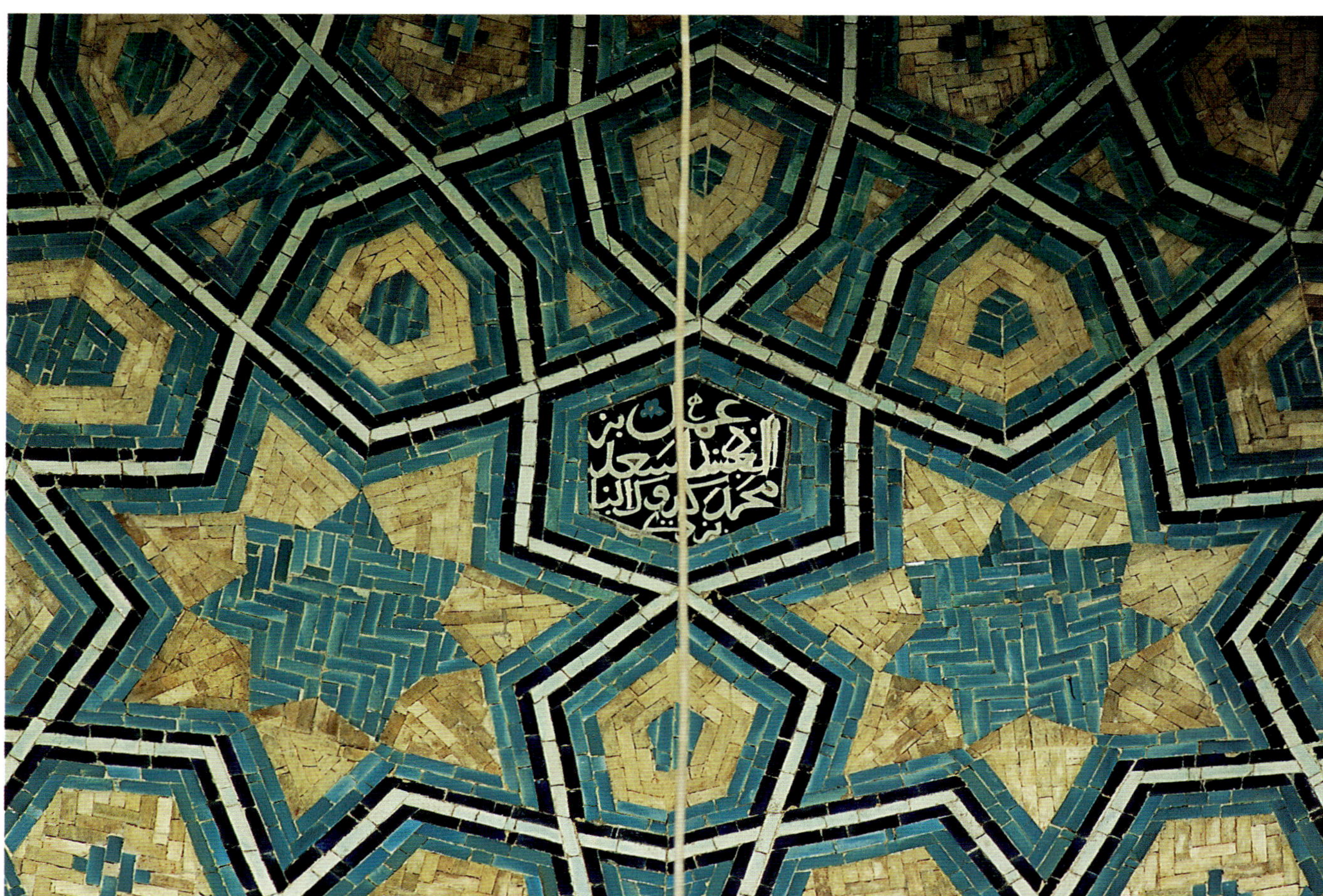

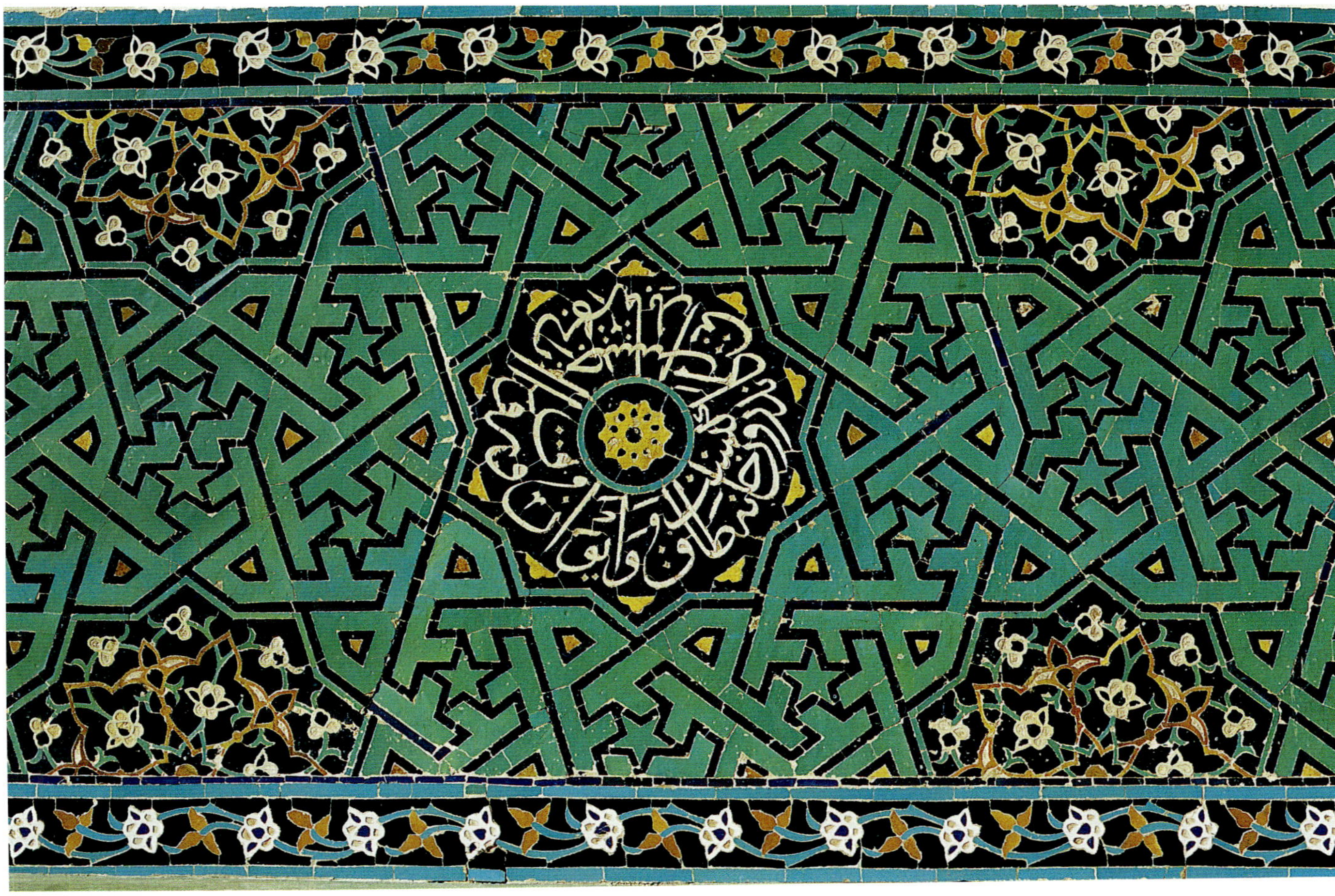

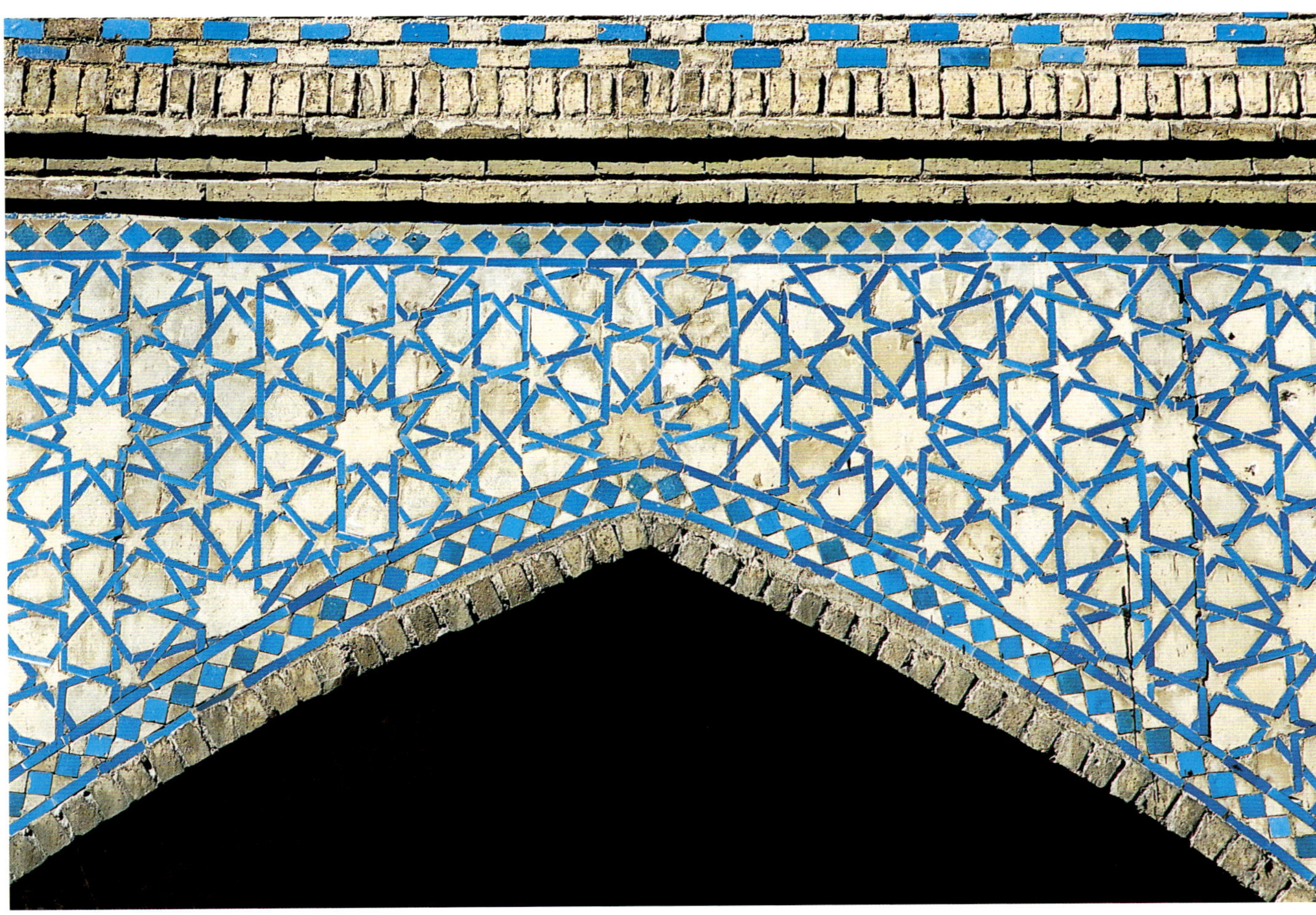

FRIDAY MOSQUE, KERMAN (IRAN), 1349

♦ Detail of the entrance *pishtaq* with a cut-tile mosaic panel showing a pair of peacocks flanking a vase.

♦ Cul-de-four vault lined with a cut-tile mosaic composing an interlace pattern interspersed with fleurons and stars.

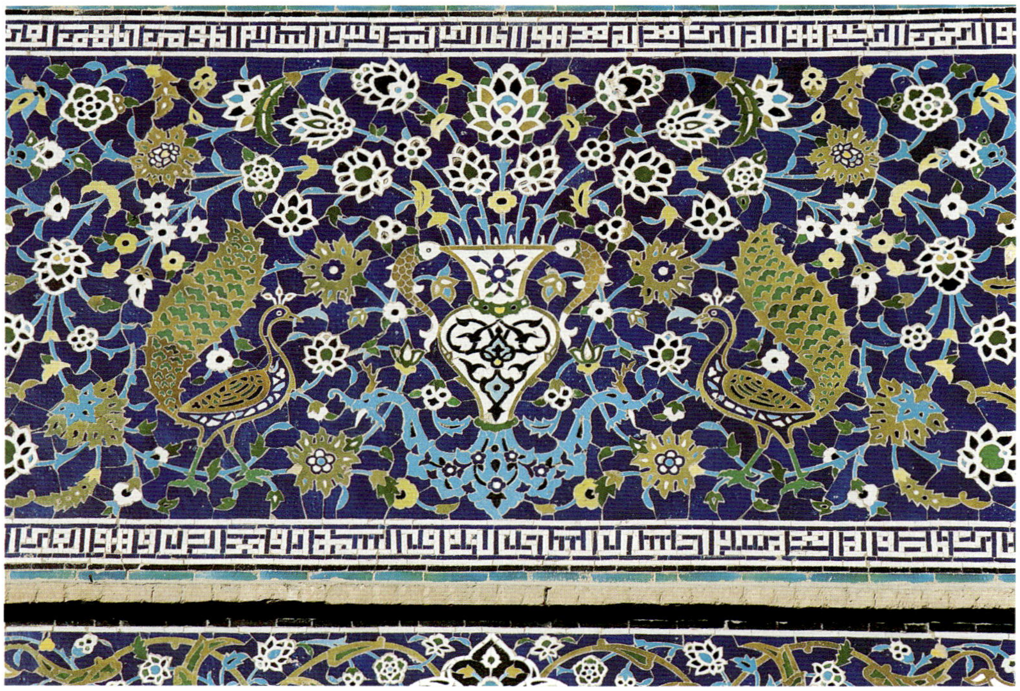

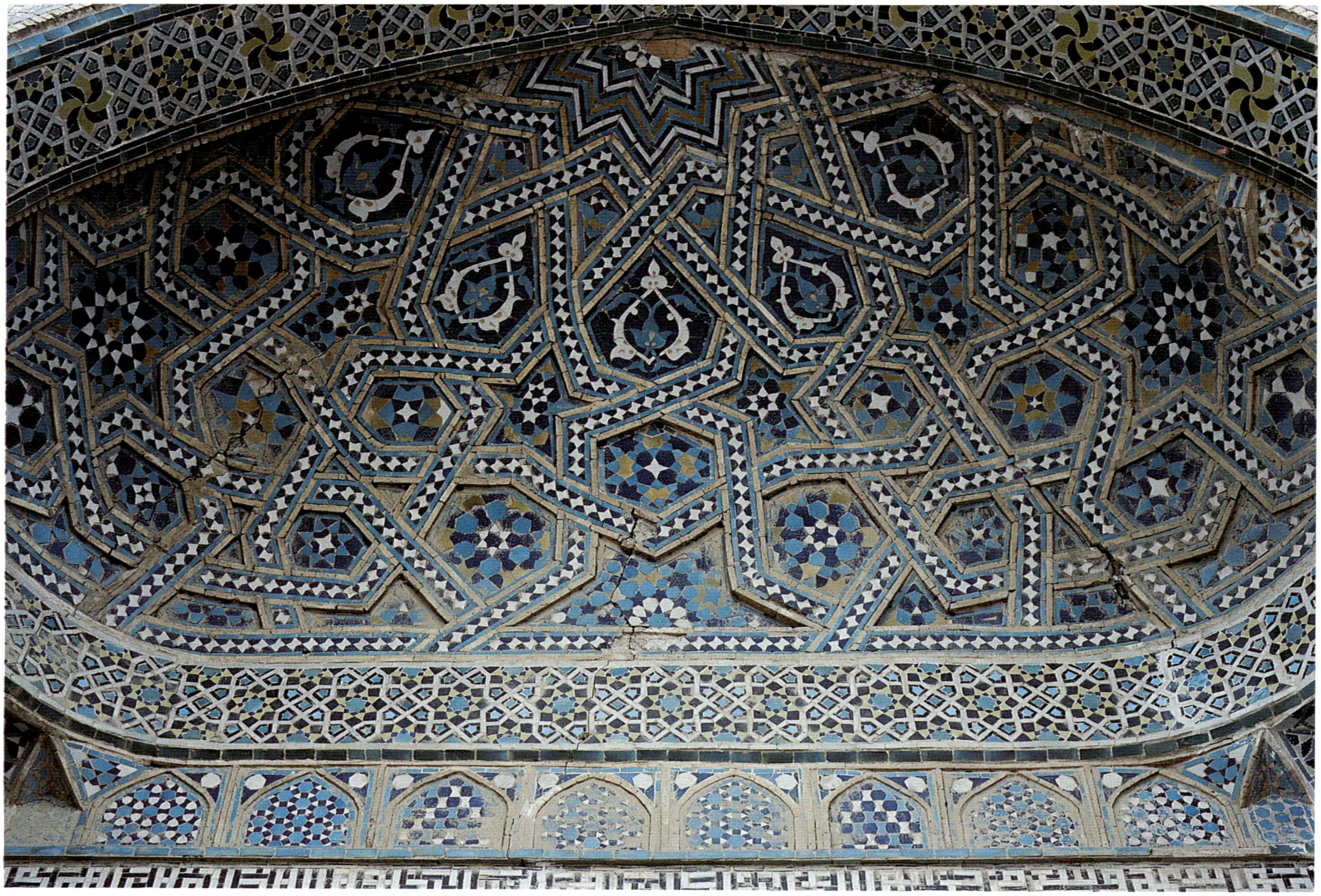

Central Asia in the Fourteenth Century: Early Large-Scale Polychrome Decorations

Architecture in central Asia under Mongol domination is characterized by the sudden and unexpected advent of polychrome underglaze-painted ceramics. It should be noted, however, that chronologically and geographically, the development of this type of ceramic proved rather uneven. To all intents and purposes contemporary with Abu'l-Qasim's text outlining the manufacture of polychrome tiles, the tiles decorating the double cenotaph at Khiva (a locality in the Khwarazm) are probably the earliest large-scale deployment of this type of cladding.

The small mausoleum of Sayyid `Ala al-Din (c. 1305) houses a ceramic masterpiece (one that some authorities prefer to date to the nineteenth century): a pair of twinned cenotaphs in the shape of little coffins standing on a sizable base that is itself placed on a pedestal and flanked by colonnettes at the corners. The front of the base presents a pair of compartments bordered by a molding mounted with twin curvilinear fleurons painted under a colorless transparent glaze with an interlace of split palmettes in the center and lotus flowers on the spandrels. These compartments are ringed by ceramic tiles decorated in overblown lotus flowers, flowerets, and trilobed trails, also underglaze and in slight relief, the whole in reserve on a cobalt ground. The decoration on the facade is repeated on the two sides. The top of the whole unit is crowned by a majestic entablature clad in underglaze-painted tiles with, in white reserve against a cobalt ground tinted with turquoise highlights, a frieze in plaited-Kufic *alafiya* motifs. In addition to cobalt and turquoise blue on a white ground, ceramists employed other colors: black served to underline the design, gray appeared on certain relief areas, while scattered touches of a yellowy green also made an appearance. As for the smaller cenotaphs, they also present floral motif decoration painted under a clear colorless glaze in white reserve on a cobalt ground with some sections in slight relief. The sides exhibit a depressed rectangular compartment set with large ovals with indented borders charged with a lotus flower in reserve on a turquoise ground. The ovals stand out against a split palmette interlace composition in reserve on a cobalt ground. The entire compartment is bordered by a frieze ornamented with flowerets and trefoil trails in reserve on a cobalt ground. The underglaze-painted palmettes emerge in very shallow relief in white reserve on a gray vermiculated ground. Finally, at the top of the cenotaphs, inset keel-arches bordered by a braid of *lam-alif* and by a ribbon adorned with white rosettes on a turquoise ground, two panels are inscribed with further specimens of Arabic calligraphy.

At the beginning of the fourteenth century, the Khwarazm was occupied by the Chagataids. This fact allows one to relate the architectural decorations carried out under their auspices to the production of the relatively poorly documented wares with underglaze "polychrome" decoration commonly known as "Saray Berke."[45]

In the same area, a few decades after the building of the cenotaph at Khiva, the mausoleum of Najm al-Din Kobra was erected on the outskirts of the town of Kunya Urgench. This building also displays astonishing underglaze decorative work, some of which resembles that found on the Khiva cenotaph. As an inscription on its facade attests, the construction was rebuilt under Qutlugh Timur, son of Najm al-Dawla wa'l-Din (1321–36) and vassal to Ghiyath al-Din Muhammad Uzbek (1312–41), a descendant of Jochi and eighth khan of the Golden Horde.

The generous continuous inscriptional bands, together with the tiles that feature a lobed fleuron and a floral decor in which underglaze *grand feu* colors dominate, also illustrates the use of tried and tested techniques. The trim-looking frontage is framed against a brickwork base by an epigraphic frieze in white, cursive "Mongolian" lettering, the loops of which are picked out in turquoise on a cobalt ground. Above the arch of the *pishtaq*, the pediment and spandrels are lined with hexagonal tiles with an underglaze-painted stellar motif. In addition, a second wide horizontal epigraphic band runs across the head of the pediment, inscribed in particular with the name of Qutlugh Timur. At the top of the facade, equilateral pointed niches alternate with terracotta tiles with finely carved decoration and ceramic tiles painted black under a transparent glaze tinged with turquoise; the tiles are very similar to those found in the mausoleum of Khwaja Ahmad in Shah-i Zinda built a few decades later. Lower down on the frontage, the intrados of the *pishtaq* arch is clad in hexagonal tiles bordered with palmette ribbonwork. The door is framed by an epigraphic frieze with tiles bearing a curvilinear fleuron itself furnished with all-over, low-relief floral motifs (peonies, lotus flowers) painted white on a cobalt ground enriched with touches of turquoise. This type of plant composition brings to mind the decorations on the Yeşil Türbe at Bursa, executed almost a century later (c. 1420). Reminiscent of Khiva, the large fleuron is here underscored by cyma recta molding; the ornament bears a leaf-scroll interlace with split palmettes on a gray ground. Lastly, below the entrance, the tympanum presents a composition based on an undulating scroll painted on hexagonal tiles, in white with a hint of turquoise on

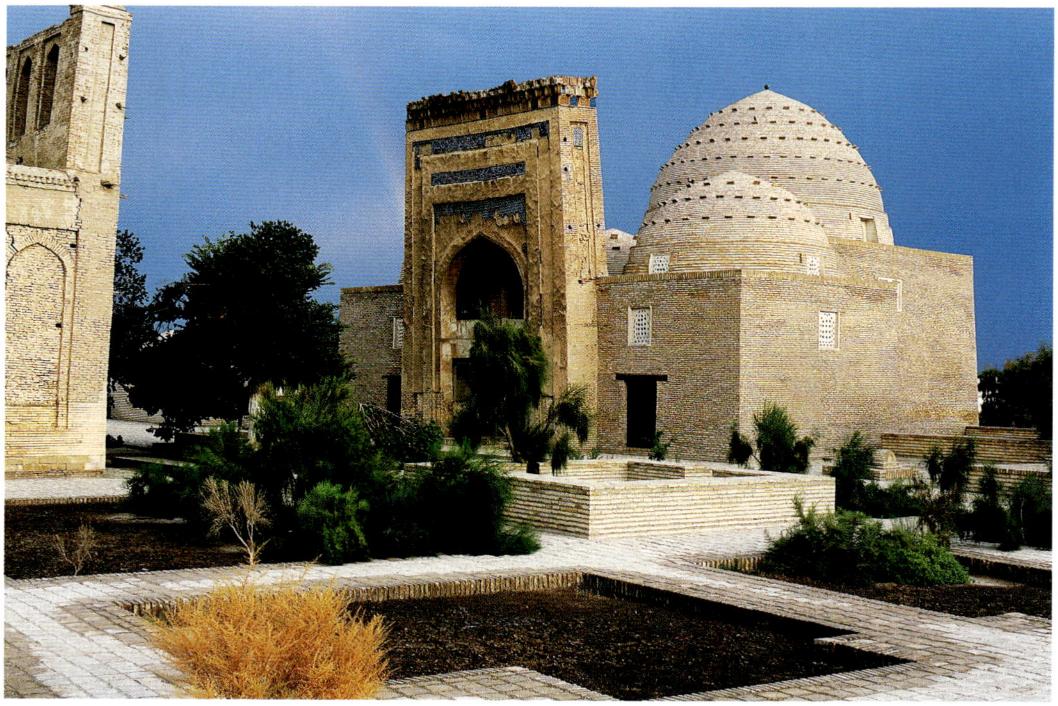

♦ Mausoleum of Najm al-Din Kobra, Kunya Urgench (Turkmenistan), c. 1321–36. A general view of the monument as recently restored.

a cobalt ground; the composition is edged by an inscription in plaited Kufic.

Curiously, after brilliant if fitful beginnings in the Khwarazm, underglaze polychrome decoration seems to have lost momentum: following the mausoleum of Najm al-Din Kubra, only very few monuments use underglaze painting on a large scale, although timid attempts do appear on the facade of the mausoleum of Khwaja Ahmad in the Shah-i Zinda, Samarkand (c. 1350). The two bands bordering the substantial epigraphic frieze are embellished with rectangular tiles decorated in relief eight-pointed stars, whose projecting edges are painted white; black-painted floral motifs emerge from under a clear glaze, turquoise-tinted inside the stars and cobalt without.

Difficult to date (mid-fourteenth century?), the cenotaph of Qutham ibn `Abbas is a masterpiece. For the most part, the decoration consists of tiles with a cobalt ground adorned with gilded motifs underlined in red and with white-slip trails, although some sections testify to high-fire polychrome decoration, notably the almond-shaped roundels featuring lotus flowers (finished in low-fired gold leaf) located on the third tier of the cenotaph. In addition, the horizontal borders of each of the three tiers are lined with small rectangular plates decorated with blooms in yellow, red ocher, cobalt, turquoise, and almond green against a white ground. Similar tiles are to be found on the skirting in the mausoleum of Shad-i Mulk Aqa in the same necropolis, built after 1371. It is not inconceivable that these tiles were fired at low temperature (*petit feu*, onglaze), in particular for the red ocher.

At Bukhara, a foretaste of achievements to come in the Shah-i Zinda at Samarkand is offered by the mausoleum of Buyan Qoli Khan (a prince of the Mongolian dynasty of Chagatai who died in 1358). Its frontage was formerly richly decorated, although most of the glazed ceramic elements were unfortunately taken down at some point and are today dispersed in several collections (notably in London and Hamburg). With a rectangular floor plan measuring only 7.5 by 8.5 meters at ground level, the proportions of the monument are unspectacular. Its attraction lies primarily in its decoration. A lofty facade *pishtaq* serves to mask the cupola of the central hall. Formerly, a large, wide epigraphic band framed the entire door, but this inscription, together with the broad horizontal band topping the *pishtaq*, have disappeared. Only the sections of the ceramic inscription located on the extrados of the arch remain in situ: the characters of the Arab text stand out in turquoise blue against a leaf-scroll ground of darker hue. The epigraphic frieze was bordered by a sequence of alternately white and turquoise *banna'i* brickwork. The spandrels to either side of the arch are ornamented with palmette leaf-scrolls of sophisticated workmanship snaking round a central fleuron; executed in relatively high relief, these ceramics are painted in predominantly white and turquoise hues. The intrados is embellished by a band of stars set in a raised geometrical interlace pattern

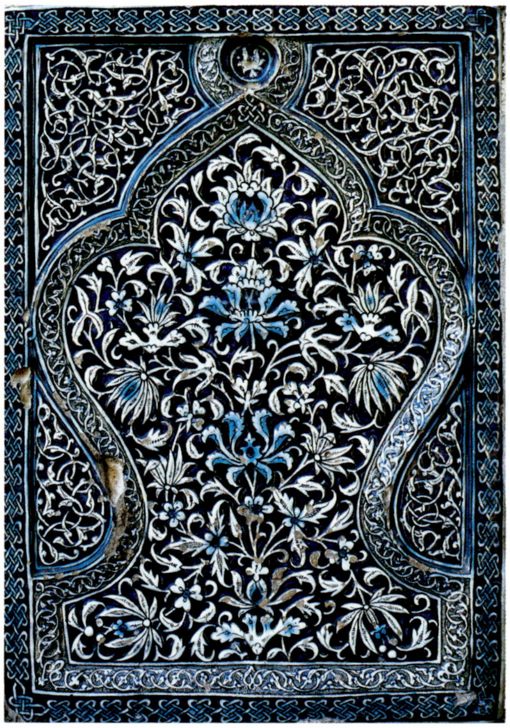

FACADE OF THE MAUSOLEUM OF NAJM AL-DIN KOBRA, KUNYA URGENCH (TURKMENISTAN), C. 1321–26

♦ Beginning of the frieze ornamenting the interior of the *pishtaq* decorated with a fleuron on a stone-paste tile in shallow relief underglaze-painted in *grand feu* enamel.

FOLLOWING DOUBLE PAGE

♦ Underglaze-painted low-relief tile decorated in interlaced palmettes and flowering branches. The plant motifs and the volute-like cartouche display a Far Eastern influence.

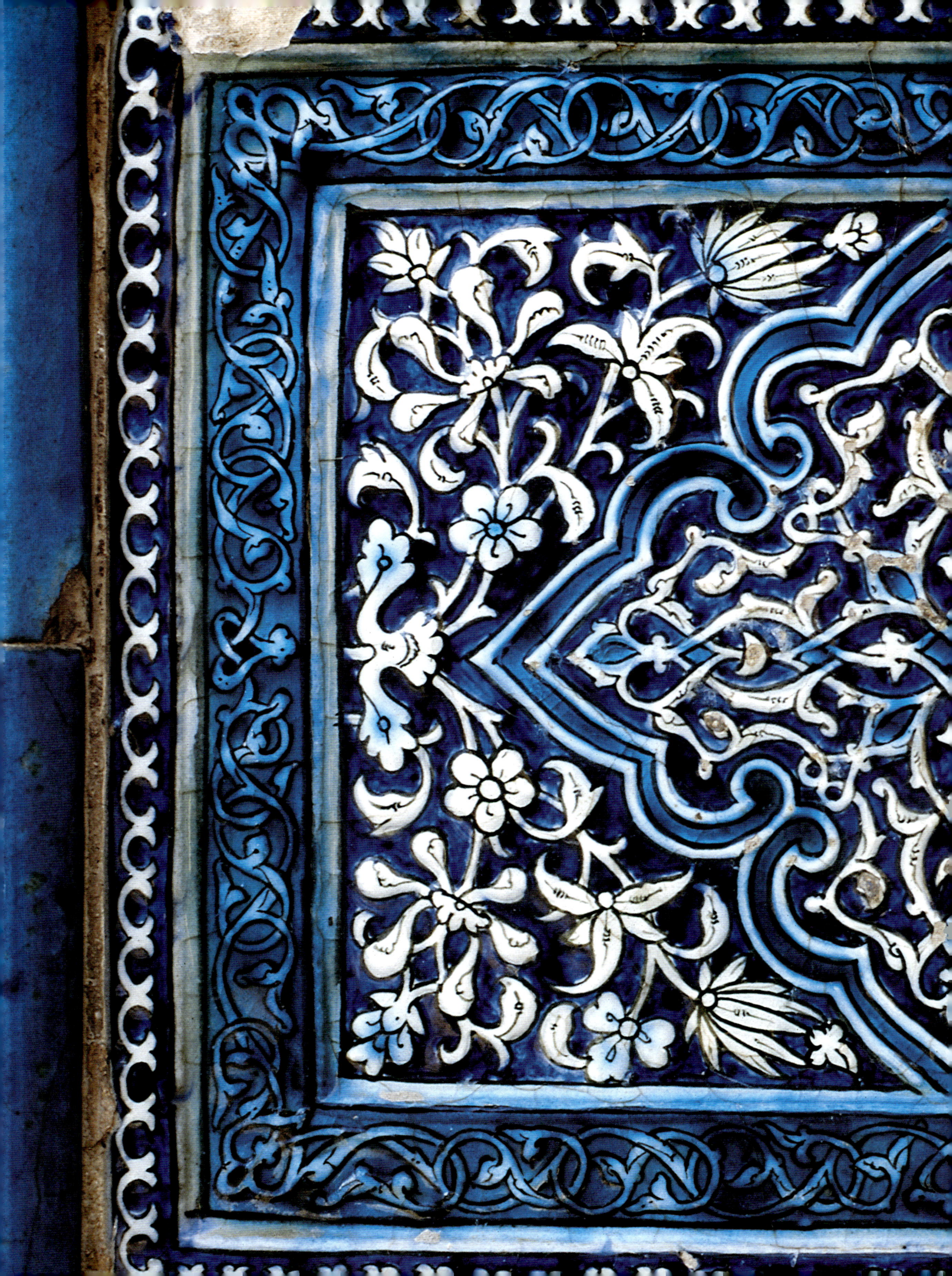

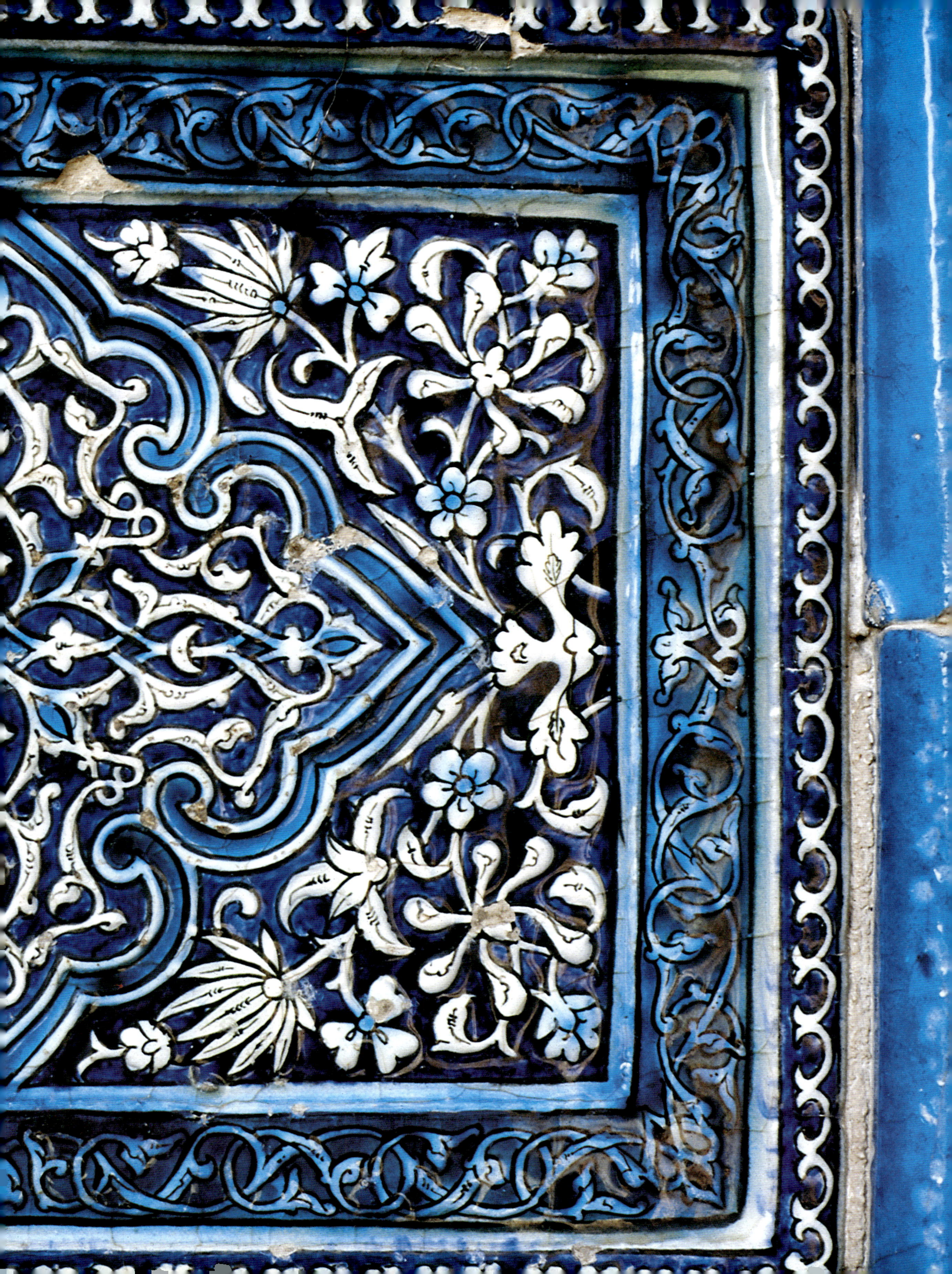

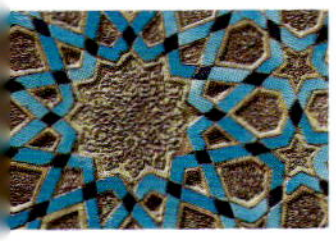

MAUSOLEUM OF TUGHABEG KHANUM, KUNYA URGENCH (TURKMENISTAN), C. 1370

♦ Detail of the interior of the cupola of the mausoleum showing the extraordinarily rich palette (the red is particularly striking) and the unparalleled delicacy of the patterns, with local gold-leaf highlights.

FACING PAGE

♦ With its central twenty-four-pointed star motif, the cupola of this magnificent mausoleum is the supreme masterpiece of cut-tile mosaic work.

bordered by a broad strip of white, turquoise, and cobalt *banna'i*. At one time incorporating a pattern of polygons and stars in relief that mirrored certain elements within the monument, the decoration of the tympanum above the door is in a bad state of disrepair.

The mausoleum known as that of Tughabeg Khanum in Kunya Urgench belongs to a wholly different category. The design of its ceramic decoration relies on polychrome mosaic, an approach that would recur—with the occasional variation in terms of the glazes—in the construction of several buildings at the Shah-i Zinda, in particular the mausoleum of Shirin Beyk Aqa (1385) and in the Tuman Aqa complex (1405). In its ceramic mosaic decoration, especially that of the inside of the glorious cupola, the mausoleum of Tughabeg Khanum represents the high point of the art. The cut-tile motifs of the utmost delicacy and the particularly brilliant colors, high-fired directly onto the tiles, are deployed in a vast palette ranging from cobalt blue, turquoise, a lighter blue, chromium green, and straw and lemon yellow to white, as well as a brick red of an intensity seldom attained elsewhere. To complete the otherworldly atmosphere, the decorators also applied light touches of *petit feu* gold leaf to the glaze. According to Golombek and Wilber, this mausoleum built in the 1370s supposedly serves as a resting place for two princes of the short-lived Sufi dynasty, Husayn and Yusuf, although local tradition allots it to a female occupant, the eponymous Tughabeg Khanum (around 1330–40), probably on the basis of an account by the celebrated traveler Ibn Battuta, who stayed at the site in 1335.

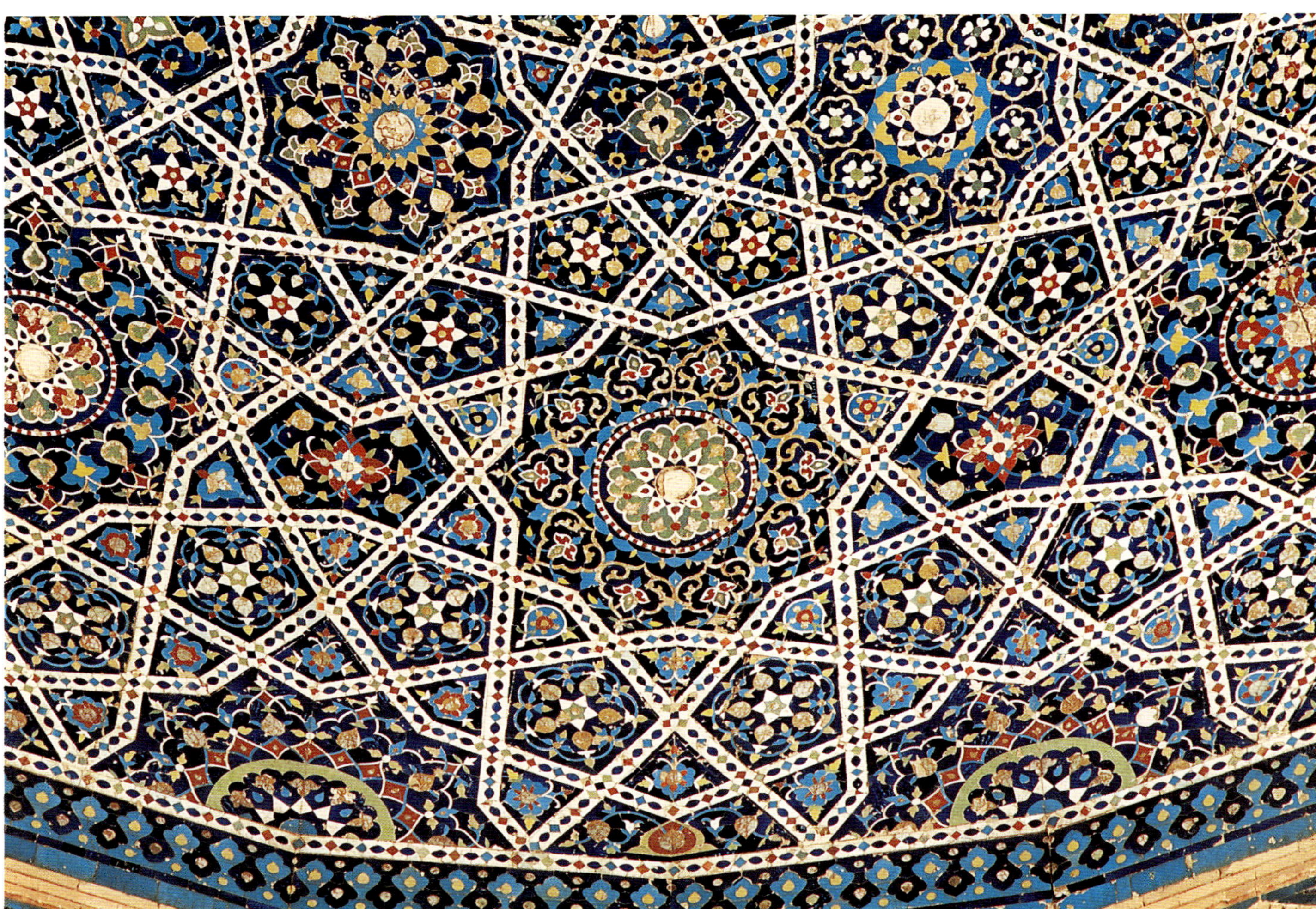

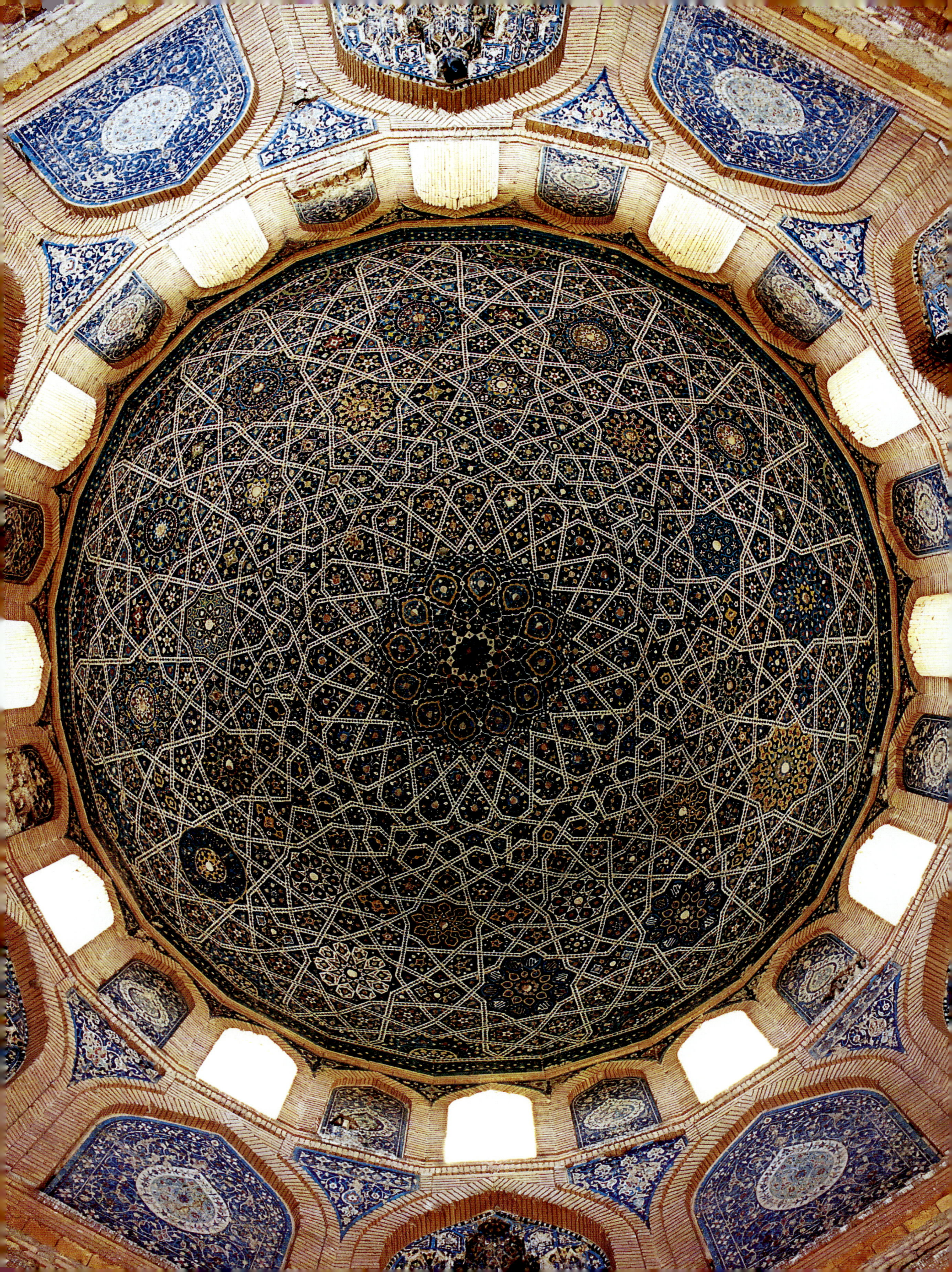

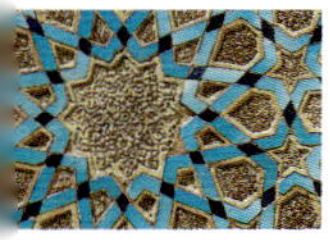

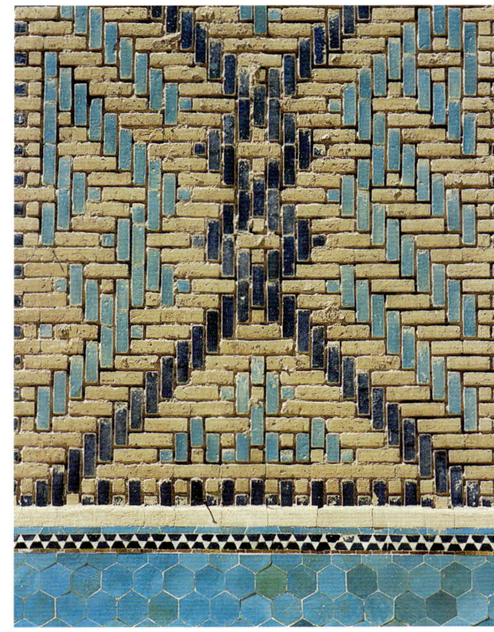

Form and Color: Timurid Architecture

♦ Mir Chaqmaq Mosque, Yazd (Iran), 1437. Wall facing in *banna'i* brickwork.

The Timurid dynasty owes its name to its founder, Timur (Temür), also known as "Timur the Lame" (Timurlenk, from which stem "Tamerlane" or "Tamburlaine"). Born at Kish (today Shahr-i Sabz), by the 1370s Timur had established himself as a force to be reckoned with in what was left of the tottering kingdoms of the Chagataids. In a few short decades, Timur had seized central Asia and Iran, taking Delhi in 1398, and even defeating the Ottoman Sultan Bayezit (Bajazet) in 1402 (battle of Ankara). The great conqueror passed away in 1405, on the verge of organizing a further campaign to China. The dynasty he set up, with its splendid court, dominated the entire fifteenth century, its influence extending far beyond the frontiers of the empire proper.

Enthusiastic patrons of the arts, Timurid princes promoted architecture and funded other artistic activities, such as painting and manuscript illumination. It was under their aegis that some of the greatest masterpieces of what is reductively termed the "Persian miniature" were created. One of the most remarkable facts about Timurid art is that it seems to have achieved perfect coherence in every field; indeed it was during this era that a rarely paralleled degree of organization was attained in royal workshops. These outlets provided at one and the same time the "conceivers"—architects, mathematicians, and engineers—and the "designers" responsible for executing the decoration, be it an art object, an illuminated manuscript, or an entire architectural complex. Based primarily on Persian traditions allied with central Asian models, in particular those from the Khwarazm, Timurid architecture attained a perfect symbiosis between color and form.

Dating from between 1389 and 1399, the mausoleum of the illustrious Khoja Ahmad Yasavi in Turkestan (Kazakhstan) was an important pilgrimage center rebuilt by Timur in honor of the much venerated sepulcher within. Although its dimensions are atypical for a mausoleum, it is nevertheless characteristic of a number of monuments built under the reign of Timur, whose most conspicuous feature is precisely their enormous size. The immense meeting hall capped with a turquoise cupola was used for ritual gatherings of Sufi dervishes; the whole complex numbers no less than twenty contiguous rooms, a mosque and a library among them. The external decoration of the building is characterized by the use of *banna'i* bricks in conjunction with cruciform and gammadion motifs on the wall within which appear inscriptions in Kufic script. Above the mausoleum proper, a smaller cupola is adorned with ridges or gadroons, dressed with tiny colored squares.

The Shah-i Zinda necropolis in Samarkand houses the tombs of several members of Timur's family clustered around the cenotaph of Qutham ibn 'Abbas. It is probable that the origin of the cemetery dates back to the eleventh century, and that it grew in size from the time of the Qarakhanids with the construction of a since vanished *madrasa*. Following the Mongol conquest in the first half of the fourteenth century, it expanded further, a process that continued until Timur eventually seized overall power. From the 1370s, several mausoleums housing in particular the remains of female members of the reigning family were erected in the necropolis. The majority of these mausoleums are not in fact characterized by hugely imposing proportions (the facades are approximately 10 meters wide). However, the variety of the techniques deployed, in conjunction with the diversity of the motifs used in the decoration—combining floral and geometrical elements with epigraphic compositions in Persian and Arabic—make the necropolis one of the greatest achievements of the art of architectural ceramics.

The oldest Timurid mausoleum in the necropolis is the one built around 1371 for a prematurely deceased princess, Shad-i Mulk Aqa. It is also the most extraordinary of all in terms of both ceramic technique and variety of motifs. All the techniques of architectural revetment (save that of metallic luster) are deployed in the service of the lamented princess's monument: carved elements covered with monochrome glaze, large underglaze-painted tiles (at the top of the facade arch), medallions decorated with low-fired enamels—each detail of the decor, exterior as well as interior, is carried off superbly. The signatures of two craftsmen (masters Zayn al-Din and Shams al-Din Fakhkhar) appear on the *pishtaq*.

It is not known who is buried in the mausoleum, which is named after Master (Ustad) `Ali Nasafi, one of the craftsmen who worked on the decor in collaboration with Master (Ustad) `Ali Tuki-kub, whose signature appears symmetrically to that of `Ali Nasafi's on the corner colonnettes flanking the doorway. Built around 1380, this small monument is covered in an enamel decoration partitioned by a black line, with low-fired red and gold highlights, in geometric interlace and star panels over which run quotations from the Qur`an and the names of the twelve Shi`ite *imams*.

Virtually contemporary, the frontage of a mausoleum known as that of Ulugh Sultan Begum in the Shah-i Zinda, Samarkand, is datable to around 1385[46] and deploys an astonishing array of decoration of geometric elements in cobalt blue glaze set off by red slip and gold forming star designs. The

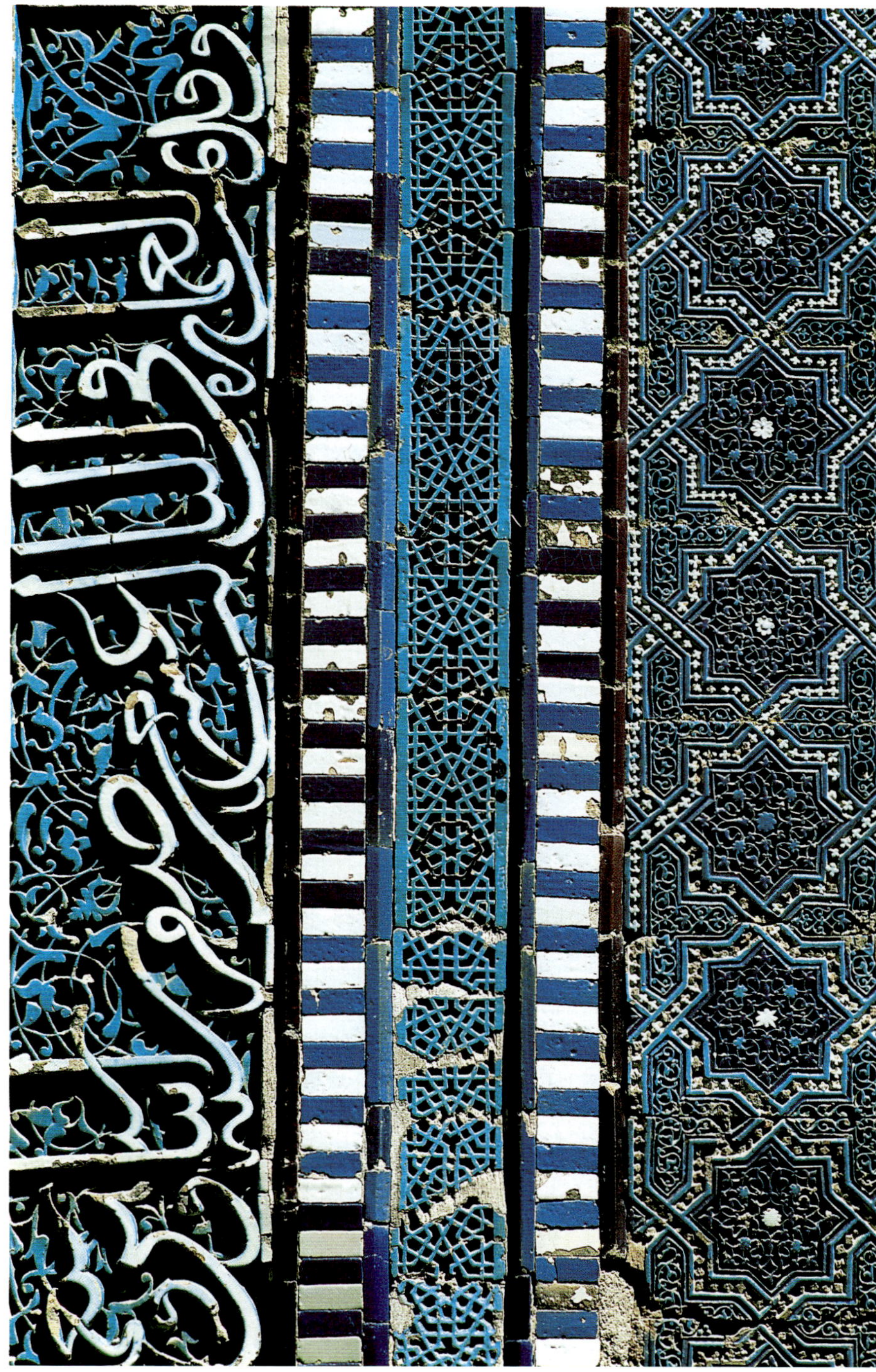

♦ Mausoleum of an anonymous lady in the necropolis of the Shah-i Zinda in Samarkand (Uzbekistan). The high-relief inscription in white characters on a turquoise blue leaf-scroll ground provides a date corresponding to December 24, 1360.

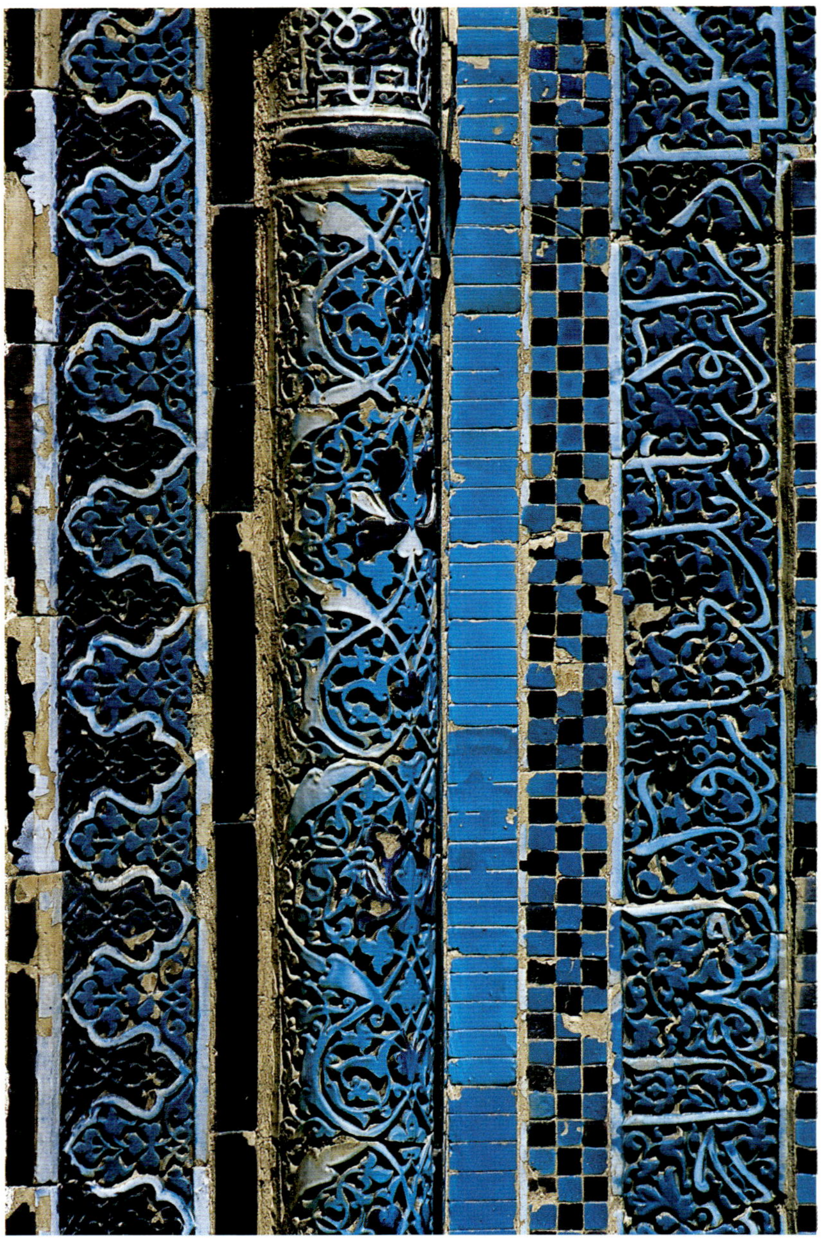

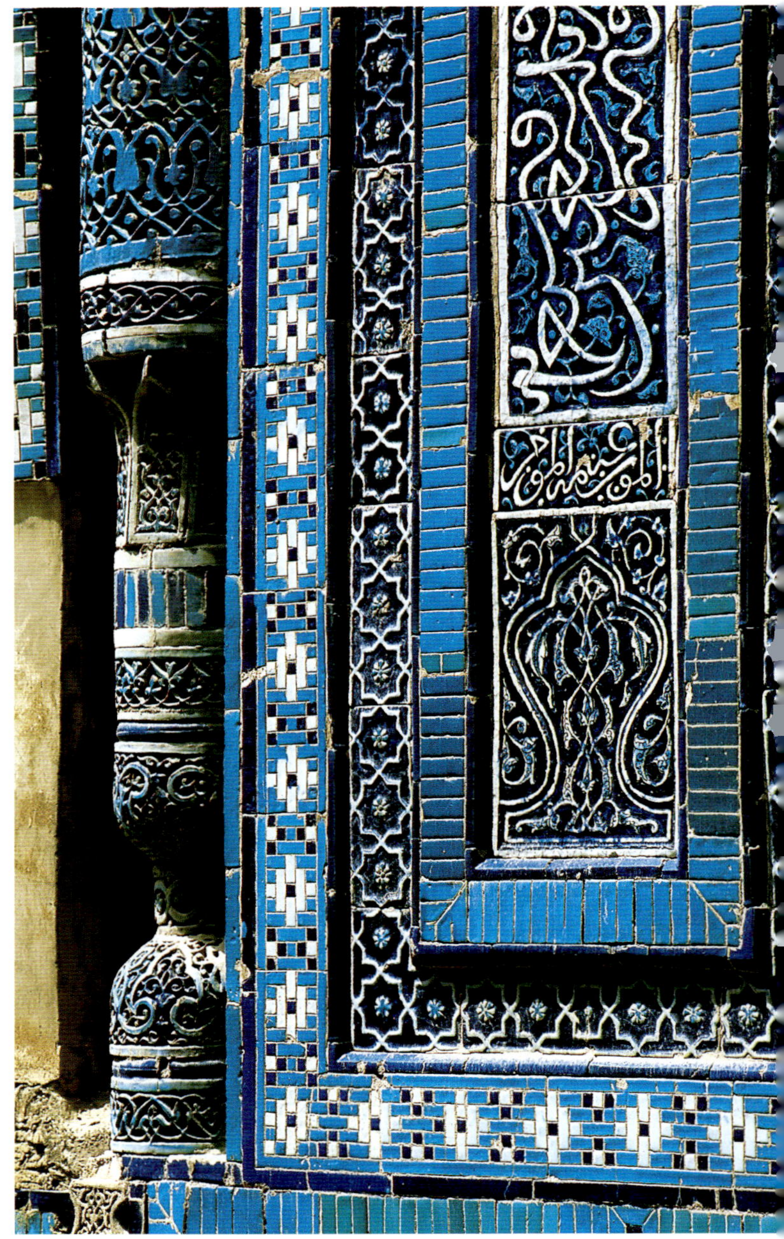

MAUSOLEUM OF AMIR HUSAYN TUGHLU TEKIN, SAMARKAND (UZBEKISTAN), 1376

♦ Persian verse inscription in glazed ceramics carved in high relief: "In this obscure tomb, with no friends, no-one at all / I place all my hopes in your mercy—and that suffices!"

MAUSOLEUM OF SHAD-I MULK AQA AT THE SHAH-I ZINDA, SAMARKAND (UZBEKISTAN), C. 1371

♦ Detail of the facade flanked by corner colonnettes, here showing the final section of an Arabic inscription giving the date of the death of the princess, a niece of Emperor Timur.

FACING PAGE

♦ Engaged corner colonnette of the *pishtaq*, bearing on the base the signatures of Zayn al-Din and Shams al-Din Fakhkhar, one of the artists who worked on the decoration.

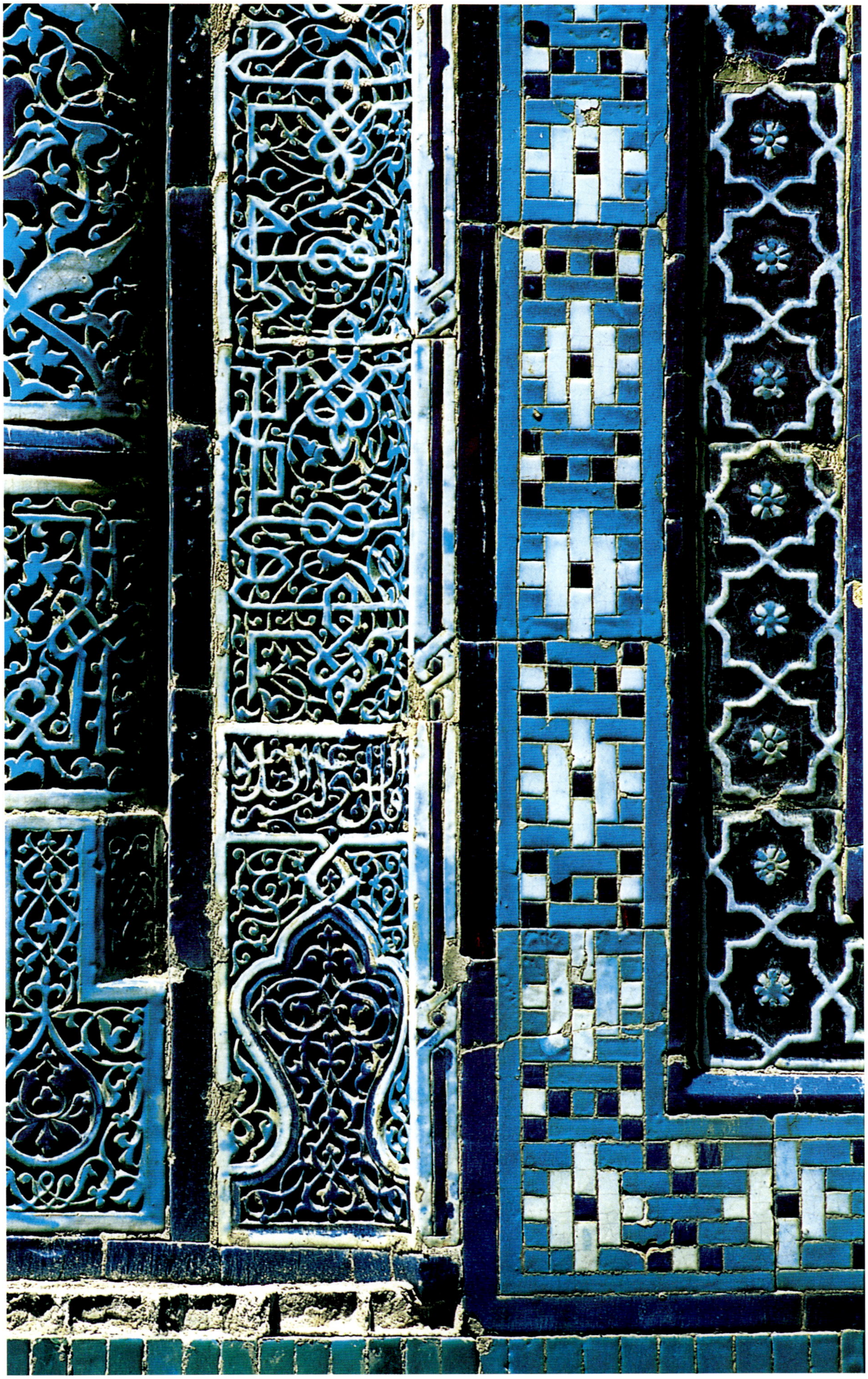

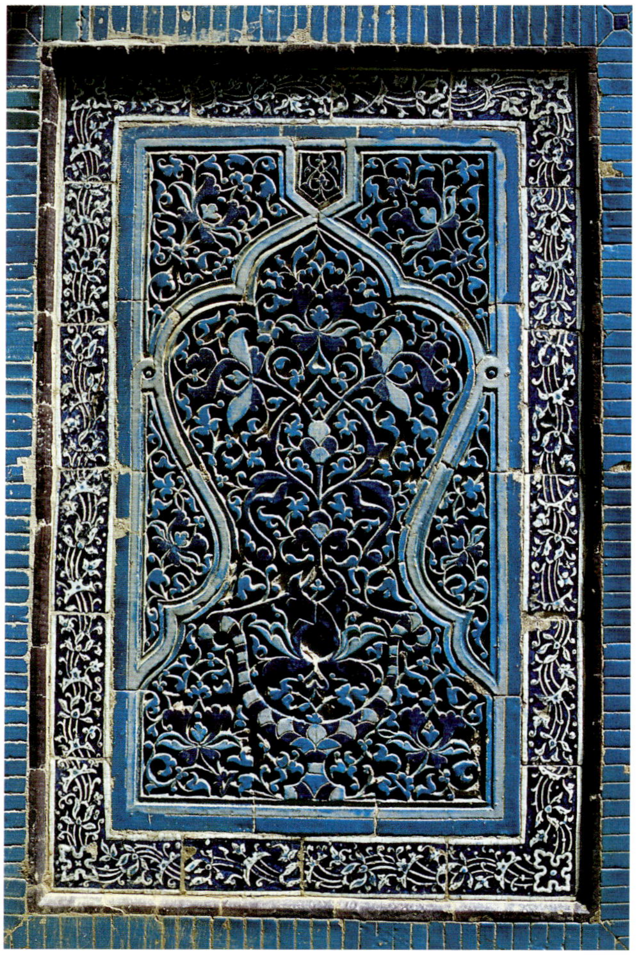

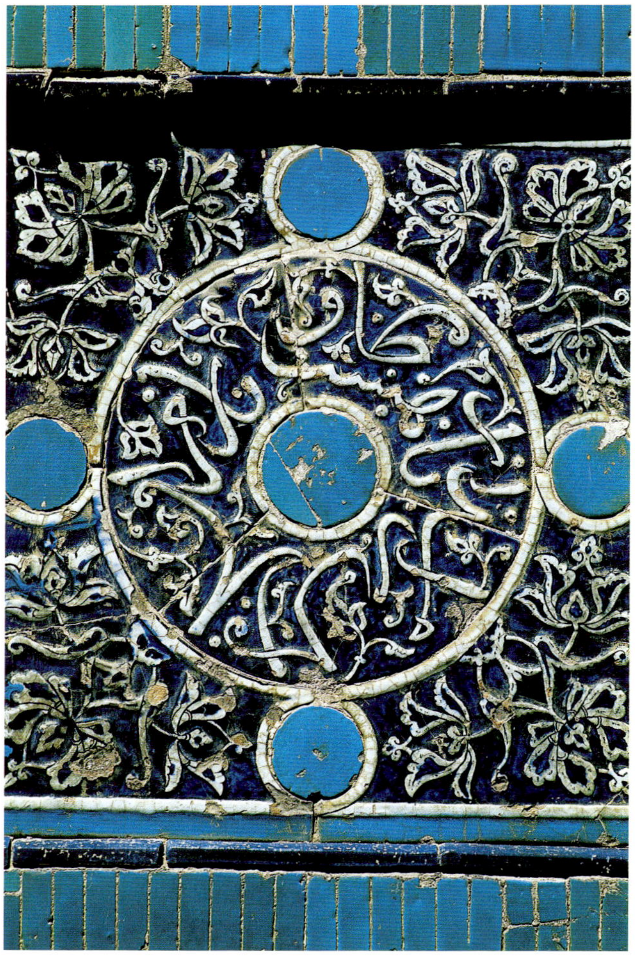

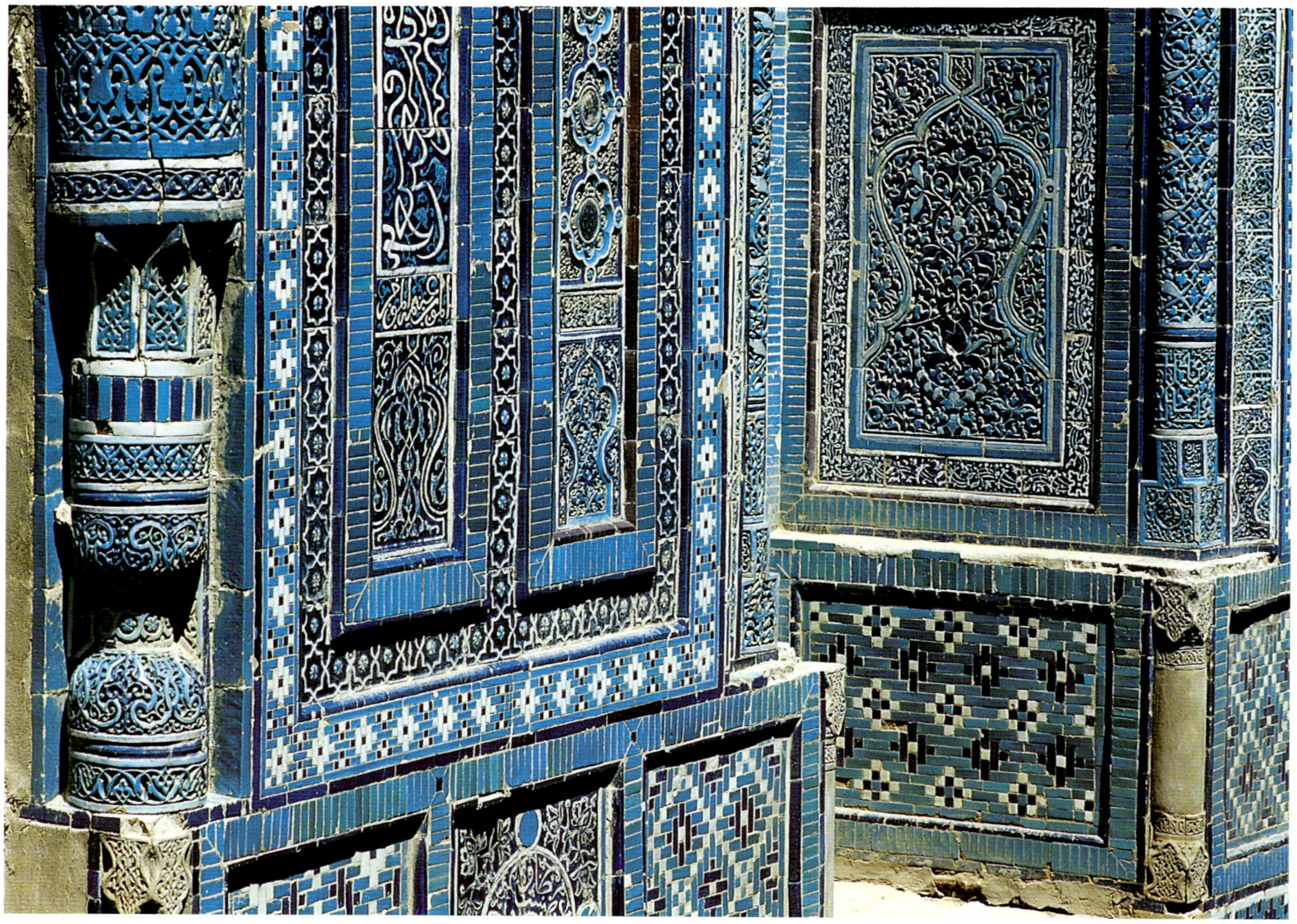

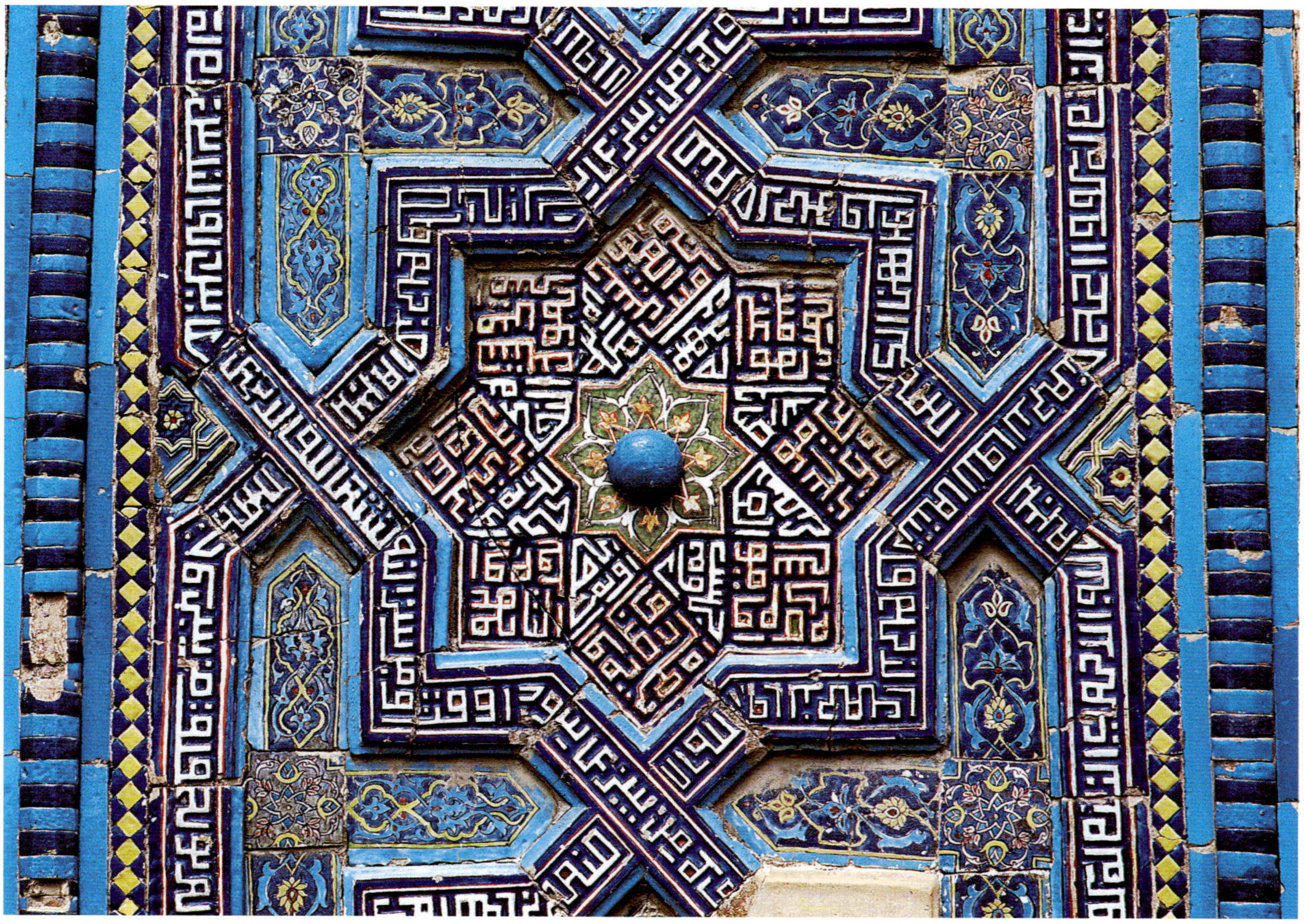

MAUSOLEUM OF SHAD-I MULK AQA AT THE SHAH-I ZINDA, SAMARKAND

FACING PAGE

♦ Carved ceramic tile with *grand feu* glaze, bordered with an underglaze-painted frieze showing floral motifs inspired by Far Eastern models.

♦ Panel (one of a pair to either side of the facade) comprising underglaze-painted tiles with floral motifs and verses by the Persian poet Sa'di: "As long as you have a vault and a roof, think not of heaven."

♦ The facade decoration includes carved ceramics, underglaze polychrome tilework (inscriptional band), and painted *petit feu* stars and lobed medallions.

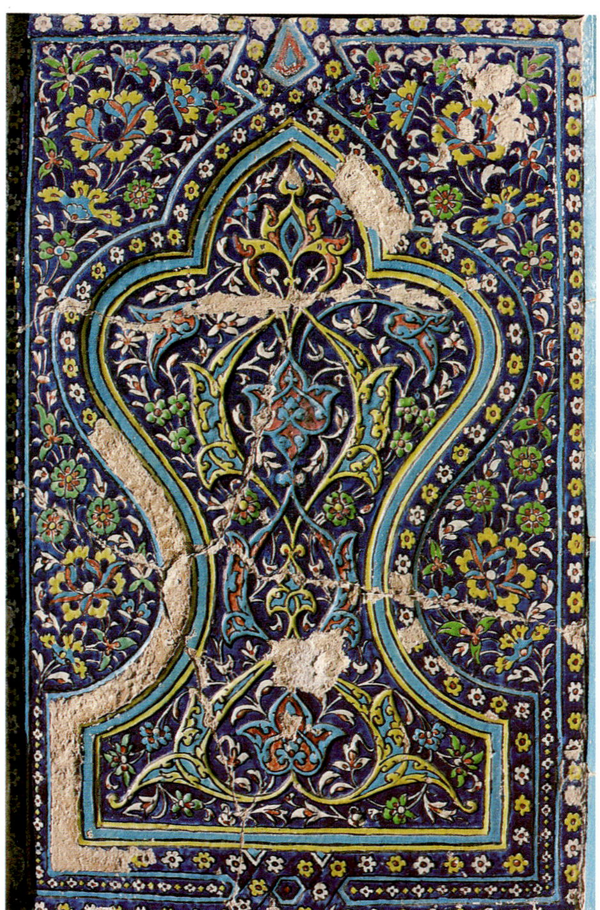

MAUSOLEUM OF USTAD 'ALI NASAFI AT THE SHAH-I ZINDA, SAMARKAND (UZBEKISTAN), C. 1385

ABOVE AND LEFT

♦ Decoration on the facade. Composition of *petit feu* decorated tilework. The eight-pointed stars contain Kufic script recording the names of the twelve Shi'ite *imams*.

♦ Underglaze polychrome ceramic panel enhanced with a rich palette of *petit feu* onglaze color.

technique used recalls that of so-called *lajvardina* ceramics.

Following Timur's rise to power in the 1370s, the technique of using polychrome tiles underwent something of a revival. Various techniques were used, as can be seen in the Shah-i Zinda, at the mausoleum of Shad-i Mulk Aqa, as well as in the mausoleums of the Amir-zade, of Tughlu Tekin, and in that bearing the name of Ustad `Ali Nasafi mentioned above. Examples also appear in other large-scale Timurid monuments at Samarkand (the so-called Bibi Khanum Mosque) and at the Shahr-i Sabz. In the complex of Sultan Sa`adat in Termez, the intrados of the central *iwan* is lined with "black line" hexagonal tiles bearing in the center a red slip boss with touches of gold leaf. Dating in all probability from the time of the repairs carried out at the beginning of the fifteenth century, these tiles—in spite of their rather rudimentary handiwork—exhibit an original design.[47]

In its external decoration, the mausoleum for Timur's sister, princess Shirin Beyk Aqa, constructed in 1385, makes exclusive use of cut-tile mosaic arranged around the entrance into elegant plant motifs together with an epigraphic scheme that quotes the "Sayings of Socrates." It has occasionally been advanced that the adoption of this decorative technique was due to the arrival of Iranian craftsmen, but it is clear—judging by the dazzling example of the mausoleum known as that of Tughabeg Khanum in Kunya Urgench—that craftsmen from the Khwarazm had no need of lessons from anyone in this domain. The mausoleum and mosque of Tuman Aqa (one of Timur's wives), built around 1405, also incorporates cut-tile mosaic decoration.

The latest Timurid mausoleum in the necropolis is undoubtedly the one which was for long wrongly known as that of Qadizada Rumi (after the name of an astrologer who practiced at the court of Ulugh Beg). When the vault was opened, scholars were able to ascertain that in fact the burial chamber was intended for an anonymous woman—perhaps a nurse to one of the Timurid princes—whose corpse was buried with others in a collective tomb. The necropolis's distinctive silhouette gave rise to its current name of the "tomb with the double dome," and this is the best-known view of the necropolis, with its two turquoise domes.

Near these sepulchers of modest size, the vast tomb of Timur, called the Gur-i Mir, is striking for its proportions. The mausoleum itself is enclosed within a complex that initially included a *madrasa* and a hospice (*khanqa*), which today lie in ruins around the court. The mausoleum is capped by an ample ribbed cupola entirely covered in colored tiles resting on buoyant *muqarnas* corbels with ceramics girdling the drum. At a later date, Timur's grandson, Ulugh Beg, commissioned the splendid cut-tile mosaic entryway from an Isfahan artist. At the outset, this large tomb was intended to house the remains of another grandson of the great conqueror who died before him, Prince Muhammad. The tomb became a dynastic vault and houses, in addition to the last-named prince and his grandfather, the sultans Shah Rokh and Ulugh Beg, as well as other princes from

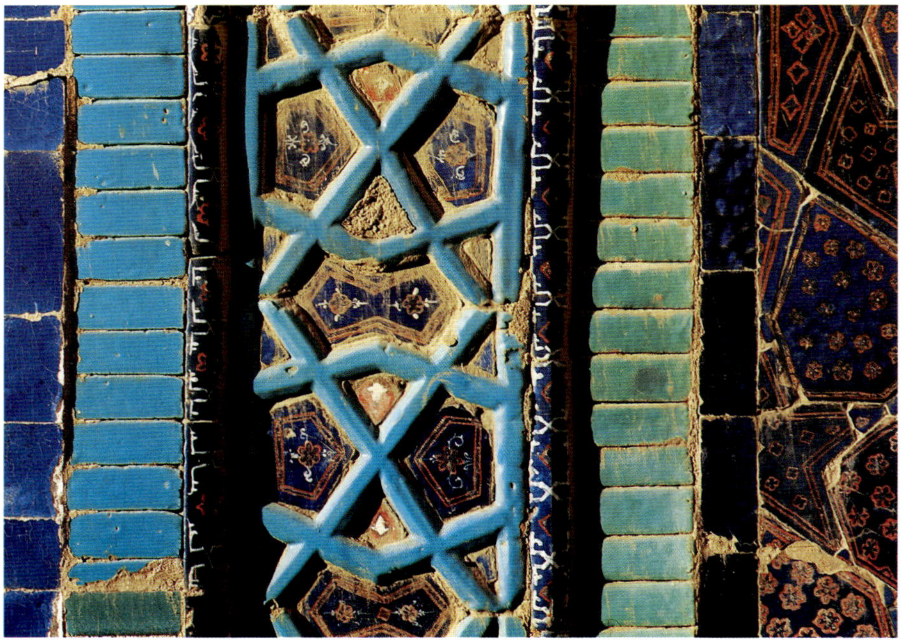

♦ Decoration in cobalt glazed tiles, embellished with *petit feu* motifs of the so-called *lajvardina* type. Anonymous mausoleum (no. 2) known as that of Ulugh Sultan Begum in the Shah-i Zinda, Samarkand (Uzbekistan), c. 1385.

the same family. A significant symbol of the dynasty, over the years the tomb was augmented and restored.

The opulence of the Timurid court is undoubtedly best revealed in its palaces, but unfortunately not one has survived intact. Surviving descriptions, however, such as an account by the ambassador of the king of Castile, Don Ruy González de Clavijo, recount in detail the wonders of the gardens of Samarkand and their fine buildings decorated with tiles of azure and gold. In Timur's birthplace of Shahr-i Sabz, only the two gigantic pylons with an impressive ceramic decor standing at the entrance to the Aq Saray Palace (the White Palace) still stand. The decorations—a juxtaposition of cut-tile mosaic and polychrome tilework—carry the signature of a single individual: Muhammad Yusuf al-Tabrizi. Undoubtedly this ascription relates

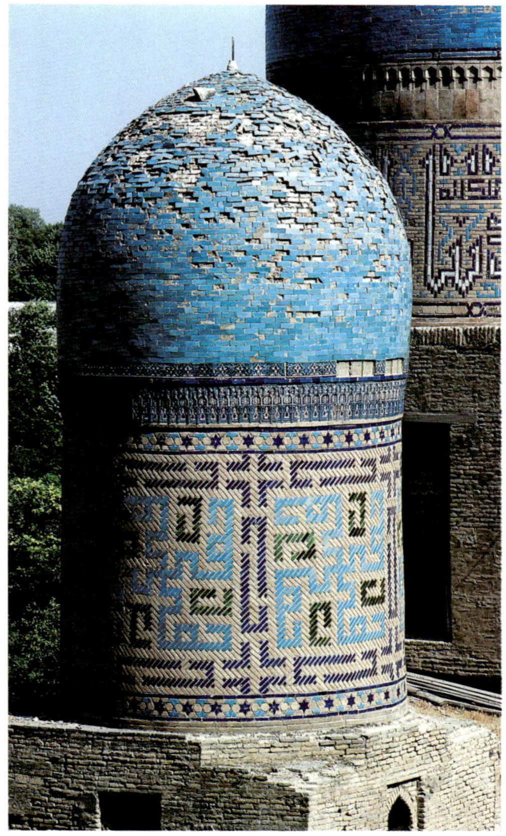

♦ Double-domed mausoleum known as that of Qadizada Rumi in the Shah-i Zinda, Samarkand (Uzbekistan), c. 1425. The *banna'i* brick decoration on the larger of the two drums displays a *hadith* of the Prophet: "A grave is the least of the dwellings of the beyond, yet the best on this earth."

♦ Cut-tile mosaic forming a grid pattern of interlaced borders and stars inset with palmettes and floral motifs. Tuman Aqa funerary complex in the Shah-i Zinda, Samarkand (Uzbekistan), c. 1405.

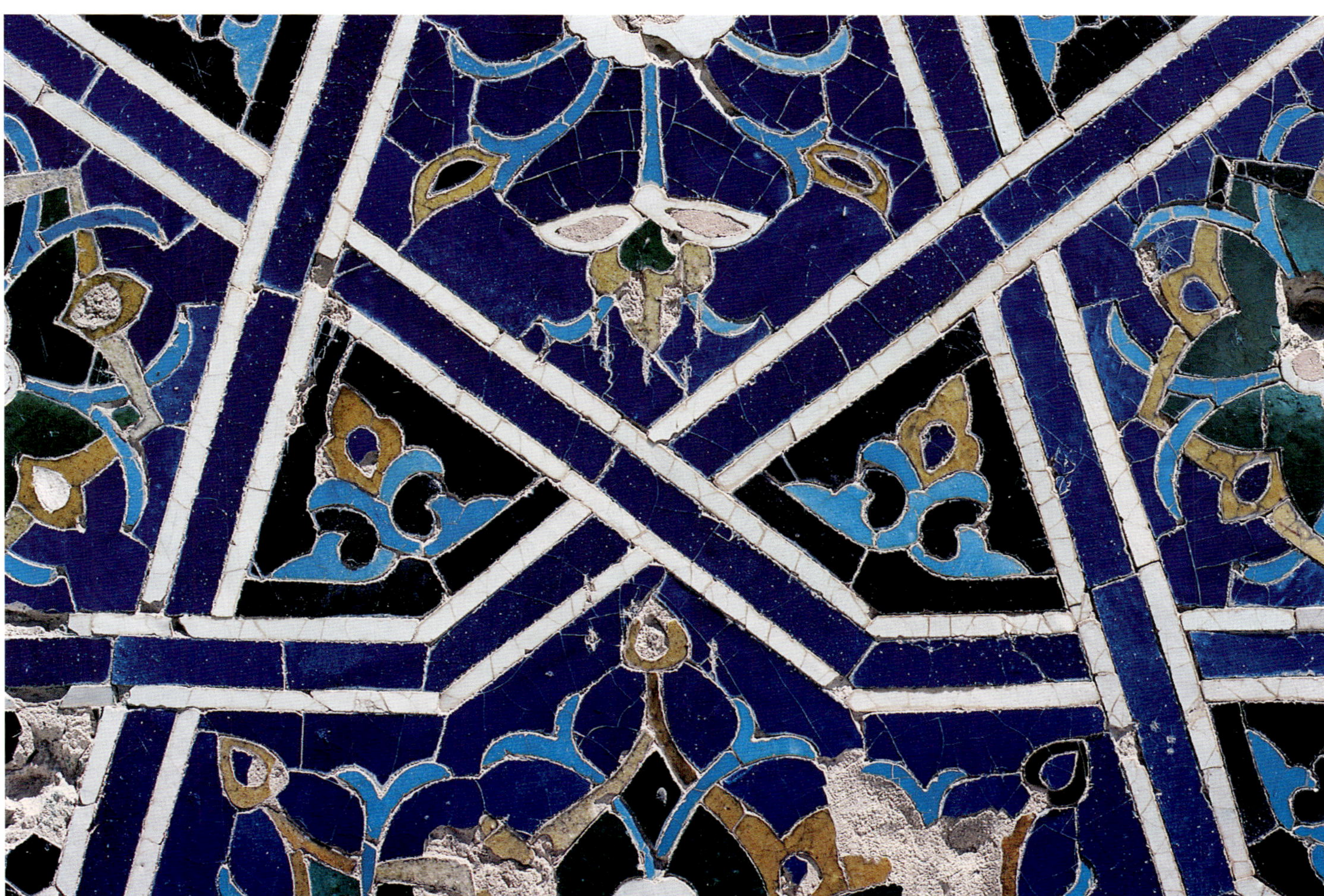

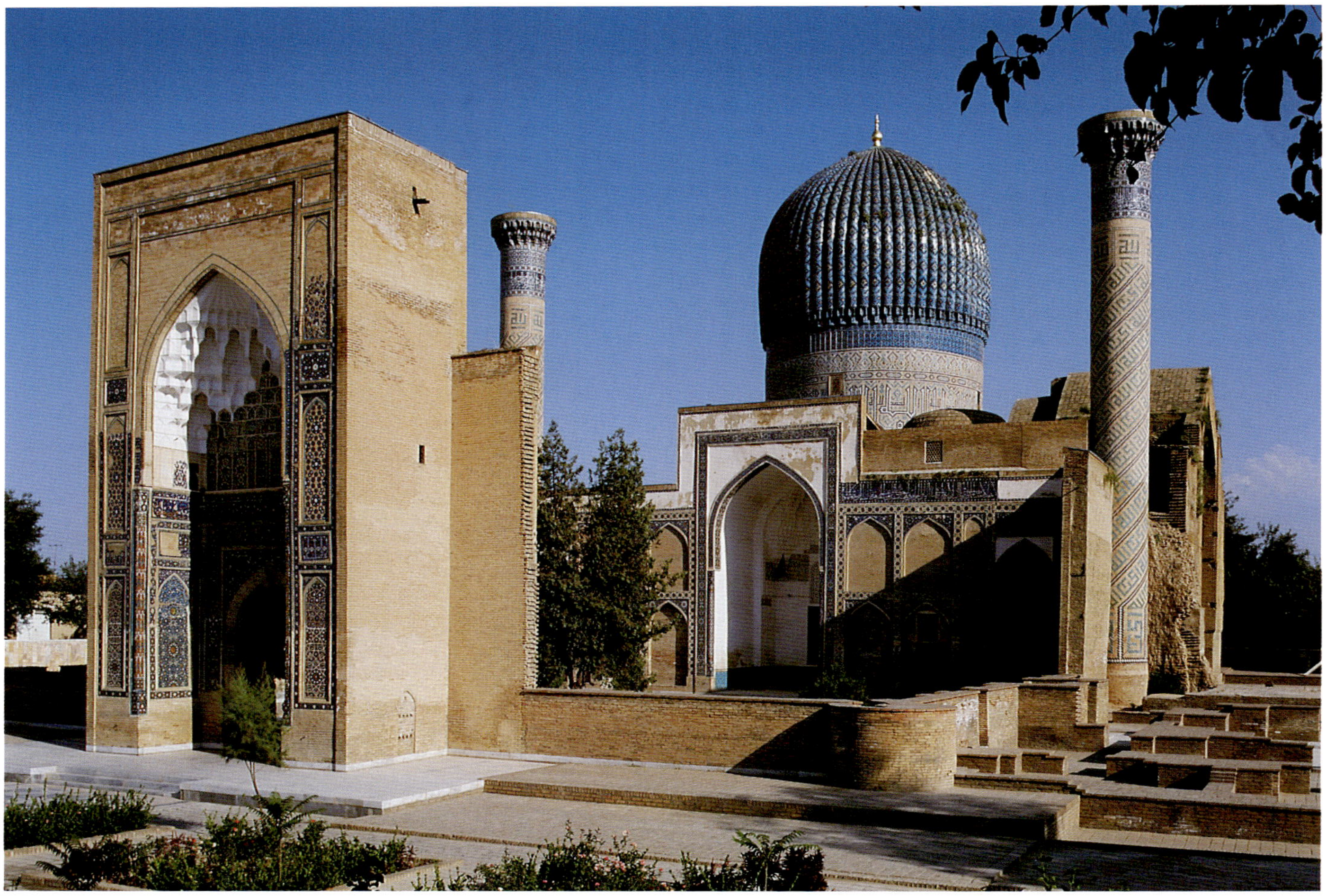

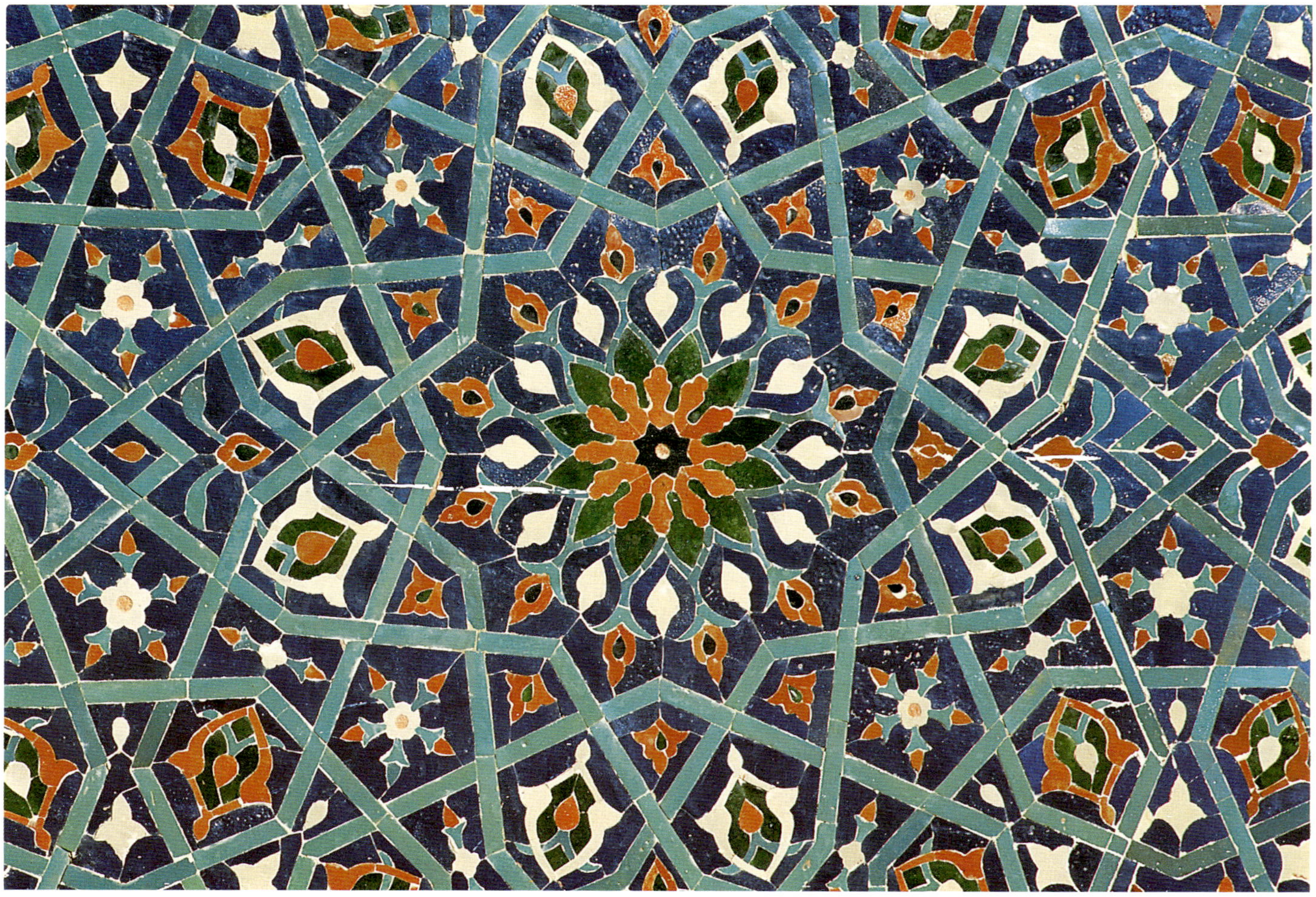

solely to the mosaic work, since, according to the sources, the polychrome tiles were made by artists of the Khwarazm.[48]

Commenced in 1399 after the conqueror's return from the Indian campaign, the Great Mosque at Samarkand (known as the Bibi Khanum Mosque) provided a suitable reflection of his blatant megalomania. The original plan of the mosque reverted in part to the idea of the four-*iwan* court but adapted to a model seen in India, the mosque of Muhammad Shah Tughluq in Delhi (the Begumpuri *masjid*). Entry is gained though a gigantic vaulted gate: in the line of axis and on the other side of the court lies a prayer hall crowned by an impressive dome and framed by engaged minarets. On either side of the court, rooms crowned by domes with gadroons connect to the remainder of the building by galleries borne on stone columns. The project was grandiose and the decoration on a par with the demands of its august patron; however, hardly had work been completed in 1404 than the devastation began. The problems arising from the over-ambitious construction were exacerbated by the prevailing tectonic and seismic conditions. The restoration of this gigantic monument, which was started as early as the turn of the twentieth century, has accelerated—if not always with an equal degree of success—in recent years.

The *madrasa* of Prince Ulugh Beg was built at the time that he held the governorship of Samarkand, between 1417 and 1420. It too conforms to the generally accepted four-*iwan* court plan; its majestic gateway, adorned with a pediment decorated with a star pattern and flanked by minarets at the corners, exemplifies the prince's taste for astronomical observation. Tragically, the observatory built in Samarkand was demolished following Ulugh Beg's assassination at the hands of his own son. Ulugh Beg also erected *madrasas* in other cities, in particular Bukhara and Gijduvan. The Gök Gunbad Mosque in Shahr-i Sabz also dates from the reign of Ulugh Beg (1435–36). Heavily restored today, only the prayer hall remains, although it too has an entirely rebuilt pediment.

Timurid architecture flowered elsewhere than in central Asia, on the territories that are today Iran and Afghanistan, for example. Numbering among some of the finest examples of Timurid art, monuments in Afghanistan have suffered much from ill-treatment in recent decades. The complex of Gawhar Shad, wife of Shah Rokh, built in Herat in 1417, which benefited from the assistance of one of the greatest architects of the time, Qawam al-Din of Shiraz, was called "one of the noblest ornaments of the court of Shah Rokh" by its contemporaries. The *madrasa* was finished in 1432, whereas the *musalla*, unfinished at the death of the architect in 1438, was almost entirely destroyed in 1885. The *madrasa* of Gawhar Shad also includes a mausoleum with a ribbed dome decorated externally in ceramic, principally in underglaze-painted tiles.

GUR-I MIR, SAMARKAND (UZBEKISTAN), BEGUN C. 1400

FACING PAGE

♦ Mausoleum of the Timurid family.

♦ Panel of cut-tile mosaic forming a twelve-pointed star pattern.

♦ Aq Saray Palace, Sahr-i Sabz (Uzbekistan), end of the fourteenth century. Only the colossal entrance pylons survive of this grandiose palace. The lower part of the structure is lined with tiles, while the upper reaches are decorated in *banna'i* brickwork.

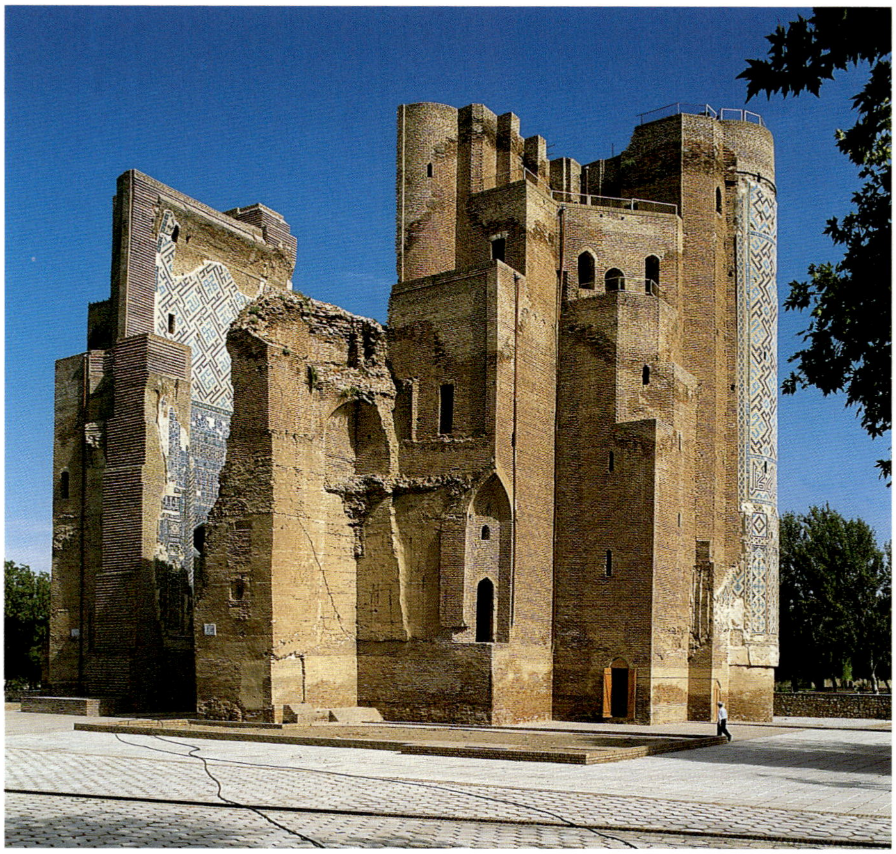

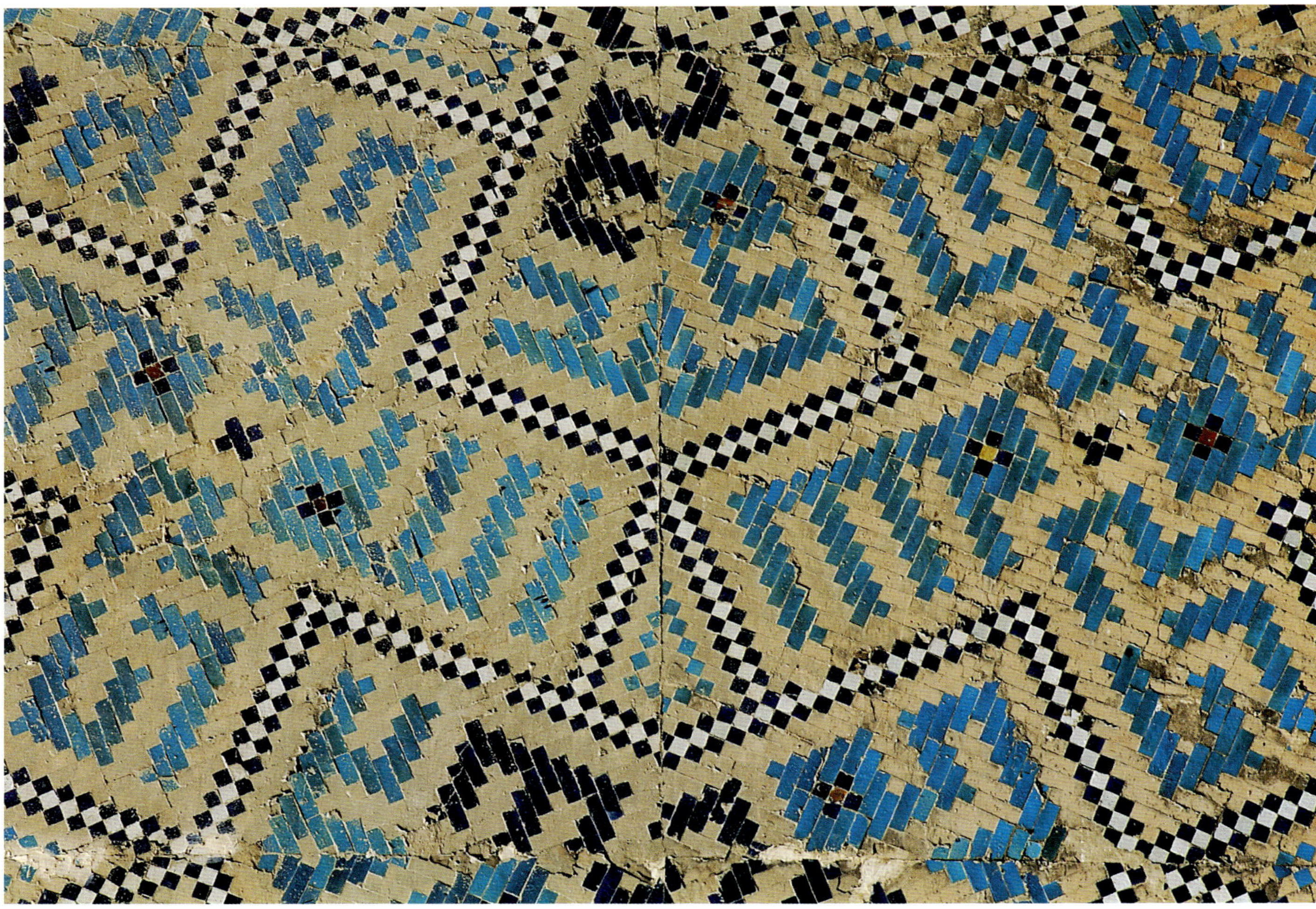

♦ *Madrasa* of Ulugh Beg, Samarkand (Uzbekistan), 1417–20. *Banna'i* brick wall revetment with motifs in the form of the *shahada* (Islamic profession of faith).

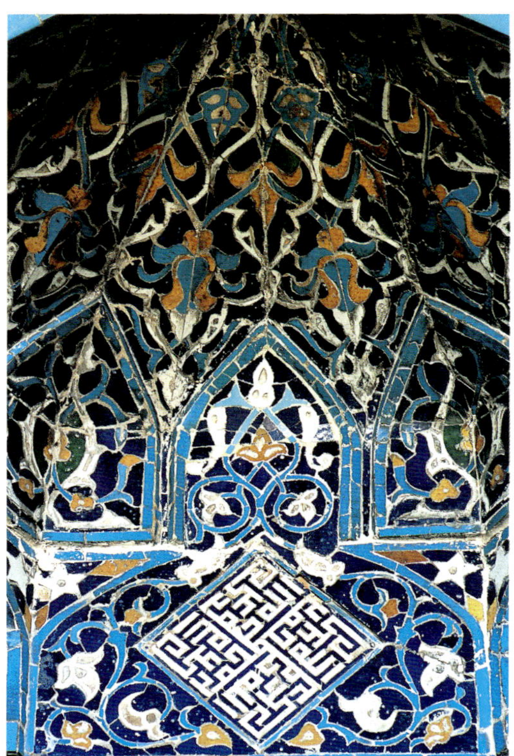

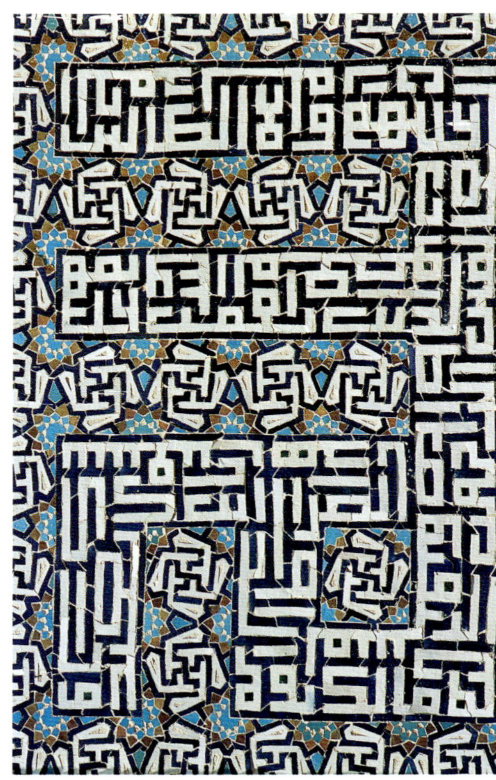

MIR CHAQMAQ MOSQUE, YADZ (IRAN), 1437

RIGHT

♦ Conch of the *mihrab* lined with cut-tile mosaic. The square in the middle repeats four times in labyrinthine Kufic the names of Allah, Muhammad, and `Ali.

♦ Inscriptional panel. The words in an angular and highly interlocked Kufic spell out the name of Allah.

FACING PAGE, TOP

♦ Mosque of the Shah, Mashhad (Iran), erected in 1451 by the Emir Malik Shah. The two brick minarets display a decoration inlaid with floral motifs and religious inscriptions in cut-tile mosaic.

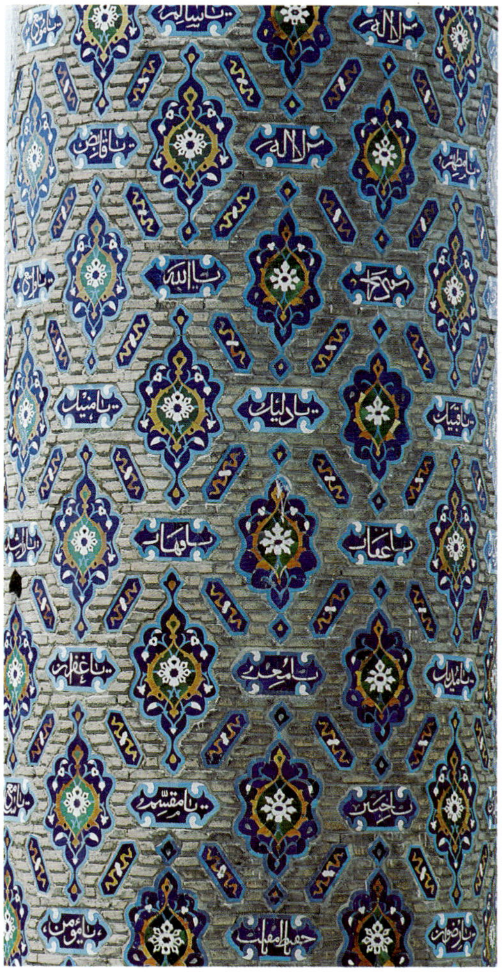

The mosque commissioned by Gawhar Shad to honor the sanctuary of the *imam* Reza at Mashhad is also the work of the Shiraz master Qawam al-Din. Enclosed within the sanctuary complex, the mosque presents no external frontage, but the great court, flanked by its four *iwans* (that of the prayer hall is bounded by cylindrical minarets), releases an explosion of color greatly enhanced by the extensive use of ceramic decoration comprising intricate twisting leaf-scrolls and epigraphic friezes. In Khargird, Khurasan, a splendid *madrasa* was built, most probably under the patronage of Shah Rokh, between 1438 and 1445. The harmoniously proportioned main facade incorporates a significant quantity of ceramic decoration, most conspicuously in the form of large polychrome "black line" stars, the vast majority of which have unfortunately disappeared.

Several "painter-designers" (*naqqash*) from the royal libraries also participated in these programs of monumental decoration. One of the most celebrated cases is that of Khwaja Mirak Naqqash, painter by appointment to the court of Herat, who worked on the decoration of the congregational mosque of that city.[49] Other less renowned artists, equally going by the professional title of *naqqash*, also made their marks in projects other than manuscript painting.[50]

♦ Gök Gunbad Mosque at Shahr-i Sabz (Uzbekistan), 1435–36. Although the monument has been completely restored in the last few years (both dome and facade have been entirely refurbished), the lower parts remain original.

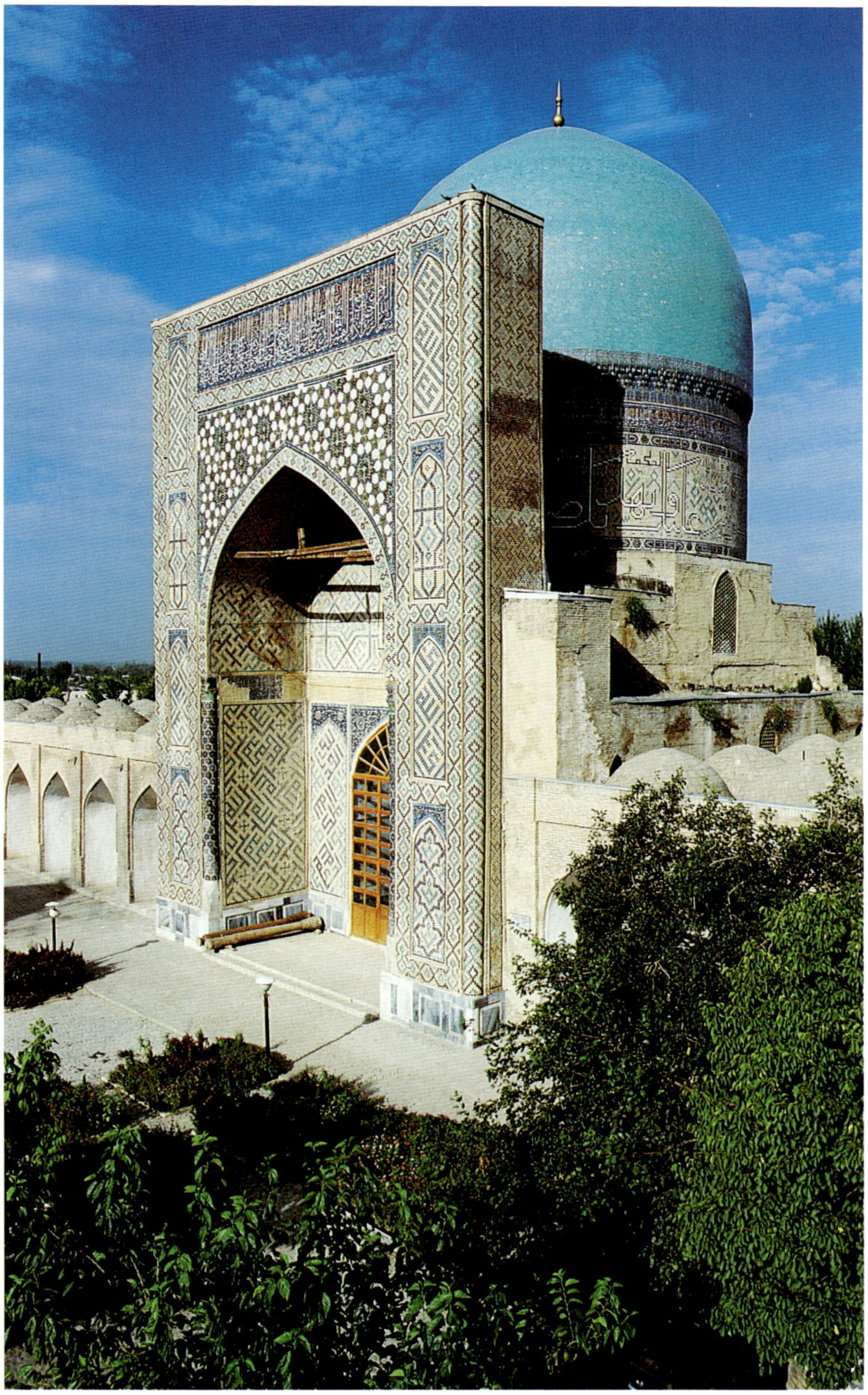

Central Asia under Uzbek Dominion

At the beginning of the sixteenth century, the Timurid empire in central Asia fell into the hands of the Uzbeks under the leadership of the Shaybanid khan. The Shaybanid capital, Bukhara, acquired its present-day appearance essentially during the reign of the most powerful of these khans, `Abdallah Khan II. Many religious and secular monuments sprung up at this time, among them mosques, *madrasas*, and caravansaries. A significant role was accorded ceramic decoration in these constructions, which tended to be designed in accordance with a principle of symmetry—especially visible in the facades. For instance, in 1514 the Great Mosque of Bukhara, with its venerable Kalan minaret, was entirely rebuilt.

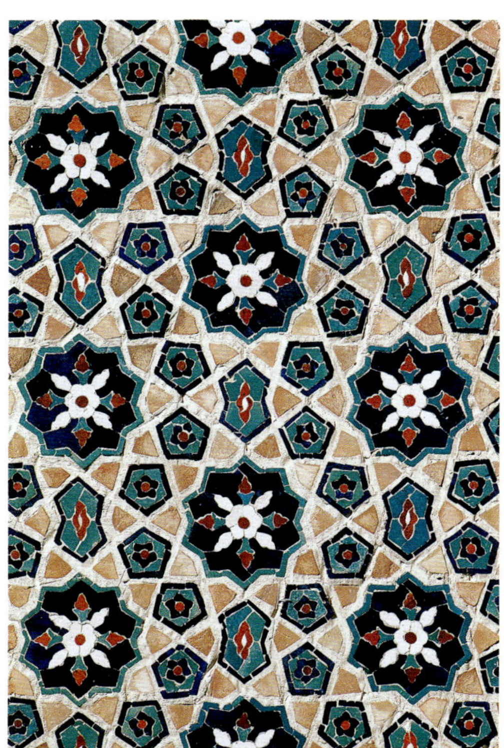

♦ Wall facing showing a ten-pointed star pattern in cut-tile mosaic. Mausoleum of Zengi Ata, Tashkent (Uzbekistan), founded at the end of the fourteenth century.

Facing this construction, on the opposite side of a vast square, is the Mir-i `Arab *madrasa*, erected in 1535–36. The arrangement of two monumental buildings mirroring one another is known as *kosh* (couple). It recurs in the west of the Pay-i Kaylan complex, where two *madrasas* face one another, that of the Mother of Khan (Madar-i Khan, 1566–67) and that of `Abdallah Khan (1588–90). The same idea lies behind the construction of the Char Bakr funerary complex, five kilometers to the west of the city, where `Abdallah Khan founded a necropolis (1560–63) incorporating a mosque and a *khaneqa*, the two domed buildings being connected by a chambered gallery.

The Lab-i Hauz complex at Bukhara was initiated by the construction of the Kukeltash *madrasa* (1568–69) bordering one of the sides of the public pool (*hauz*). During the following century, two new monuments were built to further frame the pool: the *khaneqa* and the Nadir Divan Begi *madrasa*, completed in 1620 and 1622 respectively. The *madrasa*, its gateway decorated by the recently restored gigantic facing *simorghs* (a fabulous bird redolent of a Chinese-style phoenix) was, according to one anecdote that has come down to us, initially designed to house a caravansary. The story goes that the emir had been invited to the official inauguration of the building; on taking leave of his host, and rather the worse for drink, the honored guest mistakenly announced: "I thank you for this marvelous *madrasa*." Following this misunderstanding, Nadir Divan Begi, unwilling to contradict the emir's will, decided to transform the building into a *madrasa*.

This taste for architectural ensembles also recurs in Samarkand, in and around Registan Square. In 1619 the governor of the city, Yalangtush, demolished the dilapidated *khaneqa* Ulugh Beg had built opposite the Timurid prince's *madrasa*, and ordered the construction of a *madrasa* known by the name of Shir-dar ("with lions"; in reality "with tigers"), which was finally completed in 1636. Under the entrance *iwan* to the *madrasa*, an inscription on a floral panel in cut-tile mosaic appears on which can be read the following pronouncement: *In `amal-i Muhammad `Avaz-i Samarqandi* ("This is the work of Muhammad `Avaz of Samarkand").[51] A certain `Avaz Muhammad is known to be one of the painters to have participated in the illumination of a manuscript of the *Khamsa* by Nezami dated 1668–71. Consequently, the question arises as to whether the artist whose name appears on the *madrasa* might be the same as the painter. In any event, the name of Muhammad `Avaz-i Samarqandi should be taken as that of a *naqqash* ("painter-designer") celebrated in the field of architectural decoration. The recent publication of the "Topkapi Scroll" provides a welcome opportunity to reexamine drawings executed by sixteenth- and seventeenth-century Uzbek artists for monuments at Bukhara.[52]

At the rear of the square stands a more recent *madrasa* erected between 1646 and 1660, known as Tala-kari (or Tila-kari, meaning "golden"). The majestic gateway is embellished with a pediment on which two rosettes essentially yellow in color emerge from a sky-blue ground. On the other hand, the major role in the interior decor is taken by painting, with gold (the origin of the name of the *madrasa*) used extensively.

The *madrasa* of `Abd al-`Aziz in Bukhara was constructed by the emir of the same name in 1651–52 to stand opposite the one Prince Ulugh Beg had built in the city. On either side of the facade, which opens into a lofty vault hung with *muqarnas*, are two large, identical cut-tile mosaic panels bearing a floral composition. Crafted in a style reminiscent of Indian work at the Chini-ka Rauza at Agra (c. 1640), the lower half of the composition on the panel to the right-hand side includes an inscription that stretches over two cartouches. According to L. Y. Mankovskaya, who informs us that the names of the master craftsmen responsible for the monument are inscribed on the frontage (notably, that of the chief architect, Muhammad Salih, and the calligrapher, Muhammad Amin),

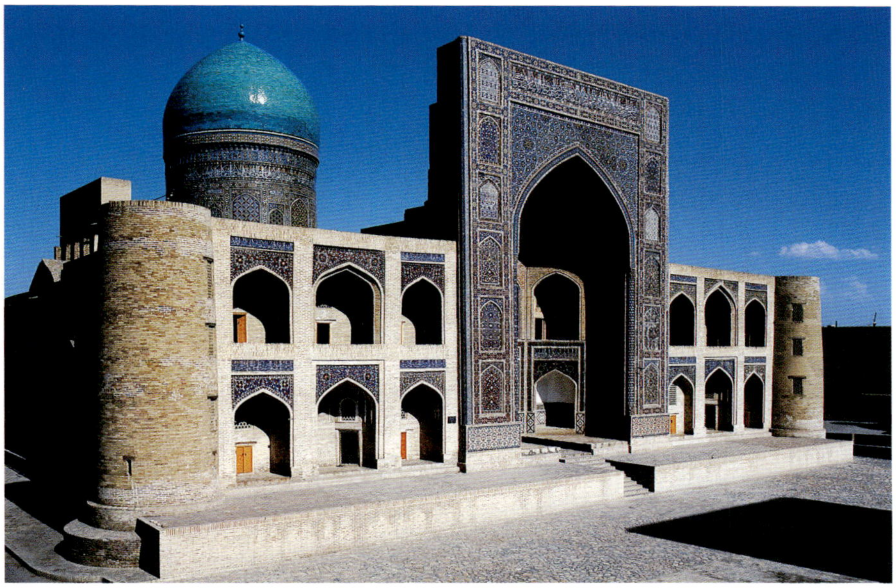

♦ Facade of the Mir-i `Arab *madrasa*, Bukhara (Uzbekistan), 1535–36, built opposite the Great Mosque.

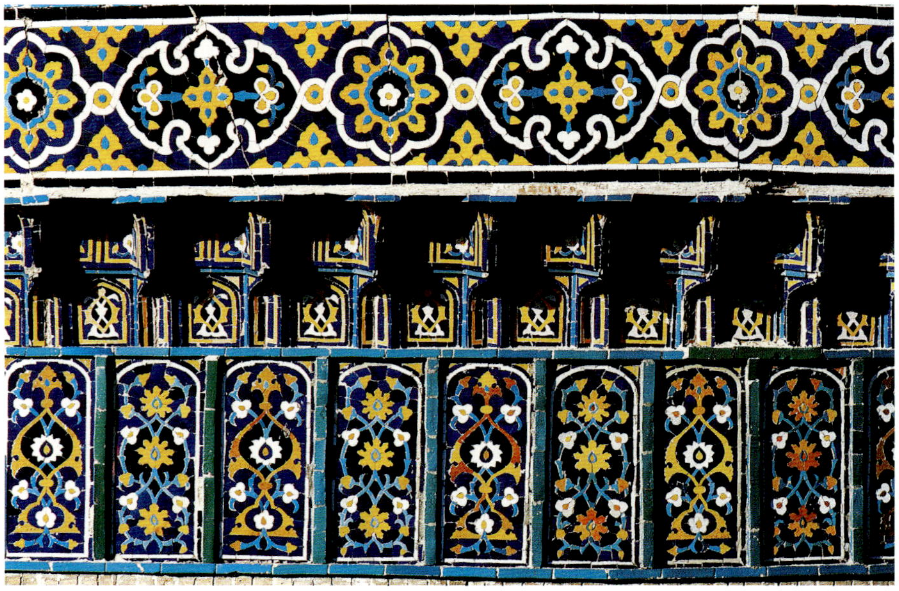

♦ Overhanging cornice with *muqarnas* clad in cut-tile mosaic. Mir-i `Arab *madrasa*, Bukhara (Uzbekistan), 1535–36.

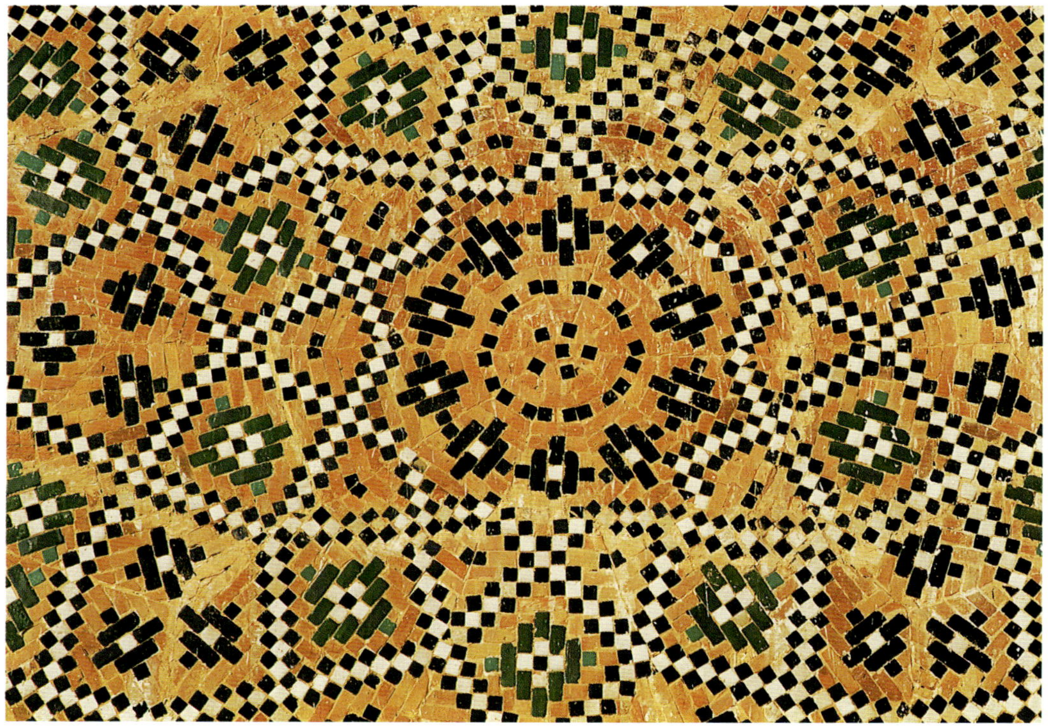

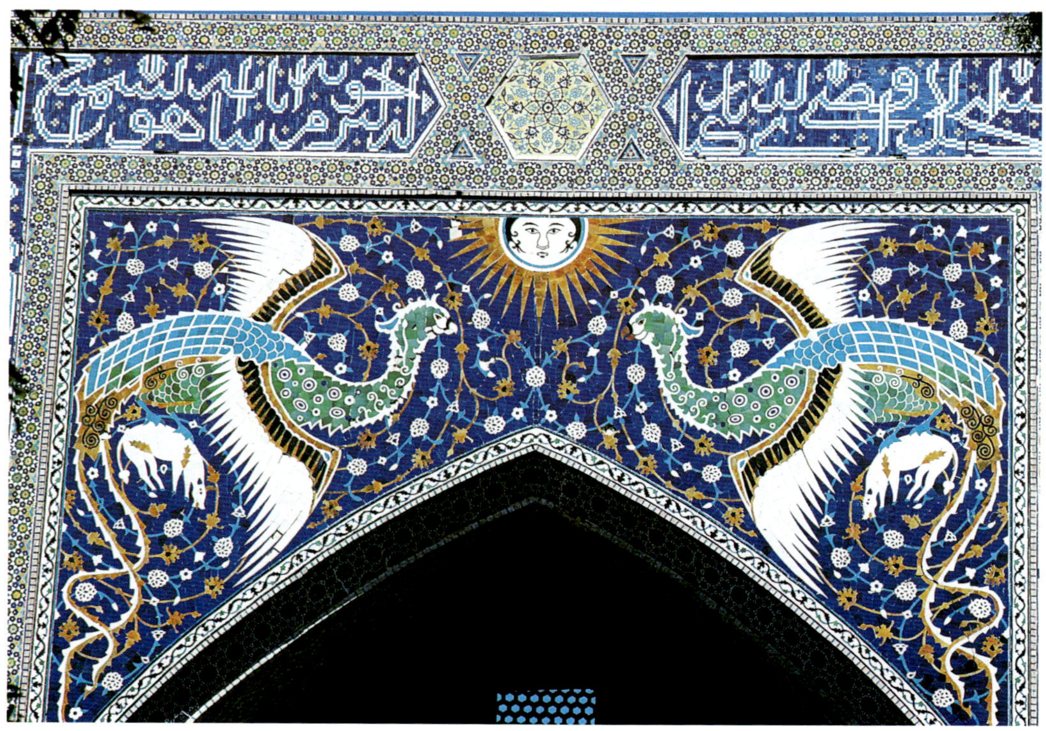

FACING PAGE

♦ Detail of the cut-tile mosaic employing motifs inspired by Timurid forms. Shir-dar *madrasa*, Samarkand (Uzbekistan), 1639.

RIGHT

♦ Facade decoration in the style of *banna'i* brickwork, consisting of a series of tiny elements of square and oblong shape arranged into a ten-branched star motif. `Abdallah Khan *madrasa*, Bukhara (Uzbekistan), 1588–90.

♦ *Pishtaq* arch flanked by *simurghs* (mythical birds). *Madrasa* of Nadir Divan Begi, Bukhara (Uzbekistan), 1622. This *madrasa* was still in a state of extreme disrepair at the turn of the twentieth century, but has since been much restored.

BELOW

♦ Wall clad in alternating unglazed and *banna'i* bricks forming inscriptions in angular Kufic. The window in the center has an openwork screen set with elements in ceramic. Shir-dar *madrasa*, Samarkand (Uzbekistan), 1639.

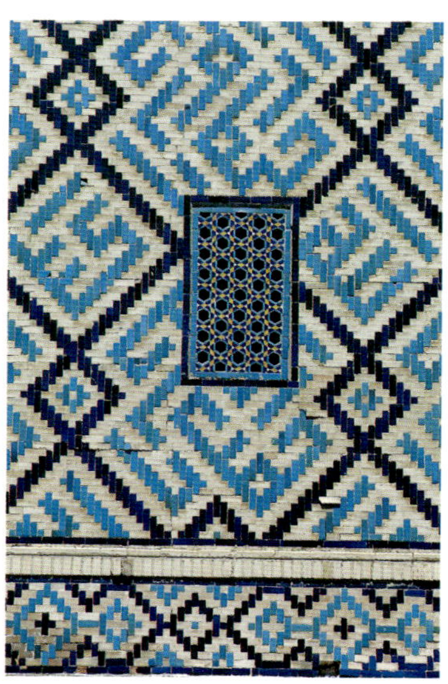

the name on the text of the panel would be Mim Khakan, son of Muhammad Amin.[53] Actually, the first cartouche has been partially damaged and might be read *band khaqani va din* ("slave of the *khaqan* and of religion"); the second clearly bears the name "Hajji Muhammad Amin." Clearly, the inscription on the two panels follows on logically (rather than being a name split over two cartouches) and even rhymes. Rather more disconcerting is the fact that Muhammad Yusuf Munshi, in his description of the *madrasa*, indicates that the inscriptions were executed by a certain Mawlana Muhammad Amin, and the question arises as to whether the calligrapher is related to the painter of the same name or if they are instead two different artists with the same name. The relevant passage runs: "Among the constructions [of `Abd al-`Aziz Khan] there is the *madrasa* in the town of Bukhara opposite that of the sovereign–martyr Mirza Ulugh Beg Gurkan. The exterior and interior are decorated with ceramic tiles (*kashi*) and its vault rises in elevated

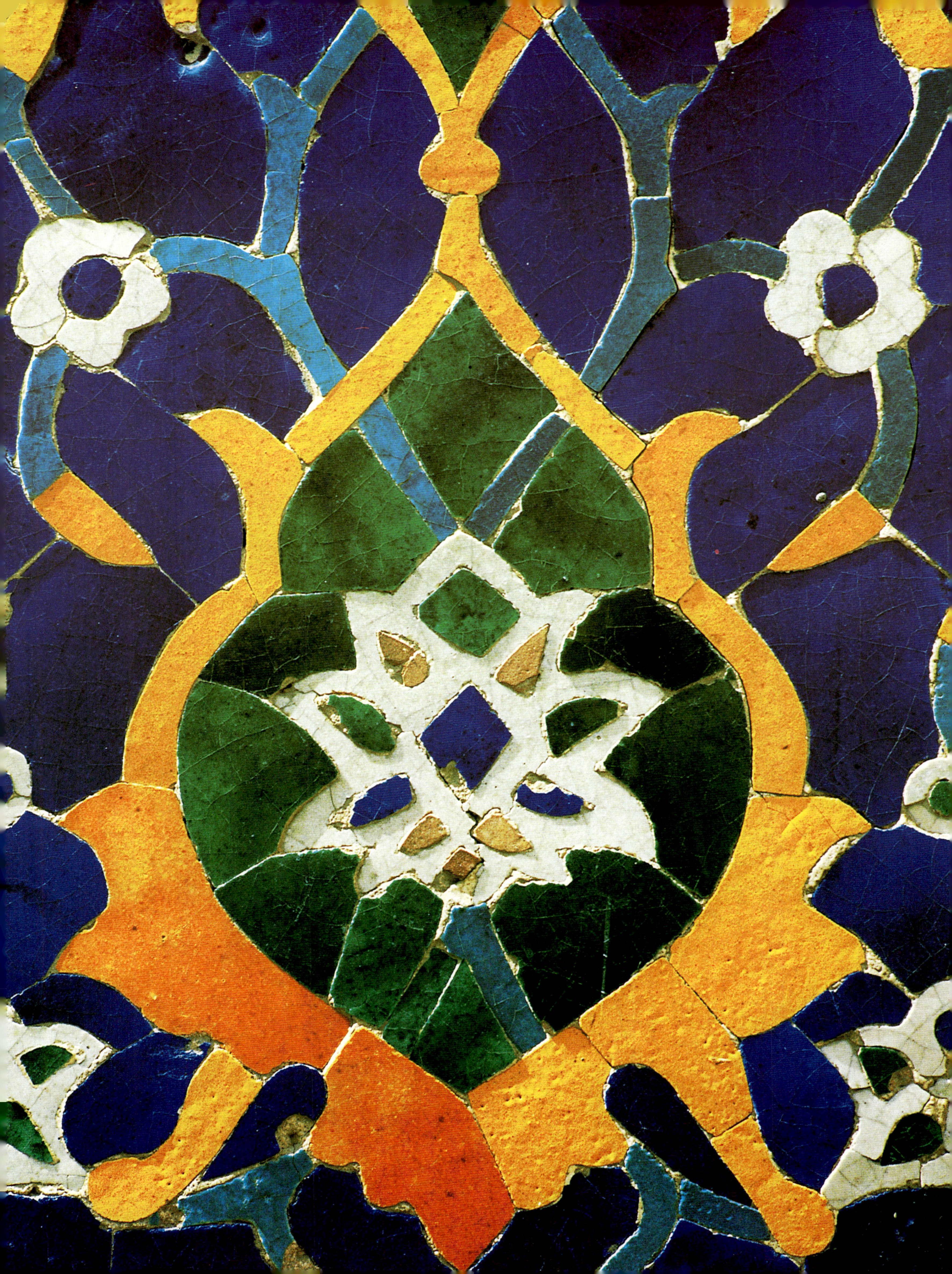

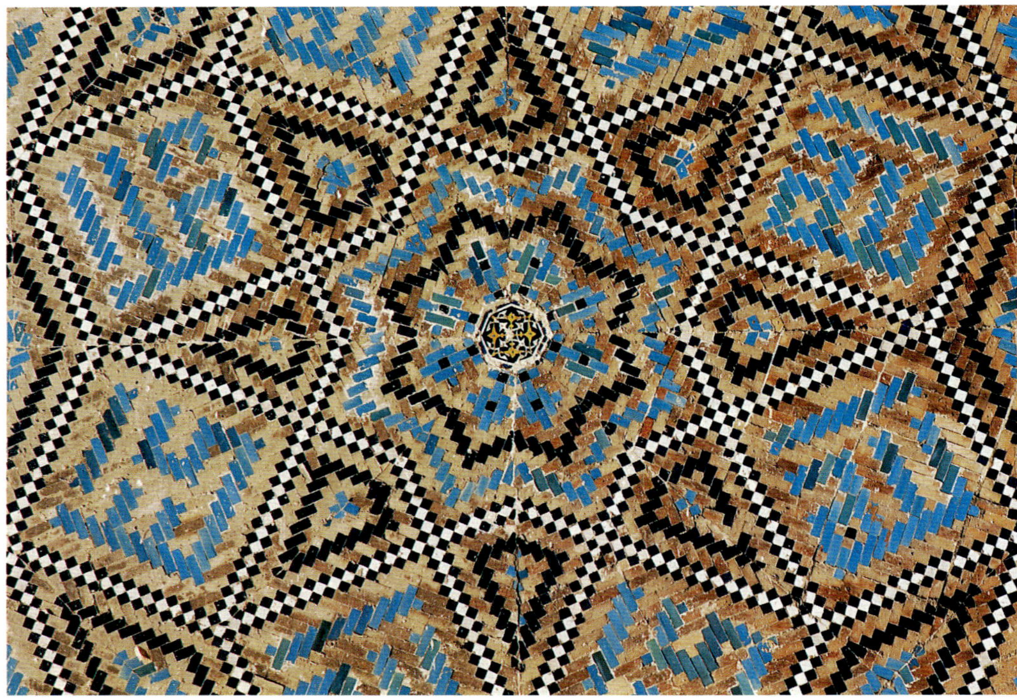

♦ Wall decorated with square and oblong elements arranged into an eight-pointed star. Shir-dar *madrasa*, Samarkand (Uzbekistan), 1639.

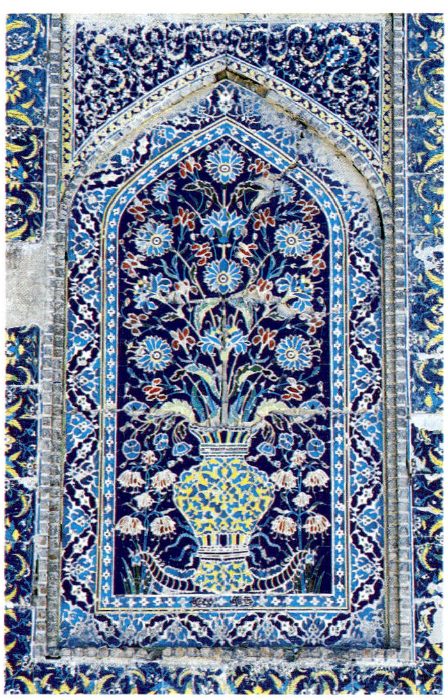

BELOW

♦ Cut-tile mosaic showing flowers in a vase. Niche on the facade of the *madrasa* of ʿAbd al-ʿAziz Khan, Bukhara (Uzbekistan), 1651–52. The style displays an Indian influence. The cartouche beneath the vase bears the signature of the artist, Hajji Muhammad Amin.

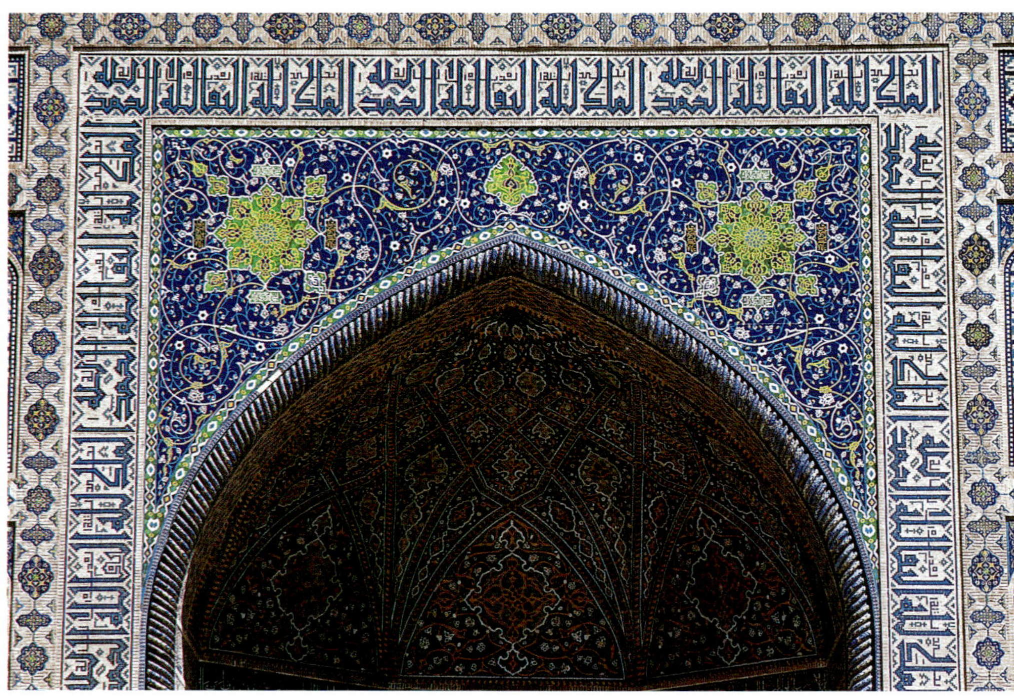

ABOVE, RIGHT

♦ Cut-tile mosaic lining the facade of the entrance *pishtaq* of the Tala-kari *madrasa*, Samarkand (Uzbekistan), 1646–60.

perfection like the chrysolite vault of the sky. The inscriptions were written in Thuluth script by the inestimable Mawlana Muhammad Amin who—despite poor eyesight—was foremost among the masters in calligraphy and other artists of his time."[54]

In addition to compositions in cut-tile mosaic, the interior of the *madrasa* comprises substantial areas of painted decoration. On the upper reaches of the prayer hall walls (to the right on entering) are tiny niches decorated with floral motifs painted blue on a white ground. Here, as outside, Indian influence is probable.

The painted mural decorations of central Asia in Timurid and Uzbek times have until now received scant attention from researchers.[55] Recent publications, such as those of Lisa Golombek, show the wealth of information that can be garnered from analyzing these paintings.[56] In particular, the

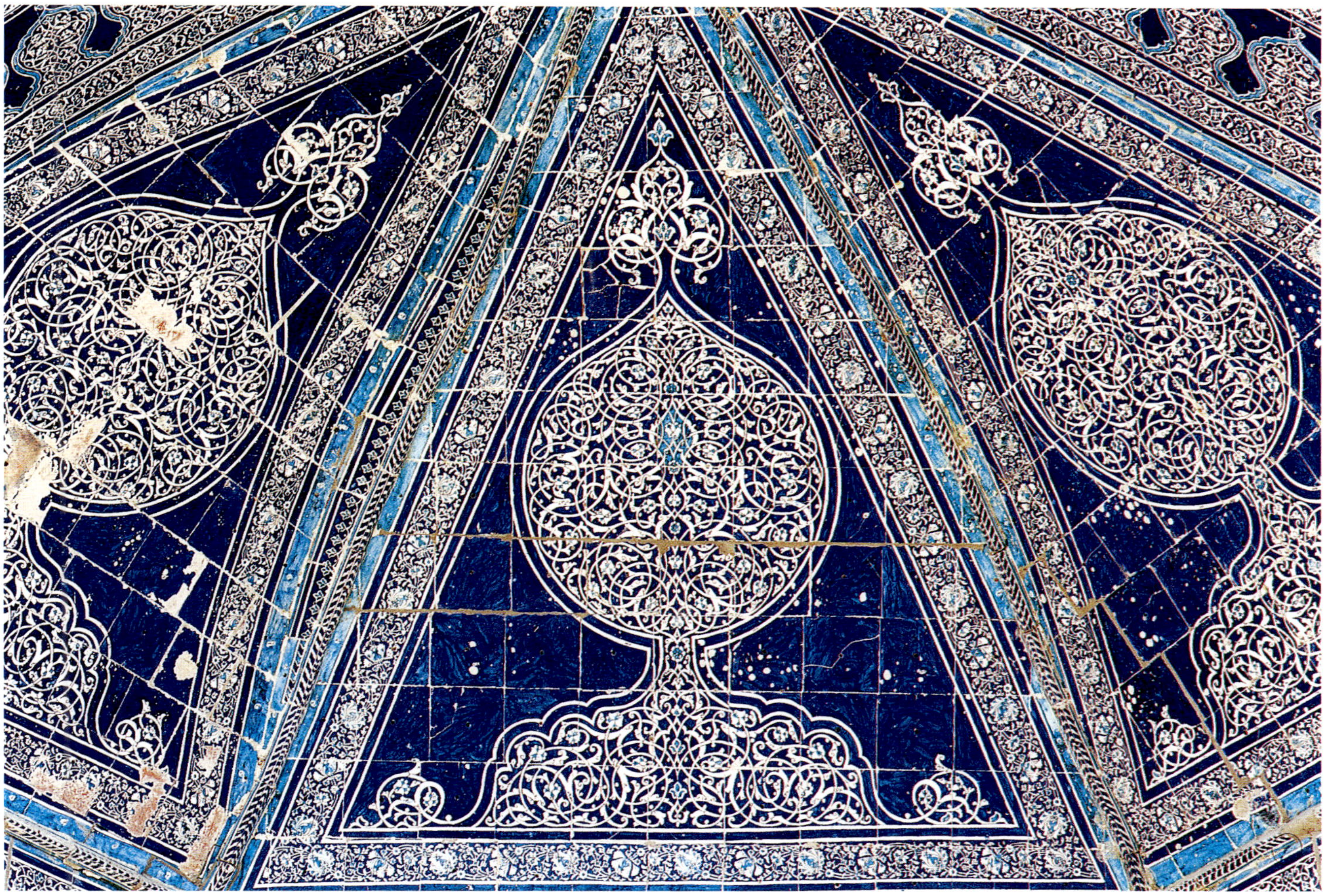

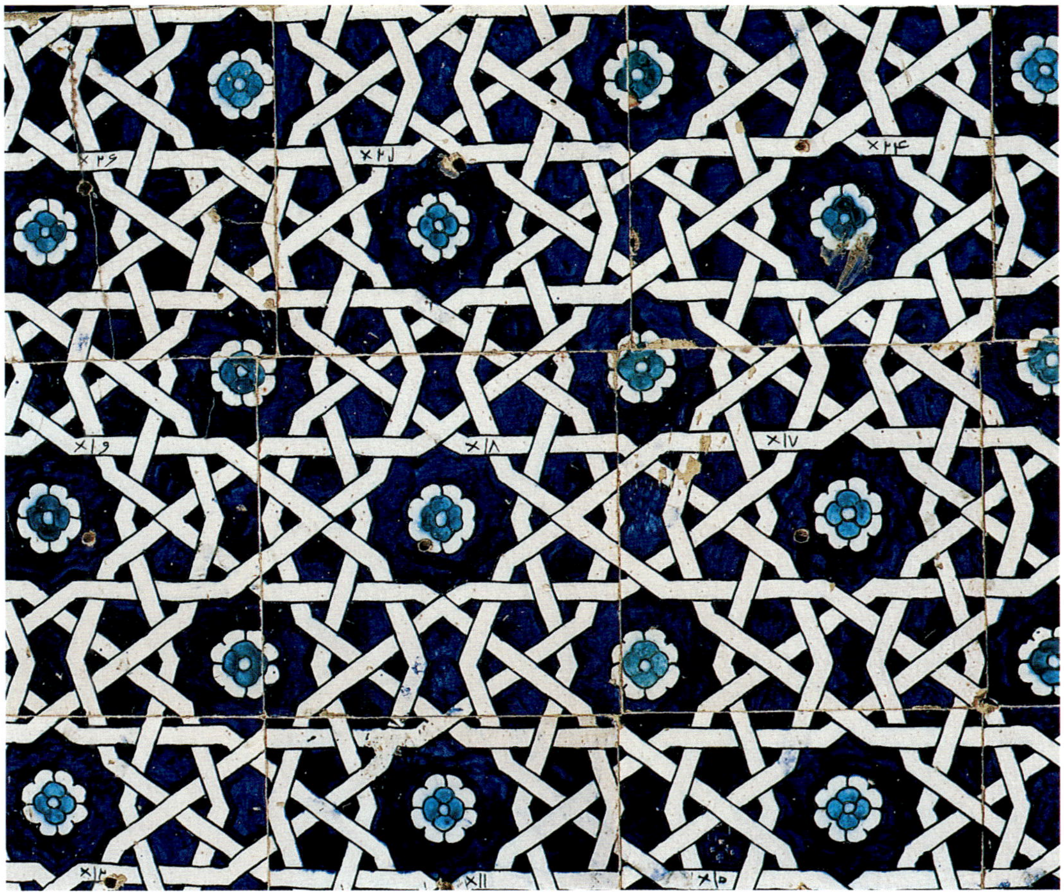

♦ Decoration of the vault over the entrance *pishtaq*. *Madrasa* of Muhammad Amin Khan, Khiva (Uzbekistan), 1851–55.

♦ Underglaze-painted tile decoration dating from the nineteenth century. Mausoleum of Pahlavan Mahmud, Khiva (Uzbekistan), founded in the fourteenth century.

FOLLOWING DOUBLE PAGE
♦ Panel of underglaze-painted tiles with an interlace leaf-scroll motif. Mosque of the Citadel, Khiva (Uzbekistan), 1838. The intricacy of the pattern meant that the craftsman had to number the tiles to facilitate assembly.

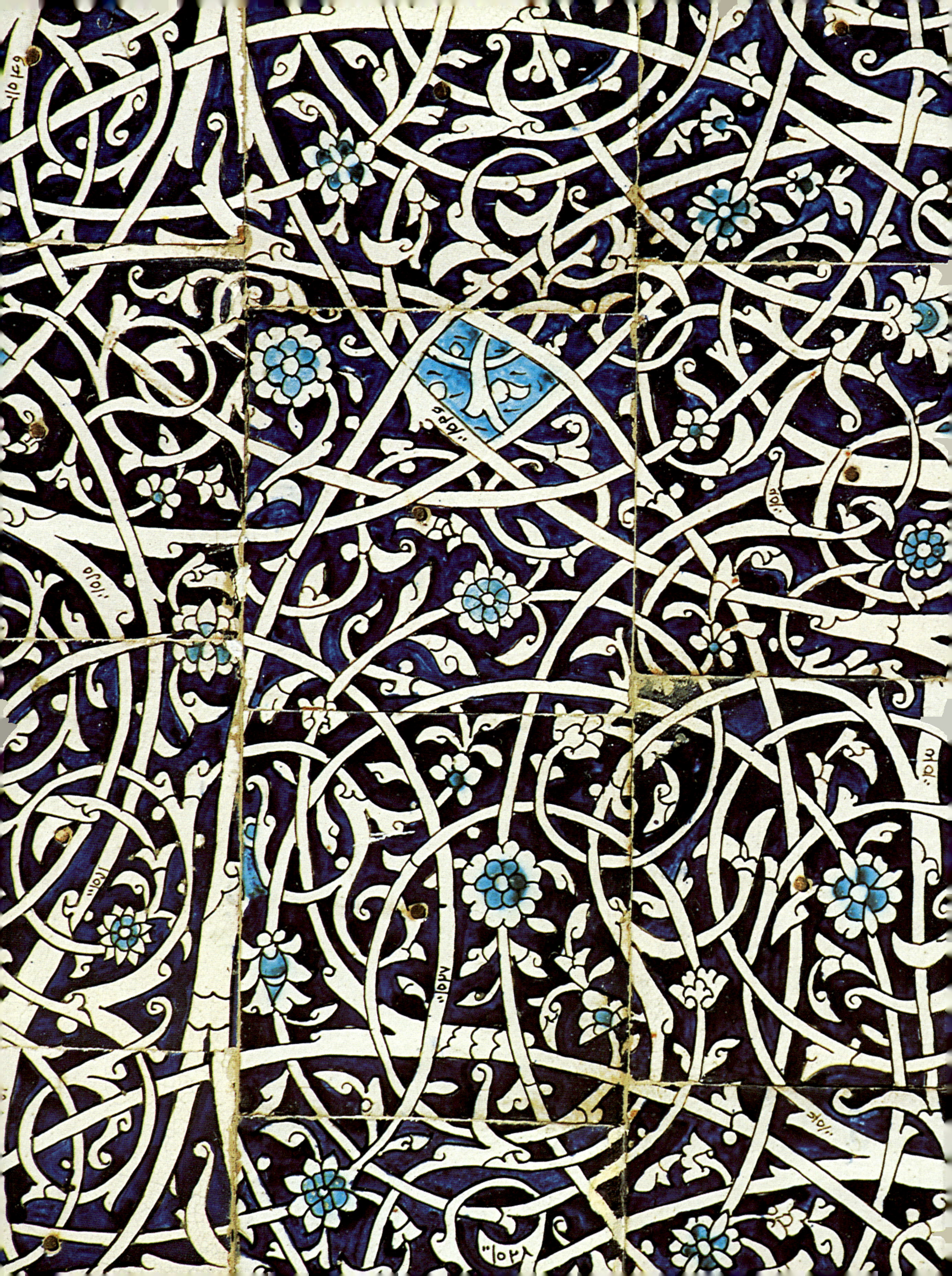

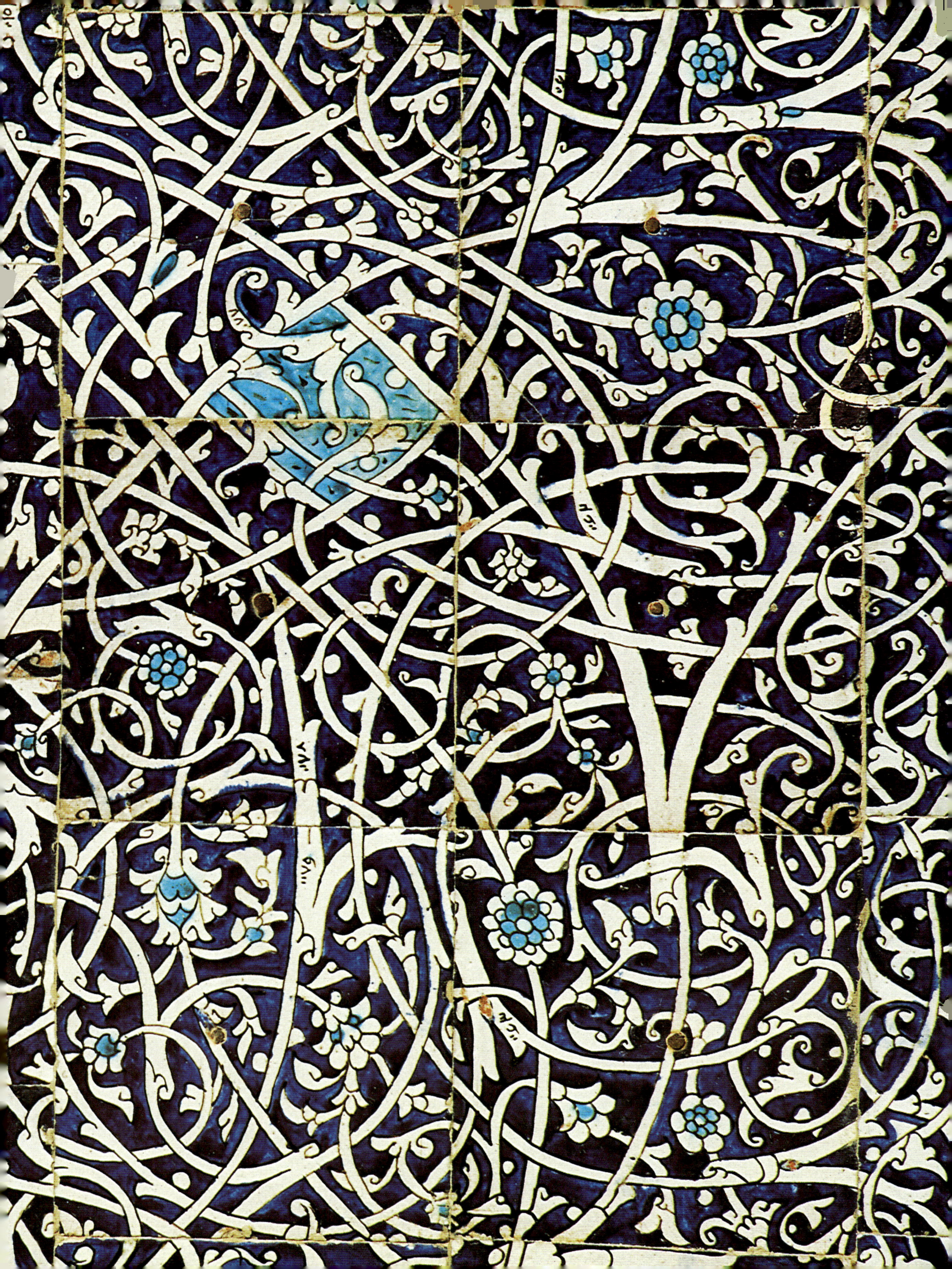

MOSQUE OF THE CITADEL, KHIVA (UZBEKISTAN), 1838

TOP TO BOTTOM

♦ Underglaze polychrome tile.

♦ Bands framing a large panel of underglaze-painted tiles embellished with decorative floral scrollwork and palmettes.

♦ Framing bands in underglaze-painted tilework.

♦ Framing bands and panel in underglaze-painted tilework.

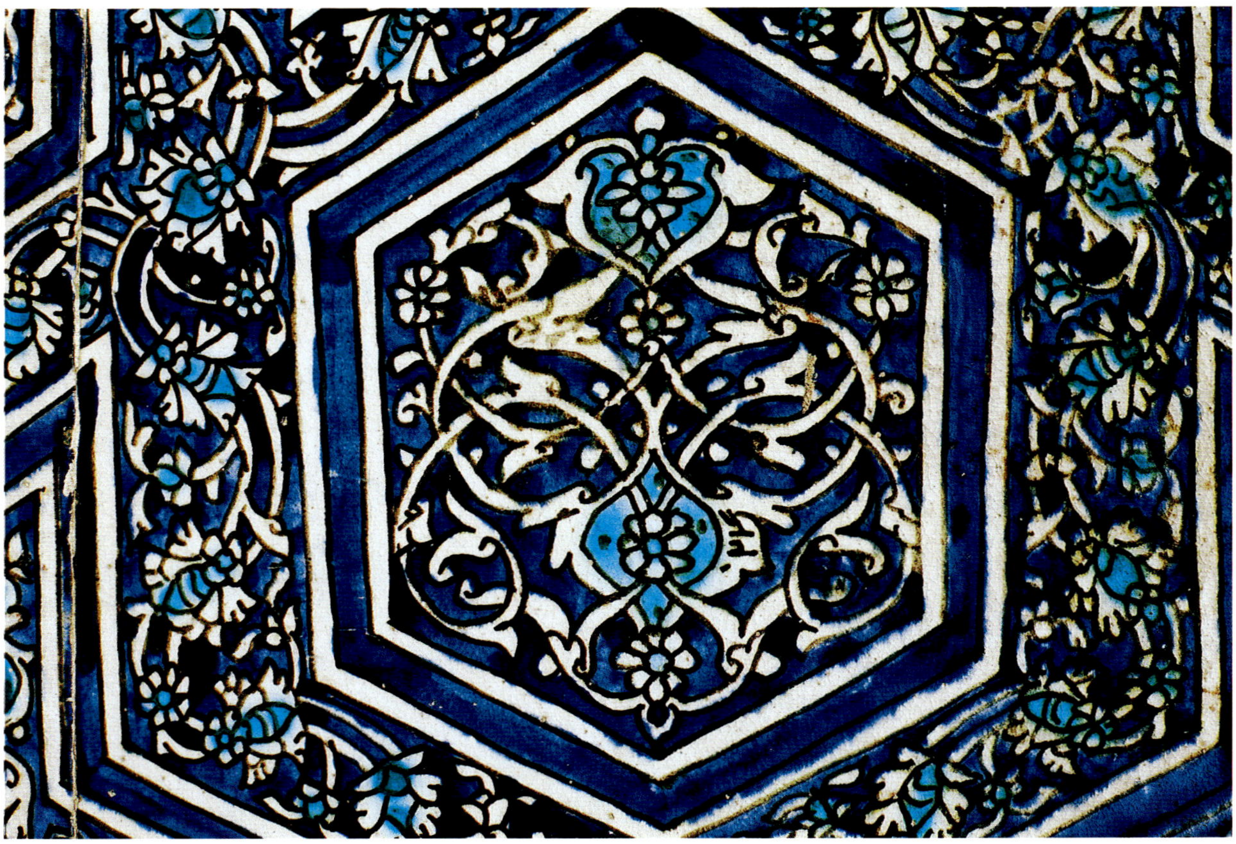

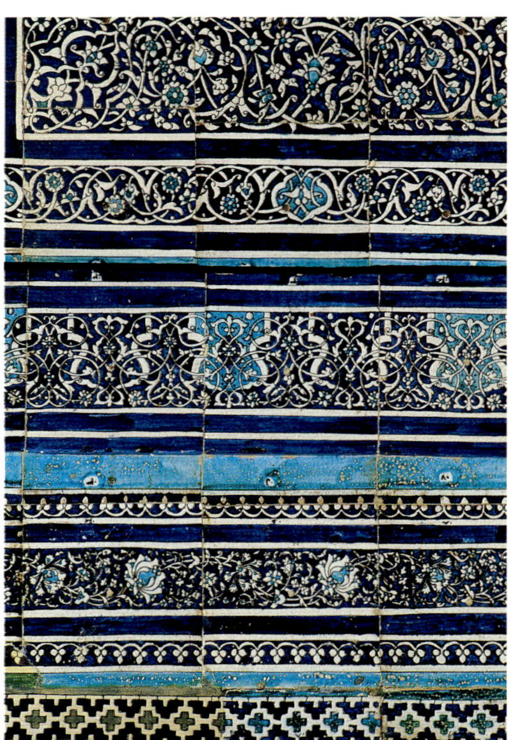

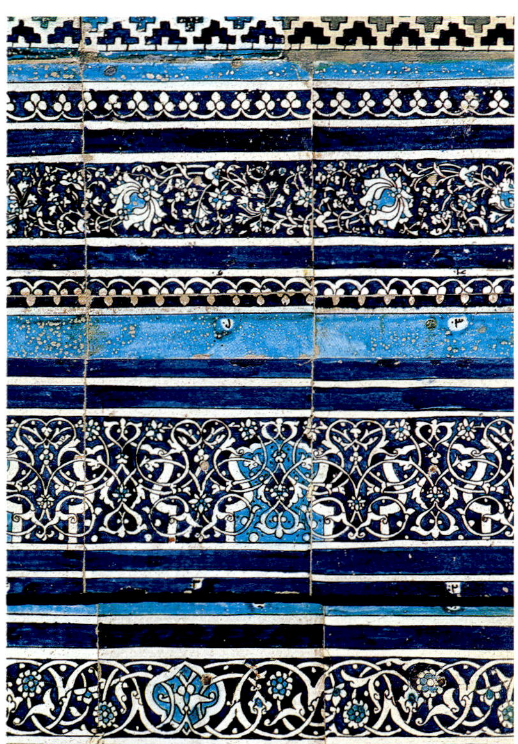

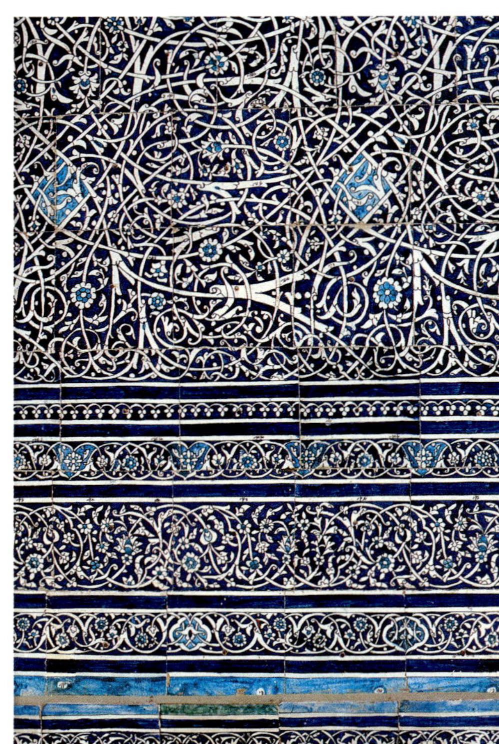

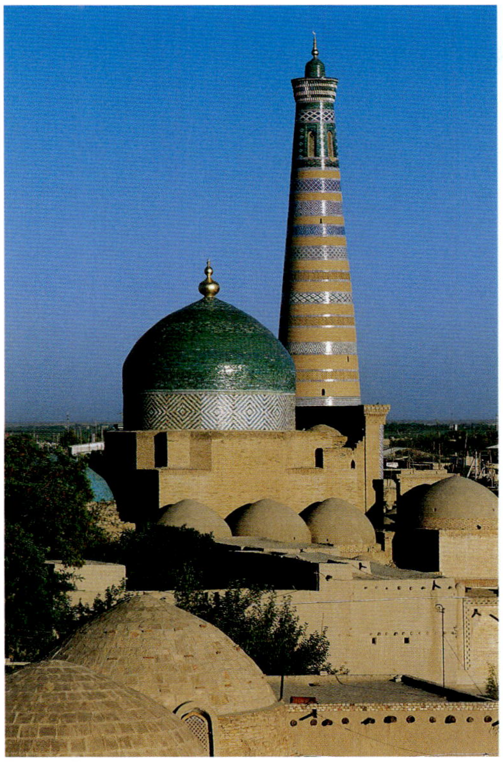

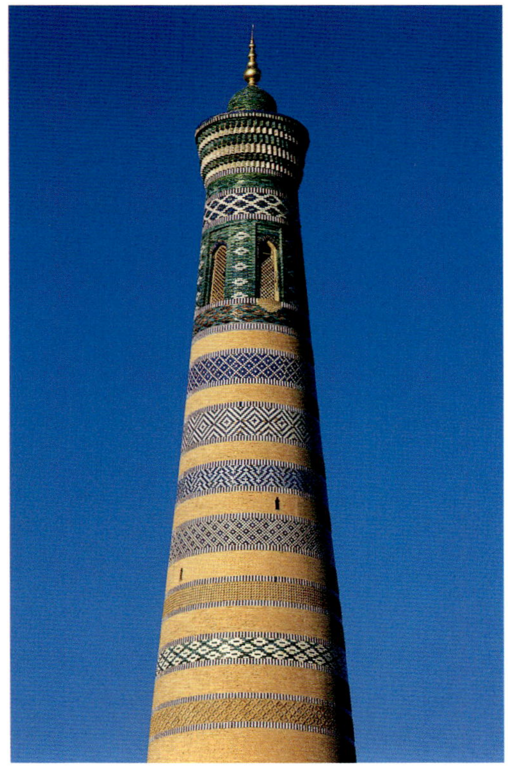

♦ *Madrasa* and minaret of Islam Khoja, Khiva (Uzbekistan), built between 1908 and 1910.

♦ Built of brick and decorated with colored *banna'i* forming geometrical bands, the minaret of Islam Khoja soars to a height of 44.6 m.

parallels between the murals and blue- and white-painted ceramics appear self-evident. There is no doubt that Chinese porcelain was the principal source of inspiration for such blue-and-white ceramics.[57] Additionally, it is recorded that Sultan Ulugh Beg himself possessed in Samarkand a "House of Porcelain" (the since vanished Chini-khana) that housed his personal collections. "Landscapes" began figuring on this porcelain from at least the mid-fourteenth century,[58] with depictions of architecture (pagodas) appearing at a later stage (perhaps in the course of the sixteenth century).[59] Nevertheless, the question of whether mural motifs in blue and white were directly taken from ceramic examples or whether the influence was indirect, remains unanswered.

By the mid-sixteenth century the Khiva khanate had won its autonomy. The majority of monuments surviving today, however, are of a later date, a prime example being the impressive ramparts girdling the city that date from 1842. Many Khiva monuments are characterized by ceramic ornament, predominantly in blue and white. The motifs, primarily nonfigurative arabesque scrolls, stem from the unbroken masterly tradition of underglaze polychrome ceramics. We have already mentioned the mausoleum of Sayyid 'Ala al-Din in Khiva (date uncertain), as well as the decorations of the mausoleum of Najm al-Din Kobra (around 1330). Most of these tiles bear the signature of Master 'Abdallah Djinn, so named because of his "diabolical" (and so "*djinn*-like") skill in draftsmanship. On its gate, the *madrasa* of Allah Quli Khan (1834) displays elegant spandrels, while skillfully crafted motifs clad the entrance *pishtaq*. The palace of the old citadel, which incorporates many ceramic-covered surfaces, was constructed in several phases; in its current state, the dates of 1838 (for the mosque) and 1855 appear inscribed on the foundation stone. The *madrasa* of Muhammad Rahim Khan II (1847–1910), a munificent patron and versifier who wrote under the nom de plume of Feruz, is located south of the old citadel and bears a date of 1871. The *madrasa* and minaret of Islam Khoja (44.6 meters high) were both erected between 1908 and 1910 and number among the very last constructions of the khanate period at Khiva.

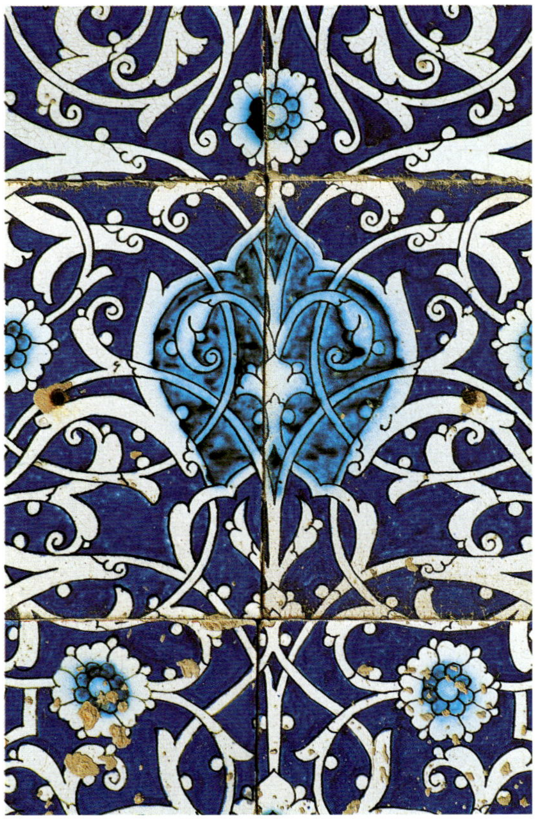

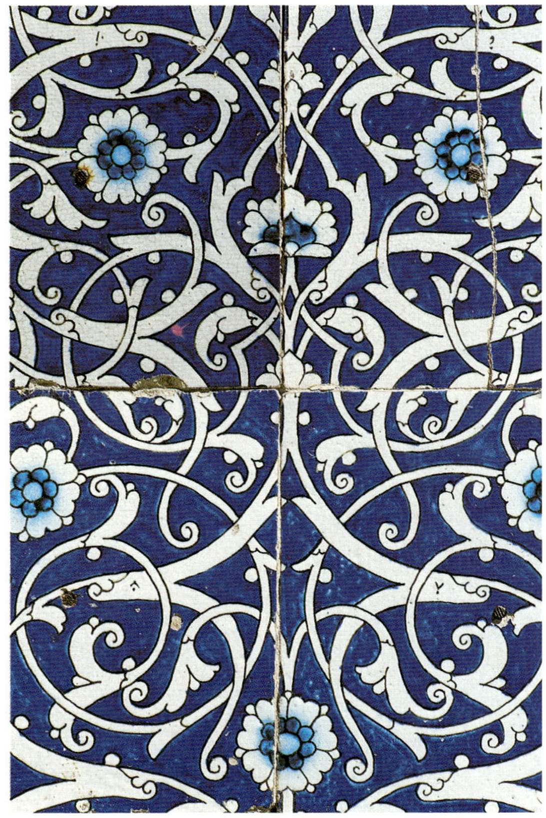

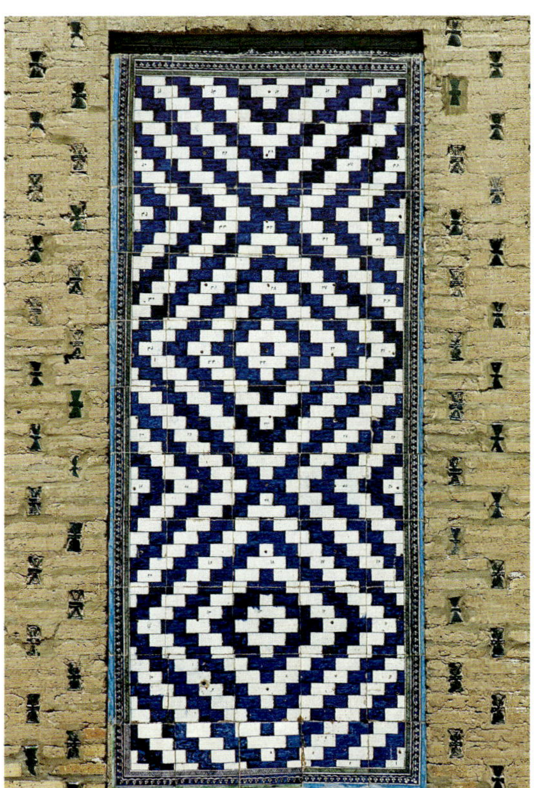

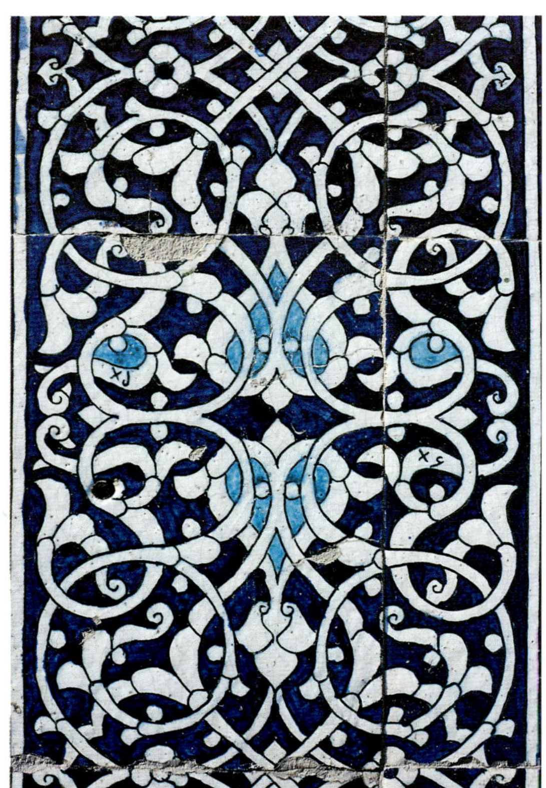

TASH-HAVLI PALACE, KHIVA (UZBEKISTAN), 1831–41

LEFT

♦ Mural decoration of underglaze-painted tilework in a basketweave pattern.

♦ Detail from a tile border with scrollwork palmette motif.

FACING PAGE, TOP

♦ Underglaze-painted tile panel with a star and geometric interlace pattern.

♦ Detail of a panel decorated with a double lattice pattern with coiling leaf-scroll border.

FACING PAGE, BOTTOM RIGHT

♦ Panel of underglaze-painted tiles with a double lattice pattern.

MADRASA OF ISLAM KHOJA, KHIVA (UZBEKISTAN), 1908–10

LEFT

♦ Detail of underglaze-painted tile panel.

♦ Underglaze-painted tile panel with scrollwork palmette motif.

FACING PAGE, BOTTON LEFT

♦ Upper part of frontage and underglaze-painted tilework banding. *Madrasa* of Muhammad Rahim Khan, Khiva (Uzbekistan), 1871.

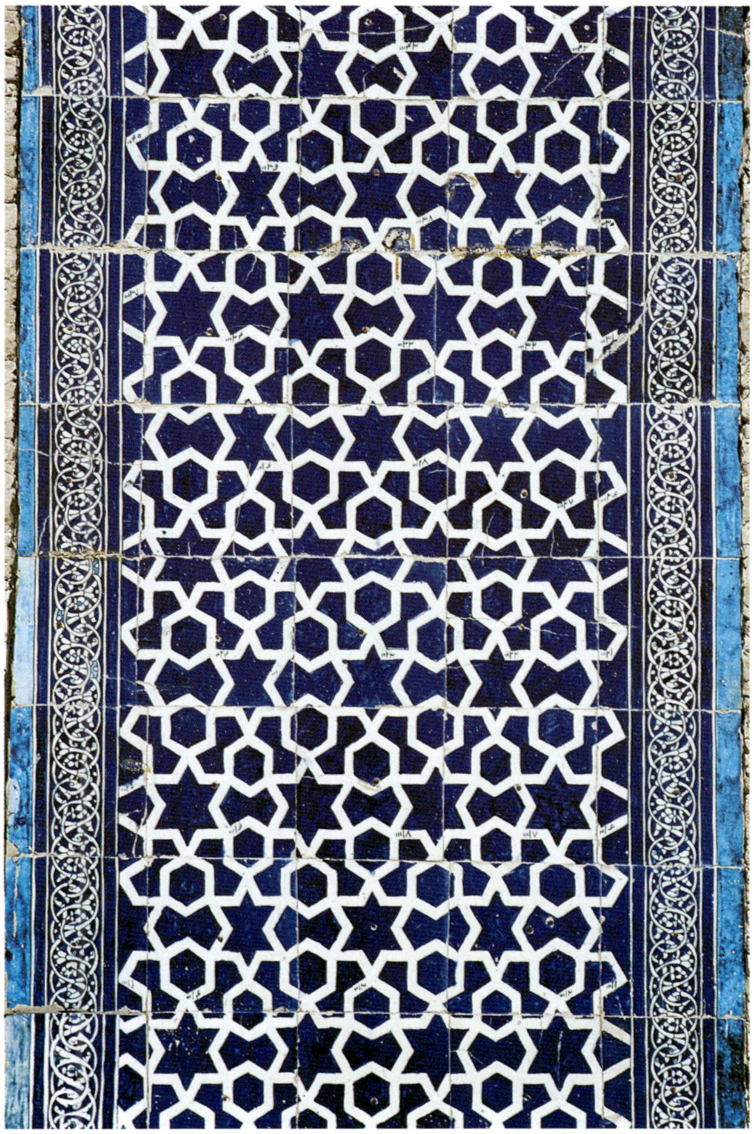

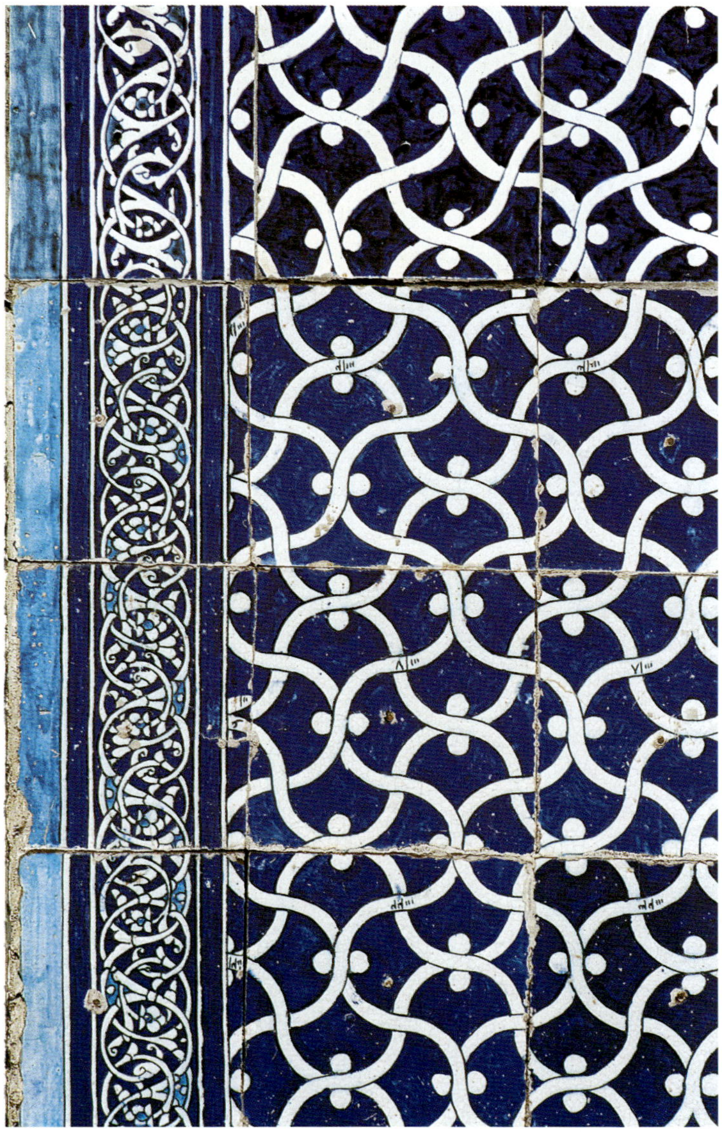

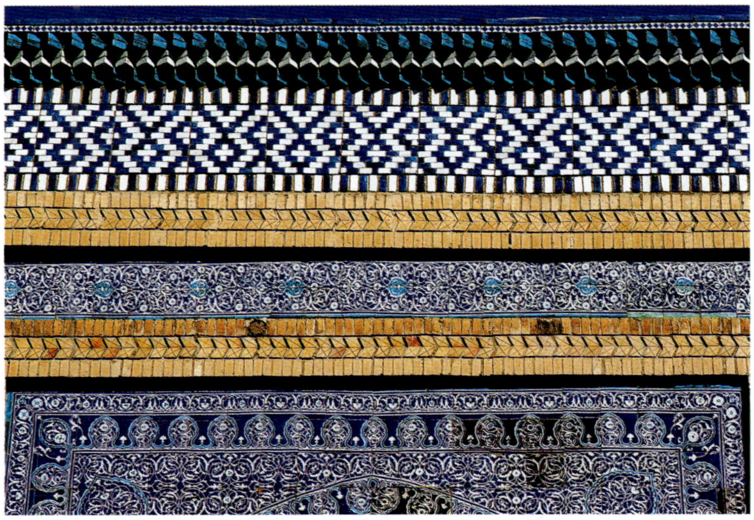

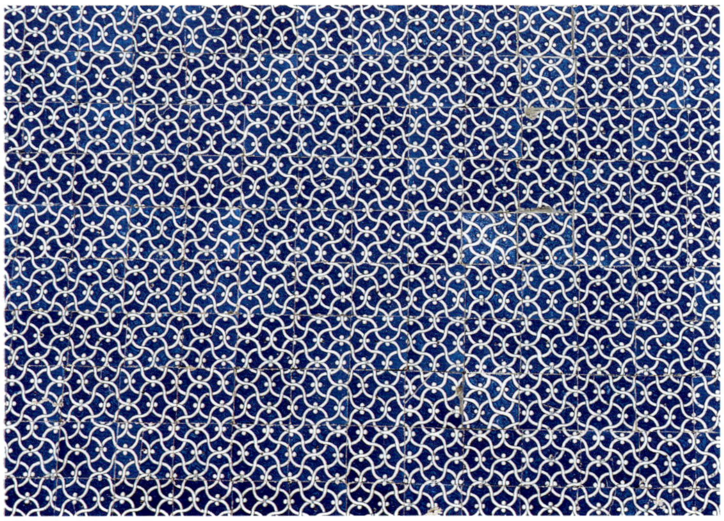

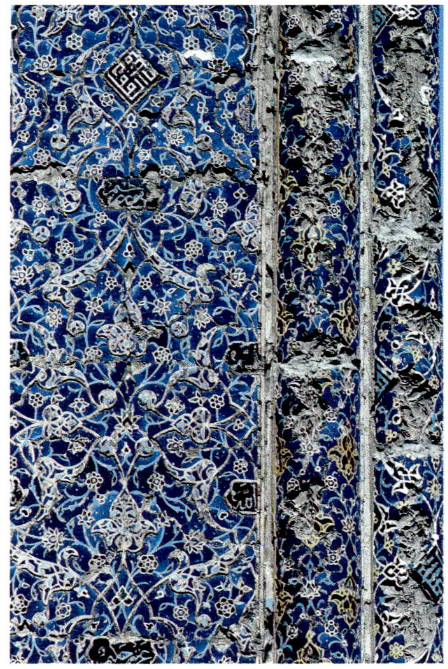

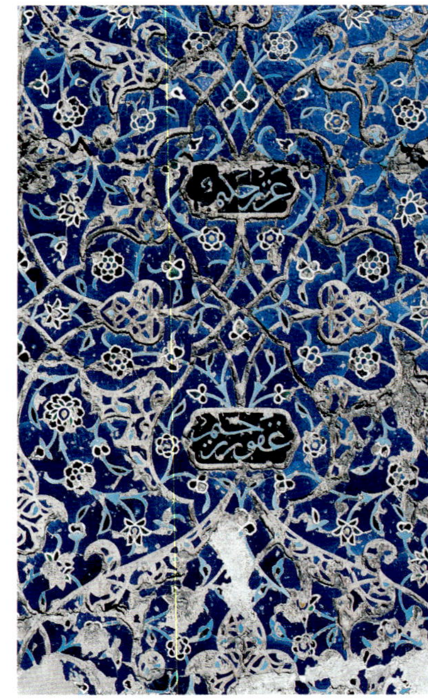

MASJID-I KABUD OR BLUE MOSQUE, TABRIZ (IRAN), 1465

RIGHT

♦ Detail of the wall fittings showing mosaic medallions and cartouches.

FAR RIGHT

♦ Detail of the mosaic decoration. The inscriptional cartouche records divine epithets (here: "the Compassionate" and "the Merciful").

BELOW

♦ Cut-tile mosaic decoration forming interlacing palmettes strewn with flowers and bearing epigraphic cartouches in Thuluth and Kufic scripts.

BOTTOM

♦ This cut-tile and inlay mosaic decoration (*kashiyi mu`arraq*) is considered the finest in all Iran.

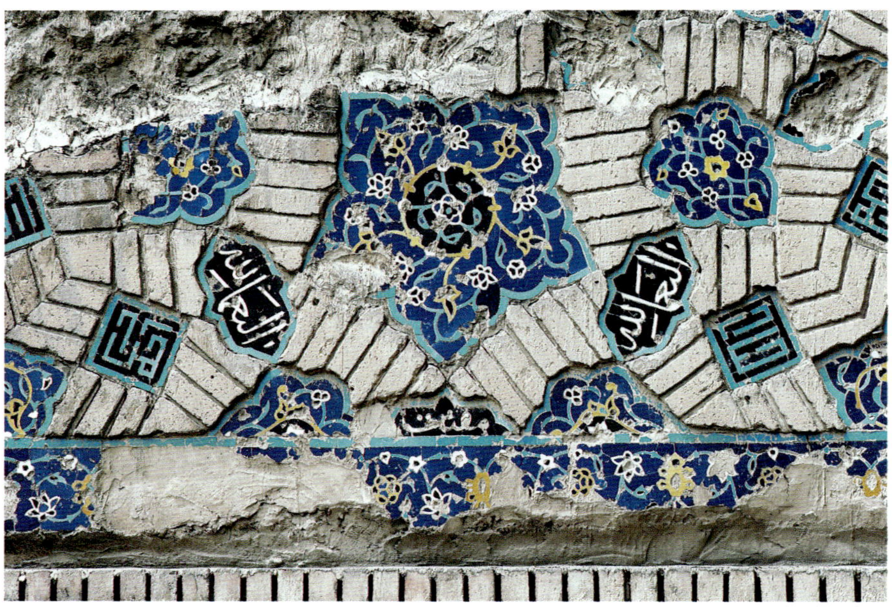

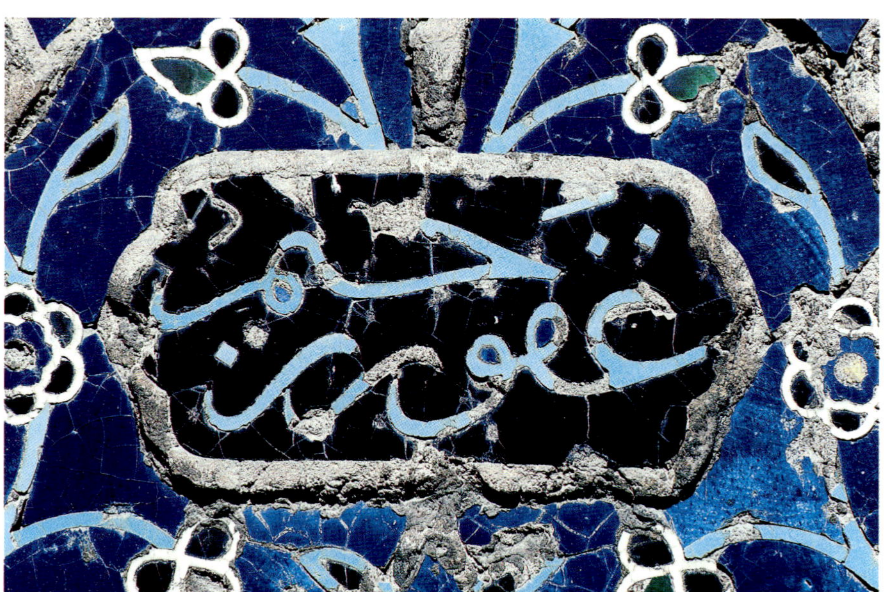

The Azure Casket: Iran under the Turkmen

The fifteenth century was a period of upheaval in the history of Iran, a time during which the territory of the Timurids, themselves increasingly pushed eastward, fell under the dominion of the Turkmen confederations. It was initially the Qara Qoyunlu or "Black Sheep" (1380–1468) who held the upper hand on the political scene, but they were eventually ousted by the "White Sheep," the Aq Qoyunlu (1378–1508), in the second half of the century. The most prominent member of this latter dynasty was Uzun Hasan (1453–78), who spent part of his life fighting the Ottomans, and even formed an alliance with the late Byzantine rulers at Trebizond (Trabzon) by wedding the Princess Despina. It was during his reign that the Blue Mosque in Tabriz (also called the Masjid-i Kabud or Buqa`-i Muzaffariyya, 1465) was erected whose cut-tile mosaics are widely regarded as one of the supreme achievements of the art.

The Blue Mosque of Tabriz, which unfortunately is substantially damaged, was instigated by Abu al-Muzaffar Jahanshah, a prince from the rival Qara Qoyunlu dynasty.

The ground plan of this edifice is rather unusual: the prayer hall, which at the outset was roofed over, once possessed a central dome that sprung from eight massive piers forming an octagon four corners of which were occupied by additional pillars, thus creating a square-shaped space with twelve apertures opening on to an ambulatory.[60] This space in turn was capped by small domes around the entire circumference, except on the side of the *qibla*, where a domed sanctuary stands in front of the *mihrab* and in line with the main entrance. Like the interior, the gateway was fully clad in an intricate pattern of masonry bricks alternating with inlay tile mosaics of the utmost richness. The entrance portal (*pishtaq*) presents engaged columns—alternately plain and twisted—supporting an elegant blind arcade and lined in mosaic, mainly cobalt blue, with white, turquoise, yellow, green, and brown completing the palette. Certain decorations with alternating vegetal and calligraphic motifs are executed in shallow relief. An inscription in ceramic mosaic gives the name of a calligrapher, Ni'mat Allah b. Muhammad al-Bawwab, who is coincidentally mentioned in the collection of biographies of the leading Persian calligraphers by a chronicler of the Safavid period, Qazi Ahmad Qumi.[61] The dados are highly original, being lined with monochrome cut tiles assembled in geometrical patterns comprising thin strips in contrasting colors (cobalt and white; turquoise and black).

During the reign of Uzun Hasan, the venerable Friday Mosque at Isfahan (which we have already discussed) underwent a new phase of ceramic decoration, in particular to the side of the south *iwan*, where the addition of the monumental *muqarnas* dates from 1475. In these *muqarnas*, plain brick is employed in combination with turquoise and cobalt glazed *banna'i* and arranged in juxtaposed geometrical figures and broad panels in a labyrinthine Kufic script. It was also perhaps at this time that the two minarets flanking the *iwan* of the prayer hall were erected and clad using the same decorative techniques. In fact—as an inscription in cut-tile mosaic dating from 1447 attests[62]—the mosque had already undergone some restoration and decorative work not long before Uzun Hasan's rule.

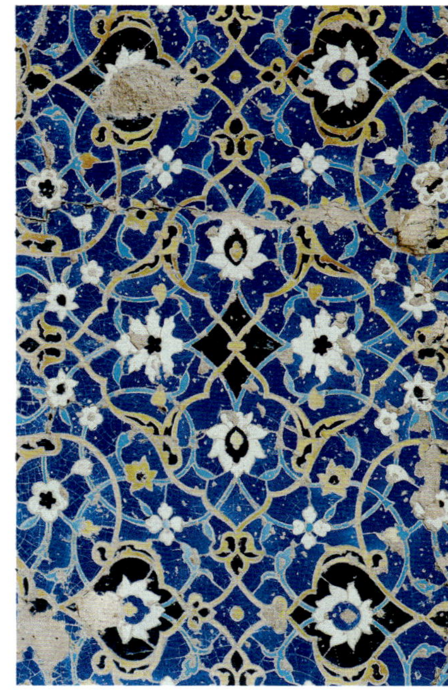

♦ Cut-tile mosaic, Qubbah-i Sabz (Green Dome), Kerman (Iran), end of the fifteenth century. Although extensively damaged, this building still has scattered remnants of extremely delicate tilework.

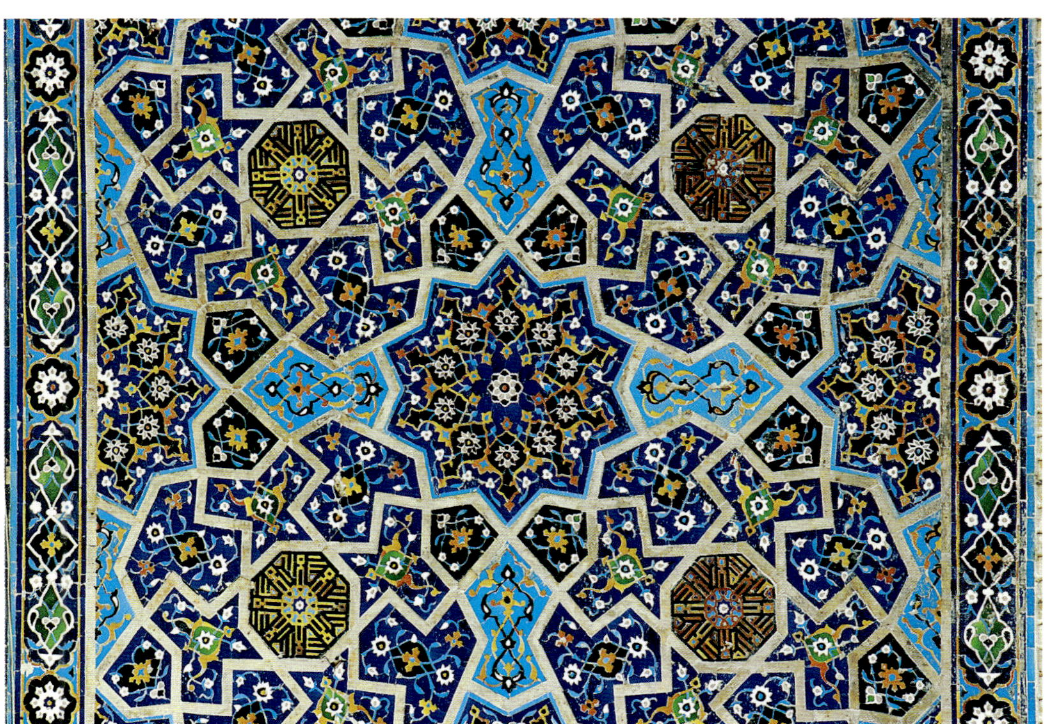

FRIDAY MOSQUE, ISFAHAN (IRAN)

LEFT

♦ Wall panel with geometric interlace set with cut-tile mosaic star and polygon motifs.

FOLLOWING DOUBLE PAGE

♦ South *iwan* leading to the prayer hall. The decoration of large *muqarnas* embellished with *banna'i* bricks forming epigraphic motifs in Kufic dates from the time of the refurbishment ordered by Uzun Hasan in 1475.

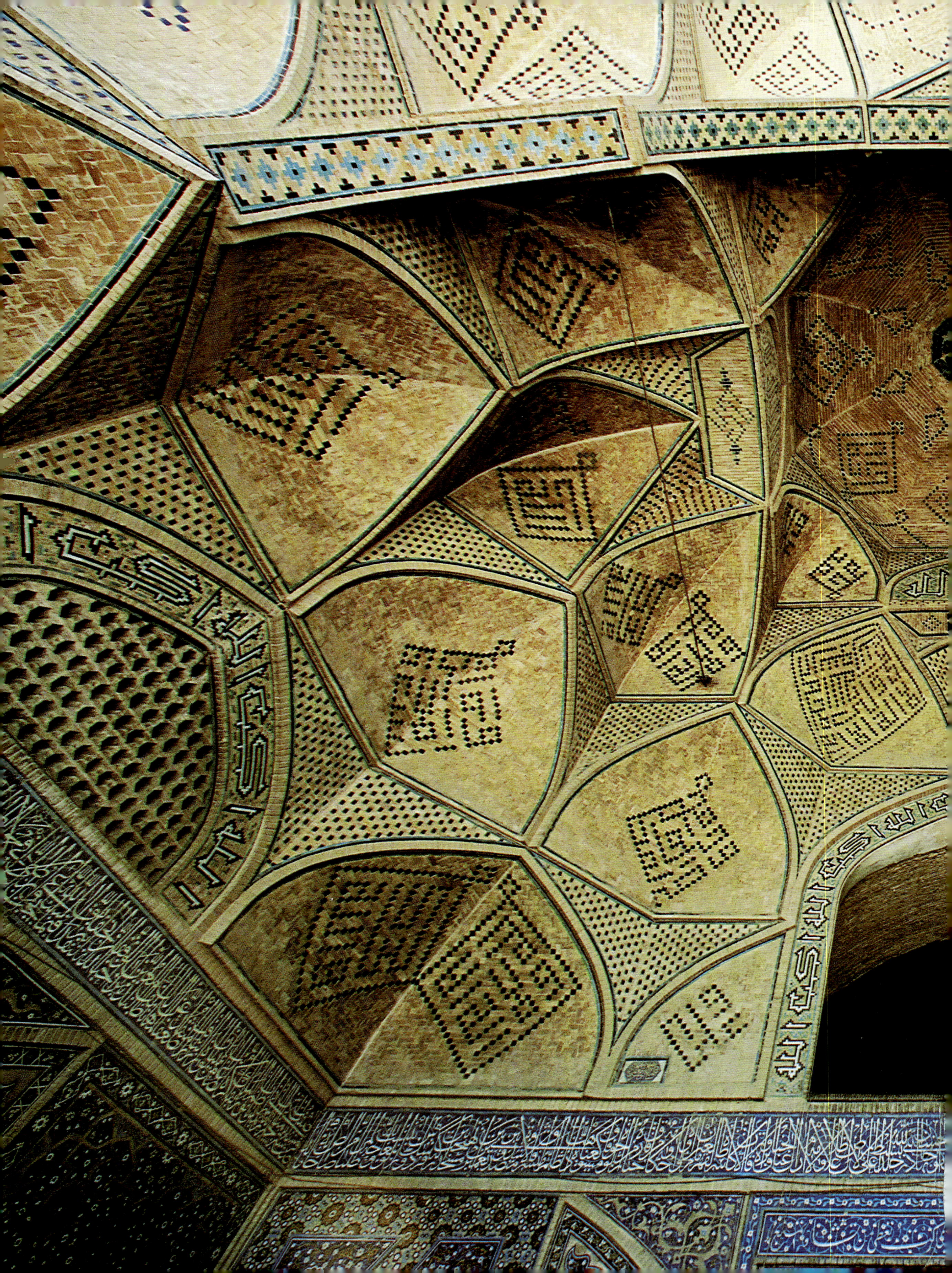

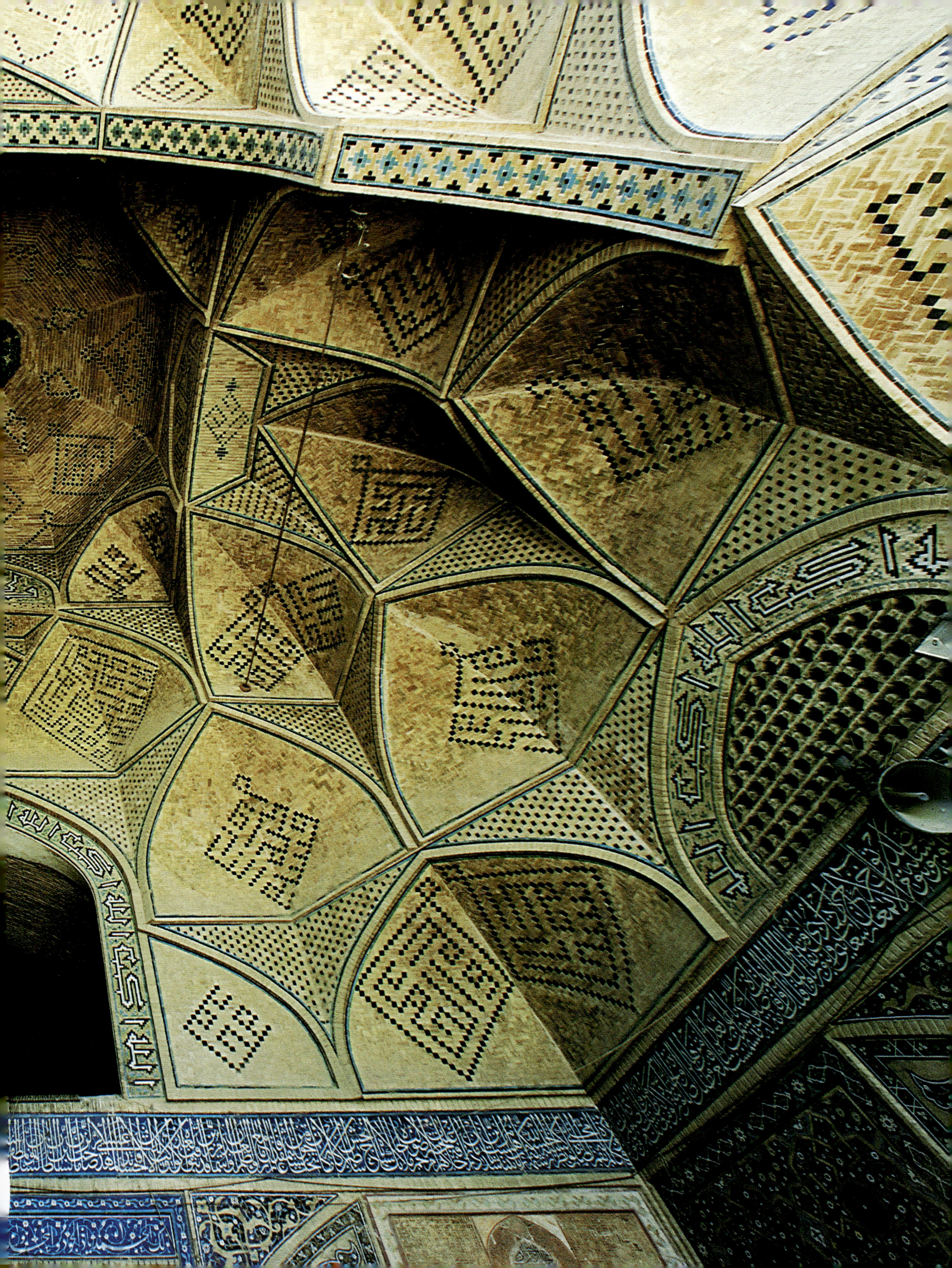

Angels and Arabesques: Iran under the Safavids

The origin of the Safavids is obscure. Some historians maintain that they are Kurds, while others are of the opinion that they are Turkmen. What is certain is that the dynasty was founded by a mystic, the Sufi Shaykh Safi al-Din (died 1334), whose followers gathered round a sanctuary in the town of Ardabil in Azerbaijan. Although the order he founded might initially have been Sunni, during the fifteenth century the Safavids evolved into a majority Shi`ite community. The era witnessed an intense propaganda effort aimed at the ruling Turkmen confederations of the Black and the White Sheep.

It was in 1501 that one of the descendants of Shaykh Safi, Isma`il ibn Haydar—under the name of Isma`il Shah—seized power and wrested Azerbaijan from the White Sheep. Over the next ten years the shah took control of the entire Iranian territory, thereby laying the foundations for an empire that was to survive—with ups and downs—until 1786. The most significant repercussion after the rise to power of the Safavid dynasty was the consolidation of Shi`ism as the state religion. Hitherto the dominant official religion in Iran had frequently been Sunnism. This fact is all the more critical since it was sanctioned by the standing of the Safavid monarchy, which claimed `Alid descent (i.e., from `Ali, the Prophet's son-in-law and founder of the line of the Shi`ite *imams*), and even went so far as to allege near-divine status.

Safavid history was punctuated by a series of sometimes serious conflicts with two major neighboring powers: the Ottoman empire to the west and the Mughals to the east. Their most eminent ruler, Shah `Abbas I, whose reign saw the zenith of the Safavid dynasty in political and cultural terms, was an approximate contemporary of Elizabeth I of England, Philip II of Spain, Ivan the Terrible, and Henry IV of France. Following the death of Shah `Abbas II in 1666, Safavid power gradually waned and the country was overrun in a sequence of Afghan incursions. During the eighteenth century, Iran was dominated by the figure of Nadir Shah, a plenipotentiary minister who had acted for the Safavid kings (deposed in the intervening period) before placing himself on the throne. On his death, Persia entered an era of chaos from which the Qajar dynasty eventually extricated itself at the end of the century. This new dynasty witnessed the arrival of printing, and thus of the press, and it seemed that an age of industrialization might be dawning, but in fact Iran soon became a pawn in the power games between Britain and Russia.

The first Safavid capital was set up at Tabriz. As the city lies near the Ottoman empire, it was occupied and ransacked many times, to the point that few monuments of importance from this period have come down to modern times. The fate of the dynasty's second capital, Qazvin, founded by Shah Tahmasp (1524–76), was less checkered, and many constructions from the Safavid period are known, although they too have

♦ Cut-tile mosaic inscriptional panel in labyrinthine square Kufic beneath the west *iwan* of the Friday Mosque, Isfahan (Iran). The square in the center bears the signature of the calligrapher Muhammad Mu`min ibn Muhammad Amin. The frieze in Thuluth script running above the panel is executed in polychrome "black line" tiles.

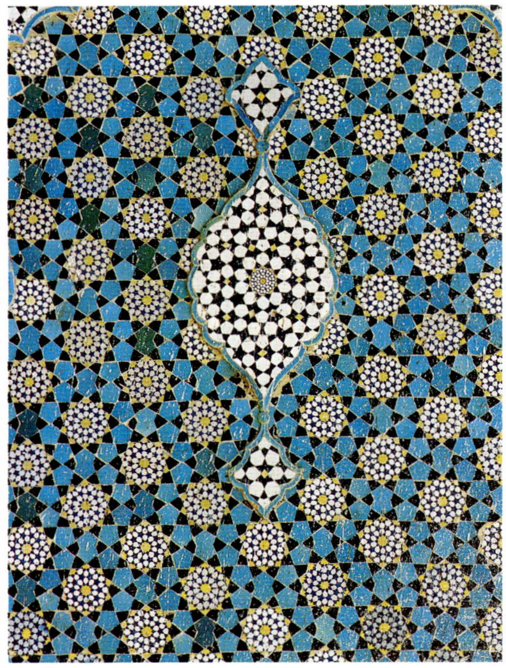

FRIDAY MOSQUE, ISFAHAN (IRAN)

♦ Panel beneath the west *iwan* dating from the time of Shah Sultan Husayn I, 1694–1722.

♦ Facade of the south *iwan*, from the time of Shah ʿAbbas II and dated 1659–60.

♦ Decoration on the upper sections of the entrance portal.

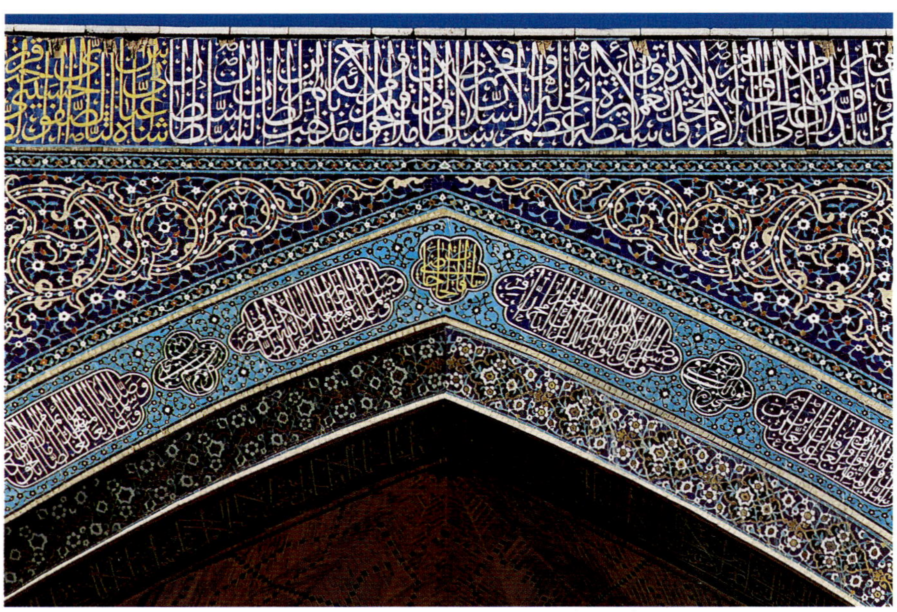

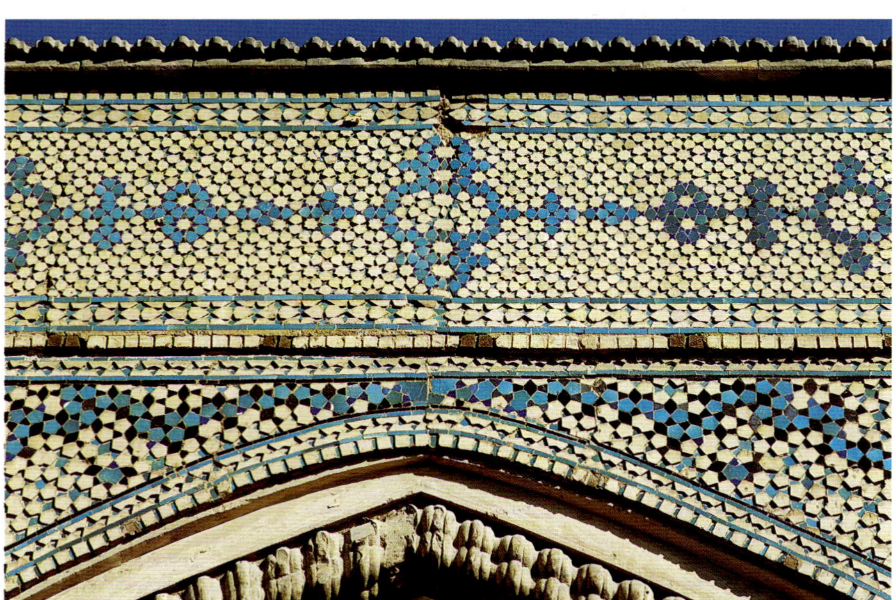

often been disfigured by careless restoration work or through being diverted from their original purpose.

It was essentially in yet a third capital, Isfahan, that Safavid art was able to flourish in its true splendor. Founded in ancient times, Isfahan possessed a long history, as testified by the Sasanid fire temple overlooking the city from the top of a hill. The capital of the Seljuqs (1038–1194), Isfahan witnessed a long succession of kings and chief ministers. Over the centuries, the remarkable Friday Mosque, a veritable architectural jewel around which the whole city was centered, was the subject of countless additions and embellishments. Several sovereigns of the Safavid dynasty were involved in this ongoing process. In particular, they were responsible for the present appearance of the mosque's courtyard with its decorative ceramics executed primarily in *bannaʾi* brickwork and cut-tile mosaic. Rectangular in plan, the court is organized around four *iwans* that open at the center of each of the four sides. The *iwans* are connected by a gallery with two superposed arcades.

The *iwan* to the south has been subjected to several restorations since being built at the time of the Seljuqs. It was undoubtedly under Uzun Hasan, around 1475, that the billowing *muqarnas* were added and the two minarets erected. During the Safavid period, under Shah Tahmasp (1524–1576), the facade of this *iwan* was clad in new ceramic decoration. An inscription bearing the name of the sovereign placed at the vault springing runs: "On the date of the year 938 [A.D. 1531–32], written by Kamal al-Din Husayn Hafez-i Haravi Mithqal." The same date recurs on a Quʾranic inscription also executed in ceramic on the head of the arch in the *iwan*. At the end of the broad epigraphic band on the wall can be seen an inscription in Taʿliq with the mention: "Written on the date of the year 938 by the hand of Yusuf the Poor, son of Taj al-Din

Banna`-i Isfahani."[63] Another inscription, at the summit of the *iwan* frontage wall dating from A.H. 1070/A.D. 1659–60, bears the name of Shah `Abbas II (1642–66) and the signature of the calligrapher Muhammad Riza al-Imami al-Adhami of Isfahan.[64] Finally, also dating from the time of Shah `Abbas II, a tile embedded in the wall attests to the name of Ustad Ibrahim ibn Ustad Isma`il Banna`-i Isfahani.[65]

The *iwan* to the east, dubbed the Iwan-i Shagerd ("the *iwan* of the pupil"), contains more restrained decoration, in particular the *muqarnas*, which are more numerous and smaller in size. The *iwan* decorated most recently is undoubtedly that to the west, known as the Iwan-i Ustad ("the *iwan* of the master"); like the southern *iwan*, it is adorned with large *muqarnas*. The arch spandrels, as well as two flanking piers, are lined entirely in an angular Kufic script executed in the last years of the seventeenth century. A broad epigraphic band in Thuluth rings the *iwan*; dating from the reign of Shah Sultan Husayn I (1694–1722), it bears the year A.H. 1112/A.D. 1700–1. In the center of another broad calligraphic composition on the right wall, inscribed in an angular, labyrinthine Kufic, figures the signature of Muhammad Mu`min ibn Muhammad Amin. At the highest point of the *iwan* stands a small construction capped by a pyramidal roof called a *guldasta*, from which the faithful were called to prayer. Finally the northern *iwan*, called "the *iwan* of the dervishes," bears rather less elaborate decoration executed essentially in *banna`i* brickwork. Behind this *iwan* is situated the splendid Seljuq dome of Taj al-Mulk (1088).

In 1598, Shah `Abbas I (1587–1629) decided to abandon Qazvin and repair to Isfahan, at which time it seems that several town-planning projects were proposed. The project finally selected envisaged developing the city toward suburbs located south of the Friday Mosque. The central focus was to be an immense precinct known as the "royal square."

Isfahan's main buildings are arranged around this immense open space: to the north lies the entry to the bazaar; opposite to the south is the Shah or Royal Mosque (1612); to the east stands the mosque-oratory of Shaykh Lutfallah (1602) and facing this the `Ali Qapu pavilion (the "Sublime Porte" or "Lofty Door") that dominates the entrance to a palatial complex, the Naqsh-i Jahan ("Design of the World"). The conception of this ensemble and its gigantic proportions were truly revolutionary. For the sake of comparison, it might be recalled that the Place de la Concorde in Paris, for example, was laid out only in the time of Louis XV.

The immense plaza in Isfahan was intended to be a multi-purpose space, used for sports such as polo (the national pastime beloved of the Safavids) and archery, for markets, and as a meeting place. As one eighteenth-century French traveler observed, "The Maydan-i Shah (new *maydan*, royal square) can pass for one of the most beautiful squares in the whole universe. It is oblong in shape, 710 paces from the rising to the setting Sun and 210 from south to north. It is encircled by a channel whose banks are lined in a shiny black stone. These banks are a foot high and wide enough for people to walk three or four abreast. The channel discharges into a large, many-sided pool lying at the northernmost end of the *maydan*. Between the channel and the buildings set around the square lies a space of some twenty paces, bordered by a further course of stonework that abuts the foot of the houses. This whole space is planted with trees of large size whose crowns tower above the dwellings." This description is all the more interesting as it takes us back to a time when the square appeared very different from how it does today, with its modern landscaping.

The first monument to be built on the square was probably the Shaykh Lutfallah Mosque. Smaller than the earlier Friday

♦ Panel in "black line" polychrome ceramic decorated with a floral mandorla with vegetal scroll pendants. Shaykh Lutfallah Mosque, Isfahan (Iran), 1602–19.

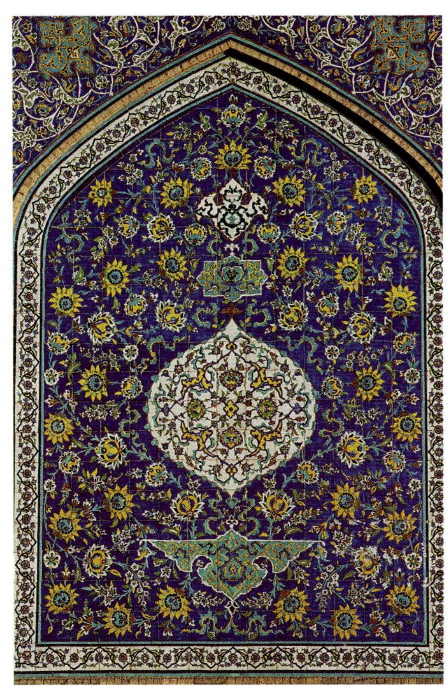

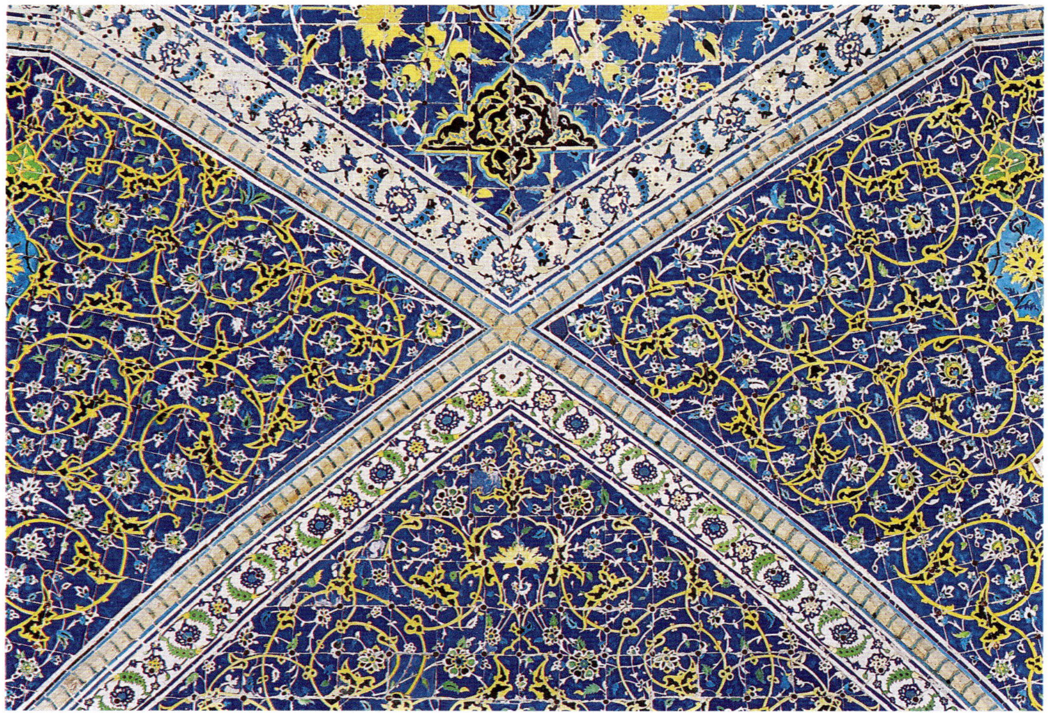

♦ Detail of the vault of the Masjid-i Shah or Royal Mosque, Isfahan (Iran), completed 1627. The vault consists of intersecting arches with banded ribs and is entirely lined in "black line" polychrome tiles.

SHAYKH LUTFALLAH MOSQUE, ISFAHAN (IRAN), 1602–19

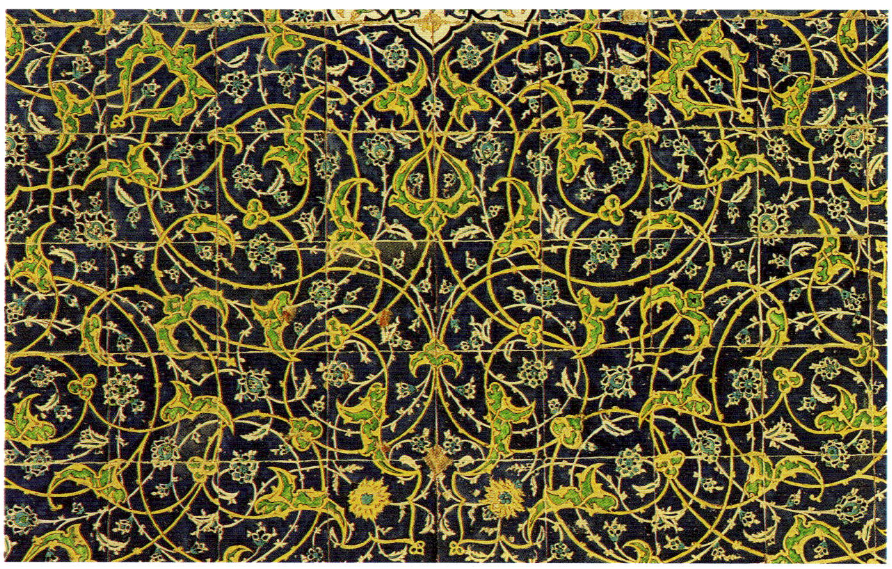

♦ Panel composed of "black line" polychrome tiles decorated with arabesques on a cobalt ground.

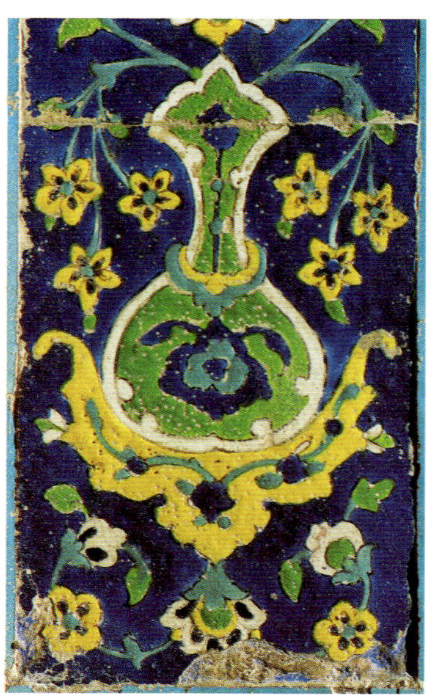

♦ "Black line" polychrome tile.

Mosque and the Shah Mosque built a few years later, it has no court. From an elegant gateway whose arch is decorated with stalactites, one arrives at the prayer hall through a passage forming a dogleg in order to conform to the orientation of the edifice demanded by liturgy. The oratory itself is crowned by an elegant dome on a drum and lit by windows with grilles.

Like the internal surfaces, the facades are all clad with ceramic tiling that is predominantly cobalt blue, turquoise, and yellow. The relatively unusual exterior cladding of the dome is characterized by an unglazed brick base from which emerge motifs of palmette scrolls and arabesques executed in white, turquoise, and cobalt glazed tilework.

The frontage is arranged around a broad *pishtaq* whose vault is adorned with *muqarnas*, the arch surround being banded by a fine turquoise torsade. A sizable horizontal inscription above the door records the name of Shah `Abbas and is signed by one of the greatest calligraphers of the time, `Ali Riza `Abbasi from Tabriz (dated A.H. 1012/A.D. 1603–4).[66] On the intrados beneath the entrance arch, a further signature inscribed in polychrome ceramic tilework records the name of another figure, perhaps that of the architect, Muhammad `Ali Mi`mar-i Isfahani. To both sides of the portal beneath a set-back vault of *muqarnas*, magnificent panels, mainly in cut-tile mosaic and divided predominantly into blind arches, spread across the entire facade and over the two lateral returns. These panels present a splendid diversity of motifs, in which the dominant cobalt tone offers a sonorous foil to isolated white, turquoise, yellow, and brown notes.

The decoration of the cupola within is staggeringly fine. Comprised of a pattern of mandorlas that progressively decrease

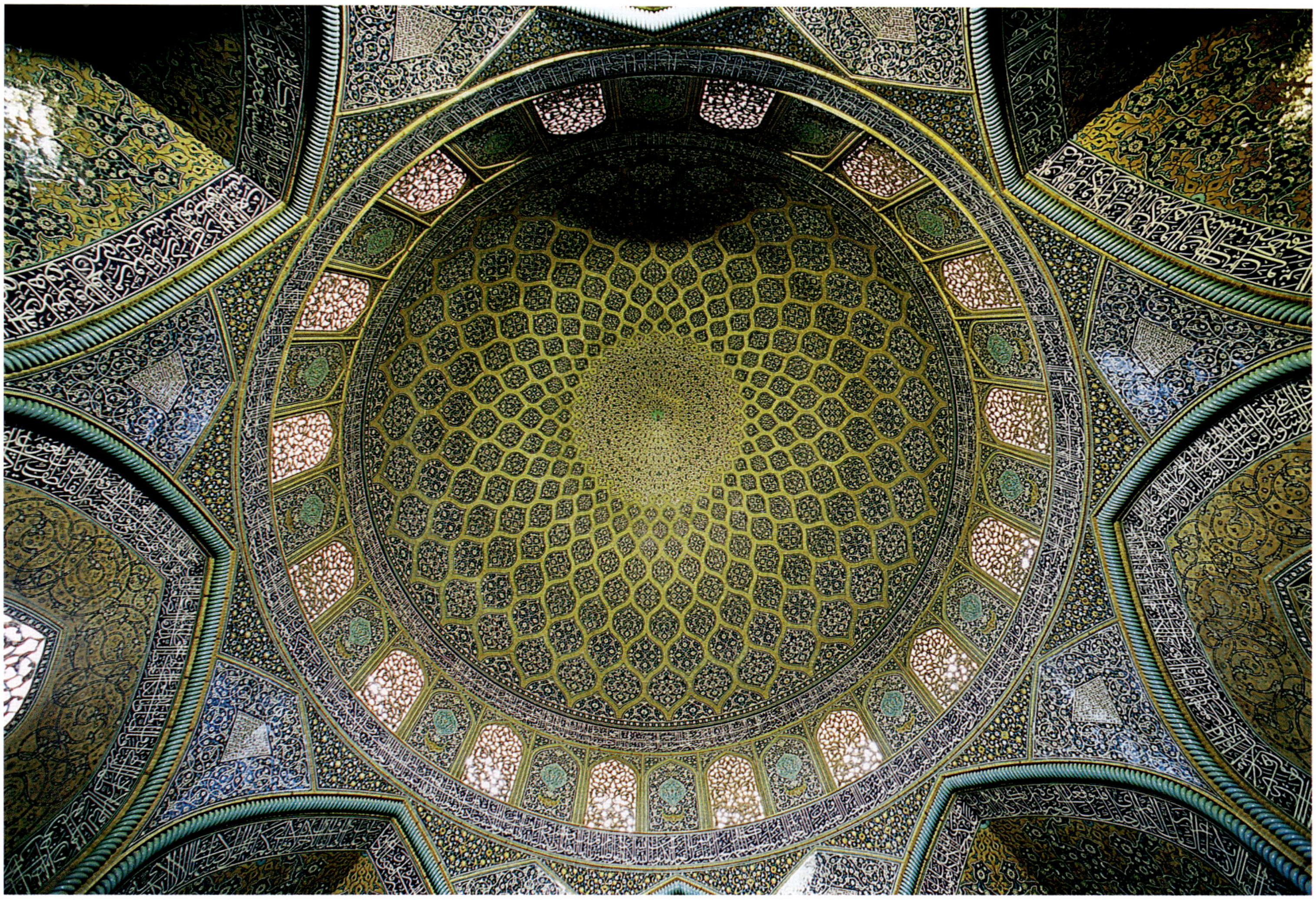

in size with height, the center presents a wide, circular, radiant medallion redolent of the *shamsa* ornaments ("sunburst medallion") of manuscript illumination. The inscription banding the drum of the cupola inside is signed `Ali Riza `Abbasi and is dated A.H. 1025/A.D. 1616.[67] The upper reaches of the wall display cut and inlay tile decoration extending over a ground of unglazed brick.

On the magnificently decorated *mihrab* another signature can be read, that of Muhammad Riza ibn Husayn Banna`-i Isfahani and the date, A.H. 1028/A.D. 1618–19. According to Homa`i-ye Shirazi, this name belonged to the mason;[68] however, in spite of this appellation "mason" (that possibly pertained to his father), Muhammad Reza ibn Husayn Banna`-i Isfahani might be well the creator of the *mihrab*'s decoration. The date of the start of work is given as A.H. 1011 or 1012/A.D. 1602–3, depending on the authority.[69] A.H. 1028/A.D. 1618–19 must therefore represent the year in which the decorative scheme was completed. Finally, the dados are faced with polychrome "black line" tiles with leaf-scroll arabesque designs on a cobalt ground interspersed with ovals on a white ground.

Built ten years later, the Shah (Royal) Mosque, or Masjid-i Shah, conformed to an even more ambitious design. Its vast proportions, its onion dome, and its four minarets offer a stunning contrast to the small-scale, intimate surroundings of the Shaykh Lutfallah Mosque. For the Shah Mosque, the architect opted for the quintessentially Persian layout of a four-*iwan* court, a type of plan that had been arrived at gradually over the centuries and that had been epitomized in the twelfth century at

♦ Cupola of the prayer hall, Shaykh Lutfallah Mosque, Isfahan (Iran). The inscription running round the drum is signed by the calligrapher `Ali Riza `Abbasi and is dated 1616.

FOLLOWING DOUBLE PAGE

♦ Detail of a panel of polychrome "black line" tiles adorned with plant motifs. Masjid-i Shah or Royal Mosque, Isfahan (Iran), completed 1627.

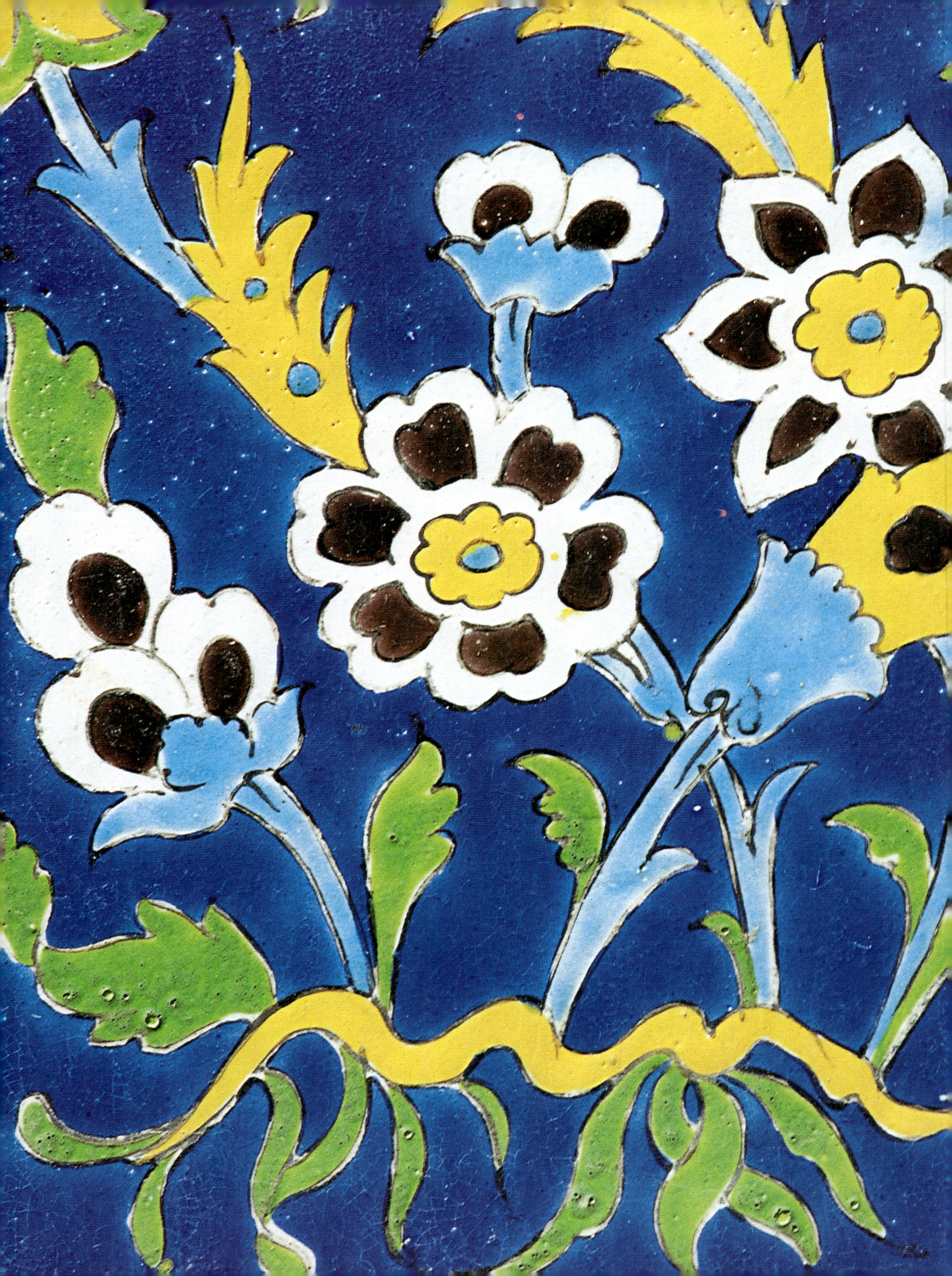

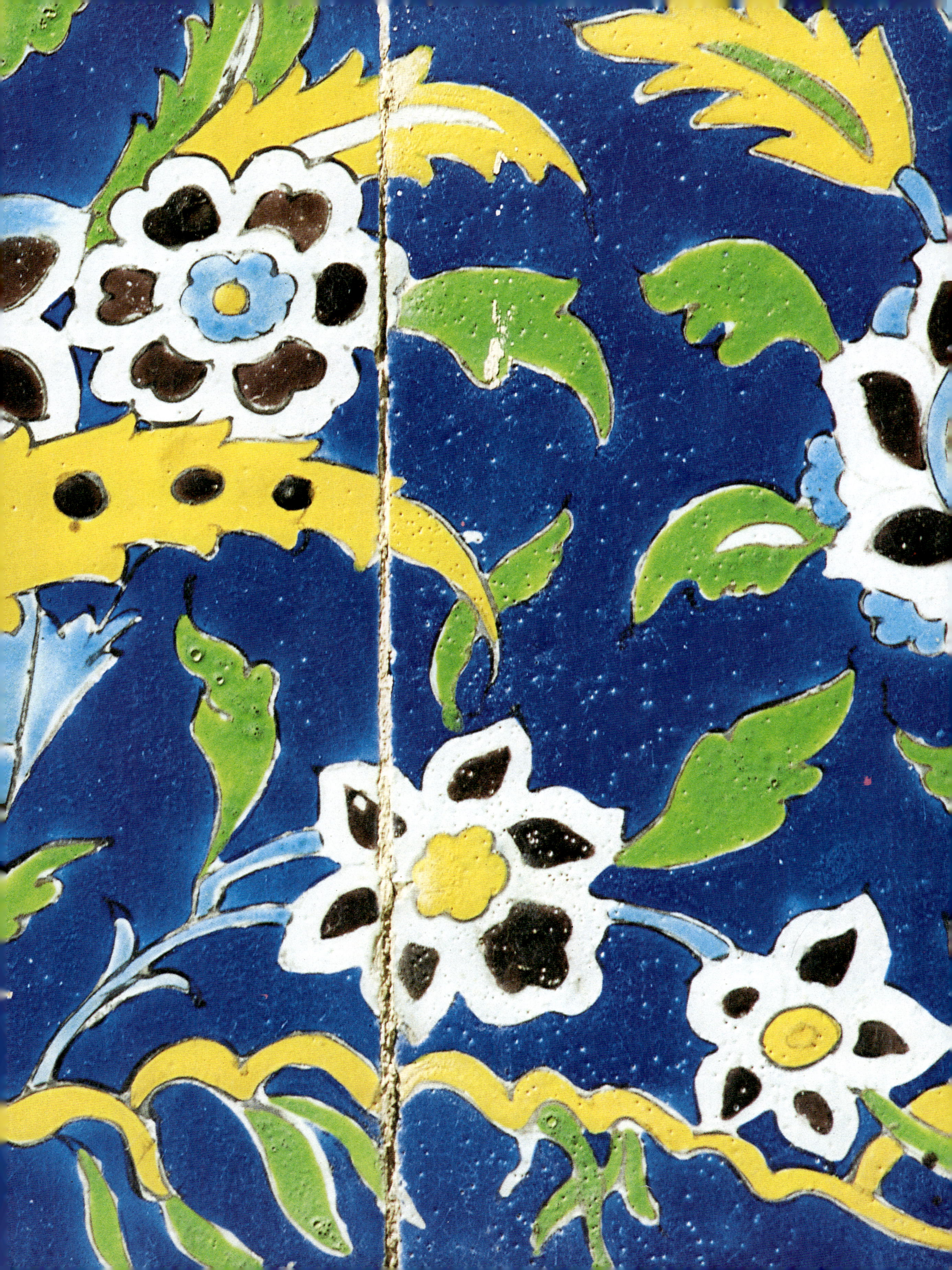

♦ Half-dome decorated with cut-tile mosaic arabesques and a geometric pattern. Mausoleum of Khwaja Rabi`a, Mashhad (Iran), founded at the beginning of the seventeenth century.

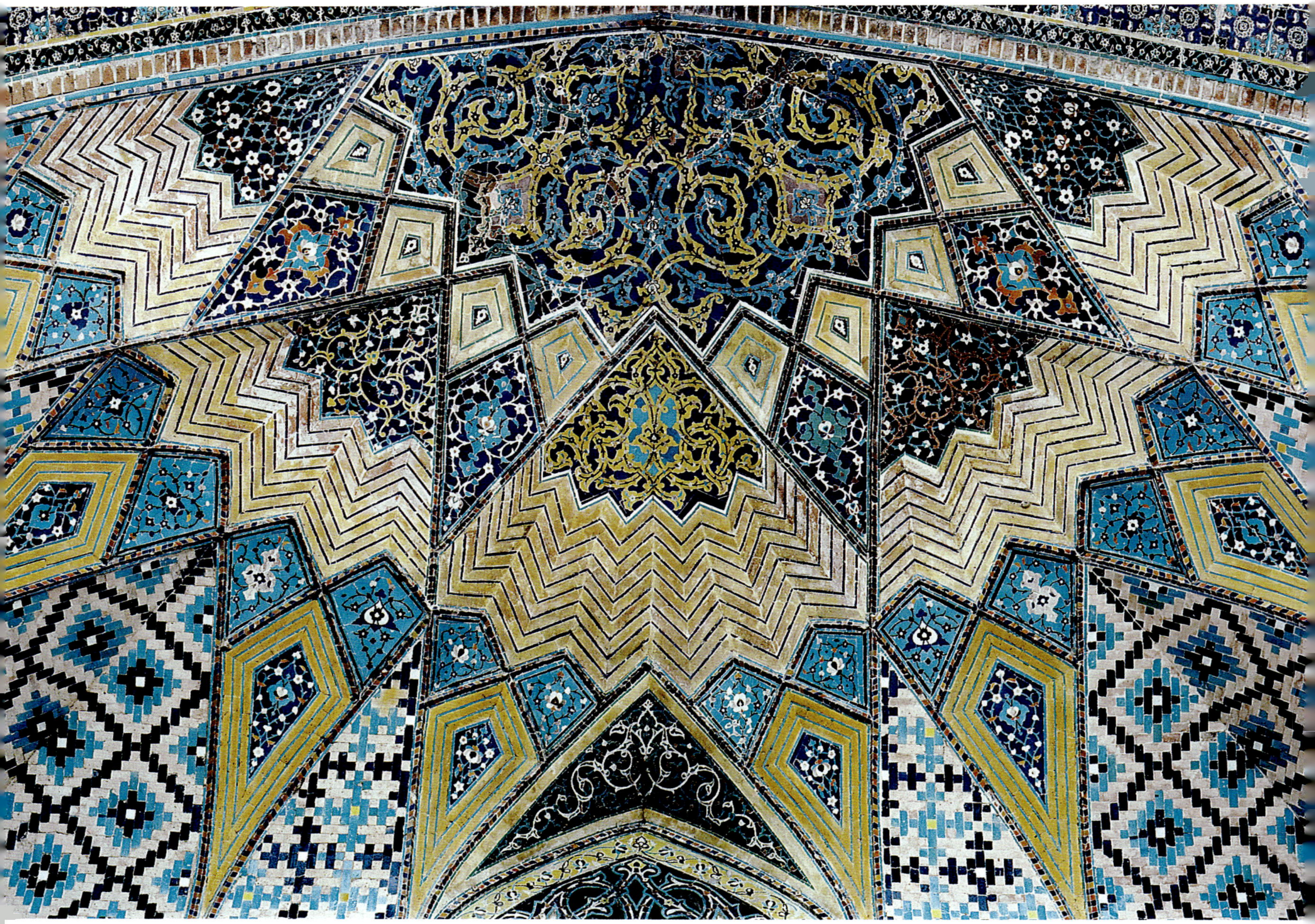

♦ Panel of polychrome "black line" tiles with epigraphic cartouches in a design of floral trails. Friday Mosque, Qom (Iran), rebuilt in the early seventeenth century under Shah `Abbas.

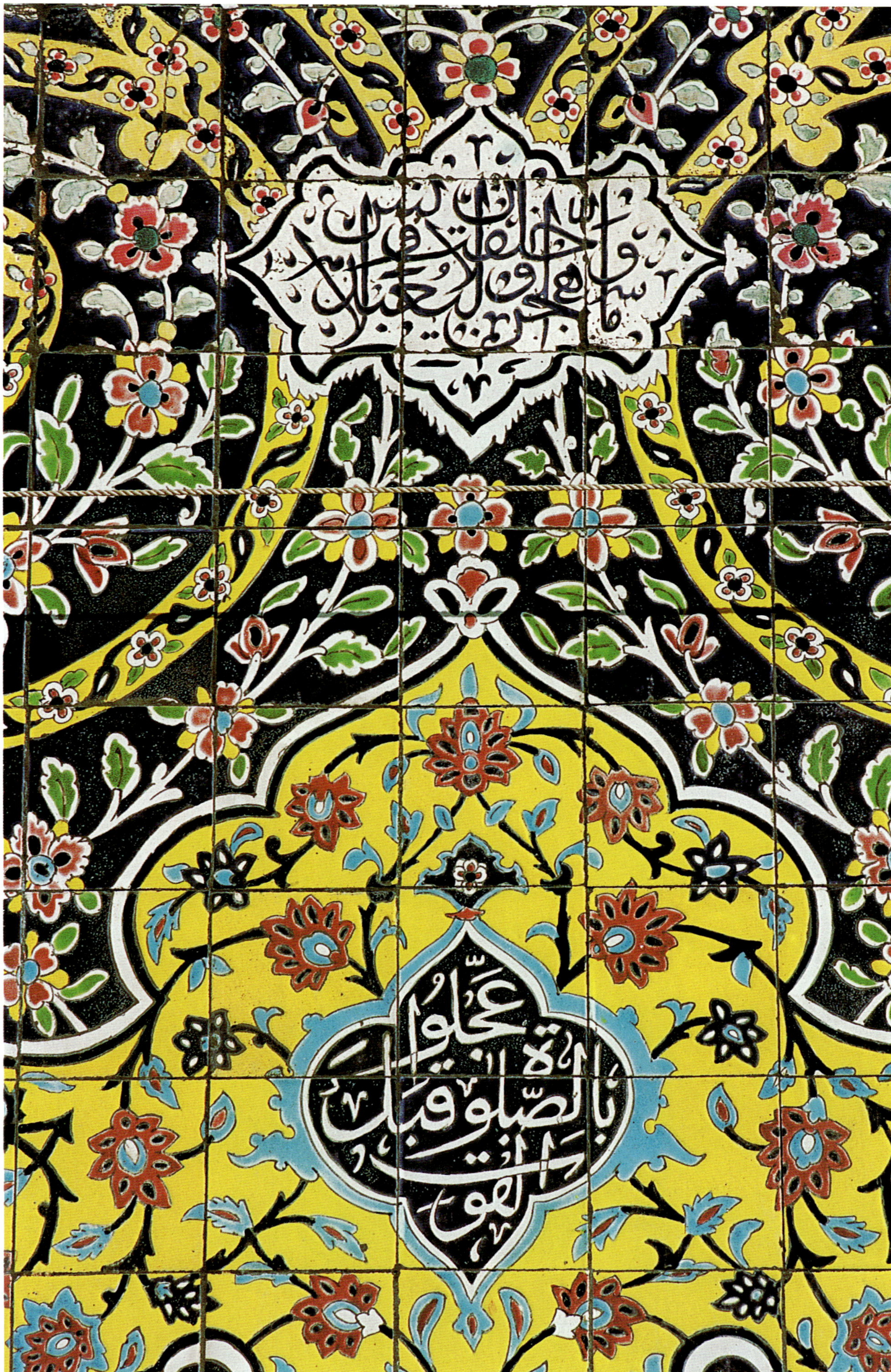

MASJID-I SHAH OR ROYAL MOSQUE, ISFAHAN (IRAN), COMPLETED 1627

♦ Panel and border in polychrome "black line" tilework.

♦ Prayer hall cupola lit by eight grille-covered windows decorated with a dazzling radial *shamsa* motif similar to those found in manuscript illumination.

FACING PAGE

♦ The pattern at the center of the prayer hall cupola in polychrome "black line" tilework is remarkable for its delicate lines and bright coloring.

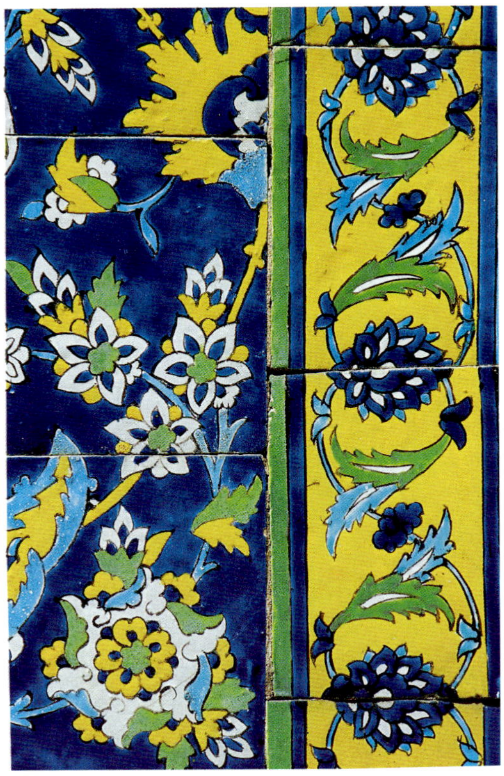

the ancient Friday Mosque at Isfahan. As with the Shaykh Lutfallah Mosque, the ritual necessity of an orientation toward Mecca forced the architect to offset the interior in relation to the gateway opening on the *maydan*. The court is thus sheltered from those beyond its walls by an angled passage from which the visitor suddenly emerges into a breathtaking tour de force of decoration. Unlike the venerable Friday Mosque, the Masjid-i Shah was conceived as a single whole. Moreover, here the architect could draw on a vast fund of knowledge accumulated during the previous centuries to produce a masterpiece whose harmonious splendor derives not only from the homogeneity of the ensemble but also from the use of complex modular units founded on an arrangement

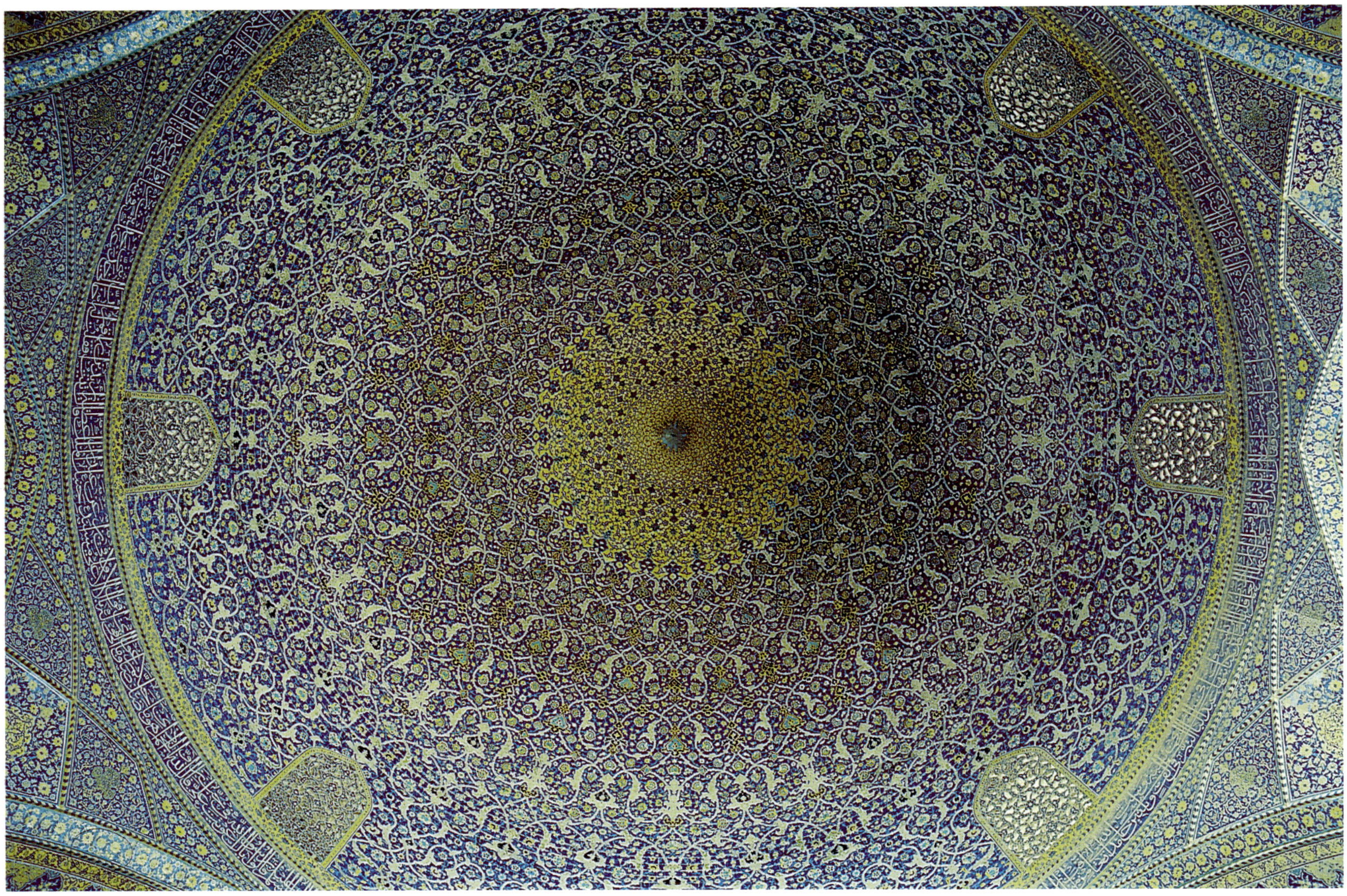

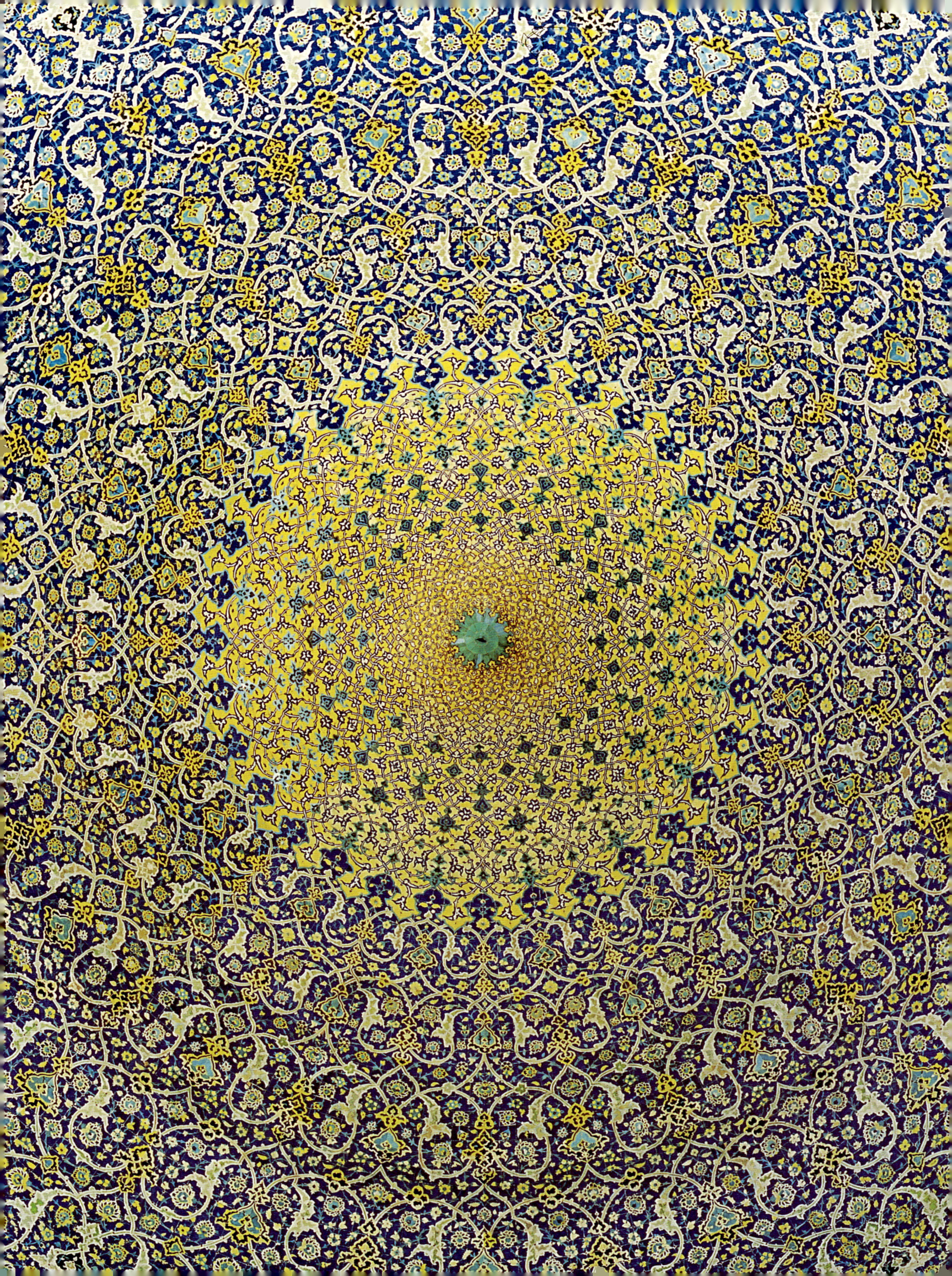

of golden sections. Here too, all the outer facades display great inventiveness in ceramic decoration, with a predilection for "black line" polychrome tilework.

These polychrome *haft-rangi* ("seven colors" in Persian) tile decorations rely on a technique close to that of *cuerda seca*, demonstrating the degree of mastery that Iranian ceramists had attained by the end of the sixteenth century. As described above, the majority of earlier ceramic decorations consist of a mosaic of cut out and reassembled tiles; this technique, although slower in execution, at least poses no problems in firing. The crucial question was how to obtain true polychromy without the colors encroaching on one another or bleeding during firing. The base of these *haft-rangi* tiles is a stone-paste (frit) body

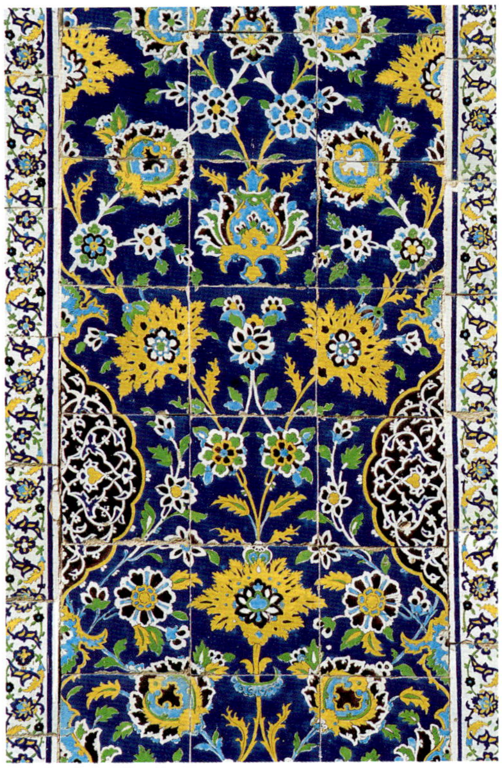

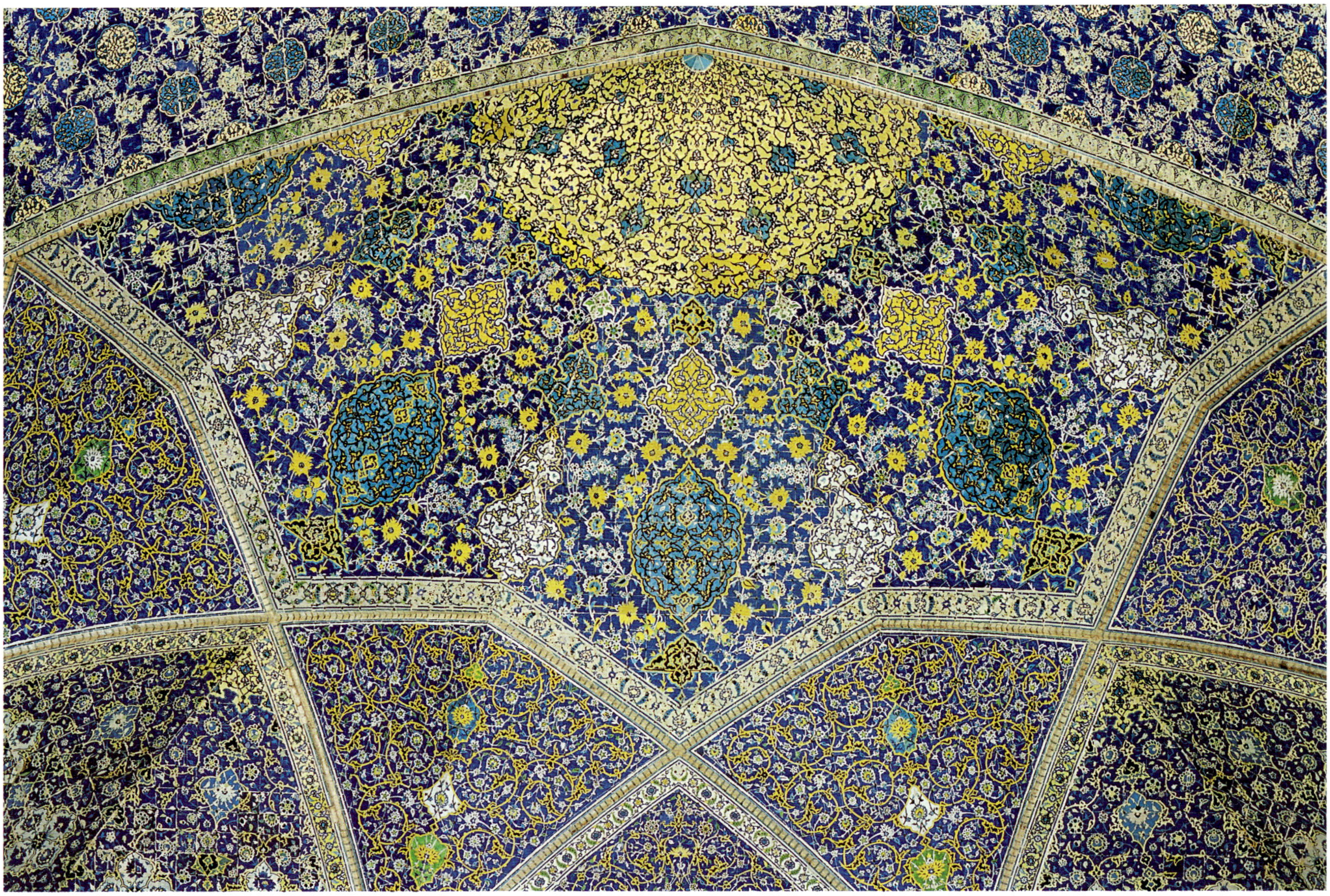

MASJID-I SHAH OR ROYAL MOSQUE, ISFAHAN (IRAN), COMPLETED 1627

♦ Panel in polychrome "black line" tilework decorated with an exuberant floral pattern.

♦ Interior of the half-dome decorated with a radiating pattern featuring mandorlas and floral scrollwork pendentives.

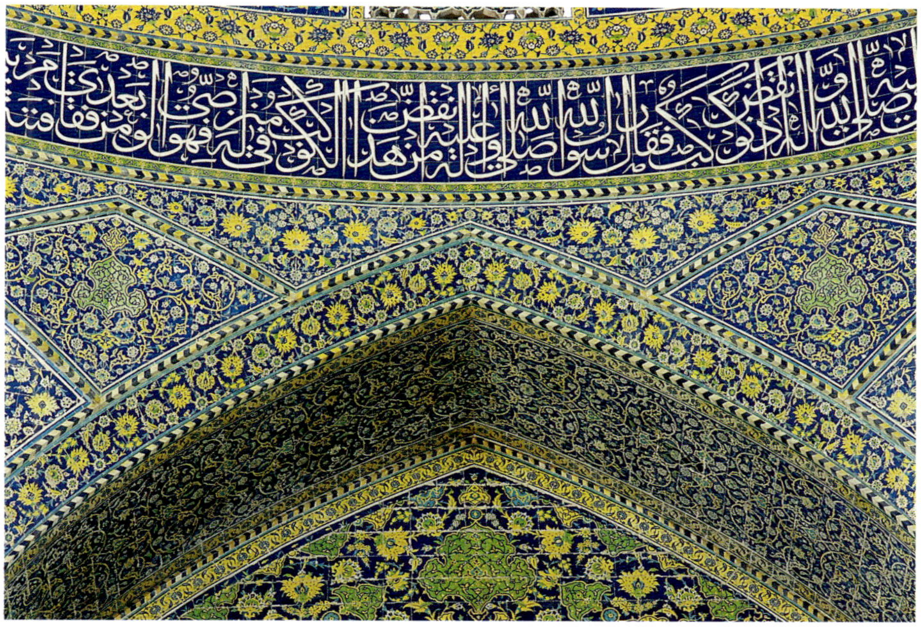

MASJID-I SHAH OR ROYAL MOSQUE, ISFAHAN (IRAN), COMPLETED 1627

♦ Inscriptional frieze around the base of the drum supporting the prayer hall cupola.

♦ Dome on squinches completely covered in polychrome "black line" tilework.

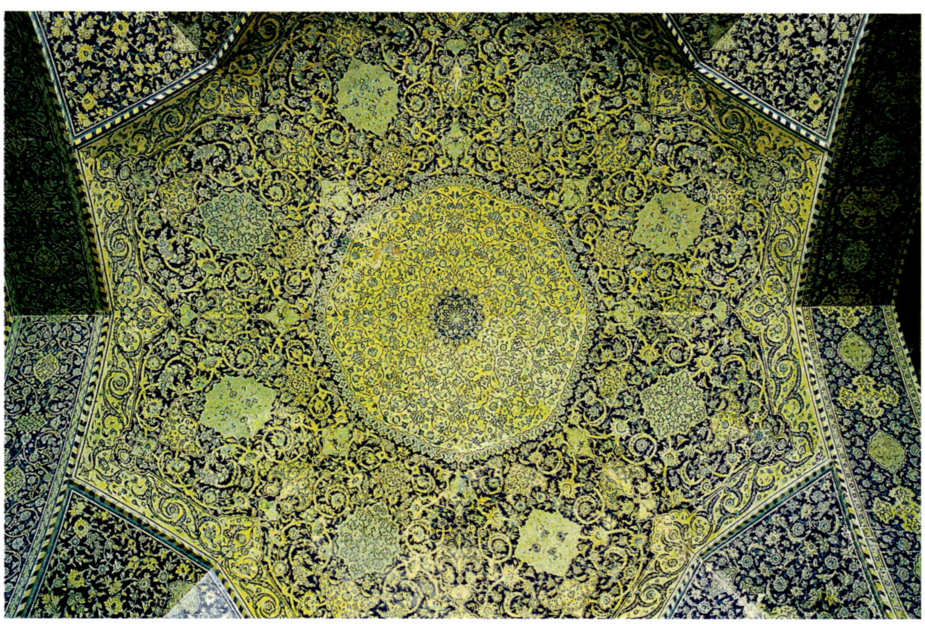

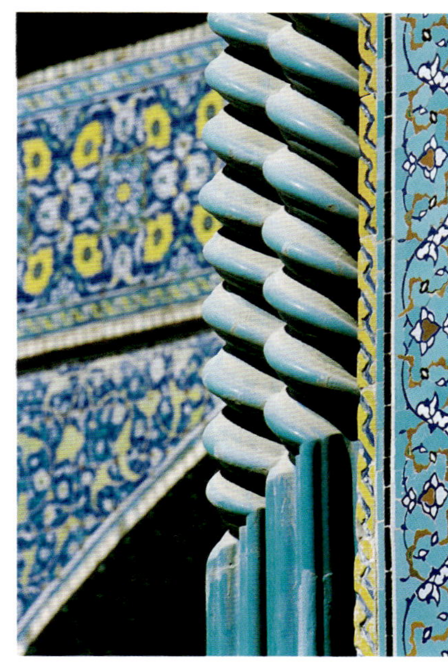

♦ Entrance *pishtaq* framed by turquoise-colored double torsades.

♦ Entrance *pishtaq* adorned with *muqarnas* lined in cut-tile mosaic.

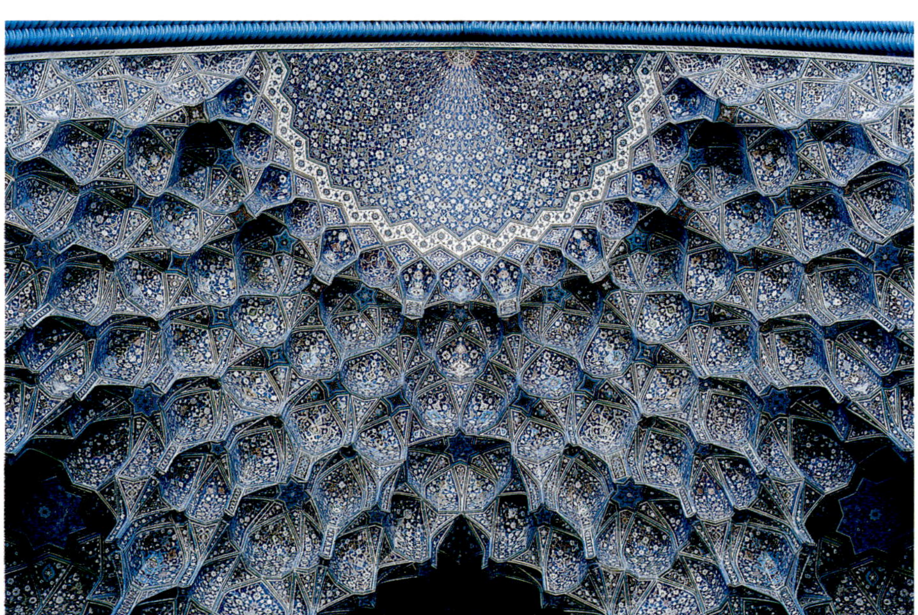

FOLLOWING DOUBLE PAGE

♦ Close-up of the motif at the center of the prayer hall cupola.

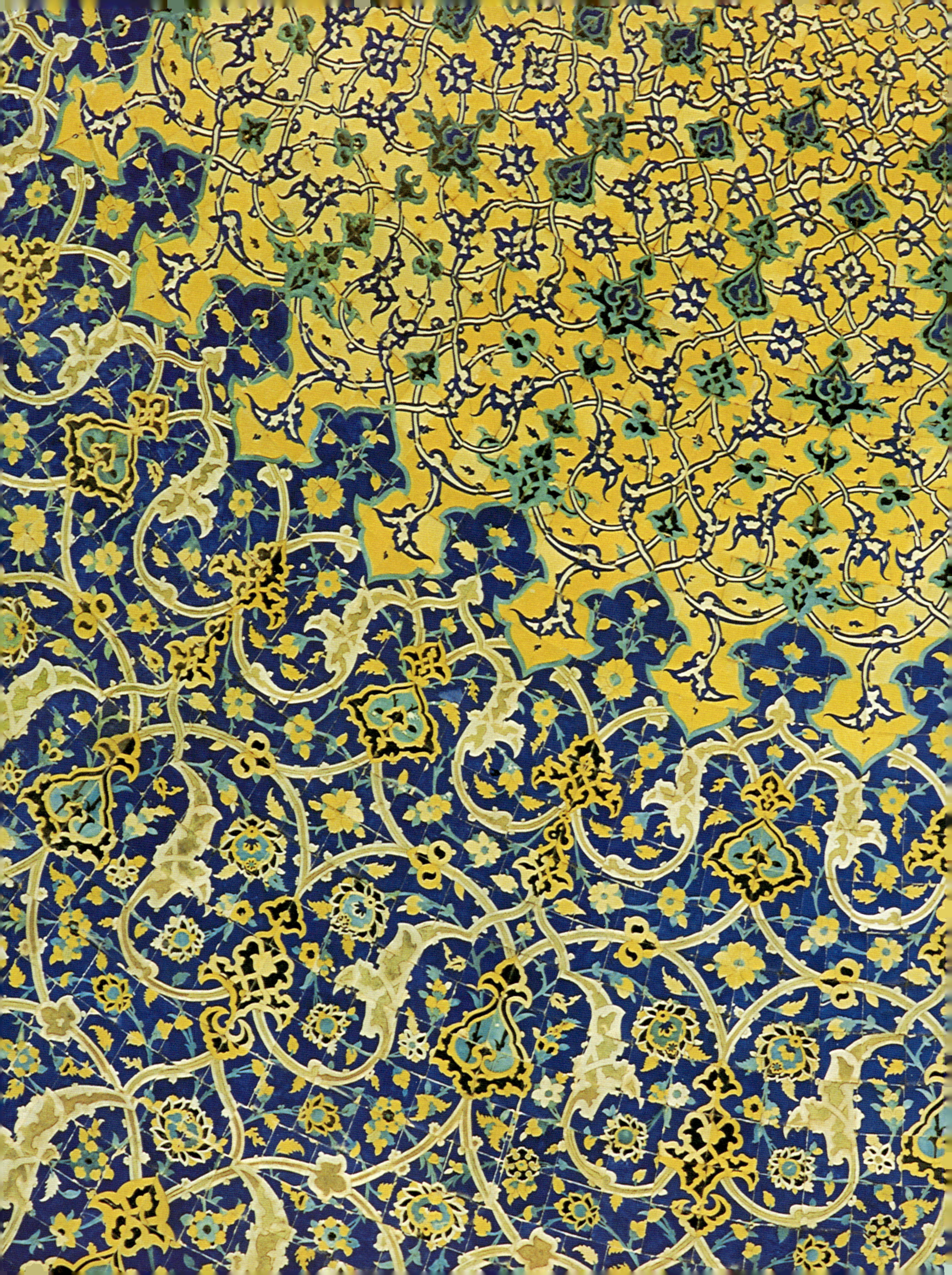

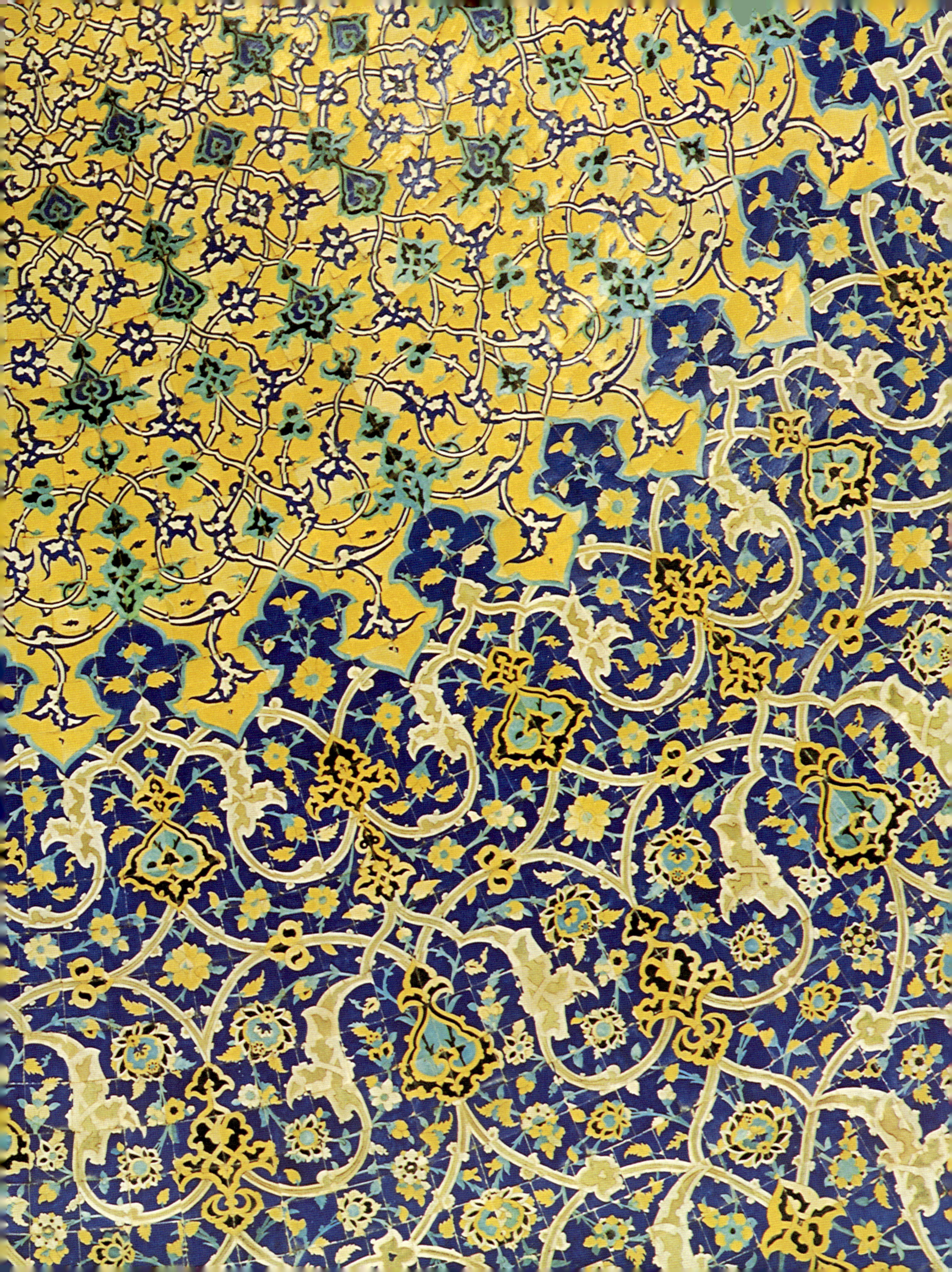

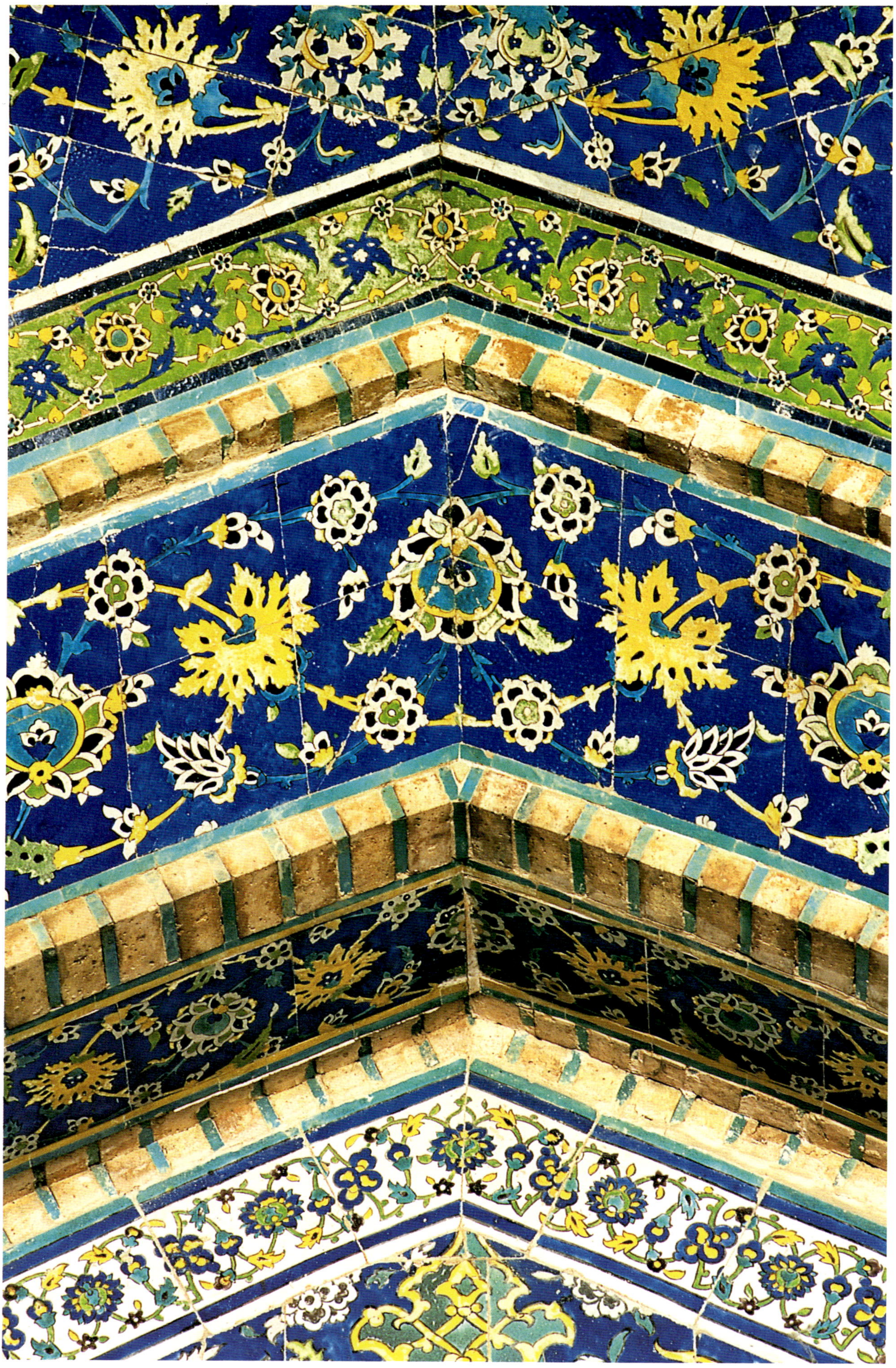

on which is applied a white enamel opacified with quartz. Thus, strictly speaking, this is not earthenware as the body is not a (tin-enameled) clay-paste. The colored glazes were separated by a poorly fusible black line that prevents the colors from mixing in the kiln. The earliest essays in polychrome tile-work date from the mid-thirteenth century (such as the star tiles at the palace in Kubadabad at Beyşehir), but, since the technique was difficult and costly, large surfaces were only rarely covered at that time. Certain authors consider that Shah `Abbas's craftsmen, in choosing a technique that consisted in cladding large surfaces in ceramic tilework—and not in mosaic—were simply taking the easy option. This assessment fails to take account of the centuries of effort that first had to be acquired to master the technological skills required.

The facade, set back slightly from the perimeter of the square, opens into a marvelous *pishtaq* that is straddled by a half-dome furnished with *muqarnas* and flanked by minarets. A broad horizontal epigraphic band, executed in ceramic and inscribed in white Thuluth script on a cobalt ground, is signed by Muhammad Riza al-Imami. In turquoise characters, the inscription also mentions the name of Shah `Abbas himself, together with that of architect `Ali Akbar al-Isfahani.[70]

Rising externally to 54 meters, the cupola above the prayer hall is the highest in the city. It is covered entirely in ceramics, with a double ribbon of arabesques, one white and the other yellow, applied to a turquoise ground. The drum is ringed by a Thuluth frieze in white on cobalt recording the name of Shah `Abbas and a date, A.H. 1037/A.D. 1627.

The decorative motifs inside the mosque are of unprecedented diversity, alternating large panels of polychrome tiles (for the flat portions) with cut-tile mosaic for the concave zones. Most of the decor relies on floral arabesque patterns, leaf-scrolls, and bouquets. Other motifs are more surprising, incorporating living creatures, such as birds, gazelles, ibex, and panthers. The double-shelled cupola within the prayer hall in front of the *mihrab* towers 38 meters high. A marvel of sophistication demonstrating exquisitely delicate handling, the decorative medallion in the center that spreads like a sunburst over the ample interlacing pattern surrounding it is once more redolent of Persian manuscript illumination. Inside the mosque, Homa`i-ye Shirazi noted two signatures in the name of the tilemaker, Master Qawam al-Din.[71] In the part of the mosque dating from Shah Sulayman's reign, an inscription of Muhammad Reza al-Emami, dated A.H. 1078/A.D. 1667–68, also provides the name of the architect, Qasim al-Banna` al-Isfahani.[72]

In accordance with Shah `Abbas's plan, the city continues to the west of the *maydan* as a long avenue bordered by gardens—the so-called Chahar Bagh ("Four Gardens"). The avenue provides an axis around which the palatial "garden city" is articulated. It is no surprise to read Pierre

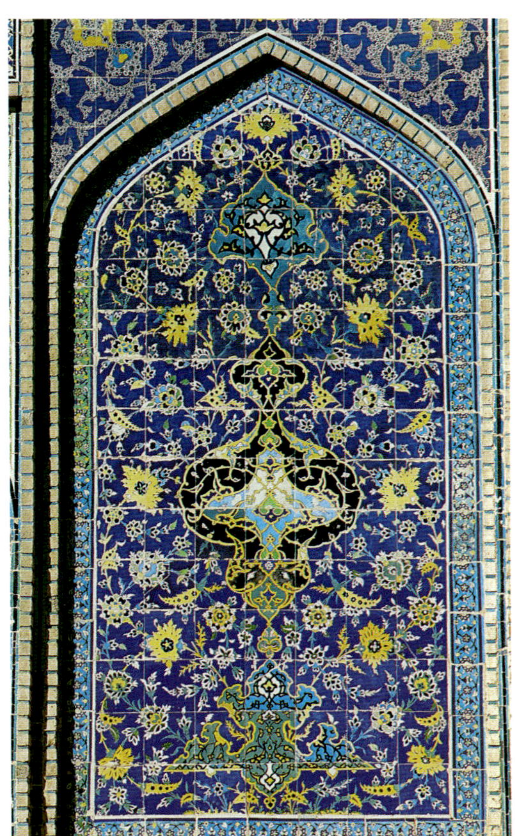

MASJID-I SHAH OR ROYAL MOSQUE, ISFAHAN (IRAN), COMPLETED 1627

FACING PAGE

♦ A series of archivolts each decorated with floral patterned banding.

LEFT

♦ Panel in polychrome "black line" tilework containing a fleuron pattern with vegetal scroll pendants.

Loti reacting to this avenue in the following terms: "In former times it was a promenade unique of its kind, something like an Isfahan Champs-Élysées."

For the most part, Safavid palaces are not grandiose constructions but buildings of modest proportions, often located in the middle of a garden. The `Ali Qapu pavilion, or "Sublime Porte," overlooking the royal square from a high terrace functioned at one and the same time as an official tribune, an audience hall in which the king received ambassadors, and as an entry to the enclosure housing the palaces located west of the Naqsh-i Jahan square. This palace-cum-portal underwent several construction phases; begun in 1609, it originally incorporated an entrance set back from the precinct onto which it opened. The projecting part of the edifice that supports the elegant timber-columned terrace is actually a subsequent addition dating from 1664. The spandrels astride the entrance arch and the side arches—as well as the window arches of the facade to the garden side—are decorated in brightly colored ceramic elements. A horizontal band surmounting the lintel over the entryway mentions the name of Nasir al-Din Shah Qajar and bears the date A.H. 1274/A.D. 1857–58, implying that, like a considerable number of monuments in Isfahan, the `Ali Qapu underwent restoration work even before the present day.[73]

Opposite the Royal Mosque on the other side of the square stands the entrance to the Qaysariya Bazaar (1605–17). Both spandrels above the portal arch are prettily decorated with a cut-tile mosaic motif representing a Sagittarius figure (undoubtedly restored more than once). Some authors propose that the motif refers to the month during which the door was executed.

Shah `Abbas seems to have devoted much time and energy to erecting public buildings in cities all over the kingdom. One of these was the bazaar at Kashan (1600–1), where the cupola vaulting the crossing of the two main galleries is bedecked with *muqarnas* and lined with scintillating multicolored ceramics.

Among the buildings forming the palatial complex, an edifice known as the Chihil Sutun, or Palace of the Forty Columns (completed in 1647), still stands. It owes its name to the twenty tall timber shafts decorating its facade that are reflected in the long pool opposite. The columns bear a flat roof that forms a deep porch to the front of the palace. The ceiling is entirely

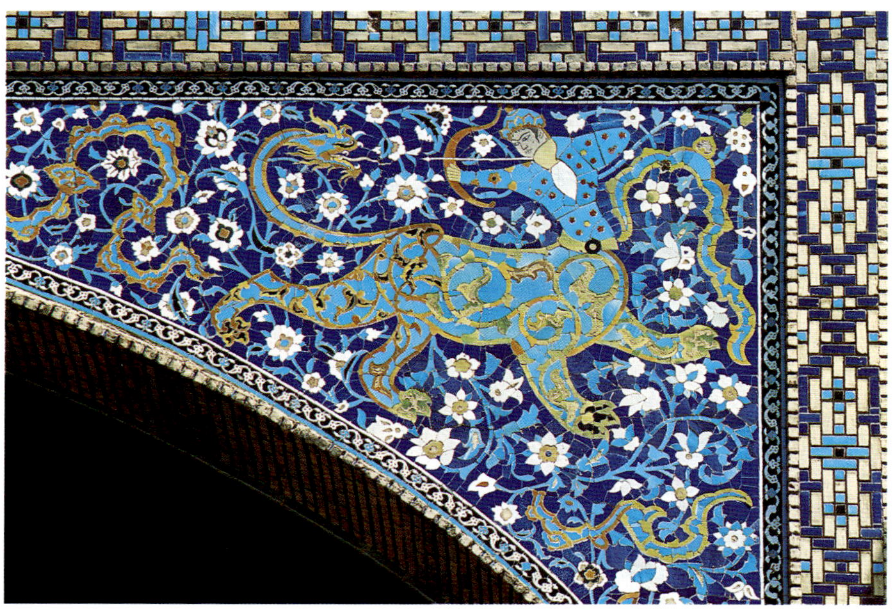

♦ Spandrel decorated by a motif representing a figure of Sagittarius in cut-tile mosaic. Entrance to the Qaysariya Bazaar on the Isfahan *maydan* (Iran), 1605–17.

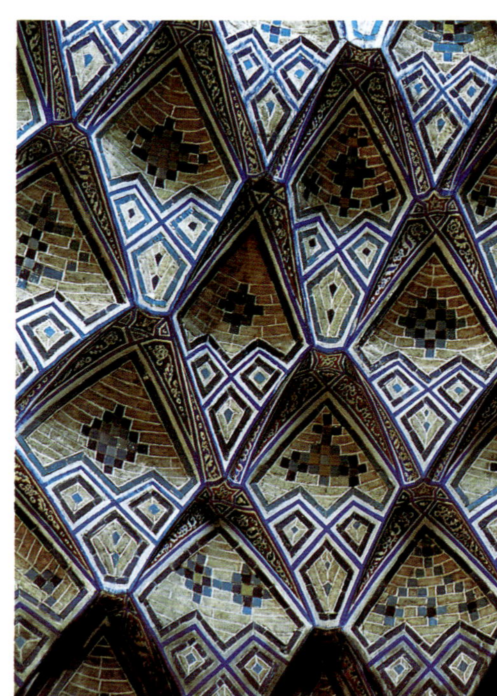

BAZAAR IN KASHAN (IRAN), FOUNDED 1600–1

RIGHT

♦ Detail of the *muqarnas* in the cupola, which are decorated with geometrical elements in *banna'i* fashion.

FACING PAGE

♦ Cupola decorated with *muqarnas* at the intersection of two passages.

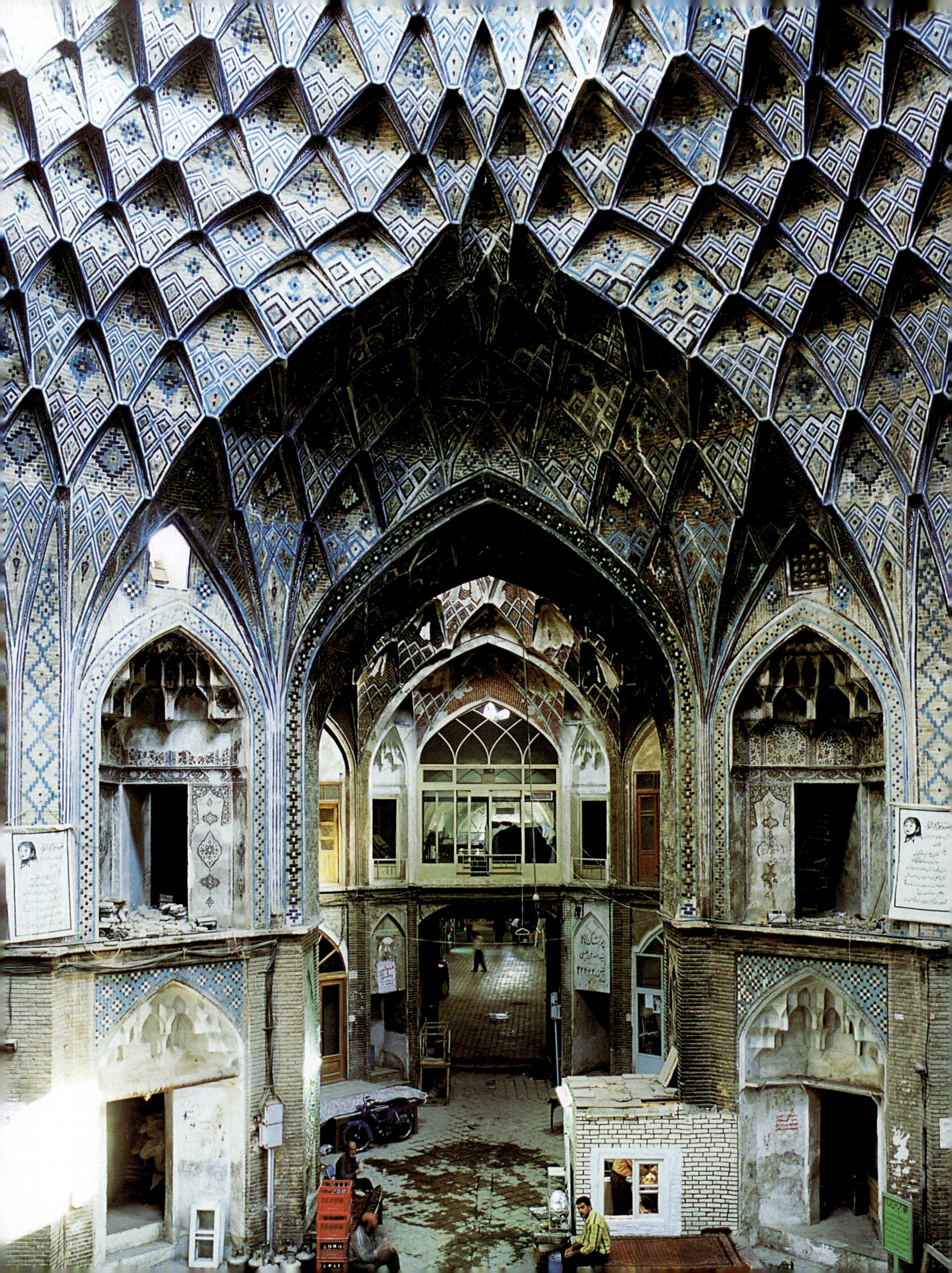

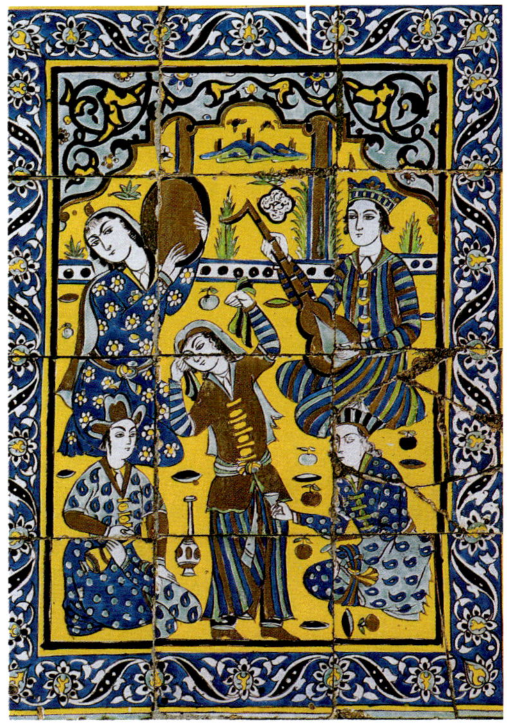

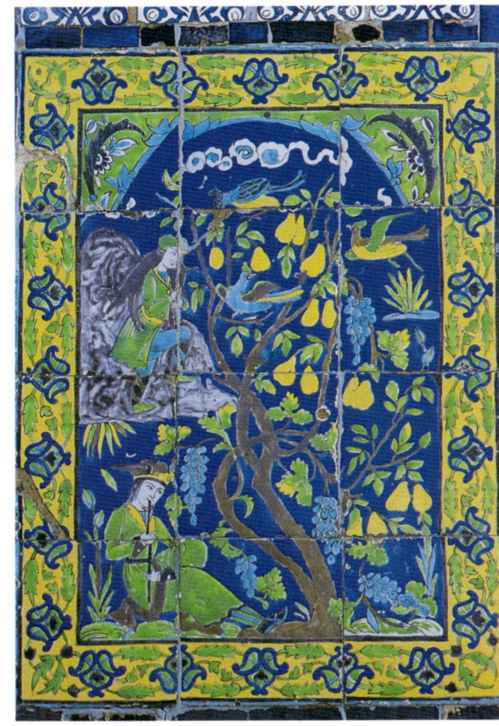

PALAIS D'ORIENT, TUNIS (TUNISIA)

♦ Panel in the Safavid style depicting the feast of King Manuchehr, the hero of Firdusi's *Book of Kings*.

♦ Safavid-style panel in polychrome "black line" tilework showing an idyllic country scene.

FACING PAGE

♦ Detail of the same panel portraying a flute-player.

FOLLOWING DOUBLE PAGE

♦ Detail of the Safavid-style panel depicting musicians and dancers.

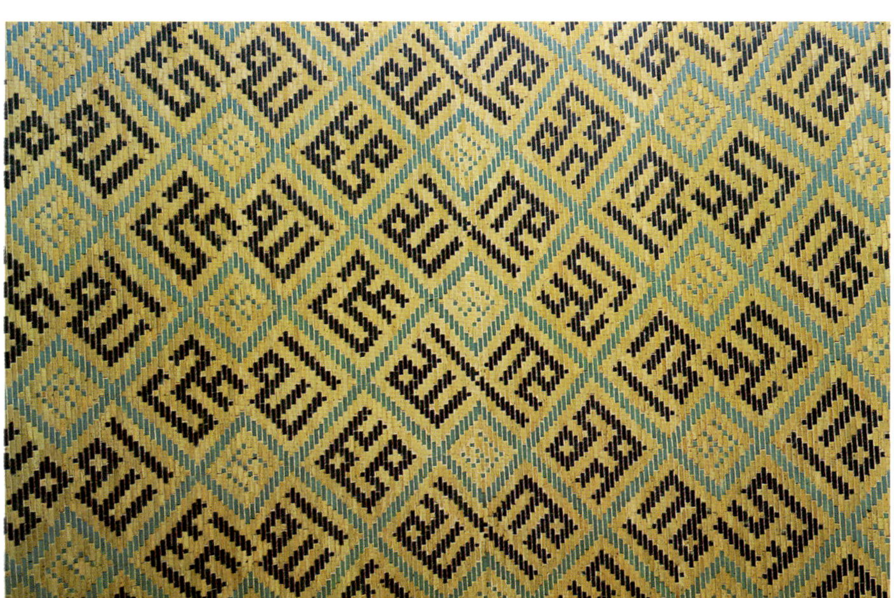

♦ Intrados of a vault decorated with *banna'i* bricks arranged to form the names of Allah, Muhammad, and `Ali in Kufic script. Hakim Mosque, Isfahan (Iran), 1656–57.

lined in beveled mirrors framed by an array of square compartments. The porch precedes an *iwan* capped by a half-cupola whose cells are lined with mirror-glass mounted in a metal setting; the *iwan* leads to an amply proportioned oblong room with a triple cupola. On both sides of this large hall lie two apartments whose walls are decorated with a number of recently restored paintings. Some of these are patently influenced by European models, while others, in a style characteristic of the early-seventeenth-century Isfahan school, were painted by Riza `Abbasi, one of the foremost artists at the court of Shah `Abbas. Originally, the external spandrels of the palace were decorated with a number of ceramic panels. It is possible that the large figure panels in a style of painting resembling a diluted version of Reza `Abbasi's that are today to be found in the Victoria and Albert Museum, London, and at the Louvre came from this palace. These large compositions were probably executed from cartoons by the great painter or by his school.

In *Le Tour du Monde* (1887), Jane Dieulafoy described the gardens formerly connecting this palace to that of the "Eight Paradises": "To repair from the Chihil Sutun to the Hasht Bihisht or 'Eight Paradises,' one starts by walking along a pool connecting two gardens of a typically Persian stamp. English parks whose grassy lawns are dotted with baskets of flowers or clumps of trees, or French eighteenth-century gardens, with their stiff, severe lines, can give little idea of the place. The *baghs* (gardens) sown beneath tall, pollarded plane trees are like fields covered in close-planted flowers, with total want of regard for color or species. These long

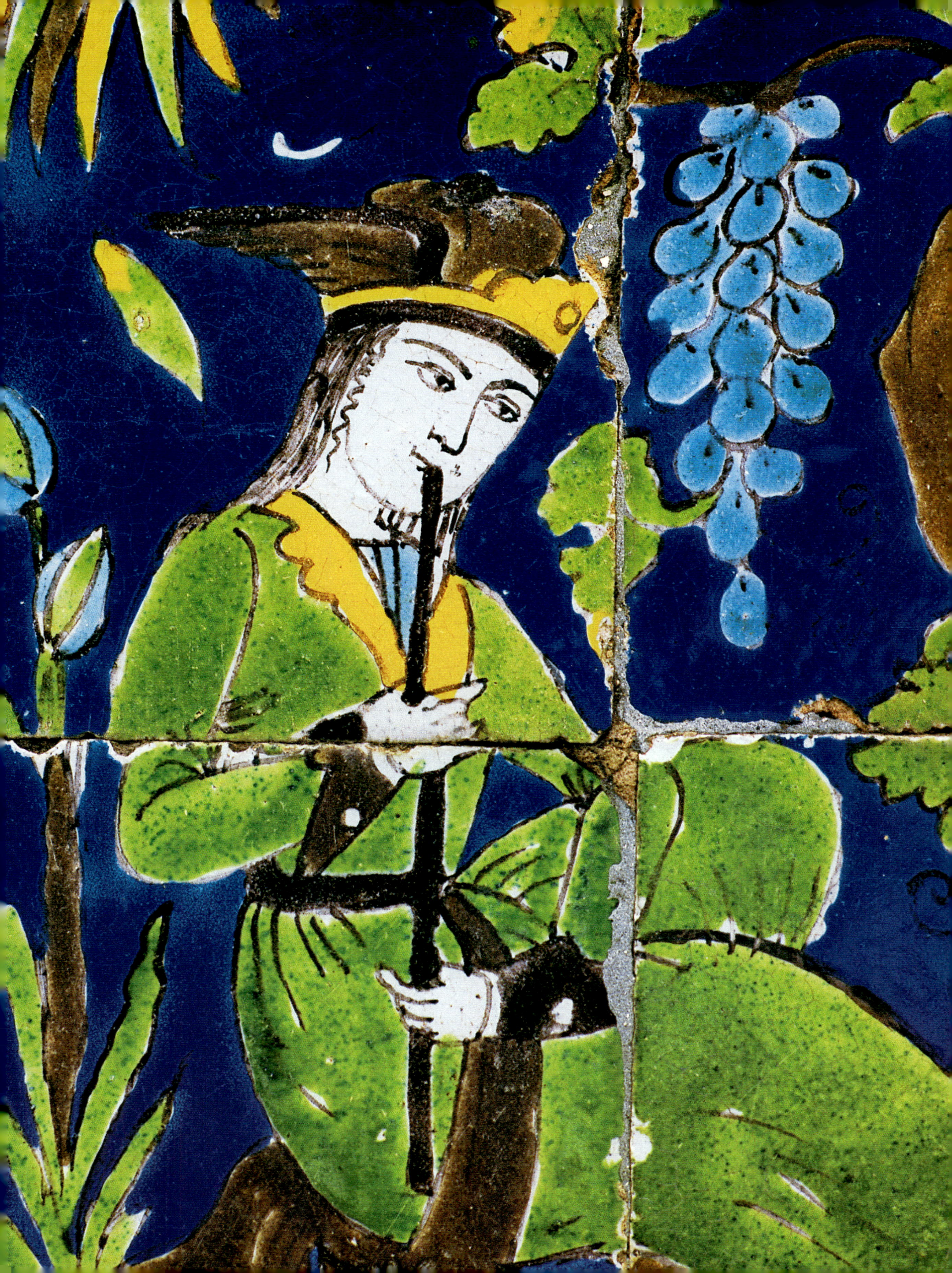

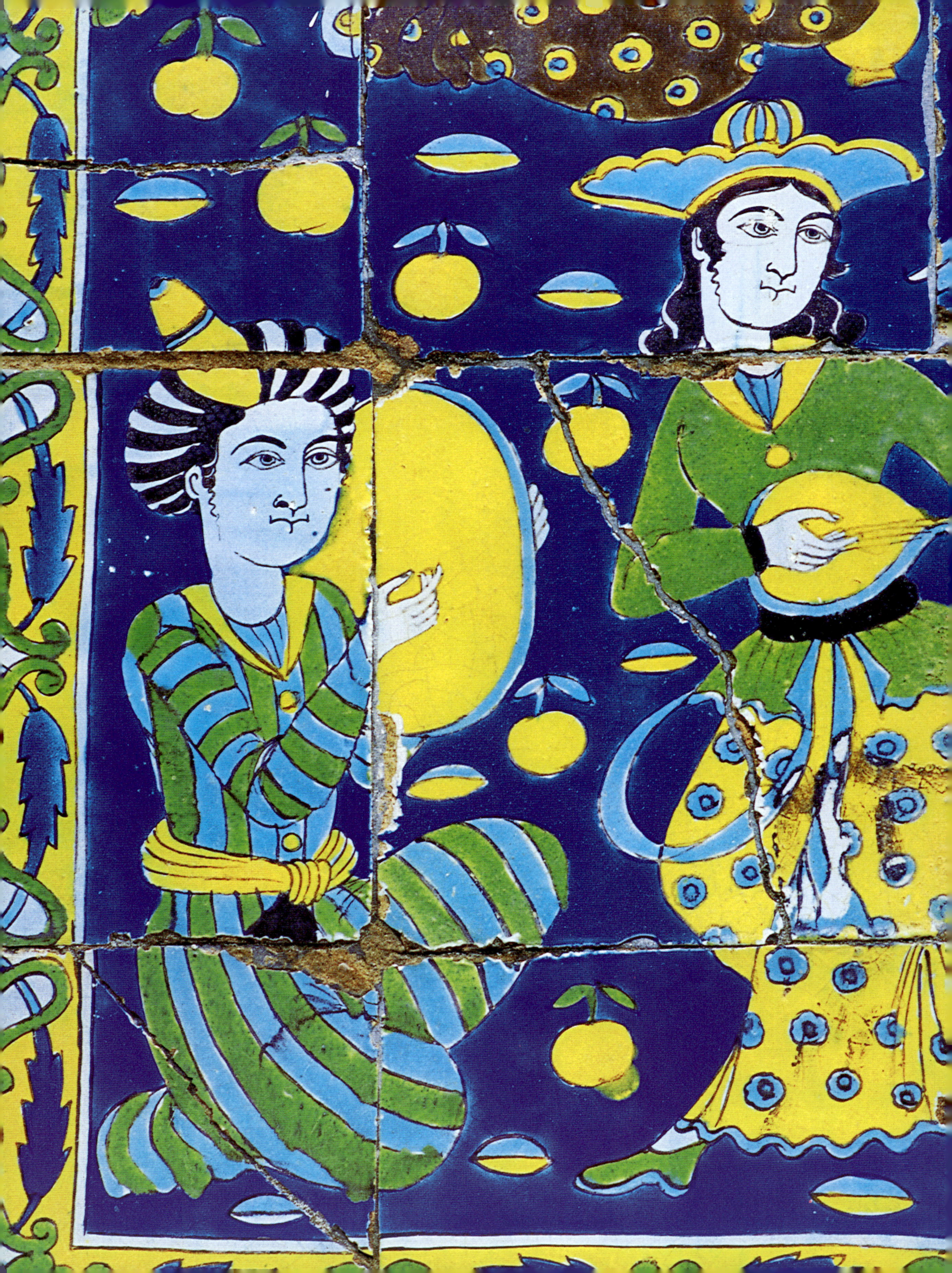

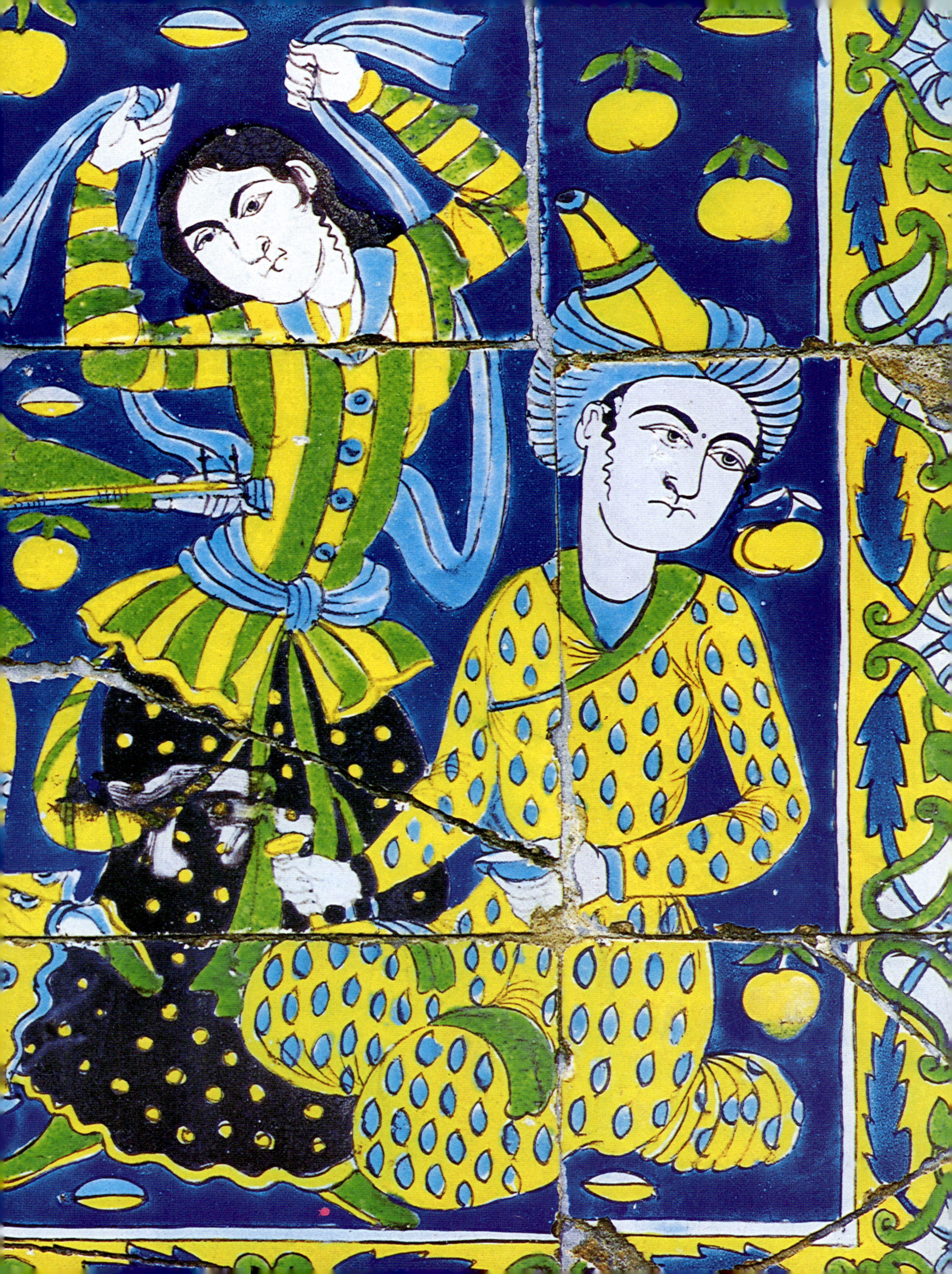

parterres appear strange indeed, and if, investigating them closely, one can reproach their want of order, one is forced to concede that, seen from afar and under a blazing sun, the effect produced is charming, with each flower looking brighter than the scintillating butterflies that brush them with their wings." The era of Shah `Abbas II (1642–66) was also marked by the building of numerous monuments in Isfahan, notably the Hakim Mosque with its remarkable ceramic tilework, some of which is dated A.H. 1067/A.D. 1656–57.

Built under Shah Sulayman (1667–94), the Hasht Bihisht or "Eight Paradises" pavilion is undeniably one of the finest achievements in all Safavid palace architecture. Its central plan (a square whose corners are lopped off to leave an irregular-shaped octagon) is composed of four eight-sided rooms—with a further story housing four identical chambers above—surrounding a central octagonal hall. The edifice is cowned by a cupola topped by a lantern. This quadripartite division of space is echoed in the layout of the parterres in the garden where the pavilion stands and alludes to the Four Rivers that crisscross Paradise.

The building possesses four facades presenting two tiers of arcades. The main entrance lies to the north while the *iwan* spans the whole elevation, including on the east and west sides; only the south entrance stops at the first arcade tier. In all, the building counts forty-nine arcades all adorned with spandrels decorated in "black line" polychrome ceramic. This extraordinary ensemble—restored in the 1970s—represents one of the most attractive examples of Safavid figurative art in architectural ceramics that remains in situ.[74] The spandrels show elements from the fabulous bestiary of Persia, as well as scenes with angel-like creatures or other figures; certain panels were restored at an early period and are now adorned with bouquets of flowers in a style inspired by Mughal India. Small bouquets are also to be found lining the pool in the pavilion's northern *iwan*.

At the time of his journey to Isfahan, Pierre Loti noted the state of dilapidation into which the city-cum-garden had fallen: "Tscharbag is a place of indescribable melancholy. The plane trees, their crowns branchless, stand like dying giants. Overrun by funereal weed, the flagstones gape. The basins have long since run dry or turned to festering pools. The flower beds have all disappeared and the last

MADAR-I SHAH *MADRASA*, ISFAHAN (IRAN), 1704–14

♦ Dado decorated with stars and hexagons in cut-tile mosaic.

♦ Vault in the west court *iwan*, decorated in cut-tile mosaic with mandorla-like shapes and inscriptions written in Kufic on a plain brick ground.

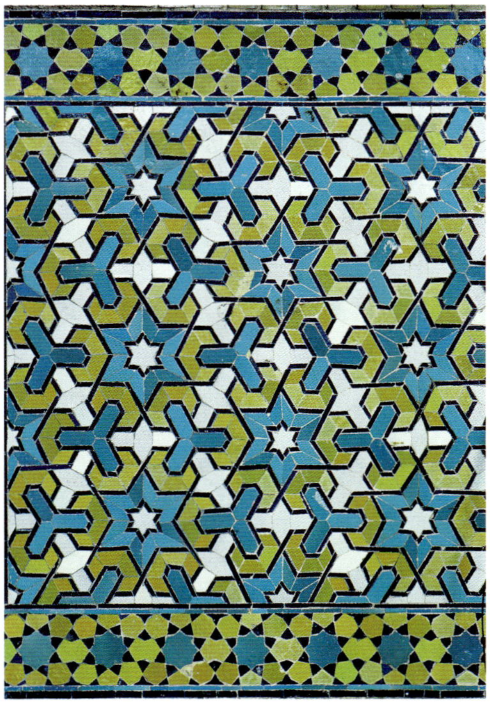

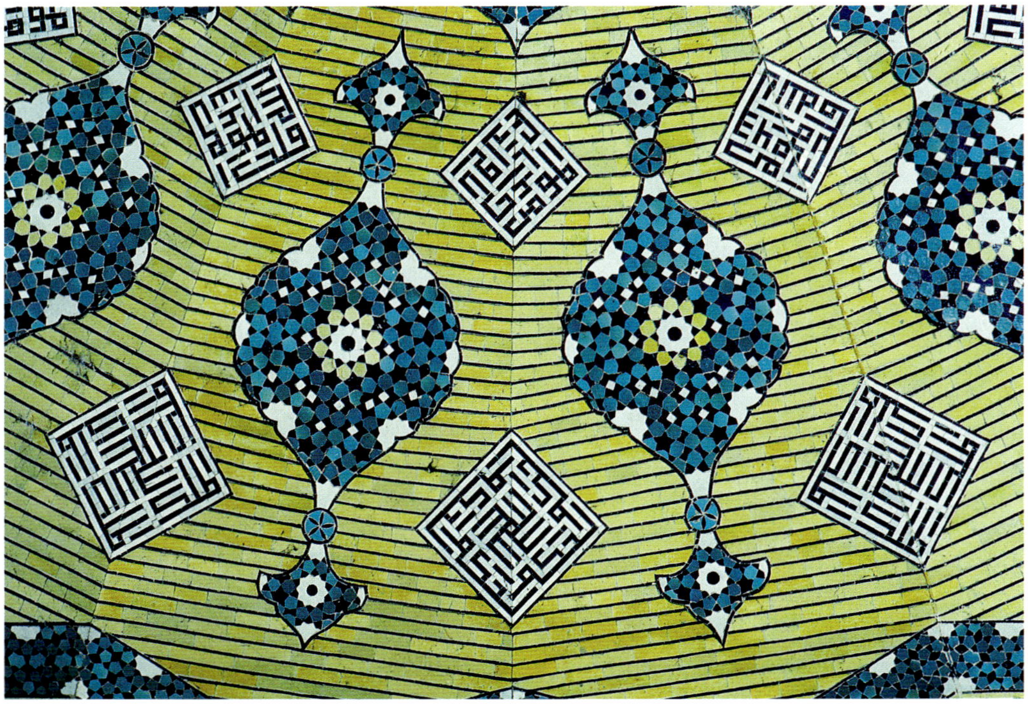

rose-trees grown rank and wild. Any chance passer-by can just walk into the few palaces still standing where delicate ceilings crumble to dust. Hardly had the Afghans arrived than they fanatically started to deface the paintings on earthenware plaques depicting elegant ladies."

Fortunately, since Loti's time the majority of the Safavid monuments preserved have undergone intensive restoration work. In the Palace of the Eight Paradises itself, whole sections of ceramic decoration that had lain hidden under "rococo"-style stucco applied in the nineteenth century gradually came to light. Murals in the `Ali Qapu and the Chihil Sutun have also been painstakingly refurbished. Some palaces were in a state of total collapse by the early years of the twentieth century and we can only gain an idea of their long-lost splendor through descriptions or from engravings.

Of later date, and located on the edge of the great promenade of the "Four Gardens," the Madar-i Shah ("Mother of the Shah") *madrasa* was built between 1704 and 1714. Through the superb portal surmounted by stalactites one arrives at a court surrounded by cells for the students. The garden, crossed by a stretch of the Chahar Bagh canal, is fabulously poetic. The prayer hall, located on the southern side of the court, is capped by a turquoise cupola of great elegance covered in intricate arabesque garlands. Here too ceramic decorations predominate and, as Pierre Loti was to describe it, "The walls enclosing the garden are, from top to bottom, simply one immense mosaic in every shade of blue imaginable." Immediately next door, the caravansary that today has been converted into a luxury hotel formerly used to raise funds for the religious institution next door.

Virtually contemporary, the Armenian church-cathedral of Vank (1702–15) in the suburb of Djolfa also harbors some beautiful examples of Safavid ceramics. The most notable features are the dados formed from polychrome tiles on which figure *inter alia*—and most especially behind the shrine—angels in a surround of serrated leaves and interwoven floral trails. Older dados—dating in fact from 1664—are populated by a teeming menagerie, including ducks, phoenix, gazelles, and ibex, set off against a rather garish yellow or turquoise ground. Predating the cathedral, the Church of St. George (1610) also contains a pictorial panel dating from 1619 above the north door. This depiction of the Adoration of the Magi undoubtedly represents one of the earliest known examples in a Safavid context of a historiated panel presenting human figures.

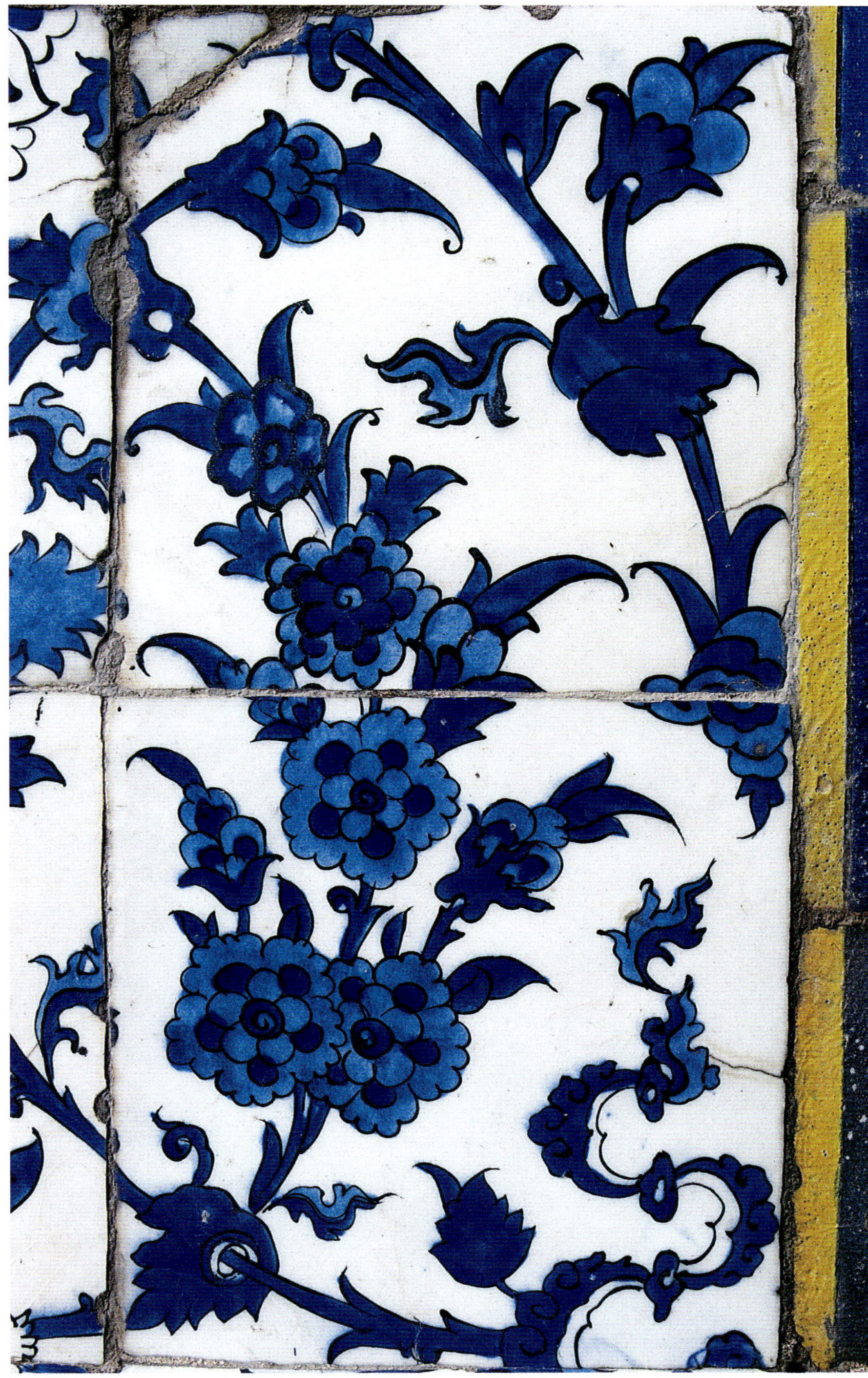

♦ Blue-and-white underglaze-painted ceramic panel dating from the seventeenth century. The pattern recalls those found on ceramic wares produced in the same region of central Iran. Friday Mosque, Kerman (Iran), 1349.

Irises and Roses: Iran of the Zands and the Qajars

Starting with the Afghan invasions in 1722, the Safavid empire gradually disintegrated, plunging the territory of Iran into a period of upheaval from which two rival and short-lived dynasties eventually struggled free. In 1736, General Tahmasp Quli Khan proclaimed himself king under the name Nadir Shah (1736–47), thereby usurping the crown of the Safavid sovereigns, although their authority lingered on nominally to 1786. Nadir Shah's tumultuous reign was marked in particular by an Indian campaign (1738–39), during which the Mughal empire was severely undermined and the treasure of Delhi plundered and much of it spirited off to Iran. Following Nadir Shah's assassination in 1747, his successors retreated primarily toward the Khorasan, establishing their capital at Mashhad. That dynasty in turn perished in 1795 under pressure from another fledgling power, the ascendant Qajars. The death of Nadir Shah also provided the opportunity for another dynasty to come to the fore in the province of Fars in the south of the country, with Shiraz as its capital. Initially adopting the title of regent in the name of the Safavid puppet Isma'il III, in 1750 Karim Khan Zand went on to found a dynasty that was to reign over southern Persia until 1794.

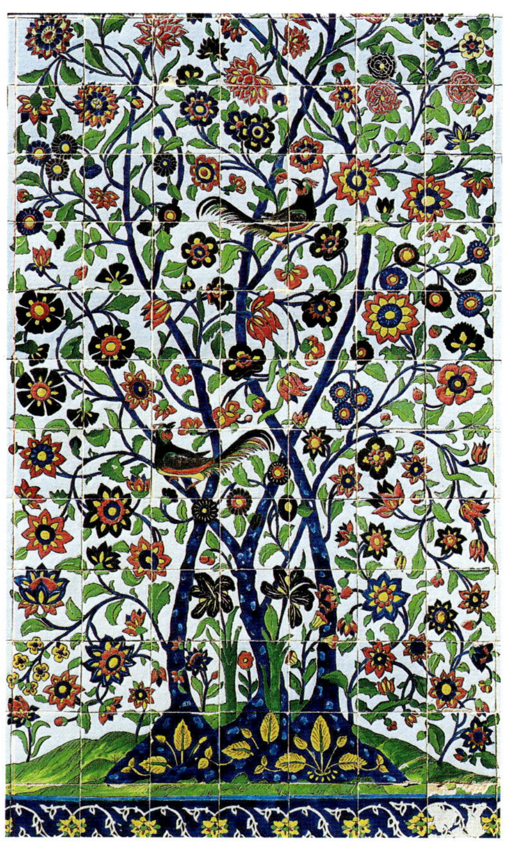

PAVILION OF KARIM KHAN ZAND, SHIRAZ (IRAN), MID-EIGHTEENTH CENTURY

♦ Panel showing pheasants roosting among flowering trees.

FACING PAGE, TOP

♦ A spandrel of polychrome ceramic tiles depicting the reigning prince as King Solomon listening to the hoopoe, a messenger sent by Balqis, Queen of Sheba.

Shiraz was selected as the capital by Karim Khan (1750–79) and during the reign of this regent (the *vakil*), the city was endowed with many monuments, most of which are preserved today. Karim Khan Zand's charming pavilion dating from the middle of the eighteenth century (today the Pars museum) presents a square plan with its corners severed to generate an irregular octagon. The long sides, which open up into wide bays in the center, are flanked by panels over two levels lined in polychrome ceramics, with, in the lower zone, flowering trees brimming with birds and, above, plentiful bouquets flanked by a pair of peacocks. The spandrels on the shorter sides of the octagon are more narrative in nature and include, in particular, scenes of hunting. At this time the range of colors employed expanded with the addition of pink, the emblematic color of the rose of Shiraz.

Describing the ceramics in the Vakil Mosque at Shiraz (1773–74), Pierre Loti noted: "Various blues dominate in the earthenware revetment and are blended with a little yellow, a little green, just enough in fact to make the overall color resemble old turquoise from afar. From out of this ensemble, branches of iris and rose burst forth here and there; the master enamelers as if haphazardly strewed them among the large religious inscriptions in white script on a royal-blue ground that frame the doors and run the whole length of the friezes."

The Vakil Mosque presents a plan indebted to antique examples, with a spacious prayer hall supported by five rows of massive twisted columns capped by capitals of Sasanid inspiration. The hypostyle opens into a large *iwan* adjoining the court; the two solitary *iwans* are flanked by small minarets betraying hints of an Indian influence. The ceramic panels decorating the mosque have often been restored; on the prayer-hall *iwan*, for instance, one can read the date A.H. 1244/A.D. 1828.

Located hard by the mosque, the Vakil *madrasa* dates from the time of Shah `Abbas (1615), although it was restored under Karim Khan Zand, and again by the Qajars. It too possesses some beautiful floral ceramic tile panels. Finally, the *vakil* was also responsible for rebuilding the bazaar with beautiful domed galleries and caravansaries, among which the Saray-i Moshir, since converted into a "tea house."

The Qajar dynasty originated in the northeast of Iran. It was Aqa Muhammad Khan, governor of Azerbaijan in 1757 and the first sovereign crowned in 1779, who established the capital at Teheran. The dynasty reached its apogee during the reign of his successor, Fath `Ali Shah (1797–1834). In order to forestall the Russian advance in the north of the country, diplomatic

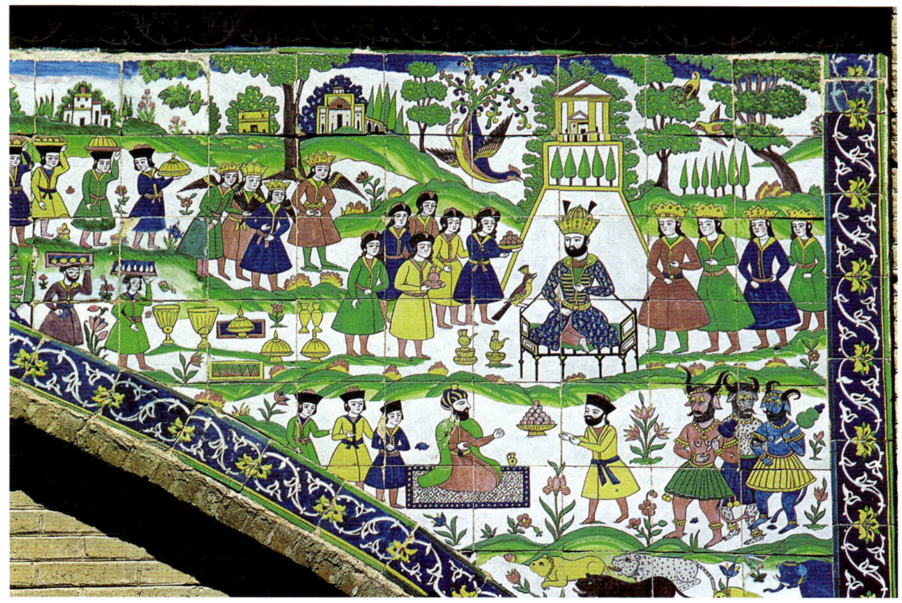

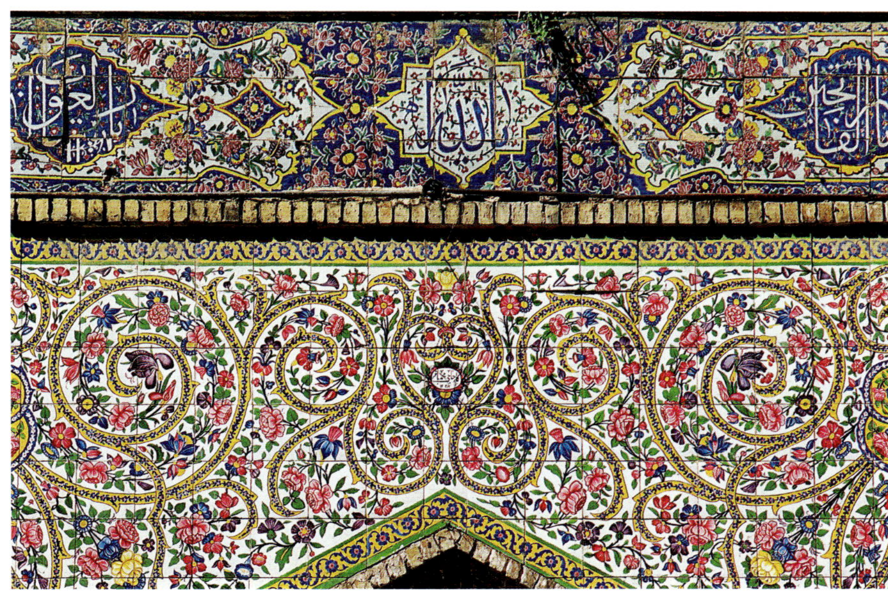

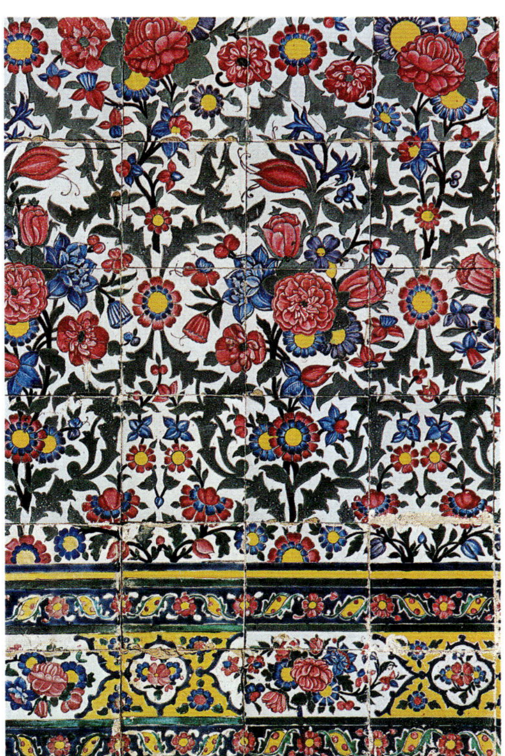

VAKIL MOSQUE, SHIRAZ (IRAN) FOUNDED 1773–74

ABOVE

♦ Polychrome ceramic decoration with the signature Hajji Muhammad Baqir and the date A.H. 1247/A.D. 1831–32.

LEFT

♦ Polychrome "black line" ceramic tile panel. The Shiraz palette is characterized by the appearance of the color pink.

VAKIL MOSQUE, SHIRAZ (IRAN), FOUNDED 1773–74

♦ Panel in polychrome ceramic. The vase that seems to explode into bloom clearly shows a Western influence.

♦ The irises, poppies, and flowering branches inspired Orientalist traveler Pierre Loti's enchanting descriptions of the mosque.

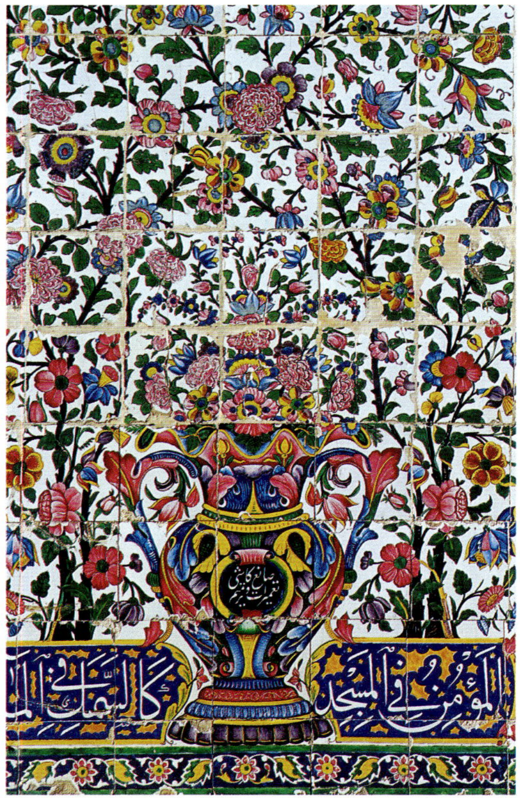

FACING PAGE

♦ Detail of a polychrome ceramic tile panel with a floral pattern. Aqa Bozorg *madrasa*, Kashan (Iran), 1851–52.

relations were forged with Napoleon I and with the British. The protracted reign of Nasir al-Din Shah Qajar (1848–96) was typical of the way the dynasty's sovereigns would do all in their power to counter the territorial ambitions of the Great Powers. From the end of the nineteenth century, however, the kingdom was beset by political movements which, in 1906, eventually obtained a constitution and a parliament. Consequently the Qajar sovereign became little more than a puppet, to the point that an obscure army officer promoted commander-in-chief of the army was able to dispatch him easily. So it was that, in 1924, Riza Khan declared himself king and founded the ephemeral Pahlavi dynasty (1924–78).

Although it was in the reign of Aqa Muhammad Khan that Teheran was chosen

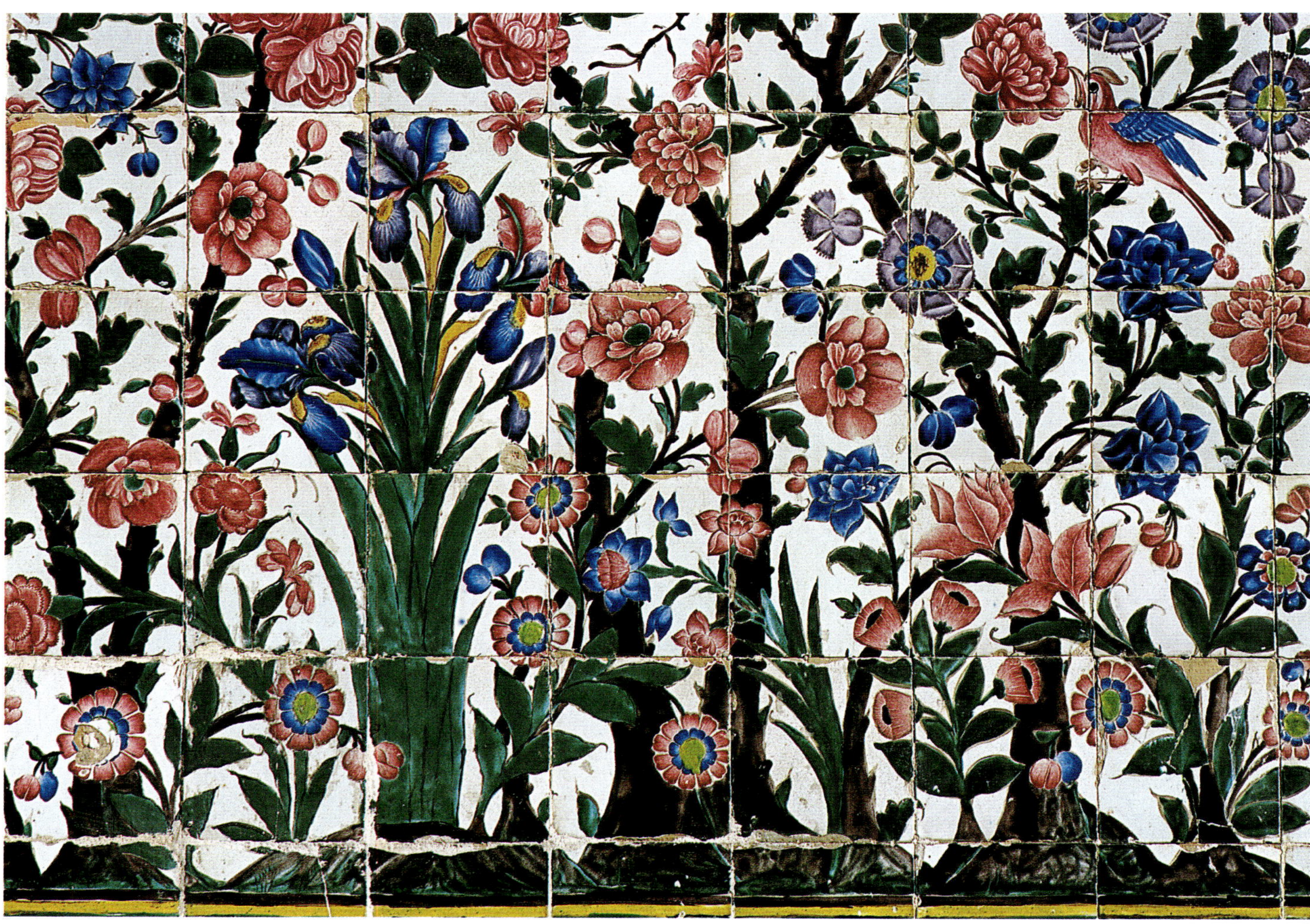

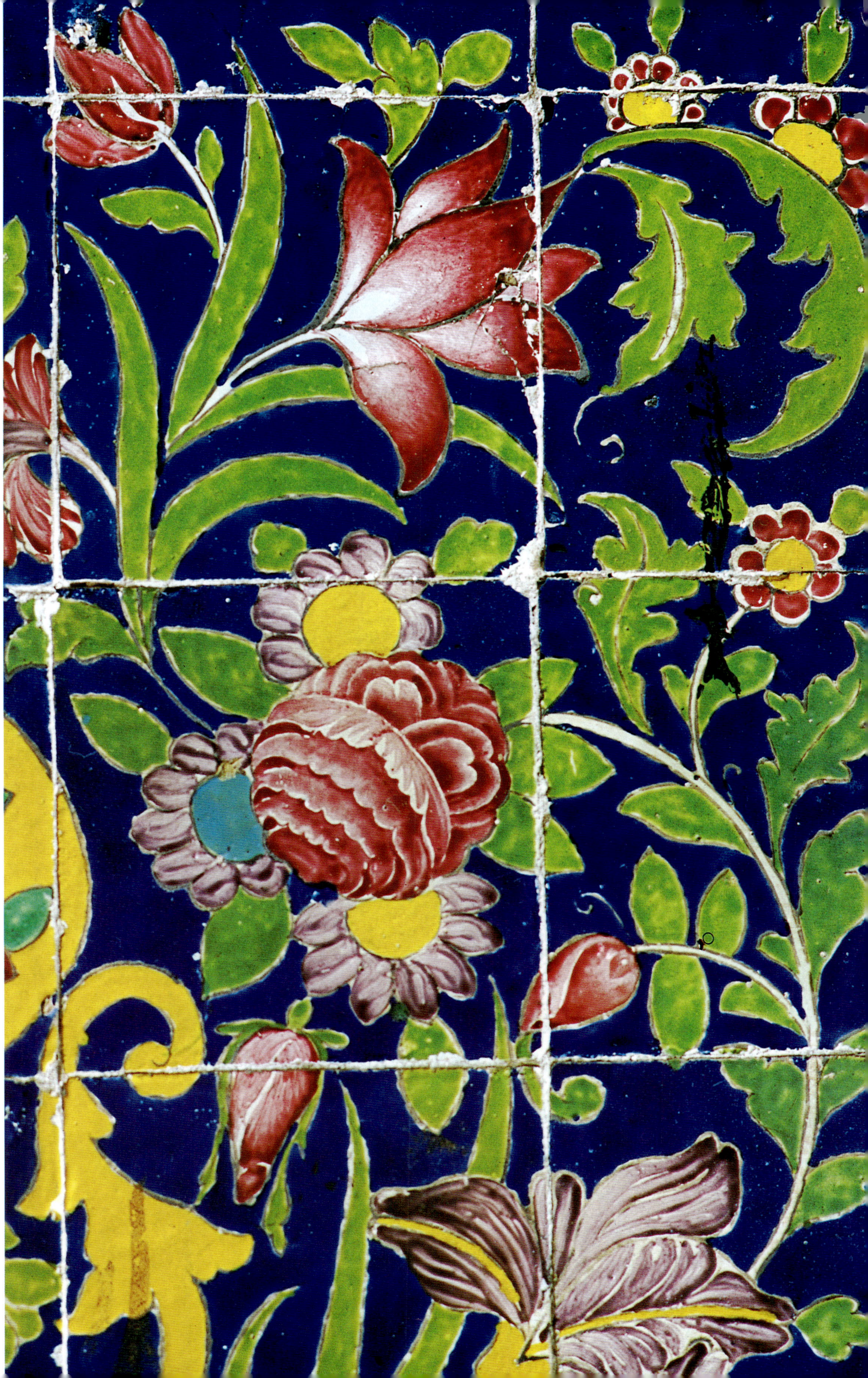

as the new dynasty's capital, it was above all during the rule of Fath `Ali Shah that the city was adorned with its principal monuments, most notably with the construction of the Gulistan Palace. This building is all that remains of an ancient citadel (*arg*) founded in Safavid times. The houses and palaces as they appear today primarily bear the stamp of the Nasir al-Din Shah Qajar period, but with some later additions. Thus, the Palace of the Marble Throne (Takht-i Marmar) is almost the only one to have preserved the character it had at its construction in 1806. Other buildings, such as the Emarat-i Badgir ("House of the Wind Towers"), also built under Fath `Ali Shah, were extensively renovated under Nasir al-Din Shah Qajar, being faced with a great wealth of ceramics. Begun in 1865, the Shams al-Emare is undoubtedly the most significant building in the whole palace complex; with its twin towers crowned by kiosks, it represents the epitome of mid-nineteenth-century Qajar architecture, in which ceramics played a significant role in the decoration of exposed surfaces. Narrative episodes, including elements from Firdusi's *Shah-Name*, and charming scenes like that of the band of musicians framing the main staircase, alternate with floral compositions and landscape views treated in a "European" style with a sometimes naïve brush.

Palatial architecture of the Qajar period can be appreciated in other examples preserved in provincial capitals. The vast garden of the Bagh-i Eram preserved at Shiraz, for example, is today a model of the parks with kiosks typical of the Qajar epoch. Although it must have been begun around 1795, the central pavilion was clearly the product of a number of subsequent phases in its construction. The lunettes adorning the principal facade are decorated with narrative scenes depicting heroic exploits from Firdusi's *Shah-Name* alongside equestrian portraits of Nasir al-Din Shah Qajar. The final interventions on

AQA BOZORG *MADRASA*, KASHAN (IRAN), 1851–52

♦ Polychrome ceramic tile panel decorated with a vase of leafy blooms.

♦ Polychrome ceramic border tiles decorated with irises and birds.

FACING PAGE

♦ Cupola over squinches forming a star pattern. The structural lines are painted to contrast with the natural brick.

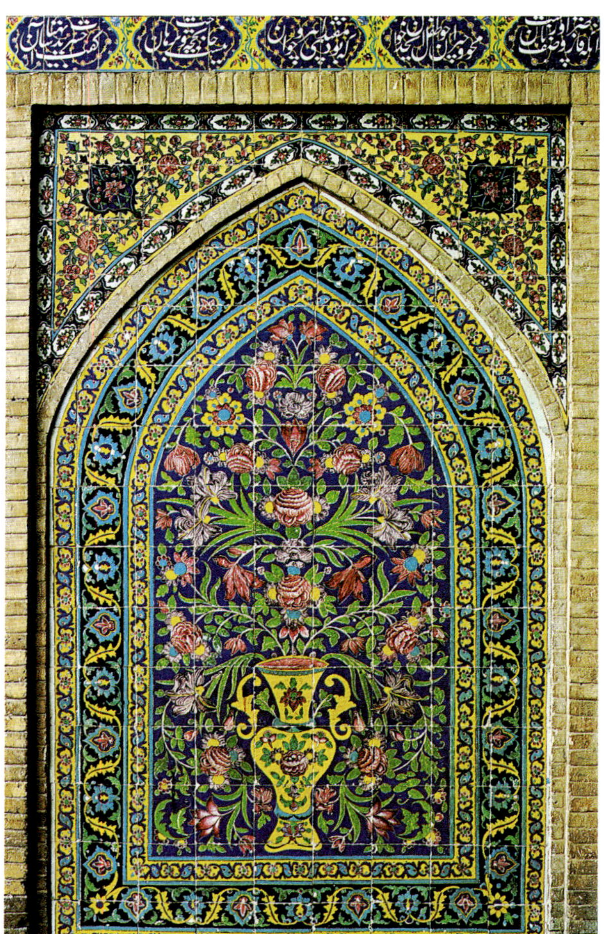

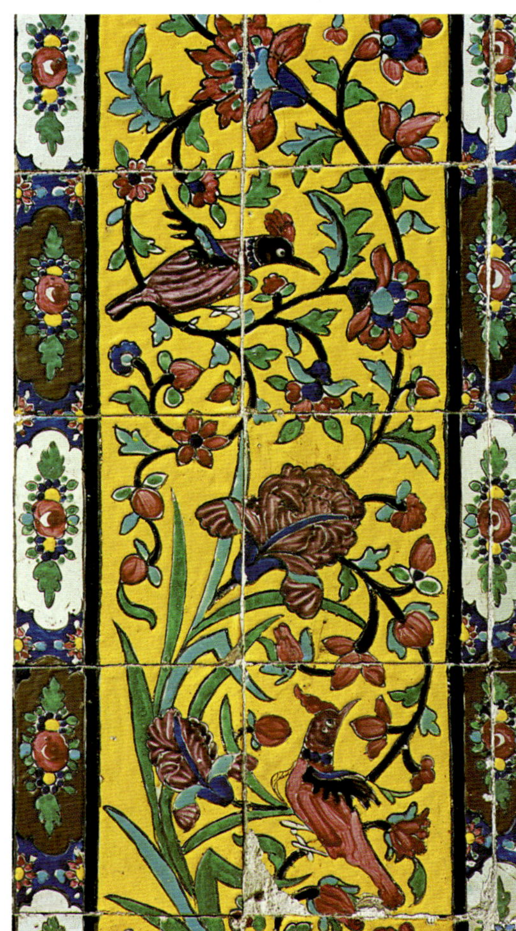

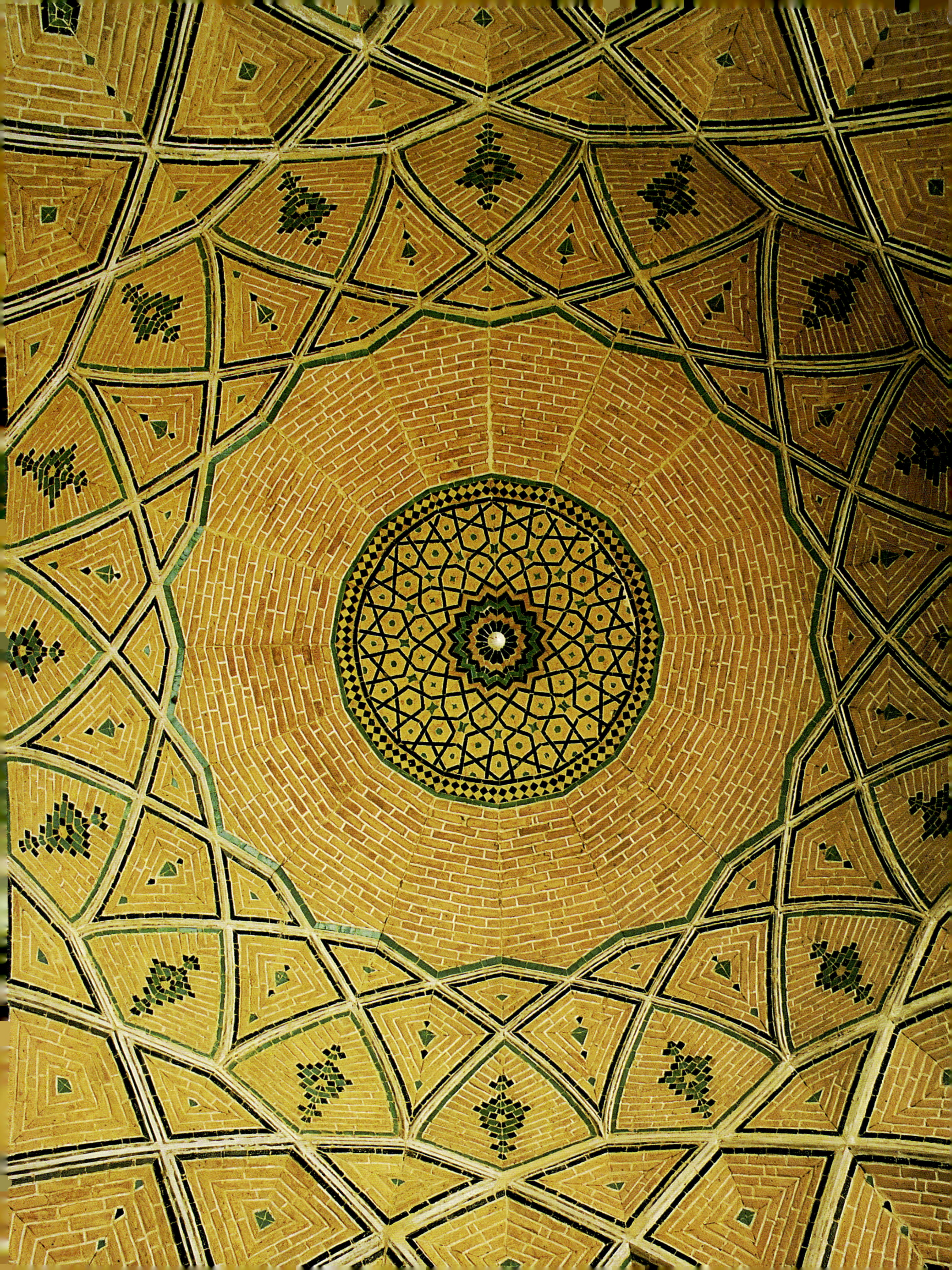

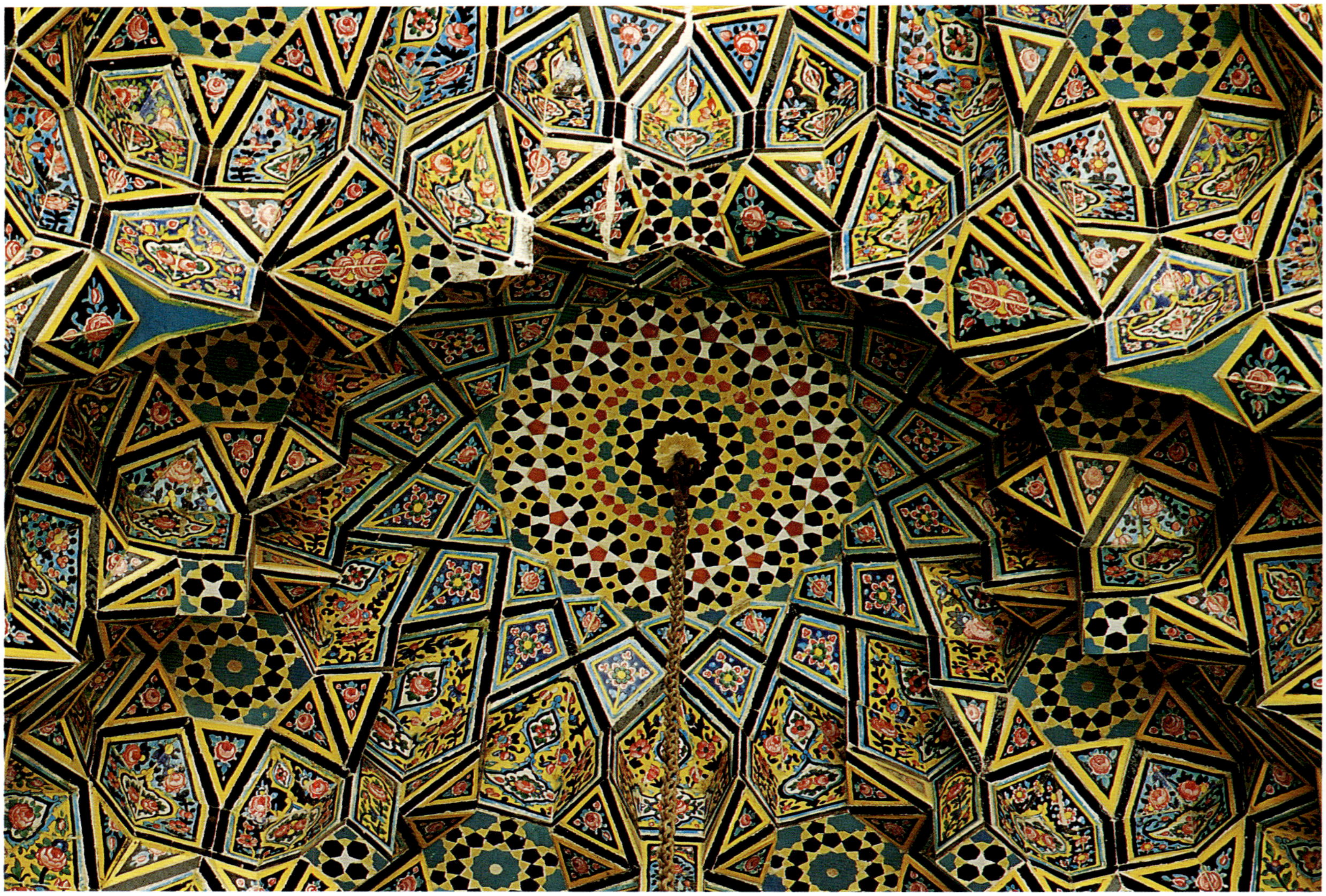

NASR AL-MULK MOSQUE, SHIRAZ (IRAN), MID-NINETEENTH CENTURY
♦ Cupola adorned with *muqarnas* lined with polychrome ceramic tilework and cut-tile mosaic.
♦ The prayer hall contains twelve massive twisted-shaft piers in imitation of those of the Vakil Mosque. The vaults are decorated in ceramic.
FACING PAGE, TOP AND CENTER
♦ Dome embellished with cut-tile mosaic *muqarnas*.
♦ Detail of ceramic-lined ribbed vault structure.

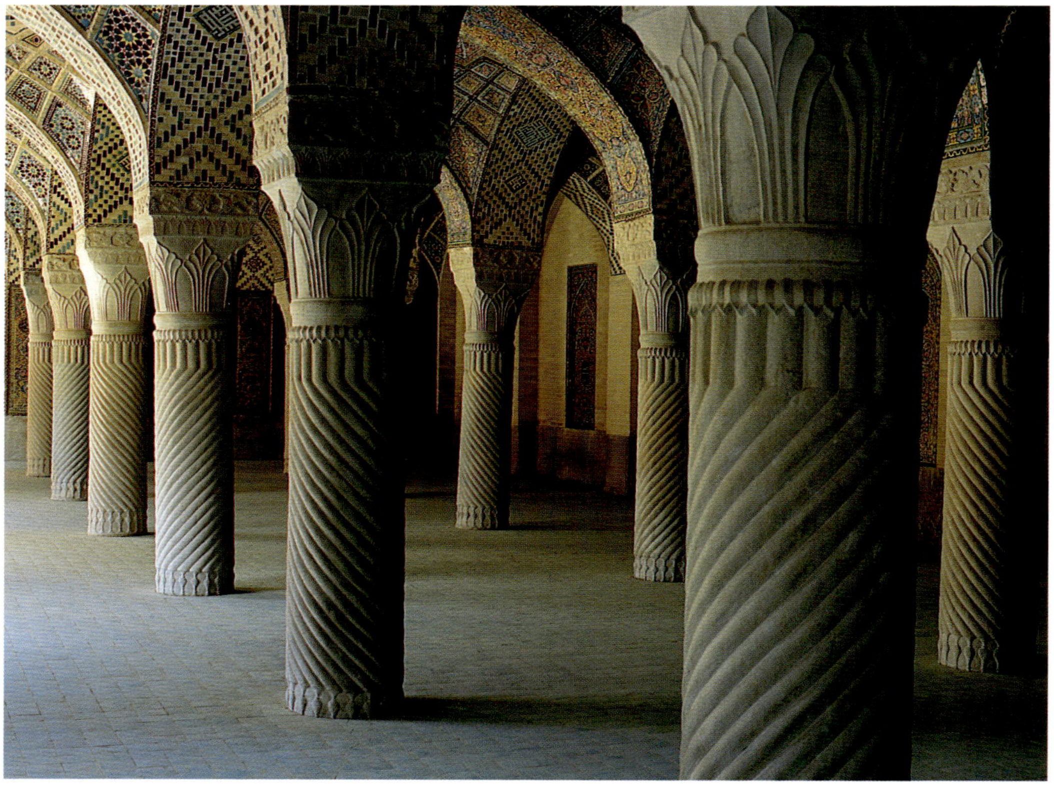

this house and its gardens date from as late as 1925. Of a similar type of design, and also located in Shiraz, the Qavvam Residence, better known under the name of Naranjestan, was begun around 1870. There, the central lunette on the main garden front presents the armorial bearings of Iran—the lion and the sun (*shir-o khorshid*)—as well as angels supporting the imperial crown.

Qajar sovereigns did not neglect religious architecture. Fath `Ali Shah, for example, founded countless "royal mosques" in Qazvin (1808), Teheran (started in 1809), and Semnan (1826–27). The Aqa Bozorg mosque and *madrasa* in Kashan were erected in 1851–52 and contain many examples of polychrome tiles in the brightest colors. The Sepah Salar *madrasa* in Teheran begun in 1878 is a characteristic example of the mildly ostentatious taste that characterizes this religious architecture. The polychrome ceramic panels decorating the main entrance incorporate a dense decor of acanthus leaves, vases, pearls, and rocaille in the middle of which nestle little still-life paintings with fruit and flowers that issue directly from Western models. The Nasir al-Mulk Mosque in Shiraz is a further glorious example of nineteenth-century architecture in which both the stone piers and ceramic decoration strive to imitate the Vakil Mosque. Its *muqarnas* vaults are covered in pink- and yellow-toned ceramic that creates a beautiful effect.

The later Rukn al-Mulk Mosque at Isfahan dates from the first years of the twentieth century; nevertheless it displays some charming decorations, among them inscriptions on a cobalt ground dated A.H. 1321/A.D. 1903–4.

A final characteristic of the time was the marked predilection for monumental city gates, frequently bedecked in tilework. Teheran, for instance, possessed a considerable number, although the majority have since vanished. The Bagh-i Melli gate (1922), one of the very few to have survived in the capital, is simply the most recent manifestation of this tradition. Fortunately, a number of provincial towns have preserved their great entryways, such as the gate at Semnan (1884), its decoration overrun by a veritable battalion of tiny soldiers painted with delectable artlessness.

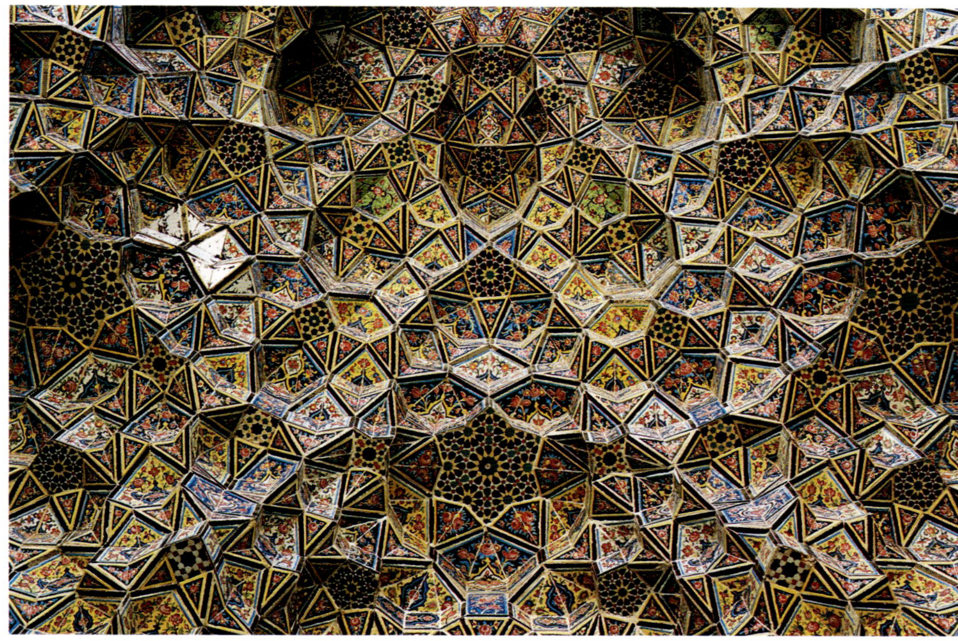

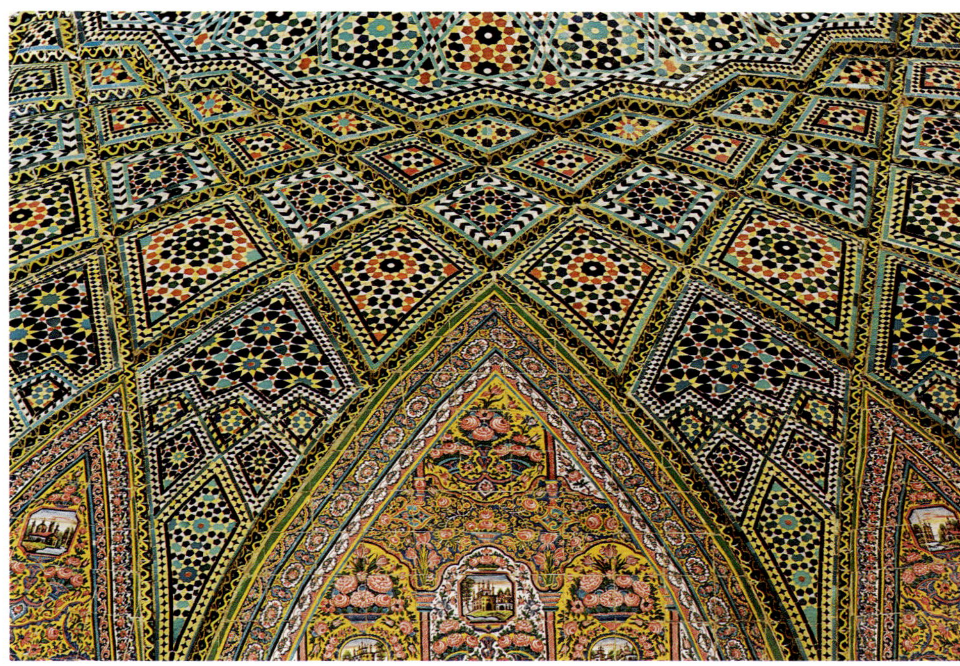

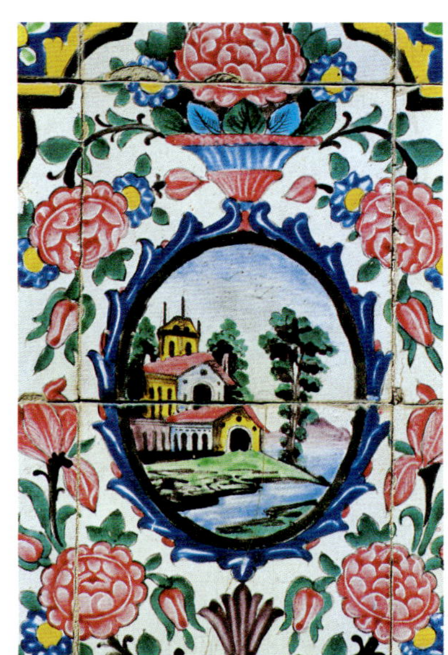

NASR AL-MULK MOSQUE, SHIRAZ (IRAN), MID-NINETEENTH CENTURY

♦ Small medallion containing a landscape painted in the European style in a floral frame with roses and irises.

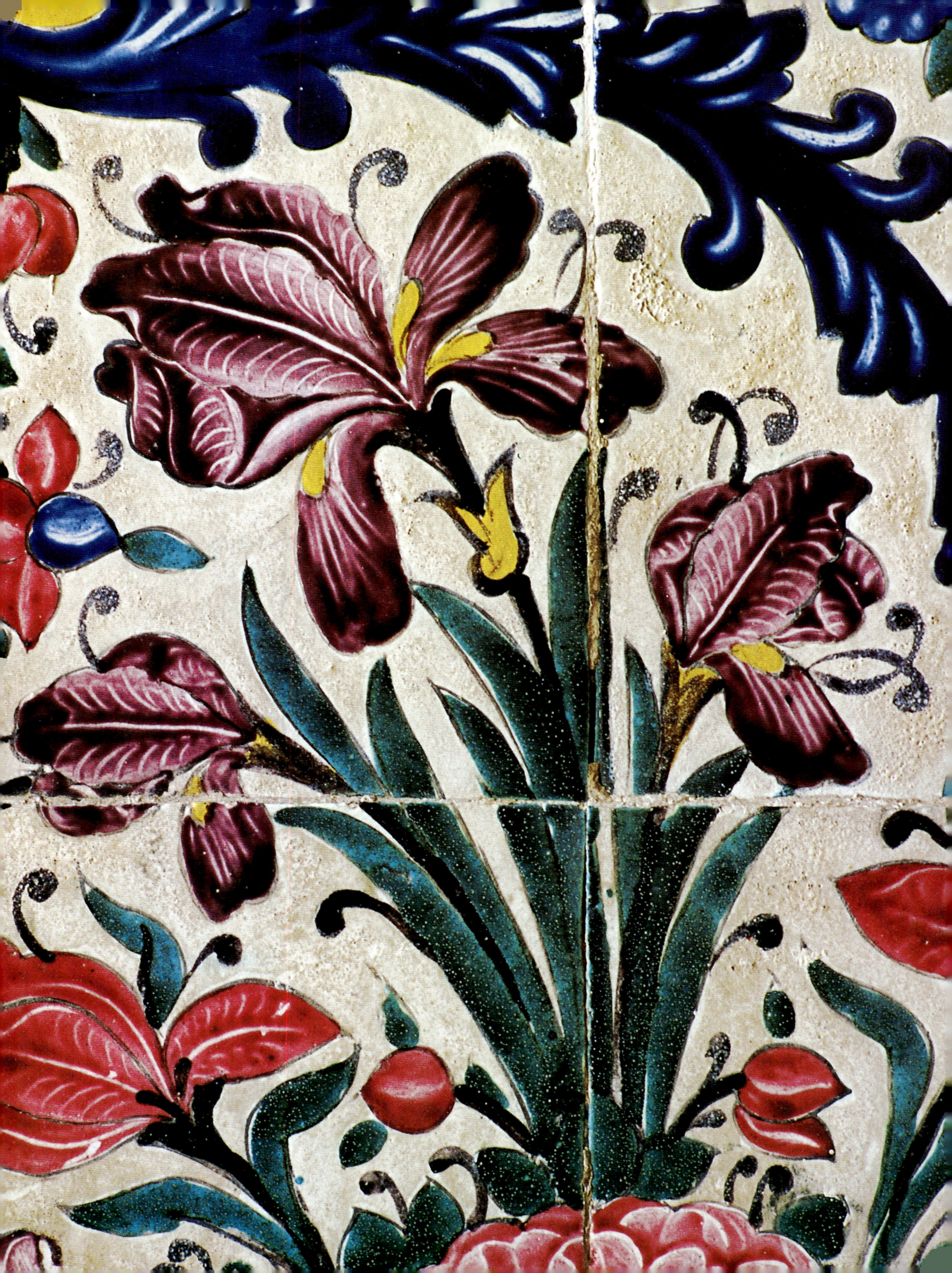

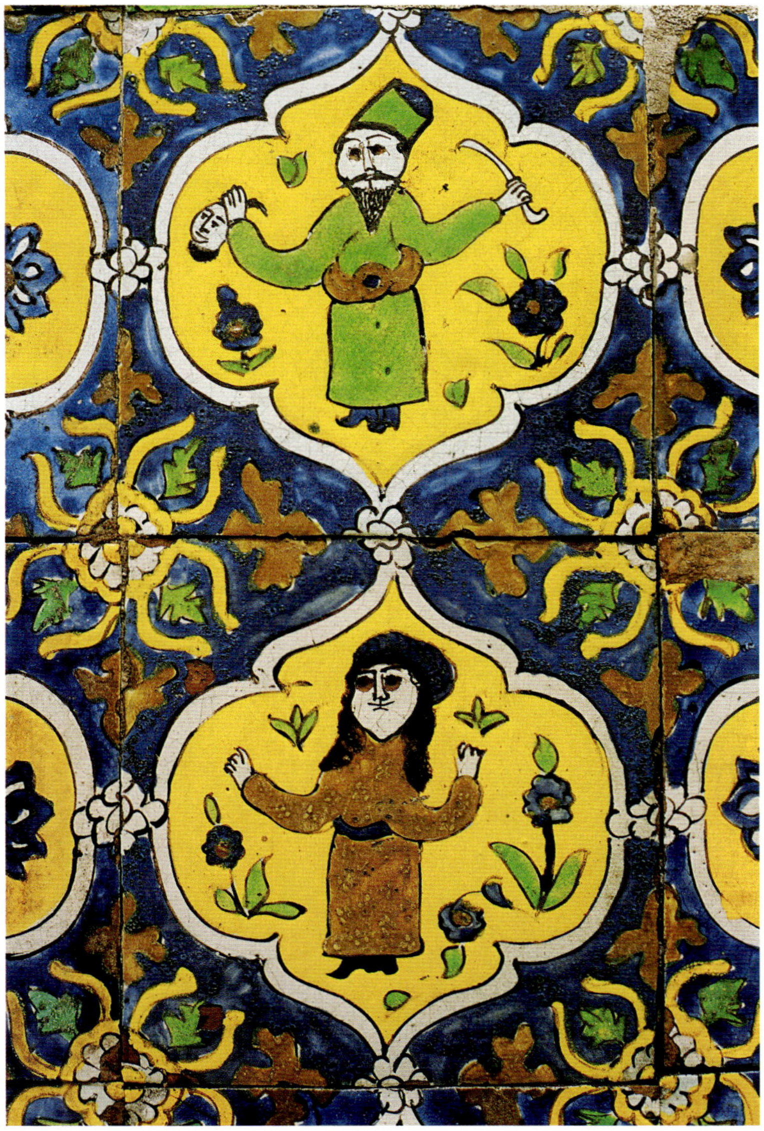

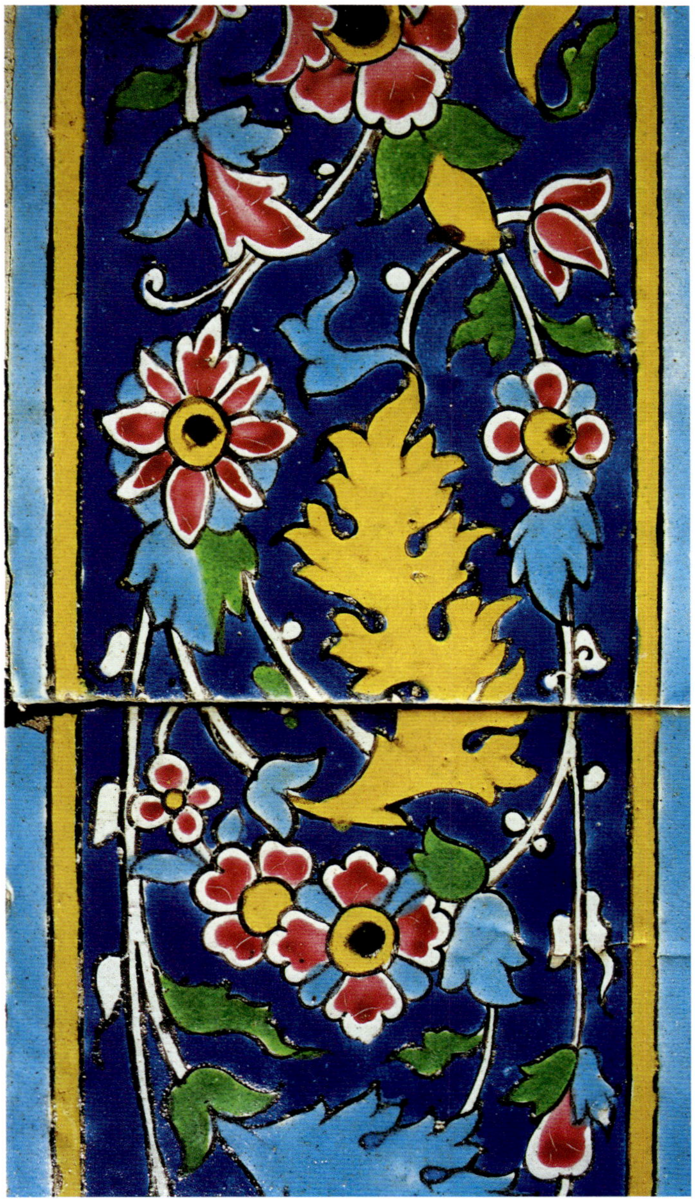

♦ Polychrome ceramic tile panel showing medallions, alternating rosettes and figures rendered in a charmingly naïve style. Hamman Khan, Kashan (Iran), mid-nineteenth century.

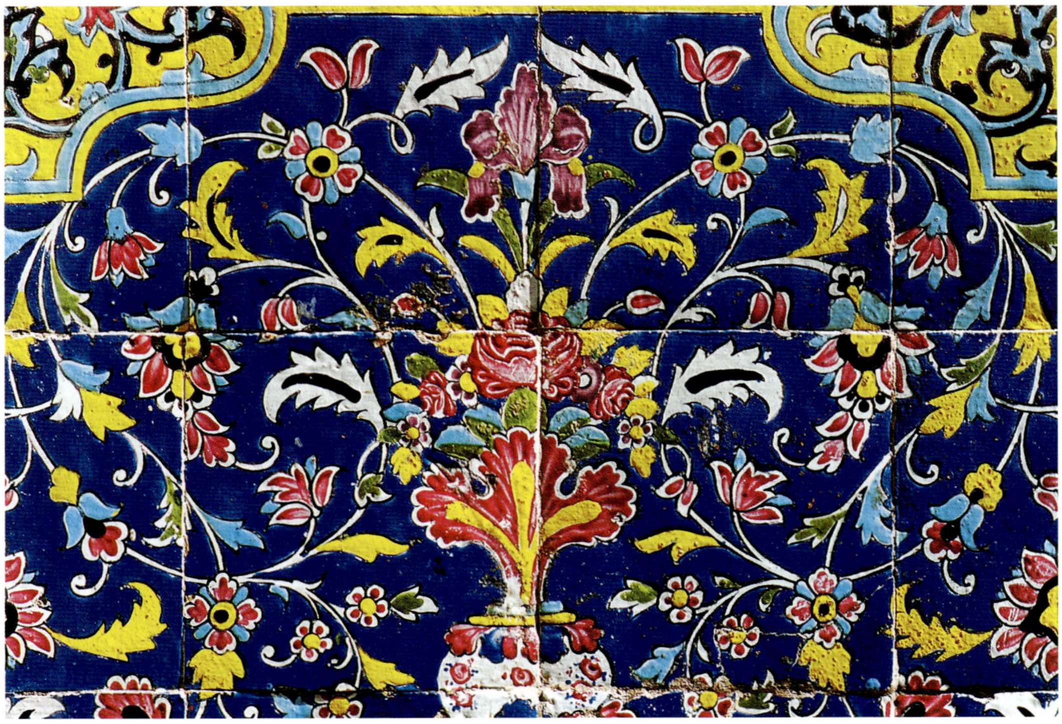

RUKN AL-MULK MOSQUE, ISFAHAN (IRAN), 1903

ABOVE AND LEFT

♦ Polychrome tilework border decorated with flowered stems.

♦ Polychrome "black line" ceramic tile decoration showing various blooms in a vase.

FACING PAGE

♦ Polychrome floral decor, Nasr al-Mulk Mosque, Shiraz (Iran), mid-nineteenth century. The naturalistic treatment of these iris stems demonstrates the influence of European art.

FOLLOWING DOUBLE PAGE

♦ Detail of the decor illustrated at left.

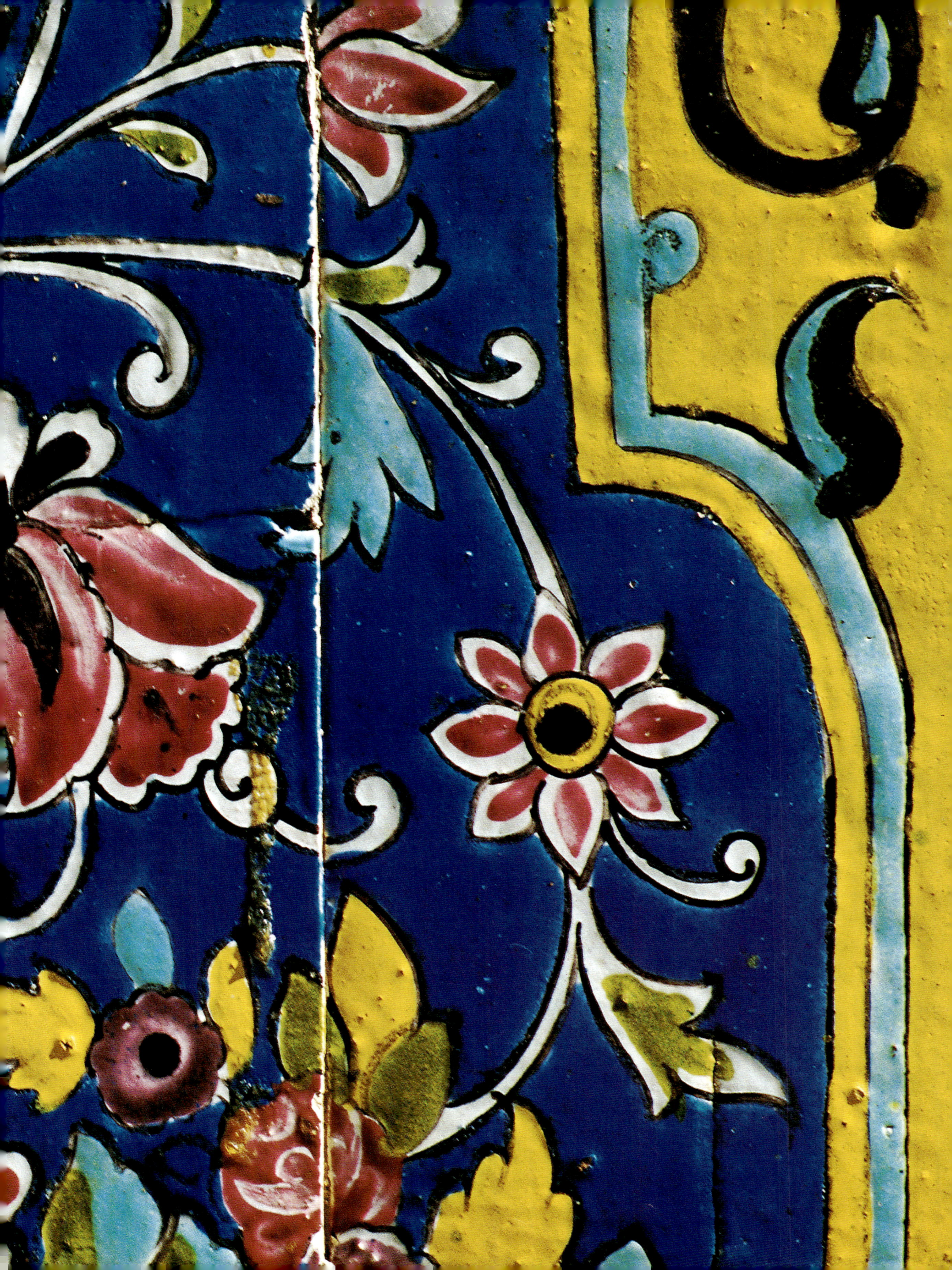

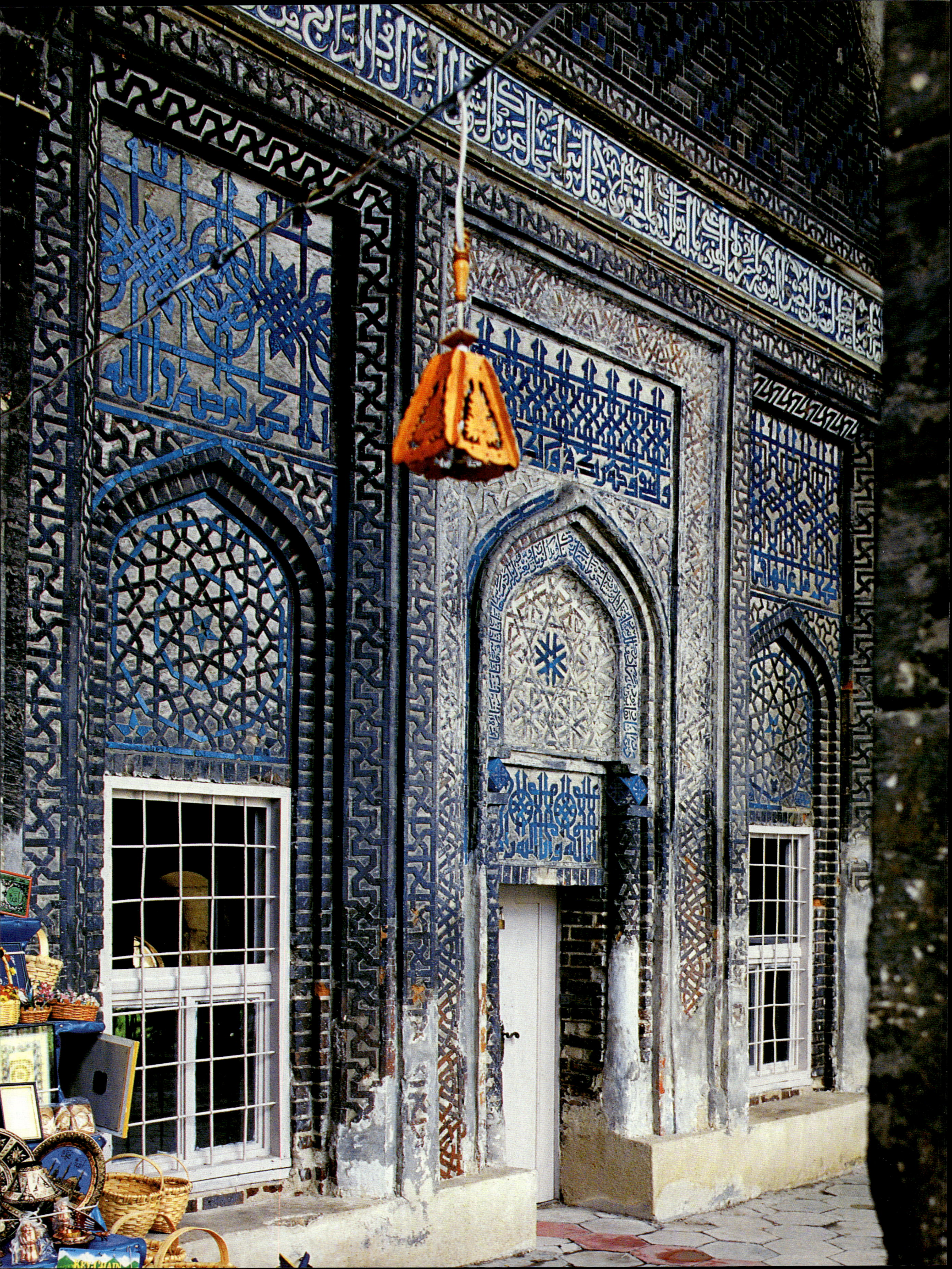

IV

Anatolia and the Levant from the Seljuqs to the Ottomans

PAGE 176

♦ Brick facade covered with ceramic inserts predominantly turquoise in color. Keykavus complex, Sivas (Turkey), 1219–20.

Turquoise Mosaic and Underglaze Stars: the Seljuqs of Rum

♦ Sarcophagi in the *türbe* of Kiliç Arslan, Konya, 1156–92. The sarcophagi are covered in tiles with an inscriptional relief decoration, white on a blue cobalt background.

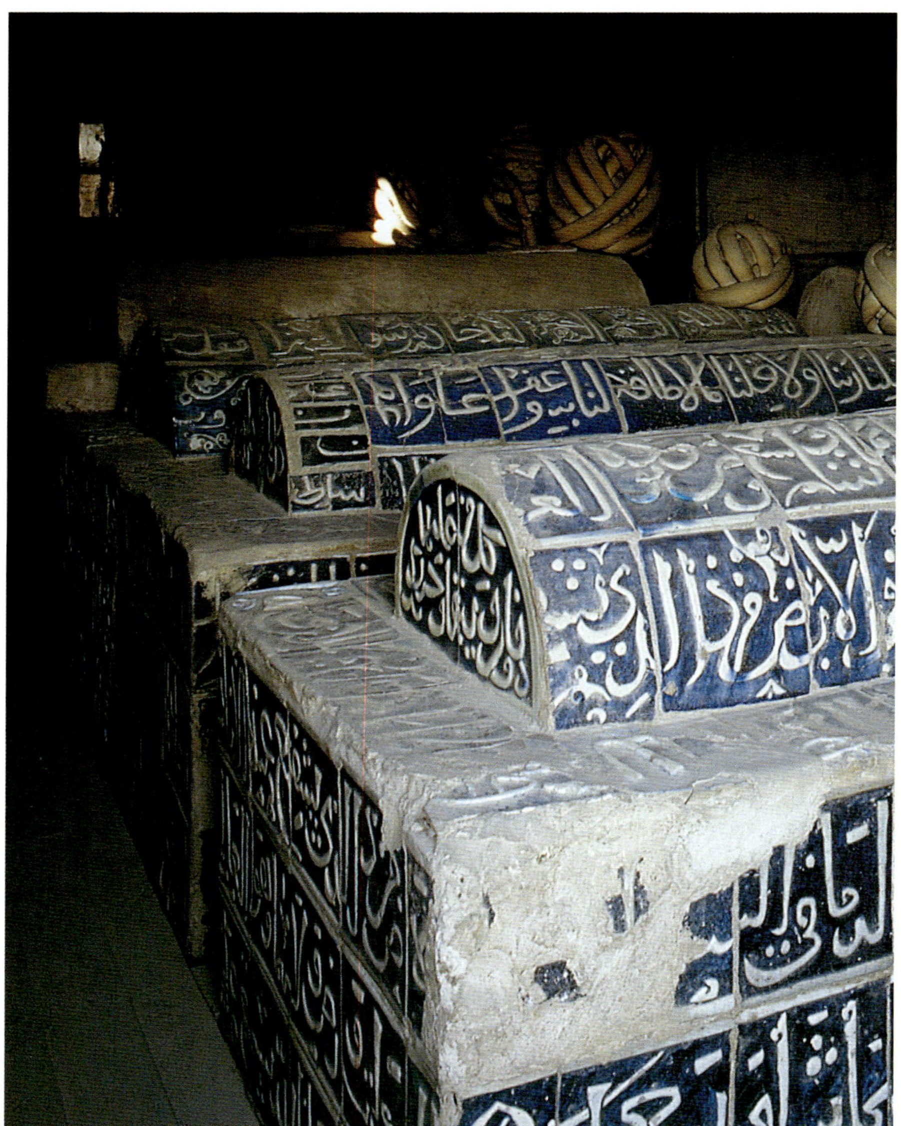

During the Seljuq invasions, and especially following the decisive battle of Manzikert (1071), Byzantine Anatolia was left open to incursions by Turkish populations. After the fall of the Seljuq kingdom of Iran, the dynasty's power base shifted into the hands of an offshoot that established its capital at Konya on the edge of the Anatolian Plateau: this was the Seljuq sultanate of Rum that for a time even survived the Mongolian invasions, until it was finally extinguished only in 1308.

One of the earliest achievements of the Seljuqs of Rum in the field of architectural ceramics was the astonishing ensemble of sarcophagi in the *türbe* of Kiliç Arslan next to the `Ala al-Din Mosque at Konya. Dated between 1156 and 1192, these sarcophagi are covered with ceramic tiles carrying inscriptions and small palmettes in relief standing out white on a blue cobalt ground.

It was during the thirteenth century that ceramic decoration in Anatolian architecture became more prevalent throughout the major cities of the kingdom, such as Sivas, Tokat, Malatya, Kayseri, and, naturally Konya itself. It is, however, interesting to note that in this region, contrary to the situation on the Iranian plateau, architecture was primarily built in masonry, with the effect that ceramic decoration was concentrated in the interior rather than on the facade, with the exception of a few brick constructions. This tendency is particularly true of minarets, such as those of the Inje Minareli *madrasa* at Konya (1264), the Çifte Minareli *madrasa* at Sivas (1272), and the Great Mosque in Afyon (1272).

TÜRBE OF KILIÇ ARSLAN, KONYA, 1156–92

♦ Dome on fan-shaped squinches lined in an all-over cut-tile mosaic.

♦ Transitional zone leading to the cupola ringed by a double inscriptional frieze: bottom, a band in plaited Kufic; above, a band inscribed in the Thuluth style.

♦ The cupola squinches are decorated with a composition of stars and polygons inside large triangles that are bordered by trails of palmettes standing out against the white facing.

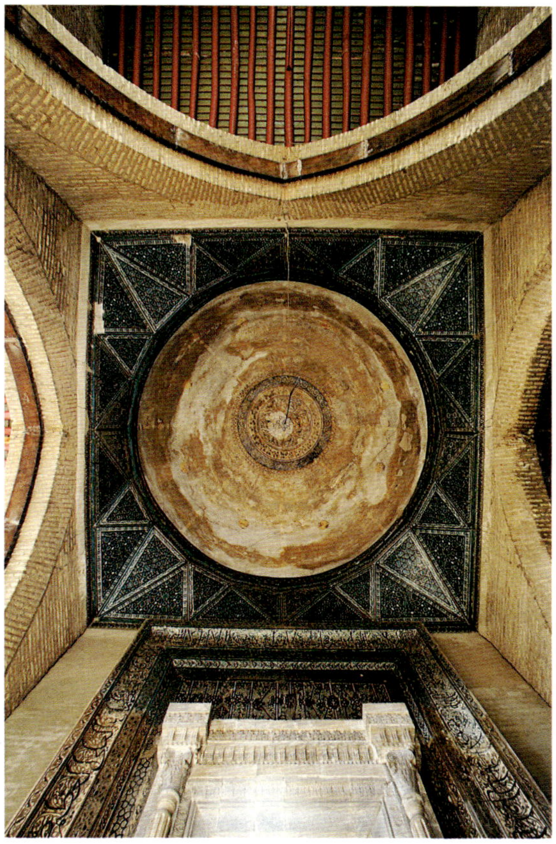

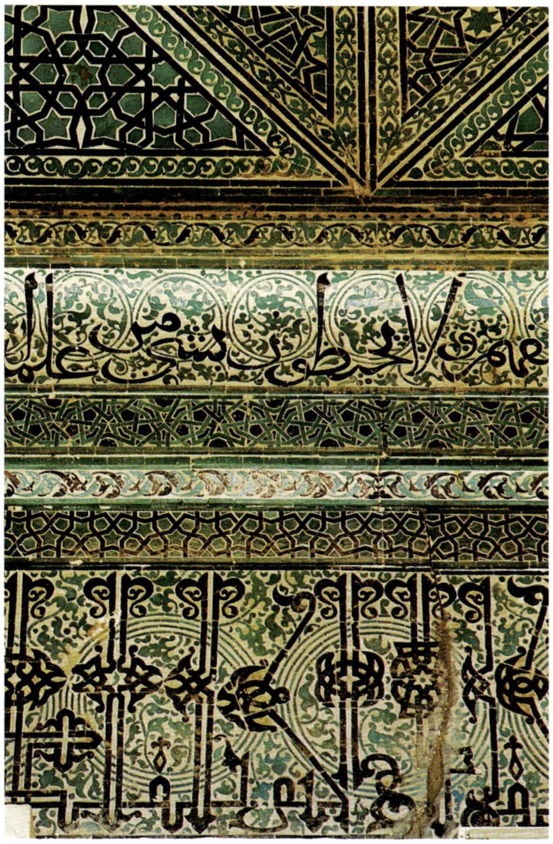

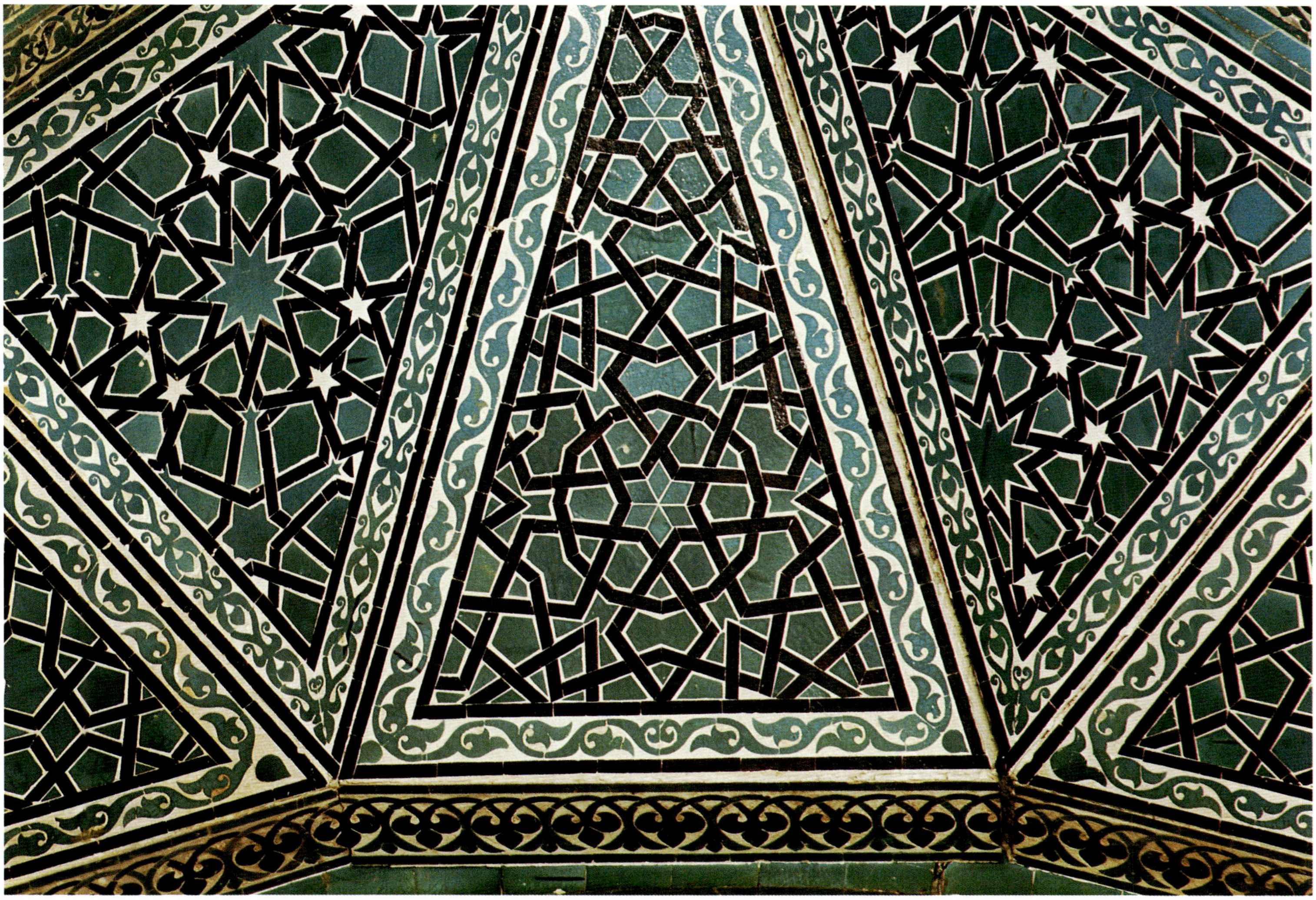

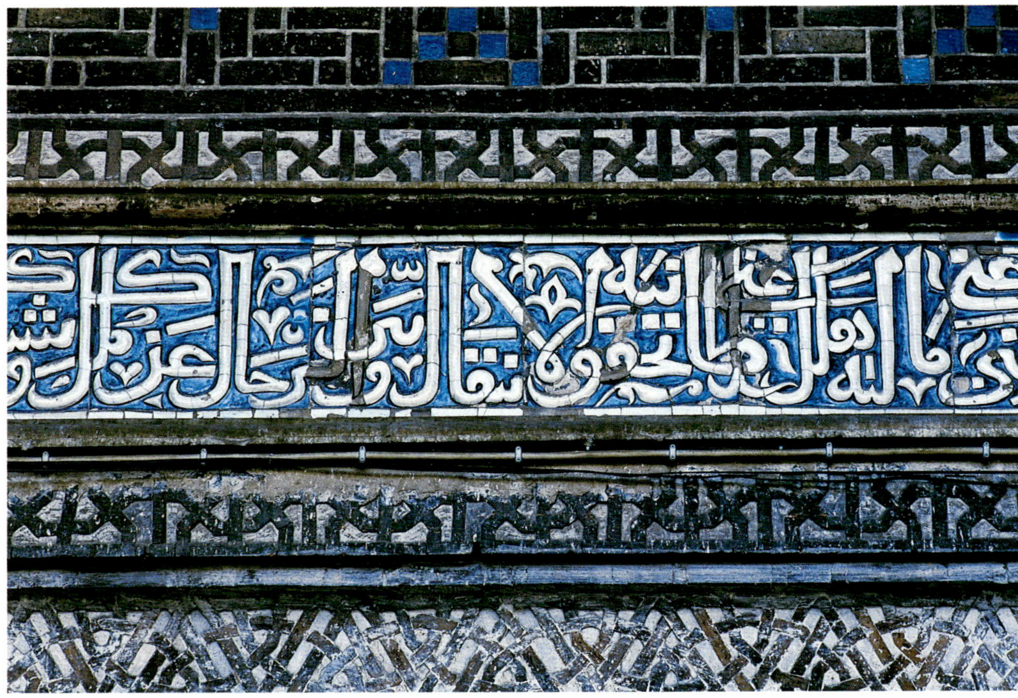

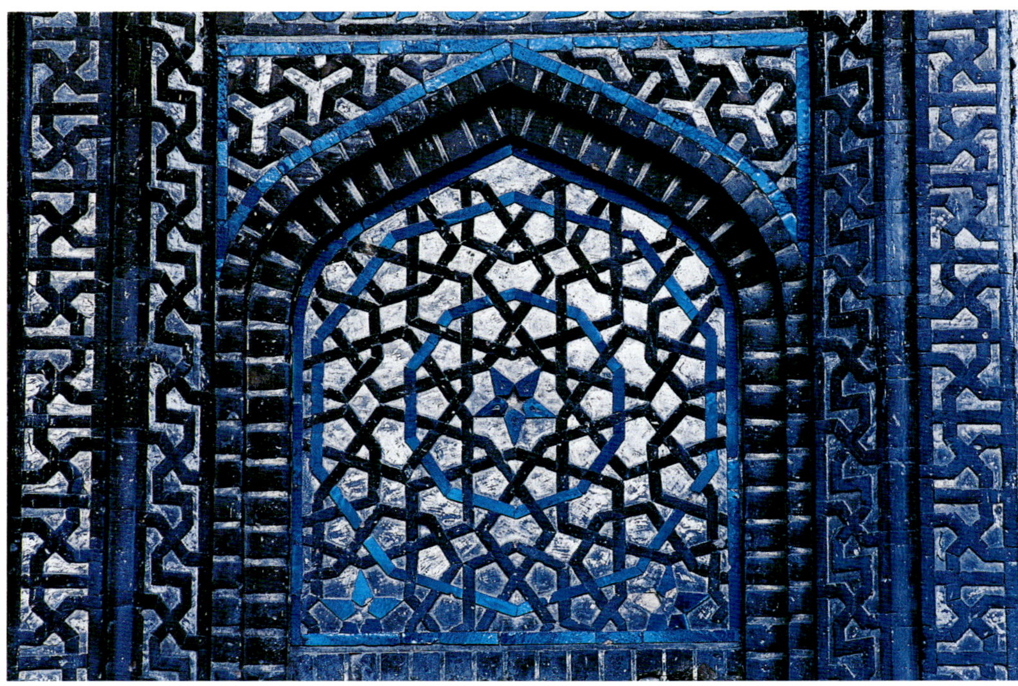

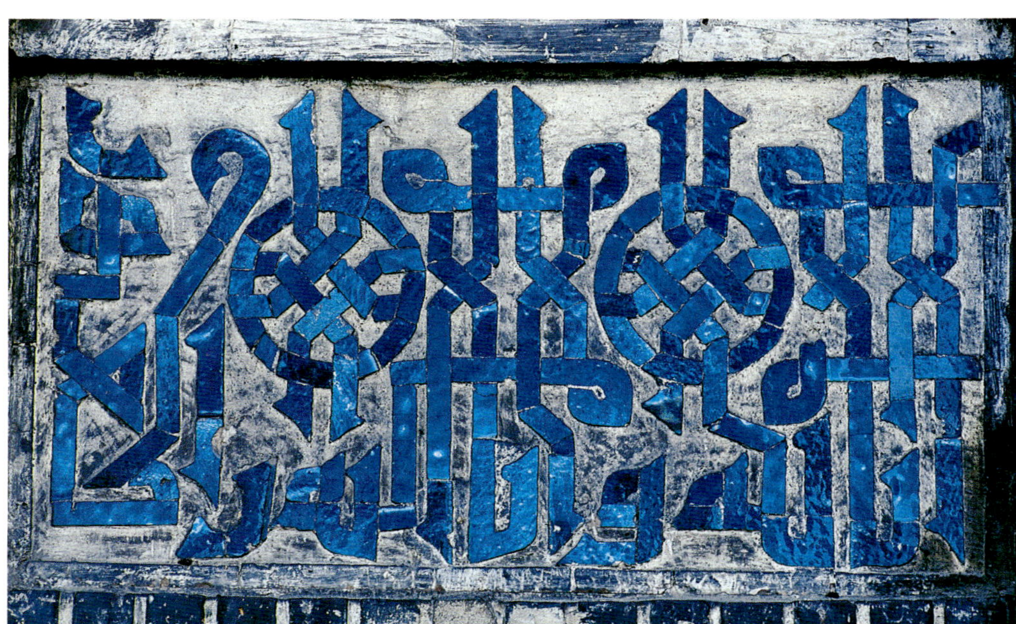

KEYKAVUS COMPLEX, SIVAS (TURKEY), 1219–20

♦ Detail of the facade with ceramic tile inscriptional band decorated in relief.

♦ Detail of the facade: blind arch dressed in an interlace pattern with a five-pointed star at the center. The colored ceramic decoration contrasts strongly with the white of the facing wall.

♦ Inscription in plaited Kufic script over the entrance.

Sometimes a lower portion of a monument was constructed out of stone, while bricks were chosen for the vaulted zones, for example at the Keykavus Hospital at Sivas (in 1219–20). The main gate of the building is impressively decorated in geometrical interlace and Kufic inscriptions formed from areas of turquoise and manganese-violet rod tiles. Similarly, the vaults of the Great Mosque of Malatya (1247) show unglazed brick alternating with turquoise *banna'i*, while the heads of the arches are embellished with a calligraphic band in cursive style executed in cut-tile mosaic. More rarely, revetment panels comprising square or hexagonal monochrome tiles line the dados and the arch lunettes, as at the Gök *medrese* at Malatya (1247) or the one in Tokat (1270).

However, it is in the realm of interior decoration that Anatolian ceramic craftsmen excelled. One of the finest specimens of such decoration is the star vault adorning the cupola of the Karatay *madrasa* at Konya (1251). Executed entirely in turquoise, black, and white cut-tile mosaic, the decoration of the cupola presents an intricate geometric interlace motif that generates twenty-four-pointed stars. A sizable epigraphic frieze in plaited Kufic girdles the drum, while the corner squinches are built in accordance with the "fan" scheme peculiar to Anatolia. The perimeter of the square room bears a frieze of Kufic calligraphy decorated with interlace ribbon; adorning the dados, hexagonal turquoise tiles line the upper reaches of the walls.

Dated 1258, the *mihrab* of the Sahip Ata Mosque in Konya is also of exemplary finesse. The dados are clad in hexagonal turquoise tiles, to which cling small cobalt triangles forming six-pointed stars. In the arched *muqarnas* zone, the tympanum displays a palmette arabesque pattern, as well as a wide variety of geometrical designs that extend over each cell. The mosque in Ankara known as the Arslanhane Cami dates from around 1289. Its splendid wood ceiling is supported by reused ancient columns, while beautiful cut-tile mosaics ornament the *mihrab*. Stars, interlace patterns, and basketweave motifs treated in turquoise and black cut-tile mosaic also appear on the *muqarnas* in the *mihrabs* of the slightly later Eshrefoglu Mosque at Beyşehir (1297–99) and the

♦ Turquoise, cobalt, and black cut-tile mosaic panel presenting a calligraphic frieze, together with a strip with geometric interlace and a palmette leaf-scroll ribbon. Gök *medrese*, Tokat (Turkey), 1270.

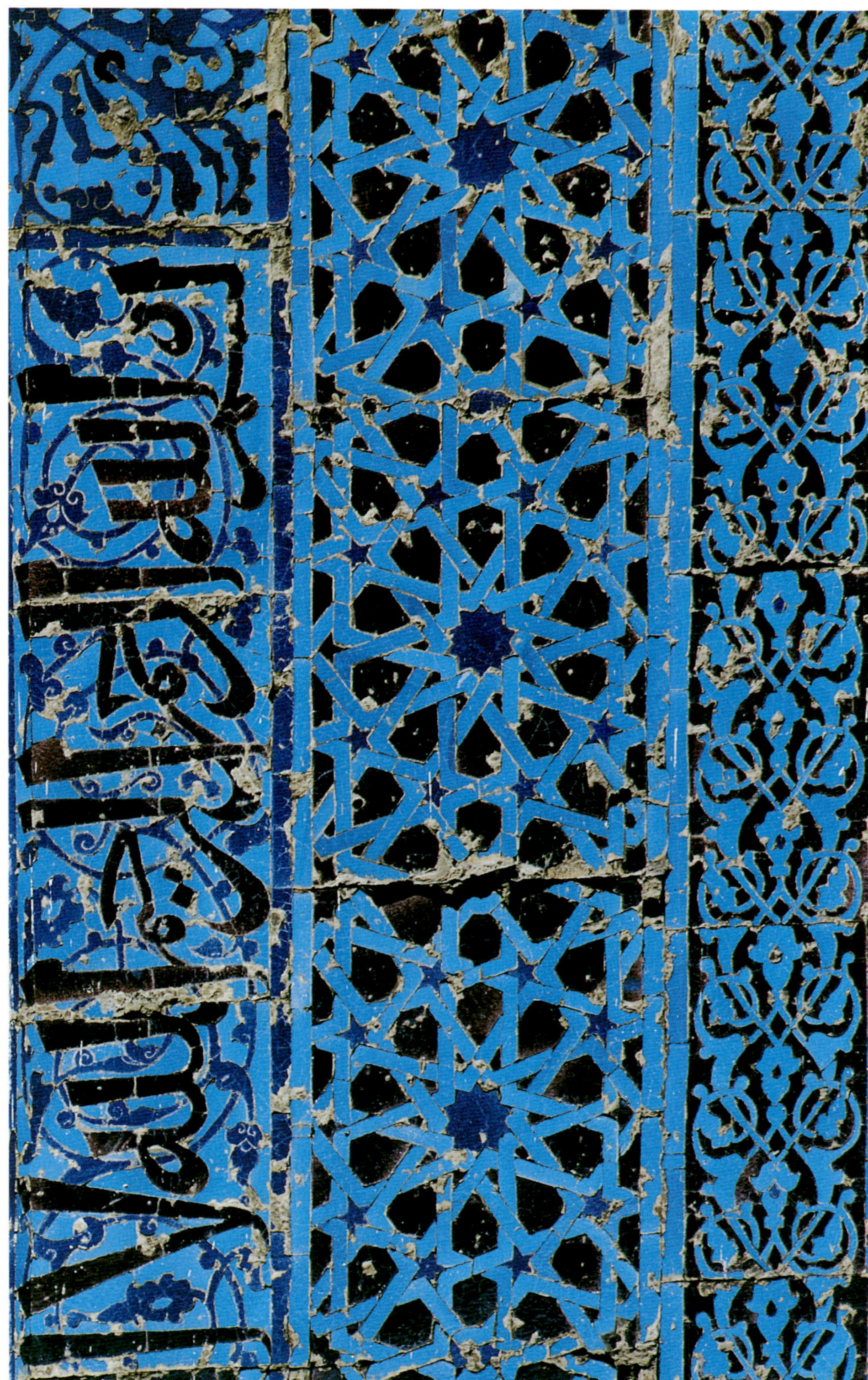

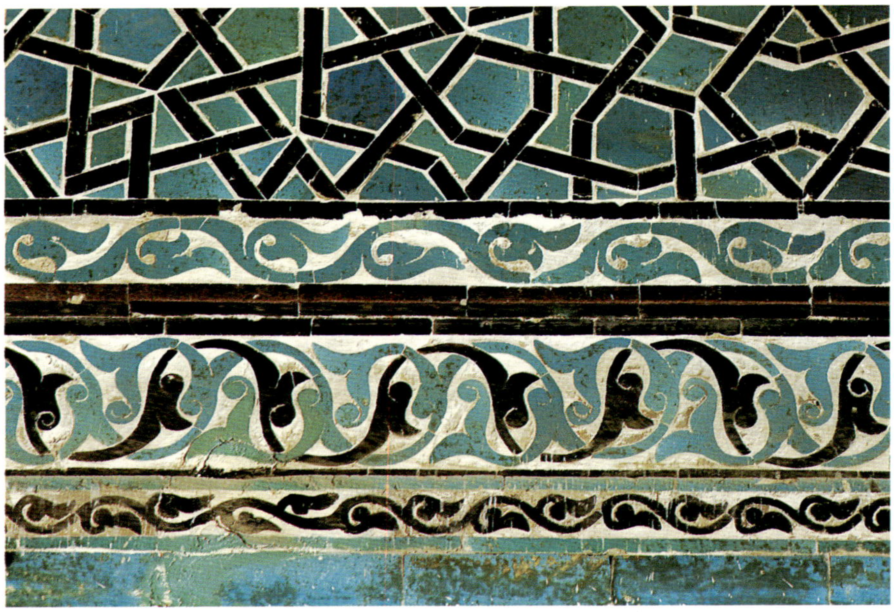

♦ Triple frieze of palmettes along the base of the cupola of the central hall. Karatay *madrasa*, Konya (Turkey), 1251.

Sirçali Mosque, Konya (end of the thirteenth century). The cut-tile signature of the artist appears on the wall of this latter mosque: "Work of Muhammad ibn Muhammad Utman al-Banna of Tus."[75] In nearly all cases, the contrasting white area is not a glaze but a terracotta facing, occasionally coated with primer.

Although the phenomenon was confined primarily to palace decoration, the period of the Seljuqs of Rum also saw the advent of underglaze-painted tiles, as well as lusterware tiles and those of the *mina'i* type, often arranged in cross and star patterns. Pieces in *mina'i* have been discovered only at the palace of `Ala al-Din at Konya dating from the reign of Kiliç Arslan II (1156–92). The most remarkable site in terms of the diversity and originality of tilework remains Kubadabad Palace, built on the shores of Lake Beyşehir to the southwest of Konya. Completed in 1236, this palace was used as a summer residence by Sultan Ala `al-Din Kaykubad. The many discoveries made at this site (and now deposited in the museum of the Karatay *madrasa* in Konya) include a number of underglaze-painted stars. A vast gamut of animated motifs parade over these tiles—including figures, birds, and fabulous beasts—painted in manganese, cobalt, and turquoise under a colorless or turquoise-tinted clear glaze. These tiles are among the first masterpieces of underglaze-painted architectural ceramics, although it is not known who the tilemakers were. While some general features recall Iranian Kashan production, they display characteristics of a specific style that combines contributions from northern Syrian potters (in particular from Raqqa) and elements from

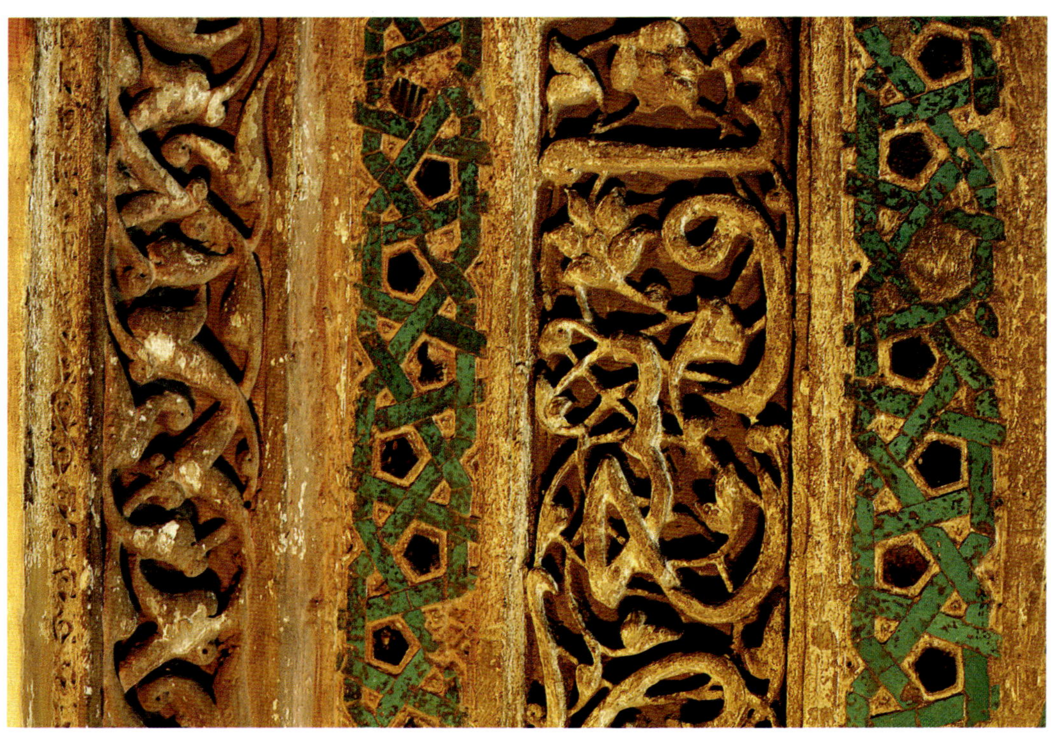

♦ Cut-tile mosaic decoration with inscriptional frieze. Arslanhane Cami, Ankara, c. 1289.

SIRÇALI *MADRASA*, KONYA (TURKEY), END OF THIRTEENTH CENTURY

FACING PAGE, FROM LEFT TO RIGHT AND TOP TO BOTTOM

♦ Cut-tile mosaic inscriptional banding, geometric interlace, and palmette trails decorating the facade.

♦ Niche decorated in cut tilework.

♦ Head-to-tail fleuron frieze in cut tile.

♦ Cut-tile mosaic wall panel.

♦ Cut-tile mosaic star motifs applied to a geometric interlace pattern.

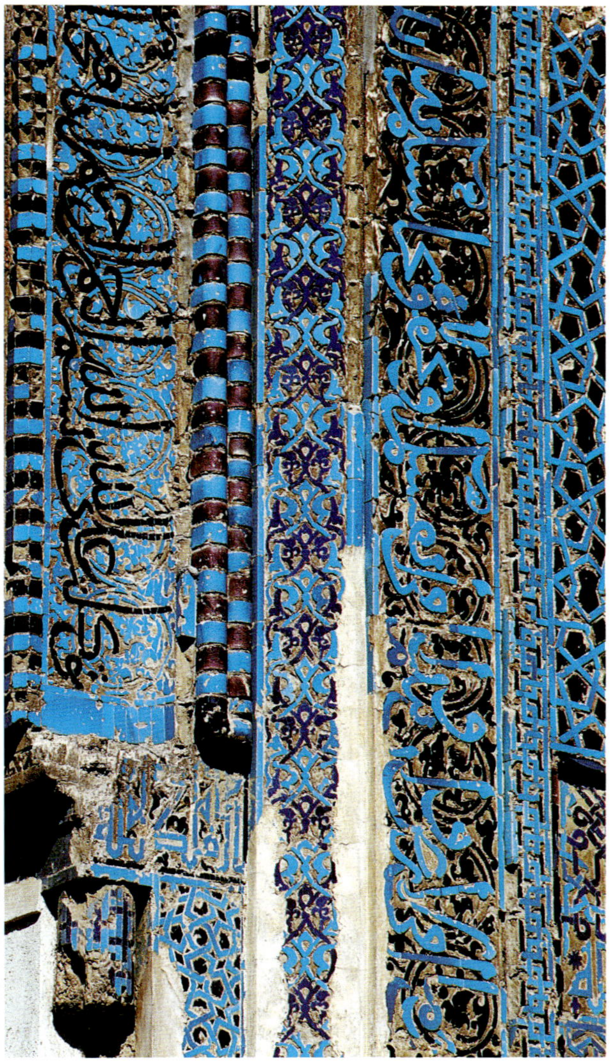

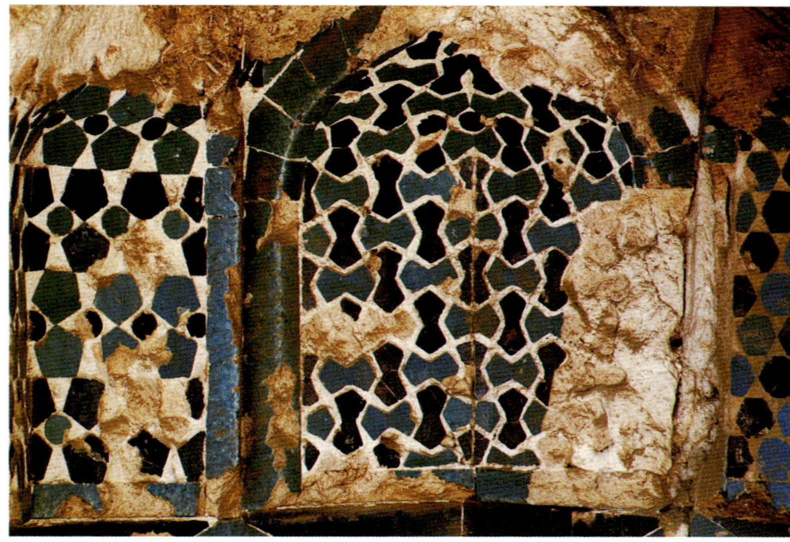

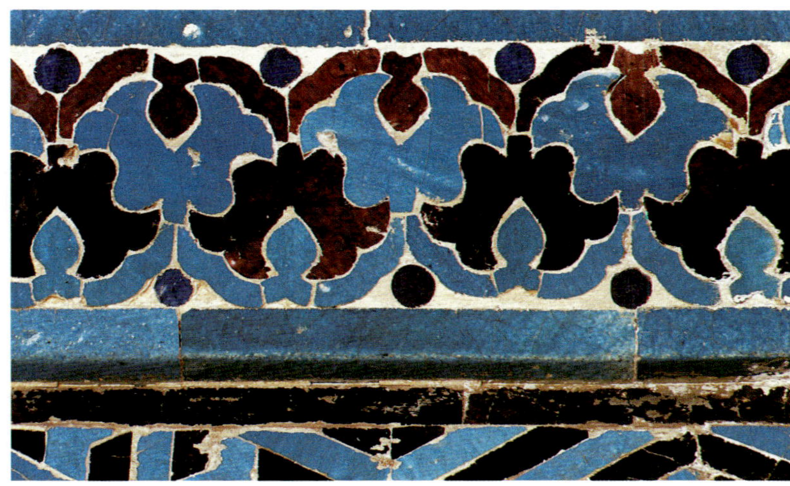

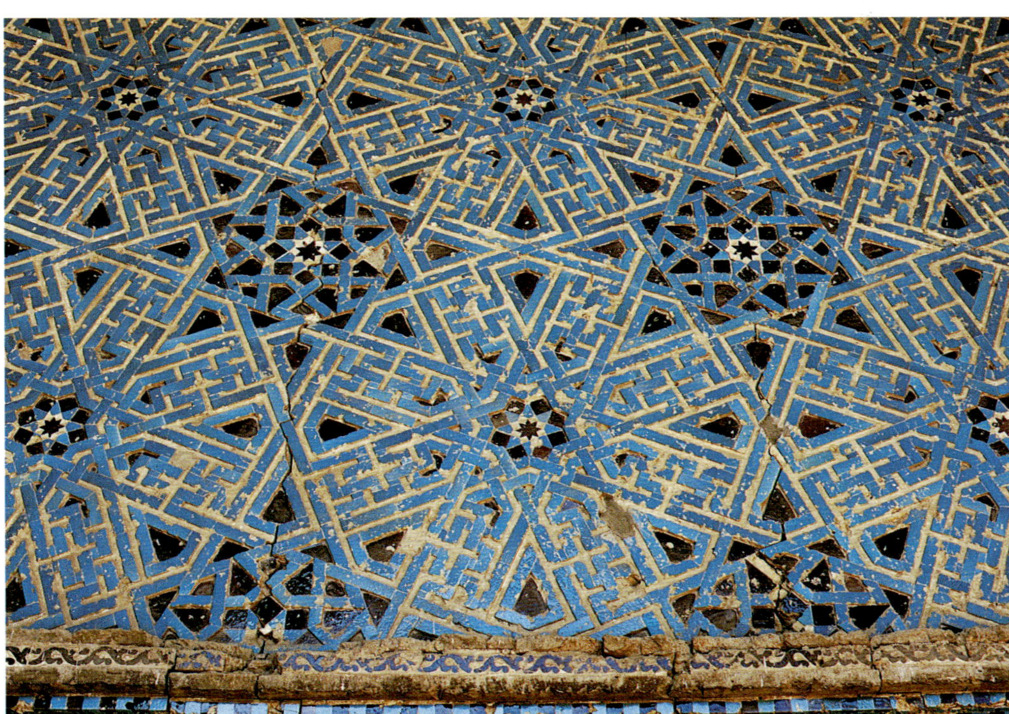

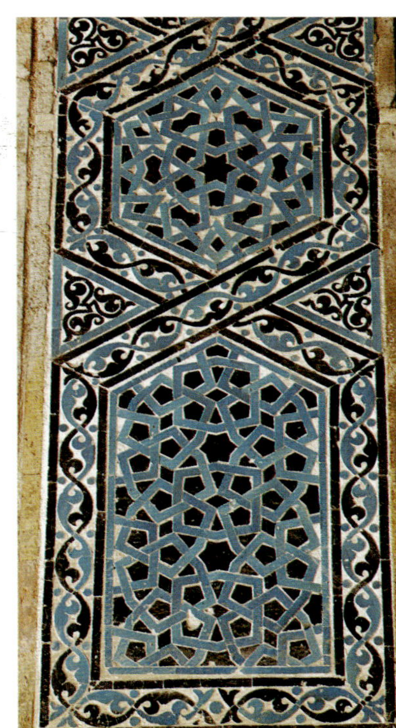

♦ Underglaze-painted star pattern enclosing a seated prince. This star, together with a series of similar pieces, comes from Kubadabad Palace on the shores of Lake Beyşehir, and dates from the first half of the thirteenth century. Museum of the Karatay *madrasa*, Konya.

the Byzantine bestiary. It is probable that these tiles were manufactured locally with the aid of potters from Raqqa. Curiously, although Raqqa was well known as a center for the manufacture of underglaze- or luster-painted tableware, tile production in these workshops seems to have been somewhat limited. Scattered examples of luster-decorated or underglaze-painted tiles have been unearthed on the site of a Syrian palace, Qasr al-Banat (end of the twelfth–beginning of the thirteenth century), whose figurative style, like that at the palace of Beyşehir, calls to mind pieces from Kashan. It is likely that other palaces also had ceramic decorations, in particular in Antalya, Alanya, Akşehir, and Kayseri; archeological investigations will surely confirm this hypothesis at some point in the future.

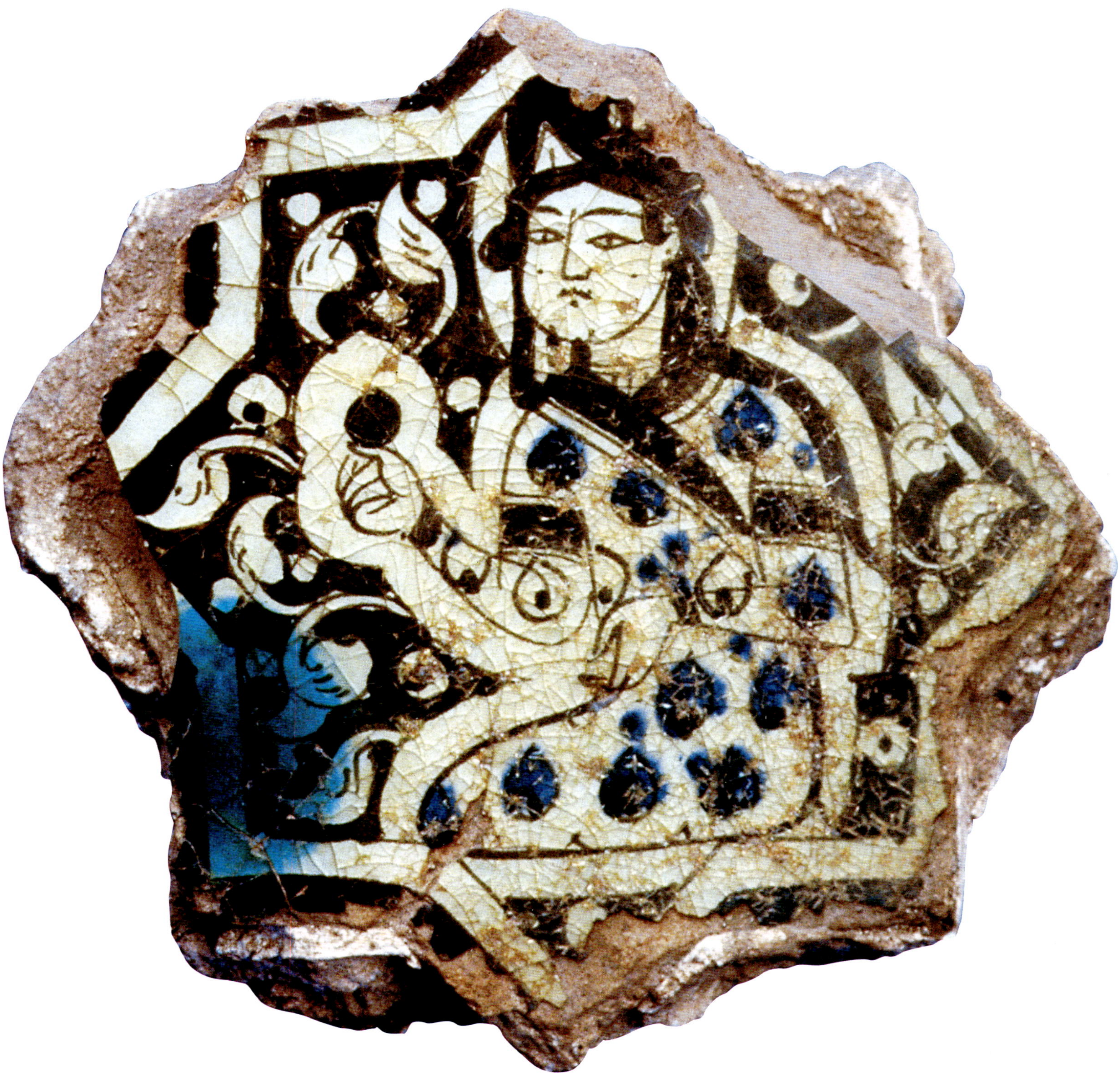

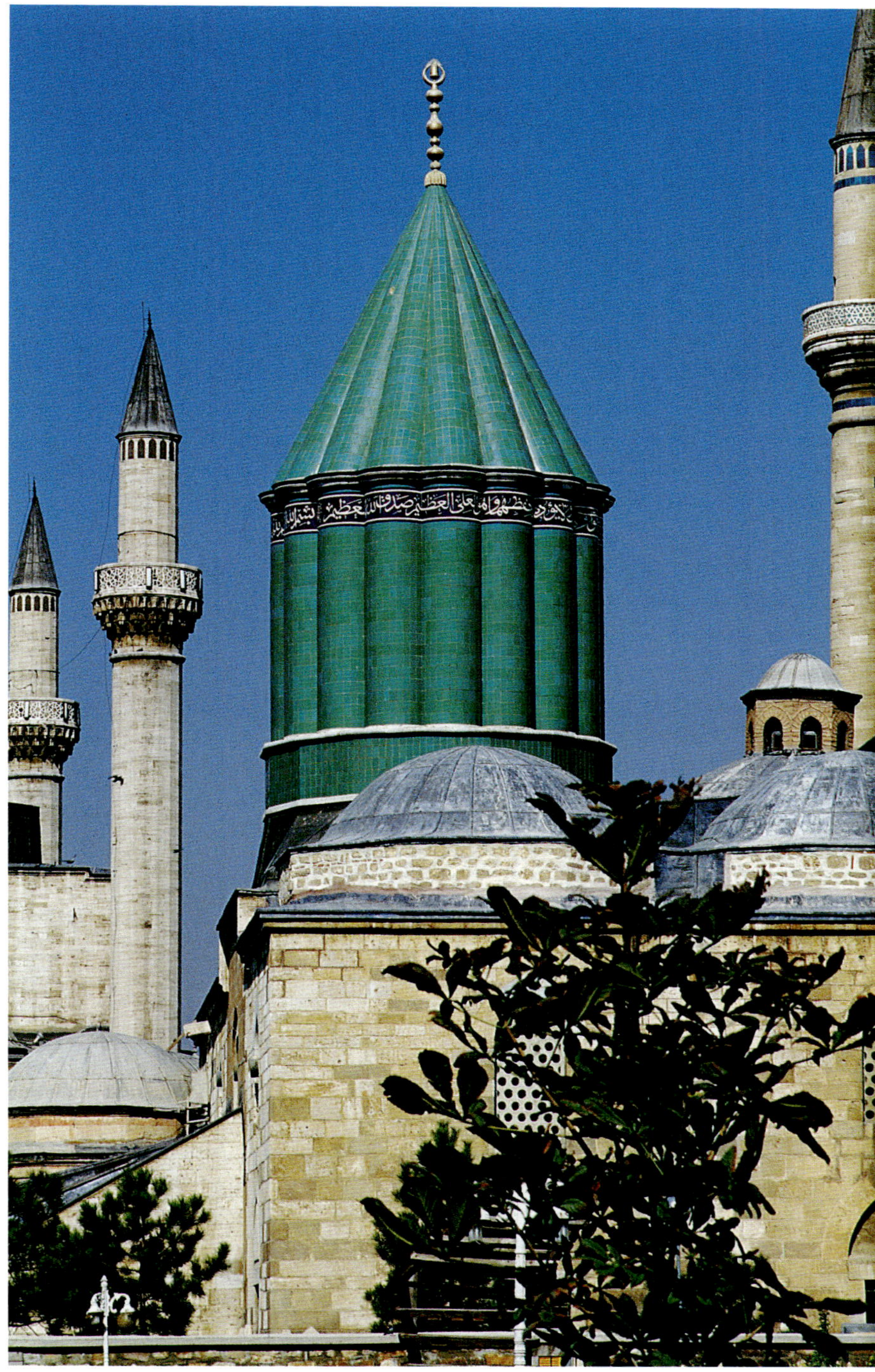

♦ Tall, lobed, ceramic-clad tower dominating the tomb and *tekke* (whirling dervish community) of Jalal al-Din (Jallaludin) Rumi (known as Mevlana in Turkey), Konya, founded in the thirteenth century. The complex (now converted into a museum) was restored and refurbished in the sixteenth century under Suleyman the Magnificent.

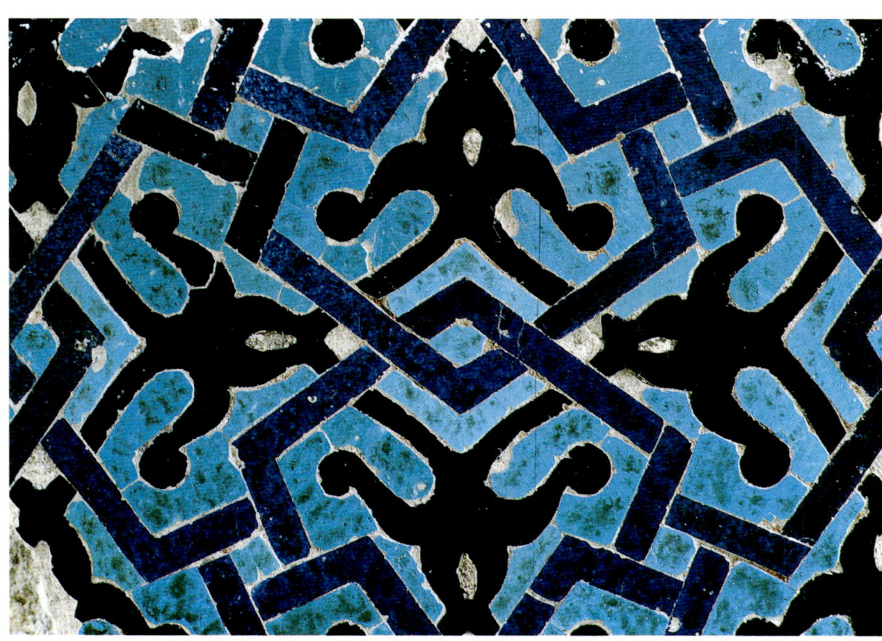

♦ Cut-tile mosaic panel originally from a monument at Konya (Turkey), thirteenth century. Iznik Museum.

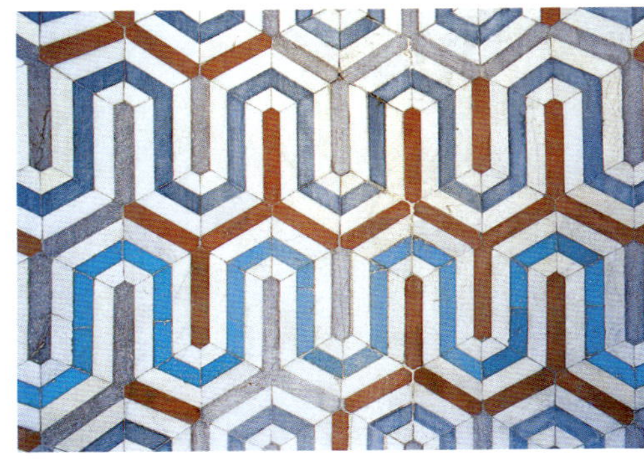

♦ *Mihrab* decoration of turquoise stone and ceramic inlay motifs. Mithqaliyya *madrasa*, Cairo (Egypt), founded in 1374.

♦ Prayer hall *mihrab*, Aqsunqur Mosque, Cairo (Egypt), 1346. The *qibla* wall is lined with Ottoman tiles dating from restoration work carried out in 1652.

Egypt and Syria under the Mamluks

The Mamluks emerged around 1250 in Ayyubid territory, which they soon annexed for themselves. Their victories against the Mongolian advance, as well as against the Crusaders (capture of Saint-Jean d'Acre in 1291), conferred on them immense prestige throughout the Muslim world. Moreover, after the assassination of the caliph of Baghdad, Mustaʿsim, in 1258, the Sultan Baybars I returned the caliphate to Cairo. Thereafter the city became the heart of the Sunni Muslim world, remaining so until the arrival in Egypt in 1517 of the Ottomans, who transferred the seat of the caliphate to Constantinople.

Mamluk architecture, whether found in Egypt or in Syria, is primarily constructed in masonry, relying on colored-marble facing for decoration. Consequently, ceramic decoration was less frequently found there than it was in lands where

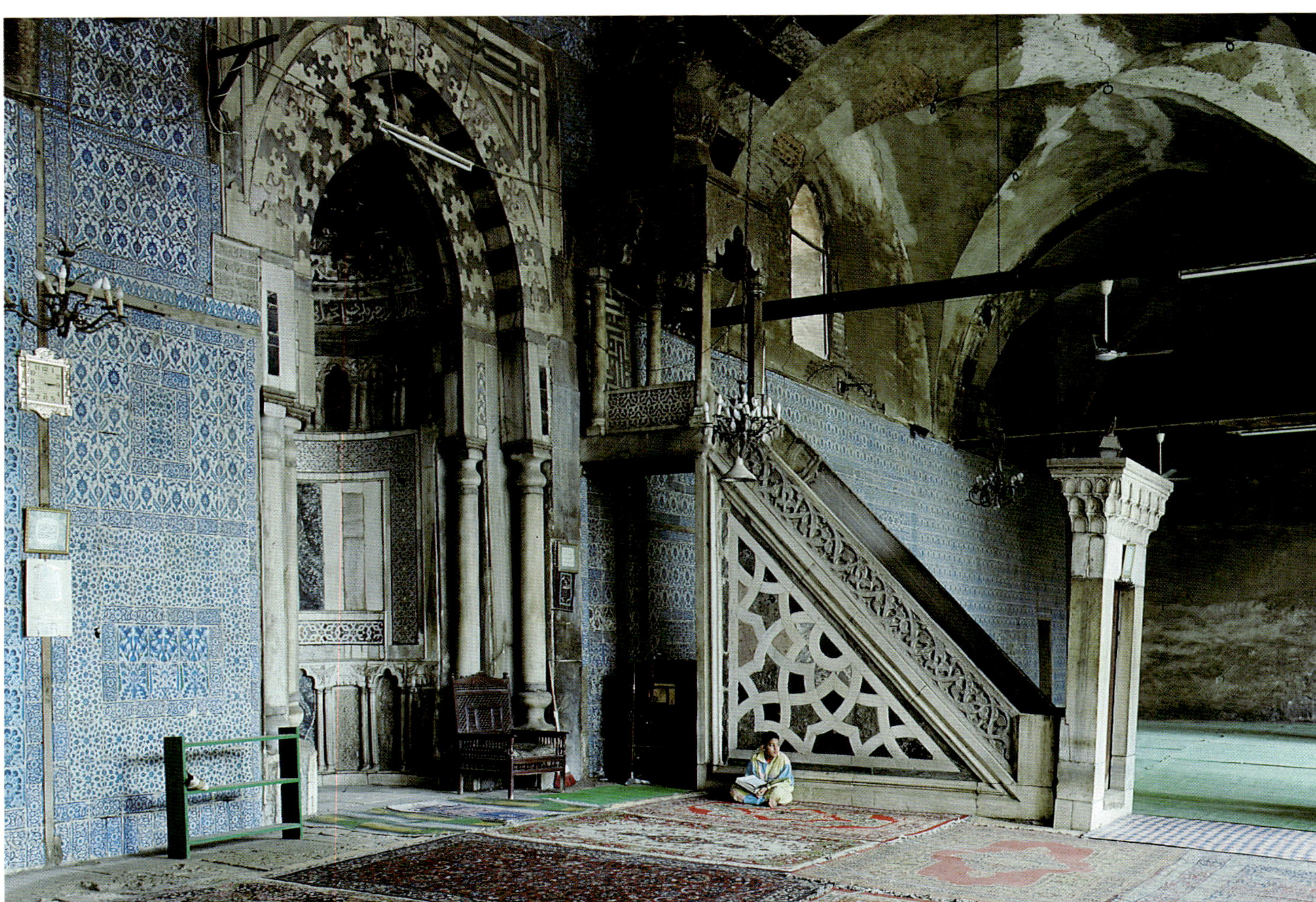

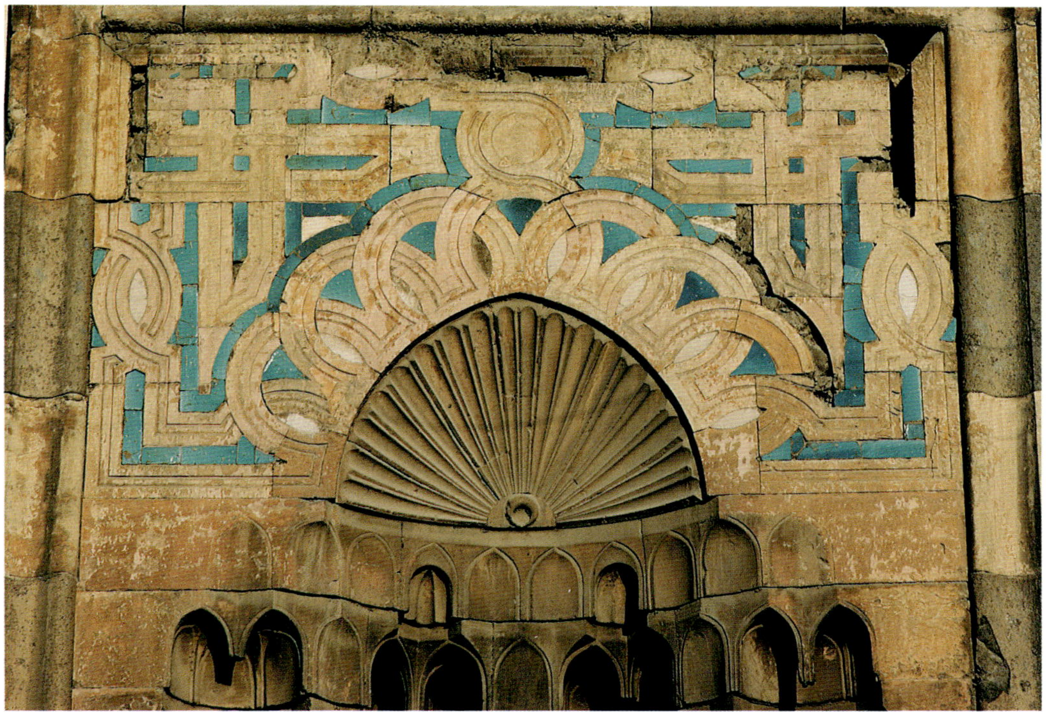

♦ Decoration of the doorway executed in colored stone marquetry ornamented with turquoise ceramics. Mausoleum of the Amir Arak, Damascus (Syria), 1349.

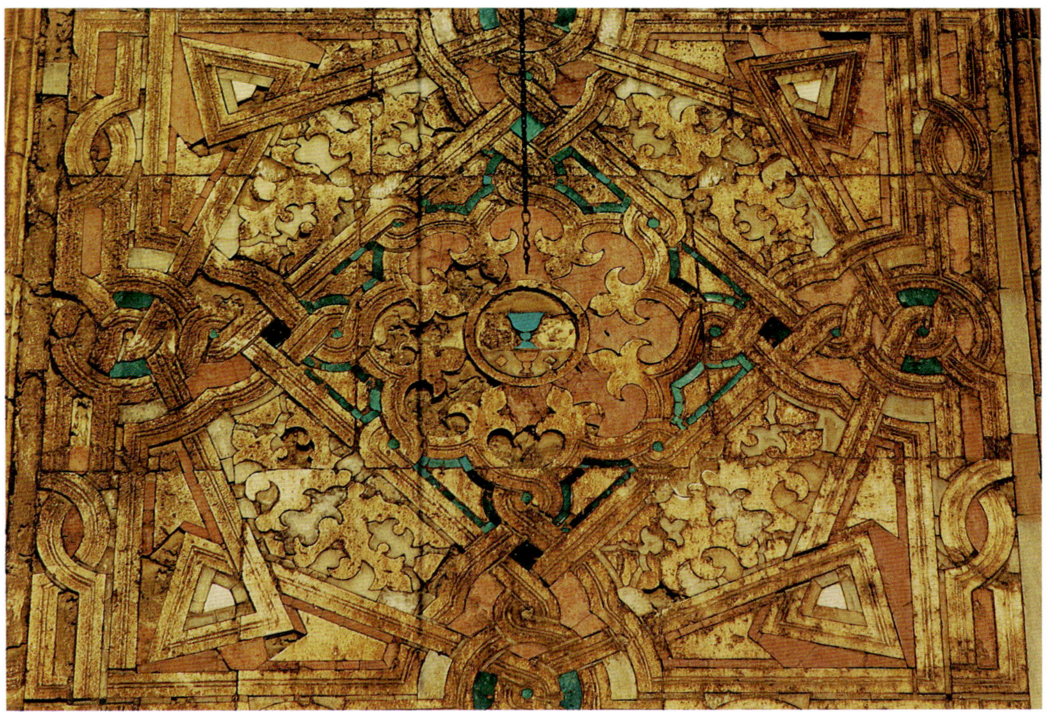

♦ Decoration in stone inlay adorned with turquoise ceramics. Taynabiyya *madrasa*, Damascus (Syria), end of the fourteenth century.

brick-built constructions were the rule. Nevertheless, substantial monuments displaying remarkable ceramic decorative schemes do exist. Sometimes, only touches of colored ceramic are dotted about the decorative stonework. Thus, in *mihrabs* such as that of the funerary hall in the complex of Sultan Hasan, Cairo (1356–59), slim turquoise-colored colonnettes can be seen among a riot of colored and partly gilded marble. The same small turquoise colonnettes recur on the *mihrab* of the Mu`ayyad Mosque (1415–20), where the *qibla* wall presents a tour de force of marble inlay. On the wall of the *mihrab* in the prayer hall of the Mithqaliyya *madrasa*, Cairo (founded by Amir Mithqal in 1374), turquoise ceramic strips appear among the ornamental marquetry.

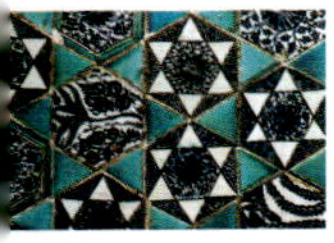

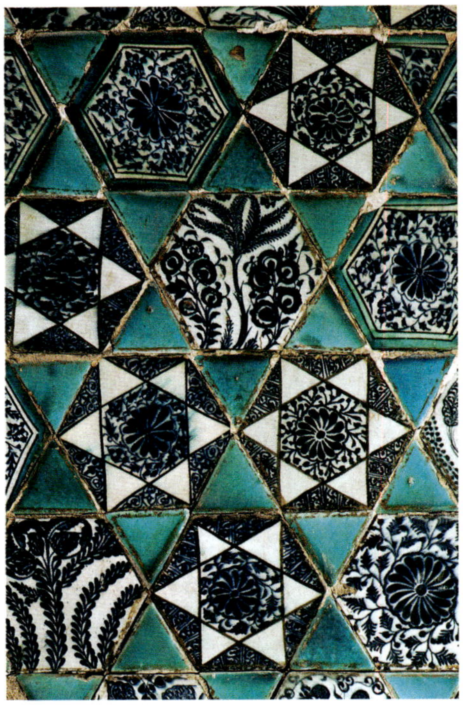

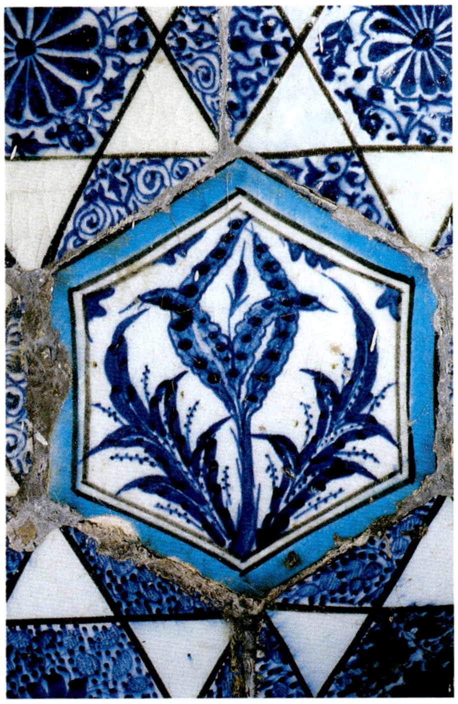

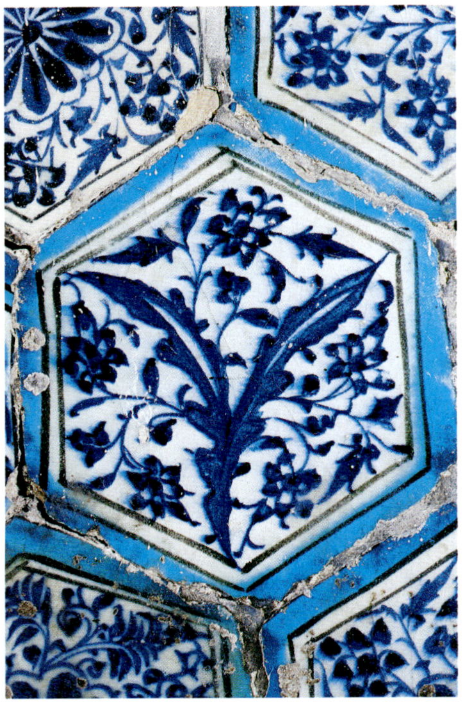

ABOVE LEFT

♦ Panel of blue-and-white underglaze-painted hexagonal tiles arranged with turquoise triangle spacers to form six-pointed stars. Mausoleum of Ghars al-Din al Khalil al-Tawrizi, Damascus (Syria).

MOSQUE OF GHARS AL-DIN AL KHALIL AL-TAWRIZI, DAMASCUS (SYRIA)

ABOVE CENTER

♦ Detail of underglaze-painted hexagonal tiles with a leafy plant design.

ABOVE RIGHT

♦ Blue-and-white underglaze-painted tile, a type of decoration inspired by Chinese blue-and-white ceramics.

FACING PAGE

♦ Underglaze-painted hexagonal tile adorned with a ewer.

FOLLOWING DOUBLE PAGE

♦ Blue-and-white underglaze-painted hexagonal tilework panel.

In Damascus there are other monuments in which the decoration, in cut and dressed stone, exploits the resources of the additional colors that ceramics allows. Examples include the mausoleum of Amir Arak (1349) and the Taynabiyya *madrasa* (end of the fourteenth century).

The mosque of Aqsunqur in Cairo, founded in 1346 by the Emir Shams al-Din Aqsunqur, did not originally incorporate ceramic decoration. It was only in 1652 that Ibrahim Agha al-Mustahfizan had it restored and clad in Ottoman tiles (probably from Iznik), which later earned it the name of "Blue Mosque."

The Damascus mausoleum of Ghars al-Din al Khalil al-Tawrizi, a vizier who died in 1430, is surely the prime example of Damascus ceramic production in Mamluk times. The tomb is located at the center of a square hall with large windows on three sides and the entrance portal on the fourth side. The walls between the windows and the doorway, as well as the recesses above the lintels, are wrapped in hexagonal blue-and-white underglaze-painted tiles. Appreciably smaller than their Ottoman counterparts at Edirne (see below), they are set out horizontally in conjunction with turquoise triangular tiles. The adjacent mosque also contains a frieze of hexagonal tiles and two panels of square ones; on one of these panels, representing a *mihrab*, an artist's signature appears that different authorities have deciphered variously as "work of ʿIsa al-Tawrizi" or "work of Ghaibi al-Tawrizi."[76] It is surely the latter version that is the more acceptable, since this potter's name (in truth, more probably a workshop sobriquet) is known from dozens of blue-and-white decorated ceramic shards that have been found, particularly at Fustat (today a district of Cairo). It is intriguing to note that both the patron of the tomb and the artist who signed the work were originally from Tabriz, in Iranian Azerbaijan.

These hexagonal tiles present an immense variety of motifs, vegetal for the most part, which are painted with singular suppleness of line. Certain tiles are decorated with objects, such as an ewer, while a few others depict birds. This taste for blue and white naturally recalls the two-color Chinese porcelain that was prized at Muslim courts. Lisa Golombek has compared the decorations painted in a number of Timurid mausoleums dating from the

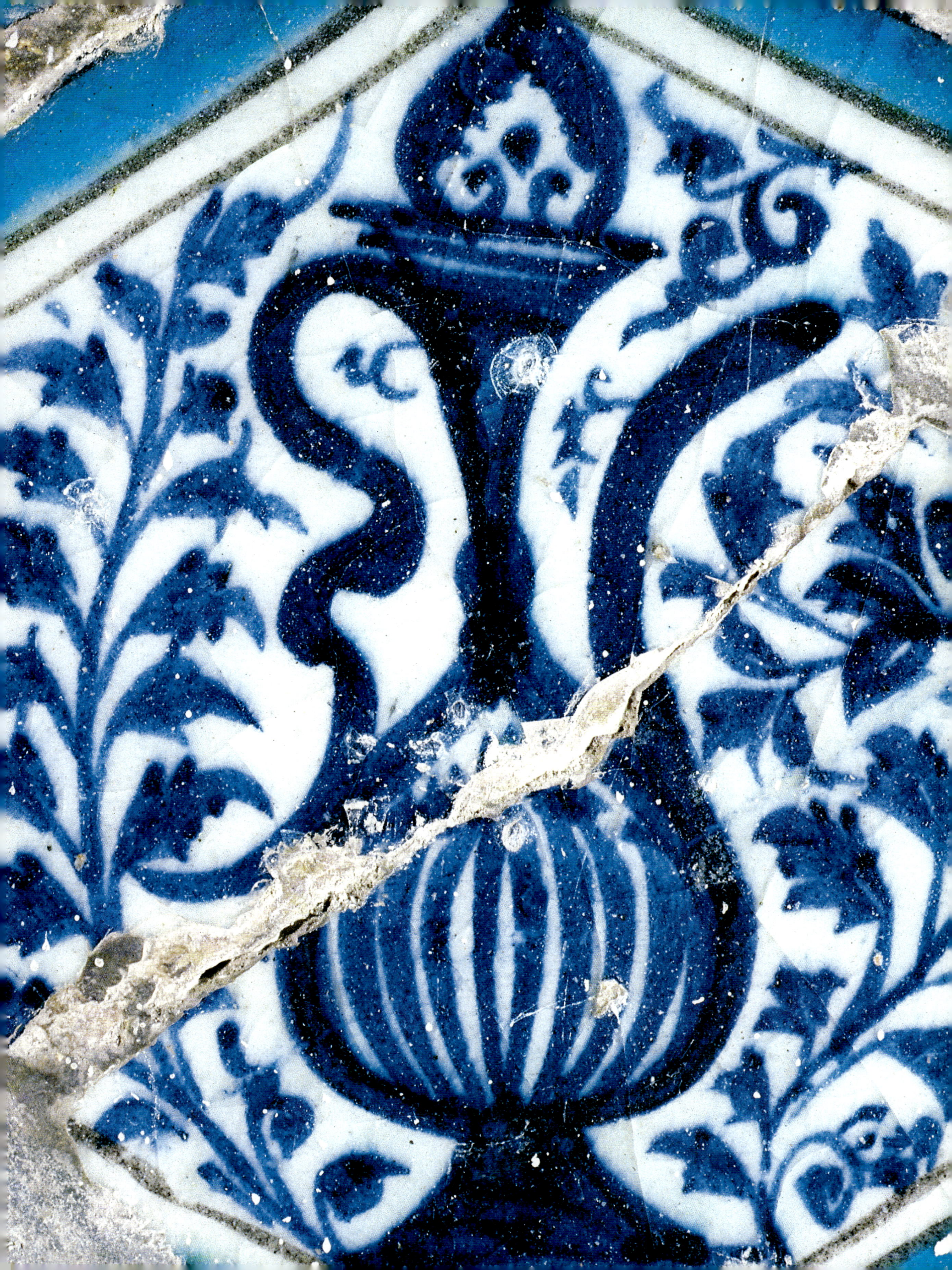

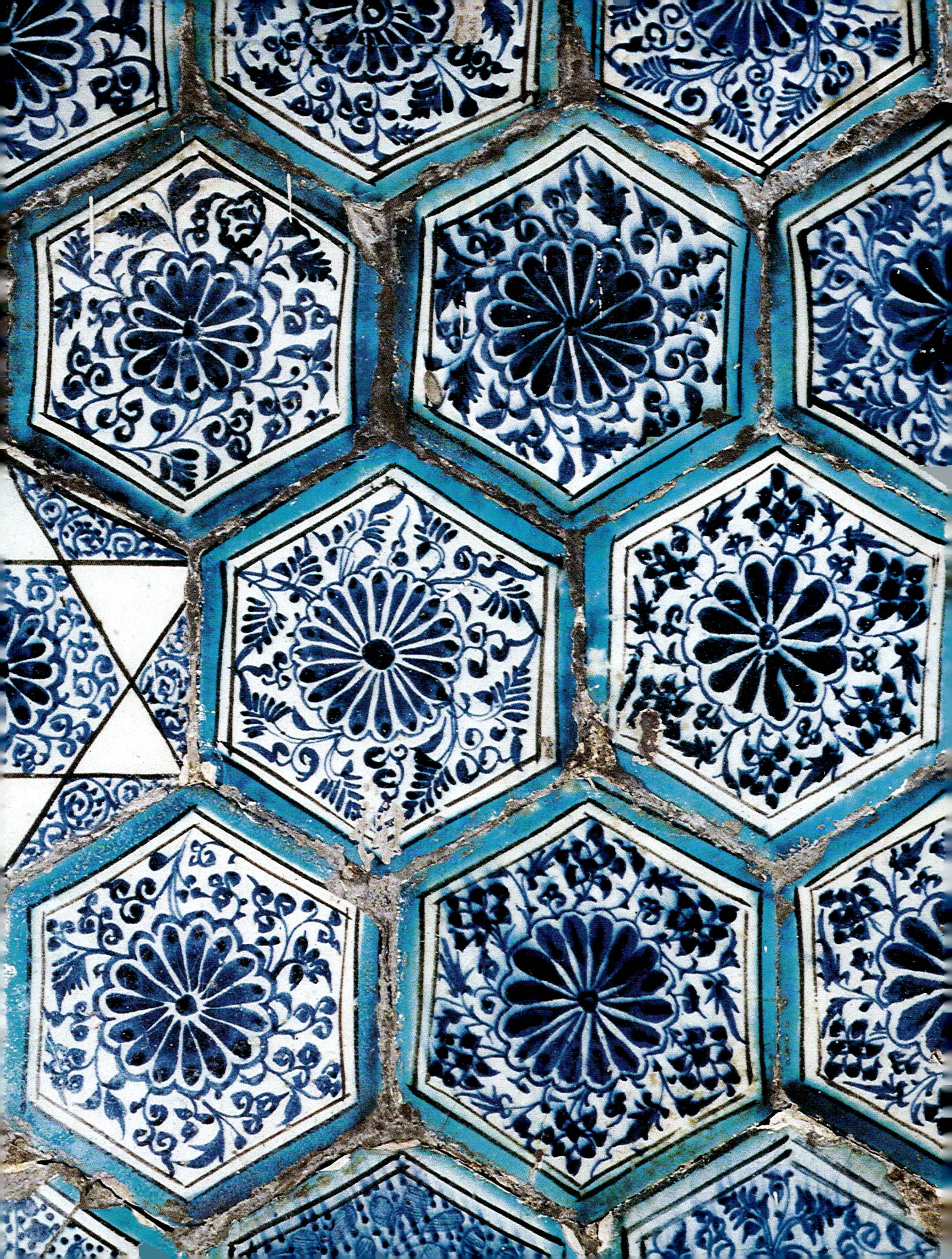

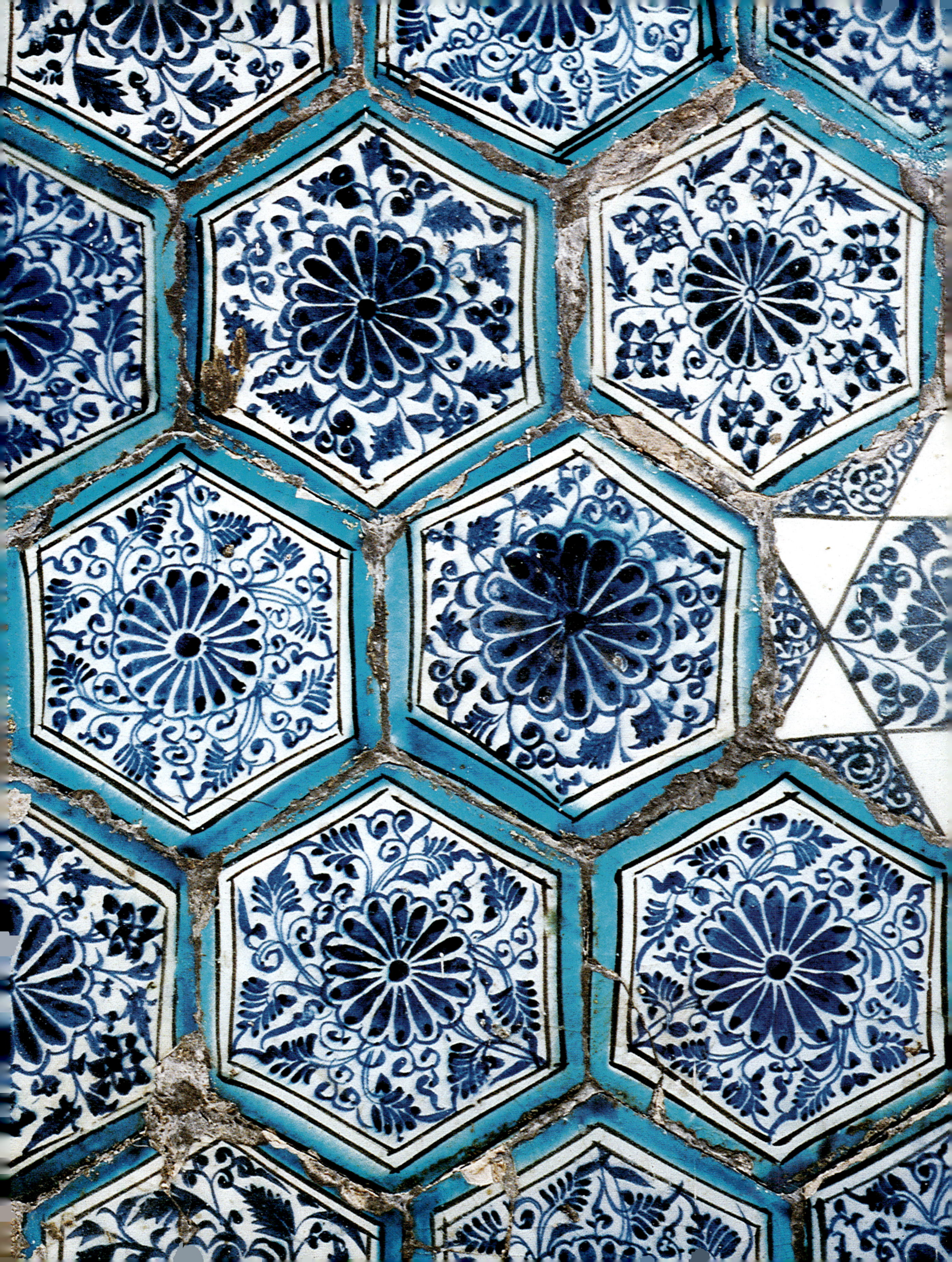

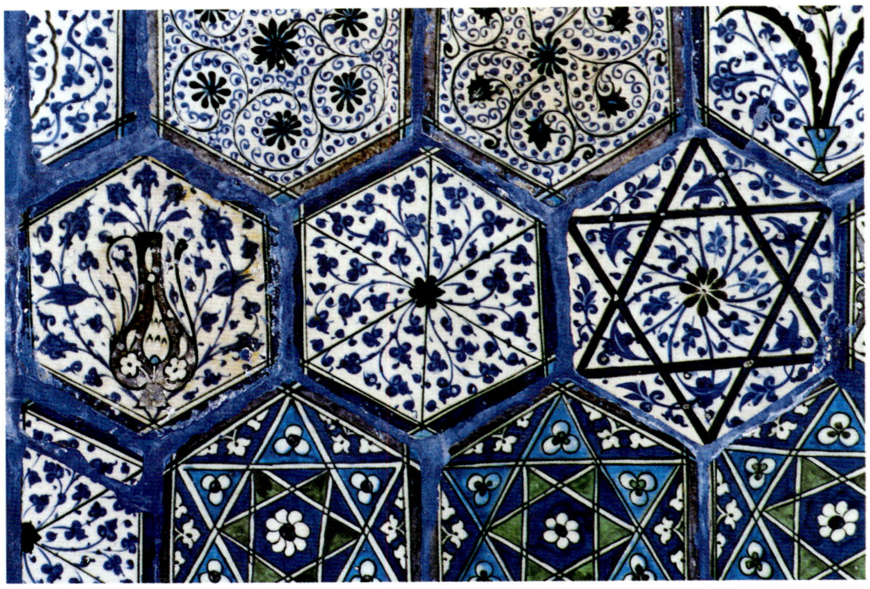

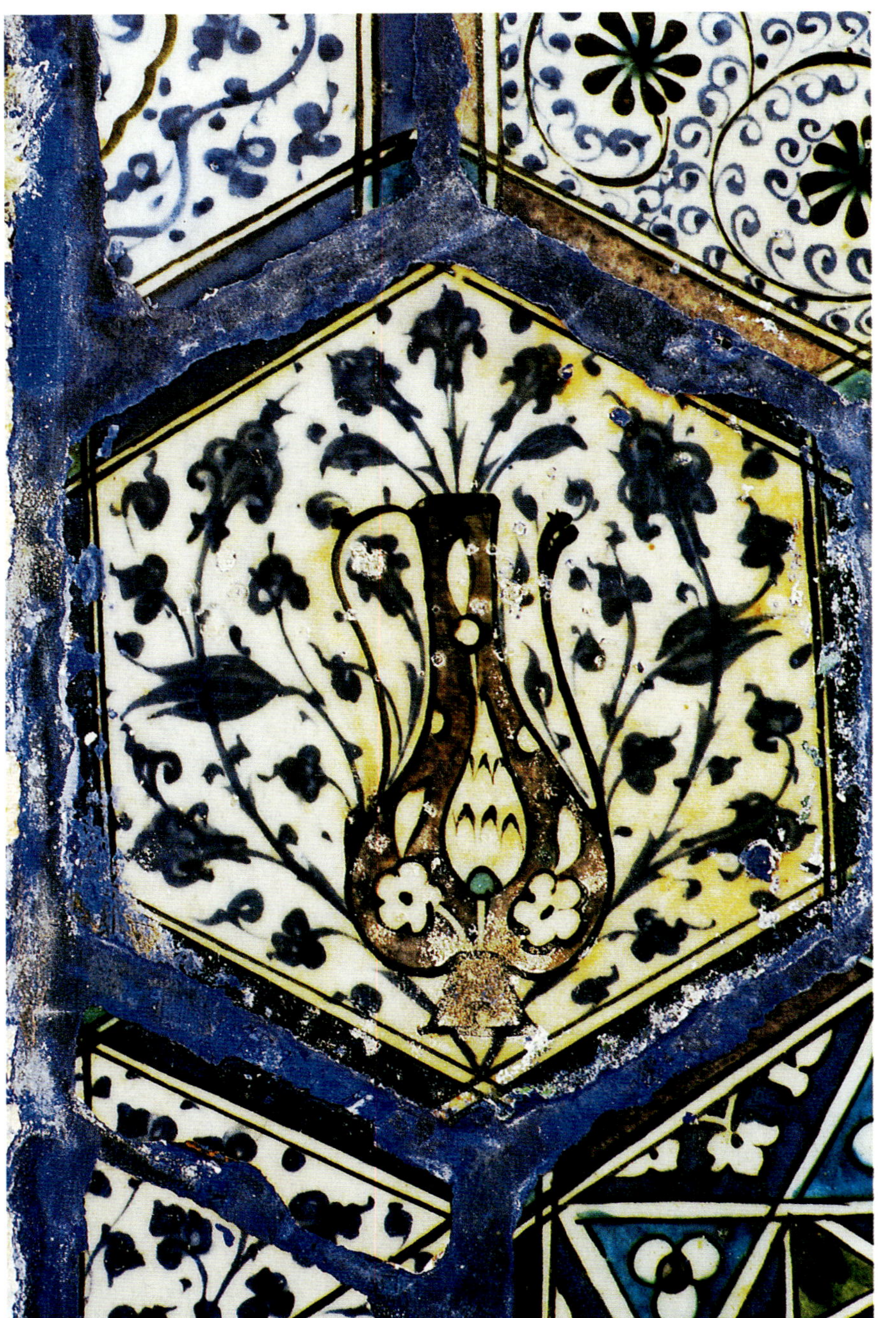

end of the fourteenth and beginning of the fifteenth century with blue-and-white decorated ceramic tiles produced elsewhere, particularly in Damascus.[77] It is her contention that these Timurid murals proved a ready source of inspiration for Syrian tile decorations. This fact would be explained by the return to their Near Eastern homelands of craftsmen exiled to central Asia by Timur. Tiles similar to those from Damascus resurface in the Qutaysh Mosque at Saida (Sidon, dating from the fifteenth century) in Lebanon. Grouped on a wall panel to the left of the entrance, these tiles measure 19 centimeters in diameter; in addition to cobalt blue, they also present highlights of turquoise, black, and manganese violet. Several hexagonal and square tiles are preserved at the Museum of Islamic Art, Cairo, together with an arch-shaped panel comprising four tiles from a fountain bearing an inscription in the name of Sultan Qa`it Bay (1468–96).[78]

QUTAYSH MOSQUE, SAIDA (LEBANON), FIFTEENTH CENTURY

♦ Panel of underglaze-painted hexagonal tiles in the style of ceramics commonly ascribed to Damascus.

♦ Underglaze-painted hexagonal tile in cobalt and black on a white clay slip decorated with a vase and blooms.

FACING PAGE

♦ Blue-and-white underglaze-painted hexagonal tile panel dating from the mid-fifteenth century in the Museum of Islamic Art, Cairo. The Chinese-inspired plant and animal forms are wedded to typically Islamic motifs, such as the triple-domed construction on one tile reminiscent of a mosque.

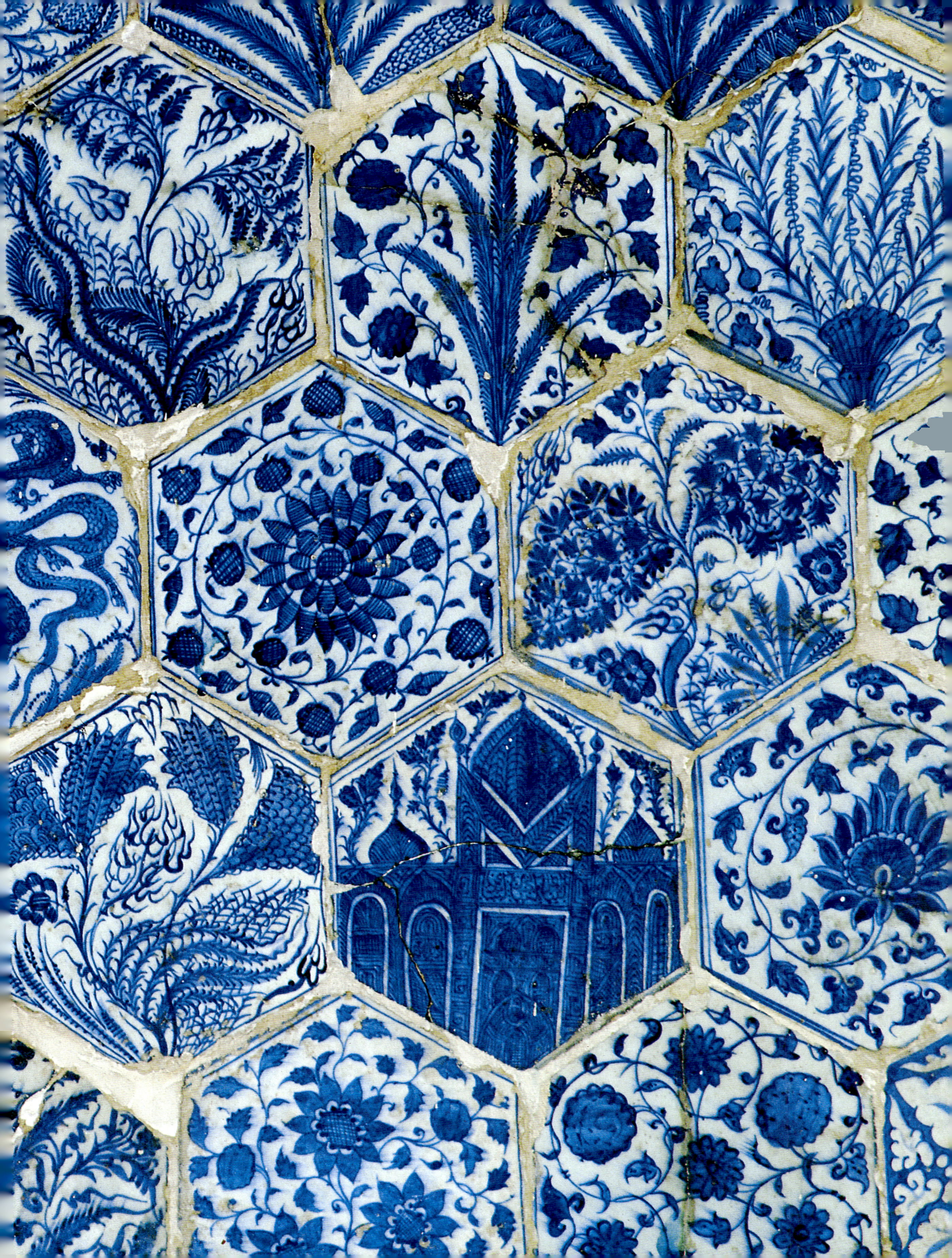

The "Masters of Tabriz" and Ottoman Anatolia in the Fifteenth Century

The Ottomans descended from one of the many Turkmen groups that swept into Anatolia in Seljuq times. After the fall of the Seljuqs of Rum, the Ottomans established themselves to the west of Anatolia, in ancient Bithynia, a province contiguous with the Byzantine empire. The name of the dynasty derives from that of their ancestor, Osman I (1281–1324), whose successor, Orhan (1324–60), seized the town of Bursa in 1326 and made it his capital. This process of expansion continued under Murad I (1360–89), who took Andrinople (today Edirne) in 1366 and, by establishing the city as his European capital, thus began the conquest of Thrace. As for Bayezit I (1389–1402), he received the title of sultan from the `Abbasid caliph in Cairo; however, his defeat at the hands of Timur at the battle of Ankara in 1402 put a stop to Ottoman expansion. The reign of Mehmet (Muhammad) II, known as the Conqueror, was marked by the capture of Constantinople in 1453. Following this success, a spate of conquests began, with Ottoman power reaching its zenith under Suleyman II, known as the Magnificent (1520–66).

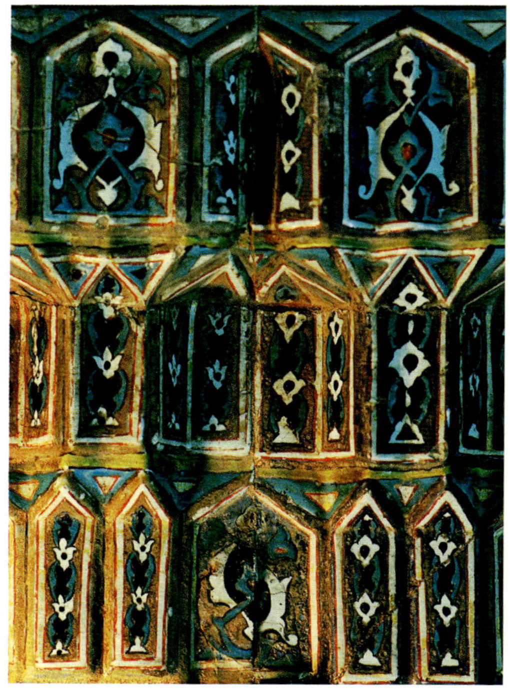

The origins of Ottoman architecture are rooted in various intersecting influences derived from the heritage of the Seljuqs of Rum and borrowings from Byzantine architecture and Timurid decorative arts. The earliest Ottoman mosques were built to various plans, the types chosen hesitating between the Bedouin, the hypostyle, and the domed, reminiscent of both the mausoleums and the smaller covered mosques of Iran. The Green Mosque at Iznik (Yeşil Cami, 1378) displays an ample central cupola on a square ground plan, in front of which is a hall and porch with columns. The mosque's name derives

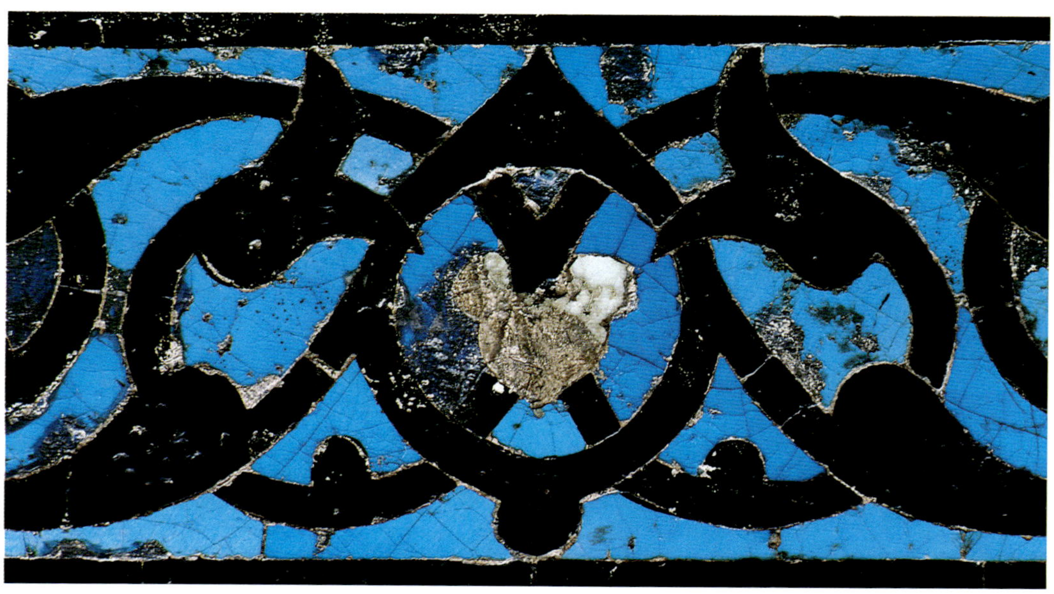

ABOVE

♦ *Muqarnas* zone of the *mihrab*, lined in "black line" polychrome tiles decorated with *petit feu* gilding. Yeşil Cami, Bursa (Turkey), completed in 1420.

RIGHT

♦ Detail of the intrados of the entrance arch set with cut-tile mosaic. Yeşil Türbe, Bursa (Turkey), 1421.

from the minaret covered with green glaze tiles to the left.

Composed of a mosque, a *madrasa*, and a *türbe* (mausoleum), the complex of Mehmet (Muhammad) I (1403–21) at Bursa (Yeşil Külliye) is certainly one of the finest achievements in fifteenth-century Ottoman art. The Yeşil Cami (Green Mosque) was designed by the architect Hajji Ivaz ibn Ahi Bayezit; according to an inscription on the doorway, it was he who, in 1412–13, designed the building for Sultan Mehmet I. In reality, the building as left in 1419–20 was not complete, because the portico that was to protect the facade was never built. The plan of the mosque corresponds to the inverted T type that can be seen in other mosques of the period. A vestibule leads to two side chambers and a staircase allows access to the imperial loge located on an upper floor. The prayer hall occupies two square-shaped spaces, each roofed by a generous dome; the two central spaces are flanked by a pair of rooms each vaulted with a cupola. The ceramic decoration, in particular on the floor in the imperial loge, around the two ground-floor alcoves, and in the *mihrab*, is of great beauty. These decorations were carried out under the direction of `Ali ibn Ilyas ibn `Ali, called Naqqash (Nakkas) `Ali (*naqqash* meaning the "painter-designer"), who put 1421 as the date of completion of work. Other signatures appear, such as those of Muhammad "the Mad" on the sultan's loge and "the Masters of Tabriz" on the *mihrab*.

Located almost directly opposite the mosque, the *türbe* of Mehmet I, known by the name of Yeşil Türbe (Green Tomb), was completed after the death of the sultan by Hajji Ivaz. Built on an octagonal plan, its form is different from that of the older

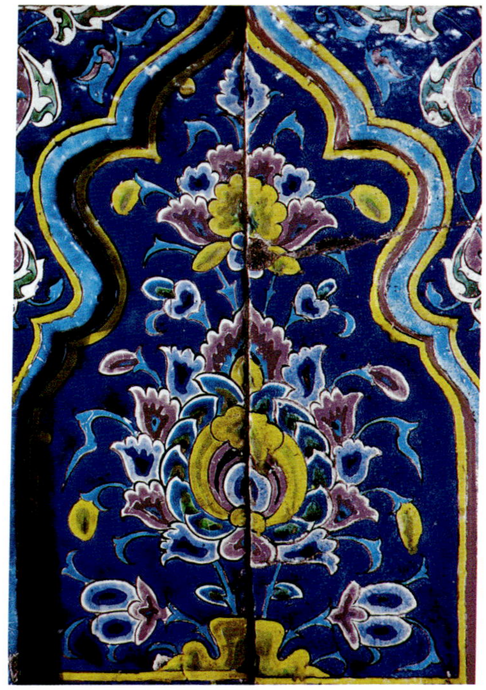

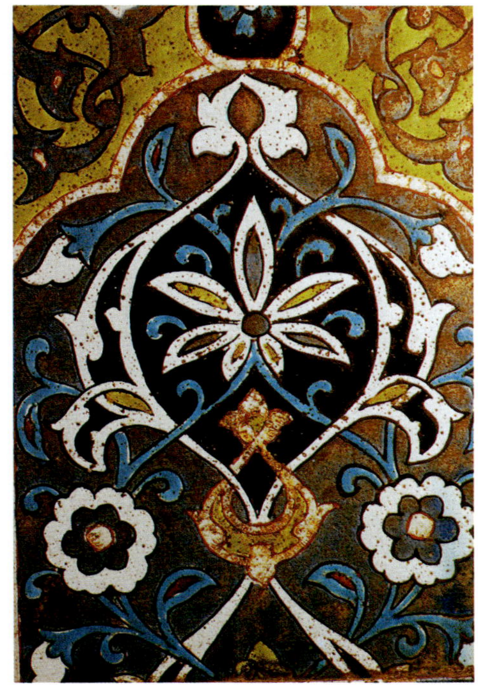

ABOVE LEFT

♦ Trefoil niche in the basement of the cenotaph decorated in "black-line" polychrome tiles featuring a floral composition painted with exceptional skill. Yeşil Türbe, Bursa (Turkey), 1421.

ABOVE RIGHT

♦ Detail of a "black line" polychrome tile with traces of *petit feu* gold decoration. *Mihrab* of the Yeşil Cami, Bursa (Turkey), completed in 1420.

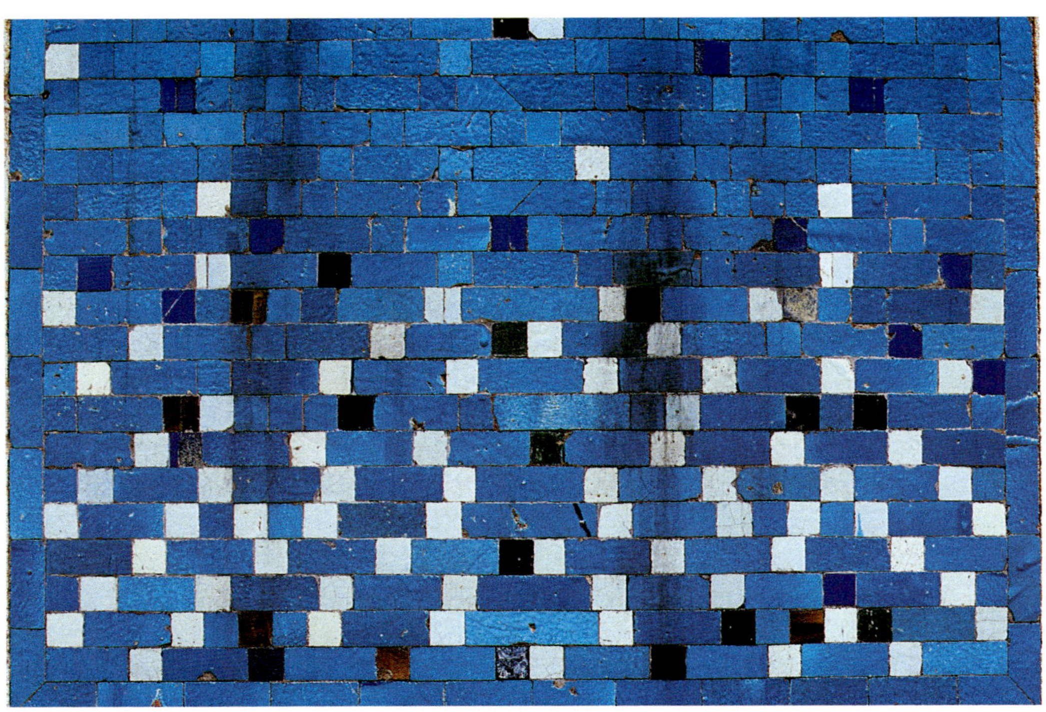

♦ Detail of the facade of Mehmet I's *türbe*. Yeşil Türbe, Bursa (Turkey), 1421. Apparently uniform, the turquoise tilework covering the monument incorporates subtle color variations that create a shimmering effect.

MURADIY MOSQUE, EDIRNE (TURKEY), 1435–36

FACING PAGE, FROM TOP TO BOTTOM AND LEFT TO RIGHT

♦ Blue-and-white underglaze-painted hexagonal tile. As at Damascus, the motifs are clearly inspired by Chinese porcelain.

♦ Here, geometrical severity predominates over Far Eastern patterns.

♦ Although the firing of many tiles seems to have been controlled to perfection, in the example here the cobalt has fused beneath the glaze, smearing the design slightly.

♦ Dado lined in blue-and-white underglaze-painted hexagonal tiles arranged with turquoise triangles to form a six-pointed star design.

♦ Panel of the *mihrab* in "black line" polychrome ceramic. The extremely high quality of these tiles is apparent above all in the masterly way the tonal values are varied.

mausoleums at Bursa, as does its exterior cladding, which is composed of turquoise blue tiles bordered with stonework. The earliest major Ottoman monuments of the fifteenth century were still largely decorated in tiles with a monochrome glaze. The same is true of the external revetments referred to above, as well as the large panels inside the mausoleum here and in other funerary buildings of the city, such as the mausoleums of princes Şehzade Ahmed (1429) and Djem (1479). For the internal decoration, the monochrome, often hexagonal tiles are coated in turquoise or cobalt glaze, sometimes finished with a gold-painted design (tomb of Prince Djem, Green Mosque). Similarly, dados and lunettes in the Muradiye Mosque (1424–27) in Bursa built by Murad II are for the most part decorated in monochrome tiles arranged into geometrical figures.

In parallel with the development in the first decades of the century of this type of ceramic decoration—relatively simple from a technical point of view—true polychrome ceramics also started appearing. Certain decorations, such as the *mihrab* of Yeşil Türbe, show a total mastery of the art of "black line" tile manufacture. Inside the niche with its *muqarnas*, a magnificent panel showing fanciful flowers frames a mosque lamp flanked by two candelabras—a direct reference to the Qu`ran *sura* "The Light" (*al-Nur, sura* 24), in which God is compared to a lamp burning in an alcove. Separated by a black line, the paints display an extended range of colors, with, in addition to traditional turquoise, cobalt, white, and manganese, touches of pink and pistachio green, as well as the odd glint of gold. Timurid taste emerges clearly in these creations, but the technique on the other hand differs markedly from the primarily underglaze-painted polychrome decors favored in central Asia. This obviously raises questions relating to the process by which the technology was transferred and to the identity of the master craftsmen behind these Ottoman pieces. The appearance of polychrome glazed decorations in Ottoman Anatolia was certainly closely related to the development of this technique in Timurid central Asia. The role played by the "masters of Tabriz" in the decoration of the Green complex in Bursa has already been referred to.[79] It is interesting to note that these "masters"—who undoubtedly also carried out the decorative schemes at the Muradiye at Edirne (see below), as well as the *mihrab* of the *imaret* of Karamanoglu Ibrahim Bey dated 1433 (today preserved at the Çinili Köşk, Istanbul)—reappear in the sixteenth century in Constantinople. Again it was another artist from Tabriz, `Abdallah Tabrizi, who designed the new decoration for the Dome of the Rock in Jerusalem that had been commissioned by Suleyman between 1545 and 1552.[80]

The Muradiye Mosque in Edirne (1435–36) initially formed part of a complex housing a community of whirling dervishes. The interior, in particular the *mihrab*, are decorated in ceramics of singular beauty. The *mihrab*, executed in "black line" polychrome tiles and relief decoration, has similarities to the decoration at Bursa described above. On the other hand, the sequences of blue-and-white hexagonal tiles decorating the dados are more original; perhaps they are forerunners of some of the so-called "Damascus" group discussed previously. Laid with the tip pointing downward, these hexagonal tiles are arranged in patterns in combination with turquoise triangles; each panel is framed by a rectangular ceramic border, also blue-and-white underglaze-painted.

Some hexagonal tiles to be found in parts of the Ottoman empire can be plainly identified as the work of Iznik workshops, while others can be assigned to workshops in Damascus or Cairo. One last group, recently identified, came from the imperial workshops of Constantinople. Various tiles of this kind, often hexagonal

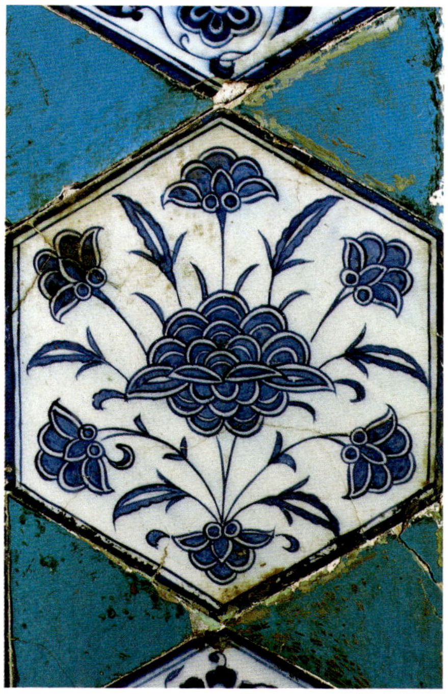

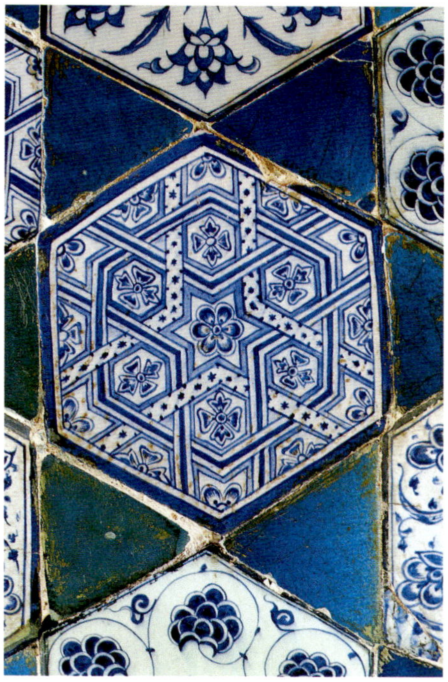

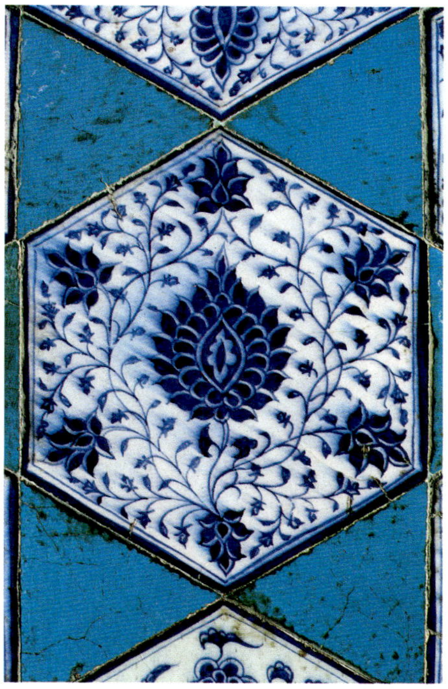

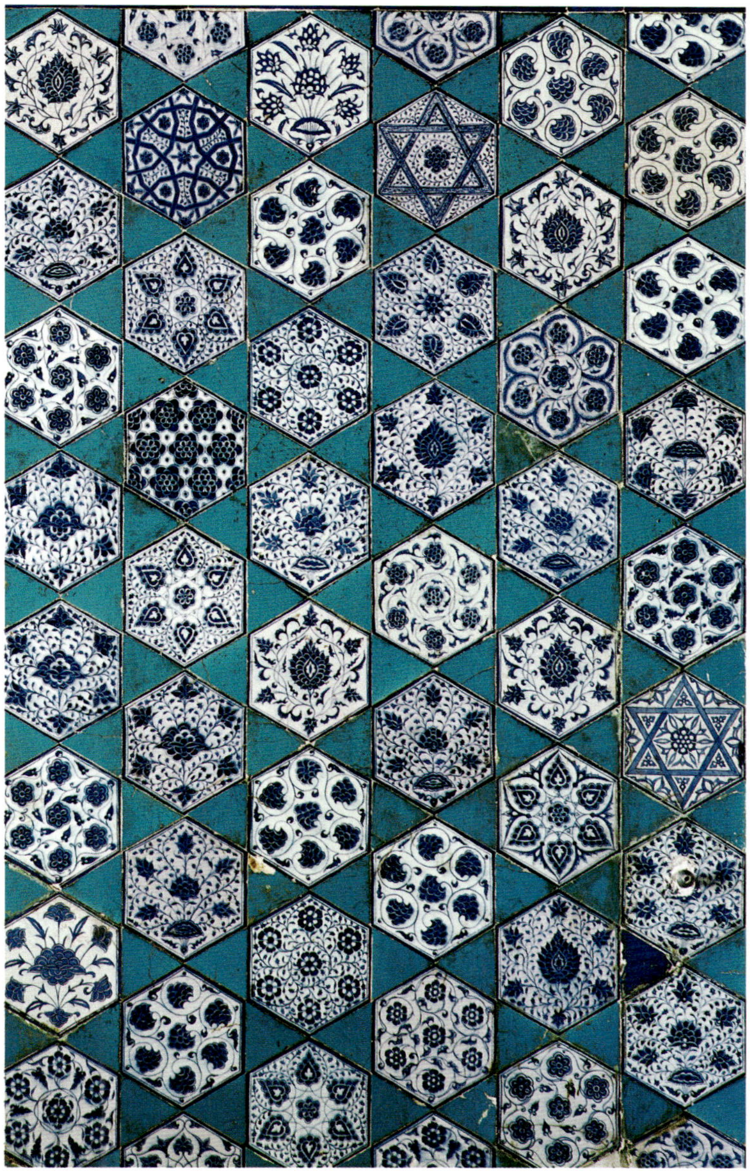

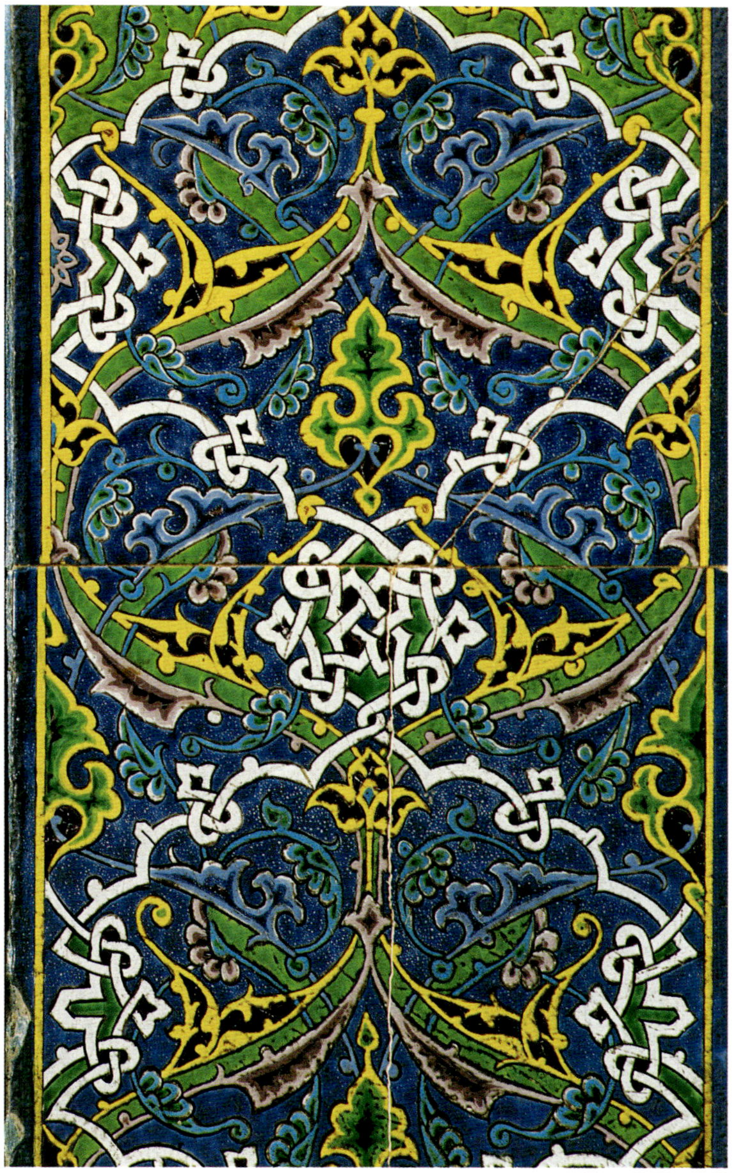

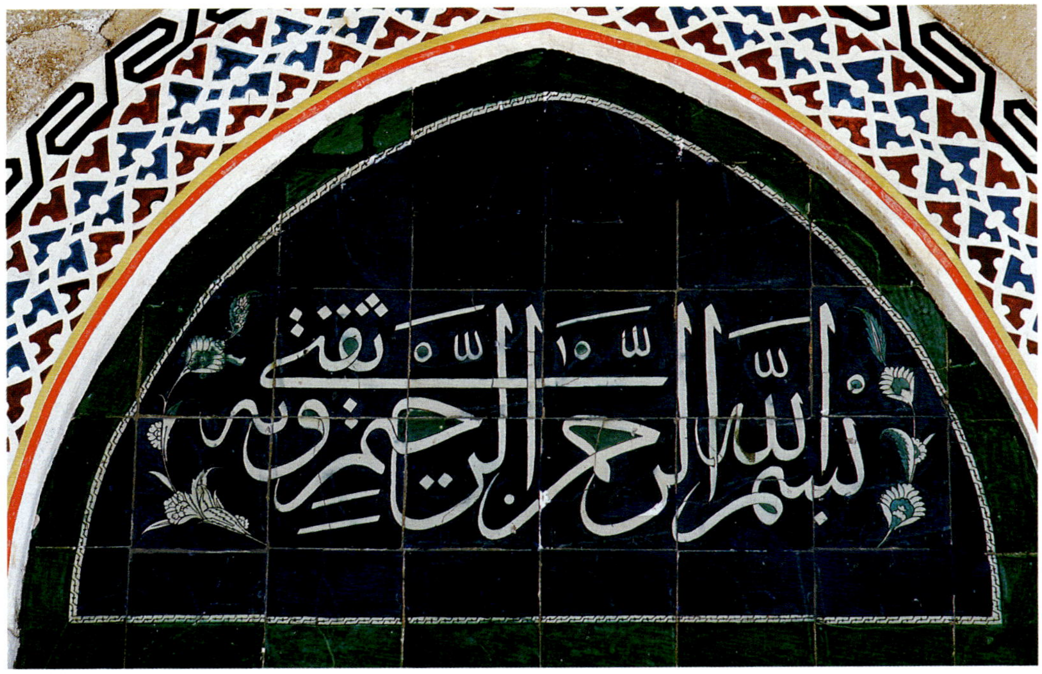

♦ Lunette lined with polychrome tiles inscribed with a Thuluth inscriptional decoration. Mosque of Bayezit II, Amasya (Turkey), 1468.

♦ Stone facade of the *türbe* of Mahmud Pasha, Istanbul (Turkey), 1463. This is one of the rare examples in Istanbul of turquoise and cobalt ceramic pieces inset to form a star pattern.

and presenting minor differences in size, paste, and motifs according to provenance, are found decorating many Ottoman monuments, such as the Üç Şerefeli Mosque, also at Edirne (1437–48), or the Mosque of the Valide at Manisa (1522).

Ceramic decorations were relatively rare on the facades of buildings in Constantinople, although there are noteworthy exceptions, in particular the *türbe* of Mahmud Pasha located next to the mosque of the same name near the Great Bazaar. In this *türbe*, constructed in 1463, ceramic tiles are incorporated into the building's stonework. In the same way, a few years after the seizure of Constantinople, Mehmet the Conqueror had a number of residences built in what was to become the palace enclosure of the Topkapi Saray. One of these pavilions, the Çinili Köşk, completed in 1473, owes its name "Tiled Pavilion" to the ceramic cladding of the facade, with its portico borne on stone columns. Today, this handsome edifice—one of the very few Ottoman residences of the fifteenth century to have survived virtually intact—houses a valuable collection of ceramics. The decoration of the frontage combines small rectangular monochrome tiles, not unlike Timurid *banna'i* brickwork, and cut-tile mosaic, notably for the broad inscriptional bands around the main entrance. These mosaic decorations are also found combined with hexagonal tiles on certain dados, as in the Green Mosque at Bursa.

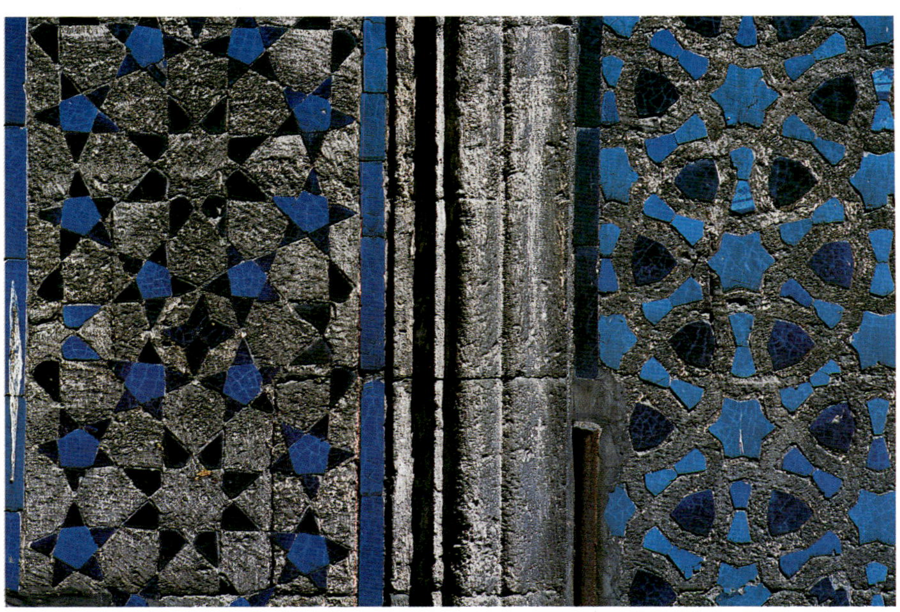

In 1486, Bayezit II (1481–1512), successor to Mehmet the Conqueror, built a complex including a mosque, a *madrasa*, and a small *türbe* in Amasya. The tympanums (or lunettes) above the windows of the mosque are filled in with beautiful epigraphic tiles with a white script on a cobalt blue ground.

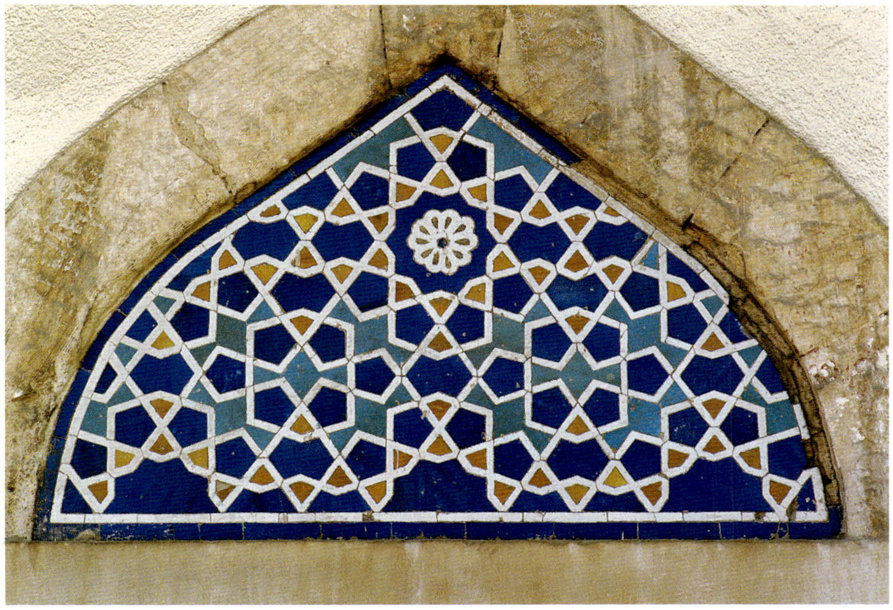

MURADIYE MOSQUE,
BURSA (TURKEY), 1424–26

♦ Lunette filled with a geometric composition in cut-tile mosaic: the petals of the white rosette are gouged out.

♦ Geometric variations in monochrome white, turquoise, and cobalt tilework.

♦ The decoration of the dados in the mosque plays on the opposition between areas containing geometric patterns and large plain panels of an intense yet restful turquoise.

BELOW

♦ Panel bearing a geometric pattern in monochrome white, turquoise, and cobalt.

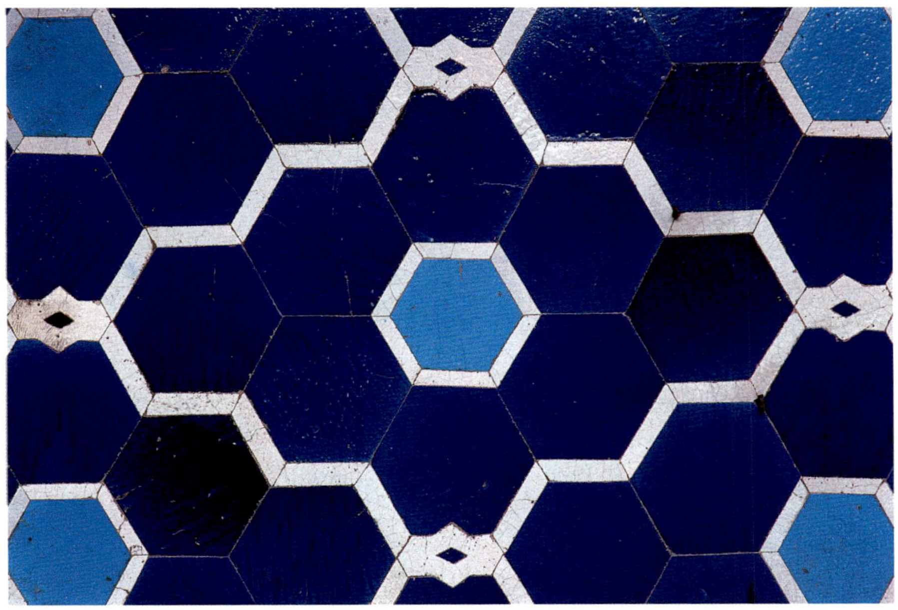

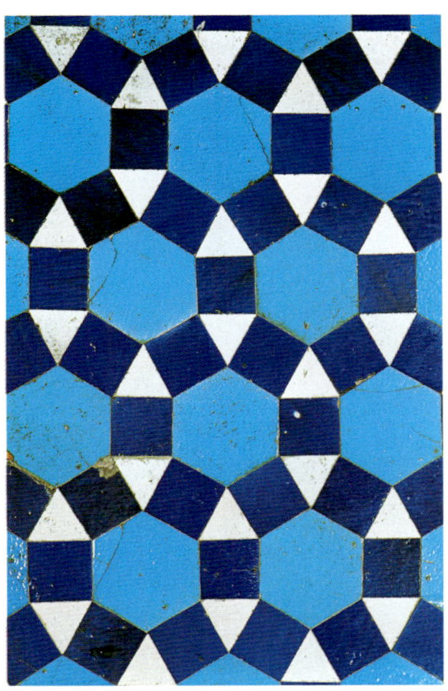

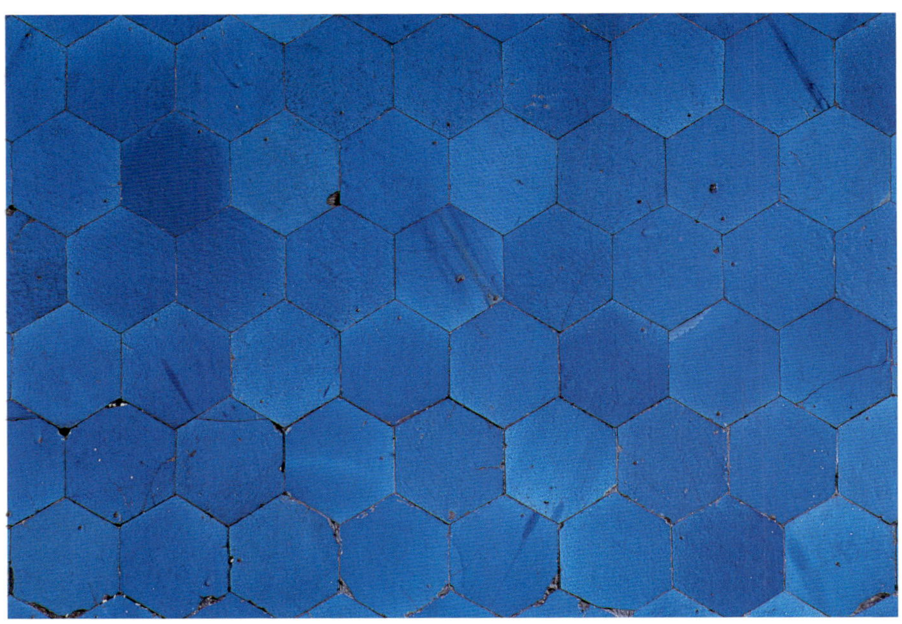

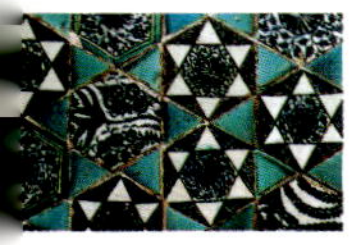

The Golden Age of Ottoman Architecture

Sixteenth-century Ottoman architecture is dominated by the exceptional architect Sinan. Born around 1490, Sinan is surely the only architect of the Muslim world who bears comparison with figures from the Italian Renaissance such as Michelangelo. The age at which Sinan learned his trade as an architect is not recorded: probably born of Christian stock, he was recruited by the Janissaries in around 1512. In 1526, he entered the imperial cavalry and served Sultan Suleyman in Austria and Baghdad, and on expeditions to Corfu and Puglia in 1537. A year later, he was appointed architect of the Darül-Saadet ("dwelling of happiness"). For fifty years until his death in 1588, Sinan drew up plans for countless buildings and supervised innumerable construction sites. In his buildings, particularly his mosques, external form reflects both the internal space and the structural system of the load-bearing elements. Although the constructions of Sinan and his successors are mostly of masonry—with a marked preference for elaborate stone carving—ceramic cladding is nevertheless far from absent, particularly in interiors and on the sheltered frontages of porticos. However, contrary to the practice in Timurid architecture, there is no interrelationship here between form and color, as the ceramics are entirely confined to the decorative role of providing a sumptuous wrapping for every available surface.

♦ "Black line" polychrome tiles decorating the facade of the ʿArz Odasi (audience hall) in the Topkapi Saray, Istanbul (Turkey). Although the building was completed in 1585, the tiles date from the early sixteenth century.

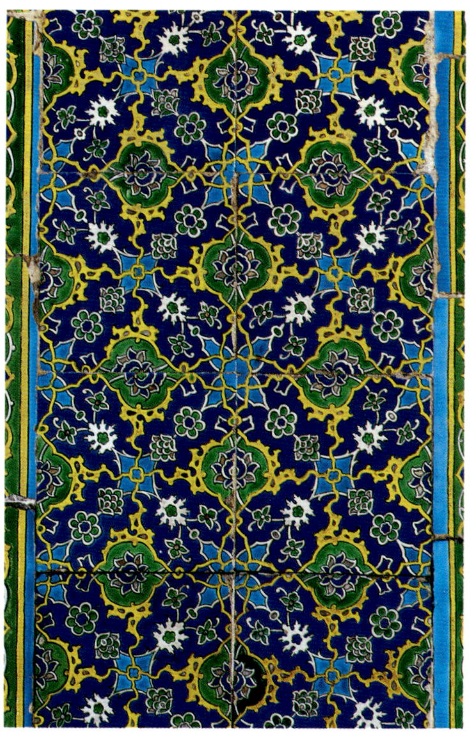

One of the earliest examples of architectural ceramics in the sixteenth century was the decoration of the *türbe* of Selim I in the Selimiye complex in Istanbul. This complex was built in 1522 on the orders of Suleyman to honor the memory of his father, Sultan Selim, called "Yavuz" ("the Grim"). The panels framing the entrance to the tomb are set with "black line" polychrome tilework. This decoration seems to be a continuation of the "Timurid" tradition that flourished in Bursa and Edirne. The panel located to the right of the entrance bears a central arabesque scrollwork motif on a cobalt ground laid out in a blind arcade. This central compartment is framed by a broad border decorated with a geometric interlace motif. An epigraphic frieze provides the date A.H. 929/A.D. 1522. Opposite the *türbe* of Selim I stands another mausoleum built for the sons of Suleyman. This building displays star-shaped tiles, also decorated in "black line" polychromy, but unusually these are set at a certain distance from one another against a ground of mortar and powdered brick.

These tiles were probably manufactured in the imperial ceramics workshop at Constantinople, whose existence is attested by a number of archive documents. These documents contain interesting information concerning what is often called the *cuerda seca* technique. The output of these workshops is in fact relatively well known and can

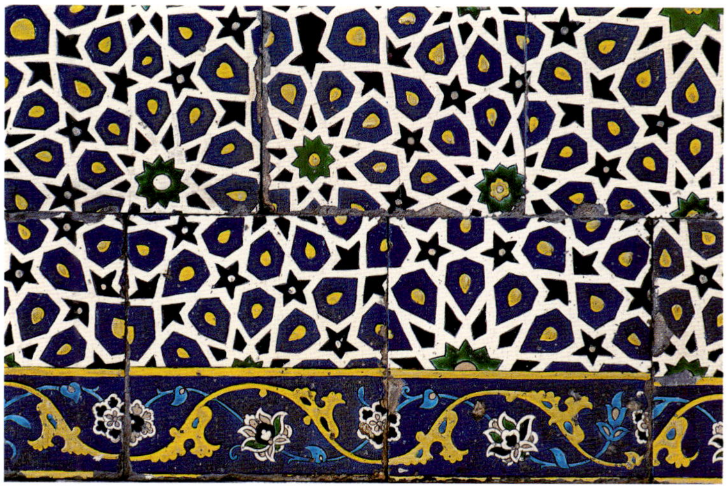

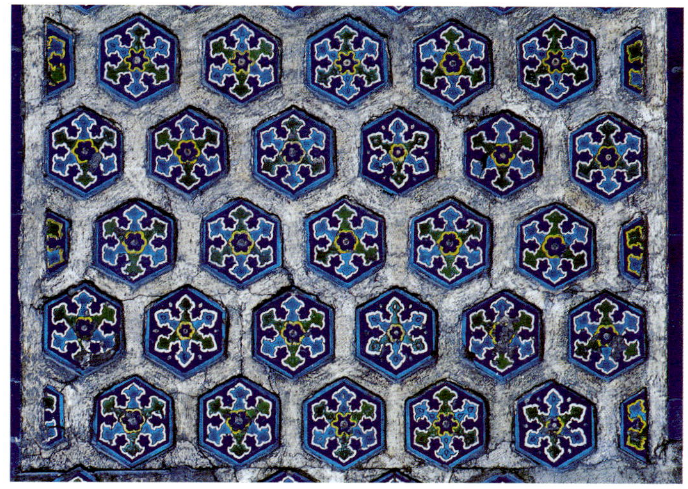

therefore be compared with the list of materials that has come down to us. Moreover, as Gülru Necipoglu has shown, in the same period the techniques used in Constantinople and Iznik differed. It would be useful at this point to reexamine the materials mentioned in these documents: they appear in the form of a list, with the quantity and price of each item for a period covering the years 1527 to 1528.[81] The use to which each ingredient might have been put, however, is not always clear. The materials mentioned include quartz, silica slip, potter's clay, cullet (necessary for the manufacture of frit, more than 4 tons of which was used in two years), and soda. As regards metal oxides and dyes, minerals such as cobalt, litharge (plumbous oxide), antimony sulfide, copper, tin, iron, and ceruse (white lead) are cited. The several types of adhesive added to glue the oxides to the body prior to firing are also cited in the documents. Ingredients used in the manufacture of paste and frit can also be deduced from these lists. On the other hand, although colors such as cobalt blue and antimony yellow appear in this list, one is struck by a number of rather surprising absences: there is very little copper (less than 13 kilograms in two years) and no manganese whatsoever. There is also no apparent trace either of *mozarrad* (chromite), the material used for the "black line" that features on tiles often described as being of the *cuerda seca* type. It is of course possible that these ingredients do not appear in the accounts because stocks had been acquired previously. Another salient feature is the enormous consumption of lead, in the form both of oxide (litharge) and carbonate (white lead). The lead ended up in frits and glazes, although, as has been seen in the account given by Abu'l-Qasim, in certain cases it was also used to "gray" colors. Tin was employed solely as an opacifer.

Charles Kiefer has defined these ceramics as "cloisonné enamels with an alkali lead glaze painted over a slip on a stonepaste body fritted with alkali lead,"[82] an analysis that corresponds to the ingredients quoted above. The drawing Kiefer provides of a section of one of the tiles from Selim I's *türbe*[83] shows that the slip separates the oxides of different colors, creating little pits; the ridge separating them is painted in a black line that Kiefer describes as "not very fusible." Actually, it is not only the low fusibility of this black pigment which is effective, but also the fact that it is not very vitreous, resulting in the matt surface that contrasts so strikingly with the brilliantly colorful glazes. Indeed, unlike polychrome underglaze-painted designs, these decorations do not display a surface glaze, which is why Kiefer describes them as "cloisonné enamels."

The tiles of the tomb of prince Mehmet (1543), which are similar in style to those

♦ "Black line" polychrome tilework panel forming a star pattern with a leaf-scroll border. *Türbe* of Selim I, Istanbul (Turkey), 1522.

♦ Panel incorporating intriguingly spaced "black line" polychrome tiles that contrast strikingly with the neutral color of the facing. *Türbe* of the sons of Suleyman, Istanbul (Turkey), c. 1522.

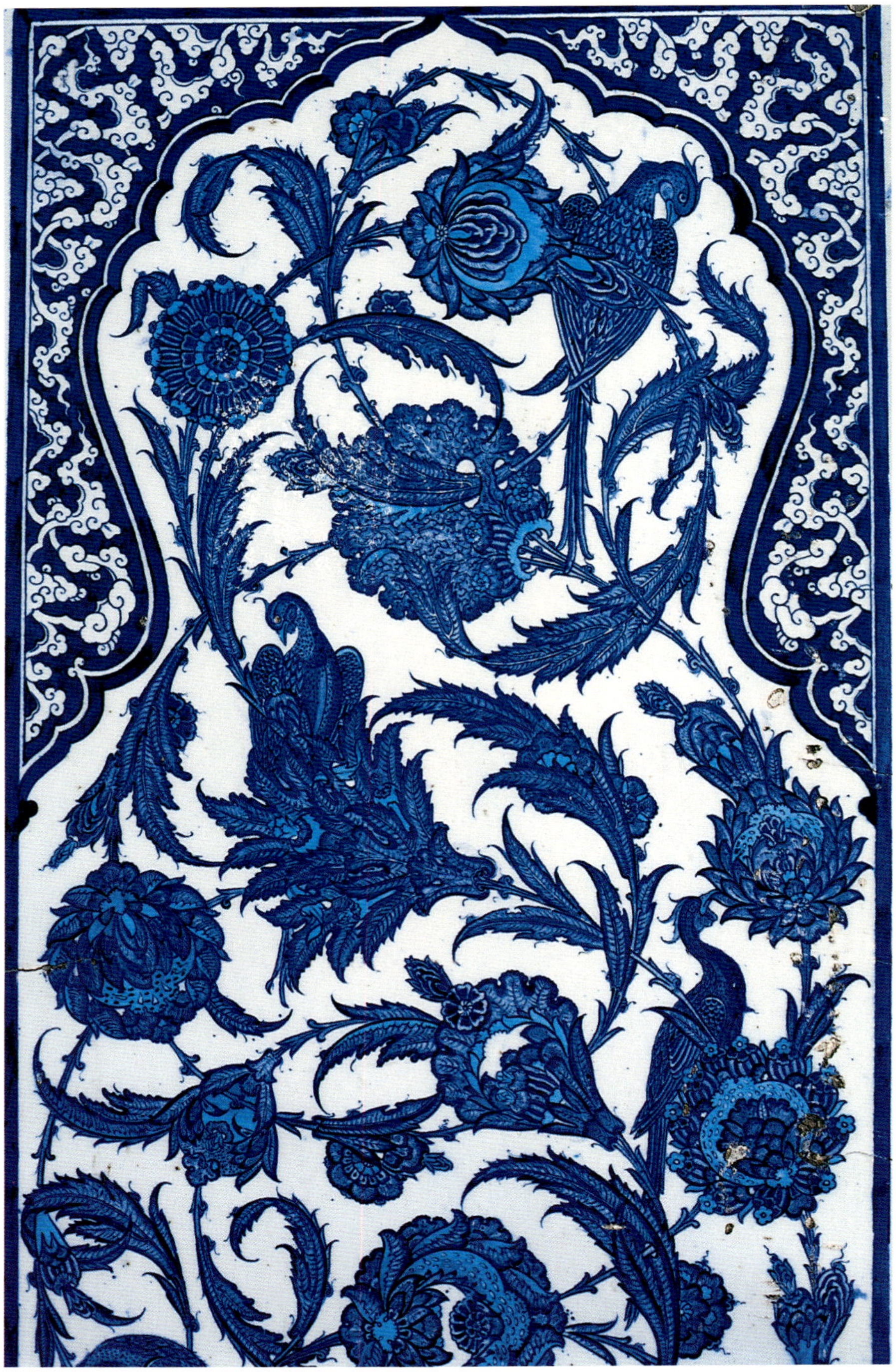

♦ One of four panels framing the door to the Sünnet Odasi (Circumcision Kiosk), c. 1527–28, at the Topkapi Saray, Istanbul (Turkey). A tour de force of draftsmanship, these large panels (125 cm high) are of exceptional quality.

of the *türbe* of Selim I, are undoubtedly the last examples of this type of Constantinople manufacture. It was around this date that tiles from workshops in Iznik seem to have taken over the market, supplanting tiles from the imperial ateliers. The fourteen lunettes above the bays in this *türbe* bear an inscription that records the "Verse of the Throne" from the Qu`ran. Long panels divided into compartments extend up the walls to the drum of the cupola and are decorated in arabesques and geometrical interlace of great beauty.

Similar tiles can be found in "black line" panels scattered over several parts of the Topkapi Palace, where they were relaid. Arranged in groups of four, these tiles, decorated with repetitive designs, combine in all-over compositions with turquoise, green, yellow, mauve, and white star and flower motifs on a cobalt ground. This is the case with the dado flanking the doorway to the `Arz Odasi (Audience Hall, built in 1585 by Davut Aga), as well as the facade of the Sünnet Odasi (Circumcision Kiosk, sixteenth century), and again in niches in the much later Baghdad Kiosk (1639).

Constantinople workshops were most likely responsible for another astonishing creation: a series of blue-and-white painted tiles of varying sizes datable to the years 1527–28 arranged into the large composite panels seen on the facade of the Sünnet Odasi. Four spectacular panels of an unusually large format (125 centimeters high) stand in pairs on either side of the doorway: one (on the right-hand side) frames a generously proportioned composition of flowering branches in Iznik polychrome ceramic (around 1570); the other (on the left) is a panel decorated with the aforementioned "black line" technique. On the four panels painted blue and white, fantastic animals such as the fabulous quadruped with the head of a dragon (often called the *ki`lin*), together with more "realistic" birds, such as pheasants, disport themselves among a graceful, luxuriant sweep of serrated leaves and imaginary flowers, all handled with extraordinary delicacy. Above the panel on the right-hand side, a large rectangle is decorated with tiles showing cloud motifs. The higher parts of the wall are lined with hexagonal tiles set horizontally, painted in cobalt with touches of turquoise in a swirling interlace of flowers and palmettes.[84] The decor is completed with tiles forming cartouches and rosettes inset into the door frame.

The Miracle that is Iznik

In the course of various excavation programs undertaken in the town of Iznik (the old Byzantine Nicea), a number of ceramic objects dating from the Byzantine era have been unearthed showing that, even before its capture by the Ottomans in 1331, the city was already a significant center for pottery manufacture. The earliest Ottoman ceramic product to be made at Iznik, often incorrectly described as coming from Miletus, employed a reddish clay paste. So-called "Miletus ware" seems, however, to have been limited to crockery. For the period between around 1350 and 1450, tilemaking was essentially restricted to monochrome pieces intended to be cut up for mosaics, as well as blue-and-white-painted squares and hexagons sometimes finished with gold leaf. From the second half of the fifteenth century, Iznik potters started adopting stone-paste, devoting particular care to the development of the white silica slip used as a ground for the decoration. In the field of architectural ceramics, the earliest major pieces of the period are the blue-and-white-painted tiles, often rectangular, used as edging. An example of this type of border can be seen in the mausoleum of Şehzade Ahmed (1429) at Bursa.

Around the end of the 1540s, Iznik potters added green to their palette—often with light, sage overtones—together with the mauve, brown, and aubergine hues of manganese. The decorative repertory also diversified, broadening sufficiently to incorporate budding flowers, blooming roses, pomegranates, vases, as well as fish-scale motifs. This period of Iznik manufacture is known as the "Damascus" group. Not only was a proportion of Iznik production traded through the Syrian capital, but craftsmen in Damascus were soon trying to imitate pieces intended for the imperial court. The baths of Yeni Kaplica at Bursa, restored by Rüstem Pasha in 1552–53, are one of the very few monuments that still contain ceramic tilework from this period with its full range of characteristic colors intact. Another panel of tiles from this period features in the mosque of Ibrahim Pasha built in 1550 in Istanbul.

It was not until the mid-sixteenth century, however, following imperial commissions from Suleyman, that the "Iznik miracle" truly got underway. At that time, potters added to the already broad spectrum of colors typical of the "Damascus" group emerald green and, above all, the famous red, produced from a slip rich in hematite (iron oxide) applied in a thick layer to form a relief beneath the lead-based glaze. This enlarging of the chromatic range corresponded to an upswing in creativity in the design of motifs, with swirling leaves and

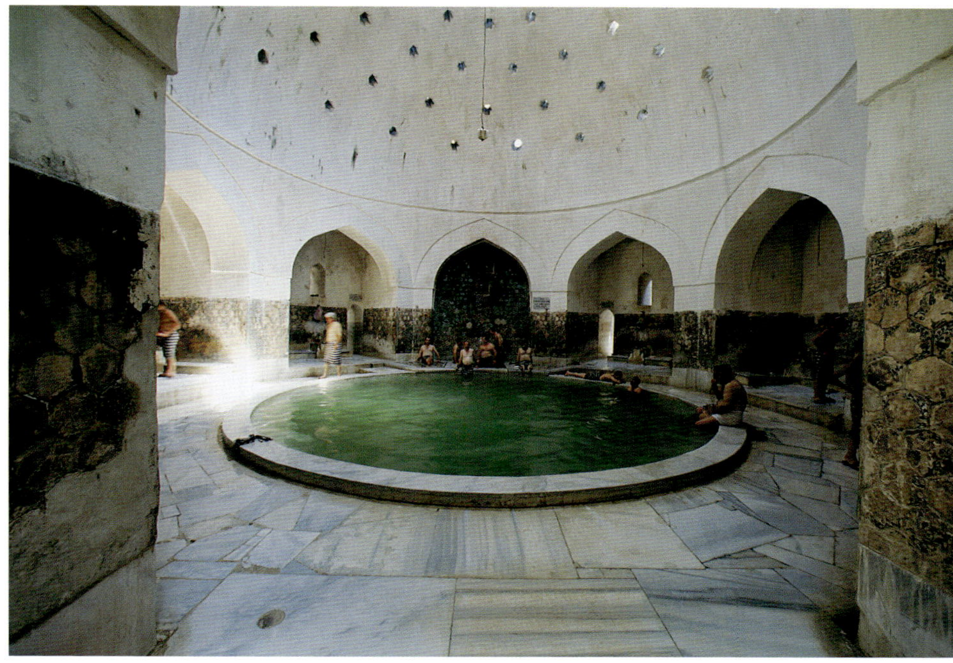

♦ Baths of Yeni Kaplica at Bursa (Turkey). This *hammam* was restored in 1552–53 and is adorned with so-called "Damascus" tiles made in Iznik.

RÜSTEM PASHA MOSQUE, ISTANBUL (TURKEY), 1561

FACING PAGE

♦ Detail of a panel festooned with branches of plum tree blossom.

BOTTOM, FROM LEFT TO RIGHT

♦ Iznik tile decorated with tulips and carnations; the border shows an undulating motif imitating tiger skin, also sometimes known as "Buddha's lips."

♦ Border tile panel with *saz* leaves coiling around long twisting stems, and, on each side, mandorla motifs with *hataī* style clouds surrounded by floral arabesques.

♦ Iznik tile panel. The central field is decorated with branches from a flowering fruit tree.

flowers now alternating with the stiffer stems of tulips and hyacinths. This rich period corresponds approximately to the reign of Suleyman the Magnificent (1520–66), under whose aegis the master architect Sinan was to create some of his finest and most important buildings.

The Süleymaniye, the imperial mosque built by Sinan, is often regarded as his first large-scale masterpiece. The external form Sinan created here corresponds precisely to divisions within the interior space and to the structural function assigned to the buttresses, arches, and vaults. Even the Hagia Sophia, whose plan inspired that of the Süleymaniye, never, in its original state, expressed the full complexity of its internal layout in its external structure. The central cupola rises 53 meters from the ground and possesses a diameter of 26.5 meters. The central space is formed by a cube surmounted by a hemisphere. The latter is borne on supports that lie beyond the median square, thus conveying an extraordinary impression of space. It should be noted, however, that ceramics do not play a very important role in the decoration of the Süleymaniye. There are polychrome calligraphic panels bordered by Iznik tiles showing plant motifs above the low windows of the prayer hall portico. Also, the large stone-built main *mihrab* is encircled by round calligraphic designs (after models supplied by the master calligrapher Ahmet) and plant motifs. Here, the main emphasis is on light and whiteness. The *türbe* of Suleyman (1566–67) next to the mosque, as well as that of his favorite wife Haseki Hürrem (1557–58; better known in the West by the name Roxelana), are adorned with significant quantities of Iznik tiles.

It is undoubtedly in mosques of more modest proportions that the genius of Iznik artists found its best expression. Monuments like the mosque of Rüstem Pasha (1561) and that of Sokollu Mehmet Pasha (1571–72), for instance, both designed by Sinan, together represent the high-water mark in the history of the Iznik workshops. The Rüstem Pasha Mosque belonged to a new and experimental phase in Sinan's career. Here the architect placed the cupola on an octagonal base that in turn stood on a square hall flanked by domed side aisles with three bays. The most original aspect of the design is the transitional zone of the central cupola, which is ringed by four half-cupolas. Quite apart from its highly

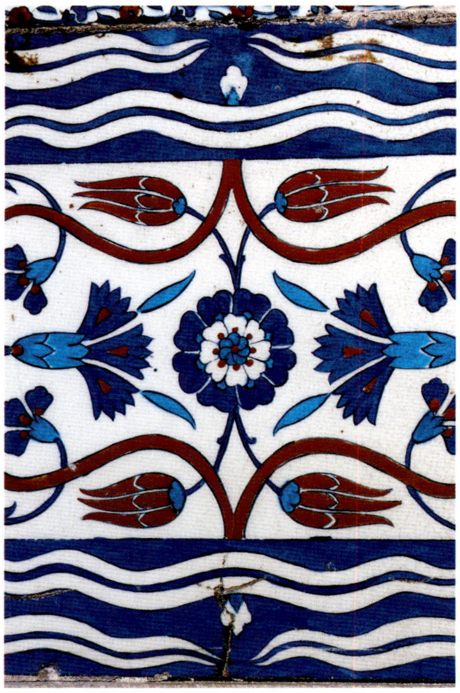

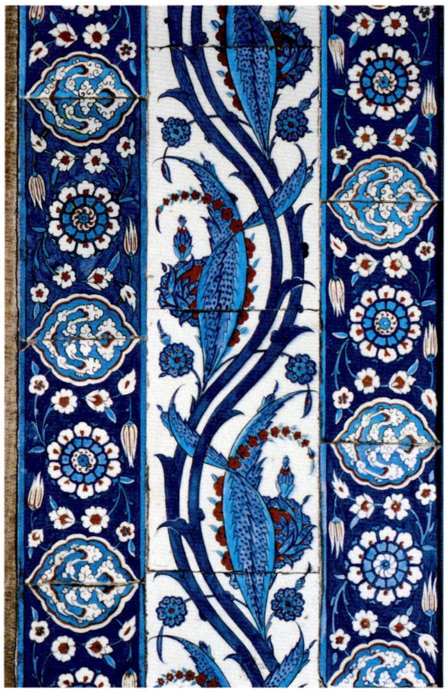

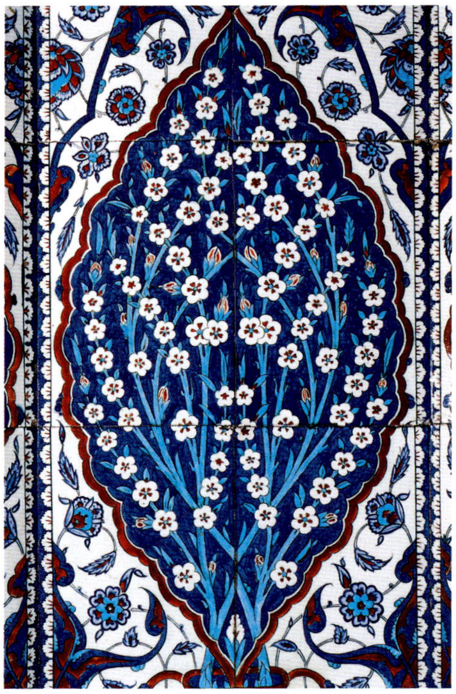

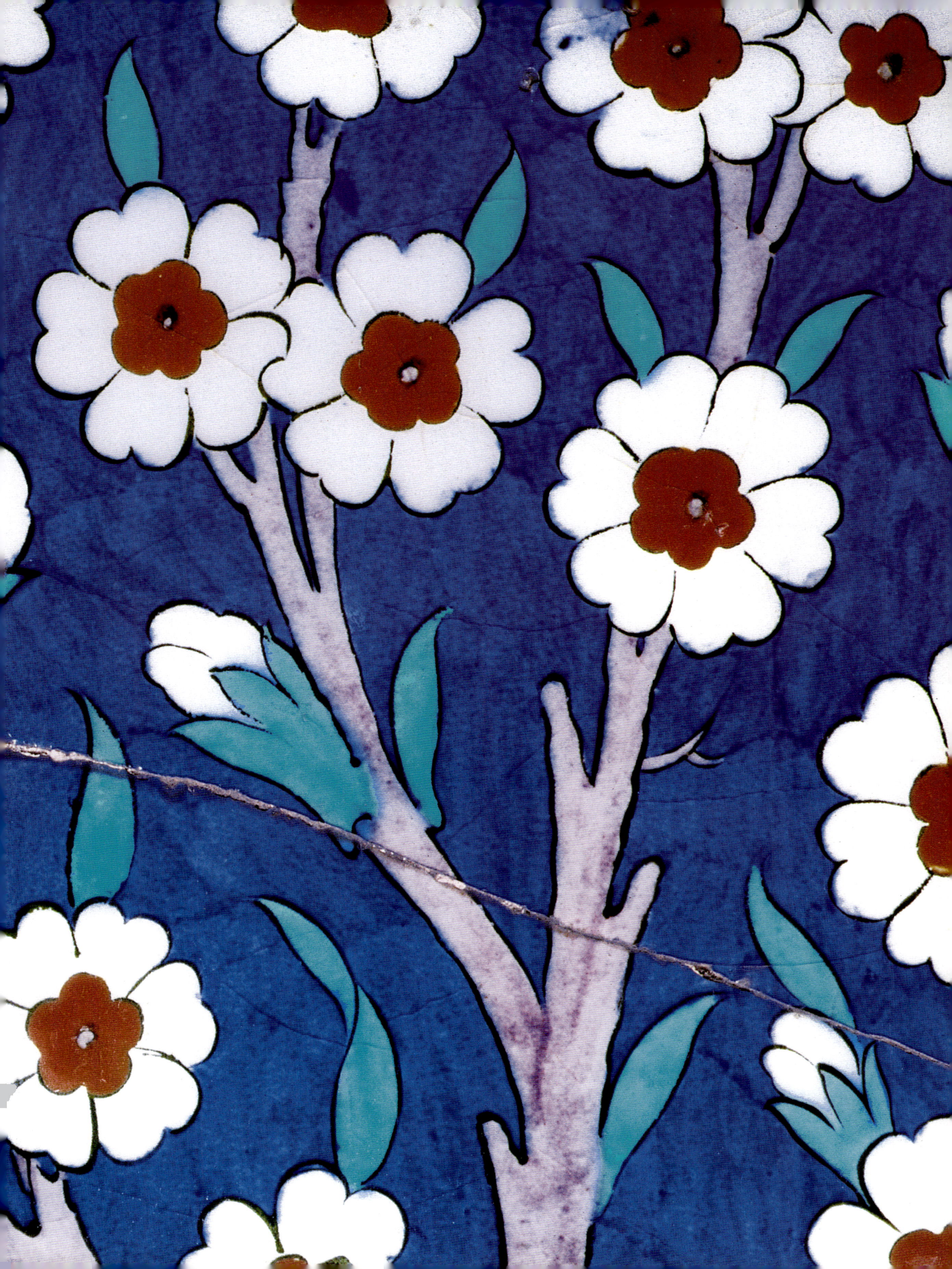

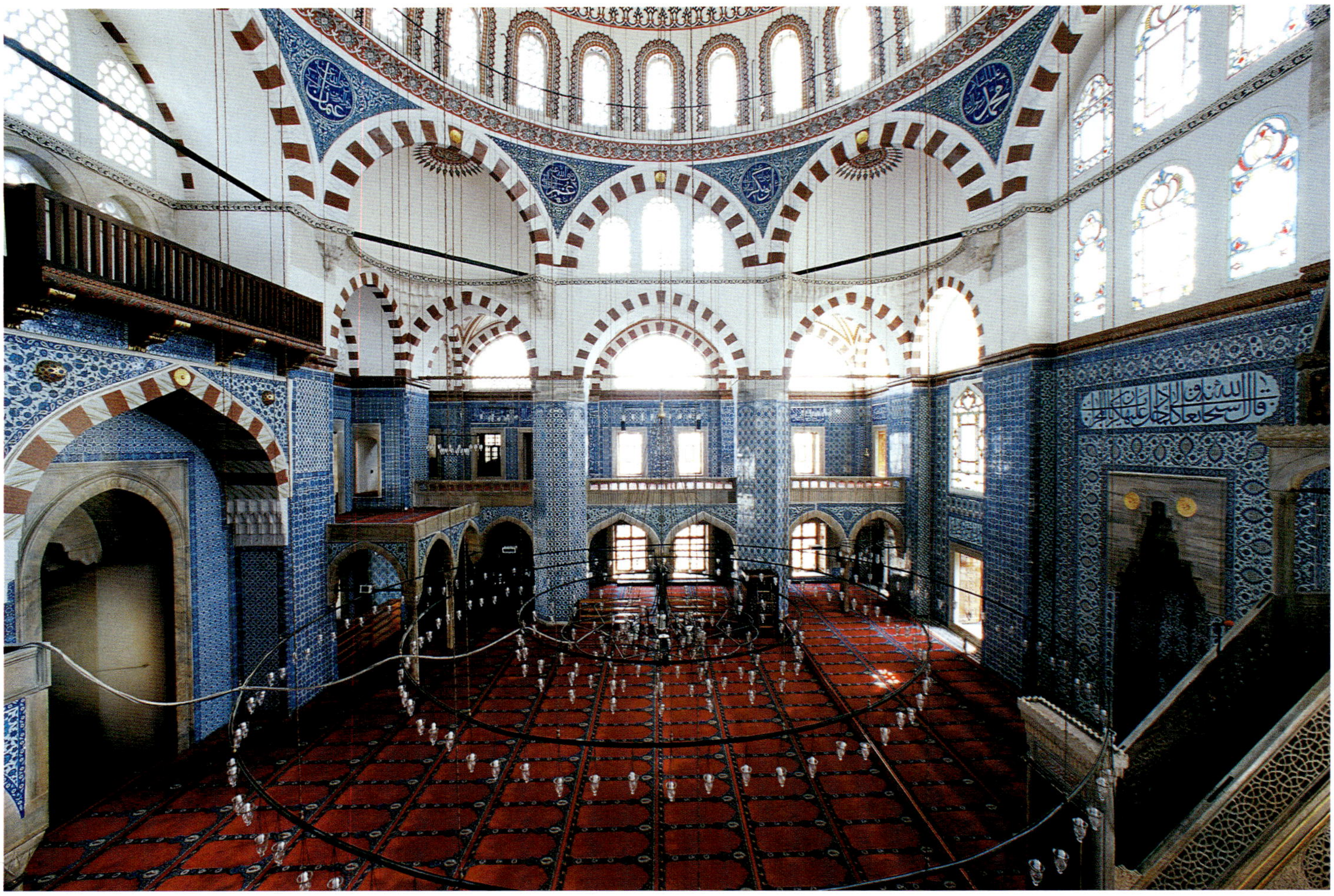

♦ Interior of the Rüstem Pasha Mosque, Istanbul (Turkey), 1561.

effective and ingenious design, the building is also remarkable for the abundance and quality of its Iznik ceramic cladding. The great panels decorating the entrance portico to either side of the prayer hall door have suffered much from neglect and deliberate damage (especially the right-hand panel, which is today made up of tiles from various places). Luckily, the decoration inside the prayer hall is much better preserved. Here the tiles cover the entire surface of the walls from the ground to the third window level in a manner that diverges from Sinan's customary approach. Indeed, such large expanses of polychromy are unusual in Ottoman architecture altogether. Nevertheless, the tiles in the Rüstem Pasha Mosque surely represent one of the finest ensembles of Iznik tiles from the period of its greatest glory. The sheer variety and number of motifs, combined with the supreme quality of the colors (including a silica white-slip ground of extraordinary purity setting off the vibrant colored paints) make this mosque a showcase that is unrivalled anywhere else.

The architectural complex of the Sokollu Mehmet Pasha Mosque in Istanbul (1571–72) is immediately intriguing in the way it responds to the challenge of the steeply sloping site. The mosque is best appreciated by entering the main entrance situated on the lower half of the slope and climbing the steps of a vaulted passage leading to the court. Once more, the architect's talent reveals itself in a harmonious layout of architectonic volumes. The plan is here based on a hexagon that supports a central cupola borne on six piers, with two half-cupolas providing counter-thrust. As a result, the internal space is thus endowed with extraordinary unity. Here, unlike at the Rüstem Pasha Mosque, the polychrome possibilities offered by Iznik tilework are underplayed.

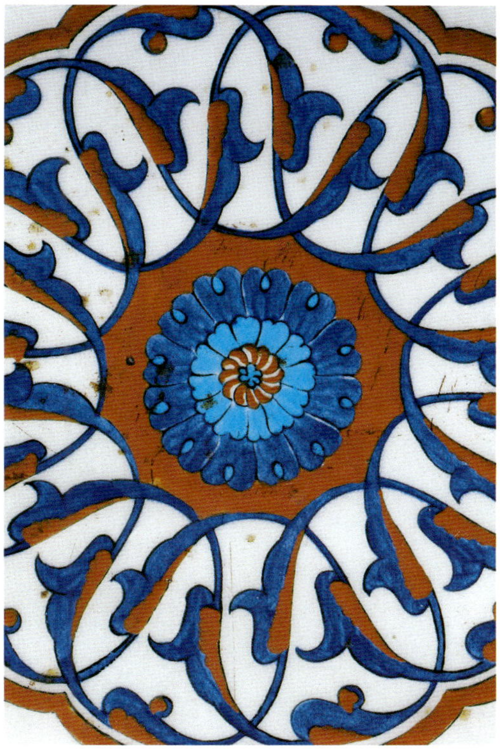

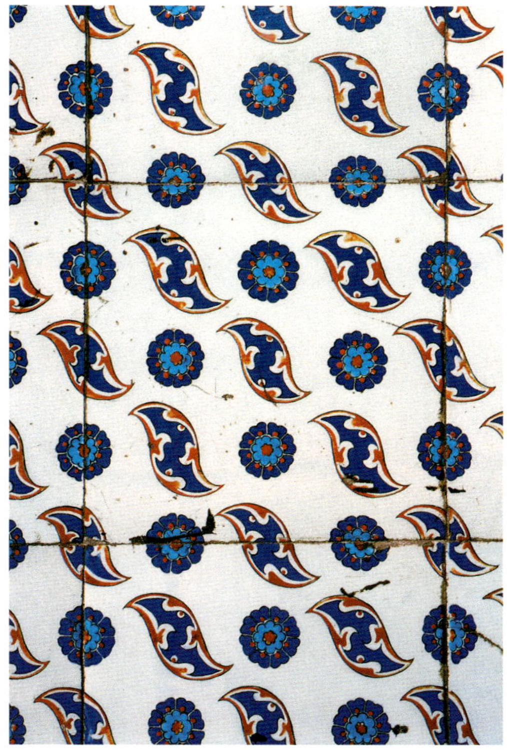

RÜSTEM PASHA MOSQUE, ISTANBUL (TURKEY), 1561

♦ Central motif consisting of a rotating pattern of palmettes ringing a rosette.

♦ The repetition of a simple fleuron unit and a motif formed of two interlocked palmettes over a dazzlingly white ground exerts a hypnotic fascination.

♦ Iznik designers did not limit themselves to naturalistic depictions of flora, as this strange-looking tulip poking its head through a greenish rock demonstrates.

♦ Detail of an Iznik tile with a floral motif. The famous "Iznik red" was used both in a thick coat to provide saturated color and diluted to give graded tones.

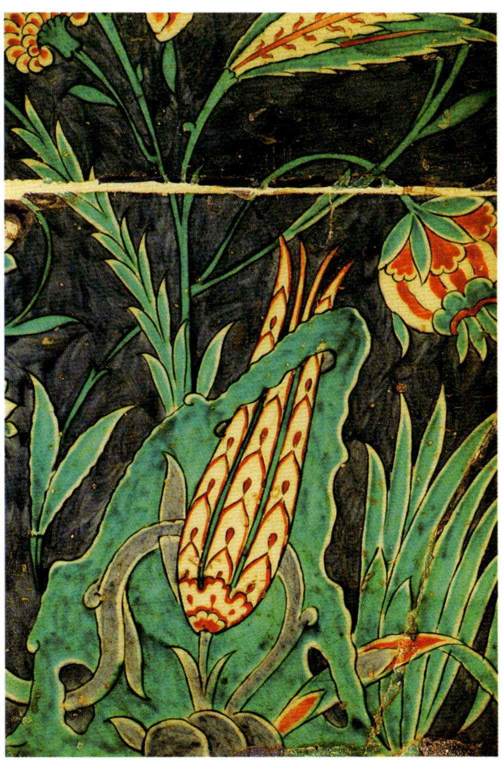

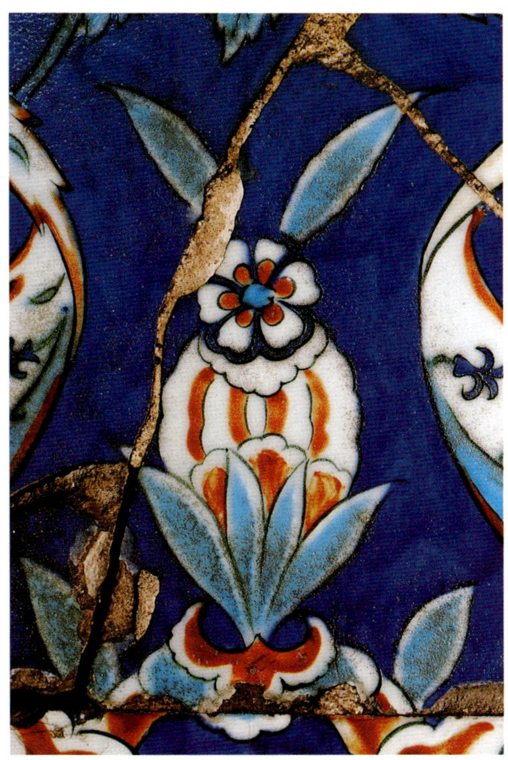

The ceramic decoration is especially remarkable where it frames the gray marble *mihrab*. On both sides of the niche, two large panels show an intricate swirl of flowers and serrated leaves whose bright tones stand out against a pure white ground. Above, a series of calligraphic cartouches include in particular two discs in *jali* script in a style close to those at the Süleymaniye. Finally, the pyramidal dome over the *minbar* is also clad with tiles on which the famous Iznik red blazes with undiminished fire.

Sinan's final masterpiece was the Selimiye Mosque at Edirne (1569–75). With its cupola rising 43 meters above the ground and its exceptionally beautiful tilework, this mosque is an architectural

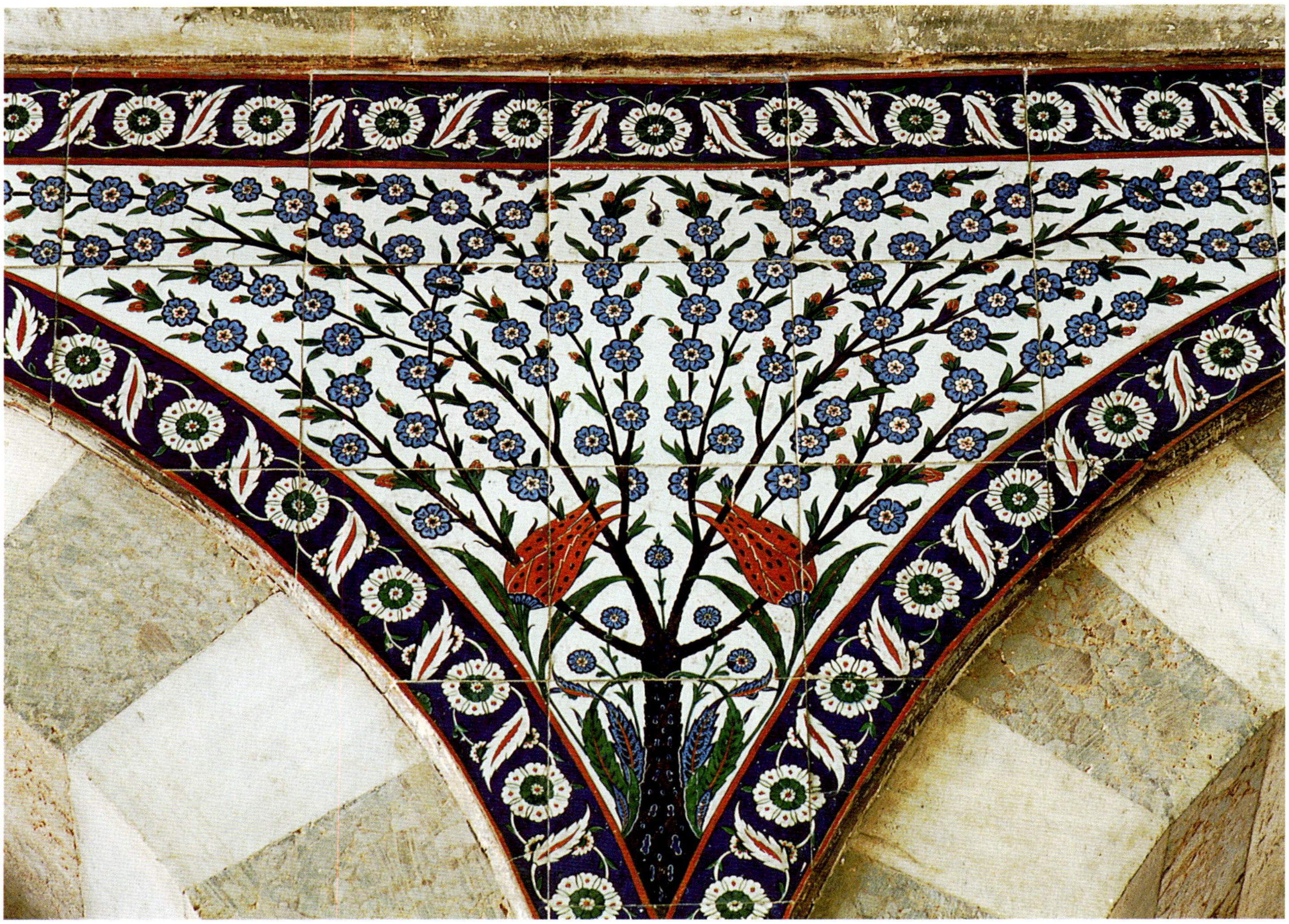

SELIMIYE, EDIRNE (TURKEY), 1569–75

♦ Sinan's masterpiece is dotted with Iznik tile decorations, such as this spandrel billowing out over two arches in the vast expanse of the prayer hall.

♦ One of the charms of Iznik decorative flora is the way identifiable species such as the carnation and the tulip are combined with wholly imaginary rosettes.

FACING PAGE

♦ The imperial loge in the mosque is lined with sumptuous tiles bearing motifs in the form of bouquets that are sometimes, as in this illustration, held in place by little ties in the shape of a cloud.

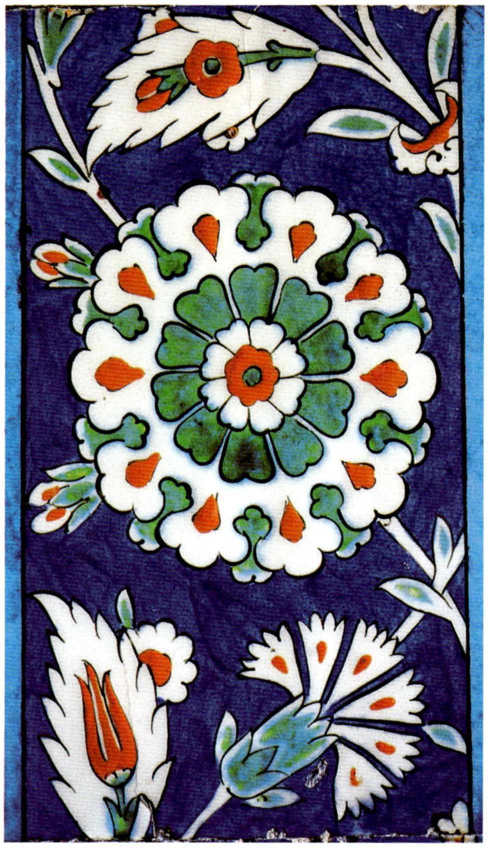

wonder. The central dome dominates the interior of the building, giving an impression of extraordinary spaciousness. The emphasis on natural lighting in the interior, achieved by means of a numerous large windows, allows one to appreciate more readily the luminosity and clarity of the architectural layout. It was undoubtedly inconceivable for Sinan to cover such surfaces with polychromy, whether painted or executed in Iznik tilework. Thus, as in the Sokollu Mosque, the use of ceramics is restricted. The most striking areas of tilework are in the center of the *qibli* wall and around the imperial loge (located on the floor above and to the left of the main *mihrab*). The loge also contains a *mihrab* framed by a marvelous example of tilework that is festooned with brightly colored bunches of flowers. However, the gray marble *mihrab* in the middle is

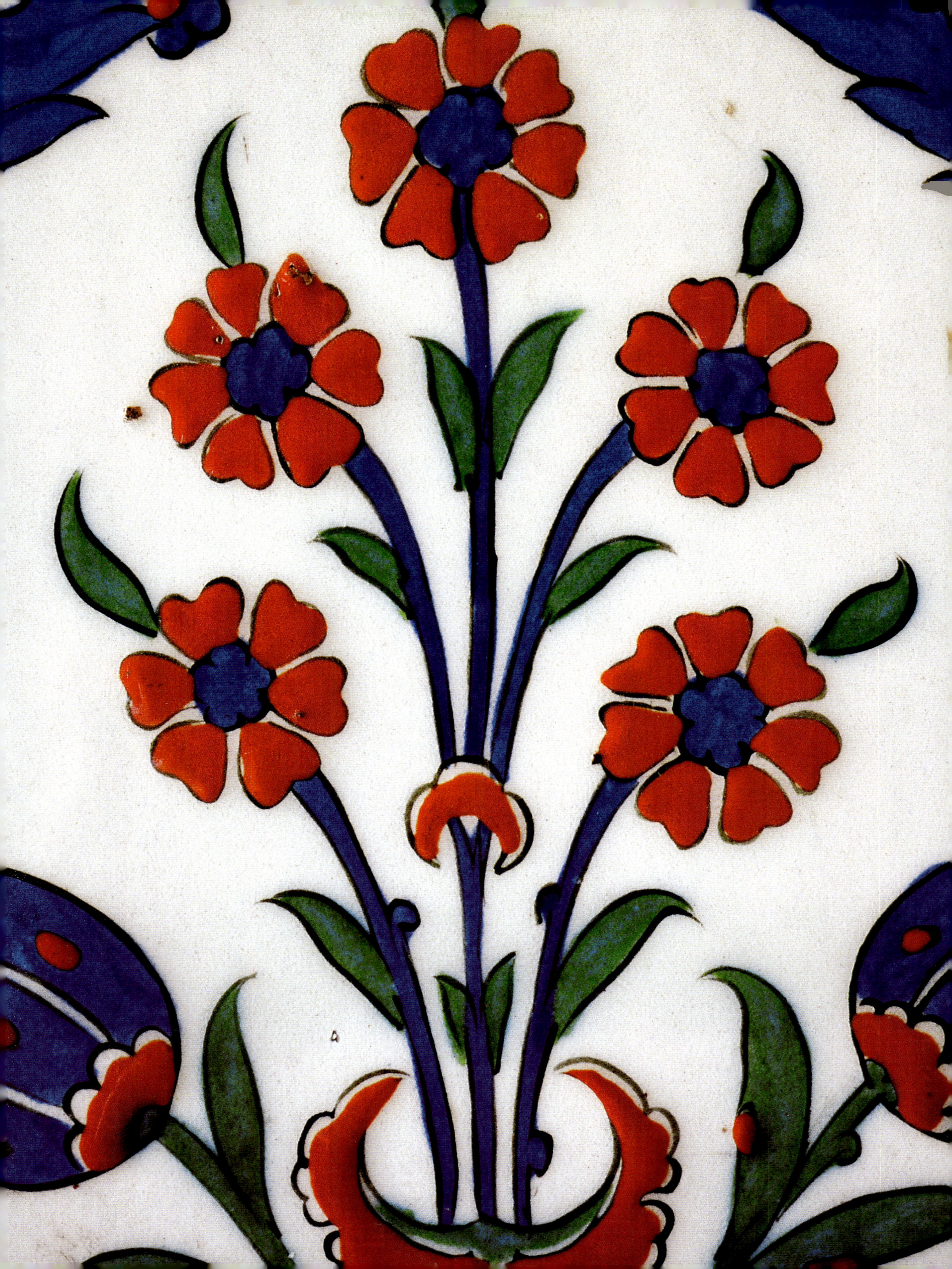

TÜRBE OF SELIM II, ISTANBUL (TURKEY), 1574

♦ Iznik tile panel decorated with floral arabesques surrounding a mandorla ornament containing a plum tree in bloom. The border and corner pieces are adorned with "cloud bands" in the *hata'i* style.

♦ Central motif of the flowering plum tree. In spite of its apparent symmetry, the design displays astonishing compositional subtlety, as well as a perfect mastery of coloring.

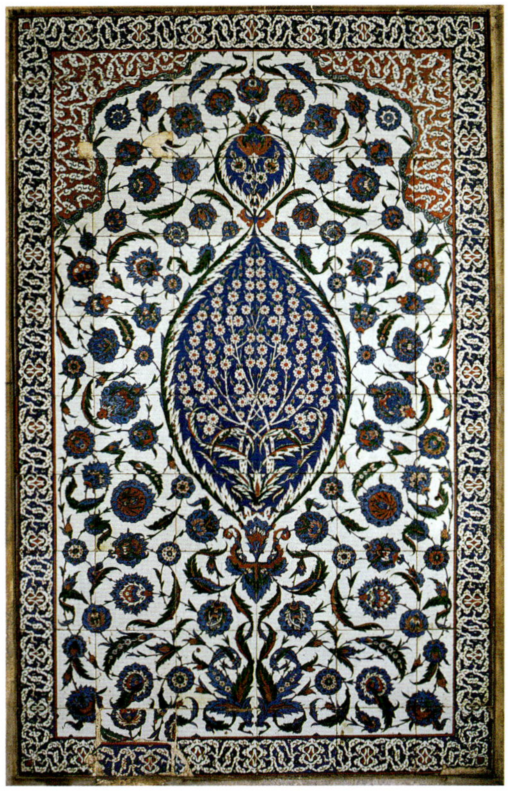

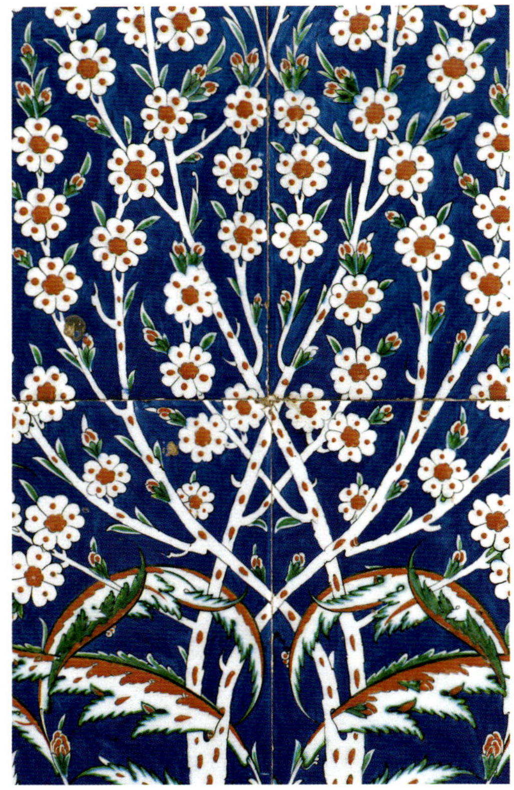

flanked, not by ceramic panels, but by rectangular windows to let in the daylight. A long inscriptional frieze extends right across the rear wall, while lunettes similarly set with calligraphy run above the lower window.

The *türbes* of Selim II (1574) and of Murad III (1595) in the Hagia Sophia complex also present some beautiful Iznik ceramic panels.

We have already mentioned a few of the ceramic decorations in the Topkapi Palace, but this immense site naturally contains a host of other examples. The oldest parts of the ensemble date from the time of Mehmet the Conqueror, while some additions and modifications are due to interventions by Sinan, such as the famous kitchen ranges and the bedchamber of Murad III (1574–95). The latter, rebuilt by

TÜRBE OF MURAD III, ISTANBUL (TURKEY), 1595

♦ Iznik tile panel decorated with *saz* leaves arranged symmetrically.

♦ Detail of a border pattern showing alternately reversed fleurons.

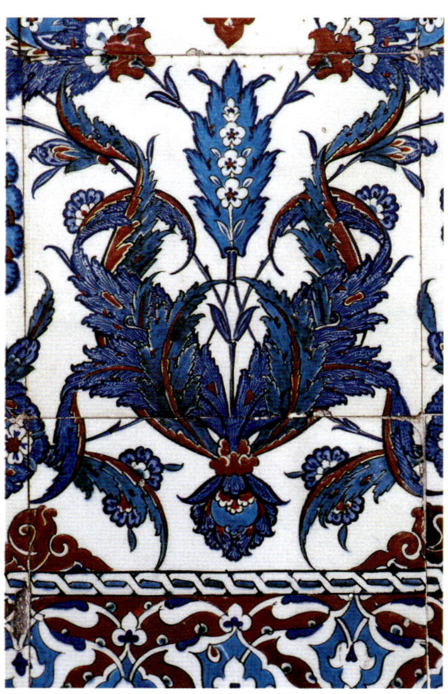

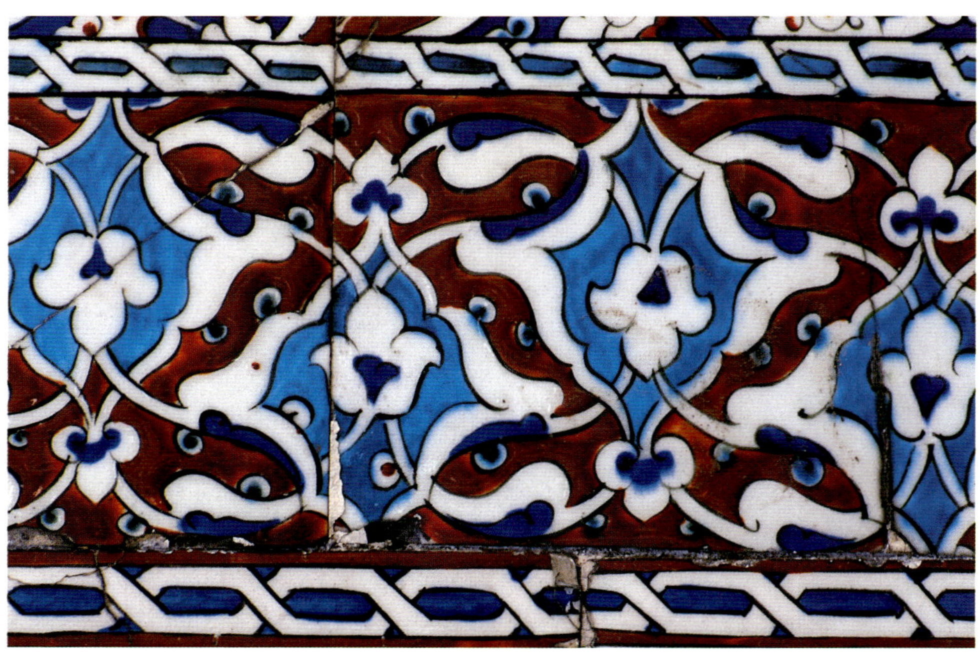

the architect in 1578 after a fire, is a splendid room comprising masonry-framed niches and a large bronze fireplace (*ocak*) bordered by superb Iznik tiles in a floral pattern, as well as a substantial frieze in Thuluth-style calligraphy running round the entire room. The cupola, however, is painted. Other decorations from the finest flowering of Iznik are scattered in various places in the palace, where they can be found next to fading or dulled compositions dating from later periods. A case in point is a big panel decorated with a splendid flowering fruit tree flanked by bunches of tulips, the whole on a blue cobalt ground and in an arched frame of a predominantly turquoise and red hue. This panel was initially intended to decorate a royal *hammam*, as an inscription in Persian (dated, unusually, to A.H. 982/A.D. 1574–75) above it attests.

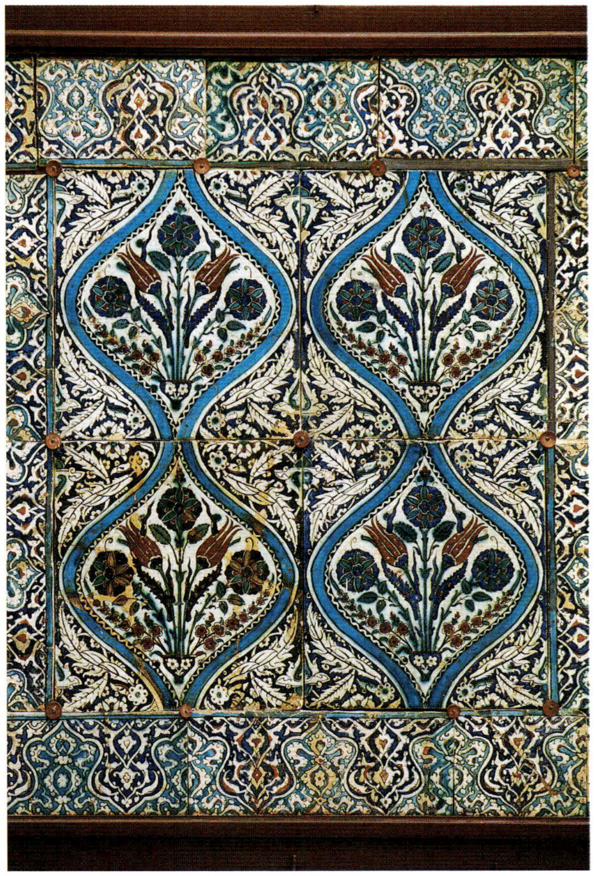

♦ Panel of late-sixteenth-century Iznik tilework in the Museum of Islamic Art, Cairo.

♦ Bedchamber of Murad III, Topkapi Saray, Istanbul (Turkey).
The walls and the insides of the niches are lined with Iznik tiles; the decoration on the fountain's marblework is painted.

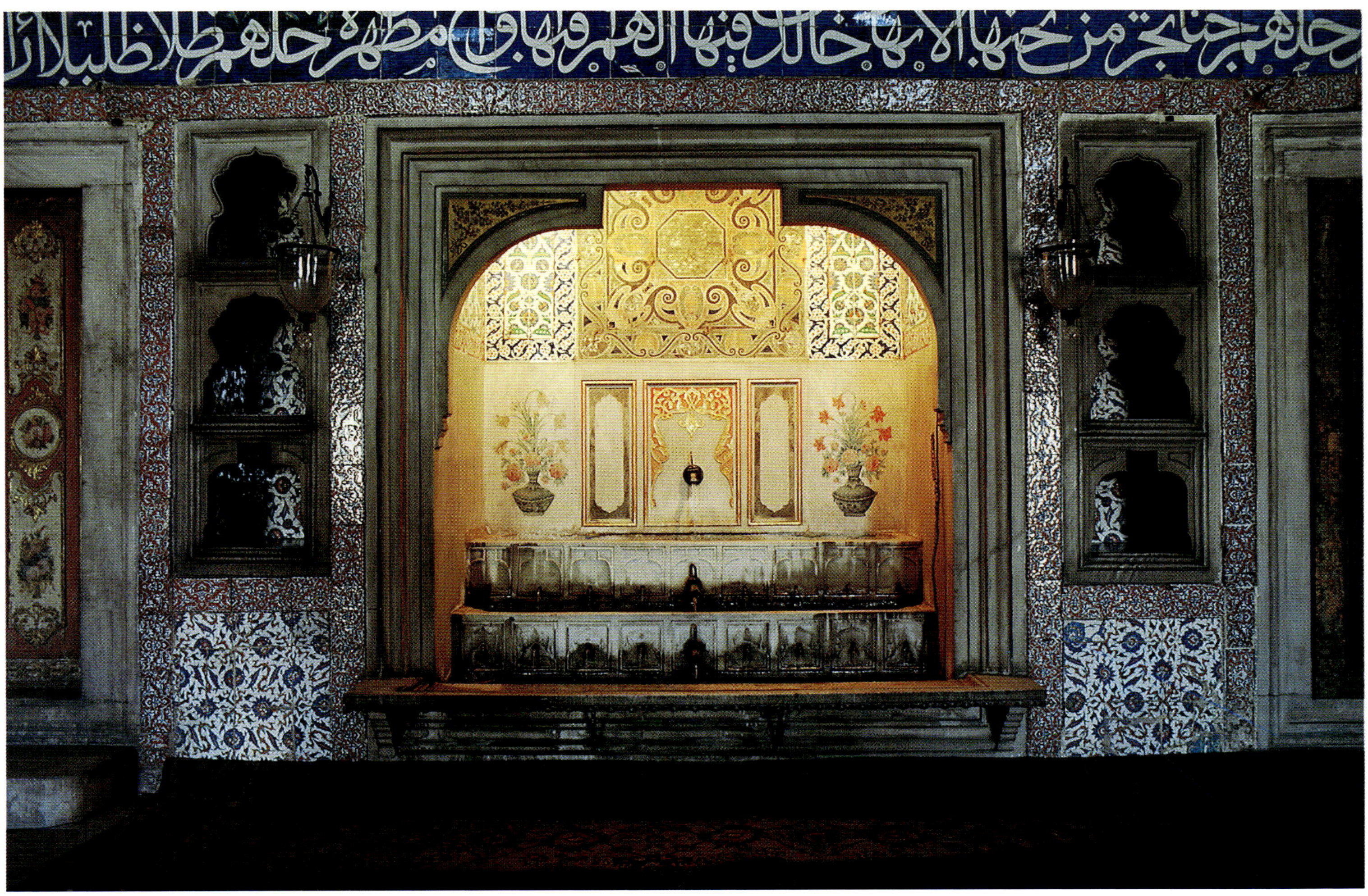

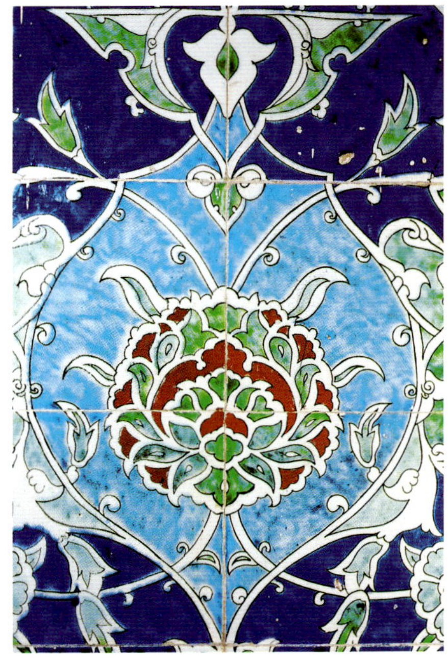

♦ Underglaze-painted tiles. Süleymaniye Mosque, Damascus (Syria), 1554. Although the draftsmanship and handiwork are reminiscent of Iznik work, the style and quality of these ceramics are readily identifiable as Damascus.

Damascus, Syria, and Palestine in Ottoman Times

The restoration of the Dome of the Rock in Jerusalem occupies a somewhat peculiar place among the many civil engineering projects undertaken by Suleyman the Magnificent. It is known that the sultan asked the master potter `Abdallah of Tabriz to oversee restoration work on the venerable monument, cladding the upper parts of the facade in ceramic tiling; some of the tiles used are dated between 1545 and 1552.[85] In addition to the grilles of the window bays on the first tier, the ceramic decorations comprise palmette patterns arranged in radial compositions, friezes of merlon motifs charged with flowers, as well as a substantial Thuluth calligraphy frieze at the top of the wall. Curiously, certain types of tile encountered at the Dome of the Rock are also found in residences in Aleppo, Syria, such as the Bayt Jumblat, the inference being that the potters who had worked in Jerusalem then moved on to Syria.

In 1554, around the same time as the Dome of the Rock was being restored, Suleyman ordered the construction of a mosque and a *madrasa* in Damascus, the Süleymaniye. It was as a consequence of this project that tile production began in the city. These so-called "Damascus" tiles

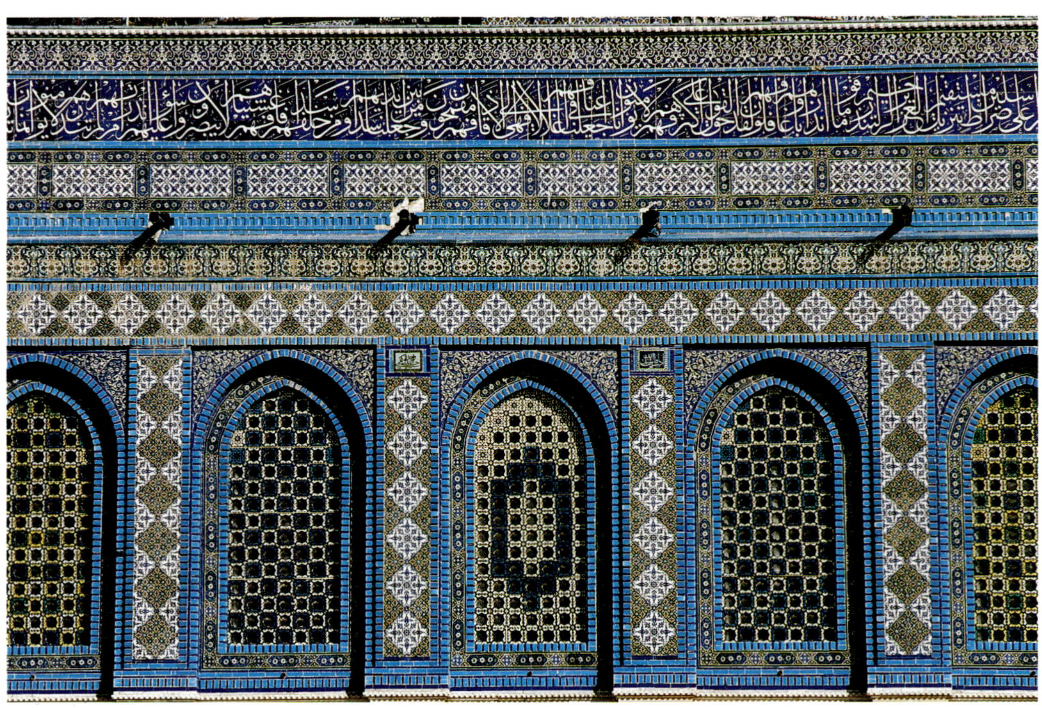

♦ Dome of the Rock, Jerusalem (Israel). Constructed in 691 under the Umayyad caliph `Abd al-Malik, this first masterpiece in the history of Islamic architecture was brilliantly restored between 1545 and 1552, in the reign of Suleyman the Magnificent. It was during this restoration that the ceramics cladding the upper part of the facade were added.

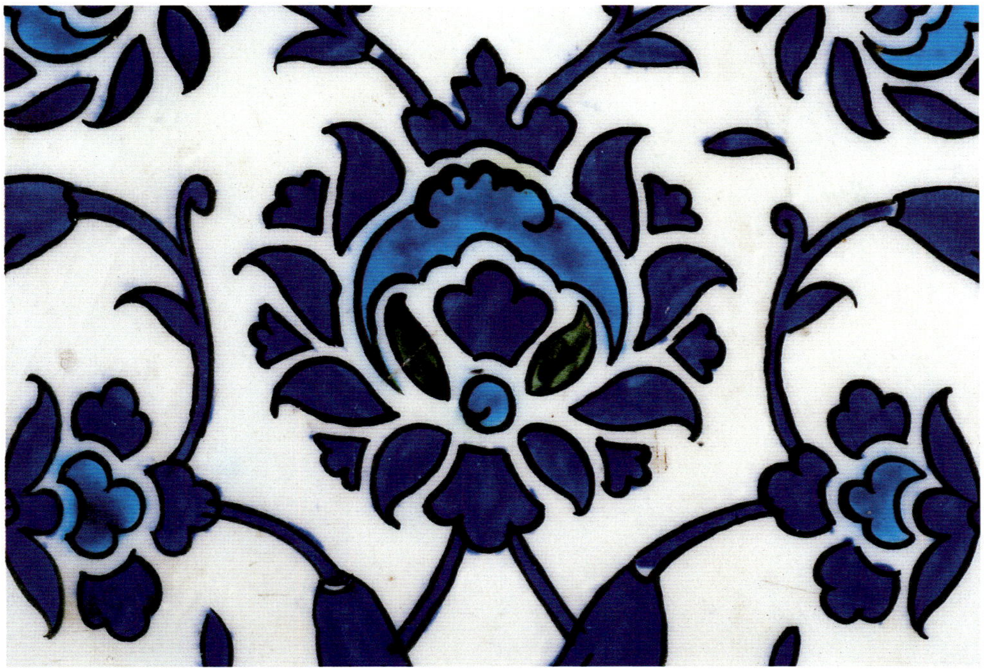

LEFT

♦ Mausoleum of Saladin, Damascus (Syria). Floral pattern tile underglaze-painted on a white siliceous slip ground.

BELOW LEFT

♦ Lunette inlaid with Damascus tiles. Takiyya in the Süleymaniye complex, Damascus (Syria). The building itself is made of masonry (the black and white voussoirs of the arch can clearly be seen at the top).

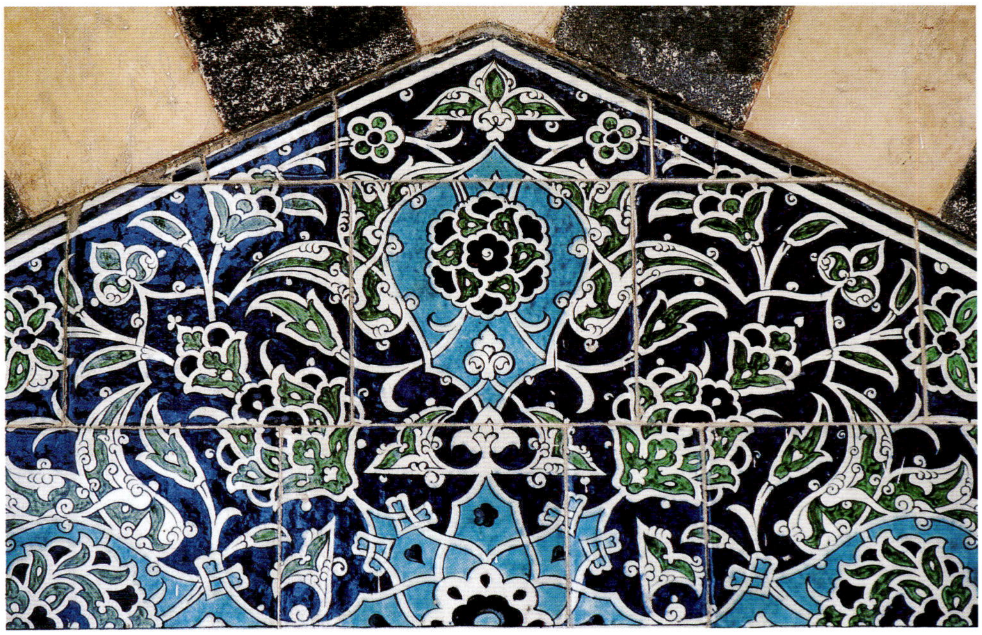

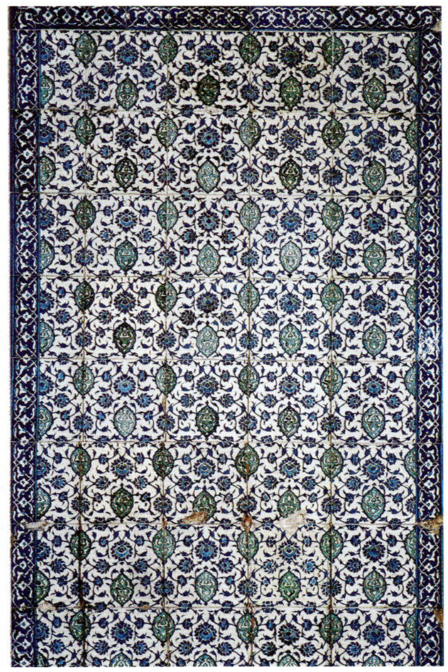

often draw on decorative motifs from the Iznik repertory. However, they are executed with a certain freshness, sometimes verging on the naïve, that stems from the fact that production at Damascus was probably less strictly supervised than the tilework carried out for the prestigious Ottoman court. It is not even unusual to see live animals among all the floral designs, in particular birds such as parrots or peacocks, something rarely found in the imperial commissions fulfilled by the Iznik workshops.

In addition to the decorations of the Süleymaniye of Damascus, those in the Darwishiyya Mosque (1571) in the same city also deserve a mention. The panel of

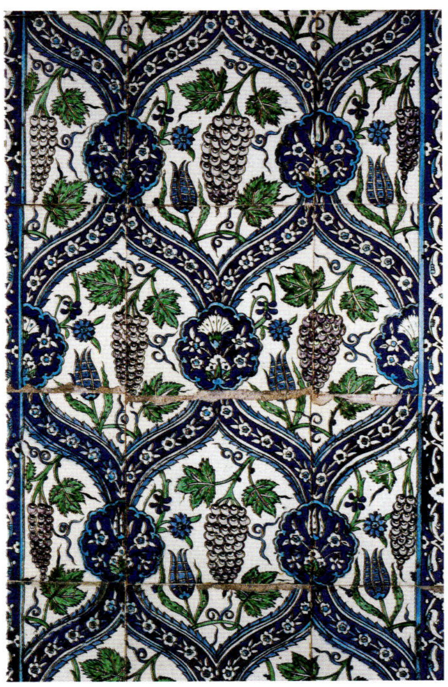

ABOVE

♦ Panel of Damascus tiles featuring a pattern of mandorlas and floral trails. Süleymaniye Mosque, Damascus (Syria).

LEFT

♦ A panel decorated with vine tendrils and tulips in a lattice of rosettes containing bunches of flowers. Darwishiyya Mosque, Damascus (Syria), 1571.

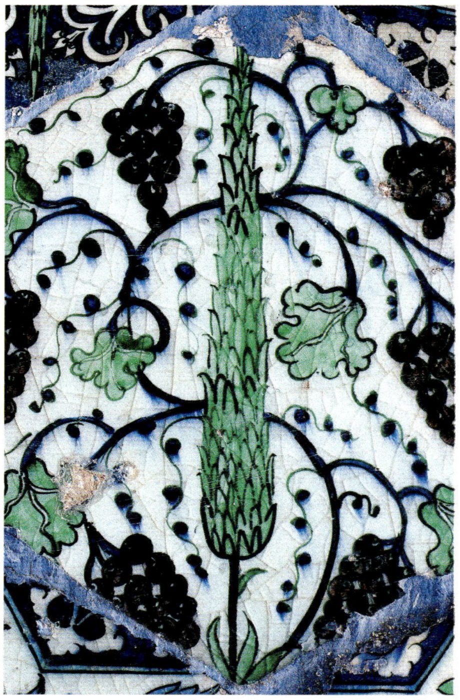

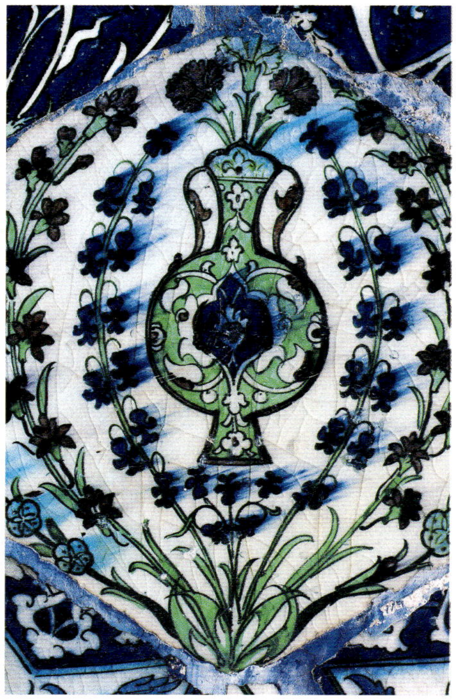

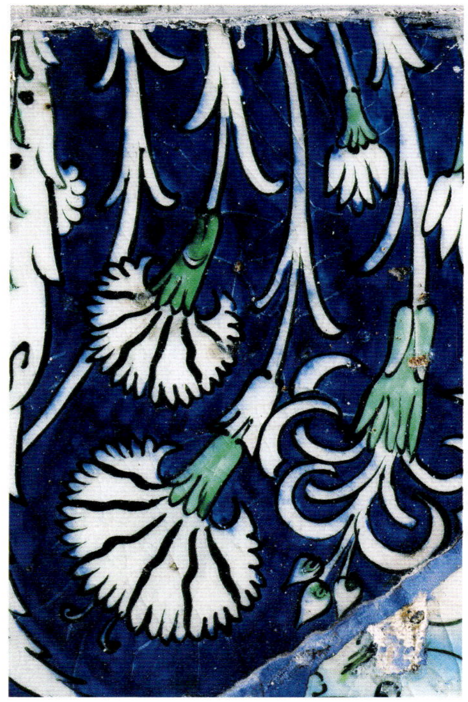

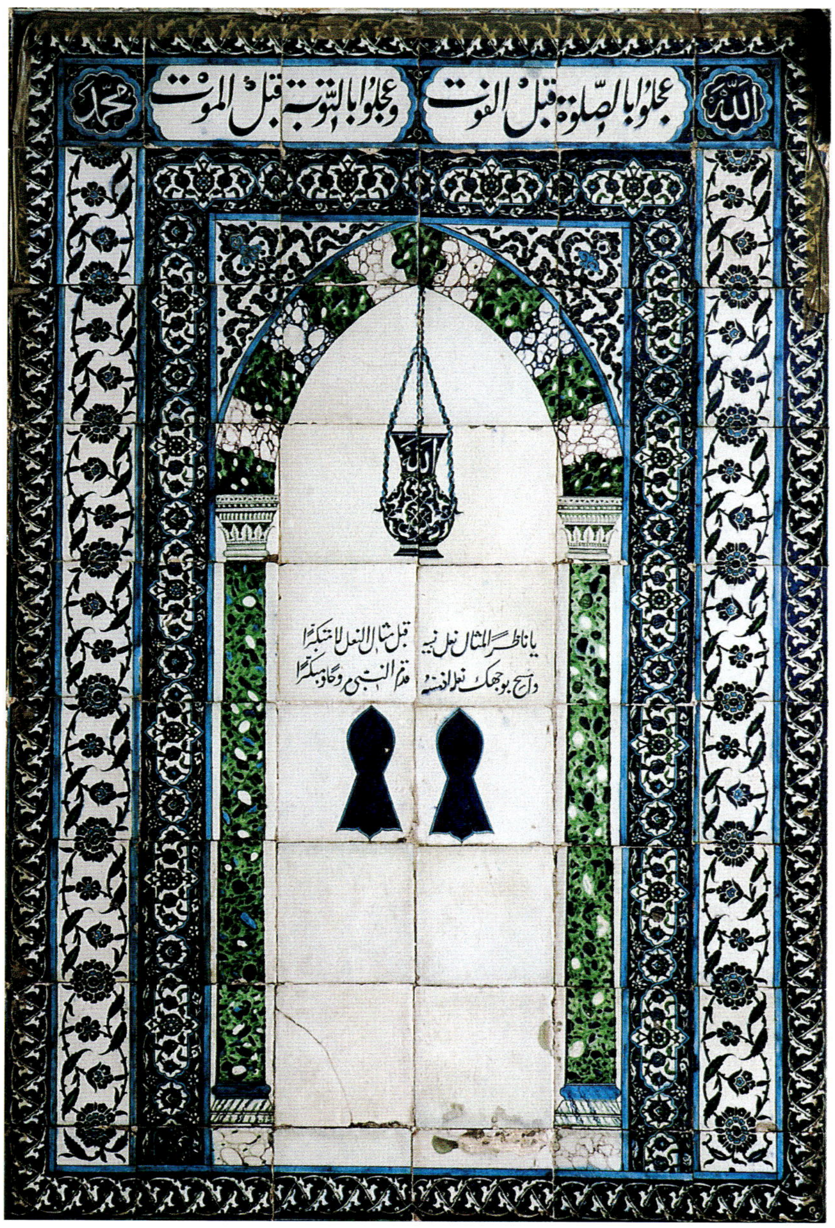

DARWISHIYYA MOSQUE, DAMASCUS (SYRIA), 1571

♦ Underglaze-painted tile displaying a cypress surrounded by vine branches. The sage green and manganese colors are characteristic of Damascus ceramics.

♦ Hexagonal tile showing a vase ringed by flowers.

♦ Detail of an underglaze-painted tile decorated with carnations.

LEFT

♦ Panel of Damascus tilework representing a *mihrab* with the lamp (a reminder of the *sura al-Nur*, "The Light") and the imprint left by the Prophet's sandals.

FACING PAGE

♦ Arrangement of hexagonal tiles. In the middle is a cypress on which a bird perches. A clumsy hand—or that of an iconoclast—has seen fit to obliterate the animal's head.

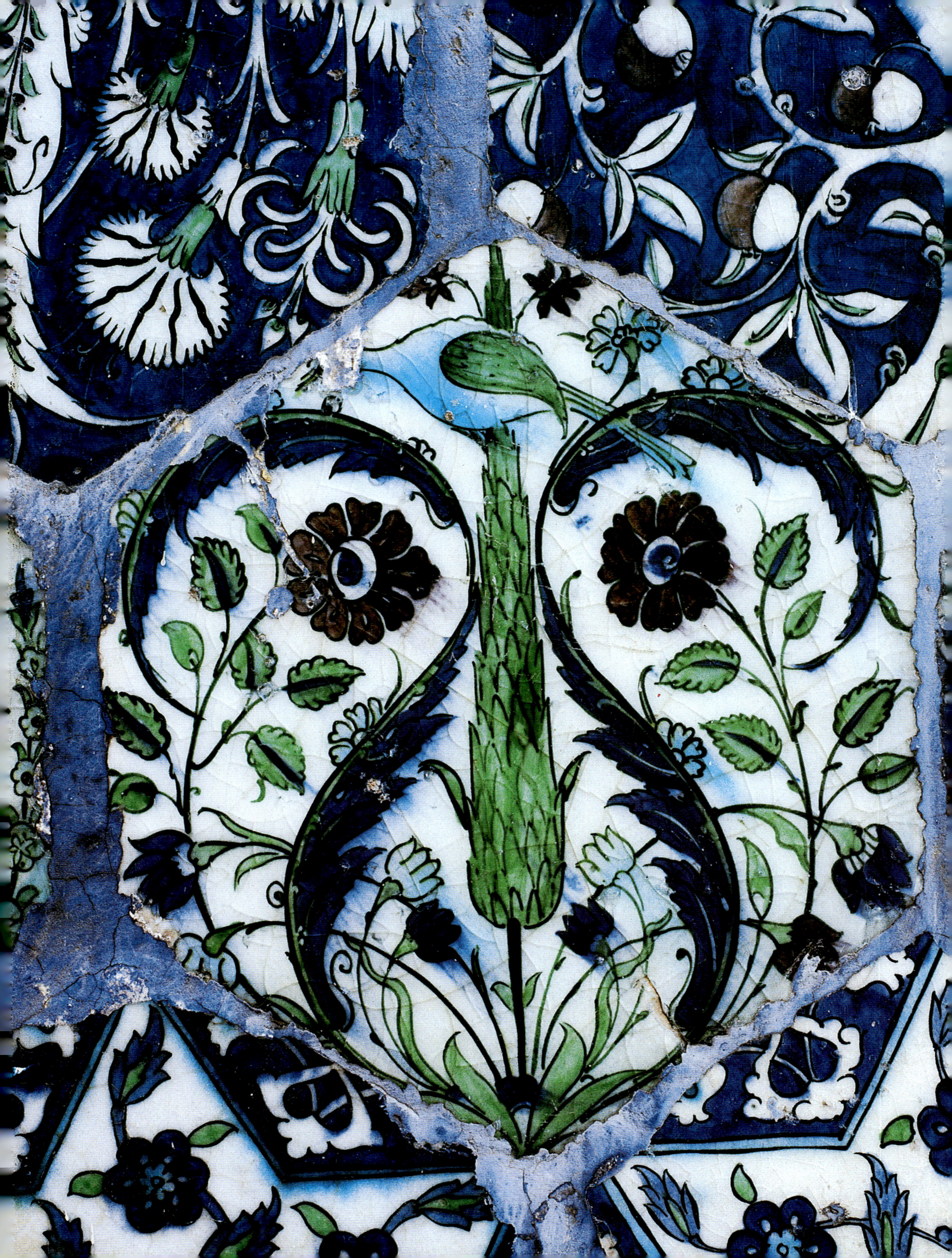

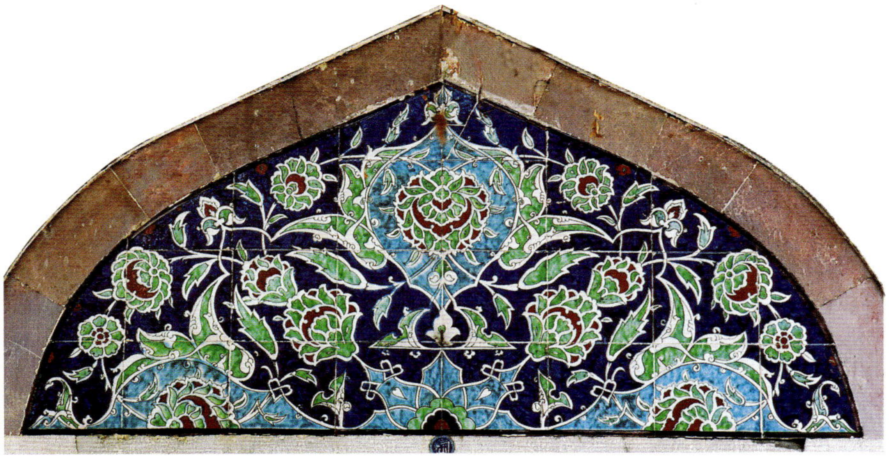

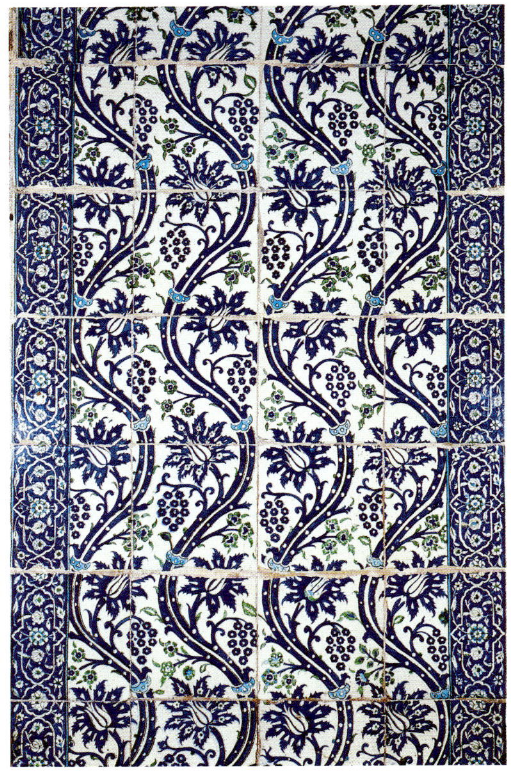

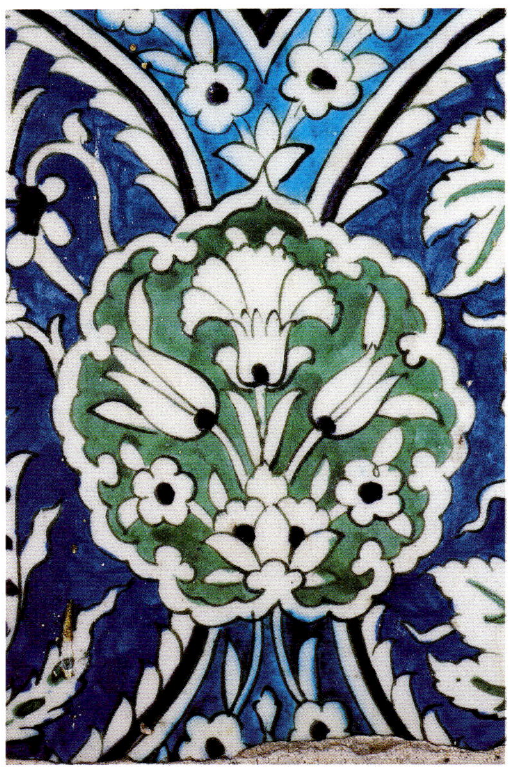

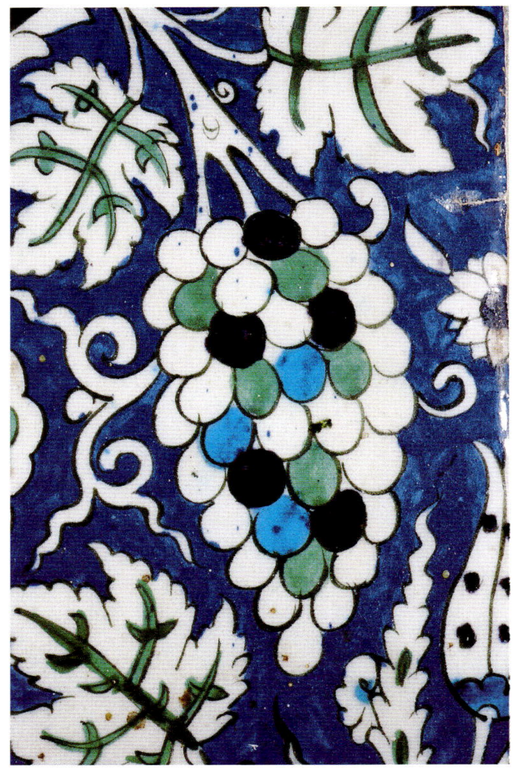

DARWISHIYYA MOSQUE,
DAMASCUS (SYRIA), 1571

♦ Lunette clad with Damascus tiles forming a design of arabesques and flowers.

♦ A panel in the prayer hall and flowers.

SINAN PASHA MOSQUE,
DAMASCUS (SYRIA), 1586

♦ Detail of an underglaze-painted tile showing a bouquet of flowers in a roundel.

♦ Underglaze-painted tile ornamented with a grape, vine, and tulip design.

the *mihrab* in this mosque is decorated with the motif of a conch hung with a mosque lamp standing within a multiple framework made up of turquoise and cobalt floral patterns on a white ground. The niche is represented by a blind arcade supported by columns in imitation green porphyry and two-color white and green barred voussoirs. In addition to the lamp, the imprints of the Prophet's sandals (*na'l*) are also portrayed. The dados are lined with hexagonal tiles often with vegetal designs (cypress, vine branches, bunches of grapes) sometimes populated by birds, amounting to a more brightly "colorful" version of the pieces produced at Damascus during the previous century. Of slightly later date, the Sinan Pasha Mosque (1586) in Damascus displays an imaginative approach to the treatment of traditional motifs such as bunches of grapes and tulip branches.

The range of colors in Damascus work includes cobalt, turquoise, a soft-hued green, and the aubergine tint of manganese; it is this characteristic spectrum, also used in Iznik in the 1540s, that gave rise to the sometimes erroneous term "Damascus" that is applied to these ceramics. Syria, and in particular the workshops of Damascus, made tiles almost continuously from the sixteenth to the nineteenth centuries, although the finest creations date from the first century of production. In following centuries, manufacture became increasingly standardized and lifeless.

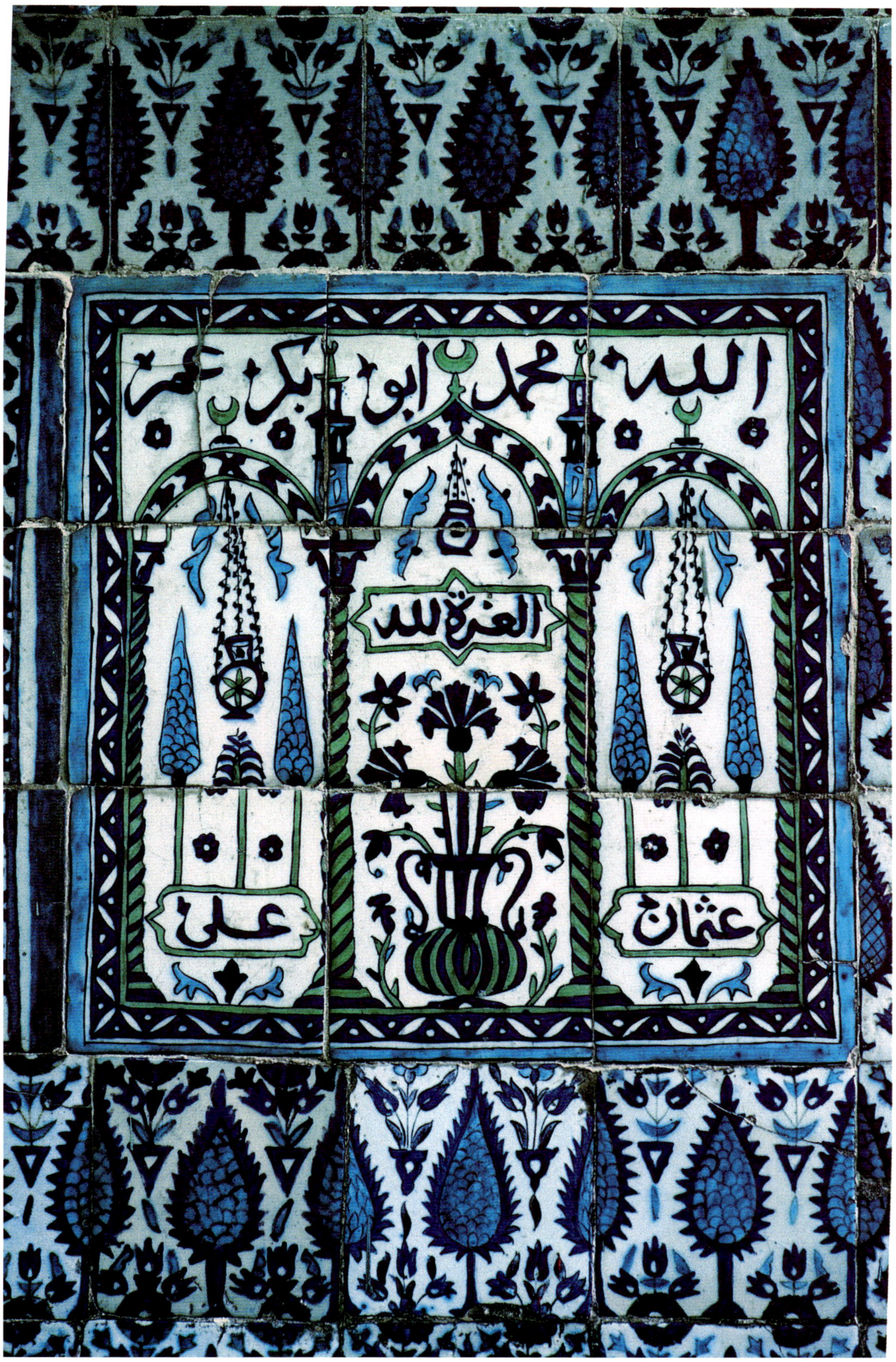

♦ Panel showing a simplified view of the mosque at Medina. The calligraphy records the names of Allah, Muhammad, and the first four caliphs. Mausoleum of Muhiy al-Din ibn ʿArabi, Damascus (Syria).

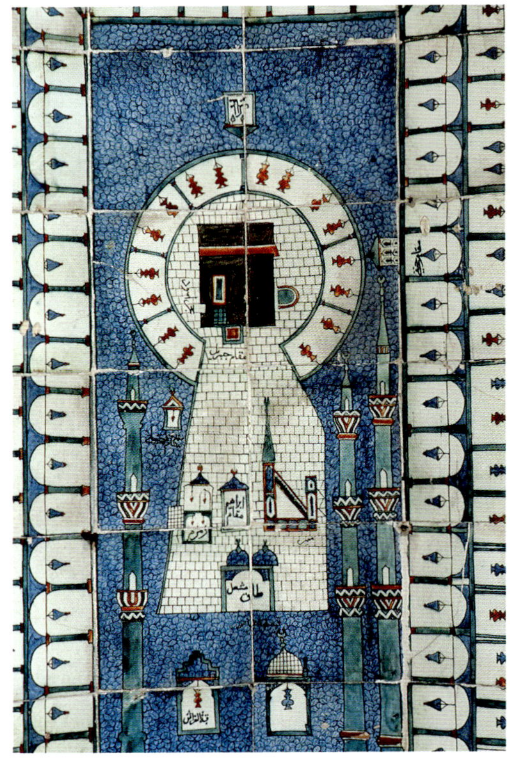

TOPKAPI SARAY, ISTANBUL (TURKEY)

RIGHT

♦ Panel of Iznik tiles portraying Mecca and the Ka'ba, the quarters of the eunuchs.

FACING PAGE

♦ Panel of Iznik tiles representing the holy places on the pilgrimage and the encampment of the Hajj.

BELOW

♦ Hall in the harem with its bronze fireplace (*ocak*). The walls are completely clad in Iznik tiles.

Ottoman Ceramics of the Seventeenth and Eighteenth Centuries

From the 1600s on, Iznik ceramics deteriorated rapidly: the white ground of the silica slip became grubby-looking, the oxides tended to fuse under the glaze, and the famous red tarnished, resulting in a less vivid tone. Architecturally, however, the seventeenth-century Ottoman empire did bequeath some stupendous and delicately decorated masterpieces.

The Sultan Ahmet I Mosque, better known as the Blue Mosque, was started in 1609 on the orders of the sultan himself and under the supervision of the architect Mehmet Aga, undoubtedly a pupil of the great Sinan. The plan reworks that of one of Sinan's earliest designs, the Şehzade Mosque (1543), from which it borrows the pyramidal structure centered on a large dome flanked by four half-domes with harmonious volumes. The mosque's unmistakable silhouette is of course characterized by its six minarets. The interior of the prayer hall is borne on four sturdy fluted cylindrical pillars; the impression of space is enhanced by the very large number of apertures, which were originally adorned with Venetian glass especially ordered by the sultan. The name "Blue Mosque" stems partly from the stencil paintings (in all probability of a later date) covering the upper sections of the walls and vaults. Among the countless ceramic panels decorating the mosque, some date back to the heyday of Iznik, that is to say before 1600, and seem to have been relaid. The majority of the tiles, however, were very probably special ordered and thus reflect the onset of the decline in Iznik manufacture. Among panels from this period (similar examples are also to be found in the Topkapi Palace), compositions presenting cypresses bordered by fantastical vine fronds are entirely typical.

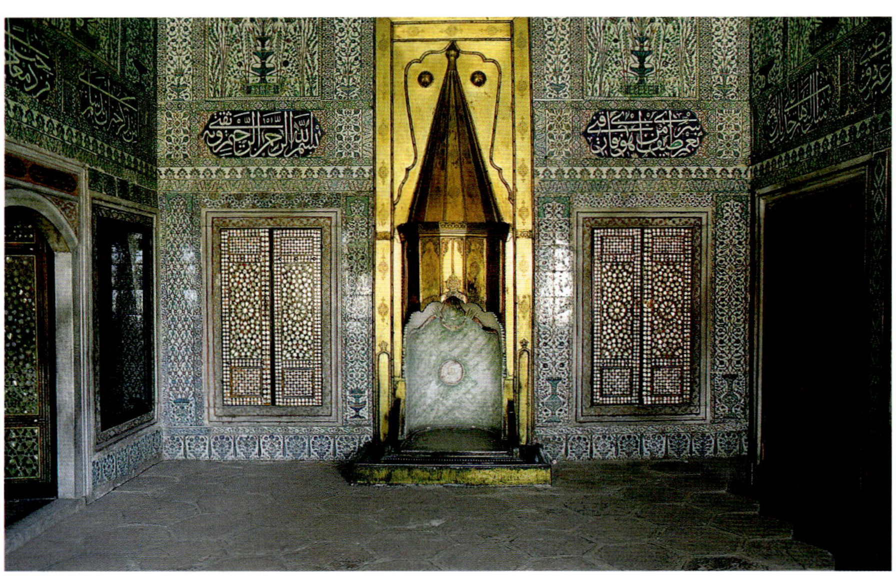

The reign of Murad IV (1623–40) was marked by the construction of several residences—notably in the Topkapi Palace complex—often considered the consummate expression of Ottoman palace art.

The Baghdad Kiosk, located at the northeastern end of the fourth court, is a small

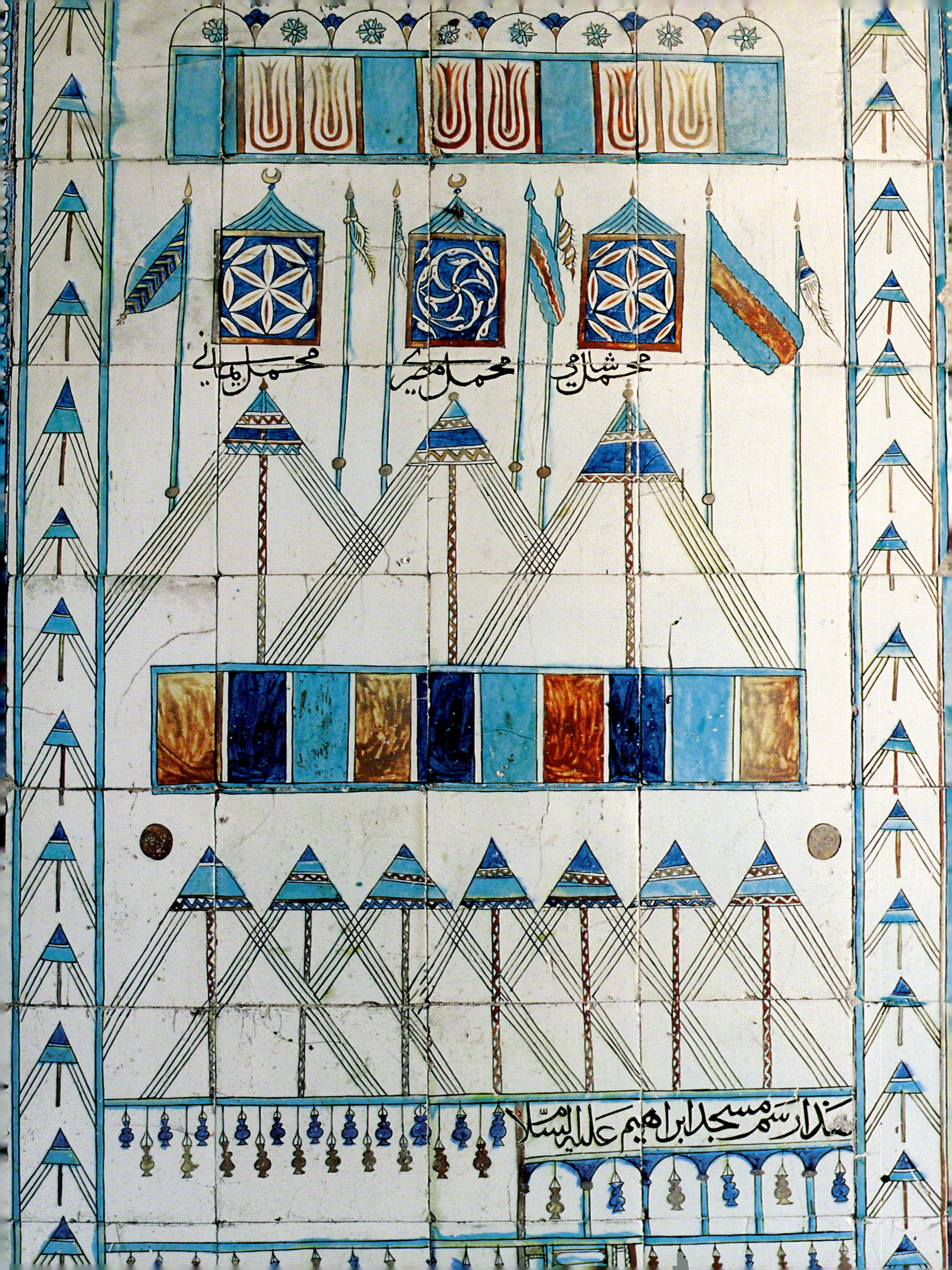

محمل يماني
محمل مصري
محمل شامي
منار سمت مسجد ابراهیم علیه السلام

♦ Marble fountain framed in panels of floral Iznik tiles. Topkapi Saray, Istanbul (Turkey).

♦ Panel of mid-seventeenth-century Iznik tiles representing the Ka`ba at Mecca, today in the Museum of Islamic Art, Cairo.

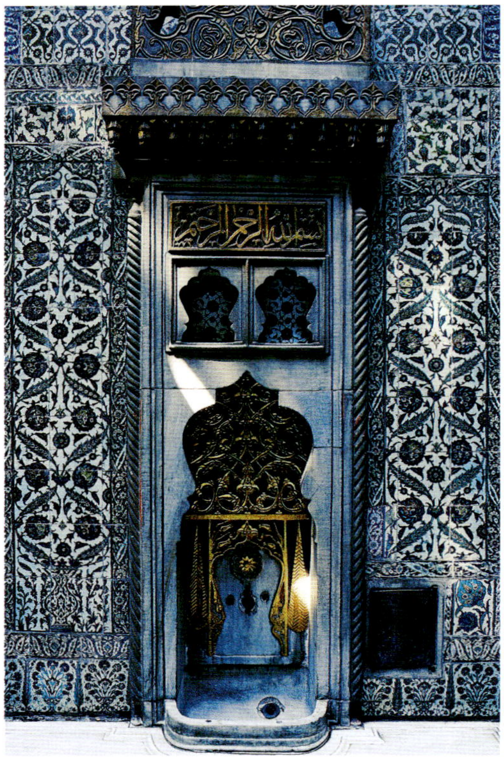

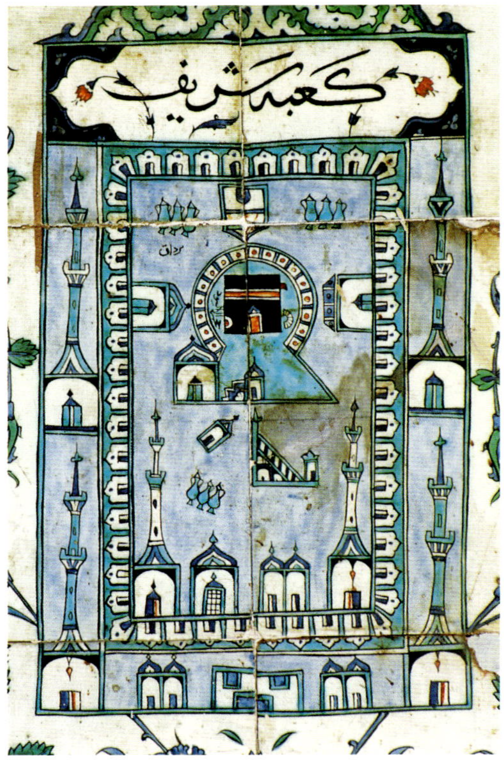

octagonal building with a dome featuring four porches and a circular gallery. The kiosk was erected by Murad IV to commemorate the capture of Baghdad in 1638. Inside, a fireplace (*ocak*) with a bronze hood dominates the central room. The latter has four arms that contain niches decorated with "black line" tiles (older recycled tiles as has already been mentioned) and wall cupboards with mother-of-pearl shutters fitted beneath the windows, which have grilles set with colored glass. The broad calligraphic frieze stretching between the two tiers of windows quotes verse 256 from the second *sura* of the Qur`an, known as the "Verse of the Throne." All the spaces between the high windows are lined in ceramic tiles, which often have repeated motifs. On either side of the fireplace, as above the sofa, splendid cobalt and turquoise panels within a series of arches are adorned with elegant serrated leaves and fantastic flowers on which roost birds whose outlines merge into the vegetation. In spite of the marginally dulled colors, these compositions represent a belated Indian summer in Iznik tile production.

A vast court, occupied essentially by a pool, links the Baghdad Kiosk to that of Erevan (the Revan Köşkü, also constructed under Murad IV in 1635 to celebrate the capture of the city) and to the Sünnet Odasi mentioned above. Overlooking the Bosphorus and the Golden Horn, this group of pavilions and courts is surely one of the most attractive parts of the Topkapi.

YENI CAMI, ISTANBUL (TURKEY)

♦ Inscriptional panel in Thuluth script on a cobalt ground.

♦ Iznik tiles with a floral design. The seventeenth-century colors are less vibrant compared with those manufactured in the sixteenth; even the white ground had started to lose its purity.

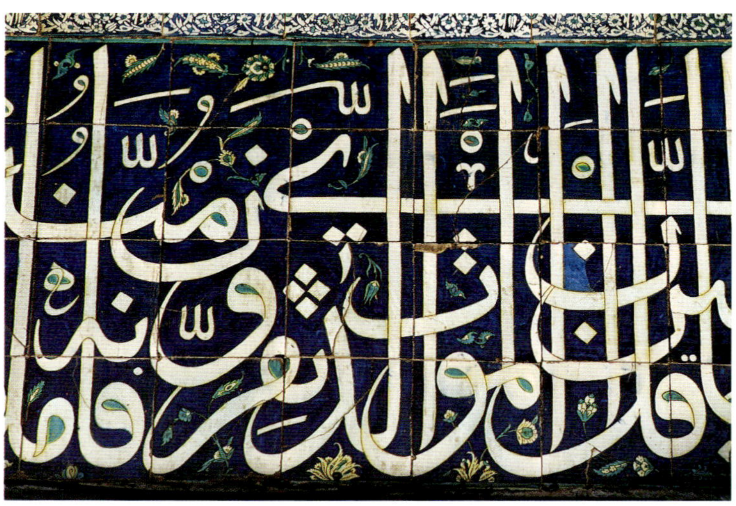

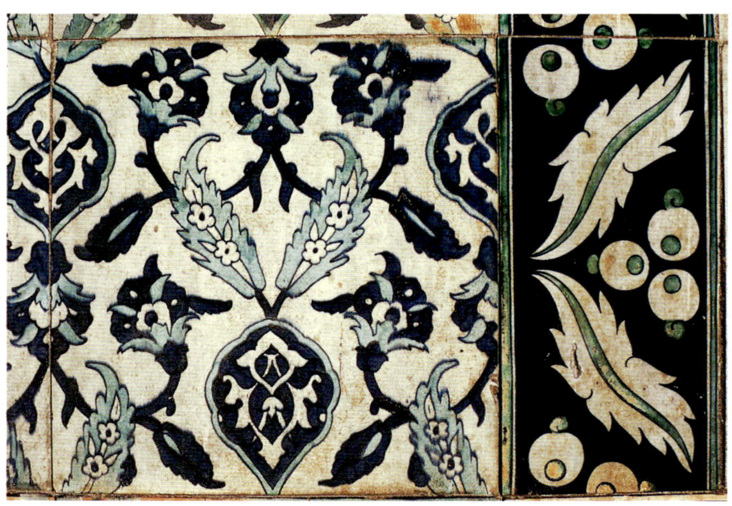

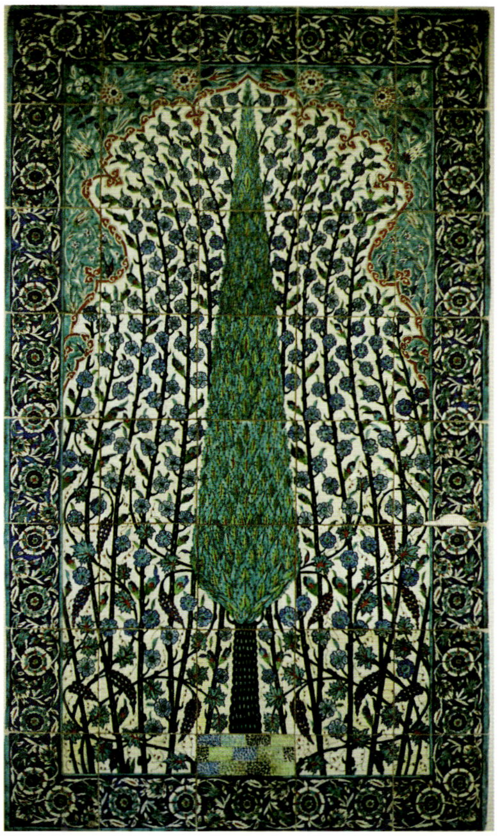

During the seventeenth century, the town of Kütahya emerged as a serious competitor to the Iznik workshops, in particular as regards wares. Indeed, when Iznik production came to an abrupt halt at the end of the century, Kütahya found itself in a position to take up the baton. Kütahya is a city lying 200 kilometers to the east of Istanbul on the edge of the Anatolian plateau. Ceramic manufacture is attested from the sixteenth century on and it clearly continued during the seventeenth, but it was only from the eighteenth century that pottery from the Kütahya workshops became well documented. These ceramics are characterized in particular by the appearance of the color yellow, hitherto absent from the Iznik palette. The tiles incorporated a vast repertory of motifs, in both polychromy and blue-and-white. Dominated by the Armenian community, production from the Kütahya workshops was often demonstrably intended for a Christian clientele. In fact, it is not so rare to find icons with a Christian theme among tiles from this center; the best-known series was executed for the decoration of the Armenian Cathedral of St. James in Jerusalem (1718–19). In the nineteenth century, kilns in Kütahya began imitating old Iznik models. After the end of World War I, a group of potters from Kütahya set up in Jerusalem in order to manufacture the tiles required for restoring the Dome of the Rock, and these two centers (Kütahya and Jerusalem) have remained active to our day. One example of these later productions in the Ottoman taste appears on ornamental panels in the American Colony Hotel in Jerusalem.

During the nineteenth century, many Iznik pieces started arriving in Europe by way of the island of Rhodes, a fact that accounts for these ceramics being described occasionally as "Rhodian pottery" (or "Rhodian earthenware"), although they are not produced on that island and are not even earthenware.

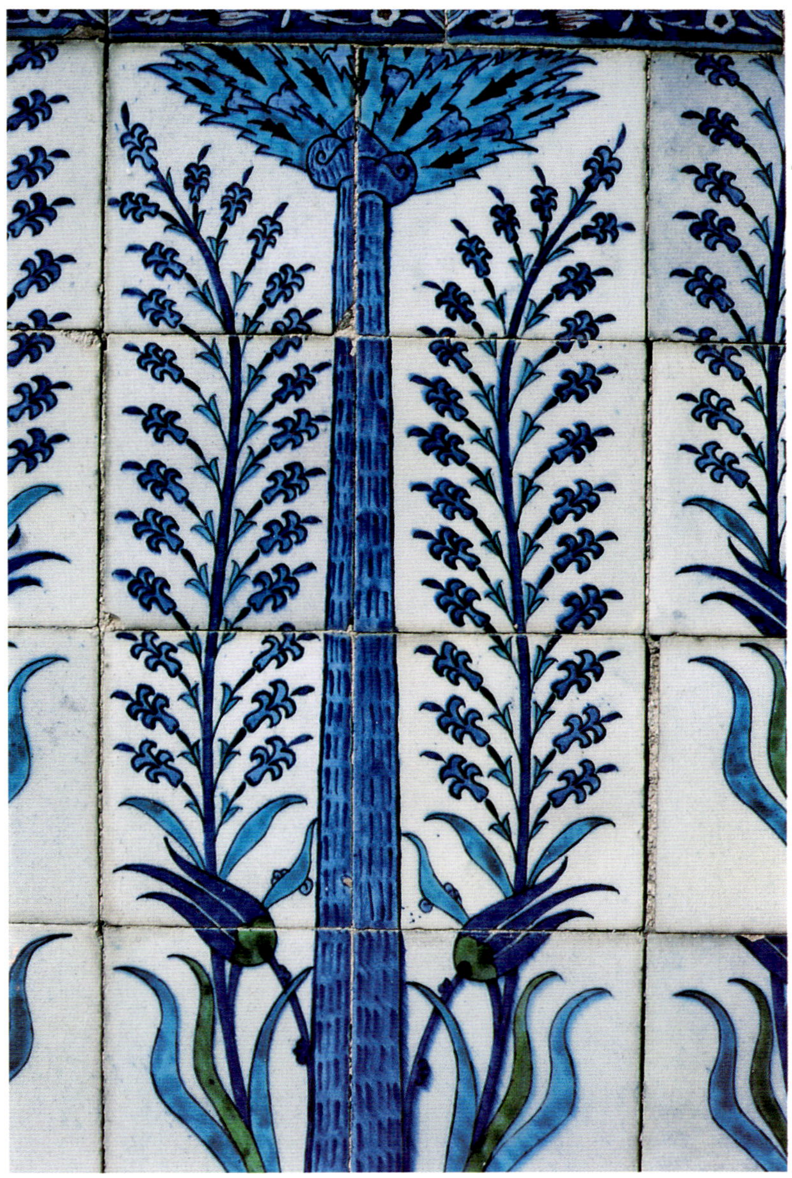

AMERICAN COLONY HOTEL, JERUSALEM (ISRAEL)

♦ Panel of tiles in the Iznik manner decorated with a cypress tree and flowering tendrils.

♦ Panel of tiles in the Iznik manner, with hyacinths and tulips flanking the trunk of a cypress tree.

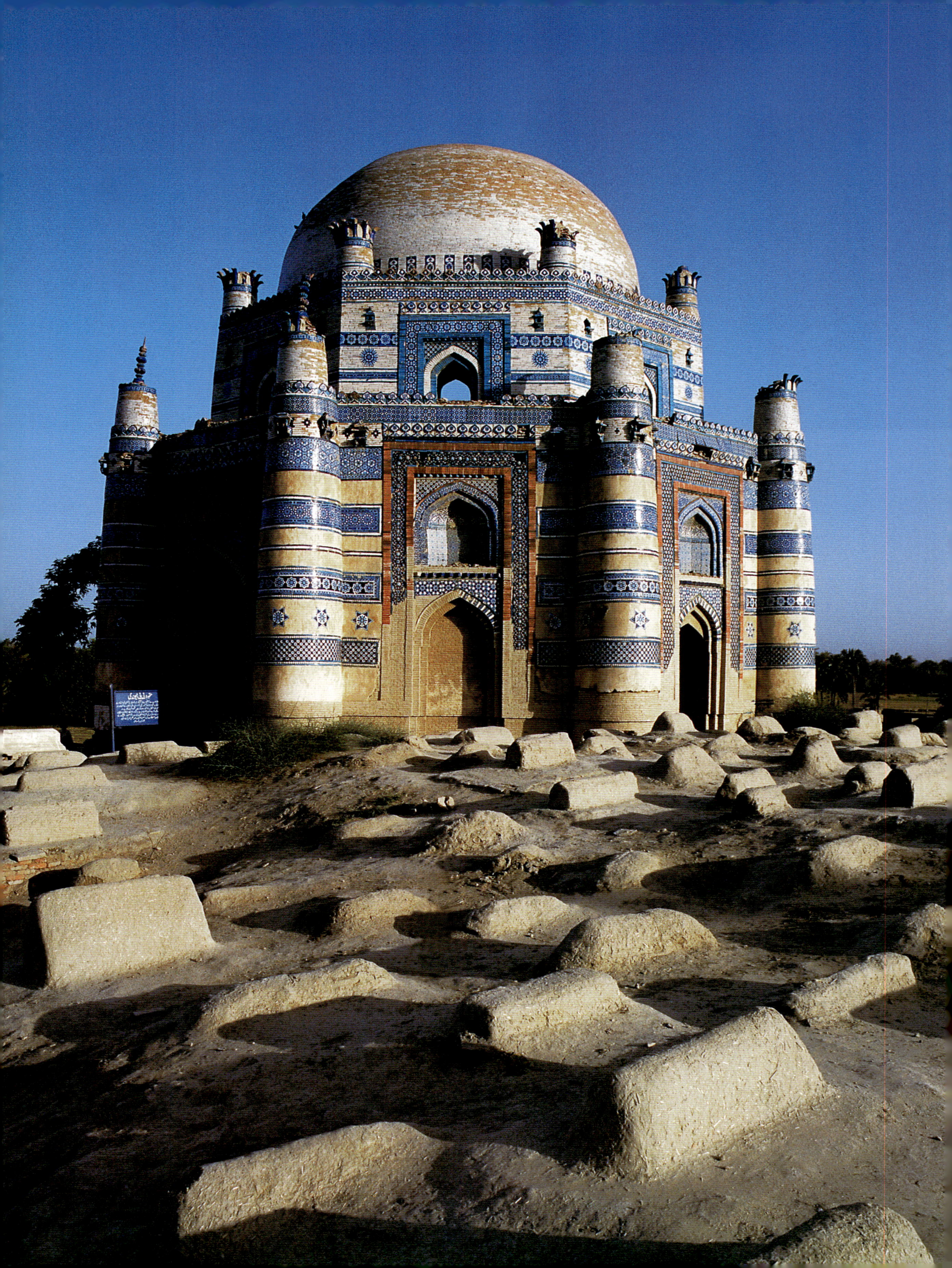

V

The Indian Subcontinent under Islamic Rule

India possesses very little glazed ceramic, especially when compared with Iran or central Asia. There are numerous reasons for this. In the first place, in the Hindu tradition terracotta is considered impure, so crockery made of it can be used only once; metal is thus preferred for tableware.[85] Moreover, as has been noted with respect to central Asia and Iran, glazed ceramic tiles are found primarily in conjunction with brick-built architecture. In areas where brick construction predominates, the number of workmen already engaged in working with clay was such that part of the workforce could turn their hand to more specialized tasks. Supervised by technicians and benefiting from the infrastructures, be they rudimentary, already in place (extraction of raw materials, fuel, kilns, etc.), more elaborate items could then be produced.

Architecture in the central Indian provinces—contrary to that in Iran or central Asia, or even to that found on the Indian subcontinent's flood plain (Bengal, Sind, or the Punjab)—is, however, primarily stone-built.[87] Naturally this type of architecture favors decoration in masonry. However, a few Indian monuments, for the most part Muslim, do display ceramic decoration. To date, no specialized study of the subject has been made, however, and no systematic catalogue of Indian tilework has yet been drawn up.[88] In addition, a substantial number of such decorative schemes have now completely disappeared and it is only by examining the marks left by the tiles in the mortar that the ceramics can be reconstituted to any degree. A further problem is caused by the fact that, divorced from their original context, detached tiles preserved in museums and collections are often difficult to date with any precision.

Tile revetments in India are of several types, differing according to region and following a more or less chronological progression. The oldest type of tile attested in the context of architectural decoration is the turquoise-blue tile (*firuze'i*) dating from the end of the Khalji era that is found in alternation with masonry facing, although they are only used over relatively small surfaces. This alternate use of stone and turquoise can be compared with the brick and *banna'i* work found in the Seljuq monuments of Maragha, such as the Gunbad-i Surkh ("the Red Tomb," 1147–48) and the Gunbad-i Kabud (the "Blue Tomb" 1196–97). At a later date, as the chromatic range became richer, *banna'i* tiles of various colors appeared, arranged in geometrical compositions.

The mosaic made up of cut tiles—and no longer bricks—represents a more sophisticated stage in the art of architectural decoration and such tilework could be arranged to create a multitude of designs. This technique, which first appeared in Iran in the mid-fourteenth century, is very laborious and labor-intensive, however: the decor first has to be painstakingly assembled from tiny ceramic elements fired in the form of plates of various colors, and these are subsequently cut out in accordance with the design and inlaid. Finally, painted tiles (*kashi-ye haft-rang*) entailed more complex techniques in the kiln, but affixing them to the wall was an easier operation, the decoration and the architectural forms being decided upon prior to firing.

The technique of glazed ceramics is undoubtedly of Iranian or Mesopotamian origin (as is glazed brick); nevertheless, traces are to be found in the Indian subcontinent from the Kushan epoch onwards (late first to third century A.D.). Indeed, excavations at Shah-ji-ki-Dheri near Peshawar have unearthed glazed bricks with inscriptions in Kharosthi script.[89] Nonetheless, recourse to tilework prior to the Muslim period remained sporadic, while colored decorations on the facades of buildings only became widespread at the time of the sultanate of Delhi.

PAGE 222

♦ Mausoleum of Bibi Jawindi, Uch (Pakistan), 1493. This magnificent mausoleum with its dazzling turquoise tiles dominates the surrounding landscape.

India's Earliest Contact with Islam

Although the first sultan of Delhi ascended to the throne only in 1206, India had already been the object of more than one Muslim incursion. Between the Arab conquest of Sind in 711 and the rise of the Ghurids at the end of the twelfth century, however, the surviving historical material—particularly in the realm of art—is extremely fragmentary. Indeed, very little is known of the earliest Muslim monuments on the subcontinent, since the Indus plain—the very epitome of a buffer zone—has suffered to such a great extent from invasion and plunder in the past that the discovery of any archeological remains represents something of a miracle. Several military campaigns had been undertaken by the Arabs against India, but the expedition that signaled the onset of Arabo-Muslim penetration into the subcontinent was the one headed by Hajjaj ibn Yusuf, governor of Iraq, in 711, the same year coincidentally that the Arabs reached Gibraltar. We know the name of at least three cities founded or rebuilt under Arab rule in Sind (currently part of Pakistan): Daybal, Mansura, and Multan. In autumn 711, General Muhammad ibn Qasim arrived at the port of Daybal. After seizing the city, he built the first mosque on the subcontinent and settled some four thousand Arab families in a new district. Excavations carried out between 1958 and 1965 in Banbhore (believed to correspond to ancient Daybal) have unearthed a mosque [90] that conforms to a plan similar to that of the old mosque at Kufa (Iraq), albeit smaller (measuring approximately 37 meters on a side). The pillars around the central court and the roof were probably of timber. An inscription that some scholars consider spurious dates from 727, that is to say only forty years after the construction of the mosque at Kufa. If this inscription is authentic, the mosque of Banbhore would be the oldest Muslim vestige in the Indian subcontinent.

After the recall of Muhammad ibn Qasim, Sind relapsed into chaos. The town of Mansura "the Victorious" only saw the light of day in 737, under the governance of one of Muhammad ibn Qasim's sons. The city was to become the Arab outpost in Sind from which expeditions could be launched so as to safeguard the integrity of the province. The actual location of Mansura was rediscovered at the beginning of the twentieth century by Henry Cousens at the site of Brahmanabad.[91] One of the buildings unearthed by the archeologist was a large stone-built construction that Cousens considered to be the Friday mosque of Mansura, together with three other small mosques. Arab historians describe Mansura as a town measuring a mile down one side, surrounded rather like an island by an arm of the Indus, heavily populated and commercially active. Mansura leather, especially shoes, were highly regarded in Baghdad, even by the family of the caliph.

The ancient capital of the Punjab, Multan, was also overrun by Muhammad ibn Qasim, although no vestiges of its Arab period have yet been brought to light. Today Multan remains a city of some size and contains many monuments from subsequent periods.

If monuments from the period remain rare, the caliphate province of Sind was nevertheless a significant center for the arts in the Muslim world. The province served in fact as a channel through which Indian knowledge, particularly in the fields of mathematics (the cipher for zero, for example) and astronomy, were transmitted to the rest of the Muslim world. It was also through its Arab province that India eventually influenced the West, particularly in the areas of music, literature, and mysticism, and through the introduction of the game of chess.

A further significant aspect of cultural life in Arab Sind was the development of schools of Hadith.[92] These diverse intellectual achievements are probably indicative of significant craft and artistic production in Sind, but sadly not a single artifact survives. By 960, the Ghaznavids, soldiers of Turkish serf origin, had began to supplant the Iranian Samanid dynasty, and Mahmud (992–1030), the greatest king of the Ghazni dynasty and a vigorous standard-bearer for Muslim orthodoxy, launched an invasion of Sind. In point of fact, this was less a genuine territorial conquest than a series of incursions into the north of India. Indeed, the only Indian possession that the Ghaznavids were to hold on to for any length of time was the Punjab, with its capital at Lahore. It was during the reign of Mahmud that Ghazni (currently in Afghanistan) became a brilliant capital, its court numbering poets, panegyrists, and historians, as well as men of science and philosophers. A significant proportion of the treasure plundered in India undoubtedly made its way to Ghazni, most of the gold being apparently melted down and minted into coin. In addition, there were many craftsmen among the prisoners seized as trophy and taken to Ghazni, and they exerted a considerable influence on artistic life among the Ghaznavids. If nothing has survived of the spoils from Mahmud's Indian campaigns, the *History of India* by the great scholar and scientist Biruni, then attached to the court of Ghazni, has come down to the present-day. According to Schimmel, this treatise represents the "earliest attempt ever undertaken to objectively study a foreign culture."

Following the death of Mahmud, relentless incursions by the Seljuqs into Khorasan forced the Ghaznavids to fall back to the Punjab. By the mid-eleventh century, the Ghaznavid empire had been reduced to its Indian province. So it was that Lahore became a thriving center for the arts where the worlds of Iran, India, and central Asia could converge. Once again though, one can only hope to gain the sketchiest idea of the splendor of the Ghaznavid capital since no "hard evidence" survives, the whole city having been razed to the ground in 1217 by the armies of Genghis Khan, before suffering a similar fate at the hands of Tamerlane in 1398. Isolated Muslim settlements seem to have existed at several locations on the subcontinent prior to the setting up of the sultanate of Delhi. Thus, the site of Bhadreshvar in Gujarat contains a mausoleum built in 1159, making it the oldest dated Muslim monument in present-day India.[93]This edifice is known as the mausoleum of Ibrahim or Dargah La'l Shahbaz. Although its funerary function can be regarded as innovative, the architectural techniques deployed and the decoration are more or less typical of indigenous craftsmanship.

In 1186, Mu'izz al-Din ibn Sam, ruler of the Ghurids, crushed the last Ghaznavids and annexed the Punjab. It was one of his generals, Qutb al-Din Aybak, who, on the death of his master, founded the sultanate of Delhi itself. Although remnants of Ghurid architecture are still poorly known, it can be supposed that monuments from the early years of the sultanate of Delhi had at least some relationship to Ghurid art.

Rediscovered only in 1957, the remarkable minaret at Djam in Afghanistan is built entirely out of brick.[94] It was erected during the reign of Ghiyath al-Din Muhammad ibn Sam (1163–1202), whose titular inscription it bears. The tapering and isolated form of this minaret is strongly reminiscent of other constructions of the type, such as the Qutb Minar at Delhi (begun in 1199), the minarets of Ghazni (late eleventh century) or the Kalan of Bukhara (1127).

Ghurid princes built superb palaces on the Ghaznavid ruins at the site of the ancient city of Bost, also in Afghanistan.[95] It is with the help of these vestiges that one can picture what Ghaznavid and Ghurid palaces in Lahore may have looked like. Certain elements of their architecture recur later in monuments built by the sultans of Delhi.

The Sultanate of Delhi

The city of Delhi is built on the site of an old Hindu town, Qila Rai Pithora, on whose ruins Qutb al-Din Aybak laid the foundations of a new eastern capital in 1192. There survive a number of significant monuments dating from this early period. The Friday mosque—called the Quwwat al-Islam ("Power of Islam")—appears today as a succession of rectangular courtyards embedded one in the other, although in point of fact the original mosque, begun in 1193, was a rectangle 60 meters by 42 meters. It was built with the *spolia* of twenty-seven Hindu and Jain temples, in the form of a ring of colonnades around a central court. The recycled columns were placed in pairs one atop the other, so as to attain the approximate height of mosques built with columns raised in the traditional manner. In 1199, a finely worked stone screen in the shape of five pointed arches was erected in front of the prayer hall (on the western side pointing toward Mecca). These "Persian" arches offer a surprising contrast to the earlier colonnades that bear stone beams and a roof of flagstones laid flat in traditional Indian fashion.

The Qutb Minar was also begun in 1199, at which time it was located outside the mosque on the southeastern corner. Nowadays, it overlooks the mosque from a height of 73 meters. Although it functions in its own right as the mosque's minaret, it also symbolizes the "power of Islam" by its sheer height, rather in the way of an Indian "tower of victory." The minaret as it appears today presents four balconies and terminates in a lantern; however, only the first three balconies are original. On the first level, the cross-section presents moldings alternately rounded and pointed in profile. The second tier is characterized by a corbeled balcony and, above it, a section marked by gadroons; the third level is star-shaped in section. We have already noted the connection between the Qutb Minar and the minaret at Djam, Afghanistan, but this was not so much a case of borrowing as an example of the adaptation of an architectural form, since the materials and construction techniques employed remain quite distinct. This opposition between brick construction, typical of the Iranian plateau, and masonry architecture, characteristic of India, is one of the crucial distinctions between these two regions.

The Quwwat al-Islam Mosque was enlarged on a number of occasions, in particular by Iltutmich in around 1220–29. It was probably also around the same time that he had his own mausoleum built in the northwestern corner of the mosque. A notable feature of this stone mausoleum, which is square in plan and was at one time spanned by a dome on squinches, is the richness of its carved decoration. The mausoleum marks an important stage in the creation of a specific architectural idiom, as this was probably the first building in sultanate architecture to contrast white marble and sandstone.

♦ The Qutb Minar, Delhi (India), begun in 1199, stands 73 m high. Its form is an adaptation of that of the Ghurid minarets, which were constructed in brick and decorated in ceramic, although stone alone is employed here. The `Ala'i Darwaza can be seen at the foot of the minaret.

Sultan `Ala al-Din Khalji (1296–1316) was also noteworthy as a builder. In an attempt to outdo the Qutb Minar, `Ala al-Din decided to erect a minaret twice its height, but his ambition was never realized. However, he did manage to enlarge the Quwwat al-Islam Mosque for a third time, constructing on the south facade a gateway known by the name of `Ala'i Darwaza, or "Sublime Porte." Of square plan, this monumental gateway was topped by a cupola. The three external projecting facades are decorated in a white marble inlay that stands out against the red sandstone. The broad entrance—a pointed arch slightly horseshoe in shape, supported by corner colonnettes—is bordered by a frieze of lotus buds, while the windows are adorned with openwork masonry grilles. The sophisticated execution and harmonious proportions of the building make the `Ala'i Darwaza one of the supreme achievements of sultanate architecture. One of the only monuments from the reign of the same sovereign that conserves ceramic tilework (of turquoise color) is the *idgah* `Ala al-Din had constructed at Rapri.[96]

Founder of a new dynasty, Ghiyath al-Din Tughluq was also the builder of a new city: Tughlaqabad (1320–25). The site selected lay eight kilometers from the Qutb Minar and about the same distance from the Yamuna. A large rocky outcrop supplied the raw materials for the construction of the fort, and served as its foundations. To the east, a dam was built to close off the natural basin between this rock and the hills opposite, and this basin fills at the time of the monsoon. To its western edge, an embankment-cum-bridge links the fortress to Ghiyath al-Din's tomb.

This gigantic enclosure seems to have been built to withstand a long siege; supplies of water were ensured by cisterns and attics for grain storage were fitted out in the towers. Nonetheless, the whole immense ensemble was probably hardly ever inhabited. In fact, the reign of Ghiyath al-Din Tughluq proved short. In 1325, on returning from a military campaign to the Lakhnauti, he was crushed to death when a timber pavilion his son, Muhammad Shah, had had erected in his honor collapsed on the guests below. Ghiyath al-Din's mausoleum stands on a fortified island on the lake in Tughlaqabad. Square in plan, it is immediately identifiable by its strongly sloping external walls and by its two-color stonework—red sandstone alternating with white marble. Three gateways with "Persian" arches bordered by a lotus-bud motif open on to the funerary hall proper. The prominent dome, covered in white marble and resting on an octagonal drum, foreshadows, in form and material, and by the fleuron on its summit, many Mughal cupolas to come. This tomb is contemporary of that of Rukn-i `Alam at Multan, a construction that is also ascribed to Ghiyath al-Din.

As described by Ibn Battuta, Delhi was a city comprising four contiguous townships. The first, built by the Chauhan kings at the end of the tenth century, was "Old" Delhi; the second, known as Siri, was built by `Ala al-Din Khalji (1296–1316); the third, Tughlaqabad, was the work of Ghiyath al-Din Tughluq (1320–25); while the fourth, Jahanpanah (literally, "refuge of the world"), was founded by Muhammad Shah and eventually engulfed the three earlier cities.[97]

The reasons behind the construction of Tughlaqabad and its abandonment by Muhammad Shah four years afterward remain obscure. Be that as it may, Muhammad ibn Tughluq (1325–51) was to build an additional palace-citadel on the other side of the Tughlaqabad dam that he called `Adilabad. These two citadels do not seem to have replaced the towns of Delhi and Siri and they continued to increase in size, a fact that induced Muhammad ibn Tughluq to have yet another large fortification constructed precisely to link "old" Delhi to Siri. This enclosure was christened

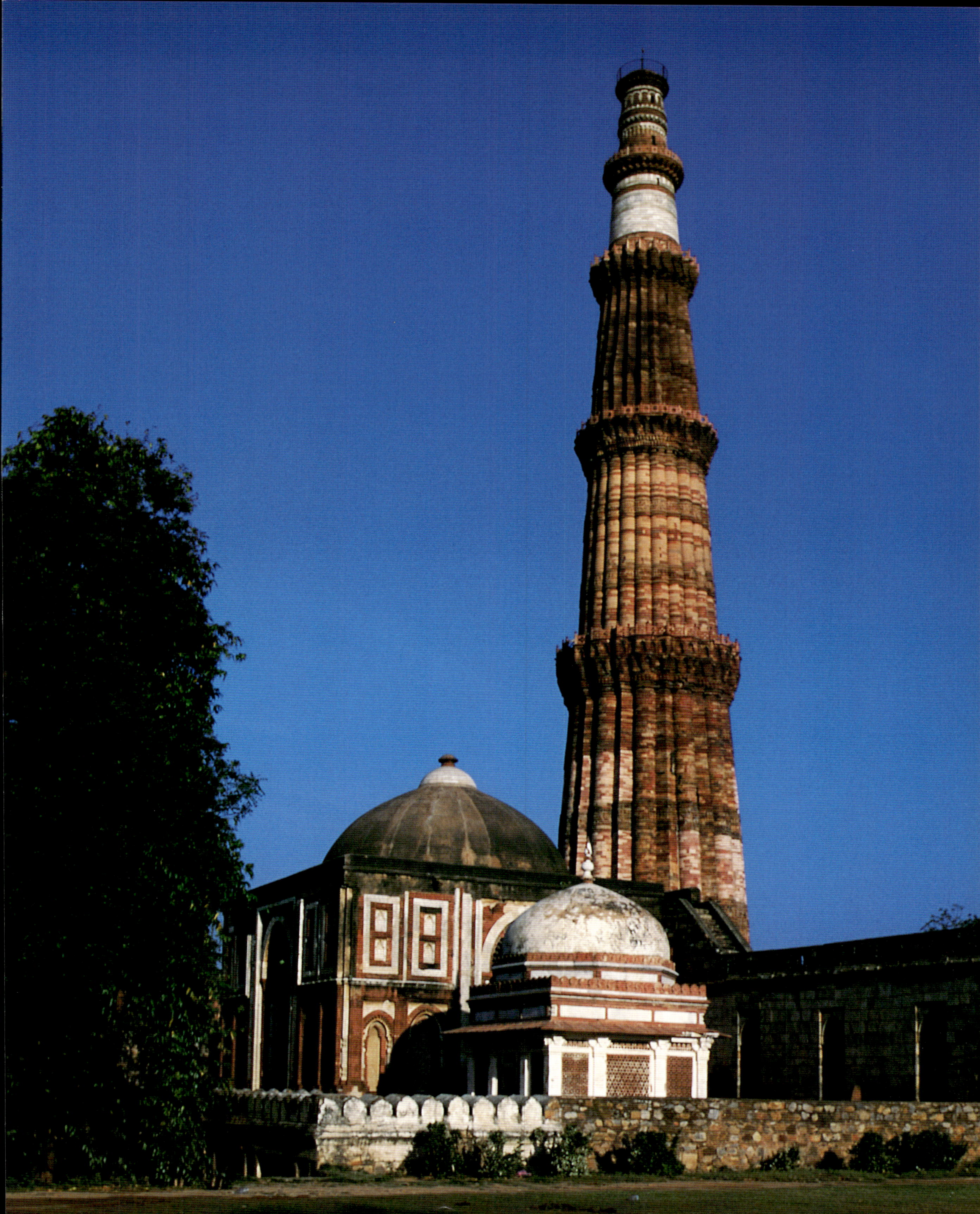

♦ Mausoleum of Rukn-i ʿAlam, Multan (Pakistan), 1320–24. This magnificent tomb was probably commissioned by the sultan of Delhi, Ghiyath al-Din Tughluq.

"Jahanpanah." Its northwestern rampart was bordered by a large reservoir, the Hauz-i Khas, while an ingenious seven-arched bridge-cum-dam was built to span a drainage channel to the east side of the fortified wall.

Plum in the middle of the city towers the great mosque of Jahanpanah, known today as the Begumpuri *masjid*. Almost square in plan (90 by 94 meters), it reflects an obvious Iranian influence. It is undoubtedly the first building in Muslim India to adopt the "Iranian" four-*iwan* mosque plan. In spite of the clear link with Iranian models, however, the building materials employed are typically Indian. Indeed, the whole building is constructed in stone, rendered in places with a coat of mortar. Small turquoise ceramic tiles enliven a construction that would other-wise be rather austere. The court is bor-dered by porticos supported on stone columns and punctuated by broad *iwans*; the one belonging to the prayer hall facing

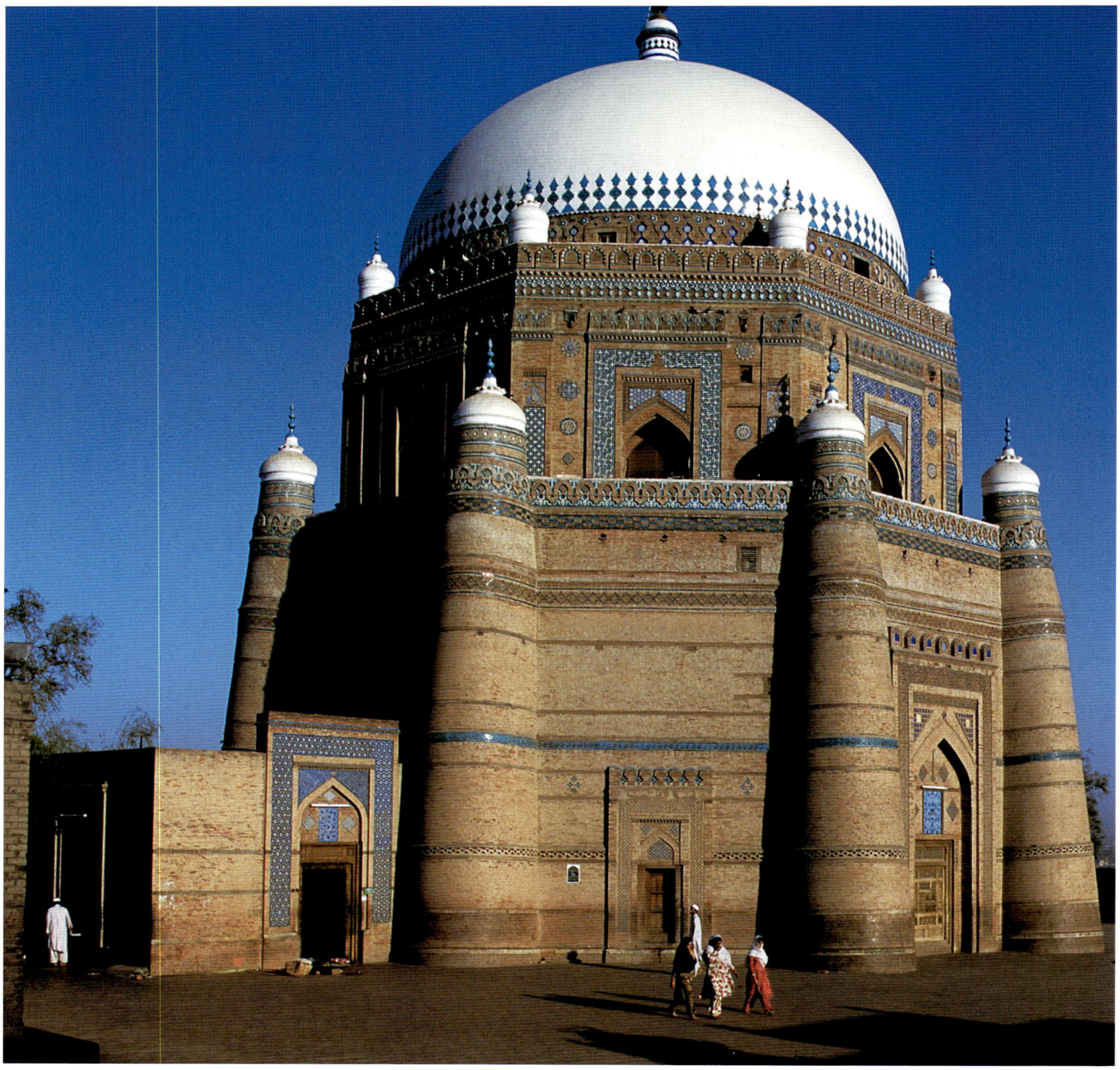

the main entrance is flanked by minarets in the form of truncated cones characteristic of Tughluq architecture.

Tamerlane certainly saw this mosque and possibly drew inspiration from some elements for the Bibi Khanum, his monumental mosque at Samarkand. Specific reference might be made to the engaged minarets on either side of the *iwan* in the prayer hall and the monumental entryway, as well as the use of columns and carved stone dados, somewhat rare in the Iranian world. This is an interesting phenomenon, since it demonstrates the mechanism of lively artistic interchange that operated in this part of the Muslim world.

With the advent of the reign of Firuz Shah (1351–88) a new period dawned. This sovereign, who was responsible for irrigation projects on a truly massive scale, was also to choose a new site for the city on the shores of the Yamuna (Jumna) River. In "old" Delhi itself, he busied himself repairing the ancient reservoirs of Iltutmich and `Ala al-Din. The latter reservoir is known today by the name of the Hauz-i Khas and in its current state shows the hand of Firuz Shah, the king who refurbished it in 1352. In addition, he added, to the southern and western sides, a series of buildings over several floors that house, among other things, a *madrasa* and his own tomb.

At the time of its construction, the palace in the new city, nowadays called Firuz Shah Kotla, stood on the shores of the Yamuna. The Archaeological Survey of India has proposed rebuilding the royal enclosure by recycling material from the many extant ruins.[98] Two relatively well-preserved buildings are particularly interesting. The first is a *baoli* (a kind of well-cum-reservoir) designed to collect seepage water from the nearby river and thus provide a supply of drinking water. Galleries on several levels surround the tank, while above a terrace bordered by balustrades bears two elegant *chhatri* (kiosks with columns). The rather unusual layout of this *baoli* arouses the suspicion that it may have originally served as a pleasure palace where refreshment could have been taken.

The other interesting building in Firuz Shah's palace is what appears to be a curiously shaped four-tier pyramid topped by a monolith-like column. The column dates in fact from the time of Ashoka, as indicated by the inscriptions. This building seems to foreshadow other palatial residences, such as the Panch Mahal at Fatehpur Sikri. It should be added that excavations undertaken in the palace have unearthed no less than seventy-two pieces of Chinese porcelain dating from the fourteenth century, the majority of which bear inscriptions in Persian identifying them as wares from the royal kitchens.[99]

Thus, shortly before Tamerlane's invasion of 1398, a style of architecture had emerged in the sultanate of Delhi which, if hardly of great unity, was nonetheless rather original. Technically, it relied primarily on the use of stone, unlike the architecture of the Iranian invader whose constructions, as we have seen, were in brick. In formal terms, it combined both typically Muslim elements and borrowings from styles closer to home. Thus, although new and unprecedented forms, such as the Persian arch and the dome on squinches, did indeed emerge in India, traditional forms also persisted, with stone lintels, awnings (*chajja*), and *chhatri* being incorporated into prototypically Islamic constructions such as mausoleums and mosques.

The sack of Tamerlane dealt a fatal blow to the Delhi sultanate, not only through the massacres and destruction that followed in the wake of the great conqueror's offensive, but also because of the evaporation of all strong political power. Many artists and craftsmen were forced to go to Samarkand, while others, bereft of patronage, elected to make their way to any number of the new courts that were being established in provinces formerly dependent on the sultanate.

Architecture under the Lodi Dynasty

SHISHA GUNBAD, DELHI (INDIA), LATE FIFTEENTH CENTURY

FACING PAGE

♦ The frieze of turquoise and cobalt tiles visible above the doorway makes it obvious why the vernacular name of this tomb signifies "glazed dome."

BELOW

♦ Monochrome glazed tilework adds touches of color to the stone facade of this anonymous tomb.

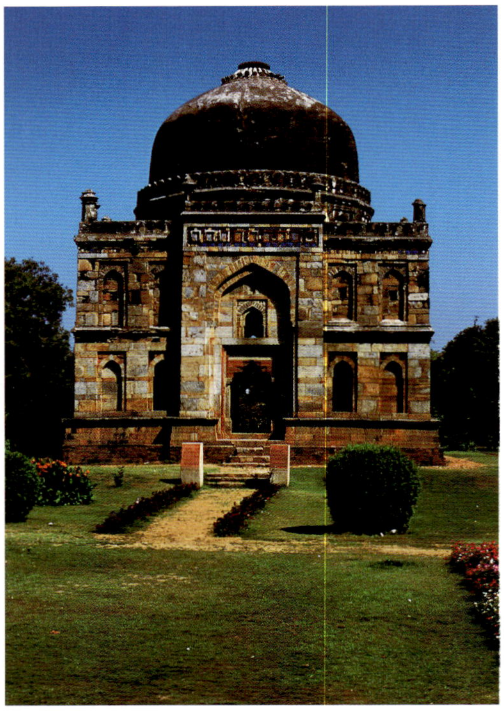

In the fifteenth century, the kings of the Lodi dynasty (1451–1526) preferred Agra, founded by Sikandar Shah Lodi (1489–1517), to Delhi, which became a sort of city-cum-necropolis because all the sovereigns of the dynasty were buried there. Delhi's equivocal status as capital-necropolis continued under the early Mughals—and during the intervening Suri period—until the foundation of Shahjahanabad (the Delhi of Shah Jahan), inaugurated in 1648.

Architecture in the Lodi era seldom conveys the grandeur of Tughluq monumentality. At this time, foreign elements were being introduced and gradually absorbed by local architects, who forged a style dubbed *pathan* (or "Afghan") by the British colonial power. Under the Lodis, the use of ceramic decoration in turquoise blue (and sometimes also cobalt) tilework gradually began to spread.

The Shisha Gunbad in Delhi, for instance, a tomb on a square plan that probably dates from the reign of Sikandar Shah Lodi, is adorned with a band of blue tiles of alternating turquoise and cobalt running along the top of the walls. In 1920, J. P. Vogel described the tiles of this tomb as being "decorated with bands of deep-blue square tiles and a few tiles in three colors, blue, green and white, apparently inscribed."[100]

Located in the middle of a square garden ringed by high walls, the tomb of Sikandar Shah Lodi (who died in 1517) is an octagonal building surrounded by a gallery whose sides are pierced by three arcades. The *chhatri* that decorated the roof of the gallery appear to have disappeared. The monument at one time bore substantial colored decoration only scattered remnants of which survive today (inlaid stucco rosettes on the arch spandrels). The interplay between architectural volumes and colors, either painted or inlaid with turquoise cut-tiles, permitted the creation of a wide variety of motifs enhanced by the use of ceramics. Flanked by a pair of *chhatri*, the doorway to the enclosure was also decorated up to the main arcade with tiles set into the mortar, although almost none of these remain today. From the same period, the small pavilion known as the Jahaz Mahal (or "ship palace") because of its location on the side of the Hauz-i Shamsi reservoir, also incorporates turquoise-blue tiles set into the stone or mortar.[101]

The Man Mandir Palace in the fort of Gwalior, located in northern Madhya Pradesh state, was built under Maharajah Man Singh (1486–1516) during the reign of Sikandar Shah Lodi. Although erected for a Hindu sovereign, the palace nevertheless contains a good deal of ceramics, in particular in the form of additional turquoise, yellow, and green glazed elements inlaid into the masonry facade. A surprising frieze showing a line of yellow ducks *passant* over a turquoise ground appears in the center of the wall of the main facade. Beneath the battlements and alternating with bas-relief elephants carved in stone, figure tigers and banana trees made up of a yellow and blue mosaic encrusted in the sandstone. Between the two registers, a band of blind niches sets off the contrast between the stone and the turquoise blue color. Ceramics also feature in the decoration of the palace's central court, although in smaller quantities. They appear in bands running above the openings, forming geometrical motifs that alternate with the stone reliefs.

It is interesting to note that the preoccupation with ornament and color visible here is seldom evident in the decoration of other Mughal palaces built subsequently, although the Lahore Fort, one of the finest examples of Mughal architecture, constitutes an important exception to this tendency (see below). The ceramic decoration of Man Mandir Palace

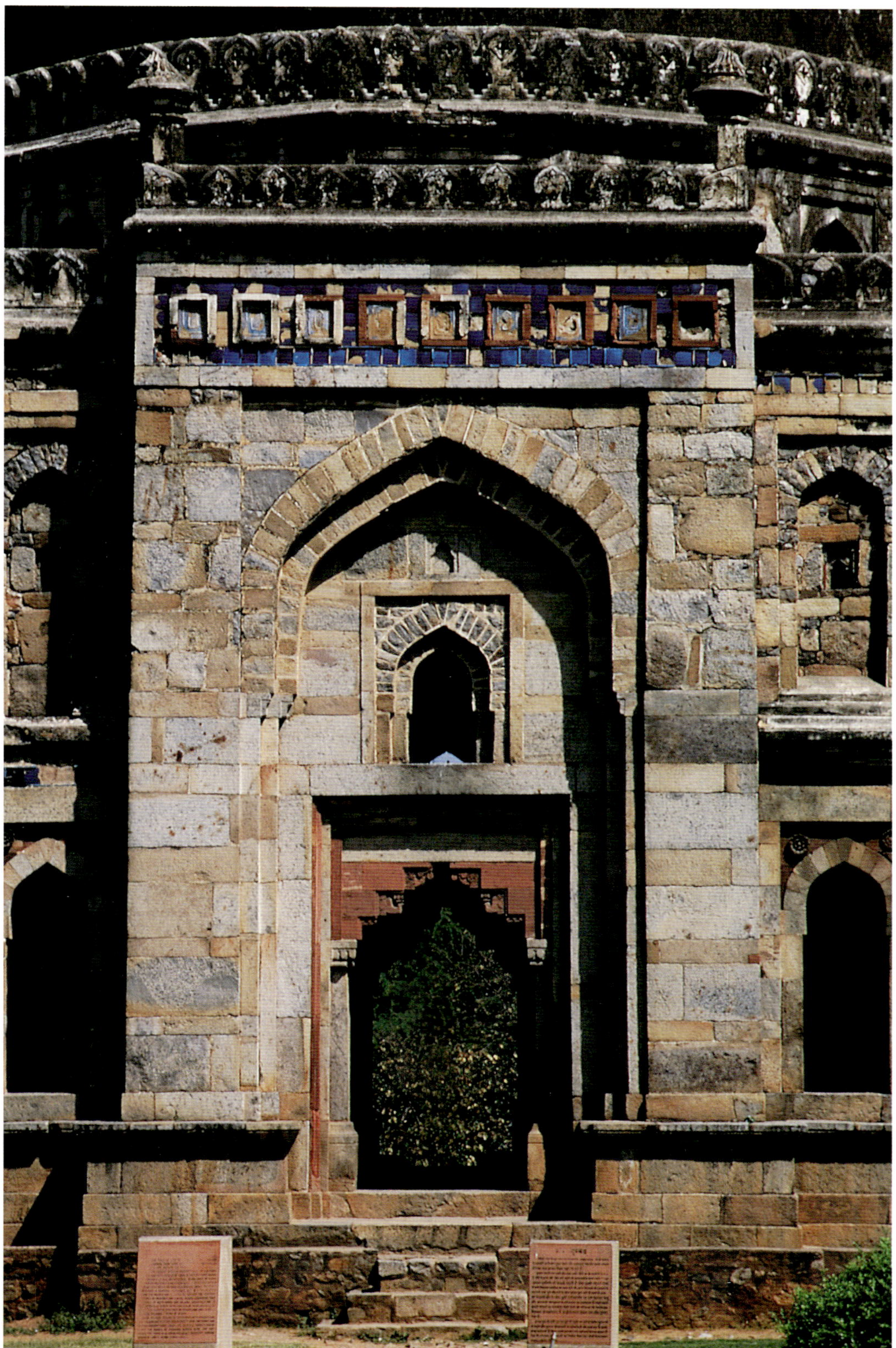

FOLLOWING DOUBLE PAGE

♦ Man Mandir, Gwalior (India). Constructed at the end of the fifteenth century by a Rajput prince, Man Singh (1486–1516), this palace is an exceptional example of pre-Mughal palatial architecture employing ceramics to decorate its facade.

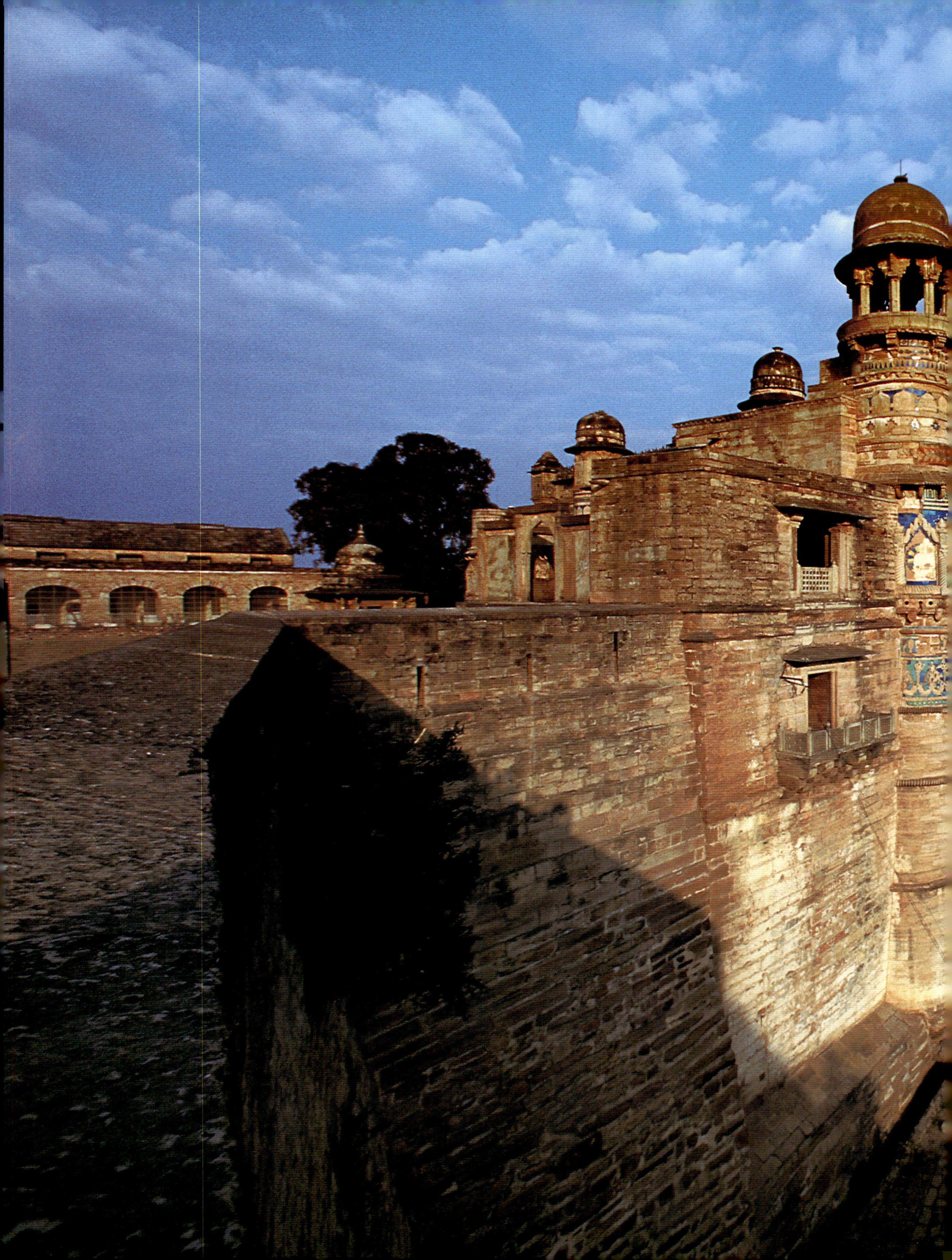

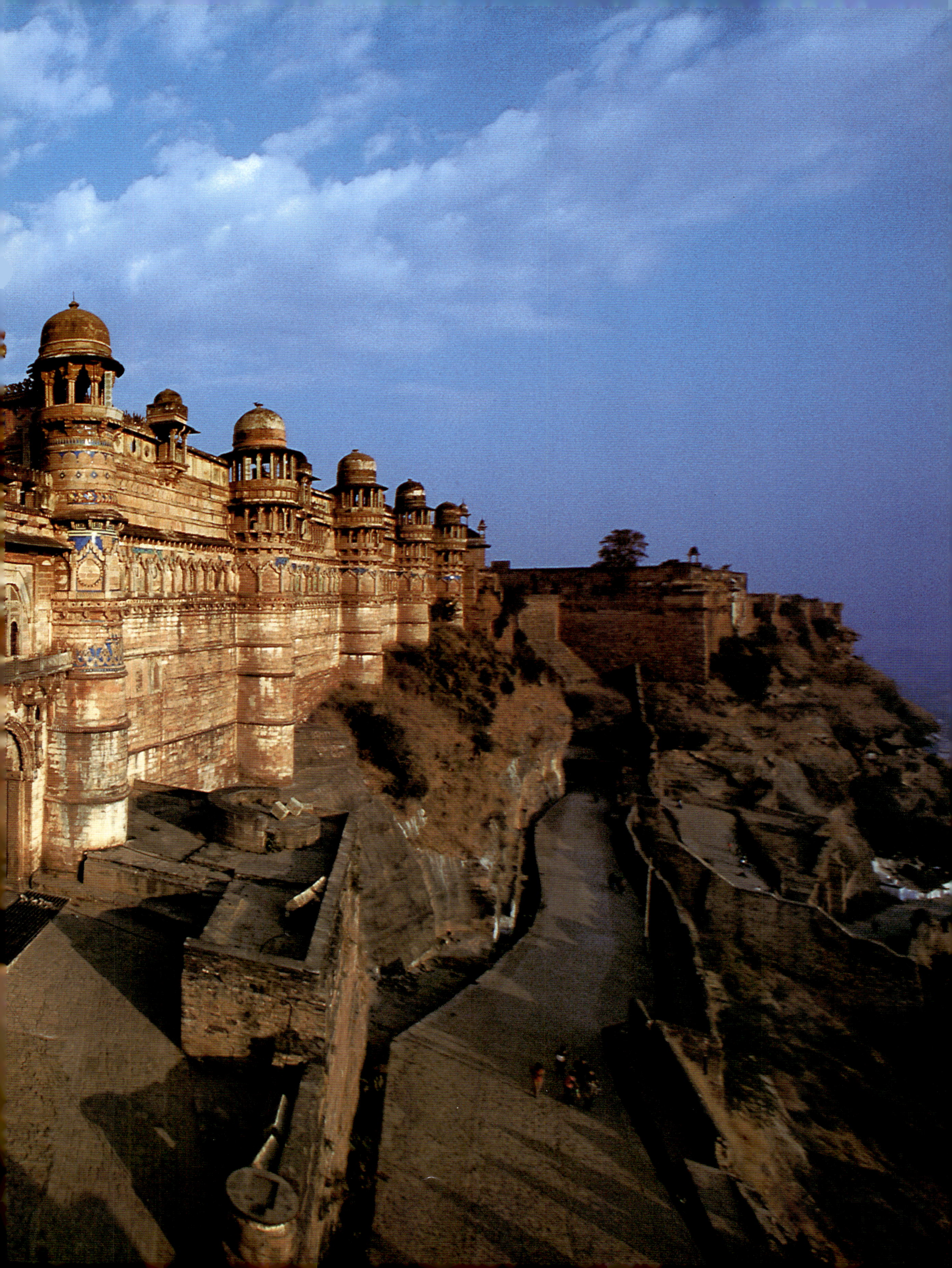

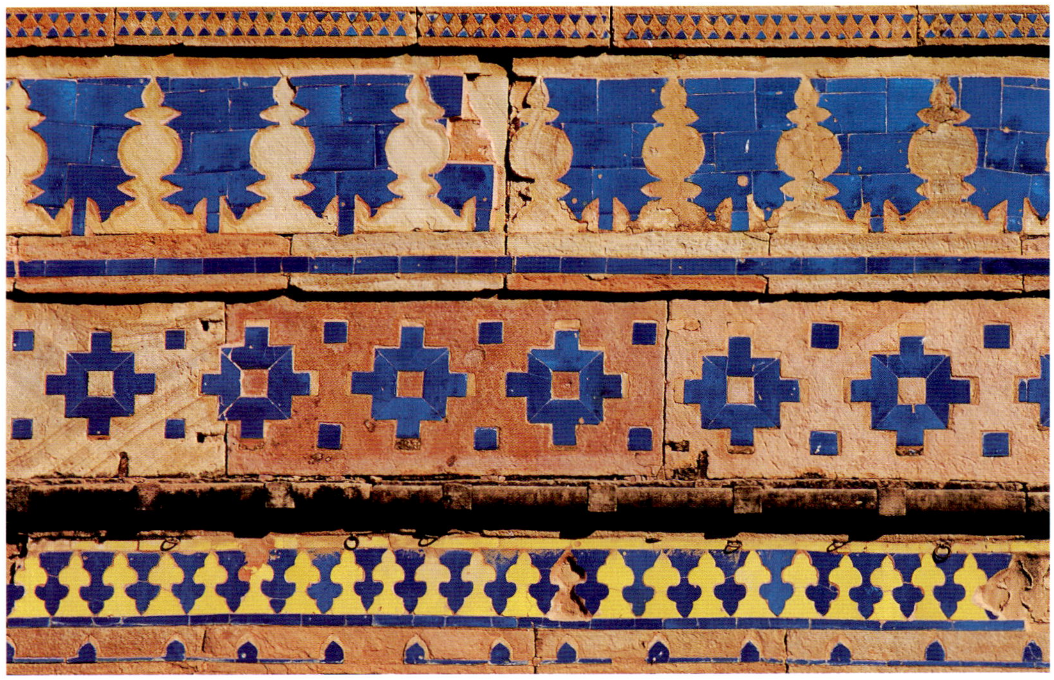

ABOVE

♦ Detail of the facade showing friezes of fleurons and crosses. Man Mandir, Gwalior (India), late fifteenth century. It is highly likely that the Rajput prince employed Muslim craftsmen to execute ceramic decoration of this type.

RIGHT

♦ Detail of the facade showing two parrots facing one another to either side of a central fleuron.

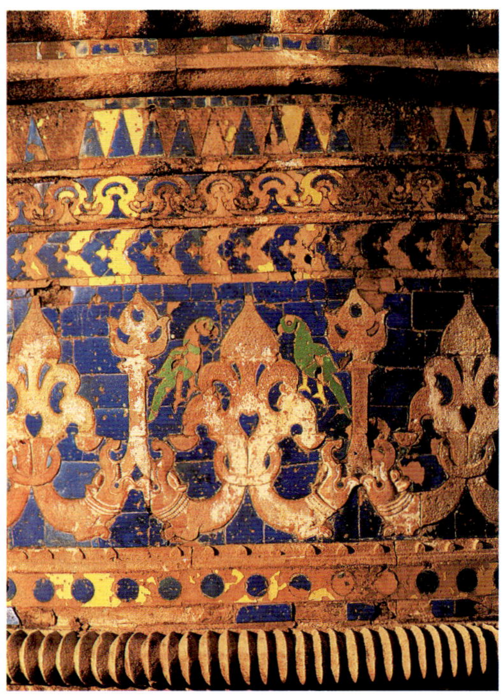

is approximately contemporary with that found a little to the southwest, in Malwa. It is consequently not impossible that the rajah brought in Muslim craftsmen from this area. The taste for additional touches of color in masonry architecture is also observed—albeit on a smaller scale—in the Rajput palaces of Orchha (c. 1600) and Datia (c. 1620), as well as at the fort of Ranthambor (besieged by Akbar in 1569, and rebuilt by the Rajputs following the death of Aurangzeb Alamgir).

The Independent Sultanates

As the sultanate of Delhi crumbled in the wake of the Timurid invasion at the end of the fourteenth century, a number of other princely states emerged. They were to express their individuality in extremely varied ways, by calling upon local traditions or on the contrary by importing both stylistic models and architects from Persia, Egypt, or Iraq.

Bengal

At the time of the sultanate of Gaur, the absence of building stone in Bengal, as in the Punjab, furthered the continuance of a brick-constructed architecture in the pre-Muslim tradition. This necessity meant that the use of ceramic tiles seems to have been slightly more widespread than in Delhi. The oldest enameled tiles from this area are those found on the tomb known as Eklakhi, which is assumed to be that of Sultan Jalal al-Din of Gaur (who died in 1431).[102]

A specific type of ceramic tile emerged in Gaur at the end of the fifteenth century, several specimens of which are now preserved in the Victoria and Albert Museum, London.[103] Some of these tiles are molded in relief and painted in underglaze colored in releif and painted in underglaze colored enamel, a decoration comparable to that of Timurid tiles from Herat or Samarkand. A second type of tile was designed specifically to cover architectural moldings (openings and door frames); painted blue and white, they appear on the tower called the Firuz Minar ("turquoise minaret") in Gaur, among other places. A final type is represented by tiles in the shape of a niche or spandrel that present, on an even ground, polychrome-painted decoration of the "black line" type in the time-honored Timurid tradition.[104] In addition, other monuments in Bengal—such as the mosques of Tantipara and Lotan—also bear ceramic decoration.[105]

The Deccan

Following the conquest of Daulatabad by `Ala al-Din Khalji, the Deccan became a transition zone in which Yadavas and Khaljis, Tughluqs and the subjects of Vijayanagar fought for supremacy. In 1347, `Ala al-Din Bahman Shah laid the bases of the Bahmanid kingdom in Gulbarga (1347–1527). Under his successors, continual conflicts with the kingdom of Vijayanagar resulted in the forced settlement of populations of Persians, Arabs, and Turks, known as *affaqi* ("emigrants"). In terms of architectural ceramics, however, this immense south Indian province occupies pride of place.

Mahmud Gawan originally came from Gilan in Iran. Arriving in India at the Bahmani court of Bidar, he occupied various posts before becoming vizier to Muhammad Shah Bahmani III (1463–82). In 1472 he had a *madrasa* built at Bidar, a monument that numbers among the most remarkable in the entire city. On the one side, its court borrows its plan from the classical "Iranian" four-*iwan* model, with two tiers of cells. However, the bulbous shape of the prayer hall dome, undoubtedly the first of this form in India, is more comparable to that of Gawhar Shad at Herat. The extensive use of ceramics on the facade is surprising in a region that at that time had little tradition in such decoration. The decor includes small glazed bricks in the manner of Timurid-period *banna`i*, used in particular to clad the minarets, although only the one to the northeast remains standing today. A large-scale calligraphic frieze in Thuluth script executed in cut-tile mosaic runs right around the building. As for the arch spandrels, they are lined in polychrome "black line" tiling. The large epigraphic frieze and the other ceramic decorations are of the highest quality, rivaling even the central Asian Timurid heritage that served as their starting point, suggesting that they might have been created by immigrant artists.

Staying in Bidar, the palace and the mausoleum of `Ala al-Din Ahmad II (1436–58) also possessed important ceramic decoration. The spandrels of the entrance to the Takht Mahal ("throne room") were decorated with the *shir-o khorshid* motif ("lion and sun," although, as at the Shir-dar *madrasa* in Samarkand, they are actually tigers). The decoration, today in an extreme state of disrepair, was carefully surveyed by G. Yazdani in 1947.[106] Unusually, the decorative ground is formed by turquoise blue hexagonal tiles, the subjects being composed of blue, yellow, and brown rectangles.

The extraordinarily beautiful panels that graced the Divan-i `Am palace probably date from the restoration of the building undertaken in 1463, after the sack of Bidar by Mahmud Khalji of Malwa. Although severely damaged today, the restoration proposed by Yazdani enables us to see the astonishing virtuosity of these decorations, which take the form of large colored panels with complex arabesques reminiscent of wall hangings. As for the sovereign's tomb, the vestiges of the cut-tile mosaic decoration that survive—in particular on the intrados of the facade archway—are of the highest quality.

At Golconda, the southern facades and the spandrels of some of the niches at the mausoleum of the sultan Ibrahim (died 1580) also preserve elements of decorative cut-tile mosaic. The French traveler Jean Thévenot, who visited the area in 1667, noted in his account the presence of colored ceramic decorations adorning the tomb.

Another monument remarkable for its tile decoration survives at Hyderabad: the Ashur Khana. Although the monument itself was built in 1598, the ceramic mosaic decoration actually dates to 1612. The ornamental panels that, where preserved, reach almost 3 meters in height display an exuberant design of flowers and serrated leaves spouting from vases, together with the sinuous outlines of trees and calligraphic cartouches, all executed in glazes of vibrant turquoise, emerald green, saffron yellow, and coral red.

The Chini Mahal at Daulatabad owes its name "Porcelain Palace" to the blue-and-white ceramic cladding on the facade. According to J. Burton-Page, although the building is Bahmani in terms of architectural style, it has occasionally been ascribed to the period of the Nizam Shahi dynasty (1491–1633). The tiles remaining on the facade are underglaze-painted, the decoration emerging as a white reserve on the blue cobalt ground. The interiors of the niches on either side of the main entrance are also decorated with white interlace on a blue ground; the border motifs are composed of a sequence of white medallions over a blue ground. In their two-tone color scheme and decorative style, these tiles are quite different from the other Indian tiles discussed here, appearing closer to those in other "china houses," such as that of Ulugh Beg in Samarkand. The style and all-over effect of the floral composition recall textile art and imply a date somewhere in the second half of the sixteenth century.

Malwa

Khalji architecture in Malwa presents many examples of ceramic revetment executed in various techniques. The earliest literary testimony of *kashi* (ceramic tilework) from Mandu is certainly that of `Ali ibn Mahmud Kirmani.[107] In several places he mentions the presence of Iranian artists and men of letters at the court of Mandu. He observes, for example, that in A.H. 845/A.D. 1442 a number of Persian craftsmen executed inscriptions and decorations in *kashi* on the walls of the Bambihisht *madrasa*: "Persian craftsmen made inscriptions in Thuluth and *mohaqqeq* characters executed in ceramic tiles (*kashi-kari*) on the door, walls, and at the top of the ceiling of surpassing beauty; they deployed such skill in laying out the interlace that the engineers could hardly believe their eyes; they made the colored ceramic designs on the dome ceiling."[108] This *madrasa*, which later became the Khalji mausoleum, has unfortunately been almost entirely destroyed and nothing remains of the ceramic decoration.

In Mandu—as in Delhi—the most common type of ceramic tile is the square monochrome tile, generally turquoise, or more rarely cobalt blue. The polychrome effects are obtained by juxtaposing tilework and stone (pink calcareous sandstone or, more rarely, marble). These tiles are sometimes arranged in the form of stars or diamonds, or else cut out and fitted into architectural niches. This type of decoration is to be found in the Friday Mosque and Malik Mughith's Mosque, among others. A different type of decoration (observed at the Jahaz Mahal and Dai-ka Mahal) takes the form of an array of tiles of various colors (in particular turquoise, cobalt, yellow, white, and green), cut out and inlaid in repeat patterns.

The third type of tile encountered in Mandu is painted. Rare in central India, especially in pre-Mughal times, there are traces of such tiles in the palace *hammam*, at the Chishti Khan-ka Mahal, and at the Malkom-ki Kothi. The only type of tile missing is thus glazed brick, i.e., *banna'i*, which is hardly surprising considering that we are concerned here with masonry architecture.

The majority of these monuments cannot be precisely dated and, moreover, the decoration of a number of them may well have been added at a later date. To be able to identify the motifs and assign them to a chronology, it is therefore necessary to compare or link them to architecture from other areas or to other arts.

Founded in 1432, as an inscription on the entrance attests, Malik Mughith's comprises a square court bordered by galleries. The entrance, at the top of a flight of steps, used to be capped by a dome supported on columns that has since caved in. The base of this cupola contains a considerable number of pink sandstone panels inlaid with cut-tile turquoise elements arrayed in a geometrical interlace pattern. This sort of alternating design recalls the turquoise stars on bricks at Maragha, although the architectural forms and the building materials are at a far remove from those of the Iranian world. The *mihrabs* in this mosque are also adorned with turquoise niches.

The most majestic monument in Mandu is undoubtedly the Friday Mosque (*jame`*). Built on an earthwork almost 5 meters high, its imposing plan is a square whose sides measure 97.4 meters. The entrance projects from the facade and consists of a square room crowned by a dome. The exterior revetment on the base of the dome's drum is embellished with a crenellated "sugarloaf" motif in light relief, the interstices of which are inlaid with turquoise tile plaques. This type of decoration is also found, among other places, on the walls of the Man Mandir at Gwalior. Inside the domed hall, a narrow band with a star and diamond motif in blue tiles runs above the windows. Opposite the entrance portal, a

♦ Ceramic friezes, Man Mandir, Gwalior (India), end of the fifteenth century. Ceramic decoration is something of a rarity in the stone architecture of central India. The crenellation and cross motif inlaid with turquoise tilework shown here, however, also appears at Mandu (although without the frieze of ducks).

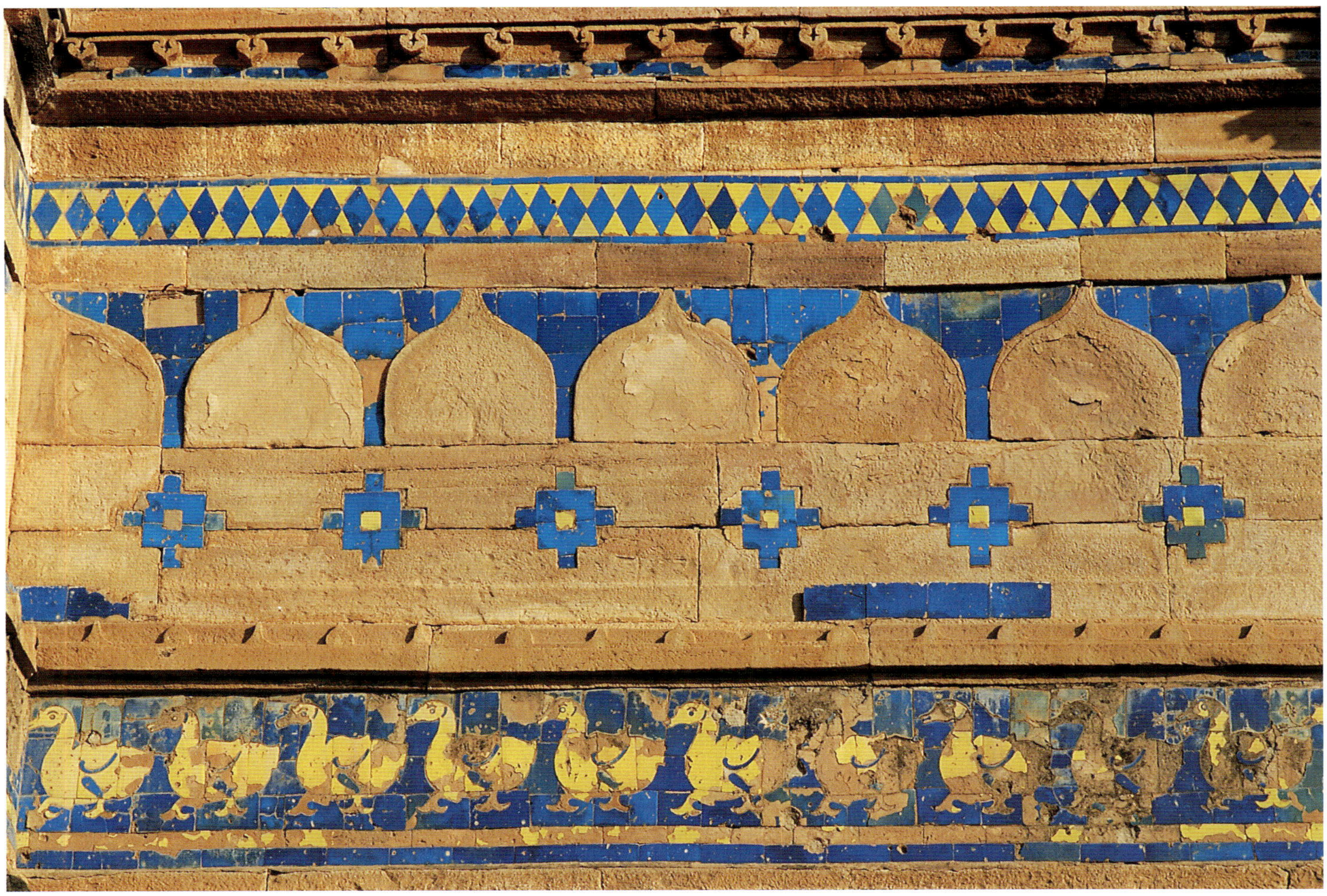

second door opens onto the mosque's courtyard, the whole perimeter of which is ringed by galleries pierced by arcades. The *qibla* wall is decorated by a large black stone *mihrab*, above which appear more "sugarloaf" crenellations bordered by turquoise tilework. The monuments located within the royal enclave (*dowlat-khane*) include a *hammam*. It should be noted that *hammams* were rare before Mughal times, although there is also one in Bidar near the royal palace dating from the same period.[109] Its location close to the mosque of Dilavar and to the center of the ancient *dowlat-khane* would seem to indicate that its construction should be assigned to the last years of the reign of Hushang or to that of Mahmud, but the absence of systematic excavations makes such dates hypothetical.[110]

The principal hall of the *hammam* in the *dowlat-khane* is octagonal and topped by a cupola pierced by stellar apertures. All eight sides bear arches whose spandrels are decorated with polychrome tiles of the "black line" type. Although these tiles have suffered serious damage, the motifs, underscored in black and forming a floral interlace pattern in turquoise, cobalt, and yellow on a white ground, remain visible. In design, these tiles recall those from mausoleums in the Shah-i Zinda at Samarkand, although the latter differ in having a blue ground.[111]

A similar decoration appears on some tiles at Mazar-i Sharif (c. 1480) and in the mausoleum of Abu Nasir Parsa at Balkh (end of the fifteenth century), but once again on a blue ground.[112] It is clear that this kind of floral arabesque decoration on a white ground employing the "black line" technique remained rare, especially in the first half of the fifteenth century.

The *Ma`ather-e Mahmudshahi* relates that artists from the Khorasan took part in the construction of a "gilded palace" (*kushk-i zarrin*) lying between the two lakes in the royal enclave, the Munj Talao and Kaphur Talao.[113] It is likely that this "gilded palace" is the building today called Jahaz Mahal ("ship palace"). This palace is a long, two-storied construction nearly 130 meters in length, although its width measures only 15.2 meters and its height 9.7 meters. In its current state, the building bears traces of additions and restoration work, notably on the large staircase of the main facade, which must surely date from the time of Jahangir's stay in the area in 1617.[114] The opposite ends of the building are crowned by little pavilions with triple domes. In the center of the facade facing the Munj Talao, there is a square, two-tiered turret also capped with a dome. The facade was at one stage lined with a colored decoration, fragments of which can still be seen. The mortar on the exterior of the walls at the Jahaz Mahal, in particular on the middle tower, bears the imprint of cut-tilework in the shape of a letter S. This same assemblage can also be seen well preserved inside the tower, in the cupola of the lower hall, the S's there being in alternate blue, green, and yellow. The interior of the cupola on the upper story is decorated with a frieze bearing an interlace pattern displaying the same color scheme. A broad string course decorated in mosaic inlay with a pattern of head-to-tail fleurons girdles the drum of the central dome; both the outline and internal surface of these fleurons was once bedecked in polychrome cut-tilework. Below this, there was a narrow frieze of chevrons, but today only the imprint remains. A little lower still, just above the *chajja* (eaves), the inlaid ceramic elements were arranged in a frieze of rosettes alternating with multi-lobed cartouches. Practically all of the colored glaze on this ceramic has disappeared—except for the occasional bright flash of blue or yellow—and nowadays only the terracotta support remains visible. An illustration in a manuscript of the *Candayana* at present in the Prince of Wales Museum, Bombay, shows architectural decoration in which crenellated friezes alternate with ones decorated with fleurons. Indeed, the similarity between these two types of decoration supports the attribution of this manuscript to Mandu. In addition to the S and chevron tiles and to the mosaic fleuron friezes, other large tilework panels, in all probability *haft-rangi*, decorated the middle tower, as well as the space between the lintel and the balcony of the central door to the palace, on the Kaphur Talao side. Of the original decoration, whose opulence was the reason for its ancient name of "gilded palace," only some white stucco florets and the impress of tiles in the mortar remain today.

The Jal Mahal ("water palace") is a rectangular building with two parallel vaulted galleries and a floor giving on to a balcony. The whole building was once covered with a marble revetment that today survives solely around an isolated doorframe facing the lake. The top of the facade presents a series of large stone rhombus shapes inlaid with blue ceramic to form epigraphic cartouches inscribed with a mazelike Kufic. The text within these cartouches is rather hard to read but can be classified as a sovereign inscription (*al-sultan al-`azam . . .*), a style of inscription very rare in India. Indeed, to date, this is the only known example. It is on the other hand rather frequent in the Iranian world and in central Asia, and appears (among other places) inside the cupola of the *jami`* mosque (Friday Mosque) at Varamin (1322–26) and in the shrine of Ansari at Gazurgah, near Herat (1428),[115] as well as in Samarkand. The four corners of each cartouche present alternating designs in high relief showing five-pointed stars and cloud forms resembling Chinese *ch`i*. The blue ceramic inlay that once decorated these cells has almost totally vanished. Whereas in Iran or in central Asia the labyrinthine Kufic inscriptions were executed in *banna`i*—or sometimes in inlaid tile mosaic—ceramic decoration here is inset into the stone. Apart from the calligraphic frieze on the tomb of Darya Khan (see below), very few examples of epigraphic decoration remain in Mandu. The inscriptions in *kashi* on the Bambihisht *madrasa* mentioned in *Ma`ather-e Mahmudshahi* have not survived, the only remains on the monument being the inscriptions in stone inlay. On the level of the dados on an upper floor of the palace, imprints of geometrical figures impressed into the mortar once again suggest the use of tiles; these would have formed a composition of triangles and trapezoids in a stellar decoration of Timurid type. Apart from an insignificant blue fragment, however, only imprints remain; at a later stage, moreover, the walls were rendered with plaster that covered up the design.

The Dai-ka Mahal is a tomb that stands on a spacious terrace that was formerly occupied by other buildings. To the western edge of the terrace lies a mosque whose ceiling betrays traces of ceramic tiling. The tomb proper is square in plan, capped by a dome whose form recalls the architecture of the Deccan. The monument possesses arched windows in the middle of each wall; inside, above those openings, stands a long line of sixteen blind niches decorated with inlaid turquoise tiles. Above this, around the base of the drum, runs a circular band ornamented with a tile frieze of turquoise and yellow head-to-tail fleurons.[116]

The tomb known today as the Dai-ki Chotti Bahen-ka Mahal stands on a double terrace. Laid out to an octagonal ground plan, the walls of the tomb are pierced by four arched openings facing in the direction of the four cardinal points; the four other walls are decorated with blind windows. At the top of the octagon formerly stood a *chajja*, of which only the corbels remain. Above, the sides of the octagon bifurcate to form a sixteen-sided drum on which rests the dome. This building, whose stone facings in places incorporate carved rosettes and small niches, once contained an extensive colored decorative scheme.

The sixteen-faced drum supporting the dome, for example, is decorated with a frieze comprising a pattern of festooned fleurons in which turquoise tiles alternate with white tiles underglaze-painted in cobalt tracery. In former times, the whole cupola was lined in a turquoise-blue revetment of which today only scant traces remain. This type of decoration is reminiscent of the great domes of central Asia, such as that crowning the Bibi Khanum Mosque and on one of the two cupolas of the mausoleum of Qadizada Rumi in Samarkand. However, whereas in the latter the fleuron frieze adjoins the turquoise cladding of the cupola, here the band is separated from it by a cable motif carved into the masonry.

The external revetments on domes in Mandu have all but vanished, although a considerable number still show almost imperceptible scraps of color that leads one to suppose that the majority were once turquoise. Examples include the cupolas of the central tower at the Jahaz Mahal, the pavilion known as Baz Bahadur, and the two octagonal pavilions in Nalcha.

The tomb known as Darya Khan—the name of an officer in the service of Mahmud II (1510–26)—was surely one of the most sumptuous *kashi* monuments in all Mandu. Square in plan, the monument possesses a central dome flanked by four smaller domes standing at each corner. Although today only the minutest traces subsist, one can still make out, in particular on the west facade, significant quantities of rectangular paneling bearing the imprint of underglaze-painted tiles; in places tiny fragments of color remain affixed to the support. Just beneath the *chajja*, a sizable epigraphic frieze used to run round the whole tomb. Today, the frieze, of which only a very few fragments remain, consists of white Thuluth characters on a cobalt ground crisscrossed by turquoise tracery and bordered by yellow bands. Below this, a band of small stone "sugarloaf" crenellations is edged by cut and inlaid tiles. Although practically nothing of the decoration has survived, the remnants conserved today testify to work of the highest quality.

The Chishti Khan-ka Mahal is a group of constructions standing on a cliff edge in a fairly remote location; severely damaged, the ensemble is organized around a courtyard the north and south wings of which can still be seen. One of the rooms in the south wing preserves traces of a rich ornamental scheme in which fresco and ceramic alternate. The tops of the walls are painted with trails in the shape of clouds; above, at the base of the drum of the small dome that roofs the room, runs a frieze of tiles that have almost entirely lost their glaze. In spite of their pitiful state, these tiles still present traces of the original enamel in a motif of interlace white ribbonwork forming a rosette, the dominant hues being blue and yellow. To my knowledge this type of tile exists nowhere else in India, although it is vaguely reminiscent of early sixteenth-century tilework from Constantinople. Above the tile frieze, thick ribs painted cobalt blue intersect up on the cupola, and the webs at the intersection of the blue bands were originally frescoed over. Although the construction may date from the Mughal period, the tilework bears no resemblance to any produced in that era.[117]

The Malkom-ki Kothi is a little-known monument in the village of Nalcha ten kilometers from Mandu. Although today situated some 500 meters distant, the kiosk once formed part of the palace and garden ensemble around Nalcha's lake. Its architectural style suggests it was built during the reign of Mahmud's successor, Ghiyath al-Din Khalji. It incorporates a flat-roofed rectangular building together with two brick-built octagonal domed pavilions that were formerly richly decorated with *kashi*. Between the summit of the arched window bays and the cupola above, nets of tiles painted turquoise, cobalt, and green framed three levels of *haft-rangi* panels that have now entirely disappeared. The middle register, however, presents a frieze of white and cobalt-blue head-to-tail fleuron motifs. Above the *chajja*, at the base of the cupola, on one of the faces of the octagon, one panel of painted tiles still displays the odd fragment of tilework. A yellow "cloud" pattern can be discerned, accompanied by a white interlace motif underscored in turquoise on a cobalt ground, in a design reminiscent of decorative arts from the Timurid era. It should be noted, however, that the "cloud" pattern itself is seldom met with in Timurid tilework, and its origin should probably be sought in the art of the manuscript, since this motif is frequently found on bindings and in illuminations. In the decoration found on ceramic tiles of the "black line" type, such "clouds" patterns are more frequent in Iznik tilework than that of Indian or Iranian regions. The non-standard size of these tiles and the regular, scrolling trail pattern imply that these panels were designed specifically for the monument.

The issue arises as to where and when the tiles in Mandu were executed and how they came to be used in a region dominated by stone building. It should be realized at the outset that no excavation campaign has as yet been carried out in Mandu. It is impossible to know, for example, if pottery kilns existed in Mandu itself. In spite of the successive occupations of the site, secure dates for the monuments have not yet been published. In Delhi, Gwalior, and in many monuments in Mandu, only tiles inset into the stone or the mortar can be found, adding notes of turquoise or yellow. In other monuments in Malwa and the Deccan, however, sizable panels of tiles were affixed to buildings constructed in stone and mortar. This method is poorly adapted to damp climates and the torrential rains of the monsoon; indeed, as we have seen, most monuments once clad in *kashi* have today lost much of their decoration. Moreover, setting up workshops specializing in ceramic painting in areas without brickyards required significant financial outlay, not only to recruit skilled craftsmen to construct the furnaces and to obtain the necessary raw materials and fuel, but more especially to obtain the considerable technical expertise that certain types of underglaze firing require. If `Ali ibn Mahmud Kirmani's account is to be believed, the craftsmen who carried out the *kashi* decorations in Mandu (at least as far as Mahmud Khalji's *madrasa* is concerned) were of Iranian extraction and adapted their stylistic repertory to suit local tastes.[118]

As has been demonstrated, certain motifs employed on Mandu tilework originated in the decorative arts of Iran and central Asia, but the forms were altered. A significant factor in this connection was Mahmud Khalji's campaign in Bidar (1461–63), a district that contains masterpieces in the art of *kashi*. The gateway of the Takht Mahal with its imposing *shir-o khorshid*, the large polychrome tile panels of the Divan-i `Am, and the *madrasa* of Mahmud Gawan show the extent to which Bidar had developed an output of ceramic tiles unique in all India. Other documents also attest to the fact that Mahmud Khalji brought with him painters and craftsmen such as Mawlana Mughith al-Din Naqqash and Mawlana Muhammad Almas Tarrash (a diamond-cutter) to Mandu.[119] In all probability, by opting deliberately for ceramic decoration in a number of monuments, Mahmud Khalji was keeping faith with the supreme artistic achievements of his time. If reference to an Iranian influence might be overstating the case, the decision to decorate in *kashi* a style of architecture so different from that built in Iran certainly suggests a pronounced taste for quotation. This practice, in defiance of the unfavorable climatic conditions and the technical limitations, would have bestowed a measure of prestige on constructions in the region.

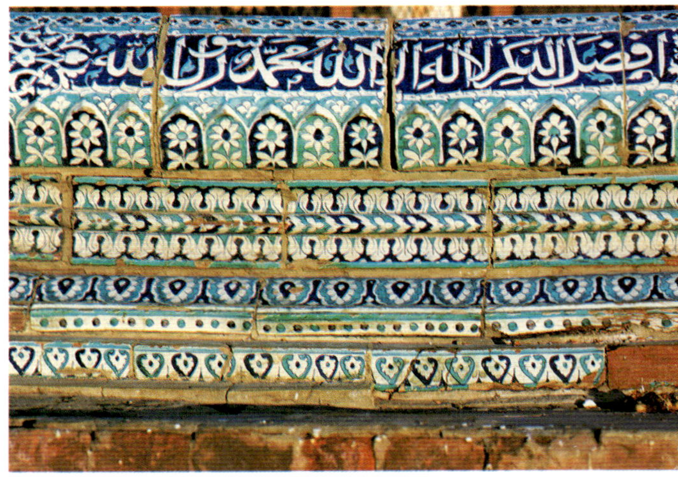

Blue and White in Sind and Punjab

TOMB OF BAHA' AL-DIN ZAKARIYA, MULTAN (PAKISTAN), 1262

ABOVE RIGHT

♦ The cenotaph of the much-revered figure buried in the tomb has recently been restored. The blue-and-white tile cladding bears the stamp of the "baroque" Mughal style of the eighteenth century, although it actually dates from the mid-twentieth.

BELOW

♦ Cenotaph finial. An inscription in Urdu provides a date of A.H. 1368/A.D. 1948–49, i.e., after Pakistan's independence.

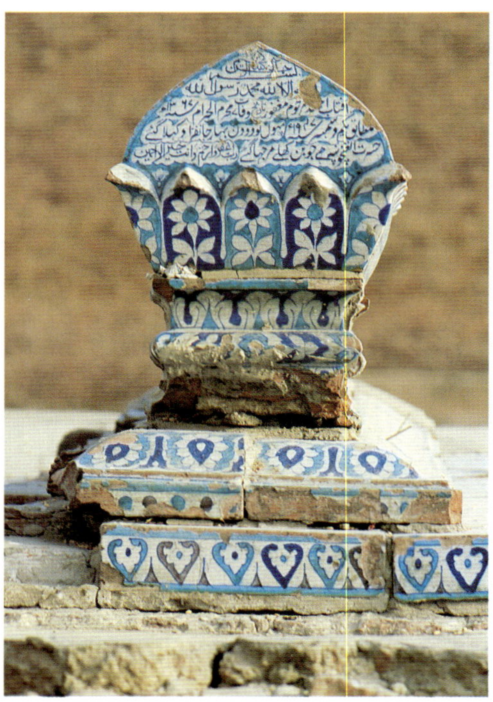

Buildings in the Indus valley, like those in nearby Iran, are primarily constructed out of brick, so ceramic revetment was more widely used than in central India. In reality, early constructions in the area appear very different nowadays from how they must have when first built. These changes are due to the restoration work undertaken in the past to safeguard the most venerated monuments, restorations that—in particular with regard to ceramic decorations—make exact dating a problematic task.

The earliest funerary monuments in the Indus valley did not incorporate glazed decors at all, ornamentation consisting of terracotta decoration and shapes built up from brick construction, as can be seen on the mausoleum of Shaykh Sadan near Multan (end twelfth–beginning of the thirteenth century).[120] Glazed tiles were undoubtedly used for the first time in this area in the small mausoleums at Adheri, where ceramic plaques decorated in molded relief and covered with a turquoise glaze are inlaid into a brick construction.[121]

Shah Yusuf Gardizi's tomb at Multan, constructed shortly after his death (1152), is a near-cubic single-story building. Today it is lined in ceramic tiling, most of which is painted in blue on a white ground, although part of it presents a molded relief decor. It is probable that most of the tiles were in fact made relatively recently, although they might replicate ancient models.

The tombs of Baha` al-Din Zakariya (or Shah Baha` al-Haqq, 1262), Shadna Shahid (1270), and Shams al-Din Tabrizi (1276; heavily restored in 1779), all three in Multan, present a quadrilateral ground plan with the walls sloping inwards, a second octagonal tier, and a dome on a drum studded with blue-and-white tiles.[122] These three tombs foreshadow a larger-scale construction in the same city, the mausoleum of Rukn-i `Alam. Erected, according to archival sources, by command of the sultan of Delhi, Ghiyath al-Din Tughluq, between 1320 and 1324 to honor the memory of a saintly personage, the mausoleum is thus contemporary with that of the sultan himself at Delhi. The two tombs differ fundamentally, however, in both materials and design, that in Delhi being built in stone and of relatively modest proportions, while the salient characteristic of the construction in Multan is a feeling of mass. The octagonal plan of a diameter of 27.5 meters is flanked by semicircular towers in the corners; the overall height is 35 meters and the internal diameter of the dome is 15 meters. Built essentially in brick with additional features in carved timber, the monument is decorated in diaperwork with touches of color provided by glazed ceramic. The monument stands on a substantial base with sloping sides up to the first tier, imparting a strong feeling of permanence and stability, while the

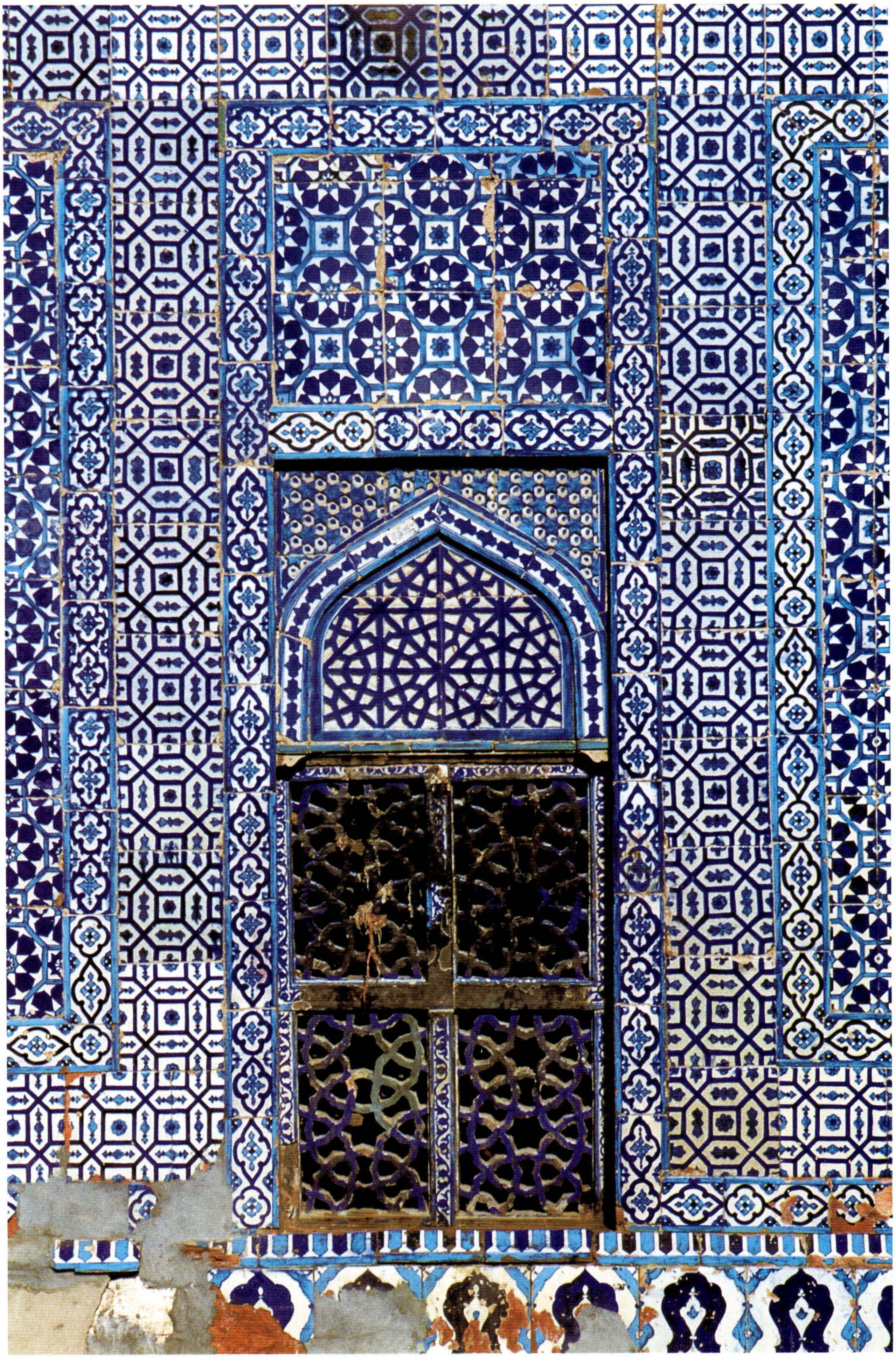

TOMB OF SHAH YUSUF GARDIZI, MULTAN (PAKISTAN)

♦ The individual buried in this monument died in 1152. The tilework seen cladding the tomb today, however, was added at a later stage and is still being restored and embellished.

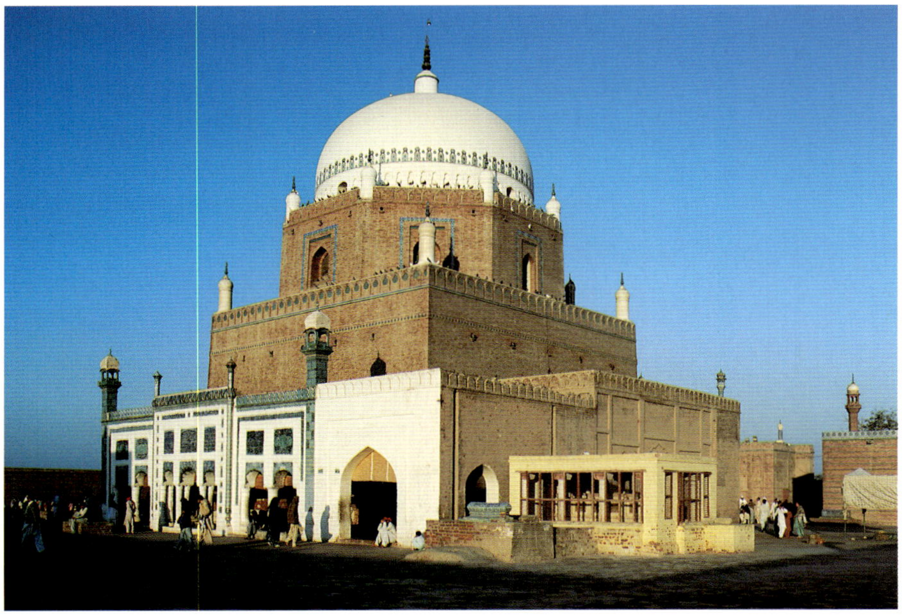

TOMB OF BAHA' AL-DIN ZAKARIYA, MULTAN (PAKISTAN), 1262

♦ The severe, massive architectural forms of this brick-built construction are enlivened by discreet touches of colored ceramic.

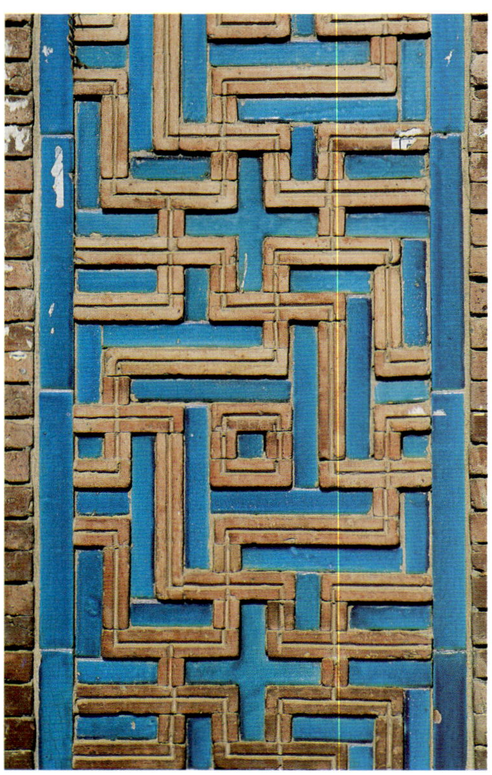

second level crowned by an ample cupola bestows a certain elegance.

Several later buildings resemble the mausoleum of Rukn-i `Alam, such as the tomb of Bibi Jawindi at Uch (1493). In this case, however, the first tier, though still octagonal and flanked by engaged towers, is more liberally decorated, featuring broad ceramic bands with cobalt and turquoise glazes on a white ground. Unfortunately, only half the elevation of the building remains. The mausoleum of Baha` al-Din Halim, also in Uch and dating from around the same time, is in a similar tradition; in spite of frequent restoration work, the monument is today in a dilapidated state. Its painted ceramic decoration in turquoise and cobalt on a white ground continues a tradition in Multan and Sind that has persisted, with varying degrees of success, to the present day. Other monuments, such as the tomb of Sayyid `Abd al-Wahhab Shah in Dera Din Panah and that of Taher Khan Nahar (early sixteenth century) in Sitpur, continued to conform to the general form of Rukn-i `Alam's mausoleum. Built in 1606, the tomb of Mirza Janibeyg Tarkhan Bin in Makli Hill presents an octagonal plan capped by a dome painted today in white. A brick-built monument, it possesses finely decorated external dados composed of blue and white hexagonal tiles, which are bordered by friezes showing plant motifs.

During the seventeenth and eighteenth centuries, the regions of Sind and Punjab were influenced artistically by the Mughal court, and this is reflected in the evolution of the decorative vocabulary of ceramic tilework. Mughal naturalistic floral elements (such as tulips, poppies, and baskets of fruit), originally derived from Western herbals, pop up on decors in Multan executed in the range of colors typical of the area (turquoise, cobalt, and white), as found on the tomb of Bibi Pak Daman (seventeenth century), that of Musa Pak (sixteenth–seventeenth centuries), and in the Taunsa Sharif Mosque near Dera Ghazi Khan (eighteenth century). Indeed, this ceramic art heritage has endured to this day.

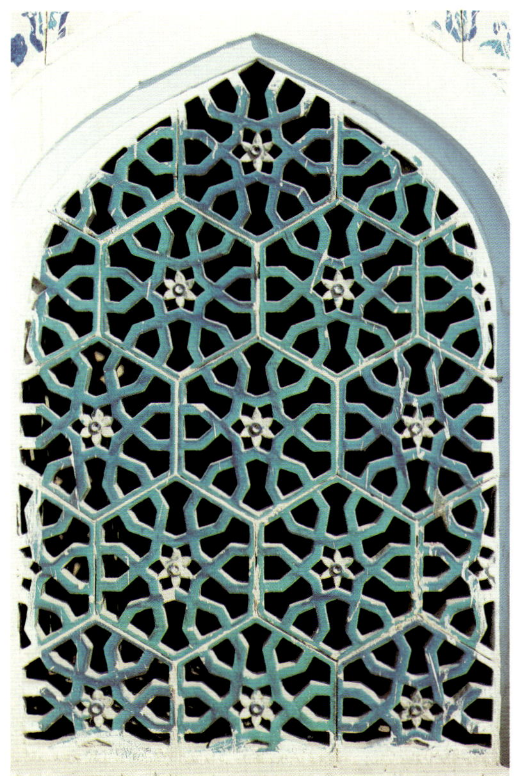

♦ Window with grille of turquoise blue glazed ceramic. Tomb of Shams al-Din Tabrizi, Multan (Pakistan). Constructed in 1276, the monument was restored in 1779.

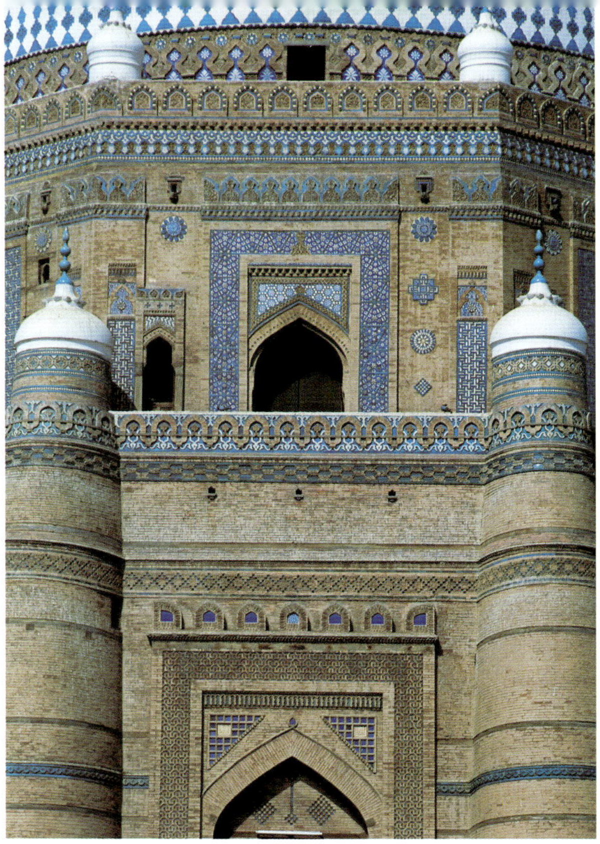

MAUSOLEUM OF RUKN-I ʿALAM, MULTAN (PAKISTAN), 1320–24

♦ Clad in ceramic tiles of considerable elegance, this sturdy brick construction is inspired by mausoleums in Iran and central Asia.

♦ This interlace geometric motif derives from the interplay between the plain brickwork and inset turquoise glazed ceramics.

♦ A panel showing an array of intersecting polygons. The interstices are set with turquoise and cobalt underglaze-painted ceramic elements on a white ground.

♦ A charming bouquet of flowers added to the monument at a late stage and betraying the influence of Mughal art from Lahore.

♦ The top of the facade has crenellations with elements in molded terracotta bordered by cut tilework.

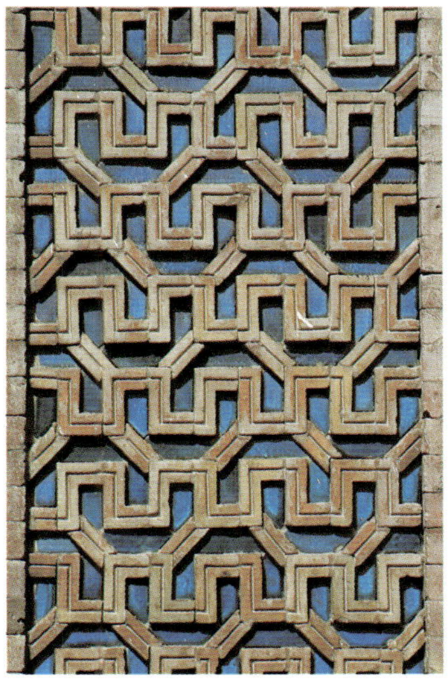

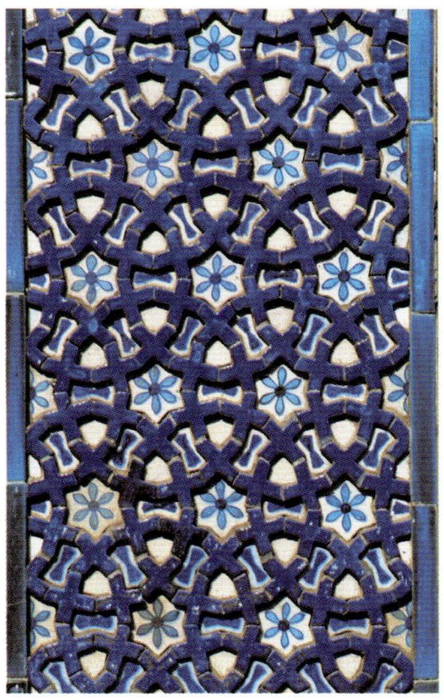

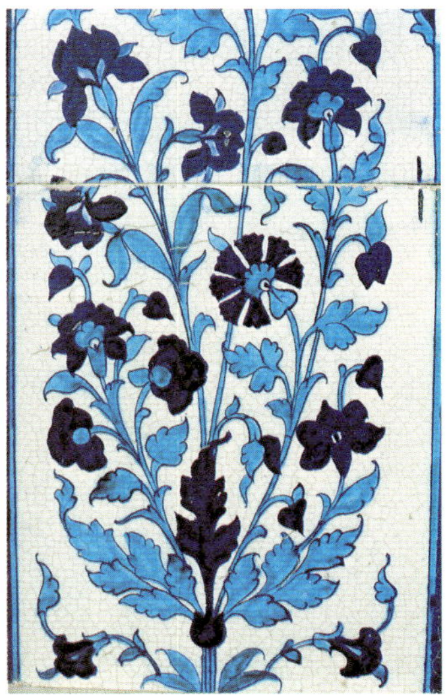

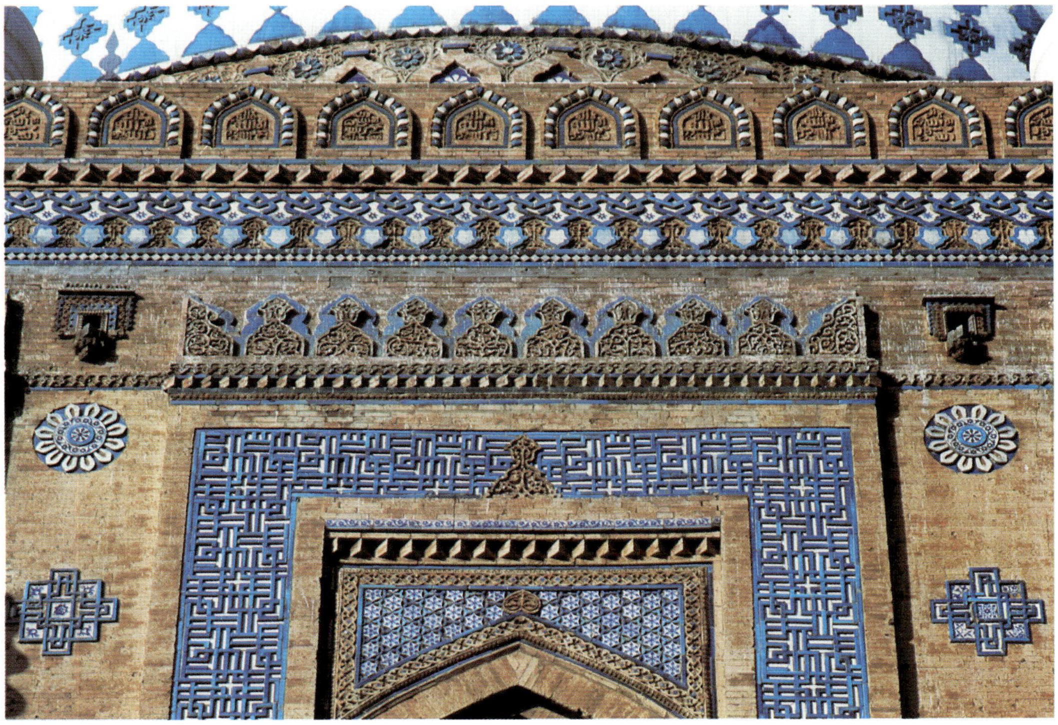

FOLLOWING DOUBLE PAGE

♦ Detail of the main facade, mausoleum of Bibi Jawindi, Uch (Pakistan), 1493. An extraordinary variety of motifs are employed; most of the tiles are decorated under the glaze.

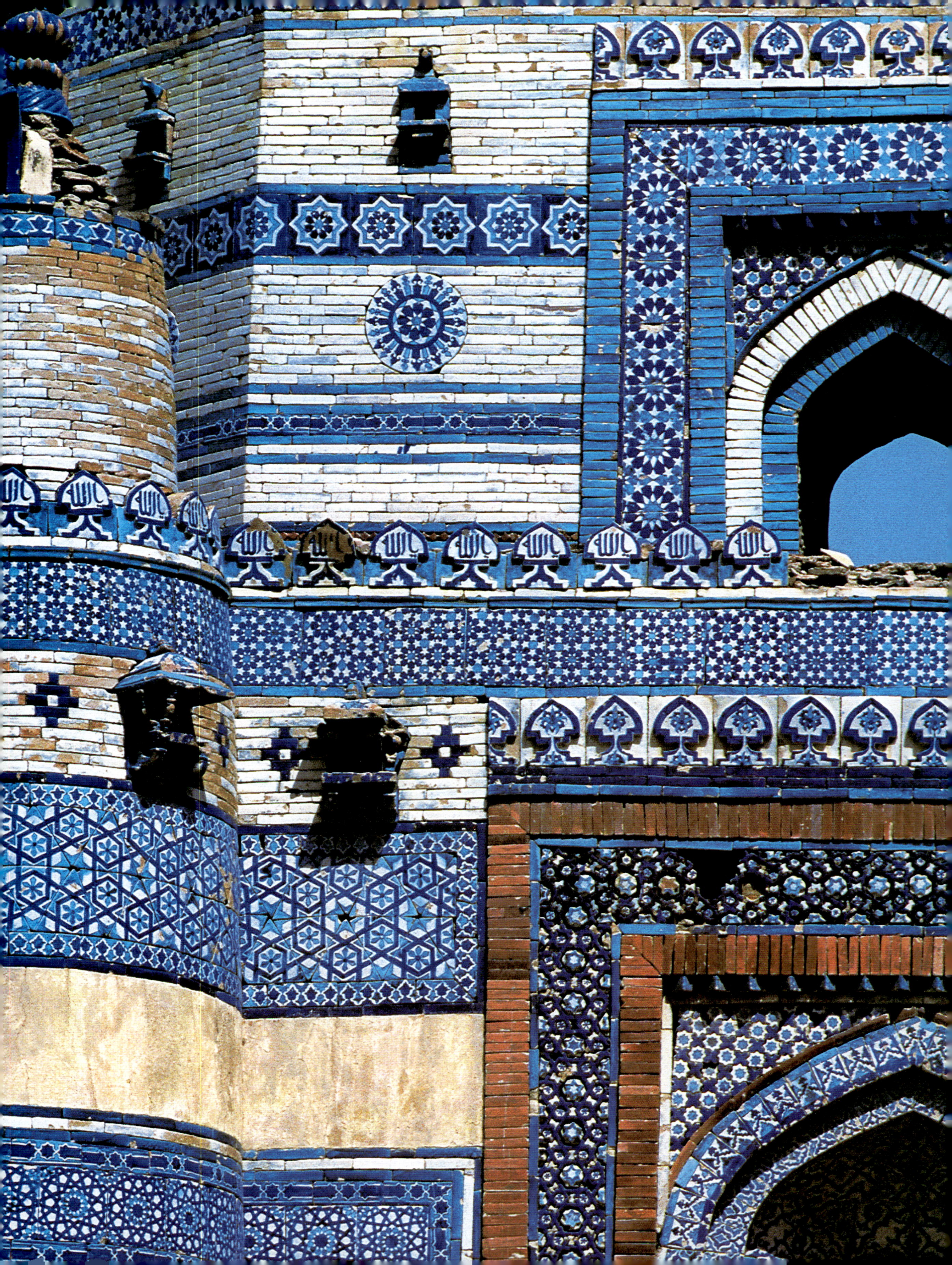

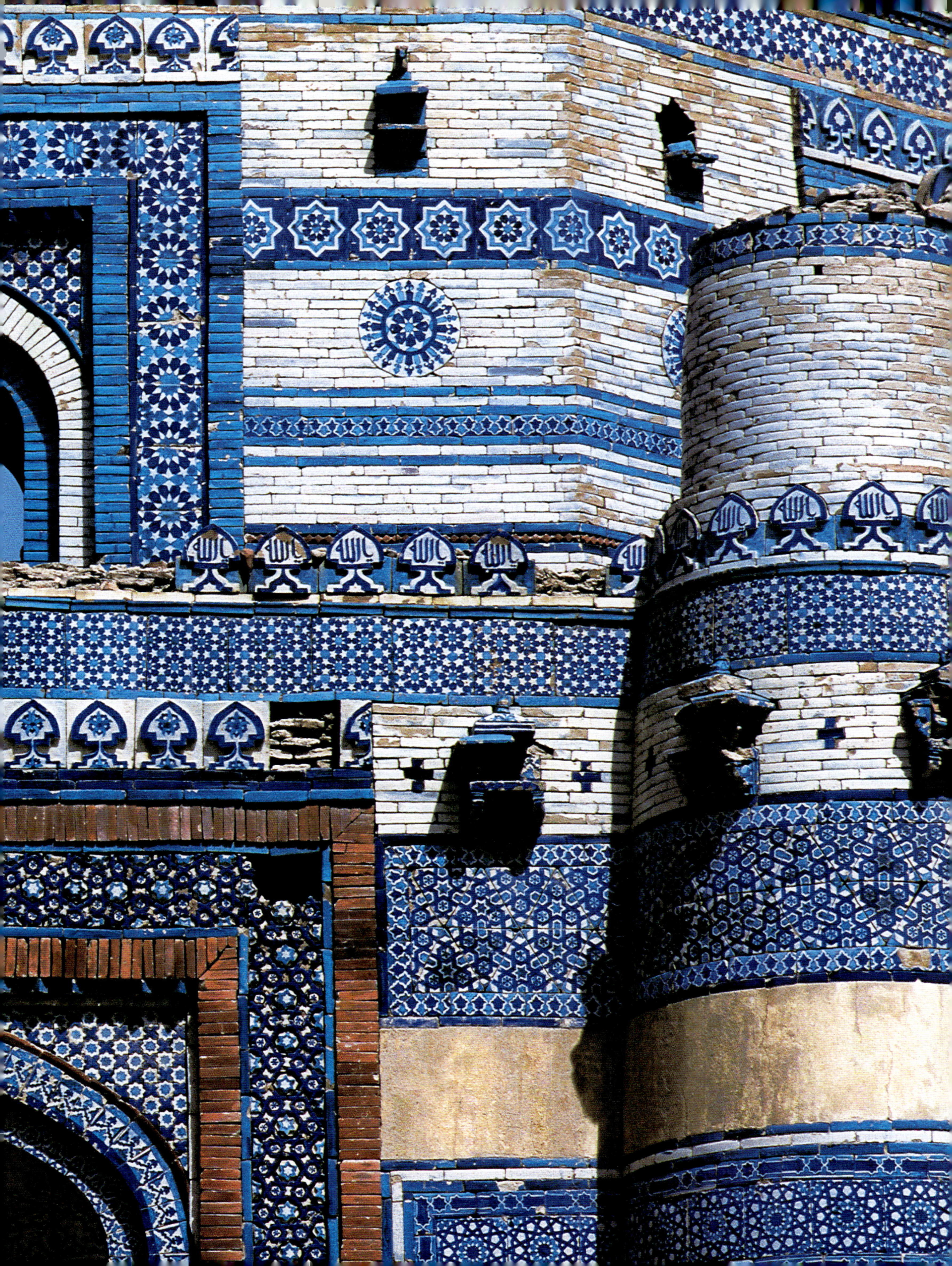

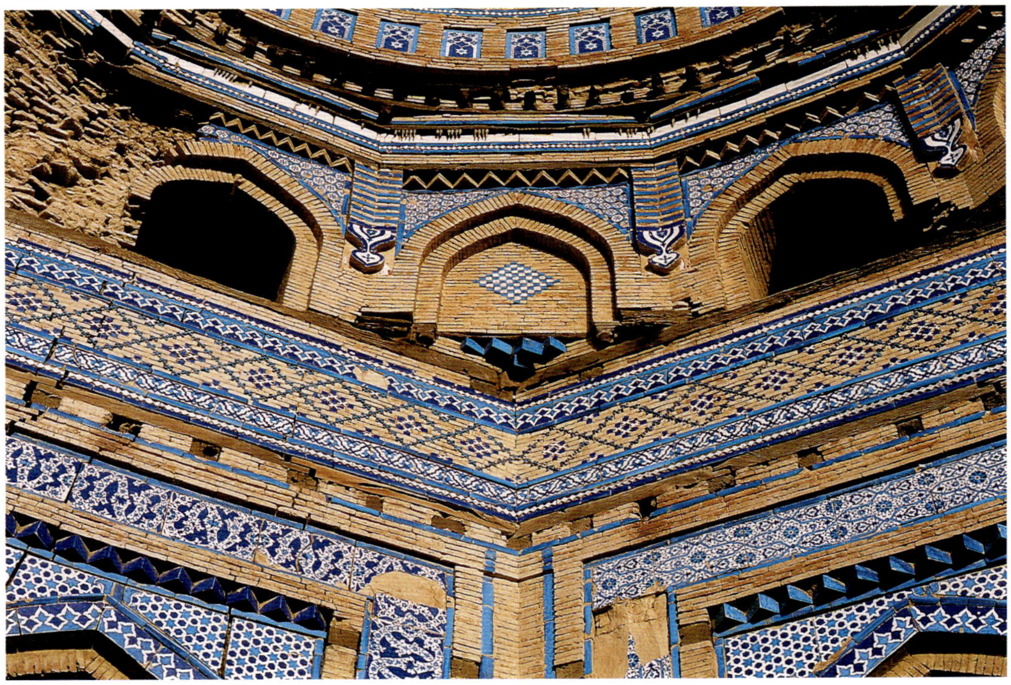

♦ Interior of the funerary hall, mausoleum of Baha' al-Din Halim, Uch (Pakistan), end of the fifteenth century. Built entirely in brick, it is decorated by large quantities of ceramics either of the *banna'i* type or underglaze-painted.

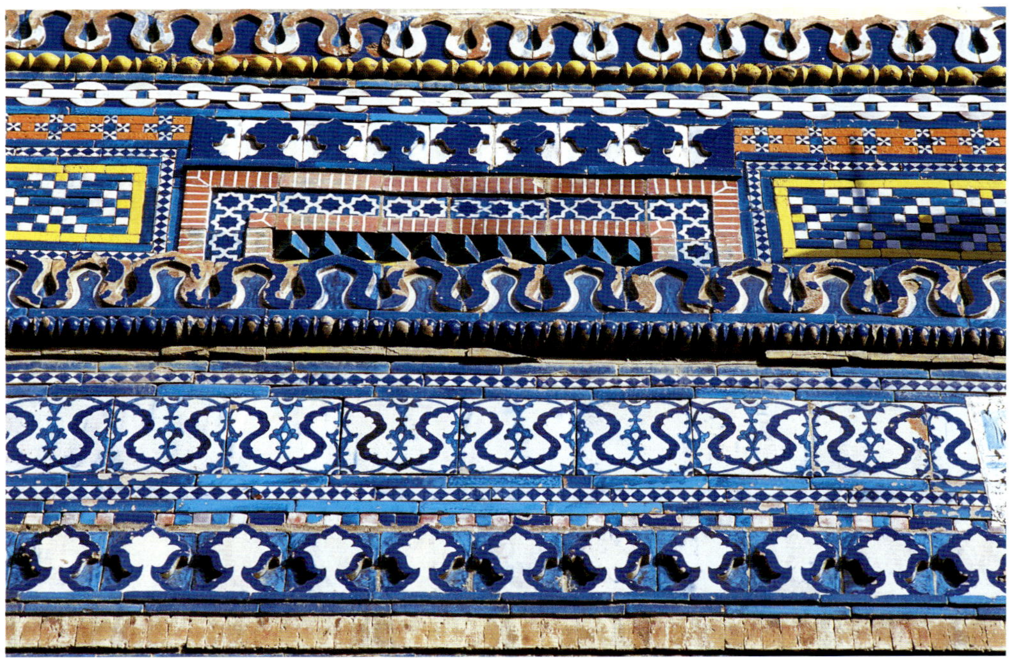

♦ Mausoleum of Taher Khan Nahar, Sitpur (Pakistan), early sixteenth century. The traditional color scheme of white and blue is here enlivened by hints of yellow and orange.

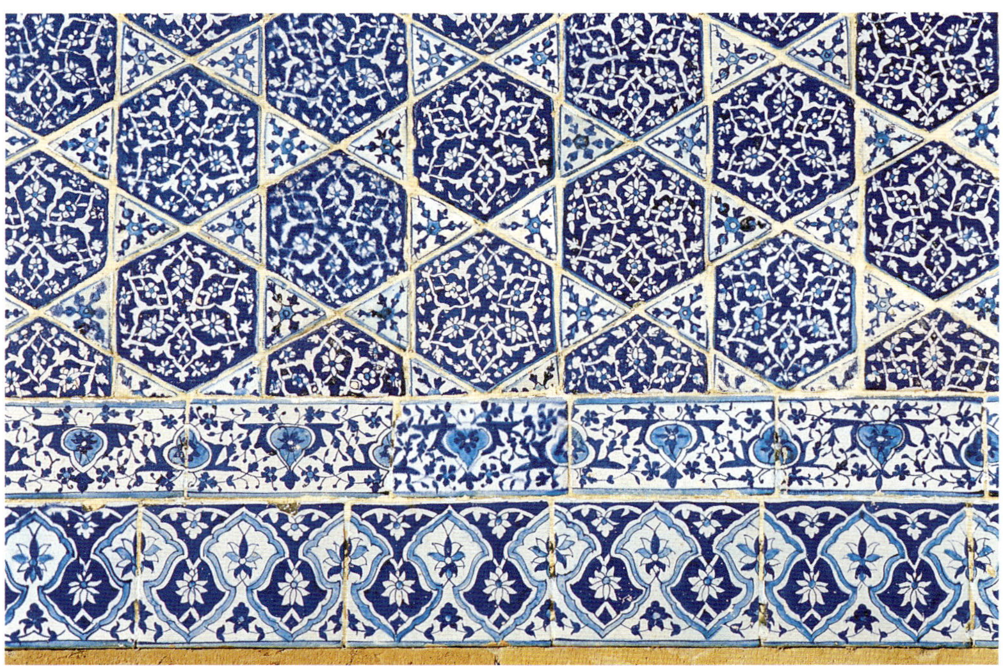

♦ Hexagonal and triangular tiles with underglaze painting decorating the external dados of the tomb of Mirza Janibeyg Tarkhan Bin, Makli Hill (Pakistan), 1606.

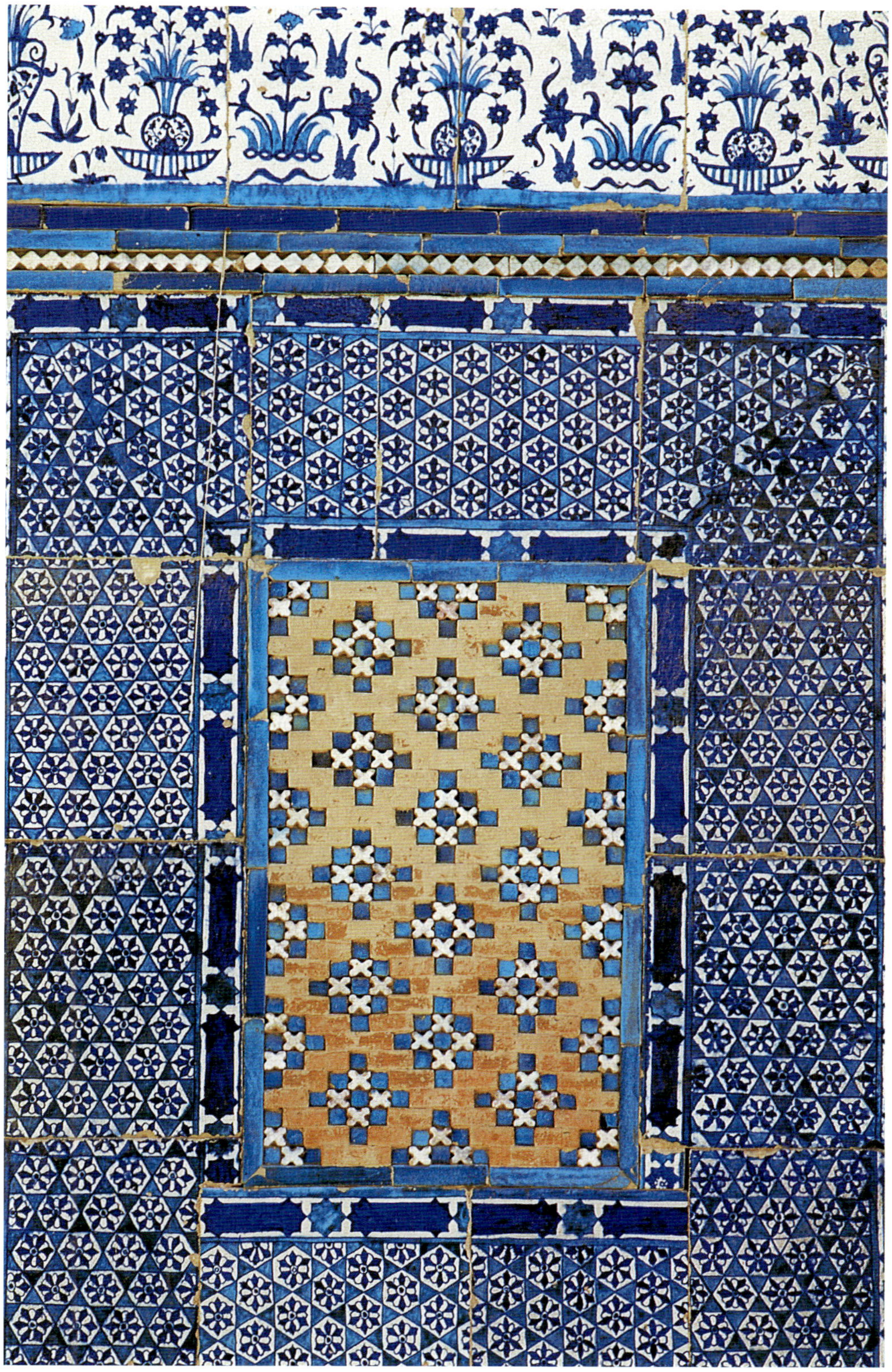

MOSQUE OF JALAL AL-DIN SURKH BUHKARI, UCH (PAKISTAN)

♦ Wall panel clad in underglaze-painted tiles: the frieze at the top with its vases teeming with flowers recalls the later Mughal style.

BELOW LEFT

♦ Here, the traditional fleuron frieze has lotus flowers in reserve on a cobalt ground.

BELOW

♦ Brick facing studded with cross shapes comprising blue squares in combination with white quatrefoil elements. Tomb of Jahanpasht, Uch (Pakistan).

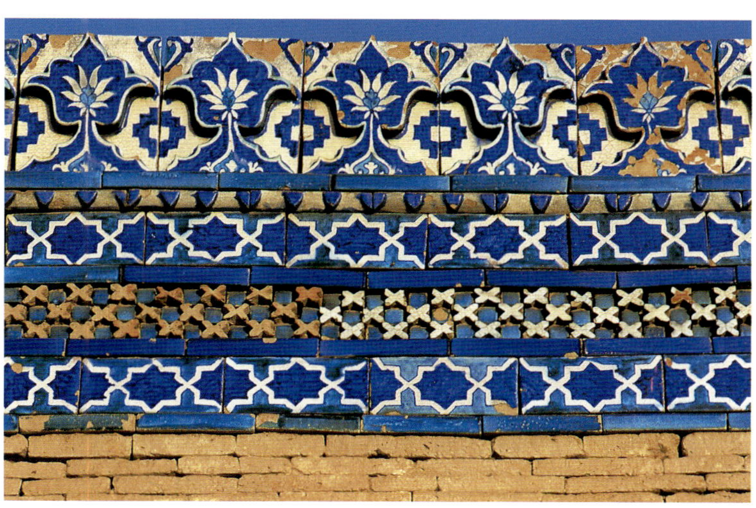

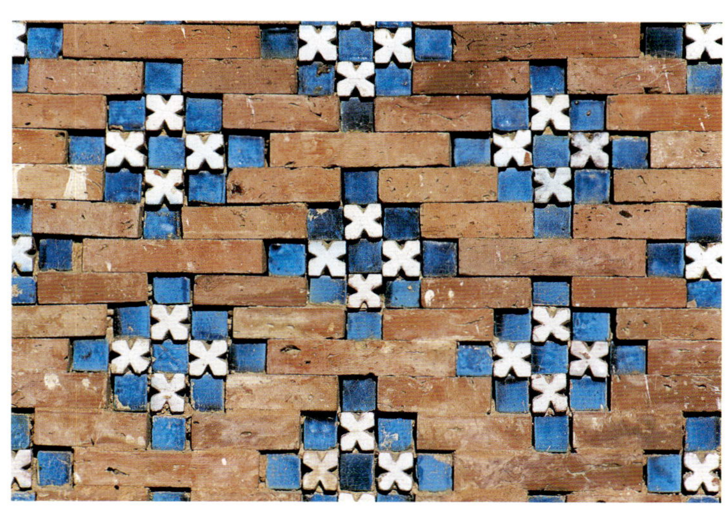

RIGHT

♦ Niche lined with star-shaped tiles around a central rectangle containing lines of poetry in Persian. Tomb of Sultan `Ali Akbar, Multan (Pakistan).

BELOW

♦ Turquoise and cobalt underglaze-painted tiles on a white ground, above a frieze containing a passage from a Persian poem. Sawi Mosque, Multan (Pakistan).

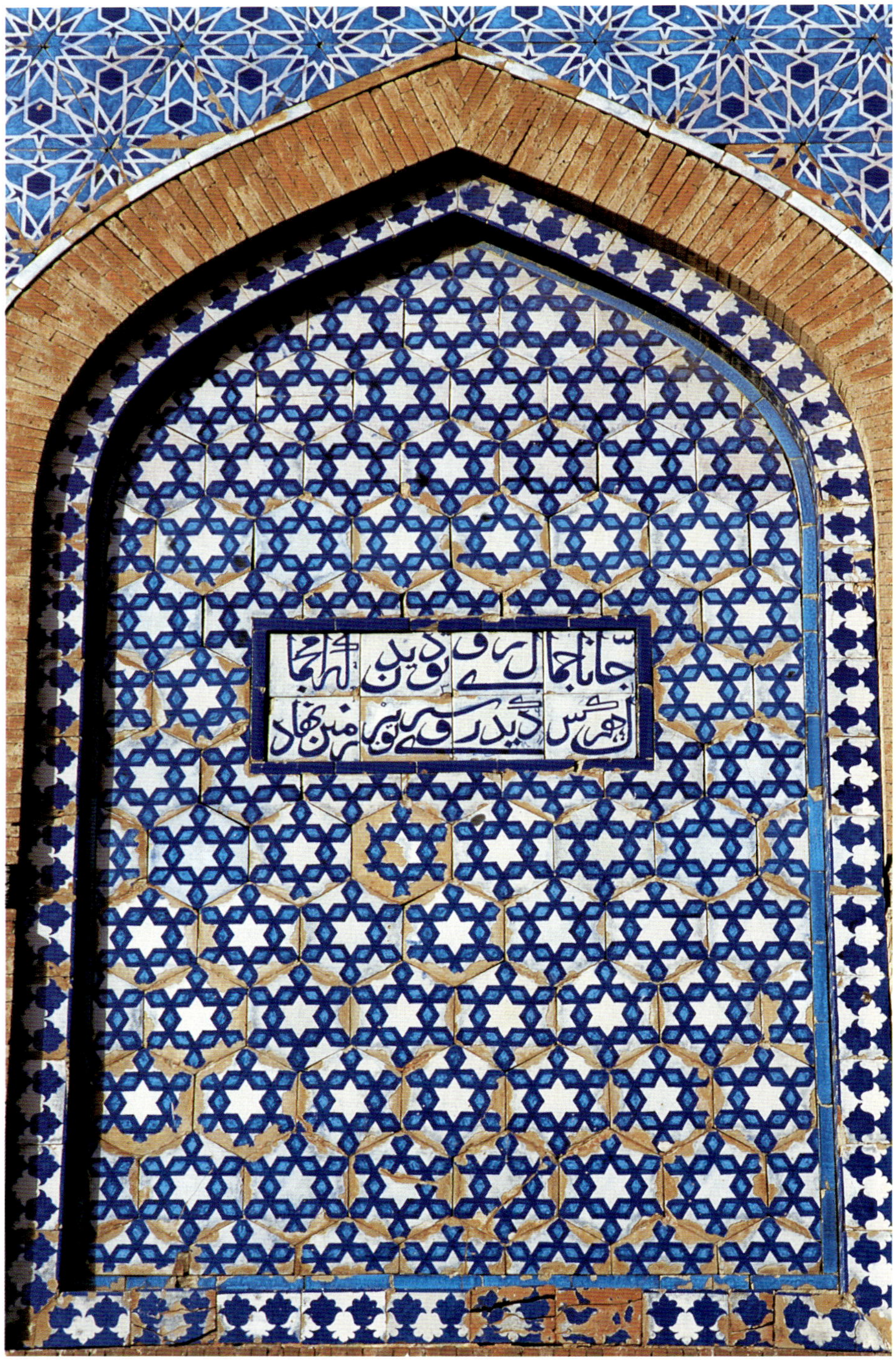

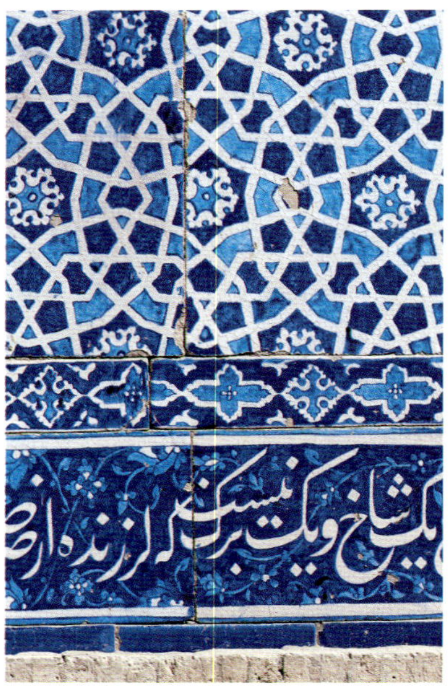

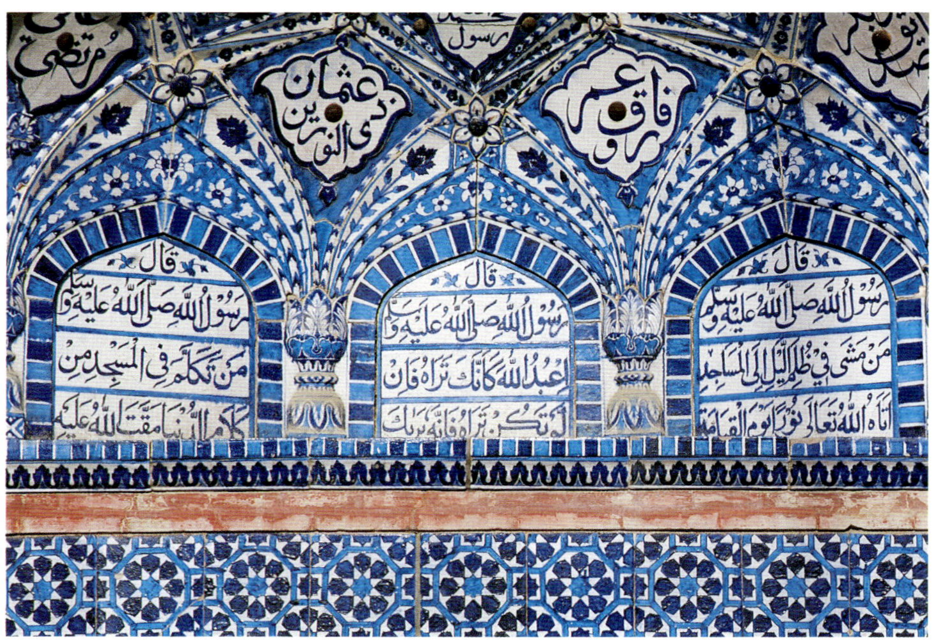

♦ Blind arcade, Durrani Saddzai Mosque. The decoration, in particular the leaves from which each arch springs, was influenced by eighteenth-century "baroque" Mughal models.

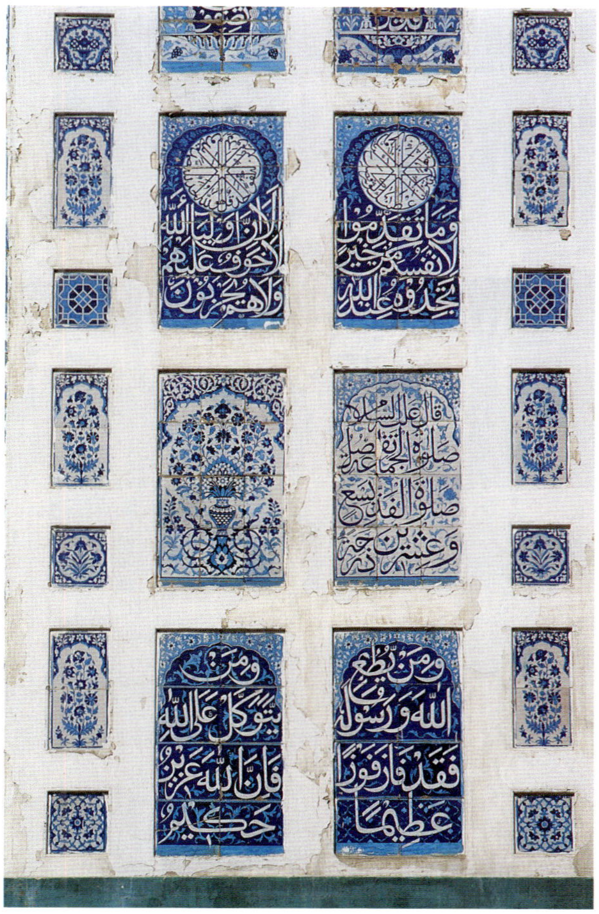

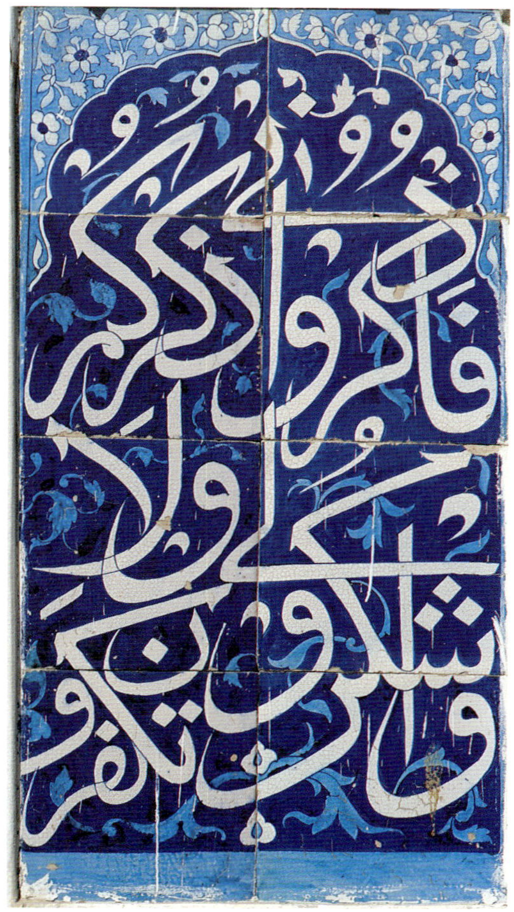

IDGAH MOSQUE, MULTAN (PAKISTAN)

TOP, LEFT TO RIGHT

♦ The wall is divided into compartments set with panels presenting underglaze-painted tiles with a calligraphic and floral pattern.

♦ Panel with an inscriptional motif in Arabic on a ground of turquoise foliate arabesque.

BOTTOM, LEFT TO RIGHT

♦ Underglaze-painted tile decorated with the facade of a mosque complete with monumental gateway and minarets at the corners; above, branches of pomegranate and mango both laden with fruit.

♦ Detail of an inscriptional tile inscribed with the name of Allah.

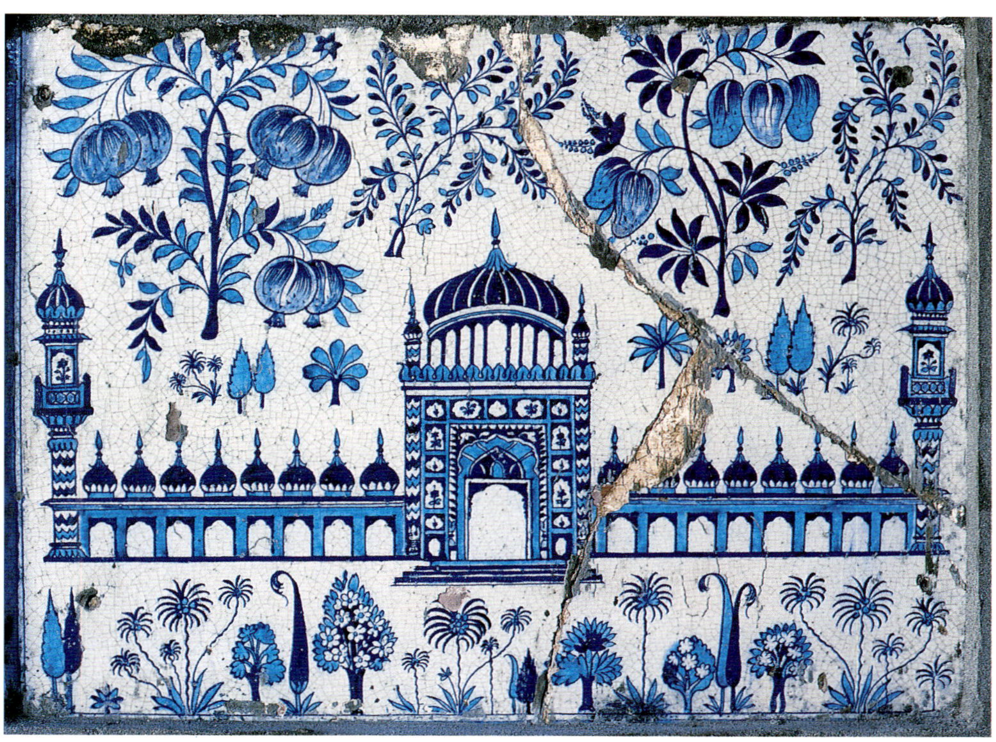

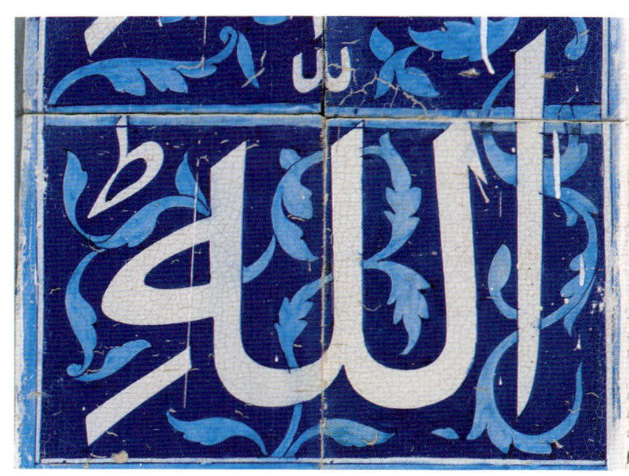

Architecture under the Mughals

Tamerlane's descendant Babur, founder of the Mughal dynasty that lasted from 1526 to 1857, appears to have spent half his life on the battlefield and the other half designing gardens. Heir to a long Timurid tradition and infatuated with the gardens of his ancestors in Samarkand and Herat, Babur created dozens during his reign. Unfortunately, only scant remnants of these "paradises"—such as the garden of Dholpur—have come down to us.[123] It was through this intermediary that the "Persian style" of garden first appeared on the Indian subcontinent; it soon became the rule as Hindu princes copied Mughal models in countless locations.

One of the earliest monuments of the Mughal period decorated with ceramics is undoubtedly the tomb of Shaykh Fazlullah, known as Jamali, a poet who lived in the reign of Sikandar Shah Lodi and died during that of Humayun in 1535–36. Both his tomb and mosque are situated very near the Qutb Minar, in the south of Delhi. The tomb is built to a rectangular plan and has a flat roof. The mural decoration inside is of a richly ornamental style, with turquoise ceramics inlaid in the wall alternating with motifs painted on plaster that recall manuscript illumination. Reinforcing this resemblance to the art of the manuscript, verses by the poet appear painted round the interior of the base of the cupola. Among the monuments of the early Mughal sovereigns decorated in ceramic, the Talaqi Darwaza (gate) to the Purana Qila (1534) in Delhi and the tomb of the martyrs of Humayun's campaigns in the Gujarat, at Hisar (1537–38), should also be mentioned.

Few striking examples of architectural ceramics have come down to us from the reign of Akbar, especially when compared with those from the reign of Jahangir. The Khayr al-Manazil Mosque (1561), the door to the tomb of Humayun (1565), and the decoration on the *chhatri* of the surrounding wall to the west side of the tomb should not be overlooked, however. A cut-tile mosaic calligraphic panel dated A.H. 1003/A.D. 1595 survives in the Calico Museum, Ahmedabad, although its exact origin is not specified.

The earliest large-scale masterpiece of Mughal architecture is undoubtedly the tomb of Humayun. This monarch, a son of Babur, ascended to the throne in 1530. Ten years later, he was driven out by Shir Shah Suri, an Afghan general who was to found his own dynasty of short duration (1540–55). Installed back on the throne of India, Humayun had little time to savor his glorious return, however, perishing in an accident in 1556. Begun ten years after his death, his tomb is a splendid pink sandstone monument embellished with white marble and a stone of a yellow ocher color. It stands at the center of a vast "Persian" garden, or *chahar-bagh* (literally, "four gardens"). The garden is laid out in a square enclosure whose space is divided into four parts, each one divided in turn into four parterres; these multiple divisions appear as a network of small channels connected to pools. This quadripartite garden design refers to Paradise as described in the Qu`ran: a garden traversed by four rivers of wine, milk, honey, and water. Built on the command of Akbar (1556–1605) by the Iranian architect Mirak Mirza Ghiyath, the tomb was envisaged as a pantheon for the Indian branch of the Timurid line. In architectural homage to the great Timurid mausoleums at Herat and Samarkand, the monument borrows many features from the central Asian vocabulary (centralized design surmounted by a dome flanked by little cupolas), but local elements are not entirely lacking: pink sandstone replaces brick, ceramic tilework gives way to marble cladding, and, last but not least, *chhatri* spread out from the terraces. Curiously, the tombs of Akbar and Jahangir depart from this model, and one has to await Shah Jahan and his Taj Mahal at Agra to see this type of plan reappear and attain perfection.

Adjoining the tomb of Humayun are several other constructions decorated in ceramics. The oldest perhaps is the mausoleum known as the Nila Gunbad, or "Blue Dome." Located outside the enclosure of Humayun's gardens, to the southeast, this building of octagonal plan surmounted by a cupola lined with turquoise tiles may have preceded the construction of the tomb of Humayun. The Sabz Burj ("Green Tower") also undoubtedly dates to the first years of the Mughal period. The dome of this tomb, which is of an irregular octagonal plan (four large sides and four small), is today covered in cobalt blue tiles, although this crass choice of color (they were surely originally turquoise) is due to recent restoration. Finally, to the southwest of Humayun's garden enclosure lies a building resembling a caravansary known by the name of the `Arab Saray. Local history has it that the building was once used to shelter Arab monks coming from Mecca at the request of Humayun's widow; the east entrance of the building is an addition from the time of Jahangir and bears some traces of a ceramic decor in cut-tile mosaic.

The *dargah* of Nizamuddin lies not far from the tomb of Humayun. Many individuals wished to be buried around the tomb of this much-revered saint. Among the many monuments surrounding the enclosure of the *dargah*, that of Ataga Khan merits special attention. Ataga Khan was the husband of Jiji Anga, wet-nurse to

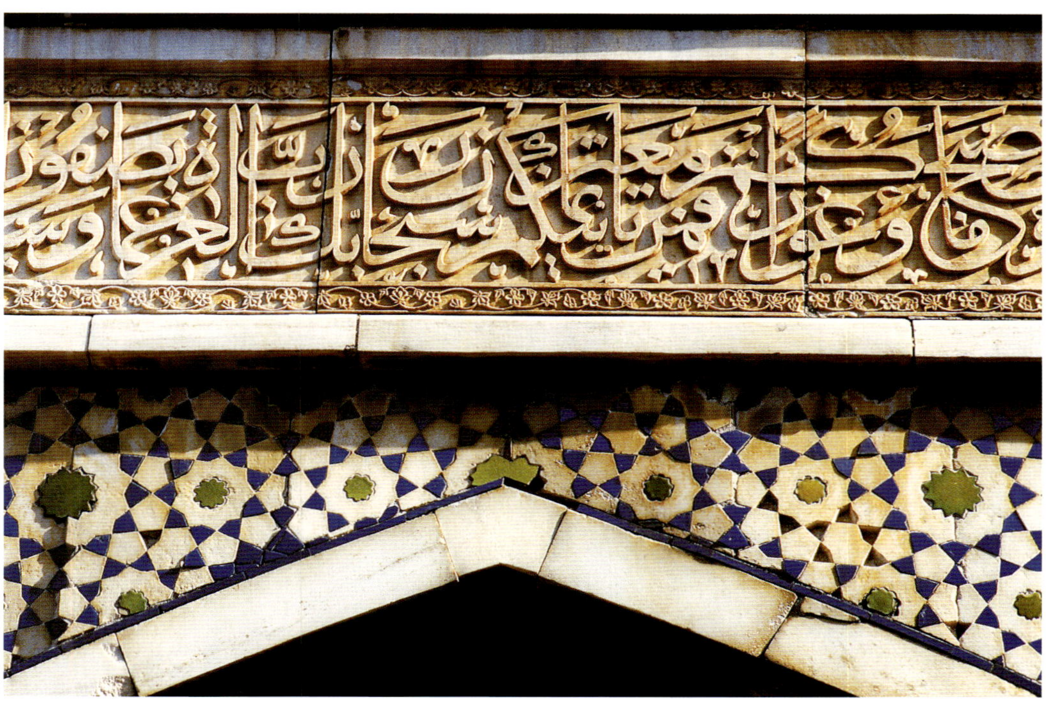

♦ Star pattern above a doorway. Tomb of Ataga Khan, Delhi (India), 1566–67. This small-scale but perfectly proportioned tomb is an architectural jewel. The two tones of the pink sandstone and the white marble are enhanced by the touches of color lent by the green and cobalt blue elements set into the marble.

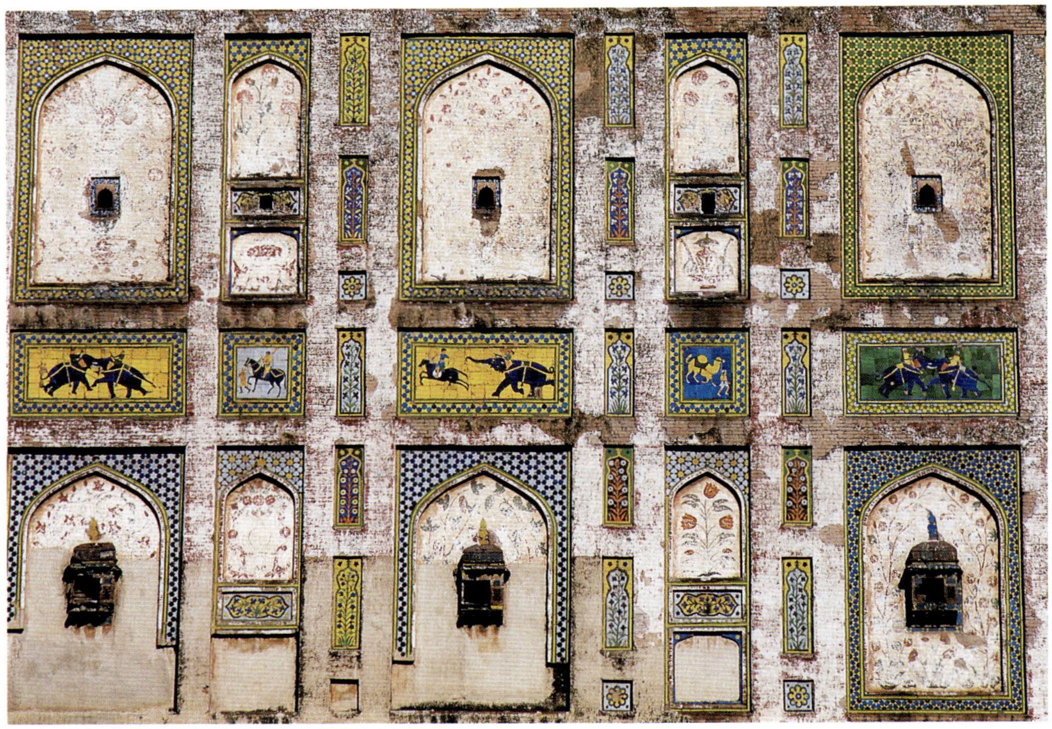

LAHORE FORT (PAKISTAN), COMPLETED IN 1631
♦ View of the outer wall divided into compartments and decorated in cut-tile mosaic panels.
FACING PAGE
♦ Floral pattern cut-tile mosaic panel within an arch. The taste for a measure of naturalism in the treatment of the flowers derived from the influence of Western herbals, which became known in India through engravings.

Akbar, and foster brother to the emperor, who was killed in 1562 by yet another foster brother of Akbar, Adham Khan. An inscription records that the tomb was completed in A.H. 974/A.D. 1566–67. Of tiny proportions (a square 6 meters on each side), the tomb is an architectural gem. The interplay between alternating pink sandstone and white marble on the external decoration is enhanced by additional notes of color provided by the blue and green ceramic elements inlaid into the stone. The wall to the west side of the enclosure, in the direction of Mecca, bore significant amounts of cut-tile mosaic adorning the *mihrab*-like blind niches, forming geometrical compositions in a star pattern that unfortunately are severely damaged today. Akbar went on to build a new capital—Fatehpur Sikri—where architectural forms are mostly very different from preexistent Timurid models (and thus practically bereft of ceramics). Fatehpur Sikri is distinguished by the strange forms and sometimes unexpected functions of many of its constructions. The bizarre-looking pavilion called the Diwan-i Khass, or "private audience hall," is a prime example. This square building consists of a single space extending over two tiers with a massive central pillar supporting a circular platform linked to the four corners of the hall by elevated passageways disposed crosswise. Like all the buildings of the palatial complex at Fatehpur Sikri, this pavilion is built entirely out of red sandstone, although the forms and techniques recall those used in timber construction. In spite of its name, nothing is known about the true purpose of the building. The whimsical city of Fatehpur Sikri existed for only a short time: founded in 1570, it was abandoned in about 1585 in favor of Agra, then Lahore.

The architecture of the reign of Jahangir, who succeeded Akbar in 1605, is marked by the development of sumptuous gardens, Shalimar at Srinagar and the garden of Nishat in Kashmir numbering among the most beautiful examples. Each garden appears as a vast walled quadrilateral enclosure; the natural slope of the ground is arranged into a series of terraces traversed by channels and little water stairs punctuated by pools. The constructions found in these gardens generally take the form of little pavilions or parapets straddling the waters. The majority of these

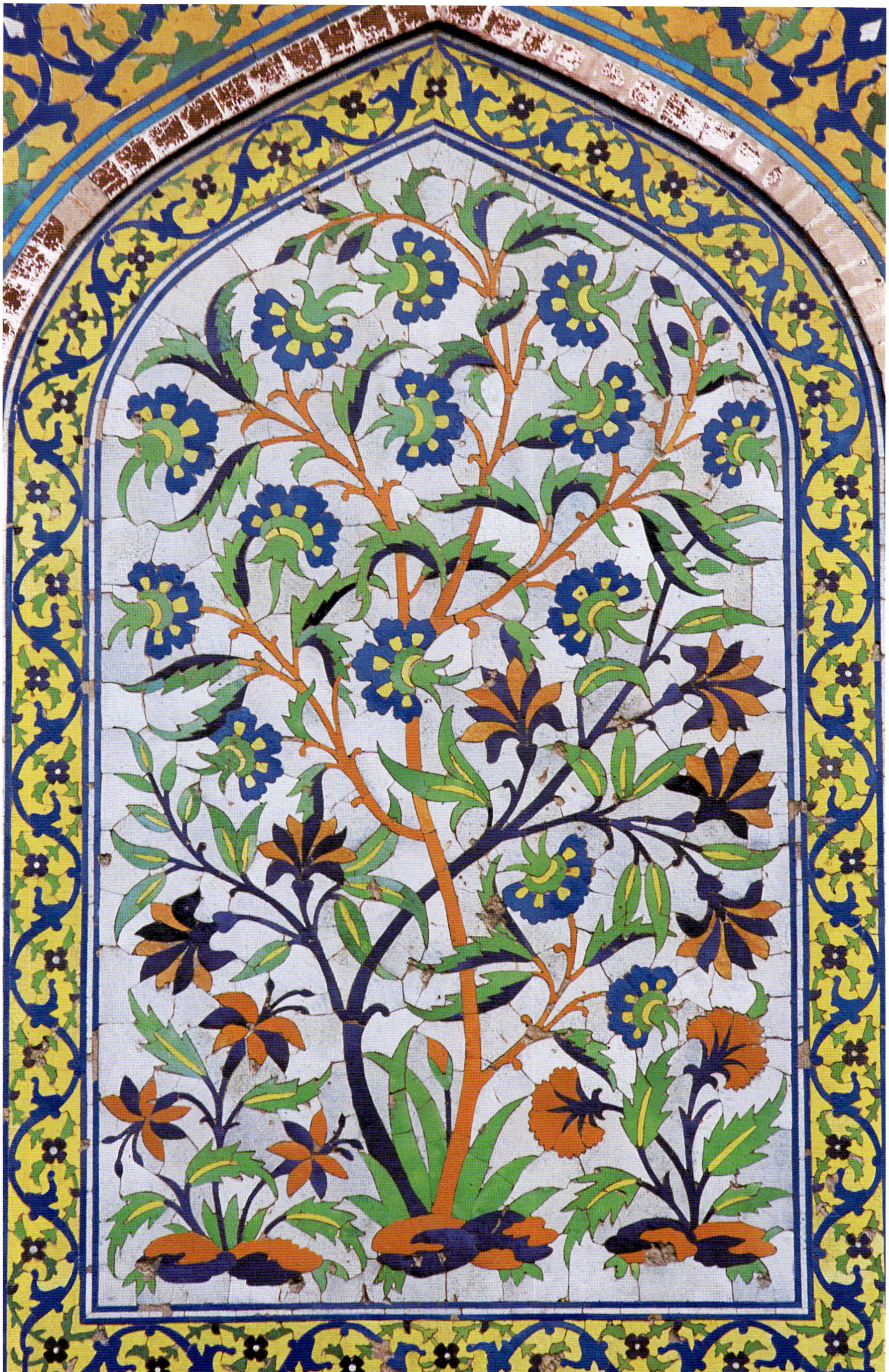

LAHORE FORT (PAKISTAN), COMPLETED IN 1631

TOP TO BOTTOM

♦ The parrot perching on the upper cornice seems to be peering down at the little scene showing horsemen in the middle register.

♦ A panel of cut-tile mosaic representing a military parade.

♦ A panel of cut-tile mosaic showing a skirmish between camels.

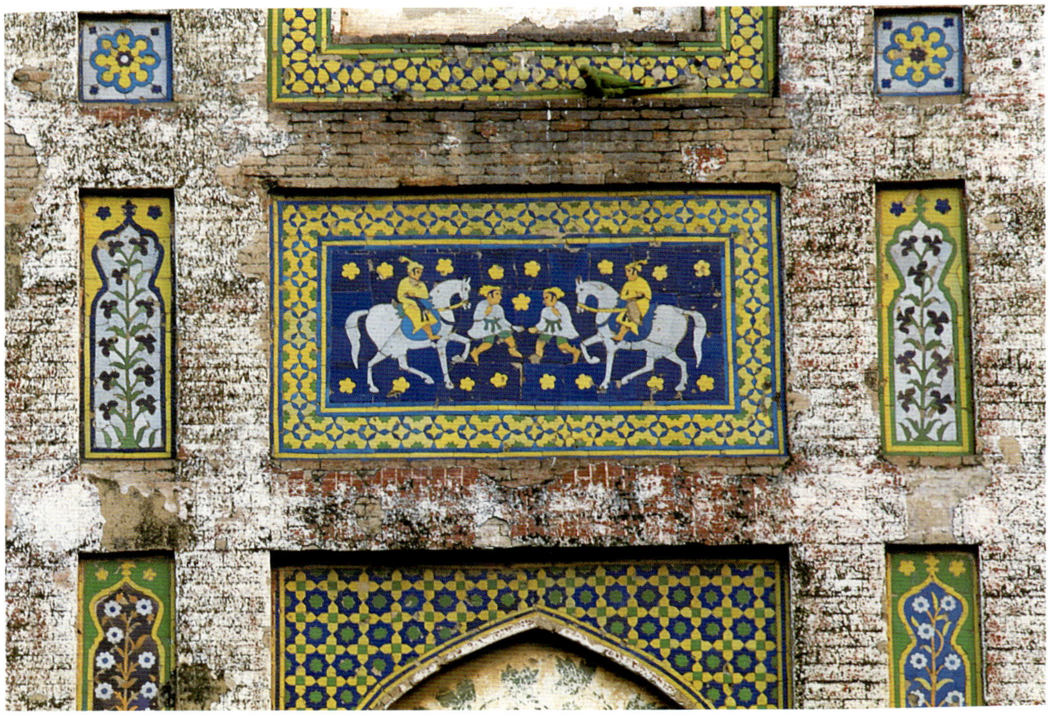

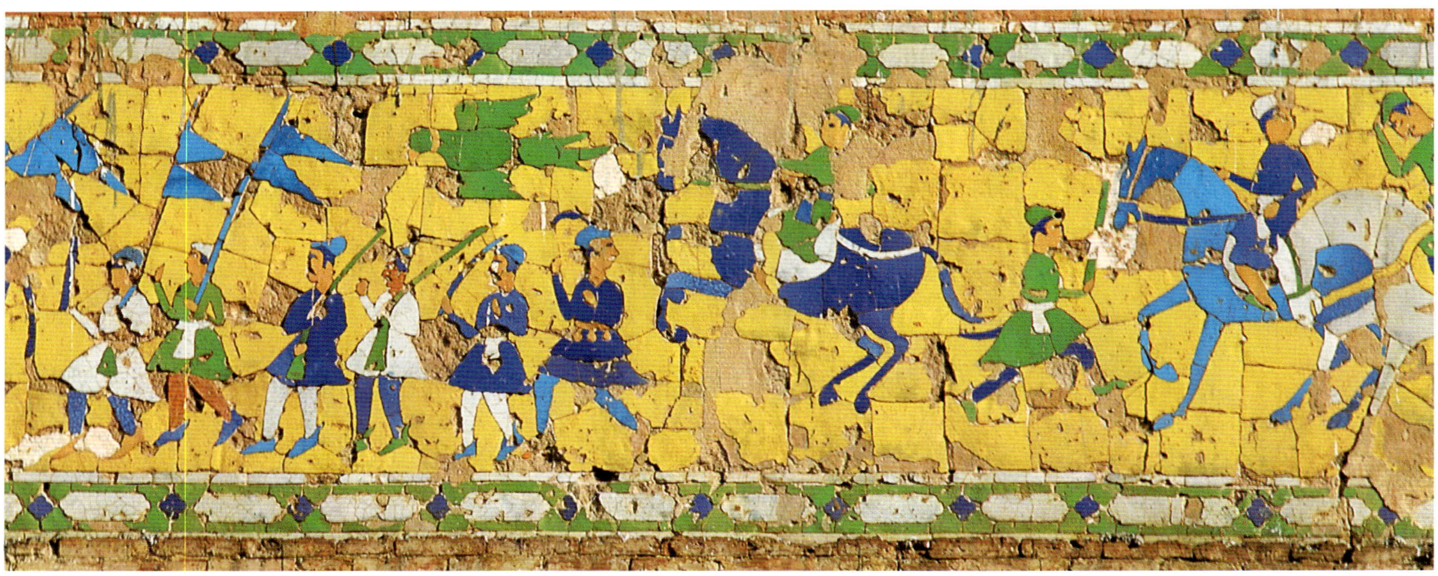

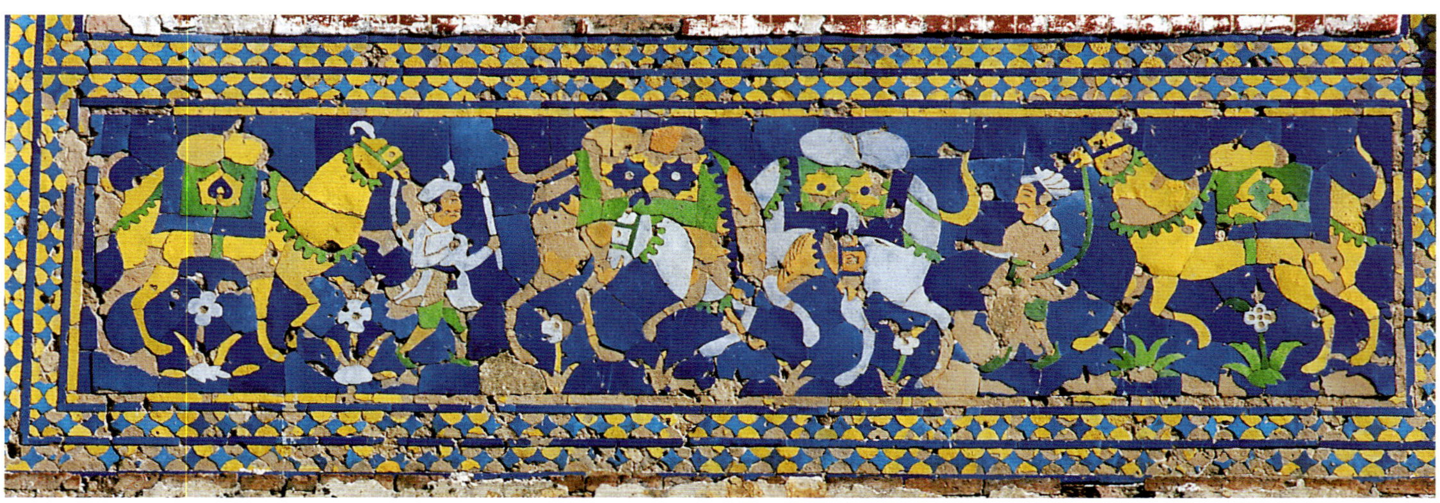

extensive parks were used essentially as encampments, and the tents housing the court were erected over the various terraces in accordance with a rigid hierarchical system. The lowest level would accommodate the guards, officers, and craftsmen, the middle terrace was used for public audiences, while the upper terrace was reserved for the harem.

Among other projects during his reign, Jahangir undertook rebuilding work on the fort at Lahore. Begun in 1624, the outer wall was completed only in 1631 under his successor Shah Jahan. The ramparts, built essentially in brick, incorporate square or rectangular compartments, some of which are ornamented with blind arcades. The surfaces of these compartments are decorated with scenes that portray—with exceptionally engaging freshness—life at the Mughal court: visible to any passer-by, elephant fights, military parades, and polo matches executed in cut-tile mosaic adorn the walls. The general design is clearly inspired by a style of court painting that reached its zenith under Jahangir and Shah Jahan. Transposed to wall mosaics, however, the handling is obviously less detailed than it would be on paper. With their limited palette that renders the color scheme somewhat unrealistic, these miniature genre scenes possess a unique savor.

It was under Shah Jahan (1628–57) that architecture attained its greatest sophistication. First Agra, then Lahore, and later Delhi—dubbed Shahjahanabad for the occasion[124]—were adorned with sumptuous palaces in which white marble vies for effect with the pink sandstone. It was undoubtedly in Shah Jahan's reign that the monumental entryway known as the Amar Singh Gate (named in honor of Prince Amar Singh Rathor of Jodhpur) was added to the Red Fort at Agra. Although constructed out of red sandstone, the towers flanking the door are decorated with panels in mosaic ceramics with stellar and

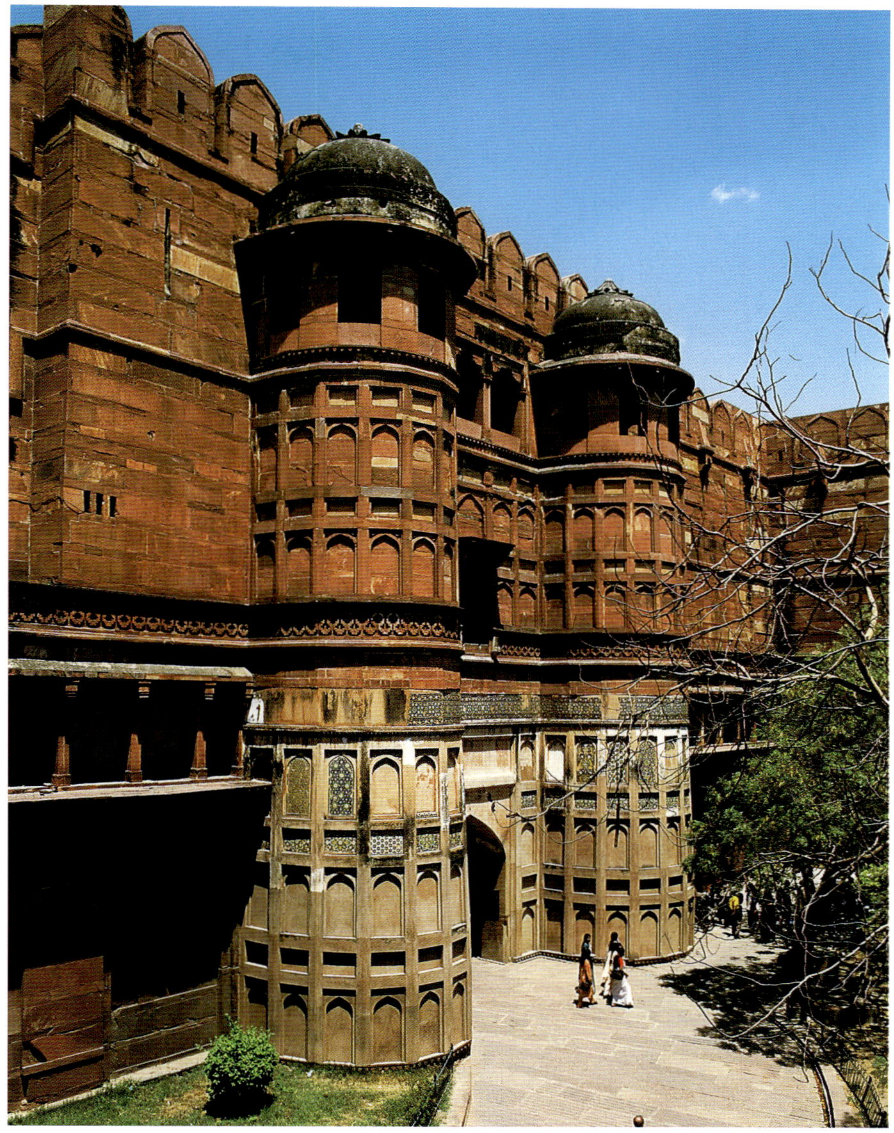

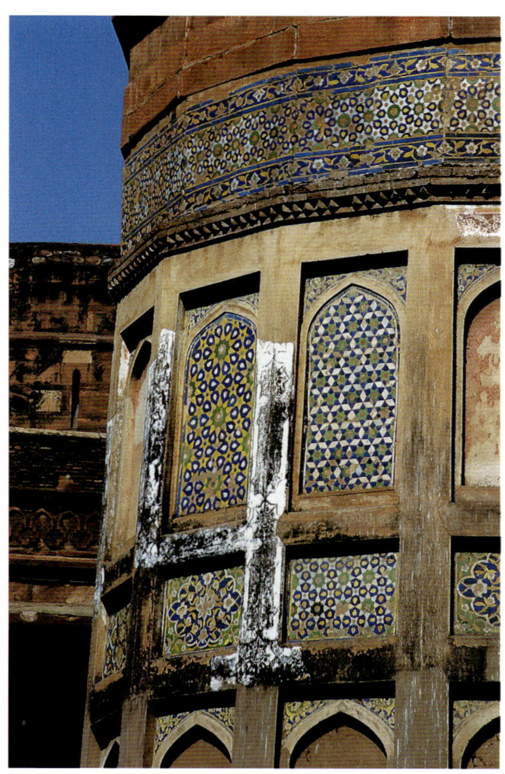

AMAR SINGH GATE, RED FORT, AGRA (INDIA), SEVENTEENTH CENTURY

♦ Like the rest of the outer wall, the gate is built of red sandstone. The facade is brightened by polychrome panels and bands.

♦ Detail of an upper frieze and niches set with cut-tile mosaic.

floral motifs, which also run in horizontal bands above the doorway.

One of the wonders of world architecture, the Taj Mahal was built by Shah Jahan as a final resting place for his wife Mumtaz Mahal, who had died in 1632. Situated on a terrace to the rear of a gigantic garden with a watercourse in the background, the white marble monument nestles in a verdant bower. Completing the complex, to either side of the tomb, stand two identical red sandstone mosques. What makes this mausoleum particularly magnificent is not just the richness of its materials (white marble encrusted with hard stone), but the supremely harmonious proportions of the whole.[125] The sense of uplift is enhanced by a high drum supporting an especially bulbous cupola. Four minarets placed at the corners of the terrace seem to encase the tomb in an invisible but almost tangible structure. In addition to dissimilarities in proportion and the exclusive use of white marble, the Taj Mahal differs from the tomb of Humayun by the presence of large epigraphic bands signed by the greatest calligrapher of the time, `Abd al-Haqq of Shiraz.

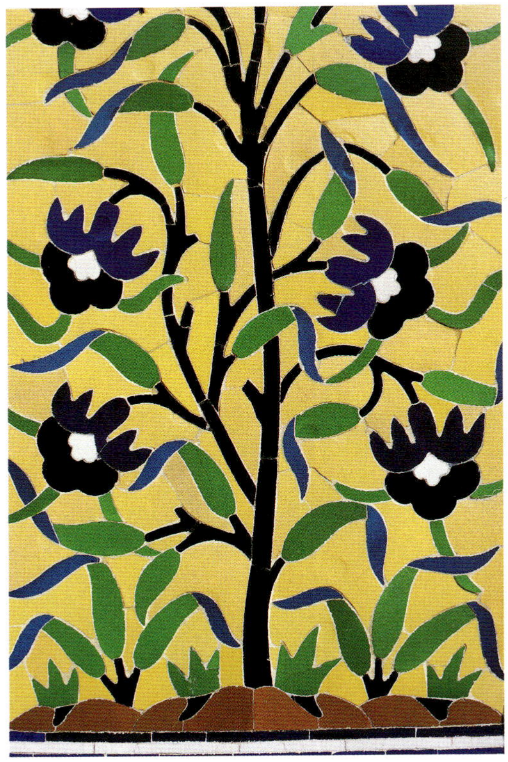

MOSQUE OF WAZIR KHAN, LAHORE (PAKISTAN), COMPLETED IN 1634–35

RIGHT

♦ Cut-tile mosaic panel decorated with flowering stems.

BELOW, FROM LEFT TO RIGHT

♦ Cut-tile mosaic panel showing a vase filled with cut flowers.

♦ Cut-tile mosaic panel with an inscription in Persian in the *nasta`liq* style on a blossom-strewn ground.

♦ Cut-tile mosaic panel decorated with an Arab inscription in Thuluth script.

FACING PAGE

♦ The brick wall is divided into compartments containing plant motifs executed in cut-tile mosaic.

The mosque of Wazir Khan in Lahore (completed in 1634–35) is undoubtedly the richest Mughal monument in terms of ceramic decoration. It was commissioned by Hakim `Ali al-Din, a physician originally from Chiniot in the Punjab who distinguished himself at Shah Jahan's court and who, in 1620 (when already a prince), had

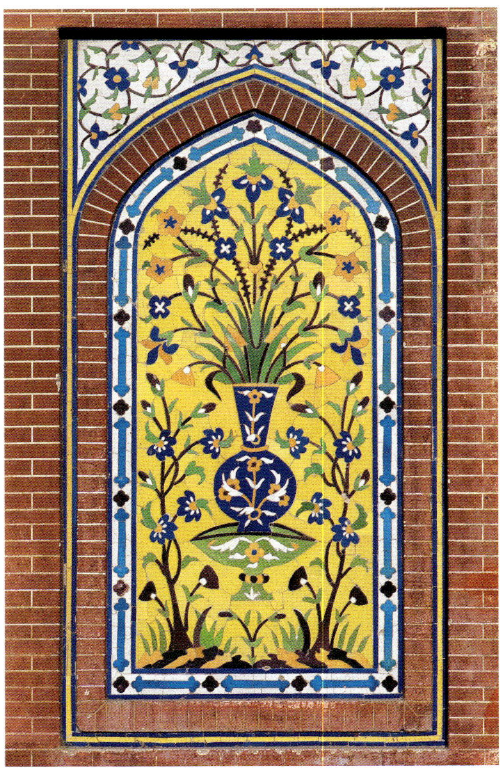

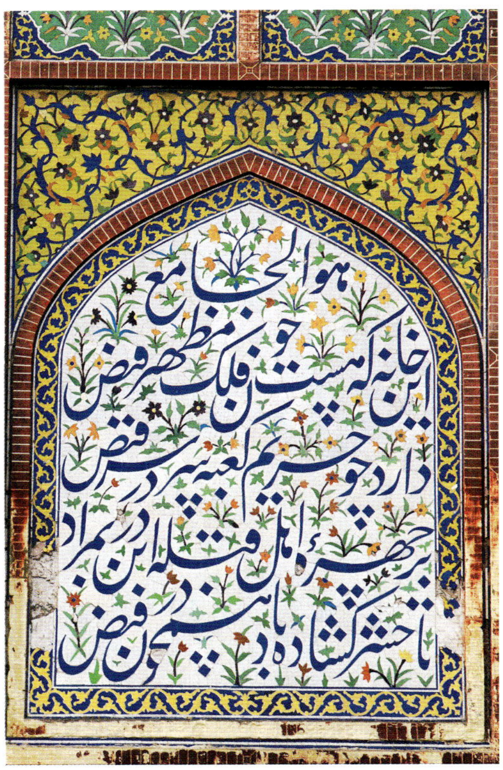

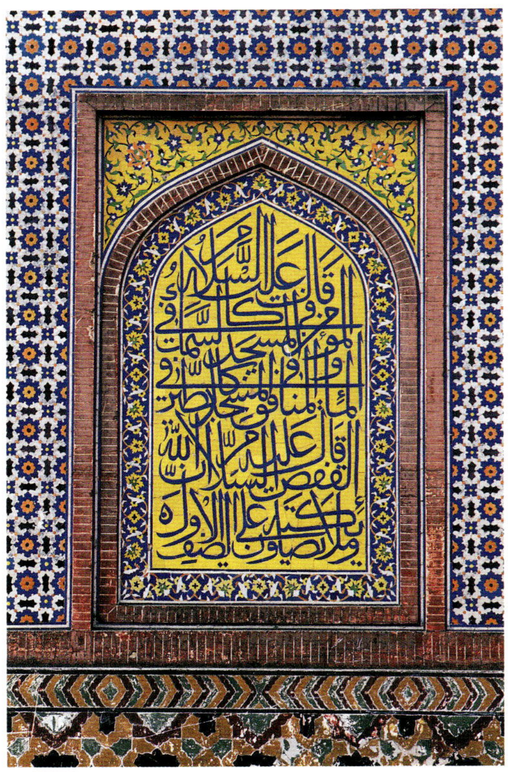

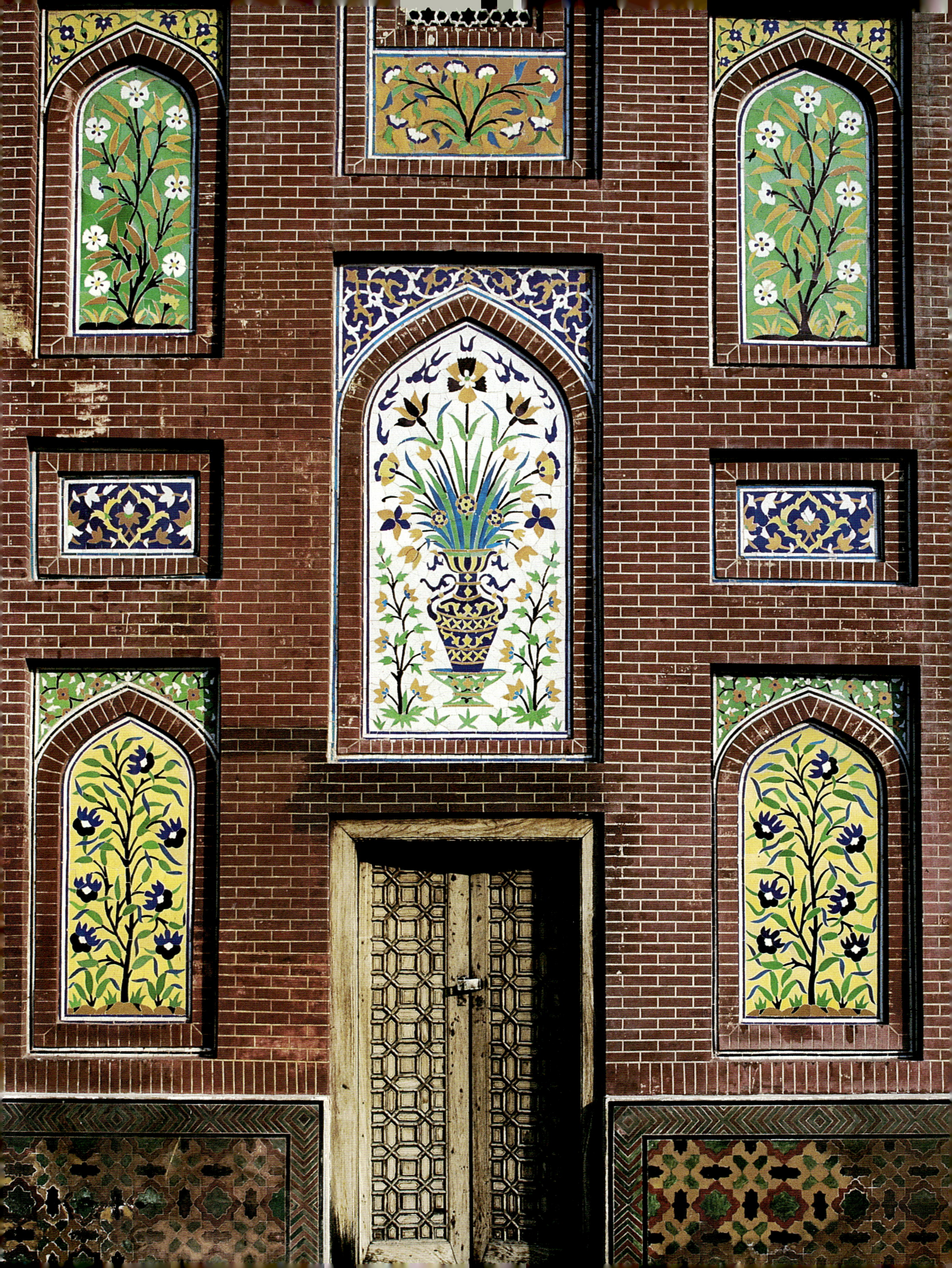

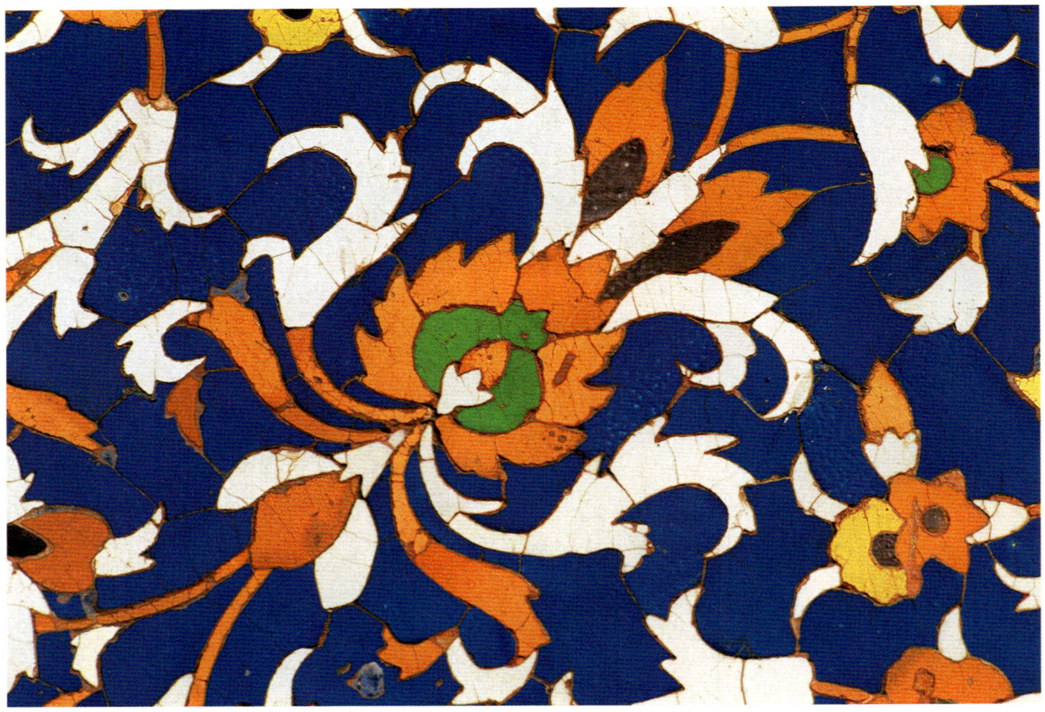

MOSQUE OF WAZIR KHAN, LAHORE (PAKISTAN), COMPLETED IN 1634–35

♦ Detail of a cut-tile mosaic showing an imaginary species of flower in flaming colors.

BELOW

♦ Iris stems beneath the branch of a tree.

FACING PAGE

♦ The flora seems halfway between naturalism and the fantastic.

BOTTOM RIGHT

♦ Cut-tile mosaic wall panel. Shalimar Bagh, Lahore, (Pakistan), 1636–42. From a wrought-iron-style trellis sprout graceful bouquets of flowers that echo the real flower beds in the garden.

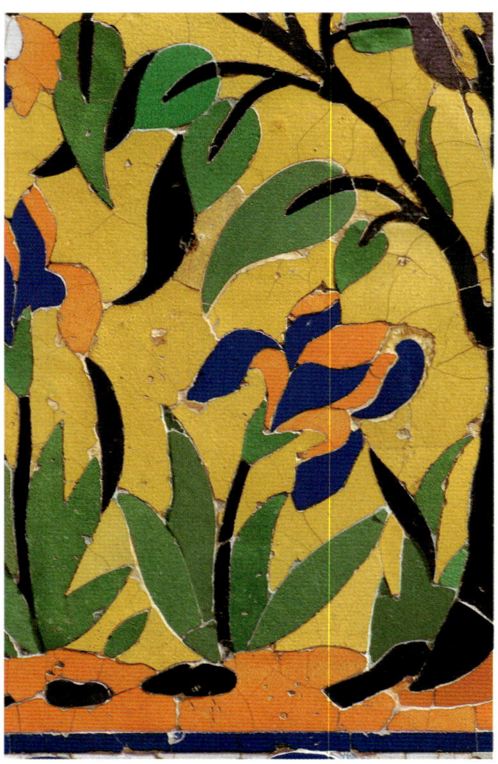

been granted the title of *wazir khan*. In 1631, he was appointed governor of the Punjab. Built entirely of brick, the mosque presents a rectangular plan (85 by 48 meters) flanked by four minarets at the corners. The main entryway to the east side is lined in cut-tile mosaic, decoration. An inscription, executed in ceramics, gives a date of A.H. 1045/A.D. 1635 for the completion of the project. The facade of the prayer hall and the four minarets also contain a large number of cut-tile mosaic panels. The epigraphic friezes are in the *nasta`liq* style, with trails and geometric interlace patterns, which are combined with an abundant vegetal decor, often treated with that dose of naturalism that had been in vogue in contemporary Mughal art since the arrival of engraved plates from Western herbals.

Built between 1636 and 1642, the Shalimar Bagh in Lahore is one of the most beautiful and best-preserved gardens. A canal, only completed in 1648 by order of the governor `Ali Mardan Khan, supplies the water for the basins and fountains. The construction of this garden was followed by that of the Chauburji Bagh, laid out by Princess Jahanara in 1646, and by the Gulabi Bagh, planted in 1671. In this way, Lahore was soon ringed by a belt of gardens offering delightful viewing points, water features, and the most sophisticated ornaments. These pleasure gardens were not the only green spaces in the city, since the various funerary constructions were also surrounded by parks. In this area of the Punjab, architectural ceramics were particularly frequent. Thus, the powerful queen Nur Jahan, the inexhaustibly wealthy wife of Jahangir, possessed a vast garden in Lahore called the Bagh-i Dilgusha. On the death of her husband in 1627, she ordered the construction of a sumptuous tomb there. Both the queen (who died in 1645) and her brother Asaf

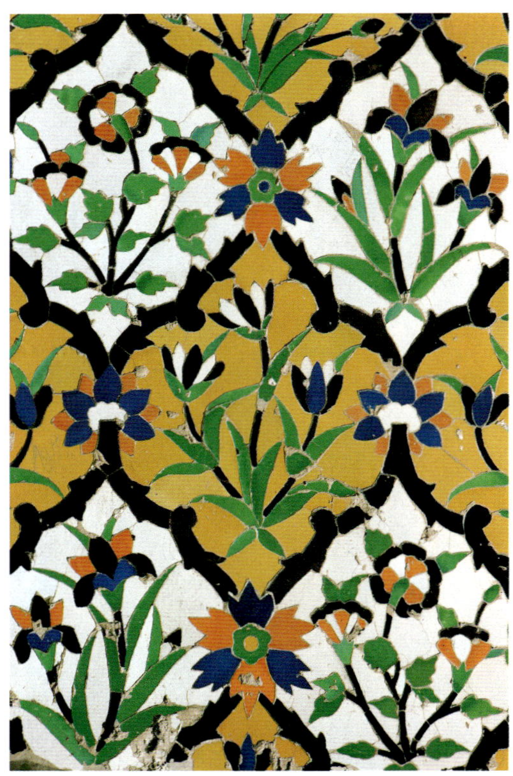

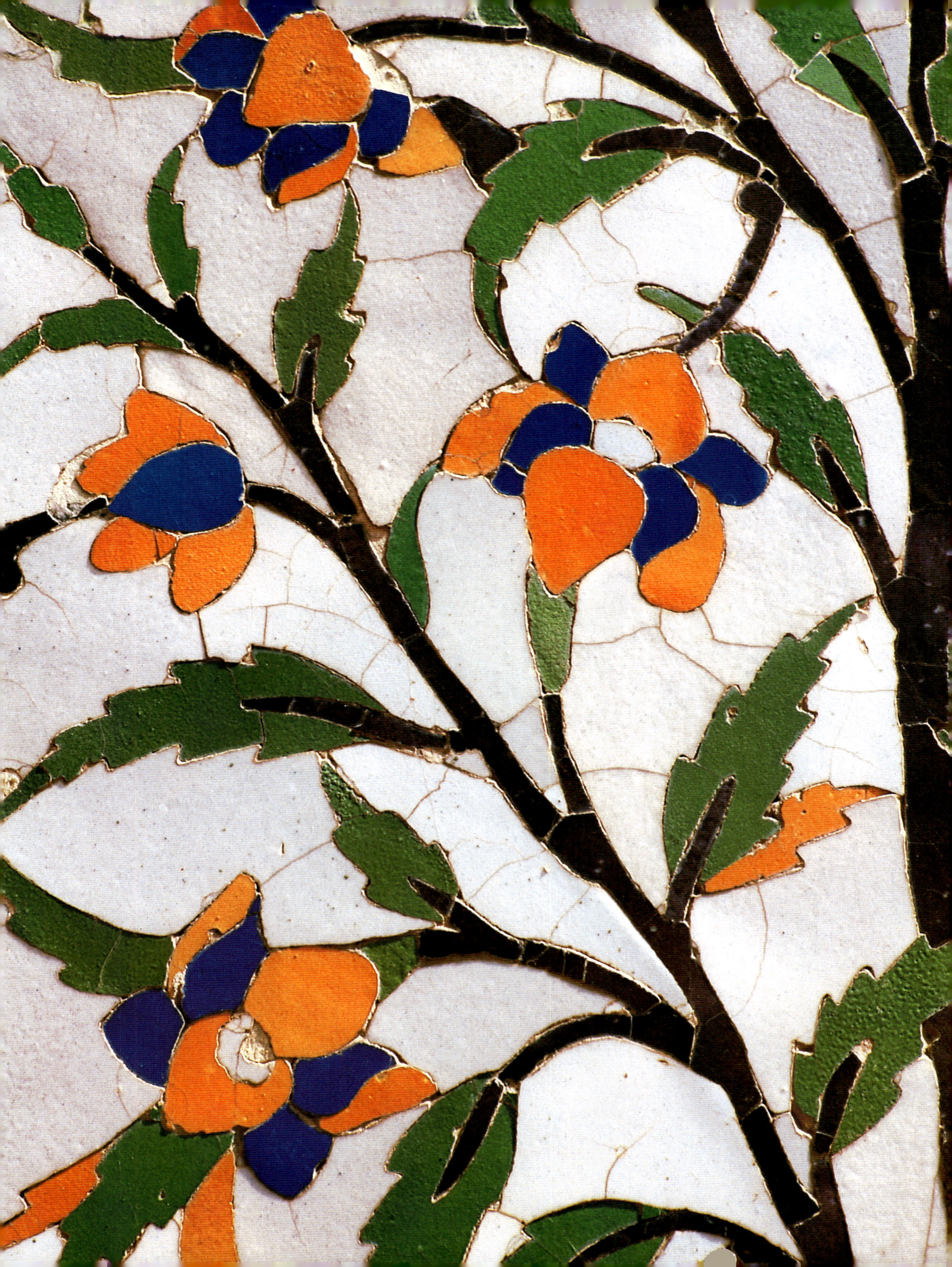

♦ Part of a vault lined entirely in cut-tile mosaic with a floral pattern. Mausoleum of Asaf Jah, Lahore (Pakistan), c. 1641.

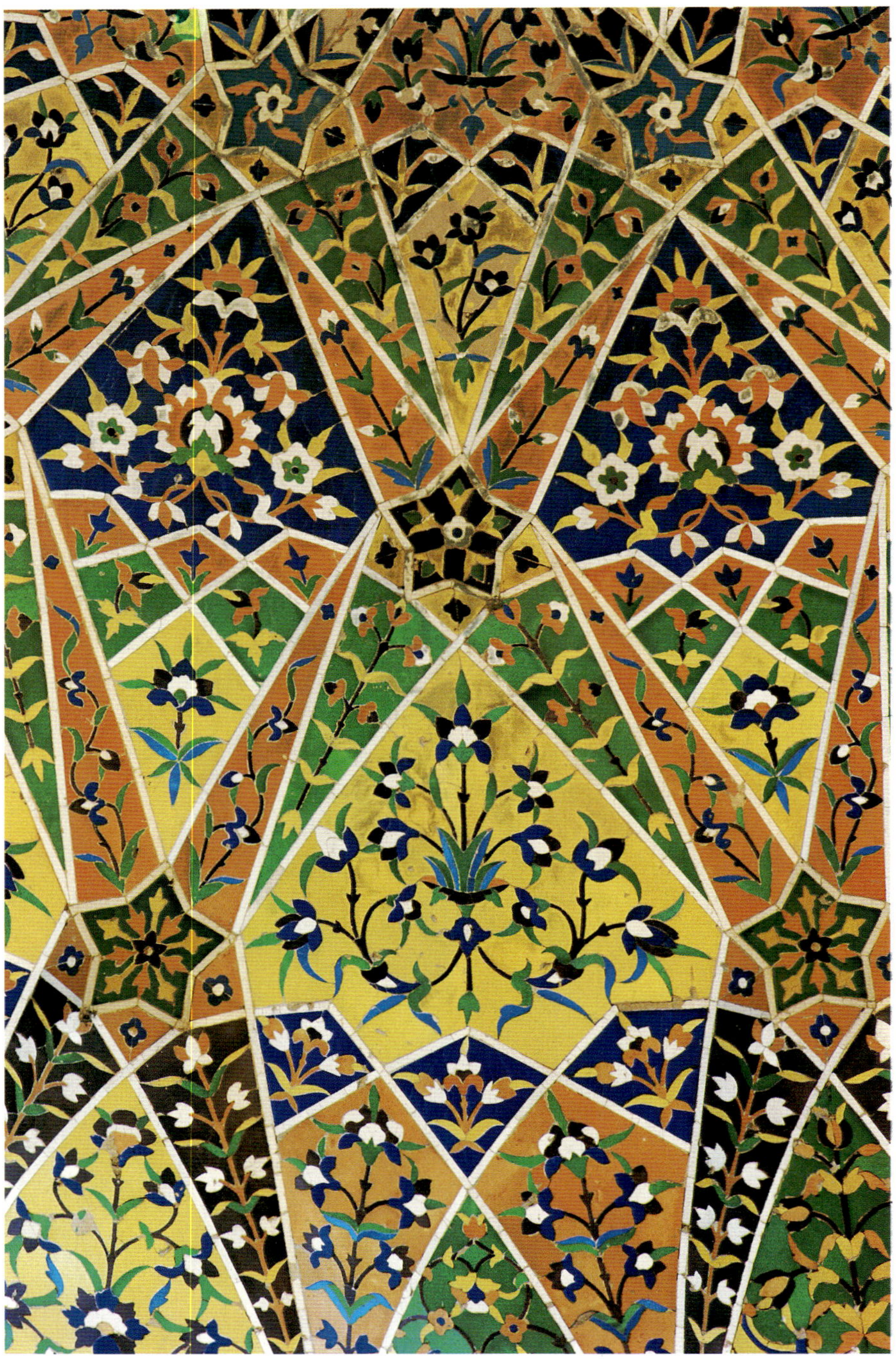

Jah were also buried at the Bagh-i Dilgusha in other tombs.

The Chini-ka Rauza, or "porcelain tomb," in Agra, a masterpiece of Indian cut-tile mosaic, stands to the north of the tomb of Itimad al-Daulah on the banks of the Yamuna. It was more than likely commissioned by Afzal Khan, a high-ranking officer at the imperial court who died at Lahore in 1639. The title of *afzal khan* was bestowed on him by Jahangir, his original name being Mirza Shukr Allah Ahmed from Shiraz. Arriving in India in the company of his brother, `Abd al-Haqq (later elevated to Amanat Khan), he initially attended the court of Khan-i Khanan at Burhanpur, before joining that of Jahangir. The two brothers were sons of a calligrapher from Shiraz named Qasim. The tomb is built to a square plan and is topped by a large single central dome with four small pinnacles at the corners. The external surfaces were at the outset lined with ceramics treated in the way of mosaic. The great archways, opening in the way of *iwans* toward the interior, were ringed by long epigraphic bands with cobalt Thuluth script on a white ground. The remaining walls of the facade were covered in square or rectangular compartments, decorated with blind arcades bearing floral motifs (poppies, lilies, amaryllis, narcissi, and irises). The range of colors includes white, yellow, turquoise, green, cobalt, manganese violet, and black. It is probable that the inscriptions, and maybe the tomb itself, were designed by the younger brother of the deceased. Curiously, whereas during his lifetime it was the elder of the two brothers, Shukr Allah, who enjoyed the more enviable position at court, it is the younger who is the better known today. He first became renowned for the execution of the inscriptions at the mausoleum of Akbar at Sikandra in 1613. In 1632, Shah Jahan bestowed on him the title of Amanat Khan. In 1636–37, he signed the monumental inscriptions on his greatest masterpiece, the Taj Mahal, only to withdraw into the Punjab near Amritsar in around 1640, where he designed a small complex around a caravansary. He died in around 1645.

The Great Mosque at Thatta (also called the Abdel Kafu Jami`a), completed in 1647 under Shah Jahan, is built to a plan inspired by "Persian"-style mosques. Built essentially out of brick, its ceramic decoration both outside and inside is particularly rich. Fronted by a dome on finely decorated squinches, the *mihrab* presents an epigraphic frieze painted white on a

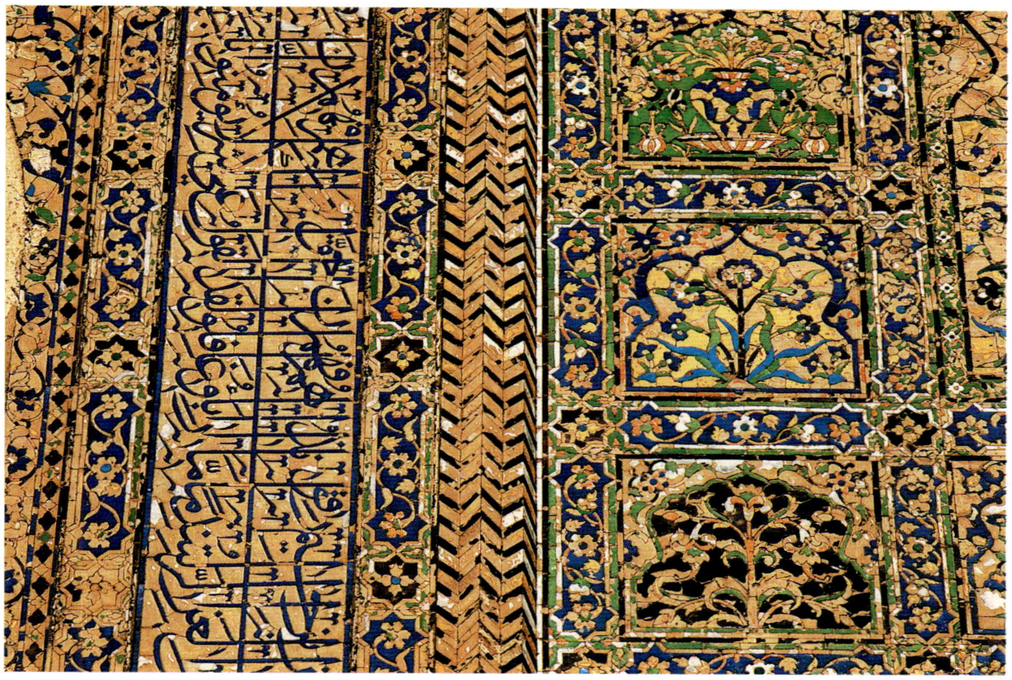

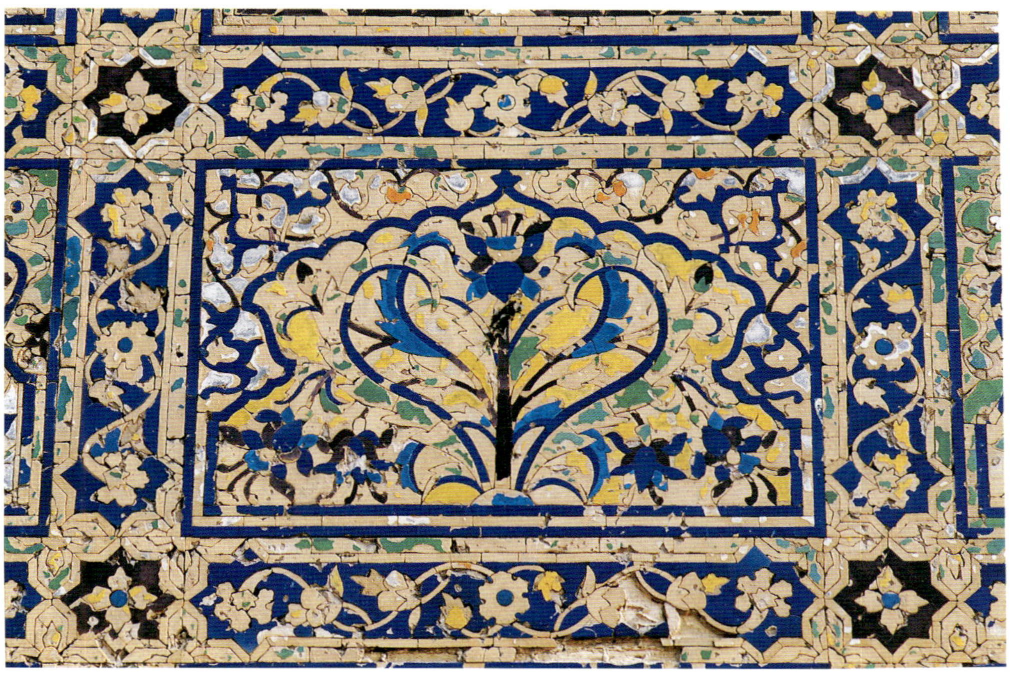

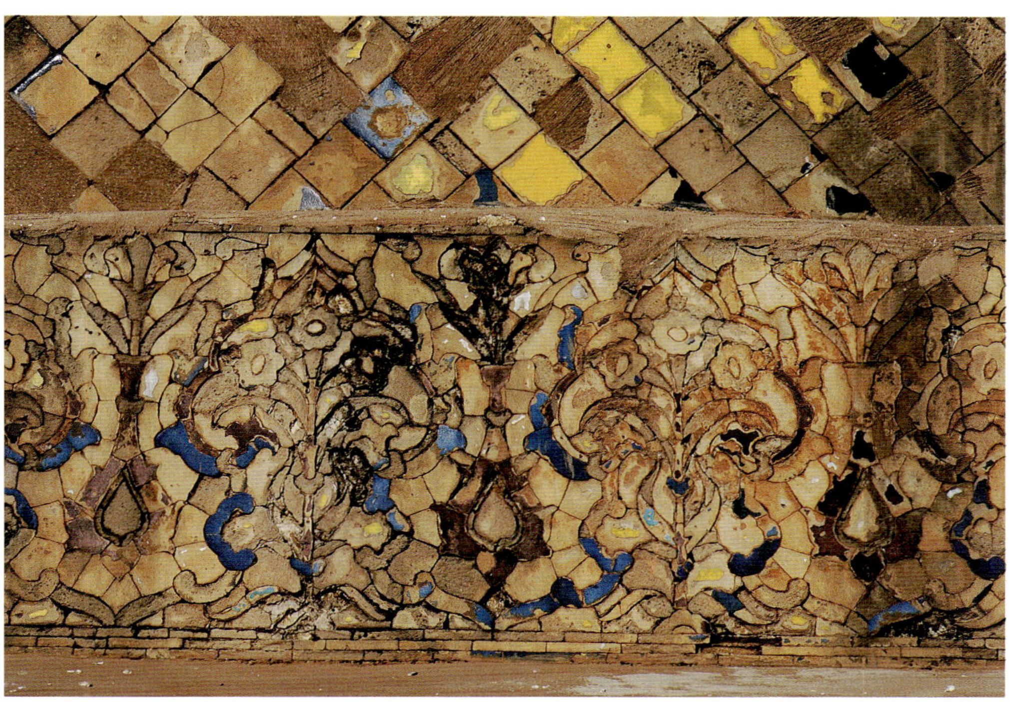

CHINI-KA RAUZA, AGRA (INDIA), C. 1640

FROM TOP TO BOTTOM

♦ This magnificent mausoleum standing on the banks of the Yamuna in all likelihood served as the tomb of Afzal Khan, a notable at the Mughal court. His brother, Amanat Khan, was a renowned calligrapher responsible for, among other works, the inscriptions on the Taj Mahal. All the facades of the monument were originally covered in cut-tile mosaics.

♦ Detail from a compartment on the main facade decorated with flowering stems in a false curtain arch.

♦ Cut-tile mosaic border with a fleuron and floral bouquet pattern.

GREAT MOSQUE, THATTA (PAKISTAN), 1647

♦ View of the *qibla* wall with, in the center, the main *mihrab* of the prayer hall.

♦ Dome on squinches in the prayer hall lined with tiles in a star pattern.

FACING PAGE, BOTTOM

♦ Star pattern above a frieze of underglaze-painted squares.

FOLLOWING DOUBLE PAGE

♦ Detail of the squinches with painted tiles lining the interstices.

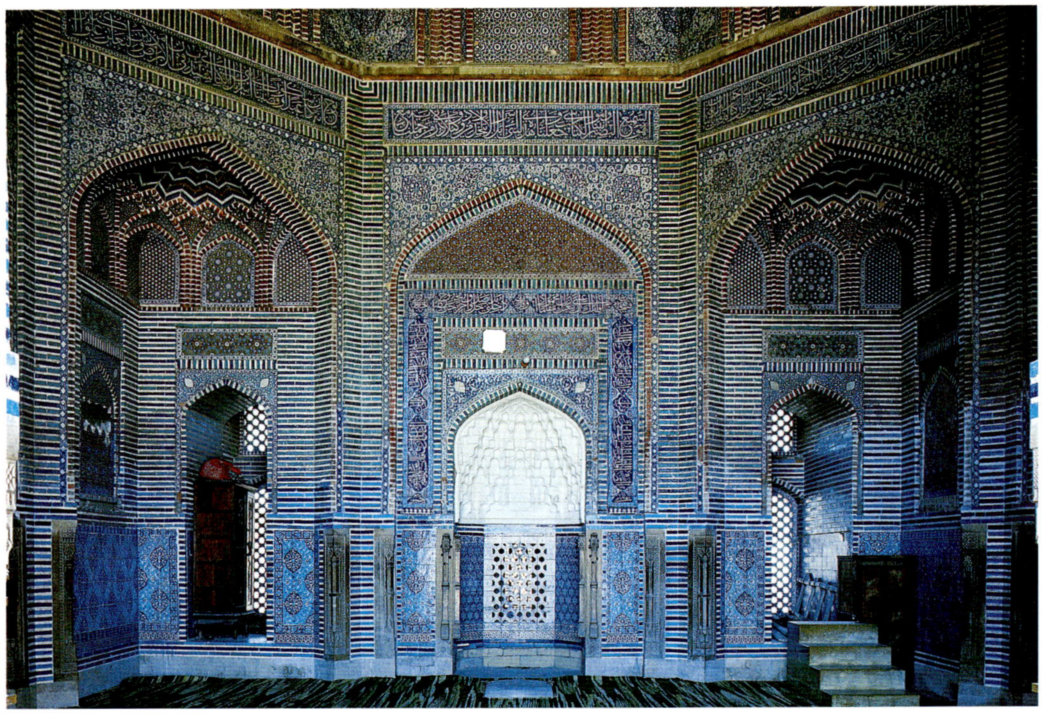

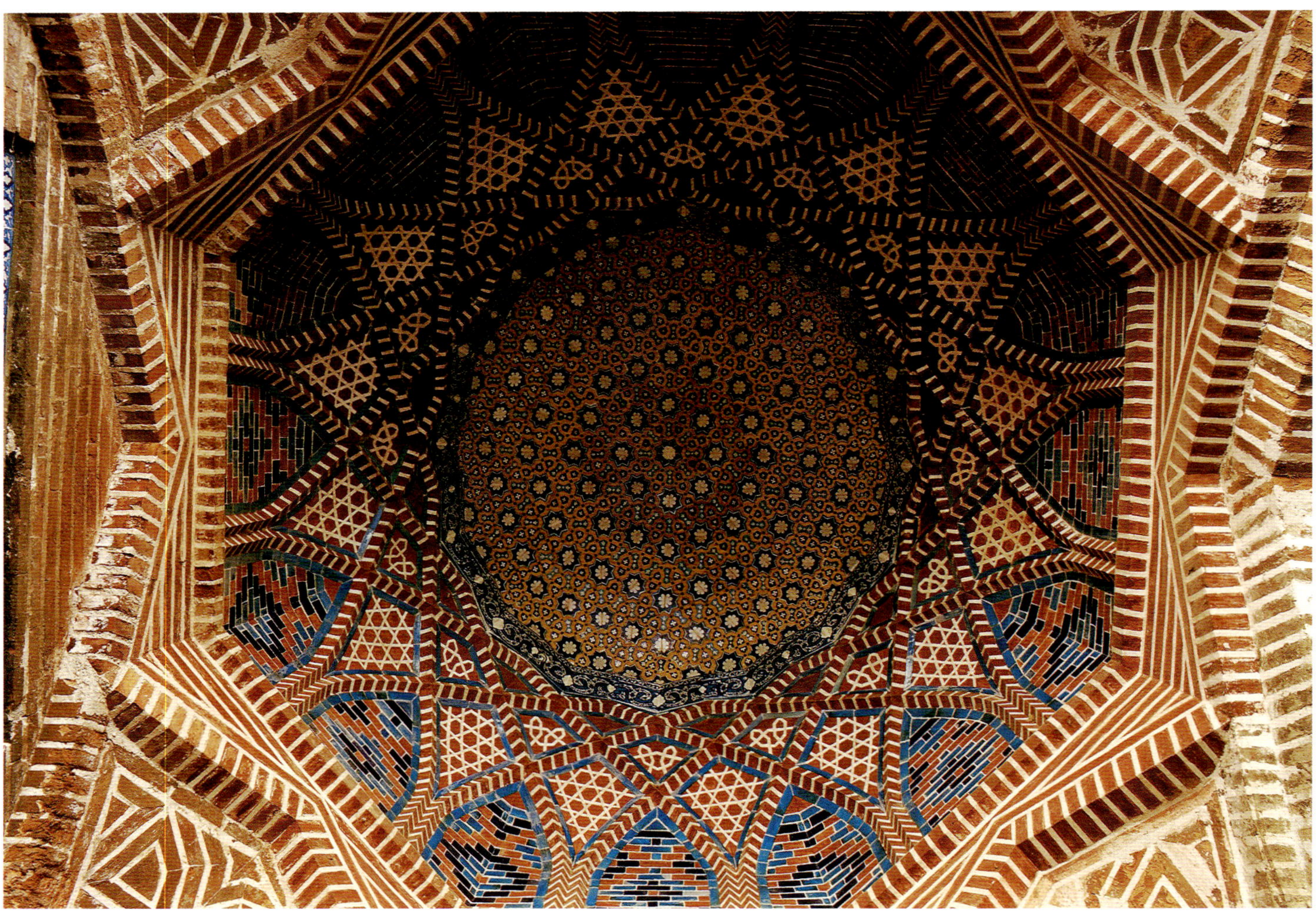

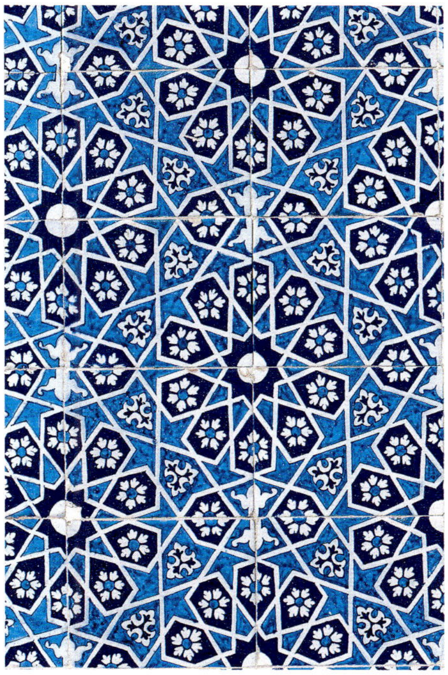 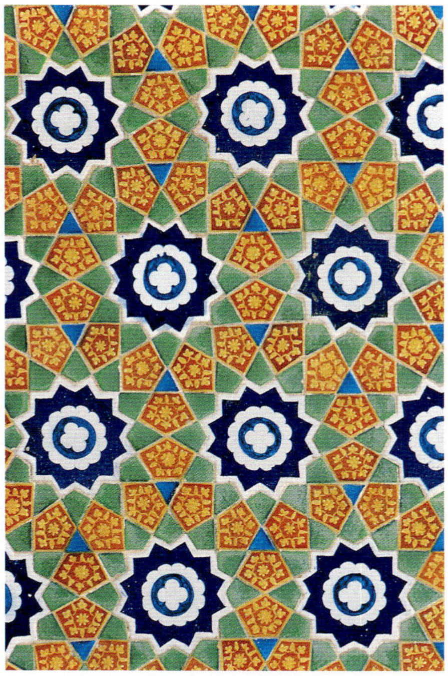 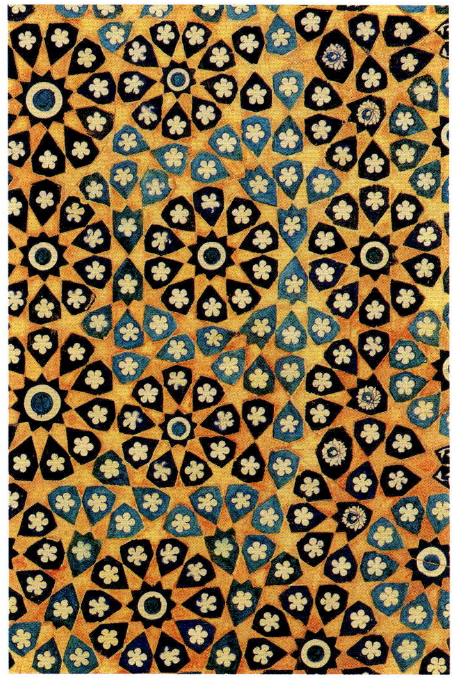

cobalt ground above a dado comprised of an array of predominantly turquoise and cobalt tiles.

The tomb of the wife of Aurangzeb Alamgir, the Bibi-ki Maqbara at Aurangabad (1678) reverted to the model of the Taj Mahal, without, however, managing to attain the same effect in terms of materials and proportions. Nevertheless, the polychrome tiles on the archway opening onto the beautiful gardens surrounding the tomb are of the highest quality. Of the "black line" type, they are decorated with blossoming stems on a white ground.

The *dargah* of Qutb Sahib houses the tomb of Khwaja Qutb al-Din Bakhtyar Kaki from Ush (in Ferghana); a disciple of Mu'in al-Din Chishti from Ajmer, he died in 1236 during the reign of Iltutmich. Originally very simple, the tomb has been repeatedly embellished over the centuries, the latest additions dating from 1944. On the west wall of the courtyard, Emperor Aurangzeb had ceramic decorations mounted, rather in the way of a *qibla* wall. The *mihrab* is contained in a deep niche that is framed by a star design in turquoise, yellow, green, and cobalt cut-tilework; the spandrels of the niche are decorated in blue and white. To the other side of the wall, a series of polychrome tiles—of rare quality for this type of production in India—show floral motifs (lilies and poppies) on a mustard-colored or green ground within tiles shaped like a mandorla. Unfortunately, these walls have often been repainted with scant regard for the ceramics and are in a deplorable state.

After Nadir Shah's invasion and the subsequent collapse of Mughal dominion, the Rajput principalities seized the opportunity to regain something of their former power. The City Palace at Udaipur contains a strange series of ceramic tiles in which Delft blue-and-white rub shoulders with cut-tile mosaic made locally and with industrial tiles—most probably of English manufacture—in a taste reminiscent of ceramics from Sarreguemines.

ABOVE

♦ Panel of underglaze-painted tiles with star and floral motifs.

♦ Small independent elements arranged according to a strict rhythm that allows for countless variations on the star and flower pattern.

♦ Panel of small elements (some underglaze-painted) fitted together with only the odd lotus flower relieving the unremitting sequence of rosettes and stars.

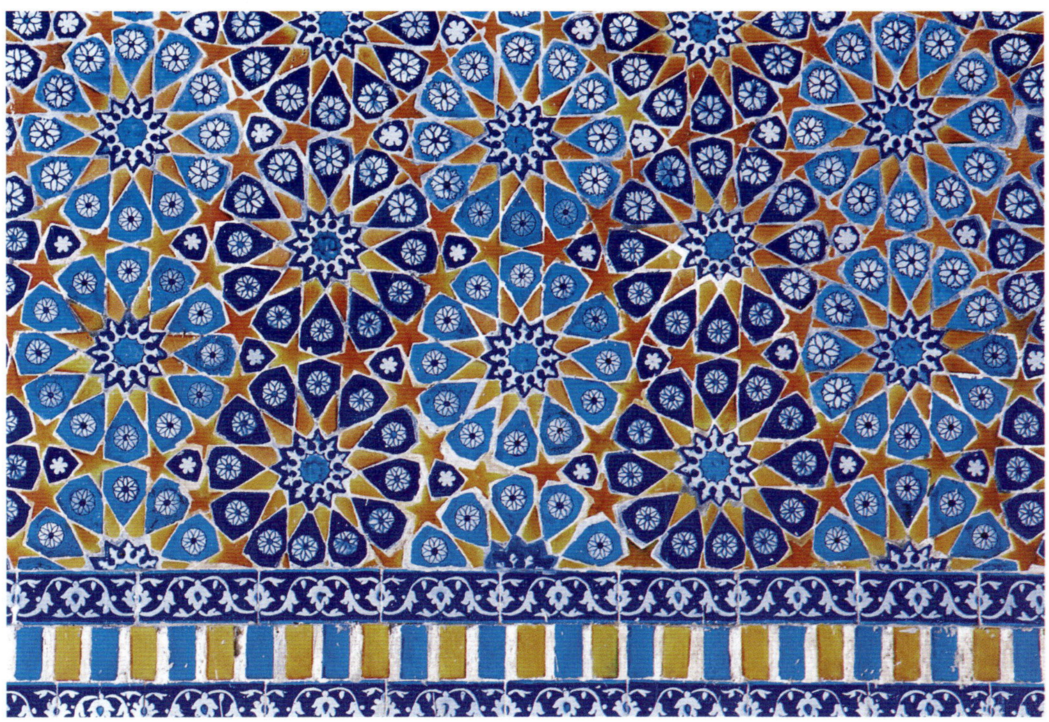

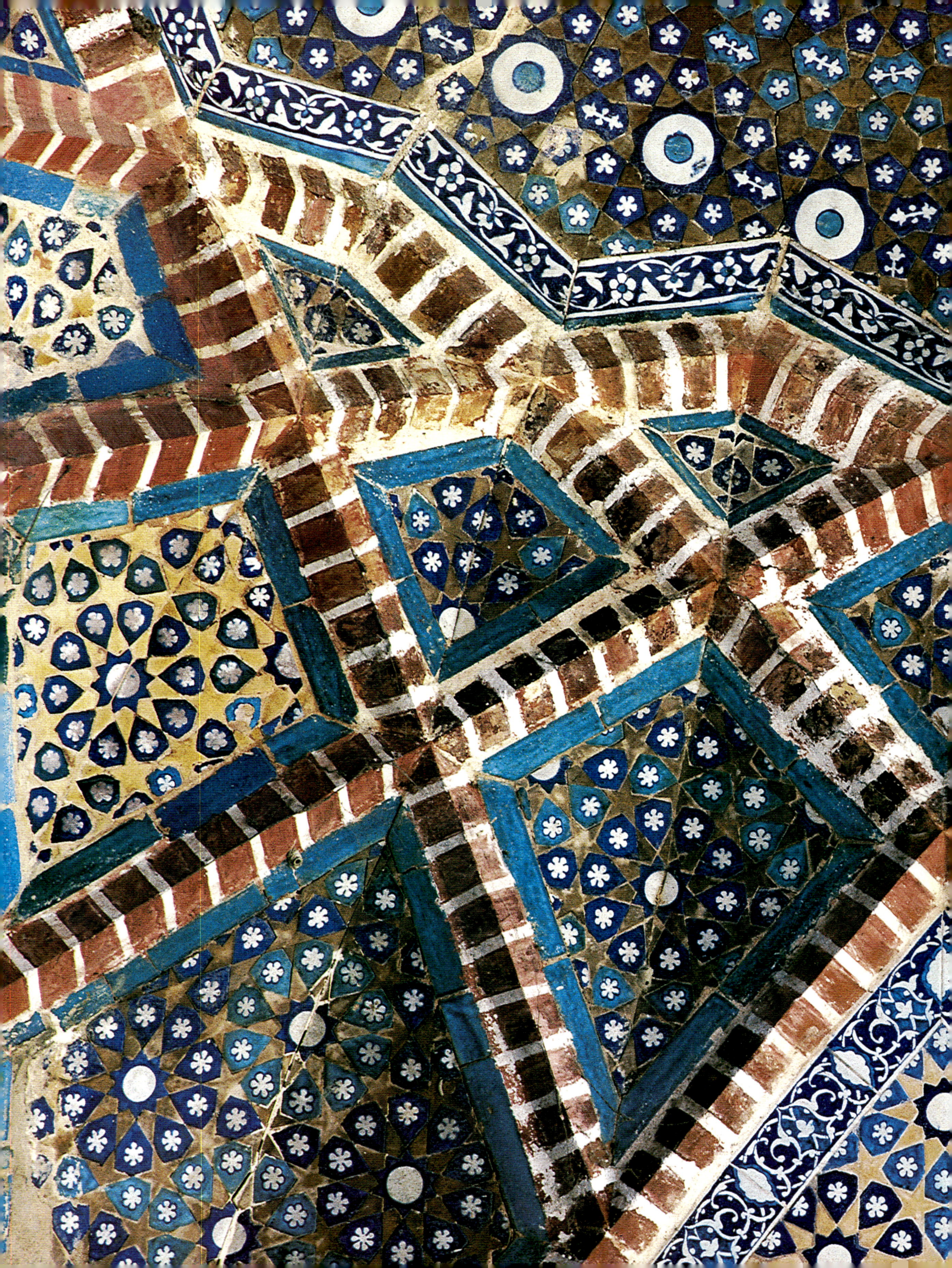

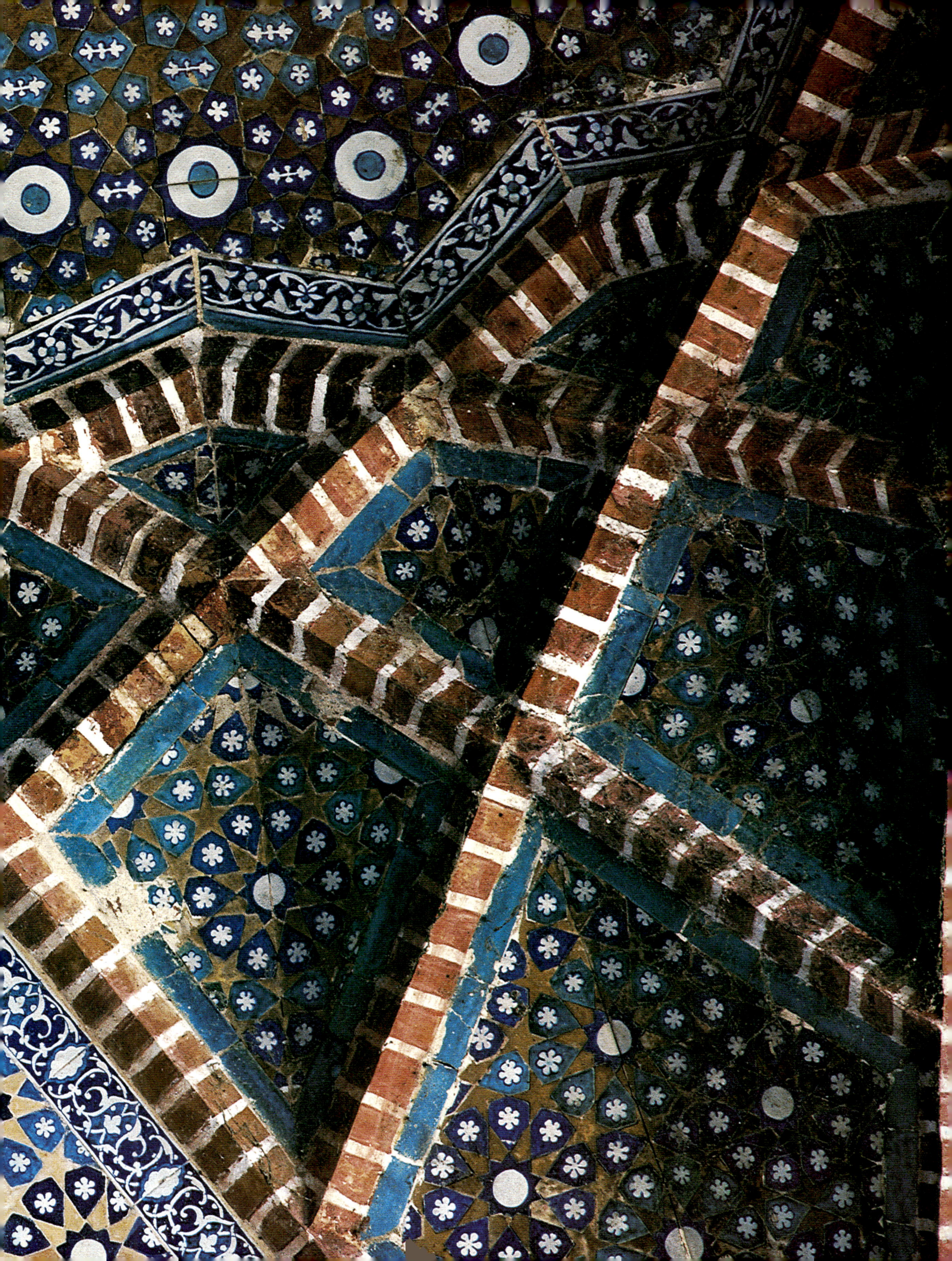

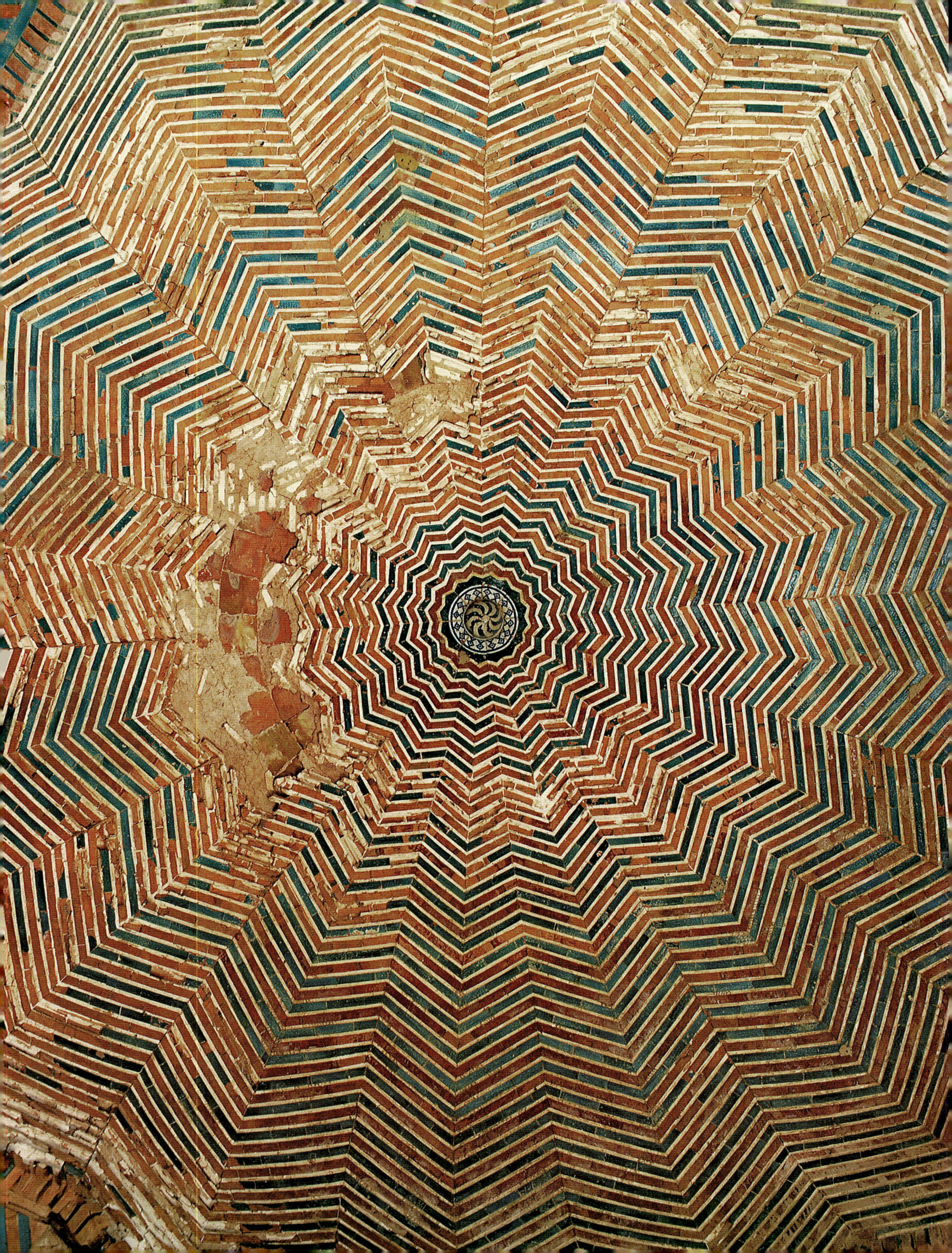

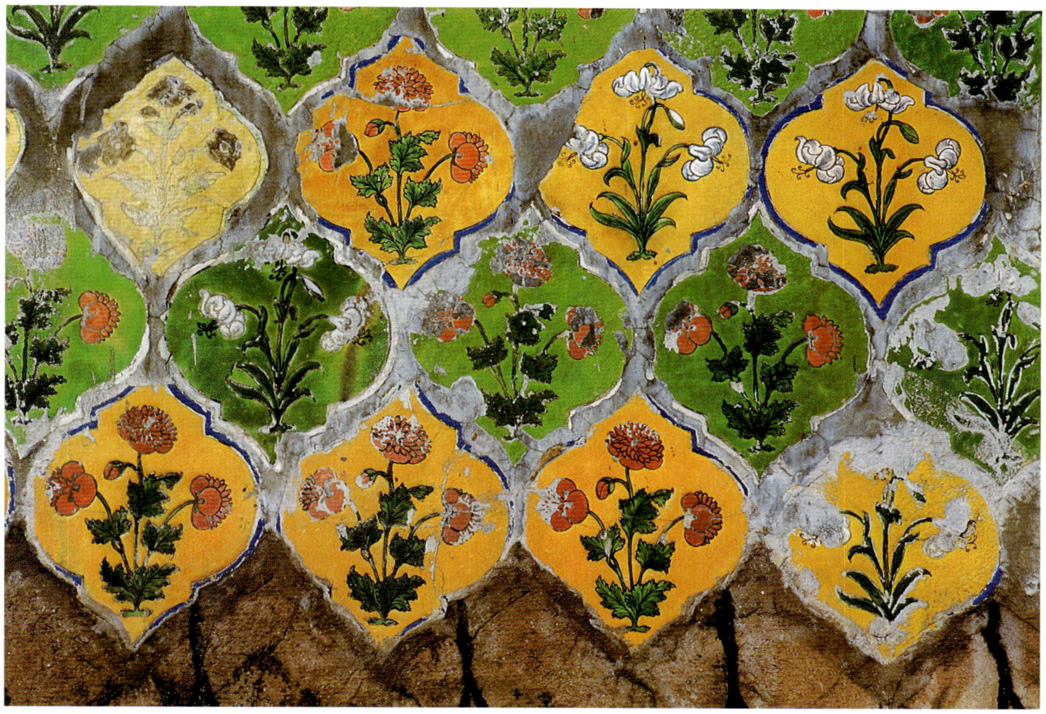

DARGAH OF QUTB SAHIB, DELHI (INDIA)

♦ Although founded in ancient times, this tomb belonging to a saint was restored on numerous occasions. These "black line" tiles decorated with poppies and amaryllis were probably applied to the walls of the sanctuary during the reign of Emperor Aurangzeb (1658–1707).

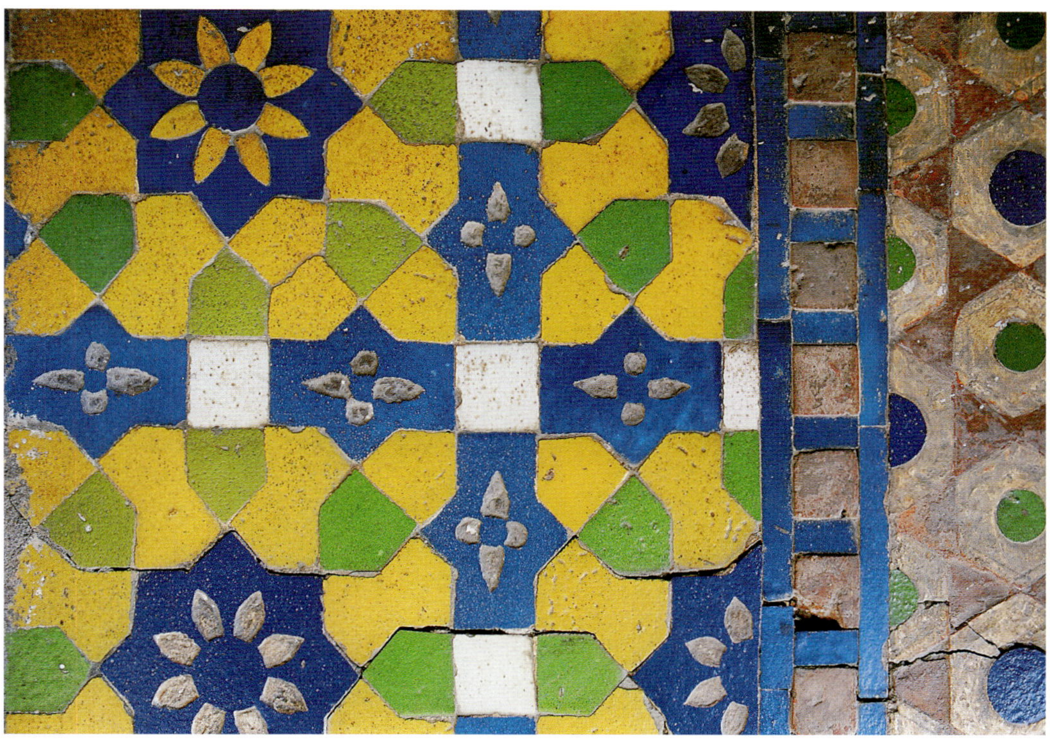

♦ Detail of a composition of tiles, some of which have been carved and scored to create floral motifs.

For the most part, India under British rule produced little in the way of ceramic masterpieces. Nineteenth-century Jaipur, however, is something of an exception,[126] producing pieces that returned to the blue-and-white palette of Multan and Sind. In 1866, Maharajah Sawai Ram Singh II (1835–80) founded the Jaipur School of Art. Under his aegis and that of his successor, Sawai Madho Singh II (1880–1922), ceramic manufacture in the Rajasthani capital improved greatly in quality, the Jeypore Exhibition of 1883 revealing many of the most beautiful pieces produced. Some slightly later examples can be seen today in the Rambagh Palace at Jaipur, built under Sawai Man Singh II (1922–49), in particular in the Polo Bar fountain and in the dressing room of the Maharani (today part of the "Maharani Suite").

FACING PAGE

♦ Cupola with chevron pattern and central rosette. Tomb of Diwan Shurja Khan, Thatta (Pakistan).

Notes

1. Tusi, 1969, p. 152.
2. Abu al-Qasem Kashani, 1966, pp. 346–47; and Allan, 1973, p. 114.
3. That is to say, adding gold leaf.
4. Kashani, 1966, p. 347; and Allan, 1973, pp. 114–15 and 120. The variant noted here also appears in Allan's translation.
5. Allan, 1973, p. 120.
6. See Watson, 1994, pp. 170–80. The same author also points out other names that appear on pieces in *mina'i*, such as Bu Tahir Husayn, Husayn, `Ali ibn Yusuf, and Mohammad ibn Abi'l-Hasan al-Muqri.
7. Soustiel, 1985, p. 198.
8. Kashani, 1966, pp. 345–46; see also Allan, 1973, pp. 114 and 119.
9. See Soustiel, 1985, *tesson* (shard) no. 62, fragment from the edge of a Sultanabad-type cup, analyzed by C. Kiefer (C.K. 0795).
10. See especially "Introduction to the analogous and corresponding figures" (in Persian), manuscript at the Bibliothèque Nationale de France, ancien fonds persan no. 169, fols. 180 to 199.
11. Published by Necipoglu, 1995. This publication contains not only a complete facsimile of the scroll, but also some valuable studies, in particular concerning the geometry and decorative motifs of Islamic art.
12. See Qazi Ahmad Qomi, 1959, p. 56. As will be seen in connection with Turkmen and Safavid Iran, this writer also records the names of a whole series of calligraphers who became famous for their monumental inscriptions, in particular those executed in ceramics.
13. Necipoglu, 1990, pp. 136–70.
14. Quoted from V. Porter, 1995, p. 25.
15. See *Le Vert et le brun*, 1995, pp. 82–83, no. 32.
16. Gestoso y Pérez, 1904, p. 68.
17. Quoted by Torres Balbás, 1947, vol. 4, p. 179.
18. Quoted by Bargebuhr, 1968, pp. 190–91, after Lafuente y Alcántara, 1859.
19. *Vanités de faïence. Entre Provence et Languedoc, carreaux de céramique espagnols xve-xviiie siècles*, 2000, p. 18.
20. Marchesi, Thiriot, and Vallauri (eds.), 1997, pp. 307–12.
21. *Vanités de faïence*, 2000, p. 104.
22. Quoted from Golvin, 1995, p. 229.
23. Ibid., pp. 199ff., for the history of the dynasty of the Beni Zayyan rulers of Tlemcen, Golvin refers to the chronicle written by Al-Tanasi, published and translated by Bargès, Paris, 1852.
24. Ibid., p. 201.
25. Ibid., 1995, p. 258.
26. Hedgecoe and Damluji, 1993. See in particular the chapiter "Zillig: un glossaire," pp. 231–41.
27. *Vanités de faïence*, 2000, pp. 104–6.
28. Ibid., p. 106.
29. Venture de Paradis, quoted by Broussaud, 1930, p. 6.
30. Ibid., p. 7.
31. Ibid., p. 1.
32. Ibid., p. 3.
33. Ibid., p. 13.
34. Diego de Haedo, 1612, p. 7.
35. Broussaud, 1930, p. 14.
36. Ibid., p. 15.
37. Ibid., p. 17.
38. "Rapport de fouille 1993," *Les Cahiers d'Achir*, no. 3, 1994, p. 4.
39. See Mélikian-Chirvani, 1996.
40. Museum für Islamische Kunst, acquired in 1966; see Soustiel, 1985, p. 98.
41. Metropolitan Museum of Art, no. 12.44; the inscription reads "[month of *shawwa*] year 707/March-April 1308." Reproduced in Blair, 1986, fig. 53.
42. Legs Fernand Dol, 1942. The inscription reads: "this was written in" [*wa kataba dhalika fi*].
43. Blair, 1987, fig. 20.
44. On this monument, see Wilber, 1969, no. 98, p. 183.
45. Soustiel, 1985, pp. 204 and 376, *tesson* (shard) no. 63. See also Grekov and Iakoubovsky, 1939, pl. V; and Lane, 1957, pp. 13–15 and pl. 5.
46. Golombek and Wilber, 1988, vol. 1, p. 245.
47. Ibid., no. 51, p. 283; the authors of the catalog describe these tiles as "haft rangi hexagonal tiles, painted with vegetal designs."
48. Ibid., p. 272.
49. Ibid., pp. 317–18, who cites Khwandamir, fols. 176–77.
50. One example is Soltanshah Naqqash, who decorated the ceiling on the mosque at Torbat-i Shaykh Jam in 1362 (ibid., p. 347) or Sayyid Mahmud Naqqash, who signed an inscription in tile mosaic in the winter prayer hall of the Friday Mosque at Isfahan in A.H. 851/A.D. 1447 (ibid., p. 379).
51. Bulatov and Shishkin, 1986, make the point (pp. 118–19), that the *madrasa* was built by command of Yalangtush Bahadur, under the direction of the architect `Abd-allah Jabbar, and the decoration was executed by Muhammad `Abbas [*sic*].
52. Necipoglu, 1995; see in particular pp. 9–14. These documents, conserved at the IO in Tashkent, were published by Baklanov in 1947: "Arkhitekturnye Chertezhi Uzbekskogo Mastera XVI veka," *Soobshcheniia Instituta Istorii i Teorii Arkhitektury, Akademii Arkhitekturi SSR*, 4, pp. 1–21.
53. Mankovskaja and Pulatov, 1991, p. 79.
54. Monshi, 1956, p. 109; Persian text: manuscript IO Tashkent no. 609, fol. 329.
55. Reference may be made, however, to a "classic" work on the subject: Pugachenkova and Rempel', 1958.
56. "The Paysage as Funerary Imagery in the Timurid period," 1993, pp. 241–52.
57. Examples of porcelain pieces copied by Syrian potters have been recorded from at least the fourteenth century. See for instance the "lotus bouquet" dish discovered at Hama, dating from the second half of the fourteenth century now in the National Museum at Damascus; reproduced in Soustiel, 1985, no. 249.
58. See especially the examples showing the "Three Friends" or the gardens with a balustrade, rockery, banana trees, etc.; reproduced in Krahl, 1986, nos. 562ff.
59. See for example, ibid., nos. 851 and 854, dating from the mid-sixteenth century.
60. Golombek and Wilber, 1988, pp. 407–9. Jahanshah, killed in an ambush in 1467–68, is supposed to be buried in this mosque.
61. Qazi Ahmad Qomi, 1959, p. 67.
62. Gabriel, 1935, p. 35.
63. Homa'i-ye Shirazi, 1996, p. 354; Mehrabadi, 1973, pp. 541 and 588. See also Gabriel, 1935, pp. 30–31.
64. Gabriel, 1935, p. 31.
65. Homa'i-ye Shirazi, 1996, p. 354. Mehrabadi, 1973, p. 540.
66. Mehrabadi, 1973, p. 699; the complete inscription is given on p. 703.
67. Text published in Mehrabadi, 1973, p. 704.
68. Homa'i-ye Shirazi, 1996, p. 353.
69. Mehrabadi, 1973, p. 694.
70. Ibid., p. 666.
71. Homa'i-ye Shirazi, 1996, p. 361.
72. Ibid., 1996, p. 354.
73. Galdieri, 1979, pp. 152–53.
74. An entire book has been devoted to these ceramic decorations: Luschey-Schmeisser, 1978.
75. Noted in Öz, 1957, p. 10 and pl. III; this author dates the mosque to 1242.
76. For the "`Isa al-Tawrizi" reading, see especially Carswell, "Six Tiles," in Ettinghausen, 1972, p. 100. As for V. Porter, she adopts the classic reading of "Ghaibi al-Tawrizi," in *Islamic Tiles*, p. 96.
77. Golombek, 1993, pp. 241–52.

78. An excellent study of tiles from Damascus, Saida, Cairo, and Edirne appears in Carswell's modestly entitled article, "Six Tiles," in Ettinghausen, 1972, pp. 99–124.
79. See Bernus-Taylor, 1997, pp. 251–66.
80. Necipoglu, 1995, p. 137. In the same article, the writer also mentions the names of other ceramists from Tabriz, such as Habib Tabrizi, the head of the *cema`at-i kashigeran* (the ceramists' community); see p. 139.
81. Quoted from Necipoglu, 1995, pp. 159–64.
82. Kiefer, 1956, pp. 15–31. It should be observed, however, that Kiefer states the tiles were made at Iznik, a hypothesis rejected today.
83. Ibid., p. 16, F.
84. See Soustiel, 2000, pp. 64–65.
85. V. Porter, 1995, p. 103.
86. Enamel-painted wares are not totally absent from India. Nevertheless, as Soustiel (1985, p. 238) has noted, no general study has yet been published on the subject.
87. On this, see the article by Rötzer, 1989, pp. 51–78.
88. R. Nath, 1970, covers vast fields, not only ceramic tilework, but also stone mosaic, stucco, and wall paintings. Three important monographs on specific examples of *kashi* decoration are given in a series published by the Archaeological Survey of India between 1901 and 1920: Smith, *Moghul Colour Decoration of Agra (Description of the Chini-ka-Rauza at Agra)*; Cousens, *Portfolio of Illustrations of Sind Tiles*; Vogel, *Tile-Mosaics of the Lahore Fort*.
89. D. B. Spooner, *A.S.I. Annual Report*, 1908–9, p. 55; Nath, 1970, p. 7.
90. Khan, 1969, pp. 24–30.
91. Cousens, 1903–4, pp. 133–44; Cousens, 1908–9, pp. 79–87; Cousens, 1929, pp. 50–51.
92. See M. Ishaq, *India's Contribution to the Study of the Hadith*, Dacca, 1955.
93. See Shokoohy, 1988.
94. Maricq and Wiet, 1959.
95. Schlumberger, 1978.
96. A. C. L. Carlleyle, *Archaeological Survey of India. Annual Report 1871–1872*, Calcutta, 1874, vol. 4, p. 219–20.
97. Ibn Battuta, 1990, vol. 2, p. 355.
98. See Brown, 1942, pl. XIV.
99. Smart, 1975–77, pp. 199–230.
100. Vogel, 1920, p. 56; this scholar referred to the description of the monument given by H. C. Fanshawe in his *Delhi, Past and Present* (1902, p. 244), although I have not found any mention of three-color tilework in this study; the polychrome tiles, moreover, seem no longer to be visible on the monument today.
101. Other monuments of the time, also in Delhi, show the typically sparing use of turquoise tiles. Instances include the Moth-ki Masjid, constructed by Miyan Bhuwa, Sikandar Lodi's vizier, the Nili Masjid (1505–6), and the *chhatri* at the *baoli* known as Rajon-ki Bain, dated 1506.
102. Guy and Swallow, 1990, p. 46.
103. Ibid., fig. 31. See also Khan and Stapleton, 1931.
104. As well as the collections at the Victoria and Albert Museum already mentioned, the British Museum additionally possesses a number of specimens of Bengal tiles; See V. Porter, 1995, pp. 87–88 and fig. 80.
105. Brown, 1942, p. 42.
106. Yazdani, 1947, p. 37.
107. Author of the chronicle of Mahmud Khalji, the *Ma`ather-e Mahmudshahi* (A.H. 872/A.D. 1467–68), was, as his *nisba* implies, of Iranian origin.

108. Kermani, 1968, p. 45.
109. See Yazdani's plan in Crowe, 1986, p. 42.
110. Y. Porter, 1994, pp. 23–36.
111. Nemtceva and Schwab, 1979, p. 71, fig. 86: the mausoleum known as "Anonymous 2." See also Bulatov and Shishkin, 1986, ill. no. 113: the tomb known as `Ali Nasafi (1380).
112. See for example Auboyer, 1968, pl. 127 and 131.
113. Kermani, 1968, p. 58.
114. Jahangir Padshah, 1989, pp. 385 and 397.
115. See Seherr-Thoss, 1968, pl. 58 and 65.
116. The monument is briefly described by Patil, 1982, pp. 46–47.
117. Patil (1982, p. 54) provides no date for this monument. An individual named Shaykh Maudud Chishti is quoted by Jahangir Padshah; this king gave him the title of Chishti Khan in 1617 when he was living at Mandu (*Tuzuk-e Jahangiri*, trans. Rogers, p. 379). Although there may be a connection between this person and the building concerned, it has not been determined that he was actually responsible for its construction.
118. Rötzer, 1989, writes (p. 74): "When these men [the invading Moslems] settled in India, they did not transplant the construction techniques they had been used to in the past but invented new ones in accordance with the materials available and their cost."
119. Kermani, 1968, p. 97.
120. See Kervran, 1996, pp. 133–71.
121. Gangler, 1993, pp. 161–62.
122. As in the case of the tomb of Gardizi, the dates provided for these monuments correspond to those of the deaths of the dignitaries entombed within; see P. Brown, 1942, p. 34.
123. See Moynihan, 1979, pp. 103–9.
124. See Nicholson, 1991.
125. See especially the diagrams published in Begley and Desai, 1989, pp. 68–72.

Map of the Islamic World

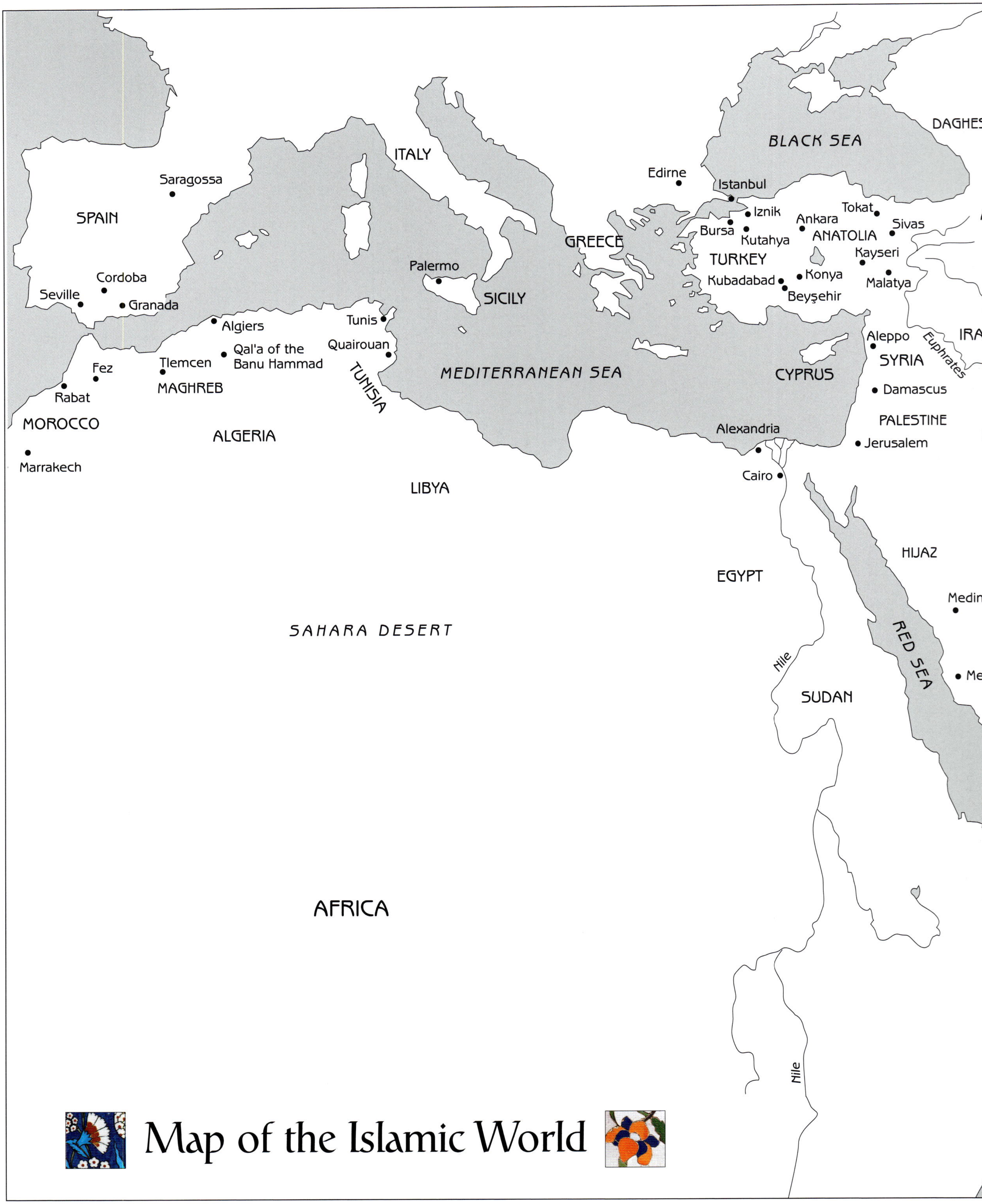

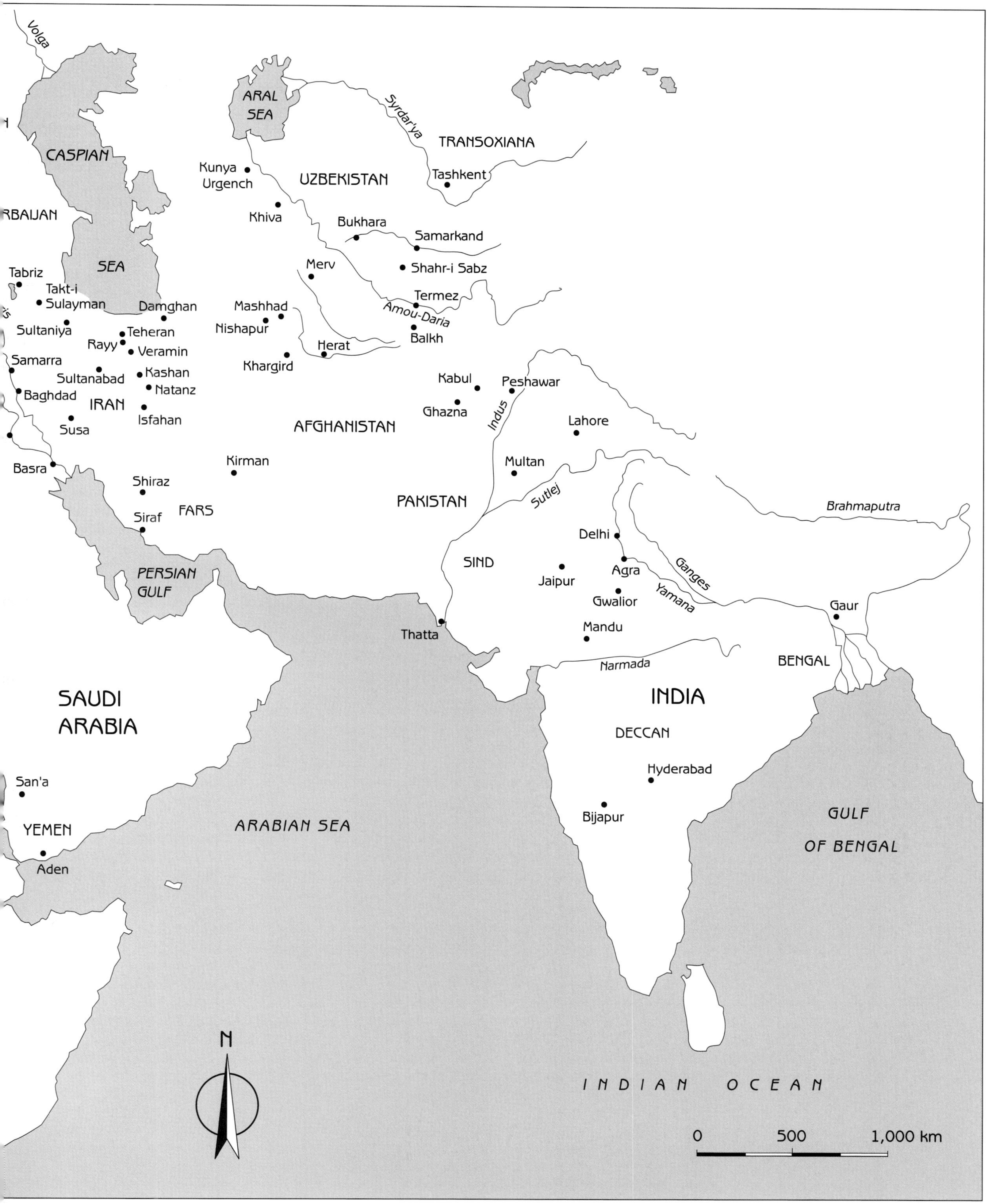
Volga
ARAL SEA
Syrdar'ya
TRANSOXIANA
CASPIAN SEA
Kunya Urgench
UZBEKISTAN
Tashkent
RBAIJAN
Khiva
Bukhara
Samarkand
Tabriz
Merv
Shahr-i Sabz
Takt-i Sulayman
Damghan
Mashhad
Termez
Amou-Daria
Sultaniya
Teheran
Nishapur
Balkh
Rayy
Veramin
Herat
Samarra
Khargird
Kashan
Kabul
Peshawar
Sultanabad
Natanz
Baghdad
IRAN
Ghazna
Indus
Susa
Isfahan
AFGHANISTAN
Lahore
Kirman
Multan
Basra
Shiraz
Sutlej
PAKISTAN
Brahmaputra
Siraf
FARS
Delhi
SIND
Ganges
Agra
Jaipur
PERSIAN GULF
Gwalior
Yamana
Gaur
Mandu
Thatta
Narmada
BENGAL
SAUDI ARABIA
INDIA
DECCAN
Hyderabad
San'a
Bijapur
GULF OF BENGAL
YEMEN
ARABIAN SEA
Aden
N
INDIAN OCEAN
0
500
1,000 km

Chronology of the Islamic World

HISTORICAL EVENTS

622 Muhammad's exile to Medina (Hegira) Beginning of the Islamic period
632 Death of the Prophet
633–40 Muslim conquest of Syria–Palestine and Iraq
642 The Muslims conquer Lower Egypt
651 Invasion of western Iraq
661 Assassination of `Ali
661–750 Rule of the Umayyads at Damascus
710–11 Muslim armies reach the Indus and invade Spain
750–1258 Reign of the `Abbasids at Baghdad
800–909 The Aghlabids control Ifriqiya
819–1005 The Samanids rule in the Khurasan and Transoxiana
836–88 The `Abbasid capital is transferred to Samarra
868–905 The Tulunids rule in Egypt
909–1171 The Fatimids reign in Tunisia, Egypt, Sicily, and Palestine
932–1062 The Buyyids control Iran and Iraq
977–1186 Rule of the Ghaznavids in Afghanistan, the Khurasan, Iran, and northern India
992–1211 The Qarakhanids rule in Transoxiana
1038–94 The Seljuqs reign in Iran
1056–1147 The Almoravids rule in Spain and North Africa
1071 Battle of Mantzikert
1077–1307 The Seljuqs of Rum control Anatolia
1095–99 First Crusade
1147–1269 Rule of the Almohads (in North Africa and Spain)
1147–48 Second Crusade
1171 Saladin unseats the Fatamid caliphate
1172–1200 Reign of the Khwarazm-Shah Tekesh
1182–1192 Third Crusade
1194 The Khwarazm Shahs overthrow the Seljuqs of Iran
1196–1465 Reign of the Marinids in Morocco
1206–1526 Rule of the sultans of Delhi
1220 The Mongols invade Transoxiana
1230–1492 Reign of the Nasrids of Granada
1248 Seville falls to the Christians
1250–1517 The Mamluks rule in Egypt and Syria
1256–1353 Reign of the Ilkhanids in Iran
1258 The Mongols seize Baghdad. End of the `Abbasid caliphate
1281–1924 Ottoman rule in Anatolia, Balkans, and the Near East
1317 Death of the Ilkhanid Uljaytu
1326 The Ottoman sultan Orhan takes Bursa
1366 The Ottoman capital is transferred from Bursa to Edirne
1370–1506 Reign of the Timurids in Iran and Transoxiana
1398–99 Timur's campaign in India and sack of Delhi
1402 Battle of Ankara opposing Bayezit and Timur
1404 The Castilian ambassador Clavijo visits Samarkand
1453 The Ottomans take Constantinople
1453–78 The reign of the Aq Qoyunlu Uzun Hasan
1487 The Portuguese round the Cape of Good Hope
1492 Granada taken by the Christians. Christopher Columbus reaches America
1498 Vasco de Gama lands at Calicut
1501–1732 The Safavids reign in Iran
1511–1659 Reign of the Sa`dis in Morocco
1517 Ottoman conquest of Syria, Egypt, and the Yemen
1520–66 Reign of Suleyman II the Magnificent
1526–1858 Reign of the Mughals in India
1529 The Ottomans lay siege to Vienna
1534 The Ottomans take Baghdad
1571 Battle of Lepanto at which the Ottomans are defeated
1588–1629 Reign of the Safavid Shah `Abbas I
1609–14 The Moriscos are expelled from Spain
1617 The Roman traveler Pietro della Valle visits Persia
1619 Establishment of the Dutch trading post at Batavia
1683 Second Ottoman siege of Vienna
1736–95 Nader Shah sets up the Afshar dynasty in Iran
1739 Delhi pillaged by Nader Shah
1750–94 Reign of the Zands in southern Persia
1779–1924 Reign of the Qajars in Iran
1797–1834 Reign of the Qajar Fath `Ali Shah
1798 Napoleon invades Egypt
1858 The Mughal Bahadur Shah II is deposed
1914–18 World War I
1924 Ottoman caliphate abolished

ARCHITECTURE AND CERAMICS

635–38	Construction of the mosques at Basra and Kufa
670	Construction of the first mosque at Qairouan
692	Dome of the Rock at Jerusalem completed
706–15	Construction of the mosques at Damascus, Medina, and al-Aqsa
762	Round city of Baghdad built
784	Construction of the Great Mosque at Cordoba
827	Reconstruction of the mosque at Qairouan commenced
836	Beginning of the construction of the Jawsaq al-Khaqani palace at Samarra
857	Foundation of the Qarawiyin Mosque at Fez
876–79	Mosque of Ibn Tulun at Fustat
905–43	Tomb of Isma`il the Samanid at Bukhara
936	Work begun on the city-palace at Madinat al-Zahra near Cordoba
961	Al-Hakam works on the mosque at Cordoba
969	The Fatimids found the city of Cairo
970	Foundation of the al-Azhar Mosque in Cairo
990	Foundation of the al-Hakim Mosque in Cairo
1006–7	Tomb of Gunbad-i Qavus
c. 1058	Minaret of the mosque at Damghan
1077–88	Friday Mosque at Isfahan refurbished
1099–1115	Construction of the palace of Mas`ud III at Ghazni
1127	Kalan minaret at Bukhara
1156–92	*Türbe* of Kiliç Arslan at Konya
1157	Tomb of Sultan Sandjar at Marv
1179	Date of the oldest luster-painted object from the Seljuq period
1183–84	Saladin begins building the citadel at Cairo
1194	The Gunbad-i Kabud at Maragha
before 1199	Minaret built at the Kutubiyya in Marrakech
1200	Tomb of Tekesh at Kunya Urgench
1251	*Madrasa* Karatay at Konya
1267	Panel of lusterware stars at Damghan (Louvre)
1271	Gök *madrasa* at Sivas
1284	Complex of Sultan Qalawun in Cairo
1307–13	Tomb of Uljaytu at Sultaniya
1320–24	Tomb of Rukn-i `Alam at Multan
1323	Construction of the *medersa* al-Attarin in Fez
c. 1330	Mosque of Muhammad Tughluq at Delhi
1333–54	Construction of the Patio de la Alberca complex in the Alhambra
1351	Masjid-i `Atiq at Shiraz
1371	Mausoleum of Shad-i Mulk Aqa at Samarkand
1403–21	Green Complex at Bursa
1404	Construction begins at Aq Saray palace at Shahr-i Sabz
1405	Gur-i Mir at Samarkand
1417	Construction work starts on the Gauhar Shad at Herat
1430	Mausoleum of Ghars al-Din al-Tawrizi at Damascus
1441	Work starts on the Jahaz Mahal at Mandu
1465	Blue Mosque at Tabriz
1472	*Madrasa* of Mahmud Gawan in Bidar
1473	Çinili Köşk, Istanbul
1486–1516	Man Mandir at Gwalior
1522	*Türbe* of Selim I at Istanbul
1538	Dados at the Casa de Pilatos at Seville
1561	Mosque of Rüstem Pasha, Istanbul
1565	Ben Yussef *medersa* and mosque, Istanbul. Tomb of Humayun in Delhi
1569–75	Selimiye Mosque at Edirne
1602	Work commenced on the Shaykh Lutfallah Mosque at Isfahan
1609	Blue Mosque begun in Istanbul
1624–31	Fort at Lahore
1632	Work begun on the Taj Mahal at Agra
1651–52	*Madrasa* of `Abd al-`Aziz Khan at Bukhara
1773–74	Vakil Mosque at Shiraz
1806	Takht-i Marmar, Gulistan in Teheran
1830–57	Mehmet `Ali Mosque in Cairo
1908–10	*Madrasa* and minaret of Islam Khoja, Khiva
1922–49	Rambagh Palace in Jaipur

Glossary

alafiya (Spanish, from the Arabic *al-`afiya*). Inscriptional motif formed from the first letters of *al-`afya*, meaning "good health." In traditional Islamic decorative arts, this formula may be repeated endlessly until the words lose their meaning and become a mere decorative motif.

alicatado (Spanish, from the Arabic *al-qata`a*, "cut"). Cut-tile mosaic.

artesonado (Spanish). Timber-coffered ceiling, occasionally decorated in marquetry.

ataurique (Spanish, from the Arabic *al-tawriq*). Decorative motif in a palmette interlace pattern.

azulejo (Spanish, from the Arabic *al-zellij*). Ceramic tile. Today the term principally (although not exclusively) designates painted soft-paste tiles.

band-i rumi (Persian). Geometric interlace pattern.

banna`i (Persian). Enamel-painted monochrome brick often used in an alternating diaper pattern with plain brick.

black line. A type of polychrome decoration characteristic of the Islamic East (from Turkey to India). Unlike *cuerda seca*, it is applied principally on stone-paste covered with a silica slip. The metallic oxides are mixed with a frit and the motifs underscored with a very slightly vitreous black line, mostly chromite (*mozarrad*), which prevents the colors from bleeding or mixing during firing.

chajja (Hindi). The stone portico or eaves protecting the facade of a building. A characteristic of Indian architecture.

chhatri (Hindi). Small domed pavilion standing alone or crowning a larger edifice.

clay. In Islamic ceramics, one of the two main materials used to make tiles (the other is stone-paste). Clay is more or less red in color depending on its composition and the firing conditions; it is frequently covered with a tin enamel. *See also* **stone-paste.**

coloring oxides. Except for antimony, all the oxides used to color ceramics come from the range of metals classified in period four of the periodic table (transition elements: chrome, manganese, iron, cobalt, copper). Their highly variable oxidation means that at high firing temperatures a wide range of colors can be obtained. For these colors to be effective, the oxides must be mixed with frit (in the case of "cloisonné" paints of the *cuerda seca* or "black line" types). For underglaze-painted decoration they are used without flux and applied to the ground (enamel or slip) with the aid of an adhesive.

cuenca y arista (Spanish, "hollow and ridge"). Type of tile molded before firing with hollows and ridges to keep the colored paints separate and minimize bleeding.

cuerda seca (Spanish). Polychrome painted decoration in which the different paints are kept apart by a line made up of a mixture of manganese oxide and an oily substance that vaporizes on firing. A distinction is made between *cuerda seca parcial* (partial) and *cuerda seca total* (complete) depending on the type of ground (painted or not) and the surface taken up by the pattern.

eslimi (Persian). Decorative motif composed of palmette interlace, the equivalent of *tawriq* in the Muslim West.

frit. Vitreous material obtained by heating silica (sand or powdered quartz) mixed with one or more fluxes (sodium carbonate, lead). Frit is used as an ingredient for hard-paste bodies as well as in glazes.

glaze. Glassy substance composed of silica and a flux (lead, sodium carbonate: alkaline fluxes). These can be termed lead or alkaline glazes depending on their composition. Glaze can be transparent (clear) and colorless, or else opacified and colored.

gunbad (Persian). Originally the term for a dome, it is also used to refer to funerary constructions capped by a dome.

haft-rang (Persian; literally, "seven-colored"). Polychrome-decorated ceramics. In the Seljuq period, the term designated ceramics painted with high-fired oxides (cobalt, copper, iron, manganese), decorated with colored slips, and finished with *petit feu* gold-leaf. In the Safavid epoch, the term was applied to polychrome "black line" designs.

hazar-baf (Persian; literally, "thousand weave"). All-over decorative motif, most commonly executed in *banna`i* brickwork diaper in imitation of basketweave patterns.

iwan (Arabic pronunciation, or *ivan*; from Persian *eyvan*). Large vaulted hall, closed on three sides with the fourth usually opening onto a courtyard or garden.

kashi (Persian). Ceramic tiles. Originally, the term was used to refer to tiles from the city of Kashan in central Iran, which was the major center of production, especially for pieces decorated in luster.

khaneqa (Persian). Charitable institution (sometimes reduced to serving merely as a hospice) that provided help, shelter, and food for members of the Sufi brotherhoods.

khata`i (Persian; "from Cathay"). Decorative floral motif composed of leaf and branch trails with floral scrollwork by Far Eastern models (in particular "blue-and-white" Chinese porcelain).

khatim (Arabic, "seal"). Star with a variable number of points or branches (*khatim thmaniya*, eight-pointed star, for example).

Kufic (from the Arabic *kufi*). One of the earliest scripts to be used on monuments, this style of calligraphy, originally from the city of Kufa, is characterized by its angular appearance and an absence of diacritics. As it evolved in various regions, Kufic diversified: some styles have ascenders crowned by palmettes (floriated or flowery Kufic), while in others the flourishes intertwine (plaited Kufic). The style occurs frequently in brickwork facings, where colored *banna`i* bricks are arranged in interlocking patterns to form labyrinthine inscriptions.

lajvardina (from *lajvard*, the Persian for lapis lazuli or cobalt). A technique adopted in the second half of the thirteenth century and into the fourteenth during the Mongol era in which a soft-fired decoration on slip (red, white, or black) with gold leaf was applied over a cobalt blue ground.

madrasa (Arabic; *medersa* in Morocco). Institute of tertiary education (and not simply a Qur`anic school, as often defined) in which the traditional Muslim sciences are taught.

maqsura (Arabic). Space in front of the *mihrab*, often capped by a dome, that in former times was closed off and reserved for the sole use of the caliph.

mihrab (Arabic). In a mosque, a niche (conch) indicating the direction (*qibla*) to which prayers should be addressed. The *mihrab* first appeared in 706 in the reign of Caliph al-Walid I, who built a niche for the mosque at Medina in Arabia.

mina`i (Persian, meaning "enameled"). A relatively recent term designating decorated ceramics fired at low temperatures, also called *haft-rang*.

minbar (Arabic). Pulpit used particularly for the *khutba* (sermon) delivered at Friday prayers.

mo`arraq (Persian, "inlaid"). Cut-tile mosaic; the equivalent of *zellij* in the Maghreb.

mozarrad (Persian). Chromite. A black mineral composed of chromium oxide, iron, and magnesium, used particularly in "black line" decoration.

Muhaqqaq (Arabic). Cursive calligraphic style derived from Naskhi and characterized by limited downstrokes that tend to lie horizontally just below the line.

muqarnas (Arabic). Corbels covered in "stalactites," especially in the vaulted areas of archways or in cupolas. This device, which became widespread in the twelfth century almost throughout the whole Muslim world, is one of the most characteristic features of Islamic architecture.

naqqash (Arabic). Draftsman, painter, or designer. In the field of architectural ceramics, the *naqqash* designed and drew the cartoons.

Naskhi (Arabic). Cursive calligraphic style developed in tenth-century Baghdad. The style is especially prevalent, even nowadays, for copying manuscripts (the Qur`an in particular). Regional variations have led to the emergence of local styles, such as the Maghribi in North Africa and Spain.

low-firing (soft-firing, *petit feu*). Low-temperature kiln firing (sometimes utilizing saggars or cases) that makes it possible to incorporate materials particularly sensitive to higher temperatures, such as unglazed slips or gold leaf. *Mina`i* (or *haft-rangi*) and *lajvardina* ware are forms of low-fired decoration.

petit feu (French; literally, "little fire"). *See* **low-firing.**

pishtaq (Persian; literally, "in front of the arch"). The vaulted entrance to a building.

qibla (Arabic). Ritual orientation of prayer in the direction of Mecca, often given material form by a *mihrab* in the mosque.

sahn (Arabic). Courtyard, in particular in mosques and *madrasas*.

saz (Turkish, from the Persian). Decorative style inspired by the arts of the Timurids that appeared in the Ottoman world in the second half of the fifteenth century, employing broad serrated leaves or palmettes.

sgraffito (or *sgraffiato*, Italian). Decoration incised into the piece to reveal the (plain) body beneath the colored glaze. *See also* ***taqshir.***

shamsa (from Arabic *shams*, meaning "sun"). Motif used in illumination forming a circular radiating medallion.

sharrafa (Arabic). Crenellated pattern superposed above another motif.

slip. Unlike enamels, slips (engobes) are not vitreous materials but clayey substances used both to provide a coating for ceramic bodies (that are then glazed) and also in the application of underglaze (high-fired) or onglaze (low-fired) decoration.

stone-paste. In Islamic ceramics, one of the two main materials used to make tiles (the other is clay). Siliceous (stone) paste (fritware) appeared in the East in the twelfth century. It contains only 10 to 20 percent clay, the rest being made up of quartz and frit. *See also* **clay.**

taqshir (Arabic, "scaled"). A process of removing the layer of colored oxide by scratching in *sgraffito* the motif, which then appears on the plain body beneath.

tawriq (Arabic). Palmette interlace pattern (known as *ataurique* in Spanish; *eslimi* in the Muslim East).

Thuluth (Arabic). Cursive calligraphic style characterized by the length of the upstrokes and much used (especially from the twelfth century onward) in monumental inscriptions.

türbe (Turkish, from Arabic). Tomb, mausoleum.

zawiya (Arabic). Religious institution devoted to teaching often composed of a mystic order gathered around a sanctuary in which the patron of the brotherhood is buried.

zellij (Arabic). Tiles cut and arranged into a mosaic (or marquetry). The term is the equivalent in the Maghreb of the *kashi-ye mo`arraq* (inlaid tilework) of the Persian-speaking East.

Bibliography

Sources: texts, translations, and studies

`Ali b. Mahmud Kermani. *Ma`ather-e Mahmudshahi*, edited by N. H. Ansari. Delhi, 1968.

Abu al-Qasem Kashani. *`Arayes al-javaher va nafayes al-atayeb*, edited by I. Afshar. Teheran, A.H. 1345/1966.

Allan, James W. "Abu`l-Qasim's Treatise on Ceramics," *Iran*, XI (1973): 111–20.

Biringuccio, Vannoccio. *The Pirotechnia of Vannoccio Biringuccio. The Classic Sixteenth-Century Treatise on Metals and Metallurgy*. New York, 1989.

Biruni, Abu Rayhan. *The Book Most Comprehensive in Knowledge on Precious Stones*, translated by H. M. Said. Islamabad, 1989.

———. *Kitab al-jamahir fi ma`rifat al-jawahir*, edited by Yusof al-Hadi. Teheran, A.H. 1374 /1995.

Clément-Mullet, J. "Essai sur la minéralogie arabe," *Journal asiatique*, no. 11 (1868): 163–73.

Dayton, J. E., and J. Bowles. "Abul Qasim of Kashan and the Problem of Persian Glazing," *Annali Istituto Orientale di Napoli*, no. 37, fasc. II: 143–52.

Hamd-Allah Mostwfi-ye Qazvini. *The Geographical Part of the Nuzhat al-Qulub*, translated by G. Le Strange. Leiden and London, 1919.

Ibn Battuta. *Voyages*, translated by C. Defremy. Paris, 1858. New edition, Paris, 1990.

———. *Travels in Asia and Africa 1325–1354*, translated by H. A. R. Gibb. London, 1929.

Ibn Ikhwah (Muhammad b. Ahmad al-Qurashi). *Ma`alim al-qurbat fi ahkam al-hisbat*. Persian translation by J. Sho`ar. *A`in-e shahrdari*. Teheran, A.H. 1347/1968. Translation of chapter LVI into French in *La céramique musulmane de l'Égypte* by A. B. Baghat and F. Massoul. Cairo, 1930.

Ibn Taymiyya. *Public Duties in Islam: the Institution of the Hisba*, translated by Muhtar Holland. Leicester, 1985.

Jahangir Padshah. *Tuzuk-e Jahangiri. Memoirs of Jahangir*, translated by A. Rogers and H. Beveridge. Reprint. Delhi, 1989.

Javaher-name, anonymous, fifteenth century, edited by Taqi Binesh; *Farhang-e Iran Zamin* no. 12, Teheran (A.H. 1343/1964): 273–97.

Kahle, P. "Bergkristalle, Glas und Glasflüsse nach dem Steinbuch des Al-Biruni," *Zeitschrift der Deutschen Morgenländlische Gesellschaft*, 90 (1936): 322–56.

Khwandamir, Habib al-Siyyar, edited by J. Homa`i. 4 vols. Teheran, A.H. 1333/1954.

Mansur, Muhammad Ebn-i. *Gowhar-name*, edited by M. Sotude, *Farhang-e Iran Zamin*, 4, 3 (1956): 185–312.

Monshi, Muhammad Yusof. *Tarikh-e Moqim Khan*, translated into Russian by A. A. Semionov. Tashkent, 1956.

Nasrabadi, Muhammad Tahir. *Tazkere-ye Nasrabadi*, edited by Vahid-e Dastgerdi. Teheran, n.d.

Naumann, R. "Brennöfen für Glazurkeramik," *Istanbuler Mitteilungen*, no. 21 (1971): 173–90.

Özergin, M. Kemal. "Temürlü sanatina ait eski bir belge, Tebrizli Ca'far'in bir Arzi," *Sanat Tarihi yilligi*, no. 4 (1976): 471–518.

Parsay, A. "Teymuri dar ketabkhane-ye baysanghori-ye Harat," *Honar-o mardom*, 175 (1977): 42–50.

Piccolpasso, Cipriano. *I tre libri dell'arte del vasaio*, edited by G. Vanzolino. Pesaro, 1879.

Porter, Yves. "Textes persans sur la céramique," in *La science dans le monde iranien*, edited by Z. Vesel. Teheran, 1998.

Qazi Ahmad Qomi. *Tazkere-ye khoshnevisan va naqqashan. Golestan-e honar*, translated by V. Minorsky, *Calligraphers and Painters*, Washington, D.C., 1959.

Ritter, H., J. Ruska, F. Sarre, and R. Winderlich. "Orientalische Steinbücher und persische Fayencetechnik," *Istanbuler Mitteilungen des Archäologischen Instituts des Deutschen Reiches*, no. 3 (1935): 16–48.

Tazkerat al-moluk, anonymous, edited and translated by V. Minorsky. London, 1943.

Thackston, Wheeler M. *A Century of Princes. Sources on Timurid History and Art*. Cambridge (Mass.), 1989.

Tusi, Nasir al-Din. *Tansukh-name-ye Ilkhani*, edited by Modarres-e Razavi. Teheran, A.H. 1348/1969.

General works and monographs

Al-Hassan, A.Y.,and D. R. Hill. *Sciences et techniques en Islam. Une histoire illustrée*. Paris, 1991.

Atil, Ehsin. *Ceramics from the World of Islam*. Exh. cat. Washington, D.C., 1973.

Bernus-Taylor, Marthe. *Les arts de l'Islam*. Paris, 1993.

Blair, Sheila, and Jonathan Bloom. *The Art and Architecture of Islam, 1250–1800*. New Haven, 1995.

Bosworth, C. E. *The Islamic Dynasties*. Edinburgh, 1980.

Caiger-Smith, Alan. *Lustre pottery. Techniques, Tradition and Innovation in Islam and the Western World*. London, 1985.

Creswell, K. A. C. *Early Muslim Architecture*. 2 vols. Oxford, 1932 and 1940.

Crowe, Yolande. "Khazaf," in *Encyclopédie de l'Islam*. Vol. 4. New edition. Leiden, 1978.

Curatola, G., ed. *Eredità dell'Islam. Arte islamica in Italia*, exh. cat. Venice, 1993.

Dreaming of Paradise. Islamic Art from the Collection of the Museum of Ethnology, exh. cat. Rotterdam, 1993.

Ettinghausen, Richard, and Oleg Grabar. *The Art and Architecture of Islam, 650–1250*. New Haven, 1987.

Fehervari, Geza. *Pottery of the Islamic World in the Tareq Rajab Museum*. Kuwait, 1998.

Forbes, R. J. *Studies in Ancient technology*. Vol. 3. Leiden, 1965.

Golvin, Lucien. *Essai sur l'architecture religieuse musulmane*. 3 vols. Paris, 1974–78.

———. *La madrasa médiévale*. Aix-en-Provence, 1995.

Grabar, Oleg. *The Formation of Islamic Art*. Reprint. New Haven, 1987.

Gratuze, B., I. Soulier, M. Blet, and L. Vallaury. "De l'origine du cobalt: du verre à la céramique," *Revue d'archéométrie*, no. 20 (1996): 77–94.

Gratuze, B., I. Soulier, J.-N. Barrandon, and D. Foy, "De l'origine du cobalt dans les verres," *Revue d'archéométrie*, no. 16 (1992): 97–108.

Greber, E. *Traité de céramique*. Paris, 1950.

Heyd, W. *Histoire du commerce du Levant au Moyen Age*. Leipzig, 1885–86; reprint, vol. 2, Amsterdam, 1959.

Hillenbrand, Robert. *Islamic Architecture. Form, Function and Meaning*. New York, 1994.

Irwin, Robert. *Islamic Art in Context: Art, Architecture and the Literary World*. New York, 1997.

Krahl, Robert. *Chinese Ceramics in the Topkapi Saray Museum. II. Yuan and Ming Dynasty Porcelains*. London, 1986.

Lane, Arthur. *Later Islamic Pottery: Persia, Syria, Egypt, Turkey*. London, 1957.

———. *Guide to the Collection of Tiles in the Victoria and Albert Museum*. London, 1960.

Launay, L. de. *Gîtes minéraux et métallifères*. 3 vols. Paris and Liège, 1913.

Marchesi, H., J. Thiriot, and L. Vallauri. *Marseille, les ateliers de potiers du XIIIe s. et le quartier de Sainte-Barbe, Ve-XVIIe siècles*. Paris, 1997.

Moulierac, Jeanne. *Céramiques du monde musulman: collections de l'Institut du Monde Arabe et de J.-P. Croisier*. Paris, 1999.

Necipoglu, Gülru. *The Topkapi Scroll: Geometry and Ornament in Islamic Architecture. Topkapi Palace Museum Library MS H.1956*. Santa Monica, 1995.

Öney, Gönül. *Ceramic Tiles in Islamic Architecture*. Istanbul, 1987.

Pigments et colorants de l'Antiquité et du Moyen Age. Teinture, peinture, enluminure: études historiques et physico-chimiques. Paris, 1990.

Piotrovsky, Mikhail B., and John Vrieze. *Art of Islam. Heavenly Art, Earthly Beauty*, exh. cat. Amsterdam, 1999.

Porter, Venetia. *Islamic Tiles*. London, 1995.

Porter, Yves. "Origines et diffusion du cobalt utilisé en céramique à l'époque médiévale. Étude préliminaire," in *La céramique médiévale en Méditerranée: Actes du VIe congrès de l'AIEMC2*, November 13–18, 1995, Aix-en-Provence (1997): 505–12.

Ragheb, Y. "Les premiers monuments funéraires de l'Islam," *Annales islamologiques*, IX (1970): 21–36.

Seherr-Thoss, Sonia P. *Design and Color in Islamic Architecture*. Washington, D.C., 1968.

Sourdel, Dominique and Janine. *La Civilisation de l'Islam classique*. Paris, 1968.

Sourdel-Thomine, J., and B. Spuler. *Die Kunst des Islam*. Berlin, 1973.

Soustiel, Jean. *La céramique islamique: guide du connaisseur*. Fribourg, 1985.

Soustiel, Jean, and Marie-Christine David. *Sur la route des découvertes*. Paris, 1988.

Tournefort, Pitton de. *Relation d'un voyage du Levant*. Paris, 1717.

Le vert et le brun, de Kairouan à Avignon: céramiques du xe au xve siècle. Exh. cat. Marseille, 1995.

The Islamic East: Iraq, Iran, Afghanistan, central Asia

Auboyer, J. *L'Afghanistan et son art*. Paris, 1968.

Bagherzadeh, F., A. Saurat, and M. Sato. *Oriental Ceramics. The World's great Collections*. Vol. 4. Tokyo, 1978.

Bahrami, Mehdi. *Recherches sur les carreaux de revêtement lustré dans la céramique persane du XIIIe au XVe siècle*. Paris, 1937.

———. "Contribution à l'étude de la céramique musulmane de l'Iran," *Athar-e Iran*, III, 2 (1938): 209–29.

Baklanov, N. B. "Arkhitekturnye Chertzhi Uzbekskogo Mastera xvi veka," in *Soobshcheniia Instituta Istorii i Teorii Arkhitektuty, Akademii Arkhitekturii SSR*, no. 4 (1947): 1–21.

Blair, Sheila. *The Ilkhanid Shrine Complex at Natanz, Iran*. Cambridge (Mass.), 1986.

———. "The Epigraphic Program of the Tomb of Uljaytu at Sultaniya: Meaning in Mongol Architecture," *Islamic Art*, II (1987): 43–96.

———. *The Monumental Inscriptions from Early Islamic Iran and Transoxiana*. Leiden, 1992.

Blake, Stephen P. *Half the World: the Social Architecture of Safavid Isfahan, 1590–1722*. Costa Mesa, 1999.

Brikalova, V. G. "Sharkija, Benaket, Shahrukhija," in Y. F. Burjakov, *Drevnii i srednevekovii gorodvostocnogo Maverannakhra*. Tashkent, 1990.

Bulatov, V., and G. Shishkin. *Samarkand, a Museum in the Open*. Tashkent, 1986.

Burjakov, Y. F., ed. *Drevnii i srednevekovii gorod vostocnogo Maverannakhra*. Tashkent, 1990.

Carboni, Stefano, and T. Masuya. *Persian Tiles*. New York, 1993.

Centlivres-Demont, Micheline, *Une communauté de potiers en Iran. Le centre de Meybod, Yazd*. Wiesbaden, 1971.

Chardin, Jean. *Voyages du chevalier Chardin en Perse et autres lieux de l'Orient*, edited by L. Langlès. 7 vols. Paris, 1811.

———. *Travels in Persia*. Reprint. New York, 1988.

Curatola, G., "Sui 'Bianchi e blu' cinesi: Il problema della provenienza del cobalto," *Incontri tra Occidente e Oriente*, III, Venice (1979): 1–13.

Ettinghausen, Richard. "Important Pieces of Persian Pottery in London Collections," *Ars Islamica*, II, 1935.

———."Dated faience," in *A Survey of Persian Art*, edited by Arthur U. Pope. Vol. 4. Oxford, 1939.

Gabriel, Albert. "Le Masdjid-i Djum'a d'Isfahan," *Ars Islamica*, II, 1 (1935): 12–44.

Galdieri, Eugenio. *Esfahan: `Ali Qapu, an Architectural Survey*. Rome, 1979.

Godard, Yedda. "Pièces datées de céramique de Kashan à décor lustré," *Athar-e Iran*, II (1937): 309–37.

Golombek, Lisa. "The *Paysage* as Funerary Imagery in the Timurid Period," *Muqarnas*, no. 10 (1993): 241–52.

Golombek, Lisa, R. B. Mason, and G. A. Bailey. *Tamerlane's Tableware. A New Approach to the Chinoiserie Ceramics of Fifteenth- and Sixteenth-Century Iran*. Costa Mesa, 1996.

Golombek, Lisa, and Donald Wilber. *The Timurid Architecture of Iran and Turan*. 2 vols. Princeton, 1988.

Hillenbrand, Robert, ed. *The Art of the Saljuqs in Iran and Anatolia*. Costa Mesa, 1994.

Homa`i-ye Shirazi. *Jalal al-din, Tarikh-e Esfahan: mojeld-e honar va honarmandan* , edited by M. Banu Homa`i. Teheran, A.H. 1375/1996.

Karimi, Fateme, and M. Y. Kiani. *Honar-e sofalgari-ye dowre-ye eslami-ye Iran*. Teheran, A.H. 1364/1986.

Kiani, M. Y. *The Islamic City of Gurgan*. Berlin, 1984.

Ladame, G. "Les ressources métallifères de l'Iran," *Schweizerische mineralogische und petrographische Mitteilungen*, 25 (1945): 195–97.

Lentz, Thomas, and Glenn Lowry. *Timur and the Princely Vision*. Los Angeles, 1989.

Loti, Pierre. *Vers Isfahan*. Paris, 1904.

Loukonine, V., and A. Ivanov. *L'art persan*. St. Petersburg, 1995.

Luschey-Schmeisser, Ingeborg. *The Pictorial Tile Cycle of Hasht-Behesht in Isfahan and its Iconographic Tradition*. Rome, 1978.

Majidzadeh, Y. "The Development of the Pottery Kiln in Iran from Prehistoric to Historical Periods," *Paleorient*, 3 (1977): 207–21.

Mankovskaja, L. Y., and T. Pulatov. *Bukhara, a Museum in the Open*. Tashkent, 1991.

Maricq, A., and G. Wiet. *Le minaret de Djam. La découverte de la capitale des sultans ghorides, xiie-xiiie siècles*, Mémoire de la Délégation Archéologique Française en Afghanistan (D.A.F.A.), XVI, Paris, 1959.

Mason, Robert B. "Mediaeval Iranian Lustre-Painted and Associated Wares: Typology in a multidisciplinary Study," *Iran*, XXXV (1997): 103–35.

Mason, Robert B., and Lisa Golombek. "Differentiating Early Chinese-Influenced Blue and White Ceramics of Egypt, Syria, and Iran," *Archaeometry* (1990): 465–74.

Mason, Robert B., and Edward J. Keall. "The 'Abbasid Glazed Wares of Siraf and the Basra Connection: Petrographic Analysis," *Iran*. 29 (1991): 51–66.

Melikian-Chirvani, A.-S. *Les frises du Shah-name dans l'architecture iranienne sous les Ilkhan*. Paris, 1996.

Mukminova, R. G. "Craftsmen and Guild Life in Samarqand," in *Timurid Art and culture*, edited by L. Golombek and M. Subtelny. Leiden, 1992.

Naraghi-Mirfendereski, F., M. A. Mirfendereski, and A. F. Zonuni. *Ceramica nell'architectura in Persia*. Florence, 1992.

Naumann, R. *Takht-i Suleiman*. Munich, 1976.
———. *Die Ruinen von Takht-e Suleimen und Umgebung*. Berlin, 1977.
Nemtseva, N. B., and Y. Z. Schwab. *Ansambl' Shakh-i zinda. Istoriko-arkhitekturnyi ocherk*. Tashkent, 1979.
O'Kane, Bernard. *Timurid Architecture in Khurassan*. Costa Mesa, 1977.
Pickett, Donald. "Inscriptions by Muhammad Rida al-Imami," *Iran*, 22 (1984): 91–102.
———. "The Significance of the Friday Mosque, Ushturjan, in the History of Persian Tilework," in *The Art of the Saljuqs in Iran and Anatolia*, edited by Robert Hillenbrand. Costa Mesa, 1994.
Pope, Arthur U., ed. *A Survey of Persian Art*. 6 vols. Oxford, 1939.
———. "A Note on Porcelain in Persia," *Bulletin of the Iranian Institute*, 6, nos. 1-4, and 7, no. 1 (December 1946): 119–20.
Pope, John A. *Chinese Porcelain from the Ardabil Shrine*. Washington, D.C., 1956.
Porter, Yves. "Shangarf et Lazhvard dans le monde iranien," *Res Orientales*, V (1993): 147–57.
———. "Technologie et mécénat: matériaux et modes de production de la céramique iranienne "médiévale," in *Matériaux pour l'histoire économique du monde iranien, Cahiers de Studia Iranica*, edited by R. Gyselen and M. Szuppe. Paris, 1999.
Pugachenkova, G., and L. I. Rempel`. *Vydajushchiesja pamjatniki arkhitektury Uzbekistana*. Tashkent, 1958.
Quchani, `Abd-allah. *Katibeha-ye sofal-e Neyshabur*. Teheran, A.H. 1364/1986.
———. *Ash'ar-e farsi-ye kashiha-ye Takht-e Soleyman*. Teheran, Ha.h. 1371/1992.
———. "Sefalgaran-e Kashan va she'r-e farsi," *Nashr-e danesh*, 14, 6 (A.H. 1373/1994): 31–41.
Rafi`i Mehrabadi, A. *Athar-e melli-ye Esfahan*. Teheran, A.H. 1352/1973.
Scarce, J. M. "Function and Decoration in Qajar Tilework," in *Persian Art and Culture of the 18th and 19th Centuries*. Edinburgh, 1979.
Schlumberger, Daniel. *Lashkari Bazar. L'architecture*, Mémoire de la Délégation Archéologique Française en Afghanistan (D.A.F.A.), XVIII, 1 A, Paris, 1978.
Shishkin, V. A. "Nadpisi v ansamble Shakhi-Zinda," *Zodchestvo Uzbekistana. Material' i issledovanija*. Vol. 2: *Ansambl' Shakhi-Zinda*. Tashkent, 1970.
Takibayeva, S. S. *Taini nebesnoi glazuri*. Alma Ata, 1987.
Terres secrètes de Samarcande. Exh. cat. Paris, 1992.
Watson, Oliver. *Persian Lustre Ware*. London, 1985.
———. "Documentary *mina`i* and Abu Zaid's Bowls," in *The Art of the Saljuks in Iran and Anatolia*, edited by Robert Hillenbrand. Costa Mesa, 1994.
Welch, Anthony. *Shah `Abbas and the Arts of Isfahan*. New York, 1973.
Whitehouse, David. "Excavations at Siraf: Fourth Interim Report," *Iran*, IX (1971): 1–18.
Wilber, Donald. *The Architecture of Islamic Iran, the Ilkhanid Period*. New York, 1969.
———. "Builders and Craftsmen of Islamic Iran: the Earlier Periods," *Art and Archaeology Research Papers* (1976): 31–39.
Wilkinson, C. K. *Nishapur, Pottery of the Early Islamic Period*. New York, 1974.
Wulff, H. E. *The Traditional Crafts of Persia*. Cambridge (Mass.), 1966.

The Maghreb and Spain

Ainaud de Lasarte, J. "Cerámica y vidrio," *Ars Hispaniae*, X, Madrid (1952).
Alvaro Zamora, Isabel. *Cerámica aragonesa*. Saragossa, 1982.
Bargebuhr, Frederik P. *The Alhambra*. Berlin, 1968.
Barrucand, Marianne (text), and Achim Bednorz (photographs). *L'architecture maure en Andalousie*. Cologne, 1992.
Broussaud, A. *Les carreaux de faïence peints de l'Afrique du Nord*. Paris, 1930.
Les Cahiers d'Achir, Revue du Musée national des Antiquités d'Alger, no. 3, *Rapport de fouille 1993*, Algiers, 1994.
De Haedo, Diego. *Topographía de Argel*. Valladolid, 1612.
Frotingham, A. W. *Lusterware of Spain*. New York, 1951.
Gestoso y Perez, José. *Historia de los barros vidriados sevillanos*. Seville, 1904.
Golvin, L. *Recherches archéologiques à la Qal`a des Banu Hammad*. Paris, 1965.
Gonzales Marti, M. *Cerámica del levante español, siglos medievales: Loza*. Barcelona, 1944.
Hedgecoe, John, and Salma Samar Damluji. *Zillig, l'art de la céramique marocaine*. Paris, 1993.
Hill, Donald, and L. Golvin. *Islamic Architecture in North Africa*. London, 1976.
Lafuente y Alcántara. *Inscripciones árabes de Granada*. Madrid, 1859.
Marçais, George. *Les faïences à reflets métalliques de la Grande Mosquée de Kairouan*. Paris, 1928.
Pérez Camps, J. *La cerámica de reflejo metálico en Manises, 1850–1960*, exh. cat. Valencia, 1998.
Torres Balbás, Leopoldo. *Arte almohade, arte nazarí, arte mudéjar*. Madrid, 1947.
———. *Artes almorávide y almohade*. Madrid, 1955.
Vanités de faïence. Entre Provence et Languedoc, carreaux de céramique espagnols XVe-XVIIIe siècles. Exh. cat. Arles, 2000.

Egypt, Syria, and the Turkish world

Aslanapa, O. *Osmanlilar Devrinde Kütahya Cinileri*. Istanbul, 1949.
———. *Türkische Fliesen und Keramik in Anatolien*. Istanbul, 1965.
———. *Turkish Art and Architecture*. New York, 1970.
Atasoy, N., and J. Raby. *Iznik. The Pottery of Ottoman Turkey*. London, 1989.
Atil, Ehsin. *Renaissance of Islam: Art of the Mamluks*. Washington, D.C., 1981.
Baghat, A., and F. Massoul. *La céramique musulmane de l'Égypte*. Cairo, 1930.
Barrucand, Marianne, ed. *L'Égypte fatimide: son art et son histoire*. Paris, 1999.
Bernus-Taylor, Marthe. "Le décor du 'complexe Vert' à Bursa, reflet de l'art timouride," in *Cahiers d'Asie centrale*, nos. 3-4 (1997): 251–66.
Carswell, John. "Six Tiles," in *Islamic Art in the Metropolitan Museum of Art, New York*, edited by Robert Ettinghausen. New York, 1972.
———. *Kütahya Tiles and Pottery*. Oxford, 1972.
Garcin, Jean-Claude, et. al. *Palais et maisons du Caire*. 2 vols. Paris, 1983.
Henderson, J. "Glass Production in Raqqa, Syria. New Evidence for an Interim Assessment," *Annales du 13e Congrès de l'Association internationale pour l'histoire du verre*, Lochem (1996): 257–68.
Jenkins-Madina, Marilyn. "Fatimid Decorative Arts: the Picture the Sources Paint," in *L'Égypte fatimide, son art et son histoire*, edited by M. Barrucand. Paris, 1999.
Kiefer, Charles. "Céramiques musulmanes d'Anatolie," *Cahiers de la céramique et des arts du feu*, no. 4 (1956): 15–31.
Konya et le règne des Seldjoukides. Exh. cat. Amiens, 1999.
Meinecke, M. *Fayencedekorationen seldschukischer sakralbauten in Kleinasien*. Tübingen, 1976.
Necipoglu, Gülru. "From International Timurid to Ottoman: a Change of Taste in Sixteenth Century Ceramic Tiles," *Muqarnas*, 7 (1990): 136–70.
Öz, Tahsin. *Turkish ceramics*. Ankara, 1957.
Raby, Julian. "Diyarbakir: a Rival to Iznik, a Sixteenth Century Tile Industry in Eastern Anatolia," *Istanbuler Mitteilungen*, nos. 27–28, 1977–78.
Rogers, Michael. "Kara Mehmed Çelebi, Kara Memi and the Role of the

ser-naqqash," in *Soliman le Magnifique et son temps*, edited by G. Veinstein. Paris, 1992.

Soustiel, Laure. *Splendeurs de la céramique ottomane*. Exh. cat. Paris, 2000.

Ünsal, B. *Turkish Islamic Architecture in Seljuk and Ottoman Times 1071–1923*. London, 1959.

The Indian subcontinent

Begley, W. E., and Z. A. Desai. *Taj Mahal, the Illumined Tomb*. Cambridge (Mass.), 1989.

Brown, Percy. *Indian Architecture, Islamic Period*. Bombay, 1942.

Chaghatay, M. Abdullah. *The Wazir Khan Mosque, Lahore: History and Architecture*. Lahore, 1975.

Cousens, Henry. "Brahmanabad-Mansura in Sind," *Archaeological Survey of India, Annual Reports* (1903–4): 133–44.

———. *Portfolio of Illustrations of Sind tiles*. London, 1906.

———. "Excavations at Brahmanabad," *ASIAR* (1908–9): 79–87.

———. *The Antiquities of Sind*. Calcutta, 1929.

Crowe, Yolande. "Some Glazed Tiles in 15th Century Bidar," in *Facets of Indian Art*, edited by R. Skelton. London, 1986.

Fanshawe, H. C. *Delhi, Past and Present*. Delhi, 1902.

Gangler, Anette. "Islamische Grabbauten im Pandschab," in *Die Gärten des Islam*. Exh. cat. Stuttgart, 1993.

Guy, J., and D. Swallow. *Arts of India: 1550–1900*. London, 1990.

Kervran, Monik. "Entre l'Inde et l'Asie centrale: les mausolées islamiques du Sind et du sud Penjab," *Cahiers d'Asie centrale*, nos. 1–2 (1996): 133–71.

Khan, `A.`A., and H. E. Stapleton. *Memoirs of Gaur and Pandua*. Calcutta, 1931.

Khan, F. A. *Banbhore*. Karachi, 1969.

Kipling, John Lockwood. "Mooltan Pottery," *Journal of Indian Art*, 1, 1884.

Moynihan, Elizabeth. *Paradise as a Garden*. London: Scholar Press, 1979.

Nabi Khan, A. *Uchchh, History and Architecture*. Islamabad, 1980.

Nath, R., *Colour Decoration in Mughal Architecture*. 3rd edition. Bombay, 1970.

Nicholson, Louise. *Inde, le Fort Rouge*. Delhi and Paris, 1991.

Patil, D. R. *Mandu*. New Delhi, 1982.

Porter, Yves. "Khalji Architecture in the Light of the Ma'ather-e Mahmudshahi," in *Confluence of cultures*, edited by F. Nalini Delvoye. Delhi, 1994.

———. "Décors émaillés dans l'architecture de pierre de l'Inde centrale: les monuments islamiques de Mandu, XVe-XVIe siècles," *Archéologie islamique*, 7 (1997): 121–46.

Rahman, A. *Islamic Architecture of Pakistan, an Introduction*. Peshawar, 1981.

Rötzer, Klaus. "Architecture de pierre dans le Dekkan et le Malwa avant l'époque moghole," *Techniques et culture*, no. 14 (1989): 51–78.

Shokoohy, M., *Badreshvar. The Oldest Islamic Monuments in India*. Leiden, 1988.

Smart, Ellen. "Fourteenth Century Chinese Porcelain from a Tughlaq Palace in Delhi," *Transactions of the Oriental Ceramic Society* (1975–77): 199–230.

Smith, E. W. *Moghul Colour Decoration of Agra, Description of the Chini-ka-Rauza at Agra*. London, 1901.

Vogel, J. P. *Tile-Mosaics of the Lahore Fort*. London, 1920.

Yazdani, G. *Mandu, the City of Joy*. Oxford, 1929.

———. *Bidar*. Oxford, 1947.

Proper Name Index

Page numbers in *italics* indicate illustrations

Site Index

Page numbers in *italics* indicate illustrations

Photo credits

All photos are by Gérard Degeorge except:

page 30, bottom: Réunion des Musées nationaux, photo Hervé Lewandowski
page 34: Bildarchiv preussischer Kulturbesitz, photo Georg Niedermeiser
page 36: Magnum Photos, photo Erich Lessing
page 37: Musée des Arts décoratifs, Paris, photo Laurent Sully-Jaulmes, all rights reserved
page 39: Christie's Images Ltd
page 64: Union centrale des Arts décoratifs, Paris, photo Laurent Sully-Jaulmes, all rights reserved
page 90: Réunion des Musées nationaux, photo Hervé Lewandowski
page 93: Réunion des Musées nationaux, photo Hervé Lewandowski
page 184: Sipa Presse, photo Eriem

ILLUSTRATIONS ON PAGES 2 AND 4

♦ Geometric interlace pattern on a twelve-pointed star. Al-`Attarin *medersa*, Fez (Morocco), completed 1325.

♦ Detail of a border with serrated *saz* leaves. Rüstem Pasha Mosque, Istanbul (Turkey), completed 1561.

Translated from the French by David Radzinowicz
Copy-editing: Bernard Wooding
Typesetting: Studio X-Act
Color separation: PPDL, Boulogne, France

Originally published as *L'art de la céramique dans l'architecture musulmane*

ISBN: 2-0801-0876-X
FA 0876-02-VII
Dépôt légal: 07/2002

Printed in Italy by Grafedit

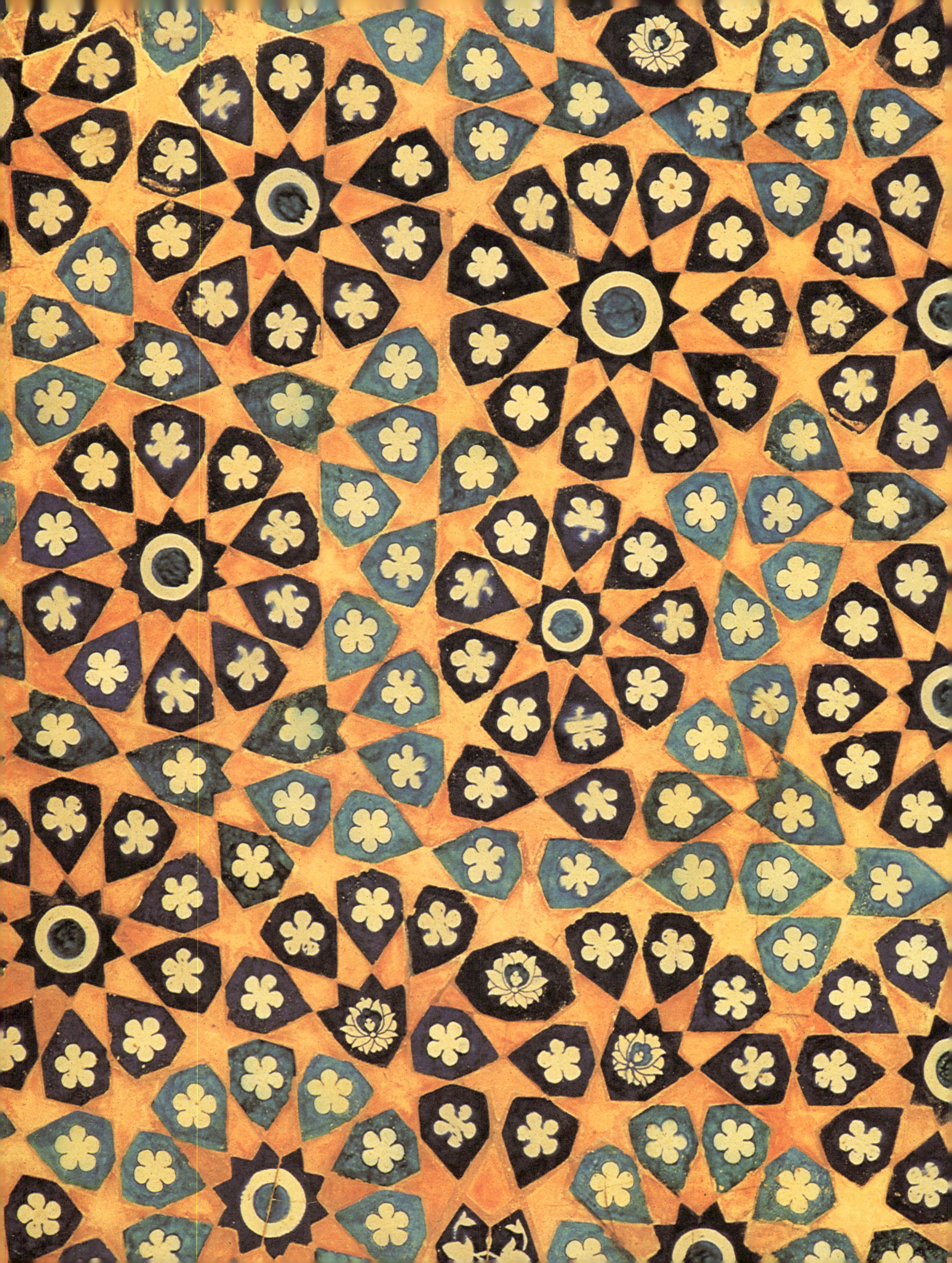